10

Recd & Delivered out *Issue*
the 10th July ~~~~~~ ~~ Ditto ~~~~ ~~~~

Date		Loaves of Bread	Pease		Porke		Beef		Numbr of Pers: vicualled		To whom deliver'd for every Class
Months	days		Bush	Quarts	Bar	weight	Oxen Sheep	Weight	Adult	under age	
July	10th	51	2	11		75					Artopaeus: Fame
		31	1	15		47					Nectacer Tower Frig
		87	4	6		129½					Christn Kurtz. Mary
		73	3	13		109.					Christn Worms Hartwell
		64	2	31		95					Fucks: Baltimore
		60	2	26		90					Gerlach Sam & Elizn
		21	1			32					Schmidt Sarah
		109	5	3½		163½					Kneskern Lyon Leith
		496	23	9½	3½	741					
	11	51									
		31									
		87									Ditto for ye Same
		73									
		64									
		60									
		21									
		109									
		496									

The Palatine Families
of New York
1710

VOLUME I

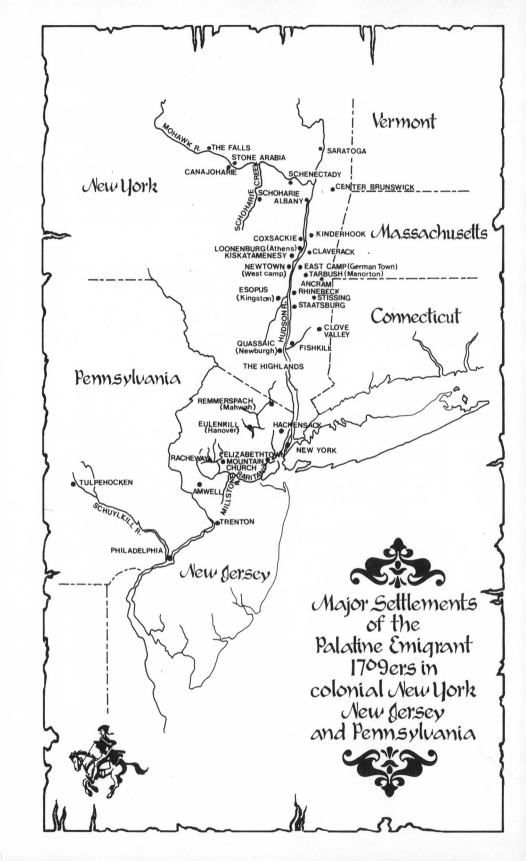

Major Settlements of the Palatine Emigrant 1709ers in colonial New York New Jersey and Pennsylvania

The Palatine Families
of New York

*A Study of the German Immigrants
Who Arrived in Colonial New York in 1710*

Volume I

by

Henry Z Jones, Jr.

PICTON PRESS
ROCKLAND, MAINE

The original account of provisions distributed 10 & 11 July 1710 including the list of ships and listmasters, shown here on the endpapers, was found by Philip Otterness in the New York Department of State at the end of Deed Book 13 Box 6.

This book is the 3rd in a series of five books on Palatine families by Henry Z Jones, Jr. (*Westerwald to America* with Annette Kunselman Burgert and *Even More Palatine Families* with Lewis Bunker Rohrbach). The books in the series are: *Westerwald to America, Palatine Families of Ireland, The Palatine Families of New York, More Palatine Families, Even More Palatine Families*.

Available from:
Henry Z Jones, Jr.
PO Box 261388
San Diego, CA 92196-1388
http://www.hankjones.com

Also available from:
Picton Press
PO Box 1347
Rockland, ME 04841
Visa/ MasterCard orders (207) 596-7766
http://www.pictonpress.com

Manufactured in the United States of America
Printed on 50# acid-free paper

TABLE OF CONTENTS

VOLUME I

VOLUME II

TO

"THE PALATINES" . . . . . .

IN TRIBUTE

Want to know more about the Palatines?

Also available, the acclaimed companion volume to this set:

More Palatine Families by Henry Z Jones, Jr. (1991)
ISBN 0-9613888-3-8

Contact the author:

Henry Z Jones, Jr.
PO Box 261388
San Diego, CA 92196-1388

THE PALATINES' STORY

The background of the great "Palatine" emigration of 1709 has been well-chronicled by such past scholars as Julius Goebel, Sr., Friedrich Kapp, Sanford H. Cobb, F. R. Diffenderffer, and especially Dr. Walter A. Knittle. By mainly utilizing state papers and official government records found in major repositories and libraries in Europe and America, these noted historians did fine work and broke new ground to give us "the big picture" of this great exodus of Germans to the new world.

My own fifteen year Palatine project, however, has approached this same subject-matter from more of a genealogical rather than an historical point of view (although, of course, both go hand in hand). I have studied the emigrants themselves as much as the emigration, and thus have developed strong feelings for the people involved as well as the events. The more I discover about the Palatines from this personal perspective, the more my admiration and respect for these courageous Germans grow, as I see how, after generations of oppression and hardship, in 1709 they finally reached the limit of their endurance and "took the risk" to find a better life in America.

Excellent historical background material on the Palatines, largely unexplored by previous researchers, has been found in the 17th and 18th century churchbooks of the towns and villages where the emigrants resided. These old registers are treasure-troves of data on the local level, for ever so often the Pastors, after recording a baptism, marriage, or burial entry in their churchbooks, would comment on important matters of the day affecting their congregations. Their notations often were written with such poignancy that they capture the spirit of the times and the flavor of life in the local Palatine community better than any other sources I have seen. For example, the churchbooks often reflect the devastation and havoc caused by the repetitive wars fought on German territory - a major factor leading to the 1709 emigration. The Pastor at <u>Partenheim</u> near Alzey wrote:

> 1635 after March: Shortly after this time, we were ruined and destroyed throughout the land by the Swedish and Emperor's [armies], so that we could not come back again until the year [16]37.

Some years later, the Pastor at <u>Westhofen</u> noted:

> 1665: In the month of October, the parish was scattered by the Mainz-Lothringian invasion, and the following children were baptised outside the area...
> From October 1665 to 1669, this churchbook, along with my other best books, were taken to Worms for security...

The plundering continued, as recorded by the Pastor at <u>Kröffel-bach</u>:

> On Friday 21 Dec 1688, a large French force came here
> to Cröffelbach, plundered everything here and at Ober-
> quembach, Oberwetz, Niederwetz, Reichskirchen [Reis-
> kirchen] and other villages in the Wetterau, demanded
> a contribution, and left again for Cassel bey Maintz
> [Castel near Mainz] and there crossed over the Rhine.
> I took flight and, through God's help, escaped their
> hands.

One year later, the Pastor at <u>Ginsheim</u> echoed his colleague:

> Because of the soldiers remaining so long in our land,
> with the French occupying the city of Mainz for two
> yrs., the German people have a right to complain about
> the [troop] movements back and forth in these parts:
> the Saxon and Bavarian armies are encamped in Nieder-
> feld with 24,000 horse and foot [soldiers], the Hess-
> ians are on the other side of Mainz, and the Emperor's
> and [the] Lothringian troops are on the other side of
> the Rhine below the city.

The churchbooks themselves sometimes did not survive, as noted
by the Pastor at <u>Sprantal</u>:

> Because in 1693 with the French invasion of Wirtem-
> berg every churchbook - as well as baptism and
> marriage record -   met with misfortune, this new
> one has been set up by me, the duly called Pastor
> here, and in it at the beginning is shown in orderly
> fashion all citizen/inhabitants with their families
> and the surviving wives and ch., the time of their bapt-
> isms, marriages, and burials as later consecrated by
> me, so that each [subsequent] Pastor at the death of
> any one of these [inhabitants] can easily set out and
> record their life history without further research.

It is obvious from these contemporary, local accounts that
the 1709ers' families had been living for generations in an
area fraught with near-constant wars, which made battlefields of
villages, towns, and whole regions.

Besides being at the mercy of invading armies, many of these
unfortunate Germans were taxed unmercifully by whatever local Prince
had jurisdiction over their particular geographic region, and by
1709 many poor Palatines were bled dry financially by their
Lords. This was another reason for the exodus, as evidenced by a
portion of a letter written back to Germany in 1749 by Johannes[1]
Müller, an emigrant who finally settled in the Mohawk Valley of
colonial New York:

> Is it still as rough [in Germany] as when we left [in
> 1709]? As far as we are concerned [in America], we
> are, compared to taxes in Germany, a free country! We
> pay taxes once a year. These taxes are so minimal that
> some spend more money for drinks in one evening when
> going to the pub. What the farmer farms is his own.
> There are no tithes, no tariffs, hunting and fishing

are free, and our soil is fertile and everything grows...

But perhaps the straw that broke the camel's back was the devastating and bitterly-cold winter of the year 1709. Throughout southern Germany, Pastors abruptly stopped their normal recording of baptismal, marriage, and burial entries in order to mention the terrible weather conditions burdening their congregations. The Pastor at Berstadt wrote:

> [In the yr. 1709] there has been a horrible, terrible cold, the like of which is not remembered by the oldest [parishioners] who are upwards of 80 years old. As one reads in the newspapers, it spreads not only through the entire country, but also through France, Italy, Spain, England, Holland, Saxony, and Denmark, where many people and cattle have frozen to death. The mills in almost all villages around here also are frozen in, so that people must suffer from hunger. Most of the fruit trees are frozen too, as well as most of the grain...

The Pastor at Runkel noted:

> [1709] Right after the New Year, such a cold wave came that the oldest people here could not remember a worse one. Almost all mills have been brought to a standstill, and the lack of bread was great everywhere. Many cattle and humans, yes - even the birds and the wild animals in the woods froze. The Lahn [River] froze over three times, one after the other...

At Diedenbergen another entry:

> [27 Oct 1708] Before Simon Juda [Day], an usually heavy snow fell which broke many branches off the trees, especially in the forests because the leaves were still on the trees, and the snow weighed heavily on them. Then on the day after New Year's, 2 Jan 1709 and for three days [thereafter], we had continuous rain and later snow. Because of the great cold, the Main froze over in four days, the Rhine in eight days, and they remained frozen for five weeks. During this time there was a great lack of wood and flour, since most mills were frozen in. The fodder for cattle was used for two purposes [the humans had to eat it too], and many a piece [of land?] was ruined. One could read in the newspapers of many complaints and much damage in all European countries.

And at Selters, even more:

> From the 6th to the 26th of January [1709], there was such a raging cold, the likes of which has not occurred in 118 yrs. according to the calculations of the mathemeticians at Leipzig. A great many trees have frozen, the autumn sowing has suffered great damage, and this yr. there will be no wine at all.

Residents of the various Duchies of southern Germany then were in a terrible state from the ongoing wars, oppressive taxation, and devastating winter - all of which contributed to their desire to emigrate from their "forsaken Egypt," as Johannes[1] Müller of the Mohawk called his former European homeland in his 1749 letter.

Interestingly enough, religious persecution does not seem to have been a major factor in the exodus. Many of the Palatines seemed quite flexible in their religious affiliation; they attended whichever church was geographically convenient or even politically expedient. For example, the 1709er Johannes[1] Heiner was baptised a Catholic, married in the Reformed church, then became a prominent Lutheran lay leader in the Hudson Valley. Also, many emigrants who were noted in Germany and shortly after their arrival in America as Catholics ("Episcopal" is Kocherthal's term for Catholic) soon turned up as full-fledged Protestants in Lutheran and Reformed churchbooks of colonial New York. It is interesting to note that Neuwied and Isenburg, two of the prime German regions of origin for New York settlers, both had atmospheres of religious toleration in the late 1500's - perhaps a contributing factor to the later, theologically flexible viewpoint of many of the 1709ers.

The British government exploited the Palatines' dissatisfaction by waging an advanced and clever public relations campaign extolling the virtues of life in the new world which also fueled the fires of emigration. This was accomplished by the circulation throughout southern Germany prior to 1709 of the so-called "Golden Book," which painted America (called "The Island Of Carolina" or "The Island Of Pennsylvania") almost as the promised land of milk and honey. Its effect is revealed by a marvelous series of manuscripts entitled "Questions And Answers Of Emigrants Who Intend To Go To The New Island, Actum 23 May 1709," found in the Staatsarchives Wiesbaden (Nassau-Weilburg File Abt. 150, No. 4493); these documents are a boon for the genealogist, as they give the name, age, religion, place of birth, length of marriage, and number of children among their statistics for each prospective emigrant. They also enhance our view of the daily lives of the Palatines, as each man is asked several personal questions relating to his reason for leaving as well as how he will finance his journey. The heart-rending responses to the queries are set forth in such a straight-forward, conversational way by the Palatines that they almost seem to make the emigrants come alive again. It is hard not to feel their despair and not be moved by their cautious hope for a better life in a new country. When asked how he first came upon the idea to emigrate and who first gave a reason for the emigration, Christian Schneider aged 25, Lutheran, married 2 years with no children stated:

People from Altenkirchen. English agents at Frankfurt and writings brought by them.

Johannes Willig aged 32, Lutheran, born in this country (Nassau-Weilburg), married 8 years with 1 daughter, replied:

> Because he's poor and has nothing more than he can earn by hard labour, he seeks something better. At Grossen Linden he had a book about the Island.

When he was asked the same question, Johannes Linck aged 30, Lutheran, born Cöpern in Hamburg an der Höhe, married 6 years with 1 son and 1 daughter, answered:

> He cultivated in the winter and the grain was bad. He knows he can no longer feed himself. He had heard of books about the Island and resolved to go there. First heard of this from people from Darmstadt who are going.

Hanß Georg Gäberling aged 40, Lutheran, came here from Lindheim an der Straße, married 16 years with 3 daughters, responded:

> Poverty drives him to it, in spite of working day and night at his handwork. Otherwise he has no special desire to emigrate. He heard of books in Braunfels and at Altenkirchen which Schoolmaster Petri at Reiskirchen brought to the village on his deer-hunting.

Georg Philip Mück aged 32, Lutheran, born in this country, married 8 years with 1 son and 2 daughters, similarly replied:

> Poverty brought him to it. He can hope for no harvest which the wild animals have eaten. There have been people from the Pfalz in the village, and he heard about it from them first.

Johannes Flach aged 30, Catholic, came to Nassau-Weilburg, married 10 years with 3 sons, noted:

> Poverty and no expectation of [ever obtaining] land. Wild animals have eaten everything. Has heard most about it at Frankfurt. He and G. Stahl bought a book for 3 Batzen in which there is writing about the Island.

When asked another question, whether he received advice about this and from whom, Philip Adam Hartmann aged 31, Lutheran, born in this country, married 8 years with 1 daughter, responded:

> No [advice]. Only from God, because people so advise it.

And to this same query, Philips Petri aged 42, Lutheran, born in this country, married 12 years, 2 sons and 2 daughters, answered:

> No one advised him, but people everywhere are talking about it!

Another question was asked as to what he actually knows about the so-called New Island? Christian Schneider replied:

> Nothing, except that it is undeveloped and could be built up with work.

Johannes Willig added:

> The place is a better land, if one wants to work.

Philip Adam Hartmann responded to the same query:

> By work one could earn in one yr. enough to live on for two years.

Georg Philip Mück answered:

> The Queen of England will give bread to the people until they can produce their own.

And Valentin Nomsboth aged 37, Reformed, came from the Braunfels area, married 12 years with 2 sons, said:

> There is supposed to be a good land there, and, in a few years, one can get both bread and land.

The prospective emigrant was then asked who told him such and under what circumstances? Christian Schneider answered:

> From a book from English agents with a carpenter from Essershausen, but he hasn't read it. The carpenter quoted from it to him.

The emigrant was then asked a final question. From where does he think he will get the means for this journey? Johannes Willig said:

> He wants to sell what little he has.

Hanß Georg Gäberling noted:

> He wants to sell his livestock.

Johann Philip Hetzel aged 36, Lutheran, married 16 years with 4 daughters and 2 sons, answered:

> He wants to sell his few sheep.

Wentzel Dern aged 40, Lutheran, born in this country, married 14 years with 3 sons and 4 daughters, answered:

> He wants to sell his cow, but leave his other possessions with friends.

Johann Wilhelm Klein aged 25, Lutheran, married since Christmas, gave an important response:

> The Queen will advance it to the people.

Johann Adam Fehd aged 30, Lutheran, born in this country, married with 1 son, put his trust elsewhere:

> He must have God's help!

But perhaps the most important yet most intangible factor in the emigration was the character and psychological make-up of

the 1709ers themselves. They seemed to have within their souls
some special spark, some sense of daring and adventure which enabled them to gamble their lives and families on an unknown fate
and set forth across a mighty ocean to a strange land. Several
emigrants were noted in churchbooks prior to 1709 as "vagabondus"
and thus were already on the move. Some exhibited a genuine
landhunger and a desire to better their lot even before leaving
Germany, as exemplified by a few of the responses to the Nassau-
Weilburg questionaires. And then there were those hearty souls
who found their way to colonial N.Y. who were simply dreamers,
as shown by this rather caustic comment of the Pastor of Welter-
od:

> [1709] In this year the winter was terrible cold and be-
> cause of its fury the spring crops of nut, cherry, and
> apple trees are almost gone...
> A particularly deceptive spirit this year broke out a-
> mong many people, especially those more or less lazy
> and indolent fellows who left their fatherland with
> wife and children to travel to England from where they
> were to be transported to Carolina in the West Indies
> or America, about which land they allowed themselves
> to dream again of great splendors where one should al-
> most believe that breakfast bread would rain into
> their mouths. Moreover, they would not let themselves
> be deterred from their calm delusion through more ac-
> curate respresentation of the facts. Out of my cong-
> regation here, for example, a single, miserably lazy
> fellow babbled about this with his wife and 3 children
> then left from here - namely Johann Curt Wüst from
> Strüth. There were others there who came back again
> after repenting of their foolishness, but he is not
> found among them.

I say, "Thank God for the dreamers!"

One of the discoveries in my finding over 500 of the 847 New
York Palatine families in their German homes is the fact that so
many emigrants originated in areas outside the boundaries of what
we think of today as the Palatinate. Many New York settlers were
found in the Neuwied, Isenburg, Westerwald, Darmstadt, and Nassau
regions as well as the Pfalz - proving again that the term
"Palatine" was more of a generic reference (meaning "Germans"
in general) rather than a literal description of their precise,
geographic origins. The Pastor of Dreieichenhain, midway between
Darmstadt and Frankfurt, substantiates the widespread origins of
the 1709ers in an utterly fascinating entry in his churchbook:

> The year 1709 began with such severe and cold weather
> and lasted such a long time that even the oldest peop-
> le could not remember ever having experienced such a
> winter; not only were many birds frozen and found dead,
> but also many domesticated livestock in their sheds.
> Many trees froze, and the winter grain was also very
> frozen...

In this year 1709 many thousands of families from Germany, especially from Upper and Lower Hessen, from the Pfalz, Odenwald, Westerwald, and other dominions, have departed for the so-called New America and, of course, Carolina. Here, from out of the grove, (..) families have departed with them [the families being those of Johann Henrich Michael Vatter, Friedrich Filippi, Christoffel Schickedantz, Christoffel Jost, and Tobias Schilfer]. [Here are] details of those who have joined together here and there in Germany and departed in 1709 for the New World:

From the Pfalz	8,589 persons
From Darmstadt area	2,334
From Hanau, Ysenburg, and neighboring Grafschaften and Wetterau districts	1,113
From Franckenland	653
From the Mainz area	63
From the Trier area	58
From the Bishopric of Worm, Speyer, and neighboring Grafschaften	490
From the Kassel area	81
From the Zweibrücken area	125
From the Nassau area	203
From Alsace	413
From the Baden countryside	320
Unmarried craftsmen	871
	(15,313)

Not all of these people went farther than to England and Ireland; very few got to America. And because England and Ireland didn't suit them, they all, except those who died on the way, returned, as did some of the above mentioned Hanau families, and that after two years. The Catholics, however, were all sent back.

Just how and where this village Pastor obtained these numbers and his information intrigues me greatly, but no source is revealed in the Dreieichenhain churchbook. However, the extract does indeed give a good, although undoubtedly incomplete, picture of the overall geographic breakdown of the origins of the emigrants from contemporary eyes.

The first trickle of German emigrants left for New York with Pastor Joshua Kocherthal in 1708 and settled near Newburgh on the Hudson River. Then, about February or March 1709, large groups began leaving their German homes for Rotterdam and thence to England. There are records of their departure. Some obtained letters of recommendation or birth certificates from officials to bring with them on their trip, such as Gerhardt[1] Schäfer and Ulrich[1] Simmendinger. Others tried to dispose of their property in an orderly and legal manner and obtain lawful permits to emigrate, such as

Peter[1] Wagener of <u>Dachsenhausen</u> and the many 1709ers who left the
Nassau-Dillenburg region. As these Germans left their homes, very
often the local Pastors made mention of their departures in their
churchbooks. For instance, the registers at <u>Bonfeld</u> in the Kraichgau have an entire page detailing the emigrants from the village
(such as Jost[1] Hite, Simeon[1] Vogt, and Hans Michael[1] Wagele) in
1710 as well as later years. The Pastor at <u>Wiesloch</u> noted that
Conrad[1] Dieffenbach emigrated with the family of Georg Bleichardt[1]
Hauck to the West Indies 15 May 1709, the minister at <u>Leonbronn</u>
mentioned that Margaretha, Lorentz[1], and Georg[1] Däther went to
England, and the <u>Treschklingen</u> register   augmented the <u>Bonfeld</u>
churchbook by stating that Hans Jost Heid (Jost[1] Hite) emigrated
with wife and child with other people to Pennsylvania in the so-
called new world in 1709. Sometimes such a churchbook entry was
quite a story filled with intrigue, as at <u>Massenheim</u>:

> Let it be known that this Spring many people left the
> country for English America, namely the Island of Car-
> olina, including also from here Matthaeus Koch and his
> wife Christina together with their 4 children who went
> thither and with them his mother Johann Henrich Aul's
> wife, between 60 and 70 years of age. [Frau Aul, the
> mother of Matthaeus Koch,] went secretly in the night,
> forsaking husband and children here and going to Eng-
> land, without doubt to find her grave in the ocean.
> On 27 Nov 1710, Johann Henrich Aul, a master cooper
> whose wife left him and went with her two sons of a
> 1st marriage to English America, married to Anna Mar-
> garetha Freund; Herr Aul was freed [from his first
> wife] as she had been cited by the government in
> three principalities and has not appeared.

The trip down the Rhine to Holland took anywhere from four
to six weeks. A personal account of an emigrant's journey from
Alsheim to London in 1709, from the Stauffer notebooks kindly
sent to me by Klaus Wust, describes in detail what probably was
a typical route:

> In the year 1709, I, Hans Stauffer, removed on the 5th
> of Nov with wife and children Jacob, 13 yrs., Daniel 12
> yrs., Henry, 9 yrs., Elizabeth with her husband Paulus
> Friedt and one child, Maria by name, and myself, eight,
> we set sail from Weissenau on the 8 day of Nov. At
> Bingen we remained one day, and we left on the 10th day
> of Nov. At Hebstet, we set sail on the 11th day of Nov.
> Neuwied, we set sail on the 12th day of Nov. At Erbsen,
> we set sail on the 13th day of Nov and came to Millem.
> There we had to remain one day. On the 15th day, we
> left Millem. At Eisen we lay two days. On Nov 17th we
> sailed away [to Erding].
> And on the 20th day of Nov, we left Erding and sailed
> half an hour under Wiesol. And on the 21st we went to
> the shore. There we had to remain until the wind be-
> came calm. And on the 22nd of Nov, we sailed as far
> as Emrig. There we had to remain until the wind be-
> came calm. And on the 24th of Nov, we left Emrig and

came to Schingen Schantzs, and sailed to Arm. During
the night [we sailed] to Rein and on the 28th of Nov
to Wieg, and thence we came to Ghert on the 29th of
Nov. On the first day of Dec, we came to Amsterdam.
And on the 17th of Dec we left Amsterdam and sailed
half an hour before the city. There we had to remain
until the wind became favorable and calm. And on the
19th day of Dec, we came to Rotterdam. There we had
to wait until the tide was ready for sailing. Thirt-
een days we had to remain. On the 29th of Dec we
sailed from Rotterdam nearly to Brielle. There we
had to remain until the wind was favorable. On the
20th day of Jan we left Brielle and sailed to London.
We sailed six days on the sea to London.

As the Germans assembled in Holland awaiting transportation to
England, ever so often they participated in a baptism performed
by a Dutch Pastor of their host country. For example, at the
christening of a child of Jeremias Schletzer sponsored by eventual New York settlers Benedict[1] Wennerich and Maria Elisabetha[2]
Lucas in April of 1709, the Pastor of the Rotterdam Lutheran
Church noted that the party was from the Palatinate, professing
to go to Pennsylvania; and at the baptism of a child of Dirck
Luijckasz (Dieterich[1] Laux?) in September 1709, the Pastor of Rotterdam Reformed Church recorded that the parents were outside the
Eastgate, coming from the Pfalz, and going to England. Similar
entries concerning these German emigrants are found in the Rotterdam Catholic registers and the Brielle Reformed churchbooks.

The Palatines encamped outside Rotterdam were in a miserable
condition, and shacks covered with reeds were the only shelter
they had from the elements. The Burgomaster of Rotterdam took
pity on them and appropriated 750 guilders for distribution among
the destitute. Meanwhile, the British government employed three
Anabaptist Dutch merchants, Hendrik van Toren, Jan van Gent, and
John Suderman, to supervise the loading and sailing of the emigrants to England (the five Rotterdam Embarkation Lists are a pro-
duct of their labours); but the Palatines continued to arrive in
Holland in increasing numbers at the rate of nearly a thousand
per week. On 14 June 1709, James Dayrolle, British Resident at
the Hague, informed London that if the British government continued to give bounty to the Palatines and encourage their migra-
tion, half of Germany would be on their doorstep, for they were
flying away not only from the Palatinate, but from all other
countries in the neighborhood of the Rhine!

Things were clearly getting out of hand. The immigrants
were coming over so fast that it was impossible to care for them
and dispose of them. The British, victims of their own too-succ-
essful p.r. campaign, tried to turn back many Palatines, especially the Catholics, and by late July refused to honor their

commitments to support the German arrivals. Many of those arriving after that date, if not sent back, made their way to England by private charitable contribution or at their own expense; this latter group probably never was catalogued or enrolled on any shipping list as were the earlier arrivals at Rotterdam.

The Palatines arriving in England beginning in May 1709 continued to have problems there. London was not so large a city that 11,000 alien people could be poured into it conveniently without good notice or thorough planning. The Government attempted to cope with the trying situation but was hard put to provide food and shelter for the emigrants. 1,600 tents were issued by the government for the Palatine encampments formed at Blackheath, Greenwich, and Camberwell; others were quartered at Deptford, Walworth, Kensington, Tower Ditch, and other areas. Pastor Fred Weiser has sent on a genealogical source indicating the Palatine's travail in London: some interesting marginal notes found in the family record of the 1709er Arnold Altlander/Altlanden family of Plänig near Alzey mention that one of the children born in 1706 "fell blessedly asleep in the Lord Christ and was buried at Derthforth near London," while another child born in 1708 "was buried in London on the heath." Palatine deaths in England were not uncommon as their places of shelter were as crowded and unhealthy as they had been in Holland. Occasionally an emigrant's marriage or baptism was recorded in a British source, such as the Savoy German Lutheran Churchbook in London; this material has been transcribed and published by John P. Dern in his valuable London Churchbooks And The German Emigration Of 1709. Mr. Dern and his late colleague Norman C. Wittwer also found several Palatine baptisms (including one in Johann Peter[2] Zenger's family) registered at St. Nicholas Church in Deptford.

While the emigrants waited in England, the Board of Trade ordered two German Pastors, Pfr. John Tribbeko and Pfr. Georg Andrew Ruperti, to compile a record of those encamped in London. Their rolls are known today as the four London Lists, but they cease in June 1709 when the Palatine emigration simply got too big to chronicle. The longer they lingered, the worse conditions became for the 1709ers; so, as in Rotterdam, they had to depend on alms and charity to survive in their camps at Blackheath and environs. At first the London populace looked on the Palatines in a rather kindly way, but gradually the novelty of their presence wore off. As the poorer classes of Londoners realized the emigrants were taking their bread and reducing their scale of wages, mobs of people began attacking the Palatines with axes, hammers, and scythes, and even the upper classes became alienated

from the Germans, fearing they were spreading fever and disease.
To alleviate the situation, groups of Palatines (labelled "Catholics," although some definitely were not) were sent back to Holland from whence they were to return to Germany. Dr. Knittle has
published two such "Returned To Holland Lists" dated 1709 and
1711. Working from a clue found in the Groves Papers at the Public
Record Office in Belfast, I employed Peter Wilson Coldham to search
for similar lists dated 1710, which eventually were found in the
Treasury Papers in the London Public Record Office and published
by John P. Dern and myself in 1981 in Pfälzer-Palatines as a tribute to the late Dr. Fritz Braun of the Heimatstelle Pfalz.

The dispersal of the Palatines continued. Some were sent to
other parts of England where, rather than receiving their expected
grants of land, they were made daylabourers and swineherds. Others
were dispatched to Ireland, where many became tenants of Sir Thomas Southwell near Rathkeale in County Limerick (my small book
The Palatine Families Of Ireland concerns these 1709ers and their
descendants). Then, some emigrants were sent to North Carolina
where they joined the Swiss settlement of Christopher von Graff-
enried, while a few others went to Jamaica and the West Indies.
Plans also were instituted to transport a group of Germans to
the Scilly Isles, but this scheme appears to have come to naught.

Of the 13,000 Germans who reached London in 1709, only an
estimated quarter came on to New York. The idea of sending
the Palatines there sprang from a proposal sponsored by Governor-
Elect Robert Hunter of New York, probably made originally by the
Earl of Sunderland. It was their thought that the 1709ers be used
in the manufacture of naval stores (i.e. tar and pitch) from the
pine trees dotting the Hudson Valley and thus earn their keep in
the colony. It also was acknowledged that a strong Palatine presence in the new world would act as a buffer against the French
in Canada and strengthen the Protestant cause in British America.
No real time-limit to the length of service of the Germans was
specified, but it was apparent they were to be employed until
the profits had not only paid their expenses, but also repaid
the government for their transportation and settlement. They al-
legedly signed a covenant to this effect in England which noted
that, when the government was repaid, forty acres of land would be
given to each person, free from taxes and quit rents for seven
years.

Most of the Palatines boarded ships for New York in December
1709, but the convoy really never left England until April of
1710. The German emigrants sailed on eleven boats, and Gov-
ernor-Elect Hunter accompanied the group. The voyage was a terrible

one for the Palatines: they were crowded together on the small vessels, suffered from vermin and poor sanitation, and were forced to subsist on unhealthy food. Many became ill, and the entire fleet was ravaged by ship-fever (now known as typhus) which eventually caused the deaths of many passengers. John P. Dern will publish the results of his research with Norman C. Wittwer on the Palatines' journey to America, the convoy that accompanied them, their route of travel, etc., which will greatly enhance our knowledge of this little-known aspect of the 1709er story.

The Palatines who arrived in the summer of 1710 found that colonial New York was hardly the paradise propounded in the Golden Book back in Germany. The New York City Council protested the arrival of 2,500 disease-laden newcomers within their jurisdiction and demanded the Germans stay in tents on Nutten (Governor's) Island offshore. Typhus continued to decimate the emigrants. Altogether about 470 Palatines died on the voyage from England and during their first month in New York. Many families were broken up at this time; Hunter apprenticed children who were orphans as well as youngsters whose parents were still alive! The Governor's record of his payments for the subsistence of the 847 Palatine families 1710 - 1712 survives today as the so-called Hunter Subsistence Lists.

On 29 September 1710, Governor Hunter entered into an agreement with Robert Livingston, Commissioner of Indian Affairs, to purchase a tract of 6,000 acres on the east side of the Hudson for the purpose of settling Palatines there to manufacture naval stores. In October, many of the Germans began going up the river, clearing the ground, and building huts on the Livingston Tract. Gradually, small, distinct settlements appeared at East Camp called Hunterstown, Queensbury, Annsbury, and Haysbury; the villages on the west side of the Hudson were Elizabeth Town, George Town, and New Town. Other 1709ers remained in New York City, and many of this group eventually made their way to New Jersey.

The Palatines grew increasingly dissatisfied with their status, which bordered on serfdom, and strongly demanded the lands promised them in London. Their rebellion was put down by the Governor, who disarmed the Germans and put them under the command of overseers and a Court of Palatine Commissioners, who treated them again as "the Queen's hired servants." Dissension continued, as the Palatines bickered with their commissaries and found fault with the irregular manner in which they were being subsisted with inferior food supplies. The situation grew worse due to trouble in the naval stores program: the knowledgeable James Bridger was replaced with Richard Sackett who seemed to know little about tar-making. In

1711, many Palatines took part in an abortive British expedition against the French in Canada, further delaying tar extraction.

To add to this sad state of affairs, in England the Whigs, who had largely sponsored the Palatine settlement in New York, were superseded in office by the Tories, who proceeded to disparage the 1709er Whig project and bring about a House of Commons investigation and censure in 1711. Hunter then lost financial backing in his efforts to support the Germans and had to withdraw the Palatine subsistences in September 1712. After all the British promises, the Germans were abandoned to suffer their own fate, although the Governor still attempted to keep some control over them by requiring the Palatines to obtain permits if they wished to move elsewhere in New York or New Jersey. Johann Friederich[1] Hager, the Reformed German clergyman sent to minister to the Palatines by the Society For The Propagation Of The Gospel in London, described their terrible plight in a poignant letter dated 6 July 1713 written to the Society:

> Pray do not take it ill that I trouble you with these lines. I have written several times, but I do not know whether the letters have come to hand. Thus have I likewise received none from my father, I do not know how long since, and therefore cannot be sure whether he is alive or dead.
>
> The misery of these poor Palatines I every day behold has thrown me into such a fit of melancholy that I much fear a sickness. There has been a great famine among them this winter, and does hold on still, in so much that they boil grass and ye ch. eat the leaves of the trees. Such amongst them have most suffered of hunger as are advanced in yrs. and too weak to go out labouring. I have seen old men and women crie that it should have almost moved a stone. I am almost resined with this people. I have given the bread out of my own mouth to many a one of these, not being able to behold their extreme want. Where I live there were two old people that, before I could be informed of their necessitous condition, have for a whole week together had nothing but Welsh turnips, which they did only scrape and eat without any salt or fat or bread; and in a word, I cannot describe the miserable state they are reduced to, and above all that, have we no hope of any alteration; for one hears no news here, nobody receives any letters, which also hinders me now from drawing a Bill of Exchange for my half year's salary, due Ladyday 1713. The knife is almost put to my throat, whilst I am in a foreign country without either money or friends to advance one any. I had sown and planted some ground at my own charges, but it has now twice been spoiled. I have served hitherto faithfully as Col. Heathcote and others can bear witness with a good conscience and should I now be forsaken in this remote land without any pay, or means of subsistence, having neither received anything hitherto from my people nor anything being to be expected from them for the time to come. They cry out after me: I should by no means forsake them for they should otherwise be

quite comfortless in this wilderness. Sir, I entreat
you to recommend my case as much as possible, for I do
not know where to turn myself otherwise...

Having been left to their own resources, the more restless
and adventurous of the Germans stole away in late 1712 to the
Schoharie Valley, which at one time was a land considered for Palatine settlement. They bought lands from the Indians there, but
also bought more trouble as the Native-Americans' title to this
property was dubious and led to years of litigation. Slowly, the
Palatines carved homes out of the frontier, and eventually seven,
distinct villages were settled in the Schoharie region. Frank E.
Lichtenthaeler in his excellent article "The Seven Dorfs Of Schoharie" has identified them as:

Named by Conrad Weiser's Journal	Named by Simmendinger:
1) Kniskern-dorf	Neu-Heidelberg
2) Gerlachs-dorf	Neu-Cassel
3) Fuchsen-dorf	Neu-Heessberg
4) Schmidts-dorf	Neu-Quunsberg
5) Weisers-dorf (Brunnendorf)	Neu-Stuttgardt
6) Hartmans-dorf	Neu-Ansberg
7) Ober Weisers-dorf	

The Palatines had not been permitted to bring their Hudson Valley
tools with them to Schoharie, so they fashioned ingenious substi-
tutes: branches of a tree for a fork used in haymaking, a shovel
from a hollowed-out log-end, and a maul from a large knot of wood
- examples of their determination and imagination.

By the time of their naturalization in 1715, the 1709ers were
spread out in colonial New York to a large extent. About this time,
Ulrich[1] Simmendinger began gathering family data concerning his
compatriots which he would eventually publish in 1717 upon his
return to Germany (see his section for further details). Simmendinger's fascinating pamphlet detailed the families at East Camp,
those at Rhinebeck and on the west side of the Hudson (lumped together in his "Beckmansland" locale), the Germans in the Schoharie
settlements, those in New York City, and groups in New Jersey at
Hackensack and on the Raritan. These latter New Jersey Germans (whom
Dr. Knittle erroneously put as Schoharie residents of Kniskerns-
dorf) settled in the colony after subsistence was withdrawn in
1712. N.J. Lutheran congregations in fairly close association were
formed at Millstone, Rockaway, and an area known as "The Mountains." Excellent data on them may be found in John P. Dern's Albany Protocol, Simon Hart and Harry J. Kreider's Lutheran Church
In N.Y. And N.J. 1722 - 1760, and Norman C. Wittwer's The Faithful And The Bold.

Troubles with the New York colonial government continued as
Hunter made plans to clear the Palatines from their Schoharie

settlements. In 1718, Johann Conrad[1] Weiser, Gerhardt[1] Walrath, and Wilhelm[1] Scheff were sent to London to plead the Palatine cause; however, the lack of agreement among the three delegates, their lack of financial resources, and Hunter's powerful influence in London made their case ineffective, and they returned to New York. Finally, in 1722/23, Hunter's successor, Governor William Burnet, purchased land in the Mohawk Valley for some of the Palatines, and they eventually settled in this area on the Stone Arabia and Burnetsfield Patents. About this time, fifteen German families left the Schoharie Valley to settle in the Tulpehocken region of present-day Berks County, Pennsylvania. Others continued to follow, and by 1730 the 1709er emigrant families were found in New York, New Jersey, Pennsylvania, Delaware, Maryland, Virginia, Connecticut, and the Carolinas.

This, then, is a necessarily brief background of the Palatine story. I especially recommend Dr. Walter A. Knittle's book <u>Early Eighteenth Century Palatine Emigration</u>, which has helped me greatly, for a fuller picture of their travails and dispersal. That the Palatines survived in America is no less a miracle than is their emigration! They left hardships in Germany to find new hardships here. The 1709ers never found the promised land of milk and honey of the Golden Book, but they did find a wilderness ready to be tamed and transformed into liveable communities by perseverance and hard work. Their story is a tribute to their fortitude and quality of character which enabled them to find the inner strength to meet the terrible difficulties they faced in their new life in a new world. The Palatine families of New York met the challenge head on and not only survived, but established a secure and important place in American life.

MY PALATINE PROJECT

My interest in genealogy began at the age of eight, when I
first started climbing the family tree. Since that time, the
hours I have spent pouring over dusty books in old libraries and
peering at faded images on microfilm have been among the happiest
of my life. Like so many of us, I have learned over the years
that genealogy is not only a comfort and companion, but also a
challenge; it gives us the opportunity to exercise our intellect,
trust our instincts, and, by getting in touch with the past,
leave a worthwhile legacy for the future. It is in this spirit
that I have tried to chronicle and honor the Palatine families
of New York.

By way of background, I first discovered my German roots in
1960, after a boyhood of tracing the English and Danish lines of
my ancestry. I found that my great-grandfather Isaac Hillman, a
California gold-rush '49er from Troy, New York, descended from
Abraham Bergmann/Barkman, a Palatine who was settled on the
Southwell Estate in County Limerick, Ireland, in 1709. Plunging
into Palatine research for the first time, I studied the few accessible source materials on the subject only to find virtually
no genealogical information had been published on the Irish group
as a whole. For five years, then, I collected as much documented
data as I could on these 1709ers in the Emerald Isle and in 1965
published the results of my digging in a small book The Palatine
Families Of Ireland.

Feeling very much at home in the Palatine milieu, my atten-
tion turned towards those Germans who went to colonial New York
in 1710. I noticed that here, too, no comprehensive genealogical
study had been written. Determined to fill this void, in December 1969, I began work on my project to document all 847 New York
Palatine families found on the Hunter Subsistence Lists. Most all
extant "Palatine" entries from New York churchbooks for the period
from 1710 to 1760 (and in many cases to 1776) were posted on family groupsheets. In doing this I utilized either a microfilm of
the original register itself or an accurate and careful transcription of the churchbook, such as those published by Royden
Vosburg, the New York Genealogical & Biographical Society in its
Record, or (especially) Arthur C. M. Kelly in his excellent Palatine Transcripts series. To these notations of baptisms, marriages, burials, confirmations, memberships, and communions, I
added genealogical data from wills, administrations, orphan's
court proceedings, deeds, land patents, censuses, tax lists,

and military records. Each color-coded groupsheet eventually
emerged as a fully-documented biography of an individual Palatine
couple and their offspring. By 1981 when I began typing my manuscript, over 17,000 of these groupsheets had been completed.

As I immersed myself in New York Palatine source materials,
I soon realized that published versions of sailing lists and subsistence lists needed to be double-checked for both accuracy and
content. When microfilms of the Rotterdam Sailing Lists, the London Census of Palatines of 1709, and the Hunter Subsistence Lists
finally arrived from the Public Record Office in London, they
were a revelation to me because printed versions were found to
contain errors and omissions when compared to the unalphabetised
original manuscripts. For example, The Rotterdam Sailing Lists
had been published by Dr. Knittle as five alphabetised lists
of emigrants; however, in the originals, each of these five parties was divided into even smaller lists of shiploads of Palatines, giving unalphabetised groups of passengers on the tiny vessels labelled with each ship's Captain's name. More importantly,
the same _groups_ of 1709ers at Rotterdam largely turned up together again on the unalphabetised London Census taken later that
year. When the Journal section (which has never been printed) of
the Hunter Subsistence Lists 1710 - 1712 was examined, many of
the same families found at Rotterdam and London in 1709 were
still clustered together in colonial New York! These connections
were reenforced when Palatine baptismal entries in New York were
studied; usually the sponsors to those baptisms were the same
1709ers recorded in proximity to the child's parent's names in
Rotterdam, in London, and in the pages of the Journal of the
Hunter Lists.

Armed with such interesting observations, I turned my eyes
towards Germany. I believed that all these associations in Holl-
and, England, and America strongly suggested some sort of common
geographic origin among certain Palatines prior to emigration.
In other words, I felt if I knew the exact ancestral home of
one family in a certain group, chances are other 1709ers in that
same group eventually would be found in the same village or region overseas. With this in mind, I then examined all extant
Palatine materials and extracted all firm points of origin given
in them for the emigrants. I continued careful study of the
juxtaposition of names on all unalphabetised documents as well
as sponsorships and the names of witnesses to wills and deeds.
Besides the actual copying-down of all this information, I sometimes would just sit in front of a microfilm reader for hours
and subliminally absorb the patterns of origin the proximity of

the names suggested. I found this sort of research of great value, as sometimes the subconscious "sees" more than the intellect
can ever hope to discover.

To test my contention that neighbors emigrated with neighbors and settled near them in America where they continued to re-
late to their same old friends, in 1973 I employed the eminent genealogist Carla Mittelstaedt-Kubaseck to go literally village-to-
village for me in Germany, seeking the 847 New York Palatine families in geographic areas I had theorized they eventually would
be found. Dear Carla has been a Godsend! She is highly skilled
at transcribing old manuscripts which often are written in difficult and faded 17th and 18th century German script, has the pro-
digious memory necessary to recall names and statistics relating
to all 847 families, and possesses the stamina and perseverance
required to sift through the literally thousands of churchbooks
and civil documents pertaining to the Palatines. Due to her dili-
gent searches under my direction, over 500 of the 847 families
on the Hunter Lists and more than 450 of the later (1720 - 1760)
immigrants to New York and New Jersey have been pinpointed and
then traced in Europe.

Carla's experiences seeking the 1709ers are an adventure in
themselves. She has had to deal with Pastors who did not know
where their old churchbooks were, as no one had asked for them in
years. Sometimes she ran into an obstinate local cleric who could
not understand why she would want to study "these poor people,"
so that she had to appeal to his Bishop or Dekan to gain access to
the registers. She found that during World War II some crucial
books had been destroyed, misplaced, or lost; and in one case,
even burned for fuel shortly after the war! She endured searches
in cold cellars, musty archives, and sometimes even in a room full
of frolicking children with a Pastor's wife nosily looking over
her shoulder at her. On the other hand, Carla has met countless
co-operative Pastors and archivists who have expressed great interest in the searches and have even invited her into their homes
on a cold night for dinner and good conversation. Early-on in our
efforts, some scholars said an investigation of this scope "could-
n't be done"; they have happily been proved wrong - in no small
part thanks to the skills and dedication of my friend, Carla Mittelstaedt-Kubaseck.

In the course of this long project, certain genealogical les-
sons have been learned, and some old axioms validated and reenforced. I would like to pass along just a few of these to help
other researchers on their own quests:

1) <u>STUDY THE NEIGHBORS</u>

As shown before, rarely did a Palatine come alone to colonial America; he usually emigrated with several neighbors from
Germany and then associated with these same people in the new
world. And such interrelationships did not end with the migrating
first-generation 1709ers; their second-generation children often
married only into those families who originated in geographic
regions near their parents' homes overseas (e.g. Hermann[2]
Segendorff married Maria Catharina[2] Schneider in America, both
families' roots being within a few miles of each other at Heddesdorf and Hachenburg in Germany). Thus, in seeking the unknown
ancestral home of a bride, I have found it useful to search for
her family in the overall European geographic region of her husband and vice versa. Also, clues to the roots of many of those in
the second wave of German emigrants to New York and New Jersey between 1720 and 1760 may be found in seeing just which families
they settled near, sponsored, and married into when they came to
the new world (e.g. Wilhelm Holtzapfel, who arrived in New York
in the late 1720's, married into the 1709er Schu family in New
York, and both groups eventually were found in the Flammersfeld/
Hachenburg locale overseas).

Besides an immigrant's neighbors often holding the key to
his European origin, they also can be important in solving
other genealogical puzzles. Rural communities in 18th and early
19th century America were very small by our 20th century standards; rarely would a young man go outside his local home area
looking for a prospective bride. Thus, very often when seeking
the maiden name of a Palatine's wife, I eventually have found
her family residing on a farm adjoining her husband's family's
land: - showing once more that neighbors often married neighbors
in early America and proving again that sometimes for good genealogical results to find out about <u>one</u> family, we really have
to study <u>all</u> the families in a geographic region, ethnic group,
or specific time-frame.

2) <u>STUDY THE SPONSORS</u>

We who have German (or Dutch) lines in our ancestry are
really blessed in that sponsors are usually named along with the
parents in most 17th and 18th century baptisms. The importance
of these names in the churchbooks cannot be minimized, for being
a godparent in a German family was a great honor and responsib-
ility. Sponsors very often were close relatives of the child
being baptised: grandparents, uncles, aunts, cousins, etc.

The child usually was named for one of the sponsors at the baptism; if the baby's name is different from the sponsor's, this sometimes may reflect the Christian name of a dead or absent grandparent. Related sponsors are especially crucial in sorting out families with common surnames, such as Schmidt, Becker, Müller, and Schneider, and, as such, have been invaluable to my project.

If a sponsor was not a relative, very often he or she was an old friend from Germany. Kocherthal baptised a child of Hieronymus Weller 2 Feb 1712, and the sponsors were Johann Müller, Johann Friederich Hager, and Margaretha Martin - all of whom resided within a few kilometers of each other near Siegen in Germany.

Genealogists, then, should treat baptismal sponsors names with great respect, knowing that these entries provide excellent clues to expanding our knowledge of a German family and its origins.

3) USE ORIGINAL SOURCES

Published versions of important Palatine source materials have been found to contain errors and omissions when compared with the originals. However, contemporary genealogists should not be too hard on well-intentioned researchers of the past. In many cases, they did not have our modern inexpensive and accessible photocopying and microfilming equipment, but instead had laboriously to copy voluminous rolls and lists by hand under unpleasant conditions. They did their best, just as we are doing our best in this era of new technology. Here are a few comments on the accuracy and content of certain 1709er documents in printed form when compared to the original manuscripts:

a) The Rotterdam Sailing Lists of 1709.
   As noted previously, Dr. Knittle published alphabetised lists of five parties of Palatines, when in actuality the originals break down each of the parties into smaller, unalphabetised lists of passengers and give the names of each ship's Captain. There are also 1709ers omitted from this printed transcription, such as the Dutchess County, New York settler Lorentz[1] Deder (Laurents Deder) in the 5th party.

b) The London Census of Palatines of 1709.
   There are many errors in the published versions which are found in the New York Genealogical & Biographical Record and later Mac Wethy's Book of Names. Some ages are printwrongly: Christian Egler in the 3rd arrivals is 38 years old, not 28; Jacob Eschwein's son in the 4th arrivals is

5 not 15 years old; and Georg Tachstetter's son in the 4th group is 1/3 not 3 years of age. Then, there are numerous errors in spelling: John Hern in the 4th arrivals is John Herr, and Jacob Merzel in the same group is Jacob Magel. Mistakes occur in other areas also: the family of Nicol Rupp is mixed up with the emigrant Berger family in the 4th arrivals; Francis Bohne in the 3rd group did have a wife noted; Christian Riegel in the 4th arrivals was a Lutheran, not a Catholic; and John Quirinus Neidhofer in the 1st group had an added occupation of linenweaver mentioned in his listing. The most glaring error found in printed transcriptions of these lists is the omission of all of page 6 of the 4th arrivals which contain several emigrant families.

c) The Hunter Subsistence Lists 1710 - 1712.

All previously printed versions have totally ignored the unalphabetised Journal section of these lists. Dr. Knittle omitted both some added notations (implied marriages, etc.) which clarify certain familial relationships and the "middle" subsistence numbers (between the first and last entries) for each of the 847 families. Mac Wethy's version of the Ledger section leaves out certain names (e.g. Ludolph Coring), as does the booklet The Palatines of New York State (which also gives erroneous double-entries for Georg Ludwig[1] Koch).

d) The West Camp Census of 1710/11.

The version of this roll in Documentary History of New York, Vol. III, erroneously transcribes Philip[1] Helmer as "Philip Kelmer," thus creating an ancestor who never existed for the Hudson Valley Kilmers and cheating the Helmer family of an important listing.

e) The Simmendinger Register.

Dr. Knittle alphabetised and combined the entries on this fascinating census, but the originals show unalphabetised households in the various Palatine settlements (some families still in the same groups they were with at Rotterdam and London). Knittle also attributed the locale of "Auf dem Rarendantz" to Kniskerndorf in the Schoharie Valley, when, in fact, this region was on the Raritan River in New Jersey. There are also minor spelling corrections to be made: "Hanss Jurg Kern" was Hanss Jurg[1] Hahn and "Johann David Lieffland" actually was the emigrant Johann David[1] Ifflandt.

One genealogical compilation that has muddied the waters for

all of us studying the 1709ers is I. Daniel Rupp's <u>A Collection</u>
<u>of upwards of Thirty Thousand Names of German, Swiss, Dutch,</u>
<u>French, and other Immigrants in Pennsylvania from 1727 to 1776.</u>.
The Pennsylvania material encompassing the major portion of his
book is not in question here, but his Appendix VII entitled
"Names Of Male Palatines, Above Twenty-one Years Old, In Livingston Manor, N.Y., In The Winter 1710, And Summer 1711" has misled
genealogists for years. Careful study reveals that, for some unknown reason, Prof. Rupp combined the West Camp Census of 1710/
11, the lists of soldiers in the 1711 Canadian expedition, <u>and</u> the
1723 and 1728 Tulpehocken, <u>Pennsylvania,</u>_petitioners in his roll
which was labelled <u>New York</u>...1710/11! Thus, many of the names
on this list have been given a New York origin when in fact
they went directly to Pennsylvania prior to 1723/1728. Among
the names he has given for whom no record can be found in colonial New York are Johan Peter Pacht, Christian Lauer, Georg Kirchner, Andreas Kapp, Jacob Löwengut, Johannes Noäcker, and Jacob
Katterman.

Other books to use with great caution in regard to veracity
in matters Palatine are <u>The Cady Records</u> chronicling Schoharie
County families, <u>The Blue Book of Schuylkill County, Pennsylvan-</u>
<u>ia,</u> and many of the biographical sections dealing with <u>early</u>
generations in the "glory volumes" published for various counties
in the late 19th century.

4) <u>REMEMBER EVEN ORIGINAL SOURCES MAY BE WRONG</u>

Having emphasized the value of sources contemporary with
the event, I must say that ever so often even these old documents
have been found to contain errors. For example, Pastor Joshua
Kocherthal's West Camp Lutheran Churchbook contains several mistakes in the marriage section of the original register. After arriving in New York a second time in 1710, Kocherthal obviously can
not be expected to have had a close relationship with all of his
parishoners. Many of them came from regions other than his Kraichgau home area of Germany. Thus, he occasionally wrote down the
wrong geographic home of a Palatine bride or groom, such as on 26
April 1715 when he recorded the ancestral home of Georg[1] Deder
(Jerg Thater) as "Lehn berg," when in actuality it was Leonbronn.

There are also other items to watch out for. Spelling errors abound in nearly every New York Palatine churchbook. The
Pastor was at the mercy of whoever was giving him the baptism
or marriage data, and if that person had a different dialect or
was of another nationality (e.g. an English minister or a Dutch
dominie writing down particulars concerning a German baptism), the

churchbook entry often was far afield from the correct spelling
of a surname or location. Then too, sometimes a Pastor would re-
verse the order of the parents and sponsors in the baptismal entries without so-noting the change. I first noticed this in studying a few entries at Red Hook Lutheran Church in the 1740's and
1750's when elderly Palatine couples seemed to begin having children at too old an age; they were actually the sponsors at these
events, and the categories were transposed in the register. Paul
Prindle, Nancy and Arthur Kelly, and I are preparing a detailed
study of such occurences for eventual publication.

One other instance of potential error in original sources
is in gravestone/burial records. In my experience, rarely does
an 18th century gravestone "agree" with the actual date or even
year of baptism found in the old churchbooks. As some colonists
grew older, they often added years to their actual ages, or, in
some cases, probably never knew them; also, many times a deceased
person's children furnished the stone-cutter or Pastor with erroneous information. Thus, gravestones should not be accepted always as containing absolutely true data.

5) STUDY NAMING AND SPELLING PATTERNS

Every ethnic group has certain unique customs in regard to
naming and spelling, and nowhere is this fact more true than
in the families of emigrant Germans. As mentioned before, every
astute genealogist should be open to all possible spelling variations of an 18th century German name. My all-time favorite example of this is in a Hudson Valley churchbook where the common
surname "Schäfer" is spelled as "Ztephyr!"

Sound-alike consonants contribute to the variety of spellings: "D" and "T" often interchange (e.g. "Diel" can be "Thiel,"
"Däther" can be "Teeter"); "C", "G", and "K" often have a similar
sound (e.g. Henrich[1] Glock was known as Henrich "Glock," "Clock,"
and "Klock"); letters "B" and "P" often transpose (e.g. "Ludwig[2] Batz" was known as "Ludwig Potts," "Johannes[1] Benroth" was
"John Penrod"); and letters "V" and "F" do the same ("Arnold[1]
Falck" was recorded periodically as "Arnold Valk"). There appears
to have been no "correct" way to write down a German name - it
all depended upon just who was doing the writing!

Knowing the myriad of Christian names and their variants and
nicknames can be extremely helpful in any search. We all know
that many men named "Johannes" also were known as "Hans," and
women named "Margaretha" were often called "Gretchen." My study
has made me realize how frequently these other variants were
also used:

IF SOMEONE WAS BAPTISED AS:	HE/SHE WAS OFTEN KNOWN AS:
1) Adolf	Adam (but rarely vice-versa)
2) Anthonius	Teunis/Tönges/Dönges
3) Barbara Elisabetha	Barvalis
4) Conrad	Curt
5) Elisabetha Margaretha	Lisgret
6) Friederich	Fritz
7) Georg	Yury/Jurie
8) Gerhardt	Garrett
9) Gertrude	Charity
10) Ludwig	Lewis
11) Melchior	Michael (but rarely vice-versa)
12) Theobald	David (but rarely vice-versa)

We also must remember other idiosyncrasies of the times. "Junior" in the 18th century did not necessarily mean that "Junior" was the son of "Senior" of the same name. It often was a term used to denote that someone was simply younger in age than another person of the same name who also resided in the same small community. Thus there were two 1709ers named Nicolaus[1] Rau often called "Senior" and "Junior," but "Nicolaus Junior" was <u>not</u> son of "Nicolaus Senior": he was an orphan boy younger than the senior Nicolaus Rau.

Then, too, German parents can have similarly named children: both a "Catharina" and an "Anna Catharina", and a "Peter" and a "Johann Peter" may be in one family; and, hard as it is to comprehend by our 20th century standards, ever so often a German couple had two children named exactly the same - both of whom survived! (See the section on #291 Johannes[1] Häner for examples of this in several generations.)

Beginning in 1780 and continuing until at least ca. 1860, the "middle initial" in a three-part name <u>usually</u> meant the first letter of the Christian name of that individual's father. (I must add with some caution, however, that this appears to apply only to <u>New York</u> Dutch and German families; my friends Dr. Arta Johnson and Annette Burgert, specialists in Pennsylvania research, tell me this custom does not hold true in that region.) Thus Georg <u>C</u>. Löscher was probably the son of someone named Conrad, Carl, or Christian, etc. Sometimes the full name of one's parent was used: "Johann<u>es</u> Peter Schmid" (not "Joha<u>nn</u> Peter," which is an entirely different name) was son of Peter Schmid, and "Catharina Jacob Failing" was the daughter of Jacob Failing. This particular custom affords an excellent clue in extending a family line.

6) USE INDICES WITH CAUTION

Indices or registers or calendars to certain 18th century documents and collections often have serious errors and omissions in their coverage. For example, such guides to Palatine data in New York Colonial Manuscripts have been known in published versions for years. However, when I examined these wonderful sources in person in Albany in 1976, I noted much data had never been catalogued: what was on page 20 of Volume LV, for instance, was correctly calendared, but the person indexing had missed the marvelous genealogical tidbits (e.g. "Tree boards for Peter Klein's coffin, 29 March 1711") on pages beyond page 20, the uncalendared pages 20a through 20j, thus omitting ten pages of valuable additional materials. Other instances of this have occurred, such as the "Palatines Returned To Holland, 1710 Lists," which I discovered only through a cryptic reference in the Groves Papers in Belfast, Northern Ireland, as these papers had never been correctly calendared.

Indices to published books also can be deceptive. I am sure we have all had the experience of checking the index to a large genealogical volume, and then finding out much later that the book actually had three or four separate additional indices which were easy to overlook. Published computer indices are often quite erroneous when compared to the original document. My colleague John P. Dern reports that 36% of a published Frederick County, Maryland 1850 Census was in error, and 52% of a published 1830 Census of Maryland was wrong or had omissions. David Kendall Martin made his own study of an 1800 Census Index for Clinton County, New York (published in The American Genealogist, Vol. 54, pp. 53-54, January 1975) and found 56 out of 799 families left out and others badly misplaced. Remember, computers are at the mercy of whoever is feeding the data into them; some firms hire people to do this who have no skills in reading 17th - 19th century handwriting and can only guess at a spelling of a name. I always recommend great caution when utilizing these research tools. There is still nothing better than your own first-hand look at the original sources to evaluate the data.

7) USE FAMILY TRADITIONS AS GUIDES, NEVER GOSPEL

Family traditions, although well-intentioned, can be misleading when accepted without reservation and should be scrutinized very carefully. For example, I would venture to say that a very high percentage of the 847 Palatine German families (dare I say upwards of 70 - 80%!!??) have a tradition of Dutch not

German origin which eventually has been completely disproved by
contemporary 17th - 18th century documentation. This common
myth possibly found its origin in several ways: 1) technically,
the last continental European point of departure for the 1709ers
was indeed a Dutch one - Rotterdam in Holland; 2) thinking that
one's ancestors were Dutch may have come from a mishearing or
misunderstanding of the word "Deutsch" (German); 3) the traumas
of World Wars I and II made some descendants reluctant to claim
German roots; and 4) intermarriages with Dutch families over the
years may have confused the correct lines of ancestry. Indeed
this latter factor, what I call "crossover lines," is a very common occurence; in my experience, a family tradition often has a
germ of truth in it, but it has at some point been attached to
the wrong ancestor.

The tradition of noble birth or royal blood is always an
intriguing one, but in the case of the 500 "Poor Palatines" found
so far in Germany has absolutely no merit whatsoever. Very often
American descendants of families who eventually achieved wealth
or acquired large landholdings in the new world attributed "blue
blood" to their ancestors in Europe; however, careful German research has failed to substantiate any such traditions (the Jost[1]
Hite and Zeller families come to mind in this regard). I have always felt it took more intestinal fortitude and character to come
to America without the "silver spoon."

Another common tradition usually proved false is the old
genealogical chestnut "three brothers came to America..." This,
again, often has a bit of truth behind it, but it usually refers
to the later generations and their geographic dispersal rather
than to the first emigrant ancestor himself.

8) FOLLOW YOUR INTUITION AS WELL AS YOUR INTELLECT IN GENEALOGICAL SEARCHES

In my years of genealogical study, I cannot tell you how
many times following "a hunch" has led to all kinds of amazing
discoveries! I believe we all have this gift of a "sixth sense,"
which can be developed over the years if only we will learn to
trust our intuition. This is neither the place nor time to examine why this occurs, but it is important to stress that it does
happen and often. I have experienced this phenomenon - the sense
of knowing where to look - many times in my eleven years of German investigations with Carla, and I urge all researchers to allow themselves to be "led" in all their genealogical pursuits.
IT WORKS!!!

ACKNOWLEDGEMENTS

For the past fifteen years, I have had the pleasure of making the acquaintance of a large and distinguished group of people who share one, common bond: a deep and abiding interest in the Palatines and their story. Without their support, encouragement, and counsel, these volumes could never have been written. My relationship with many of these individuals has grown over the years from a simple correspondence to a close, personal friendship, and indeed the most wonderful side-benefit of this project has been the opportunity to meet, in person and by mail, some of the nicest and brightest people I have ever known.

To name them all would almost take another 1,300 pages, but I would especially like to thank the following individuals for their assistance:

John P. Dern, who has shared his wide experience and knowledge of matters Palatine with me for the entire duration of this project. His keen, analytical mind especially helped me in evaluating data on and structuring the New Jersey 1709ers, and his skills at translating some of the old and faded German documents found by Carla Mittelstaedt-Kubaseck in Europe were truly invaluable. John was the editor of Pastor Berkenmeyer's Albany Protocol, cited often in these volumes. He also generously kept me abreast of his ongoing investigations in English archives on his latest project, chronicling the Palatines' journey from a nautical aspect. Whenever a "find" was made concerning a 1709er in Germany via my project, John was always the first person I would tell, because I knew he CARED so much. Our relationship has spurred me on to dig deeper and set my sights higher in the course of this Palatine project, and much of what appears on these pages is the result of the input and encouragement of John Dern.

Norman C. Wittwer, Jr., who had no peer when it came to expertise regarding the New Jersey Germans. Norm was literally a "walking encyclopedia" of local history, and his multitude of friends had an ongoing crusade to make him write down the wealth of historical data he carried around in his head! He theorized probable relationships among the New Jersey Palatine families long before my German discoveries substantiated the connectives. This fine man died on Christmas Day, 1982, and his posthumous book The Faithful And The Bold, a study of those colonists who participated in the first worship service of the Zion Lutheran Church in Oldwick, New Jersey, is a tribute to his scholarship. It was the <u>heart</u> of Norm Wittwer, however, which touched me the most: whether it was trudging around the old cemeteries of Hunterdon County with him in the rain or being the lucky recipient of one of his lengthy and informative late-night telephone calls, I always felt so much better after being in contact with him; his goodness shown through!

<u>David Kendall Martin</u>, who, with his wife Pat, probably has more Palatine 1709er ancestors than anyone else I can think of. His detailed studies of several of his ancestral families, such as the Zimmermanns, the Schnells, the Failings, and the Clappers, have been very helpful to me in sorting out these complex groups. David's talents as a teacher have been put to good use in this project, and his suggestions and "red-penciling" have been most welcome. David Martin is yet an-other good example of how genealogy can turn a correspondent into a valued friend.

<u>Pastor Frederick S. Weiser</u>, the guiding light of the Pennsyl-vania German Society and the Weiser Family Association, who, for many years, has taken time from an unbelievably heavy schedule to send me genealogical materials on those 1709ers who settled in colonial Pennsylvania. These gems of informa-tion help form the cornerstones of the chapters on many of the families found in these volumes. Besides my appreciation of his scholarly contributions, I shall always be grateful to Fred for inviting me to partake of one of the best meals I have ever eaten - a Pennsylvania Dutch feast personally cooked by the good Pastor himself in his own kitchen!

<u>Annette K. Burgert</u>, who has done such an excellent job of researching the origins of the Palatine emigrants who went directly to Pennsylvania. Annette is a true "kindred spirit," in that we are both reenforcing each other's work by proving that the Germans came to America, whichever colony, in <u>groups</u> - the saving grace of both our projects! Her publica-tions, such as her <u>Eighteenth Century Emigrants - The North-ern Kraichgau</u> for the Pennsylvania German Society, will bene-fit genealogists for years to come.

<u>Arthur C. M. Kelly</u>, who has made New York colonial church-books accessible at long last to researchers everywhere. His fine <u>Palatine Transcripts</u> series enabled me to have nearly every register I need close at hand in my own home library. In addition, Art and Nancy Kelly opened their home to me on several visits to the beautiful Hudson Valley and showed me

the sights and historical landmarks of "Palatine Country."

Wayne V. Jones, who has been generous in sharing the results
of his own researches and always has been so supportive of
my efforts. Wayne not only has investigated his direct ancestral lines, but also has made detailed studies of many of
the allied and collateral lines barely touching his own family tree. As his in-depth searches covered quite a few of the
847 families who arrived in 1710, his fine work helped me
greatly in constructing many chapters of this book.

Dr. Kenn Stryker-Rodda, who has given me the benefit of his
counsel from years of experience in genealogy. He also was
kind enough to share certain New York Lutheran churches' membership and communion records with me early on in my efforts,
long before they were eventually published, and these materials
were of great use in assisting me sort out the early generations of Palatines in colonial New York.

Effingham P. Humphrey, Jr., who, from his vantage point of
being a former editor of The Pennsylvania Genealogical Magazine, has broadened my horizons and helped acquaint me with
aspects of genealogy far beyond the limits of research I
initially set for myself. As Eff is a noted critic and re-
viewer, he has been of immeasurable assistance in helping me
with the format and structure of these volumes. In addition,
his welcome letters have enlivened and brightened my days
and contributed to making genealogy so much fun for me during the past years.

Arta F. Johnson, a brilliant scholar specializing in German
families and former editor of The Palatine Immigrant, whose
books on German research have been helpful to everyone
in the field. However, it is Arta's pun-filled treatises on
imaginary ancestors (such as the humorous Begin With The
Beerswiggers) which endear her to all of us genealogical
scholars who sometimes are in need of some serious "lightening up."

Lewis Bunker Rohrbach, whose multi-volume study of the complex Rohrbach families is a model of just what good genealogies should be. Lew's background in the financial world has
been of great help to me personally, as he shared his business
acumen and experience via suggestions on just how I should
publish and then market these books.

Ralph H. Weller, who has allowed me to use his excellent trans-
scriptions of the Simmendinger Register and of records of

cemeteries in the Montgomery, Orange County, New York area. Throughout the duration of my project, Ralph continued to send me wonderful tidbits of data on all the Montgomery families which were extremely helpful in structuring the groups who resided in this particular settlement.

Klaus Wust, my co-author with Ralph Connor of The German Origins Of Jost Hite, Virginia Pioneer, who shared with me some of his vast knowledge regarding those Germans who settled in the southern colonies in the 18th century. His Shenandoah History series continues to be the prime source of reliable information on the Virginia Germans.

Others who gave me valuable help, especially in the area of New York historical and genealogical research, were:

Van Buren Lamb, Jr., my first genealogical mentor, who helped whet my appetite for research when I was a young boy.

Kathryn Schwartz Callaghan, a dear friend, so knowledgeable about her many Hudson Valley Palatine lines.

Elaine B. Liepshutz, always generous in sharing her expertise regarding the East Camp settlement.

William Kiessel, a Renaissance man, interested in just about everything historical, always supportive of my research.

Walter V. Miller, late historian of Columbia County, a genunine treasure-trove of Hudson Valley lore.

Hazel C. Patrick, a vital force behind the Herkimer County Historical Society and expert on Mohawk Valley families.

David Jay Webber, a bright young man representative of the high skills of the next generation of Palatine scholars.

Nancy Kelly, the good right hand of Arthur Kelly and, more than that, a recognized Palatine scholar in her own right.

William J. Embler, late owner of Half Moon Books, helpful in tracking down elusive source materials on the 1709ers.

Rev. Gordon Proper, an enthusiastic collector of Hudson Valley records and good friend.

William Barker, one of the new breed of genealogists whose talents extend to the computer.

Sue Van Wie, interested in many of the Palatine families, so generous in sharing her years of research with me.

Rosabelle Leetham, who always made me feel good about this project and its potential value to future generations.

__Paul W. Prindle__, a noted genealogist with many Palatine lines, always supportive and interested.

Additional genealogists of note who have been of great assistance include:

June B. Barekman, Clifford M. Buck, Frank J. Doherty, Gerde Haffner, Darby G. Livingston, William P. Mc Dermott, Maryly B. Penrose, Doris Dockstader Rooney, Kenneth Scott, Elisabeth Sharp, Deanna Vosburgh Smith, Frances Spencer, Michael Tepper, Ernest Thode, and Jean D. Worden.

I am indebted to the following specialists in Pennsylvania Palatine research:

Raymond M. Bell, Ed Berge, Schuyler C. Brossman, Marie K. Graeff, John W. Harper, Earl Ibach, Larry Neff, Frank and Helen Seubold, John F. Vallentine, and Don Yoder.

New Jersey experts who gave of their time and expertise include:

Roxanne K. Carkhuff, Donald Sinclair, and Fred Sisser III.

Canadian researchers who have helped with United Empire Loyalist materials and Palatine data include:

Dr. E. K. Fitzgerald, Dexter Hawn, Major Donald C. Holmes, Eula Lapp, John Ruch, and Thomas B. Wilson.

Besides the many German ministers who were kind enough to make their churchbooks accessible to this project, other German genealogists and archivists who gave special assistance include:

Dr. Fritz Braun, Pastor Hans Fritzsche, Dr. Hellmuth Gensicke, Herr Kätsch, Dr. Friedrich Krebs, Alfred Laun, Karl Scherer, Heinz Schüler, Baron Karl Friedrich von Frank, and Friedrich R. Wollmershäuser.

Besides Carla Mittelstaedt-Kubaseck, my chief German genealogist, among those who have done professional reasearch and special investigations for me are:

Kenneth Brown, Peter Wilson Coldham, Dr. John Dahl, Charles M. Hall, and Hendrik O. Slok.

Major financial contributors to my ongoing German searches for extended periods of time include:

The Hayner Family Association, Wayne V. Jones, Rosabelle Leetham, The Mattice Family Reunion, John Dorrance Morrell, The Snell - Timmerman Family Reunion, Myron F. Steves, and The Weiser Family Association.

Innumerable librarians and archivists have helped me over the years, both by mail and on my personal visits, including the staff at:

The Adriance Memorial Library, Herkimer County Historical Society, Holland Society of New York (especially Louis Duermyer), LDS Libraries around the world (especially the Westwood Branch, and David F. Putnam, Jr. and Kip Sperry of the Salt Lake City Main Library), Library of Congress, Montgomery County Department of History and Archives (especially Violet D. Fallone), New York Genealogical & Biographical Society (especially Carol S. Day and Mary Lou Thomas), New York Historical Society, New York State Library at Albany (especially James Corsaro in Manuscripts and History Section), and the Old Stone Fort Museum, Schoharie, New York.

The following large group of individuals was very important to the success and completion of my researches; for they supported my project by contributing funds to help continue my village-to-village investigations in Europe in return for my sending them pre-publication discoveries on their German ancestors! Among these donors were:

Kenneth Abbott, Mrs. James Adams, Margaret B. Adams, Marolyn N. Adams, Elizabeth Aikman, Marjorie C. Alderks, Dale T. Alexander, Patricia A. Allen, Lt. Col. Ervan I. Amidon, Doris Anderson, W. Cary Anderson, Helen Apgar and the Apgar Association, Norma Arnett, Blythe M. Artman, Debra Ashton, F. Jack Auringer,

Arthur C. Badorf, Naida E. Bahling, Lindsley R. Bailey, Anne M. Baines, Thelda Baker, Audrey J. Balcom, Marian G. Banker, Eleanor Baribault, Col. J. P. Barnes, Margaret Barnes, Edwin D. Barnhart, Sondra Barrett, Ann Bartle, Ernest F. Barton, Fonda Baselt, Eleanor Dice Batchelder, Paul Bateman, Carlton Baxter, Judith B. Baxter, Richard K. Beamer, Gertrude Beard, Bea Beck, Glyn Beesley, Corrine E. Bengtson, Frances M. Bellinger, Dr. Frederick Bellinger, Jane Bellinger, Terry D. Belk, Tom Bellis, James O. Bemesderfer, Tami Bendel, Carol J. Benner, Richard H. Benson, Emma S. Berg, Camilla A. Berger, Mrs. D. Betts, Ervin F. Bickley, Jr., Lora Lee Blackburn, George H. Blakeslee, William E. Bloss, William H. Blue, Georgia Bohle, O. J. Bonawit, Barbara Borst, Howard E. Boswell, Jr., Jane Bottorff, Thomas Bouck, Donald Bougher, Bill Bowman, Bob Bowman, C. Philip Boyce, M. Carolyn Boyd, Robert J. Boyd, P. F. Boyer, Samuel H. Boyer, Martin H. Brackbill, David C. Brecht, Jean Brewer, Mildred Briggs, Valoe Brink, Dee C. Brown, Jr., Mabel Warner Brown, Norvil L. Brown, Theodore L. Brownyard, Richard K. Brugler, Shirley Buirch, Mildred O. Burcalow, Mrs.

William T. Burchell, Joyce I. Burg, Virginia Burns, Bradley Burrell, Natalie R. Burrows,

Wayne R. Cain, Christa R. Caldwell, Karen Campola, Clifford R. Canfield, George F. Capes, Mrs. Emerson Capps, Donna E. Carlberg, Mr. and Mrs. Richard E. Carey, James J. Carmichael, Audrey Casari, Edwin T. Case, Mr. and Mrs. Everett Case, Bernice Chapman, Evelyn Haas Charlebois, Ellie Chellis, Pattie H. Chrisman, James N. Churchyard, Reetha Clancy, Charles H. Clapper, Ralph G. Clark, Rita Clark, Sara Clawson, Mrs. F. R. Cleaver, W. I. Clements, Glenn Cline, Charles W. Cockerline, Richard E. Coe, Frederick G. Cole, Maurice E. Comfort, Jean Condon, Ralph Connor, Wesley Contryman, Robert R. Cook, George E. Cookingham, Ford L. Coolman, Maynard A. Coons, Walter V. Corey, Meryl M. Courtenay, Robert J. Couzynse, Elsie Cox, Alfred S. Cramer, Joseph L. Cramer, Marilyn J. Cramer, Katherine Crapser, Gary A. Craver, Gordon Crouse, Valerie H. Cullison, James R. Cumming, Millard R. Curtis,

T. Dafoe, Marion H. Damiano, Madeleine K. Daniels, Marie Davidson, Winona F. Davies, Jean Day, Roberta Daymon, G. Donavan Dean, Rear Admiral B. W. Decker, Phyllis H. Decker, Calvert L. Dedrick, F. V. Dedrick, Elizabeth T. Dehn, Janice Sheidy DeLong, Joan DeLong, Jean C. Denison, Rita R. DePew, Barbara Desai, Beulah S. DeSanchez, Bruce Despain, Alice Dice, Mrs. E. M. Dickinson, Ray Dieffenbach, Donald Dills, Nancy E. Dixon, Richard Dodge, Ruth S. Dowty, Gladys Doyle, Jean P. Dreher, Jane Duffy, Marietta Duncan, Edwin C. Dunn, Elizabeth A. Dutton, Laura E. Dwyer, Hazel Dygert,

Ruby Wagley Eason, Paul I. Edic, Mrs. Alfred Ehrig, Mr. and Mrs. Edward Ekert, David N. Ellis, John Ely, Norman C. Emerick, Ward R. Emigh, Oran S. Emrich, Laura C. Enders, Frances B. Engelsen, Shirley M. Eoff, Gwenn F. Epperson, Annette Ercanbrack, S. R. Ercanbrack, Louise Erekson, George Evans, Frankie Evenhouse,

David Faris, George Goodrich Farrell, David Faux, Marjorie Fennell, Winnie Layman Fernstrom, Barbara Ferree, Elaine Feuz, Rev. J. W. Files, Gerald F. Fisher, Bernice Fitchett, V. E. Flanders, Helen Fleming, Marge Fleming, Donald Fletcher, H. R. Fletcher, Mary H. Fletcher, Katie Flory, Marie Forehan, Margaret S. Foster, Brian O. Fox, Claire E. Fox, Charles H. Fraleigh, Frances C. Francis, Leslie Francis, Gayle B. Frandsen, Mary Elizabeth Fraser, Mary Frashuer, June E. Frech, Stanley C. Freeman, Mr. and Mrs. Robert L. French, Mrs. Reese Fryer, William D. Frymire, Betty Fullerton, Ruth Coan Fulton, Dennis L. Funk,

Rob Gamble, Alice Stupp Garbutt, Muriel E. Gartner, Ardith Gau, Esther Gerhart, Roe Ann Sampson Gooch, Pauline M. Good, Margaret M. Goodwin, Richard J. Goodwin, Herbert C. Gould, John P. Gould, Cdr. W. H. Graham, Dr. Roberta Grahame, Elizabeth F. Grange, Alice L. Green, Holly K. Green, Christine Gregg, Norna Groff, Alice M. Gruber, Angus M. Gunn, Jr., Jerry Guyn,

Mark Haacke, Marjorie Haan, Eva Hoy Haelen, Donna J. G. Hafer, Alfred Arthur Hagedorn, Kenneth D. Haines, Nellie M. Hall, Patricia Haller, Dorothy G. Hamilton, Marjorie B. Hamlin, W. B. Hampshire, Rosetta F. Hancock, Louise Hanne, Carleton Z. Hanor, Edward G. Harnsberger, Rev. Harvey E. Harsh, Richard Hart, Dr. David J. Harter, Harley D. Haton, Anna F. Harvey, Martha Harvin, Douglas L. Haverly, Myrtle R. Hawken, David G. Hayner, Florence Hayner, Jennie A. Hayner, Martha Hays, Lorraine S. Healton, Eileen R. Heggen, Dorothy G. Helmer, Hugh J. Helmer, Frank Hendershot, William E. Hendershot, Janet Henjum, Frank O. Henning, Jr., Roberta Miller Herbert, Adella Travers Herring, Bernice F. Hess, Edwin P. Hess, Laurence L. Hill, Mauna Rae Hinton, Clifton Hite, Ken Hite, E. C. Hoagland, Stephanie A. Hochuli, David Hodder, Betty J. Hoffman, C. William Hoffman, Laurelynn Holladay, Mrs. Lloyd M. Holliday, Julia O. Holmes, William P. Holowesko, Herman L. Holsopple, Doris Hoover, Gary T. Horlacher, Edgar S. Housel, Fred Houts, Mildred Howard, Mrs. Neil W. Huffman, Mrs. Arthur Hunt, Charles and Harriet Hunt, Cynthia N. Hurd, Marie Hutchens, Mary Alice Hyatt,

Earl W. Ibach, Gladys Ingram, Bland Isenbarger, Lee B. Iverson,

Mrs. H. C. Jackman, Ruth H. Jensen, Joan E. Jephcott, G. Owen Johnson, Mary E. Johnson, Carl C. Johnston, Raymond S. Johnston, Don E. Jones, Ruth Harrison Jones, Helen Josefsberg, Rosemary A. Joy,

Lois Kabbe, Dennis A. Kastens, Martha H. Keate, Donald A. Keefer, Dr. Oreon Keeslar, Earl R. Keesler, Mildred N. Kell, Jane A. Kellam, Harry L. Keller, Russell E. Keller, Henry R. Kelly, J. Wesley Kemp, Bettina H. Kesteloot, Alberta Killie, Elizabeth J. Kilmer, Glenn Kilmer, Lawrence H. Kilmer, Sterling Kimball, Peggy Posson Kindall, Dr. E. L. Kinney, Riley H. Kirby, Dorthie Kirkpatrick, John Kitzmiller, Rev. Fred Klopfer, Craig P. Knapp, Janet Dunn Knox, Helen Kocher, Marion Harter Kofmehl, Norma P. Krom, Edward Kryder, Ray Kuehne, John W. Kuhl, Margaret Kwadrat,

La Verta Langenberg, Eugene D. Larson Sara La Roche, Zylphia K. Lassell, Lorna J. Laughton, Joan Lautensack, C. Edward Lawson,

Donald O. Lawyer, Mary Posson Lay, Eva Layton, Phyllis H. Leedom, Joy Lehmann, Alice Lenker, Julia G. Lesh, Blanche Lindquist, Roderick W. Link, E. Douglas Lince, Homer Loucks, Dorothy M. Lower, Gayford R. Lowrance, Peggy Lugthart, Bernice Lupinetti, Ruth Lupo,

Donald H. Mac Donald, Andrew B. W. Mac Ewen, Ann H. Mack, Joseph Linn Marino, Lawrence S. Markell, Mr. and Mrs. Louis C. Masten, Rear Admiral M. D. Matthews, Paul M. Mattice, Virginia Mattice, Ada Zellers May, Gerald A. May, Mildred F. Mc Chesney, Carol Mc Craw, Senator James A. Mc Dermott, Juanita Mc Entire, Dr. Samuel D. Mc Fadden, Dale Mc Intosh, Leslie Mc Laughlin, Jeannette Mattice Mc Morris, David Mc Neal, Nanette Meals, Shirley A. Mearns, Muriel Meeker, Roberta Meraz, Paul Merikle, Ejvor Merkley, Kory L. Meyerink, Carol M. Meyers, Mary K. Meyer, Agnes I. Michaels, Dorothy A. Mighell, Condra Miller, Doris Miller, Dorothy C. Miller, Dorothy Wallace Miller, Edmund Miller, Sharon L. Miller, Virgil G. Miller, Mrs. George F. Mills, Jeannine Minisci, John F. W. Minke III, Calvin Minkler, Robert A. Minkler, Viola E. Moak, Peytie Moncure, Austin H. Montgomery, Jr., Betty Montoye, Dr. George Moore, Barry C. K. Moravek, John D. Morrell, G. H. Morrissey, Joseph C. Mumpower, Colleen E. Murphy, Sandy Musselman, Laurel A. Mussman, Beatrice P. Myers, Gerry Myers, Marcus G. Myers, Nancy J. Myers, Judge Paul I. Myers,

Mrs. Curtis Nellis, Irene I. Nelson, Frederick T. Newbraugh, Elizabeth M. Newton, Dee Nicholson, Peg Bauder Nielsen, Ellen van Nieuwenhuyzen, Marya D. Nill, Mary Lee Northrop, Sharon Nuttall,

Elsie O'Brien, Ruth W. O'Connor, Irene Oestrike, Reva J. Oines, Shirley O'Neil, Charles M. Otstot, Shirley M. Overbagh, Theodore S. Overbagh, Al Overbough, Clara Styers Overton, Barbara E. A. Owens, Mae Z. Oxenreider,

Janis Pahnke, Emily D. Park, Lois Shaffer Pawson, Joyce Paynter, A. Delbert Peterson, Charles P. Phillips, Laura N. Phillips, Robert Pierce, Frederick T. Pike, Barbara Platt, Lois M. Plowman, Velma Pomeroy, Marilyn E. Pope, Harold F. Porter, Jr., James L. Powell, Eileen Lasher Powers, Noreen Pramberg, Donald Preston, Ruth Thomas Priest, Helen Prill, Lewis G. Proper, Kay Prothers, Josephine P. Pultz, David Putnam, Jr.,

Helen S. Race, Clara L. Radz, Janice Ramsay, Mildred Traver Ramsay, Joseph C. Ramsey, Jean Rand, Lynne Rankin, R. M. Ransom, Carol Raphael, Lucille H. Rasmussen, Mrs. John J. Ravert, Phyllis Raut, Dr. William J. Reals, Marilyn Rector, Hazel M. Reddick, Carter Reed, Herbert P. Reed, Martha G. Reed, Virginia F. W. Reichelt, Elaine Loucks Restad, Michael K. Reynolds, Donna M.

Rhodes, Jeanne Rhodes, Mrs. Lyle Richards, Betty Richmond, Willis Rickert, Richard Rider, Mary Jane Rieth, Bob Riffenburgh, James Rivenburg, Mrs. Edward Robenalt, Brian Roberts, Shirley A. Robinson, Virginia Rodefer, Dennis B. Rodgers, Doris Dockstader Rooney, Mrs. William Rossman, Delos A. Rowe, John S. Rowe, James S. Ruoff, Donna Valley Russell, George Ely Russell,

Mollie Sackman, Mrs. Sidney Salzman, Joe Anne Sanford, William B. Saxbe, Jr., Beryl V. Schindler, Margaret Dopp Schliepp, Marilyn Schneider, William J. Schock, Catherine M. Scholl, Herbert A. Schrader, James O. Schuyler, Roberta Stanulewich Schwartz, Alden M. Scrum, Jane Sekela, Harold A. Senn, Mrs. David Serviss, Esther Serviss, Milo Barrus Shaffer, Dorothy G. Shamblin, Charlotte Sharer, David Nathan Sharp, Dennis A. Shaver, Earl G. Shaver, Gloria L. Shaw, Cyrus N. Shearer, Mary Elizabeth Sheppard, John A. Sherman, Clarence R. Shirey, Morris A. Shirts, James W. Short, Hazen Shower, Harold V. P. Shultis, Lynn Shultis, Allan Signor, Bernice Silcott, Carolyn G. Simmendinger, Katharine C. Simonds, Mr. and Mrs. William J. Six, Ada Smith, Charlotte Smith, Curtis E. Smith, Dee Smith, Edwin E. Smith, Elaine Smith, Elsie Smith, Helen J. Smith, Ken Smith, Richard C. Smith, Roberta S. Smith, Shaler G. Smith, Jr., Vona E. Smith, Walter B. Smith II, Jean Snedeger, Charlotte J. Snyder, Jane Snyder, H. Martin Soward, Margaret Spalsbury, Dyan Kaye Sparling, William D. Speece, Barbara W. Speed, Maryann Stalpers, Charlotte Hilts Steele, Julie Steitz, Jean F. Rose Stephenson, T. S. Sterling, Marjorie R. Smeltzer Stevenot, Mrs. James Stevens, Lois Stewart, Ralph F. Stoudt, Eleanor W. Straffin, Charles M. Strope, Marilyn Stubbs, John Stufflebeam, Kenneth E. Stufflebeam, Lee N. Stufflebeam, Jr., Linda Stufflebean, Darryl L. Stup, William C. Summers, Carol Swinehart, Lillian Moore Swingle, H. R. Swisher, Doyle P. Swofford, Francis J. Sypher,

Donald E. Teeter, Fred W. Teetsell, Mrs. Norman Terando, Bonnie Kent Thomas, Howard Thomas, Shirley Thompson, Betty Thornburg, David L. Thurber, George G. Tillapaugh, W. C. Tinkess, R. L. Tinklepaugh, Joy C. Torgeson, Barry E. Tracy, Lavina M. Travers, Robert W. Trimmer, Rodney W. Trimmer, Irvin L. Trautman, Wallace Trumper, Dorothy H. Truscott, Dorothy J. Turner, Kathleen Turner, Shirley Turner,

Eunice Unger,

Robert W. Van Alstine, Andrew B. Van Hooser, William Van Trump, Anita B. Van Vliet, Ruth D. Van Vliet, Betty Ball Vickery, Kathleen Voshall,

Mrs. Donald P. Wache, Clinton Wagner, Dorothy E. Wahl, Herman W. Walborn, Marjorie H. Walburn, Mrs. John P. Warden, Betty L. Wardle, John Waldorf, Mrs. Donald H. Waldroff, Dorothy Wallace, Nellie B. Walrath, Steve Walrath, Theo F. Walrath, Don and Lois Walrod, C. Loral R. Wanamaker, Kathryn F. Warncke, Lois M. Warner, Peter A. Warner, Thomas Weatherwax, Richard B. Weaver, Calvin Weddle, Harry M. Weese, Fred Westcott, Alice A. Whitbeck, Dorothea D. White, Lenellen R. Whitehead, C. G. Whitely, Roger N. Whiting, Elizabeth Wiegand, Helen L. Wikoff, Josephine Jacks Wilde, Rayelle S. Williamson, Francis L. Wilson, Marion Wilson, Lyle G. Wimmer, Frank H. Wisner, Mrs. C. M. Witthoft, John F. Wolever, Terry Wolever, Karen H. Wolzanski, Patricia I. Woodstrup, Shirley Woodward, Marian L. Worrall, Helen G. Wright, Tom Wright, William E. Wright, F. C. L. Wyght,

James W. Yerdon, Pat Yott, Bernard C. Young, Eunice H. Young, Martin G. Young, Richard G. Young,

January Z. Zeh, Harvey B. Zeh, Mildred Zekoll, G. Thomas Zellers, Janet C. Zern, Robert R. Zhe, Chester G. Zimmer, Carolyn H. Zoller, Dorothy Zollweg.

****

I also wish to extend my thanks to Carla Mittelstaedt-Kubaseck, my chief German researcher, for service beyond the call of employment! Carla really has made my project, her project, and the trials and tribulations she encountered "on the hunt" are detailed in the chapter entitled "My Palatine Project."

Finally, I want to extend my appreciation to my family. My parents, Henry Z and Anne Jones, have seen my interest in genealogy grow since my boyhood, and I am grateful for their nurturing influence over the years. Most of all, however, I must thank my wife Lori Spring Jones and my daughter Amanda Falene for their understanding and loving support. During the past fifteen years I have been engaged in this project, much time and energy have had to be directed towards the completion of these volumes at the expense of my wife and daughter. As I jokingly remark when I lecture, whenever the question arose as to whether I would spend my paycheck to put food on the table to feed my "starving family" or to use my funds to pay for foreign research, like every good genealogist worth his salt, the choice was easy ... the money went to genealogy!!!; but, in all seriousness, Lori never once complained that so much of the family budget was necessarily spent on German genealogical research. In this way, she has given more than anyone else to this effort, and it is deeply appreciated!

SOME HINTS FOR USING THIS BOOK

The Palatine families of New York were recorded alphabetic-
ally in the Ledger Section of the Hunter Subsistence Lists; on
these rolls, each family was assigned a certain number from #1
through #847. As this was the original manner in which the families were registered upon their arrival, I decided to keep this
format in structuring my book.

In order to save space in the text, I have abbreviated several common genealogical terms as follows:

```
b.....................born
bpt...................baptised
bur...................buried
ca....................about/approximately
Cath..................Catholic
cem...................cemetery
ch....................children
chbk..................churchbook
Co....................County
conf..................confirmed
d.....................died
d/o...................daughter of
e.....................east
HJ....................(see below)
km....................kilometer(s)
Luth..................Lutheran
md....................married
mss...................manuscript(s)
nat...................naturalized
n.....................north
Ref...................Reformed
s.....................south
s/o...................son of
sp....................sponsor(s)/sponsored
w.....................west
wid/o.................widow/widower of
w/o...................wife of
yr(s).................year(s)
```

I have used the "HJ" citation (which stands for my own in-
itials) when, after careful study of all available materials, I
strongly believe someone "belongs" in a family structure even
though a certain baptism or marriage entry is no longer extant
to prove it, or simply to note that a particular connective or
statement is my own opinion based on this evaluation of the data.

I have seen too many genealogical books where fact and opinion are blurred, so perhaps have over-emphasized the distinction between the two; but I would rather be _over_-cautious in this regard than mislead and confuse future generations of Palatine scholars.

I have tried my best to chronicle the second and, in many cases, the third generation of Palatine descendants in the new world using extant church and civil records. The reader must note, however, that several important churchbooks which would have cleared up many genealogical questions have been missing for centuries: the early 18th century registers of Pastors Hager, van Dieren, and Ehle come to mind in this regard. The loss of church records is particularly severe for families in New York's Mohawk Valley and in New Jersey, and I urge descendants of these settlers to be wary of unsubstantiated connectives regarding their ancestors found in some of the older genealogical publications. Due to the loss of these churchbooks, realistically, the lists of children and grandchildren of the first generation 1709ers which follow cannot be considered to be complete. Hopefully, private sources (family Bibles, diaries, letters, etc.) will be found to fill in some of the gaps and clarify certain tenuous family structures.

Palatine childrens' baptisms are taken, in many families, to 1776, but not beyond that date; thus, in some groups, churchbooks after 1776 should be examined for further baptisms in the third generation. I have listed _only_ the children whose names are known by firm documentation; thus, some second generation offspring who are unnamed at Rotterdam and London in 1709 (many of whom undoubtedly died on the voyage to America) are not reflected in my sections on the second generation in the new world. All spellings are _as found_, whenever possible; this accounts for the wide variations so common with the times.

Working from my files, collections, and 17,000 documented family groupsheets has taken me four years just to type and index these volumes (this is probably the last, big genealogical compendium that will be written with_out_ the aid of a computer or word processor!); during these last years, Carla Mittelstaedt-Kubaseck has continued to search village-to-village for me in Germany. The results of her latest investigations are to be found in the two _Addenda Sections_. I urge my readers not only to study the main genealogical section for pertinent chapters on families of interest, but also to examine the alphabetised and unalphabetised Addenda for even more material to enhance and expand their lines.

I. [handwritten 1709 German manuscript — list of emigrants]

Herborn. Matthias _____ in Herborn mit Weib und — 5. Pers.
Johann Henrich _____ mit Weib — — — 4. —
Johann Henrich _____ und Mutter mit Weib — 2. —
Johann Conrad _____ mit Weib und — — 5. —
Nicol _____ mit Weib und — — 3. —
Johann Jost Wilhelmi mit Weib und — — 3. —
Johan Marcus _____ mit Weib und — — 3. —
_____ mit Weib und — — 4. —

Offenbach. Johann Andreas _____ mit Weib und — 4. —
Johann Henrich _____ mit Weib und Kind — 6. —
Hans Georg _____ mit Weib und — —

Jost Roda, Johann Henrich Schmidt, Conrad
_____, Conrad _____ von Offenbach
noch zwei Bäst, Johann Henrich _____ und
Johann Nicol Bäst mit Weib und — 3. —

Biden. Johann Conrad _____ mit Weib und — 5. —

Schönbach. Johann Jost Schmidt mit Weib und — 4. —
Jost Henrich Bast mit Weib und — 5. —
Jost Georg Bast mit Weib und — 1. —

Medenbach. _____ , Johann Jacob _____
_____ mit ihren Weibern und — 6. —

von Gonsdorf und _____. Johann _____ Müller und
Merkenbach. _____ mit ihren Weibern und — 3. —

Amdorf. Jost _____ mit Weib und — 2. —

_____. Simon _____ und Johann _____ Bast
mit 2 Weibern und Kindern — 8. —
Jost Gilt mit Weib und — 1. —

_____. Johann Friedrich Maul mit Weib und — 2. —

_____. Johann Adam Bast, Jost Henrich Bast _____
_____ , Johann _____ Bast
mit 4 Weibern und — 12. —

Rabenscheid. Henrich Thomas mit Weib und — 6. —

Summa 35 Mann, 3? Weiber, 107 Pers.

A document dated 1709 mentioning certain emigrants from the Nassau Dillenburg region, among them members of the Maul, Thomas, Bäst, Stahl, Petri, and Funck families who settled in colonial New York.

A list of emigrants from the town, found in the back of the Bonfeld church-book. Members of the Hayd (Hite), Wageli, Vogt, and Wimmer families are noted in the section dated 1710.

Photo courtesy of Klaus Wust.

The church at Bonfeld in the Kraichgau.

Interior view of
the emigrant's
ancestral church
at Bonfeld.

Emigrants from the Alzey/Oppenheim region recorded near one another on Captain Wilken's ship in the third party of Palatines at Rotterdam in 1709. Members of the Braun, Schmidt, Lesch, and Mattheus families are listed here.

Husbandmen and Vinedressers.

Names.	age.	wife.	Sons. numb.	age.	Daughters. numb.	age.	Religi.
1 Henry Mick	35	1	1	9	1	12	Refor.
	0	0	1	5	1	7	
1 Werner Spiess	50	1	1	11	1	14	Refor.
	0	0	1	5	1	9	
1 Daniel Schmidt	33	1	1	2	1	4	Refor.
1 Balzar Lesch	38	1	1	14	1	9	Luth.
	0	0	1	8	0	0	
	0	0	1	2	0	0	
1 John Jacob Walter	41	1	1	7	1	10	Refor.
1 John Weitz	35	1	1	6	1	8	Luth.
	0	0	1	1	0	0	
1 Henry Mathes	42	1	1	8	1	13	Refor.
	0	0	1	6	1	10	
	0	0	1	1	1	6	
1 Israel Brodhauer	43	1	1	6	1	9	Luth.
	0	0	1	1	1	3	
1 John Zeg	42	1	1	1	0	0	Cath.
	0	0	1	6	0	0	
	0	0	1	½	0	0	
1 Ignatius Spehd	28	1	1	2	0	0	Cath:
1 John Wagner	46	1	1	6	0	1	Cath:
	0	0	1	2	0	0	
1 Henry Kuhn	53	1	1	8	1	10	Luth.
1 John Simon Köhler	42	1	1	6	1	2	refor.
	0	0	0	0	1	2 month
18 In all 66.			13	24	16		

Many of the same Alzey/Oppenheim emigrants noted together on the
London census of Palatines later in 1709. Members of the Lesch, Schmidt,
Mattheus, and Zeh families are registered here. Courtesy of the Public Record Office, London.

		Name						
		Brought Forward		466	179	317	6	2
160		Ulrich Schmidt	£ 3 4 10 for 4	2		3	4	10
35		Niclaus Drumbaur	£ 1 1 — for 2	3		1	1	
215 48		Zacharias Flugler for his wife Gertrude Haasin	£ — 11 6 for 1	—			11	6
46		Frantz Finck	£ 1 6 — for 2	—		1	6	
43		Johannes Faeg	£ 3 12 — for 6	—		3	12	
28		Anna Maria Demuthin	£ 1 10 6 for 1	—			10	6
123		Samuel Muller	£ 1 16 6 for 2	—			16	6
159		Peter Schmidt for his Wife Margretha Elisabeth Coblentzerin	£ — 7 — for 1	—			7	—
86		Johann Georg Klug	£ 1 12 2 for 2	1		1	12	2
37		Johann Ernest Emichen	£ 1 19 10 for 2	2		1	19	10
19		Valentin Bressler	£ 3 1 8 for 4	2		3	1	8
171		Martin Seubert	£ 2 3 4 for 2	2		2	3	4
159		Niclaus Schmidt	£ 4 — 2 for 6	1		4	—	2
59		Niclaus Haas	£ 2 16 6 for 3	3		2	16	6
19		Johann Jost Braun	£ 2 2 4 for 3	5		4	2	4
103		Balthasar Lesch	£ 2 13 10 for 3	2		2	13	10
210		Johannes Zehe	£ 1 16 — for 3	—		1	16	
110		Henrich Matheus	£ 3 15 — for 4	3		3	15	—
113		Johannes Menges	£ 2 10 10 for 3	2		2	10	10
60		Peter Hagedorn	£ 3 18 — for 7	—		3	18	—
114		Henrich Mess	£ — 14 — for 2	—			14	—
12		Andreas Bergman	£ 1 14 6 for 3	—		1	14	6
27		Conrad Darrey	£ — 13 — for 1	—			13	—
64		Johann Wilhelm Hasel	£ — 4 6 for 1	—			4	6
108		Albrecht Dietrich Marterstock	£ — 13 — for 1	—			13	—
195		Andreas Weixnecht	£ 2 7 8 for 3	1		2	7	8
87		Ludwig Knab	£ 1 1 8 for 1	1		1	1	8
97		Peter Lampman	£ 2 16 4 for 3	2		2	16	4
183		Johann Georg Stumpff	£ 1 14 8 for 2	1		1	14	8
63		Anna Maria Harttmännin	£ — 13 — for 1	—			13	—
109		Johann Conrad Martin	£ — 17 6 for 1	1			17	6
94		Matheus Gundy	£ 1 7 — for 3	—		1	7	—
112		Johann Georg Nauser	£ 2 7 8 for 3	1		2	7	8
138		Johann Paul Reitschuff	£ — 2 — for 1	—			2	—
174		Johannes Speder	£ — 2 — for 2	—			2	—
57		Johann Friederich Gonderman	£ 2 16 4 for 3	2		2	16	4
51		Johann Philipp Fuchs	£ 3 19 6 for 7	—		3	19	6
25		Ludolph Coring	£ 3 6 — for 5	2		3	6	
84		Helena Kleinin	£ 1 1 8 for 1	1		1	1	8
122		Johann Conrad Muller	£ 1 14 8 for 2	1		1	14	8
61		Johann Wilhelm Hainbuch	£ 1 6 — for 2	—		1	6	—
170		Johann Adam Segendorff	£ 2 1 — for 4	—		2	1	—
		Borne Forward		579	220	396		

The Schmidt, Haas, Braun, Lesch, Zehe, and Matheus families from the Alzey/Oppenheim area recorded together on the 4 August, 1710 Hunter Subsistence list. Notice how families enrolled near each other at Rotterdam and London remained in proximity even on American lists.

A view of the church at Lorsbach, ancestral home of the 1709ers Henrich Barthel, Abraham Berg, and Henrich Pfeiffer. Note how this structure resembles the one at Arheilgen.

The church at Arheilgen, home of the New York settler Conrad Schauermann.

The town of Lang
Göns, where the
family of Johann
Wilhelm Kieffer
originated.

Interior view of the old church at Breithardt, home of the
emigrants Conrad and Ottilia Gerlach.

The Protestant
Church at Auerbach,
ancestral home of
the Batz (Potts)
family of the Hudson
Valley.

From a drawing by Wilhelm
von Harnier in 1835.

A scenic view of the Modau Valley near Nieder Ramstadt, home of the
emigrants Johann Peter Appelmann, Johann Peter Pfuhl, Nicolaus Ruhl,
and Johann Peter Heiser.

From a water-color by Carl Schweich, 1851

The church at Kettenbach/Taunus, home of the emigrants Martin and Philip Zerbe, and Jost Hermann.

The old church and burial ground at Dickschied, the original German home of the Schoharie Valley Gerhardt Schäffer family.

The church of Adelshofen, where notations concerning the emigrant Castner, Casselmann, and Weidknecht families are found.

A view of Sinsheim, home of Ludwig Wanner and other 1709ers.

The Westhofen Protestant Church, home of the Ludwig Streit family.

An old picture of the town of Alzey, which was a point of origination for many emigrant 1709ers.

Laubenheim, the village that was an ancestral home of the emigrant Scherp, Bender, Stoppelbein, Sponheimer, and Minckeler families.

Daubhausen, the point of origin for the Huguenot Bruier family who arrived with the Palatines in 1710.

Dienheim, the village near Oppenheim that was home to the emigrants Henrich Mattheus, Nicolaus Bason, and Johann Jacob Caputski.

Henry Z Jones, Jr.   Carla Mittelstaedt-Kubaseck.

Henry Z Jones, Jr. and Carla Mittelstaedt — Kubaseck meeting in 1976 to plan their German village-to-village searches.

JOHN PETER ABELMAN (Hunter Lists #1)

The ancestral home of the N.J. Appleman family was 6109 Nieder-Ramstadt (5 km. s.e. of Darmstadt; Chbks. begin 1636). On 13 Feb 1700 Johan Peter Appelmann md. Anna Magdalena Diekerhoff there "hochzeit gehalten und in der Betstunde sich cop. lassen." The Nieder-Ramstadt registers show Anna Magdalena Dickerhofin bpt. 11 Nov 1677 (no parents mentioned) and conf. in 1690; a Hans Clas and a Hans Paul Dickerhoff lived nearby at Waschenbach at that time, and either man could have been Anna Magdalena's father (HJ). Hans Peter Appelman and wife with 3 ch. were listed on Capt. Francois Warens' ship at Rotterdam 3 July 1709 (Rotterdam Lists); they were recorded five names away from Niklaas Roel, a N.Y. 1709er who also came from Nieder-Ramstadt, and seven names from Johan Peter Kneskern, an emigrant from 6107 Reinheim - 5 km. farther e. (HJ).

John Peter Abelman first appeared on the Hunter Lists 4 Aug 1710 and had 2 pers. over 10 yrs. of age and 1 under 10; the family showed 2 pers. over 10 yrs. of age on 24 Dec 1711. Peter Ableman aged 42, and Anna Margareta Ableman aged 32 were in N.Y. City in 1710/11 (Palatines In N.Y. City). Peter Appleman's name was entered on a N.J. colonial store account in 1735/36 (Janeway Account Books). The will of Peter Appleman, yeoman and weaver, of Somerset Co., N.J. was dated 27 May 1742 and probated 6 Aug 1745 (N.J. Wills: Lib. D, p. 311). Johann Peter[1] Abelmann and his wife Anna Magdalena had ch.:

1) Johann Peter[2], b. 2 April 1701 - sp.: Johan Peter Weber - miller at the Wambacher mill (Nieder-Ramstadt Chbk.).
2) Johann Michael[2], b. 2 April 1702 - sp.: Johan Michael Mertz, single man (Nieder-Ramstadt Chbk.).
3) Elisabetha[2], b. 19 Dec 1703 - sp.: Xstina Elisabetha - surviving d/o Joh. Mertz from Franckhausen (Nieder-Ramstadt Chbk.).
4) Anna Catharina[2], b. 4 Dec 1705 - sp.: Anna Cath. - w/o Nickel Engelhard (Nieder-Ramstadt Chbk.). The child was bur. 7 May 1706, aged 5 months (Nieder-Ramstadt Chbk.).
5) Maria Catharina[2], b. 13 March 1707 - sp.: Anna Elisabeth - w/o Sebastian Götz (Nieder-Ramstadt Chbk.). The child was bur. 4 Aug 1707 (Nieder-Ramstadt Chbk.).
6) Johann Daniel[2], b. 26 July 1708 - sp.: Johan Daniel Huhtman (Nieder-Ramstadt Chbk.).
7) Johann Balthasar[2], b. 25 March 1714 at the Raritons - sp.: Baldus Pickel (N.Y. City Luth. Chbk.). Baltas Appleman of Somerset Mountains appeared in the Janeway

store accounts 1735-40. Balzer Appelman signed a list
of 22 Raritan people who wanted to go to the Anglican
church 12 Feb 1740 (Hamburg Luth. Ministerial-Archiv
III, A-2-k, Nr. 41-44). He received the land where his
father lived in his father's 1742 will. The will of
his brother John[2] Appleman gives some of Balthasar's
ch.:
  i) Peter[3], in will.
  ii) Elisabeth[3], who md. Jacob Wyckoff, in will.
  iii) John[3], in will.
  iv) Christian[3], in will. There was a Christopher Ap-
      pleman with wife Margaret in the records of St.
      James Episc. Ch., Delaware, Warren Co., N.J.
8) Johannes[2], b. 3 May 1716 and bpt. at Nine Mile Run -
   sp.: Matthias Reinbold and wife Anna Eva (N.Y. City
   Luth. Chbk.); d.y.
9) Johannes[2], b. 5 April 1718 and bpt. at Middlebosch -
   sp.: Jurgen Kremer and wife Elisabeth (N.Y. City Luth.
   Chbk.). He md. 1st Ursula Teeple d/o Lucas Teeple
   (Will of Lucas Teeple) and md. 2nd an Elizabeth ____.
   John Appleman was entered on a subscription list for
   building a Luth. church at Bedminstertown (Pluckemin)
   7 Dec 1756. He often was mentioned in Pfr. Muhlenberg.'s
   Journals. His will written Aug 1801 and probated 14
   March 1807 (N.J. Wills: Lib. 1319 R) named no ch. but
   only nieces and nephews of deceased brothers.
10) Matthias[2], named as deceased brother in will of John[2].
    Matth: Appelman was bur. at "Blokemin" 15 Sept 1784
    (Zion Luth. Chbk., Oldwick, N.J.). Ch. from will of
    John[2]:
    i) David[3], in will.
    ii) Lena[3], in will.
    iii) Catherine[3], in will.

An unplaced Andreas Applemann and wife Maria Otelia had a
son Johann Lenard bpt. 5 weeks old 12 Sept 1731 at Raghgeway -
sp.: Joh: Schwalbe and wife Anna Catharina (New York City Luth.
Chbk.). He might have some connection with the Andres Abel of
Rocksberg, Morris Co., N.J. who made his will 28 Feb 1751 and
named wife Maria and sons Mathias, Paul, Michael and Andreas;
the will was proved 23 April 1751, and an inventory taken 9 April 1751 by Baltis Bickel and Jacob Shipman (N.J. Wills: Lib. 7,
p. 60).

JOHN BALTHASAR ANSPACH (Hunter Lists #2)

An old Pa. family tradition gave 6374 Steinbach/Taunus (9 km. w. of Frankfurt and 14 km. s.e. of Anspach; Chbks. begin 1676) as Balthasar Anspach's village of origin. The father of the emigrant was Johann Jacob Anspach, who d. in that region before 1700. The ch. of Johann Jacob Anspach, smith at Steinbach, were:

  Anna Catharina, bpt. 9 May 1682 - sp.: his sister-in-law
  Anna Catharina.
+ Balthasar, bpt. 26 Aug 1683 - sp.: Johann Balthasar Bender,
  single man.
  Anthonius, bpt. 1 Dec 1687 - sp.: Anthonius, s/o Johann
  Caspar Bach.
  "A son",bur. 16 May 1695.
  Anna Ursula, bpt. 29 March 1696 - sp.: Ursula, d/o Johann
  Niclas Soltzbach - Gerichtsverwandten and Kirchenältesten.
  She d. 29 Aug 1724.

The first entry for John Balthasar[1] Anspach on the Hunter Lists was on 4 Oct 1710 with 2 pers. over 10 yrs. of age in his household. Baltz Anspach of Hunterstown was a Palatine volunteer in the Canadian expedition of 1711 (Palatine Volunteers To Canada). Baltus Annsbach was nat. 3 Jan 1715/16 (Albany Nats.). He was on the roll of the independent company of the Manor of Livingston 30 Nov 1715 (Report of the State Historian, Vol. I, p. 522). Balthasar Anspach with wife and children were at Hunterstown ca. 1716/17 (Simmendinger Register), and Baltis Auspah was a freeholder of Albany Co., "northpart Livingston", in 1720 (Albany Freeholders, 1720). Paltus Unsf signed a petition dated 10 Feb 1725 and stated he had been in the Tulpehocken, Pa. region since spring of 1723 (Colonial Records of Pa., Vol. III, p. 323). Edgar H. Berge's excellent study of original landowners in the Tulpehocken area showed Johann Balthasar Anspach living almost due no. of Stouchsburg on a 402 acre farm - probably the largest farm in the area; he purchased the land from Casper Wistar on 11 Dec 1741 for the sum of £160, 16 shillings (Die Shilgrut, Vol. VI, Nr. 1). He was on the 1743 Tulpehocken list of names and bur. there 5 Dec 1748 in his 65th yr. (Tulpehocken Chbk.). His wife was named Anna Maria, and she was probably the "Mrs. Anspach, widow" who was bur. 16 March, 1750 (Tulpehocken Chbk.). Their issue were:

  1) Johann Peter[2], b. 25 Feb 1715 - sp.: Johann Peter
     Schmidt (West Camp Luth. Chbk.). He md. 4 April 1738
     Magdalene Bockenmeyer (Burkemayer) (Stoever Chbk.).

John Peter Anspach d. 25 May 1797, aged 82, and his
wife d. 10 Sept 1785, aged 65 (Christ Church Cem., Tulpehocken). Ch.:

   i) <u>Maria Barbara</u>[3], conf. 1753, aged 14¼ yrs. (Tulpe-
      hocken Chbk.).

  ii) <u>Catharina</u>[3], conf. 1760, aged 17 yrs. (Tulpehocken
      Chbk.).

 iii) <u>John</u>[3], b. 21 Nov 1745 - sp.: John Anspach and wife
      Anna Elisabeth (Tulpehocken Chbk.).

2) <u>Johann Georg</u>[2] (HJ), who appeared on the 1743 Tulpehock-
en church list. His wife was Anna Catharina, and she
probably was the "Anna Catharina, relict of ____ Anspach, who md. Jacob Katermann on Easter Tuesday 1745
(Tulpehocken Chbk.)." Known issue:

   i) <u>Johann Jacob</u>[3], conf. 1754, aged 15 yrs. (Tulpe-
      hocken Chbk.).

3) <u>Maria Barbara</u>[2], b. 28 Jan 1719 - sp.: Henrich Schaester and Anna Maria Propert (West Camp Luth. Chbk.).
She md. Hermann Batorf (Tulpehocken Chbk.).

4) <u>Johannes</u>[2], b. 26 Sept 1721 at Taar Boss - sp.: Johannes
Gans and wife Gertruyd (New York City Luth. Chbk.). He
was on the 1743 Tulpehocken list and md. Pentacostal
Tuesday 1744 Elisabeth Fischer, single d/o Sebastian
Fischer (Tulpehocken Chbk.). Johannes Anspach of Tulpehocken made his will 21 Jan 1777, and it was probated
10 May 1777 (Berks Co. Wills: Vol. 2, p. 289). Ch.:

   i) <u>Paul Jacob</u>[3], b. 25 March 1745 - sp.: Jacob Fisch-
      er and wife Maria Elisabeth (Tulpehocken Chbk.).

  ii) <u>John Peter</u>[3], b. 6 Jan 1747 - sp.: John Peter Ans-
      pach and wife (Tulpehocken Chbk.).

 iii) <u>Maria Elisabeth</u>[3], b. 5 July 1750 - sp.: Jacob
      Fischer and wife (Tulpehocken Chbk.).

  iv) <u>John Jacob</u>[3] (Will).

   v) <u>John Adam</u>[3] (Will).

  vi) <u>Eva Christina</u>[3] (Will).

 vii) <u>Johannes</u>[3] (Will).

5) <u>Leonard</u>[2], who md. 15 Nov 1748 as son of Balthes Anspach Anna Maria Etsberger, orphan d/o Jacob Etsberger
(Tulpehocken Chbk.). She may be the Mary Anspach who
was bur. 25 Nov 1816, aged 87-8-4 (Womelsdorf Luth.
Chbk.). Leonard was on the 1743 Tulpehocken Chbk.
list. Orphan's Court Records of Berks Co. (Vol. 2, p.
104) listed his surviving ch. 25 March 1774 as follows:

    i) John[3], b. 10 Oct 1749 - sp.: John Anspach and wife
       (Tulpehocken Chbk.).

   ii) Peter[3].

  iii) Philip[3].

   iv) John Jacob[3].

    v) Anna Catharina[3].

   vi) Margaret[3].

  vii) Elizabeth[3].

 viii) Maria[3].

CONRAD ANTHES' WIDOW (Hunter Lists #3)

Conrad Anthes's Widow often was mentioned on the Hunter
Lists 1710 - 1712 near other emigrants who originated in the
Pfalz (i.e. Mattheus Kuntz, Michael Brack, and Peter Klopp) (HJ).
Hans Conrad Anthes and wife Anna Margaretha were found at 6554
Meisenheim (20 km. s.w. of Bad Kreuznach; Chbks. begin 1607,
Ref.). Hanß Conrad Antes from Breidheim (Breitenheim) was conf.
in 1684, aged 18 yrs. Conradt Anthes md. 11 July 1691 Anna Marg-
aretha Stöblin (?); her surname in the marriage entry is diffi-
cult to read, but a 1708 bpt. called her Steckelin.

Conrad Anthes's Widow first appeared on the Hunter Subsistence Lists 4 July 1710 with 3 pers. over 10 yrs. of age and 1
under 10 yrs.; her last listing was 13 Sept 1712 with 2 pers.
over 10 yrs. and 1 under 10 in the household. The ch. of Conrad[1]
Anthes and Anna Margaretha were:

  1) Anna Elisabetha[2], bpt. 21 Aug 1691 - sp.: Philip Anthes
    ..., Cathr. - w/o Conradt Anthes, and Anna Elisabeth -
    d/o Thomas Schiel (Meisenheim Chbk.).

  2) Johann Jacob[2], bpt. 30 July 1692 - sp.: Conrad Gießler,
    Hans Jacob Gießler, and Juditha - ... Hans Michel Anthes
    ... from Breidenh. (Meisenheim Chbk.).

  3) Johann Nicolaus[2], bpt. 8 Feb 1694 - sp.: Hans Conrad Anth-
    es, Nickel Gudemann ..., and Frau Maria Fürstenwärter
    (Meisenheim Chbk.).

  4) Susanna[2], bpt. 21 June 1695 - sp.: Hans Georg Anthes -
    cooper, Anna Elisabeth - w/o Philip Anthes, and Susanna
    - d/o Abraham Herman (Meisenheim Chbk.).

  5) Anna Elisabetha[2], bpt. 4 Oct 1697 - sp.: Peter Geres,
    Anna Cathrina - w/o Conrath Antheß the younger, and Anna
    Elisabetha - w/o Peter Hertz, all living at Breitenh.
    (Meisenheim Chbk.).

  6) Johann Wendel[2], bpt. 10 Jan 1700 - sp.: Joh. Asmus Anthes
    - s/o the cooper here, Hans Wendel Schill, and Anna Engel

- w/o Hans Adam Einrich (Meisenheim Chbk.).

7) <u>Johannes</u>[2], bpt. 11 March 1702 - sp.: Anna Margreth ...
(Meisenheim Chbk.). The bpt. entry adds "+" (HJ).

8) <u>Johann Conrad</u>[2], bpt. 2 Aug 1704 - sp.: Conrad Geißer -
Gemeinsmann, Hans Adam Mohr - Gemeinsmann, and Anna Marg.
- w/o Johan Gers (?), Gemeinsmann (Meisenheim Chbk.).

9) <u>Philipp Jacob</u>[2], b. 19 May 1708 - sp.: Hans Jacob Geißler,
Philipp Anthes - Gemeinsmänner at Breitenau, Elisabeth
Ottilia - w/o H. Velten Heyes teacher's ..., and Maria
Catharina - w/o Hans Wilh. Schiel, Gemeinsmann (Meisen-
heim Chbk.).

JACOB ARNOLD (Hunter Lists #4)

German searches revealed several individuals with the same
name as the 1709er Jacob[1] Arnold: 1) a Johan Jacob Arnold md.
Dom. XX Trin.: 1705 Veritas (?) Ritterstorf at 5900 <u>Siegen</u>; 2) a
H. Joh. Jacob Arnoldt md. Sybilla Elisabetha Weinrich 18 May 1702
at 6472 <u>Altenstadt/Wetterau</u>; and 3) a Johann Jacob Arnold, s/o
Balthasar Arnold of Ladenburg, md. Maria Elisabetha Schefer, d/o
H. Hans Jacob Schefer - citizen here, 25 March 1704 at 6713 <u>Frein-
sheim</u> and had a daughter Dina bpt. 15 Feb 1705 there. However, no
firm connective between these men and the N.Y. family has been
established (HJ).

Jacob Arnold made his initial appearance on the Hunter Lists
4 July 1710 with 4 pers. over 10 yrs. The family was recorded with
6 pers. over 10 yrs. 4 Aug 1710, 3 over 10 on 31 Dec 1710, and
5 pers. over 10 yrs. 24 June 1711. ___ Arnold: 1 man, and 2 women,
were in Ulster Co. in 1710/11 (West Camp Census). Jacob Arnold
and wife Elisabetha were at Beckman's Land ca. 1716/17 (Simmendinger Register). Jacob Aarnhout and wife Maria Margareta sp. Johan Parleman at Remobuch in 1720 (N.Y. City Luth. Chbk.). The ch.
of Jacob[1] Arnold were:

1) <u>Christina</u>[2] (HJ), conf. at Newtown Easter 1713 (West Camp
Luth. Chbk.).

2) <u>Peter</u>[2] (HJ), conf. 1717, date and place struck through
(N.Y. City Luth. Chbk.). The will of a Peter Arnout of
Goshen, Orange Co. was dated 20 March 1764 and probated
10 June 1764 (Fernow Wills #22).

A later Jacobus Arnold with wife Anna Margaretha is found
in the Albany Ref. Chbk. 1739 - 1759; however, sp. suggest that
he was a later arrival in colonial N.Y. (HJ).

JOHN ADOLPH ARTHOPOEUS (Hunter Lists #5)

Johann Adolph Artopaeus was found among a prominent family of clergymen at 5580 Traben-Trarbach (16 km. e. of Wittlich; Chbks. begin 1609 at Trarbach). The earliest known forefather of the American line was Herr Johann Nicolaus Artopoeus, Pfarrer and Inspector at Trarbach, who d. 29 April 1666, aged 62 yrs.; his wife Johannata Elisabetha d. 12 June 1642, aged 33 yrs. Their ch. were:

> Johann Jeremias, b. 11 Jan 1634 - sp.: H. Jeremias Heidericum Orthium (?) - Pfarrer at Castellaun, and H. Johannum Pauschium - Pfarrer at Kirn ...
>
> Jacobus Joachimus, b. 7 Oct 1635 - sp.: Jacobus Schneit, Joachimus Brunovius, and Ottilia - wid/o Michael Artopoe.
>
> + Johann Valentinus, b. 9 June 1637 - sp.: Joh. Valentinus Corvinus ..., Leonhardt Glitzer - Pastor Wolfensis, H. Hans Jacob Meurer - Bürgermeister, and Regina Maria - w/o H. Johannis Glitz.

Herr Joh. Valentinus Artopoeus, Pfarrer at Rood (Roth) in Ambt Castellaun and s/o H. J. Nicolaus Artopoeus - Pfarrer and Inspector, md. Anna Margaretha, d/o Albert Pistoris - citizen and church-censoris here, 5 May 1663. Anna Margretha, d/o Albert Pistoris and wife Margretha, was bpt. Petri & Pauli: 1646; Albert Pistoris d. 10 June 1674. The ch. of Herr Johann Valentinus Artopoeus and wife Anna Margaretha were:

> Johanna Elisabetha, bpt. 6 April 1673 - sp.: Elisabeth - ... Johann Artopoeus, Brigitta Elisabetha Adam, and Johannes Beust (?).
>
> + Johann Adolph.

Johann Adolph Artop., s/o the late H. Joh. Valentin Artop. - formerly Pastor at Pferdsfeld, md. Martha Catharina, single d/o the late H. Johannes Franck (?) - formerly Pastor at Lotzhausen, 22 May 1691. Johann Adolph Artopaeus, citizen, brewer, and widower, md. (2nd) 29 Jan 1704 Barbara Elisabetha, wid/o the late Nickel Kaass - citizen and shoemaker. Barbara Elisabeth, d/o the late H. Philipp Daniel Metzler, md. Hans Nicolaus Kaass, widower, 9 Feb 1694; Nickel Käss was bur. 20 May 1703, aged 56 yrs. Herr Philips Daniel Metzler md. Maria Agnes Nebel 15 Nov 1664.

John Adolph[1] Arthopoeus made his initial appearance on the Hunter Lists 1 July 1710 with 3 pers. over 10 yrs. of age; his last entry was 4 Aug 1710 with the same numbers. Joh. Adolph Artopoeus, Jonathan Chamboray, and wife Barbara Elisabetha sp. Johann Jacob Schnitt in 1710 at N.Y. (West Camp Luth. Chbk.); I believe that the wife Barbara Elisabetha in this entry belongs to Johann

Adolph[1] Arthopoeus and not Chamboray (HJ). The ch. of Johann Adolph[1] Arthopoeus were:

1) <u>Johann Adolph[2]</u>, bpt. 29 Jan 1692 - sp.: H. Adolph Henrich Weyland, Hans Matthes Franck, and Anna Margaretha Artopaeus ... (Traben-Trarbach Chbk.).

2) <u>Sophia Maria[2]</u>, bpt. 12 April 1693 - sp.: H. Georg Wilhelm Duncker, Magd. Anna Ebner, and Maria Catharina Finck (Traben-Trarbach Chbk.).

3) <u>Regina Maria[2]</u>, bpt. 19 Dec 1694 - sp.: H. Joh. Jacob Artop. - Pastor at Idar, Regina Margaretha Wagner, Hans Peter ..., and Maria Engel ... (?) (Traben-Trabach Chbk.).

4) <u>Philip Daniel[2]</u> (HJ), aged 13 when he was bound to Jno. Johnston of N.Y. as a Palatine orphan 21 Sept 1710 (Apprenticeship Lists). The child's unusual combination of Christian names suggests the possibility that he might be an adopted s/o Johann Adolph[1], named for his 2nd wife's father Philips Daniel Metzler and from her 1st marriage to Nickel Kaass (HJ).

5) <u>Daniel[2]</u> (HJ), 12 yrs. of age when bound to Jno. Johnston of N.Y. 21 Sept 1710 (Apprenticeship Lists). He also may have been adopted (HJ).

PHILIPP ASMER (Hunter Lists #6)

The German home of the Asmer family was given by Joshua Kocherthal 31 Jan 1714 when Peter Christian of Madagascar, a servant of Master John Von Loon, md. Anna Barbara, wid/o Philipp As(m)er of Langen on the Bergstrasse (West Camp Luth. Chbk.). The emigrant was documented at 6073 <u>Egelsbach</u> near Langen (12 km. n. of Darmstadt; Chbks. begin 1650). Although not mentioned on an inhabitant list of 1705, the registers there noted Philips Aßmer and wife Anna Barbara there in 1709.

Philipp Asmer made his initial appearance on the Hunter Rolls 4 July 1710 with 2 pers. over 10 yrs. of age in the family. John P. Dern's <u>Albany Protocol</u> details the history and genealogy of Peter Christian and Asmer's widow. Anna Barbara Asmer Christian d. by Feb 1716, when Peter Christian md. 2nd Elisabeth Brandemoes, a Paltser woman (N.Y. City Luth. Chbk.). A child of Philipp[1] Asmer and Anna Barbara was:

1) <u>Anna Barbara[2]</u>, b. 19 Jan 1709 - sp.: Anna Barbara - w/o Joh. Wilhelm Schlapp (Egelsbach Chbk.).

AGNES BACHES (Hunter Lists #7)

Agnes, wid/o Sebastian Backus of Roth by Bingen, md. Just
Henrich Schaster 5 Sept 1710 (West Camp Luth. Chbk.). The entries for 6531 Roth (8 km. w. of Bingen) are contained in the
chbks. of 6534 Stromberg (4 km. farther w.; Chbks. begin 1646).
Sebastian Backes, single man from Roth, md. Agnes Seibert, single girl from Wartenstein in May 1706. Their ch. were:

1) Johan Philippus[2], b. at Roth and bpt. 3 April 1707 -
   sp.: Philipp ... from Ober Haußen, Johan Mattheus Meyer
   - single man from Genheim, and Anna Christina Maltzing
   from here.

2) Anna Elisab.[2], bpt. 11... 1708 - sp.: Johannes Culmann,
   Susanna Backes, and Anna Elisab. Seibel from Ob.hausen.

(Susanna) Agnes probably was the d/o Hans Cunradt Seibert from
Schweppenhausen who md. 24 Jan 1665 Elisabeth Barth; among
their ch. were Johan Niclaus - bpt 17 March 1667, Joh. Philipp
- bpt 13 Aug 1671, Anna Margaretha - bpt. 15 Jan 1674, Johann
Jacob - bpt. 5 Aug 1676, Anna Sabina - bpt 18 Oct 1684, and
Hanß Peter - bpt. 17 April 1688. The family name appears to
have been written both Seibert and Seibel at Stromberg and environs. A fascinating letter "to Susannah Agnes Schafferin -
living in Rhynbeck, Dutchess Co., in the Colony of N.Y. in
North America, written from Oberhausen 20 March 1750" recently
has come to light and, as translated by Ottilie E. Hoss of Red
Hook, N.Y., reveals much information on the Seibert/Seibel family who stayed behind in Germany:

> "Greetings to you, beloved sister Susannah Agnes:
> Your letter of 5 Dec 1749 was received on 11 March
> 1750, and we were very happy to receive the good news of
> your well-being, also of your six children's. We also
> received the sad news that for the second time you be-
> came a widow which saddened our hearts greatly, and we
> are asking God that He may on you and on your beloved
> children in future years graciously bestow His Bless-
> ings. As far as we are concerned and the all around
> surroundings - your beloved mother d. in 1716 and your
> father changed time with eternity in 1719. Your bro-
> ther Niskemann (?) d. unmarried, also your brother Con-
> rad who was three yrs. married and left one son. Your
> brother Culmann and wife also died; they left five ch.
> - four daughters and one son - who are still living,
> two are married and the others are yet single. Your
> brother Phyllip d. a short time ago. He had by his
> first marriage one daughter, who also is married and
> has seven ch. By his second marriage he had four ch.
> One son d., one son and one daughter are married and
> one daughter is single. Your brother Nicolaus is still
> living. His first wife d., from whom he had two sons -
> both living and married. The oldest one has five ch.,
> the younger one two, both living and married. In his
> second marriage he had no ch. May God protect and

bless them both. Your sister Elizabeth Catherina is
still living. Her husband Felix has d. They had two
ch., one son who d. and left two ch, one daughter is
still living and has three ch. Your brother Jacob is
also still living as long as God keeps him. He is married the second time. In his first marriage he had
nine ch: two daughters are still living - the rest d.
in childhood. The two living daughters are both in
their second marriage. In your brother's second marriage, he had six ch., two d. - four are still living
at home. He now lives at Gonnweyler (Hennweiler?)
where he exchanged his house and grounds with someone
from there. As far as we are concerned (our life and
support) so are you dear sister well informed that
many brothers make the belt tied, as the saying goes.
In the inheritance we have put your name on a paper,
ours also, but later on - when we didn't know whether
you were living or dead, we divided it amongst us,
but with the understanding that if you should be living, we would return it to you. If you want your inheritance now, we are all willing to give it back to
you. Should you decide to leave it to us as is, we
would not only give our devoted thanks to you, but
also to our heavenly father and your children and cousins. You surely know that all of us here are toiling
and sweating hard to keep existing. But we thank God
for being still able to do this. The land is used up
so much that hardly an existance is possible and the
township is growing so fast. In Oberhausen are forty
churchmembers and in Gonnweyler eighty. The land is
in smaller portions now, and there is really nothing
to praise about. We don't know of anything more to
write from here. We commit you and your beloved ch.
into the hands of Almighty God; and we could wish
nothing more than to see you and your children. But
if not in our lifetime so do we have the eternal hope
to see you in Heaven.

So we are (all of us) sending you a thousand
Greetings! Your beloved brothers and sister,

John Nicholas Söybol, Jacob Söybol and Elisabeth
Catherina (nee Söybol)

P.S.: If you will honor us with another letter to let
us know if you received this, we are eternally thank-
ful.

Sebastian[1] Baches' widow Agnes Baches was listed only once
on the Hunter Lists on 4 Oct 1710 with 1 pers. over 10 yrs. of
age in the household.

JOHANNES BÄHR (Hunter Lists #8)

The ancestral home of Johannes[1] Bähr was recorded in the
West Camp Luth. Chbk. when Johann Beer, widower of Dicksener in
commune Oppenheimer in the Pfaltz, md. 4 Dec 1711 Magdalena,
wid/o Lucas Haug of Lichtenberg in the commune Zweybrucken.
The actual village of origin was 6501 Dexheim (4 km. w. of Oppenheim; Chbks. begin 1675, Ref.). The earliest known ancestor
of the American line was Hans Georg Bähr, whose wife Elisabetha

was bur. 24 Aug 1687. Their ch. were:

> Susanna, bpt. 31 Dec 1676 - sp.: Susan, single d/o the
> late Stephan Scherle. She was bur. 1 Sept 1689.
> + Johannes.
> Marinus, bpt. 20 March 1681 - sp.: Marinus Krug - citizen
> here. He was bur. 29 Oct 1689.

Johannes Bähr, s/o the late Hans Georg Bähr - formerly citizen
at Dexheim, md. 24 Feb 1699 Helena Schneider, single d/o the
late Peter Schneider - formerly citizen at Holtzheim in the
Grafschaft Braunfels. 6301 Holzheim (10 km. s. of Gießen;
Chbks. begin 1653) was the ancestral home of Helena Schneider
Bähr, and the registers there show that Johann Peter Schneider
was bur. on the 2nd day Witsuntide 1692, and that Juliana - w/o
Johann Peter Schneider - was bur. 12 March 1699. Helena, w/o
Johannes Bär of Dexheim, was bur. 10 March 1705, aged 37 yrs.

John Bähr aged 38, with his wife, and sons aged 8, 6, and
3, Ref., husbandman and vinedresser were enrolled in the 1st
arrivals at London in 1709 (London Lists). Johannes Bähr was
reported on the Hunter Lists 1 July 1710 with 2 pers. over 10
yrs. of age and 2 under 10. The 4 Aug 1710 entry read 2 pers.
over 10 and 3 under 10 until 24 June 1711 when 3 pers. over 10
and 1 under 10 were noted. Johannes Bähr and Magd: Haukin with
6 pers. over 10 and 2 under 10 were listed 24 Dec 1711. Johannes Baer aged 40, Anna Baer aged 27, John Fred. Baer aged 10,
and John Jacob Baer aged 4 were in N. Y. City in 1710/11 (Palatines In N. Y. City). Johannes Bär with his wife and 4 ch.
were on the Raritan ca. 1716/17 (Simmendinger Register). There
was a John Bear taxed for land at Shawongonck in 1720/1 (Ulster
Co. Tax Lists). The ch. of Johannes[1] Bähr bpt. at Dexheim:

> 1) Friederich[2], b. 6 April 1701 - sp.: Friedrich Bär - al-
> so inhabitant at Dexheim.
> 2) Johan Georg[2], b. 11 Feb 1703 - sp.: Joh. Georg Christ,
> servant at the time at Mrs. Schmidt's. Hans Jerick
> Paer aged 8, son of Johan[S] Paer, was bound to Rich[d]
> Smith of Smithtown 26 Sept 1710 (Apprenticeship Lists).
> 3) Johann Jacob[2], b. 3 Nov 1706 - sp.: Johann Jacob Jäger,
> the baker of the community. A Jacob Pear of Papack near
> Hannis Hager and James Mc Cain bought items for Lanah
> Peer in N.J. in 1739 (Janeway).

JACOB BÄHR'S WIDOW (Hunter Lists #9)

The German home of the 1709er Jacob Bähr was at 5905 Ober-
Fischbach (8 km. w. of Siegen; Chbks. begin 1670). The family

descends from <u>Johannes Bär</u>, who d. at Niederndorf 1 March 1724,
aged 79 yrs.; his 1st wife Agnes d. at Niederndorf 8 June 1707,
aged 63 yrs. Johannes Bär, shepherd and widower, md. 20 June
1710 Anna Catrin, d/o the late Gerlach Schmidt from Oberheus-
ling, and Anna Catharin , wid/o the late Johannes Bär d. 31
July 1724, nearly 56 yrs. old. Issue from 1st marriage:

> <u>Johannes</u>, b. 1672 - bur. 1676.
>
> <u>Hana</u>, b. 1675 - md. Johannes Hoffmann 1696.
>
> + <u>Jacob</u>, bpt. 17 Nov 1678 - sp.: Jacob Cuntz at Oberfischb.
>
> <u>Eberhard</u>, b. 1681.
>
> <u>Else Margrethe</u>, b. 1687.
>
> <u>Anna Ela</u>, b. 1690.

Jacob Bär, s/o Johannes Bär from Niderndorff, md. Anna Gela,
d/o the late Hans Jacob Siebel from Oberfischbach 25 Jan 1704.
Hans Jacob Seibel, widower from Niederfischbach, md. Sept 1670
Catharina, wid/o Henrich Bruder; Anna Gela Siebel was the
"daughter" bpt. 15 June 1676 to this couple and sp. by Gela,
wid/o Henrich Loos at Heusberg. Hans Jacob Siebel d. 26 Nov
1694. The last reference found in Germany of Jacob[1] Bär was on
an inhabitant list of Oberfischbach dated 1708 when Jacob Bär,
his wife Gela and son Hermannus were mentioned as aus dem Land
(out of the country).

Jacob Bähr, recorded next to Peter Giesler and Hyeronimus
Weller who also were emigrants from Oberfischbach, was on the
Hunter Lists 4 Aug 1710 with 2 pers. over 10 yrs. of age and 2
under 10. The 31 Dec 1710 list mentioned Jacob Bähr's widow
with 2 pers. over 10 yrs. and 3 under 10; the 24 June 1711 list
noted Jacob Bähr's widow Elizabeth with only 2 pers. over 10
yrs. of age in the household. The name Elizabeth suggests a
2nd marriage for the emigrant Jacob Bähr. Elisab. Bayherin:
1 woman and 1 boy 8 yrs. and under were at West Camp in 1710/11
(West Camp Census). The ch. of Jacob[1] Bähr and Anna Gela were:

1) <u>Johann Diederich</u>[2], bpt. 15 Feb 1705 - sp.: Hans Diedrich Schneider, single. The child d. 1705, aged ¼ yrs.
   (Oberfischbach Chbk.).

2) <u>Hermannus</u>[2], bpt. 24 Oct 1706 - sp.: Hermannus Bruder
   (Oberfischbach Chbk.) Harmanus Bear was noted in the King-
   ston Trustees Records (Book 4, p. 213), and in land
   records in 1754 when Jury Wilhelm Dederick of West Camp
   deeded property to Harmanus Beer (Albany Co. Deeds,
   Vol. 7, p. 341). Hermannus Beer, son of the late Jacob
   Beer, md. 2 May 1729 Maria Magdalena Wixheuser, d/o
   Peter Wixheuser of Newtown, at Newtown (N.Y. City Luth.

Chbk. and Loonenburg Luth. Chbk.). Their ch. were:

    i) <u>Wilhelmus</u>[3], b. 17 Dec 1732 and bpt. Kisket. - sp.:
Johan Wilhelm Elig and his father Andreas Elig,
and Eva Maria Hertel (Loonenburg Luth. Chbk.).

   ii) <u>Christina</u>[3], b. 11 May 1735 and bpt. Kisket. - sp.:
Henr. Fees and wife Christina (Loonenburg Luth.
Chbk.). She md. Wilhelm Dieterich by 1764 (HJ).

  iii) <u>Annatje</u>[3], b. 30 March, 1738 and bpt. Newton - sp.:
Hannes Hertel and Anna Julia Becker (Loonenburg
Luth. Chbk.). She md. Simon Rockefeller by 1763
(HJ).

   iv) <u>Adam</u>[3], b. 17 Nov 1740 and bpt. Newton - sp.: Adam
Hertel and wife Gertrud (Loonenburg Luth. Chbk.).
Adam Behr md. 12 Nov 1763 Anneke (or Janneke)
Spaan (Loonenburg Luth. Chbk.) and had issue bpt.
at Germantown Ref., Katsbaan Ref., West Camp
Luth., and Loonenburg Luth. churches. Adam d. 20
Nov 1828, aged 88 yrs. (West Camp Luth. Cem.).

    v) <u>Georg</u>[3] (HJ), md. 19 June 1763 Catharina Maurer
and had ch. bpt. at Germantown Luth. and Ref.,
West Camp Luth., Katsbaan Ref., and Loonenburg
Luth. churches.

   vi) <u>Margriet</u>[3], bpt. 1 Nov 1743 - sp.: Jacob Eigenaar
and wife Margriet Maures (Katsbaan Ref. Chbk.).
She md. Wilhelm Rockefeller by 1768 (HJ).

Hermanus Behr, widower of Newtown, md. Maria Eva
(Spohn), wid/o Frid Martens, 5 May 1747 (Loonenburg
Luth. Chbk.). Issue of 2nd marriage:

  vii) <u>Jacob</u>[3], b. 5 June, 1748 and bpt. Kisket. - sp.:
Philip Spoon and Lisabeth Spoon (Loonenburg Luth.
Chbk.).

 viii) <u>Mareitgen</u>[3], bpt. 1 April 1750 - sp.: Adam Span
and Mareitgen Span (Germantown Ref.). She md.
Wilhelm Breyn by 1772 (HJ).

   ix) <u>Catharina</u>[3], bpt. 11 July 1752 - sp.: Pieter Laux-
er Catharina; in their place Adam Spaan Mareitje
(Loonenburg Luth. Chbk.). Cath. Bear, late relict of Ludwigh Russel, d. 1842, aged 91 (West
Camp Luth. Cem.).

    x) <u>Henrich</u>[3], b. 10 July 1754 - sp.: Joh. Birgert and
Liesabeth (Loonenburg Luth. Chbk.). (Confusing b.)

   xi) <u>Liesabeth</u>[3], b. 3 March 1757 - sp.: Willem Behr
and Christina Behr (Loonenburg Luth. Chbk.).

The mother on the last four bpts. was called Maria.

14

ANNA CATHARINA BALLIN (Hunter Lists #10)

On 5 Sept 1711 Pastor Kocherthal recorded the marriage of
Christoph Bellross, of Schwerin in the duchy of Mecklenburg,
and Maria Ottila Ball, d/o the late Johann Ball of Magenheim in
the commune Altzeyer, Pfaltz (West Camp Luth. Chbk.). The Ball
ancestral village proved to be 6719 Mauchenheim (4 km. s.w. of
Alzey; Chbks. begin 1580, Ref.). The earliest known ancestor
of the American line was Hans Ball, who was bur. 27 March 1676.
His wife Margret d. 9 July 1666. Church records show Hans Bahl
was a Gemeinsmann in 1628 in the village, and Ältester in 1654.
Ch. of Hans Ball and Margret were:

> Susanna, bpt. Dom. Quasimodogeniti: 1620 - sp.: Susanna,
> w/o Hans Philips Eichenlaub.
> Appolonia, bpt. 29 April 1621 - sp.: Appolonia, single d/o
> Wendel Bollenbach. The child d. 24 Aug 1621, aged 18
> weeks.
> Anna Maria, bpt. 29 Sept 1622 - sp.: Anna Maria, w/o Hans
> B...
> Catharina, bpt. 24 Oct 1624 - sp.: Catharina, w/o Thoma
> Schuchart.
> + Johan Valentin, bpt. 16 July 1625 - sp.: Valentin Bollen.
> Margaretha, bpt. Feb 1629 - sp.: Johan Danfulser (?) and
> his wife Marg.
> Elisabeth, bpt. 23 Jan 1631 - sp.: Elisabeth, d/o Georg
> Ramser.
> Hans Martin, as s/o Hans Ball md. Aug-Sept 1655 Anna Mar-
> ia Knebel, d/o the late Hans Christ Knebel. Martin Ball
> d. 22 March 1702, and his widow Maria was bur. 23 Jan 1710
> aged ca. 80 yrs.
> Hans Henrich, as s/o Hans Ball md. 15 April 1662 Cathar-
> ina, d/o Johannes Gülcher.

The American line was carried on by Johan Valentin Ball and his
wife Margaretha Heintz who had ch.:

> + Johannes, bpt. 22 June 1654 - sp.: Joh. Gülcher.
> Samuel, b. 14 April 1656 - sp.: H. Samuel Pitisen, s/o
> H. Samuel Pitisen (?) - the Pastor at Mauchenheim.
> Hans Jacob, b. 29 July 1658 - sp.: Hans Jacob Voltz from
> Melsheim (Mölsheim).
> Melchior, b. 9 June 1660 - sp.: Melchior from Kettem (Ket-
> tenheim - ?).
> Maria Barbara, b. 8 Sept 1661 - sp.: Maria, w/o Hans Jacob
> Vols from Mölßheim.
> Margaretha, b. 5 Nov 1664 - sp.: Marg., w/o Hans Bell.

<u>Hans Henrich</u>, b. 11 Dec 1667 - sp.: Hans Henrich Ball.
<u>Elisabeth</u>, bpt. 5 July 1668 - sp.: Elisabeth, wid/o Velten
Heintz.
The Mauchenheim chbk. mentioned that six ch. of Hans Valentin Ball d. during five weeks in 1666 during an outbreak
of pestilence.

Johannes[1] Ball's widow first was noted on the Hunter Lists
as Anna Catharina Ballin on 30 June 1710 with 3 pers. over 10
yrs. of age and 1 under 10; her last entry was 25 March 1711
with 4 over 10 yrs. of age in the family. The ch. of Johannes[1]
and Anna Catharina (Adam? - HJ) Ball bpt. at Mauchenheim were:

1) <u>Anna Maria</u>[2], bpt. 25 May 1687 - sp.: Ottilia, w/o Nicklas Hoffmann from Offenheim (Mauchenheim). Since this
child's baptismal sp. was named Ottilia, I believe that
her full name may have been Anna Maria Ottilia, and it
may have been she who md. Christoph Bellross in 1711.

2) "<u>A son</u>"[2], bpt. uff Cantate 1699 - sp.: Peter Adam, the
brother-in-law of the father from Offenheim. Due to
the sp. named Peter, this child probably was the Peter
Ball who carried on the family name in the Schoharie
Valley (HJ). Johan Peter Baal was nat. at Albany 13
March 1715/16 (Albany Nats.). John Pieter Ball was a
member at the Schoharie Ref. church 1 April 1743 and d.
by 4 Nov 1753. He and his wife Anna Margaretha had ch.:

   i) <u>Anna Dorothea</u>[3] (HJ), who md. Johann Peter Fischer
   by 1751 (HJ).

   ii) <u>Catharina Elisabeth</u>[3] (HJ), who joined the Schoharie
   Ref. church 14 May 1740.

   iii) <u>Johannes</u>[3]. He joined the Schoharie Ref. church 14
   May 1740 and md. by 1749 Maria Dietz. He md. 2nd
   as widower and s/o the late Piter Ball on 20 Aug
   1768 Geertuid Smid, d/o Johannes Smid of Dietz
   (Schoharie Ref. Chbk.). Johannes Ball was Chair-
   man of the Committee of Safety in Schoharie during
   the revolution and had nine ch. by his 1st wife
   and ten ch. by his 2nd wife (<u>Simm's History of
   Schoharie</u>, p. 213).

   iv) <u>Jacob</u>[3], bpt. 20 March 1733 - sp.: Jacob Endes and
   Elisabetha Sophia (Schoharie Luth. or Ref. Chbk.).
   Jacob Ball, s/o the late Piter Bal, md. Maria El-
   isabeth Mann, d/o Piter Mann, after banns of 4 Nov
   1753 (Schoharie Ref. Chbk.). He had joined the
   Schoharie Ref. church 15 April 1750. Jacob[3] was a

tory at Beaverdam (<u>Simm's History of Schoharie</u>, p. 209) and a member of Butler's Rangers at Niagara in Canada (<u>Loyalists In Ontario</u>, p. 14).

v) <u>Johann Friederich</u>[3], b. 13 July 1737 and bpt. Schohari - sp.: Henrich Schneider, and Gertrude, d/o Niclas Eckers (Loonenburg Luth. Chbk.). He md. Eva Zee, d/o Johannes Zee, 12 Sept 1767 (Schoharie Ref. Chbk.).

vi) <u>Johann Henrich</u>[3] (HJ), a member at Schoharie Ref. church March 1752. He md. 22 Feb 1763 Maria Elisabeth Thijts (Dietz? - HJ) (Schoharie Ref. Chbk.).

vii) <u>Johann Georg</u>[3], bpt. 15 May 1740 - sp.: Jurrie Eo.. and Maria Eva -ils (Schoharie Ref. Chbk.). He md. Elisabetha Dietz 21 Oct 1763 (Schoharie Ref. Chbk.).

<u>HENRICH BARTHEL</u> (Hunter Lists #11)

Elisabetha Bartel, d/o Henrich Bartel of Hunterstown - of the commune of Epstein in the duchy of Darmstad, md. 20 June 1716 Peter Schmid, widower of Hunterstown - of Borstein in the earldom of Eisenburg (West Camp Luth. Chbk.). The Bartels were documented near 6239 <u>Eppstein/Taunus</u> at 6238 <u>Lorsbach</u> (15 km. e. of Wiesbaden; Chbks. begin 1639, Luth.) and at 6270 <u>Heftrich</u> (15 km. n.e. of Wiesbaden; Chbks. begin 1649). The father of the emigrant 1709er Henrich Barthel was <u>Mattheus Barthold</u>, cowherd at Langenhain. He had two known ch.:

+ <u>Henrich</u>, conf. as "Hennig" in 1676 (Lorsbach).

<u>Sophia Margareth</u>, conf. 1679 (Lorsbach).

Henrich Bartold and Maria Catharina were md. at Langenhain 21 June 1686; her father was said to be Hans Hack from Andernach (so entered in the Lorsbach registers). Henrich Bartel and his wife did penitence at Langenhain 29 March 1687 (Lorsbach). Henrik Bartel and wife with 5 ch. were listed on Capt. Robbert Bulman's ship leaving Holland for London in June 1709 (Rotterdam Lists). Henrich Bartel aged 45, with his wife, sons aged 17, 14 and 9, daughters aged 20 and 6, Luth., husbandman and vinedresser were in London 15 June 1709 (London Lists).

Henrich Barthel first appeared on the Hunter Subsistence Lists 1 July 1710 with 4 pers. over 10 yrs. of age and 1 under 10. Heinrich Bartel and Anna Catharina with 2 ch. were at Hunterstown ca. 1716/17 (Simmendinger Register). Hendrik Bartel was mentioned on Palatine Debtors Lists of 1718, 1719 ("of Hunterstown"), 1721, 1722 and 1726 (Livingston Debt Lists).

Henrig Bardel was a Palatine willing to remain at the Manor in
1724 (<u>Documentary History of N.Y.</u>, Vol. III, p. 724). He was
alive as late as Feb 1734, when he was on a list of families at
Queensbury with his wife Maria Catharina (Rhinebeck Luth. Chbk.)
The ch. of Henrich[1] Barthel and Maria Catharina were:

1) <u>Anna Elisabetha</u>[2], b. 31 Jan 1687 eight weeks earlier
   than usual - sp.: Anna Christina Barthold and Anna Ließ-
   betha Grüning from Hurt (Lorsbach Chbk.). She md. Peter
   Schmid 20 June 1716 (West Camp Luth. Chbk.).

2) <u>Hans Jacob</u>[2], bpt. 1 Aug 1690 - sp.: H. Schultz of Lorsbach and Johann Caspar Schäffer - s/o the smith at Langenhain (Lorsbach Chbk.). Johann Jacob Bartel was conf.
   in 1707 (Heftrich Chbk.).

3) <u>Andreas</u>[2] (HJ), the son aged 17 in the London 1709 Census of Palatines who was conf. 30 April 1711 in the new
   German colony by Pastor Kocherthal (West Camp Luth.
   Chbk.). Andreas Bartel was nat. 22 Nov 1715 (Albany
   Nats.). He was noted on Palatine Debtors Lists of 1718,
   1719 and 1726 (Livingston Debt Lists) and was a Palatine
   willing to remain at Livingston Manor in 1724 (<u>Document-
   ary History of N.Y.</u>, Vol. III, p. 724). Andris Bartull
   was recorded in the Middle Ward in 1726/7 (Dutchess Co.
   Tax Lists). He md. Sophia Elisabeth Mertz and had ch.:

   i) <u>Maria Catharina</u>[3], b. 31 Oct 1719 at Hunterstown
      and bpt. Lonenburg - sp.: Parents and Maria Kuni-
      gunda Merssin (New York City Luth. Chbk.). She
      was conf. Dom. 6 Trin: 1737 at Theerbosch (Loonen-
      burg Luth. Chbk.) and md. Johannes Thater by 1743
      (HJ).

   ii) <u>Elisabetha</u>[3], mentioned as daughter on 1734 list
       (Rhinebeck Luth. Chbk.). She was conf. 7 May 1743
       at Theerbosch (Loonenburg Luth. Chbk.) and md. 3
       May 1746 Frans Seel (Loonenburg Luth. Chbk.).

   iii) <u>Wilhelm</u>[3], b. latter part of Nov 1721 at Camp
        Queensberry - sp.: Willhelm Hagedoorn and Engel
        Winnecker (New York City Luth. Chbk.). He md.
        Gertraud Rees (HJ).

   iv) <u>Johannes</u>[3], bpt. 17 Aug 1729 - sp.: Johannes Kleyn
       and Anna Catreyn (Kinderhook Ref. Chbk.). Joh.
       Bartel aged 19 was conf. at Theerbosch 5 Feb 1748/
       9 (Loonenburg Luth. Chbk.). He md. Gertraud Alt-
       hauser by 1753 (HJ) and had ch. bpt. at Manorton
       Luth., Linlithgo Ref., and Schoharie Luth. churches.

v) <u>Margareta</u>³, b. 23 April 1732 - sp.: Peter and Lis-
abets Schmid (Loonenburg Luth. Chbk.). Margreta
Barteln was conf. at Theerbosch 5 Feb 1748/9
(Loonenburg Luth. Chbk.) and md. Jacob Bauer by
1751 (HJ).

vi) <u>Anna</u>³, b. 4 Dec 1734 - sp.: Andres Schurtz and
wife Cath. (Rhinebeck Luth. Chbk.).

vii) <u>Johan Philip</u>³, b. 27 Jan 1738 - sp.: Philip Balth:
Bartel and wife Maria (Loonenburg Luth. Chbk.).
He md. Jannitge Decker by 1766 (HJ) and had ch.
bpt. at Manorton Luth. and Linlithgo Ref. churches.

viii) <u>Magdalena</u>³, bpt. 19 May 1741 - sp.: Stoffel Ring
and Magdalena (Germantown Ref. Chbk.).

ix) <u>Andries</u>³, bpt. 1 Oct 1743 - sp.: Andries Scherts
and wife Catharina Steiver (Linlithgo Ref. Chbk.).
He md. Christina Bauer 16 June 1770 (N.Y. Marriage
Lic.).

4) <u>Philip Balthasar</u>² (HJ), the son aged 14 on the 1709
London Census of Palatines who was conf. at Queensburg
23 March 1712 (West Camp Luth. Chbk.). Philip Bartel
was nat. 22 Nov 1715 (Albany Nats.). Baltus Bartull
was taxed in the Middle Ward 1726-28 (Dutchess Co. Tax
Lists). He was mentioned as a Palatine Debtor 23 Feb
1726 (Livingston Debt Lists) and appeared on the 1734
list of Queensbury families (Rhinebeck Luth. Chbk.).
Philip Balthasar Bartel md. 6 May 1725 Maria (Kunigunda)
Mertz and had issue:

i) <u>Henrich</u>³, bpt. 21 Aug 1726 - sp.: Hendrick Bartel
and Cath Spyckerman (Linlithgo Ref. Chbk.). He
was conf. at Theerbos 2 Sept. 1744 (Loonenburg
Luth. Chbk.) and md. Anna Scheffer, d/o Jacob
Scheffer, 31 July 1746 (Rhinebeck Luth. Chbk.).
A Henrich Bartel d. 1805 (Churchtown Luth. Chbk.).

ii) <u>Peter</u>³, bpt. ½ yr. old 5 May 1728 at Kamp - sp.:
Peter Schmid and wife Liesabeth (New York City
Luth. Chbk.). He was conf. 2 Sept 1744 at Theer-
bos (Loonenburg Luth. Chbk.). He md. 1st Geesje
Kohl by 1753 (HJ) and had issue at Linlithgo Ref.
and Claverack Ref. churches. Peter md. 2nd 4 Oct
1762 Eleanor Vredenburg (Claverack Ref. Chbk. and
N.Y. Marriage Lic.) and had ch. bpt. at Manorton
Luth. and Churchtown Luth. churches.

iii) <u>Catharina</u>³, mentioned as a daughter in 1734 at the

Rhinebeck Luth. church. She was conf. 2 Sept 1744
at Theerbos (Loonenburg Luth. Chbk.) and md. Johannes Mohr by 1748 (HJ).

iv) Andries[3], bpt. 14 Nov 1731 - sp.: Andries Barthel
and Sophia (Germantown Ref. Chbk.). He was conf.
5 Feb 1748/9 aged 17 at Theerbosch (Loonenburg
Luth. Chbk.).

v) Johann Philip[3], b. 26 Dec 1733 - sp.: Philip Spickerman and Anna Elisabetha Rosm... (Rhinebeck Luth.
Chbk.). He md. Catharina Ham by 1760 (HJ) and had
issue bpt. at Linlithgo Ref. and Manorton Luth.
churches. Capt. Philip Bartle d. 25 March 1804
aged 73 (Cem. in field, no. side Route 21, Harlem-
ville, town of Hillsdale). Papers in the estate of
Philip Bartle, dec. of Hillsdale, were issued to
Philip Bartle Jr. of Claverack 23 April 1804 (Columbia Co. Admin. Book B).

vi) Johannes[3], b. 7 Feb 1736 - sp.: Joh: Sch(ne)id and
Cath: Schertz, daughter (Rhinebeck Luth. Chbk.).
He md. Margaretha Lott by 1761 (HJ) and had ch.
bpt. at Churchtown Luth., Gallatin Ref., and Pine
Plains churches.

vii) Maria[3], bpt. 4 weeks old 7 May 1738 at Teerbosch -
sp.: Anton Michel and Catharina Barteln (Loonenburg Luth. Chbk.). She md. Andreas Schertz by
1761 (HJ).

viii) Elisabeth[3], bpt. 17 Aug 1740 - sp.: Pieter Schmid
and Lisabeth Bardel (Linlithgo Ref. Chbk.)

ix) Johann Frans[3], b. 19 Jan 1743 - sp.: Andreas Bartel and Sophia (Loonenburg Luth. Chbk.).

x) Frans[3], bpt. 29 Jan 1744 - sp.: J. Frans Diel and
Barbara Scheetz (Germantown Ref. Chbk.).

xi) Anna[3], bpt. 15 Feb 1747 - sp.: Wilhelm Bartel and
Catharina Schmidt (Germantown Ref. Chbk.).

5) Maria Margretha[2], b. 10 Aug 1704 - sp.: Philipp Jacob
Kolb - citizen here, Anna Margaretha - w/o Adam Peter
Scharff, and Anna Maria - w/o Hans Adam Weiand (?).
In this baptismal entry Henrich Bartel was called a
woodcutter (Heftrich Chbk.). Maria Margaretha Barthel sp.
Martin Zerb in 1715 (West Camp Luth. Chbk.).

ANNA DOROTHE BARTHELIN (Hunter Lists #12)

Anna Dorothe Barthelin appeared once on the Hunter Lists

on 4 Aug 1710 with 1 pers. over 10 yrs. of age in the household.

ANNA BARTHIN (Hunter Lists #13)

Anna Barth may have been related to the emigrant Henrik Bart and wife with 5 ch. on Capt. Robbert Bulman's ship in the 4th party of Palatines at Rotterdam (Rotterdam Lists); this family was enrolled as Henrich Bart aged 54, with his wife, son aged 22, daughters aged 18, 16, 14, and 12, Ref., linen and clothweaver at London in June 1709 (London Lists).

Anna Bartin (so entered) with 3 pers. over 10 yrs. of age appeared on the Hunter Lists 24 Dec 1711. A Margarieta Baar md. 8 Jan 1715 Joannes Roelefsen Van der Werke (Albany Ref. Chbk.). A Magdalena Baart md. 25 Sept 1718 Dirck Van der Karre (Albany Ref. Chbk.). There was a Thomas Barth with ch. bpt. at Albany Ref. church in 1721 and 1724. An Anna Margaretha Bart md. Caspar Rieth by 1729 and lived near Reed's church in Berks Co., Pa. (HJ). Any or all of these individuals may have been in the family of the emigrant Anna Barthin.

NICOLAS BASON (Hunter Lists #14)

Nicolaas Basing and Maria his wife of Gondersheim were members of the New York City Ref. church 28 Aug 1711, and then noted as "departed" (N.Y. City Ref. Chbk.). The search for the family began at 6521 Gundersheim (20 km. s.w. of Oppenheim), and the emigrant finally was found at 6505 Nierstein (5 k.m. n.w. of Oppenheim; Chbks. begin 1607, Ref.) and at 6501 Dienheim (2 k.m. s. of Oppenheim; Chbks. begin 1689/90, Ref.). An earlier Niclaus Bason, Gemeinsmann from Gaintzheim (Geinsheim), and his wife Margaretha had a daughter Anna Gertrudt bpt. 12 Dec 1672 at the Oppenheim Luth. church, and he may have been related to the 1709er. Nicolaas Batyn, his wife and 2 ch. were recorded on Capt. Borwood's ship sailing for London 23 May 1709 (Rotterdam Lists). Nicol Bason aged 34, with his wife, and sons aged 6 and 4, Ref., husbandman and vinedresser were in the 2nd arrivals at London in 1709 (London Lists).

Nicolas Bason first appeared on the Hunter Lists 4 Aug 1710 with 1 pers. over 10 yrs. of age and 2 pers. under 10. The entry for 29 Sept 1711 shows 2 pers. over 10 yrs. of age and 2 pers. under 10, suggesting that Nicolas remarried by that date (HJ). Nicolaus Bassan, his wife and 4 ch. were on the Raritan 1716/17 (Simmendinger Register). Inventory of the personal estate of Nicholas Bason of Somerset Co., N.J. was made 11 March 1727/8 (N.J. Wills: Lib. B, p. 80). The ch. of the

1709er Nicolas[1] Bason and his 1st wife Maria Catharina were:

1) Reichard[2], b. 27 July 1700 to Johan Niclas Basson, in-
    habitant and day-labourer here - sp.: Reichard Zimmer-
    mann. This child d. 15 Aug 1700, aged 3 weeks (Nier-
    stein Chbk.).

2) Hans Jörg[2], b. 4 June 1703 - sp.: Hans Jörg Es...heim
    from Gundersheim (Nierstein Chbk.).

3) Conrad[2], b. 21 Jan 1706 to Johann Nickel Basson at Rud-
    elsheim - sp.: Conrad Meyer, Gemeinsmann at Rudelsheim
    (Dienheim Chbk.). A Conrad Bazoon, 56, b. in N.Y., was en-
    rolled in Cornelius Van Debaregh's Co. for the city and
    county of Albany 17 May 1762 (Report of the State Hist-
    Historian, Vol. II, p. 675). Conrat Passoon made his
    first appearance on Dutchess Co. Tax Lists in 1739/40.
    He md. Catharina Heip and had issue:

    i) Johann Henrich[3], b. 8 March 1736 - sp.: Henrich
        Blas and wife (Rhinebeck Luth. Chbk.).

    ii) Niclas[3], bpt. 4 weeks old 20 Aug 1738 at Rhinebeck
        - sp.: Niclas Philip and wife Christina (Loonen-
        burg Luth. Chbk.).

    iii) Elizabeth[3], bpt. 27 May 1740 - sp.: Pieter Weever
        and Eliz. Wever (Germantown Ref. Chbk.).

    iv) Peter[3], bpt. 10 July 1743 - sp.: Pitter Bitzor and
        Cattarina, his wife (Red Hook Luth. Chbk.). He
        md. Elisabeth Becker 20 April 1767 (Red Hook Luth.
        Chbk.) and had ch. bpt. at Red Hook and Katsbaan.

    v) Gertraud[3], bpt. 11 May 1746 - sp.: Jacob Berringer
        and Gertaraud Schneider (Red Hook Luth. Chbk.).
        She md. Wilhelmus Becker by 1766 (HJ).

    vi) Antonius[3], bpt as Altoni 19 April 1749 - sp.: An-
        toni Klump and Catharina Klump (Germantown Ref.
        Chbk.).

    vii) Magdalena[3], bpt. 22 Sept 1751 - sp.: Wilhelm Bet-
        zer and Madalen (Germantown Ref. Chbk.).

By his 2nd wife Maria Nicolas Bason had ch.:

4) Maria Lies[2], bpt. 3 June 1714 - sp.: Jacob Moer and El-
    isabet Laurence (Somerville Ref. Chbk.).

5) Madalena[2], bpt. 22 Aug 1716 - sp.: Kasper Haltbeg and
    wife (Somerville Ref. Chbk.).

6) Marieya[2], bpt. 29 July, 1718 - sp.: Frans Lukas (Somer-
    ville Ref. Chbk.). Mother on this entry Madeleen Casan.

7) Rosina[2], bpt. 23 April 1720 - sp.: Robbert Bolmer and
    wife Rosina (Somerville Ref. Chbk.).

8) Anna[2], bpt. 3 June 1722 - no sp. (Somerville Ref.Chbk.).

9) <u>Margarietje</u>[2], bpt. 12 April 1724 - no sp. (Somerville
Ref. Chbk.).

<u>JOST HENRICH BÄST</u> (Hunter Lists #15)

The European home of Jost Henrich Bäst was 6348 <u>Herborn</u>
(8 km. s. of Dillenburg; Chbks. begin 1638). The earliest known
forefather of the American family was <u>Niclas Bast</u>. He md. Elisabeth (--), lived at Amroff (Amdorf) and had issue:
+ <u>Niclass</u>, bpt. 23 May 1641 - sp.: Francken Clasgen at Amroff
and Barbara, w/o Johannes Bast at Ockersdorf.
Claus Bast, s/o the late Niclaus Bast from Amrof, md. Dom. XV:
1664 Anna, d/o Jost Wetz from Hirschberg. They had ch.:
<u>Catharina</u>, bpt. 3 Dec 1665.
<u>Anna Margreth</u>, bpt. 19 Sept 1668.
+ <u>Jost</u>, bpt. 10 Nov 1671 - sp.: Jost Wetz from Hirschberg,
the grandfather of the child.
<u>Adam</u>, bpt. 16 Aug 1674 to Nicolau Bast's widow - sp.: Adam
Rumph.
Jost Henrich Bast, s/o the late Claass Bast at Herbach, md. 14
Jan 1696 Anna Dorothea Hayman, d/o the late Johann Jost Hayman
at Herbach. Johann Jost Heumann, s/o the late Jost Peter Heumann, md. Dom. XX: 1659 Elisabeth, d/o Christ Diebes (?). Dorothea, d/o Johann Jost Heymann and Elisabeth at Herbach, was
bpt. 23 Aug 1668 - sp.: Dorothea - d/o Tonges Adams from Roden-
berg, and Johannes Lang. Jost Henr. Bast, his wife and 5 ch.
of Hörbach petitioned to leave Germany in 1709 (Nassau-Dillenburg Petitions). Johannes Heimann and his wife bought goods
from Jost Henrich Bast and his wife Anna Dorothea just prior to
their departure on 23 June 1709 (Protokoll über Immobilienkäufe
ü. Verkäufe wie andere Vermögenssachen 1708-1720 in the Archiv
der Stadt Herborn, p. 39). Joost Hendrig Bast and wife with 5
ch. were in the 6th party of Palatines at Rotterdam 27 July
1709 (Rotterdam Lists).

John Henrich Bast made his first appearance on the Hunter
Lists 4 July 1710 with 2 pers. over 10 yrs. of age and 2 pers.
under 10 in the family. The 24 Dec 1711 entry shows the household increasing to 2 pers. over 10 yrs. and 3 pers. under 10;
he was called Johann Henrich, Jost, Henrich, and Jost Henrich
at various times in the journal section of Hunter. Hendrick
Bast was in Col. Thomas Ffarmar's Regt., 7th Company, in N.J.
in 1715 (<u>Report of the State Historian</u>, Vol. I, p. 537). Just
heinrich Bost, his wife and 5 ch. were on the Raritan 1716/17
(Simmendinger Register). Henry Bost of Somerset Co. took up 150

acres of land in May 1720 (N.J. Deeds, Trenton, Lib. E, p. 308).
Hendrick Bost was nat. 8 July 1730 (N.J. Nats.). He was a freeholder of Amwell in 1741 (Hunterdon Co. Freeholders). Henry
Baest of Amwell, Hunterdon Co., yeoman wrote his will 19 Jan
1743/4, and it was proved 20 Feb 1743/4 (N.J. Wills: Lib. 5, p.
19). Jost Henrich[1] Bast and his 1st wife Anna Dorothea had ch.:

1) Anna Elisabeth[2], bpt. 8 Nov 1696 - sp.: Paulus Kreuter
   - ploughman at Herbach, and Anna Elsbeth, d/o the late
   Johann Jost Heyman at Herbach (Herborn Chbk.)

2) Anna Margaretha[2], bpt. 21 Sept 1699 - sp.: Theiss Bast
   at Herbach, and Anna Cath., w/o Johannis Heymann (Herborn Chbk.).

3) Johann Jost[2], bpt. 23 Nov 1704 - sp.: Joh. Jost Rump -
   teacher at Sehlbach, and Anna Maria, w/o Henrich Caspar
   Schelts (?) (Herborn Chbk.). Joseph Bost of N.J. was nat.
   8 July 1730 (N.J. Nats.) and was a freeholder of Amwell
   in 1741 (Hunterdon Co. Freeholders). The will of Joseph Boss Sr. of Amwell Township was written 18 April
   1758 and proved 23 May 1758 (N.J. Wills: Lib. 9, p.
   155). In the will he named his wife Catrin and ch.:
     i) Joseph[3].
    ii) Nicholas[3].
   iii) John[3].
    iv) Elisabeth[3], md. a Ties.

4) Anna Juliana[2], b. 23 Oct 1708 - sp.: Georg Bast - citizen at Herborn, and Anna Juliana, w/o Johannes Bast
   at Herbach (Herborn).

5) Anna Maria[2], b. 22 Nov 1711 - sp.: Johannes Müller, Anna Elisabetha Stahl, and Anna Julian Maul (West Camp
   Luth. Chbk.).

The 2nd wife of Jost Henrich[1] Bast was named Mary, and she may
have been the mother of his other ch. named in his will:

6) Johannes[2]. The will of a John Boss of Amwell was written 25 June 1788 and proved 17 Sept 1791 naming a wife
   Elizabeth and nephew Joseph Boss (N.J. Wills: Lib. 32,
   p. 328).

7) Ann[2], md. Tunes Hoppay (Anthonius Hoppach - HJ).

8) Godfrey[2], a minor in his father's will. The will of
   Godfrey Boss of Amwell was written 8 Nov 1804 and proved
   6 Feb 1805 (N.J. Wills: File 2132J). Ch. from will:
     i) Mary[3].
    ii) Elizabeth[3], md. Peter Fox.
   iii) Sarah[3], md. William Lair as his 1st wife.
    iv) Anna[3], md. William Lair as his 2nd wife.

9) <u>Henry</u>[2], named as a minor in his father's will.

JACOB BÄST (Hunter Lists #16)

Jacob[1] Bäst first appeared on the Hunter Lists 4 July 1710
with 2 pers. over 10 yrs. of age in his household; he was recorded next to Georg Bäst and two names from Johann Henrich
Bäst on the roll. The proximity of names suggests some sort of
relationship in Germany between the emigrant Bästs. At 6348
<u>Schönbach</u> (5 km. s.w. of Herborn; Chbks. begin 1614) a Johan
Jacob Bast md. 21 Jan 1705 Margreth, d/o Johannes Kurtz from
Schönbach, and this couple had a son bpt. 21 March 1705 there
named Johann Jost. As the emigrant 1709er Georg Bäst came from
Schönbach also, this may have been our Jacob[1] Bäst's 1st marriage (HJ). The Hunter Lists go on to show that Jacob's family
decreased to 1 pers. over 10 yrs. of age 24 June 1711 and then
increased back to 2 pers. over 10 13 Sept 1712; this indicates
his marriage to his 2nd wife Anna Christina Bitzer was between
24 June 1712 (his last entry with only 1 pers. in the household)
and 13 Sept 1712 (HJ). Jacob Bast of Annsberg was a Palatine
volunteer to Canada in 1711 (Palatine Volunteers To Canada).
Jacob Best was nat. 17 Jan 1715/16 (Albany Nats.). Jacob Bast
and his wife Anna Catharina with 1 child were at Hessberg ca.
1716/17 (Simmendinger Register). Jacob Pest was a Palatine
Debtor on lists dated 1718, 1719 ("on our land"), and 1721 (Livingston Debt Lists). He and his wife Anna Christina Bitzer were
alive as late as 1759 (Germantown Ref. Chbk.) and had ch.:
1) <u>Jacob Jr.</u>[2]. He md. Catharina Berringer, who d. 29 Sept
   1747, aged 30 yrs. and leaving 3 ch. (Germantown Ref.
   Chbk.). Issue from 1st marriage:
     i) <u>Jacob</u>[3], b. 15 June 1741 - sp.: Jacob Best and
        Christina, grandparents (Loonenburg Luth. Chbk.).
        He may be the Jacob Best with wife Catharina Mel-
        lenton in the Schaghticoke Chbk. in 1773 (HJ).
    ii) <u>Conrad</u>[3], bpt. 5 Dec 1742 - sp.: Conrad Berringer
        and Anna Elizabeth Berringer (Red Hook Luth. Ckbk.).
        A Conrad Pest and wife Catharina Diel were in the
        Rensselaer Co. area at Centre Brunswick in the
        1770's (HJ).
   iii) <u>Adam</u>[3], bpt. 14 March 1746 - sp.: Adam Betzer and
        Catharina Betzer (Germantown Ref. Chbk.).
   Jacob Jr. md. 2nd 11 June 1748 Anna, d/o Hannes Taat,
   (Germantown Ref. Chbk.) and had ch:
    iv) <u>Elizabeth</u>[3], bpt. 23 July 1749 - sp.: Hannes Taat

and Elisabeth Taat (Germantown Ref. Chbk.).

    v) <u>Adam</u>[3], bpt. 7 July 1754 - sp.: Adam Snyder and
Catrina Snyder (Germantown Ref. Chbk.).

    vi) <u>Catharina</u>[3], bpt. 21 Oct 1756 - sp.: Christian
Philip and Catharina Thadt (Germantown Ref. Chbk.).

    vii) <u>Christina</u>[3], bpt. 4 Feb 1759 - sp.: Jacob Best Sr.
and wife Christina Petzer (Germantown Ref. Chbk.).

    viii) <u>Johannes</u>[3], bpt. 9 Aug 1761 - sp.: Johannes Taet
and wife Elisabeth Ruyter (Linlithgo Ref. Chbk.).

    ix) <u>Annatje</u>[3], b. 22 July 1764 - sp.: Izaac and Catharina Vosburg (Albany Ref. Chbk.).

2) <u>Johannes</u>[2], md. Eva Launhardt. The will of Johannes
Best of Clermont was dated 10 Dec 1787 and probated 27
March 1788 (Columbia Co. Will Bk. A), mentioning his
ch. and brother Harmon Best. Issue:

    i) <u>Johannes</u>[3], bpt. 19 May 1741 - sp.: Pieter Launer
and Catharina (Germantown Ref. Chbk.).

    ii) <u>Jacob</u>[3], bpt. 20 Oct 1742 - sp.: Jacob Best and
wife Christina Bötzer (Germantown Ref. Chbk.).
A Jacob Best md. Jannetje Vredenburgh by 1772 (HJ).

    iii) <u>Catharina</u>[3], bpt. 22 Jan 1745 - sp.: Jacob Best and
Catharina Beringer (Germantown Ref. Chbk.). She
probably md. Jacob Decker (HJ).

    iv) <u>Eva</u>[3], bpt. 1 Jan 1747 - sp.: Peter Scherp and wife
(Germantown Ref. Chbk.).

    v) <u>Johannes</u>[3], b. 24 April, 1751 - sp.: Johannes Petrie and Chapyta Ham (Claverack Ref. Chbk.). He
took out a license to marry Margaretha Musick 14
Dec 1772 (N.Y. Marriage Lic.). Johannes Best d.
25 Oct 1820, aged 69 yrs., and his wife Margaretha
d. 5 Oct 1831, aged 78 yrs. (Livingston Cem.).

    vi) <u>Petrus</u>[3], bpt. 31 May 1753 - sp.: Pieter Launert
and wife Catharina Spoon (Germantown Ref. Chbk.).

    vii) <u>Benjamin</u>[3], bpt. 8 Oct 1755 - sp.: Joh: Michael and
wife Anna Margaretha Kuhn (Germantown Ref. Chbk.).

    viii) <u>Lisabeth</u>[3], bpt. 9 April 1758 - sp.: Herman Best
and wife Marilis Rorich (Linlithgo Ref. Chbk.).

    ix) <u>Jeremias</u>[3], bpt. 22 Feb 1761 - sp.: Jurie Rosman
and wife Lena Lesscher (Linlithgo Ref. Chbk.).

    x) <u>Wilhelmus</u>[3], bpt. 20 Nov 1763 - sp.: Willem Bartel
and wife Geertruy Rees (Claverack Ref. Chbk.).

    xi) <u>Anna</u>[3], bpt. 18 May 1766 - sp.: Dirk Jansen and Anna
Best (Linlithgo Ref. Chbk.).

3) <u>Anna Maria</u>[2], born 9 March 1720 at Central Camp on East

Bank - sp.: Johan Jacob Thengs, Anna Maria Dietrich, and Agnes Dietrich (New York City Luth. Chbk.). Maria Best joined the Red Hook Luth. Church 21 May 1739. She md. Henrich Enters by 1743 (HJ).

4) Elisabeth², b. 2 April 1722 at Camp Queensberry - sp.: Johann Peter Philipp and Elisabeth Betzer (New York City Luth. Chbk.). She joined the Red Hook Luth. Church 21 May 1739. Elisabeth md. Henrich Berringer by 1740 (HJ).

5) Georg², (HJ), md. 11 May 1743 Maria Magdalena Hoff (Germantown Ref. Chbk.). They had ch.:

    i) Catharina³(HJ), who probably md. Markus Plattner (HJ).

    ii) Christina³, bpt 8 Sept 1746 - sp.: Jacob Best and wife (Germantown Ref. Chbk.).

    iii) Jacob³, bpt. 12 Feb 1749 - sp.: Jacob Best and Annetjen Best (Germantown Ref. Chbk.). He md. Eva Schmidt 4 July 1769 (Linlitgho Ref. Chbk.) and had ch. bpt. at Manorton Luth. and Germantown Ref. He may have been the Jacob Best, dec'd of Livingston, who had administration papers issued to George J. Best of Clermont, 17 Nov 1808 (Columbia Co. Admin. Bk. B).

    iv) Elisabeth³, bpt. 22 Sept 1751 - sp.: Harmes Best and Maria Elisabeth Best (Germantown Ref. Chbk.). She md. Henrich Schmidt by 1775 (HJ).

    v) Johannes³, bpt. 17 April 1757 - sp.: Joh: Lesscher and Catharina Lesscher (Germantown Ref. Chbk.). A John I Best d. 10 May 1835, aged 79 (Livingston Cem.).

    vi) Hendrik³, bpt. 2 March 1760 - sp.: Hendrik Hoef and wife Antje Minkelaer (Linlithgo Ref. Chbk.).

    vii) Petrus³, bpt. 20 March 1763 - sp.: Pieter Ham and wife Cathrina Louwrie (Linlithgo Ref. Chbk.).

    viii) Maria³, bpt. 11 May 1766 - sp.: Johannes Klum and wife Maria Bernhard (Germantown Ref. Chbk.).

6) Johann Hermann², bpt. 4 weeks old 28 Nov 1725 - sp.: Hermann Betzer, father-in-law, and Catharina Betzer (West Camp Luth. Chbk.). He md. Maria Elisabetha Rohrig and had ch.:

    i) Christina³, bpt. 28 Dec 1746 - sp.:"Christina"(Germantown Ref. Chbk.). A daughter of Hermann Best d. 1 Jan 1747, aged 10 days (Germantown Ref. Chbk.).

    ii) Eva³, bpt. 13 Dec 1747 - sp.: Jurg Rorig and Eva

(Germantown Ref. Chbk.). She md. Jacob Miller 3
Oct 1770 (Germantown Ref. Chbk.).

   iii) Anna[3], bpt. 11 June 1749 - sp.: Jacob Best Jr. and
Anna (Germantown Ref. Chbk.).

   iv) Catrien[3], bpt. 3 Feb 1751 - sp.: Adam Pitier and
Catryn Vonk (Linlithgo Ref. Chbk.).

   v) Georg[3], bpt. 31 May 1753 - sp.: Jurg Best and wife
Mareitje Hoof (Germantown Ref. Chbk.). He md. 5
Feb 1773 Maria Mussig (Germantown Ref. Chbk.).
Georg d. 19 Aug 1811, aged 58-2-19, and his wife
Maria d. 7 Feb 1800, aged 43-11-21 (Leesville Cem.,
Schoharie Co.). The will of George Best of Sharon
was dated 2 April 1811 and probated 26 Oct 1811
(Schoharie Co. Will Bk. A).

   vi) Maria[3], bpt. 23 March 1755 - sp.: Marcus Kuhn and
Maria Lescher (Germantown Ref. Chbk.).

   vii) Elisabetha[3], bpt. 26 Dec 1756 - sp.: Henrich Berringer and wife Elisabetha Best (Germantown Ref.
Chbk.).

   viii) Johannes[3], bpt. 4 Feb 1759 - sp.: Joh: Best and
wife Eva Launert (Germantown Ref. Chbk.).

   ix) Christina[3], bpt. 17 Aug 1760 - sp.: Niclaes Dick
and wife Christina Herder (Linlithgo Ref. Chbk.).

   x) Magdalena[3], bpt. 6 Feb 1763 - sp.: Willem Bitser
and wife Magdalena Dunsbach (Linlithgo Ref. Chbk.).

   xi) Jacob[3], bpt. 12 Oct 1766 - sp.: Jacob Dekker and
wife Catharina Best (Germantown Ref. Chbk.).

7) Anna[2], bpt. 14 Aug 1732 - sp.: Wilhelm Holtzappel and
Anna (Germantown Ref. Chbk.).

GEORG BÄST (Hunter Lists #17)

The German home of Georg Bäst was 6348 Schönbach (5 km.
s.w. of Herborn; Chbks. begin 1614). Joh. Georg Best, his wife
and 1 child petitioned to leave Schönbach in 1709 (Nassau-Dillenburg Petitions). A document dated 23 June 1709 stated that
Joh. Georg Bast and his wife Anna Catharina from Schönbach appeared and said that they had sold to their cousin Johann Jost
Rumpf - now teacher at Hörbach - their inheritance, as well as
what she had received as a child; and also two cows for ca. 110
räd. with the proviso that the buyer would take care of their
mother in food and clothing so long as she lives. Furthermore,
they sell to him their horse and equipment for 10 rth., with the
condition, however, that he will take them and their things to

Neuwied (Protokoll über Immobilienkäufe u. Verkäufe wie andere
Vermögenssachen 1708-1720 in the Archiv der Stadt Herborn, p.
50). Johan Hirg Best, his wife and 1 child were in the 6th party sailing from Rotterdam in 1709 (Rotterdam Lists).

Georg Bäst first appeared on the Hunter Lists 4 July 1710
with 1 pers. over 10 yrs. of age and 1 pers. under 10 in the
family. On 4 Oct 1710 the entry read 2 pers. over 10 yrs of
age, suggesting that he md. his 2nd wife Anna Donsbach between
the two dates (HJ). Jurian Best was enrolled in the foot company of the Marbletown militia under Capt. Wm. Nottingham in Ulster Co. in 1715 (Report of the State Historian, Vol. I, p. 562).
Jury Best was nat. 8 and 9 Sept 1715 (Kingston Nats.) and taxed
in 1718-1721 at Marbletown (Ulster Co. Tax Lists). He was a
sp. at Rochester in 1727 (Kingston Ref. Chbk.). The ch. of
Georg[1] Bäst and his wife Anna Donsbach bpt. at Kingston Ref.
Church were:

1) Anna Christina[2], bpt. 27 July 1712 - sp.: Johan Willem
   Snyder and Anna Catryn. She md. Hermanus Decker (HJ).
2) Pieter[2], bpt. 31 Oct 1714 - sp.: Pieter Van Leuven and
   Catryna Snyder.
3) Eva[2], bpt. 1 July 1716 - sp.: Jan Biks and Eva Brink.
4) Niclaas[2], bpt. 1 Feb 1719 - sp.: Niclaas De Pue and
   Wyntjen Roosa. He was a sp. at Deerpark Ref. Church in
   1741.
5) Jacob[2], bpt. 5 Feb 1721 - sp.: Cornelis Ennes and Marytjen Van Etten.
6) Margriet[2], bpt. 10 March 1723 - sp.: Hendrik Donsbeg
   and Margriet Kaggen.

ANNA BATTORFFIN (Hunter Lists #18)

Peter Petturf, his wife and 5 ch. were recorded on Capt.
Francois Warens's ship in Holland 3 July 1709 (Rotterdam Lists).
He was listed near Niklaas Roel and Hans Peter Appelman, and
next to Johan Peter Kneskern - all N.Y. settlers who originated
near the town of Darmstadt.

Anna Battorff made her 1st appearance on the Hunter Lists
30 June 1710 with 3 pers. over 10 yrs. of age in the household;
4 Aug 1710 the family had 5 pers. over 10 yrs. and 4 Oct 1710
4 pers. over 10. On 24 June 1711 after listing 5 pers. over 10
again a notation added"Johann Georg Zeller's son and An: Battorff" while his entry read "Anna Battorffin and John Zeller."
On 29 Sept 1711 her entry read"Anna Battorffin" with 3 pers.
over 10 yrs of age; Zeller's read "Johann Georg Zeller and An:

Battorffin." Anna Battorffin with 1 pers. over 10 yrs. was noted
24 June 1712. Anna Badtorffin, a widow with 2 ch., was near the
Zöllers at Neu-Ansberg ca. 1716/17 (Simmendinger Register). Her ch.:

1) Catharina Elisabetha[2] (HJ), conf. 23 March 1712 at Queensberg (West Camp Luth. Chbk.) and md. Christ. Wm. Walborn (HJ).

2) Martin[2] (HJ), a sp. to Henrich Ohrendorf at Schoharie in
   1717 (West Camp Luth. Chbk.). He md. Maria Elisabetha (undoubtedly Walborn - HJ) and moved to Pa. Their ch. were:

   i) Credelis[3], bpt. 2 June 1718 - the parents being from
      Scoharry - sp.: Christian ... (Schenectady Ref.
      Chbk.). The bpt. name of this girl was either Marg-
      aretha Elisabetha or Catharina Elisabetha, the latter
      name if the full sponsors were Christian Wilhelm Wal-
      born and his wife Catharina Elisabetha (HJ).

   ii) Hermann[3] (HJ), md. 1st Maria Barbara Anspach (HJ) and
       2nd Catharina Elisabetha Rieth (per Annette Burgert).

   iii) Johann Adam[3] (HJ), md. Anna Elisabetha Zeller (HJ).
        See Berks Co. Administrations Vol. I (1757) and Orph-
        an's Court Proceedings Vol. I, p. 9, for more on him.

   iv) Christian[3] (HJ), md. Eva Regina (Kastnitz?) (HJ).

   v) Georg Peter[3], md. as s/o Martin[2] 1 Nov 1748 Eva Elis-
      abetha Rieth (Tulpehocken Chbk.).

   vi) Anna Catharina[3] (HJ, per Annette Burgert), md. Chris-
       toph Noecker (HJ).

   vii) Maria Margaretha[3], b. 10 Oct 1729 and conf. Quasimodo-
        geniti: 1745. She md. John Weiser (Tulpehocken Chbk.).

   viii) Henrich[3], conf. 3 June 1750, aged 18 yrs. (Tulpehocken
         Chbk.). He md. Anna Maria Saltzgeber (per A. Burgert).

   ix) Martin[3], conf. 1751, aged 16½ yrs. (Tulpehocken Chbk.)
       He md. Barbara Elisabetha Saltzgeber (per A. Burgert).

   x) Maria Elisabetha[3], conf. Easter 1752, aged 15 yrs.
      (Tulpehocken Chbk.). She md. Simon Koppenheffer (per
      Annette Burgert).

   xi) Eva[3] (HJ, per Annette Burgert), md. Michael Koppen-
       heffer (HJ).

ANNA CATHERINA BATZIN (Hunter Lists #19)

Anna Catharina, wid/o Fridrich Batz of Aurbach in Hessen-
Darmstadt, md. Gabriel Hoffmann, widower of Wollstein near
Creutzenach in the Pfaltz 11 Sept 1711 (West Camp Luth. Chbk.).
The actual village of origin of the Batz/Potts family was Auer-
bach near 6140 Bensheim (22 km. s. of Darmstadt). The Auerbach

registers begin in 1660 and show that Friedrich Batz, formerly
a soldier in H. Hauptmann Zincken's Company md. 9 May 1698
Catharina (--). Fredrig Bots, his wife and 3 ch. were listed
10 June 1709 on Capt. John Howlentzen's ship in Holland (Rotterdam Lists). Friederik Batz aged 28, his wife, sons aged 5
and 3, daughter aged 8, Luth., husbandman and vinedresser were
in the 4th arrivals in England in 1709 (London Lists).

Anna Catherina Batzin made her first appearance on the
Hunter Lists 30 June 1710 with 1 pers. over 10 yrs. of age and
1 pers. under 10 yrs; the 24 June 1711 entry added that she
md. to Gabriel Hoffmann. Anna Cath Batzin aged 38 and John
Ludwig Batzin aged 7 were in N.Y. City in 1710/11 (Palatines In
N.Y. City). The ch. of Friederich and Anna Catharina Batz were:

1) Anna Barbara[2], bpt. 1 Nov 1701 - sp.: Anna Barbara,
   d/o H.Schultheiss Elgart (Auerbach Chbk.).

2) Johann Ludwig[2], bpt. 13 July 1704 - sp.: Joh. Ludwig
   Elgarth, s/o H. Schultheiss Elgarth (Auerbach Chbk.).
   Lodwick Pats was taxed in the North Ward of Dutchess
   Co. in 1732 and 1733 (Dutchess Co. Tax Lists). He was
   one of the elders and/or deacons of the Germantown Luth.
   Church in 1741 (Settlers And Residents, Vol. I, p. 12).
   Lodewick Batts was noted on an undated list of freehol-
   ders of East Camp (Livingston Papers). The will of
   Lodowick Batz of German Camp, yeoman, was dated 21
   March 1785 and probated 8 Jan 1798 (Columbia Co. Will
   Bk. A). He md. Rebecca Hoffmann and had issue:

   i) Johann Friederich[3], bpt. 24 Sept 1727 - sp.:
      Christian Haver and Geertruy (Kinderhook Ref.
      Chbk.). He was conf. 15 July 1744 at Camp (Loon-
      enburg Luth. Chbk.) and md. 18 June 1752 Catharina
      Hagedorn (Germantown Ref. Chbk.). Administration
      papers in the estate of Frederick Potts of Liv-
      ingston were issued to Wm. F. Potts of Livingston
      13 May 1790 (Columbia Co. Administration Bk. A).

   ii) Henrich[3], on 1734 church list (Rhinebeck Luth.
       Chbk.). He was conf. at Camp with Johann Frieder-
       ich[3] 15 July 1744 (Loonenburg Luth. Chbk.). Cath-
       arina Donsbach, widow of Henry Potts, d. 15 Oct
       1755, aged 20 yrs. and 7 months (Germantown Ref.
       Chbk.).

   iii) Johann David[3], on 1734 church list (Rhinebeck Luth.
        Chbk.) and conf. 21 Jan 1749/50 at Theerbosch
        (Loonenburg Luth. Chbk.). A David Pots sp. at

Albany Ref. Church in 1752.

iv) Anna Catharina[3], b. 13 Dec 1731 and bpt. Rhynbek -
sp.: Peter Dreber and wife Cath. (Loonenburg Luth.
Chbk.). Cathar. Patz was conf. at Theerbosch 21
Jan 1749/50 (Loonenburg Luth. Chbk.).

v) Anna Margareta[3], b. 14 June 1733 - sp.: Joh. Georg
Forster and wife Maria Margreta (Rhinebeck Luth.
Chbk.). She md. Philip Klum Jr. 5 Nov 1751 (Ger-
mantown Ref. Chbk.).

vi) Georg[3], b. 4 Sept 1734 and bpt. as "Georg Adam" -
sp.: Joh. Georg Forster and wife Maria Margreta
(Rhinebeck Luth. Chbk.). He md. 31 Jan 1758 Veronica Lescher (Germantown Ref. Chbk.). George
Batz was enrolled in Capt. Frederick Kortz's Company at East Camp in 1767 (Report of the State
Historian, Vol. II, p. 870).

vii) Christina[3], named in her father's will. She md.
Conrad Lasher.

viii) Johann Wilhelm[3], bpt. 7 weeks old 26 May 1739 at
Teerbosch - sp.: Wilhelm Hagedorn and wife Maria
(Loonenburg Luth. Chbk.). He md. Veronica (--),
and the Churchtown Luth. Chbk. noted that the wife
of William Batz d. 5 Oct 1804.

ix) Anna Barbara[3], bpt. 25 Feb 1741 - sp.: Willem Hagendorn and Maria Barbara Diederich (Linlithgo Ref.
Chbk.). She md. Georg Lasher (Will).

x) Johannes[3], md. as s/o Ludwig 18 Nov 1766 Elsjen
Schneider, d/o Joh. Peter Schneider (Germantown
Ref. Chbk.). They had ch. bpt at Germantown Ref.,
Germantown Luth., and Red Church-Tivoli Churches.
Johannes Batz was listed on Capt. Frederick Kortz's
Company at East Camp in 1767 (Report of the State
Historian, Vol. II, p. 870). The will of John
Bate, yeoman of East Camp in the Co. of Albany,
was dated 9 Nov 1775 and probated 22 Feb 1790
(Columbia Co. Will Bk. A).

3) Johann Niclas[2], bpt. 27 May 1707 - sp.: Johann Niclas
Wald - lime burner here 'uffm fürsl. Kälkhof.' (Auerbach Chbk.).

CHRISTIAN BAUCH (Hunter Lists #20)

Christian Baug and wife with 3 ch. were in the 6th party
sailing from Holland 27 July 1709 (Rotterdam Lists); he was listed near N.Y. 1709ers Mattys Bron, Johann Bernhardt and Johan

Nikel Jung.

Christian Bauch first was mentioned on the Hunter Lists 4 July 1710 with 2 pers. over 10 yrs. of age and 2 pers. under 10; the last entry for the family in Hunter noted 4 pers. over 10 yrs. and 1 under 10 yrs. on 13 Sept 1712. Christian Bauch of Haysbury was a soldier in 1711 (Palatine Volunteers To Canada). A Christiaen Lang was nat. 17 Jan 1715/16 (Albany Nats.); as no other N.Y. German was so-named, this may have been Bauch (HJ). Christian Bauch and Anna Dorothea with 5 ch. were at Neu-Stuttgardt ca. 1716/17 (Simmendinger Register). Christian and several of his sons were listed on Pastor Sommer's roll of Schoharie Luth. families ca. 1744/5 (Schoharie Luth. Chbk.). The Old Christian Bauch d. 17 Dec 1752, and Anna Dorothea Bauch d. 19 Jan 1747, aged 68 yrs. (Schoharie Luth. Chbk.). Ch. of Christian[1] and Anna Dorothea Bauch were:

1) Johann Christian Jr.[2] (HJ), conf. at Tschoghari in the so-called Weisert's-dorp in 1720 (New York City Luth. Chbk.). The wife of Christian Jr. was Ottilia Becker. The Old Christian Bauch d. 2 May 1768 (Schoharie Luth. Chbk.). The Sommers list shows the following ch.:
    i) Friederich[3].
    ii) Johannes[3], crossed out on the 1744/5 list, but probably the Johannes Bauch who md. Eva Schäfer 6 June 1759 (Schoharie Luth. Chbk.) (HJ).
    iii) Wilhelm[3], probably md. Elisabeth Mattheus 2 April 1758 (Schoharie Ref. Chbk.) (HJ).
    iv) Maria Magdalena[3], bpt. 18 Oct 1732 - sp.: Fredrik Bekker and Cathrina Zenger (Schoharie Ref. Chbk.). Banns 17 Oct 1753 to marry Johannes Beckker (Schoharie Ref. Chbk.).
    v) Elisabetha[3].
    vi) Margaretha[3], b. 29 Sept 1736 and bpt. Schohari (Loonenburg Luth.Chbk.).

2) Johann Friederich[2] (HJ), md. Magdalena Ecker. The Old Johan Friederich Bauch d. 20 July 1767 (Schoharie Luth. Chbk.). Their ch. were:
    i) Johann Christian[3], md. 23 Aug 1743 Christian Elisabetha Rickert, eldest d/o Ludwig Rickert (Schoharie Luth. Chbk.). Some family sources give dates of 9 Feb 1723 - 13 April 1786 for Johann Christian[3] and 6 Oct 1726 - 1791 for his wife (N.Y. D.A.R. Bible Records, Vol. 19, p. 80). Several of their ch. were Loyalists and d. in Williamsburg, Ontario.

   ii) <u>An un-named daughter</u>[3] (HJ).

  iii) <u>Anna Eva</u>[3], md. 3 July 1744 Adam Braun (Schoharie
      Luth. Chbk.),as 2nd daughter.

   iv) <u>Anna Dorothea</u>[3], bpt. 18 Oct 1732 - sp.: Niclas
      Feek, and Anna Dorothea, w/o Christ. Baug (Scho-
      harie Ref. Chbk.).

    v) <u>Johann Friederich Jr.</u>[3], bpt. 1 Feb 1734/5 - sp.:
      Will. Baugh and Elis. Maritje (Schoharie Luth. or
      Ref. Chbk.). He md. 7 April 1761 Catharina In-
      goldt (Schoharie Luth. Chbk.), and several of his
      ch. appear to have gone to Canada (HJ).

   vi) <u>Henrich</u>[3], b. 9 Feb 1737 and bpt. at Schohari - sp.:
      Christian Bauch and wife Anna Dorothea (Loonenburg
      Luth. Chbk.).

  vii) <u>Johannes</u>[3], bpt. 29 Sept 1739 - sp.: Johannes Law-
      yer and Elisabeth Lawyer (Schoharie Ref. Chbk.).

 viii) <u>Anna Maria</u>[3] (Sommers List).

   ix) <u>Peter Nicolas</u>[3], b. 18 Oct 1743 - sp.: Peter Nico-
      las Sommer - Pastor at Schoharie, and Maria Mag-
      dalena Ingold (Schoharie Luth. Chbk.); d. 1746.

    x) <u>Barend</u>[3], b. 6 April 1746 - sp.: Christian Bauch
      Jr. and his wife (Schoharie Luth. Chbk.).

3) <u>Anna Margretha</u>[2], bpt. 21 Aug 1710 at N.Y. - sp.: Lorentz Henrich and Maria Marg. Kurtz (West Camp Luth.
   Chbk.). She md. Johann Jost Mattheus (HJ).

4) <u>Johann Wilhelm</u>[2], one of the 1st four ch. born in Schoharie (<u>Simm's History Of Schoharie</u>, p. 51). The dates
   on his tombstone in Middleburgh Cem. read 1711-1799.
   He md. Anna Elisabeth (--) and had ch.:

    i) <u>Anna Dorothea</u>[3], b. 25 Feb 1744 - sp.: Anna Doro-
      thea and Christian Bauch Sr. (Schoharie Luth.
      Chbk.). She d. 26 May 1746, aged 2 yrs - 3 months
      (Schoharie Luth. Chbk.).

   ii) <u>Maria</u>[3], b. 28 Sept 1745 - sp.: Hieronymus Kräusler
      and wife. She d. 20 July 1746 aged 10 months less
      7 days (Schoharie Luth. Chbk.).

  iii) <u>Johannes</u>[3], b. 3 June 1747 - sp.: Johannes Bauch
      and wife (Schoharie Luth. Chbk.). He d. 31 Dec
      1830, aged 83-6-23(Schoharie Cem., Schoharie Co.).

   iv) <u>Maria</u>[3], b. 18 June 1749 - sp.: Hieronymus Kräusler
      and his wife (Schoharie Luth. Chbk.).

    v) <u>Dorothea</u>[3], b. 18 Aug 1751 - sp.: Jacob Veeg and
      wife (Schoharie Luth. Chbk.).

   vi) <u>Christian</u>[3], b. 18 Oct 1753 - sp.: Christian Bauch

and Anna Matthes (Schoharie Luth. Cem.). He d.
1836 (Middleburg Cem.).

vii) Elisabeth³, b. 23 Jan 1756 - sp.: Friederich Bauch
Jr. and Elisabeth Kräusler (Schoharie Luth. Chbk.).

viii) Johann Wilhelm³, b. 28 July 1758 - sp.: Johann
Friederich Bauch and wife. A little boy, Johann
Wilhelm Bauch, d. 6 Oct 1760 (Schoharie Luth.
Chbk.).

ix) Wilhelm³, b. 29 June 1762 - sp.: Adam Braun - s/o
Johannes, and Margareth Kräusler.

5) Maria Margaretha² (HJ), md. Georg Henrich Stubenrauch
30 May 1738 (Loonenburg Luth. Chbk.).

6) Johannes², md. as youngest s/o Christian Bauch 12 Feb
1744 Elisabeth Bellinger, youngest d/o Henrich Bellinger (Schoharie Luth. Chbk.). Family records noted
dates for Johannes as 7 April 1720 - 4 Sept 1784 and
14 Sept 1726 - 11 Sept 1786 for Elisabeth (N.Y.D.A.R.
Bible Records, Vol. 19, p. 78). Their ch. were:

i) Thomas³, b. 30 April 1744 - sp.: Christian Bauch
Sr. and his wife (Schoharie Luth. Chbk.).

ii) Johannes³, b. 17 April 1746 - sp.: Henrich Bellinger and wife. He d. 3 March 1747, aged 11 months,
14 days (Schoharie Luth. Chbk.).

iii) Anna³, b. 6 March 1748 - sp.: Matthes Werner and
wife (Schoharie Luth. Chbk.).

iv) Nicolas³, b. 24 Nov 1749 - sp.: Johan Balthasar
Borst and wife (Schoharie Luth. Chbk.).

v) David³, b. 18 April 1752 - sp.: Johann Wilhelm
Bauch and wife (Schoharie Luth. Chbk.).

vi) Anna Dorothea³, b. 2 Oct 1754 - sp.: Jost Matthes
and wife (Schoharie Luth. Chbk.).

vii) Cornelius³, b. 13 June 1758 - sp.: Johannes Zahe
and his wife (Schoharie Luth. Chbk.).

viii) Elisabeth³, b. 30 Sept 1761 - sp.: Jurgen Henrich
Stubrach and wife (Schoharie Luth. Chbk.).

MATHIAS BAUM modo JNO. JOST BAUM (Hunter Lists #21)

The first entry of Mathias Baum on the Hunter rolls was 1
July 1710 with 3 pers. over 10 yrs. of age in the family; on 4
Oct 1710 the household increased to 4 pers. over 10 yrs. On 25
March 1711 Johann Jost Baum was entered on Hunter with 1 pers.
over 10 yrs; the size increased once again to 2 pers. over 10
on 25 March 1712, then decreased to 1 pers. again 24 June 1712.

There was an Antony Böhm conf. 25 Oct 1719 at Remerbuch
(New York City Luth. Chbk.) who md. in Dec 1719 Margaretha Lein;
he was a single man b. in Flammersveld, Germany, and she a single woman b. in Darmstadt (Hackensack Ref. Chbk.). Their first-
born child was named <u>Jost</u>, b. 7 Sept 1720 at Remobuch - sp.:
Jost Brandorff and wife Magdalena (New York City Luth. Chbk.).
As Jost Brandorff often was listed very near the Mathias Baum
family in Hunter and as "Jost" was chosen as a baptismal name,
perhaps Antony Böhm may have been related to this Matheus/Jost
Baum group (HJ).

ADAM BAUMANN (Hunter Lists #22)

Adam Baumann, widower and butcher of Bacherach-on-the-
Rhine, md. Anna Margretha, wid/o Johann Kugel of Unter-Owisheim
in the commune Maulbronner, duchy of Wurtemberg 6 March 1711
(West Camp Luth. Chbk.). The Baumann home was 6533 <u>Bacharach</u>
(33 km. w. of Wiesbaden; Chbks. begin 1577, Ref.). Mr. Wayne V.
Jones of Houston, Texas, a descendant of the Bacharach Baumanns
and a noted genealogist, has been most generous in sharing his
German findings on the family. The earliest known direct ancestor of the American line was <u>Wilhelm Bauman</u>, d. 9 July 1622
and md. Helena Magdalena (--). His son was <u>Peter Bauman</u>, bpt.
28 April 1581, md. 22 June 1615 Christina Rössler, bpt. 15 Nov
1592 as d/o Jacob Rössler and wife Barbara Ritter - who had md.
11 May 1579. The line was carried on by Peter and Christina
Bauman's son <u>Johann Peter Baumann</u>, who md. 6 Oct 1652 Anna Magdalena Sommer. She was the d/o Hans Wilhelm Sommer (s/o Frantz
Sommer and Elisabeth Katharina) who md 5 June 1625 Sophia Conradt (d/o Philip Conradt and Elisabeth Thill). Two ch. of
Johann Peter Baumann and Anna Magdalena Sommer were:

> <u>Anna Catharina</u>, bpt. 28 Jan 1658. She md. Walrath Wolle-
> ben, founder of one of the N.Y. Wolleben families.
> + <u>Johann Adam</u>, bpt. 8 Oct 1665 - sp.: Johann Adam Sturz - a
> clerk of the customs office of Bacharach.

Johann Adam Baumann, s/o of the late cooper Johann Peter Baumann of Bacharach, md. Susanna Catharina Dresch, single d/o the
late shoemaker Nicolaus Dresch of Bacharach, on 17 Feb 1688.

Adam Baumann's first entry on the Hunter Lists was 4 July
1710 with 4 pers. over 10 yrs. of age and 2 pers. under 10 yrs.
He sp. Antoni Schayt in 1712 and Hans Michel Etich in 1713 at
Schenectady Ref. Church. Adam Baumann, his wife Maria Margr-
retha and 5 ch. were at Neu-Quunsberg ca. 1716/17 (Simmendinger
Register). Ch. of Adam[1] Baumann with his two wives:

1) <u>Margretha Elisabeth</u>², bpt. 12 Jan 1690 - sp.: Sara Elisabetha - w/o Henop, and Margretha Elisabetha - w/o Schippert (Bacharach Chbk.).

2) <u>Anna Margretha</u>², bpt. 9 Nov 1692 - sp.: the d/o Hans Michael Mußkopf and Johann Christoffel - s/o the turner of Simmer(n) (Bacharach Chbk.).

3) <u>Elisabetha Catharina</u>², bpt. 4 April 1695 - sp.: Anna Elisabetha - w/o Hans Peter Baumann, and the w/o Michael Baumann (Bacharach Chbk.).

4) <u>Henrich Peter</u>², bpt. 27 July 1698 - sp.: Hans Peter - s/o Hans Peter Baumann, Henrich Luther - s/o Matheus Henop, and Fronica Catharina - d/o Johann Jacob Hail (Bacharach Chbk.).

5) <u>Maria Sybilla</u>², bpt. 12 Sept 1700 - sp.: Christina Sybilla - w/o Johann Adam Scheib, a hunter of Rheinollen, and Maria - d/o Conrad Tresch, a citizen and shoemaker of Hanau (Bacharach Chbk.).

6) <u>Maria Margaretha</u>², bpt. 11 Feb 1703 - sp.: Maria Margaretha - d/o the late Johann Philipp Hessert (Bacharach).

7) <u>Johann Adam</u>² (HJ), probably the patentee of Lot #14 on the north side of the Mohawk River 30 April 1725 (Burnetsfield Patent).

8) <u>Jacob</u>² (HJ), probably the patentee of Lot #27 on the south side of the Mohawk River 30 April 1725 (Burnetsfield Patent). He made his will 6 January 1757 (Bowman Papers, Dept. of History & Archives, Fonda, N.Y.).

9) <u>Susanna</u>², (HJ), md. Robert Flint 1 Jan 1732 (Schoharie Ref. Chbk.).

10) <u>Maria Catharina</u>², b. 9 June 1717 and bpt. Schoharie - sp.: Johann Henrich Spohn and wife (West Camp Luth. Chbk.).

<u>The Baumann/Bowman Family of the Mohawk, Susquehanna and Niagara Rivers</u> by Maryly B. Penrose, C. G. is an excellent, in-depth study of this U.S.A./Canadian family.

ANNA MARGRETHA BAUMÄNNIN (Hunter Lists #23)

Although called "Baumännin" in the ledger, "Anna Margretha Baumin" with 1 pers. over 10 yrs. of age was entered 4 Oct 1710 in the journal section of the Hunter Lists; on 24 Dec 1711 she was named Magdalena Baumännin with 3 pers. over 10 yrs of age. Magdalena Baumin, a widow aged 29 with Johan Niclaus Baumin aged 15 were in N.Y. City ca. 1710/11 (Palatines In N.Y. City). Thus Magdalena¹ Baumin had a child:

1) <u>Johann Nicolaus</u>[2]. He first was mentioned in the Dutchess Co. Supervisor's Records in the North Ward in 1727/
   28; his entries continued until 1737/8 (Dutchess Co. Tax
   Lists). He md. Catharina (--) and had ch.:

      i) <u>Anna Magdalena</u>[3], bpt. 13 April 1729 - sp.: Michael
          Heyntjen and Magdalena Heyntjen (Kingston Ref.
          Chbk.).

     ii) <u>Gertraud</u>[3], bpt. 6 weeks old 13 Jan 1732 at Rhynbek
          - sp.: Niclas Rauw and wife Gertraud (Loonenburg
          Luth. Chbk.).

    iii) <u>Nicolaus</u>[3], b. 8 Jan 1733/4 - sp.: Nicol Rau and
          wife Gertraud (Rhinebeck Luth. Chbk.).

There was a Johannes Boom and wife Anna or Anna Barbara
who had ch. bpt. at the Kinderhook Ref. Church 1722-35; they also had Niclas Rauw as a baptismal sp. to one of their ch. in
1731 which hints at a relationship to Johann Nicolaus[2] (HJ).

ANNA MARIA BAUMARSIN (Hunter Lists #24)

Anna Maria, wid/o Henrich Baumann of Upstatt near Brustel
in the commune of Speur, md. Johann Adam Sollner, widower and
miller of Eppingen in the Pfaltz 25 Oct 1710 (West Camp Luth.
Chbk.). The Henrich Baumann ancestral village probably was
7521 <u>Ubstadt-Weiher</u> (3 km. n. of Bruchsal) (HJ).

Anna Maria Baumarsin made her first appearance on the Hunter Lists 1 July 1710 with 1 pers. over 10 yrs. of age; her
final entry with just 1 pers. over 10 was 4 Oct 1710.

ANNA MARGRETHA BAYERIN (Hunter Lists #25)

Anna Margretha Bayerin was entered on the Hunter Lists 30
June 1710 with 2 pers. over 10 yrs. of age in the family; her
last notation was 4 Aug 1710 with 2 pers. over 10 yrs. Due to
her juxtaposition with other 1709ers in Hunter's journals, it
appears that #58 Johann Jacob Beyer replaced her on the rolls
4 Oct 1710 (HJ).

ANDREAS FRIDERICH BECK (Hunter Lists #26)

Jacob Bickman and his wife, with Andries Fredrig, Justina
Magdalena, Anna Christina, Abraham, Maria Dorta and 2 other ch.
in the family were in the 2nd party in Holland 23 May 1709
(Rotterdam Lists). John Jacob Beck aged 50, with his wife, son
aged 18, daughters aged 20, 13, 10, 8, and 6, Luth., husbandman
and vinedresser, and also a hunter, were in the 2nd arrivals at

London 27 May 1709 (London Lists). The German home of the Beck
family was near 6450 Hanau: Andreas Friederich Beck lived near
and was sp. to Theobald Scherer and his wife Justina Magdalena
Beck in Dutchess Co,; Justina Magdalena Wiegand, d/o Johannes
Wiegand of Hanau, md. Hans Theobald Scherer, s/o Bernhard Scherer of Oberamt Gernsheim, 7 Aug 1709 in England (London Churchbooks and the German Emigration of 1709, by John P. Dern, p.
24). Thus Johann Jacob Beck probably md. the wid/o Johannes
Wiegand somewhere near Hanau, as Justina Magdalena was called
Beck and Pik in America, and Wiegand in London (HJ).

Andreas Friderich Beck made his first appearance on the
Hunter Lists 4 Aug 1710 with 1 pers. over 10 yrs. of age and 2
under 10. The family listing was 2 over 10 yrs. of age and 1
under 10 on 31 Dec 1710, and then 2 over 10 yrs. 25 March 1711.
Perhaps the Johanna Maria Beck conf. Easter 1715 at Queensberg
(West Camp Luth. Chbk.) was a younger sister of Andreas Friederich[1] Beck. Andries Frederick Pech's entries in the South
Ward of Dutchess Co. began in 1717/18 (Dutchess Co. Tax Lists).
The Supervisor's records of Dutchess Co. noted that he was an
overseer of ye common ways back in ye woods in the South Ward
in 1726. Surviving ancient documents relating to him are num-
bered #3764 and #950 (Dutchess Co. Ancient Docs.). He md.
Veronica (--) and had issue:

1) Elisabeth[2], b. summer 1712 in Dutchess Co. and bpt. at
   Pieter Lassen's in Langerack - sp.: Pieter Jansen Nor-
   man, and in his place Joh: Milltler and Mary Jansen
   Normans (New York City Luth. Chbk.).

2) Christina[8],(HJ), conf. 1733 at Pieter Lassing's in the
   Highland (New York City Luth. Chbk.).

PETER BECKER (Hunter Lists #27)

The European home of Peter Becker was the Neuwied region.
The emigrant was documented in the registers of 5450 Nieder-
bieber (2 km. n. of Neuwied; Chbks. begin 1655) and at 5450
Altwied (3 km. farther n.; Chbks. begin 1706). The father of
Peter[1] was Johannes Becker at Wiedt; his wife d. April 1687 at
Wiedt together with her newborn child (Niederbieber). Their
ch.:

Maria Elisabetha, md. the N.Y. 1709er Valentin Falckenburg
7 Feb 1702 (Niederbieber).

Johann Paulus, called brother of Johann Peter Becker 1708
(Altwied).

+ Peter, recorded as son of the late Johannis Becker at

Wiedt when he sp. Valentin Falckenberg 1708 (Niederbieber).
Johan Peter Bekker sailed on Capt. Robbert Lourens's ship from
Holland to England 5 June 1709 (Rotterdam Lists). Peter Becker
aged 28, Ref. was in the 3rd arrivals in London 1709 (London
Lists); his future wife Anna Elisabetha Hasch was on the same
small boat at Rotterdam and, as Elizabeth Haas aged 21, Ref.,
was listed near him at London (Rotterdam and London Lists).

Peter Becker made his first appearance on the Hunter Lists
4 July 1710 with 2 pers. over 10 yrs. of age, showing he had
md. Anna Elisabetha Haas in London or on the voyage across the
Atlantic (HJ). On 24 June 1711 their family increased to 2
pers. over 10 yrs. and 1 under 10 yrs. of age. Peter Becker:
1 man and 1 woman were enrolled in the 1710/11 census of Ulster
Co. Palatines (West Camp Census). He was nat. 8 and 9 Sept
1715 (Kingston Nats.) and recorded at Beckmansland with Elisabeth ca. 1716/17 (Simmendinger Register). The Kingston Trustees Records mention Peter and Elisabetha Backer in Bk. 7, p.
136. The ch. of Peter[1] Becker and Anna Elisabetha Haas were:
1) <u>Anna Veronica</u>[2] (HJ), md. Johannes Kilmer by 1734 (HJ).
2) <u>Johann Christian</u>[2], b. 2 Jan 1714 - sp.: J. Veltin Falckenburg, J. Christian Dietrich, and Amelia Klein
   (West Camp Luth. Chbk.). He md. Anna Emmerich 1 Sept
   1735 (Katsbaan Ref. Chbk.). Christian Backer of Ryne-
   beck Prect. dated his will 11 Jan 1780,and it was probated 29 May 1780 (<u>Fernow Wills</u> #177). Their ch. were:
   i) <u>Anna</u>[3], bpt. 6 Feb 1737 - sp.: Johannes Em... (Kat-
      sbaan Ref. Chbk.). She md. Henrich Schuch (HJ).
   ii) <u>Elisabetha</u>[3],(the child's name being torn out on
       the page - HJ) bpt. 26 Dec 1738 - sp.: Pieter Bak-
       ker and Elisabeth Bekker (Katsbaan Ref. Chbk.).
       She md. Henrich Ahlendorff by 1761 (HJ).
   iii) <u>Margaretha</u>[3], b. 20 Feb 1740 and bpt. Kisket. - sp.:
        Hendryk Brouwer and Margreta, his wife (Loonenburg
        Luth. Chbk.). She md. Philip Schafer by 1762 (HJ).
   iv) <u>Petrus</u>[3], b. 20 Sept 1741 and bpt. Kisket. - sp.:
       Peter Becker and Gritje Emmerichs (Loonenburg Luth.
       Chbk.). He probably md. Sarah Ellen by 1770 (HJ).
   v) <u>Maria</u>[3], bpt. 26 Dec 1743 - sp.: Willem Brouwer and
      Maria Emmerich (Katsbaan Ref. Chbk.). She md. Jo-
      hannes Schmidt by 1761 (HJ).
   vi) <u>Wilhelmus</u>[3], b. 31 May 1746 and bpt. Kisket. - sp.:
       Wilm. Emmerich and Lisabeth Brandauw (Loonenburg
       Luth. Chbk.). He md. Gertjen Basson by 1766 (HJ).

vii) <u>Catharina</u>³, bpt. 11 April 1748 - sp.: Hans Jurg
Elig and wife Catharina Emmerich (Katsbaan Ref.
Chbk.). She md. Jeremiah Fredenburg by 1772 (HJ).

viii) <u>Gertrud</u>³, b. 15 June 1750 and bpt. Newton - sp.:
Godfr. Wulf and wife Gertrud (Loonenburg Luth.
Chbk.).

ix) <u>Johannes</u>³, bpt. 18 May 1752 - sp.: Johannes Maul
and Elisabeth Tromboor (Red Hook Luth. Chbk.).

x) <u>Henricus</u>³, bpt. 27 Feb 1757 - sp.: Henricus Martin
and Elisabetha Emmerich (Red Hook Luth. Chbk.).

3) <u>Anna Juliana</u>², b. 10 Oct 1716 and bpt. as Anna Justina
- sp.: Anna Juliana Weller, Anna Eva Menges, and Hieronymus Scheib (West Camp Luth. Chbk.). She md. Johann
Wilhelm Funck by 1743 (HJ).

4) <u>Antonius</u>² (HJ), a sp. of Wilhelm Funck and Anna Juliana²
Becker in 1747 (Germantown Ref. Chbk.). He md. Anna
Eva Dick and d. 20 Sept 1808 in Therbush (Churchtown
Luth. Chbk.). Their ch. were:

i) <u>Wilhelm</u>³, bpt. 16 April 1745 - sp.: Wilhelm Herder
and Maria Herderin (Germantown Ref. Chbk.).

ii) <u>Christina</u>³, bpt. 26 Dec 1746 - sp.: Nicolaus Dick
and Christina (Germantown Ref. Chbk.).

iii) <u>Johann Henrich</u>³, bpt. 17 April 1755 - sp.: Hendrick Bernhard and Anna Maria Herder (Linlithgo
Ref. Chbk.).

5) <u>Gertruyd</u>², bpt. 12 Nov 1721 - sp.: Mathys Jong and
Geertruy Hertel (Kingston Ref. Chbk.). She md. Godfrey De Wulvin by 1743.

6) <u>Maria Elisabeth</u>², bpt. 12 April 1724 - sp.: Joh: Pieter
Overpag and Maria Lies Meyer (Kingston Ref. Chbk.).

7) <u>Johann Peter</u>², b. 20 June 1727 and bpt. at Kisket. -
sp.: J. Peter Sachs, Hermannus Behr, and Annetje Weyd
(Loonenburg Luth. Chbk.). He md. Margaretha Emmerich
1 Oct 1745 after banns were published at Katsbaan
(Kingston Ref. Chbk.). Their ch. were:

i) <u>Lisabeth</u>³, b. 6 Aug 1746 and bpt. Newton - sp.:
Pieter Becker and Lisab., grandparents (Loonenburg
Luth. Chbk.). She md. Petrus Basson 20 April 1767
(Red Hook Luth. Chbk.).(HJ).

ii) <u>Johannes</u>³, b. 2 Nov 1748 and bpt. Newton - sp.:
Hendryk Brouwer and Marg., grandparents (Loonenburg Luth. Chbk.).

iii) <u>Petrus</u>³, b. 3 Nov 1750 and bpt. Newton - sp.: Hans

Jurge Elig and wife Cath. (Loonenburg Luth. Chbk).

iv) Catharina³, bpt. 26 Dec 1752 - sp.: Godfried Wulfin and wife Geertruy Bekker (Katsbaan Ref. Chbk.).

v) Wilhelmus³, b. 18 Jan 1755 - sp.: Wilhelmus Emerich and Margaretha (Loonenburg Luth. Chbk.).

vi) Annaatje³, b. 18 Nov 1757 - sp.: Christian Becker
and Annaatje (Loonenburg Luth. Chbk.).

vii) Margaretha³, b. 19 April 1760 - sp.: Wilhelmus Emmerich and Margareth (Loonenburg Luth. Chbk.).

viii) Marya³, b. 6 Sept 1762 - sp.: Johann Elig and Maria Broodbeek (Loonenburg Luth. Chbk.).

JOHN FRIDERICH BECKER (Hunter Lists #28)

Johann Friderich Becker was recorded next to Anna Catharina Becker 30 June 1710 on the Hunter Lists; Anna Catharina
came from 5409 Dörnberg (11 km. s.w. of Diez) according to her
marriage entry in Kocherthal (West Camp Luth. Chbk.). There
was a Joh. Friedrich Becker, s/o Hans Jürg, who md. Anna Clara
Barabam, d/o Reinhard, 10 July 1709 in London (London Churchbooks and the German Emigration of 1709, by John P. Dern, p.
23); Frederick Becker aged 23, single, Luth., husbandman and
vinedresser was in the 2nd arrivals at London (London Lists).
This man noted in London was not our N.Y. 1709er (HJ).

Johann Friderich Becker first appeared on the Hunter Lists
with 1 pers. under 10 yrs. of age on 30 June 1710. The entries
then become confusing, as Johannes Becker with 2 pers. over 10
yrs. was listed 4 Oct 1710, and Johannes Becker with 4 pers.
over 10 was noted 24 June 1711. The final Hunter listings
show Johannes Becker with 4 pers. over 10 yrs. of age and 1
pers. under 10 through 1712 (with Peter Becker heading the
last entry 13 Sept 1712). Friedrich Becker and Anna Elisabetha
Beckerin were at Hackensack ca. 1716/17 (Simmendinger Register).
Frederick Becker was in Capt. Charles Laroexs's Company of Militia in 1738 (Report of the State Historian, Vol. I, p. 581).
Frederik Bekker and his wife Catherina Zenger joined the N. Y.
Ref. Church 26 Aug 1729 (N.Y. City Ref. Chbk.) and sp. Christian Bauch and his wife Ottilia Bekker, along with a Magdalena
Bekker, at Schoharie in 1732 (Schoharie Ref. Chbk.). The ch.
of Johann Friederich¹ Becker and wife Catharina Zenger (md. 16
Sept 1727 at the N.Y. City Ref. Church) were:

1) Johanna², bpt. 13 Nov 1728 - sp.: Pieter Senger and
widow Johanna Senger (New York City Ref. Chbk.).

2) Elisabetha², bpt. 10 Jan 1731 - sp.: Joh^s Jacob Signer

and Elisabet Bekker, both single (N.Y. City Ref. Chbk.).
3) <u>Frederik²</u>, bpt. 15 April 1733 - sp.: J. Peter Zenger
and his wife Catharina Maúlin (N.Y. City Ref. Chbk.).
4) <u>Catharina²</u>, bpt. 18 July 1736 - sp.: Jan Vredenbúrg and
Maria Maul, both single (N.Y. City Ref. Chbk.).

MARIA BECKERIN (Hunter Lists #29)

Maria Beckerin with 1 pers. over 10 yrs. of age was registered 4 July and 4 Aug 1710 in the Hunter Lists.

ELIZABETH BECKERIN 1ST (Hunter Lists #30)

Elizabeth Beckerin 1st was mentioned 30 June 1710 on the
Hunter Lists with 1 pers. over 10 yrs. of age.

ELIZABETH BECKERIN 2D JUNR. (Hunter Lists #31)

Elizabeth Beckerin 2d Junr. was noted with 1 pers. over
10 yrs. of age 30 June and 4 Aug 1710. Elisabetha, wid/o Johann
Michael Becker of Creitzenech in the Pfaltz, md. 27 Sept 1710
Ludwig Schmidt, widower of Michelbach near Giesen in Hesse
Darmstadt (West Camp Luth. Chbk.). Elisabetha Becker's German
home probably was 6550 <u>Bad Kreuznach</u> (HJ).

ANNA CATHARINA BECKERIN (Hunter Lists #32)

It is interesting to note that Pastor Joshua Kocherthal
recorded three Becker marriages on the same day - 27 Sept 1710:
1) Elisabetha Becker, #31 cited above, 2) Anna Catharina, d/o
Johann Henrich Becker of Weerheim in the commune of Dillenburg,
md. Abraham Lauck of the commune of Epstein in Darmstadt, and
3) Anna Catharina, wid/o Johann Becker of Durnberg near Dietz
in the commune of Schemburg, md. Christian Hauss, widower and
carpenter of Alten Staeden near Wetzler in the duchy of Solm.
The ancestral village of the 2nd bride was 6393 <u>Wehrheim</u> (40
km. e. of Dietz), and the home of #32 - the 3rd bride - was
5409 <u>Dörnberg</u> (11 km. s.w. of Dietz). There may have been a
relationship between the last two brides due to the proximity
of their geographic regions of origin; indeed it is possible
that Johannes Becker of Dörnberg and Johann Henrich Becker of
Wehrheim were one and the same man (HJ). Henrich Becker, s/o
Frideric Becker of Ohren, md. Anna Elisabetha Graulich, d/o Johannes Graulich, 30 Jan 1691 at Niederbrechen Catholic Church,
and had ch. Catharina bpt. 1693 and Johannes bpt. 1699; 6259
<u>Niederbrechen</u> is located between Wehrheim and Dörnberg, and

Ohren, home of Frideric Becker, was also the village of origin
for several N.Y. Laux 1709ers. Hendrich Becker aged 53, sons
aged 20, 19, 15, and 11, daughters aged 22, 18, 16, and 13,
Cath., husbandman and vinedresser, were in the 3rd arrivals in
England 2 June 1709 (London Lists) and may have been related to
Anna Catharina[1] Becker (HJ).

Anna Catharina Beckerin with 2 pers. over 10 yrs. of age
and 2 pers. under 10 made her first appearance on the Hunter
Lists 30 June 1710, next to Johann Friderich Becker. The 4 Aug
1710 entry read 2 pers. over 10 and 1 under 10, and her 4 Oct
1710 listing noted 1 pers. over 10 yrs. of age and 2 under 10;
the journal added that she md. John Christian Haus. Due to the
mysterious Johannes Becker in #28 Johann Friderich Becker's entries who is unplaced as yet in a Becker family structure, a
list of the ch. of Anna Catharina[1] Becker is difficult to determine - but possible issue might have been:

1?) <u>Johann Jacob[2]</u>, md. as s/o Johann Becker of Darmbach in
the earldom of Runckel to Maria Elisabetha Laux, d/o
Johann Just Laux of Weiher in the earldom of Runckel
on 24 Jan 1716 at Schoharie (West Camp Luth. Chbk.).
As Kocherthal made mistakes in the spelling of several
German locales in his registers, perhaps Darmbach was
5409 <u>Dörnberg</u> (HJ); Weiher in this entry was Weyer, a
few km. e. of Niederbrechen. Johann Jacob Becker and
Maria Elisabetha were at Neu-Cassel ca. 1716/17 (Simmendinger Register).

2?) <u>Ottilia[2]</u>, md. Christian Bauch Jr. (HJ).

3?) <u>Anna Margaretha[2]</u>, conf. at Tschoghari in the so-called
Weiserts-dorp in 1720 (N.Y. City Luth. Chbk.). She md.
1st Johannes Ingoldt and 2nd Anthony Widmer (HJ).

4?) <u>Maria[2]</u>, conf. at Tschoghari in the so-called Weiserts-
dorp in 1720 (N.Y. City Luth. Chbk.).

5?) <u>Magdalena[2]</u>, sp. to Christian Bauch Jr. and Ottilia
Becker in 1732 (Schoharie Ref. Chbk.).

6?) <u>Johannes[2]</u>, sp. with Maria Margretha (Laux) Wagner to
Johannes Leer in 1712 (West Camp Luth. Chbk.).

Unplaced Beckers include the Johannes Becker and wife Anna
Elisabetha who had a son Johannes b. 5 Feb 1712 - sp.: Johann
Straub and Anna Barbara Gunterman (West Camp Luth. Chbk.), and
the Jacob Becker with his wife and ch. at Wormsdorff ca. 1716/17
(Simmendinger Register). There were also early Beckers in Pa.,
such as Anna Maria Becker who md. Johann Zeller, Peter Becker's
wife who d. 10 May 1748, and Maria Catarina Becker 1706-1745

(Tulpehocken Chbk. and Tulpehocken Cem.).

ANNA DOROTHE BECKERIN (Hunter Lists #33)

Although called Anna Dorothe on the ledger, Maria Dorothe
Beckerin first appeared on the Hunter Lists 4 Oct 1710 with 1
pers. over 10 yrs. of age. On the 24 Dec 1711 journal entry
she was Catharina Beckerin with 1 pers. over 10 yrs. of age.

MAGDALENA BECKERIN (Hunter Lists #34)

Conrad Becker, s/o the late Sebastian Becker of Altzheim
on the lower Rhine in the commune of Altzheim in the Pfaltz, md.
at Schoharie Sabina Mattheus, d/o the late Henrich Mattheus of
Dinheim..., 4 June 1717 (West Camp Luth. Chbk.). The Becker
home town was 6526 Alsheim (10 km. s. of Oppenheim; Chbks. begin
1668, Ref.). The earliest known ancestor of the American family was Hans Eckert Becker, a butcher who d. 26 May 1687, aged
55 yrs. He may have been s/o Apollonia Becker, a widow who d.
21 May 1677, aged 73 yrs. (HJ). Hans Eckert md. Elisabetha
Bethner (? - hard to read) and had ch.:

> Maria Elisabetha, conf. 1678, aged 15 yrs. She md. Johan-
> nes Wilhelm 10 Nov 1685.
>
> + Sebastian, conf. 16 March 1681, aged 18 yrs.
>
> Johann Peter, conf. 16 March 1681, aged 14½ yrs.
>
> Ottilia, bpt. 14 April 1667 - sp.: Jost and Ottilia Baltz-
> hauser. Conf. 1684, aged 15 yrs.
>
> Christoffel, bpt. 9 May 1669 - sp.: Christoffel Beyer, the
> Sand-miller.
>
> Anna Margreth, conf. Easter 1688, aged 16½ yrs.
>
> Hans Conrad, conf. Easter 1688, aged 14½ yrs.
>
> Anna Catharina, b. 29 June 1677 - sp.: Anna Catharina, w/o
> Michel Ohnmöth
>
> Maria Ottilia, bpt. 11 Nov 1680.
>
> Josephus, b. 24 May 1683 - sp.: Joseph Unnöth, s/o Georg
> Unnöth.

Sebastian Becker, s/o the Gerichtsverwandten Hans Eckhard Becker, md. Magdalena, d/o the late Henrich Weyland from Erksdorf
in Fürstenthumb Cassel, 5 Dec 1686. Although the family is not
found on surviving passenger lists of 1709, a strong tradition
among the Schoharie Becker descendants tells of how the emigrant
ancestor went ashore at Plymouth, England while the Palatines
were lying at anchor awaiting a fair wind or sailing orders to
take them to America. After making necessary purchases of supplies, a gale of wind capsized his small boat as he was return-

ing to the larger vessel, and Becker and five others were drowned (Simm's History of Schoharie, p. 40).

Magdalena Beckerin made her first appearance on the Hunter
Lists 30 June 1710 with 2 pers. over 10 yrs. of age and 2 pers.
under 10 in the household. Magdalena, widow with 2 ch., and
Conrad Becker were recorded next to each other on the Simmen-
dinger Register of 1716/17 at Neu-Stuttgardt. The ch. of
Sebastian and Magdalena Becker were:

1) <u>Michael²</u>, b. 8 Dec 1687 - sp.: Michael Göbel, s/o the
late Laurentz Göbel here (Alsheim Chbk.).

2) <u>Justus²</u>, b. 9 Feb 1691 - sp.: Herr Justus Fay... (Alsheim Chbk.).

3) <u>Conrad²</u>,, md. as s/o Sebastian Becker 4 June 1717 Sab-
ina Mattheus, d/o the late Henrich Mattheus (West Camp
Luth. Chbk.). A child of Conrad Becker of Albany was
carried into the woods by a slave belonging to John
Layer Esq. and murdered 31 May 1741 (Zenger's N.Y.
Weekly Journal, 22 June 1741). Sabina Becker was on
Pastor Sommer's list of Schoharie families ca. 1744/5
(Schoharie Luth. Chbk.). Their ch. were:

  i) <u>Johann Nicholas³</u> (HJ), banns registered 25 Sept
  1742 to marry Elisabeth Schafer (Schoharie Ref.
  Chbk.). The will of John Nicholas Becker of Mid-
  dleburgh was written 17 March 1800 naming a son
  Conrad among others; it was probated 14 June 1800
  (Schoharie Co. Will Bk. A).

  ii) <u>Sebastian³</u>, s/o Coenraad Beckker 19 Oct 1749 when
  banns registered to marry Anna Maria Schafer, d/o
  Henrich Schafer (Schoharie Ref. Chbk.).

  iii) <u>Johannes³</u>, joined the Schoharie Ref. Church 1 April 1743 as s/o the late Conrad Becker. Banns
  registered 17 Oct 1753 to marry Magdalena Bauch,
  d/o Christian Bauch (Schoharie Ref. Chbk.).

  iv) <u>Friederich³</u>, s/o "C. B." when banns registered to
  marry Anna Heeger, d/o Henderick Heeger 14 Jan
  1756 (Schoharie Ref. Chbk.).

  v) <u>Catharina³</u>, bpt. March 1736/7 - sp.: J. Marten
  Borst and Catharina Borst (Schoharie Luth. or Ref.
  Chbk.).

Three unplaced Beckers in the Schoharie Valley were related: 1) Johannes Becker md. Anna Maria Kneskern, 2) Wilhelm Becker md. Anna Dorothea York, and 3) Anthony Becker md. Charlotta Margaretha Berninger. All had ch. 1730-60 at Schoharie Ref.

Church. Perhaps they were ch. of the Johannes Becker mentioned
on #28 John Friderich Becker's account on the Hunter Lists (HJ).

ELIZABETHA BELLIN - JNO. FRID: BELL, HER SON (Hunter Lists #35)

Elisabetha Bell often was recorded on the Hunter Lists near
other 1709ers who originated near 5450 Neuwied (i.e. Jacob Manck,
Paulus Duntzer and Johann Christoph Fuchs). A family matching
known data from American sources was documented at 5450 Niederbieber (2 km. n. of Neuwied; Chbks. begin 1655). Lothari Bell
and wife Elisabetha had 4 ch. bpt. at Niederbieber. Sp. to their
issue had many connections to American emigrants: 1) the Rema-
gens md. into the 1709er Dieterichs, 2) the Neitzerts md. into
the Fuchs family, and 3) the Falckenburgs md. into the Beckers
and were 1709ers themselves.

Elizabeth Bellingin made her initial appearance as #40 on
the Hunter Lists on 4 July 1710 with 2 pers. over 10 yrs. of
age; her entries as #40 stop 4 Aug 1710. As #35 she was enrolled
4 Oct 1710 with 2 pers. over 10 yrs. (in this one entry she was
called Johann Friderich Bell's widow, which I believe was in error - HJ). She was Elizabeth Bellin on most of the 1711 notations in Hunter. Beginning 25 March 1712 Friderich Bell was
head of the family with 3 pers. over 10 yrs. of age and 1 pers.
under 10; the last entry for Friderich was 13 Sept 1712 with 4
pers. over 10 yrs. and 1 pers. under 10 in the household. The
ch. of Lotharii Bell and Elisabetha bpt. at Niederbieber were:

1) Maria Elisabetha[2], bpt. 15 March 1685 - sp.: Maria Elisabetha - d/o the late H. Wilhelm Clauer the Pastor at
   Honnenfeld, Maria - d/o Hans Thönges..., and Johannes -
   s/o the late Wilh. Remagen at Segendorf.
2) Wilhelmus[2], bpt. 7 Nov 1686 - sp.: Wilhelmus Im...,
   Georg Friedrich...son, and Catharina - w/o Theis Fritsch
   here .
3) Christina[2], bpt. 27 Jan 1689 - sp.: Hupert Bösch at N.B.,
   and Christina - d/o the late H. Joh. Wilh. Neitzert of
   Niederbieber.
4) Johann Friederich[2], bpt. 3 Jan 1692 - sp.: Friedr. Sensebach - citizen at Neuenwiedt, Joh. Peter - s/o Johannes
   Falckenberg at O. B., and Anna Marg. - wid/o Joh. Caspar
   Schönauer at N. B. (Niederbieber). Johann Frederick Bell
   md Anna Maria (--). Frederick Bell of Hunterstown was
   a soldier in 1711 (Palatine Volunteers To Canada). He
   was nat. 11 Oct 1715 (Albany Nats.). Johann Friederich
   Bell and wife Anna Maria with 4 ch. were at Neu-Quunsberg

ca. 1716/17 (Simmendinger Register). Frederick Pell
and Anna Mary Bell each were patentees on the n. side
of the Mohawk 30 April 1725 (Burnetsfield Patent). He
was dead by 1760 when his daughter Gertraud md. as d/o
Friederich Bell, deceased - formerly school-teacher at
Burnetsfield (Stone Arabia Ref. Chbk.). Issue:

   i) Johann Jacob[3], b. 28 July 1712 - sp.: J. Michael
      Herder, Jacob Weber, and Anna Eva Thomas (West Camp
      Luth. Chbk.). A Jacob Bell was on Capt. Conrad
      Frank's Company in the Mohawk region in 1767 (Re-
      port of the State Historian, Vol. II, p. 850).

  ii) Georg Henrich[3] (HJ), a Captain in the Mohawk area
      in 1767 (Report of the State Historian, Vol. II,
      p. 848). He md. Catharina Herkimer and was men-
      tioned in the will of Nicholas Herchheimer 7 Feb
      1777 (Fernow Wills #849). Georg Henrich[3] d. 24 Ap-
      ril 1807, aged 79 yrs. and 1 month (Herkimer Ref.
      Chbk.). He had ch. bpt. at Stone Arabia Ref. and
      Germantown Ref. Churches.

 iii) Gertraud[3], md. 7 Feb 1760 as d/o Friederich Bell
      to Johannes Helmer (Stone Arabia Ref. Chbk.).

     There were other Bells in the Mohawk Valley related to Jo-
hann Friederich Bell, possibly additional sons: 1) Johann Dieterich Bell d. 24 Aug 1812, aged ca. 79 (Herkimer Ref. Chbk.),
2) Thomas Bell had ch. bpt. at Stone Arabia Ref. Church in the
1760's, 3) Melger and Phillips Bell were in Capt. Mark Petry's
Company 26 Feb 1757 (Report of the State Historian, Vol. II, p.
781/2) and 4) Fredrick Bell was enlisted in Capt. Conrad Frank's
Company in 1767 (Report of the State Historian, Vol. II, p.
850/1) (HJ).

                NICOLAUS BELLINGER (Hunter Lists #36)
                JOHANNES BELLINGER (Hunter Lists #37)
                 MARCUS BELLINGER (Hunter Lists #38)
                HENRICH BELLINGER (Hunter Lists #39)

     The ancestral towns of the Mohawk and Schoharie Bellinger
families were 1) 6497 Steinau an der Straße (5 km. s. of
Schlüchtern; Chbks. begin 1689, with a water-damaged Protocol
1597-1681), 2) 6458 Rodenbach (6 km. e. of Hanau; Chbks. begin
1600, Ref.), 3) 6456 Langenselbold (27 km. e. of Frankfurt;
Chbks. begin 1563), and 4) 6451 Hüttengesäß (4 km. n. of Langenselbold). My German findings revealed that all the emigrant
Bellingers of 1709 were related, but not in the way previously

thought. The earliest known ancestor of the American line was
<u>Hans Bellinger</u>, called a citizen of Steinau an der Straße at a
son's marriage in 1664 (Rodenbach). He was a communicant at Rodenbach in 1667 and 1668. His wife was named Anna, and she was
a communicant with her son Dieterich at Rodenbach in 1668; Hans
d. before 1679 when his widow was mentioned at Steinau. Anna,
wid/o Hans, was bur. 3 July 1698 as Diederich Bellinger's mother (Rodenbach). Ch. of Hans and Anna Bellinger were:

+ <u>Dieterich</u>

<u>Margreth</u>, conf. 1665, aged 16 (Rodenbach).

<u>Anna Maria</u>, conf. as d/o Hans from Steinau on Christmas in
1664 (Rodenbach).

<u>Johannes</u>, conf. on Christmas 1667 (Rodenbach). He md. 16
Feb 1679 Elisabeth, d/o Peter Seelig of Belling (Schlüchtern Chbks.).

+ <u>Nicholaus</u> (HJ).

Dieterich Bellinger, single fellow from Steinau - 18 yrs. old,
was a communicant at Rodenbach on Whitsutide 1662, and again in
1663, 1665, 1666 and 1668 (with his mother Anna). On 25 Feb
1664 Dieterich Bellinger, s/o Hans Bellinger - citizen of Steinau
an der Straße, md. Barbara, d/o Michel Geysen or Gessen of Klat-
tingen near Lotharingen near Metz (Rodenbach). Dieterich Bellinger was bur. 25 June 1722, aged 78 yrs; Barbara, his wife, was
bur. 3 April 1695, aged 60 yrs. (Rodenbach). They had ch.:

+ <u>Johannes</u>, bpt. 17 Nov 1664 - sp.: Johannes, s/o Conrad Bach
(Rodenbach).

<u>Johann Wilhelm</u>, bpt. 25 March 1666 - sp.: Johann Wilhelm,
s/o Christian Hauburg Praetoris, aged 11 yrs. (Rodenbach).

<u>Elisabetha</u>, bpt. 12 Dec 1667 - sp.: Maria Elisabetha, d/o
Johann Schöpf (Rodenbach).

<u>Johann Theobald</u>, bpt. 3 July 1670 - sp.: Theobald, s/o Con-
rad Merk (Rodenbach).

<u>Anna Margaretha</u>, bpt. 29 Feb 1680 - sp.: Anna, d/o Peter
Gebel. She d. 29 March 1680 (Rodenbach).

<u>Friederich</u>, a sp. at Langenselbold in 1691. He md. Elis-
abetha, d/o Hans Schäfer, 28 Oct 1695 (Langendiebach Chbk.).

The line was carried on by the 1709er Johannes Bellinger, bpt.
at Rodenbach 17 Nov 1664. He sp. the emigrant Nicolaus Bellinger in 1688 (Langenselbold). On 24 April 1690 Johannes Bellinger, s/o Dietrich Bellinger at Niederrodenbach, md. Anna Margretha, d/o Hans Kuhn (Langenselbold). Anna Margaret, d/o Hans
Kuhn and his wife Catharina, was bpt. 11 Aug 1661 - sp.: Anna
Margaretha,...Heinrich Kuhn from Lüden (Langenselbold). Anna

Margaretha was a sister of the N.Y. emigrant Samuel Kuhn, which explains their close connection after their arrival in the colonies. Johannes Bellinger was called a carpenter in 1699 (Langenselbold) and was listed as having one horse at Hüttengesäß 3 March 1701 (Birstein Archives).

Johannes Bellinger made his first appearance on the Hunter Lists 4 Aug 1710 with 4 pers. over 10 yrs. of age in the family; the household increased to 5 over 10 yrs. 4 Oct 1710. He was listed among some carpenters with Frederik Bellinger in a Palatine Debt Book dated 1712/13 (Livingston Papers). Johannes Bellinger and his wife Anna Maria Margretha with 2 ch. were at Neu-Quunsberg ca. 1716/17 (Simmendinger Register). Johannes Pellinger was a patentee on the n. side, and Margaret Pellinger his wife was a patentee on the s. side of the Mohawk 30 April 1725 (Burnetsfield Patent). The ch. of Johannes[1] Bellinger and Anna Margaretha all bpt. at Langenselbold were:

1) <u>Johann Friederich[2]</u>, b. at Hüttengesäß and bpt. 13 Sept 1691 - sp.: Friedrich Bellunger - the father's brother from the village of Niederrodenbach. Fred Bellinger of Queensbury was a soldier in 1711 (Palatine Volunteers To Canada) and was nat. 22 Nov 1715 (Albany Nats.). Johann Friederich Bellinger, his wife Anna Elisabetha and 3 ch. were at Neu-Heessberg ca. 1716/17 (Simmendinger Register). Ffrederick Pellinger was a patentee on the s. side of the Mohawk 30 April 1725 (Burnetsfield Patent). He and Johannis Hess received land from Lewis Morris Jr. in 1732 (Albany Co. Deeds, Vol. 6, p. 348). He md. Anna Elisabeth (--).

2) <u>Philipp[2]</u>, b. at Hüttengesäß and bpt. 16 Dec 1694 - sp.: Philipps Schmied, s/o the late Bernhard Schmied of the
...

3) <u>Johann Peter[2]</u>, b. at Hüttengesäß and bpt. 30 April 1697 - sp.: Johann Peter Frantz of Rodenbach in the vicinity. He was nat. 31 Jan 1715/16 (Albany Nats.). Peter Pellinger and Margaret his wife each were patentees on the n. side of the Mohawk 30 April 1725 (Burnetsfield Patent).

4) <u>Johann Adam[2]</u>, b. at Hüttengesäß and bpt. 15 Jan 1699 - sp.: Adam Schröder.

Nicolaus Bellinger, sp. strongly suggest, was another s/o Hans Bellinger of Steinau an der Straße (HJ). Like his nephew Johannes[1] Bellinger (#37 in Hunter), Nicolaus[1] (#36 in Hunter) also md. a d/o Hans Kuhn. The Pastor at Langenselbold wrote at length concerning the marriage in his register:

50

Nicolaus Bellinger and Anna, d/o Hans Kuhn, were md 25
Nov 1685 as per the order of the noble government. She
had md. some yrs. ago (11 June 1674 - HJ) Jörg Brüning
at Hüttengesäß; but she was not compatable with him, so
Brüning went from her and she from him. She went away
with this Nicolaus Bellinger and had an illegitimate
child - a little son, so that the aforementioned Jörg
Brüning has contracted another marriage. After all
this, however, the above-mentioned Bellinger has remained as a stranger... She sent a request to the
honourable government to let them stay in the country,
and this finally has been permitted by the aforementioned
honourable government which ordered me to marry them
with prior-published penitence and to avoid further
trouble and also to legitimize the rearing of this blameless child.

Nicklas Böllinger and Samuel Kuhn both had 1 horse and ½ carts
30 Sept 1693 at Hüttengesäß (Birstein Archives). Another list
mentioned that he had 3 horses with Jost Henrich Kuhn (Birstein
Archives #6125).

Nicolaus[1] Bellinger made his first appearance on the Hunter Lists 4 Aug 1710 with 6 pers. over 10 yrs. of age; on 4 Oct
1710 the family decreased to 4 over 10 yrs. After several fluctuations, the household had 3 pers. over 10 yrs. through the yr.
1712. Nicolaus Bellinger, widower with 1 ch., was at Neu-Ansberg
ca. 1716/17 (Simmendinger Register). Issue bpt. Langenselbold:

1) Marcus[2] (HJ), most probably the illegitimate child b.
   prior to their marriage. He first appeared on the Hunter Lists as #38 4 Oct 1710, recorded next to Niclaus
   Bellinger; as Nicolaus's family decreased Marcus[2] began
   his entries. On 24 June 1711 Marcus was registered next
   to Niclaus and Henrich Bellinger; on 24 Dec 1711 he had
   4 pers. over 10 yrs. of age and 1 under 10 in his family. He sp. his uncle Samuel Kuhn in 1714 (West Camp
   Luth. Chbk.). Marcus Bellenger of Annsberg was a Palatine soldier to Canada in 1711 (Palatine Volunteers To
   Canada) and was recorded with his wife Anna and 5 ch.
   next to his brother Heinrich Bellinger at Neu-Ansberg
   ca. 1716/17 (Simmendinger Register). Markus Bellinger,
   widower living at Huntersfield, md. Maria Margaretha
   Zee, single girl, 11 Oct 1737 (Loonenburg Luth. Chbk.);
   the Schoharie Ref. Chbk. noted the banns.

2) Henrich[2], b. at Hüttengesäß and bpt. as Henrich Philips
   16 Jan 1687 - sp.: Henrich Philips Feuersteiner. He
   appeared with his father as Niclaus and Henrich Bellinger on the Hunter Lists 24 June 1711; his entries alone
   began 24 Dec 1711 next to Nicolaus[1] and Marcus[2] Bellinger. On 24 June 1711 he was noted with 2 pers. over 10

and 1 pers. under 10 yrs. He sp. Hartmann Windecker in
1711 (West Camp Luth. Chbk.) and was a Palatine soldier
that yr. (Palatine Volunteers To Canada). Heinrich Bellinger, his wife Anna Maria and 2 ch. were at Neu-Ansberg
ca. 1716/17 (Simmendinger Register). He settled in the
Schoharie region (HJ).

3) Anna Barbara[2], bpt. as a twin 16 Jan 1687 - sp.: the d/o
   Samuel Neidat. She was bur. 19 Jan 1691, aged 4 yrs.

4) Johannes[2], b. at Hüttengesäß and bpt. 19 Dec 1688 - sp.:
   Johannes, s/o Diettrich Bellinger at Nieder Rodenbach.

5) Dieterich[2], b. at Hüttengesäß and bpt. 18 Feb 1694 - sp.:
   Dietrich Bellinger of Nied Rodenbach.

6) Barbara Elisabetha[2], b. at Hüttengesäß and bpt. as a
   twin 18 Feb 1694 - sp.: Barbara, w/o H. Niklas Ziegen.
   She probably md. Hartmann Windecker as his 2nd wife (HJ).

7) Margaretha Elisabetha[2], b. at Hüttengesäß and bpt. 14 Jan
   1698 - sp.: the d/o Johannes Jeckel at Nied Rodenbach.

Since several of the Ref. Chbks. covering the Mohawk region
in the early 18th century are missing, connective links between
the early generations of Bellingers are difficult to make. Although he didn't have access to the aforementioned German background on the family, Commander Lyle Frederick Bellinger's re-
markable Genealogy of the Mohawk Valley Bellingers and Allied
Families published by the Herkimer Co. Historical Society in 1976
helps fill the void created by the lost church registers and is
an excellent source of additional data on the family.

ELIZABETH BELLINGIN (Hunter Lists #40)

Elizabeth Bellingin with 2 pers. over 10 yrs. of age made
her first appearance on the Hunter Lists 4 July 1710 and her last
on 4 Aug 1710. Her entries were continued on #35 in Hunter as
Elizabetha Bellin - Jno. Frid: Bell, her son.

GEORG BENDER (Hunter Lists #41)

A Jörg Bender was found at 6451 Hüttengesäß along with other
1709ers who settled in the Mohawk Valley (i.e. the Bellingers,
Samuel Kuhn, Wörner Deichert, etc.). As Jörg sp. Hartmann Windecker and his wife Barbara Elisabetha (Bellinger - HJ) at Schoharie in 1716 (West Camp Luth. Chbk.), the Hüttengesäß Jörg Bender merits close scrutiny (HJ). Hüttengesäß entries were recorded
in the registers of 6456 Langenselbold (27 km. e. of Frankfurt;
Chbks. begin 1563) and revealed the earliest known forefather of
the Hüttengesäß Jörg Bender to have been Velten Bender who d. at

Hüttengesäß and was bur. 19 March 1679, aged 75 yrs. On 28 Jan 1664 <u>Lorentz Benner,</u> s/o Velthen Bender (sic) of Hüttengesäß, md. Magdalena, d/o Johann Koch. The had ch.:

>   <u>Maria</u>, bpt. 17 Dec 1665 - sp.: Maria, d/o Conrad Ruth.

>   <u>Adam</u>, bpt. 14 June 1668 - sp.: Adam, s/o the Baumwiesen Hoffmann.

> ?+ <u>Geörge</u>, b. at Hüttengesäß and bpt. 26 Jan 1670 - sp.: Geörge Stromb.

>   <u>Anna Christina</u>, bpt. 11 May 1673 - sp.: Christina, d/o H. Johann Krähen.

>   <u>Philips</u>, bpt. 19 Oct 1678 - sp.: the father's brother Philipps.

Lorentz Bender md. as a widower 17 March 1681 Anna, d/o Hans Jörg Zimmermann of Michelstadt in the Odenwald. On 1 Oct 1696 Jörg Bender of Hüttengesäß, s/o Lorentz Bender, md. Anna Maria, d/o Johannes Becker of Rommelshausen under the jurisdiction of Friedberg. The registers of 6472 <u>Oberau/Altenstadt</u> (12 km. n.w. of Langenselbold; Chbks. begin 1665) show that Johan Becker, widower and inhabitant of Rommelhausen, md. 1 March 1666 Kunigund Wegfarth, d/o Henrich Wegfarth of Heßenland; their daughter Anna Maria was bpt. there 1 Feb 1670.

Georg Bender first was entered on the Hunter Lists 4 Aug 1710 with 2 pers. over 10 yrs. of age and 1 under 10 yrs.; the family increased to 2 over 10 yrs. and 2 under 10 on 4 Oct 1710. The last notation was for 3 pers. over 10 yrs. and 1 under 10 on 13 Sept 1712. George Bender of Hunterstown was a soldier in 1711 (Palatine Volunteers To Canada). Jurry Beenner was nat. 11 Oct 1715 (Albany Nats.). Anna Maria Bender sp. Adam Klein and Johann Peter Kneskern in the Schoharie Valley in 1716 (West Camp Luth. Chbk.); she may have d. shortly thereafter (HJ) as the Simmendinger Register ca. 1716/17 recorded Georg Bender and his wife Maria Dorothea with 2 ch. at Neu-Heidelberg. Jurch Bender received land in the Staley Patent (34,000 acres on the s. side of the Mohawk River) 24 Sept 1724. Maria Dorothea Benner was noted on Pastor Sommer's list of Schoharie families ca. 1744/5. The ch. of Georg[1] Bender, <u>probably</u> of Hüttengesäß, were:

> 1?) <u>Anna Maria[2]</u>, b. at Hüttengesäß and bpt. 6 Aug 1697 - sp.: the w/o Joh. Caspar Müller (Langenselbold Chbk.).

> 2?) <u>Philips[2]</u>, nat. 31 Jan 1715/16 (Albany Nats.). He md. a Margaretha (--) and sp. Piter Louwis in 1752 (Stone Arabia Ref. Chbk.). It is interesting to note that there was a Philips Bender, brother of Georg of Huttengesaß (HJ).

> A Wm. Bender was enrolled in Capt. Marx Petry's Company at

Bornets Field 9 May 1767 (<u>Report of the State Historian</u>, Vol. II, p. 856).

VALENTIN BENDER (Hunter Lists #42)

Valentin Bender, Peter Stoppelbein, Kilian Minckeler, Jacob Scherp and Johann Georg Sponheimer all came as a group to colonial N.Y. from 6531 <u>Laubenheim</u> (10 km. n. of Bad Kreuznach; Chbks. begin 1659). The earliest known ancestor of the Rhinebeck Benners was <u>Esaias Bender</u>, Oberschultheiß at Laubenheim, who d. 12 May 1677, aged 60 yrs; his widow Anna Margaretha d. 7 March 1688. His son was <u>Johannes Bender</u>, md. as Johannes Bende 18 Oct 1669 Ottilia from Bosenheim; sp. show her surname was Schick (HJ). Johannes Bender the elder, Gerichtsverwandter, was bur. 10 Jan 1712, aged 63 yrs. and 1½ months. Otilia Bender, wid/o the late Joh. Bender, was bur. 10 March 1719, aged 71 yrs. and 3 months. They had ch.:

> <u>Hans Velten</u>, d. 14 Dec 1681, aged 10 yrs. and 10½ months.
>
> <u>Esaias</u>, bpt. 31 Aug 1673 - sp.: H. Oberschultheiß Esaias Bender and his wife at Laubenheim.
>
> <u>Johann Adam</u>, bpt. 14 March 1675 - sp.: Conrad Adam and his wife here.
>
> <u>Johanneth</u>, bpt. 9 April 1676 - sp.: Emmerich Schick, Schultheiß at Bosenheim and his wife - the mother's parents.
>
> <u>Maria Johanneth</u>, bpt. 2 Dec 1677 - sp.: Christoffel Schick and his wife, inhabitants at Boßenheim.
>
> <u>Anna Elisabetha</u>, bpt. 17 Aug 1679 - sp.: Hans Veltin Schick and his wife Elisab. at Boßenheim. The child d. 26 Aug 1679, aged 14 days.
>
> <u>Görg Emmerich</u>, bpt. 2 April 1681 - sp.: the father, owing to the weakness of the child. The child d. 5 April 1681, aged 3 days.
>
> + <u>Johann Veltin</u>, bpt. 7 Sept 1682 - sp.: his brother-in-law from Bosenh.
>
> <u>Christophorus</u>, bpt. 11 Jan 1684 - sp.: Christophorus Schick and his wife Maria from Boßenheim.
>
> <u>Georg Emmerich</u>, bpt. 7 March 1688 - sp.: Emmerich Schick, Chur-Pfälz, Oberschultheiß at Bosenheim.

Hanß Velten Bend md. 30 Sept 1706 Anna Margaretha Stoppelbein at Laubenheim. Falentÿn Binder, his wife and 1 child were passengers on Capt. Powell's vessel in the 2nd party sailing 23 May 1709 from Holland to England (Rotterdam Lists). Valentin Binder aged 25 and his wife, Ref., cooper and brewer, were in the 2nd arrivals at London 27 May 1709 (London Lists).

Valentin Bender first appeared on the Hunter Lists 1 July
1710 with 2 pers. over 10 yrs. of age and 1 pers. under 10; on
4 Aug 1710 the family decreased to 2 pers. over 10 yrs. Valinten
Bendor: 1 man and 1 woman were at West Camp in 1710/11 (West Camp
Census). Valatin Bender was nat. 8 and 9 Sept 1715 (Kingston
Nats.). Felter Pinner was in the foot company of militia for the
town of Shawangunk under the command of Capt. Nicolas Hoffman in
Ulster Co. in 1715 (<u>Report of the State Historian</u>, Vol. I, p.
564). Valentin Binder, his wife Anna Maria Margreta and 1 child
were at Beckmansland ca. 1716/17 (Simmendinger Register). Fall-
entyn Penner first was mentioned in the North Ward on tax rolls
in 1717/18 and continued until 23 Jan 1727/8 when the widow of
Fallentyne Bender, deceased was noted; his widow continued to be
listed as late as Feb 1758, but was not found in the June 1758
roll (Dutchess Co. Tax Lists). A document relating to Marg: Penner was dated 1738 and numbered 2482 (Dutchess Co. Ancient Docs.).
The ch. of Valentin[1] Bender and Anna Margaretha were:

1) <u>Johann Christoffel[2]</u>, bpt. 19 Feb 1708 - sp.: Johannes
   Stoppelbein, Christoffel Bend, and Anna Catharina Enck
   - all single (Laubenheim Chbk.)

2) <u>Anna Maria[2]</u>, bpt. 9 Dec 1711 - sp.: Willem and Mary West
   (Kingston Ref. Chbk.). She md. Zacharias Schmidt (HJ).

3) <u>Johannes[2]</u>, bpt. 20 March 1715 - sp.: Joh: Rouwe and Cat-
   rina Rouwe (Kingston Ref. Chbk.). He made his first ap-
   pearance on Rhinebeck tax rolls in 1741/2 (Dutchess Co.
   Tax Lists). Johannes had banns published at Rhineback
   and md. Magdalena Streit 27 May 1740 (Kingston Ref. Chbk.).
   He md. 2nd Elisabeth Ben 4 Sept 1767 (Germantown Ref.
   Chbk.); she d. 11 Aug 1803, aged 85 (Red Hook Luth. Chbk.).
   Issue from 1st marriage:

   i) <u>Hans Veltin[3]</u>, bpt. 2 March 1742 - sp.: Frederick Maul
      and Margriet Benner (Red Hook Luth. Chbk.). He
      joined the Red Hook Church 9 June 1759 and md Alida
      Weydman (HJ). He d. 13 July 1833, aged 91-6-18
      (Red Hook Luth. Cem.).

   ii) <u>Catharina[3]</u>, bpt. 12 Aug 1744 - sp.: Friederich Streit
       and Catterina Maul (Red Hook Luth. Chbk.). She md.
       Johannes Hamm (HJ).

   iii) <u>Friederich[3]</u>, b. 16 Nov (?) 1746 - sp.: Friedrich
        Streit and wife Catharina (Rhinebeck Luth. Chbk.).
        He md. Neeltjen Heermans (HJ).

   iv) <u>Anna Margaretha[3]</u>, b. 17 June 1749 - sp.: Henrich Ben-
       ner and wife Catharina (Rhinebeck Luth. Chbk.). She
       md. Georg Reisdorf (HJ).

     v) <u>Henrich</u>³, b. 16 Aug 1751 - sp.: Henrik Bender and
Catrina Bender (Rhinebeck Flats Ref. Chbk.).

    vi) <u>Johannes</u>³, b. 6 Oct 1753 - sp.: Johannes Akkert and
his wife (Rhinebeck Flats Ref. Chbk.).

   vii) <u>Jacobus</u>³, bpt. 15 Feb 1756 - sp.: Jacobus Maul and
Anna Torothea Trumbauer (Red Hook Luth. Chbk.).

  viii) <u>Anna Maria</u>³, bpt. 13 Aug 1758 - sp.: Zacharias
Schmidt and Anna Maria Bender (Red Hook Luth. Chbk.).

    ix) <u>Georg</u>³, b. 19 Oct 1760 - sp.: Han Georg Streit and
wife Elisabeth (Rhinebeck Luth. Chbk.).

     x) <u>Petrus</u>³, bpt. 11 Dec 1763 - sp.: Jost Bauer and wife
Elisabeth Maul (Red Hook Luth. Chbk.). Peter Benner
d. 2 Dec 1842, aged 78-11-21 (Red Hook Luth. Cem.).

    xi) <u>Ludewig</u>³, bpt. 29 June 1766 - sp.: Ludwig Streit
and Anna Maria Felder (Red Hook Luth. Chbk.).

4) <u>Johann Henrich</u>², b. 4 Oct 1717 - sp.: J. Henrich Schaester and his wife Agnes (West Camp Luth. Chbk.). He made
his first appearance on Rhinebeck/North East tax rolls
in 1743/4 (Dutchess Co. Tax Lists) and md. Catharina
Bitzer (HJ). They had ch.:

     i) <u>Anna Margaretha</u>³, 6 May 1741 - sp.: Pieter Bitser
and Anna Margretha Benner (Red Hook Luth. Chbk.).
She joined the church 4 June 1756 and md. 20 Jan
1761 Zacharias Voland (Red Hook Luth Chbk.).

    ii) <u>Catharina</u>³, bpt. 12 Aug 1744 - sp.: Pitter Bitzer
and wife Cattarina Phillip (Red Hook Luth Chbk.).
She md. 7 Feb 1762 Friderich Streit (Red Hook Luth.
Chbk.).

   iii) <u>Anna Maria</u>³, b. 14 Jan 1747 - sp.: Zacharias Schmidt
and wife Anna Maria (Rhinebeck Luth. Chbk.). She
md. Philip Staats 7 Jan 1765 (Red Hook Luth. Chbk.).

    iv) <u>Christina</u>³, b. 12 Nov 1749 - sp.: Zacharias Philip
and Christina Beltzer (Rhinebeck Luth. Chbk.). She
md. Petrus Mohr 16 Dec 1770 (Red Hook Luth. Chbk.).

     v) <u>Anna</u>³, b. 27 Jan 1752 - sp.: Johannes Bender and Mag-
dalena Stryt (Rhinebeck Flats Ref. Chbk.). She probably md. Philip Mohr 10 Oct 1774 (HJ) at Red Hook.

    vi) <u>Magdalena</u>³, bpt. 18 May 1755 - sp.: Wilhelm Bitzer
and Magdalena Donsbach (Red Hook Luth. Chbk.).

   vii) <u>Henrich</u>³, bpt. 10 Sept 1758 - sp.: Henrich Deithardt
and Catharina Benner (Red Hook Luth. Chbk.). He d.
3 June 1817, aged 58-9 months (Upper Red Hook Cem.).

5) <u>Catharina</u>², bpt. 28 Aug 1720 - sp.: Barent Nol and Catrina
Penhamer (Kingston Ref. Chbk.). She md. Henrich Teder (HJ).

PETER BENDER'S WIDOW (Hunter Lists #43)

Although called Peter Bender's widow on the ledger, the journal section of the Hunter Lists named the head of the household as Peter Bender with 3 pers. over 10 yrs. and 1 pers. under 10 yrs. of age on 1 July and 4 Aug 1710.

ANNA MARIA BENDERIN (Hunter Lists #44)

Anna Maria Benderin made her first appearance on the Hunter Lists 4 Oct 1710 near the same names where #43 Peter Bender formerly was enrolled. Her initial entry was with 3 pers. over 10 yrs. of age and 2 pers. under 10, and her final notation on 25 March 1712 was for 1 pers. over 10 yrs. and 1 pers. under 10 yrs. of age. Anna Maria Benderin - widow aged 44, Eva Catharina Benderin aged 12, and John Matheus Benderin aged 8 were in New York City in 1710/11 (Palatines In New York City). Anna Maria Bigi, wid/o Hans Peter Pender of the Pfalz, joined the New York Dutch Ref. Church 29 May 1711 (N.Y. City Ref. Chbk.). The ch. of Peter[1] Bender and his wife Anna Maria were:

1) Johann Matheus[2], nat. as Matthias Benter of N.Y., a boy of 14 yrs., cooper, on 14 Feb 1715/16 (Minutes of the Mayor's Court of N.Y. City: 142). He sp. Jurgen Maurer at Claverack in 1720 (N.Y. City Luth. Chbk.). Mattheus Bender joined the church 17 Feb 1730 in N.Y. City (N.Y. City Ref. Chbk.). There was a will for a Mathias Bender of New Hanover Twp., Philadelphia Co., Pa. written 25 June 1743 (Philadelphia Co. Wills Bk. G, p. 165); however, Annette K. Burgert's excellent Eighteenth Century Emigrants ... The Northern Kraichgau, p. 52, shows this latter man originated in Ittlingen and went direct to Pa.
2) Eva Catharina[2], md. as Eva Binder 3 June 1722 Johannes Lesser (Löscher - HJ) (N.Y. City Ref. Chbk.).

There may have been other issue of Peter and Anna Maria since the Simmendinger Register shows Anna Maria Benderin, a widow with 5 ch., in Neu-Yorck ca. 1716/17 (HJ).

CHRISTIAN BERCK (Hunter Lists #45)

Christian Berg's only entry on the Hunter Lists was on 4 Oct 1710 with 1 pers. over 10 yrs. of age. Johann Christian Berg was conf. Easter of 1714 by Pastor Kocherthal (West Camp Luth. Chbk.). Christian Berck was nat. 31 Jan 1715/16 (Albany Nats.). He made his first appearance on Dutchess Co. Tax Lists in Dec 1722. He was noted on the St. Peter's Family List of

ca. 1734 with his ch. (Rhinebeck Luth. Chbk.). Dutchess Co. Ancient Documents noted him in 1740 in connection with an assault
at Kingston (#1721 and #1751) and at Rhinebeck in 1759/60 regarding a forced entry (#4505 and #3300). Papers in the estate
of Christian Bergh late of Rhinebeck were issued to John Bergh,
eldest s/o the deceased 2 March 1785 (<u>Genealogical Data from Administration Papers</u>, by Dr. Kenneth Scott, p. 23). <u>History of
Rhinebeck</u> by Edward M. Smith has much material on the family,
including what look to be dates from the old family Bible (HJ).
Christian Berg md. 7 Aug 1722 Anna Margaretha Wohlleben, both
being single, b. in Germany and residing in Dutchess Co. (Kingston Ref. Chbk.). They had ch.:

1) <u>Anna Margaretha</u>², bpt. 6 weeks old 27 Jan 1726 at Rein-
bek in Bekman's land - sp.: Velbke Wolleben and Anna
Margareta Weldmanns (N.Y. City Luth. Chbk.). Margariet
Berg joined the Rhinebeck Flats Ref. Church 17 Sept
1742. She md. Friederich Hillegass by 1746 (HJ).

2) <u>Maria Barbara</u>², on the 1734 St. Peter's List (Rhinebeck
Luth. Chbk.). She joined the Red Hook Luth. Church in
1743 and md. Martin Dopp by 1745 (HJ).

3) <u>Johannes</u>², on the 1734 St. Peter's List (Rhinebeck Luth.
Chbk.). He joined the Rhinebeck Flats Ref. Church 29
March 1755 and md. 12 April 1759 Elisabetha Wust (Rhine-
beck Flats Ref. Chbk.).

4) <u>Catharina</u>², bpt. 15 March 1730 - sp.: Albartus Schryver
and Catrina Hekker (Kingston Ref. Chbk.). She md. Michael Prua 22 April 1755 (Rhinebeck Flats Ref. Chbk.).

5) <u>Johann Peter</u>², b. 20 Nov 1733 - sp.: Peter Treber and
Catharina (Rhinebeck Luth. Chbk.).

6) <u>Johann Martin</u>², b. 4 Nov 1735 - sp.: Joh. Mart. Wedman
and Maria Demot (Rhinebeck Luth. Chbk.).

7) <u>Adam</u>² (HJ), md. Helletje Redleft (Radcliffe). They
joined the Rhinebeck Flats Ref. Church 15 Feb 1771.
They had ch.:

   i) <u>Anna Margaretha</u>³, bpt. 26 June 1763 - sp.: Christian Berg and wife Anna Margaretha Wolleber (Red
   Hook Luth. Chbk.).

   ii) <u>Joachim</u>³, bpt. 11 Nov 1764 - sp.: Corneles Redle
   and Helentie Hoogeboom (Red Hook Luth. Chbk.). Je-
   hoiakim Bergh d. 20 Dec 1840, aged 77 (Rhinebeck
   Ref. Cem.).

   iii) <u>Heletien</u>³, bpt. 7 Sept 1766 - sp.: Johannes Redly
   and wife Neeltien Schermehoorn (Red Hook Luth.
   Chbk.).

    iv) <u>Maria</u>³, bpt. 11 Nov 1770 - sp.: Marten Dop and Maria
        Barbara Berg (Rhinebeck Flats Ref. Chbk.).

    v) <u>Neeltjen</u>³, bpt. 8 Nov 1772 - sp.: Rudolf v: Hoeven-
        berg and Elisabeth Reddleft (Red Hook Luth. Chbk.).

    vi) <u>Catharina</u>³, bpt. 11 Sept 1774 - sp.: Michel Brua
        and wife Catharina Berg (Red Hook Luth. Chbk.).

8) <u>Christian</u>², bpt. 23 Jan 1743 - sp.: Johannes Weisman and
  Engel Van Etten (Red Hook Luth. Chbk.). He md. Catharina
  Van Bunschoten 23 April 1762 (Rhinebeck Flats Ref. Chbk.)
  and had issue:

    i) <u>Christian</u>³, b. 30 April 1763 - sp.: Christian Berg
      Sr. and wife Anna Margaretha (St. Paul's-Rhinebeck
      Chbk.).

    ii) <u>Tones</u>³, bpt. 14 July 1765 - sp.: Tones Binschoten
      and wife Elisabeth Du (mon) (Red Hook Luth. Chbk.).

    iii) <u>Johannes</u>³, bpt. 9 Jan 1767 - sp.: Johannes Berg and
      wife Elisabeth Wust (Red Hook Luth. Chbk.).

    iv) <u>Ellen</u>³ (?), bpt. 12 March 1769 - sp.: Solomon V:
      Binschooten and Neeltjen (Red Hook Luth. Chbk.).

    v) <u>Petrus</u>³, bpt. 20 June 1773 - sp.: Michel Brua and
      wife Catharina Berg (Rhinebeck Flats Ref. Chbk.).

    vi) <u>Anna Margaretha</u>³, bpt. 30 April 1775 - sp.: Zach-
      arias Top and Anna Margaretha Top (Red Hook Luth.
      Chbk.).

<u>JOHANNES BERG</u> (Hunter Lists #46)

    Johannes Berg first was entered on the Hunter Lists 30 June
1710 with 2 pers. over 10 yrs. of age and 1 pers. under 10 in
the household. The notation in the journal for 4 Oct 1710 diminished to 2 pers. over 10 yrs. of age with none under 10; as
#45 Christian Berck was recorded that same date on Hunter for
the only time, and as Christian obviously was quite young - being
conf. in 1714 by Kocherthal - these Hunter listings may hint that
at one time Christian Berck #45 was part of the family of Johannes
Berg #46, but left 4 Oct 1710 (HJ). The last Hunter entry for
24 Dec 1711 recorded Johannes Berg's widow with 3 pers. over 10
yrs. of age in the family. Johannes Berg's wife, Episcopal,
joined the Luth. church 19 July 1710 (West Camp Luth. Chbk.).

    There were several unplaced Bergs in colonial N.Y.: a Jo-
hanna Berk joined the N.Y. City Ref. Church 21 Nov 1722, an
Anna and Maria Bork joined the same congregation 25 May 1731,
and an Anna Mag(dalena) Burke paid money to the Luth. church in
1727 (Protocol of the N.Y. City Luth. Church).

ABRAHAM BERG (Hunter Lists #47)

The obituary of Old Abraham Berg written by Pastor Sommer
4 May 1765 in the Schoharie Luth. Chbk. read:

> He was b. at Langen Hahn, under the government of the
> Electorate of Hessen-Darmstadt, in the yr. 1677. In
> the 26th **yr.** of his age he was md. with Catharina
> Homberg, legitimate d/o Thomas Homberg. They spent 6
> yrs. of married life in Germany, and (--) came to this
> country in the yr. 1709, with the first High-Germans.
> They (have) together in their married life begotten,
> with the Lord's blessing, 10 ch., 2 in Germany and 8
> in this country, 3 sons and 7 daughters. (There were)
> after his death still 6 living, namely 1 son and 5
> daughters. He had 24 grandchildren and 2 great-grand-
> children living, and he brought his venerable age up
> to 88 yrs.

The ancestral home of the family was 6238 Langenhain (10 km. e.
of Wiesbaden), the entries for this village being at 6238 Lorsbach (3 km. farther e.; Chbks. begin 1639, Luth.). The earliest
known forefather of the Schoharie Bergs was Johann Henrich Berg.
He md. 6 March 1660 Anna Margretha Müller and had ch.:

Anna Christina, bpt. 27 Oct 1661 - sp.: Anna Cath. - d/o
Matthias Hieronymus, Anna Christina - d/o Andreas Michel,
Hans Henrich Schneider - all at Lorsbach.

Maria Dorothea, bpt. 2 Oct 1664 - sp.: Anna Dorothea - w/o
Georg Kirchner and Hans Heintz (sic), and Johannes Roth at
Langenhain. She was conf. 1679.

Anna Margaretha, b. 11 March 1667 - sp.: Anna - w/o Johannes
Schmähl (?) at Lorsbach, Anna Margreta - w/o Jacob Franck
at Langenhain, and Johannes Dierlam from Meichen (?). She
was conf. 1681.

Anna Maria Clara, b. 2 Feb 1670 - sp.: Anna Clara - w/o Johan Henrich Zabel, Anna - w/o Joh. Antonius Zubrod at Delckenheim, and Maria - w/o Johannes Roth.

Anna Margaretha, w/o Joh. Henrich Berg, was bur. 19 Feb 1673,
aged 30 yrs. and 16 weeks. Joh. Henrich Berg md. 2nd Anna Maria
- d/o Peter Billgram at Wildsachsen, called "des Rölpen" on 7
Sept 1675. J. Henrich Berg d. in Langenhain and was bur. 26 March
1694, aged ca. 60 yrs. Issue with 2nd wife:

Johan Lucas, bpt. 2 Advent 1677 - sp.: Joh. Caspar Bilgram
at Wallau, Lucas ... from Dietenbergen, and Anna Margreth...

+ Johann Abraham, b. 2.p.Trin: 1679 - sp.: Abraham Kirchner
at Langenh., Joh. Enders Becker at Lorspach, and Anna Catharina - w/o Andreas Lotz the hunter.

Anna Maria, b. 20 July 1688 - sp.: Maria - the Schultzen's
wife, and Anna Maria - Abraham Kirchner's...

Johann Andreas Henrich, b. 21 May 1692 - sp.: Johs. Roht,
Andreas Lotz, and Henrich Schäfer.

Johann Abraham Berg, s/o the late Henrich Berg at Langenhayn, md.
Anna Catharina, youngest d/o Thomas Homberger the cowherd, 19 Jan
1706. (#322 Thomas Homburger was also a N.Y. settler - HJ).

Abraham Berg made his first appearance on the Hunter Lists
30 June 1710 with 2 pers. over 10 yrs. of age; the family increased to 2 pers. over 10 yrs. and 1 pers. under 10 yrs. on 24
June 1711. Abraham Berk was nat. 17 Jan 1715/16 (Albany Nats.).
Abraham Berg, his wife Anna Catharina, and 3 ch. were at Neu-
Heidelberg ca. 1716/17 (Simmendinger Register). Pastor Berkenmeyer wrote of meeting the emigrant in 1734:

> (Mrs. Peter Kniskern) then told me that they had no past-
> ure. She persisted in this, even after I had told her my
> name. Finally she said that neither her husband nor
> Scheffer were deacons, but that Abraham Berts was. His
> house I had passed on the left coming into Scoghary.
> Her husband arrived with a gun on his shoulder, but his
> wife called to him to go over the stream and drive the
> beasts out of the grain. I said I would hold service
> tomorrow.
>
> I then went to Abraham Berts. Although he was unknown
> to me, he admitted us willingly and, despite his lame-
> ness, took word to some of the neighbors that evening.
> We received a kindly welcome. The big problem was
> that he could not say where the service could be held.
> The Lutheran church at Weiserdorp was too far away...
> (Albany Protocol, p. 98).

Abraham Berg was noted on Pastor Sommer's list of Schoharie Luth.
families ca. 1744/5 (Schoharie Luth. Chbk.) and was a freeholder
of Albany Co. at Schoharrie in 1763 (Albany Co. Freeholders).
The old widow Catharina Berg d. 31 July 1771, aged 99 yrs. (Schoharie Luth. Chbk.). The ch. of Abraham[1] Berg and Anna Catharina
were:

1) <u>Maria Catharina[2]</u>, bpt. 9 Dec 1706 - sp.: Anna Cath...
   Christoph Caspary, and Maria Margretha...J. Adam Pinckel
   - single from Delckenheim (Lorsbach Chbk.).

2) <u>Margaretha Elisabetha[2]</u>, bpt. 11 Nov 1708 - sp.: Anna
   Margaretha... and Maria Lies...for them, their mothers
   (Lorsbach Chbk.).

3) <u>Johann Philip[2]</u>, a son in Pastor Sommer's 1744 list (Schoharie Luth. Chbk.). He md. Christina Fuchs 25 Oct 1748
   (Schoharie Luth. Chbk.). He was commissioned a Lieut.
   in the N.Y. Militia in 1748 (<u>Report of the State Histor-
   ian</u>, Vol. II, p. 786). Johannes Lawyer and Phillip Berg
   of Schoharie were grantors to Jacob Zeimer 27 Oct 1753
   (Albany Co. Deeds, Vol. 7, p. 103). The will of a Philip
   Berg was proved 9 Feb 1790 (Albany Co. Wills, Bk. 1, p.
   229). He and Christina had issue:

   i) <u>Catharina[3]</u>, b. 3 Sept 1749 - sp.: Abraham Berg and

wife (Schoharie Luth. Chbk.).
- ii) <u>Anna Eva</u>[3], b. 15 Feb 1752 - sp.: Jacob Sternberger and his wife (Schoharie Luth. Chbk.).
- iii) <u>Maria Elisabetha</u>[3], b. 17 March 1754 - sp.: Niclas Yorck and his wife (Schoharie Luth. Chbk.).
- iv) <u>Anna Margaretha</u>[3], b. 16 May 1756 - sp.: Philip Merckel and Margaretha Kayser (Schoharie Luth. Chbk.).
- v) <u>Johann Abraham</u>[3], b. 13 July 1759 - sp.: Abraham Berg and his wife (Schoharie Luth. Chbk.). He d. 21 April 1835, aged 77 yrs. (Schoharie Cem.).
- vi) <u>Johann Philip</u>[3], b. 17 Dec 1761 - sp.: Philip Freymeyer and Catharina Sternberg (Schoharie Luth. Chbk.).
- vii) <u>Christina</u>[3], b. 16 Dec 1764 - sp.: Johannes L. Lawyer and Christina Sternberg (Schoharie Luth. Chbk.).
4) <u>Maria Elisabetha</u>[2], md. Nicholas York (<u>Fernow Wills #2158</u>).
5) <u>Anna Maria</u>[2] (HJ), md. Conrad Frymeier 20 Oct 1739 (Schoharie Ref. Chbk.).
6) <u>Anna Elisabetha</u>[2], 3rd d/o Abraham at her marriage 3 April 1744 to Matthes Baumann (Schoharie Luth. Chbk.).
7) <u>Elisabeth</u>[2] (HJ), md. Lorentz Lawyer 27 Oct 1747 (Schoharie Luth. Chbk.).
8) <u>Maria Barbara</u>[2] (HJ), sp. strongly suggest md. Barend Keyser (HJ).

<u>ANDREAS BERGMAN</u> dead (HUNTER LISTS #48)

The bpt. of a Johannes Andreas, s/o Johan Cleopha Bergmann and wife Catharina Magdalena, on 12 Nov 1684 was found at 6701 <u>Kallstadt</u>; however the baptismal age differs greatly from the age given on the London Lists (HJ). Andreas Bergman, his wife, and 2 ch. were on Capt. Robbert Lourens's ship 5 June 1709 in Holland (Rotterdam Lists). Andreas Bergman aged 32, with his wife and a daughter aged 3, carpenter, Luth. were in England in 1709 (London Lists).

Andreas Bergman made his first appearance in the Hunter Lists 1 July 1710 with 3 pers. over 10 yrs. of age in the family. The last entry was for 1 pers. over 10 yrs. on 24 Dec 1711; the notation on this date added that the widow married Peter Hamm. Indeed, Hamm's listing on 25 March 1712 read Peter Hamm and Andr: Bergman's widow. Andreas Bergman of Queensbury was a soldier on the Canadian expedition of 1711 (Palatine Volunteers To Canada). He probably d. on the trip (HJ).

<u>CONRAD BERINGER</u> (Hunter Lists #49)

Conrad Beringer's initial entry on the Hunter Lists was for
1 pers. over 10 yrs. of age on 4 Oct 1710. The next notation
showed 2 pers. over 10 yrs. of age and 1 pers. under 10 yrs. on
31 Dec 1710; probably between 4 Oct and 31 Dec 1710 he md. his
wife Anna Elisabetha Stahl (HJ). On 25 March 1712 the family had
2 pers. over 10 and 2 pers. under 10 yrs. of age registered.
Coenraed Barringer was nat. 17 Jan 1715/16 (Albany Nats.). Conrad Bernger, his wife Anna Elisabeth and 5 ch. were at Hunderston ca. 1716/17 (Simmendinger Register). Coenradt Bellinger was
a Palatine Debtor in 1718, in 1719 (at Kingsberry) and 1721 (Livingston Debt Lists). He first appeared on Dutchess Co. Tax Lists
in 1722 as Johannes Berenger, seve maker, and later as Johannes
Counrate Perenger into the 1740's. On 10 Dec 1729 he signed as
a representative of the Ref. members of the church at Rhinebeck
(History of Rhinebeck, by Edward Smith, p. 92). The ch. of Conrad[1] Beringer and his wife Anna Elisabetha were:

1) Friederich[2] (HJ), on Rhinebeck Tax Lists beginning 1738/9
   (Dutchess Co. Tax Lists). He md. Anna Margaretha Zufeldt;
   many of their ch. moved to Rensselaer Co. (HJ). Issue:

   i) Conrad[3], bpt. 17 Oct 1736 - sp.: Conrad Berger and
      Anna Elisabeth Staal (Kingston Ref. Chbk.). He was
      noted 8 Oct 1757 as a member at Red Hook Luth. Church.

   ii) Hans Georg[3], bpt. 11 May 1738 - sp.: Jurge Zufelt
       and Cathrina Zaam (Red Hook Luth. Chbk.). He was a
       member in 1756 at Red Hook , and md. Elisabetha
       Beem (HJ). The will of George Barrenger, late of
       Greenbush, was written 9 July 1809 and recorded 17
       Oct 1816 (Rensselaer Co. Will Bk. 5).

   iii) Zacharias[3], bpt. 9 March 1740 - sp.: Coenraad Wyn-
        gaard and Margrietje Berringer (Kingston Ref. Chbk.).
        He was a member at Red Hook Luth. 8 Oct 1757. Along
        with his brothers Jury, Jacob and Johannis, Zachar-
        ias was listed in Capt. Abraham Van Aernam's Company
        in the Colony of Rennselaer Wyck in 1767 (Report of
        the State Historian, Vol. II, p. 812). He md. Anna
        Feller (HJ). The will of Zacharias Berringer, late
        of Greenbush, was written 3 July 1812 and recorded
        30 Nov 1816 (Rensselaer Co. Will Bk. 5).

   iv) Catharina[3] (HJ), md. Oct 1762 Petrus Scharp Jr.
       (Albany Ref. Chbk.). She joined the Red Hook Luth.
       Church 4 June 1756.

   v) Elisabetha[3], bpt. 16 Sept 1744 - sp.: Conrad Berrin-
      ger and Anna Elisabeth Stall (Red Hook Luth. Chbk.).

   vi) Jacob[3], bpt. 12 Oct 1746 - sp.: Jacob Beringer and

his wife Gertraut Schneider (Red Hook Luth. Chbk.).
Jacob Barringer d. 25 July 1828, aged 82; his wife
Kath. d. 23 Aug 1834, aged 71-2-19 (Columbia Cem.
in the Ref. Church, Herkimer Co.).

   vii) Johannes[3], b. 6 Oct 1748 - sp.: Georg Tromper and
wife Lena (Rhinebeck Luth. Chbk.).

  viii) David[3], bpt. 25 Dec 1750 - sp.: David Reichart and
Anna Elizabeth Schaefer (Red Hook Luth. Chbk.).

    ix) Philip[3], bpt. 24 April 1753 - sp.: Philip Voland
and Eva Switzelaar (Red Hook Luth. Chbk.). Mr.
Philip Baringer, a respectable old gentleman of
Greenbush, was killed instantly by lightening...
(Albany Balance, 8 Aug 1809)

     x) Anna Maria[3], bpt. 7 Dec 1755 - sp.: Zacharias Schmidt
and Anna Maria Benner (Red Hook Luth. Chbk.).

    xi) Christina[3], bpt. 27 Aug 1758 - sp.: Cornelius Mul-
ler and Cristina Nier (Red Hook Luth. Chbk.).

2) Maria Elisabetha[2], b. 30 Dec 1711 - sp.: Maria Elisabetha
Schlitzler (West Camp Luth. Chbk.). She md. Henrich
Schafer by 1734 (HJ).

3) Johann Henrich[2], b. 21 Sept 1714 - sp.: Johannes Rosch-
mann and wife Anna Elisabetha (West Camp Luth. Chbk.).
He made his first appearance on Rhinebeck rolls in 1740/1
(Dutchess Co. Tax Lists) and md. Elisabetha Best. Issue:

    i) Conrad[3], bpt. 2 March 1740 - sp.: Coenraad Bervin-
ger and Elisabeth Staal (Kingston Ref. Chbk.). He
md. Anna Margaretha Schmidt 23 Jan 1764 (Red Hook
Luth. Chbk.). She was bur. 17 Dec 1825, aged 81
(Nassau-Schodack Cem., Rensselaer Co.).

    ii) Jacob[3], bpt. 19 April 1742 - sp.: Jacob Best and
Christina Bitzer (Red Hook Luth. Chbk.).

  iii) Elisabetha[3], bpt. 14 Oct 1744 - sp.: Hennerich
Schever and Elisabeth Beringer (Red Hook Luth. Chbk.).
She md. at Red Hook 4 April 1763 Peter Schmidt.

   iv) Henrich[3], bpt. 26 April 1747 - sp.: Henrich Enters
and Anna Maria Enters (Red Hook Luth. Chbk.). He md.
at Red Hook to Sarah Bohm 19 Jan 1772.

    v) Johannes[3], bpt. 1 Aug 1749 - sp.: Godfriet Gressel-
bregt and Anna Maria Berringer (Rhinebeck Flats Ref.
Chbk.). He md. Elsjen Blass 17 Nov 1772 (Germantown Ref. Chbk.). He d. 5 Dec 1815, aged 67 yrs,
and she d. 10 May 1822, aged 72 yrs. (Germantown
Ref. Cem.).

   vi) Anna[3], b. 10 June 1751 - sp.: Frederik Bhyringer

and Margriet Bhyringer (Rhinebeck Flats Ref. Chbk.).

    vii) Petrus[3], b. 28 Jan 1754 - sp.: Henrik Treber and
Eva Akkert (Rhinebeck Flats Ref. Chbk.).

  viii) Anna Catharina[3], bpt. 26 Oct 1755 - sp.: Hen: Benner and Catharina Petzer (Red Hook Luth. Chbk.).

     ix) Helena[3], bpt. 24 Sept 1758 - sp.: Jacob Best Jr.
and Anna Thath (Red Hook Luth. Chbk.).

      x) Jacob[3], bpt. 13 May 1761 - sp.: Willem Botser and
wife Magdalena Donsbach (Red Hook Luth. Chbk.).

     xi) Johann Georg[3], b. 19 March 1763 - sp.: Georg Schnei-
der and Catharina (Rhinebeck Luth. Chbk.).

4) Catharina[2] (HJ), md. Jacob Best Jr. (HJ).

5) Jacob[2] (HJ), first appeared on Rhinebeck rolls in 1740/1
(Dutchess Co. Tax Lists). A bond for Jacob Berringer
survives in Dutchess Co. Ancient Documents (#3266) dated
1753. He md. Anna Gertraud Schneider and had ch.:

      i) Anna Catharina[3], bpt. 4 Jan 1741 - sp.: Frederich
Berringer, Anna Margriet Zuvelt and Catharina Schneider (Kingston Ref. Chbk.). She md. Abraham Kohl (HJ).

     ii) Conrad[3], bpt. 2 March 1742 - sp.: Conrad Berringer
and Lisabeth Stahl (Red Hook Luth. Chbk.). He md.
Gertraud Overbach (HJ).

   iii) Anna[3], bpt. as Antgen 19 Feb 1744 - sp.: Wilm.
Schneider and Gertaraut Bitzer (Red Hook Luth.Chbk.).

    iv) Johannes[3], b. 27 May 1748 - sp.: Johannes Feller and
wife Anna Barbara (Rhinebeck Luth. Chbk.).

     v) Petrus[3], bpt. 11 March 1750 - sp.: Pieter Sherf and
Evje Schneider (Red Hook Luth. Chbk.).

    vi) David[3], b. 5 July 1751 - sp.: David Reichard and El-
isabetha (Rhinebeck Luth. Chbk.). He md. Elisabetha
Kempel (HJ).

    vii) Wilhelm[3], bpt. 20 Nov 1753 - sp.: Henrich Bender and
Catharina Botzer (Red Hook Luth. Chbk.).

  viii) Jacobus[3], bpt. 4 July 1756 - sp.: Georg Klumm and
Anna Maria Schneider (Red Hook Luth. Chbk.).

6) Maria[2], bpt. 5 Aug 1722 - sp.: Jury Teeter and Marytjen
Meyer (Kingston Ref. Chbk.). She md. Gottfried Gisel-
brecht (HJ).

7) Margaretha[2] (HJ), a sp. at Kingston Ref. Church to Frederich Berringer in 1740.

8) Johannes[2] (HJ), a sp. at Germantown Ref. Church in 1749
and at Rhinebeck Luth. Church in 1747. Dutchess Co. Ancient Documents show a bond for Joh: Barringer of Beekman in 1751 (#2486 and #2487).

JOHANNES BERLEMANN (Hunter Lists #50)

An old family tradition placed the ancestral home of the
Berlemann-Parliament family at 6501 Partenheim (15 km. n. of Al-
zey;Chbks. begin 1590 with severe gaps). The marriage contracts
of 6501 Jugenheim (1 km. farther n.) revealed that the earliest
known ancestor of the N.J. family was Henrich Berlemann: Jacob
Berlemann, s/o Henrich Berlemann from Ladbergen in the Grafschaft
Tecklenburg, md 2 Feb 1661 Elisabeth Heep, d/o M. Melchior Heep.
Some other Heeps in the registers came from Kurhessen Dudenhofen,
so perhaps Melchior Heep originated there also (HJ). The ch. of
Jacob Berlemann, tailor at Partenheim, and wife Anna Elisabetha
bpt. at Partenheim were:

Anna Katharina Apollonia, bpt. 2 April 1665 - sp.: Wilhelm
Pfernen (?), Joh. Hatterß daughter...
Hans Philip, bpt. auff Thoma: 1666 - sp.: the s/o Joes Vel-
tin Ulmer.
Anna Barbara, bpt. 13 Dec 1668 - sp.: Adam Hilbersheimer,
and Barbara - w/o Christian Brandt.
Anna Lisa, bpt. 18 Sept 1670 - sp.: Hanß Miner's wife Lisa,
and Anna - w/o Philip Klippel.
+ Johannes, bpt. 11 Aug 1672 as a twin - sp.: Johan Jochs and
Johan Westerberger.
Anna Catharina, bpt. 11 Aug 1672 as the other twin - sp.:
Anna Catharina Soror...
Maria, bpt. 9 Dec 1677 - sp.: Maria - w/o Hans Hambach.
There was a Hans Jacob Berleman with wife Margaretha who had ch.
at Partenheim bpt. 1685 and 1694 who was related somehow to the
aforementioned family (HJ). Johan Peerelman and wife, with 3 ch.
were in the 5th party at Rotterdam on the ship of Capt. Francois
Warens 3 July 1709 (Rotterdam Lists).

Johannes Berlemann made his first appearance on the Hunter
Lists 4 July 1710 with 1 pers. over 10 yrs. of age; on 4 Aug 1710
the family was noted with 2 pers. over 10 and 2 pers. under 10.
Johannes[1] Berlemann's wife in America was Anna Catharina Stier;
he may have been md. to someone else in Germany. His ch. were:

1) Jacob[2], s/o John Berliman 6 Nov 1710 when bound to Henry
Wileman of N.Y.; he was aged 11 when bound to Nathl. Kay
of Rhode Island 19 April 1711 (Apprenticeship Lists).
He md. and had issue in Rhode Island (HJ).
2) Edward[2], bpt. 2 Sept 1711 - sp.: Edwaert Earle (Hackensack Ref. Chbk.). He md. an Anna (--) and had ch. at
Pompton Plains Ref. Church.
3) Johannes[2], bpt. 16 Aug 1713 - sp.: Jan Evertse and wife

Maria Barbara (Hackensack Ref. Chbk.).

4) Elisabeth[2], b. 10 June 1716 - sp.: Michael Schurt and
wife Elisabeth (New York City Luth. Chbk.). She md. Wilhelm Felten (HJ).

5) Maria Catharina[2], b. April 1718 near Remobuch - sp.: Niclaes Meysinger and wife Anna Catharina (New York City
Luth. Chbk.).

6) Maria Margaretha[2], b. 17 Oct 1720 - sp.: Jacob Aarnhout
and wife Maria Margareta (New York City Luth. Chbk.).

7) Georg[2], bpt. as Juriaen 17 Feb 1723 - sp.: Johannis Mot
and wife Jorriae (Hackensack Ref. Chbk.).

GEORG LUDW: BERNER (Hunter Lists #51)

Johann Georg Berner, widower and carpenter of grosten As-
tach in Wurtenberg, md. 29 Aug 1710 Maria Barbara Dausweber, d/o
the school teacher Johann Melchior Dausweber (West Camp Luth.
Chbk.). The Berner village of origin was 7152 Großaspach (26 km.
n.e. of Stuttgart; Chbks. begin 1693/4). A Hanß Georg Berner
was found there with wife Margaretha; he was a carpenter. Johan
Berner, his wife and 3 ch. were at Rotterdam in the 6th party in
1709 (Rotterdam Lists).

Georg Ludwig Börner made his first appearance on the Hunter
Lists 1 July 1710 with 1 pers. over 10 yrs. of age and 3 pers.
under 10 yrs. After that date he was called Georg or Johann
Georg on the rolls, which often fluctuated as to the number of
pers. in the household. His last entry on the Hunter Lists was
13 Sept 1712 with 2 pers. over 10 yrs. and 1 pers. under 10 yrs.
Hans Jury Barner was nat. 13 March 1715/16 (Albany Nats.). A
mss. regarding two planks for the coffin of Joh: Georg Berner's
child was found dated 1711 (N.Y. Colonial Mss.: Vol. 55, p. 21).
The ch. of Hanß Georg Berner and wife Margaretha were:

1) Anna Maria[2], bpt. 16 Dec 1702 - sp.: Jerg Ulmer the cartwright and his wife, and Hanß Jacob Übelin the tailor
and his wife (Großaspach Chbk.). The child d. 1703.

2) Hanß Jerg[2], bpt. 13 July 1704 - sp.: Jerg Ulmer the cartwright and his wife, and Hanß Jacob Übelin the tailor
and his wife (Großaspach Chbk.).

3) Margaretha Catharina[2], bpt. 22 Feb 1706 (Großaspach Chbk.).

A Johan Jurrie Purmer had a son Johann Baltus bpt. 11 Sept
1709 - sp.: Johan Coenradt Reijffenbergher (Feijffenbergher?) and
Anna Maria Top (Brielle Dutch Ref. Chbk. in Holland); the mother
at this bpt. in 1709 was called Elsje, however, so it probably
wasn't the Großaspach family (HJ).

JOST BERNHARDT (Hunter Lists #52)

The village of origin of the Jost Bernhardt family was 6112 Groß-Zimmern (12 km. e. of Darmstadt; Chbks. begin 1640). The earliest known ancestor of the N.Y. group was Philip Jacob Bernhardt; his wife Anna Sara d. 29 Dec 1692. The ch. of Philip Jacob Bernhardt and wife Anna Sara (Leber? - HJ) were:

Caspar, md. as s/o Philip Bernhardt 28 Dec 1695 to Anna - d/o Peter Hornung.

Carl, md. as s/o Philip Bernhard 9 Dec 1697 to Anna Margaretha, d/o Martin Buschbaum.

Georg, b. 20 Nov 1675 - sp.: Görg, s/o Caspar Hottesen.

+ Johannes, b. 9 Sept 1678 - sp.: Johannes Leber at Dieburg - "infantin (?) avus."

Gustavus (HJ), a sp. there in 1708.

Anna Margaretha, b. 16 Aug 1682 - sp.: Anna Marg. - w/o Wendel Philips, citizen here. Anna Margaretha, d/o (--) Bernhard the Spielmann (street-player or fiddler) had an illeg. son Gustavus, bpt. 30 Sept 1708 - sp.: her brother Gustavus. This is most interesting as Johannes[1] Bernhardt of colonial N.Y. was nicknamed "Spielmann" (HJ).

+ Johann Jost

Johann Jost Bernhard, s/o Philipp Jacob Bernhard md. 15 Sept 1707 Elisabeth, d/o Johann Diederich the shoemaker; a notation in the Groß-Zimmern registers added that this couple left for the Island of Carolina in the year 1709. Elisabeth, d/o Johannes Dieterich and wife Magdalena, was bpt. 3 Aug 1684 - sp.: Elisabeth - w/o the young Gerhard Hard. Jozep Bernhard and his wife were in the 6th party of Palatines in Holland in 1709 (Rotterdam Lists)

Jost Bernhardt first appeared on the Hunter Lists 4 July 1710 with 2 pers. over 10 yrs. of age; the family increased to 2 pers. over 10 yrs. and 1 under 10 on 24 June 1711 and then decreased down to 1 pers. over 10 on 24 Dec 1711. Just Bernhard, his wife Elisabeth and 1 child were at Neu Yorck ca. 1716/17 (Simmendinger Register). They had ch.:

1) Samuel[2], b. 8 Feb 1715 at Kreupel Bos on L. I. and bpt. at Newtown (N.Y. Luth. Chbk.). He was in Capt. Van Horne's Company of the militia in N.Y. City in 1737/8 (Report of the State Historian, Vol. I, p. 588). Rev. Knoll reported that Samuel Bernhard, Hans Jurgen Schwarz and wife Sara, and Liesabeth Bernhard took communion 12 July 1741 at Rachway and Leslie's Land, N.J. (Luth. Church in N.Y. and N.J., p. 169). He signed Rev. Weygand's call in 1749 and was an elder in the New Germantown, N.J. church (Early Germans

of N.J., p. 264).

2) Sarah[2], b. 28 Sept 1717 near Prekel, L. I. and bpt. N.Y.
   - sp.: Michel Pfeffer and wife Anna Maria (N.Y. City
   Luth. Chbk.). She md. Georg Schwartz 21 June 1738 (N.Y.
   City Ref. Chbk.).

JOHANNES BERNHARDT (Hunter Lists #53)

The ancestral home of Johannes Bernhardt also was 6112 Groß-
Zimmern. He was b. 9 Sept 1678, s/o Philip Jacob Bernhardt and
Anna Sara (for more on them see #52 Jost Bernhardt). Two different entries for Johan Bernhart, his wife and 2 ch. were found in
the 6th party in Holland in 1709 (Rotterdam Lists).

Johannes Bernhardt made his first appearance on the Hunter
Lists 4 July 1710 with 2 pers. over 10 yrs. of age and 2 pers.
under 10 yrs; he was enrolled on this unalphabetized list only
two names from Jost Bernhardt. His last notation on Hunter was
13 Sept 1712 with 3 pers. over 10 yrs. of age and 3 under 10 yrs.
Johannes Bernhard of Annsberg was a soldier in 1711 (Palatine
Volunteers To Canada). Joh. Bernhard and Anna Eulalia with 5
ch. were at Wormsdorff ca. 1716/17 (Simmendinger Register). He
delivered a letter of Rev. Hager 26 Sept 1717 (Livingston Papers,
Reel#3) and was mentioned as a Palatine Debtor in 1718, 1721 and
1726 (Livingston Debt Lists). A deposition of Anna, w/o Joh:
Bernard (signed "Anna Eulalia") recorded that she was ca. 36 yrs.
of age in 1721/2 (Livingston Papers, Reel #4). Like his father
in Germany, Johannes was nicknamed "Spielmann" (West Camp Luth.
Chbk., 1725). Pastor Berkenmeyer mentioned him in a visit to
East Camp 1 Sept 1732:

> Similarly, Hannes Bernhard requested that, due to the
> fact he was ill, that Han(neman) Saalbach was deaf,
> that H. Heiner was away, and that Sam Miller was the
> only active church official, a new election might be
> planned to be held tomorrow (Albany Protocol, p. 41).

Johannes Bernhardt was d. by late Feb 1733 when Berkenmeyer mentioned his widow (Albany Protocol, p. 47). Anna Berhartin, widow, with her children were listed on the St. Peter's Luth. Family
List ca. 1734 (Rhinebeck Luth. Chbk.). The 1st wife of Johannes[1]
Bernhardt was named Anna Maria, and they had ch.:

1) Elisabetha[2], b. 22 Sept 1710 at N.Y. - sp.: Elisabetha
   Berenhard (West Camp Luth. Chbk.). She was conf. Miser-
   cordia Sunday 1726 at Kamp (N.Y. City Luth. Chbk.). She
   md. Johannes, s/o Joh. Christ Kurtz, on 26 Nov 1726 (N.Y.
   City Luth. Chbk.).

Johannes[1] md. 2nd Anna Eulalia, wid/o Johann Dieterich Hausmann

(HJ) and had ch.:

2) <u>Johann Jost</u>[2] (HJ), conf. with Liesabet Bernhard and Eva Hasman together on Misericordia Sunday 1726 at Kamp (N.Y. City Luth. Chbk.). He md. Maria Christina Hemer and had issue:

    i) <u>Johannes</u>[3] (HJ), md. 12 May 1754 Christina Huyck - both resided Hosunk (Albany Ref. Chbk.).

    ii) <u>Johann Henrich</u>[3], bpt. 8 weeks old 9 June 1734 at Newton - sp.: Hans Jurge Loscher and Anna Eulalia Bernhard (Loonenburg Luth. Chbk.). He md. Anna Elisabetha and had ch. b. at Hoseck bpt. in the Schoharie Luth. Church.

    iii) <u>Jacob</u>[3], b. 6 Sept 1735 - sp.: Joh: Jacob Jager and Maria Elisabeth Emerich (Rhinebeck Luth. Chbk.). He md. Anna (--) and had ch. bpt. at Albany Ref. and Schoharie Luth. Churches.

    iv) <u>Maria</u>[3], bpt. as Mareitie 24 Jan 1739 - sp.: Johannes Korts and Lisabeth Bernhard (Linlithgo Ref. Chbk.). She md. Johannes Klumm 19 Dec 1758 (Germantown Ref. Chbk.).

    v) <u>Johann Friederich</u>[3], b. 25 Dec 1739 and bpt at Goghkem. (Ancram) - sp.: Frider Proper and wife Maria Susanna (Loonenburg Luth. Chbk.). He md. Sophia Zeal (HJ).

    vi) <u>Anna Catharina</u>[3], b. 2 April 1741 and bpt. Goghkem. (Ancram) - sp.: Adam Hoof and wife Cathar. (Loonenburg Luth. Chbk.).

    vii) <u>Elisabetha</u>[3], bpt. 5 June 1745 at Hosek - sp.: Peter Lampman, Jr. and wife Lisabeth (Loonenburg Luth. Chbk.).

    viii) <u>Maria Christina</u>[3], bpt. 27 May 1746 - sp.: Jacob Pulver and Maria Christ. Pulver (Germantown Ref. Chbk.).

    ix) <u>Jost</u>[3], bpt. 2 Aug 1747 - sp.: Henrich Hoff and wife (Germantown Ref. Chbk.).

    x) <u>David</u>[3], bpt. 7 June 1752 - sp.: David Pots and Catrina Daats (Albany Ref. Chbk.).

3) <u>Johannes</u>[2], on the 1734 St. Peter's List (Rhinebeck Luth. Chbk.). Hannes Bernhard was conf. 3 May 1729 at Kamp, aged 14 yrs. (N.Y. City Luth. Chbk.). He md. at Camp 21 March 1738 Maria Gertraud Rau (Loonenburg Luth. Chbk.). He settled in the North East and 9 Partners section of Dutchess Co. (see Dutchess Co. Ancient Docs. #4260 and #5729) and had issue:

    i) <u>Nicolaus</u>[3], b. 25 March 1740 and bpt. Goghkem. (Ancram) - sp.: Hannes Rauw and wife Catharina (Loonenburg Luth. Chbk.).

    ii) <u>Maria Gertrude</u>[3], b. 25 Oct 1741 and bpt. at Camp -
        sp.: Nicolas Rau and Maria Gertrude, grandparents
        (Loonenburg Luth. Chbk.).

   iii) <u>Georg</u>[3], bpt. 29 Jan 1744 - sp.: George Barnhardt Jr.
        and Marytche Rau (Germantown Ref. Chbk.).

    iv) <u>Johann Jacob</u>[3], b. 8 June 1745 and bpt. Rhinebeck -
        sp.: Jacob Laan and wife Grit (Loonenburg Luth. Chbk.).

     v) <u>Philip</u>[3], b. 16 Feb 1747 - sp.: Philip Rhraw and Sophia
        Loth (Rhinebeck Luth. Chbk.).

    vi) <u>Johann Hermann</u>[3], bpt. 2 April 1749 - sp.: Hermann Kuhn
        and Anna Catharina Kuhn (Gallatin Ref. Chbk.).

   vii) <u>Catharina</u>[3], b. 12 Jan 1750 and bpt. Ancram - sp.:
        Wilhelm Rhau and Catharina Cuntz (Rhinebeck Luth.
        Chbk.).

Johannes[2] probably md. 2nd to Cornelia Ketter (HJ) and had
ch.:

  viii) <u>Wilhelm</u>[3], bpt. 13 Nov 1757 - sp.: Wilhelm Milius and
        Gertruyd Silvernagel (Gallatin Ref. Chbk.).

    ix) <u>Christoph</u>[3], bpt. 13 May 1765 - sp.: Willhelm Schleu-
        der (?) and wife Maria (Pine Plains Chbk.).

4) <u>Anna Elisabetha</u>[2], b. 30 July 1715 - sp.: Elisabetha Hast-
   mann and Henrich Schaester (West Camp Luth. Chbk.). An
   Anna Elisabetha Bernhard was conf. with Hannes Bernhard
   3 May 1729 at Kamp, aged 12 (N.Y. City Luth. Chbk.).
   Elisabetha was on the 1734 list with widow Anna Bernhardt
   (Rhinebeck Luth. Chbk.).

5) <u>Maria Christina</u>[2], on 1734 list (Rhinebeck Luth. Chbk.).
   She md. Jacob Pulver (HJ).

6) <u>Catharina</u>[2], on 1734 list (Rhinebeck Luth. Chbk.). She
   md. Simon Kool Jr. (HJ).

7) <u>Johann Georg</u>[2], b. 27 Sept 1722 at Camp Queensberry - sp.:
   Hans Jurgen Loscher and Christina Roorbach (N.Y. City
   Luth. Chbk.). Johan Jurgen Bernhard, s/o the late Jan
   Bernhard - his mother (being) Anna Elatia, now md. to
   Hinrich Leithen residing at Bedfort, was conf. DNIA 1
   p. Trin.: 1739 at P. Lassing's (N.Y. City Luth. Chbk.).
   He md. Joachimina Cornelissen 23 Aug 1749 (N.Y. City Luth.
   Chbk.) and had issue:

     i) <u>Hannes</u>[3], b. 4 May 1750 and bpt. at Pieter Lassing's
        - sp.: Hannes Romer and Catharina (N.Y. City Luth.
        Chbk.).

    ii) <u>Cornelis</u>[3], b. 25 July 1752 - sp.: Willem Lessing and
        Mareitje (Loonenburg Luth. Chbk.).

   iii) Annaatje³, b. 11 Nov 1755 - sp.: Johannes Scherer
and Liesabeth (Loonenburg Luth. Chbk.).

   iv) Jeremia³, b. 24 Oct 1757 - sp.: Andrees Lassing and
Catharina (Loonenburg Luth. Chbk.).

   v) Maria³, b. 9 May 1760 - sp.: Andrees Wiederwachs
and Annaatje (Loonenburg Luth. Chbk.).

   vi) Petrus³, b. 1 Sept 1762 - sp.: Jacob Laun and Margaretha (Loonenburg Luth. Chbk.).

   vii) Anna Elisabeth³, b. 5 May 1764 - sp.: Alexander
Wiederwachs and Liesabeth Wiederwachs (Loonenburg
Luth. Chbk.).

8) Maria Margaretha², b. 27 Nov 1725 - sp.: Johann Emich
Saalbach, called Hannemann, and wife Maria Marg. (West
Camp Luth. Chbk.). She was on the 1734 St. Peter's List
(Rhinebeck Luth. Chbk.) and conf. at Pieter Lassing's
DNIA p.t.: 1741 (N.Y. City Luth. Chbk.). She md. Jacob
Laun (HJ).

9) Maria Philippina², b. 16 March 1728 and bpt. at Kamp -
sp.: James Ogelby and wife Anna Catharin, Frid. Maul
and wife Anna Ursula (N.Y. City Luth. Chbk.). She was
conf. in prayerhouse at Pieter Lassing's in 1743 (N.Y.
City Luth. Chbk.). She md. Peter Hamm (HJ).

ULRICH BERNHARDT (Hunter Lists #54)

Ulrich Bernhardt first appeared on the Hunter Lists 4 July
1710 with 2 pers. over 10 yrs. of age in the family. On the 4
Aug 1710 roll he was separated by 5 names from #52 Jost Bernhardt
of Groß-Zimmern. An Ulrich Bernhard, single pants-maker and s/o
the late Hans Bernhardt, md. 5 March 1685 Maria Magdalena, d/o
the late Herr Hans Wolff Martenstein, at 6525 Westhofen, but no
proof exists that he was the emigrant 1709er (HJ). Johann Ulrich
Bernhard sp. Wilhelm Simon in 1711 (West Camp Luth. Chbk.). Ulrich Bernhard and Elisabetha were at Hunderston ca. 1716/17 (Simmendinger Register). Olrig Bernat was a Palatine willing to remain at Livingston Manor 26 Aug 1724 (Documentary History of N.Y.,
Vol. III, p. 724).

GERHARD BERTER & ANNA BERTIN (Hunter Lists #55)

Gerhard Berter appeared once on the Hunter Lists 4 Oct 1710;
Anna Berthin was noted 29 Sept 1711. Both entries had 1 pers.
over 10 yrs. of age.

A Hendrik Porter, orphan aged 14, was bound to Garret Van
Horne of N.Y. 28 Sept 1710 (Apprenticeship Lists). Maria Borter

md. Andreas Eichler 7 Dec 1730 (N.Y. City Luth. Chbk.). There were Börders found near Neuwied at 5455 Rengsdorf among other 1709ers who emigrated from Germany to colonial N.Y. A Magdalena Burder aged 22, Ref. and a Johann Burder aged 16, Ref. were in the 3rd arrivals at London in the midst of Palatines originating near Neuwied (London Lists).

JACOB BERTRAM (Hunter Lists #56)

Jacob Bertram first appeared on the Hunter Lists 1 July 1710 with 3 pers. over 10 yrs. of age in the family. His last entry was 24 June 1712 with 2 pers. over 10 yrs. of age.

There was a Joseph Bertram at Hackensack who had a daughter Maria bpt. in 1733 and a son Jan bpt. in 1735 (N.Y. City Luth. Chbk.). The will of Joseph Bartram of Saddle River, Bergen Co. was proved 11 Oct 1760 (N.J. Wills: Lib. G, p. 325).

HERMANN BETZER (Hunter Lists #57)

The European home of the Hudson Valley Betzer-Pitcher family was 5238 Hachenburg-Altstadt (37 km. n.e. of Koblenz; Chbks. begin 1661). The earliest known ancestor of the American line was Daniel Bitzer, d. by 1666. Peter Bitzer, s/o the late Daniel Bitzer from Nister, md. 12 Jan 1666 Ann Els, d/o Peter Zimmermann also from Nister. Peter and Ann Els Bitzer had ch.:

"A Child", bpt. 1 May 1666 - sp.: Anna... - w/o Wilhelm Fischer at Nister, Johann Wilhelm - single s/o Johannes..., and Marg. - w/o Wilhelm Dornebusch at Merkelbach.

+ "A Child", bpt. uff. Astri-monday: 1669 - sp.: Hans Hermann - s/o Peter Zimmermann, Johannes Braun - both from Nister, and Anna Maria Rorbach from Hachenburg. Due to the primary male sponsor, this child was our emigrant 1709er (HJ).

"A Child", bpt. 7. Trin.: 1671 - sp.: Anna Christin - d/o Johann the miller, Eva - d/o Peter Zimmermann, and Thiel - single brother of the child's father. Due to the female sp., this child was the Eva Betzer who md. the N.Y. settler Johannes Schu (HJ).

Ann Els, wid/o the late Peter Bitzer from Nister, md. Peter Jung, s/o the late Daniel Jung from Hattert on Exaudi 1677. Hermann[1] Bitzer md. an Elsa Maria (--). The many sp. of the Frantz family to their ch. suggest that she may have been the "child", sp. by an Elsa Maria, bpt. Jubilate 1666 to Johannes Frantz; Johannes Frantz, s/o Henrich Frantz at O.H., md Anna Maria, d/o Martin Müller at O.H., 19 Nov 1663 (HJ). Johan Herman Bötser, his wife and 8 ch. were in the 6th party at Rotterdam, recorded near an Anna

Maria Botser, a Johan Peter Timmerman, and N.Y. 1709ers Johan Diderig Schniter, Johan Klein, Johan Schu, Kristian Meyer, and Hans
Jacob Dinges (Rotterdam Lists).

Hermann Betzer made his first appearance on the Hunter Lists
4 July 1710 with 5 pers. over 10 yrs. of age and 2 pers. under
10 yrs. The last entry on Hunter was 13 Sept 1712 with 5 pers.
over 10 yrs. and 1 pers. under 10. He was a soldier in the Canadian expedition of 1711 (Palatine Volunteers To Canada). Harma
Betser was nat. 17 Jan 1715/16 (Albany Nats.). Hermann Betzer
and Elsen Maria with 3 ch. were at Wormsdorff ca. 1716/17 (Simmendinger Register). He was on Palatine Debtors Lists dated 1718,
1719 (at Annsberry), and 1721 (Livingston Debt Lists). Herman
Betzer was a Palatine willing to remain at Livingston Manor 26 Aug
1724 (Documentary History Of N.Y., Vol. III, p. 724). He signed
a receipt mentioning Pastor Hager 29 July 1722 (Livingston Papers).
The ch. of Hermann[1] and Elsa Maria all bpt. Altstadt were:
1) "A young daughter"[2], bpt. 17. Trin.: 1693 - sp.: Johann
   Kreiss..., Anna Maria - the child's mother's single sister, and Christine - single d/o Johann Frantz. Sp. suggest this was Anna Christina Betzer who md. Jacob Best
   Sr. (HJ).
2) "A Young daughter"[2], bpt. 6.p.Trin.: 1695 - sp.: Johann
   Daniel - single s/o Peter Schmitt, Elsbeth - single d/o
   Johann Frantz, and Stina Cathrin Hütt - single d/o Adam.
3) "A young son"[2], bpt. 3.p. Epiph.: 1697 - sp.: Peter Jung
   - Sendschöffe, Peter - single s/o Johan Frantz, and Anna
   Gertraut - w/o Martin Frantz - all of Ober Hattert. Sp.
   show this child was named Peter Betzer (HJ). Peter Betser
   was nat. 17 Jan 1715/16 (Albany Nats.). Peter Pitser
   was a Palatine Debtor in 1721 and 1726 (Livingston Debt
   Lists). Pieter Pittsier of Dutchess Co. and Anna Catrien,
   his wife, deeded 7 pieces of land to Tiel Rockevelt 15
   Oct 1751 (Albany Co. Deeds: Vol. 7, p. 1). He md. Anna
   Catharina Philips and had ch.:
   i) Maria Catharina[3], b. middle of Sept 1720 at Annsberry
      and bpt. at Camp - sp.: Joh. Peter Phlipps and Maria
      Catharina Putserin (N.Y. City Luth. Chbk.). She md.
      Henrich Benner (HJ).
   ii) Wilhelm[3],md. as s/o Peter 5 Nov 1748 Magdalena Dons-
       bach (Germantown Ref. Chbk.). The will of William
       Pitcher, yeoman of Rhinebeck, was dated 13 Jan 1800
       and proved 7 May 1800 (Dutchess Co. Will Bk. B).
   iii) Magdalena[3] (HJ), md. Wilhelm Klum (HJ)
   iv) Gertraut[3] (HJ), md. 1st Conrad Pulver and 2nd Frid.

Stickel (HJ).

    v) <u>Christina</u>[3] (HJ), md. Johannes Schmidt (HJ).

   vi) <u>Elisabetha</u>[3], bpt. 1 Nov 1736 - sp.: Willem Phillips
and Lisabeth Best (Red Hook Luth. Chbk.). She md.
14 Feb 1758 Andreas Stickel (Red Hook Luth. Chbk.).

  vii) <u>Adam</u>[3] (HJ), md. Anna Maria Richter. The will of
Adam Bityer of Rhinebeck Prec. was dated 30 May 1768
and probated 12 Sept 1768 (<u>Fernow Wills</u> #128).

4) <u>"A daughter"</u>[2], bpt. 27 June 1700 - sp.: Maria Magdalena -
d/o Johann Leyendecker, Gertrudt - w/o Martinus Greis
from Ober Hattert, and Johannes Schuch - brother-in-law
of the father. A d/o Hermann Betzer md. Johann Wilhelm
Schneider and, due to the sp. names, this child may have
been that <u>Anna Gertraud Betzer</u>; if so, she md. at a very
young age (HJ).

5) <u>"A son"</u>[2], bpt. 26 April 1702 - sp.: Johannes Frantz from
Obber Hatteroth, Johann Adam Hintz (Kurtz?)...from Oberhatteroth, and Anna Christina - w/o Daniel Kreiss. Due
to the names of the sp., this child was <u>Adam Betzer</u> (HJ).
An old declaration survives regarding Adam Pitser (Dutchess Co. Ancient Docs. #276). The will of Adam Pitsier
of Dutchess Co. was dated 10 May 1760 and probated 30 May
1768 (<u>Fernow Wills</u> #1313). He md. 23 Nov 1725 with banns
to Catharina Funck (Linlithgo Ref. Chbk.). Issue:

    i) <u>Peter</u>[3], bpt. 4 June 1727 - sp.: Pieter Petsier and
Catrien (Linlithgo Ref. Chbk.). He md. 9 Dec 1746
Elisabetha Linck (Germantown Ref. Chbk.).

   ii) <u>Hermanus</u>[3], bpt. 5 weeks old 21 Sept 1728 at the Camp
- sp.: Herman Pezard and Gertaud Funk (N.Y. City
Luth. Chbk.). He md. Elisabetha Kuhn (HJ).

  iii) <u>Jacob</u>[3], bpt. 14 Aug 1732 - sp.: Jacob Bys and his
wife Christina (Germantown Ref. Chbk.). He md.
Gertraud Klum (HJ). Jacob Pitcher d. 22 Feb 1804,
aged 76 yrs. (Germantown Ref. Chbk.).

   iv) <u>Johannes</u>[3], bpt. 6 Aug 1734 - sp.: Johannes Philipp
and Catharina (Germantown Ref. Chbk.).

    v) <u>Wilhelm</u>[3] (HJ), md. Anna Margaretha Schmidt (HJ).
They had ch. bpt. at Germantown Ref., Red Hook, Germantown Luth., and Rhinebeck Luth. Churches.

6) <u>"A daughter"</u>[2], bpt. 1 Jan 1704 - sp.: Johann Christ. Leyendecker, Agnesa Elisabeth Zimmermann from Niester, and
Klara - w/o Johann Henrich Jung from Obberhattert.

7) <u>"A daughter"</u>[2] , bpt. 29 Sept 1705 - sp.: Anna Margaretha -
w/o Gerhard Schneyder, Johann Pitter Korst (?) - all from

Obberhatteroth, and Maria - w/o Theiss Dünschman...

8) "A son"[2], bpt. Oct 1707 - sp.: Tönes Bietzer..., Johann
   Marten Müller, and Anna Elisabeth Licht - w/o Hans Gerhard from Obberhatteroth.

9) Catharina[2] (HJ), md. Johannes Philip (HJ).

10) Elisabetha Catharina[2] (HJ), md. Peter Weber (HJ).

11) Johann Theiss[2] (HJ), on the Dutchess Co. Tax Lists 1732-
    1738/9. He md. Anna Margaretha (--) and had ch.:
    i) Gertraud[3], bpt. 17 April 1732 - sp.: Christian Haber
       and Gertraud (Germantown Ref. Chbk.).
    ii) Peter[3], bpt. 16 March 1735 - sp.: Peter Pulver and
        Susanna (Red Hook Luth. Chbk.).
    iii) Johann Wilhelm[3], b. 16 Feb 1739 and bpt. Teerbosch
         - sp.: Wilhelm Kuhn and wife Lisabeth (Loonenburg
         Luth. Chbk.).

An Anna Maria Betzerin was recorded next to Johannes (and
Eva Betzer) Schuh at Wormsdorff ca. 1716/17 (Simmendinger Regis-
ter); she may have been the Anna Maria Botser noted near Johann
Hermann[1] at Rotterdam in 1709 (HJ).

JOHANN JACOB BEYER (Hunter Lists #58)

Johann Jacob Beyer first was noted on the Hunter Lists 4
Oct 1710 with 1 pers. over 10 yrs. of age; he appears to have re-
placed #25 Anna Margretha Bayerin on these rolls (HJ). Jacob
Bayer was nat. 17 Jan 1715/16 (Albany Nats.). He was on Palatine
Debt Lists dated 1718, 1719 (at Kingsberry), 1721 and 1726 (Liv-
ingston Debt Lists). Jacob Berjer was a Palatine willing to re-
main at Livingston Manor 26 Aug 1724 (Documentary History of N.Y.,
Vol. III, p. 724). He was on the St. Peter's List of 1734
(Rhinebeck Luth. Chbk.). He md. Anna Margaretha Dieterich (HJ),
and they were sp. to many bpts. along the Hudson until 1754.

SUSANNA BEYERIN dicta BEURIN (Hunter Lists #59)

Susanna Baurin made her first appearance on the Hunter Lists
30 June 1710 with 1 pers. over 10 yrs. of age and 1 pers. under
10 yrs. The surname was spelled Bayerin on 4 Aug and 4 Oct 1710.
Susannah Beijerin, a widow aged 30, and Susannah Maria Beijerin,
aged 1, were in N.Y. City in 1710/11 (Palatines In N.Y. City).
Anna Susanna Lamp, widow of Joh[S] Hendrik Beierds of the Pfalz
joined the N.Y. City Ref. Church 29 May 1711; a notation added
after this entry read "does not come to church." (N.Y. City Ref.
Chbk.).

JOHANNES BIERMANN (Hunter Lists #60)

A Johan Berman and his wife were on Capt. Jno. Untank's ship in the 5th party in Holland in 1709 (Rotterdam Lists).

Johannes Biermann made his first appearance on the Hunter Lists 30 June 1710 with 1 pers. over 10 yrs. of age and 2 pers. under 10 yrs. in the household; the entries diminished to 1 pers. over 10 yrs. on 4 Aug 1710 and then 1 pers. over 10 yrs. and 1 pers. under 10 yrs. on 4 Oct 1710. The notations then fluctuated in 1711, ending with 3 pers. over 10 yrs. and 1 under 10 yrs. on 13 Sept 1712. Johannis Beerman was nat. 22 Nov 1715 (Albany Nats.). Johann Biermann with his wife and 3 ch. were at Neu-Ansberg ca. 1716/17 (Simmendinger Register). Johannis Beerman and Mary Beerman were each patentees on the n. side of the Mohawk River 30 April 1725 (Burnetsfield Patent). Johannis Peerman granted land to Joh: Kaspar in 1741/2 and again in 1767 (Albany Co. Deeds: Vol. 8, p. 474). The N.Y. Mercury reported on 2 March 1761 that Catharine Bearman, w/o Johannis Bearman of Burnetsfield, was not to be trusted or bought from, and that her husband would not pay her future debts (Genealogical Data From Colonial N.Y. Newspapers, p. 78).

JOHANNES BLASS (Hunter Lists #61)

Johan Blasch, his wife and 2 ch. were in the 6th party of Palatines sailing from Holland to England in 1709 (Rotterdam Lists). Anna Maria, wid/o Adam Blast of Alt-zaborn in the Pfaltz, md. Martin Stein of Langen, Stalz Thuringen 27 Feb 1711 (West Camp Luth. Chbk.); perhaps Johannes[1] Blass may have been related to this Blast family of 6753 Alsenborn (HJ).

Johannes Blass made his first appearance on the Hunter Lists 4 July 1710 with 2 pers. over 10 yrs. of age and 1 pers. under 10 in the family; the household was reduced to 2 pers. over 10 yrs. on 31 Dec 1710. The entry for 29 Sept 1711 read Johannes Blass and Peter Klein's widow; a special notation 24 Dec 1711 read for his wife, Peter Klein's widow. The last entry for the family on Hunter was 13 Sept 1712 with 3 pers. over 10 yrs. and 2 pers. under 10. Johannes Blass of Annsberg was a Palatine soldier in 1711 (Palatine Volunteers To Canada). Johannes Blass, his wife and 4 ch. were at Quunsberg ca. 1716/17 (Simmendinger Register). He was on Palatine Debtors Lists dated 1718, 1721, and 1726 (Livingston Debt Lists) and was a Palatine willing to remain on the manor 26 Aug 1724 (Documentary History of N.Y., Vol. III, p. 724). He d. 6 Dec 1749, aged 70 yrs. (Germantown Ref. Chbk.). By his 1st wife in Germany he had issue:

1) <u>Johann Henrich</u>[2] (HJ), nat. 17 Jan 1715/16 (Albany Nats.).
He md. 21 Dec 1725 Elisabetha Catharina Blees (Plies)
(Linlithgo Ref. Chbk.). They had ch.:

    i) <u>Johannes</u>[3], b. 23 Oct 1726 and bpt. at Jacob Schu-
macher's at Kamp - sp.: Johannes Plass and Agnesa
Flora Plass (N.Y. City Luth. Chbk.).

   ii) <u>Johann Emmerich</u>[3], b. 17 April 1728 and bpt. at Loon.
- sp.: Emmerich Plass, (maternal) grandfather, and
Cath. Plass, (paternal) grandmother (Loonenburg
Luth. Chbk.). He md. 15 Nov 1753 Anna Gertraudt
Rockefeller (Germantown Ref. Chbk.) (HJ).

  iii) <u>Johannes</u>[3], b. 27 Feb 1730 and bpt. at Loon. - sp.:
Johannes Kleyn and Anna Margareta (Loonenburg Luth.
Chbk.). He was probably the Hannes Plass conf. in
Feb 1744/5 at Loonenburg Luth. (HJ). He md. 25
April 1749 Geesche Jansen (Loonenburg Luth. Chbk.),
and they had ch. bpt. at Loonenburg Luth., Rhine-
beck Flats Ref., and Churchtown Luth. Churches.

   iv) <u>Anna Eva</u>[3], b. 15 Nov 1735 - sp.: Wilhelm Blass -
father..., and Anna Eva Dik - brother...(Rhinebeck
Luth. Chbk.)

    v) <u>Anna Elisabetha</u>[3], b. 4 Dec 1737 and bpt. at the Camp
- sp.: Jo. Mich. Plass and Anna Liese Miller (Loonenburg Luth. Chbk.).

   vi) <u>Anna Eva</u>[3], bpt. 8 weeks old at Teerbosch 13 April
1740 - sp.: Wilhelm Link and wife Eva, and in place
of the father Jac. Scheffer (Loonenburg Luth. Chbk.).
There was an Anna Eva Plass who md. Petrus Heiser
by 1760, and this may have been her (HJ).

  vii) <u>Anna Maria</u>[3], b. 7 July 1742 and bpt. at the Camp -
sp.: Kilian Stoffelbein and Anna Marg Palss (Loonenburg Luth. Chbk.).

 viii) <u>Agness Flora</u>[3], bpt 15 May 1744 - sp.: Emmerich Blass
and Anganisse Flora Blass (Germantown Ref. Chbk.).

   ix) <u>Elisabetha</u>[3], bpt. 28 Aug 1748 - sp.: Henrich Schmidt
and Lisabeth Blass (Germantown Ref. Chbk.).

    x) <u>Petrus</u>[3], bpt. 2 Dec 1750 - sp.: Peter Plass and Sil-
ge Maria Plass (Germantown Ref. Chbk.).

   xi) <u>Michael</u>[3], bpt. 27 Jan 1753 - sp.: Michael Plass and
Elisabeth Rockefeller (Linlithgo Ref. Chbk.).

  xii) <u>Maria Magdalena</u>[3], bpt. 6 March 1757 - sp.: Joh:
Caspar Ruher (minister) and Maria Magdalena Jacobina
Engel, his wife (Germantown Ref. Chbk.).

By his 2nd wife Elisabetha, Johannes[1] probably had ch.:

2) <u>Peter²</u> (HJ), who md. Celia Maria Link (HJ) and had ch.:

    i) <u>Johann Wilhelm³</u>, b. 12 Jan or June 1735 - sp.: Joh:
Wilhelm Link and wife Anna Maria (Rhinebeck Luth.
Chbk.). He md. 16 March 1757 Anna Elisabetha Holz-
apfel (Germantown Ref. Chbk.) and d. 6 April 1757
(Germantown Ref. Chbk.).

    ii) <u>Johannes³</u>, md. as s/o Peter Blass to Gertraut Holz-
apfel 5 Dec 1758 (Germantown Ref. Chbk.).

    iii) <u>Elsje³</u>, bpt. 23 Jan 1739 - sp.: Teunis Schoe and
Elsje Dings (Linlithgo Ref. Chbk.).

    iv) <u>Peter³</u>, md. as s/o Peter Blass 19 Nov 1765 Eva Leik
(Germantown Ref. Chbk.).

    v) <u>Catharina³</u>, bpt. 26 Jan 1741 - sp.: Willem Plas and
Catharina Link (Germantown Ref. Chbk.).

    vi) <u>Margaretha³</u>, bpt. as Cretha 16 April 1745 - sp.: Jost
Henrich Dunsbach and Cretha Dunsbach (Germantown Ref.
Chbk.).

    vii) <u>Anna Maria³</u>, bpt. 25 Jan 1747 - sp.: John Emerich
Plass and Anna Maria Linck (Germantown Ref. Chbk.).
She md. Georg Kuhn (HJ).

    viii) <u>Philipp³</u>, bpt. 9 March 1749 - sp.: Philipp Linck and
Lisabeth Blass (Germantown Ref. Chbk.). He md. in
Dec 1771 Margaretha Dieterich (Germantown Ref. Chbk.).

    ix) <u>Henrich³</u>, bpt. 28 July 1751 - sp.: Henrick Plas and
Elisabeth Plas (Linlithgo Ref. Chbk.).

Peter Blass, widower, md. Barbara Kurz, widow, 17 May
1758 (Germantown Ref. Chbk.).

3) <u>Johann Wilhelm²</u>, b. 17 July 1714 and bpt. as s/o Johann
and Elisabetha Plass - sp.: J. Wilhelm Schneider and Magdalena Philipp (West Camp Luth. Chbk.). He md. Magdalena
Müller and had ch.:

    i) <u>Henrich³</u>, bpt. 24 April 1748 - sp.: Henrich Blass and
Lish-Catharina Blass (Germantown Ref. Chbk.).

    ii) <u>Elsge³</u>, bpt. 12 March 1751 - sp.: Martinus Schoets
and Anna Els. Shoets (Germantown Ref. Chbk.).

    iii) <u>Petrus³</u>, bpt. 22 Oct 1752 - sp.: Peter Plas and wife
(Gallatin Ref. Chbk.).

    iv) <u>Michael³</u>, bpt. 19 July 1755 - sp.: Michael Plas and
Elisabeth Plas (Linlithgo Ref. Chbk.).

    v) <u>Elisabetha³</u>, bpt. 26 June 1757 - sp.: Herman Best and
wife Maria Eliesabetha Rohrig (Germantown Ref. Chbk.).

    vi) <u>Wilhelm³</u>, bpt. 25 May 1760 - sp.: Hendrik Philip and
wife Elisabeth Caspar (Linlithgo Ref. Chbk.).

    vii) <u>Magdalena³</u>, bpt. 28 March 1762 - sp.: Pieter Coopar and Magdalena Stoppelbeen (Linlithgo Ref. Chbk.).

    viii) Catharina[3], bpt. 6 May 1764 - sp.: Pieter Krain and
        wife Catharin Lescher (Germantown Ref. Chbk.).

    ix) Maria[3], bpt. 28 May 1767 - sp.: Georg Dekker and wife
       Marytien Schurtz (Germantown Ref. Chbk.).

By his 3rd wife Anna Catharina (sp. suggest she may have been a
Hagedorn - HJ), Johannes[1] had ch.:

    4) Maria Gertraud[2], b. beginning of Nov 1720 at Queensberry
       and bpt. at Camp - sp.: Maria Gertrud Hagedorn (N.Y. City
       Luth. Chbk.). She md. Michael Stoppelbein (HJ).

    5) Johann Michael[2] (HJ), md. Anna Elisabetha Rockefeller and
       had ch.:

        i) Jacob[3], bpt. 24 May 1747 - sp.: Jacob Scherp and Lis-
          abeth Conrad (Germantown Ref. Chbk.).

        ii) Elsgen[3], bpt. 3 Jan 1749 - sp.: Hans Christ. Rocker-
          felder and Gret Blass (Germantown Ref. Chbk.). She
          probably md. Johannes Finger (HJ).

       iii) Maria[3], bpt. 2 Dec 1750 - sp.: Peter Plass and Silge
          Maria Plass (Germantown Ref. Chbk.). She probably
          md. Jacob Finger (HJ).

       iv) Eva[3], bpt. 26 Sept 1752 - sp.: Simon Rokenfeller and
          Gertje (Germantown Ref. Chbk.).

        v) Johannes[3], bpt. 16 April 1754 - sp.: Johannes Plas Jr.
          and Anna Maria Roggefeller (Germantown Ref. Chbk.).

       vi) Peter[3] (HJ), bur. as Peter M. Blass 22 Jan 1832, aged
          87-11-22 (Germantown Ref. Cem.); he md. Catharina
          Finger (HJ).

       vii) Elisabeth[3], bpt. 7 March 1756 - sp.: Henrich Blass and
          Eliesa Catharina Plies (Germantown Ref. Chbk.).

      viii) Philippus[3], bpt. 4 May 1758 - sp.: Diel Rockenfeller
          and wife Anna Gerd: Alsdorff (Germantown Ref. Chbk.).

       ix) Wilhelm[3], bpt. 13 April 1760 - sp.: Willem Rockenfel-
          ler and Griet Rockenfeller (Linlithgo Ref. Chbk.).

        x) Michael[3], bpt. 13 Nov 1762 - sp.: Niclaes Shurz and
          wife Marytje Shutz (Linlithgo Ref. Chbk.).

    6) Elisabetha Catharina[2], b. 18 March 1728 and bpt. Kamp - sp.:
       Peter Hagedorn and wife Liese Catharina (N.Y. City Luth.
       Chbk.). She md. 16 April 1750 Bernhard Schmidt (Germantown
       Ref. Chbk.).

    7) Anna Maria[2], bpt. 20 Dec 1732 - sp.: Peter Stoppelbein, Anna
       Maria Schoplein and Ottila Maria Stoppelbein (Germantown
       Ref. Chbk.).

    8) Johann Christophel[2], b. 12 May 1734 - sp.: Joh: Christoffel
       Hagedorn and wife (Rhinebeck Luth. Chbk.).

9) <u>Johann Jacob[2]</u>, b. 1 April 1736 - sp.: Joh: Henrich Schmid and wife Anna (Rhinebeck Luth. Chbk.).

10) <u>Barbara[2]</u> (HJ), md. Johannes Schaer (HJ).

11) <u>Johannes Jr.[2]</u> (HJ), a sp. at Germantown Ref. in 1754.

12) <u>Margaretha[2]</u> (HJ), a sp. at Loonenburg Luth. in 1742, who may have been the Anna Margaretha Plass who joined the Germantown Ref. Church 11 May 1743 (HJ).

<u>JOHN HENRICH BÖHLER</u> (Hunter Lists #62)

Henrig Bieler sailed from Holland to England in 1709 (Rotterdam Lists). Henry Behler aged 30, Ref., cooper and brewer, was in the 3rd arrivals at London 2 June 1709 (London Lists).

John Henrich Böhler made his first appearance on the Hunter Lists 30 June 1710 with 1 pers. over 10 yrs. of age in his household. On 4 Oct 1710 the family increased to 2 pers. over 10 yrs., and on 31 Dec 1710 the entry noted 3 pers. over 10 yrs. of age and 3 under 10 yrs. Johann Heinrich Poler of Alt-Zheim on the lower Rhine md. Susanna, wid/o Johann Paul Clotter of Berchenheim by Weinheim in the Pfaltz, 24 Aug 1710 (West Camp Luth. Chbk.); thus the ancestral village of the family was 6526 <u>Alsheim</u> (HJ). Johann Henrich Poeler's wife, Epis., joined the church at N.Y. 19 July 1710 (West Camp Luth. Chbk.).

<u>HENRICH BÖHM</u> (Hunter Lists #63)

Henrich Böhm first appeared on the Hunter Lists 4 July 1710 with 2 pers. over 10 yrs. of age in the family. On 4 Aug 1710 the household increased to 5 pers. over 10 yrs., and on 4 Oct 1710 the notation read 3 pers. over 10 yrs. of age. Hans Henrich Boehm or Behm was nat. 8 and 9 Sept 1715 (Kingston Nats.). Hendrick Beem was in the foot company of militia for Shawangunk under the command of Capt. Nicolas Hoffman in Ulster Co. in 1715 (<u>Report of the State Historian</u>, Vol. I, p. 564). Heinrich Böhm, his wife and ch. were at Beckmansland ca. 1716/17 (Simmendinger Register). Henrich Beam was on the tax rolls of Kingston, Ulster Co. 1718/19-1720/21 (Ulster Co. Tax Lists). He first was mentioned on Dutchess Co. rolls in 1723/24 and was continued until March of 1732 when the widow of Hendrick Beem, deceased was recorded (Dutchess Co. Tax Lists). 4 acres of his farmland were set aside for a church at Rhinebeck in 1724 (<u>History of Rhinebeck</u>, p. 92). He md. 1st Maria Apollonia (Schoole - HJ) and 2nd Julianna (--) (Banns given at Kingston Ref. Church 7 April 1721). Issue from 1st wife:

1) <u>Maria Dorothea[2]</u> (HJ), md. Wilhelm Douwty 10 Dec 1715 (Kingston Ref. Chbk.).

2) <u>Georg</u>[2] (HJ), md 14 Nov 1719 Elisabeth Hertel (Kingston
   Ref. Chbk.). Gorg Beam was nat. 8 and 9 Sept 1715 (Kingston Nats.). Jury Beem was in Capt. Wittaker's company
   of the Ulster Co. militia in 1715 (<u>Report of the State</u>
   <u>Historian</u>, Vol. I, p. 557). Jurian Beam was taxed in
   Kingston in 1720/1 (Ulster Co. Tax Lists) and was a defendant in a suit involving two hogs running in the
   street against the Trustee's orders in 1725 (Kingston
   Town Court Records). His ch. were:

   i) <u>Henrich</u>[3], bpt. 25 Sept 1720 - sp.: Hendrich Beem and
      Apolonia Schoole (Kingston Ref. Chbk.).

   ii) <u>Adam</u>[3], bpt. 9 Dec 1722 - sp.: Adam Herten and Geer-
       truy Smit (Kingston Ref. Chbk.).

   iii) <u>Wilhelm</u>[3], bpt. 1 March 1724 - sp.: Willem Douty and
        Nenny Beam (Kingston Ref. Chbk.). He md. 30 Sept
        1746 Rebecca Freer (Rhinebeck Flats Ref. Chbk.) and
        had ch. bpt. at Rhinebeck Flats Ref., Kingston Ref.,
        and Red Hook Luth. Churches. The will of William
        Beam of Rhinebeck Precinct was dated 26 March 1783
        and probated 19 Nov 1793 (Dutchess Co. Will Bk. A).

   iv) <u>Adam</u>[3], bpt. 22 May 1726 - sp.: Johannes Schram and
       Catrina Weet (Kingston Ref. Chbk.). He md. 24 Sept
       1747 Catharina Freer (Rhinebeck Flats Ref. Chbk.)
       and had ch. bpt. at Rhinebeck Flats Ref., Albany Ref.,
       and Kingston Ref. Churches.

   v) <u>Georg</u>[3], bpt. 28 July 1728 - sp.: Cheerles Tangerly
      and Marytjen Keeteltas (Kingston Ref. Chbk.).

   vi) <u>Albert</u>[3], bpt. 4 March 1733 - sp.: Albert Beem and
       Marytjen Hartken (Kingston Ref. Chbk.).

   vii) <u>Zacharias</u>[3], b. 15 June 1735 and bpt. Newton - sp.:
        Wilhelm Brandauw and wife Liese Catharina (Loonen-
        burg Luth. Chbk.).

   viii) <u>Elisabeth</u>[3], bpt. 23 Oct 1737 - sp.: Lodewyk Smith
         (Readington Ref. Chbk.).

3) <u>Albert</u>[2] (HJ), md. 23 Aug 1721 Anna Margaretha Beeshaar
   (Kingston Ref. Chbk.). Johan Albert Beam was nat. 8 and
   9 Sept 1715 (Kingston Nats.). He was a defendant regarding unpaid rent in 1731 (Kingston Town Court Records) and
   mentioned in the Kingston Trustees Records (Bk. 2, pg 340).
   Albert Beein was in the foot company of the Ulster Co.
   militia in 1738 (<u>Report of the State Historian</u>, Vol. I,
   p. 603). His ch. were:

   i) <u>"An un-named child"</u>[3], who accompanied the parents
      to their marriage (Kingston Ref. Chbk.).

ii) <u>Maria</u>[3], bpt. 27 Aug 1721 - sp.: Jan Oet and Hille-
gonda Slegtenaar (Kingston Ref. Chbk.). A Marreitje
Beam md. Jacob Teerpenning 25 May 1746 (Kingston
Ref. Chbk.).

iii) <u>Magdalena</u>[3], bpt. 13 Jan 1723 - sp.: Juriaan Beem and
Magdalena Peeshaar (Kingston Ref. Chbk.). She md.
Henrich Eckhardt 24 Sept 1743 (Rhinebeck Flats Ref.
Chbk.).

iv) <u>Christina</u>[3], bpt. 24 Jan 1725 - sp.: Willem Bolk and
Christina Beeshaar (Kingston Ref. Chbk.).

v) <u>Anna</u>[3], bpt. 11 Feb 1728 - sp.: Willem Douwdie and
Anna Beem (Kingston Ref. Chbk.). She md. Gerrit
Teerpenning 20 Sept 1750 (Kingston Ref. Chbk.).

vi) <u>Hendrich</u>[3], bpt. 4 March 1733 - sp.: Barent Peesharing
and Magdaleen Peesharing (Kingston Ref. Chbk.).

vii) <u>Elisabetha</u>[3] (HJ), md. Henricus Dijo 13 Oct 1753 (Kingston Ref. Chbk.).

viii) <u>Margaretha</u>[3], bpt. 25 April 1736 - sp.: Tammes Zett-
iwik and Elisabeth Sevel (Kingston Ref. Chbk.).

ix) <u>Albartus</u>[3], bpt. 3 Sept 1738 - sp.: Jan Maklien and
Eva Smit (Kingston Ref. Chbk.).

SOPHIA BOLLIN (Hunter Lists #64)

Anna Sophia, wid/o Lastar Bohl of Maller near Coblentz, md.
Peter Pfuhl, widower and cabinetmaker of Nider-Rammstadt in Darmstadt, 27 Sept 1710 (West Camp Luth. Chbk.). Caspar Boll aged 40,
with his wife, and a daughter aged 4, Luth., husbandman and vinedresser, were in the 4th arrivals in England (London Lists). Sophia Bollin first appeared on the Hunter Lists 30 June 1710 with
1 pers. over 10 yrs. in the family; her last entry was 4 Oct 1710
with 1 pers. over 10 yrs.

FRANTZ BONN (Hunter Lists #65)

Frans Bonn, his wife and 3 ch. were enrolled on Capt. Robb[t]
Breem's ship Mary And Elisabet on 5 June 1709 (Rotterdam Lists).
Francis Bohne aged 39, with his wife, sons aged 10 and 9, and a
daughter aged 5, Catholic, husbandman and vinedresser, were in
the 3rd arrivals at London in 1709 (London Lists).

Frantz Bonn made his first appearance on the Hunter Lists 4
Aug 1710 with 2 pers. over 10 yrs.; Frantz Lefebure dicta Bonn was
noted with 3 pers. over 10 yrs. 4 Oct 1710 and with 1 pers. over 10
24 Dec 1711. Maria Barbara Kras, wid/o Frans Poore of Twee Brugge
uit Swede, md. Daniel Thevoe 27 Feb 1711 (N.Y. City Ref. Chbk.).

NICLAUS BONENSTIEHL (Hunter Lists #66)

Niklaas Penenstehl, his wife and 2 ch. were in the 5th party sailing from Holland to England 3 July 1709 on the ship captained by Jno Ünthank (Entank) (Rotterdam Lists).

Niclaus Bonestiel made his first appearance on the Hunter Lists 4 Oct 1710 with 2 pers. over 10 yrs. of age; on 24 Dec 1711 the family was recorded with 2 pers. over 10 yrs. and 1 under 10. On 25 March 1712 Niclaus had 1 pers. over 10 yrs. of age and 1 under 10 yrs.; on 24 June 1712 he was registered with 3 pers. over 10 yrs. of age and 1 pers. under 10 yrs. These entries suggest that Niclaus Bonestiehl md. his 2nd wife Anna Margaretha Kuhn in mid-1712 (HJ). Niecolas Bonnesteel was nat. 17 Jan 1715/16 (Albany Nats.). Nicolaus Bohnenstiel and Margretha with 2 ch. were at Hunderston ca. 1716/17 (Simmendinger Register). Nicholas Boonsted was a Palatine Debtor in 1718, 1719 (of Hunterstown) and 1721 (Livingston Debt Lists). He made his first appearance on the tax rolls in 1722 and was continued in Rhinebeck Precinct until June 1767 (Dutchess Co. Tax Lists). Michael Bonestell asked for a piece of ground to build a church on behalf of the Luth. congregation of Rhinebeck 4 Nov 1729 (History of Rhinebeck, p. 98). Jacob Van Kampen granted land to Nicholas Bonestel and Phillip Lonehert of Reynebeeck 17 Nov 1738 (1st Dutchess Co. Deed Bk., p. 353), and John Van Renselaer granted land to Nicholas Bonesteel of Rynbeeck in 1751 (Albany Co. Deeds: Vol. 6, p. 423). Some old documents were found relating to him dated 1748-58 (Dutchess Co. Ancient Docs., #659, 661, 2479, 2480, 2481, and 3789). Niclaus[1] Bonenstiehl and Anna Margaretha Kuhn had ch.:

1) Elisabetha[2] (HJ), conf. with Susanna Bohnenstiel 24 May 1732 at Rhynbek (Loonenburg Luth. Chbk.). She md. Balthasar Simon (HJ).

2) Susanna Margretha[2], b. 5 Nov 1714 - sp.: Susanna Margretha Schneider (West Camp Luth. Chbk.). She also was conf. 24 May 1732 at Rhynbek (Loonenburg Luth. Chbk.). She md. Andreas Michel 30 May 1739 at Camp (Loonenburg Luth. Chbk.).

3) Anna Barbara[2] (HJ), md. Michel Simon (HJ).

4) Nicolaus[2], b. 17 March 1722 at Rheinbeeck - sp.: Nickel Kuntz and wife (N.Y. City Luth. Chbk.). He was conf. 13 April 1740 at Theerbos (Loonenburg Luth. Chbk.). Niclaus Jr. made his first appearance on Rhinebeck/North East tax rolls in 1744/5 and continued to 1763 (Dutchess Co. Tax Lists). He was in Capt. Abraham Van Aernam's Company above Poesten Kill in 1767 (Report of the State Historian, Vol. II, p. 813). The will of Nicholas Bonistiel of Troy

was written 26 Nov 1806 and recorded 5 Sept 1809 (Rensselaer Co. Will Bk. 3). Niclaus[2] md. Anna Elisabetha Treber and had ch.:

i) Anna Margaretha[3], bpt. 4 Sept 1743 - sp.: Nicklas Bonestiel and wife Anna Elisabeth (Red Hook Luth. Chbk.). She md. Henry Simons Jr. (Will).

ii) Catharina[3], bpt. 7 April 1745 - sp.: Pitter Treber and wife Catterina (Red Hook Luth. Chbk.). She md. Abraham Simons (Will).

iii) Anna Maria[3], b. 17 Oct 1746 - sp.: David Bohnenstiel and Anna Maria Treber (Rhinebeck Luth. Chbk.). She md. Killien Rickard (Will).

iv) Johannes[3], b. 1 Jan 1749 - sp.: Johanne Treber and Barbara Simon (Rhinebeck Luth. Chbk.).

v) Elisabeth[3], b. 1 Oct 1750 - sp.: Balthas Simon and wife Elisab. (Rhinebeck Luth. Chbk.).

vi) Frederick[3] (Will).

vii) Nicolaus[3], bpt. 26 May 1754 in a confusing entry - sp.: Nicolaes Boonestell and Elizabeth Boonesteel (Red Hook Luth. Chbk.).

viii) Philipus[3], bpt. 22 Dec 1755 - sp.: Philip Bonenstiehl and Elisabetha Hagedorn (Red Hook Luth. Chbk.).

ix) Lodowick[3] (Will), d. 14 Nov 1841 (?), aged 81-8-25 (Bonesteel Cem., Grafton, Rensselaer Co.).

x) Henrich[3], b. 8 May 1761 - sp.: Henrich Simmon and Elisabeth Simmon (Rhinebeck Luth. Chbk.).

xi) Anna[3], b. 23 June 1766 - sp.: David Bohnestiel and Anna Barbara (Churchtown Luth. Chbk.). She md. Jeremiah Smith (Will).

xii) Magdalena[3], b. 20 Jan 1770 - sp.: Jerg Roschman and Magdalena (Manorton Luth. Chbk.). She md. Henry Wager (Will).

5) Johann David[2], b. 27 April 1726 at Rheynbek - sp.: Joseph Reichard and wife Anna Maria (N.Y. City Luth. Chbk.). David Bohnenstiel was conf. 10 April 1743 at Kamp (Loonenburg Luth. Chbk.) and was in Capt. Jeremiah Hogeboom's Company in 1767 (Report of the State Historian, Vol. II, p. 864). He md. Anna Barbara, d/o Peter Hagedorn, 1 April 1749 (Rhinebeck Luth. Chbk.). The will of David Bonesteel of Claverack was dated 4 Nov 1790 and probated 22 Jan 1791 (Columbia Co. Will Bk. A). Issue:

i) Elisabeth[3], b. 9 May 1750 and bpt. Teerbosch - sp.: Peter Bohenstiel and Lisab. Hagedorn (Loonenburg Luth. Chbk.).

     ii) <u>Catharina</u>³, bpt. 20 July 1755 - sp.: Jurie Heyner
       and Catharina Heyner (Linlithgo Ref. Chbk.).

    iii) <u>David</u>³, b. 27 Jan 1765 - sp.: Johannes Kunz and Anna
       (Churchtown Luth. Chbk.).

     iv) <u>Jacob</u>³ (Will).

      v) <u>Mary</u>³ (Will).

6) <u>Johann Peter</u>² (HJ), conf. 21 Oct 1744 at Rhynbek (Loonen-
burg Luth. Chbk.). Peter Bonestel was in Capt. Jeremiah
Hogeboom's Company in 1767 (<u>Report of the State Historian</u>,
Vol. II, p. 864). He md. Anna Elisabetha Simon and had ch.:

     i) <u>Johannes</u>³, bpt. 27 March 1756 - sp.: Joh: Simon and
      Maria Barbara Hentgen (Red Hook Luth. Chbk.).

     ii) <u>Anna Margaretha</u>³, bpt. 15 Jan 1758 - sp.: Niclaus
      Bonenstiehl and Anna Marg: Kuhns (Red Hook Luth. Chbk.).

    iii) <u>Elisabeth</u>³, b. 27 May 1765 - sp.: Jerg Finckel and
      Elisabeth (Churchtown Luth. Chbk.).

     iv) <u>Anna</u>³, b. 30 March 1768 - sp.: Jacob Schmidt and El-
      isabeth (Churchtown Luth. Chbk.).

7) <u>Johann Philip</u>², b. 18 Jan 1730 at Haneman Saalbach's at
Kamp - sp.: Philipp Kuns and wife Maria Liese (N.Y. City
Luth. Chbk.). He was conf. 3 Nov 1745 at Rhynbek (Loon-
enburg Luth. Chbk.). Record of him was found in Dutchess
Co. Ancient Docs. #5854, 12735, 12754 and 10196. He md.
Elisabetha Hagedorn and had ch.:

     i) <u>Anna</u>³, b. 16 Jan 1752 - sp.: Michael Simon and wife
      Anna Barbara (Rhinebeck Luth. Chbk.).

     ii) <u>Nicolaus</u>³, b. 21 Nov 1753 - sp.: Nicolaus Bohnenstiel
      and wife Anna Elisabetha (Rhinebeck Luth. Chbk.).

    iii) <u>Jacobus</u>³, bpt. 23 May 1756 - sp.: Jacobus Maul and Anna
      Dorothea Trumbauer (Red Hook Luth. Chbk.).

     iv) <u>Henrich</u>³, b. 20 Feb 1762 - sp.: Henrich Michel and
      Elisabeth Simmon (Rhinebeck Luth. Chbk.).

     v) <u>Jeremias</u>³, b. 20 May 1767 - sp.: Jerg Bennet and wife
      Gertraut (Rhinebeck Luth. Chbk.).

     vi) <u>Elisabeth</u>³, b. 2 Oct 1769 - sp.: Petrus Treber and
      Elisabeth Marta (Rhinebeck Luth. Chbk.).

    vii) <u>Magdalena</u>³, b. 28 Feb 1772 - sp.: Georg Eckert and
      Anna Maria (Rhinebeck Luth. Chbk.).

   viii) <u>David</u>³, b. 20 Dec 1775 - sp.: David Bohnestiel and
      Anna Barbara (Rhinebeck Luth. Chbk.).

8) <u>Johann Friederich</u>², b. 6 March 1732 and bpt. at Rhynbek -
sp.: Jo. Frid. Meyer and wife Anna Barbel (Loonenburg Luth.
Chbk.). Frid: Bohnenstiel, aged 16, was conf. at Theerbosch 5 Feb 1748/9 (Loonenburg Luth. Chbk.). He was in

Capt. Abraham Van Aernam's Company above Poesten Kill in
1767 (<u>Report of the State Historian</u>, Vol. II, p. 813).
He md. Catharina Mayer and had ch.:

    i) <u>Anna Margaretha</u>[3], bpt. 1 Jan 1757 - sp.: Nicolaus
       Bonenstiehl and Anna Margaretha Kuhn (Red Hook Luth.
       Chbk.).

   ii) <u>David</u>[3], b. 6 March 1761 - sp.: David Bohnestiel and
       Barbara (Churchtown Luth. Chbk.).

  iii) <u>Johannes</u>[3], b. 7 March 1767 - sp.: Jerg Finckel and
       Elisabeth Bohnestiel (Churchtown Luth. Chbk.).

   iv) <u>Georg</u>[3] - a twin, b. 7 March 1767 - sp.: Hannes Bar-
       tel and Margaretha (Churchtown Luth. Chbk.).

JOHANNES BONROTH (Hunter Lists #67)

There were Bonroths documented at 5270 <u>Gummersbach</u> and 5238
<u>Hachenburg</u>, but no firm connective links to the American settler
were found. Johannes Bonroth made his first appearance on the
Hunter Lists 4 July 1710 with 1 pers. over 10 yrs. of age. On 4
Oct 1710 the family increased to 4 pers. over 10 yrs. of age.
Johannes Bonroth of Annsberg was a soldier in 1711 (Palatine Volunteers To Canada). There was a Johannes Conrad and wife Gertraud
with 3 ch. at Neu-Ansberg ca. 1716/17 (Simmendinger Register);
they may have been our Bonrath family (HJ). Johannes Poenradt
and his wife Gertruy were each patentees on the n. side of the
Mohawk River 30 April 1725 (Burnetsfield Patent).

There were Penrods in Frederick Co., Md. and Somerset Co.,
Pa. who may have been descendants of the Mohawk Valley Bonraths
(HJ).

JACOB BORN & his sister (Hunter Lists #68)

Jacob Born was first mentioned on the Hunter Lists 4 July
1710 with 2 pers. over 10 yrs. of age. The entry for 4 Aug 1710
recorded Jacob Born's widow with her sister, 2 pers. over 10 yrs.
of age.

LUDWIG BÖRSCH (Hunter Lists #69)

A Ludwig Beesch, his wife and 1 child were on Capt. Jn⁰ Untank's ship sailing 3 July 1709 (Rotterdam Lists).

Ludwig Börsch made his first appearance on the Hunter Lists
1 July 1710 with 2 pers. over 10 yrs. and 1 pers. under 10; the
entry for 24 June 1711 gave the family 4 pers. over 10 yrs. and
2 under 10. The 29 Sept 1711 entry named Henrich Börsth as head
of the family, which may have been an error (HJ). Ludwig Buers

aged 32, Maria Cath. Buers aged 28, and Catharine Buers aged 3, were in N.Y. City in 1710/11 (Palatines In N.Y. City). Lodwick Pares and Catharine Pears were each patentees on the Mohawk 30 April 1725 (Burnetsfield Patent). **The wife of Ludwig[1] was Catharina** Lapping (N.Y. City Ref. Chbk.), a relative of #434 Agnes Lappin (HJ). The ch. of Ludwig Börsch (Bertsch, Peerts) were:

1) <u>Catharine[2]</u>, aged 3 yrs. in 1710/11 (Palatines In N.Y. City).
2) <u>Anna Maria[2]</u>, bpt. 3 Jan 1711 (West Camp Luth. Chbk.) and 10 Jan 1711 (N.Y. City Ref. Chbk.) - sp.: Conrad Friedrich and wife Anna Maria Wysing.
3) <u>Johann Ludwig[2]</u>, b. 31 March 1713 - sp.: Johann Cuntz and wife Maria Catharina (West Camp Luth. Chbk.). He may have been the Ludwig Bors who sp. Heinrich Dups at Swatara in 1741 (Stoever Chbk.).

A Catharina Bärsen and her mother were in the congregation at the Fall ca. 1744 (Schoharie Luth. Chbk.). An Adam Pears was a freeholder at the Falls in 1763 (Albany Co. Freeholders).

JONAS BÖRSCH (Hunter Lists #70)

Jonas Börsch was listed once on the Hunter Lists on 29 Sept 1711 with 3 pers. over 10 yrs. of age and 2 pers. under 10 yrs. in the household.

JACOB BORST (Hunter Lists #71)

Jacob Borst first appeared on the Hunter Lists 4 July 1710 with 2 pers. over 10 yrs. of age. The family increased 24 June 1711 to 2 pers. over 10 yrs. and 1 under 10 yrs. and grew again 13 Sept 1712 to 2 pers. over 10 yrs. of age and 2 under 10 yrs. A letter from Robert Livingston Sr. to Robert Livingston Jr. mentioned Jacob Burst the Palatine 13 April 1711 (Livingston Papers, Reel #3). Jacob Borst and Anna Maria with 3 ch. were at Neu-Cassel ca. 1716/17 (Simmendinger Register). In discussing whether or not the Schoharie Valley Lutherans would adhere to the church constitution, Pastor Berkenmeyer wrote in 1743:

> Mr. Jacob Borst sought all kinds of evasions, but the others, Mr. Kniskern and Mr. Stuberauch, resolved to do so. Hereupon the first (Borst) also signed, and, having witnessed this, the remaining elders of Albany signed too. (<u>Albany Protocol</u>, p. 299).

Jacob Borst and his family were recorded on Pastor Sommer's list of Schoharie Lutherans ca. 1744. The Old Jacob Borst fell asleep in the Lord 2 Jan 1757, and his wife Maria d. 3 Aug 1753, aged 67 yrs. The ch. of Jacob[1] Borst and his wife Maria were:

1) Jacob[2], bpt. 25 March 1711- sp.: Wm. Jorick and his wife, Henrich Lorenz, Marg. Weishard, and Anna Maria Ziperlin (West Camp Luth. Chbk.). He md. 15 March 1748 Anna Elisabet Reinhardt (Schoharie Luth. Chbk.). He was a freeholder at Schoharrie in 1763 (Albany Co. Freeholders) and in Capt. Thomas Ackeson's Company of the militia in 1767 (Report of the State Historian, Vol. II, p. 846).

2) Johann Martin[2], b. 1 March 1714 on Col. Schuyler's Flatts in Albany Co. and bpt. at Albany - sp.: Jacob Beyer and Eva Scherts (N.Y. City Luth. Chbk.). He was on the 1744 Schoharie Luth. roll and d. 20 May 1746, aged 32 yrs. (Schoharie Luth. Chbk.). He md. Catharina Mathyse, who remarried to Hend: Oÿens 18 Aug 1747 after Johann Martin's death (Schoharie Ref. Chbk.). Issue:

   i) Johannes[3], bpt. 6 weeks old 10 Oct 1736 at Schohari - sp.: Hannes Laeyer Jnr. and Anna Maria Scherry (Loonenburg Luth. Chbk.). He md. 13 Dec 1763 Catharina Mercki (Schoharie Luth. Chbk.).

   ii) Henrich[3], bpt. 9 Dec 1738 - sp.: Hendrick Mathyse and Sobina Mathyse, weduwe van bek (Schoharie Ref. Chbk.).

   iii) Maria[3], bpt. 7 March 1741 - sp.: Jacob Borst and Maria, his wife (Schoharie Ref. Chbk.).

   iv) Catharina[3], bpt. 20 May 1743 - sp.: Johan Eckkerzon and his wife (Schoharie Ref. Chbk.).

   v) Anna[3], b. 10 Nov 1745 - sp.: Jost (--) and his wife (Schoharie Luth. Chbk.).

3) Johann Balthasar[2] (HJ), enrolled next to Jacob Burst on Capt. Thomas Ackeson's Company of the militia in 1767 (Report of the State Historian, Vol. II, p. 846). He md. Maria (--) and had ch.:

   i) Maria[3], b. 6 Dec 1743 - sp.: Jacob Borst and his wife Maria (Schoharie Luth. Chbk.).

   ii) Michael[3], b. 2 April 1745 - sp.: Michel Borst and Maria Magdalena Ingoldt (Schoharie Luth. Chbk.).

   iii) Elisabetha[3], b. 9 Dec 1746 - sp.: Johannes Bauch and his wife (Schoharie Luth. Chbk.).

   iv) Jacob[3], b. 3 Oct 1748 - sp.: Jacob Borst Jr. and wife (Schoharie Luth. Chbk.).

   v) Jost[3], b. 18 April 1750 - sp.: Jost Borst and Maria Werner (Schoharie Luth. Chbk.).

   vi) Sophia[3], b. 2 Jan 1752 - sp.: Christian Zähe and wife (Schoharie Luth. Chbk.).

   vii) Johannes[3], b. 19 March 1754 - sp.: Johannes Borst and

Anna Bellinger (Schoharie Luth. Chbk.).

   viii) <u>Catharina</u>³, b. 12 April 1759 - sp.: Johannes Zähe
and wife (Schoharie Luth. Chbk.).

4) <u>Michael</u>², on the 1744 Sommer's list (Schoharie Luth.
Chbk.). He md. 16 Nov 1749 Anna Elisabeth Löwenstein
and d. 13 May 1758 (Schoharie Luth. Chbk.). Issue:

   i) <u>Maria</u>³, b. 2 Dec 1750 - sp.: Jacob Borst and his
wife (Schoharie Luth. Chbk.).

   ii) <u>Peter</u>³, b. 28 Nov 1751 - sp.: Peter Löwenstein and
wife (Schoharie Luth. Chbk.). He d. 22 Feb 1840,
aged 90 yrs. (Middleburg Cem.).

   iii) <u>Elisabetha</u>³, b. 15 April 1753 - sp.: Johannes Borst
and Sophia Ingold (Schoharie Luth. Chbk.).

   iv) <u>Michael</u>³, b. 25 Sept 1754 - sp.: Johan Balthasar
Borst and wife (Schoharie Luth. Chbk.). "A little
boy" d. 7 Oct 1754 (Schoharie Luth. Chbk.).

   v) <u>Philippus</u>³, b. 10 Dec 1755 - sp.: Jost Borst and
wife (Schoharie Luth. Chbk.).

   vi) <u>Anna</u>³, b. 19 April 1758 - sp.: Michel Friederich Jr.
and Abelona Löwenstein (Schoharie Luth. Chbk.).

5) <u>Johannes</u>², on the 1744 Sommers list (Schoharie Luth.
Chbk.). He was a Corporal in Capt. Thomas Ackeson's Comp-
any in the militia of 1767 (<u>Report of the State Historian</u>,
Vol. II, p. 845) and a freeholder of Schoharrie in 1763
(Albany Co. Freeholders) along with brothers Jacob and
Battis. He probably was the Johannes Borst who md. 4 Jan
1761 Catharina Rickert (Schoharie Luth. Chbk.).

6) <u>Johann Jost</u>², on the 1744 Sommers list (Schoharie Luth.
Chbk.). He md. 20 Nov 1753 Margaretha Sternberg, who d.
11 Nov 1756 (Schoharie Luth. Chbk.). They had ch.:

   i) <u>Maria</u>³, b. 20 May 1754 - sp.: Lambert Sternberg and
his wife (Schoharie Luth. Chbk.).

   ii) <u>Catharina</u>³, b. 3 Aug 1755 - sp.: Lambert Sternberger
and his wife (Schoharie Luth. Chbk.).

   iii) <u>Jacob</u>³, b. 30 Oct 1756 - sp.: Michel Borst and his
wife (Schoharie Luth. Chbk.).

Jost md. 2nd 10 Oct 1758 Catharina Fuchs; a Jost Borst d.
30 July 1784 (Schoharie Luth. Chbk.). Issue from 2nd
marriage:

   iv) <u>Jost</u>³, b. 20 Dec 1760 - sp.: Henrich Borst - s/o
Joh. Martin, and Maria Borst - d/o Michel (Schoharie
Luth. Chbk.).

   v) <u>Margaretha</u>³, b. 17 Oct 1762 - sp.: Johannes Borst
and wife (Schoharie Luth. Chbk.).

    vi) <u>Anna</u>[3], b. 3 Oct 1764 - sp.: Peter Warmuth and wife
       (Schoharie Luth. Chbk.).

   vii) <u>Peter</u>[3], b. 30 March 1766 - sp.: Johann Peter Sommer
      and Christina Sternberg (Schoharie Luth. Chbk.).

  viii) <u>Elisabetha</u>[3], b. 11 July 1768 - sp.: Nickel Matthes
      and wife (Schoharie Luth. Chbk.).

    ix) <u>Wilhelm</u>[3], b. 2 Sept 1770 - sp.: Anton Witmer and
      wife (Schoharie Luth. Chbk.).

    x) <u>Johannes</u>[3], b. 5 May 1772 - sp.: Johan(nes) Lawyer
      Bellinger and wife (Schoharie Luth. Chbk.).

   xi) <u>Eva</u>[3], b. 28 Feb 1774 - sp.: Pitter Borst and wife
      (Schoharie Luth. Chbk.).

  7) <u>Elisabetha</u>[2], on the 1744 Sommer's list (Schoharie Luth.
Chbk.). She d. 24 Dec 1746, aged 26 yrs. (Schoharie Luth.
Chbk.).

  8?) <u>Henrich</u>[2], possibly the sp. to Michael Hilsinger in 1758
(Schoharie Luth. Chbk.).

JACOB BÖSHAAR (Hunter Lists #72)
JOHN JACOB BÖSHAAR (Hunter Lists #73)

The German home of the Böshaar family was 6660 <u>Zweibrücken</u>
(28 km. e. of Saarbrücken; Chbks. begin 1607, Ref.). The earliest
known ancestor of the American family was <u>Hanß Albrecht Boßhaar</u>.
Hanß Jacob Bößhaar, s/o the late Hanß Albrecht Bößhaar at Breit-
enbach, md. 20 Jan 1681 Anna Gertrudt, d/o the late Hans Lux Meyer, Court-gardener at Zweibrücken. Anna Gertrud, d/o Hanß Laux
Mejers, gardener, and wife Benigna, was bpt. 17 Oct 1647; Anna
Gertrud, w/o Johann Jacob Böshaar, d. 4 March 1693, aged 45 yrs.
and 4 months. Hanß Jacob Bößhaar, citizen and cooper here, widower, md. Christina, d/o the late Samuel Maurer - citizen and
linenweaver at Hornbach, 30 July 1693. Jacob Boesshaar, a cooper
from the town of Zweibrücken, was an emigrant from the Duchy of
Zweibrücken in 1709 (<u>Emigrants from the Palatinate to the American Colonies in the 18th Century</u>, p. 31). Hans Jacob Peeshoor,
his wife, and 6 ch. were in the 6th party sailing on the ship of
Captain Johan Facit 3 July 1709 (Rotterdam Lists).

    Jacob Böshaar made his first appearance on the Hunter Lists
4 July 1710 with 6 pers. over 10 yrs. and 2 pers. under 10 in the
family; the 4 Oct 1710 entry called him Johann Jacob Böshar.
There is a mss. relating to him at the Albany State Library (N.Y.
Colonial Mss.: Vol. 58, p. 63a-d). Johan Jacob Besharn was nat.
31 Jan 1715/16 (Albany Nats.). Jacob Boshair was taxed £5 at
Hurley in 1718/19 (Ulster Co. Tax Lists). He was d. before 6 Dec

1719 when his widow md. Wilhelm Bolk (Kingston Ref. Chbk.). Hanß
Jacob[1] and his 1st wife Anna Gertraudt had ch.:

1) <u>Hanß Jacob[2]</u>, bpt. 10 Nov 1681 - sp.: Hanß Jacob Küfer from
   Odweiler, and Fr. Anna Margreth - w/o H. Joh. Balthasar
   Bruch (Zweibrücken). He came to America with his parents
   and was first entered on the Hunter Lists as #73 John Jacob Böshar 24 Dec 1711 with 2 pers. over 10 yrs. of age
   in his family; his last entry was 13 Sept 1712 with 3 pers.
   over 10 yrs. of age. Jacob Bsheere was nat. 22 Nov 1715
   (Albany Nats.). Johann Jacob Boßheren, his wife Anna
   Catharina and 2 ch. were at Neu-Heessberg ca. 1716/17
   (Simmendinger Register) and had ch.:

   i) <u>Johann Georg[3]</u>, b. 17 March 1717 and bpt. at Schoharie
      - sp.: Johann Georg Stump and wife (West Camp Luth.
      Chbk.). He md. Catharina Stump and d. in 1787 in
      Bethel Twp., Berks Co., Pa. (HJ).

2) <u>"A child"[2]</u>, bpt. March 1684 - sp.: Friedrich Ludwig Meier
   - tailor, the w/o Hanß Velten Küffer at Breidenbach, and
   Charlotta Kunigunda - single d/o H. Hanß Kilian Otth
   (Zweibrücken).

3) <u>Anna Margaretha[2]</u>, bpt. 23 March 1687 - sp.: Balthasar
   Bruch, Elisabeth - d/o Jörg Adam Eckeler (?), and Anna
   Margaretha - w/o Jörg Dietz (Zweibrücken). The child d.
   20 July 1687 (Zweibrücken).

Hanß Jacob[1] and his 2nd wife Christina Maurer (called "Wever" at
Kingston Ref. Church, due to her father's occupation -HJ) had ch.:

4) <u>Johann Georg[2]</u>, bpt. 7 June 1694 - sp.: Hanß Jörg Koch -
   citizen and merchant, Ulrich Maurer - citizen and weaver
   at Hornbach, and Anna - w/o the town-miller Hans Balth.
   Weber (Zweibrücken). Jorg Boshaaer or Boshaer was nat.
   8 and 9 Sept 1715 (Kingston Nats.). Johan Gorg Boshair
   was taxed £2 at Hurley in 1718-21 (Ulster Co. Tax Lists).
   He md. Maria Elisabetha Wennerich 7 Aug 1716 (Kingston
   Ref. Chbk.) and moved to Lancaster Co., Pa. (HJ). Issue:

   i) <u>Anna Margaretha[3]</u>, bpt. 5 May 1717 - sp.: Zymen Helm
      and Margrita Besa (Kingston Ref. Chbk.). She md.
      Christian Lang and d. March 1794 in Earl Twp, Pa. (HJ).

   ii) <u>Jacob[3]</u>, bpt. 22 June 1718 - sp.: Jacob Pesor and
       Dorothea Beem (Kingston Ref. Chbk.). He md. Judith
       (--) and d. 1778 in Hanover Twp., Pa. (HJ).

   iii) <u>Balthus[3]</u>, bpt. 31 July 1720 - sp.: Baltus Wenrig and
        Magdalena Wenrig (Kingston Ref. Chbk.). He md. 6 Feb
        1739 Johanna Dorothea Weider (Stoever Chbk.) and 2nd
        Anna Maria Schaeffer 23 March 1747 (Stoever Chbk.).

The will of Baltzer Baishor of Leacock Twp. was written 3 Feb 1789 and probated 19 Nov 1791 (Lancaster Co. Will Bk. F, p. 332).

iv) <u>Matheus</u>[3], bpt. 31 Dec 1721 - sp.: Matheus Wendel and Catrina Snyder (Kingston Ref. Chbk.). He md. Apollonia Hengerer 13 Oct 1745 (Trinity Ev. Luth. Chbk., New Holland, Pa.) and d. 30 May 1807 in E. Hanover Twp., Dauphin - now Lebanon Co., Pa. (Zion Ev. Luth. Chbk., Jonestown, Pa.).

v) <u>Magdalena</u>[3] (HJ), md. Jacob Ulm (Woolham) and moved to Berkeley Co., West Va. (HJ).

vi) <u>Georg</u>[3] (HJ), md. 12 March 1745 Charlotta Hetzer (Hefer) (Trinity Ev. Luth. Chbk., New Holland, Pa.) and moved to N.C. (HJ).

vii) <u>Johannes</u>[3], b. 11 Oct 1732 - d. 16 April 1814 in Bethel Twp., Lebanon Co., Pa. (HJ). He md. 1st Anna Maria Lang and 2nd Rosina, widow Ward (HJ).

viii) <u>Bernhardt</u>[3] (HJ), md. 1st Caroline (--) and 2nd (?) Catharine (HJ). His will was written 27 Oct 1799 and probated 21 April 1800 (Berkeley Co., West Va. Will Bk. 3, p. 284).

5) <u>Johann Daniel</u>[2], bpt. 22 July 1696 - sp.: Johan Daniel Bruch - pharmacist, Johan Niclaus Ehrmann - citizen and merchant, and Anna Margareth...(Zweibrücken). He d. 30 June 1699.

6) <u>Johann Bernhard</u>[2], bpt. 18 May 1698 - sp.: Niclaus Dahl - citizen and baker, Bernhard Koch - landlord "Hirsch", and Maria Elisabeth - w/o Henrich Maurer - linenweaver (Zweibrücken). He first appeared on tax rolls in the North Ward in 1725/6 and continued until 1738/9 in Rhinebeck (Dutchess Co. Tax Lists). A 1736 mss. for Barent Breshaar of Rhinebeck survives (Dutchess Co. Ancient Docs. #79). He md. Mary (--) and had issue:

i) <u>Jacob</u>[3], bpt.one month old at Rynbek 15 Aug 1727 - sp.: William Bolk and wife Christyne (N.Y. City Luth. Chbk.).

7) <u>Anna Margaretha</u>[2], bpt. 11 Feb 1701 - sp.: Johan Balth. Zölner - brewer, Anna Marg. - w/o H. Hanß Jörg Bietz, and Anna Marg. - w/o Christian Koch - tanner (Zweibrücken). She md. Albertus Beem 23 Aug 1721 (Kingston Ref. Chbk.). Anna Margret Böhm, born Besbooren - her stepfather is William Bolk - joined the church 15 Aug 1726 (N.Y. City Luth. Chbk.); this took place at Rynbek.

8) <u>Johann Wilhelm</u>[2], bpt. 20 Nov 1703 - sp.: Wilhelm Kurz -

-shoemaker, Hanß Jörg Kleinsch - citizen and shoemaker, and Loysa - w/o Peter Trautmann - citizen and merchant. He d. 27 April 1704 (Zweibrücken).

9) <u>Maria Catharina[2]</u>, bpt. 22 Feb 1705 - sp.: Johan Paul - s/o Peter Neuschwanger the shoemaker, Anna Catharina - w/o Velten Wahm (?) the nailsmith, and Eva Maria - w/o Johan Otten Jungler. the landlord (Zweibrücken).

10) <u>Magdalena Elisabetha[2]</u>, bpt. 20 June 1706 - sp.: Henrich Maurer - citizen and weaver, Magdalena - w/o Hanß Jacob Römer, and Eva Elisabeth - w/o H. Johan Niclaus Dahl (Zweibrücken). She md. 9 Aug 1735 Johannes De Graaf (Kingston Ref. Chbk.).

Mrs. Frances C. Francis of Washington, D. C. was most kind in sharing her documented data on the Pa. and W. Va. descendants of Jacob[1] Böshaar.

There were other unplaced members of the family in colonial N.Y. and N.J.: a Jacob Pescheerer and wife Barbara had ch. at Somerville Ref. Church 1725-31, and he may have been the Jacob Bescherer of Roxbury, Morris Co., N.J. who wrote his will 24 Nov 1751 (N.J. Wills: Lib. F, p. 13). A Johannes Pescheerer sp. this Jacob 12 Jan 1729 (Somerville Ref. Chbk.). A Jacob Tofharn was nat. 8 and 9 Sept 1715 (Kingston Nats.), and he may have been connected with the other N.Y. Böshaars (HJ).

DANIEL BOUSCHE 2[d] (Hunter Lists #74)

A Daniel Buschert, his wife and 8 ch. were on Capt. Jan Duk's ship in the 4th party of Palatines sailing 10 June 1709 (Rotterdam Lists). Daniel Boset aged 59 with his wife, sons aged 14 and 5, daughters aged 21, 19, 13, 11, 9, and 1 month, linen and cloth-weaver, Ref. were in the 4th arrivals in England (London Lists).

Daniel Bousche 2[d] made his first appearance on the Hunter Lists 1 July 1710 with 2 pers. over 10 yrs. of age in the family. The family appears to have been continued under #96 in Hunter (HJ).

ANNA CATHARINA BRACHIN (Hunter Lists #75)

An Anna Catharina, d/o Johannes Brack, was bpt. in 1697 at 6551 Roxheim, but no proof exists that she was the emigrant (HJ). A Katrina Bruckin with 5 ch. was in the 5th party in Holland (Rotterdam Lists).

Anna Catharina Brachin appeared once on the Hunter Lists on 4 October 1710 with 1 pers. over 10 yrs. of age in the family.

JOHN MICHAEL BRACK (Hunter Lists #76)

Johann Michel Brack of Klein-Odenbach in the commune of Mei-
stenheim, district of Zweybrucken, md. Anna Maria Schley, d/o Johann Michel Schley of Hettenbach, Rhenish Earldom on 3 Jan 1717
(West Camp Luth. Chbk.). The Brack village of origin was 6759
Odenbach (4 km. s.w. of Meisenheim; Chbks. begin 1566, Ref.).
Hans Conrad Brack from Schlitz (Scheitz?) in the Berner Gebith,
widower and daylabourer, md. Agnes, d/o the late Hans Michel Heyel 29 Oct 1678. Hans Michael Heyel the elder or Censor was bur.
1 Oct 1677, aged 82 yrs; his wife was named Ottilia (HJ). The ch.
of Hans Conrad Brack and his wife Agnes were:

Magdalena Catharina, bpt. 8 Aug 1679 - sp.: Hans Peter Heyel
- brother of the mother in childbed, and Magdalena Catharina
- w/o Benedict Feyerabend the shoemaker from Meisenheim.
Hanß Conrad, bpt. 22 June 1683 - sp.: Ottilia - wid/o Hans
Michel Heyel and mother of the mother in childbed, (her)
brother Hans Conrad Heyel, and Johannes Braß - s/o the late
Joh. Braß. A note added "is dead."
Hans Jacob, bpt. 3 Jan 1685 - sp.: Hans Christoph Heyel -
teacher at Oberndorf and brother to the mother in childbed,
Hans Jacob Rimpi the smith, and Caecilia - young w/o Hans
Conrad Heyel.
+ Hans Michael, bpt. 8/18 April 1687 - sp.: Hans Michel Mohr
from Roß Becherbach, and Anna Elisabet, d/o (?) Michel Cro-
benberg.
Hans Michel Prak, his wife and 1 child were in the 5th party of
Palatines on Capt. Jan Coate's ship in 1709 (Rotterdam Lists).

John Michael Brack made his first appearance on the Hunter
Lists 4 July 1710 with 2 pers. over 10 yrs. of age in his family.
The household diminished to 1 pers. over 10 yrs. on 24 Dec 1711
and then rose again to 3 pers. over 10 on 25 March 1712; the last
entry read 2 pers. over 10 yrs. of age on 13 Sept 1712. Hans Michall Brack was nat. 22 Nov 1715 (Albany Nats.). Michael Brack and
Anna Maria with 3 ch. were at Hunderston ca. 1716/17 (Simmendinger
Register). He appeared on Palatine Debt Lists in 1718 and 1721
(Livingston Debt Lists). He was not willing to remain at Livingston Manor 26 Aug 1724 (Documentary History of N.Y., Vol. III, p.
724). By his wives (both named Anna Maria) he had issue:

1) Maria Catharina[2], bpt. 18 April 1715 - sp.: Johann Roschmann and Maria Catharina Drum (West Camp Luth. Chbk.).
2) Johann Gerhard[2], b. 14 Feb 1721 at Camp - sp.: Andreas
Barthol, Joh: Gerhard Winecker, and Maria Magd. Meyer
(N.Y. City Luth. Chbk.).

WILHELM BRANDAW (Hunter Lists #77)

Johan Willem Brando, his wife and 1 child were on Capt. Robbert Bulman's ship in Holland in June of 1709 (Rotterdam Lists).
William Brandau aged 30, his wife, and a son aged 3, Ref., baker,
were in England later that year (London Lists).

Wilhelm Brandaw made his first appearance on the Hunter Lists
4 Aug 1710 with 2 pers. over 10 yrs. and 1 pers. under 10 yrs.;
the family increased in size 25 March 1712 to 2 pers. over 10 yrs.
and 2 pers. under 10 yrs. of age. ---Brandau: 1 man; 1 lad 9-15;
and 1 woman were in Ulster Co. in 1710/11 (West Camp Census).
Wilhelmus Brandau was nat. 8 and 9 Sept 1715 (Kingston Nats.).
Joh. Wilhelm Branthau, Mar Elisabet and 3 ch. were at Beckmansland ca. 1716/17 (Simmendinger Register). He was a Palatine Debtor
in 1726, and his entry 13 Dec 1747 read Wilhelmus Brando, deceased,
debt passed to his son Nicholas (Livingston Debt Lists). He md.
Maria Elisabetha (called Elisabeth Catharina once in 1717 - HJ)
and had issue:

1) Nicolaus[2], nat. 8 and 9 Sept. 1715 (Kingston Nats.). He
   md. 5 Nov 1726 Elisabetha Klein (Kingston Ref. Chbk.) and
   had ch.:

   i) Elisabetha[3], b. 7 Oct 1727 and bpt. at Kiskatom - sp.:
      Hannes Brandau and Liesabeth Reuter (West Camp Luth.
      Chbk.). She md. 1 Sept 1747 Peter Schumacher (Loon-
      enburg Luth. Chbk.).

   ii) Hieronymus[3], b. 31 Oct 1730 and bpt. Kisket. - sp.:
      Hieronymus Klein and Christina Kreisler (Loonenburg
      Luth. Chbk.). He md. in 1754 Anna Lehmann (Catskill
      Ref. Chbk.). Mr. Jeronimus Brando d. Nov 1812, aged
      84 yrs. (Catskill Recorder of 18 Nov 1812). They had
      ch. bpt. at Loonenburg Luth., Catskill Ref., and
      Katsbaan Ref. Churches.

   iii) Henrich[3], bpt. 7 June 1733 - sp.: Hennerich Graed
      and Maria Catharina Dietterich (Catskill Ref. Chbk.).

   iv) Amalia[3], b. 27 Jan 1736 and bpt. Kisket. - sp.: Peter
      Borghart and wife Amalia (Loonenburg Luth. Chbk.).

   v) Catharina[3], b. 18 Jan 1739 and bpt. Kisket. - sp.:
      Martin Borchard and Catharina Spaan, standing for
      the parents (Loonenburg Luth. Chbk.).

   vi) Petrus[3], b. 29 March 1741 and bpt. Kisket. - sp.:
      Peter Borghard and wife Amalia (Loonenburg Luth.
      Chbk.). He md. Maria Dieterich (HJ).

   vii) Anna[3], b. 11 June 1743 and bpt. evening before 27 Aug
      at Christian Becker's house (Loonenburg Luth. Chbk.).

The sp. were Christian Beckker and wife Anna.

   viii) <u>Valentin</u>[3], bpt. 21 April 1747 - sp.: Valentin Fierer and wife Catharina Schram (Katsbaan Ref. Chbk.).

2) <u>Johannes</u>[2], b. 16 Feb 1712 - sp.: Johannes Franck (West Camp Luth. Chbk.). He was on a Palatine Debtor's List 13 Dec 1747 (Livingston Debt Lists). He md. Jannetje Van Schayk 30 Nov 1737 (Loonenburg Luth Chbk.). The will of Johannis Brandow of Cocksakie District, yeoman was written 11 Jan and proved 26 April of 1786 (<u>Fernow Wills</u> #202). They had ch.:

   i) <u>Wilhelmus</u>[3], b. 18 Sept 1738 - sp.: Wilhelm Brandau and Liesabeth, grandparents (Loonenburg Luth. Chbk.). He md. Eitje (--) (HJ).

   ii) <u>Arend</u>[3], b. 22 Dec 1739 - sp.: Arend Van Schayk and Mary, grandparents (Loonenburg Luth. Chbk.).

   iii) <u>Elisabetha</u>[3], b. 11 Sept 1743 and bpt. Kisket. - sp.: Hannes Hendr. Schermerhoren and wife Christina (Loonenburg Luth. Chbk.).

   iv) <u>Maria</u>[3], b. 4 Oct 1745 - sp.: Michiel Van Schayk and wife Lena (Loonenburg Luth. Chbk.).

   v) <u>Zacharias</u>[3], b. 28 Feb 1749 - sp.: Frederyk Brandau and wife Marytje (Loonenburg Luth. Chbk.).

   vi) <u>Gritje</u>[3], b. 21 April 1751 - sp.: Frieder Wormer and wife Gritje (Loonenburg Luth. Chbk.).

   vii) <u>Arent</u>[3], bpt. 25 Aug 1753 - sp.: Laurens Van Wormer and Judikje Van Wormer (Coxsackie Ref. Chbk.).

   viii) <u>Nicolaus</u>[3], b. 5 June 1755 - sp.: Cornelius Van Schaak, Matty Brandau, Casper V: Hoesen and Mareitje (Loonenburg Luth. Chbk.).

   ix) <u>Christina</u>[3], b. 5 June 1755 (twin).

3) <u>Johann Friederich</u>[2], b. 1 Jan 1715 - sp.: Fridrich Streit and Elisabetha Krantz (West Camp Luth. Chbk.). He md. 5 Dec 1737 Maria Gradt at Bak oven (Loonenburg Luth. Chbk.). He was a Sergeant in Capt. Cornelius DuBois Company at Caskill 9 April 1767 (serving along with relatives Petrus Brandoe, Hendrieck Brandoe and Hieronimus Brandoe) (<u>Report of the State Historian</u>, Vol. II, p. 876, 878). The will of Frederick Brandow was proved 10 July 1789 (Albany Co. Will Bk. 1, p. 203). His ch. were:

   i) <u>Elisabetha</u>[3], b. 3 March 1739 and bpt. at Newton - sp.: Gotfried Brandau and Lisabeth Graad (Loonenburg Luth. Chbk.).

   ii) <u>Elisabetha</u>[3], bpt. 30 May 1740 - sp.: Johannes Diederich and Catharina Brando (Catskill Ref. Chbk.).

  iii) <u>Maria</u>[3], bpt. 22 March 1742 - sp.: Henrich Graat and
    Mareitje Diederich (Katsbaan Ref. Chbk.).

  iv) <u>Catharina</u>[3], bpt. 26 Aug 1744 - sp.: Johannis Brando
    and Jannitie Van Schaek (Rhinebeck Flats Ref. Chbk.).
    She md. Wilhelm Dieterich (HJ).

   v) <u>Anna</u>[3], bpt. 5 April 1747 - sp.: Friderick Dedrick
    and Eva Grad (Germantown Ref. Chbk.).

  vi) <u>Sara</u>[3], bpt. 27 Aug 1749 - sp.: Jurg Johan Oberbach
    and Elisabeth Lehman (Germantown Ref. Chbk.). She
    md. Peter Oberbach (N.Y. Marriage Lic. 24 Nov 1773).

  vii) <u>Wilhelmus</u>[3], bpt. 16 Feb 1752 - sp.: Wilhelmus Ber-
    gen and Catharina Bergen (Coxsackie Ref. Chbk.).

 viii) <u>Margaretha</u>[3], bpt. 17 Dec 1758 - sp.: Nicolaes Brando
    and Elizabeth Brando (Catskill Ref. Chbk.).

4) <u>Anna Christina Elisabetha</u>[2], b. 8 Nov 1717 - sp.: Elisabetha Krantz, Anna Christina Streit, and Jan Bertsch
 (West Camp Luth. Chbk.). She md. 3 Dec 1739 Hannes Schermerhorn, s/o Hendrich (Loonenburg Luth. Chbk.).

5) <u>Gottfried</u>[2] (HJ), md. 10 March 1740 in de Groote Inbogt
 Catharina Oberbach (Loonenburg Luth. Chbk.). He was in
 Capt. Jacob Halenbeck's Company of the militia in 1767
 (<u>Report of the State Historian</u>,Vol. II, p. 829). His
 branch of the family settled in Greenville, N.Y. (<u>History</u>
 <u>Of Greene Co., N.Y.</u>, p. 294), and his will was proved 16
 May 1792 (Albany Co. Wills Bk. 2, p. 55). Issue:

   i) <u>Maria</u>[3], bpt. 5 Jan 1741 - sp.: Christian Overbach
    and Mareitje Overbach (Katsbaan Ref. Chbk.). She
    md. Stephan Landtmann (HJ).

   ii) <u>Elisabetha</u>[3], bpt. 28 Sept 1742 - sp.: Willem Brando
    and Lisabeth Brando (Katsbaan Ref. Chbk.).

  iii) <u>Catharina</u>[3], bpt. 28 Sept 1742 - sp.: Johannes and
    Lisabeth Overbach (Katsbaan Ref. Chbk.).

  iv) <u>Anna</u>[3], bpt. 25 Nov 1747 - sp.: Joan Jurg Overbach
    and Annatgen (Germantown Ref. Chbk.).

   v) <u>Petrus</u>[3], bpt. 7 May 1749 - sp.: Johan Jurg Oberbach
    and Annatgen (Germantown Ref. Chbk.).

  vi) <u>Catharina</u>[3], bpt. 13 Oct 1751 - sp.: Frederick Brando
    and Maria Brando (Catskill Ref. Chbk.).

  vii) <u>Anna</u>[3], bpt. 18 (?) Nov 1753 - sp.: Pieter Souser and
    Mareytje Souser (Catskill Ref. Chbk.).

 viii) <u>Sara</u>[3], bpt. 23 July 1758 - sp.: Johannes Diderik
    and Elizabeth Overpach (Catskill Ref. Chbk.).

6) <u>Catharina</u>[2], bpt. 23 Oct 1720 - sp.: Pieter Mouwer and
 Catrina Mouwer (Kingston Ref. Chbk.).

JOST BRANDORFF (Hunter Lists #78)

The Brandorff family was documented at 5429 Ködorf (7 km. s.e. of Nassau; Chbks. begin 1655). The probable father of the emigrant Johann Jost[1] was Ludwig Brandorff from Rupperhaußen (?) in the Grafschaft Zigenhayn who md. 10 Sept 1679 Maria Dorothea, d/o the late teacher Andreas Zorn...; the marriage entry stated that Ludwig was 30 yrs. old at the time. Maria Dorothea Zorn at Kirtorf was conf. in 1675 and was bur. 24 July 1694 aged 32 yrs. and 11 days. Ludwig Brandorff, p.t. Hessicher Schultheiß, was bur. 19 Sept 1702, aged 56 yrs. Joh. Jost Brandorff md. Anna Magdalena Faßbänner 12 April 1703. Anna Magdalena, d/o Valentin Faßbänder at Bremberg, was bpt. Thoma Day: 1670 - sp.: Mathias Herold, Peter Faßbander at Alten Dietz, Magdalena - d/o Goar Maxsainer, and Anna Margreth - d/o Peter Anthony at Bremberg. Anna Margaretha, w/o Valentin Fasbänder from Bremburg, was bur. 6 July 1698, aged 56 yrs. Joost Brandeürf, his wife and 4 ch. were on Capt. William Koby's (Colebÿ) vessel in Holland in 1709 (Rotterdam Lists).

Jost Brandorff was noted once on the Hunter Lists on 1 July 1710 with 3 pers. over 10 yrs. of age and 1 pers. under 10 yrs. in the household. He and his wife Magdalena sp. Anthony Bohm at Remobuch in 1720 (N.Y. City Luth. Chbk.) and had ch.:

1) Maria Margaretha[2], bpt. 4 March 1706 - sp.: Joh. Christian Steinborn, Joh. Christophorus - the cowherd in Gutenacker, Anna Margaretha Fahring, and Maria Catharina Ebsteiner (Ködorf Chbk.).

2) Johannes[2], bpt. 28 March 1709 - sp.: Johannes Wöll, Johannes Horn, Anna Margaretha Neidhöfer, and Anna Marie Ebsteiner (Ködorf Chbk.).

JOHN JOST BRAUN (Hunter Lists #79)

The ancestral German home of the N.Y.-Pa. Braun family was Udenheim (14 km. n.e. of Alzey; Chbks. burned in 1945). A list of inhabitants of Udenheim in 1687 and 1688 revealed that Johann Jost Braun, aged 27 yrs. in 1687, was born in Thuringia and came in serfdom to Udenheim. His (1st) wife Anna was 43 yrs. old in 1687 had 4 ch. by her 1st husband (un-named): in 1687 they were Hans Adam aged 20, Elisabeth aged 18, Johannes aged 16, and Hans Jacob aged 11 ("Einwohnerverzeichnis von Udenheim, Rheinh." in Hessische Familienkunde, Band 5, p. 119-124). Jost Braun, a Lutheran, was a resident of Udenheim in 1698 (Alzey Census of 1698). Johannes Joost Broun, his wife and 7 ch. were on Capt. Thomas Wilkens's ship Providens 10 June 1709 in Holland (Rotterdam

Lists). John Braun aged 39, with his wife, sons aged 12, 9, 4, and 1, daughters aged 7, 5, and 3, Luth., husbandman and vinedresser, were in England in 1709 (London Lists). Johann Jost[1] Braun was surrounded by other 1709ers originating near Alzey-Rheinhessen at London and Rotterdam: i.e. Henrich Matthes, Balthasar Lösch, Johann Adam Bubenheiser, and others; it is interesting that Jost was listed near Lorentz Kröll, b. 1682/3, on the 1687/88 Udenheim list, and was entered next to Lorentz Graehl, b. 1682, at London in 1709 (London Lists) (HJ).

John Jost Braun first appeared on the Hunter Lists 1 July 1710 with 3 pers. over 10 yrs. of age and 5 pers. under 10 yrs. The last entry for the family in Hunter read 5 pers. over 10 yrs. of age and 3 pers. under 10 yrs. His 2nd wife was named Magdalena, and was listed as "Magdalena Braun, the mother" in the family of Johannes Braun at Schoharie in 1744 (Schoharie Luth. Chbk.). In colonial N.Y. the family often interacted with the 1709ers Johann Philip Kreisler and Nicolaus Feller, both of whom md. daughters of one Benedict Braun of Udenheim (Guntersblum Chbks.). The Old Braunen d. 20 Aug 1752 (Schoharie Luth. Chbk.); this was probably Jost's wife Magdalena (HJ). The ch. of Jost[1] were:

1) Johann Philip[2] (HJ), conf. by Pastor Kocherthal 30 April 1711 at the new German colony (West Camp Luth. Chbk.). He was an early settler at Tulpehocken, Pa. and eventually resided on a 267 acre farm in Plumpton Manor which he purchased from John Page on 5 Dec 1739 (Edgar Berge's article in Die Shilgrut, Vol. VI, No. 1). Philip Braun d. 16 Aug 1767, aged 74 yrs., and his wife Elisabetha Magdalena Lösch d. 31 March 1769, aged 63 yrs. (Cem. near Tulpehocken, Pa.); there are some minor differences in the several transcriptions of these dates (HJ). Issue:

   i) Jacob[3], mentioned in the will of Jacob Kopf (Philadelphia Co. Wills Bk. F, p. 279). He probably md. Ursula (--) and had ch. at Tulpehocken (HJ).

   ii) Philip[3], conf. 14 May 1749 (Tulpehocken Chbk.). He md. Dorothea (--). The will of Philip Brown of Tulpehocken was written 15 Dec 1774 and probated 9 Feb 1775 (Berks Co. Will Bk. 2, p. 188).

   iii) Adam[3], con.f 14 May 1749 (Tulpehocken Chbk.). He md. as s/o Philip 4 June 1751 Anna Barbara Nagel (Tulpehocken Chbk.). The will of Adam Brown of Tulpehocken was written 5 Aug 1786 and probated 21 Sept 1786 (Berks Co. Will Bk. B, p. 157).

   iv) Johann Georg[3], conf. 14 May 1749 (Tulpehocken Chbk.).

The will of George Braun of Heidelberg was written 3 March 1783 and probated 29 March 1783 (Berks Co. Will Bk. A, p. 50).

  v) <u>Susanna Philippina</u>[3], conf. 14 May 1749 (Tulpehocken Chbk.).

  vi) <u>Anna Eva</u>[3], conf. 14 May 1749 (Tulpehocken Chbk.).

 vii) <u>Johannes</u>[3], conf. 1751, aged 17½ (Tulpehocken Chbk.). The will of John Brown of Tulpehocken was written 22 Dec 1783 and probated 9 Feb 1784 (Berks Co. Will Bk.B, p. 90).

viii) <u>Johann Martin</u>[3], conf. 1751, aged 15½ (Tulpehocken Chbk.).

  ix) <u>David</u>[3], conf. 1751, aged 14 yrs. and 5 months (Tulpehocken Chbk.).

2) <u>Maria Apollonia</u>[2] (HJ), conf. Easter 1716 at Albany (N.Y. City Luth. Chbk.).

3) <u>Johannes</u>[2] (HJ), the (--) Braun on Pastor Sommer's 1744 list (Schoharie Luth. Chbk.). He d. 16 Oct 1754 (Schoharie Luth. Chbk.) and md. Maria Elisabetha Freymeyer. Issue:

   i) <u>Johann Adam</u>[3], on 1744 Sommer's list (Schoharie Luth. Chbk.). He was a freeholder at Schoharrie in 1763 (Albany Co. Freeholders).

  ii) <u>Johann Michael</u>[3], bpt. 25 Dec 1731 - sp.: Johann Michael Freymeyer and Anna Elisa. (Schoharie Ref. Chbk.). He probably was the Michel Braun who md. 11 April 1758 Anna Matthes (Schoharie Luth. Chbk.).

 iii) <u>Maria Magdalena</u>[3], bpt. 16 July 1735 - sp.: John Frederik and Maria Magdalena (Schoharie Ref. Chbk.).

  iv) <u>Conrad</u>[3], bpt. 3 March 1738 - sp.: Coenraad Vrymayer and Anna Maria (Schoharie Ref. Chbk.).

   v) <u>Margaretha</u>[3], on 1744 Sommer's list (Schoharie Luth. Chbk.).

  vi) <u>Elisabetha</u>[3], bpt. 23 May 1740 - sp.: Michael Vrymayer and Elisabeth Vrymayer (Schoharie Ref. Chbk.).

 vii) <u>Catharina</u>[3], bpt. 20 March 1743 - sp.: Jacob Feeck and Maria Catharina Vrÿmeyer (Schoharie Ref. Chbk.).

viii) <u>Johannes</u>[3], b. 28 April 1745 - sp.: Johannes Freymaurer and Magdalena Feg. The ch. d. 23 June 1745, aged 8 weeks (Schoharie Luth. Chbk.).

  ix) <u>Anna Maria</u>[3], b. 31 May 1747 - sp.: Lorentz Lawyer and Margareth Fremauer (Schoharie Luth. Chbk.).

4) <u>Adam</u>[2], called s/o Johann Jost at his 2nd marriage in 1744 (Schoharie Luth. Chbk.). He appeared on the 1744 Sommer's list and d. 12 Jan 1757 (Schoharie Luth. Chbk.). Adam md.

1st Anna Eva Freymeyer, who d.6 Oct 1743, aged 32 yrs.
and some days (Schoharie Luth. Chbk.). They had ch.:

    i) Michael[3], on the 1744 Sommer's list (Schoharie Luth.
       Chbk.).

   ii) Catharina[3], md. as d/o Adam 7 Dec 1752 John Van der
       Hyden (Schoharie Ref. Chbk.).

  iii) Elisabetha[3], bpt. 20 Oct 1739 - sp.: Willem Bauch
       and Maria Magdalena (Schoharie Ref. Chbk.).

   iv) Johannes[3], bpt. 19 Oct 1740 - sp.: Hannes Brouwn and
       Maria Elis. Vrymeyer (Schoharie Ref. Chbk.). He md.
       5 May 1770 Magdalena Zeh (Zähe) (Schoharie Luth.
       Chbk.) and was at Niagara in 1783 (The Ontario Reg-
       ister, Vol. I, No. 4).

    v) "A Child"[3], d. at birth with the mother 6 Oct 1743
       (Schoharie Luth. Chbk.).

   vi) Magdalena[3], on 1744 Sommer's list (Schoharie Luth.
       Chbk.).

Adam[2] md. 2nd Anna Eva Bauch 3 July 1744, who d. 14 March
1747 (Schoharie Luth. Chbk.). They had ch.:

  vii) Maria[3], b. 23 Sept 1744 - sp.: Friederich Bauch and
       his wife (Schoharie Luth. Chbk.).

 viii) Margaretha[3], b. 9 July 1745 - sp.: Hieronymus Kräus-
       ler and his wife (Schoharie Luth. Chbk.).

   ix) Eva[3], b. 29 Dec 1746 - sp.: Fridrich Bauch and wife
       (Schoharie Luth. Chbk.).

Adam[2] md. 3rd Anna Maria Hofer 30 June 1752 (unless this
was the Adam[3], s/o Johannes - HJ). Issue:

    x) Adam[3], b. 1 Oct 1753 - sp.: Adam Kräusler and Mag-
       dalena Braun (Schoharie Luth. Chbk.).

   xi) Jost[3], b. 7 Sept 1755 - sp.: Jost Borst and his wife
       (Schoharie Luth. Chbk.).

There were other early Brauns in the Tulpehocken region of
Pa. who may have been related to Johann Jost Braun: a Johannes
Braun md. 9 Nov 1740 at Tulpehocken Eva Kueffer (Stoever Chbk.)
and a John Wendel Braun md. 27 Aug 1739 at Tulpehocken Maria Elisabetha Knopf (Stoever Chbk.).

JOHN PAUL BRAUN (Hunter Lists #80)

Paul Braun was found on the Hunter Lists among 1709ers originating near Alsheim and Oppenheim (i.e. Johannes Franck, Niclaus Rauch, Johann Henrich Böhler, and Magdalena Becker). Braun
himself was documented at 6504 Oppenheim (20 km. s.e. of Mainz;
Chbks. begin 1650, St. Sebastian Luth.). Johannes Paulus Braun,

s/o Simon Braun - inhabitant at Werheim 'im churtrierschen Gebieth', md. Anna Catharina, d/o the late Johannes Becker - citizen here, 10 May 1707.

John Paul Braun made his first appearance on the Hunter Lists 30 June 1710 with 2 pers. over 10 yrs. of age; the family increased to 4 pers. over 10 yrs. and 4 under 10 24 Dec 1711, but this probably should have been entered under #79 Johann Jost Braun's household (HJ). Paulus Braun and his wife were auf dem Rarendantz ca. 1716/17 (Simmendinger Register). Paul Brauwn subscribed 6 sh. N.Y. money from the Mühlstein congregation in N.J. to the N.Y. Luth. Church building fund in 1727 (N.Y. City Luth. Protocol, p. 89). Paul Braun, Thomas Eheman and Niclas Pickel from Racheway did not accompany the Racheway group to the Mountains at Peter Kasner's on Monday 13 Sept 1731 for the continued deliberations there in drawing up a call for Daniel Falckner's replacement, but they stated their decision that they would be in agreement with whatever the parish decided (Albany Protocol, p. 11). Paul Braun and wife Anna Catharina sp. Daniel Schoemaker at Raritons in 1716 (N.Y. City Luth. Chbk.) and had ch.:

1) Maria Susanna[2], b. 5 July 1708 - sp.: Maria Susanna - w/o Hans Peter Schad, servant...(Oppenheim Luth. Chbk.).

CASPAR BRENDEL (Hunter Lists #81)

Kasper Brandleÿn, his wife and 2 ch. were on Capt. George Bronwell's (Brouwel) ship the Ridschert and Samuel 5 June 1709 in Holland (Rotterdam Lists). Caspar Brandlin aged 42, his wife, a son aged 4, a daughter aged ½, Cath., husbandman and vinedresser, were at London later that year (London Lists).

Caspar Brendel made his first appearance on the Hunter Lists 30 June 1710 with 2 pers. over 10 yrs. of age and 2 pers. under 10 yrs.; the 4 Aug 1710 entry read 2 pers. over 10 yrs. and 1 under 10. On 29 Sept 1711 the notation mentioned Caspar Brendel's widow with 1 pers. over 10 yrs. of age and 1 pers. under 10. Caspar Brendel and wife Anna Agatha had issue:

1) Anna Margaretha[2], bpt. 2 May 1710 by Mr. Rohrbach on the ship Leon; sp.: Anna Margretha Gobel (West Camp Luth. Chbk.). Anna Margaretha Brendell md. Nicolaus Rausch 3 Jan 1732 (Kinderhook Ref. Chbk.).

VALENTIN BRESSELER (Hunter Lists #82)

Valentine Presler aged 40, with his wife, sons aged 6, 4, and 1½, daughters aged 10 and 8, Roman Catholic, husbandman and vinedresser, were in the 1st arrivals in England in 1709 (London Lists).

Valentin Bresseler made his first appearance on the Hunter Lists with 4 pers. over 10 yrs. of age and 2 under 10 yrs. on 1 July 1710; the last entry for the family was 13 Sept 1712 with 5 pers. over 10 yrs. of age and 2 under 10 yrs. Johan Valentyn Bressler and wife Anna Christiana of the Hoogduidsche Kerk joined the N.Y. City Ref. Church 1 June 1714. They had been listed earlier at N.Y. City as Valtin Bressler aged 41, Christina Bressler aged 36, Anna Eliz Bressler aged 14, Anna Gertrude Bressler aged 12, Andreas Bressler aged 9, Anthony Bressler aged 5, and Maria Agnes Bressler aged ½, in 1710/11 (Palatines In N.Y. City). Faletyn Presser was in the North Co. of Col. Aug. Graham in the Richmond Co. militia in 1715 (Report of the State Historian, Vol. I, p. 548). The ch. of Valentin[1] Pressler and wife Anna Christina France were:

1) Anna Elisabetha[2] (Palatines in N.Y. City).

2) Anna Gertrude[2] (Palatines in N.Y. City).

3) Andreas[2] (Palatines in N.Y. City). Andries Preslaar, single man b. Germany, md. 21 April 1723 Antje Wels, single woman b. Staten Island (N.Y. City Ref. Chbk.).

4) Anthony[2] (Palatines in N.Y. City) and called s/o Valentine Presler when apprenticed to Theunis Montaine 25 Aug 1721 (Indentures of Apprentices 1718-27, p. 144). Anthony Preslaer was in the foot company of the Highland in Ulster Co. in 1738 (Report of the State Historian, Col. I, p. 615). He figured in a court case vs. Thomas Ellison in 1742 in the Kingston Court of Common Pleas. He md. a Neeltje (--) and had ch.:

   i) Johan Matthias[3], bpt. ca. 1 yr. old 18 June 1729 at Qvassayk-kill in B. Mynder's barn - sp.: Johan Matthys Kienberg and wife Anna Maria (N.Y. City Luth. Chbk.).

   ii) Adriantje[3], b. 27 May 1730 and bpt. Qvassayk-kil - sp.: Ariantje Quik and Lenard Lieuves (N.Y. City Luth. Chbk.).

   iii) Mattheus[3], b. 20 May 1735 and bpt. at Pieter Lassings - sp.: Mattheus Van Keur and Coecilie or Seeltje, his wife (N.Y. City Luth. Chbk.).

   iv) Thomas[3], bpt. 18 June 1738 aged 1 yr. old today - sp.: Thomas Quick and wife Mareitje (N.Y. City Luth. Chbk.).

   v) Anna Margaretha[3], b. 18 Jan 1741, bpt. Pieter Lassings - sp.: Ludewig Muller and Anna Magdalena (N.Y. City Luth. Chbk.).

   vi) Joseph[3], b. 28 April 1742 and bpt. at Pieter Lassings

sp.: Joseph Simsens and Seidje Trewilliker (N.Y. City
Luth. Chbk.).

5) <u>Maria Agnes</u>[2] (Palatines in N.Y. City).

6) <u>Hans Georg</u>[2], bpt. 4 Dec 1713 - sp.: Hans Juria Pechor and
Elizabeth Roseboom (N.Y. City Ref. Chbk.).

7) <u>Martinus</u>[2], bpt. 25 July 1716 - sp.: Johannes Keÿser and
Elizabeth Kerlag (N.Y. City Ref. Chbk.).

8) <u>Peter</u>[2], bpt. 8 Sept 1717 - sp.: Pieter Van Pelt and wife
Sara (Port Richmond, Staten Island Ref. Chbk.).

There was a Johannes Breslar and wife Elisabeth Kermer who
had a son John bpt. 12 Feb 1758 - sp.: Bastian Kortregt and Rachel
Dekker (Deerpark Ref. Chbk.) who may have been related to Valentin
(HJ). The estate of John Presler, late farmer at New Paltz, was
probated 17 Jan 1798 (Ulster Co. Administration Bk. B).

ANTHONI BRETTER (Hunter Lists #83)

Teunis Prettert, his wife and 2 ch. were on Capt. John Encrist's ship in Holland 3 July 1709 (Rotterdam Lists). The German home of the family was 6754 <u>Otterberg</u> or its environs: estate
papers of Maria Shieler, Roman Catholic w/o Anthony Prattor, mentioned Magdalena Prattor - now w/o John **Michael** Sweyer and d/o
Johannes Prattor who lived at Otterberg near Kaiserslautern - as
heir at law of Anthony[1] and Maria, since they had no ch. (Lancaster Co., Pa. probate records, per Pastor Fred **Weiser** and Annette Burgert).

Anthoni Bretter made his first appearance on the Hunter
Lists 1 July 1710 with 1 pers. over 10 yrs. of age; the 24 June
1711 entry noted 2 pers. over 10 yrs. of age. Minutes of the
Board of Property show a signed warrant to Anthony Pretter of
East Jersey for 300 acres of land near Conestoga dated 16 9ber
1716 (<u>Pa. Archives</u>, Ser. 2, Vol. XIX). Antoni Breder and his
wife were auf dem Rarendantz ca. 1716/17 (Simmendinger Register).
Minute Bk. I dated 19 3mo. 1725 shows a memorandum stating that
Anthony Bretter produced a receipt under James Logan's hand for
£30, which the said Bretter acknowledged was paid equally between
himself and John Fredericksffulls for 300 acres of land called
the Black Walnut Bottom, to be divided and held equally between
them (<u>Pa. Archives</u>, Ser. 2, Vol. XIX). Anthony Bretter took the
Oath of Allegiance in 1739 (<u>The Statutes at Large of Pa.</u>, Vol. IV,
p. 328). He had 189 acres on a branch of Mill Creek when he d.
ca. 1746 (Lancaster Co. Deed Bk. B, p. 401 and Deed Bk. D, p. 85)
which came to Magdalena Prattor Sweyer upon his death; Mary's will
was dated 14 March 1748 and proved 14 April 1748 (Lancaster Wills).

GEORG BRIEGEL (Hunter Lists #84)

Georg Briegel made his first appearance on the Hunter Lists
4 July 1710 with 2 pers. over 10 yrs. of age; the family increased
to 2 pers. over 10 yrs. and 1 pers. under 10 on 29 Sept 1711.
The 25 March 1712 entry noted 1 pers. over 10 yrs. and 1 pers.
under 10, and the last entry 13 Sept 1712 read 2 pers. over 10
yrs. of age. Geo. Breigel of Queensbury was a soldier in 1711
(Palatine Volunteers To Canada). Hans Jorg Priegel was nat. 8
and 9 Sept 1715 (Kingston Nats.). Johann Georg Brugel, his wife
and ch. were at Heessberg ca. 1716/17 (Simmendinger Register).
Jurie Priegel was constaple and collector of the North Ward in
1720, and on Dutchess Co. Tax Lists 1717/18 through 1725/26 (Dutchess Co. Tax Lists). He and an Eva Priegel sp. Jury Scheever in
1724 (Kingston Ref. Chbk.). A Joh. Georg Brigel was a member at
Tulpehocken in 1743 (Tulpehocken Chbk.).

ANNA MARGRETHA BRILLIN (Hunter Lists #85)

The European home of the Palatine Brill family was 6589 Eckersweiler (7 km. n.w. of Kusel); the entries concerning the family
were found at 6587 Baumholder (10 km. n. of Kusel; Chbks. begin
1679, Ref.) and at 6799 Pfeffelbach (4 km. w. of Kusel; Chbks. begin 1571). The earliest known ancestor of the N.Y. line was Peter
Zimmermann (Brill). Hans Simon Brill, s/o the late Peter Zimmermann at Pfeffelbach, md. 17 Nov 1647 Maria, d/o the late Peter
Weyrich from Schwartzerden (Pfeffelbach). The wife of Peter Weyrich was named Margretha; Peter Weyrich's mother-in-law Barbel
was bur. 29 March 1628. A Johannes Weyrich was bur. 23 Feb 1627
who may have been father to Peter (HJ). The ch. of Hans Simon
Brill, shepherd, and Maria Weyrich bpt. at Pfeffelbach were:

> Appolonia, bpt. 28 May 1648 - sp.: Clauß Chumbt im Thal,
> Gödtmann Heß - shepherd at Reichw., Kunigunda - wid/o Pan-
> cratis at Schwarzerden, Sibylla from Dietel Kopf, and Appol-
> onia Beyerlin - d/o the late shoemaker at Pf.
> Anna Elisabetha, bpt. 13 Jan 1650 - sp.: Job Bessering (?)
> from Reichweiler, Nickel Thiel at Cörborn, Agnes - w/o An-
> dreas Schramm at Cörb, Cath. - w/o Simon Dhiel at Cörb, and
> Anna Elis.- surviving d/o Diebald Gerlach at Pf.
> Hanß Dieboldt, bpt. 26 Jan 1652 - sp.: Hans Dieboldt Rech at
> Pf., Johannes Thomas from Reichweiler, Kunigunda from Schwar-
> tzerd., and Barbara - w/o Godtmann Weyrich at Reichw.
> Wilhelm Daniel, bpt. 17 Feb 1654 - sp.: Wilhelm Röhl at Rohr-
> bach, Daniel Aulenbacher im Thal, and Sibylla from Dietel
> Kopf. He was bur. 10 March 1658.

Hanß Nickel, bpt. 17 Feb 1654 (twin) - sp.: Nickel Becker
at Pfeffelb., Hans Jacob Kohl at Rohrb., and Margaretha -
wid/o Johannes Müller at Pfeffelb.

+ Johannes, bpt. 20 Jan 1657 - sp.: Johannes Bast - Sergeant,
Johannes Gerlach, and Margaretha - w/o Nickel Thiel at Cö-
born.

A Child, bpt. 6 Oct 1659 - sp.: Bast Pfeiffer - citizen at
Cassell (?), Salome - w/o Johannes Müller at Langenbach, and
Cath. - d/o Nickel Diel at Cörborn.

Johannes[1] Brill md. Margaretha (--) and lived 1686-1691 at Eck-
ersweiler and 1700-1703 at Ruschberg (Baumholder Chbk.). Johannes
Brill, his wife, and 3 ch. were in Holland 5 July 1709 on Capt.
Frans Robbenson's ship Egear (Rotterdam Lists).

Anna Margretha Brillin made her first appearance on the Hunter Lists 1 July 1710 with 2 pers. over 10 yrs. of age and 1 pers.
under 10 yrs. in the family; she was called Anna Margretha, Anna
Maria and Anna Brillin at various times on Hunter in 1710-11.
The ch. of Johannes and Margaretha Brill bpt. at Baumholder were:

1) Hanß Nickel[2], bpt. 10 Feb 1686 - sp.: Hans Albert - Censor
at Eckersweiler, Hans Nickel Müller from Pfeffelbach,
Maria - w/o Hans Nickel Köhler the Censor at Mettw., and
Apollonia - w/o Nickel Schäfer at Mettw.

2) Johann Fritz[2], bpt. 15 Feb 1688 - sp.: Fritz Gerhard from
Oberalben, Johannes Köhl from Mettweiler, Barbel - Sei-
moth (?) Weyrich's wife from Reinweiler (?), and Agnes -
w/o Theobald Brill from Pfeffelbach.

3) Nickel[2], bpt. 14 Feb 1690 - sp.: Nickel Welsch at Eckersweiler.

4) Elisabeth[2], (twin) bpt. 14 Feb 1690 - sp.: Anna Elisabeth
- w/o Jacob Künsel.

5) Maria Salome[2], bpt. 20 Sept 1690 - sp.: Hans Welsch here,
Salome - w/o Jacob Köhl at Berschweiler, and Maria Salome
- w/o Bast Müller at...

6) Margaretha[2],, (twin) bpt. 20 Sept 1690; they died in the
night after the baptism.

7) Hanß Adam[2], bpt. 3 Dec 1691 - sp.: Hans Adam Becker from
Reichweiler, Hans Nickel Braun (?) at Fohren, and Margaretha - w/o Nicklaß Weyerich from Reichw.

8) Theobald[2] (HJ), probably named for his paternal uncle
Hans Theobald (Dieboldt) (HJ). Dewaeld Pryl was nat. 3
Jan 1715/16 (Albany Nats.). He was sometimes known as
David Brill and was so-named in his first appearance
on Dutchess Co. Tax Lists in 1723/4. He was a surveyor

of fences in the South Ward in 1725 (Dutchess Co. Super-
visors Records). His wife was Catharina Bek, and she was
conf. at P. Lassings 13 Sept 1730 as the wife of Dewald
Brill (N.Y. City Luth. Chbk.). Issue:

  i) Johannes[3], bpt. 6 May 1724 - sp.: Ary Kool and Mary-
     tjen Pik (Poughkeepsie Ref. Chbk.).

 ii) Elisabetha[3], b. 25 Jan 1726 - sp.: Hannes Dewald Scher
     and Eva Pril (N.Y. City Luth. Chbk.).

iii) Catharina[3] (HJ), conf. together with Hannes and El-
     isabeth Brill 12 June 1743 at Backway (N.Y. City Luth.
     Chbk.). She md. Jacob Rosener 1 Oct 1745 (HJ).

 iv) Jacob[3], b. 26 May 1730 and bpt. Pieter Lassings - sp.:
     Hannes Berger and wife Anna Maria (N.Y. City Luth.
     Chbk.). Sargant Jacob Brill was in Capt. Peter Van-
     denburgh's Co. in 1755 (Report of the State Historian,
     Vol. I, p. 683).

  v) Johanna[3], b. 2nd Sunday after Trinity 1732 and bpt.
     Pieter Lassings - sp.: Philip Salomon Vlegeler and
     wife Margaretha (Loonenburg Luth. Chbk.).

 vi) Christina[3], b. New Year's Day 1735 and bpt. at P.
     Lassings in the Highland - sp.: Hans Busch and wife
     Christina (N.Y. City Luth. Chbk.).

vii) Anna Maria[3], b. May 1737 and bpt. at Niclaus Emig's
     in Kove at Bachwaij - sp.: Hans Jacob Scherer and
     wife Maria Magdalena (N.Y. City Luth. Chbk.).

viii) Helena[3], b. 29 July 1739 - sp.: Hannes Uhl and wife
     Lena (N.Y. City Luth. Chbk.).

 ix) David[3], b. 14 Feb 1742 and bpt. Pacquesien - sp.:
     Niclaas Walther and Sophia (N.Y. City Luth. Chbk.).

  x) Petrus[3], b. 13 June 1744 and bpt. Bachway - sp.: Pet-
     rus Scherer and wife (N.Y. City Luth. Chbk.). Peter
     Brill d. 1 May 1812, aged 70 yrs. (Vander Burgh Cem.,
     town of Beekman, Dutchess Co.).

9) Anna Eva[2], bpt. 30 Dec 1700 - sp.: Adam Wentz at Rusperg,
   Nickel Welsch here, Eva - w/o Michel Welsch, and Anna
   Maria - w/o Hans Nickel Leicht (?) at Mehbockel (?).   Eva
   Brill md. Johannes Jung in Dutchess Co, N.Y. (HJ).

10) Hanß Nickel[2], bpt. 9 Sept 1703 - sp.: H. Nickel Albert -
    Schultheiß at Berschweiler, Anna Cath - H. Joh. Barthel
    Rauscher's wife, Hans Nickel Meiß from Linden, and Anna
    Catrina - w/o Ludwig Metzger. Hans Nickel, the little
    s/o Johannes Prill at Rusperg was bur. 9 March in the
    year 1708.

HELENA BRILLEMÄNNIN (Hunter Lists #86)

There were Brüllmanns found at 6308 <u>Griedel</u> and 6309 <u>Münz-enberg</u>, but no connective link to the N.Y. family was found.

Helena Brillemännin made her first appearance on the Hunter Lists 4 Oct 1710 with 3 pers. over 10 yrs. of age in the house-hold; the 24 Dec 1711 entry showed 1 pers. over 10 yrs. of age. Magdalen Brilman aged 12, an orphan, was bound to Lancaster Symes of N.Y. 20 Nov 1710 (Apprenticeship Lists). Helena Brilmannin aged 17, orphan, was in N.Y. City in 1710/11; an "x" was entered after her name (Palatines In N.Y. City).

ANNA GERTRUD BROMWASSER (Hunter Lists #87)

Herman Bornwaßer, his wife, and 1 child were on Capt. John Howlentzen's ship in Holland 10 June 1709 (Rotterdam Lists). Herman Brunnwaßer aged 31, with his wife, a son aged 1 yr., Luth., husbandman and vinedresser, were in England later that year (London Lists).

Anna Gertrud Bromwasser was entered 4 Aug 1710 with 1 pers. over 10 yrs. of age on the Hunter Lists; she was called Maria Bromwasser on 24 Dec 1711 in Hunter. Some 1710 Hunter entries placed her with #241 Henrich Klock, but these are confusing (HJ). Maria Cath Bornwaserin, widow, aged 26, was in N.Y. City in 1710/11 (Palatines In N.Y. City).

MATHEUS BRONG (Hunter Lists #88)

Mattheus Brunck, widower and blacksmith of Andel in the earl-dom of Veldenz, md. 15 Nov 1710 Anna, wid/o Sebastian Wormser of Bubach in the commune of Lichtenberg, county of Zweybruck (West Camp Luth. Chbk.). The German home of the Broncks then was 5550 <u>Andel</u> (HJ). Matheus Brong made his first appearance on the Hunter Lists 4 July 1710 with 3 pers. over 10 yrs. of age; the 24 June 1711 entry read 3 pers. over 10 yrs. and 1 pers. under 10, and the remaining notations gave 4 pers. over 10 yrs. of age. Matheis Bronck aged 50 - works in ye Govr. Gard., Anna Christina Bronck his daughter aged 22, and John Hendrick Bronck his son aged 16 were in N.Y. City ca. 1710/11 (Palatines In N.Y. City). His widow Anna md. Johann Planck 29 May 1716 (West Camp Luth. Chbk.).   Ch. from 1st marriage:

1) <u>Anna Christina</u>[2] (Palatines In N.Y. City)
2) <u>Johann Henrich</u>[2] (Palatines In N.Y. City), nat. 8 and 9
   Sept 1715 (Kingston Nats.).

Issue from 2nd marriage to Anna:

3) <u>Nicolaus</u>[2], b. 28 Feb 1713 - sp.: Niclaus Jung (West Camp
   Luth. Chbk.). A Nicolaus Bronk md. Catharina Schram 3
   Dec 1757 (Loonenburg Luth. Chbk.); it is difficult to de-
   termine if this was the s/o Mattheus[1] or a member of the
   Dutch Bronck family of Greene Co. (HJ).

HENRICH BRUCHLE (Hunter Lists #89)

John Henry Bruchly aged 32, with his wife, sons aged 4 and
2, Ref., cloth and linenweaver, were in the 1st arrivals at London in 1709 (London Lists).

Henrich Bruchle made his first appearance on the Hunter Lists
4 Aug 1710 with 1 pers. over 10 yrs. of age; the entry for 4 Oct
1710 showed 2 pers. over 10 yrs., and the notation for 31 Dec
1710 gave the household 2 pers. over 10 yrs. and 1 pers. under
10. The last two entries in 1712 showed 2 pers. over 10 yrs. of
age. Heinrich Brugler and Magdalena with 1 child were at Quunsberg
ca. 1716/17 (Simmendinger Register). Hendrik Breakle was on Palatine Debt Lists in 1718, 1719 (at Kingsberry) and 1721 (Livingston Debt Lists). The administration papers of Henry Bruckler
were probated in 1747 in Pennsylvania (Philadelphia Co. Administrations Bk. F, p. 145). Ch. with wife Anna Magdalena:

1) <u>Johann Jacob</u>[2], b. 29 Oct 1714 - sp.: Jacob German and Anna
   Catharina Mueller (West Camp Luth. Chbk.). The estate
   papers for Jacob Brickly, deceased, of Manheim were granted
   to a friend Conrad Minnich, as the widow renounced on 6
   April 1796 (Berks Co. Administrations Bk. 5, p. 77).
2) <u>Anna Magdalena</u>[2], (a twin) b. 29 Oct 1714 - sp.: same
   (West Camp Luth. Chbk.).
3) <u>Anna Margaretha</u>[2], b. 20 April 1720 at Central Camp on the
   East Bank - sp.: Anna Magdalena Finckler (N.Y. City Luth.
   Chbk.).

Papers in the estate of a Paul Bruckle were granted to Catharine Bruckle in 1772 (Berks Co. Administrations Bk. 3, p. 81,
also in Berks Co. Orphans Court records detailing his children);
he may have been connected with Henrich[1] (HJ).

SUSANNE BRUYERE (Hunter Lists #90)
JEANNE BRUYERE (Hunter Lists #91)

The ancestral German home of the Bruyere family was 6331
<u>Daubhausen</u> (7 km. s. of Herborn; Chbks. begin 1685, Huguenot).
The founders of family #90 were Pierre Bruere and wife Susanne
Tiebaud who md. in 1691. Family #91 was begun by Jaques Bruier

de Chervey en Champagne who md. 29 June 1690 Louise Dousset du dit
Chervey.

#90 Susanne Bruyere first appeared on the Hunter Lists on 1
July 1710 next to Jeane Bruyere; Susanne had 2 pers. over 10 yrs.
of age in her family. Pierre Bruere and Susanne Tiebaud had ch.:
1) Jeanne[2], b. 9 March 1694 at Greifenthal - sp.: Jaques
   Bruere and Jeanne Tibaud (Daubhausen).

Jaques Bruier (Bruere) and wife Louise Dousset had issue:
1) "A son"[2], b. in Greifenthal and bpt. 6 April 1691 - sp.:
   Jean Robin and Susanne Bruere (Daubhausen).
2) Jeanne[2], b. in Greifenthal and bpt. 11 March 1693 - sp.:
   Jean Hugon and Jean Doucet (Daubhausen). This child became the head of the household of family #91 on the Hunter Lists. Jeanne Bruyere was enrolled next to Susanne
   Bruyere 1 July 1710 with 2 pers. over 10 yrs. of age and
   1 pers. under 10 in his family. Jeane Bruiere aged 18,
   Jacque Bruiere aged 15, and Susannah Bruiere aged 6, were
   in N.Y. City in 1710/11 (Palatines In N.Y. City).
3) Jaques[2], b. 24 Feb 1695 in Greifenthal - sp.: Isac Doucot
   and Anne Robin (Daubhausen). James Bruere aged 14, an
   orphan, was bound to Rip Van Dam of N.Y. 21 March 1711
   (Apprenticeship Lists). There was a Jacob Breuer who md.
   Lea Beeckmans at the N.Y. City Luth. Church in 1711, but
   this groom was not our emigrant, as he was b. in N.J. (HJ).
4) Susanne[2], b. 25 March 1704 - sp.: Abraham Doucot and Susanne Einget (?) (Daubhausen).

JOHANN GEORG BUFF (Hunter Lists #92)

George Buff aged 28, with his wife, a daughter aged 1, Luth.,
husbandman, was in the 1st arrivals in England in 1709 (London
Lists).

Johann Georg Buff was registered once on the Hunter Lists
on 1 July 1710 with 2 pers. over 10 yrs. of age in his family.
Georg Buff, his wife and 2 ch. were auf dem Raredantz ca. 1716/17
(Simmendinger Register). He was mentioned in the N.Y. City Luth.
Protocol in 1727. He was a Luth. leader at Rareton in 1731 (Luth.
Church in N.Y. and N.J., p. 15). He md. Maria Selfs or Selus
(Van Vleq's Chbk.) and had issue:
1) Jannet[2], bpt. 18 Nov 1711 at Sammeny - sp.: Paulus Van
   Vlecq and Jannetje (Van Vleq's Chbk., Bucks Co., Pa.).
2) Philippus[2], bpt. 9 Dec 1712 at Sammeny - sp.: Hendricks
   Van Dyck (Van Vleq's Chbk., Bucks Co., Pa.).

3) <u>Johann Georg</u>², b. 23 Nov 1719 and (bpt.) at Raritons at
   Baldus Pickel's - sp.: Jurgen Remer and wife Elisabeth
   (N.Y. City Luth. Chbk.).

4) <u>Elisabeth</u>², b. Spring of 1722 on the Raritons - sp.: Quirinus Neidebber and wife (N.Y. City Luth. Chbk.).

MARTIN BUCK (Hunter Lists #93)

Martin Buck made his first appearance on the Hunter Lists 30
June 1710 with 2 pers. over 10 yrs. of age and 2 pers. under 10;
the 4 Oct 1710 entry read Maria Gertrud Hamin and Martin Buck. The
family was reduced to 2 pers. over 10 yrs. and 1 pers. under 10
on 31 Dec 1710 and remained that size until 13 Sept 1712 when the
household returned to 2 pers. over 10 and 2 pers. under 10 yrs.
Marte Bok, metselaer, was mentioned in 1712/13 and, as Marte Bock,
appeared on the 1718 Palatine Debt List (Livingston Debt Lists).
Martin Boeck was nat. 8 and 9 Sept 1715 (Kingston Nats.). Martin
Buch with Nicolaus Hamen's widow and 2 ch. was at Quunsberg ca.
1716/17 (Simmendinger Register). Marttyn Bock made his first appearance in Dutchess Co. rolls in the North Ward in 1717/18; he
was listed there until 1729/30, when he was recorded in the Middle
Ward. In 1735/6 he appeared in the South Ward for the first time,
and in 1739/40 at Beekmans. Martin Buck's widow made her appearance in 1743/4 (Dutchess Co. Tax Lists). Ancient Documents survive for him in the period 1733-36 (Dutchess Co. Ancient Docs.,
#41, #64, and #47). He and wife Maria Gertraud Schmidt had ch.:

1) <u>Christina</u>², bpt. 19 Feb 1716 - sp.: Johannes Top and Christina Oels (Kingston Ref. Chbk.). An Anna Christina Bocken
   md. Barend Thalheimer 29 June 1742 (N.Y. City Luth. Chbk.).

2) <u>Henrich</u>², bpt. 26 Jan 1718 - sp.: Henderick Oel and Anne-
   lies Vrelingen (Kingston Ref. Chbk.).

3) <u>Anna Margaretha</u>², bpt. 2 Aug 1719 - sp.: Pieter Tiepel and
   Grietjen Oel (Kingston Ref. Chbk.). She was conf. DNIA III,
   p.t.: 1737 at Nic. Emig's and md. Joh. Jurgen Kuhns 9 Oct
   1739 (N.Y. City Luth. Chbk.).

4) <u>Anna Maria</u>², b. 14 Oct 1721 at Rheinbeck - sp.: Albertus
   Schreiber and A. Maria Ulin (N.Y. City Luth. Chbk.). She
   was conf. DNIA II, p.t.: 1740 at Nicolaes Emig's; an Anna
   Maria Bocken md. Laurens Emig 17 Oct 1742 (N.Y. City Luth.
   Chbk.).

5) <u>Elisabetha</u>² (HJ), conf. DNIA II, p.t.: 1740 with Anna Maria
   Bocken at Nicolaes Emig's (N.Y. City Luth. Chbk.).

6) <u>Martinus</u>², bpt. 18 June 1727 - sp.: Albartus Schryver and
   Eva Schryver (Kingston Ref. Chbk.).

7) <u>Gertraud²</u>, b. 20 April 1729 and bpt. at Rhynbek - sp.:
Jurge Ekkhard and Gertrude Switzlers (N.Y. City Luth.
Chbk.).

8) <u>Andreas²</u>, b. 13 Sept 1732 (and bpt.) Pieter Lassing's -
sp.: Andreas Frd. Beck and wife Veronica (Loonenburg Luth.
Chbk.). The estate of Andries Buck, late of Beekman, was
probated 27 April 1805 (Dutchess Co. Administration Bk. B).

ULRICH BURCKARDT dicta BRUCKER (Hunter Lists #94)

Ulrich Burckardt made his first appearance on the Hunter
Lists 1 July 1710 with 3 pers. over 10 yrs. of age in the family.
The name was Ulrich Bruckert on the 4 Oct 1710 list and thereafter;
the family size increased 24 June 1712 to 3 pers. over 10 yrs. of
age and 1 pers. under 10 yrs. Ulrich Bruckhart of Annsberg was a
soldier in 1711 (Palatine Volunteers To Canada). Ulrich Bruck-
hard joined the church at Schoharie 24 Jan 1716, called Epis(copal) at the time (West Camp Luth. Chbk.). Ulrich Burckhardt and
Anna Maria with 2 ch. were at Neu-Ansberg ca. 1716/17 (Simmendinger
Register). The ch. of Ulrich¹ Brucker and Anna Maria were:

1) <u>Margaretha²</u>, (HJ), conf. 30 April 1711 at the new German
colony - her parents being Epis(copal) (West Camp Luth.

2) <u>Elisabetha Catharina²</u> (HJ), md. Peter Schneider (HJ).

JOHANNES BURCKHARDT (Hunter Lists #95)

Johann Peter Burckhard, s/o the late Johann Burckhard of
Ober-Mockstatt in the earldom of Isenburg, md. Anna Amalia Klein,
d/o Hieronimus Klein of Flommersfeld in the earldom of Sehnish-
Hachenburg near Neuwid on 5 Nov 1717 (West Camp Luth. Chbk.). The
correct village of origin for the Burckhardts was 6479 <u>Ober-Mock-
stadt</u> (25 km. n.e. of Frankfurt; Chbks. begin 1656). The earliest
known ancestor of the N.Y. family was <u>Nicolaus Burghardt</u>. Johannes
Burghardt, s/o Nicolaus Burghardt from Gersfeld in Fuldischen land,
md. Elisabetha, d/o Johannes Schleicher - inhabitant here, 28 April
1687. Johannes Schliecher Senior was bur. 8 June 1689, aged 74
yrs.

Johannes Burckhardt made his first appearance on the Hunter
Lists 4 July 1710 with 4 pers. over 10 yrs. of age and 1 pers. under 10 yrs.; the 4 Aug 1710 list gave 3 pers. over 10 yrs., and
the 4 Oct 1710 entry read 5 pers. over 10 yrs. of age. Peter
Burckhardt took over as head of the family as of 29 Sept 1711 with
4 pers. over 10 yrs. of age. The family then dwindled down to
1 pers. over 10 yrs. of age on its last entry 13 Sept 1712. Elisabetha Burckhardt, a widow with 2 ch., was at Beckmansland ca.

1716/17 (Simmendinger Register). The ch. of Johannes[1] Burckhardt
and wife Elisabetha were:

1) Anna Margaretha[2], md. as d/o Johannes Burckhardt 1 Nov
1715 Johann Peter Sutz (West Camp Luth. Chbk.).

2) Johann Peter[2], md. as s/o Johannes Burckhardt 5 Nov 1717
Anna Amalia Klein (West Camp Luth. Chbk.). Peter Burger
was nat. 17 Jan 1715/16 (Albany Nats.). He was in the
foot company of the Ulster Co. militia at Kingston in
1738 (Report of the State Historian, Vol. I, p. 603).
His ch. were:

    i) Johann Conrad[3], b. 4 March 1718 - sp.: Conrad Mar-
    tin, Mattheus Schlemmer, and Gerdraut Kehl (West
    Camp Luth. Chbk.).

    ii) Martin[3], bpt. 18 Sept 1720 - sp.: Marthen Burger
    and Marytjen Klein (Kingston Ref. Chbk.).

    iii) Hieronymus[3], bpt. 8 March 1724 - sp.: Anderies Eli
    and Zofia Eli (Kingston Ref. Chbk.). He was conf.
    with Marten and Elisabeth Borghard at Newton 3 June
    1744 (Loonenburg Luth. Chbk.). He md. 20 June 1760
    Helena Sluiter; his marriage entry stated he was b.
    under the jurisdiction of Albany and resided in
    Rochester (Kingston Ref. Chbk.).

    iv) Johannes[3], bpt. 6 weeks old 24 or 26 Jan 1726 at
    Newtown - sp.: Johan Henr. Reuter and wife Anna Jul-
    iana, and Johan Jacob Maul and Elis. Klein (Loonen-
    burg Luth. Chbk.). He md. 3 Advent: 1752 Liesabeth
    Spoon (Loonenburg Luth. Chbk.).

    v) Anna Elizabeth[3] (a twin), bpt. same time.

    vi) Maria[3], bpt. 2 months old 24 Jan 1728 at Kiskatom -
    sp.: Friderich Maul and Maria Klein (West Camp Luth.
    Chbk.).

    vii) Nicolaus[3], b. 2 Oct 1735 at Kisket - sp.: Niclas
    Brandauw, and Cath - w/o Frid. Scheib (Loonenburg
    Luth. Chbk.).

    viii) Conrad[3], b. 23 June 1738 and bpt. Newton - sp.: Nic-
    las Brandaun and Christina Brandaun (Loonenburg Luth.
    Chbk.).

    ix) Anna[3], b. 1 Sept 1740 and bpt. at Bakoven - sp.: Phil-
    ip Spaan and Agneta Borterin (Loonenburg Luth. Chbk.).

    x) Catharina[3], b. 11 July 1743 and bpt. Kisket - sp.:
    Catharina Spoonin and Jo: Henr. Spoon (Loonenburg
    Luth. Chbk.).

3) Anna Elisabetha[2], bpt. 27 June 1697 - sp.: Anna Elisabetha
d/o Georg Bommer of Mogstadt (Ober-Mockstadt Chbk.). She was

bur. 21 April 1701, aged 4 yrs.

4) <u>Johann Martinus</u>[2], bpt. 21 Oct 1700 - sp.: Joh. Martin - s/o Johannes Frick (Ober-Mockstadt Chbk.). Martin Burghard was conf. Easter 1713 at Newtown (West Camp Luth. Chbk.). Martin Burger was nat. 8 and 9 Sept 1715 (Kingston Nats.). He made his first appearance on Dutchess Co. rolls in 1722 and his last in 1771 (Dutchess Co. Tax Lists). He md. Ursula Frölich 16 May 1721 (Kingston Ref. Chbk.) and had ch.:

   i) <u>Elisabetha</u>[3], bpt. 11 March 1722 - sp.: Jury Ekkert and Elisabeth Freling (Kingston Ref. Chbk.). She md. Emmerich Schryver 20 Oct 1738 (Kingston Ref. Chbk.).

   ii) <u>(Maria) Catalyntjen</u>[3], bpt. 31 July 1726 - sp.: Mathys Slegt, Jr. and Catalyntjen Kip (Kingston Ref. Chbk.). She md. Johannes Becker 8 Aug 1749 (Kingston Ref. Chbk.).

   iii) <u>Maria</u>[3] (HJ), md. Salomon Eckert 30 Dec 1746 (Rhinebeck Luth. Chbk.).

   iv) <u>Stephanus</u>[3], bpt. 4 months old 6 May 1729 at Rhynbek - sp.: Anna Liesabeth Frölich and Stephanus Frölich (N.Y. City Luth. Chbk.). He joined the church at Rhinebeck Flats 28 June 1751 and md. 17 Aug 1756 Rebecca Van Etten (Rhinebeck Flats Ref. Chbk.). They had ch. bpt. at Rhinebeck Flats and Red Hook Luth. Churches.

   v) <u>Martin</u>[3], bpt. 1731 - sp.: Michel Pulver and Anna Maria Klom (Red Hook Luth. Chbk.). He md. Catharina Hoogteeling (HJ) and had ch. at Red Hook Luth. and Rhinebeck Flats Churches.

   vi) <u>Eva</u>[3], on 1734 St. Peter's List (Rhinebeck Luth. Chbk.). She md. Martin Schryver 28 Aug 1750 (Kingston Ref. Chbk.).

   vii) <u>Margaretha</u>[3] (HJ), md. Benjamin Van Wageninen (HJ).

   viii) <u>Gertraud</u>[3], b. 25 Sept 1735 - sp.: Peter Frolich and Gertrude Cramer, single (Rhinebeck Luth. Chbk.).

   ix) <u>Christina</u>[3], bpt. 23 Oct 1737 - sp.: Jacob Sikner and Christina Schryver (Kingston Ref. Chbk.). She md. Jacob Pulver 9 May 1758 (Rhinebeck Flats Ref. Chbk.).

   x) <u>Johannes</u>[3], bpt. 2 Dec 1739 - sp.: Johannes Wiest and Catrina Freeling (Kingston Ref. Chbk.).

   xi) <u>Catharina</u>[3], bpt. 15 Sept 1745 - sp.: Johannes Wust and wife Catterina (Red Hook Luth. Chbk.).

5) <u>Johann Henrich</u>[2], bpt. 2 April 1707 - sp. Joh. Henrich -

s/o Joh. Henrich Ulrich (Ober-Mockstadt).

DANIEL BOUCHE 2^d (Hunter Lists #96)

Daniel Busch and his wife were listed next to Daniel Buschert and Wendel Bulfer on Capt. Jan Duk's ship in Holland in 1709
(Rotterdam Lists). Daniel Busch aged 65 and his wife, Ref. husbandman and vinedresser, were at London in 1709 (London Lists);
they were noted again near Wendel Pulver in the 4th arrivals.
Wendel Pulver md. an Anna Catharina Busch, and an Anna Catharina
-d/o Daniel Busch and Elisabetha at Wiedt - was bpt. Dom. 4 Advent: 1679 in the church at Wiedt, according to the Chbks. at
5455 Rengsdorf near Neuwied.

#96 Daniel Bouche 2^d appears to have been entered first in
Hunter as #74 Daniel Bousche 2^d (HJ). #96 made his first appearance 4 Oct 1710 with 2 pers. over 10 yrs. of age in the family.
The family increased to 3 pers. over 10 yrs. on 24 June 1711, and
then decreased to 1 pers. over 10 yrs. of age 29 Sept 1711. Two
boards for the coffin of Daniel Busch were ordered 7 April 1711
(N.Y. Colonial Mss., Vol. 55, p. 20 a-h).

DANIEL BUSCH senr (HUNTER LISTS #97)

The European home of the Dutchess Co. Busch family was 6344
Ewersbach (11 km. n. of Dillenburg; Chbks. begin 1635). The father of the emigrant 1709er was Johann Jost Busch who md. an Elisabeth (--), lived at Steinbrücken, and had ch.:
>   A Young Daughter, bpt. 5 March 1671 - sp.: Hans Jacob - s/o
>   Johannes Roth at Remmel, Johan Busch's wife, and Marg. - d/o
>   Frank Haan.
> +   Johann Daniel, b. in the evening 2 Jan 1677 - sp.: Johann
>   Daniel - s/o Andreas Beck at Ebersbach, Anna... - d/o the
>   late Hermann Becker at Steinbr., and Anna Margreth - d/o
>   Johann Jacob Wickel there.
>   Johannes, b. 23 May 1679.
>   A Daughter, b. 13 Feb 1682.

Johann Daniel, s/o Johann Jost Busch from Ebersbach, md. Anna Margaretha, d/o the late Caspar Eichert from Niederrossbach, 4 Nov
1700. Johann Daniel Busch from Ebersbach, his wife and 3 ch.,
along with his wife's sister, Hans Jacob Kisseler's daughter, left
without release in 1709 (Nassau-Dillenburg Petitions); Hans Jacob
Kesseler had md. in 1678 Magdalena, wid/o Caspar Eickert (HJ).

Daniel Busch Sr. made his first appearance 1 July 1710 with
2 pers. over 10 yrs. of age and 2 under 10; the entries appear to
have been mixed up quite often with the other Daniel Busches (HJ).

His last entry on Hunter was 13 Sept 1712 with 3 pers. over 10 yrs.
Daniel Busch of Annsberg was a soldier in 1711 (Palatine Volun-
teers To Canada). Daniel Buch was nat. 17 Jan 1715/16 (Albany
Nats.) and was a surveyor of the King's Highway for roads about
Pocghquaiek in 1724 in the South Ward (Dutchess Co. Supervisor's
Records). He made his first appearance on the tax rolls in 1718/
19 as Daniell Bossh and continued to be listed in the Fishkill
area until 1740/1 (Dutchess Co. Tax Lists). Catherine Brett of
Fishkill deeded a tenement farm, now in the possession of Daniel
Boss, to Daniel Boss 25 Sept 1727 (Dutchess Co. Deeds, p. 105).
He was listed as a member of the Fishkill Ref. Church 25 Aug 1719
and 19 Dec 1731 (Fishkill Ref. Chbk.). Issue:

1) A Son[2], b. 11 Oct 1701 at Rittershausen - sp.: Johann Henrich - s/o Jost Schäfer there, and Anna Catharina - d/o
   Johann Jost Busch at Ebersbach (Ewersbach Chbk.). Male sp.
   of the child suggests strongly that his name was Henrich
   (HJ). Johann Hend. Buch was nat.(next to Daniel Buch) 17
   Jan 1715/16 (Albany Nats.). Hendrick Boss first was taxed
   in Dutchess Co. in 1723/24 (Dutchess Co. Tax Lists). He
   md. Catharina Schawer, and the will of Henry Bush of Charlotte Precinct was dated 10 July 1780 and proved 18 Jan
   1791 (Dutchess Co. Will Bk. A). They had ch.:

   i) Maria[3], bpt. 6 May 1724 - sp.: Johannes Snyder and
      Anna Maria Keetelaar (?) (Poughkeepsie Ref. Chbk.).
      She md. Jacob Sharpsteen (Will).
   ii) Margaretha[3], b. 22 Feb 1726 at Willem Lassing's -
      sp.: Daniel Busch, the grandfather, and his wife Mar-
      grete (N.Y. City Luth. Chbk.).
   iii) Christina[3], b. 18 Aug 1729 - sp.: Ned Diamant and
      wife Christyne (N.Y. City Luth. Chbk.).
   iv) Daniel[3], b. 8 Oct 1730 at P. Lassing's - sp.: Daniel
      Busch and wife Margrete (N.Y. City Luth. Chbk.).
   v) Magdalena[3], bpt. 16 March 1735 - sp.: Johannes Bush
      and Magdalena (Red Hook Luth. Chbk.).
   vi) Catharina[3], b. 16 Nov 1740 and bpt. at Bachwaij at
      Nicolaus Emig's - sp.: Hans Uhl and wife Magdalena
      (N.Y. City Luth. Chbk.). She md. Caleb Husted (Will).
   vii) Henrich[3], b. 14 March 1743 and bpt. at Bachwaij in
      Klove (N.Y. City Luth. Chbk.).
   viii) Christina[3], b. 12 Oct 1745 and bpt. Bachway - sp.:
      Hans Dijmand and Nelt Dijmand's wife (N.Y. City Luth.
      Chbk.). She md. John Degraff (Will).
   ix) John[3] (Will).
   x) Elisabeth[3] (Will).

Henrik Busch Sr., brewer of Dutchess Co., md. 4 Jan 1756
Catharina Rykman, widow of Kingston (Kingston Ref. Chbk.).
This may have been a 2nd marriage of Henrich[2] (HJ).

2) <u>A Child[2]</u>, b. 18 Dec 1703 at Rüttershausen - sp.: Henrich
..., Johannes - s/o Hans Jacob Kesseler there, and Elsbeth - w/o Philipp Busch at Steinbrücken (Ewersbach Chbk.).

3) <u>A Son[2]</u>, b. 18 May 1705 - sp.: Johann Henrich Möller at
Steinbrücken, Anna Maria - d/o Hans Jacob Kesseler at
Ritterhausen (Ewersbach Chbk.).

4) <u>Johannes[2]</u> (HJ), who may have been the son #3 bpt. above
(HJ). He md. 1st Magdalena (--), and they sp. at Red Hook
Luth. and Fishkill Ref. 1732-35. He md. 2nd Christina
Demuth (or De Mold) and first appeared on rolls in the
South Ward in 1735/6 (Dutchess Co. Tax Lists). Johannes[2]
will was dated 5 Aug 1774, proved 1781 (<u>Fernow Wills</u> #147).

   i) <u>Daniel[3]</u>, bpt. 13 Aug 1738 - sp.: Daniel Bos and Mar-
agriet Bos (Fishkill Ref. Chbk.).

   ii) <u>Margaretha[3]</u>, bpt. 13 Jan 1741 - sp.: Philip Salomon
Vlengeler and Grietje Top (Red Hook Luth. Chbk.).

   iii) <u>Johannes[3]</u>, b. 15 May 1743 and bpt. in Klove at Bachwaij (N.Y. City Luth. Chbk.).

   iv) <u>Maria[3]</u>, bpt. 1 Dec (?) 1745 - sp.: Joost Bos and
Marya de Mold (Fishkill Ref. Chbk.).

   v) <u>Nostront[3]</u> (Will).

   vi) <u>Peter[3]</u> (Will).

   vii) <u>Zacharias[3]</u> (Will).

5) <u>Joseph (Joost)[2]</u> (HJ), md. as single man of Livingston
Manor 12 Nov 1738 Maria de Mold, single woman of Dutchess
Co. (Fishkill Ref. Chbk.). He sp. Johannes Busch in 1745
at Fishkill Ref. Church and Henrich Busch in 1743 at Bachwaij. He first appeared on Dutchess Co. rolls in 1741/2
at Beekman (Dutchess Co. Tax Lists).

There was another Henrich Busch in Dutchess Co. at the same
time as Henrich[2], s/o Daniel[1]. He md. an Anna Maria (--) and had
ch. Elisabeth b. 1734 (Rhinebeck Luth. Chbk.), Peter b. 1737,
Henrich b. 1738, Martinus b. 1741, Jacob b. 1744, and Johannes
b. 1747 (all from N.Y. City Luth. Chbk.). He may have been the
Hendrick Boss, a blacksmith, found in the rolls beginning 1729/30,
or the Johannes Hendrick Bosse found in the Middle Ward in 1733
(Dutchess Co. Tax Lists). This other Henrich appears to have been
related somehow to Henrich[2]: 1) Henrich, s/o Daniel, sp. the
other Henrich at Niclas Emig's in 1738, and 2) Elisabet De Mott
sp. the other Henrich in 1734, and Demuths were involved with
Daniel's ch. (HJ).

JOHN JACOB CAPUTSCHER (Hunter Lists #98)

Ana Margretha Capuzgi, d/o Johann Jacob - late of Erbelheim on Rhine in the duchy of Darmstadt, md. Georg Salzmann, widower of Stollberg, Upper Laussintz, electorate of Sach, on 6 Feb 1718 (West Camp Luth. Chbk.). The actual German homes of the family were 6710 Eppstein (3 km. s. of Frankenthal; entries on the family nearby at Weisenheim am Sand - Chbks. begin 1647), 6086 Goddelau-Erfelden (9 km. e. of Oppenheim; Chbks. begin 1636), and 6501 Dienheim (2 km. s. of Oppenheim; Chbks. begin 1689/90). The earliest known ancestor of the American line was Johann Jacob Caputzki Sr. He lived at Eppstein and d. bet. 1686 and 1697. He had ch.:

> Johann Friederich, md. as single s/o Johan Jacob Cabutschke
> - inhabitant at Eppstein 14 Aug 1686 to Eva Catharina Bemm,
> d/o the late Paul Bemm - Mußquetierer at Manheim (Weisenheim
> am Sand).

+ Johann Jacob Jr.

Hans Jacob Caputzki from Epstein near Franckenthal and s/o the late Hans Jacob Caputzki and Anna Magdalena, d/o Hanß Eckelman, did penitence Dom. 8 p. Trin. (25 July): 1697 (Goddelau-Erfelden); they were not found in the marriage register there, but German and American chbks. called Anna Magdalena Eckelmann the w/o Johann Jacob Caputzki (HJ). Magdalena, d/o Hans Eckelmann, was bpt. 14 June 1668 and conf. in 1682, aged 14. Hans, s/o Philipp Eggelman, md. Elisabeth, step-d/o Niclas Horst (?) 31 Oct 1651; Johannes Eckelmann, Centschöffe, Gerichtsmann, and faithful Church-Elder, was bur. 9 Aug 1707, aged 80 yrs., 2 months, less two days (all from Goddelau-Erfelden Chbks.).

Johann Jacob Caputscher made his first appearance on the Hunter Lists 1 July 1710 with 4 pers. over 10 yrs. of age and 1 pers. under 10 yrs. Jacob Kapouche was nat. 8 and 9 Sept 1715 (Kingston Nats.). Jacob Cabbutzer with wife and ch. were at Wormsdorff ca. 1716/17 (Simmendinger Register). The wid/o Jacob Kapontsier was enrolled in the North Ward 1717/18 to 1720/21 (Dutchess Co. Tax Lists). Johann Jacob[1] and Anna Magdalena had ch.:

1) Anna Margaretha[2], conf. at Rheinbeck 14 Oct 1716, her father being Ref. (West Camp Luth. Chbk.). She md. 6 Feb 1718 Georg Salzmann (West Camp Luth. Chbk.).

2) Anna Dorothea[2], b. 30 Oct 1698 at Erfelden - sp.: Anna Dorothea - d/o Johan Wilhelm Strauss, butcher at Griesheim (Goddelau-Erfelden Chbk.). She was also conf. on 14 Oct 1716 (West Camp Luth. Chbk.) and md. Thomas Evans (HJ).

3) <u>Johann Jacob²</u>, bpt. 13 Jan 1701 - sp.: Johann Jacob Mar-
   inger (?), citizen at Erbach (Erbenheim?) in Darmstadt
   (Dienheim Chbk.). The father was noted as from Rudelsheim,
   and the mother was of the Augustiner confession.

4) <u>Johann Jacob²</u>, b. 27 June 1703 - sp.: Jacob, s/o the late
   Caspar Conradt Horst (Goddelau-Erfelden Chbk.). He was bur.
   June 1704, aged 1 yr. less 4 weeks at the same church.

5) <u>Anna Magdalena²</u> (HJ), md. Martin Diehl (HJ).

6) <u>Johann Jost²</u>, b. 20 Nov 1707 - sp.: his brother-in-law
   Joh. Jost Schütz there (Goddelau-Erfelden Chbk.).

7) <u>Conradt²</u>, bpt. 4 May 1712 - sp.: Coenraat Frederick and
   Anna Maria (Kingston Ref. Chbk.).

JOHANNES CAST (Hunter Lists #99)

Johannes Cast made his first appearance on the Hunter Lists
29 Sept 1711 with 1 pers. over 10 yrs. of age. He was a Palatine
Commissioner in charge of the supplies given the settlers on the
e. side of the Hudson River (<u>Knittle</u>, p. 163-9). Many of his
letters (written in French) survive in the Livingston Papers.
Johann Kast, Commissioner, sp. Georg Hahn at Schoharie in 1717
(West Camp Luth. Chbk.).

JOHANN CONRAD CASTNER (Hunter Lists #100)
JOHN PETER CASTNER (Hunter Lists #101)

The ancestral origins of the N.J. Castner family were at
7519 <u>Elsenz</u> (10 km. s.w. of Sinsheim; Chbks. begin 1661 with
gaps). The earliest known forefather of the emigrant brothers was
<u>Peter Kastner</u>. Johannes Kastner, s/o Peter Kastner - formerly
citizen at Nieder-Flörsheim, md. Anna, d/o the late Michel Strick-
els - formerly citizen at Elsenz, 14 Nov 1676. Michel Strickel
was an elder in the community in 1662, took communion in 1672,
and d. 2 Feb 1674, aged 50 yrs. Johannes Kastner was a police-
officer in the community at Elsenz in 1683. Anna Margareta, w/o
Johann Kastner, d. 13 Nov 1701, aged 44 yrs. less 5 weeks old (Rei-
Chbk.). Johan Kastner (no wife) and 7 ch. were in the 6th party
of Palatines in 1709 (Rotterdam Lists). Johannes¹ was a smith, and
with his wife (called Anna, unless noted otherwise) had ch.:

1) <u>Johann Peter²</u>, bpt. 1 April 1678 - sp.: Hans Martin Bochler
   - Schultheiß at Tieffenbach, and Margaretha - w/o Hans Conrad Schem, dyer at Eppingen (Elsenz Chbk.). Johann Peter
   md. Veronica Bähr 8 March 1707 (Elsenz Chbk.). Heinrich Bär of
   Rifferschweil aus dem Zürch Gebieth was bur. at Elsenz on

11 June 1682, aged 39 yrs.; he may have been the father
of Veronica Bähr (HJ). Johann Peter Castner made his
first appearance on the Hunter Lists 4 July 1710 with 2
pers. over 10 yrs. of age; the entries for 4 Aug and 4
Oct 1710 showed 1 person over 10 yrs. of age and 1 pers.
under 10 yrs. The size of the family increased to 2 pers.
over 10 yrs. of age and 3 pers. under 10 yrs. 24 June 1710.
Joan Peter Kassener, widower of Keur Pals, md. 2 April
1711 Magdalena Paan Hoof, wid/o Jacob Hoof from Wirten-
bergerlandt (N.Y. City Ref. Chbk.); his 2nd wife actually
was Maria Magdalena Nuss<u>baum</u>, wid/o Jacob Off, #562 in
Hunter (HJ). A Peter Cassell was in Col. Thomas Ffarmar's
Regt. in the 6th Co. with other N.J. 1709ers in 1715 (<u>Re-
port of the State Historian</u>, Vol. I, p. 535). Peter Kass-
ner and Magdalena with 3 ch. were auf dem Rarendantz ca.
1716/17 (Simmendinger Register). Pieter Käsner subscribed
15 sh. N.J. money in 1727 (N.Y. City Luth. Protocol, p.
89). Peter was recorded on the Bedminster Twp. Tax List
in 1756 (<u>Somerset Co. Historical Quarterly</u>, Vol. 3, p.
157). The will of Peter Cassinor Sr. of Somerset Co. was
written 14 Sept 1756 and proved 1 Dec 1756 (N.J. Wills,
Lib. F, p. 391). Peter[2] had ch. with his 1st wife:

   i) <u>Georg Peter</u>[3], b. 20 July 1707 - sp.: Hans Jacob Bentz
     and Anna Maria Oettinger (Elsenz Chbk.).

  ii) <u>Georg Peter</u>[3], bpt. 8 July 1708 - sp.: Hans Jacob
     Bentz and Anna Maria Oettinger (Elsenz Chbk.).

Peter[2] and his 2nd wife Maria Magdalena had ch.:

 iii) <u>Juliana Elisabeth</u>[3], b. 17 Dec 1711 - sp.: Andreas
     Weidknecht, Juliana Motsch, and Elisabetha Flegler
     (West Camp Luth. Chbk.).

  iv) <u>Jacob</u>[3] (Will).

2) <u>Anna Margaretha</u>[2], bpt. 12 Dec 1680 - sp.: Margaretha -
   w/o Hans Conrad Schem - dyer at Eppingen, and Johannes
   Wickenhäuser - Gerichtsmann at Elsentz (Elsenz Chbk.).

3) <u>Anna Elisabetha</u>[2], bpt. 16 Dec 1683 - sp.: Hans Conrad
   Schemm - citizen and dyer at Eppingen, and Elisabeth -
   w/o Joh. Wickenhäuser - Gerichtsman here (Elsenz Chbk.).

4) <u>Maria Margaretha</u>[2], bpt. 27 Sept 1685 - sp.: Margaretha -
   w/o Conrad Schemm, and Hans Wickenhäuser (Elsenz Chbk.).

5) <u>Johann Conrad</u>[2], bpt. 23 Nov 1687 - sp.: Conrad Schemm,
   and Elisabeth - w/o H. Georg Bentz, the Schultheiß (Elsenz
   Chbk.). There was a Koenrat Gessner in Holland in the 4th
   party of Palatines (called Conrad Gesner in London in 1709)
   but it is difficult to establish if he was Conrad[2] (HJ).

Johann Conrad Castner first appeared on the Hunter Lists
4 July 1710 with 5 pers. over 10 yrs. of age in the family. The family decreased to 4 pers. over 10 yrs. 4 Aug
and 4 Oct 1710 and then to 3 pers. over 10 yrs. of age
throughout 1711; Conrad Castner was recorded with 1 pers.
over 10 yrs. of age during 1712. Conrad, Johannes and
Georg Casser, 3 brothers, were auf dem Rarendantz ca.
1716/17 (Simmendinger Register). Conrad Kasner subscribed
15 sh. N.J. money in 1727 (N.Y. City Luth. Protocol, p.
90). Conrad Carsner was a Luth. member member of the Rareton, N.J. parish who wanted to go to the Anglican church
12 Feb 1740 (Luth. Church in N.Y. and N.J., p. 155). He
was mentioned in N.J. store accounts 1735-41 (Janeway
Account Books). Johann Conrad[2] md. Rebecca (--) and had
ch.:

    i) Barbara[3], bpt. 7 May 1721 - sp.: Miindert Lefefer
       and Katrinke Van Blerke, his wife (Freehold Ref.
       Chbk.).
   ii) Margaret[3] (Janeway Account Books).

6) Johannes[2], bpt. 21 May 1690 - sp.: Hans Bentz..., and
   Maria Barbara - d/o Rudolph Frick (Elsenz Chbk.). Johannes
   Casser, with brothers Conrad and Georg, was auf dem Rarendantz ca. 1716/17 (Simmendinger Register). He subscribed
   14 sh. N.J. money to a Luth. church building in 1727
   (N.Y. City Luth. Protocol, p. 90). Johannes Kastner (along
   with John Jr., James, widow Mary, Peter - s/o John, and
   Peter Castner) contributed to the building fund of Pluckemin Luth. Church 7 Dec 1756. Pastor Henry M. Muhlenberg
   mentioned a visit to John Gasner Sr. and John Gasner Jr.
   (the Deacon) in his Journal 24 April 1760. The will of
   Johannis Castner of Bridgewater, Somerset Co. was written
   9 Feb 1765 and probated 20 May 1765 (N.J. Wills, Lib. H,
   p.510). He md. Margaret Falckner, d/o Daniel Falckner,
   and had ch.:

     i) John[3] (Will), d. 17 Sept 1778, aged 53 yrs. and 6
        months (St. Paul's Church Cem., Pluckemin).
    ii) Daniel[3] (Will), town clerk at Tewksbury, 1766/67 (HJ).
   iii) Katharina[3] (Will).
    iv) Jacob[3] (Will). He md. Catharine Neu 27 April 1760
        at Bedminster (Pluckemin) and d. 1788 (HJ).
     v) Peter[3] (Will). He lived in Bedminster or Bridgewater
        Twp. 1767, per road petition (Somerset Co. Histori-
        cal Quarterly, Vol. 7, p. 29).
    vi) Anne[3] (Will).

vii) <u>Michael</u>[3] (Will), noted in Pluckemin (Vosseler's) store records in 1768/75, and the Sutphen Day Book, Bedminster in 1774/75 (<u>Somerset Co. Historical Quarterly</u>, Vol. 6, p. 35).

viii) <u>Conrad</u>[3] (Will).

ix) <u>Ursula</u>[3] (Will).

7) <u>Johann Michael</u>[2], bpt. 4 Oct 1693 - sp.: H. Michel Waibel, the Gerichts and citizen at Hilßbach (Elsenz Chbk.). The mother in this entry was called Anna Margaretha.

8) <u>Johann Georg</u>[2], bpt. 13 Jan 1697 - sp.: the s/o Hanß Georg Bentz - the Schultheiß, and Maria Barbara Scherer (Elsenz Chbk). Jerit Castnor aged 13, an orphan, was bound to Mich[1] Hawdon of N.Y. 23 Oct 1710 (Apprenticeship Lists). Georg Casser was listed with his brothers Conrad and Johannes auf dem Rarendantz ca. 1716/17 (Simmendinger Register). Johann Georg md. Naomi Hepburn (Will of John Hepburn Jr., her brother, dated 28 Jan 1744/45 in N.J. Wills, Lib.5,p.218). Johann Georg[2] sometimes was called Jeremias (Janeway Account Books and N.Y. City Luth. Chbk.). Issue:

    i) <u>Johannes</u>[3], b. Sept 1718 at Freehold and bpt. Raritons - sp.: Hannes Kastner and Catharina Messner (N.Y. City Luth. Chbk.).

    ii) <u>Anna</u>[3], bpt. 21 April 1733/34 aged 13 yrs. at Raretons - sp.: Michael Schurz and wife Elisabeth (N.Y. City Luth. Chbk.).

    iii) <u>Maria</u>[3], bpt. 21 April 1733/34 aged 11 yrs. at Raretons - sp.: Andreas Neu and wife Maria Elisabeth (N.Y. City Luth. Chbk.).

    iv) <u>Elisabetha</u>[3], bpt. 23 Oct 1733 aged ½ yr. old less 3 days - sp.: Jurgen Kramer and wife Lisabeth (N.Y. City Luth. Chbk.).

Other possible ch. of Johann Georg[2] may have been James Castner, d. 8 Jan 1821, aged 93-9-11 (Castner-Compton Cem. on the Pott's farm n. of Somerville), and Margaret Castner, d. 17 March 1813, md. John Teeple (HJ).

9) <u>"A Child"</u>[2], b. 10 April 1701 - sp.: Hanß Benß' widow from Elsenz. The parents were recorded as Johannes Castner, citizen at Elsenz who brought his child for baptism here where it is his religion, and his wife Anna Margaretha (Adelshofen Chbk.).

<u>Early Germans of N.J.</u>, by Theodore F. Chambers has an interesting article on the Castners which should be studied, but the information therein should be used with some degree of caution (HJ).

DANIEL CHAMPANOIS (Hunter Lists #102)

Daniel Champanois made his first appearance on the Hunter Lists 1 July 1710 with 2 pers. over 10 yrs. and 2 pers. under 10 yrs. of age in the household. Daniel Bache and Champanois were enrolled together 4 Oct 1710 with 4 pers. over 10 yrs. of age; throughout 1711 the family had 2 pers. over 10 yrs. of age and 1 pers. under 10 yrs. On 25 March 1712 Daniel was noted with 1 pers. over 10 yrs. and 2 under 10; on 24 June 1712 the household was recorded with 2 pers. over 10 yrs. and 2 pers. under 10. Daniel Champenois, a native of Niort in Poitou, was in New Rochelle in 1723 with his wife Marguerite (Biographical Sketches and Index of the Huguenot Settlers of New Rochelle 1687-1776, by Morgan H. Seacord). He was noted as registering his earmark for his domestic animals in 1724 (New Rochelle Town Records, p. 148). By his 1st wife Johanna he had issue:

1) Paul[2], b. 12 Nov 1711 - sp.: Paul Burnet and Martha Bertram (West Camp Luth. Chbk.).

By his 2nd wife Marguerite he had issue:

2) Thomas[2] (HJ), md. as single man b. Nieuw Rosel 11 April 1747 Eliesabet Jurckse, single woman b. Philipsburgh (Tarrytown Ref. Chbk.). They had ch.:

    i) Maria[3], bpt. 1 May 1748 - sp.: Harmen Jurckse and his wife (Tarrytown Ref. Chbk.).

    ii) Maragriet[3], bpt. 17 April 1750 - sp.: Willum Jurckse and Marytye Jurckse (Tarrytown Ref. Chbk.).

    iii) Daniel[3], bpt. 20 June 1752 - sp.: John Sclat and Maria Sclat (Tarrytown Ref. Chbk.).

HANNS CHRISTMANN (Hunter Lists #103)

A Hans Peter Christmann and wife Anna Gertraud were found at 6521 Dalsheim (12 km. w. of Worms; Chbks. begin 1690); they had a son Johann Jacob bpt. 12 Sept 1706 which, at first glance, would appear to be a good match with known U.S. data. However, Hans Peter of Dalsheim had a son Conrad bpt. 7 July 1709 which would conflict with the emigrant Christmann being at Rotterdam in June (HJ). Hans Krisman, his wife, and 4 ch. were on Capt. John Howlentzen's ship in Holland 10 June 1709 (Rotterdam Lists). John Christman aged 41, his wife, sons aged 7 and 5, daughters aged 9 and 2, husbandman and vinedresser, Mennonite were in England in 1709 (London Lists).

Johannes Christmuller (sic) made his first appearance on the Hunter Lists 1 July 1710 with 3 pers. over 10 yrs. of age and 3 pers. under 10 yrs.; the 4 Aug 1710 entry read Johannes Christmann. On 25 March 1711 the family increased to 6 pers. over 10 yrs. of

age and 3 pers. under 10 yrs. The size of the family was 5 pers.
over 10 yrs. and 3 under 10 yrs. from 24 Dec 1711 through the
end of 1712. Johans Christman was nat. 17 Jan 1715/16 (Albany
Nats.). Hanß Christmann and Anna Gertraud with 6 ch. were at
Neu-Ans-berg ca. 1716/17 (Simmendinger Register). Johannis
Christman of the city of Albany petitioned for a license to purchase 300 acres of vacant land above Burnetsfield in the Co. of
Albany adjoining a creek 7 Nov 1728 (N.Y. Land Papers, Vol. X,
p. 73). A child of Johannes[1] was:

1) Jacob[2] (HJ), d. 29 April 1790, aged 84 yrs. and 6 months
   (Stone Arabia Ref. Chbk.); the date of death is given as
   29 April 1789 in History of Montgomery and Fulton Counties, p. 153. He md. Catharina (--) (Schoharie Luth.
   Chbk.); his obituary recorded the date of his marriage
   as 1738 (Stone Arabia Ref. Chbk.). Jacob Christman was
   enrolled in Capt. Soffrines Deychert's Co. 20 March 1757
   and in Capt. Marx Petry's Co. at Bornets Field 9 May
   1767 (Report of the State Historian, Vol. II, p. 783 &
   854). Jacob Christman was a freeholder of Canajoharrie
   in 1763 (Albany Co. Freeholders). Issue:

   i) John[3] (HJ), d. 1827, aged 93 yrs. (Albany Gazette,
      7 Dec 1827). The age at death may be in error or
      may indicate an earlier marriage for Jacob[2] (HJ).

   ii) Johann Jacob[3], bpt. 13 Aug 1744 at Cani-Scohare -
       sp.: Johan Jacob Fehling and Magdalena (--) (Scho-
       harie Luth. Chbk.). Mr. Jacob Christman d. 23 Feb
       1826, aged 85 (Utica Oneida Observer); his obituary
       noted he was a native of Herkimer and a soldier in
       the revolution; he was a brother-in-law of the late
       John Bellinger and was the first settler of what is
       now called Utica.

There are several unplaced Christmanns, including the Johannes Christmann who was a freeholder at The Falls in 1763 (Albany Co. Freeholders), and Nicholas Christman (Chrissman) who
was a soldier in Lt. Goshin Van Alstein's Co. in 1763 and in
Capt. Conrad Frank's Co. in 1767 (Report of the State Historian,
Vol. II, p. 798 & 851).

ELIZABETH CHRISTMÄNNIN (Hunter Lists #104)

Elisabeth Christmänin made her first appearance on the Hunter Lists 30 June 1710 with 1 pers. over 10 yrs. of age and 2
pers. under 10; the ages changed to 2 pers. over 10 yrs. and 1
under 10 yrs. 4 Oct 1710. The 24 June 1711 entry read 3 pers.

over 10 yrs. of age. Johann Peter Heuser and Eliz. Christmann
were listed together 24 June 1711, indicating their marriage in
that year (HJ). Elisabetha Christmann's child from her 1st marriage:

1) Anna Margaretha[2] (HJ), md. Michael Schmidt by 1733 and
noted on various chbk. entries as both Anna Margaretha
Christmann and Anna Margaretha Heuser (HJ).

BERNHARD CLEVENIUS (Hunter Lists #105)

Bernhard Clevenius made his first appearance on the Hunter
Lists 1 July 1710 with 2 pers. over 10 yrs. of age and 3 pers.
under 10 yrs. of age; the last entry 13 Sept 1712 showed 4 pers.
over 10 yrs. of age. Anna Maria, wid/o Bernhard Lifenius, md.
**Johann Adam, s/o Joh. Niclaus Starring of Wonsheim in the com-
mune of Altzey, Pfaltz,** 2 Dec 1712 (West Camp Luth. Chbk.). Bernhard[1] and Anna Maria had ch.:

1) Anna Barbara[2] (HJ), conf. as Anna Barbara Listenus at
Newtown on Easter, 1713 (West Camp Luth. Chbk.).
2) Elisabetha[2] (HJ), called Elsje Listinius, md. Georg
Gerlach (HJ).
3) Christianus[2], b. 20 Aug 1711 - sp.: Christian Aigler
(West Camp Luth. Chbk.).

HENRICH CONRAD (Hunter Lists #106)

The first entry for Henrich Conrad on the Hunter Lists was
dated 30 June 1710 with 2 pers. over 10 yrs. of age; he was called
Johann Henrich Conrad 4 Oct 1710. The family increased to 2 pers.
over 10 yrs and 1 under 10 31 Dec 1710, dwindled down to 2 pers.
over 10 25 March 1711, and then returned to 2 pers. over 10 yrs.
and 1 pers. under 10 24 Dec 1711. A Johann Connrath, Episcopal,
joined the church at N.Y. 19 July 1710 (West Camp Luth. Chbk.).
Jno. Hen. Conradt of Annsberg was a soldier in 1711 (Palatine
Volunteers To Canada). Hendrick Coenraet was nat. 17 Jan 1715/16
(Albany Nats), and Johann Heinrich Conrad and Gertraud with 2 ch.
were at Wormsdorff ca. 1716/17 (Simmendinger Register). Hans
Hend: Coenradt was a Palatine Debtor in 1718, 1719 (at Annsberry),
1721 and 1726 (Livingston Debt Lists). Johannes Henrig Conrad
was a Palatine willing to remain at Livingston Manor 26 Aug 1724
(Documentary History of N.Y., Vol. III, p. 724). Henry Conrad
had lot #197 at Germantown in 1741 (Settlers & Residents, Vol. I,
p. 32d). Hans H: Coenrat was a freeholder at East Camp in 1763
(Albany Co. Freeholders). Johann Henrich[1] md. several times:
1) in Germany; 2) as a widower of Anshausen in the duchy of

Nassau-Sieg, to Anna Gertraud Seegendorst (Segendorf - HJ), d/o
Adam of Hermandorst in the commune of Neuwied, 31 Aug 1716 (West
Camp Luth. Chbk.); 3) on 25 April 1726 Maria Barbara Hommels,
d/o the late Hans Jurge Hommels of Mussbach in the Palatinate
(N.Y. City Luth. Chbk.); and 4) Maria Margaretha (--), called
his wife in 1752 (Germantown Ref. Chbk.). From his 1st or 2nd
marriage, Johann Henrich[1] Conrad had a son:

1) Johann Philip[2] (HJ), md. Anna Margaretha Klumm. Philip
   Coenrat was in Capt. Abraham Van Aernam's Co. above Poesten Kill in 1767 (Report of the State Historian, Vol. II,
   p. 814). He was an early settler in the area near Centre
   Brunswick, Rensselaer Co. and had ch.:

   i) Johann Henrich[3], bpt. 24 May 1737 - sp.: Henrich
      Conradt and Maria Margaretha (Germantown Ref. Chbk.).

   ii) Johann Philip[3], b. 17 Sept 1739 and bpt. Teerbosch
       - sp.: Joh. Philip Glum and wife Anna Maria Veronica
       (Loonenburg Luth. Chbk.). He md. Veronica (Frony)
       Klumm and had ch. bpt. at Centre Brunswick Luth.,
       Albany Ref., and Schoharie Luth. Churches (HJ).
       The will of a Philip Conradt, late of Brunswick,
       was written 10 July 1815 and recorded 14 Sept 1815
       (Rensselaer Co. Will Bk. 5).

   iii) Catharina[3], bpt. 8 Dec 1741 - sp.: Henrich Klom and
        Catharine Schneider (Germantown Ref. Chbk.).

   iv) Adam[3], bpt. 11 Oct 1743 - sp.: Adam Klom and Elisa-
       beth Ben... (Germantown Ref. Chbk.). He md. an
       Elisabetha (--), and his will was written 22 Nov
       1815 and recorded 20 March 1816 (Rensselaer Co. Will
       Bk. 5).

   v) Engel[3], md. as d/o Philip 16 Feb 1766 Johannes
      (Georg) Klockner (Germantown Ref. Chbk.).

   vi) Margaretha[3], bpt. as Creta 8 Jan 1749 - sp.: Philipp
       Klumm and Veronica Klumm (Gallatin Ref. Chbk.).

   vii) Veronica[3], bpt. 5 Aug 1750 - sp.: Philipp Klumm and
        Veronica Klumm (Gallatin Ref. Chbk.).

   viii) Henrich[3], bpt. 18 June 1752 - sp.: Henrich Conrad
         and wife Maria Margretha (Germantown Ref. Chbk.).
         He md. Lea Bautzer and had ch. at Red Hook Luth.
         and Centre Brunswick Luth. Churches.

   ix) Johannes[3], bpt. 27 Oct 1754 - sp.: Johannes Klom
       and Veronica Lescher (Germantown Ref. Chbk.).

   x) Wilhelmus[3], bpt. 16 Dec 1756 - sp.: Wilhelm Kilmer
      and Eva Kohler (Gallatin Ref. Chbk.). He md. Chris-
      tina Brust and d. 13 Feb 1832, aged 75 yrs., and

4 months (Gilead Luth. Cem., Centre Brunswick).

    xi) <u>Eva</u>[3], bpt. 17 April 1759 - sp.: Adam Klumm and Eva
        Klumm (Gallatin Ref. Chbk.).

    xii) <u>Elisabetha</u>[3], b. 23 Feb 1761 - sp.: Adam Loescher and
         Elisab: (Germantown Luth. Chbk.).

From his 2nd marriage Johann Henrich[1] Conrad and Anna Gertraud
Segendorff had ch.:

  2) <u>Johannes</u>[2] (HJ), as Johannes Cunrath a soldier in the East
     Camp Co. 12 May 1767 (<u>Settlers & Residents</u>, Vol. I, p. 35).
     He md. 1st Catharina Ham and had issue:

     i) <u>Anna Catharina</u>[3], bpt. 28 May 1740 - sp.: Henrich
       Conrad and Catharina Ham (Germantown Ref. Chbk.).

     Johannes[2] md. 2nd Eva Hener and had issue:

     ii) <u>Johannes</u>[3], bpt. 7 Jan 1742 - sp.: Johannes Lesscher
       and Anna Maria Klom (Germantown Ref. Chbk.). He may
       have been the Johannes Conradt who md. Rachel Kohl
       and had ch. bpt. at Germantown Ref. Church (HJ).

  3) <u>Jost Henrich</u>[2], b. Sept 1720 at Annsberry and bpt. at Camp
     - sp.: Jost Henrich Toonsbach, Joh: Henrich Schaffer, and
     Maria Cath. Sagendorff (N.Y. City Luth. Chbk.).

  4) <u>Margaretha</u>[2] (HJ), a member at Germantown Ref. Church 1742.
     Margaret Conrad d. 2 June 1747, aged 22 yrs. (Germantown
     Ref. Chbk.).

From his 3rd marriage to Maria Barbara Hommel he had ch.:

  5) <u>Anna Eva</u>[2], b. 30 April 1729 and bpt. Kamp - sp.: Willem
     Lemek and wife Eva (N.Y. City Luth. Chbk.). She md. 27
     Jan 1756 Joseph Nier, widower of Rhinebeck (Germantown
     Ref. Chbk.).

  6) <u>Elisabetha</u>[2] (HJ), joined the Germantown Ref. Church 11 May
     1743. She md. Johannes Mohr (HJ).

<u>ANNA CONRADIN</u> (Hunter Lists #107)

The ancestral German home of the Schoharie Conrad family was
6475 <u>Stockheim</u> (7 km. n.w. of Büdingen), records for the village
entered in the registers of 6470 <u>Düdelsheim</u> (5 km. w. of Büdingen;
Chbks. begin 1660) and 6470 <u>Rohrbach</u> (2 km. s. of Stockheim; Chbks.
begin 1699). The earliest known ancestor of the American family
was the teacher <u>Johannes Conradt</u>. Johann Henrich Conradt, s/o the
teacher Johannes Conradt, md. 23 Nov 1689 Anna Deckmann, d/o Conrad Deckmann of Stockheim (Düdelsheim). Anna, d/o Conradt Deckmann
and his 1st wife Gela, was bpt. Dom. Oculi: 1671 (Düdelsheim).
Conrad Deckmann, s/o Peter Deckmann, md. Juliana, d/o Georg Stroh
of Stockheim, 23 Oct 1662 (Bleichenbach Chbk.). In the Fürstlich
Ysenburg und Büdingische Rentkammer Archive is a document dated

1709 which deals with the emigration of Johann Henrich Conradt
and other residents of Stockheim to the new world:

> Highly esteemed Graf, most gracious Graf and Lord:
>   Your Grace: May we subjects and obedient servants,
> named below, indicate and not avoid setting forth how
> large we measure our debts and the extreme poverty to
> which we are reduced, so that because of the (lack of)
> food we can no longer remain at Stockheim with wife
> and children.
>   Because now the Lord God has revealed a land
> where, in the same island and country, the poor people
> and the needy could cultivate their nourishment and
> could enjoy it till the end of their days, when there-
> fore our humble request and petition reaches you to be
> charitable in consideration of our debts and on account
> of our extreme poverty to permit us the favor to go to
> the Island and aforementioned land with wife and child-
> ren and on account of our conduct to permit it with an
> honest farewell (discharge).
>   As we then hope most confidently for your most gra-
> cious compliance and meanwhile remain in all respect-
> ful (?)...

Your Grace's subjects and
Obedient Servants

>   Johann Henrich Conradt
>   Peter Lambmann
>   Hardtman Windecker
>   Justus Deppich
>   Conrad Depie's widow with her daughter
>   Johann Conradt Deckmann's two sons
>   Johann Henrich and Johannes Deckmann
>   Johan Conradt Windecker
>   ----------------

>   Just as your exalted Countly (Graf-ly) Grace, our
> merciful Graf and Lord, does not wish to hinder his
> petitioners in their probable good fortune, therefore
> they are permitted to go to Carolina with wife and
> children; also the exemption certificate should be
> delivered to each, as follows:

To Johann Henrich Conradi with his wife and 4 ch.	f 15
To Peter Lampmann with his wife and 4 ch.	f 7½
To Hartman Windecker with his wife and ch.	f 8
To Justus Dewig with his wife and ch.	f 7½
To Christian Dewig's widow with her daughter	f --
To Johann Henrich Deckmann	f 5
To Johannes Deckmann	f 5
To Johan Conrad Windecker with his wife	f 7½

Documented and sealed at Marienburg, 31 Aug 1709

Carl A., G(ra)f Ysenburg

Subjects and Obedient Servant's
Request
Memorial
Several Subjects from the
Stockheim Court

      Anna Conradin made her first appearance on the Hunter Sub-
sistence Lists 30 June 1710 with 2 pers. over 10 yrs. of age and
1 pers. under 10 yrs. in the family; on that same page in the
Journal were Peter Lampman and Harttman Windecker. Her last entry

was 4 Aug 1710 with 2 pers. over 10 yrs. of age and 1 under 10.
Tradition says that Anna md. 2nd Marcus Bellinger (Hunter #38)
which may have been true, as his subsistence begins 4 Oct 1710
with 4 pers. over 10 yrs. of age in the family (HJ). The ch. of
Johann Henrich and Anna[1] Conrad were:

1) <u>Henrich</u>[2] (HJ), a freeholder at Schoharrie in 1763 (Albany
   Co. Freeholders). He md. Anna (Maria) Margaretha Staring
   (HJ) and had issue:
   i) <u>Elisabetha</u>[3] (HJ), md. Jurgen Michel Happolt 22 Jan
      1754 (Schoharie Luth. Chbk.).
   ii) <u>Anna Margaretha</u>[3], md. as d/o Henrich 10 Nov 1754
       Lambert Eeker (Schoharie Ref. Chbk.).
   iii) <u>Henrich</u>[3], bpt. 8 Aug 1735 - sp.: Henrich Bottger
        (Bellinger - HJ) and wife Anna Maria (Schoharie Ref.
        Chbk.). He md. 6 Dec 1757 Eva Richtmeyer (Schoharie
        Ref. Chbk.).
   iv) <u>Gertraud</u>[3], b. 17 March 1737 and bpt. at Schohari -
       sp.: Hannes Scheffer, Jr. and Gertrud Haring (Loon-
       enburg Luth. Chbk.). She md. Johannes Regtmeyer 13
       Jan 1757 (Schoharie Luth. Chbk.).
   v) <u>Johannes</u>[3], bpt. 8 Dec 1738 - sp.: Johannes Scheefer
      and wife Anna Maria Zoeller (Schoharie Ref. Chbk.).
   vi) <u>Anna Maria</u>[3], bpt. 14 Aug 1740 - sp.: Jacob Frederick
       Lawyer and Anna Maria Schever (Schoharie Ref. Chbk.)
   vii) <u>Anna</u>[3], bpt. 22 Dec 1743 - sp.: Johannes Schuyler and
        wife Annatie (Schoharie Ref. Chbk.).
   viii) <u>Nicolaus</u>[3], bpt. 19 July 1745 - sp.: Niclaas Staarn-
         berger and Anna Rickkert (Schoharie Ref. Chbk.).
   ix) <u>Eva</u>[3], bpt. 1 Feb 1746/47 - sp.: Coenraad Rickkert
       Jr. and Anna Eva Staringh (Schoharie Ref. Chbk.).
   x) <u>Markus</u>[3], bpt. 3 Nov 1748 - sp.: Markus Rickkert and
      Anna Scheffer (Schoharie Ref. Chbk.).
   xi) <u>Johann Philip</u>[3], bpt. as John Lips 23 Feb 1749/50 -
       sp.: John: Lips Bergh and wife Christina (Schoharie
       Ref. Chbk.).
   Henrich Conrad, widower b. Germany, md. 1 July 1755 Catharina (Böning), wid/o Stoffel Trommer (Schoharie Ref.
   Chbk.) and had issue:
   xii) <u>Georg</u>[3], b. 4 Aug 1756 - sp.: Jürgen Rickert and his
        wife (Schoharie Luth. Chbk.).
   xiii) <u>Friederich</u>[3], b. 23 Aug 1757 - sp.: Friederich Mat-
         thes and Catharina Ingold (Schoharie Luth. Chbk.).
   xiv) <u>Margaretha</u>[3], b. 3 Feb 1760 - sp.: Antony Widmer and
        Margreth Widmer (Schoharie Ref. Chbk.).

2) <u>Anna Catharina²</u>, b. 6 Oct 1700 - sp.: Anna Catharina, d/o Hen· Wendel (Rohrbach Chbk.). She md. Ludwig Rickert (HJ).

3) <u>"A Child"²</u>, d. 1 July 1704, "den 8 worden" (Rohrbach Chbk.).

4) <u>Johann Georg²</u>, b. 21 Oct 1705 at Stockheim - sp.: Johann Georg - s/o Conradt Deckmann (Rohrbach "little book of the Pastor"). He d. 20 Jan 1707 (Rohrbach Chbk.).

5) <u>Caspar²</u>, b. 4 Oct 1708 and bpt. Stockheim - sp.: Caspar Stroh at Glauberg (Rohrbach Chbk.).

<u>LUDOLFF CORING</u> (Hunter Lists #108)

Anna Catharina Curring, d/o Ludolst Curring of Hellstein in the earldom of Isenburg, md. 29 Aug 1711 Johannes Hess, a black-smith of Bleichenbach in the earldom of Hanau (West Camp Luth. Chbk.). The village of origin for the Kording family was 6486 <u>Hellstein</u> (14 km. e. of Büdingen; Chbks. begin 1689); records of the family were found also at 6486 <u>Spielberg</u> (4 km. farther w.; Chbks. begin 1653). The earliest known ancestor of the Mohawk Valley family was <u>Anthon Kording</u> of Erlingshausen/Lippe. Anthon Kording, "bürdig aus Westphalen", d. 30 Aug 1703 at Schächtelburg (Hellstein). Johann Ludtolff Cording, s/o Antoni Cording of Erlingshausen in the Graffschaft Lippe, md. 21 Oct 1685 Ottilia, d/o the late Johann Fründt of Helstein (Spielberg). Ottilia, d/o Johan Freundt from Helstein and wife Anne Appels, was b. at Hellstein and bpt. Spielberg 11 March 1666 - sp.: Ottilia, w/o Weygandt Velten of Hanau. Johann Freundt, s/o Velten Freundt from Helstein, md. An Appell, d/o Johann Gedern from Udenhain 20 April 1665. Johann Freundt from Helstein was bur. 27 July 1682. Velten Freundt from Helstein was bur. 7 Feb 1675, and Margaretha, w/o Velten Freundt from Helstein, was bur. 25 April 1665 (all Freundt entries from Spielberg Chbk.).

Ludolph Coring made his first appearance on the Hunter Lists 1 July 1710 with 6 pers. over 10 yrs. of age and 1 pers. under 10 yrs; the household gradually decreased in size until 24 Dec 1711 when the entry read 3 pers. over 10 yrs. of age and 1 pers. under 10. Ludolf Korning aged 50, Otillia aged 50, Catharina aged 16, Anna Dorothea aged 15, Conrad aged 7, and Johanna Eliz: Fucks frau aged 22, were in N.Y. City in 1710/11 (Palatines In N.Y. City). Johan Ludolph Corning was nat. 31 Jan 1715/16 (Albany Nats.). Johann Rudolph Hornig and his wife were at Neu-Heessberg ca. 1716/17 (Simmendinger Register). Ludolph Korsing and Odelia Koring, his wife, were each patentees on the s. side of the Mohawk in the Burnetsfield Patent 30 April 1725. Rodolf Caring was one of the twelve original trustees of the Fort Herkimer Church in 1730;

Berkenmeyer visited him in 1734, noting "It was fortunate that (we stayed), for shortly afterward, while we were at the home of old Lulof, who had been md. 50 yrs., a hurricane came up suddenly, which hurled more than twenty trees in our path" (Albany Protocol, p. 94). The ch. of Ludolff[1] Coring and Ottilia were:

1) Anna Apollonia[2], bpt. 5 June 1687 - sp.: Anna Apolonia, wid/o the late Johann Freundt from Helstein (Spielberg). She d. 27 May 1688, aged 1 yr. (Spielberg Chbk.).

2) Johanna Elisabetha[2], bpt. 3 March 1689 - sp.: Johann Henrich Krigk - servant at Hellstein, and his sister-in-law Anna Elisabetha Freundt (Spielberg Chbk.). She md. Christoph Fuchs (HJ).

3) Johannes[2], bpt. 27 Nov 1692 - sp.: Johannes - s/o Hans Kaufman of Schlierbach (Hellstein). He was bur. 27 June 1693 (Hellstein Chbk.).

4) Anna Catharina[2], bpt. 10 June 1694 - sp.: Cathrin Jungert - step-daughter/o J. Georg Seitz from Leisenwald (Hellstein). Maria Catharina Corhof was conf. 19 July 1710 at N.Y. (West Camp Luth. Chbk.). She md. Johannes Hess.

5) Anna Dorothea[2], bpt. 22 Dec 1695 - sp.: Anna Dorothea - w/o Johann Freundt of Gelnhausen (Hellstein). Sp. and circumstantial evidence strongly suggest she md. Thomas Schumacher (HJ).

6) Elisabetha Christina[2], bpt. 4 Dec 1698 - sp.: Elisabeth Wick (?) (Hellstein). She was bur. 11 Dec 1698 (Hellstein).

7) Johann Georg[2], bpt. 22 Aug 1700 - sp.: Johannes Schmedes ...(Hellstein Chbk.).

8) Johannes[2], bpt. 20 April 1702 - sp.: Johannes - s/o Johann Jacob Schäfer (Hellstein Chbk.).

9) Anna Margaretha[2], bpt. 23 Nov 1704 - sp.: Anna Margarethe - w/o Johann Goerge Giesen (Hellstein). An Anna Margaretha Koning md. Conrad Kuhn by 1731 in the Mohawk/Schoharie region and may have been this woman (HJ).

10) Johann Conrad[2], bpt. 9 Nov 1706 - sp.: Johann Conrad - s/o Johann Jacob Christen (Hellstein Chbk.).

11) Johann Wilhelm[2], bpt. 14 Oct 1707 - sp.: Wilhelm - s/o Johann Schäfer (Hellstein Chbk.).

The family surname was spelled Kording, Köring and Cording at Spielberg and Hellstein.

GEORG DACHSTÄTTER (Hunter Lists #109)

After studying the juxtaposition of emigrants' names in the 4th group of Palatines on the Rotterdam and London Lists, I

believe the emigrant Georg[1] Dachstätter was on Capt. John Howlentzen's ship 10 June 1709 in Holland and recorded as Hans Jeörg, his
wife, and 1 child (Rotterdam Lists). Georg Tachstetter aged 30,
his wife, and a son aged 1/3 yr., Luth., husbandman and vinedresser, were in the 4th arrivals in England (London Lists).

Georg Dachstätter made his first appearance on the Hunter
Lists 4 July 1710 with 2 pers. over 10 yrs. and 1 pers. under 10;
the family increased to 2 pers. over 10 and 2 under 10 yrs. 24
June 1711. George Dachstader of Queensbury was a soldier in 1711
(Palatine Volunteers To Canada). Jury Taxstieder was na† 3 Jan
1715/16 (Albany Nats.). George Dachstatter, his wife Anna Elisabetha, and 4 ch. were at Neu-Quunsberg ca. 1716/17 (Simmendinger
R gister). Jurgh Dacksteder and his wife Anna were each patentees
3 April 1725; he on the n. side of the Mohawk, and she on the s.
side (Burnetsfield Patent). Pastor Berkenmeyer mentioned a visit
to Dachsteder 13 Aug 1734 (Albany Protocol, p. 91), and Pastor
Sommer noted Jürgen Dachstätter at the Fall in 1744 (Schoharie
Luth. Chbk.). Jury Docksteder was a freeholder at the Falls in
1763 (Albany Co. Freeholders). The ch. of Georg[1] Dachstätter were:

1) Georg Adam[2] (HJ), probably the Adam Docksteder at Mohack
   in 1763 (Albany Co. Freeholders). He md. Anna Catharina
   Stahring (HJ).
2?) Cornelius[2] (per Doris Dockstader Rooney).
3) Henrich[2] (HJ), md. Anna Catharina Van Antwerp (per Doris
   Dockstader Rooney).
4) Johann Friederich[2], b. 14 May 1717 and bpt. at Schoharie -
   sp.: Fridrich Schaester and wife (West Camp Luth. Chbk.).
   He md. Anna Elisabetha Stahring (HJ).
5) Georg[2] (HJ).
6) Johann Leonhardt[2], noted with Georg[1] at the Fall in 1744
   (Schoharie Luth. Chbk.).
7) Christian[2] (HJ), a freeholder of Stonrabie in 1763 (Albany Co. Freeholders). He md. Catharina Nellis (HJ).
8) Barbara Elisabetha[2] (HJ), md. Johann Peter Wagener
   (Stone Arabia Luth. Chbk.).

Crucial chbks. for the Mohawk Valley are missing for the
period 1723 through 1738, making firm connectives between 1st,
2nd, and 3rd generation Dachstätters difficult. Doris Dockstader
Rooney of Dodge City, Kansas - a long-time student of the family -
has written one of the finest of all Palatine genealogies on this
extremely difficult family; I recommend her multi-volume "The
Dockstader Family" wholeheartedly as a model of careful research,
good documentation, and beautiful presentation (HJ).

JOHANN WILHELM DAHLES (Hunter Lists #110)

The ancestral home of the N.J. Dawlis family was 5450 Heddesdorf/Neuwied (10 km. n. of Koblenz; Chbks. begin 1674). A possible ancestor of the emigrant was Walther Dales, d. by 1706 (HJ). The 1st wife of Johann Wilhelm[1] Dales was Maria Catharina (--), d. 20 July 1705. Johann Willem Dales, widower and shepherd here, md. 14 Oct 1705 Johanna Margaretha, d/o the late Hermann Schmidt. Johanna Margretha, d/o Hermann Schmid, was bpt. 25 July 1675 - sp.: Johanna Margr. - w/o Tönges Hoff, Maria Gerdraut von Werth, and Philipp Melsbach. Hermann Schmid d. 6 Feb 1700. Johan Willem halles, his wife and 4 ch. were on Capt. Robbert Lourens's ship in Holland 5 June 1709 (Rotterdam Lists). William Dales aged 36, with his wife, sons aged 4 and 1, a daughter aged 6, Ref., husbandman and vinedresser, were in the 3rd arrivals in England in 1709 (London Lists).

Johann Wilhelm Dahles made his first appearance on the Hunter Lists 4 July 1710 with 2 pers. over 10 yrs. of age; the family size increased 24 Dec 1711 to 2 pers. over 10 yrs. of age and 1 pers. under 10 yrs. John Wm. Dales of Haysbury was a soldier in 1711 (Palatine Volunteers To Canada). Johan Willem Dalis was nat. 17 Jan 1715/16 (Albany Nats.) and on the roll of the independent company of the Manor of Livingston 30 Nov 1715 (Report of the State Historian, Vol. I, p. 523). Willem Dalles, his wife and ch. were at Heessberg ca. 1716/17 (Simmendinger Register). He was a Palatine Debtor in 1718, 1719 (on our land), 1721 and 1722 (Livingston Debt Lists). He came to the Amwell Valley in N.J. in 1727 and purchased 265 acres of the Benjamin Field tract from Nathan Allen; he owned a grist mill a short distance s. of Ringoes (A History of East Amwell, p. 67). William Dawlis was a freeholder of Amwell in 1741 (Hunterdon Co. Freeholders). His will was dated 2 Jan 1740 and proved 15 June 1741 (N.J. Wills: Lib. 4, p. 308). He had one child by his 1st wife Maria Catharina:

1) Elisabetha Maria[2], bpt. 11 June 1703 - sp.: Elisab. Veronica - d/o Mattheis Köcher, and Maria Magdalena - sister of the mother (Rengsdorf Chbk.).

By his 2nd wife Johanna Margaretha he had issue:

2) Johannes[2], b. 8 July 1706 - sp.: Herr Johannes Fimmel - the Schultheiss here, Johannes Söhn, and Anna Elisabetha - w/o Conrad Löwenberger (Heddesdorf Chbk.).

3) Wilhelm Antonius[2], bpt. 2 Dec 1708 - sp.: Johan Antonius Schmitt, Hans Wilhelm Müller, and Anna Elisabeth - surviving d/o Wilhelm Seuser (Heddesdorf Chbk.).

4) Hermann[2] (Will). The will of Herman Dahles of Hunterdon

Co. was written 10 Feb 1747/48 and proved 23 March 1747/
48 (N.J. Wills: Lib. 5, p. 470). His wife Catharine md.
2nd (--) Lott (A History of East Amwell, p. 91). Issue:
  i) William[3] (Will).
  ii) Margaret[3] (Will).
5) Johann Wilhelm[2], b. 18 Oct 1714 - sp.: Johann Niclaus Haas,
  Johann Wilhelm Hambuck, and Maria Catharina Segendorst
  (West Camp Luth. Chbk.). He received the new mill in his
  father's will and resided in New England Twp., Salem Co.,
  East Jersey in 1743 (A History of East Amwell, p. 102).
6) Susanna[2] (Will), md. Honust Yauger (Will).

A Catharine Dales aged 25, Ref. was listed in the 3rd arrivals in England in 1709 (London Lists). Johanna Margaretha, w/o
Johann Wilhelm[1] Dales, sp. a child of Anna Catharina Dales, d/o
the late Walther Dales in 1706 (Heddesdorf Chbk.).

ULRICH DANLER (Hunter Lists #111)

Ulrich Danler made his first appearance on the Hunter Lists
1 July 1710 with 1 pers. over 10 yrs. of age. His entry 4 Oct
1710 read 2 pers. over 10 yrs. of age and 1 under 10. Uldrich
Dandler was nat. 31 Jan 1715/16 (Albany Nats.). Ulrich Dantler
and Maria Margretha with 1 child were at Neu-Ansberg ca. 1716/17
(Simmendinger Register). Issue:
1) Anna Eva[2] (HJ). Anna Eva Tantelaar was the w/o Matth:
  Hilts in 1731 (Schoharie Ref. Chbk.); as Mattheus Hilts appeared only in this one entry, and as an Anna Eva Merckle was w/o Theobald Hilts in other Schoharie bpts., perhaps Ulrich[1] Danler md. a member of the Merckle family
  in 1710, as he was noted living next to Johannes Merckle's
  widow on Simmendinger's Register in 1716/17 (HJ).

CHRISTOPH DANNEMARCKER (Hunter Lists #112)

Kristoffel Denemarker, his wife and 3 ch. were enrolled on
Capt. William Koby's ship in Holland 6 July 1709 in the 5th party
of Palatines (Rotterdam Lists); he was listed near other N.Y.
1709ers who originated in the Nassau region (Joost Brandeurf,
Kristiaan Street, and Johann Krist Moor). Dennenmärckers were documented near Nassau at Dausenau and Bad Ems, but the emigrant
Christoph[1] has not been found yet.

Christoph Dannemarker made his first appearance on the Hunter
Lists 1 July 1710 with 3 pers. over 10 yrs. of age and 1 pers. under 10 yrs. in the household; the entry changed to 4 pers. over
10 yrs. of age 24 June 1711. Christopher Daunermarker aged 28,

Christina Daunermarker aged 28, Cath. Eliz. Daunermarker aged 8, and Anna Hargt. Danemark, wid., aged 58 were in N.Y. City in 1710/11 (Palatines In N.Y. City). Christoffel Denmarken was taxed £5 in 1718/19 and £8 in 1720/21 at Hurley (Ulster Co. Tax Lists). He and his wife Christina Elisabetha Bernhardt sp. at Deerpark **Ref., Walpeck Ref., and Red Hook Luth. Churches.** Issue:

1) Catharina Elisabetha[2] (Palatines In N.Y. City) md. 1st 9 Oct 1724 Henrich Kittel (Kingston Ref. Chbk.) and 2nd 9 July 1731 Johannes Weaver (Kingston Ref. Chbk.).
2) Anna Margaretha[2], bpt. 11 May 1712 (Kingston Ref. Chbk.). She md. Johannes Kortregt (HJ).
3) Anna Dorothea[2], b. 17 Feb 1714 at Roosendal in Sopos - sp.: Johan Wilhelm Schmidt and Anna Dorothea Bohm (N.Y. City Luth. Chbk.). She was a sp. at Walpeck in 1747.
4) Anna Magdalena[2], bpt. 12 Feb 1716 - sp.: Jacob Bushoorn and Madelina Wenderig (Kingston Ref. Chbk.). She md. Georg Trombauer 24 Oct 1733 (Kingston Ref. Chbk.) and joined the Rhinebeck Flats Ref. Church 28 June 1745.
5) Johann Christophel[2], bpt. 9 June 1717 - sp.: Juriaan Beem, Willem Douty, and Zofiya Spykerman (Kingston Ref. Chbk.); the surname of the parents was not mentioned in the bpt. entry. Christophel Dennemark, single man b. at Rosendal, md. Lea Swartwood, single girl b. at Pipeck, 26 July 1741; both lived at Smithfield (Walpeck Ref. Chbk.). They had ch.:
   i) Anna[3], bpt. 19 Oct 1743 - sp.: Bernardus Swartwood and wife Grietje Decker (Walpeck Ref. Chbk.).
   ii) Claudina Sophia[3], bpt. 13 Jan 1745 - sp.: Joh: Christoffel Denemerken and wife Christina Elisabetha Bernhard (Walpeck Ref. Chbk.).
   iii) Anna Dorothea[3], bpt. 5 April 1747 - sp.: Rodolfus (--) and Dorothea Dennemarke (Walpeck Ref. Chbk.).
   iv) Femmetje[3], bpt. 17 Sept 1749 - sp.: Benjamin Swartwout and Femmetje Decker (Walpeck Ref. Chbk.).
   v) Johann Christophel[3], bpt. 22 March 1752 - sp.: Christoffel Dennemarken and Christina Lis: Bernhard (Walpeck Ref. Chbk.).

The widow Anna Hargt. Danemark aged 58, listed with Christophel[1] in N.Y. City in 1710/11 probably was his mother (HJ). An Anna Margreet (no surname) was recorded next to Kristoffel Denemarker in the 5th party at Rotterdam in 1709 (Rotterdam Lists); this Anna Margreet probably was the same person as the Anna Hargt. registered in N.Y. City in 1710/11 (HJ).

CONRAD DARREY (Hunter Lists #113)

Koenraet Deür was a passenger on Capt. Tomas Wilkens's ship 10 June 1709 in Holland (Rotterdam Lists). Conrad Dorry aged 36, Luth., carpenter, was in the 3rd arrivals in England later that year (London Lists).

Conrad Darrey was entered twice on the Hunter Lists: on 1 July and 4 Aug 1710 with 1 pers. over 10 yrs. of age.

LORENTZ DÄTHER (Hunter Lists #114)

Jerg Thater, s/o the late Johann Thater of Lehn berg, commune Giglinger in the duchy of Wurtemberg, md. 26 April 1715 Anna Maria Meyer, d/o the late Johann Fridrich Meyer of Rohrbach near sintzen, baronate Vennig (West Camp Luth. Chbk.). This was one of several entries where Kocherthal erred in noting an emigrant's ancestral village: after years of searching throughout Württemberg and the Kraichgau, the actual Däther home was found to be not Lehn berg, but 7129 Leonbronn (14 km. n.e. of Bretten; Chbks. begin 1657, but gaps). Hanß Döther, his wife Elisabetha, and their children Lorenz, Margaretha, and Georg were on communicant lists at Leonbronn beginning in 1697; they were noted 1697-1700, and 1704-1708. Elisabetha, w/o Hß. Dötter, d. 31 July 1708. Hanß Dötter, the so-called old Nürnberger, d. 13 Jan 1709. After the entry on the 1709 communicant list for the surviving three children - Margaretha, Lorenz, and Hß. Jörg - was an added notation which read "sind in Engelland verreißt." Laurents Deder and Maria Dederin were in the 5th party of Palatines on Capt. William Newton's ship 3 July 1709 (Rotterdam Lists).

Lorentz Däther made his first appearance on the Hunter Lists 30 June 1710 with 3 pers. over 10 yrs. of age; the household always was recorded with 3 pers. over 10 yrs. on Hunter except for 4 Oct 1710 when 5 pers. over 10 yrs. were registered, and 25 March 1712 when 2 pers. over 10 yrs. were listed. Lourens Dieder was nat. 8 and 9 Sept 1715 (Kingston Nats.). Louwerens Teder made his first appearance on the tax rolls in the North Ward in 1717/18 and was continued until 1727/28 when Margreeta, wid/o Lowerence Teder deceased was noted (Dutchess Co. Tax Lists). A child of Lorentz[1] Däther was:

1) Henrich[2] (HJ), md. Catharina Benner. His first entry on the tax rolls was in 1739/40 (Dutchess Co. Tax Lists). The will of Hendrick Tieter of Rhinebeck was dated 18 Sept 1778 and probated 18 May 1785 (Fernow Wills #1742). The ch. of Henrich[2] Dieter (Titter, Doder, Deithardt, Teter et. var.) were:

    i) <u>Anna Margaretha</u>[3], bpt. 10 Aug 1740 - sp.: ... and
       Margridt Bender (Rhinebeck Flats Ref. Chbk.). She
       md. Jacob Thomas by 1761 (HJ).

   ii) <u>Johannes</u>[3], bpt. 2 March 1742 - sp.: Johannes Benner
       and Magdalena Streit (Red Hook Luth. Chbk.). He md.
       Margaretha Reiffenberger (HJ). The will of a Johannes
       Teeter of Rhinebeck was dated 15 Aug 1794 and pro-
       bated 2 March 1795 (Dutchess Co. Will Bk. A).

  iii) <u>Zacharias</u>[3], bpt. 16 Oct 1743 - sp.: Zacharias Schmith
       and wife Anna Maria (Red Hook Luth. Chbk.). He md.
       17 Dec 1770 (Annatjen) Elisabeth Wahlen (Red Hook
       Luth. Chbk.).

   iv) <u>Elisabetha</u>[3], bpt. 25 April 1747 - sp.: Henrich Ben-
       der and Catharina Bender (Red Hook Luth. Chbk.). She
       md. John Fulton (HJ).

    v) <u>Catharina</u>[3], b. 3 Jan 1750 - sp.: Johannes Schmidt
       and Catharina Pulver (Rhinebeck Luth. Chbk.).

   vi) <u>Abraham</u>[3], bpt. 15 May 1751 - sp.: Abraham Benthuisen
       and Catharina Benthuisen (Red Hook Luth. Chbk.).

  vii) <u>Henrich</u>[3], bpt. 24 April 1753 - sp.: Henrich Bender
       and Catharina Botzer (Red Hook Luth. Chbk.). He d.
       24 July 1835, aged 82-4-24 (Red Hook Luth. Cem.).

 viii) <u>Catharina</u>[3], bpt. 15 Feb 1755 - sp.: Jacob Maul and
       Anna Dorothea Tromboor (Red Hook Luth. Chbk.).

   ix) <u>Wilhelmus</u>[3], bpt. 8 April 1757 - sp.: Wilhelm Petzer
       and Magdalena Dunsbach (Red Hook Luth. Chbk.). He d.
       29 April 1841, aged 84 yrs., 1 month (Red Hook Luth.
       Cem.).

    x) <u>Philip</u>[3], b. 9 Feb 1761 - sp.: Philip Feller and wife
       Sussanna (Rhinebeck Luth. Chbk.). He d. 3 March 1833,
       aged 72 yrs., 1 month (Red Hook Luth. Cem.).

Georg Doher was nat. 8 and 9 Sept 1715 (Kingston Nats.). He
made his first appearance on tax rolls in the North Ward in 1717/
18 and his last at Rhinebeck in Feb 1761 (Dutchess Co. Tax Lists).
Pastor Berkenmeyer wrote of visiting his home at Rhynbek in 1737
(<u>Albany Protocol</u>, p. 130). Georg[1] Deter and wife Anna Maria Meyer
had ch.:

    1) <u>Maria Magdalena</u>[2], b. 7 July 1716 - sp.: Jacob Kaputzgi
       and wife Anna Magdalena (West Camp Luth. Chbk.). She md.
       Christoph Ring (Rink) at Rhinebeck 27 April 1736 (Loon-
       enburg Luth. Chbk.).

    2) <u>Johannes</u>[2], b. 11 Jan 1718 - sp.: Johann Michael Waegelin
       and his wife (West Camp Luth. Chbk.). He was on Rhinebeck
       tax rolls 1742/43 - 1768 (Dutchess Co. Tax Lists). He md.

1st Catharina Barthel and had issue:

    i) <u>Georg</u>[3], b. 27 Oct 1743 - sp.: Jurge Deter and Anna
       Maria, grandparents (Loonenburg Luth. Chbk.). He
       probably md. Anna Maria Zufeldt (HJ).

   ii) <u>Johannes</u>[3], bpt. 20 Oct 1745 - sp.: Johannes Veller
      and Anna Barbara Deter (Red Hook Luth. Chbk.).

  iii) <u>Catharina</u>[3], b. 24 Aug 1747 - sp.: Friedrich Dodter
      and Catharina Zufeld (Rhinebeck Luth. Chbk.).

   iv) <u>Sophia</u>[3], b. 31 Jan 1750 - sp.: Georg Adam Zufeld and
      wife Catharina (Rhinebeck Luth. Chbk.).

    v) <u>Anna Maria</u>[3], b. 7 Dec 1752 - sp.: Georg Toedter and
      Anna Maria (Rhinebeck Luth. Chbk.).

Johannes[2] md. 2nd Elisabeth, d/o Balthasar and Elisabetha
Loth, 10 Feb 1754 (Rhinebeck Luth. Chbk.) and had ch.:

   vi) <u>Johannes</u>[3], bpt. 26 May 1754 - sp.: Christoffel Ringh
      and Maria Magdalena Ringh (Red Hook Luth. Chbk.).

  vii) <u>Elisabetha</u>[3], b. 15 Dec 1754 - sp.: Henrik Theeter
      and his wife (Rhinebeck Flats Ref. Chbk.).

 viii) <u>Philipus</u>[3], bpt. 27 Feb 1757 - sp.: Stoffel Ring and
      Maria Magdalena Teder (Red Hook Luth. Chbk.).

   ix) <u>Henrich</u>[3], b. 16 June 1762 - sp.: Henrich Voland and
      wife Elisabeth (Rhinebeck Luth. Chbk.).

    x) <u>Magdalena</u>[3], b. 2 Jan 1766 - sp.: Joseph Reichert and
      wife Catharina (Rhinebeck Luth. Chbk.).

Note that the age-spread on some of these ch. is confusing (HJ).

3) <u>Anna Elisabetha</u>[2], b. August 1719 at Rheinbeck - sp.: Henrich Schaffer and wife Susanna Agnes (N.Y. City Luth.
   Chbk.).

4) <u>Anna Barbara</u>[2] (HJ), conf. 13 April 1740 at Theerbos (Loonenburg Luth. Chbk.). She md. Johannes Feller by 1747 (HJ).

5) <u>Henrich</u>[2], md. as s/o Georg[1] in 1747 Beletje Neher (Rhinebeck Luth. Chbk.). He made his appearance on tax rolls at
   Rhinebeck in Feb 1747/48 and may have been the Capt. Henrich whose estate was noted in 1777 (Dutchess Co. Tax
   Lists). Issue:

    i) <u>Anna Maria</u>[3], b. 7 Jan 1749 - sp.: Georg Toder and An-
      na Mara, and Anna Neher (Rhinebeck Luth. Chbk.).

   ii) <u>Rebecca</u>[3], b. 27 Oct 1750 - sp.: Frans Neher and wife
      Rebecca (Rhinebeck Luth. Chbk.). She had a license
      to marry Georg Sharp 23 April 1772 (N.Y. Marriage
      Lic.).

  iii) <u>Georg</u>[3], b. 11 Aug 1752 - sp.: Jurrien Theeter and his
      wife (Rhinebeck Flats Ref. Chbk.).

    iv) <u>Beeltje</u>[3], bpt. 9 July 1754 - sp.: Christiaen Bekker and Annatje Bekker (Red Hook Luth. Chbk.).

    v) <u>Johannes</u>[3], bpt. 22 Aug 1755 - sp.: Frans Nier and wife Rebekka (Red Hook Luth. Chbk.).

    vi) <u>Johann Henrich</u>[3], b. 18 Aug 1760 - sp.: Hanes Deder and wife Elisabeth (Rhinebeck Luth. Chbk.). The mother in this entry was not named (HJ).

    vii) <u>Elisabetha</u>[3], b. 7 Feb 1766 - sp.: Jacob Neher and wife Elisabeth (Rhinebeck Luth. Chbk.).

6) <u>Johann Friederich</u>[2], b. 26 Jan 1723 at Rheinbeek - sp.: Joh: Fried: Meyer and wife Anna Barbara (N.Y. City Luth. Chbk.). He was conf. at Rhynb. 19 June 1743 (Loonenburg Luth. Chbk.). Frederick was on Rhinebeck tax rolls from June 1748 to 1775, when his widow was listed (Dutchess Co. Tax Lists). He md. 9 Feb 1748 Catharina Zufeld (Rhinebeck Luth. Chbk.). He d. Nov 1773, aged 51 yrs. (Rhinebeck Luth. Cem.). Issue:

    i) <u>Anna Maria</u>[3], b. 15 May 1750 - sp.: Georg Toedter and his wife Anna Maria Maria Magdalena (Rhinebeck Luth. Chbk.).

    ii) <u>Elisabetha</u>[3], b. 27 Aug 1752 - sp.: Jurrien Adam Shoefelt and his wife (Rhinebeck Flats Ref. Chbk.).

    iii) <u>Catharina</u>[3], b. 6 April 1755 - sp.: Henric Theeter and his wife (Rhinebeck Flats Ref. Chbk.).

    iv) <u>Anna</u>[3], b. 22 Feb 1761 - sp.: Johannes Feller and wife Barbara (Rhinebeck Luth. Chbk.).

    v) <u>Friederich</u>[3], b. 10 July 1763 - sp.: Friderich Neher and wife Anna Maria (Rhinebeck Luth. Chbk.).

    vi) <u>Georg</u>[3], b. 16 Aug 1766 - sp.: Jerg Adam Zufeld and wife Catharina (Rhinebeck Luth. Chbk.).

    vii) <u>Jeremias</u>[3], b. 18 June 1769 - sp.: Henrich Deder and Maria (Rhinebeck Luth. Chbk.).

7) <u>Elisabetha</u>[2], bpt. 25 June 1727 - sp.: Frerik Meyer and Anna Barbara Meyer (Kingston Ref. Chbk.). She was conf. 17 June 1744 at Rhynbek (Loonenburg Luth Chbk.) and md. Jacob Neher 20 Jan 1747 (Rhinebeck Luth. Chbk.).

8) <u>Anna Maria</u>[2], b. 6 Nov 1728 and bpt. Rhynbek - sp.: Maria Barbel and husband Velten Scheffer (N.Y. City Luth. Chbk.).

9) <u>Lorentz</u>[2], b. 25 Dec 1736 and bpt. Rhinebeck - sp.: Hans Velten Scheffer and wife Maria Barbel (Loonenburg Luth. Chbk.).

A Hendrick Dieter of Dutchess Co., Luth. was nat. 17 Oct 1744 (<u>Denizations, Naturalizations, and Oaths of Allegiance in Colonial N.Y.</u>, p. 24).

JOHANN BERNHARD DATT (Hunter Lists #115)

Bernhard That aged 45, with his wife, a son aged 6, a daughter aged 2, Luth. cooper and brewer, were in the 3rd arrivals in England in 1709 (London Lists).

Johann Bernhard Datt made his first appearance on the Hunter Lists 1 July 1710 with 2 pers. over 10 yrs. of age and 2 pers. under 10 yrs. in the family; the household was listed with 3 pers. over 10 yrs. and 1 under 10 yrs. 25 March 1712. Hans Bernhardt Daet was nat. along with Johannis Daet 14 Feb 1715/16 (Albany Nats.). Bernard Tadt was a Palatine Debtor in 1721 and 1726 (Livingston Debt Lists). He and his wife Elisabetha were noted in the St. Peter's Luth. list of families in 1734 (Rhinebeck Luth. Chbk.); his wife Elisabetha signed a deposition dated 1721/22 in which she was called Elizabeth, w/o Bern. Taat, a Palatine, aged 52 yrs. (Livingston Papers, Reel #4). A child of Bernhard[1] Datt and his wife was:

1) Johannes[2] (HJ), nat. alongside Bernhardt Daet 14 Feb 1715/ 16 (Albany Nats.) and listed next to Bernhart in 1734 at St. Peter's Luth. (Rhinebeck Luth. Chbk.). Hannes Daad was conf. at Kamp Misericordia Sunday: 1726 (N.Y. City Luth. Chbk.). Pastor Berkenmeyer administered the Lord's Supper to the w/o Hannes Daat, Jr. at Camp 11 Jan 1732 (Albany Protocol, p. 33). Johannes Daet was a freeholder at East Camp in 1763 (Albany Co. Freeholders). He md. Elisabetha Reuter and had ch.:

   i) Anna[3], md. as d/o Johannes 11 June 1748 Jacob Best (Germantown Ref. Chbk.).

   ii) Anna Catharina[3], b. 21 Nov 1734 - sp.: Joh: Loscher and Anna Cath. Boener (Rhinebeck Luth. Chbk.).

   iii) Elisabetha[3] (HJ), md. Johannes Schultes by 1763 (HJ).

   iv) Maria Juliana[3], b. 4 Aug 1742 and bpt. Camp - sp.: Henr. Reuter and Juliana, the grandparents, but these being absent and the father ill, the mother and Catharina Abner (Loonenburg Luth. Chbk.).

   v) Rebecca[3], bpt. 6 April 1746 - sp.: Frans Nier and Rebekka Kool (Rhinebeck Flats Ref. Chbk.); child unnamed in bpt. entry. She md. Henrich Reuter (HJ).

   vi) Anna Margaretha[3], b. 5 Oct 1748 - sp.: Jacob Eigener and Anna M: (Germantown Luth. Chbk.). She md. Johannes Bratt (HJ).

   vii) Christina[3], bpt. 29 July 1750 - sp.: Jacob Best Sr. and Christin Best (Germantown Ref. Chbk.).

   viii) Johannes[3] (HJ), md. Christina (--) and was mentioned at Gilead Luth. Chbk. in Rensselaer Co.

   ix) <u>Henrich</u>[3] (HJ), a sp. in 1774 (Schaghticoke Ref. Chbk.).

<u>MELCHIOR DAUSWEBER</u> (Hunter Lists #116)

Johann Melchior Dausweber, widower and schoolteacher of Burshel in the commune of Marbach in Wurtenberg, md. 13 Feb 1711 Magdalena, wid/o Michael Schauer of Mastenbach in the Creichgau (West Camp Luth. Chbk.). The family was documented at 7150 <u>Backnang</u> (27 km. n.e. of Stuttgart; Chbks. begin 1629). The earliest known ancestor of the American line was <u>Hans Daußweber</u>, a smith who d. before 1637; his wife Christina d. 11 May 1637. They had ch.:

   <u>Michael</u>, d. 1629.

   <u>Michael</u>, b. 3 April 1630 and d. 2 Oct 1634.

   <u>Georg</u>, d. 11 Sept 1693.

+ <u>Hans</u>, d. 20 Sept 1693, aged 70 yrs.

Hans Daußweber, tailor, md. 28 Jan 1651 Anna Maria Maier. She was the d/o Georg Maier, tailor and Gerichtsverw., who d. 21 July 1667. Georg Maier md. 11 Feb 1623 Maria, d/o Melchior Strobel (?) from Schöckingen; Maria Maier d. 27 Nov 1679. Hans Daußweber md. 2nd 15 Oct 1689 Katharina Schlief, wid/o Georg Schlief. Hans Daußweber and his 1st wife Anna Maria Maier had issue:

   <u>Hans Georg</u>, b. 2 Dec 1651 and d. 2 March 1681.

   <u>Maria Christina</u>, b. 27 Feb 1653.

+ <u>Hans Melchior</u>, b. 1 Jan 1655.

   <u>Daniel</u>, b. 25 April 1656.

   <u>Maria Dorothea</u>, b. 2 Sept 1657.

   <u>Anna Maria</u>, b. 4 Nov 1658.

   <u>Christine</u>, b. 12 Jan 1660.

   <u>Christine</u>, b. 9 July 1661.

   <u>Marie Christine</u>, b. 2 April 1663, md. a Klenk.

   <u>Anna Margaretha</u>, b. 24 May 1664.

   <u>Johannes</u>, b. 15 Feb 1669 and d. 21 Feb 1669.

The American line was founded by the emigrant 1709er Hans Melchior, s/o Hanß Daußweber the tailor and his wife Anna Maria, bpt. 1 Jan 1655 - sp.: H. M. N. Glöckler, and Christina - wid/o H. Daniel Reckberger the Burgomaster. Johan Melgior Daustel, his wife and 3 ch. were listed next to Johan Koenraat Weiser and Jozep Reinhart (Reichardt - HJ), N.Y. settlers from the Großaspach/Backnang region, in the 6th party of Palatines in Holland (Rotterdam Lists).

Melchior Dausweber made his first appearance on the Hunter Lists 4 July 1710 with 5 pers. over 10 yrs. of age in the family. The family fluctuated in size throughout 1710-12, with separate

entries for his two daughters, his "hol" family, and then his widow. One of the notations for 25 March 1712 read Christina Daus-
weberin and sister. Melchoir Dausweber aged 55, Maria Christina
Dausweber aged 20, and Anna Maria Dausweber aged 17 were in the
1710/11 Census of Palatines remaining in N.Y. City. Melch. Tous-
weber: 1 man and 2 women were in the 1710/11 Winter Census at
West Camp (West Camp Census). Issue from his 1st marriage:

1) Johannes², bpt. 19 Sept 1678 - sp.: Andreas Vaysinger,
   Knapp, Maria Barbara - wid/o Michael Felger and her son
   Joh. Michael (Backnang Chbk.).

2) Johann Andreas², bpt. 26 Nov 1687 - sp.: H. Andreas Vaysinger des Raths, Joh. Michael Folger, and Maria Barbara
   - wid/o Joh. Michael Folger (Backnang Chbk.). Andreas
   Tausweber, young shoemaker and s/o Joh. Melchior Tausweber the Beysitzer and shoemaker here, d. 30 Nov 1707,
   aged 20 yrs. (Großaspach Chbk.).

3) Maria Barbara², md. as d/o Johann Melchior¹ 29 Aug 1710
   Johann Georg Borner from Großaspach (West Camp Luth.
   Chbk.).

4) Maria Christina² (Palatines In N.Y. City), md. 3 July
   1720 Nicolaus Neidebber (Niedhofer) (N.Y. City Luth.
   Chbk.).

5) Anna Maria² (Palatines In N.Y. City), md. She md. 1st
   Jacob Feeck and 2nd 7 Nov 1724 Zacharias Oenmaest (Ofenauf) (Tappan Ref. Chbk.).

By his 2nd wife Anna Magdalena he had a child:

6) Maria Regina², b. 24 Jan 1712 - sp.: Johann Straub and
   wife Maria Elisabeth, and Maria Regina Fridrich (West
   Camp Luth. Chbk.). Maria Regina Dausweber was conf. 28
   Feb 1733 at Theerbosch (Loonenburg Luth. Chbk.).

Magdalena, wid/o Johann Melchior¹ Dausweber, md. Paul Engel
after Dausweber's death. Paul Engel, his wife Magdalena, and his
step-daughter Maria Dausweber were recorded on the 1734 St. Peter's Luth. list (Rhinebeck Luth. Chbk.).

DANIEL DEFFU (Hunter Lists #117)

Daniel Thevoux aged 44, with his wife, a son aged 6, a daughter aged 8, Ref., husbandman and vinedresser, was in the 1st arrivals in England in 1709 (London Lists). He was originally from
Switzerland (N.Y. City Ref. Chbk.).

Daniel Teffa aged 30, Marianna Teffa aged 11, and Abraham
Teffa aged 7 were in N.Y. City in 1710/11 (Palatines In N.Y.
City). Daniel and Abrm. Thevou were nat. together 8 and 9 Sept

1715 (Kingston Nats.). Daniel Diefuh and Maria Barbara with 2 ch. were at Beckmansland ca. 1716/17 (Simmendinger Register). Daniel's 1st wife's name in Switzerland and Germany is unknown, but he md. 2nd as Daniel Thevoe, widower of Switserlandt, 27 Feb 1711 Maria Barbara Kras, wid/o Frans Poore (N.Y. City Ref. Chbk.). Issue from 1st marriage:

1) <u>Maria Anna^2</u> (Palatines In N.Y. City), md. 18 March 1724 Henrich Michel (Linlithgo Ref. Chbk.). Maria Anna De For, w/o (--) Michiln, was conf. at Kamp 3 May 1729 (N.Y. City Luth. Chbk.).

2) <u>Abraham^2</u> (Palatines In N.Y. City), nat. 8 and 9 Sept 1715 next to Daniel Thevou (Kingston Nats.). Abraham De Foon made his first appearance on tax rolls in the North Ward in 1726/27 and continued until Feb 1747/48 at Rhinebeck (Dutchess Co. Tax Lists). He md. Maria Catharina Reiffenberger and had ch.:

i) <u>Johann Ernst^3</u>, md. as s/o Abraham De Fuh 1 Feb 1749 Maria Keller (Germantown Ref. Chbk.). They had ch. bpt. at Albany Ref. and Schoharie Luth. Churches. He was known as John Defoe, was a Loyalist, and d. St. John's, Quebec, 1784 (Upper Canada Land Pets., RG 1, L3, Vol. 151, pp. 6-6d).

ii) <u>Johann Georg^3</u>, bpt. ½ yr. old 13 Aug 1727 at Kamp - sp.: Johan Jurge Scheffer and wife Anna Marie (N.Y. City Luth. Chbk.). He md. Anna Keller, and they had ch. bpt. at Loonenburg Luth., Claverack Ref., and Albany Ref. Churches. They lived at Halfmoon and then Schaghticoke.

iii) <u>Daniel^3</u>, bpt. 1 Aug 1731 - sp.: Daniel Rysbergen and Elis. Fingel (Rhinebeck Flats Ref. Chbk.). He md. Catharina Keller and had ch. bpt. at Albany Ref. and Schaghticoke Ref. Churches.

iv) <u>Johannes^3</u>, bpt. 1733 - sp.: Johan Georg Richt(--), Johannes Richter, (--) Catharina (--)(Germantown Ref. Chbk.).

v) <u>Maria Elisabetha^3</u>, b. 30 Sept 1735 - sp.: Joh: Milius and wife Maria Elisabeth (Rhinebeck Luth. Chbk.). She md. Johannes Van Derwerken (HJ).

vi) <u>Anna Margaretha^3</u>, b. 9 Feb 1738 - sp.: Johannes Reiffenberg and Anna Margreta Nitzbach (Loonenburg Luth. Chbk.). She md. Abraham Vanderkeer 6 April 1759 (Albany Ref. Chbk.) and lived in Saratoga Co.

vii) <u>Eva^3</u>, bpt. 14 April 1740 - sp.: Willem Jacobus and Eva Jacobuss (Red Hook Luth. Chbk.). She md. 12 Oct

1759 Hendrick Kazenbach (Albany Ref. Chbk.).
viii) <u>Elisabetha</u>³, bpt. 23 Aug 1742 - sp.: James Morris
and wife Elisabetha (Red Hook Luth. Chbk.). She md.
John Northern (HJ) and had ch. bpt. at Albany Ref.
and Brunswick Luth. Churches.
ix) <u>Abraham</u>³ (HJ), a Loyalist who settled briefly in
Canada and then returned to N.Y.

David Kendall Martin of West Chazy, N.Y. and Brian Roberts
of Bainbridge Island, Washington were most helpful in the prep-
aration of the Deffu section of this book.

JACOB DEMUTH (Hunter Lists #118)

Jacob Demuth made his first appearance on the Hunter Lists
1 July 1710 with 4 pers. over 10 yrs. of age and 2 pers. under 10
yrs. The household showed 5 pers. over 10 yrs. and 1 under 10 on
4 Oct 1710, 4 pers. over 10 yrs. and 1 under 10 on 31 Dec 1710,
and then 5 pers. over 10 yrs. of age 24 June 1711. Jacob Dimouth:
1 man, 1 lad aged 9 to 15, 1 woman, and 2 maids aged 9 to 15, were
in Ulster Co. in 1710/11 (West Camp Census). Jacob Teymout/Zeymout
was noted on the Ramapo Tract in N.J. in 1714 (Ramapo Tract Acct.
Bk.). Jacob Demuth and his wife with 3 ch. were at Hackensack ca.
1716/17 (Simmendinger Register); there was also a Jacob Demuth
with wife Anna Elisabetha and 3 ch. at Beckmansland mentioned
in Simmendinger. Jacob Demuth of Eulenkil and Hanover appeared
in Berkenmeyer's Protocol in 1731 (<u>Albany Protocol</u>, p. 19). He md.
1st Anna Elisabetha (Febers?); he may have been the Jacob Tymouth,
widower, who md. Barbar Parleman, widow, in 1735 (Pompton Plains
Ref. Chbk.) or the Jacob Themout, widower of Hooghwyzel, Darmstad,
Germany, who md. Barbara Thewalt, widow b. Moxter, Germany, in
1736 (Acquackanonk Ref. Chbk.). Issue with 1st wife:
1) <u>Anna Dorothea</u>² (HJ), md. Johann Peter Friederich June 1717
(N.Y. City Luth. Chbk.).
2) <u>Anna Maria</u>² (HJ), conf. at Newtown 12 June 1712 (West Camp
Luth. Chbk.). She md. Martin Van Duyn (HJ), and they were
sp. by Jacob Themoth and Elis: Febers in 1728 (Acquacka-
nonk Ref. Chbk.).
3) <u>Johann Friederich</u>² (HJ), conf. Easter 1714 (West Camp Luth.
Chbk.). Fredrik Temont, single man b. Darmstadt, md. 14
April 1722 Annatie Miller, single woman b. Hedenborgh
(Hackensack Ref. Chbk.); her full name was Anna Charlotte
Müller (HJ). Issue:
i) <u>Conrad</u>³, bpt. 4 weeks old 6 March 1733/34 on the
Eulenkill - sp.: Jacob Demuth and wife Elisabeth

(N.Y. City Luth. Chbk.).

ii) Elisabetha³, b. 29 Oct 1735 and bpt. on the Eulenkill - sp.: Pieter Friederich and wife Anna Dorothea
(N.Y. City Luth. Chbk.).

ANNA CATHARINA DEMUTHIN & FR GEORG (Hunter Lists #119)

Jerg Demuth, s/o the late Alexander Demuth of Runckel on the
Lohn, md. Margretha Dopf, d/o Peter Dopf of Metter in the commune
of Zweybrucken, 26 Oct 1714 (West Camp Luth. Chbk.). The ancestral
home of this branch of the Demuth family was 6251 Runkel (7 km.
e. of Limburg; Chbks. begin 1651). The Demuths were not found in
the Runkel registers, however.

Anna Catharina Demuthin made her first appearance on the Hunter Subsistence Lists 1 July 1710 with 4 pers. over 10 yrs. of age
in the household; on 31 Dec 1710 the family was noted with 3 pers.
over 10 yrs., and the head of the household was recorded as Johann
Georg Demuth. A Henrich Hoffmann and a G^r Demuth were listed together 24 June 1712, and this entry may pertain to #119 (HJ). The
ch. of Alexander and Anna Catharina¹ Demuth were:

1) Johann Georg², md. 26 Oct 1714 Margaretha Dopf (West Camp
Luth. Chbk.). Juryan Tymot was nat. 8 and 9 Sept 1715
(Kingston Nats.). Georg Demuth, his wife and ch. were at
Heessberg ca. 1716/17 (Simmendinger Register). Jurie De
Mont was enrolled in the North Ward in 1717/18 and con-
tinued until 20 Jan 1720/21 when the Widow of Jurie De-
month was registered (Dutchess Co. Tax Lists). His widow
(Anna) Margaretha md. 2nd Philip Salomon Flegeler (HJ).
The issue of Johann Georg² Demuth and Margaretha were:

   i) Elisabetha³, bpt. 3 July 1715 - sp.: Johannes Lamet
   and Elisabeth Lamet (Kingston Ref. Chbk.). She md.
   Johannes Reisdorff (HJ).

   ii) Christina³ (HJ), md. Johannes Busch (HJ).

   iii) Maria³ (HJ), md. Joseph Busch 12 Nov 1738 (Fishkill
   Ref. Chbk.).

   iv) Johann Peter³, b. Jan 1720 and bpt. at Rheinbeeck -
   sp.: Peter Topp and Ursulla Weidmann (N.Y. City Luth.
   Chbk.). A Peter Demoet was sp. at Rhinebeck Flats
   Ref. Church in 1746 and 1748.

2) Dieterich² (HJ), conf. at Queensberg 23 March 1712 (West
Camp Luth. Chbk.). Dederik Demoet was a Palatine Debtor
in 1718 (Livingston Debt Lists). Tedrigh Temouth was a
patentee on the n. side of the Mohawk 30 April 1725 (Burnetsfield Patent).

3) <u>Johann Jost</u>[2] (HJ), a patentee on the n. side of the Mohawk 30 April 1725 (Burnetsfield Patent). A Johan Jost
Demut was in Capt. Mark Petry's Co. 26 Feb 1757 (<u>Report
of the State Historian</u>, Vol. II, p. 782).

There were unplaced Demuths in the Mohawk region who were
probably descendants of Dieterich[2] or Johann Jost[2] (HJ): 1) Georg
Demoth, will probated 15 Oct 1791 (Montgomery Co. Will Bk. I); 2)
Johann Marcus Demuth, a soldier in Capt. Marx Petry's Co. at Bornets Field 9 May 1767 (<u>Report of the State Historian</u>, Vol. II, p.
854), and 3) John Demuth, d. 16 Nov 1810, aged 73 yrs. (Herkimer
Intelligencer of 22 Nov 1810), called an ancient and respectable
inhabitant of this town, formerly called "Damewood."

ANNA MARIA DEMUTHIN (Hunter Lists #120)

Anna Maria Demuth made her only appearance on the Hunter
Lists 4 Aug 1710 with 1 pers. over 10 yrs. of age in the family.
A Maria Deunies, wid/o Jacob Demoot, md. Peek De Wit 21 Dec 1723
at Kingston Ref. Church; she was b. in Germany and resided in
Kingston.

AGNES DEMUTHIN (Hunter Lists #121)

Agnes Demuth was entered only once on the Hunter Subsistence
Lists: on 4 Oct 1710 she had 2 pers. over 10 yrs. of age in the
household. A Johann Wilhelm Demut and his wife Eva Zabel had a
daughter Agnes bpt. 31 Jan 1694 at 5418 <u>Marienrachdorf</u> Cath.
Church, but more information is needed to determine if indeed
this was our emigrant 1709er (HJ).

As #121 Agnes Demuth had 2 pers. over 10 yrs. in her family
in 1710, perhaps she was the mother of Peter De Mott aged 13, an
orphan bound to Cornelis Wyckoff of Flatlands 17 April 1711 (Apprenticeship Lists); Peter Demuth was at Hackensack ca. 1716/17
(Simmendinger Register).

JOHN PAUL DEUBIG (Hunter Lists #122)

The ancestral village of the family was 6349 <u>Driedorf</u> (8 km.
s.w. of Herborn; Chbks. begin 1671). The earliest known ancestor
of the American line was <u>Niclas Daubig</u>. Simon, s/o Niclas Daubig
at Sechshelden, md. 2 Feb 1698 Anna Catharina, d/o the late Johann
Jacob Gross in Driedorf. Simon Deubig, his wife and 2 ch. from
Driedorf petitioned to leave Germany in 1709 (Nassau-Dillenburg
Petitions). The ch. of Simon[1] Deubig and his wife Anna Catharina
were:

1) "A Child"[2], bpt. 15 Oct 1699 - sp.: Fritz Deubig, Johann Friedr. Brand - Corporal, the w/o Johann Peter Hermann, and Ursell - w/o Johann Görg Dörner (Driedorf Chbk.). This child may have been the Johann Peter Deubig, listed as head of the family 4 Oct 1710 in Hunter and conf. as Johann Peter Tobich 12 June 1712 at Newtown (West Camp Luth. Chbk.).

2) "A Child"[2], bpt. 14 May 1703 - sp.: Johannes Gross - single, Johan Henrich Geissler - citizen from Herborn, Anna Margaretha - d/o Clas Schmits (?) from ..., and Anna Catharina - single d/o Frid. Deubig in Driedorf (Driedorf Chbk.).

3) "A Child"[2], bpt. 5 Sept 1704 - sp.: Johann Peter Hess - single, Paulus Schaff - a single man from Merkenbach, Anna Margaretha Fris - single woman, and Anna Catharina - d/o ... Möller - single (Driedorf Chbk.). This child was our emigrant #122 Johann Paul Deubig (HJ). Johann Paul Deubig made his first appearance on the Hunter Lists 30 June 1710 with 1 pers. over 10 yrs. of age and 1 pers. under 10 yrs. Jno. Paul Denbig aged 7 was an orphan bound to S. Phillips of N.Y. 22 Sept 1710 (Apprenticeship Lists).

4) "A Young Daughter"[2], bpt. Dnca Exaudi: 1706 - sp.: Johann Philipp Göbel - the Hoffman here, Abraham Cadwunckel - a carpenter 'aus dem Brandenburgischen Comat.', Anna Catharina - w/o Johann Henrich Geissler of Herborn, and Anna Susanna - w/o Joh. Jacob Lotts of Herborn (Driedorf Chbk.).

JOHANN JACOB DIETRICH (Hunter Lists #123)

Jacob Diderich, his wife and 7 ch. were noted on Capt. John Bulson's ship in Holland in 1709 (Rotterdam Lists). Jacob Dietrich aged 44, his wife, sons aged 18, 12 and 2, daughters aged 15, 12, 10 and 6, linnenweaver, Ref. were in the 3rd arrivals in England later that year (London Lists). A Jacob Dieterich was found in the Neuwied region near other Dieterich 1709ers: Jacob Dieterich, s/o the late Class Dieterich of Jahrsfeld, md. Maria Walpurg Jung, d/o the late Jonas Jung of Datzerot, on Bettag July 1683 (Rengsdorf Chbk.); this couple had a son Johann Christian b. Dom. XXV p. Trin: 1684 - sp.: Johann Christian Pinhammer and Conrad Rossbach of Datzerot (Rengsdorf Chbk.). However, other than the names, the match with known data on the American Jacob Dietrich (#123) is poor (HJ).

Johann Jacob Dietrich made his first appearance on the Hunter Lists 4 July 1710 with 6 pers. over 10 yrs. of age and 2 pers.

under 10 yrs. of age; the last notation in Hunter 13 Sept 1712
recorded 5 pers. over 10 yrs. of age and 2 pers. under 10 yrs.
Jacob Dietrich's widow with 4 ch. was at Quunsberg ca. 1716/17
(Simmendinger Register). The wife of Jacob[1] Dietrich was probably
either the Margriet Dederik or the Catryn Dederik mentioned on
the Palatine Debt Rolls in the 1718-1721 period (Livingston Debt
Lists). The ch. of Jacob[1] were:

1) <u>Nicolaus</u>[2], as Nichs Tedry aged 14, s/o Jacob Tedry, was
   bound to Thos. Wiggins of Jamaica, L. I. 9 April 1711 (Apprenticeship Lists).

2) <u>Anna Margaretha</u>[2] (HJ), md. Jacob Beyer (HJ).

3) <u>Maria Barbara</u>[2] (HJ), md. Wilhelm Hagedorn (HJ).

4) <u>Christian</u>[2] (HJ), one of the two of that name nat. 17 Jan
   1715/16 (Albany Nats.). He may have been the "Christiaen
   Dederik, Catr's" listed next to Catryn Dederik in 1721
   on Palatine Debt Rolls (Livingston Debt Lists). Christ.
   Dietrig was a Palatine willing to remain at Livingston
   Manor 26 Aug 1724 (<u>Documentary History of N.Y.</u>, Vol. III,
   p. 724). He md. 1st Gertraud Hagedorn and had issue:

   i) <u>Maria Barbara</u>[3] (HJ), md. 30 Dec 1746 Kilian Minckler
      (Germantown Ref. Chbk.).

   ii) <u>Johann Jacob</u>[3], bpt. 1732 - sp.: Jacob Beyer and Mar-
       garetha Beyer (Germantown Ref. Chbk.).

   iii) <u>Elisabetha Margaretha</u>[3] (HJ), md. 31 May 1753 Georg
        Proppert (Germantown Ref. Chbk.).

   iv) <u>Johann Wilhelm</u>[3], bpt. 4 Oct 1735 - sp.: Willen Hoge-
       doorn and Mary Barbor Hogedoorn (Germantown Ref.
       Chbk.).

   v) <u>Anna</u>[3], bpt. 24 Feb 1741 - sp.: Stoffel Hagedorn and
      Anna Barbara (Linlithgo Ref. Chbk.). She md. as d/o
      Christian 12 June 1759 Johannes Schneider (Germantown
      Ref Chbk.).

Christian[2] md. 2nd Maria Elisabetha (H)emmerich Schantz
6 Sept 1748 (Germantown Ref. Chbk.) and had issue:

   vi) <u>Philip</u>[3], bpt. 17 April 1749 - sp.: Philip Klum and
       Veronica Klum (Germantown Ref. Chbk.). He md. 23 Dec
       1770 Magdalena Kuper (Germantown Ref. Chbk.); Magdal-
       ena was bur. 26 Nov 1827, aged 76 yrs. (Stewart Farm
       Cem., Kline Kill near Ghent).

   vii) <u>Anna Margaretha</u>[3], bpt. same day 17 April 1749 - sp.:
        Jost Henrich Dunsbach and Anna Margary (Germantown
        Ref. Chbk.). It is interesting to note that there
        also were twins in the family of the emigrant Johann
        Jacob[1], as recorded on the London Lists (HJ). Anna

Margaretha³ md. Dec 1771 Philip Blass (Germantown Ref. Chbk.).

   viii) Christina³, bpt. 17 Jan 1752 - sp.: Jurich Pieter Heyser and Christina Heyser (Germantown Ref. Chbk.).

     ix) Jacob³, bpt. 16 April 1754 - sp.: Jacob Beyer and wife Anna Marg. Diederich (Germantown Ref. Chbk.). He was a Loyalist, a Sergeant in Capt. Peter Hares's Co. at Niagara in 1783 (Canadian family data from Major Donald Holmes, U. E. L.).

      x) Anna Maria³, bpt. 19 Sept 1756 - sp.: Henr. Bernhardt and wife Anna Maria Hörter (Germantown Ref. Chbk.).

   xi?) Magdalena³, a sp. in 1758 (Germantown Ref. Chbk.).

The Livingston Debt Lists also mention a Margriet and a Jury Dederik 1718, 1721 and 1726 who may have been related to the family of Johann Jacob¹ Dietrich (HJ).

JOHANN WILHELM DIETRICH (Hunter Lists #124)

The ancestral origins of Johann Wilhelm Dietrich were at 5450 Niederbieber (3 km. n. of Neuwied; Chbks. begin 1655). The earliest known ancestor of the Hudson Valley family was Simon Dieterich from Segendorff, who d. 12 Nov 1701; his wife Anna (Zirbes) was bur. 17 April 1682. They had issue:

Christianus, a N.Y. Palatine settler (Hunter #125).

Johanata, bpt. 8 June 1656 - sp.: Johanata - w/o Jonas Volpert at Seg., Anna Cath. Rehmagen there, and Daniel Ziebes - brother-in-law of the child's father, a "Leydecker" at Rengsdorf.

Magdalena, bpt. 24 Jan 1658 - sp.: Magdalena - w/o Melchior Hofmann on the middle Hahnhof, and Johannes from Leutesdorf - a servant of Christ Erschfeldts at Seg.

+ Hans Wilhelm, bpt. 15 Dec 1660 - sp.: Jacob Hundert, Wilhelm Anhausen, and Catharina - w/o ... Zirbes at Seg.

Maria, a sp. at Niederbieber in 1683.

Martin, bpt. 23 July 1665 - sp.: Geret - s/o the Hon. Adolf Noll the Gerichtsschöffe at O'Bieber, Martin - brother of Christ Albert's wife from the Rasselmühle, and Margreta - w/o Jacob Simon at Segend.

Philipp, bpt. 7 March 1669 - sp.: Philipp - s/o Hannes Fischer, and Maria Sophia - w/o Christ ... from Seg.

The 1st wife of the emigrant Hans Wilhelm¹ Dieterich was Agnes Remagen, who d. 27 June 1700 aged 37 yrs. Hans Wilhelm Dieterich, widower at Segendorf, md. 25 Nov 1700 Anna Margaretha, d/o the late Peter Neff at Niederbieber. Anna Margaretha, d/o Peter Nefs

and wife Anna Margaretha at Oberbieber, was bpt. 26 Dec 1671 -
sp.: Anna - w/o Werner Theobald, Margaretha - d/o ... Stahlschmidt,
Clemens Köhl - teacher in Feldkirchen, and ... Peter. Hans Wilhelm[1] sp. the N.Y. emigrant Georg Friederich Neff in 1702 (Neuwied Luth. Chbk.). Hans Willem Tietruy, his wife and 5 ch. were
on Capt. John Encrist's ship 3 July 1709 in Holland (Rotterdam
Lists).

Johann Wilhelm Dietrich made his first appearance on the Hunter Lists 1 July 1710 with 4 pers. over 10 yrs. of age in the family; the last entry 13 Sept 1712 read 4 pers. over 10 yrs. of age
and 1 pers. under 10 yrs. .... Dietrich: 1 man, 1 lad 9-15 yrs.,
2 boys under 8 yrs., and 1 woman were in Ulster Co. in 1710/11
(West Camp Census). John Wilhm Dedrick was nat. 8 and 9 Sept 1715
(Kingston Nats.). Johann Wilhelm Dietrich, Anna Margr. and 3 ch.
were at Beckmansland ca. 1716/17 (Simmendinger Register). The ch.
of Johann Wilhelm[1] and his 1st wife Agnes Remagen were:

1) Johannes[2], bpt. 30 Dec 1688 - sp.: Johannes - brother of
   the child's mother, and the w/o Peter Remagen (Niederbieber Chbk.).

2) Hans Henrich[2], bpt. 26 March 1690 - sp.: Hans Henrich Wanbach, and Anna Christina - w/o Johann Wilhelm Schneider
   at Rodenbach. The child d. 5 May 1690, aged 6 weeks old
   (Niederbieber Chbk.).

3) Maria Elisabetha[2], bpt. 29 March 1691 - sp.: Joh. Wilh.
   Paulus - s/o the Hofmann at the ..., Maria - w/o Christ
   Wirtges at Segendorf, and Leysa Margaretha - d/o Christ
   Schneider at Rodenbach. The child d. 25 Feb 1701, aged
   nearly 11 yrs. (Niederbieber Chbk.).

4) Christianus[2], bpt. 15 Oct 1693 - sp.: Christ. Dieterich
   - brother of the child's father at N. Bieber, Peter Remagen - brother of the child's mother, and Anna Maria -
   d/o the late Ludwig Becker at N. B. (Niederbieber Chbk.).
   Christn Dedrick (one of two of that name) was nat. 8 and
   9 Sept 1715 (Kingston Nats.). Christian Derick was in the
   foot Co. of the militia at Kingston in 1738 (Report of
   the State Historian, Vol. I, p. 604). The name of Christian Diederick appeared on Bk. 2, p. 6 of the Kingston
   Trustees Records. Christian Dederik, single man b. Germany, md. 21 Dec 1723 Margriet Schut, single woman b.
   Kingston (Kingston Ref. Chbk.); she was called a widow
   in 1761 (Katsbaan Ref. Chbk.). They had issue:

   i) Meyndert[3], bpt. 23 Jan 1725 - sp.: Jan Paarsen and
      Antjen Post (Kingston Ref. Chbk.). He md. 7 Nov 1748
      Elisabetha, d/o Gisbert Scherp (Germantown Ref. Chbk.).

Myndert Diederich (grouped with Willem, John Jr., and Hendrick Dederick) was in Capt. Cornelus Dubois Co. at Caskill in 1767 (Report of the State Historian, Vol. II, p. 878).

  ii) Catharina[3], b. 19 Nov 1727 and bpt. Kisketom - sp.: Catharina Schut and Hans Jurge Elig (West Camp Luth. Chbk.). She md. Henrich Mesick 19 Sept 1748 (Kingston Ref. Chbk.) and d. 20 Dec 1792, aged 65 (Claverack Ref. Cem.).

  iii) Johannes[3] (HJ), md. 15 Oct 1756 Anna De Witt (Kingston Ref. Chbk.). They had ch. bpt. at Katsbaan Ref. and Germantown Ref. Churches, including Lucas - a Loyalist in Capt. Peter Hare's Co., 1783, Niagara.

  iv?) Sarah[3], who possibly md. 15 Oct 1756 Salomon Schutt (Kingston Ref. Chbk.), as Johannes[3] above was md. that same day (HJ). However, this Sarah[3] may belong in the family of Friederich[2] Dieterich.

  v) Elisabetha[3] (HJ), md. Jonas Müller (HJ),

  vi) Anna[3], b. 14 May 1736 - sp.: Hisrya Du Bois and wife Annatje (Loonenburg Luth. Chbk.). She md. Johannes Jung 4 Oct 1754 (Katsbaan Ref. Chbk.).

  vii) Agnes[3], b. 16 Jan 1739 and bpt. Newton - sp.: Jo: Matthys Jung and wife Catharina (Loonenburg Luth. Chbk.).

  viii) Henrich[3], bpt. 4 Sept 1743 - sp.: Johannes Swart and Antjen Wyncoop (Kingston Ref. Chbk.).

5) Margaretha[2], bpt. 1 Nov 1696 - sp.: Hans Ludwig - s/o the late Ludwig Becker at N.B., Catharina - d/o Georg Herzog at Segendorf, and Margaretha - d/o Christ. Schneider at Rodenbach (Niederbieber Chbk.).

6) Johann Henrich[2], bpt. 2 April 1699 - sp.: Johannes Lang at Segendorf, Henrich - s/o Johannes ... at Bendorf, and Anna Maria - d/o Christ. Remagen at Segendorf (Niederbieber Chbk.). The child d. 1 June 1699, aged 2 months.

Johann Wilhelm[1] md. 2nd Anna Margaretha Neff and had issue:

7) Johann Friederich[2], bpt. 2 Oct 1701 - sp.: Georg Friedrich Nef - citizen at Neuwiedt, Johann Wilhelm - s/o the late Hans Caspar Bauer at Neuwied, and Margaretha - w/o Johannis Remagen at Segendorf (Niederbieber Chbk.). Fred[k] Dedrick was nat. 8 and 9 Sept 1715 (Kingston Nats.). On 4 Jan 1736 going to Newtown, Berkenmeyer noted "on the way, near the home of Frits Dieterich, the driver was not careful enough and turned the sleigh over, so that I hurt my left arm (Albany Protocol, p. 170)." Vredrick Dederick was enrolled in Capt. Cornelus Dubois Co. at Caskill in 1767

(<u>Report of the State Historian</u>, Vol. II, p. 878). Frederick Deiderick was a freeholder at Caters Kill and Cats
Kill in 1763 (Albany Co. Freeholders). The will of Frederick Dederick of Albany Co. was dated 6 June 1746 and
probated Feb 1764 (<u>Fernow Wills</u> #442). He md. Eva Gradt
and had ch.:

  i) <u>Johannes</u>[3], bpt. 23 Aug 1724 - sp.: Pieter Helm and
     Anna Elisabeth Kleyn (Kingston Ref. Chbk.). He md.
     Elisabetha Overbach (HJ) and had ch. bpt. at Cats-
     kill and Katsbaan Ref. Churches.

 ii) <u>Anna Margaretha</u>[3], bpt. 25 Nov 1725 at Newtown - sp.:
     Hans Wilhelm Dieterichs - the grandfather - and Anna
     Margareta - the grandmother (Loonenburg Luth. Chbk.).

iii) <u>Maria</u>[3], bpt. 3 months old 24 Jan 1728 - sp.: Jurge
     Willem Kohl and Maria Margreta Graad (West Camp Luth.
     Chbk.). She probably md. Peter Brando (HJ).

 iv) <u>Anna Catharina</u>[3], b. 29 March 1729 - sp.: Gabriel
     Graat and Maria Catharina Dieterich (Loonenburg Luth.
     Chbk.).

  v) <u>"A Child"</u>[3], bpt. 8 Nov 1730 (Katsbaan Ref. Chbk.).
     This child probably was <u>Wilhelmus</u>[3] Dieterich, whom
     sp. show to be a firm child of Friederich[2]. He. md.
     1761 Catharina Brando (Catskill Ref. Chbk.).

 vi) <u>Henrich</u>[3], bpt. 11 Dec 1733 - sp.: Gabriel Graed and
     wife Catharina (Catskill Ref. Chbk.). He md. 1760
     Catharina Kalyer (Catskill Ref. Chbk.).

vii) <u>Elisabetha</u>[3], b. 5 Feb 1736 and bpt. Newton - sp.:
     Christian Dieterich and Liesabeth Graad (Loonenburg
     Luth. Chbk.). She md. Johannes Schermerhoorn (HJ).

viii) <u>Sarah</u>[3], bpt. 12 Jan 1737 - sp.: Godfried Brandau and
     Marytie Grad (Germantown Ref. Chbk.).

 ix) <u>Peter</u>[3], bpt. 18 Aug 1740 - sp.: Johann Matheis Jonk
     and Catharina Diederich (Katsbaan Ref. Chbk.). He
     md. Catharina Corree and had issue at Catskill Ref.
     Church (HJ).

8) <u>Anna Catharina</u>[2], bpt. 8 June 1704 - sp.: Catharina - w/o
   Philipp Fuchs - miller here at N.B., Anna Christina - w/o
   Johannis Remagen, and Joh. Wilhelm - s/o Christ Remagen
   at Seg. (Niederbieber Chbk.). She md. Matthias Jung 14
   Nov 1731 (N.Y. City Ref. Chbk.).

9) <u>Ottilia</u>[2], bpt. 3 Oct 1706 - sp.: Martin Dieterich, and
   Ottilia - d/o Peter Remagen at Seg. (Niederbieber Chbk.).

10) <u>Johann Christ</u>[2], bpt. 8 July 1708 - sp.: Johann Christ Bell,
    Joh. Daniel - s/o the late Weyandt Wirttges at Seg., and

Elsa Christina - w/o Georg Braun at Seg. (Niederbieber Chbk.).

11) <u>Georg Wilhelm²</u>, b. 5 Dec 1711 - sp.: Jorg Wilhelm Kehl and Anna Maria Dorothea Deumth (West Camp Luth. Chbk.). Jury William Dederick of West Camp, Albany Co. granted land to Henderick Fees 20 March 1754, and then to Jacob Eigenaer, William Eligh and Harmanus Beer in later entries (Albany Co. Deeds: Vol. 7, pp. 309, 314, 332, and 341). Jurie W. Dederick was a freeholder at West Camp in 1763 (Albany Co. Freeholders), and he was in Capt. Cornelus Dubois Co. at Caskill in 1767 (<u>Report of the State Historian</u>, Vol. II, p. 876). The will of Jury William Diederick of the West Camp was dated 11 Nov 1786 and probated 31 Jan 1787 (<u>Fernow Wills</u> #537). He d. 13 or 15 Dec 1786, aged 75 yrs, and his wife Catharina Elisabetha Jung d. 29 Oct 1776, aged 61-1-27 (both from Old Dederick Cem., West Camp). Issue:

    i) <u>Wilhelm³</u>, b. 11 Feb 1736 and bpt. Newton - sp.: Joh. Wilhelm Dieterich and Anna Margareta, grandparents (Loonenburg Luth. Chbk.). He md. Christina Bahr and had issue bpt. at Germantown Ref. Church. Wilhelm³ d. 5 Aug 1814, aged 78-5-24, and his wife Christina d. 15 June 1800, aged 65 (both from Schoonmaker Cem., Saugerties).

    ii) <u>Matthias³</u>, b. 14 Feb 1737 and bpt. Newton - sp.: Jurge Jong and Eva Maria Jurg (Loonenburg Luth Chbk.). He md. Maria Emmerich 12 March 1761. Papers in the estate of Matthias Dederick, late of Kingston, were given to his widow Gitty, Jury William Dedericks and Benjamin Snyder of Kingston 31 Dec 1808 (Ulster Co. Admin. Bk. C). Matthias d. 19 Dec 1808, aged 71-9-19, and Maria Emmerich Diderich d. 12 Dec 1773 (Old Dederick Cem., West Camp). An item in the Kingston Plebian of 3 Jan 1809 mentioned the death of Capt. Mathew Dederick at West Camp.

    iii) <u>Jacobus³</u>, b. 26 Feb 1739 and bpt. in his father's house - sp.: Jo. Matthys Junge and wife Catharina (Loonenburg Luth. Chbk.).

    iv) <u>Anna³</u>, bpt. 5 Jan 1741 - sp.: Johannes Diederich and Catharina Diederich (Katsbaan Ref. Chbk.). She md. Jacob Kunnies (HJ).

    v) <u>Jacobus³</u>, b. 10 Aug 1742 and bpt. at Newton - sp.: Henr. Graad and wife Mar. Catharina (Loonenburg Luth. Chbk.). He md. a Margaretha Diederich (HJ).

vi) <u>Maria³</u>, bpt. 27 Sept 1744 - sp.: Willem Broun and wife Elisabeth Jong (Katsbaan Ref. Chbk.).

vii) <u>Maria³</u>, b. 5 April 1746 and bpt. Kisket. - sp.: Willem Braun and wife Lisabeth (Loonenburg Luth. Chbk.). She md. Georg Carl 5 June 1764 (Germantown Ref. Chbk.).

viii) <u>Margaretha³</u>, bpt. 11 April 1748 - sp.: Frederich Diederich and wife Eva Graat (Katsbaan Ref. Chbk.). She md. Friderich Martin 25 April 1769 (Germantown Ref. Chbk.).

ix) <u>Elisabetha³</u>, b. 27 Oct 1749 and bpt. Newton - sp.: Johannes Mussier and wife Gertruy (Loonenburg Luth. Chbk.). She md. Johannes Mohr (Will).

x) <u>Zacharias³</u>, bpt. 21 April 1751 - sp.: Willem Diederich and Sara Diederich (Katsbaan Ref. Chbk.). He md. Catharina Bahr (HJ).

xi) <u>Catharina³</u>, bpt. 27 Dec 1752 - sp.: Pieter Jong and wife Elisabeth Moschius (Katsbaan Ref. Chbk.). She md. Jeremiah Wolf (Will).

xii) <u>Sara³</u>, bpt. 25 May 1755 - sp.: Wilh: Diederich and Anna Diederich (Germantown Ref. Chbk.).

xiii) <u>Eva³</u>, bpt. 5 May 1757 - sp.: Johannes Jong and Anna-atje Diederich (Katsbaan Ref. Chbk.). She md. Johannes Falckenburg (Will).

12) <u>Maria Catharina²</u> (HJ), md. Henrich Gradt 1734 (Catskill Ref. Chbk.).

CHRISTIAN DIETRICH (Hunter Lists #125)

The 1709er Christian Dietrich also came from 5450 <u>Niederbieber</u> (3 km. n. of Neuwied; Chbks. begin 1655). He was brother to the emigrant Johann Wilhelm Dietrich (see #124) of Ulster Co. and sp. Wilhelm's son Christian there in 1693. Christianus, s/o Symon Diederich at Segendorff, md. 9 Nov 1682 Magdalena, d/o Theiss Remagen there; Magdalena was bur. 8 Dec 1696. Christianus¹ md. 2nd as a widower at Segendorf Anna Maria, d/o the late Ludwig Becker at N. Bieber, 25 March 1700.

Christian¹ Dietrich made his first appearance on the Hunter Lists 1 July 1710 with 3 pers. over 10 yrs. of age and 2 pers. under 10 yrs; he was recorded next to Johann Wilhelm Dietrich on that date in the unalphabetised list. Later entries in Hunter fluctuated widely, the last being 13 Sept 1712 with 4 pers. over 10 yrs. of age. A Christ. Dederich was nat. at Albany 17 Jan 1715/16 (Albany Nats.). Christian Dietrich, Anna Maria and 1 child were at Heessberg ca. 1716/17 (Simmendinger Register); however,

this may have been his son Christian Jr.[2] (HJ). Christiaen Dederik
Sr. and Jr. were noted on various Palatine Debt Lists in the 1720's
(Livingston Debt Lists). It is extremely difficult to sort them all
out, as four different Christian Dietrichs were living along the
Hudson in the 1720's (HJ). The ch. of Christian[1] and Magdalena
Remagen were **all** b. at Segendorf:

1) <u>Matthias[2]</u>, bpt. 4 March 1683 - sp.: Christian Remagen,
   Theiss Fritsch, and Maria - sister of the child's father
   (Niederbieber Chbk.). He was bur. 11 Jan 1684.
2) <u>Elsa Christina[2]</u>, bpt. 16 Nov 1684 - sp.: Elsa Christina -
   sister of the child's mother at Ehlingen, Agnes - d/o the
   late Wilhelm Remagen at Segendorff, and Martinus - brother
   of the child's father (Niederbieber Chbk.).
3) <u>Margaretha[2]</u>, bpt. 23 Jan 1687 - sp.: Hans Henrich Wanbach
   - a soldier, and Margaretha - sister of the child's mother
   (Niederbieber Chbk.). She md. Anthonius Schneider 2 Nov
   1715 (West Camp Luth. Chbk.).
4) <u>Agnes[2]</u>, bpt. 22 Sept 1689 - sp.: Agnes - w/o Hans Wilhelm
   Dieterich, and Christian - brother of the child's father
   (Niederbieber Chbk.). Sp. strongly suggest she md. Christophel Fritz (HJ).
5) <u>Johann Christian[2]</u>, bpt. 13 March 1692 - sp.: Christ Schneider at Rodenbach, Johannes Remagen, and Anna Margaretha
   - wid/o Joh. Caspar Schön at N. Bieber (Niederbieber
   Chbk.). He was one of the four Christian Dietrichs nat.
   at Albany or Kingston 1715/16 (HJ). Christian Dederik's
   son was a Palatine Debtor 26 Dec 1718 (Livingston Debt
   Lists). Kris Daderick and Christean Dederick were both
   freeholders at East Camp in 1763 (Albany Co. Freeholders).
   There was also one of that name of the Rhinebeck Tax Rolls
   1744/45 through 1770 (Dutchess Co. Tax Lists). Christian
   md. Anna Maria Winegar and had ch.:
   i) <u>Anna Maria[3]</u>, b. 29 Jan 1719 - sp.: Abraham Lang and
      his wife, and the w/o Fridrich Rau (West Camp Luth.
      Chbk.). She md. Nicolaus Schreiber (HJ).
   ii) <u>Engel[3]</u> (HJ), md. Philip Henrich Mohr (HJ).
   iii) <u>Anna Barbara[3]</u> (HJ), d. 23 April 1803, aged 80 yrs.
      and md. Wilhelm Mohr (HJ).
   iv) <u>Christian[3]</u>, md. as s/o Joh. Christian 7 May 1748
      Sophia Reuschtler (Rhinebeck Luth. Chbk.). They had
      ch. at Red Hook Luth. and Rhinebeck Flats Ref. Churches.
   v) <u>Anna Catharina[3]</u> (HJ), md. Jacob Mohr (HJ).
   vi) <u>Agnes[3]</u>, bpt. 3 Oct 1732 - sp.: Stophel Frelch and
      Angenilge (Germantown Ref. Chbk.). She md. Michael

Herder (HJ).

vii) <u>Anna Christina</u>[3], b. 11 June 1735 - sp.: Wendel Jager
and wife Christina Elisabet, and Anna Maria (Lue)viry
(Rhinebeck Luth. Chbk.). She md. Georg Reisdorf (HJ).

viii) <u>Wilhelm</u>[3] (HJ), md. Catharina Mohr (HJ).

ix) <u>Margaretha</u>[3], b. 29 Sept 1737 - sp.: Jurge Schneider
and Gretje Falkenburgs (Loonenburg Luth. Chbk.). She
md. Michael Puls Jr. 11 April 1761 (Rhinebeck Flats
Ref. Chbk.).

x) <u>Gerhardt</u>[3], bpt. 21 May 1739 - sp.: Gerhard Winegar
and Anna Catharina Winegar (Red Hook Luth. Chbk.).
He md. Maria Frölich (HJ).

xi?) <u>Anna</u>[3], md. Peter Segendorff (HJ).

6) <u>Johann Christoph</u>[2], bpt. 7 Oct 1694 - sp.: Christoffel Noll,
Hans Ludwig Fischer, and Maria - wid/o Wilhelm Remagen,
all at Seg. (Niederbieber Chbk.).

By his 2nd wife Anna Maria Becker he had ch.:

7) <u>Johann Wilhelm</u>[2], bpt. 20 May 1702 - sp.: Jacob Honnert -
Gerichtsschöffe at Seg., Johann Wilhelm - surviving s/o
Johannis Rockenfelder at Wiedt, and Anna Maria - d/o
Christ Remagen at Seg. (Niederbieber Chbk.).

8) <u>Johann Peter</u>[2], bpt. 16 Sept 1703 - sp.: Peter Remagen,
Johann Peter Remagen..., and Johannata - wid/o the late
Caspar Busch at Neuwied (Niederbieber Chbk.).

9) <u>Anna Gertraud</u>[2], bpt. 21 June 1705 - sp.: Hans Wilhelm
Klein at Grävenwied, Elsa Gertraudt - d/o the late Thönges
Fischer at Seg., and Anna Magdalena - d/o the late Hans
Wilh. Michels at N.B. (Niederbieber Chbk.).

10) <u>Anna Catharina</u>[2], bpt. 16 Jan 1707 - sp.: Anna Cath. - w/o
Wilhelm Wirttges, Catharina - w/o Hans Wilhelm Kämmer,
and Christ Wilhelm Fischer, all at Segendorf (Niederbieber
Chbk.).

ANNA ELIZABETH DIETRICHIN (Hunter Lists #126)

The German home of this Dieterich family was 6344 <u>Ewersbach</u>
(10 km. n. of Dillenburg; Chbks. begin 1635). Johann Peter Diderich, s/o the late couple Henrich and Annels Diderich, md. Margareth, d/o the late couple Jost Henrich Krumbs and Annels from Mandeln, 29 Jan 1688. Joh. Peter Didrich, his wife and 5 ch. were
noted on petitions to emigrate from Ebersbach in 1709 (Nassau-
Dillenburg Petitions).

Anna Catharina Dietrich with 3 pers. over 10 yrs. of age and
1 pers. under 10 yrs. was on the Hunter Lists 4 Oct 1710; later

entries in the Journal called her Anna Elizabetha. In 1710, she
was enrolled next to Elisabetha Rohrbach, who also came from Ewersbach. Anna Eliz. Dietrich aged 20, orphan, and Anna Gertrude Deitrich aged 12, orphan, were mentioned together in N.Y. City in
1710/11 (Palatines In N.Y. City). The ch. of Johann Peter[1] Diderich and Margaretha all b. Mandeln were:

1) Anna Elisabetha[2], b. 26 Dec 1689 and bpt. as Annel - sp.:
   Johannes - s/o Henrich Diederich, Elsbeth - w/o Johannes
   Leuck, and Urthe - w/o Hans Georg Krumb (Ewersbach Chbk.).

2) Johann Henrich[2], b. 11 Nov 1692 - sp.: Johann Peter Wehe,
   Johann Henrich - s/o Johann Peter Diederich, and Barb. -
   w/o Johannis Krum (Ewersbach Chbk.).

3) "A Daughter"[2], b. 22 Nov 1695 - sp.: Johann Jost Schäfer,
   Anna Christina - w/o Gottfried Leuckels, and Catharina -
   d/o Hans Georg Thebus, all at Mandeln (Ewersbach Chbk.).

4) "A Daughter"[2], b. 19 April 1698 - sp.: Jacob Blumenstiehl,
   Margreth - w/o Hermann Thilmans, and Gertrud - w/o Hans
   Jacob Frize, all at Mandeln (Ewersbach Chbk.).

5) "A Daughter"[2], b. 17 June 1701 - sp.: Jacob Franck, Catharina - w/o Johann Leuckel, and Maria - d/o Hans Gorg
   Krumme, all at Mandeln (Ewersbach Chbk.).

6) " Child"[2], b. 24 March 1704 - sp.: Johannes - s/o Hans
   Gorg Wehe, Annels - d/o Jost Krumm, and Christina - d/o
   Jost Thilmans, all at Mandeln (Ewersbach Chbk.).

7) "A Daughter"[2], b. 24 June 1708 - sp.: Hans Henrich Krum,
   Catharina - w/o Johannis Krumm, and Liess - w/o Conrad
   Diederichs (Ewersbach Chbk.).

There were several early unplaced Dieterichs also: 1) a
Gerret Didrik sp. Johannes Vrelandt and Antje Didriks in 1727
(N.Y. City Ref. Chbk.), and 2) a Jacob Diederich was in the Scho-
harie Valley in the 1740's and had ch. Wilhelmus bpt. 25 Jan
1746/47, Christina b. 28 April 1749, and Maria Margaretha bpt. 24
Dec 1750 (all at Schoharie Ref. Church).

CONRAD DIEVENBACH & HIS MOTHER ANNA (Hunter Lists #127)

The ancestral home of the Pa. Dieffenbach family was 6908
Wiesloch (10 km. s. of Heidelberg; Chbks. begin 1698, Ref.). A
possible earlier home of the emigrant might have been 6366 Berstadt,
where a son Conrad was bpt. Feb 1660 to Claus and Elisabetha Wöl-
fin Dieffenbach; the age of this child, who disappears from Berstadt, matches the emigrant Conrad's age at London (HJ). Hans Conrad Dieffenbach, widower, and Barbara Christler, d/o the late
Hans Jacob Christler "auß der Schweitz im Obern Siebenthal an d.

Lenk (?)", md. 25 Oct 1702 (Wiesloch Chbk.). A note in the register added that the family emigrated 15 May 1709 with the family
of Georg Bleichardt Hauck to the West Indies (Hauck's notation
mentioned England and the Island of Carolina also). Hans koenraad
thirffenbach, his wife, 3 ch., and Anna thirffenbachrin were in
the 4th party in Holland on Capt. John Sewell's ship (Rotterdam
Lists). Conrad Tieffenbach aged 50, his wife, daughters aged 11,
4, and 1, cooper, Ref. were in the 4th arrivals in England in 1709
(London Lists); Anna Tieffenbach aged 74, Ref., widow was also
listed in the same group (London Lists).

Conrad Dievenbach made his first appearance on the Hunter
Lists 1 July 1710 with 3 pers. over 10 yrs. of age and 1 pers.
under 10 yrs. in the household; the family size increased 4 Oct
1710 to 4 pers. over 10 yrs. of age and 1 pers. under 10, and on
25 March 1712 the entry grew to 4 pers. over 10 yrs. of age and
2 pers. under 10 yrs. An entry dated 23 Sept 1713 noted 273 days
subsistence to his mother. Johan Coenraet Jefbach was nat. 31
Jan 1715/16 (Albany Nats.). Conrad Dieffenbach, Maria Barbara,
and 5 ch. were at Neu-Ansberg ca. 1716/17 (Simmendinger Register).
A ... Dievebak was a Palatine Debtor in one of the four villages
along the Hudson 26 Dec 1718 (Livingston Debt Lists). Conrad Dif-
fenbach was at Tulpehocken by 1725, and the will of John Conrad
Tiffebough was written 22 July 1737 and probated later that year
(Philadelphia Co. Wills: Bk. N, p. 322). His ch. from his 1st
marriage were:
    1) Jacob^2 (Will).
    2) Catharina Margaretha^2, md. ... Rieth (Will).
From his marriage to (Maria) Barbara Christler he had issue:
    3) Johann Ludwig^2, bpt. 10 Sept 1704 - sp.: Johann Ludwig
       Guth at Beyerthal (Wiesloch Chbk.).
    4) Maria Elisabetha^2, bpt. 8 July 1705 - sp.: Maria Elisabeth
       Dieffenbach (Wiesloch Chbk.). She md ... Ernst (Will).
    5) Anna Elisabetha^2, bpt. 5 Aug 1708 - sp.: Anna Elisabetha
       Laumer, single (Wiesloch Chbk.).
    6) Johann Adam^2 (Will), md. Maria Sybilla Kobel 13 Aug 1734
       at Tulpehocken (Stoever Chbk.). The will of Adam Diefen-
       bach of Tulpehocken was written 2 Oct 1772 and proved 16
       Dec 1777 (Berks Co. Wills: Bk. 2, p. 322). Issue:
         i) Johann Michael^3 (Will) 1735-1797, md. Maria Margar-
            etha Anspach.
        ii) Catharina^3 (Will) 1739-1817, md. Martin Schell.
       iii) Johann Georg^3 (Will) 1741-1788, md. Eva Maria Mag-
            dalena Kapp.

iv) <u>Johann Jacob</u>[3] (Will) 1744-1803, md. Sabina Schmelzer.

v) <u>Magdalena</u>[3] (Will) 1747/48.

vi) <u>Johann Peter</u>[3] (Will), md. Catharina Lewegud.

7) <u>Anna Dorothea</u>[2], b. 27 July 1714 - sp.: Jurg Maurer and wife Dorothea (West Camp Luth. Chbk.). She md. ... Hock or Haak (Will).

Ray J. Dieffenbach of Elizabethtown, Pa., a long-time expert on his family, was most kind in sharing data on the group, including his Wiesloch findings and the dates and marriages of the ch. of Johann Adam[2].

<u>JOHANNES DIEWEL</u> (Hunter Lists #128)

Johannes Diebel first appeared on the Hunter Lists 4 July 1710 with 2 pers. over 10 yrs. of age and 1 pers. under 10 yrs.; the entry for 4 Aug 1710 read 3 pers. over 10 yrs. and 1 pers. under 10, for 29 Sept 1711 3 pers. over 10 yrs. and 2 under 10, and for N.Y. City 25 March 1712 3 pers. over 10 yrs. and 1 under 10 yrs. The family name was called Diebel in most entries, Diewel in just a few. Johannes Deible aged 38 and Anna Catharina Deible aged 7 were listed together in N.Y. City in 1710/11 (Palatines In N.Y. City). Johannes Tibel, widower of the Graafschap v. Hoogsolmes, md. 15 Feb 1711 Margritje Eringer, wid/o Anthony Smit of the Graafschap Welburg (N.Y. City Ref. Chbk.). With his 1st wife in Germany Johannes[1] Teeple had ch.:

1) <u>Georg</u>[2] (HJ), noted as a single man auf dem Rarendantz ca. 1716/17 (Simmendinger Register). He was called brother of Lucas Dibbel in a letter of Pastor Berkenmeyer 19 July 1746 (<u>Luth. Church in N.Y. and N.J.</u>, p. 318). A Juny De Tipple was in Col. Thomas Ffarmar's Regt. in 1715 in N.J. (<u>Report of the State Historian</u>, Vol. I, p. 535). Georg Dibbel subscribed £1 N.J. money in 1727 (N.Y. City Luth. Protocol). Jerry Tipple Sr. and Jr. were noted in the Janeway Account Books.

2) <u>Lucas</u>[2] (HJ), called brother of Georg by Berkenmeyer in 1746 (<u>Luth. Church in N.Y. and N.J.</u>, p. 318). Lucas Dippel was conf. 2 Aug 1719 on the Raritons (N.Y. City Luth. Chbk.). He md. 17 May 1722 Anna Maria Streit (N.Y. City Luth. Chbk.). Lucas Dibbet subscribed 15 sh. N.J. money in 1727 (N.Y. City Luth. Protocol). He and his brother often were mentioned in various proceedings of the N.J. Lutherans (see both <u>Albany Protocol</u> and <u>Luth. Church in N.Y. and N.J.</u>). The will of Lucas Teeple of Bridgewater Twp., Somerset Co. was dated 20 Aug 1764 (N.J. Wills:

Lib. L, p. 85). His obituary in the Zion Luth. Chbk. related that he was b. in Aug 1696 in Hessish, md. May 1722,
was bur. 16 Jan 1774, and fathered 12 ch., of whom 6 were
living. Ch. mentioned in his will:

   i) John[3], the eldest.

  ii) Christopher[3]

 iii) Peter[3].

  iv) Ursula[3], md. John Appleman.

   v) A Daughter[3], md. Jacob Fusler.

  vi) A Daughter[3], md. John Meyer.

3) Anna Catharina[2] (Palatines In N.Y. City), md. 22 Nov 1724
David König (N.Y. City Ref. Chbk.).

By his 2nd wife Margaretha he had issue:

4) Johannes[2], b. 1 June 1712 - sp.: Daniel Schumacher, Jost
Bernhard and wife Eva (N.Y. City Luth. Chbk.). He was
mentioned in the Janeway Account Book 1735-44.

There were other Dippel-Teeple families in the N.Y. City area
who are difficult to fit in to either #128 or #129: 1) Anna Barbara, d/o the late Philipp Dippel of Flammborn in the commune Altzeyer, md. 16 Oct 1710 Engelbertus Wollbach, widower of commune
Neustatt, Marck-Brandenburg (West Camp Luth. Chbk.) - Anna Barbara
was conf. at N.Y. City 10 Oct 1710 (N.Y. City Luth. Chbk.), and
2) Anna Margareta Dippels from the Palatinate either was conf. or
joined the N.Y. City Luth. Church in 1709.

JOHANN PETER DIEWEL (Hunter Lists #129)

Johan Peter Diepel, his wife, and 3 ch. were in the 6th party
in Holland in 1709 (Rotterdam Lists). There was a Hans Peter, s/o
Hans Valentin Deipel and wife Anna Ottilia Frölich, bpt. 16 April
1689 at 6762 Oberndorf; this village was home to the N.Y. Spohns
and some of the emigrant Frölichs, but more research is needed to
firmly determine that this child is our Rhinebeck settler (HJ).

Johann Peter Diebel made his first appearance on the Hunter
Lists 4 July 1710 with 2 pers. over 10 yrs. of age in the family;
on 4 Oct 1710 the family was recorded with 3 pers. over 10 yrs.
The last entry 24 June 1712 showed 2 pers. over 10 yrs. of age
and 1 pers. under 10. Peter Diebel: 1 man, 1 woman, and 1 maid
9-15 were in Ulster Co. in 1710/11 (West Camp Census). Johan
Pieter Dipel was nat. 8 and 9 Sept 1715 (Kingston Nats.). Peter
Diebel, Anna Catharina, and 3 ch. were at Beckmansland ca. 1716/
17 (Simmendinger Register). He was listed on North Ward-Rhinebeck
tax rolls 1717/18 to Feb 1757 (Dutchess Co. Tax Lists). His family appeared on the St. Peter's Luth. family list in 1734. He was

a Surveyor of the Highway in Rynbeek in 1749 (<u>History of Rhine-</u>
<u>beck</u>, p. 49). He md. Anna Catharina Krost or Kroest and had ch.:

1) <u>Anna Maria²</u> (HJ), conf. 14 Oct 1716 at Rheinbeck (West
   Camp Luth. Chbk.). She md. Barent Zipperle Jr. 16 May
   1721 (Kingston Ref. Chbk.).

2) <u>Anna Eva²</u>, b. 23 Nov 1711 - sp.: Eva Catharina Manck, Elisabeth Jung, Gottfrid Ruehl, and J. Balthasar Kuester
   (West Camp Luth. Chbk.). She was conf. at Beekman's Mill
   22 June 1731 (N.Y. City Luth. Chbk.).

3) <u>Anna Catharina²</u>, b. 26 March 1714 - sp.: Johann Lamert,
   Anna Veronica Manck, Maria Gerdaut Buck ... (West Camp
   Luth. Chbk.). She was conf. 22 June 1731 at Beekman's
   Mill (N.Y. City Luth. Chbk.).

4) <u>Adam²</u>, bpt. 22 Jan 1716 - sp.: Adam Ekkert, Steven Frederich, and Elisabeth Lammertd (Kingston Ref. Chbk.). Adam
   Tippel made his first appearance on tax rolls in 1739/40
   (Dutchess Co. Tax Lists). An old mss. relating to him survives dated 1767 (Dutchess Co. Ancient Docs. #6190). The
   will of Adam Dipple, yeoman of Rhinebeck, was dated 2 Jan
   1797 and probated 22 June 1799 (Dutchess Co. Will Bk. B).
   He md. Catharina Eckert and had issue:

   i) <u>Johann Peter³</u>, bpt. 1 Oct 1739 - sp.: Johan Peter
      Dippel and Christina Dippel (Red Hook Luth. Chbk.).

   ii) <u>Johann Georg³</u>, bpt. 6 May 1741 - sp.: Johan Jurge
       Eckert and Catharina Evert (Red Hook Luth. Chbk.).
       He md. 1st Susanna (--) and 2nd Catharina (--) (HJ).

   iii) <u>Johannes³</u>, bpt. 22 May 1743 - sp.: Johannis Ekkert
        and Susanna Tippel (Rhinebeck Flats Ref. Chbk.).
        He md. Catharina Henrich (HJ).

   iv) <u>Catharina³</u>, bpt. 11 Aug 1745 - sp.: Johannes Eckert
       and Eva Eckert (Red Hook Luth. Chbk.). She md. Jo-
       hannes Tremper 29 Sept 1762 (Rhinebeck Flats Ref.
       Chbk.).

   v) <u>Elisabetha³</u>, b. 3 Dec 1747 - sp.: Peter Dippel and
      Barbara (Rhinebeck Luth. Chbk.).

   vi) <u>Rebecca³</u>, b. 17 Dec 1748 - sp.: Peter Schreiber and
       wife Anna Barbara (Rhinebeck Luth. Chbk.). She md.
       Conrad Eckert (HJ).

   vii) <u>Elisabetha³</u>, b. 21 Feb 1751 and bpt. Staatsburg -
        sp.: Hans Georg Marquart and Anna Barbara Tippel
        (Rhinebeck Luth. Chbk.). She md. Johann Nicolaus
        Kramer (HJ).

   viii) <u>Jacob³</u>, b. 7 June 1753 - sp.: Friedrich Treber and
         wife Barbara (Rhinebeck Luth. Chbk.).

    ix) <u>Maria</u>³, b. 18 Sept 1755 - sp.: 18 Sept 1755 - sp.:
        Hans Akkert and Maria Stryt (Rhinebeck Flats Ref.
        Chbk.). She md. David Puls (HJ).

     x) <u>Lena</u>³, b. 27 Dec 1757 - sp.: Adam Ackkert and Lena
        Trimper (Rhinebeck Flats Ref. Chbk.).

    xi) <u>Petrus</u>³, b. 1 Feb 1759 - sp.: Pieter Akkert and Eliz-
        abeth Frolich (Rhinebeck Flats Ref. Chbk.).

    xii) <u>Leah</u>³, b. 8 March 1761 - sp.: Johan Jurrian Stryt
        and wife (Rhinebeck Flats Ref. Chbk.). She md. Dan-
        iel Pouz (Will).

   xiii) <u>Salomon</u>³, b. 30 June 1763 - sp.: Adam Ecker and wife
        (Rhinebeck Luth. Chbk.).

    xiv) <u>Anna</u>³, b. 20 Oct 1766 - sp.: Joerg Kuckenheim and
        wife (St. Paul's, Rhinebeck).

5) <u>Susanna</u>², bpt. 24 Aug 1718 - sp.: Henderik Oel, Albert
   Beem, and Catrina Everts (Kingston Ref. Chbk.). She md.
   Georg Trimper 25 May 1754 (Rhinebeck Flats Ref. Chbk.).

6) <u>Christina</u>², b. 9 March 1720 and bpt. Rheinbeeck - sp.:
   Jurgen Adam Zufeldt, Anna Eckhards, and Ursula Frolicks
   (N.Y. City Luth. Chbk.). She was conf. 3 Nov 1745 at Rhynb.
   (Loonenburg Luth. Chbk.).

7) <u>Johann Peter</u>², bpt. 17 June 1722 - sp.: Jurian Ykert and
   Catrina Everts (Kingston Ref. Chbk.).

8) <u>Barbara</u>², conf. 3 Nov 1745 at Rhynb. (Loonenburg Luth.
   Chbk.) and md. as d/o Peter and Catharina 13 July 1756
   Johann Georg Marquard (Rhinebeck Luth. Chbk.).

<u>WERNER DIEWCHERT/DEUCHERT</u> (Hunter Lists #130)

The ancestral German home of the Mohawk Deygert family was
6451 Hüttengesäß (27 km. e. of Frankfurt), home of many 1709ers
who settled in that lovely N.Y. region. The entries for Hüttengesäß are at 6456 <u>Langenselbold</u> (2 km. s. of Hüttengesäß; Chbks. begin 1563). The earliest documented forefather of Werner Deygert
was <u>Hans Deichert</u>, who was bur. 8 April, 1700, aged 63 yrs.; the
w/o Hans was Gerdraut, who was bur. 26 June 1721, aged 81 yrs.
(Hüttengesäß Chbk.). The probable father of Hans Deichert was
the Sebastian Deucher, widower of Issigheim near Hanau, who md.
an Anna (Kiese?) 8 June 1640 (Langenselbold Chbk.). The ch. of
Hans Deichert and Gertraud b. Hüttengesäß and bpt. Langenselbold:

  + <u>Wörner</u>.

    <u>Catharina</u>, bpt. 22 March 1664 - sp.: Catharina, w/o Lentz
    Dörr.

    <u>Engel</u>, bpt. 19 Aug 1666 - sp.: Engel, d/o Hans Zieg.

Hans Caspar, bpt. 12 April 1669 - sp.: the s/o Caspar Horr.

Anna Catharina, bpt. 11 Feb 1672 - sp.: Catharina - d/o Christian Rüdel.

Anna Margaretha, bpt. 26 Jan 1675 - sp.: the d/o M. Hans Rack (Rapp?).

Clas, bpt. 22 June 1676 - sp.: Clas Zig.

Anna Catharina, bpt. 14 Jan 1683 - sp.: Catharina - d/o Philipp Köhler.

Johann Martin, bpt. 4 Jan 1687 - sp.: the s/o Christian Rudel. Wörner, s/o Hans Deichert at Hüttengesäß, md. Anna Catharina, d/o Valentin Ähl, 16 Jan 1690 at Selbold. Wörner Deichert of Hüttengesäß was listed 3 March 1701 with 2 oxen and 1 cart in a mss. found at the Birstein archives; on the same roll were members of the Kuhn, Bellinger, and Bender families who later emigrated to colonial N.Y.

Werner Deuchert made his first appearance on the Hunter Lists 4 July 1710 with 5 pers. over 10 yrs. of age and 2 pers. under 10 yrs.; the family size increased to 5 pers. over 10 yrs. and 3 under 10 on 4 Aug 1710, and to 6 pers. over 10 yrs. and 3 pers. under 10 24 June 1711. Warner Dyker, mayer, was on a list from a Palatine Debt Book dated March 1712/13 (Settlers & Residents, Vol. I, p. 16). Werner Reichert of Queensbury was a Palatine soldier in the Canadian expedition (Palatine Volunteers To Canada). Warnaer Deygert was nat. 11 Oct 1715 (Albany Nats.). Warner Deickert, his wife Anna Catharina, and 6 ch. were at Neu-Quunsberg ca. 1716/17 (Simmendinger Register). He was a patentee at Stone Arabia in 1723 (Stone Arabia Patent). The ch. of Wörner Deichert and Anna Catharina Ähl bpt. at Langenselbold were:

1) Anna Magdalena[2], bpt. 25 Feb 1691 - sp.: the sister of the mother. She was bur. 30 June 1691, aged 19 weeks old.
2) Elisabetha[2], bpt. 11 Jan 1694 - sp.: Henrich Zuber's wife.
3) Johann Peter[2], bpt. 9 Aug 1696 - sp.: M. Johan Friedrich Steuchs (?)... Johan Pieter Diegert was nat. 31 Jan 1715/16 (Albany Nats.). Peter Deickert and his wife Anna Elisabetha were at Neu-Heessberg ca. 1716/17 (Simmendinger Register). Peter's[2] wife was Anna Elisabetha Fuchs, and as Peter Teygert and Elysabet Vockien they sp. Mart: Dillenbeck in 1726 (Schenectady Ref. Chbk.). He signed a deed representing the Stone Arabia Ref. congregation 27 March 1744 along with Severines Deigert (History of Montgomery & Fulton Counties, p. 155).
4) Sabina[2], bpt. 5 Jan 1698 - sp.: Sabina - w/o Peter Blum.
5) Severinus[2], bpt. 3 Oct 1700 - sp.: Severin Rohrich. Sefreen Devgert was nat. 31 Jan 1715/16 (Albany Nats.).

Severinus Deygert was a patentee at Stone Arabia in 1723 (Stone Arabia Patent) and the leader of several military companies in the Mohawk region (<u>Report of the State Historian</u>, Vol. II).

6) <u>Anna Margaretha</u>[2], bpt. 1 Nov 1702 - sp.: the w/o Johann Caspar Schade.

7) <u>Ottilia</u>[2], bpt. 18 Feb 1705 - sp.: the d/o H. Lieut. Schäfer.

8) <u>Johann Conrad</u>[2], bpt. 4 Dec 1707 - sp.: Gesell - s/o Henrich Schäffer here. He was bur. 26 Aug 1708, aged 8 months.

ANANIAS DILL ALIAS THIEL (Hunter Lists #131)

The ancestral origins of the Dutchess Co. Teal family were at 6200 <u>Wiesbaden/Erbenheim</u> (4 km. n.e. of Mainz; Chbks. begin ca. 1660, but gaps). Ananias Thiel md. Maria Catharina, d/o Emmerich Schmid 27 Sept. 1703. She was bpt. Dec 1683 to Emrich and Agnes Schmitt. Emerich Schmidt d. of weakness of old age 15 Aug 1716, aged 77 yrs; his wife Agnesa was bur. 26 April 1694, aged 54 (from a chest stabbing?). Ananias Tiell, his wife and 2 ch. were listed near others from Erbenheim (i.e. Johan Jürg Sleiger, Peter Hagedoren, Johan Salbach, and Johan Peter Focks) on Capt. Robbert Bülman's ship in Holland in 1709 (Rotterdam Lists); also near Ananias Tiel on the small boat were a Johan Tiell and a Herman Tiell and their families. Ananias Tiel aged 36, his wife, and sons aged 5 and 1, Luth. wheelwright were at London later that year (London Lists).

Ananias Diel made his first appearance on the Hunter Lists 4 Aug 1710 with 2 pers. over 10 yrs. of age and 2 pers. under 10 yrs. The family decreased to 1 pers. over 10 yrs. and 2 under 10 4 Oct 1710, and then increased to 2 pers. over 10 yrs. and 2 under 10 yrs. 25 March 1711; the last entries in June and Sept of 1712 were for 3 pers. over 10 yrs. and 2 under 10 yrs. in the household. A special entry 31 Dec 1710 read 87 days subsistence for his frow Elis: Finkin; another note in Hunter that yr. recorded Elizabeth Finchin md. to Anan: Thiel (listed next to a Frantz Finck). Ananias Tiel was nat. 22 Nov 1715 (Albany Nats.). He made his first appearance on Dutchess Co. rolls in 1717/18 in the North Ward and continued until Feb 1733/34 when his widow was listed; on these tax lists he often was called Anannieas Tiel Wagenar (Dutchess Co. Tax Lists). The ch. of Ananias Thiel and his 1st wife Maria Catharina Schmidt were:

1) <u>Johann Martin</u>[2], bpt. 3 Dec 1704 - sp.: Johann Martin Krag and Johann Conrad Rossenbecker Jr. (Erbenheim Chbk.).

Martin Tiel was nat. 17 Jan 1715/16 (Albany Nats.). He
was conf. at Rheinbeeck 8 April 1722 (N.Y. City Luth.
Chbk.). Martynus Teell made his first appearance on tax
rolls in the North Ward in 1727/28 (Dutchess Co. Tax Lists).
Martin[2] md. Anna Magdalena Caputski and had ch.:

    i) <u>Maria Catharina</u>[3], b.at Rynbek 15 March 1728 - sp.:
       Laurens Diel and Maria Catharina Suffelt (N.Y. City
       Luth. Chbk.).

   ii) <u>Magdalena</u>[3], bpt. 5 April 1730 - sp.: Hendrick Beem
       and Magdalena Beem (Red Hook Luth. Chbk.). Marlena
       Diel was conf. 21 Oct 1744 at Rhynbek (Loonenburg
       Luth. Chbk.). She md. Peter Treber (HJ).

  iii) <u>Elisabetha</u>[3], bpt. 16 Dec 1732 - sp.: Jonis Diel and
       Elisabeth Diel (Germantown Ref. Chbk.).

   iv) <u>Johann Jacob</u>[3], b. 19 Feb 1736 - sp.: Joh: Dater, and
       Anna Maria - d/o Valentin Schaffer (Rhinebeck Luth.
       Chbk.). Data on his family and his wife Elisabetha
       are found in N.Y. State D.A.R. Bible Records, Vol.
       114, p. 75).

    v) <u>Maria Barbara</u>[3], b. 30 Oct 1738 and bpt. Newton - sp.:
       Hans Veltin Scheffer and wife Maria Barbel (Loonen-
       burg Luth. Chbk.).

   vi) <u>Henrich</u>[3], bpt. 6 May 1741 - sp.: Heinrich Thiel and
       Anna Barbara Dieter (Red Hook Luth. Chbk.). He md.
       Anna Barbara Müller 3 Dec 1769 (Red Hook Luth. Chbk.).
       They had ch. at Rhinebeck Luth. and Manorton Luth.
       Churches.

  vii) <u>Maria Catharina</u>[3], bpt. 5 Feb 1744 - sp.: Lerentz
       Diel and wife Maria (Red Hook Luth. Chbk.).

 viii) <u>Lorentz</u>[3], b. 29 Feb 1748 - sp.: Laurentius Thiel
       and Maria, his wife (Rhinebeck Luth. Chbk.).

2) <u>Johann Lorentz</u>[2], bpt. 27 March 1708 - sp.: Joh. Lorenz
   Thiel, and Joh. Nicol - s/o Erasimus Merthen (Erbenheim
   Chbk.). He was nat. 19 Oct 1743 (Mss. in N.Y. Public
   Library). Louwrens Diel was a surveyor of fences in the
   North Ward in 1731, and constable there in 1732 (Dutchess
   Co. Supervisor's Records). His wife Maria was conf. 24
   May 1732 at Rhynbek (Loonenburg Luth. Chbk.). He was noted
   as having one slave in Dutchess Co. in 1755 (<u>Smith's His-</u>
   <u>tory of Rhinebeck</u>, p. 50). The will of Laurentz Deal of
   Rhinebeck Precinct was dated 21 June 1783 and probated 17
   May 1786 (<u>Fernow Wills</u> #530). Issue with wife Maria:

    i) <u>Catharina</u>[3], b. 19 Jan or 19 June 1735 - sp.: Hannes
       Lammert and Catarina Barringer (Rhinebeck Luth.

Chbk.). She md. Jacob Tremper in 1758 or 1759 (Rhinebeck Flats Ref. Chbk.).

By his 2nd wife Elisabetha Finck the ch. of Ananias[1] Tiel were:

3) <u>Johann Peter[2]</u>, b. 10 Jan 1714 - sp.: Johann Peter Hagendorn and Catharina Steiger (West Camp Luth. Chbk.).

4) <u>Johann Henrich[2]</u>, b. 15 March 1718 - sp.: Johann Lorentz Henrich and wife Regina (West Camp Luth. Chbk.). He made his first appearance on Rhinebeck tax rolls in 1741/42. The will of Henry Diel of Rhinebeck Precinct was dated 13 June 1771 and probated 20 Feb 1772 (<u>Fernow Wills</u> # 493). He md. Gertraud Neher and had ch.:

  i) <u>Elisabetha[3]</u>, bpt. 4 Sept 1743 - sp.: Elisabeth Diel (Red Hook Luth. Chbk.).

  ii) <u>Johannes[3]</u>, bpt. 24 Feb 1745 - sp.: Joseph Neher and Christina Neher (Red Hook Luth. Chbk.). He d. 13 Aug 1794, aged 48 yrs. and 6 months (Rhinebeck Luth. Cem.).

  iii) <u>Anna[3]</u>, b. 1 Jan 1747 - sp.: Zacharia Haber and wife Anna, and Christina Neher (Rhinebeck Luth. Chbk.).

  iv) <u>Carl[3]</u>, b. 11 Feb 1749 - sp.: Lorentz Thiel and wife Maria (Rhinebeck Luth. Chbk.). He md. Rebecca (--), and his estate was probated 16 Jan 1804 (Columbia Co. Admin. Bk. B).

  v) <u>Catharina[3]</u>, b. 30 June 1751 - sp.: Wilhelm Thiel and wife Hannah (Rhinebeck Luth. Chbk.).

  vi) <u>Jacob[3]</u>, bpt. 24 April 1753 - sp.: Marte Theil and Magdalena Copbutser (Red Hook Luth. Chbk.).

  vii) <u>Anna Maria[3]</u>, bpt. 26 Oct 1755 - sp.: Lorens Diehl and Anna Maria Diehl (Red Hook Luth. Chbk.).

  viii) <u>Henrich[3]</u>, b. 12 May 1758 - sp.: Christoffel Koebach and wife (Rhinebeck Flats Ref. Chbk.). He d. 9 July 1826, aged 69 yrs. at Athens (Hudson Gazette 18 July 1826).

  ix) <u>Zacharias[3]</u>, b. 2 May 1761 - sp.: Zacharias Neher and Catharina Tiel (Rhinebeck Luth. Chbk.).

  x) <u>Wilhelm[3]</u>, b. 4 Feb 1763 - sp.: Wilm. Tiel and wife Johanna (Rhinebeck Luth. Chbk.). He d. 31 March 1843, aged 80-1-27 (St. Paul's in Wurt. Cem.).

  xi) <u>Lorentz[3]</u>, b. 20 Nov 1765 - sp.: Lorentz Tiel and wife Anna Maria (Rhinebeck Luth. Chbk.).

  xii) <u>Cornelius[3]</u>, b. 26 Oct 1767 - sp.: Cornelius Miller and wife Christina (Rhinebeck Luth. Chbk.).

5) <u>Wilhelm[2]</u> (HJ), conf. 24 May 1732 at Rhynbek (Loonenburg Luth. Chbk.). He made his first appearance on tax rolls in 1741/42 (Dutchess Co. Tax Lists). Wilhelm md. Johanna

Reisly (Reuschle) and had issue:

 i) Christopher[3], b. 10 June 1744 and bpt. at Rhinebeck
    - sp.: Christopher Cremer and wife Barbel (Loonenburg
    Luth. Chbk.). He first appeared on Rhinebeck tax
    rolls in June 1768 (Dutchess Co. Tax Lists). Papers
    in the estate of Christopher Teal, deceased, of Clav-
    erack were issued to Maria Agnes Teal and Abraham
    and Andrew Teal 2 Jan 1811 (Columbia Co. Admin. Bk.
    B). Maria Agnes, wid/o Christ., d. 1831, aged 87 yrs.
    (Cem. n. of Ghent Turnpike).

 ii) Elisabetha[3], b. 10 Oct 1745 - sp.: Lisabeth Diel, the
    grandmother (Loonenburg Luth. Chbk.).

iii) Lorentz[3], b. 26 Aug 1747 - sp.: Lorentz Thiel and
    wife Maria (Rhinebeck Luth. Chbk.). Lawrence Teal d.
    1818, aged 72 yrs. (Cem. n. of Ghent Turnpike).

 iv) Anna Barbara[3], b. 17 Sept 1749 - sp.: Henrich Thiel
    and wife Gertraut (Rhinebeck Luth. Chbk.).

  v) Magdalena[3], b. 28 Aug 1751 - sp.: Andries Reisley
    and Elisabeth Tiel (Rhinebeck Flats Ref. Chbk.).

 vi) Sabina[3], b. 3 Oct 1753 - sp.: Christiaan Diederik
    and his wife (Rhinebeck Flats Ref. Chbk.).

vii) Johanna[3], bpt. 7 July 1756 - sp.: Cristoffel Kramer
    and Barbara Kramer (Red Hook Luth. Chbk.).

viii) Wilhelm[3], b. 2 Jan 1761 - sp.: Jacob Neher and wife
    Elisabeth (Rhinebeck Luth. Chbk.).

 ix) Andreas[3], b. 30 Aug 1763 - sp.: Andreas Reuschli
    and wife Barbara (Rhinebeck Luth. Chbk.). An Andrew
    Teal d. 12 Jan 1832, aged 68-1-13 (Rhinebeck Luth.
    Cem.).

WILHELM DILL (Hunter Lists #132)

Wilhelm Dill made his first appearance on the Hunter Lists
4 July 1710 with 1 pers. over 10 yrs. of age and 2 pers. under 10
in the family; on 4 Aug 1710 the family diminished in size to 1
pers. over 10 yrs. and continued at that level until the end of
1712. Jno. Wm. Dill of Annsberg was a soldier in 1711 (Palatine
Volunteers To Canada). Wilhelm Diell, his wife and 1 child were
at Neu-Yorck ca. 1716/17 (Simmendinger Register). Wilhelm Tiel md.
Sarah De Pu and had ch.:

 1) Gertraud[2], bpt. 22 July 1716 - sp.: Harme Bussing and wife
    Sara Selove (N.Y. City Ref. Chbk.).

 2) Johannes[2], bpt. 11 Aug 1717 - sp.: Jan De Lamontangne and
    Elisabeth Lamontagne (N.Y. City Ref. Chbk.).

 3) Dorothea[2], bpt. 24 Aug 1718 - sp.: Willem De Puw and Eva

Franse (N.Y. City Ref. Chbk.).

4) Elisabetha[2], bpt. 5 Nov 1723 - sp.: Tomus De Peu and
   wife Cornelia (Tarrytown Ref. Chbk.).

5) Maria[2], bpt. 27 April 1728 - sp.: Abram Lent and wife
   Maria (Tarrytown Ref. Chbk.).

ANNA CLARA DILLIN (Hunter Lists #133)

Anna Clara Dill made her first appearance on the Hunter Lists
4 Aug 1710 with 1 pers. over 10 yrs. of age in the family; her
other entries with 1 pers. over 10 yrs. were on 4 Oct 1710 and
the cumulative entry 5 Oct 1710 through 5 Oct 1711.

BARBARA DILLEBACHIN, HER SON MARTIN (Hunter Lists #134)

The ancestral home in Europe of the Dillenbach family was
Lauperswil in Switzerland. A mss. dated 12 May 1732 from Trachsel-
wald, Amtsrechnung recorded:

> Martin Dällenbach of Lauperswil has emigrated to Amer-
> ica and resides in Schaggarill. He commissions his bro-
> ther Johannes Dällenbach, who has settled in Zweibrück-
> en, to withdraw the property which he has in this coun-
> try, amounting to 13 crowns, 10 btz., from which 10 per-
> cent emigration tax is deducted. (List of Swiss Emigrants
> in the Eighteenth Century to the American Colonies, Vol.
> II, p. 41).

According to The Dällenbachs in America, by Andrew L. Dillenbeck
and Karl M. Dallenbach, Nicholas Dällenbach was the husband of
Anna Barbara Zerlin and the father of (Jorg) Martin Dillenbach.

Barbara[1] Dillebachin made her first appearance on the Hunter Lists 4 July 1710 with 2 pers. over 10 yrs. of age in the family. On 4 Oct 1710 the entry read "for himselve" and 1 pers. over
10 yrs. of age, and on 31 Dec 1710 the notation recorded 1 pers.
over 10 yrs. of age "for Martin the son." The family increased to
2 pers. over 10 yrs. of age 24 June 1711; the entry was for 3
pers. over 10 on 24 June 1712, and for 2 pers. over 10 yrs. and
1 pers. under 10 on 13 Sept 1712. The son of Barbara[1] was:

1) (Georg) Martin[2], called her son on the Hunter Lists. Martin Dilleback of Queensbury was a soldier in 1711 (Palatine Volunteers To Canada). Martin Dielenbach, Elisabetha
   and 2 ch. were at Neu-Cassel ca. 1716/17 (Simmendinger Register). He was a patentee at Stone Arabia in 1723 (Stone
   Arabia Patent). By his 1st wife Sarah Catharina (Wohleben - HJ), he had a daughter:

   i) Anna Margaretha[3], b. 1 Aug 1712 - sp.: Jacob Boe-
      schaar and Anna Margaretha Baumann (West Camp Luth.
      Chbk.).

Jorg Martin Dillenbach, widower, md. Anna Elisabetha Castelmann, d/o Johann Dietrich Castelmann, 24 Feb 1713 (West
Camp Luth. Chbk.). Their offspring were listed in Pastor
Sommer's list of families in the Mohawk region in 1744;
they were:

ii) Henrich[3] (HJ), md. 19 March 1735 Anna Margaretha Wagner (Stone Arabia Luth. Chbk.). A full list of his
ch. can be found in the Stone Arabia Luth. Chbk. in
a family list. Hendrick Delipag was a freeholder in
1763 at Stonrabie (Albany Co. Freeholders).

iii) Johann Christian[3] (Family List), md. Anna Maria Six.
Christian Dillenbag was on a roll of delinquents in
Capt. Soverinus Deyger's Co. in 1763 (Report of the
State Historian, Vol. II, p. 799). Christean Delipag
was a freeholder in 1763 at Stonrabie (Albany Co.
Freeholders). He was a Loyalist in the revolution.

iv) Anna Maria[3] (Family List).

v) Wilhelm[3] (Family List), md. Eva (--).

vi) Elisabetha[3] (Family List).

vii) Martinus[3], bpt. 1726 (?) - sp.: Jan Pieter Teygert
and Elysabet Vockien (Schenectady Ref. Chbk.). Martin
Jr., William, Dittrick and Baltes Dillenbag were all
in Capt. Soffrines Deychert's Co. 20 March 1757 (Report of the State Historian, Vol. II, p. 783). He or
his father was the Martines Tielibag registered as
a freeholder of Stonrabie in 1763 (Albany Co. Freeholders).

viii) Johann Dieterich[3] (Family List).

ix) Johann Balthasar[3] (Family List).

x) Johann David[3] (Family List).

On Pastor Sommer's 1744 family list was a Johannes Dillenbach
with wife Magdalena and a daughter Maria Elisabetha; he was separate from the family of Martin[2]. He may have been an elder son
of Martin or, more likely in my opinion, a later arrival from Germany or Switzerland (HJ).

CATHARINA DILTEYIN (Hunter Lists #135)

Hans Jacob Diltey, his wife, and 5 ch. were in the 6th party
of Palatines in Holland in 1709 (Rotterdam Lists); they were surrounded on that list by emigrants from the Siegen-Westerwald region
of Germany (i.e. Hans Willem Sneider, Bernhart Smit, Johan Maul).
The Dilthey family was prominent throughout that section, and the
name was found at Hachenburg, Flammersfeld, Siegen and Runkel.

Catharina Dildeyin made her first appearance on the Hunter Lists 4 Aug 1710 with 5 pers. over 10 yrs. of age and 1 pers. under 10; the entry for 4 Oct 1710 read 2 pers. over 10 yrs. On 24 June 1711, the family had 6 pers. over 10 yrs. of age, and the last entry 24 Dec 1711 noted 4 pers. over 10 yrs. in the household. The ch. of Johann Jacob and Catharina[1] Diltey were:

1) Frantz[2] (HJ), living with Hermann Dildein and their sister, next to Georg Dillbein and his family, at Hackensack ca. 1716/17 (Simmendinger Register). The will of Francis Dildine of New Brunswick, Middlesex Co., was written 3 Dec 1750 and proved 26 Feb 1750/51 (N.J. Wills: Lib. E, p. 510). He and his wife Maria had issue:

    i) Maria[3], bpt. 9 Oct 1720 - sp.: Jurie Tildey and wife Annatje (New Brunswick Ref. Chbk.).

    ii) Catharina[3], bpt. 15 Nov 1724 (New Brunswick Ref. Chbk.).

    iii) "A Child"[3], bpt. 5 Oct 1735 (New Brunswick Ref. Chbk.).

    iv) Magdalena[3], bpt. 31 Dec 1738 - sp.: Maria Dilden (New Brunswick Ref. Chbk.).

    v) Johannes[3], bpt. 27 March 1743 - sp.: Laurens Williamson and Maria Dildin (New Brunswick Ref. Chbk.).

    vi) Abraham[3] (Will).

    vii) Elisabetha[3] (Will).

2) Georg[2] (HJ), joined the N.Y. City Ref. Church as Joh[s] Georgius Pilday 27 May 1712. Georg Dillbein, his wife, and 1 child were at Hackensack ca. 1716/17 (Simmendinger Register). He and wife Christiana had a daughter:

    i) Elisabetha[3], bpt. 25 March 1722 (Readington Ref. Chbk.).

He and wife Anna Lefooij had a daughter:

    ii) Magdalena[3], bpt. 31 March 1731 - sp.: Christiaen Hersel and Lena Reddix (Harlingen Ref. Chbk.).

3) Hermann[2] (HJ), joined the N.Y. City Ref. Church as Joh[s] Hermannus Pilday 27 May 1712 with letters from Germany. Hermann Dildein was listed with Frantz Dilbein and their sister at Hackensack ca. 1716/17 (Simmendinger Register). Harman Dildyne, Ag[d] was a freeholder of Lebanon Twp in 1741 (Hunterdon Co. Freeholders). The will of Herman Dildine of Lebanon Twp was dated 16 Oct 1769 and proved 27 Oct 1769 (N.J. Wills: Lib. 14, p. 144). With wife Cere he had:

    i) Henrich[3], bpt. 26 Feb 1721 - sp.: Frans Tildey and wife Maery (New Brunswick Ref. Chbk.).

With wife Jannet De Voor he had:

    ii) Saertje[3], bpt. 18 May 1727 - sp.: Jacobus De Voor

and Engeltje Speets (Harlingen Ref. Chbk.).
Other ch. named in the will of Hermann[2] were:
iii) Daniel[3] (Will).
iv) Jane[3], md. (--) Savage (Will).
v) Eve[3] (Will).
vi) Hermann[3] (Will).
vii) Elisabetha[3] (Will).
viii) Rachel[3] (Will).
ix) Catharina[3] (Will).
x) Anna[3] (Will).

An Elisabetha Dilthey md. Harmen Laan by 1745; she may have been the sister of Hermann[2] and Frantz[2] mentioned by Simmendinger ca. 1716/17 (HJ). Georg[2] in all probability was the Uriah Dildine, whose will dated 17 June 1760 and probated 30 April 1761 was witnessed by a Harman Lane (N.J. Wills: Lib. 10, p. 478)(HJ).

PETER DINANT (Hunter Lists #136)

Hans Pieter Dinant, his wife, (daughter) Susanna, (son) Hans Philip, and 4 other ch. were in the 2nd party in Holland in 1709 (Rotterdam Lists). Peter Dinant aged 39, his wife, sons aged 11, 9, 7, and 5, a daughter aged 3, Ref., joiner, were in England later that year (London Lists).

Peter Dinant made his first appearance on the Hunter Lists 4 Aug 1710 with 2 pers. over 10 yrs. of age and 2 pers. under 10 yrs. of age in the family; the size diminished to 2 pers. over 10 yrs. and 1 pers. under 10 yrs. 4 Oct 1710. His wife was named Anna Margaretha, and they had ch.:
1) Susanna[2] (Rotterdam Lists).
2) Hans Philip[2] (Rotterdam Lists).
3) Susanna[2], bpt. 28 Oct 1711 - sp.: Anthony Slegt and Maria Catrina (Kingston Ref. Chbk.).

JACOB DINGS (Hunter Lists #137)

The ancestral European home of the Hudson Valley Dings family was 5239 Höchstenbach (7 km. s.w. of Hachenburg; Chbks. begin 1670, but gaps). Johan Jacob Dinges from Mündersbach md. Gerdraut Ax from Höchstenbach 20 Oct 1691. Johann Jacob[1] was probably the s/o Anna Maria Dinges, the smith's wife from Mindersbach, who d. 8 Feb 1672; Anna Gerdraut was probably the d/o Jost Henrich Ax from Höchstenbach, who d. eight days before his wife's burial on 5 May 1698. Hans Jacob Dinges, his wife, and 4 ch. were in the 6th party at Rotterdam in 1709 among others (i.e. Johan Schü, Johan Diderig Schniter, Johan Klein) from near the Hachenburg region (Rotterdam Lists).

Jacob Dings made his first appearance on the Hunter Lists 4 July 1710 with 4 pers. over 10 yrs. of age; entries for 1710-11 were somewhat erratic after that date, fluctuating between 4 pers. over 10 yrs. and 1 under 10, 5 pers. over 10 yrs., and then 4 over 10 yrs. once again. Jacob Dings of Annsberg was a soldier in 1711 (Palatine Volunteers To Canada). He sp. Wilhelm Georg, also from Höchstenbach, in the upper German colonies in 1711 (West Camp Luth. Chbk.). Johan Jacob Dings was nat. 8 and 9 Sept 1715 (Kingston Nats.). Jacob Dhons, his wife and ch. were at Heessberg ca. 1716/17 (Simmendinger Register). Hans Jacob Denkes made his first appearance on tax rolls in the North Ward in 1717/18 and continued to be listed there until 1737/38 (Dutchess Co. Tax Lists). He was surveyor of the fences in the North Ward in 1722; in 1723 he and Adam Dings witnessed the will of Margery Alsteyn (Dutchess Co. Supervisor's Records). The ch. of Johann Jacob[1] and Gertraut Ax Dings were:

1) Anna Maria[2], bpt. 26 June 1692 - sp.: Piter Becker - s/o the landlord, Maria - his sister of Rosbach, and Anna Catharina Ax at Höchstenbach (Höchstenbach Chbk.). She md. Johann Jacob Melius (HJ).

2) Johann Adam[2], bpt. 22 Sept 1695 - sp.: Adam Görg, Johann Mirten, and Eva Frey - all from Mindersbach (Höchstenbach Chbk.). Adam Ding was nat. 17 Jan 1715/16 (Albany Nats.). He made his first appearance on North Ward rolls in 1720/21 (Dutchess Co. Tax Lists). He md. Anna Eva Schu (proof of her maiden name found in the Gallatin Ref. Chbk. on a pre-Oct 1759 membership roll) and had issue:

   i) Gertraud[3], bpt. as Gerritje at East Camp and b. 3 April 1720 on White Clay's Kill - sp.: Martinus Schoe and Anna Elisabeth Things (N.Y. City Luth. Chbk.). She md. Martin Müller 2 Sept 1735 (Kingston Ref. Chbk.), unless the Gertraud who md. Müller was a younger d/o the emigrant Jacob[1] (HJ).

   ii) Johannes[3], b. 15 Feb 1722 at Camp Queensberry - sp.: Johannes Schmidt and Anna Maria Nelius (N.Y. City Luth. Chbk.). He joined the Red Hook Luth. Church 2 April 1743 and md. Anna Maria Donges (HJ). Papers in the estate of John Dings of Gallatin were issued to Peter Knickerbocker Jr. 9 June 1809 (Columbia Co. Admin. Bk. B).

   iii) Eva Gertraud[3], bpt. 11 Aug 1726 at Haneman Saalbach's at Kamp aged 10 weeks - sp.: Gertrud Denks and Peter Bauer (N.Y. City Luth. Chbk.). She appears to have

been rebaptised 29 Jan 1744 at the Germantown Ref.
Church (HJ). She md. 8 Aug 1748 Georg Kilmer (Germantown Ref. Chbk.).

    iv) <u>Elisabetha[3]</u>, md. 28 Aug 1750 Johann Georg Rohrich
       (Germantown Ref. Chbk.).

     v) <u>Maria Elisabetha[3]</u>, b. 9 May 1732 - sp.: Joh. Thys
       Smid, Phil. Kahn, Mai Liese Smids, his wife (sic)
       (Loonenburg Luth. Chbk.).

    vi) <u>Anna Maria[3]</u>, b. 23 Feb 1739 and bpt. Goghkam(enko)
       (Ancram) - sp.: Philip Kuntz and Anna Maria Milius
       (Loonenburg Luth. Chbk.). She md. Wilhelm Donges (HJ).

  vii) <u>Maria[3]</u>, b. 27 April 1741 and bpt. Goghkam(enko) (An-
       cram) - sp.: Henrich Heitzrood and wife Anna Maria
       (Loonenburg Luth. Chbk.). She md. Johannes Striebel
       (HJ) and d. 10 Feb 1808, aged 66 yrs. and 10 months
       (Dings Cem.).

3) <u>Anna Elisabetha[2]</u> (HJ), md. Martin Schu (HJ).

4) <u>Johann Theis[2]</u>, bpt. 6 Jan 1707 - sp.: Johanes Theiss from
   Minnersbach, Johan Henrich ..., and Anna **Maria** ... (Höchstenbach Chbk.).

LAZARUS DORN ALIAS TRUM (Hunter Lists #138)

Annette K. Burgert found the origins of Lazarus Dorn at 6799
<u>Ulmet</u> and 6587 <u>Baumholder</u>; a comprehensive study of his European
background will be found in the Addenda Section of this book. Lazarus Dorn aged 48, with his wife, sons aged 14 and 7, and daughters
aged 10, 9, 6, 1½, and ¼, Ref., husbandman and vinedresser, were
in the 3rd arrivals in England in 1709 (London Lists).

Lazarus Dorn made his first appearance on the Hunter Lists
1 July 1710 with 2 pers. over 10 yrs. of age and 4 pers. under 10
in the household; on 4 Oct 1710, he was noted next to Peter Heyd,
his brother-in-law from Baumholder (HJ). His entry on 25 March 1711
read 2 pers. over 10 yrs. and 3 pers. under 10. Lazarus Dhorn and
Anna Catharina with 4 ch. were at Hunderston ca. 1716/17 (Simmendinger Register). He made his first appearance on tax rolls in
1722 and continued in the North Ward until 1740/41 when his widow
was listed; her listing was passed over to Johannis Dorn in 1746/
47 (Dutchess Co. Tax Lists). The ch. of Lazarus[1] and his wife
(called Anna Margaretha at West Camp Luth. in 1715 and 1718) were:

1) <u>Maria Barbara[2]</u>, b. 13 April 1715 - sp.: Conrad Schmid and
   Maria Barbara Heydorn (West Camp Luth. Chbk.).

2) <u>Michael[2]</u>, bpt. 12 Jan 1718 - sp.: Michael Werner and wife
   (West Camp Luth. Chbk.).

3) Johannes[2] (HJ), md. as single man b. Dutchess Co. 6 Dec
1746 Elisabetha Eberhardt, single woman b. Kisketmens in
Albany Co. (Rhinebeck Flats Ref. Chbk.). Dutchess Co. Ancient Docs. #2277 show a surviving mss. for him. His ch.
Jacob, David, and Jeromy Doran were noted in a list of
scholars at the Free School in Johnstown ca. 1769 (Book
Of Names, p. 74). His ch. were:

   i) Catharina[3], bpt. 1 Aug 1749 - sp.: David Ekker and
     Eva Frolich (Rhinebeck Flats Ref. Chbk.).

  ii) Johannes[3], bpt. 23 Dec 1750 - sp.: Johannes Kremer
     and Catryn Kreemer (Rhinebeck Flats Ref. Chbk.).

 iii) Jacob[3], b. 8 Dec 1752 - sp.: Johannes Everhart and
     Catrina Stryt (Rhinebeck Flats Ref. Chbk.).

  iv) Petrus[3], b. 23 Sept 1754 - sp.: Ulrich Krebser and
     Rachel Oostrander (Rhinebeck Flats Ref. Chbk.).

   v) Jacob[3], b. 16 Oct 1756 - sp.: Henrik Akker and Mag-
     dalena Bheem (Rhinebeck Flats Ref. Chbk.).

  vi) David[3], b. 19 Oct 1758 (Rhinebeck Flats Ref. Chbk.).
     A descendant, Vona E. Smith of Coquitlain, B.C., re-
     ports that David Doran d. July 1861 at his farm in
     Cape Rich District, Ontario at a great age.

 vii) Jeremias[3], b. 5 July 1760 (Rhinebeck Flats Ref. Chbk.).

4) Hans Veltin[2], bpt. 4 Jan 1730 - sp.: Velten Woe-leven, Johannes Lammert, and Dorothea Veltin (Kingston Ref. Chbk.).

There were several unplaced Dorns found in colonial N.Y.:
1) A Thomas Doorn and wife Mally had ch. bpt. at Loonenburg Luth.
and Kinderhook Ref. Churches in the 1740's, 2) a Peter Dorn was
noted once in 1723/24 on the Dutchess Co. Tax Lists, and 3) a
Mrs. Margaret Dorne d. Oct 1817, aged 102 at Johnstown, N.Y.
(N.Y. Spectator 31 Oct 1817).

JOHANNES DÖRNER (Hunter Lists #139)

Johannes Dörner often was enrolled near emigrants from the
Neuwied-Westerwald region of Germany. In searching that area, it
was noted that a Johannes Dörner md. Anna Eva, d/o Christ Mäurer,
16 Jan 1704 at 5239 Alpenrod; also that a Johannes Dörner, s/o
Johannes Dörner at Unnau, md. Gertraut, d/o Henrich Kölsch, Dom.
16 p. Trin: 1687 at 5439 Marienberg.

Johannes Dörner made his first appearance on the Hunter Lists
1 July 1710 with 2 pers. over 10 yrs. of age and 1 pers. under 10
yrs. Johannes Dorner aged 36 and Anna Margaretta Dorner, dead,
aged 40, were in N.Y. City in 1710/11 (Palatines In N.Y. City).

JACOB DÖRNER (Hunter Lists #140)

The ancestral origins of Jacob Dörner were at 6504 Oppenheim (20 km. s. of Wiesbaden; Chbks. begin 1650, Luth.). Hans Jacob Derner, his wife, and 2 ch. were on Capt. Johan Facit's ship in Holland in 1709 (Rotterdam Lists).

Jacob Dörner made his first appearance on the Hunter Lists 30 June 1710 with 3 pers. over 10 yrs. of age; he was registered on the same page and just a few names from other 1709ers from Oppenheim and environs (i.e. Niclaus Rauch, Anna Margretha Göbelin, and Magdalena Streithin). The family size increased to 3 pers. over 10 yrs. and 1 pers. under 10 24 June 1712. Jacob Dörner, his wife and 2 ch. were at Beckmansland ca. 1716/17 (Simmendinger Register). Jacob Torner was on Palatine Debt Lists 1718, 1719, 1721 and 1722 (Livingston Debt Lists). He and his 1st wife Anna Ursula had ch.:

1) Hans Georg[2], md. as s/o Hans Jacob 9 Aug 1707 Maria Elisabetha Fuchs (Oppenheim Luth. Chbk.).

2) Christiana Sophia[2], b. 8 Feb 1696 - sp.: Christiana Sophia - w/o Master Henrich Dietmers, citizen and baker here (Oppenheim Luth. Chbk.). Jacob[1] was called from Mannheim in her baptismal entry.

3) Anna Margaretha[2], b. 24 Feb 1697 - sp.: Anna Marg. - single d/o the late Wilhelm (Witters?) (Oppenheim Luth. Chbk.). Anna Margretha Doerner was conf. 19 July 1710 at N.Y. (West Camp Luth. Chbk.). She md. Thomas Carter 27 Dec 1718 at the Pastor's lodgings at Lonenburg (N.Y. City Luth. Chbk.).

4) Anna Ursula[2], b. 7 Jan 1701 - sp.: Anna Ursula - w/o the late Wilhelm Witters, formerly Markschieffer here (Oppenheim Luth. Chbk.).

Hans Jacob Dörner, widower here, md. Anna Margaretha Düssel, d/o the late Johannes Düssels - formerly citizen and Schmidburgischer Hofmann, 10 April 1708. They may have had issue:

5?) Dorothea[2], md. Peter Daniel (HJ).

There were other Torners in the Hudson Valley in the early part of the 18th century. One Wilhelm Torner and wife Abigail had ch. at Camp in the 1720's, but he was called "an Englishman" in contemporary records (N.Y. City Luth. Chbk.).

JACOB DORNHEISER (Hunter Lists #141)

Jacob Dornheuser (sic) had but one entry on the Hunter Lists on 24 Dec 1711 with 1 pers. over 10 yrs. of age in his household.

ANNA ELIZABETH DONTZBACHIN (Hunter Lists #142)

Anna Elizabeth Donsbachin made only one appearance on the Hunter Lists on 4 Oct 1710 with 3 pers. over 10 yrs. of age in the family. She may have been the Anna Elisabeth Duntzbach who sp. Johann Grad in 1714 and Michael Honigen in 1717 (West Camp Luth. Chbk.), unless this sp. was the w/o Frantz Dontzbach #143 (HJ).

FRANTZ DONTZBACH (Hunter Lists #143)

The German home of the Dunsbach family of East Camp was 6349 Breitscheid (6 km. w. of Herborn; Chbks. begin 1636, but gaps). The earliest known ancestor of the American line was Hannes Donsbach. On 6.p. Trin: 1677 at Schönbach, Frantz Donsbach, s/o Hannes Donsbach at Breidscheidt, md. Christina, d/o the late Lutz Kolb at Rod. He md. 2nd Anna Elisabetha (--) ca. 1691-92 (HJ). Frantz Donsbach, Joh. Jost Görg, and Joh. Görg Koppenstein - each with their wife and 7 ch. - petitioned to leave Germany in 1709 from the village of Breitscheid (Nassau-Dillenburg Petitions).

Frantz Donsbach made his first appearance on the Hunter Lists 4 July 1710 with 4 pers. over 10 yrs. of age; the entry for 4 Oct 1710 read 2 pers. over 10 yrs. and 2 pers. under 10. On 24 June 1711, the household had 2 pers. over 10 yrs. and 1 pers. under 10 yrs. of age. Frans Dinsbagh was on the roll of the Independent Companie of the Mannor of Livingston 30 Nov 1715 (Documentary History of N.Y., Vol. III, p. 704). Franz Dompsback was nat. 17 Jan 1715/16 (Albany Nats.). He and his 1st wife Christina had ch.:

1) Jost Henrich[2], bpt. Dom. Qua simodogeniti: 1678 - sp.: Jost Henrich Petri from Waldaubach and Barba Georg here (Breitscheid Chbk.). A note added that the child d.
2) "A Young Daughter"[2], bpt. Dom. 22. p. Trin: 1680 - sp.: Theiss Betz at Waldaubach and Enche Jung at Birgk (Breitscheid Chbk.). As the female sp. was an Enche, which meant Anna in this region and time, perhaps this child may have been the Anna Donsbach who md. the 1709er Georg Bäst by 1712 (HJ).
3) Jost[2], bpt. Dom. 3. p. Trin: 1684 (Breitscheid Chbk.). An added notation read den 15. Jul sepultus.
4) "A Young Daughter"[2], bpt. 1. p. Epiph: 1687 - sp.: Peter Schmitt and Anna Margaretha Gross (Breitscheid Chbk.).
5) Johann Henrich[2], bpt. Dom. 19. p. Trin: 1690 - sp.: Joh. Henrich Möller in the new mill, Liess - wid/o Johann Jost Schlemmer, and the d/o Thönges Feisch (Breitscheid Chbk.). A note added that the child d.

With his 2nd wife Anna Elisabetha the ch. of Frantz[1] Donsbach were:

6) <u>Peter</u>[2], bpt. 8 Jan 1693 - sp.: Peter Petri, single, and Anna Catharina Philips (Breitscheid Chbk.). He was bur. 27 May 1694.

7) <u>"A daughter"</u>[2], bpt. 7 April 1695 - sp.: Maria Kettcherhard (?) (Breitscheid Chbk.).

8) <u>Johann Jost</u>[2], bpt. 25 April 1698 - sp.: Johann Jost Petri the Heimberger (Breitscheid Chbk.). He may have been "the son" bur. 20 March 1701.

9) <u>"A Son"</u>[2], bpt. 27 Feb 1702 - sp.: Peter Petri and Anna Elsbeth - w/o Johannes Scheff, both from Breidscheidt (Breitscheid Chbk.). "A son" was bur. 1 April 1702.

10) <u>"A Daughter"</u>[2], bpt. 27 Feb 1702 - sp.: same as above (Breitscheid Chbk.). "A daughter" was bur. 9 April 1702.

11) <u>"A son"</u>[2], bpt. 2 March 1704 - sp.: Jost Henrich Schelts - s/o Lurentz Schelt, and Catharina - d/o Joh. Jost Petri at Breitscheid (Breitscheid Chbk.). The sp. strongly sugests that this son was the East Camp resident <u>Jost Henrich Donsbach</u> (HJ). Jost Hend. Dompsbach was nat. next to Franz Dompsback 17 Jan 1715/16 (Albany Nats.). Hend: Donsbag was a Palatine Debtor 23 Feb 1726 (Livingston Debt Lists). Hendrick Dunsbagh was a freeholder in 1763 at East Camp (Albany Freeholders). The will of Joost Hendrick Dontzbach of East Camp, yeoman, was dated 7 March 1785 and probated 26 April 1790 (Columbia Co. Will Bk. A). He md. Maria Margaretha Scheffer and had issue:

    i) <u>Magdalena</u>[3], md. 5 Nov 1748 Wilhelm Betzer (Germantown Ref. Chbk.).

    ii) <u>Johannes</u>[3], bpt. 8 days old 11 Aug 1726 at Haneman Saalbach's at Kamp - sp.: Lip. Scheffer and wife Anna Elisabeth (N.Y. City Luth. Chbk.).

    iii) <u>Eva</u>[3], bpt. 3 weeks old 5 May 1728 at Kamp - sp.: Dan. Reiseberger and Anna Elis. Scheffer (N.Y. City Luth. Chbk.). The papers in the estate of Eva Duntzbach of Germantown, dec., were dated 14 Jan 1800 (Columbia Co. Admin. Bk. B).

    iv) <u>Johann Philip</u>[3], bpt. 1731 - sp.: Philip Shafer and Elizabeth Schafer (Red Hook Luth. Chbk.).

    v) <u>Catharina</u>[3], bpt. 13 April 1735 - sp.: Nicolaus Linck and Catherina Schmidt (Germantown Ref. Chbk.). She md. Adam Clum (Will).

    vi) <u>Henrich</u>[3] (Will).

    vii) <u>Maria</u>[3] (Will), md. Henry Yager (Will).

    viii) <u>Elisabeth</u>[3] (Will).

12) "A Son"[2], bpt. 10 Nov 1707 - sp.: Johann Henrich Philips, and Anna Elisabetha - w/o Jost Henrich Staals there. These godfathers were cancelled in the register, leaving alone Joh. Peter Göbel as sp. (Breitscheid Chbk.). The child d. suddenly before bpt. He had been the surviving twin of a deadborn daughter bur. 27 Oct 1707 (Breitscheid Chbk.).

JOHANN PETER DOPFF (Hunter Lists #144)

Margretha, d/o Peter Dopf of Metter in the commune of Zwey-brucken, md. Jerg, s/o Alexander Demuth late of Runckel on the Lohn 26 Oct 1714 (West Camp Luth. Chbk.). The actual village of origin for the Top family was 6759 Medard (6 km. s.w. of Meisen-heim; Chbks. begin 1639). The earliest known ancestor of the American line was the elder Hans Peter Dopp, whose widow Catharina **md.** Hans Job Weickardt 21 Nov 1678. The ch. of the elder Hans Peter Dopp were:

Catharina Margaretha, bpt. 15 July 1663.

Elisabetha Barbara, bpt. 22 April 1666.

+ Hans Peter, bpt. 8 Sept 1667.

Hans Peter Dopp, s/o the late Hans Peter Dopp, md. 14/24 Feb 1688 Anna Margaretha Bernhardt, d/o Leonhardt Bernhardt. Anna Margreta, d/o Leonhardt Bernhardt, was bpt. 5 Jan 1668; Maria Magdalena, w/o the innkeeper Leonhardt Bernhardt at Medard d. 7/17 March 1687, aged 62 yrs.

Peter Dopff made his first appearance on the Hunter Lists 4 Oct 1710 with 5 pers. over 10 yrs. of age in the family. Jno. Peter Dopff was a soldier from Queensbury in 1711 (Palatine Volunteers To Canada). Johan Peter Dopp was nat. 8 and 9 Sept 1715 (Kingston Nats.). Peter Dob, his wife and 3 ch. were at Heessberg ca. 1716/17 (Simmendinger Register). Peter Dob made his initial appearance in the North Ward on tax rolls in 1717/18 and continued at Rhinebeck until his farm was noted in 1755 (Dutchess Co. Tax Lists). He was an overseer of ye King's highway in the North Ward in 1725 (Dutchess Co. Supervisor's Records). He and his wife Anna Margaretha Bernhardt had issue:

1) "A Stillborn Little Son"[2], bur. Good Friday 1689 (Medard Chbk.).

2) Anna Margaretha[2], bpt. 5/15 Feb 1691 - sp.: Hans Job Veick-ardt, Item Anna Margaret - w/o Nickel Berendt at Cronen-berg, and Anna Elisabet - single d/o Leonhardt Bernhardt (Medard Chbk.). She md. 26 Oct 1714 Georg Demuth (West Camp Luth. Chbk.).

3) Johann Peter Jr.[2] (HJ), nat. 8 and 9 Sept 1715 (Kingston

Nats.).

4) <u>Johannes</u>[2], bpt. 5 Jan 1695 new calendar - sp.: Leonhardt
Bernhardt - Wirth, and Johannes Bernhardt - tailor, as
well as his daughter (Medard Chbk.). Johannes Dobb was
nat. 8 and 9 Sept 1715 (Kingston Nats.). He md. 14 May
1717 Maria Barbara Eckhardt (Akkert et var.) (Kingston
Ref. Chbk.). Johannes Dob made his first appearance on the
North Ward tax rolls in 1717/18 and continued until Feb
1733/4 when his widow was listed (Dutchess Co. Tax Lists).
His widow md. 12 Jan 1735 Willem Smit, and later in 1749
Urias Nelson (Rhinebeck Flats Ref. Chbk.). Johannes[2] had
issue:

  i) <u>Johann Peter</u>[3], b. 15 March 1718 - sp.: Peter Dopf
  and Christina Uhl (West Camp Luth. Chbk.). Peter
  John Dop made his first appearance on Rhinebeck rolls
  in 1740/41 (Dutchess Co. Tax Lists). Dutchess Co. Ancient Docs. survive for him (unless these are for
  his grandfather Johann Peter[1] - HJ) #119, 1734-36,
  and 1739. He md. Gertraud Kramer (HJ).

  ii) <u>Martin</u>[3], bpt. 13 March 1720 - sp.: Marthen Boek and
  Elisabeth Freelig (Kingston Ref. Chbk.). Marte Dop,
  step-son of William Smith of Rhinebeck, registered
  his livestock mark 14 May 1741 (Dutchess Co. Supervisor's Records). He md. Maria Barbara Berg (HJ).

  iii) <u>Johann Georg</u>[3], bpt. 4 Feb 1722 - sp.: Joh. Jury Ekker
  and Margriet Dop (Kingston Ref. Chbk.).

  iv) <u>Eva</u>[3] (HJ), conf. at Newton 7 March 1740/41 (Loonenburg Luth. Chbk.).

  v) <u>Margaretha</u>[3] (HJ), joined the Red Hook Luth. Church
  6 May 1741. She md. Hermann Schnuch or Schu (HJ).

  vi) <u>David</u>[3], bpt. 5 April 1730 - sp.: David Eckert and
  Catarina Eckert (Red Hook Luth. Chbk.). A 1769 An-
  cient Doc. (#6967) survives for him. He md. Rachel
  Ostrander 4 Feb 1758 (Rhinebeck Flats Ref. Chbk.).

  vii) <u>Anna Catharina</u>[3], b. 5 March 1734 - sp.: Georg Ekhart
  and wife Anna Cath. (Rhinebeck Luth. Chbk.).

5) <u>Maria Margaretha</u>[2], bpt. 21/31 March 1697 - sp.: Caspar
Jackel - Saltzmesser from Meisenheim, Maria Margaret - w/o
Thebald Tebelts, and Anna Maria - w/o his brother Hans
Nickel Tebelts (Medard Chbk.).

6) <u>Anna Catharina</u>[2], bpt. 3 Oct 1701 - sp.: Peter Wilhelm,
Nickel Gravius - s/o Jacob Gravios, and Anna Cath. - d/o
Jacob Bernhardt (Medard Chbk.).

LUDWIG DRAUTH'S WIDDOW (Hunter Lists #145)

Ludwig Drauth (no "widdow" mentioned in the journal) first appeared on the Hunter Lists 1 July 1710 and again 4 Aug 1710 with 1 pers. over 10 yrs. of age. Johannes Lodowick Troit aged 9, an orphan, was bound to Laur Van Hook of N.Y. 26 Sept 1710 (Apprenticeship Lists).

PETER DRECHSLER (Hunter Lists #146)

John Peter Drechsler aged 28, his wife, and a son aged 1, Luth., husbandman and vinedresser, were in the 1st arrivals at London in 1709 (London Lists).

Peter Drechsler made his first appearance on the Hunter Lists 4 Aug 1710 with 2 pers. over 10 yrs. of age and 1 pers. under 10 yrs. The family size increased 13 Sept 1712 to 2 pers. over 10 yrs. and 2 pers. under 10 yrs. Documents survive dealing with this emigrant at Albany (N.Y. Col. Mss. Vol. 59, pp. 61d and 64d,e,f). Pr. Drosselaer - Fery queen was noted March 1712/13 in Palatine Debt Lists (Livingston Papers in Settlers & Residents, Vol. I, p. 16). Peter Teackselar was entered in rolls for the South Ward in 1717/18 and 1718/19 (Dutchess Co. Tax Lists). Peter Trexler took the oath of allegiance to Pa. in 1730/31 (Statutes At Large Of Pa.). The will of Peter Trexler was proved in 1758 (Philadelphia Co. Will Bk. L, p. 180). The ch. of Peter[1] and Catharina Drechsler were:

1) **Anna Catharina[2]**, b. 26 Sept 1714 - sp.: Jacob German and wife Anna Catharina (West Camp Luth. Chbk.). Catarina Drechsler md. Joh: Georg Schumacher 9 Nov 1730 at Macungie (Stoever Chbk.).

2) **Margaretha[2]**, b. 26 Sept 1717 at Pachquee, back of Lange Rack and bpt. at Pieter Lassen's - sp.: Jan De Lange and Maria Elisabeth Schwitsler (N.Y. Luth. Chbk.).

John Trexler Warren's History of the John Peter Trexler Family gives other ch. to the emigrant Peter[1], such as Jeremiah[2] (who may have been named for Jeremy Schletzer, listed next to Peter Drechsler at London in 1709 - HJ), Peter[2], John[2], and Anna[2].

CATHARINA DREUTHIN (Hunter Lists #147)

The ancestral home of Catharina Dreuth most probably was 6479 Ober-Mockstadt (23 km. n.e. of Frankfurt; Chbks. begin 1656, but gaps). Catharina[1] often was noted on the Hunter Lists near other emigrant families from this town, especially the 1709ers Rheinhardt and Werner Schäffer, next to whom she was noted in 1710 and

1711. Andreas Drauth, s/o Johannes Drauth at Dauernheim, md. Catharina, d/o Johannes Culmann at Nieder-mogstadt, 10 Feb 1687. She was bur. 15 May 1703, aged 41 yrs. and 2 weeks. Andreas Drauth, inhabitant at Niedermogst., md. Anna Catharina, wid/o the late Joh. Achilles Pauli, 23 Aug 1703.

Catharina Dreuth made her first appearance on the Hunter Lists 30 June 1710 with 4 pers. over 10 yrs. of age and 1 pers. under 10 yrs.; the entry for 4 Aug 1710 read 5 pers. over 10 yrs. and 1 pers. under 10. The entry on 4 Oct 1710 read 1 pers. over 10 yrs. and 1 pers. under 10, and the family increased to 2 pers. over 10 yrs. on 31 Dec 1710. The ledger noted that she md. Henrich Korn (who was noted with Rheinhardt and Werner Schäffer on either side of him and near Catharina Dreuth 4 Oct 1710). The ch. of Andreas Drauth and his 1st wife Catharina Culman were:

1) Anna Juliana[2], bpt. 13 Feb 1697 - sp.: Juliana - w/o Johs. Lauster (Ober-Mockstadt Chbk.).

2) Joh. Nicolaus[2], bpt. 16 June 1700 - sp.: Joh. Nicolaus - s/o Joh. Culman (Ober-Mockstadt Chbk.).

ELIZABETH DREUTHIN (Hunter Lists #148)

Wörner Drauth, s/o Henrich Drauth - inhabitant here, md. Elisabeth, d/o Peter Schmidt - formerly inhabitant here, 28 July 1687 (Ober-Mockstadt Chbk.). She may have been the emigrant (HJ).

Elizabeth Dreuth was noted with 1 pers. over 10 yrs. of age 24 Dec 1711 on the Hunter Lists. The ledger added that she was in Werner Schäffer's family; this makes yet another connection between the emigrating Dreuths and the Ober-Mockstadt Schäffers (HJ). An Elisabetha Traut sp. Johann Nicolaus Michel in 1716 (West Camp Luth. Chbk.).

There was a John Traut in the 1st arrivals in England in 1709; he was aged 40 and came with his wife, sons aged 10 and 6, was a brewer and Ref. (London Lists). Emigration Materials from Lambsheim in the Palatinate, by Heinrich Rembe (courtesy of Don Yoder) noted that the Lambsheim man had a wife Catharina and a son Johannes bpt. 5 July 1699. He was a Ref. brewer accused of Pietism in 1706 and sentenced with others to cleaning the town ditches; according to the Lambsheim deed registers, he sold his house in the Kirchgasse to Adam Fauth in 1709. However, I can find no evidence that this man was a N.Y. arrival (HJ).

ANDREAS DRUMM (Hunter Lists #149)

The ancestral home of the emigrant 1709er Andreas[1] Drumm

was <u>Niederkirchen i/Ostertal</u> (4 km. e. of St. Wendel; Chbks. begin
1666, but gaps). Margaretha, w/o Endres Tromm from Marth, d. 7 Feb
1702. Andreas Trom, widower from Marth, md. Maria Magdalena, wid/o
the late Hanß Melchior Schopp from Rehweiler, 16 May 1702. Andreas
sp. his fellow emigrant Christophel Hüls at Niederkirchen in 1708.
Andreas Trumm from Marth (Sarre) was noted in Germany as an emigrant from the Duchy of Zweibrücken in 1709 (<u>Emigrants from the
Palatinate to the American Colonies in the 18th Century</u>, p. 32).
Andries Drom, his wife, and 5 ch. were noted next to Kristoffel
Hilsch on Capt. John Coate's ship in Holland 10 July 1709 (Rotterdam Lists).

Andreas Drumm first was entered on the Hunter Lists 1 July
1710 with 3 pers. over 10 yrs. of age and 1 pers. under 10 yrs.;
the family decreased to 2 pers. over 10 yrs. and 1 pers. under 10
on 4 Aug 1710. On 4 Oct 1710 the entry noted 5 pers. over 10 yrs.,
and on 31 Dec 1710 it read 4 pers. over 10 yrs. Beginning 24 June
1711, the family size was 3 pers. over 10 yrs. and 1 pers. under
10. Andreas Drom signed a document with a group of other Palatine
carpenters in 1712 (N.Y. Col. Mss.: Vol. 57, p. 27a). A letter
with the signatures of Johannes Roschmann and Andreas Trum was
dated 24 Oct 1712 (Livingston Papers, Reel #3). Johan Andries
Drom was nat. 22 Nov 1715 (Albany Nats.). Andreas Trum, Mar. Magdalena, and 5 ch. were at Hunderston ca. 1716/17 (Simmendinger
Register). And's Trum was on Palatine Debt Lists in 1718 and 1721
(Livingston Debt Lists). He made his first appearance on tax rolls
in 1723/24, was noted in the North Ward in 1726/27, and continued
to be listed until 1737/38 in that precinct (Dutchess Co. Tax
Lists). The ch. of Andreas[1] Drumm and his 1st wife Margaretha were:

1) <u>Johann Philip[2]</u>, bpt. Auf Jacobi: 1692 - sp.: Joh. Bricius
   of Achtelsbach, Philips Schu of ..., Anna Maria - w/o
   Reinhard Scherer, and Anna - w/o (--) Keller (?) (Wolfers-
   weiler Ref. Chbk.). A Philip Tromm and wife Maria Catharina were noted at the Readington Ref. Church in N.J. in
   1740.

2) <u>Maria Catharina[2]</u>, bpt. 28 Nov 1694 - sp.: Hans Adam Glock-
   ner of Buppack, Clara Catharine - d/o Hans Adam Müller the
   Judge, and Maria - d/o Hans Adam Trumb (Niederkirchen
   Chbk.). Mary Trum aged 15, d/o (--) Trum, was bound to
   Rich'd Willet of N.Y. 28 Sept 1710 (Apprenticeship Lists).

3) <u>Hans Jacob[2]</u>, bpt. 10 March 1697 - sp.: Hans Adam Glockner,
   Jacob Hans - s/o Hans Adam Muller the Presbyter, Catharina - w/o Johan Abra(ham) Scherer, and Anna Maria - w/o
   Jacob Glockner (Niederkirchen Chbk.). Jacob Drom made his
   first appearance on tax rolls in 1737/38 and continued

at Rhinebeck on the rolls until his estate was listed in
1773 (Dutchess Co. Tax Lists). He joined the Red Hook Luth.
Church 14 Sept 1741. Jacob Drom, single man b. Germany,
md. Anna Storm, single woman b. Phillipsburgh, 3 May 1724
(Tarrytown Ref. Chbk.). They had ch.:

   i) <u>Margaretha</u>[3], bpt. 10 April 1725 - sp.: Pieter Storm
     and wife Grietie (Tarrytown Ref. Chbk.). Margreda
     Drum joined the Red Hook Luth. Church 14 April 1745.
     She md. Peter Strack (HJ).

  ii) <u>Johannes</u>[3], bpt. 28 Oct 1727 - sp.: Joannis Storm and
     Zara Storm (Tarrytown Ref. Chbk.). Johannes Droom
     joined the Red Hook Luth. Church 26 April 1747. He md.
     Elisabetha Kreissler and had ch. bpt. at Red Hook
     Luth. and Rhinebeck Luth. Churches. The will of Jo-
     hannis Drum of Granger was dated 14 March 1807 and
     probated 24 July 1807 (Columbia Co. Will Bk. C).

 iii) <u>Maria</u>[3], bpt. 19 Sept 1730 - sp.: Wolfart Ecker and
     wife Marrethen (Tarrytown Ref. Chbk.). She md. Simon
     Cool (HJ).

  iv) <u>Anna</u>[3], bpt. 26 June 1733 - sp.: Dirck Storm and wife
     Eliezabeth (Tarrytown Ref. Chbk.). She joined the
     Red Hook Luth. Church 15 May 1751. She md. Wolfert
     Eckert (HJ).

Jacob[2] md. 2nd Margaretha Kuhn and had issue:

   v) <u>Andreas</u>[3], bpt. 6 Nov 1738 - sp.: Klaus Stickel and
     Margriet Trom (Red Hook Luth. Chbk.). He md. Anna
     Margaretha Kranckheyt (HJ).

  vi) <u>Veltin</u>[3], bpt. 17 Aug 1740 - sp.: Velde Koen and Cath-
     arina Wies (Linlithgo Ref. Chbk.). He md. 11 Dec 1764
     Margaretha Backes (Red Hook Luth. Chbk.).

 vii) <u>Nicolaus</u>[3], bpt. 31 Dec 1744 - sp.: Nicklas Stickel
     and Margrit Stickel (Red Hook Luth. Chbk.). He md.
     25 Oct 1764 Catharina Bautzer (Red Hook Luth. Chbk.).

viii) <u>Petrus</u>[3], bpt. 6 Oct 1747 - sp.: Peter Pulver and Sus-
     anna Pulver (Red Hook Luth. Chbk.).

  ix) <u>Jacob</u>[3], bpt. 11 March 1750 - sp.: Jacob Jager and
     Elizabeth Jager (Red Hook Luth. Chbk.).

   x) <u>Zacharias</u>[3], bpt. 5 July 1752 - sp.: Zacharias Smit
     and his wife (Rhinebeck Flats Ref. Chbk.). He md.
     Lena Bautzer (HJ).

4) <u>Hans Theobald</u>[2], bpt. 2 Feb 1702 - sp.: Hans Theobald - s/o
Simon Karst from Marth, Theobald - s/o Hans Glöckner from
Buppach, Anna Christina - d/o the late Carl Schenck, and
Anna Margaretha - d/o Hanß Nickel Hauch in Berglangenbach

184

(Niederkirchen Chbk.).

By his 2nd wife Maria Magdalena, he had ch.:

    5) <u>Anna Margaretha</u>[2], bpt. 22 Feb 1704 - sp.: Hans Adam Meyer
       from ..., Velten Follriegel (?) from Rehweiler, Hans Theo-
       bald - s/o Jacob Büttels at Marth, Marg. - w/o Nickel Mül-
       ler from Brucken, Anna Margaretha - d/o Hans Glöckner, and
       Maria Margaretha - w/o Hans Adam Müller from Leutersweil
       (Niederkirchen Chbk.). She md. Nicolaus Stickel (HJ).

    6) <u>Maria Margaretha Engel</u>[2], bpt. 18 Oct 1706 - sp.: Hans Nic-
       kel - s/o Hans Adam Müller the Judge at Marthe, Anthoni
       Becker of Hampersweiler, Anna Maria - wid/o Leonhard Schel-
       bek of Dambach in Birkenfeld, Margaretha - wid/o Jacob
       Hellrigell, Maria Cath. - d/o the late Carst, and Engel -
       d/o Joh: Abraham Scherer (Niederkirchen Chbk.).

    7) <u>Sophia Catherina</u>[2] (possibly Regina Catharina), bpt. 15
       April 1709 - sp.: Joan Nickel Gerhard from Leutersweil,
       Joan Jacob Tromb from Dambach, Eva Catharina - w/o Chris-
       tophel ... from Marth, and Regina (?) Catharina - d/o
       Hans Nickel Hauch (Zauch?) from Berglangenbach (Nieder-
       kirchen Chbk.). This entry was written badly and is dif-
       ficult to read (HJ).

    8) <u>Susanna</u>[2] (HJ), md. Peter Pulver (HJ).

<u>NICLAUS DRUMBAUR</u> (Hunter Lists #150)

Niclas Trombauer aged 33, his wife, a son aged 6, daughters
aged 3 and 3/4, Rom. Cath., husbandman and vinedresser, were in
the 1st arrivals in England in 1709 (London Lists).

Niclaus Drumbaur made his first appearance on the Hunter
Lists 4 Aug 1710 with 2 pers. over 10 yrs. of age and 3 pers. under 10 yrs.; the entry for 4 Oct 1710 read 1 pers. over 10 yrs.
of age and 3 pers. under 10. On 24 June 1711 he was recorded with
3 pers. over 10 yrs. and 2 under 10, and on 24 June 1712 with 3
pers. over 10 yrs. and 3 pers. under 10 in the household. Nicolas
Trompoor was nat. 8 and 9 Sept 1715 (Kingston Nats.). Nicolaus
Trumbohr and Magdalena with their ch. were at Beckmansland ca.
1716/17 (Simmendinger Register). Nicolas Dromboer was a freeholder
of Kingston in 1728 (Ulster Co. Freehodlers), and he appeared
in the Kingston Trustees Records (Bk. 2, pp. 72-74). The Hunter
Lists suggest that he md. twice (HJ); by his 1st wife he had ch.:

    1) <u>Johann Jacob</u>[2] (HJ), nat. next to Nicolas[1] 8 and 9 Sept
       1715 (Kingston Nats.).

    2) <u>Agnes</u>[2] (HJ), md. 28 Sept 1727 Johann Peter Sachs (Kings-
       ton Ref. Chbk.).

3) Dorothea², md. as d/o Nicolaus¹ 16 April 1730 Johann Jacob
   Maul, s/o Friederich Maul (N.Y. City Luth. Chbk.).

By his 2nd wife Magdalena Stier, the ch. of Nicolaus¹ were:

4) Anna Christina², b. 2 June 1712 - sp.: Justina - w/o Bernhard Lueckhard (West Camp Luth. Chbk.). She md. Paul
   Schmidt (HJ).

5) Anna Barbara² (HJ), md. Hans Georg Schmidt (HJ).

6) Anna Elisabetha², b. 17 March 1716 - sp.: Arnold Falck and
   his wife Elisabetha (West Camp Luth. Chbk.). She md. Johannes Maul (HJ).

7) Dieterich², b. 10 May 1718 - sp.: Dietrich Sutz and his
   wife (West Camp Luth. Chbk.).

8) Johannes², b. 5 March 1719 - sp.: Johannes Emerich and
   his wife Margretha (West Camp Luth. Chbk.). The will of
   Johannes Trumpbour of Ulster Co. was dated 3 March 1783
   and probated 28 June 1785 (Fernow Wills #1752). He d. in
   1785 and his wife Christina Fiero (Führer et var) d. 1791
   (stones in Old Trumpbour Cem., Asbury, Saugerties, N.Y.).
   They had issue:
   i) Nicolaus³, bpt. 26 July 1741 - sp.: Johannes Fierer
      and Grietje Elich (Kingston Ref. Chbk.). He md. Elis-
      abetha Schmidt (HJ).
   ii) Catharina³, bpt. 4 April 1743 - sp.: Valentin Fierer
      and wife Catharina Schram (Katsbaan Ref. Chbk.). She
      md. William Cockburn (HJ).
   iii) Maria³, bpt. 7 May 1745 - sp.: Samuel Deffenpoort and
      wife Catharina Mejer (Katsbaan Ref. Chbk.). She md.
      29 May 1765 Simon Kohl (Germantown Ref. Chbk.).
   iv) Jacob³, bpt. 26 Dec 1748 - sp.: Andries Tromboor and
      Catharina Schram (Katsbaan Ref. Chbk.). He md. Marg-
      aretha Dieterich (HJ) and d. 11 April 1824, aged 75-
      3-3 (Old Luth. Cem., West Camp).
   v) Anna³, b. 11 May 1751 - sp.: Adam Scholtz and Anna
      Schultz (Loonenburg Luth. Chbk.).
   vi) Johannes³, bpt. 10 March 1754 - sp.: Johannes Maul
      and wife Elisabeth Tromboor (Katsbaan Ref. Chbk.).
   vii) Christina³, bpt. 26 May 1754 - sp.: Jacob Maul and
      Dorite Maul (Red Hook Luth. Chbk.). (Note some con-
      flict in bpt. dates of #vi and #vii - HJ).
   viii) Paul³, bpt. 31 May 1757 - sp.: Paulus Schmidt and
      wife Christina Trombauer (Katsbaan Ref. Chbk.).
   ix) Valentin³, bpt. 21 Oct 1762 - sp.: Valentyn Viere and
      wife Christina Schram (Katsbaan Ref. Chbk.).

9) Andreas², bpt. 15 Aug 1725 - sp.: Andries Soet and Mag-

dalena Soet (Kingston Ref. Chbk.). Andreas Trumbauer
joined the Red Hook Luth. Church 14 April 1745. The will
of Andres Trumpover (Drumbauer) of Montgomery Precinct,
Ulster Co. was dated 29 Dec 1783 and probated 4 June 1784
(Fernow Wills #1749). He md. 1st Anna Margaretha Gernreich and 2nd Elisabeth Krantz (HJ). By his 1st wife he
had issue:

    i) Magdalena[3], b. 24 July 1753 - sp.: Bernerd Sipperly
       and Lena Vyl (Rhinebeck Flats Ref. Chbk.).

   ii) Petrus[3], bpt. 22 Feb 1756 - sp.: Paulus Schmidt and
       wife Catharina Gernreich (Katsbaan Ref. Chbk.).

  iii) Elisabetha[3], bpt. 31 Dec 1758 - sp.: Friederich Maul
       and Eliesabetha Muller (Red Hook Luth. Chbk.). She
       md. Mattheus Clearwater (Will).

   iv) Nicolaus[3], b. 8 April 1761 - sp.: Christiaan Shiller
       and Regina Gernryk (Rhinebeck Flats Ref. Chbk.).

    v) Margaretha[3], bpt. 26 June 1763 - sp.: Joh: Trombaur
       and wife Cristina Fuhrer (Red Hook Luth. Chbk.).

   vi) Susanna[3] (Will).

  vii) Mary[3] (Will).

 viii) Catharina[3] (Will).

   ix) Christina[3] (Will).

    x) Andreas[3] (Will).

PAULUS DUNTZER (Hunter Lists #151)

The ancestral origins of the family were at 5455 Rengsdorf
(17 km. n. of Koblenz; Chbks. begin 1677). The father of the emigrant was Wilhelm Düntzer of Melsbach, who dropped from a cherry
tree and d. in the 1st week of July 1700 in Rengsdorf. His wife
was bur. 1 May 1687. Paulus Düntzer, s/o Wilhelm Düntzer of Melsbach, md. 28 Aug 1700 Anna Emilia, d/o of Herbert Klein from Rau-
bach. Paulus Deutger, his wife, and 2 ch. were in the 3rd party
at Rotterdam in 1709, amongst the Falckenburgs, Mancks, Beckers,
and others from the Neuwied region (Rotterdam Lists).

Paulus Duntzer made his first appearance on the Hunter Lists
4 July 1710 with 2 pers. over 10 yrs. and 1 pers. under 10; the
entry for 24 June 1711 read 5 pers. over 10 yrs. of age for Paulus
Duntzer and Barbara Freyin (called his wife in Hunter 25 March
1712). The last entry noted 3 pers. over 10 yrs. for "Paulus Duntzer's family" on 13 Sept 1712. Paulus Dientzer of Haysbury was a
soldier in 1711 (Palatine Volunteers To Canada). Paul Dinser was
nat. 11 Oct 1715 (Albany Nats.). With his 1st wife he had ch.:

    1) Anna Elisabetha[2], bpt. Dom. 3. p. Trin: 1701 - sp.: Anna -

w/o J. Wilh. Moscheti, Elisab. - w/o Theis Hofmann, and
Daniel Runckel (Rengsdorf Chbk.).
2) <u>Anna Gertraud²</u>, bpt. 6 Aug 1702 - sp.: Anna Gertrud - d/o
the late Ludwig Becker, and Johannes Müller at Melsbach
(Rengsdorf Chbk.). "Paulus Düntzer's child" was bur. 12
March 1703.
3) <u>Johann Georg²</u>, bpt. 28 March 1704 - sp.: Georg Moschetus,
Johannes Kleinmann, and Elisabetha - w/o Peter Schenckelberg (Rengsdorf Chbk.).
4) <u>Anna Veronica²</u>, bpt. 27 Feb 1707 - sp.: Johannes Reinhart,
Veronica - w/o Georg Runckel from Hed., and Anna Christina
- d/o Fritz Runckel (Rengsdorf Chbk.). A little child of
Paulus Düntzer at Rengsdorf d. 7 Sept 1707.

JOHANNES EBERHARDT (Hunter Lists #152)

Johann Eberhard, widower of S. Johann near Creutzenach, md.
Sibylla Gieser, d/o Johann Gieser - late of Ober Moshel-Landsberg
in the commune of Zweybrucken, 24 July 1711 (West Camp Luth. Chbk.).
The actual village of origin was 6551 <u>St. Johann</u> (11 km. n.e. of
Bad Kreuznach). Surviving Chbks. begin early, but end in 1672,
thus data on the 1709er are difficult to come by (HJ). A Johannes
Eberhardt, s/o Johan Frantz Eberhard at St. Johann, md. Waldburga
Dückert, d/o the late Hans Dückert there, 12 May 1650 (Sprendlin-
gen Chbk.). They had 3 ch. bpt. at Sprendlingen (Johann Wendel
b. 1651, Margaretha b. 1653, and Anna Catharina b. 1655), and then
Waldburga Eberhardt d. at childbirth in 1658. There was a Catholic
Johannes Eberhardt with 4 ch. in the 2nd party at Rotterdam and
the 2nd group at London, but he was returned to Holland (P.R.O.
T1/119, pp. 136-153).

Johannes Eberhardt made his first appearance on the Hunter
Lists 4 July 1710 with 1 pers. over 10 yrs; on 29 Sept 1711 the
entry read Johannes Eberhardt and Sib. Gieserin with 3 pers. over
10. The family diminished to 2 pers. over 10 24 Dec 1711, increased
to 2 pers. over 10 and 1 under 10 on 24 June 1712, and then read
2 pers. over 10 yrs. 13 Sept 1712. Johannes Eberhard: 1 man was
in the 1710/11 Palatine Census (West Camp Census). Johanis Ever-
thert was nat. 8 and 9 Sept 1715 (Kingston Nats.). Johann Eberhard,
his wife and 2 ch. were at Beckmansland ca. 1716/17 (Simmendinger
Register). He was noted in the Kingston Trustees Records (Bk. 1,
Part C, pp. 142-44). He and his 1st wife had issue:
1) <u>Anna Catharina²</u> (HJ), conf. at Rheinbeck 14 Oct 1716 (West
Camp Luth. Chbk.). She md. Johann Georg Eckhardt 13 Feb
1721 (Kingston Ref. Chbk.).

By his 2nd wife Anna Sybilla he had ch.:

2) <u>Johann Georg²</u>, b. 7 March 1712 - sp.: Johann Georg Sponheimer and wife Anna Maria (West Camp Luth. Chbk.).

3) <u>Maria Magdalena²</u>, md. at Kisk. 4 Feb 1734 Johann Michael Planck at Kisk. (Loonenburg Luth. Chbk.).

4) <u>Elisabetha²</u> (HJ), md. as a single woman b. Kisk. 6 Dec 1746
Johannes Doorn (Rhinebeck Flats Ref. Chbk.). Her ch. sp.
in the Eckhardt family of Rhinebeck helps cement crucial
Eberhardt relationships (HJ).

JOHANN GEORG ECKLING (Hunter Lists #153)

Johann Georg Eckling made his first appearance on the Hunter
Lists 1 July 1710 with 2 pers. over 10 yrs. of age and 3 pers. under 10 yrs. The entry for 4 Aug 1710 read Johann Georg Egelin and
had 3 pers. over 10 yrs. and 3 under 10; the 4 Oct 1710 listing
noted 4 pers. over 10 yrs. and 3 under 10 yrs. of age. He and his
1st wife Anna Barbara had issue:

1) <u>Anna Barbara²</u>, b. at Hackinsack last summer and bpt. 28 Oct
1711 at Hackinsack at a meeting at Cornelius Van Hoorn's -
sp.: Andreas Van Boschkerck, and Margreta - w/o Thomas
Van Boschkerck (N.Y. City Luth. Chbk.).

Johann Georg¹ md. Johanna Wagenaer (wid/o Nicolaus E. Zenger - HJ)
and by this 2nd wife had a child:

2) <u>Johann Georg²</u>, bpt. 4 July 1713 - sp.: Jan Everse Molegh
and wife Maria Barbara (Hackensack Ref. Chbk.). George
Eckling, with the consent of his mother Hannah Carter, was
apprenticed to Mr. Bartholomew Miller 10 Sept 1723, with
Peter Zenger as a witness (<u>Indentures of Apprentices 1718-
27</u>, p. 157). He md. Sara Van Amen and had issue:

i) <u>Johanna³</u>, bpt. 11 Feb 1736 - sp.: Johan Pieter Zenger
and Johanna - w/o Sam¹ Carter (N.Y. City Ref. Chbk.).

Dutchess Co. Ancient Docs. #790 noted a mss. for a Wm. Ackley
of Frealingburgh, Bergen Co., N.J. in 1758.

ADAM ECKARDT (Hunter Lists #154)

The ancestral home of the Dutchess Co. Ackert family was 6200
<u>Wiesbaden</u> (5 km. n. of Mainz; Chbks. begin 1595). The bpts. of Adam's
ch. with his 1st wife Elisabetha Catharina were found there.

Adam Eckardt made his first appearance on the Hunter Lists 1
July 1710 with 2 pers. over 10 yrs. and 1 pers. under 10; the entries increased to 4 pers. over 10 yrs. 4 Oct 1710. His last notation mentioned 3 pers. over 10 yrs. of age on 13 Sept 1712. Adam
Eckert was nat. 8 and 9 Sept 1715 (Kingston Nats.). Adam Ecker

with his 2nd wife and ch. was at Beckmansland ca. 1716/17 (Simmendinger Register). He made his first appearance in tax rolls of
the North Ward in 1717/18; they continued until 1744/45 at Rhine-
beck/Northeast when Adam Ackert's widow was registered (Dutchess
Co. Tax Lists). His family was noted on the St. Peter's 1734 list
of families (Rhinebeck Luth. Chbk.). By his 1st wife (N.Y. Col.
Mss. Vol. 58, p. 48 noted she d. April 1712) Adam[1] had ch.:

1) Maria Barbara[2] (HJ), conf. 19 July 1710 at N.Y. (West Camp
   Luth. Chbk.). She md. 1st Johannes Dopp 14 May 1717 (Kingston Ref. Chbk.), 2nd Wilhelm Schmidt 12 Jan 1735 (Rhinebeck Flats Ref. Chbk.), and 3rd Urias Nelson in 1749 (Rhinebeck Flats Ref. Chbk.).

2) Johann Georg[2] (HJ), conf. 23 March 1712 at Queensberg (West
   Camp Luth. Chbk.). John George Eckert was nat. 8 and 9
   Sept 1715 (Kingston Nats.). He made his first appearance
   on tax rolls in 1722 and continued in the North Ward and
   Rhinebeck areas until June 1763 (Dutchess Co. Tax Lists).
   Jurrye Ekert was an overseer of ye King's Highway in the
   North Ward in 1729 (Dutchess Co. Supervisor's Records).
   An Ancient Doc. survives for him dated 1747 (#1608). His
   tombstone in the Ref. Church at Rhinebeck gives him dates
   of 1698 - 3 June 1764. He md. Anna Catharina Eberhardt
   (Evert, Ebbert et var.) and had issue:

   i) Catharina[3], b. Nov 1721 at Rheinbeck - sp.: Peter
      Dippel and wife Anna Catharina (N.Y. City Luth. Chbk.).
      Catharina - d/o Joh. Jurgen Eckhard was conf. in 1737
      (N.Y. City Luth. Chbk.). She md. Adam Dippel (HJ).

   ii) Johannes[3], bpt. 23 Aug 1724 - sp.: Johannes Dop and
      Marytjen Ekkert (Kingston Ref. Chbk.). He md. 23 Nov
      1748 Anna Maria Streit (Rhinebeck Luth. Chbk.). He d.
      19 April 1786, aged 62 yrs., and she d. 22 May 1773
      (German Church Cem., Pink's Corners).

   iii) Anna Margaretha[3], bpt. 2 April 1727 - sp.: Marthen
      Boek and Anna-Margrieta Wel-leven (Kingston Ref. Chbk.).

   iv) Eva[3], b. 19 April 1729 and bpt. Rhynbek - sp.: Adam
      Ekkhard, and Eva - w/o Albertus Schreiber (N.Y. City
      Luth. Chbk.). She md. 24 May 1748 Henrich Treber
      (Rhinebeck Luth. Chbk.).

   v) Maria Barbara[3], bpt. 1731 - sp.: John David Eckert
      and Maria Barbara Eckert (Red Hook Luth. Chbk.). She
      was conf. with Eva Eckard 3 Nov 1745 at Rhynbek (Loon-
      enburg Luth. Chbk.). She md. Friederich Treber (HJ).

   vi) Johann Georg[3], b. 25 Feb 1734 - sp.: Martin Burchart
      and wife Ursula (Rhinebeck Luth. Chbk.).

vii) <u>Johann Adam</u>[3], bpt. 1 Oct 1739 - sp.: Adam Eckert and
Anna Eckert (Red Hook Luth. Chbk.). He md. 5 March
1762 Maria Webber (Wever) (Rhinebeck Flats Ref. Chbk.).
Adam Ackard d. 8 April 1799, aged 58-6-9, and Maria
d. 28 Feb 1826, aged 86 yrs. (Rhinebeck Luth. Church
Cem.).

viii) <u>Johann Peter</u>[3], bpt. 2 March 1742 - sp.: Pieter Dippel
and Susanna Dippel (Red Hook Luth. Chbk.). He md.
Elisabetha Frölich 23 July 1762 (Rhinebeck Flats Ref.
Chbk.). Elisabeth, w/o Peter Ackert, d. 2 June 1826,
aged 82 yrs. and 5 months (Ref. Church Cem., Rhinebeck).

3) <u>Susanna Catharina</u>[2], bpt. 21 Feb 1702 (Wiesbaden Chbk.).

4) <u>Johann Nicolaus</u>[2], bpt. 11 Nov 1703; the father was called
Hofmann im Ochsen in the bpt. entry (Wiesbaden Chbk.).

5) <u>Conrad</u>[2], bpt. 5 March 1707 - sp.: Conrad Geip, Gemeinsmann
at Moßbach (Wiesbaden Chbk.).

6) <u>Johann Christian</u>[2], bpt. 2 Jan 1709 - sp.: Christian Wiß (?)
- citizen and Glaser, and Johann Heinrich Grünkorn, hie-
siger Hofmann (Wiesbaden Chbk.).

7) <u>Anna Catharina</u>[2], b. 23 March 1712 - sp.: Anna Cast (West
Camp Luth. Chbk.).

By his 2nd wife Anna Rau, Adam[1] had issue:

8) <u>Anna Elisabetha</u>[2], b. 2 Sept 1714 - sp.: Anna Elisabetha
Lambert (West Camp Luth. Chbk.). She md. Michael Weber (HJ).

9) <u>Johannes</u>[2], bpt. 13 May 1716 - sp.: Johannes Dob and Anna
Maria (Kingston Ref. Chbk.).

10) <u>Johann Peter</u>[2], b. 19 April 1717 - sp.: Johann Peter Dopf
and Anna Catharina Dippel (West Camp Luth. Chbk.). He md.
Anna Maria Wust (HJ) and had issue:

i) <u>Adam Peter</u>[3] (HJ), md. 7 Sept 1765 Maria Steenberg
(Kingston Ref. Chbk.). The estate of Adam P. Eckert,
late of Kingston, was probated 2 Feb 1792 (Ulster Co.
Admin. Bk. A).

ii) <u>Conrad</u>[3], bpt. 21 Feb 1745 - sp.: Johannis Ekkert and
Angenietie Ekkert (Rhinebeck Flats Ref. Chbk.). He d.
16 Jan 1835, aged 89-11-6 (German Church Cem., Wurtem-
burgh).

iii) <u>Johann Peter</u>[3], bpt. 13 June 1747 - sp.: Pieter Top Jr.
and Geesbury Kremer (Rhinebeck Flats Ref. Chbk.).

iv) <u>Friederich</u>[3], b. 11 Oct 1749 - sp.: Friedrich Treber
and Eva Top (Rhinebeck Luth. Chbk.).

v) <u>Johannes</u>[3], b. 13 Nov 1751 - sp.: Johannes Wust and
wife Catharina (Rhinebeck Luth. Chbk.).

vi) Maria[3], b. 8 Sept 1754 - sp.: Stephanus Wust and
Mariah Bekker (Rhinebeck Flats Ref. Chbk.).

vii) Elisabetha[3], bpt. 28 Nov 1756 - sp.: Stephanus Wüst
and Elisabeth Wüst (Kingston Ref. Chbk.).

viii) Jacob[3], b. 1 March 1759 - sp.: Johannes Wust and his
wife (Rhinebeck Flats Ref. Chbk.). He d. 4 June 1827,
aged 68-3-4 (Smith Cem., Marbletown, Ulster Co.).

11) Johann David[2] (HJ), md. 1st Eva Frölich and 2nd Maria
Ploeg 8 Nov 1761 (Kingston Ref. Chbk.). David Eecker first
appeared on tax rolls in 1738/9 and continued until June
1755 (Dutchess Co. Tax Lists). With his wife Eva, he had:

i) Elisabetha[3], bpt. 2 Dec 1739 - sp.: Pieter Freeling
and Elisabeth Ekkert (Kingston Ref. Chbk.).

ii) Stephan[3], bpt. 14 Nov 1744 - sp.: Steven Freeling and
Berbel Meyjer (Rhinebeck Flats Ref. Chbk.).

iii) David[3], b. 28 Oct 1748 and bpt. at Stattsburg - sp.:
David Sorenberger and Eva Top (Rhinebeck Luth. Chbk.).

iv) Eva[3], b. 4 March 1751 - sp.: Adam Tippel and wife
... (Rhinebeck Luth. Chbk.).

v) Salomon[3], b. 29 March 1753 - sp.: Salomon Eckard and
wife Maria (Rhinebeck Luth. Chbk.).

vi) Petrus[3], b. 9 Nov 1755 - sp.: Pieter Froelich and his
wife (Rhinebeck Flats Ref. Chbk.).

With his 2nd wife Maria, he had a child:

vii) Rachel[3], bpt. 26 Sept 1762 - sp.: Petrus Brink and
Maria Ploeg (Kingston Ref. Chbk.).

12) Eva[2], bpt. 1 Nov 1719 - sp.: Albertus Schryver and Eva
Louwerman (Kingston Ref. Chbk.).

13) Adam[2], bpt. 2 April 1721 - sp.: Pieter Tiepel and Catrina
Tiepel (Kingston Ref. Chbk.). He was conf. in 1737 (N.Y.
City Luth. Chbk.). Adam md. Anna Margaretha Althouser
and had issue:

i) Adam[3], bpt. 26 Dec 1743 - sp.: Adam Tippel and Cattarina Ekkert (Rhinebeck Flats Ref. Chbk.).

ii) Johannes[3], bpt. 14 April 1745 - sp.: Johannis Ekkert
and Marya Stryt (Rhinebeck Flats Ref. Chbk.).

iii) Anna Barbara[3], bpt. 14 June 1747 - sp.: Pieter Schryver and Anna Barbara Schever (Rhinebeck Flats Ref.
Chbk.).

iv) Martinus[3], b. 21 June 1749 - sp.: Martinus Schreiber
and Agnesa Eckardt (Rhinebeck Luth. Chbk.). He d. 18
Dec 1842, aged 93 yrs. (German Church Cem., Wurtem-
burgh).

v) Petrus[3], b. 1 June 1751 - sp.: Pieter Frylyk and

Grietje Frylyk (Rhinebeck Flats Ref. Chbk.).

    vi) <u>David</u>[3], b. 3 Sept 1753 - sp.: David Doff and Racheltje Oostrander (Rhinebeck Flats Ref. Chbk.).

    vii) <u>Johann Georg</u>[3], b. 6 Oct 1755 - sp.: Jurrien Walther-meyer and his wife (Rhinebeck Flats Ref. Chbk.). He d. 26 Nov 1845, aged 90-1-20 (German Church Cem., Wurtemburgh).

    viii) <u>Jacob</u>[3], bpt. 5 Feb 1758 - sp.: Johannes Schryver and his wife (Rhinebeck Flats Ref. Chbk.).

    ix) <u>Catharina</u>[3], bpt. 25 May 1760 - sp.: Bastiaan Brouwn and Catrina Benschoten (Rhinebeck Flats Ref. Chbk.).

    x) <u>Albertus</u>[3], bpt. 9 (March) 1766 - sp.: Albertus Schry-ver and Margaretha Frolich (Rhinebeck Flats Ref. Chbk.). He d. in Ghent 26 July 1827, aged 61 yrs. (Hudson Rural Repository 4 Aug 1827).

    xi) <u>Sara</u>[3], bpt. 11 Nov 1770 - sp.: Hans Van Etten and Zara Stoert (Rhinebeck Flats Ref. Chbk.).

14) <u>Johannes</u>[2], bpt. 17 June 1722 - sp.: Johannes Albartes Schryver and Eva Catrina Schryver (Kingston Ref. Chbk.). Hannes Eckhard was conf. at Newton 7 March 1740/41 (Loon-enburg Luth. Chbk.). There was a Johannes Eckart with wife Christina Wies in the Schaghticoke Chbk. in the 1750's who might have been this man (HJ).

15) <u>Henrich</u>[2], bpt. 8 Sept 1723 - sp.: Hendrik Oel and Anna Mar-ia Oel (Kingston Ref. Chbk.). He appeared on tax rolls in Rhinebeck from 1745/46 through 1774 (Dutchess Co. Tax Lists) He md. 24 Sept 1743 Magdalena Beem (Rhinebeck Flats Ref. Chbk.) and had issue:

    i) <u>Maria</u>[3], bpt. 14 April 1745 - sp.: Marya Beem and Salo-moen Ekkert (Rhinebeck Flats Ref. Chbk.).

    ii) <u>Anna</u>[3], bpt. 31 May 1747 - sp.: Johannes Ekker and Anna Beem (Kingston Ref. Chbk.).

    iii) <u>Anna Margaretha</u>[3], b. 1 March 1749 and bpt. Staatsburg - sp.: Albertus Boehm and wife Anna Margaretha, and Agnesa Eckard (Rhinebeck Luth. Chbk.).

    iv) <u>Agnesa</u>[3], bpt. 10 Nov 1751 - sp.: Stephanus Burger and Agnies Akkert (Rhinebeck Flats Ref. Chbk.).

    v) <u>Ursula</u>[3], b. 21 Dec 1753 - sp.: Marting Burger and his wife (Rhinebeck Flats Ref. Chbk.).

    vi) <u>Henrich</u>[3], b. 11 April 1756 - sp.: Johannes Doorn and Elisabeth Doorn (Rhinebeck Flats Ref. Chbk.).

    vii) <u>Albertus</u>[3], b. 17 Nov 1760 - sp.: Adam Akkert and Marg-reit Bheem (Rhinebeck Flats Ref. Chbk.).

    viii) <u>Magdalena</u>[3], b. 25 Jan 1763 - sp.: Marten Schryver and

wife
    ix) <u>Johannes</u>[3], b. 1 Dec 1765 - sp.: Johannes Becker and
        wife Catharina (St. Paul's Rhinebeck Chbk.).

16) <u>Salomon</u>[2], md. as s/o Adam 30 Dec 1746 Maria Burghardt
    (Rhinebeck Luth. Chbk.). He was conf. at Staatsburg 30 May
    1742 (Loonenburg Luth. Chbk.). He appeared on tax rolls
    Feb 1746/47 through Feb 1757 (Dutchess Co. Tax Lists).
    His wife Maria Burghardt Akkert's dates were 7 March 1724
    - 11 May 1790 (Teerpenning Family Ground, Esopus). They
    had ch.:
      i) <u>Martin</u>[3], bpt. 9 Aug 1747 - sp.: Marthen Borger and
        Orsetjen Freling (Kingston Ref. Chbk.). He md. Apol-
        lonia Wust (HJ).
     ii) <u>Anna Ursula</u>[3], b. 4 Dec 1749 - sp.: Friedr: Treber
        and Anna Ursula Burghard (Rhinebeck Luth. Chbk.).
        She md. Henrich De Graaf (HJ).
    iii) <u>Stephanus</u>[3], b. 17 April 1752 - sp.: Stephanis Burger
        and Margrietje Akkert (Rhinebeck Flats Ref. Chbk.).
     iv) <u>Salomon</u>[3], b. 11 May 1755 - sp.: Stephanus Wust and
        Christina Burger (Rhinebeck Flats Ref. Chbk.).
      v) <u>Anna</u>[3], b. 3 July 1757 - sp.: Johan Jurrian Burchard
        and Annatje Smith (Rhinebeck Flats Ref. Chbk.).
     vi) <u>Maria</u>[3], b. 10 June 1759 - sp.: Johannes Acquet and
        Marytje Slegt (Rhinebeck Flats Ref. Chbk.).
     vii) <u>Jeremias</u>[3], bpt. 8 Nov 1761 - sp.: Albertus Schreiber
        and Elisabeth Ekkert (Kingston Ref. Chbk.).
    viii) <u>Catharina</u>[3], bpt. 6 May 1764 - sp.: Jurg Diepel and
        Catharintje Burger (Kingston Ref. Chbk.).

17) <u>Agnesa</u>[2], bpt. 17 Sept 1727 - sp.: Hendrik Scheever and
    Angenietjen Scheever (Kingston Ref. Chbk.). She was conf.
    at Rhynbek 17 June 1744 (Loonenburg Luth. Chbk.). She md.
    David Marquardt in 1758 (Rhinebeck Flats Ref. Chbk.).

18) <u>Catharina</u>[2], bpt. 8 June 1729 - sp.: Nicel Koen and Catrina
    Freelig (Kingston Ref. Chbk.).

<u>NICLAUS ECKARDT</u> (Hunter Lists #155)
<u>GERTRUDE ECKARDTIN</u> (Hunter Lists #156)

Niclaus Eckardt made his first appearance on the Hunter Lists
31 Dec 1710 with 2 pers. over 10 yrs. of age; his last entry on
these rolls was 13 Sept 1712 with 1 pers. over 10 yrs. Nicklaus
Eckard of Queensbury was a soldier in 1711 (Palatine Volunteers To
Canada). Niccolas Eckhar was nat. 31 Jan 1715/16 (Albany Nats.).

Gertrud Eckardtin made her first appearance on the Hunter

Lists 4 Oct 1710 with 2 pers. over 10 yrs. of age and 1 pers. under 10 yrs. in the family; the notation changed to 3 pers. over 10
yrs. 24 June 1711. Gartrud Eikertin: 1 lad 9-15 yrs, 1 woman, and
1 girl 8 yrs. and under were in Ulster Co. in 1710/11 (West Camp
Census).

There was a Palatine Eckhardt family in the Schoharie region,
and one in the Mohawk area. It is difficult to establish which
1709er, Niclaus or Gertraud, was the ancestor of each of these
two groups, because Gertraud also may have had a son named Nicolaus (HJ). But, after allowing for the fact that the founder of
the family in each region may have been either Nicolaus[1] or Gertraud[1], the two family structures appear to have been...

The Schoharie Valley Eckhardt Family:

Nicolaus Eckhardt[1] and his 1st wife Anna Margaretha had ch.:

1) <u>Maria Catharina[2]</u> (HJ), d. 5 Feb 1747, aged 34 yrs. (Schoharie Luth. Chbk.).

2) <u>Maria Elisabetha[2]</u> (HJ), md. 25 Nov 1745 Johann Henrich
Dietz (Schoharie Ref. Chbk.).

3) <u>Catharina[2]</u>, md. as d/o Nicolaus 13 July 1746 Wilhelm Sy-
bert (Schoharie Ref. Chbk.).

4) <u>Maria Gertraud[2]</u>, a sp. at Schoharie called d/o Nicolaus
in 1737 (Loonenburg Luth. Chbk.). She md. Adam Dietz 25
Aug 1740 (Schoharie Ref. Chbk.).

5) <u>Nicolaus Jr.[2]</u> (HJ), md. 1st Dorothea Elisabetha (--) and
2nd Gertraud Jung (HJ).

6) <u>Jacob[2]</u>, md. 23 Feb 1750 Neeltie Fort (Schoharie Ref. Chbk.).

7) <u>Peter[2]</u>, md. 10 Jan 1751 Maria Elisabetha Rickert (Schoharie
Ref. Chbk.).

8) <u>Lambert[2]</u>, bpt. 14 Nov 1732 - sp.: Lampert Sternberger and
his wife Catharina (Schoharie Luth. or Ref. Chbk.). He
joined the Schoharie Ref. Church in March 1752. There was
a Loyalist named Lambert Acre in Canada (<u>The Loyalists
in Ontario</u>, p. 1). He md. Anna Margaretha Conrad 10 Nov 1754.

9) <u>Johannes[2]</u>, bpt. 14 Oct 1734/35 - sp.: Johannes Fink and
Catharina Seubell (Schoharie Luth. or Ref. Chbk.). He
joined the Schoharie Ref. Church in 1752 also. He md. Catharina Jung (HJ).

With his wife Maria Magdalena Horn, Nicolaus[1] had issue:

10) <u>Johann Jost[2]</u>, bpt. 20 May 1738 - sp.: Niclaas Miller and
wife (Schoharie Ref. Chbk.). He md. Margaretha Weber and
had ch. at Albany Ref. and Beaverdam Ref. Churches.

Nicolaus[1] md. 3rd as a widower b. at Swedelbach in the jurisdiction
of Kaiserslautern 1 Nov 1741 Catharina Scheid (Schoharie Ref.
Chbk.). They had children:

11) <u>Maria Margaretha²</u>, bpt. 10 Nov 1742 - sp.: Willem Dietz and Maria Margareth Zimmer (Schoharie Ref. Chbk.).

12) <u>Johann Henrich²</u>, bpt. 11 Nov 1745 - sp.: John Hendrick Dietz and Catharina Eckker (Schoharie Ref. Chbk.).

13) <u>Catharina²</u>, bpt. 21 Feb 1747/48 - sp.: Jacob Zimmer and wife Catharina (Schoharie Ref. Chbk.).

14) <u>Elisabetha²</u>, bpt. 11 Nov 1749 (Schoharie Ref. Chbk.).

15) <u>Anthony²</u>, bpt. 7 Feb 1751/52 - sp.: Anthony Scheid and wife Dorothea (Schoharie Ref. Chbk.).

16) <u>Eva²</u>, bpt. 12 Sept 1754 - sp.: Piter Man and Creed, his wife (Schoharie Ref. Chbk.).

17) <u>Anna Maria²</u>, b. 23 Jan 1757 - sp.: Friederich Schup and his wife (Schoharie Luth. Chbk.).

18) <u>Elisabetha²</u>, b. 11 Oct 1759 - sp.: Friederich Ball and Elisabeth Mann (Schoharie Luth. Chbk.).

19) <u>Wilhelm²</u>, b. 11 Nov 1761 - sp.: Jurgen Henrich Mann and wife (Schoharie Luth. Chbk.). No mother named in entry.

In this Schoharie Valley Eckhardt family belongs Magdalena Eckhardt, sp. to Gabriel Hoffman in 1713 and to Johann Leer in 1717 (both West Camp Luth. Chbk.). She md. Johann Friederich Bauch (HJ).

The Mohawk Valley Eckhardt Family:

An un-named Eckhardt (perhaps another Nicolaus - HJ) had ch.:

1) <u>Johann Georg²</u>, b. 12 Nov 1716 and d. 28 Jan 1789 (Stone Arabia Ref. Chbk.); this entry noted that he was b. in Schoharie. He md. 19 Oct 1742 Maria Elisabetha Schnell (Stone Arabia Ref. Chbk.). The will of George Aker of Palatine was dated 2 April 1787 and probated 2 April 1793 (Montgomery Co. Will Bk. I).

2) <u>Christina²</u>, conf. 1739 (Stone Arabia Ref. Chbk.).

3) <u>Adam²</u>, conf. 1748 and md. as widower Margretha Cochnat 8 May 1764 (both Stone Arabia Ref. Chbk.). The will of Adam Ecker of Mohawks District was dated 4 Jan 1776 and probated 10 Aug 1784 (<u>Fernow Wills</u> #593).

4) <u>Maria Elisabetha²</u>, conf. with Adam² 1748 (Stone Arabia Ref. Chbk.). She md. Wilhelm Deichert (HJ).

5) <u>Elisabetha Gertraud²</u>, conf. 1752 (Stone Arabia Ref. Chbk.).

6) <u>Abraham²</u>, conf. 1754 (Stone Arabia Ref. Chbk.).

7) <u>Johannes²</u>, conf. 1757 and md. 24 May 1763 Anna Elisabetha Dachstätter (Stone Arabia Ref. Chbk.). See N.Y. D.A.R. Bible Records, Vol. 135, p. 181.

I can find no relationship between the Schoharie Eckhardts and the Mohawk Eckhardts in any surviving church register I have examined (HJ).

THOMAS EHEMANN (Hunter Lists #157)

Thomas Ehmann, widower of Schornbach in Wurtemberg, md. 26 June 1711 Elisabetha, wid/o Johann Jacob Lauck of Nurstatt in Darmstadt (West Camp Luth. Chbk.). Ehmann's home was 7060 Schornbach (26 km. e. of Stuttgart; Chbks. begin 1640). The earliest known ancestor of the American line was Georg Ehmann, who was bur. 21 Nov 1682, aged 72 yrs.; his wife Magdalena was bur. 21 June 1671, aged 61 yrs. Daniel Ehemann, s/o Georg Ehmann here, md. 8 Feb 1665 Maria, d/o Georg Weber from Steinbruck. The ch. of Daniel Ehmann and wife Maria were:

    Georg, bpt. 3 Dec 1665 - sp.: Hans Winckh - Schultheiß, and Maria - w/o Hans Nehr.

    Maria, bpt. 25 Jan 1667.

    A Stillborn Child, d. 13 Aug 1668.

    Hans Conrad, bpt. 16 Aug 1669.

    Anna, bpt. 29 April 1671, md. 24 Sept 1695 Hans Wiesenauer.

    Elisabetha, bpt. 19 Nov 1674.

+ Hans Thomas, bpt. 6 Dec 1676.

    Catharina, bpt. 31 Dec 1678 - d. 19 Aug 1679.

    David, bpt. 19 Feb 1683 - d. 21 June 1683.

    Agnes, bpt. 20 Sept 1688 - d. 15 Feb 1689.

Thomas Ehemann, s/o Daniel Ehemann citizen here, md. 21 Nov 1701 Magdalena, d/o Leonhard Greiner - late citizen here. Magdalena, d/o Leonhardt Greiner and wife Euphrosina, was bpt. 6 Jan 1678 - sp.: Johann Michts (?) - Schultheiss, and Margaretha - w/o Georg Schmid. Leonhardt Greiner, citizen and widower here, md. Euphrosina, wid/o the late Hans Michel Köpff - miller at Stetten, 4 Feb 1677; Leonhardt Greiner d. 28 Oct 1678, aged 58 yrs.

Thomas Ehemann made his first appearance on the Hunter Lists 4 July 1710 with 1 pers. over 10 yrs. and 1 pers. under 10 yrs. The family increased to 3 pers. over 10 yrs. 29 Sept 1711, after several fluctuations. Thomas Ehman: 1 man and 1 girl 8 yrs. and under were in Ulster Co. in 1710/11 (West Camp Census). Thomas Ehmann, Anna Elisabetha and 1 child were at Neu-Stuttgardt ca. 1716/17 (Simmendinger Register). Thomas Theman subscribed 6 shillings N.J. money in 1727 (N.Y. City Luth. Protocol, p. 90). Peter Fischer bought 200 acres of land in East Amwell in 1731 from Thomas Emmans, who had obtained it from Joseph Arney (A History of East Amwell, p. 41). Berkenmeyer mentioned Thomas Eheman in a visit to N.J. in 1731 (Albany Protocol, p. 11). The ch. of Thomas Ehemann and his 1st wife Magdalena Greiner were:

    1) Anna Maria[2], bpt. 13 July 1702 - sp.: Hans Jerg Bronner from Monshaupten, and Maria - w/o Jacob Kurtz the Gerichts

(Schornbach Chbk.). Anna Maria Ehmann was conf. at Tschoghari in the so-called Weiserts Dorp in 1720 (N.Y. City
Luth. Chbk.).

2) <u>Johannes²</u>, bpt. 7 Aug 1703 - sp.: Hans Georg Bronner, and
Maria - w/o Jacob Kurtz the Gerichts (Schornbach Chbk.).

3) <u>Johann Georg²</u>, bpt. 14 March 1705 - sp.: as before (Schornbach Chbk.).

4) <u>Euphrosina²</u>, bpt. 28 Oct 1706 - sp.: as before (Schornbach
Chbk.).

5) <u>Johannes²</u>, bpt. 12 Nov 1708 - sp.: Hans Jerg Brunner and
Agnes Schmil (Schornbach Chbk.).

<u>ANDREAS EHLIG</u> (Hunter Lists #158)

Andreas Ellich, widower of Necke-Burcken in the commune of
Mossbach in the Pfaltz, md. Anna Sophia, wid/o Gerhard Hornung of
Newtown, 9 May 1715 (West Camp Luth. Chbk.). The German home of
this emigrant was 6957 <u>Neckarburken</u> (2 km. n. of Mosbach). Andreas
Gilig, his wife and 1 child were noted on Capt. Frans Robbenson's
ship 5 July 1709 in Holland (Rotterdam Lists). Andreas Hillig aged
26, his wife, and a son aged 2, Luth., husbandman and vinedresser,
were in England later that year (London Lists).

Andreas Ehlig made his first appearance on the Hunter Lists
4 Aug 1710 with 2 pers. over 10 yrs. of age and 1 pers. under 10
yrs.; the family grew to 2 pers. over 10 and 2 pers. under 10 yrs.
24 June 1711. Andreas Elich aged 37, Anna Rosina Elich aged 23,
and John Georg Elich aged 3 were in N.Y. City in 1710/11 (Palatines In N.Y. City). Andries Elich was nat. 8 and 9 Sept 1715
(Kingston Nats.). Andreas Ehlich and Sophia, with 3 ch. were at
Beckmansland ca. 1716/17 (Simmendinger Register). Andries Elik was
a Palatine Debtor 26 Dec 1718 (Livingston Debt Lists). Berkenmeyer
mentioned him often as a Lutheran prominent in church activities
in colonial N.Y. (<u>Albany</u> Protocol). The Kingston Trustees Records
noted him in Bk. 1, part C, pp. 94/95, Bk. 2, pp. 1/2, and Bk. 3,
pp. 299-302. Andreas¹ was alive as late as 1751 (Katsbaan Ref.
Chbk.). With his 1st wife Anna Rosina, who d. 20 March 1715 (West
Camp Luth. Chbk.), he had ch.:

1) <u>Johann Georg²</u> (Palatines In N.Y. City), nat. with his
father 8 and 9 Sept 1715 (Kingston Nats.). The Kingston
Town Court Records 1728-30 show a court case involving
Hans Ju^r Elich vs. Arenoht Valk. Johann Georg² md. 26 Feb
1732 Catharina Emmerich at Newton at the house of Hannes
Emmerich who was sick until death (Loonenburg Luth. Chbk.).
The will of Johan Yury Eligh of the Beverkil was dated 6

Dec 1780 and probated 2 Sept 1783 (<u>Fernow Wills</u> #596).
His ch. were:

    i) <u>Elisabetha</u>[3], b. 20 Jan 1733 and bpt. at Newtown - sp.:
Johann Wilhelm Elig and his father Andreas Elig, and
Elis. Emmerichs (Loonenburg Luth. Chbk.). Lisabeth
Eligs was conf. at Newton 10 Jan 1747/48 (Loonenburg
Luth. Chbk.). She md. Wilhelm Laux 11 Sept 1751 (Loon-
enburg Luth. Chbk.).

    ii) <u>Anna</u>[3], b. 18 Sept 1735 and bpt. at Newton - sp.: Phil.
Spohn and Anna Marg. Eligs, but as both hadn't commun-
ion, the parents Sophia Elig and Adam Spohn (Loonenburg Luth. Chbk.).

    iii) <u>Andreas</u>[3], b. 3 Feb 1738 - sp.: Andreas Elig and Sophia
- grandparents (Loonenburg Luth. Chbk.). Andries Eligh
was in Capt. Cornelus Dubois' Co. at Caskill in 1767
(<u>Report of the State Historian</u>, Vol. II, p. 878). He
md. Catharina Laux 26 Jan 1762 (Loonenburg Luth. Chbk.)
and they had ch. at Katsbaan Ref. and Germantown Luth.
Churches. He d. 17 Aug 1816, aged 78-6-14 (West Camp
Luth. Cem.).

    iv) <u>Johannes</u>[3], b. 11 April 1740 and bpt. at Newton - sp.:
Hannes Hertel and Catharina Spohn (Loonenburg Luth.
Chbk.). He md. Margaretha Schumacher and had ch. at
Germantown Luth. Church (HJ).

    v) <u>Jacob</u>[3], b. 28 March 1746 and bpt. Kisket. - sp.: Jacob
Eigener and wife Ann. Margr. (Loonenburg Luth. Chbk.).
The mother called Elisabeth in this entry.

    vi) <u>Catharina</u>[3], b. 3 July 1751 - sp.: Maria Marlena Lehman,
Hannes Hes Jr. and wife from Canojoharie (Loonenburg
Luth. Chbk.).

    vii) <u>Margaretha</u>[3], b. 3 July 1751 - sp.: Willem Emmrich and
Margaretha (Loonenburg Luth. Chbk.).

2) <u>Christian</u>[2], bpt. 18 March 1711 - sp.: Christian Echler and
Maria Neef (in both West Camp Luth. and N.Y. City Ref.
Chbks.).

3) <u>Anna Maria</u>[2], banns to marry pub. 9 Nov 1735 Jacob Brink
(Loonenburg Luth. Chbk.). There was some trouble regarding
this marriage (<u>Albany Protocol</u>, p. 164). Anna Maria[2] had
been conf. at Newtown in Andr. Elig's house 14 Jan 1730,
aged 17 yrs. (N.Y. City Luth. Chbk.).

By his 2nd wife Anna Sophia Hornung, Andreas[1] had issue:

    4) <u>Johann Wilhelm</u>[2], b. 7 Sept 1717 - sp.: Johann Wilhelm Leh-
mann and his wife (West Camp Luth. Chbk.). He was conf. at
Newton 1 April 1733, aged 16 yrs. (Loonenburg Luth. Chbk.).

William Ealik was a freeholder of Caters Kill and Cats Kill in 1763 (Albany Co. Freeholders). Willem Eligh was in Capt. Cornelus Dubois Co. at Caskill in 1767 (Report of the State Historian, Vol. II, p. 876). He md. 5 Jan 1736 at Kisk. Anna Margaretha - d/o Adam Spoon (Loonenburg Luth. Chbk.). The will of William Eligh of the West Camp was dated 14 Aug 1782 and probated 15 Oct 1783 (Fernow Wills #602).

5) Anna Margaretha[2], b. Nov 1720 at Newtown in Albany Co. - sp.: Johannes Emmerich and wife Anna Margareta (N.Y. City Luth. Chbk.). She was conf. at Newton Feb 1738/39 and md. Johannes Fuhrer 13 Jan 1741 (both Loonenburg Luth. Chbk.).

There was a Johannes Elig who md. Anna Gertraud (--) and had ch. Elisabetha b. 23 May 1741 and bpt. Newton (Loonenburg Luth. Chbk.), Anna Elisabetha b. 29 April 1744 (Red Hook Luth. Chbk.), and Cornelia b. 25 Sept 1750 (Rhinebeck Luth. Chbk.); it is difficult to find a connective link between this man and Andreas[1] (HJ).

ELIZABETH EIGENBROD (Hunter Lists #159)

Elizabeth Eigenbrod made her only appearance on the Hunter Lists 31 Dec 1710 with 2 pers. over 10 yrs. of age in the family. She may have been the Anna Almerodrin, widow, aged 67 mentioned in the list of Palatines in N.Y. City in 1710/11 (HJ).

A possible source for the N.Y. arrival may have been the Elisabetha, w/o Johannes Eigenbrodt, who had two ch. at 6719 Bischheim and then was deserted by her husband ca. 1708 (HJ).

CHRISTIAN EIGLER (Hunter Lists #160)

Kristiaen Figeler, his wife, and 4 ch. were recorded next to Andreas Gilig (Ehlig), a 1709er from Neckarburken, on Capt. Frans Robbenson's ship in Holland (Rotterdam Lists). Christian Egler aged 38, with his wife, a son aged 2, daughters aged 8, 7, and 4, Ref. mason and stonecutter, was in the 3rd arrivals in England in 1709 (London Lists).

Christian Eichler made his first appearance on the Hunter Lists 1 July 1710 with 2 pers. over 10 yrs.; the size increased to 2 pers. over 10 and 1 under 10 yrs. 24 June 1711. He and wife Maria Eva (who later md. Wilhelm Lehman - HJ) had a son:

1) Andreas[2], bpt. 8 April 1711 - sp.: Andreas Ellig (both West Camp Luth. and N.Y. City Ref. Chbk.). Andreas Eger was conf. 15 April 1729, aged 19 yrs. at Newton, and md. 7 Dec 1730 at Kisketamenesy Maria Borters (both N.Y. City Luth. Chbk.). They had a son:

i) <u>Andreas</u>[3], bpt. 9 March 1732 - sp.: Wilhelm Leeman
and Maria Eva (Catskill Ref. Chbk.). Andreas Eigeler
was conf. 10 Jan 1747/48 at Newton (Loonenburg Luth.
Chbk.). He md. 24 Nov 1749 Maria - d/o Friederich
Schramm (Loonenburg Luth. Chbk.). Andries Ekelaer was
a soldier in Capt. Dubois Co. at Caskill in 1767
(<u>Report of the State Historian</u>, Vol. II, p. 878).

<u>PAUL ELSASSER</u> (Hunter Lists #161)

Gertrauda, wid/o Paul Elsaster of Fishborn in the earldom of
Isenburg, md. 23 Jan 1711 Antoni Kramer, widower of Altzheim on
the lower Rhine (West Camp Luth. Chbk.). The actual European home
of the family was 6484 <u>Fischborn</u> (3 km. n. of Birstein). Entries
concerning the Elsassers were discovered at 6484 <u>Unterreichenbach</u>
(Chbks. begin 1599) and 6490 <u>Schlüchtern</u> (Chbks. begin 1577).
The earliest known ancestor of the American line was <u>Henrich Ähl-
sesser</u>. He was recorded in 1679-83 on an old family list at
Schlüchtern as inhabitant #37 with his wife Gertraud and ch.:

+ <u>Jost</u>.
 <u>Peter</u>.
 <u>Anna</u>.
 <u>Maria</u>.
 <u>Margretha</u>.
 <u>Anna Kunigunda</u>.

The 1st wife of <u>Jost Elsässer</u> was Margaretha Pfahl, who d. 21 Feb
1699 (Schlüchtern Chbk.). They had the following ch. bpt. at
Schlüchtern:

 <u>Henrich</u>, bpt. as "a son" 4 Oct 1680 - sp.: Henrich Elsässer.
+ <u>Paulus</u>, bpt. as "a son" 29 Jan 1683 - sp.: Paulus Ringeler.
 <u>Albrecht</u>, bpt. 25 Oct 1685 - sp.: Altbrecht Hadermanns...
 He was conf. 1703.
 <u>Anna Margaretha</u>, bpt. 15 Aug 1688 - sp.: Anna Margarretha -
 w/o Joh. Martin Paal. She was conf. 1703/4.
 <u>Johann Georg</u>, bpt. 21 Aug 1695 - sp.: Johann Görg Pfal and
 Thomas Pfal.

Jost Elsässer md. 2nd Anna Elisabeth Rüffer 9 Nov 1699; Jost was
bur. 12 July 1738 (Schlüchtern Chbk.). Paulus Elsässer was conf.
at Schlüchtern in 1701. Paul Elsasser, s/o Jost Elsasser of
Schlüchtern, md. Anna Dorothea, d/o Henrich Schaarman of Fischborn,
26 Sept 1708 (Unterreichenbach Chbk.).

Paul Elsasser made his first appearance on the Hunter Lists
1 July 1710 with 2 pers. over 10 yrs. of age in the household; the
entry for 24 Dec 1711 read Paul Elsasser's widow.

JOHANN ERNEST EMICHEN (Hunter Lists #162)

Johan Ernst Emick, widower of Konigsberg more recently Worms, md. Margretha, d/o Hans Carl Winter of Bach im Würtenbergschen, 21 Aug 1709 (London Chbks. and the German Emigration of 1709, by John P. Dern, p. 25). Emick's ancestral origins then were at 6520 Worms and possibly 6301 Königsberg near Wetzlar. Ernst Emichen aged 55, his wife, sons aged 9, 6, 5, and 1½, Luth., husbandman and vinedresser, were in the 1st arrivals in 1709 (London Lists).

Ernst Emichen made his first appearance on the Hunter Lists 1 July 1710 with 2 pers. over 10 yrs. of age and 2 pers. under 10 yrs.; the numbers changed to 3 pers. over 10 yrs. and 1 pers. under 10 on 4 Oct 1710, and the last entries for the family in 1712 noted 4 pers. over 10 yrs. of age. An old mss. dated 1711 recorded that one pound of butter was given for Joh: Ernst Emichen (N.Y. Col. Mss., Vol. 55, p. 29e). Johan Earnest Emegin was nat. 13 March 1715/16 (Albany Nats.). Johann Ernst Eingen and Anna Christiana with 2 ch. were at Neu-Heessberg ca. 1716/17 (Simmendinger Register). The surviving ch. of Johann Ernst[1] Emichen were:

1) Johann Adam[2] (HJ), conf. 30 April 1711 at the new German colony (West Camp Luth. Chbk.). Jerg Adam Oemich sp. Joh: Martin Seibert in 1716 (West Camp Luth. Chbk.). Adam Empie was a patentee at Stone Arabia in 1723 (Stone Arabia Patent). He md. Catharina Barbara Schmidt, d/o Adam Smit, 5 Feb 1727. Pearson's First Settlers of Schenectady gives ch.:

   i) Maria[3], bpt. 17 May 1727.

   ii) Anna[3], bpt. 27 July 1729.

   iii) Johannes[3], bpt. 3 Oct 1731.

   iv) Adam[3], bpt. 5 May 1734.

   v) Henrich[3], bpt. 12 Sept 1736.

2) Johannes[2] (HJ), nat. next to Johan Earnest[1] 13 March 1715/ 16 (Albany Nats.). Hans Emiche was conf. 1720 at Tschoghari in the so-called Fuchsen-dorp (N.Y. City Luth. Chbk.). Johannes Empie was a patentee at Stone Arabia in 1723 (Stone Arabia Patent). His family appeared on Pastor Sommer's list of his congregation at Stone Arabia and Cani-Schohare in 1744. Johannes[2] md. Elisabetha Schnell (HJ). They had ch.:

   i?) Anna Eva[3], md. Christopher Schultheiss/Schultz (HJ).

   ii?) Philip[3], listed alone but near Johannes[2] on Pastor Sommer's 1744 list at Stone Arabia. He was in Capt. Soffrines Deychert's Co. in March 1757 (Report of the State Historian, Vol. II, p. 784). He was a Loyalist and went to Canada in 1780. His petition survives in the Haldimand Papers, dated 6 Dec 1782. The will of Philip Empey was signed 4 Aug 1795 and probated 27 Feb

1796 (Surrogate's Court, Brockville and Leeds Co., Ontario, Eastern District). Philip³ md. Maria Elisabetha Barbara Schultheiss/Schultz (HJ).

    iii?) <u>Wilhelm³</u>, b. 29 April 1728 and d. 8 Dec 1803 (Anglican Church Records, Diocese of Ottawa). He also was noted separately on Pastor Sommer's List in 1744. William Empie was in Capt. Soffrines Deychert's Co. in 1757 (<u>Report of the State Historian</u>, Vol. II, p. 783). He md. Maria Margaretha Laux (HJ) and also went to Canada.

    iv) <u>Friederich³</u>, a s/o Johannes² on Sommer's 1744 List. He md. Maria Elisabetha Schultheiss/Schultz (HJ).

    v?) <u>Anna Margaretha³</u>, md. Wilhelm Casselmann (HJ).

    vi) <u>Adam³</u>, s/o Johannes² on Sommer's 1744 List. The will of Adam Empie of Stone Arabia was dated 20 Oct 1782 and probated 8 Dec 1783 (Fernow Wills #601).

    vii) <u>Johannes³</u>, a s/o Johannes² on Sommer's 1744 List. He md. Anna Maria Kilts (HJ) and was bur. in Sharon, N.Y.

    viii) <u>Anna Maria³</u>, a d/o Johannes² on Sommer's 1744 List.

    ix) <u>Johann Jacob³</u>, bpt. Nov 1752 (Stone Arabia Luth. Chbk.).

   3) <u>Elisabetha²</u> (HJ), md. Peter Krembs (HJ).

   4) <u>Christina²</u> (HJ), md. Henrich Krembs (HJ).

Dr. E. Keith Fitzgerald sent wonderful Canadian data which clarified the family structure. David Kendall Martin also was of great assistance in sorting out this group, and his excellent <u>The 18th Century Snell Family of the Mohawk Valley</u> contains more material on this complex family (HJ).

JOHN NICLAUS EMICH (Hunter Lists #163)

Johan Nicolaus Emich, s/o Hans Valtin Emich of Dannenfels in Nassau Weilburgschen, md. 4 Sept 1709 Anna Catharina Müller, d/o Henrich Müller of Staudrum (<u>London Chbks. and the German Emigration of 1709</u>, by John P. Dern, p. 25). The village of origin was 6761 <u>Dannenfels</u> (10 km. e. of Rockenhausen; Chbks. begin 1698, Luth.); certain entries on the family were found at 6719 <u>Marnheim</u> (8 km. farther e.; Chbks. begin 1648, Ref.). The earliest known ancestor of the Dutchess Co. family was <u>Hans Emich</u>, a baker in Dreisen. Two of his ch. were:

+ <u>Hans Veltin</u>, conf. as s/o Hans on Easter 1675, aged 17 yrs. (Marnheim Chbk.).

   <u>Hans Conrad</u>, conf. as s/o Hans on Easter 1675, aged 15 yrs. (Marnheim Chbk.).

The line was continued by <u>Hans Veltin Emich</u>, who d. before 1704.

He was listed at Dreisen in 1698 (Alzey Census) and had ch.:

> Hans Velten, conf. as s/o the late Velten Emich in 1704
> (Dannenfels Chbk.).
>
> + Johann Nicolaus, conf. as a minor and s/o the late Velten
>   Emich in 1706 (Dannenfels Chbk.).

Johan Nicolaas Eemig was listed next to Sebastiaen Spykerman in the 2nd party of Palatines in Holland in 1709 (Rotterdam Lists).

Johann Niclaus Emich made his first appearance on the Hunter Lists 4 Aug 1710 with 2 pers. over 10 yrs. of age; the family increased to 2 pers. over 10 yrs. and 1 pers. under 10 yrs. on the 24 June 1712 entry. Niclas Emich was nat. 8 and 9 Sept 1715 (Kingston Nats.). He made his initial appearance on tax rolls as a resident of the North Ward in 1717/18 and continued there until 1727; he was listed in the South Ward from 1728 through 1738 and at Beekman Precinct from 1739 through Feb 1761 (Dutchess Co. Tax Lists). His land near Hendrick Oul's was mentioned in the laying out of a road in 1742, and his livestock mark was registered 10 Jan 1739/40 (Dutchess Co. Supervisor's Records). A mss. dated 1751 survives for him (Dutchess Co. Ancient Docs. #2399). His wife Anna Catharina Müller may have been related to one of the emigrant Philip Müllers (HJ). They had issue:

1) Philip² (HJ), md. 16 Sept 1737 in the Highland at P. Lassing's Gertraud Lassing (N.Y. City Luth. Chbk.). The will of Phillip Emigh of Beekmantown was dated 24 March 1796 and probated 26 Feb 1799 (Dutchess Co. Will Bk. B). Ch.:

   i) Nicolaus³, b. 26 Jan 1740 and bpt. at Nicholas Emig's at Backwaij - sp.: Jo: Niclaas Emig and wife Anna Catharina (N.Y. City Luth. Chbk.).

   ii) Peter³, b. 20 March 1741 and bpt. at Pieter Lassing's in the Highland - sp.: Pieter Lassing and Cornelia (N.Y. City Luth. Chbk.).

   iii) Catharina³, b. 25 Feb 1743 and bpt. in the Klove at Bachwaij - sp.: Peter Peterson Lassing and Anna Maria (N.Y. City Luth. Chbk.).

   iv) Gertraud³, bpt. 5 Feb 1745 and bpt. at Bachway in the Klove - sp.: Georg Lahn and Gertruydt Lehn (N.Y. City Luth. Chbk.).

   v) Cornelia³, b. 25 April 1747 and bpt. at P. Lassing's in the Highland - sp.: Laurens Lassing and Cornelia (N.Y. City Luth. Chbk.).

   vi) Philip³ (Will).

   vii) Jeremiah³ (Will).

   viii) Daniel³ (Will).

      ix) <u>Elias</u>[3] (Will).

       x) <u>Lenah</u>[3] (Will).

      xi) <u>Maria</u>[3] (Will).

    xii) <u>Margaretha</u>[3], b. 10 April 1760 - sp.: Andrees Heering and Anna Margaretha (Loonenburg Luth. Chbk.).

  xiii) <u>Hester</u>[3], b. 27 June 1762 - sp.: Johannes Emig and Annaatje (Loonenburg Luth. Chbk.).

2) <u>Anna Maria</u>[2], b. 22 April 1715 - sp.: Jerg Thaeter and wife Anna Maria (West Camp Luth. Chbk.). Anna Maria and Philip Emig, both aged 20 yrs., were conf. together among the Germans at Beekman's Land in 1731 (N.Y. City Luth. Chbk.). She md. Peter Lassing Jr. on the Monday after 16 Trin.: 1735 (N.Y. City Luth. Chbk.).

3) <u>Johannes</u>[2], bpt. 7 April 1717 - sp.: Johannes Lammertsz and Anna Maria Tiepel (Kingston Ref. Chbk.). Hannes Emig was conf. DNIA III, p.t. 1737 at Niclaas Emig's (N.Y. City Luth. Chbk.). He md. Anna de Lang 7 Aug 1743 (Fishkill Ref. Chbk.). He d. 24 May 1801 (<u>Saratoga Co. Epitaphs</u> by Durkee, cited by George Olin Zabriskie in his excellent article on the family in the <u>N.Y. Genealogical & Biographical Record</u>).

4) <u>Lorentz</u>[2], b. 6 Feb 1719 - sp.: Lorentz Thaeter, and the w/o Johann Lamert (West Camp Luth. Chbk.). He was conf. DNIA III, p.t.: 1737 at Niclaas Emig's (N.Y. City Luth. Chbk.). Banns for his marriage to Anna Maria Buck were dated 5 Oct 1742 (N.Y. City Luth. Chbk.). The will of Lawrance Emeigh of Beekman, yeoman, was dated 5 Feb 1800 and probated 5 March 1804 (Dutchess Co. Will Bk. B). Issue:

      i) <u>Anna Maria</u>[3], b. 18 April 1745 and bpt. Bachwaij - sp.: Nichlaas Emig Sr. and Catharina (N.Y. City Luth. Chbk.).

     ii) <u>Nicolaus</u>[3], b. 30 Sept 1748 and bpt. in parent's house at Bachwaijer Klove - sp.: Pieter Lassing and Anna Maria (N.Y. City Luth. Chbk.).

    iii) <u>Lena</u>[3], b. 8 July 1750 and bpt. in Klove at Bachwaik at Niclaas Emig's - sp.: Pieter Janssen and Eva (N.Y. City Luth. Chbk.).

     iv) <u>Anna</u>[3], b. 30 March 1752 - sp.: Henrich Emig and Sara (Loonenburg Luth. Chbk.).

      v) <u>Lorentz</u>[3] (Will).

     vi) <u>Christina</u>[3], called Christian in Will.

    vii) <u>Georg</u>[3] (Will).

5) <u>Johann Nicolaus</u>[2], b. 30 Nov 1720 at Rheinbeeck - sp.: Christian Berg and Greetge Uling (N.Y. City Luth. Chbk.).

Niclaas, Hinrich and Eva Emig were conf. together at Nicolaes Emig's DNIA II, p.t.: 1740 (N.Y. City Luth. Chbk.).
He md. Eva (--). The will of Nicolaus Jr. was dated 8 May
1794 and probated 3 March 1810 (Dutchess Co. Will Bk. C).

6) Henrich², bpt. 29 July 1722 - sp.: Hendrik Oel and Margriet Teeter (Kingston Ref. Chbk.). He md. Sarah (--). The
   will of Hendric Emigh, yeoman, of Beekman was dated 21
   Aug 1801 and probated 11 Jan 1804 (Dutchess Co. Will Bk.
   B). Issue:

   i) Catharina³, b. 14 March 1752 - sp.: Joh: Niclaus
      Emig, Sr. and Catharina (Loonenburg Luth. Chbk.).
   ii) Nicolaus³ (Will).
   iii) Henrich³ (Will).
   iv) Margaretha³ (Will).
   v) Maria³ (Will).
   vi) Eleanor³ (Will).
   vii) Cornelia³ (Will).
   viii) Sarah³ (Will).
   ix) Rachel³ (Will).
   x) Elisabetha³ (Will).
   xi) Georg³ (Will).

7) Eva² (HJ), conf. with Niclaas and Hinrich DNIA II, p.t.:
   1740 (N.Y. City Luth. Chbk.). She md. Peter Janssen in
   the Highlands 13 June 1743 (N.Y. City Luth. Chbk.).

8) Johann Georg², bpt. 2 April 1727 - sp.: Jury Ekkert and
   Anna-Orsel Wykman (Kingston Ref. Chbk.). He md. Eva (--),
   and his will was dated 23 Feb 1799 and probated 29 Jan
   1810 (Dutchess Co. Will Bk. C). Issue:

   i) Nicolaus³, b. 25 Aug 1752 - sp.: Niclas Emig and Eva
      (Loonenburg Luth. Chbk.).
   ii) Maria Barbara³, b. 3 Oct 1754 - sp.: Pieter Dop and
       Gertruyd (Loonenburg Luth. Chbk.).
   iii) Johannes³, b. 31 Oct 1756 - sp.: Pieter Lassing and
        Anna Maria (Loonenburg Luth. Chbk.).
   iv) Johann Georg³, b. 12 Sept 1758 - sp.: Hinrich Emig
       and Sara (Loonenburg Luth. Chbk.). A Capt. George
       Ameigh d. 14 Feb 1830, aged 73 yrs. (Hudson Gazette,
       16 Feb 1830).
   v) Elisabetha³, b. 31 Oct 1760 - sp.: Philip Emig and
      Gertruyt (Loonenburg Luth. Chbk.).

9) Catharina², bpt. 8 weeks old 21 Sept 1729 at P. Lassing's
   - sp.: Peter Salomon Vlegeler and wife Margrete (N.Y.
   City Luth. Chbk.).

JOHANNES EMMERICH (Hunter Lists #164)

The ancestral origins of the West Camp Emmerichs were at 6474 Bleichenbach (22 km. n. of Hanau; Chbks. begin 1650, Ref.). and 6474 Selters (2 km. w. of Bleichenbach; Chbks. begin 1672). The tie to Bleichenbach is substantiated by Johannes Emmerich's interaction in the American colonies with his nephew, #302 Johannes Hess whom Kocherthal called of Bleichenbach: 1) Johannes Emmerich and Johannes Hess were listed next to each other on the Hunter Lists, 2) Johannes Emmerich sp. Johannes Hess in 1713 (Stone Arabia Luth. Family Book), and 3) Johannes Hess Jr. sp. Georg Elig and his wife Catharina Emmerich, d/o Johannes[1], in 1751 (Loonenburg Luth. Chbk.). The earliest known ancestor of the American family was Johann Emmerich, d. 23 Nov 1688, aged 74 yrs.; his wife Barbara d. 20 Jan 1689, aged 66 yrs. (Selters Chbk.). They had ch.:

> Johannes, bpt. 1 Jan 1652 - sp.: Johannes Emmrich of Reichelsheim (Bleichenbach Chbk.).
>
> Johann Conrad, bpt. 30 March 1657 - sp.: Conrad Emmerich, his brother from Bergheim (Bleichenbach Chbk.). D. 1665.
>
> Kunigunda, bpt. 5 June 1659 - sp.: the sister Kunigunda (Bleichenbach Chbk.). She md. Augustini Hess 20 Oct 1680 (Selters Chbk.); they were parents of the emigrant 1709er Johannes Hess.
>
> Anna Margaretha, bpt. 26 June 1662 - sp.: ... Helfrich Goddel (Bleichenbach Chbk.).
>
> + Johannes, bpt. 13 Nov 1664 (Bleichenbach Chbk.).
>
> Peter, bur. with his brother Johann Conradt 8 March 1665 (Bleichenbach Chbk.).

Johannes Emmerich made his first appearance on the Hunter Lists 30 June 1710, next to Johannes Hess; he was noted with 3 pers. over 10 yrs. of age in the household. In Aug and Oct of 1710 he was enrolled with 2 pers. over 10 yrs; on 24 June 1711 Emmerich had 2 pers. over 10 yrs. and 1 pers. under 10 yrs., and on 29 Sept 1711 the entry read 3 pers. over 10 yrs. and 1 pers. under 10. The family size diminished to 1 pers. over 10 yrs. 24 Dec 1711, and then increased again 25 March 1712 to 2 pers. over 10 yrs. and 1 pers. under 10 yrs. Joh[S] Emrich was nat. 8 and 9 Sept 1715 (Kingston Nats.). Johannes Emrich and Anna Margreta with 2 ch. were at Beckmansland ca. 1716/17 (Simmendinger Register). The w/o Johannes[1] Emmerich was Anna Margaretha (Depes? - HJ); she md. Henrich Brouwer 10 April 1735 (Catskill Ref. Chbk.), but there was much dissension among the family over the marriage (Albany Protocol, pp. 128-131). The ch. of Johannes[1] Emmerich and Anna Margaretha were:

1) Johanna Catharina², b. 17 Aug 1711 - sp.: Johann Hess and Catharina Curring (West Camp Luth. Chbk.). She was conf. at Newtown 25 Feb 1728 (N.Y. City Luth. Chbk.) and md. 26 Feb 1732 Johann Georg Elich at Newtown (Loonenburg Luth. Chbk.).

2) Elisabetha², b. 20 June 1714 - sp.: Johann Hess and wife Catharina (West Camp Luth. Chbk.). She was conf. 25 Feb 1728 at Newtown (N.Y. City Luth Chbk.) and md. 6 April 1736 Henrich Martin (Katsbaan Ref. Chbk.).

3) Anna², b. 20 July 1716 - sp.: Johann Valentin Froelich and wife Apollonia (West Camp Luth. Chbk.). She was conf. at Newton 1 April 1733, aged 16 yrs. (Loonenburg Luth. Chbk.) and md. Christian Becker 1 Sept 1735 (Katsbaan Ref. Chbk.).

4) Johannes², b. 7 May 1719 - sp.: Wilhelm Lehmann and his wife (West Camp Luth. Chbk.). Hannes Emmerich was conf. Feb 1738/39 at Newton (Loonenburg Luth. Chbk.). He md. Catharina Elisabetha Martin 26 Feb 1739 and d. 19 June 1739 (Loonenburg Luth. Chbk.); she md. 2nd Christian Führer 16 Feb 1740. They had one child:
    i) Maria³, b. 6 Feb 1740 and bpt. Cater-kill - sp.: Henrich Marten and wife Lisabeth (Loonenburg Luth. Chbk.). She md. Matthias Dieterich (HJ).

5) Anna Margaretha², b. 20 Nov 1721 at New Town in Albany - sp.: Christian Meyer and wife Anna Catharina (N.Y. City Luth. Chbk.). She md. Peter Becker Jr. 1 Oct 1745 (Kingston Ref. Chbk.).

6) Maria², b. 16 Sept 1724 - sp.: Adam Spohn and wife Anna Maria (West Camp Luth. Chbk.). She md. Georg Jung 26 March 1744 (Katsbaan Ref. Chbk.).

7) Henrich², b. 23 Dec 1726 - sp.: Johann Henrich Fesel and Christina (West Camp Luth. Chbk.).

8) Wilhelmus², md. as s/o Johannes 17 Dec 1749 Margaretha Laux (Loonenburg Luth. Chbk.). He was conf. at Newton 10 Jan 1747/48 (Loonenburg Luth. Chbk.). Wilhelmus Emmery was a freeholder of West Camp in 1763 (Albany Co. Freeholders). Wilhelmus Emmerigh was in Capt. Cornelus Dubois' Co. at Caskill in 1767 (Report of the State Historian, Vol. II, p. 877). His will was dated 12 June 1792 and probated 8 Oct 1792 (Ulster Co. Will Bk. A). He had issue:
    i) Johannes³, b. 1 May 1751 - sp.: Joh: Laux and Liesabeth (Loonenburg Luth. Chbk.).
    ii) Neeltje³, b. 10 Dec 1752 - sp.: Pieter Laux and Neeltje, in his place Jacob Eigener (Loonenburg Luth.

208

Chbk.). She md. Johannes Baker (Will).

   iii) <u>Margaretha</u>³, b. 19 March 1755 - sp.: Pieter Bekker and Margaretha (Loonenburg Luth. Chbk.). She md. Wilhelmus Wolven (Will).

   iv) <u>Petrus</u>³, b. 13 Dec 1757 - sp.: Petrus Eigener and Neeltje (Loonenburg Luth. Chbk.).

   v) <u>Wilhelmus</u>³, b. 28 May 1759 - sp.: Wilhelmy Laux and Liesabeth (Loonenburg Luth. Chbk.).

   vi) <u>Petrus</u>³, b. 18 June 1762 - sp.: Petrus Laux and Neeltje (Loonenburg Luth. Chbk.).

   vii) <u>Jeremiah</u>³, b. 19 May 1765 - sp.: Georg Elick and C: (Germantown Luth. Chbk.).

   viii) <u>Anna</u>³, bpt. 27 Sept 1767 - sp.: Adam Bahr and wife Annatien Spahn (Germantown Ref. Chbk.). She md. Nicolaus Shoemaker (Will).

JOHN MICHAEL EMMERICH (Hunter Lists #165)

Johann Michael Emerich of Delckenheim in the commune of Epstein in Darmstatt md. Elisabetha, wid/o Conrad Krantz of the commune of Zigenheim in Hesten 18 Dec 1711 (West Camp Luth. Chbk.). The actual village of origin was 6200 <u>Delkenheim</u> (5 km s.e. of Wiesbaden; Chbks. begin 1652). The earliest known ancestor of the American line was <u>Christoff Emmerich</u>, who was bur. 13 March 1683, aged 70 yrs. and 6 months; his widow Anna was bur. 22 May 1688, aged ca. 69 yrs. They had issue:

+ <u>Henrich</u>, bpt. 25 July 1652 - sp.: Henrich Pflug.
<u>Anna Christina</u>, bpt. 24 June 1655 - sp.: Christina Magdalena - d/o the Pastor at Massenheim, and Anna Marg. - eldest d/o Johann Michel.
<u>Johann Nicolaus</u>, bpt. 14 March 1658 - sp.: Nicl. Runtzheimer and Joh. Reinhard Geis, young man.
<u>Anna Maria</u>, bpt. 21 July 1661 - sp.: Anna Maria - w/o Henrich Pflug.
<u>Anna Catharina</u>, bpt. 10 Feb 1667 - sp.: Anna Cath. Cerfel (?) and Catharina - w/o Nicl. Runtzheimer.

<u>Henrich Emmerich</u> carried on the line. He was conf. in 1665 and md. 10 Dec 1678 Anna Margaretha - d/o Nicolaus Grünagel. Anna Margaretha, d/o Nicl. Grünagel, was bpt. 25 Sept 1653 - sp.: Anna - d/o Jacob Heil, and Joh. Jacob Caspar; Anna Grünagel was conf. in 1665. Nicolaus Grünagel md. Catharina (--) 7 Nov 1652, and Catharina was bur. 10 Sept 1677. Henrich Emmerich was bur. 19 Sept 1693, aged 41 yrs. and 2 months. The ch. of Henrich Emmerich and his wife Anna Margaretha Grünagel were:

<u>Anna Catharina</u>, bpt. 25 July 1680 - sp.: Maria Catharina - d/o Johann Michel, and Anna Christina - d/o Christophel Emmerich. She was conf. in 1695 and md. 3 April 1709 to the emigrant 1709er #751 Georg Henrich Stubenrauch.

+ <u>Johann Michael</u>, bpt. 2 March 1682 - sp.: Joh. Nicol Emmerich, and Johann Michael Emmerich, both single. He was conf. 1696.

<u>Elisabetha Catharina</u>, bpt. 17 Aug 1684 - sp.: Susanna Eliesab. - single d/o Johs. Betz; and Anna Catharina - single d/o the late Christoph Emmerich.

<u>Anna Maria</u>, bpt. 9 Oct 1687 - sp.: Anna - wid/o Joh. Jacob Caspar, and Anna Maria Emmerich - sister of the father.

<u>Christina Elisabetha</u>, bpt. 28 June 1692 - sp.: Elisabetha - wid/o Henrich Zabel, and Anna Christina - d/o Christoff Caspar.

Johann Michael Emmerich made his initial appearance on the Hunter Lists 4 Oct 1710 with 2 pers. over 10 yrs. of age in the family. The household diminished to 1 pers. over 10 yrs. of age 29 Sept 1711, was noted with 2 pers. over 10 and 1 pers. under 10 yrs. 24 Dec 1711, and then was registered with 2 pers. over 10 yrs. for all of 1712. Jho. Michel Emrich: 1 man and 1 woman were in Ulster Co. in 1710/11 (West Camp Census). Johann Michael Emrich and Elisabetha with 2 ch. were at Neu-Ansberg ca. 1716/17 (Simmendinger Register). Michael Emrich d. 1 June 1744 (Reed's Chbk., Tulpehocken). The will of Johes Michal Emerick of Tulpehocken was dated 10 June 1743 and probated 31 July 1744 (Philadelphia Co. Will Bk. G, p. 134). Issue:

1) <u>Anna Catharina</u>[2], b. 16 Dec 1712 - sp.: Wilhelm Kuester and Anna Catharina Stubenrauch (West Camp Luth. Chbk.).

As the will of Johann Michael[1] Emmerich does not name his ch., a complete list of his offspring with Elisabetha is difficult to determine. Probable issue were Balthas, Leonhard, Johann Adam, and Johannes Emrich conf. together Quasimodogeniti: 1745 (Tulpehocken Chbk.), Jacob Emerich - whose wife was bur. 29 Oct 1748 at the Blue Mountains (Tulpehocken Chbk.), and perhaps the Johann Georg Emrich (Emert, however, in some entries) who md. 26 April 1742 at Heidelberg (Stoever Chbk.).

ANNA MARIA EMRICHIN (Hunter Lists #166)

Georg Ludwig Leich, widower of Bernsfeld in Darmstatt, md. Maria Martha, wid/o Johann Peter Emmerich of Neustad on the Hard, 26 June 1711 (West Camp Luth. Chbk.). A soldier, Corporal Johann Peter Emmerich and his wife Maria Magdalena Rathgeber had a son

Johann Christoph b. 24 June 1699 at 6920 <u>Hilsbach</u>; this may have been an early reference to our N.Y. emigrant. Peter Emrig, his wife and 1 child were on Capt. Frans Wand's ship in Holland in 1709 (Rotterdam Lists).

Anna Maria Emrichin made her first appearance on the Hunter Lists 4 Oct 1710 with 1 pers. over 10 yrs. of age and 1 pers. under 10 in the family; her last entry was 24 June 1711 with 2 pers. over 10 yrs. of age in the household. Ana Mar. Emrichin: 1 woman and 1 maid aged 9 to 15 yrs. were in Ulster Co. in 1710/11 (West Camp Census).

JOHANNES ENGEL (Hunter Lists #167)

Johan Engel, his wife, and 3 ch. were recorded on Capt. Jan Duk's ship in Holland in 1709 (Rotterdam Lists). John Engel aged 36, his wife, daughters aged 10, 6, and 3, Rom. Cath., husbandman and vinedresser, were in the 4th arrivals in England later that year (London Lists).

Johannes Engel made his initial appearance on the Hunter lists 1 July 1710 with 2 pers. over 10 yrs. of age and 2 pers. under 10 yrs.; the last entry for the family was 4 Oct 1710 with the same numbers. Johannes Engel, Episcopal, joined the church in June 1710 under Rev. Daniel Falckner (West Camp Luth. Chbk.). The ch. of Johannes[1] Engel were:

1) <u>Christian</u>[2] (HJ), an orphan aged 12 yrs. bound to James Elmes of N.Y. 19 Feb 1711 (Apprenticeship Lists); due to the female daughters noted at London in 1709, this child may have been named Christina (HJ).

2) <u>Anna Maria</u>[2] (HJ), an orphan aged 8 when bound to Mary Robinson of N.Y. 19 Feb 1711, and then recorded as an orphan aged 11 when bound to Geo. Willocks of Elizabethtown 5 May 1714 (Apprenticeship Lists).

3) <u>Anna Elisabetha</u>[2] (HJ), an orphan aged 5 when bound to Ffrancis Salisbury of Kattskill 22 May 1712 (Apprenticeship Lists). She md. Nicolaus Schmidt 1 May 1726 (N.Y. City Luth. Chbk.).

There were other unplaced Engels in the middle colonies at an early date: 1) Anna Engelen van Sweits md. 24 July 1712 by Rev. Haeger to Jan Gardenier (Albany Ref. Chbk.), and 2) Hendrik Enkelse and wife Fronika had a son Joh: Hendrik Mattÿs bpt. 25 Dec 1722 (Hackensack Ref. Chbk.). There were many other Engels who arrived in N.J., Pa., and N.Y. in the middle of the 18th century (HJ).

MARIA ELIZABETHA ENGELIN (Hunter Lists #168)

Maria Elizabeth Engelin made her first appearance on the Hunter Lists 30 June 1710 with 1 pers. over 10 yrs. of age; the last entry for this woman was 4 Aug 1710 with 1 pers. over 10 yrs.

JOHANN PETER ENGELBERT (Hunter Lists #169)

Johann Peter Engelbert sp. Joh: Antonius Kexel in Holland in 1709 (Brielle Ref. Chbk.).

He made his first appearance on the Hunter Lists 1 July 1710 with 3 pers. over 10 yrs. of age in the family. His widow Margritie Wyndor (Margaretha Winter? -HJ) md. 19 Sept 1718 Abram Snyer (Hackensack Ref. Chbk.). The child of Johann Peter[1] Engelbert was:

> 1) Anna Maria[2] (HJ), a sp. at Hackensack in 1718. She md.
>   1 April 1721 Theunis Velten (Tappan Ref. Chbk.).

NICLAUS ENGELSBRUCHER (Hunter Lists #170)

The ancestral home of this emigrant was 6520 Worms (15 km. n. of Mannheim; Chbks. begin 1699). Nicol Engelsbrücher aged 57, his wife, a daughter aged 15, Ref., husbandman and vinedresser, were in England in 1709 (London Lists).

Niclaus Engelsbrucher made his first appearance on the Hunter Lists 4 Aug 1710 with 3 pers. over 10 yrs. of age. Michael Engelsprecher and Aña Catharina with 1 child were at Quunsberg ca. 1716/17 (Simmendinger Register). Nicolas Engelsbreker was a Palatine Debtor in 1718, 1721, and 1722 (Livingston Debt Lists). He was called a Beisaß and a Catholic, and his wife Catharina was noted as being Ref. at Worms when they had issue:

> 1) Susanna Catharina[2], b. 29 March 1707 - sp.: Suanna - d/o
>   H. Pfarrer Böhmer (Worms Chbk.).

TILLEMAN ENGSTENBURGER (Hunter Lists #171)

Tillemann Engstenberger made his only appearance on the Hunter rolls 4 Oct 1710 with 1 pers. over 10 yrs. of age in the family. Note the different spellings of his name from the journal to the ledger (HJ).

BERTRAM ENNERS (Hunter Lists #172)

The German village of origin for the Schoharie Enders family was 5419 Freirachdorf (22 km. n.e. of Neuwied; Chbks. begin 1689). The family is an old one in the area, and the name occurs quite often in churchbooks of the Dierdorf-Westerwald region.

212

Bertram Enners made his first appearance on the Hunter Lists
1 July 1710 with 3 pers. over 10 yrs. of age; the family increased
in size to 3 pers. over 10 and 1 pers. under 10 on 31 Dec 1710,
but returned to just 3 pers. over 10 yrs. 24 June 1711. Patron
Anders was nat. 17 Jan 1715/16 (Albany Nats.). Bartholomaus Endes
and wife Maria Christina and 3 ch. were at Neu-Heidelberg ca.
1716/17 (Simmendinger Register). Bertram[1] Enders and his wife Maria
Christina md. 3 June 1699 at Freirachdorf and had ch.:

1) <u>Anna Veronica[2]</u>, bpt. 19 Oct 1700 - sp.: Anna Catharina -
   w/o Christian Geier, Dietz Schwäze, and Veronica - w/o
   Jacob Enders (Freirachdorf Chbk.). She probably md. Henrich Hauck (HJ).

2) <u>Maria Clara[2]</u>, bpt. 8 Oct 1702 - sp.: Clara - w/o Johannis
   Henric Kutschid, Maria - d/o Johannes Völkers, and Ger-
   hardus Schluck from Offhausen (Freirachdorf Chbk.).

3) <u>Juliana Maria[2]</u>, bpt. 9 Aug 1705 - sp.: Peter Lehner, Juliana - w/o Peter ..., and Maria - w/o Georgius Schmid
   (Freirachdorf Chbk.).

4) <u>Johann Henrich[2]</u>, bpt. 18 Dec 1707 - sp.: Henricus Puderbach, Jacobus Enders, and Catharina - w/o Antony Jung
   (Freirachdorf Chbk.).

5) <u>Jacob[2]</u> (HJ), md. Anna Maria Sidnig (Süttenich) and had ch.:
   i) <u>Johann Henrich[3]</u>, b. 1 Sept 1736 and bpt. Schoharie -
      sp.: Henrich Hauck and Anna Veronica (Loonenburg Luth.
      Chbk.).
   ii) <u>Jacob Schneider[3]</u>, bpt. 9 Aug 1740 - sp.: Jacob Sneider
      and wife (Schoharie Ref. Chbk.). Vosburg says 1741 (HJ).
   iii) <u>Wilhelm[3]</u>, bpt. 12 July 1746 - sp.: Willem Enters and
      Elisabetha Margaretha, his wife (Schoharie Ref. Chbk.).
   iv) <u>Margaretha[3]</u>, bpt. 25 Feb 1749 - sp.: Christeyaan Sid-
      nig and wife Anna Margarith (Schoharie Ref. Chbk.).
   v) <u>Petrus[3]</u>, bpt. 11 May 1751 - sp.: Piter Hauch and Maria
      Barbara Merkel (Schoharie Ref. Chbk.).
   vi) <u>Johannes[3]</u>, bpt. 20 June 1754 - sp.: Johannes Merkel
      and Maria Hester Hauck (Schoharie Ref. Chbk.). Jo-
      hannes Entes, s/o Jacob, md. Anna Dorothea Bauch 16
      April 1780 (Schoharie Luth. Chbk.).
   vii) <u>Christian[3]</u>, bpt. 20 Sept 1756 - sp.: Christian Sit-
      tenich and Christina Hauck (Schoharie Ref. Chbk.).

6) <u>Johann Wilhelm[2]</u>, b. 11 May 1717 and bpt. at Schoharie -
   sp.: Jerg Baender, J. Wilhelm Schost, and Elisabeth Fidler
   (West Camp Luth. Chbk.). William Mentes was a freeholder
   at Schoharrie in 1763 (Albany Co. Freeholders). The will

of William Enders of Schohary, Albany Co., yeoman, was dated 29 Nov 1785 and probated 16 Feb 1786 (<u>Fernow Wills</u>
#605). He md. Elisabetha Margaretha Kneskern (HJ) and had:

   i) <u>Johann Jost</u>[3], bpt. 8 Oct 1743 - sp.: John Joost Knies-
      kern and Catharina Elisabeth (Schoharie Ref. Chbk.).
      He may have been the son John mentioned in William's
      will (HJ).

  ii) <u>Johann Wilhelm</u>[3], bpt. 12 April 1746 - sp.: Willem
      Dietz and wife Dorothea (Schoharie Ref. Chbk.). Wil-
      lem Enters, s/o Willem, md. Catharina Staarnberg 6
      Sept 1772 (Schoharie Ref. Chbk.).

 iii) <u>Maria</u>[3], bpt. 30 Dec 1747 - sp.: Jacob Enters and wife
      Anna Maria (Schoharie Ref. Chbk.). She md. Johannes
      Dietz 6 Oct 1773 (Schoharie Ref. Chbk.).

  iv) <u>Peter</u>[3], bpt. 27 April 1750 - sp.: Piter Knieskern and
      wife Elisa Barbara (Schoharie Ref. Chbk.).

   v) <u>Elisabetha</u>[3], bpt. 3 Feb 1751/52 - sp.: Henderick
      Knieskern and wife Elisabeth (Schoharie Ref. Chbk.).
      She md. Johannes Fischer 10 Oct 1773 (Schoharie Ref.
      Chbk.).

  vi) <u>Margaretha</u>[3], bpt. 29 Sept 1753 - sp.: Niclaas Merkel
      and Elisa Creed (Schoharie Ref. Chbk.).

 vii) <u>Jacob</u>[3], b. 25 Aug 1756 - sp.: Johan Jacob Werth and
      wife (Schoharie Luth. Chbk.). He md. Elisabeth Stern-
      berger 7 Oct 1781 (Schoharie Luth. Chbk.).

viii) <u>Christina</u>[3], b. 30 April 1758 - sp.: Pitter Hauck and
      Christina Enders (Schoharie Ref. Chbk.). She md. Jacob
      Kniskern 10 Feb 1782 (Schoharie Luth. Chbk.).

  ix) <u>Anna</u>[3], b. 18 March 1760 - sp.: Hannes Becker the Ger-
      man and Anna Maria, his wife (Schoharie Ref. Chbk.).

There were other early Enders-Enters in colonial N.J. and
N.Y.: 1) Henrich Enters and wife Anna Maria Best had ch. in Hudson
Valley Chbks. 1743-55, 2) Joannes Enters from Spÿtenduivel md. 21
Nov 1730 Maria Regtmeyer (Hackensack Ref. Chbk.), and 3) Johannis
Enders from Germany md. 24 Feb 1739 Zara Fosuur (Tarrytown Ref.
Chbk.).

<u>CATHARINA ERBIN</u> (Hunter Lists #173)

A document in the Staatsarchivs Wiesbaden (Nassau-Weilburg
Abteilung 150/4493, Actum d. 23 Mai 1709) revealed much data on
one Heinrich Erbe, a prospective emigrant in 1709. Erbe was noted
as being aged 63 yrs. old, a Luth., born "here", and md. 24 yrs.
with 9 ch. He said he first thought of emigrating when a carpenter

214

from Esserhaussen brought a book to Rohnstatt in which he saw particulars (of the exodus); also poverty drove him to it. He received
advice concerning this from no one and knew nothing beyond what
was in the books. In order to travel, he said, he would have to
sell something of what he owned. A Johan Hendrig Obresch, his
wife and 7 ch. were on Capt. William Koby's ship in the 5th party
and a Hans Henrig Erbs, his wife and 3 ch. were on Capt. Francois
Warens's ship in the 5th party in Holland (Rotterdam Lists); the
latter family probably returned to the continent (HJ).

Catharina Erbin made her first appearance on the Hunter Lists
1 July 1710 with 1 pers. over 10 yrs. of age and 1 pers. under 10
yrs.; she often was listed on these rolls among 1709ers from the
Nassau region (i.e. Johann Jost Laux and Johann Jacob Zimmermann).
Anna Catharina Erbin aged 44, a widow, and Eliz Catha Erbin aged
9 were in N.Y. City in 1710/11 (Palatines In N.Y. City). The child
of Catharina[1] Erb was:

1) Elisabetha Catharina[2] (Palatines In N.Y. City). Elisabeth
Erbin, a German in N.Y., was conf. or joined the church
in 1713 (N.Y. City Luth. Chbk.). She sp. Zacharias Ofenauf
in 1727 (N.Y. City Luth. Chbk.) and pledged money to the
same church that year (N.Y. City Luth. Protocol). Elisabeth
Erving md. Jacob Kien 11 Jan 1730 (N.Y. City Ref. Chbk.).

BERNHARD ERCKEL (Hunter Lists #174)

Bernhard Erkel aged 33 and his wife, Ref., husbandman and
vinedresser, were in the 1st arrivals in England in 1709 (London
Lists).

He made his first appearance on the Hunter Lists 4 Oct 1710
with 1 pers. over 10 yrs. of age in the household; the family increased to 2 pers. over 10 yrs. of age 24 June 1711. Bernhard Erkel
aged 53 and Anna Maria Erkel aged 43 were in N.Y. City in 1710/11
(Palatines In N.Y. City). Bernhard Erckelt and his wife were at
Hackensack ca. 1716/17 (Simmendinger Register).

SIMON ERHARDT (Hunter Lists #175)

John Simon Erhardt aged 46, with his wife, sons aged 6 and 3,
a daughter aged 8, Ref., husbandman and vinedresser, were in the
2nd arrivals in England in 1709 (London Lists).

Simon Erhardt made his initial appearance on the Hunter Lists
4 Aug 1710 with 1 pers. over 10 yrs. and 3 pers. under 10; the entry changed to 1 pers. over 10 and 2 pers. under 10 on 4 Oct 1710.

The notation read 2 pers. over 10 yrs. and 2 pers. under 10 on
31 Dec 1710, and the family changed to 3 pers. over 10 yrs. and
1 pers. under 10 yrs. 24 June 1711. The Erhardts were recorded
with 3 pers. over 10 yrs. and 2 pers. under 10 on 24 Dec 1711.
Symon Herhardt was nat. 3 Jan 1715/16 (Albany Nats.). Simon Erhardt and his wife Anna Margretha with 5 ch. were at Neu-Heessberg
ca. 1716/17 (Simmendinger Register). Simon Earhart was a patentee
in 1723 (Stone Arabia Patent). Symon Eerhart and Karrell Eerhart
were mentioned as grantors (among others) to William Van Schelluyne
for land at Stone Arabie 1 Sept 1734 (Albany Co. Deeds, Vol. 7,
p. 520). Simon[1] and Anna Margaretha Erhardt had ch.:

1) Carl[2] (HJ), a co-grantor with Simon[1] at Stone Arabia in
1734. A Carl or Charles Ehrhardt and wife Clara had:
   i) Theobaldt[3], bpt. 5 June 1734 at Opequon - sp.: Theobaldt Gerlach (Stoever Chbk.).
They sp. Rilie Moor in 1737 at Shenandoah (Stoever Chbk.).
2) Catharina[2] (HJ), md. Georg Haus (HJ).
3) Anna Rosina[2] (HJ), md. Georg Kuhn (HJ).
4) Maria Catharina[2], bpt. 6 Nov 1711 - sp.: Johann Niclaus
Schäffer and wife Maria Catharina (West Camp Luth. Chbk.).
This child may have been #2 Catharina aforementioned (HJ).
5) Johannes[2] (HJ), one of the first four ch. born in the Palatine Schoharie settlements (Simm's History of Schoharie,
p. 51). A Jno. Erhardt aged 50 yrs., b. Germany, carpenter, 5' 8 3/4", swarthy complexion, blue eyes, light brown
hair, enlisted in Capt. John Veghten's Co. 4 May 1761 in
the Co. of Albany (Report of the State Historian, Vol. II,
p. 633). Johannes[2] md. Christina Wies (HJ). They sp. Joh.
Michael Brant in 1745/46 (Fort Hunter Chbk.) and had ch.:
   i) Adam[3], bpt. 21 May 1751 - sp.: Adam Eccert and Catharina Bessinger (Stone Arabia Ref. Chbk.).
   ii) Wilhelm[3], bpt. 9 May 1756 - sp.: John Perry and Fran-
   cyntje Cloet (Albany Ref. Chbk.).

There were other Erhardts in the Stoever Chbk. who may have
been related (HJ): John Michael Ehrhardt md. 27 May 1740 Catharina
Elisabetha Lesch at Tulpehocken, Margaretha Ehrhardt md. Johannes
Dierdorf at Conewago 22 May 1740, and Maria Elisabetha Ehrhardt md.
Carl Thiel 24 Nov 1742 at Codorus.

HENRICH ESCHENREUTER (Hunter Lists #176)

Hendrich Escheröder aged 46, his wife, and a son aged 18,
Luth., carpenter, were in England in 1709 (London Lists).

Henrich Eschenreuter made his first appearance on the Hunter Lists 4 July 1710 with 2 pers. over 10 yrs. of age. Anna Margretha Eschenreiter, Epis., joined the church 24 June 1711 (West Camp Luth. Chbk.). She sp. Martin Netzbacher in 1715 (West Camp Luth. Chbk.). Eschrodter's widow - Maria Margaretha - was noted at Quunsberg ca. 1716/17 (Simmendinger Register).

CATHARINA ESCHOFFIN (Hunter Lists #177)

A possible town of origin for Catharina Eschoffin may have been 6251 Runkel (10 km. s.w. of Weilburg; Chbks. begin 1651). A Johann Henrich Eschhoven and wife Elisabetha had a daughter Anna Catharina b. 22 Jan 1694 - sp.: Jodocus Eschhoven and Anna Catharina Hartmänn at Runkel. A Jocobus Eschhoven md. Maria Catharina Nassauw 19 Oct 1681, and they had a daughter Anna Catharina b. 23 April 1692 - sp.: Johannes Wilhelmus Schön, Katharina - wid/o Adam Becker, and Catharina Rompel (Runkel Chbk.). Either of these two Anna Catharinas may have been our 1709er (HJ).

Catharina Eschoffin made her first appearance on the Hunter Lists 4 Aug 1710; she was called Anna Elizabetha Eschoffin once on 31 Dec 1710, but Catharina on all later dates in Hunter. Catharina Eschofin uit de Hoogduidschekerk joined the N.Y. City Ref. Church 31 Aug 1716. She md. Johannes Rÿpele 25 May 1719 (Albany Ref. Chbk.). They sp. several German families at N.Y. City Ref. Church. The will of her husband John Rypele of N.Y. City dated 18 July 1745 mentioned William Speeder (Späder), whose family was documented at Runkel.

THOMAS ESCHWEIN'S WIDDOW (Hunter Lists #178)

Anna Elisabetha, wid/o Thoma Esswein of Hart in the commune of Germersheim, md. Johann Mickler, widower of Perthenheim in the commune of Altzeyer in the Pfaltz, 10 Oct 1710 (West Camp Luth. Chbk.). The actual village of origin for the Eschweins was 6729 Hördt (18 km. s. of Speyer; Chbks. begin 1695, Cath.). Joannes Thomas, s/o Joannis Esswein of Herdens, md. 28 May 1696 Elisabetha, d/o Joannis Werner of Gunspach. Tomas Eschweiler, his wife and 2 ch. were noted 10 June 1709 on Capt. John Howlentzon's ship in Holland (Rotterdam Lists). Thomas Eschweiler was listed next to Jacob Eschwein in London in the 4th arrivals later that year: Thomas Eschweiler aged 34, with his wife, daughters aged 10 and 6, Ref., husbandman and vinedresser (London Lists).

Thomas Eschwein made his first appearance on the Hunter Lists 4 July 1710 with 2 pers. over 10 yrs. of age in his family. The entry for 4 Aug 1710 read Thomas Eschwein's wid[W] and for 4 Oct 1710 recorded Elizabeth Eschweinin, a wid[W]. The ch. of Thomas[1] Eschwein and his wife Anna Elisabetha were:

1) <u>Christina</u>[2], bpt. 9 April 1697 - sp.: Georgius Albertus Sax ... (Hördt Chbk.). She md. Hans Georg Mustiir (HJ). Her maiden name was noted both as Eswyn (Poughkeepsie Ref. Chbk.) and Midler (N.Y. City Luth. Chbk.), for her step-father Johannes Midler (Mitteler).

2) <u>Maria Elisabetha</u>[2], bpt. 13 Dec 1699. She d. Dec 1701, aged 1 yr. (Hördt Chbk.).

JACOB ESS (Hunter Lists #179)

The probable ancestral origins of Jacob Ess just prior to 1709 were at 6348 <u>Herborn</u> (22 km. n. of Weilburg; Chbks. begin 1638). Jacob Ess, s/o the late Johannes Ess formerly of Sonthofen in the Augsburg area, md. Anna Catharina Sergius, d/o the late Herr Werner Sergius - formerly Pastor at Rückeroth in the Grafschaft Neuwied, on 8 Sept 1707 (Herborn Chbk.). Hans Jacob Egh, his wife and 1 child were enrolled next to Hans Jürg Egh and his wife on Capt. Robbert Bulman's ship in Holland in 1709 (Rotterdam Lists). Jacob Ess aged 49, his wife and a daughter aged 1, R. Cath., husbandman and vinedresser, were in the 4th arrivals in England later that year (London Lists).

Jacob Ess made his first appearance on the Hunter Lists 1 July 1710 with 2 pers. over 10 yrs. of age in the household; on 25 March 1712 the family was noted with 1 pers. over 10, and then resumed the entry stating 2 pers. over 10 yrs. 24 June 1712. Jacob Ess of Annsberg was a soldier in 1711 (Palatine Volunteers To Canada). Jacob Ess and Anna Catharina lived at Neu-Ansberg ca. 1716/17 (Simmendinger Register); on the original page in this census they were listed but one name from Johannes Mühl, and the 1709er Mauls intermarried with Sergius family also.

JACOB ESWEIN (Hunter Lists #180)

Like #178 Thomas Eschwein, the roots of #180 Jacob Eschwein also were at 6729 <u>Hördt</u> (18 km. s. of Speyer; Chbks. begin 1695, Cath.). Hans Jacob Öhswein of Hördt md. 2 Feb 1699 Anna Margaretha Schneider, d/o Nicolaus Shneider of Rülsheim; the witnesses to the marriage were Thomas Liebel and Joh: Jacobus Eswein, Anwalt. Contrary to the opinion expressed by H. Minot Pitman in his <u>Snyder-Brown Ancestry</u>, the sp. at the marriage suggest the possibility that the two Eschwein emigrants, Jacob and Thomas, may not have

been brothers: Thomas[1] was s/o Joannis Esswein according to his
marriage entry, and Jacob[1] may have been s/o the attorney Joh:
Jacob Eswein, witness at his marriage (HJ). Margaretha Volker, w/o
Jacob Ohswein the attorney d. 23 Jan 1704, aged ca. 74 yrs. after
being md. 46 yrs. Jacob Eschweiler, his wife and 3 ch. were in the
4th party in Holland on Capt. John Howlentzon's ship in 1709 (Rotterdam Lists). Jacob Eschwein aged 41, his wife, a son aged 5, and
daughters aged 7 and 1, Ref., husbandman and vinedresser, were in
the 4th arrivals in England (London Lists).

Jacob Eswein made his first appearance on the Hunter Lists 1
July 1710 with 3 pers. over 10 yrs. of age and 3 pers. under 10;
the family was recorded with 2 pers. over 10 yrs. and 3 pers. under
10 4 Aug 1710. The size diminished to 2 pers. over 10 yrs. and 2
pers. under 10 yrs. 4 Oct 1710, and then increased again to 2 pers.
over 10 and 3 under 10 yrs. 25 March 1712. Jacob Eswine was nat.
31 Jan 1715/16 (Albany Nats.). Jacob Eschwein with his wife and
ch. was at Hunderston ca. 1716/17 (Simmendinger Register). Jacob
Eswin was a Palatine Debtor in 1718, 1721 and 1726 (Livingston
Debt Lists). Jacob Eschwyn, widower at Claverack, md. 27 Nov 1720
at Claverack Maria Herder, wid. at Queensberry (N.Y. City Luth.
Chbk.). They sp. Jureje Adam Smit in 1723/24 (Kinderhook Ref.
Chbk.) and Peter Herder in 1734 (Rhinebeck Luth. Chbk.). Jacob[1]
had issue with his 1st wife:

1) Anna Catharina[2], bur. 29 Nov 1707, aged 7 yrs. and 8 weeks
   (Hördt Chbk. per H. Minot Pitman).
2) Johann Jacobus[2], bpt. 16 June 1701 - sp.: Jacobus Doll and
   wife Anna Margareth Öhswein (Hördt Chbk.). He was bur.
   7 Oct 1702 (Hördt Chbk. per H. Minot Pitman).
3) Anna Margaretha[2], bpt. 15 July 1703 - sp.: Anna Margretha
   Hennig, single (Hördt Chbk.). She md. 1st Peter Schneider
   and 2nd Henrich Ells or Kells (HJ).
4) Georg Adam[2], b. 30 Jan 1706 - sp.: Jörg Adam Böhm and Anna
   Margretha Hennig, single (Hördt Chbk.).
5) Eva Catharina[2], b. 3 Sept 1708 - sp.: Hans Jörg Moser and
   wife Catharina Scherer (Hördt Chbk.).
6) Maria[2], md. as d/o Jacob 20 Oct 1738 Francis Herdyk (Loonenburg Luth. Chbk.).
7) Johann Wendel[2], b. 15 Sept 1714 - sp.: Johann Wendel Pulver
   and Justina - w/o Theobald Scherer (West Camp Luth.). He
   md. Gerritje Herdyk 28 June 1740 (Loonenburg Luth. Chbk.)
   and was mentioned by Berkenmeyer in his Protocol in 1750
   (Albany Protocol, p. 515).
8) Veronica[2], bpt. 1 Feb 1719 - sp.: Anna Maria Schneider
   (West Camp Luth. Chbk.).

PETER EYGNER (Hunter Lists #181)

Peter Eygner made his initial appearance on the Hunter Lists
1 July 1710 with 2 pers. over 10 yrs. of age in the household; the
family increased to 2 pers. over 10 yrs. and 1 pers. under 10 on
the 24 June 1712 entry. Peter Egner: 1 man and 1 woman were in Ulster Co. in 1710/11 (West Camp Census). Peter Eygenaar was nat. 8
and 9 Sept 1715 (Kingston Nats.). Peter Eygner and Anna Margretha
with 2 ch. were at Beckmansland ca. 1716/17 (Simmendinger Register). He was a member of Berkenmeyer's Church Council in 1735
(Albany Protocol, p. 115). The ch. of Peter[1] Eygner and his wife
Anna Margaretha were:

1) Johann Jacob[2], md. as s/o Pieter Eigener 6 Jan 1734 at
Newton Anna Margaretha Maurer (Loonenburg Luth. Chbk.).
His wife's dates as found on her tombstone were 13 Aug
1712 - 5 Dec 1769 (Dederick Cem., West Camp). Joh. Jacob
Eigener was conf. 15 April 1729 at Newton, aged 17 yrs.
(N.Y. City Luth. Chbk.). Jury William Dederick of West
Camp deeded land to Jacob Eigenaer of the same place, far-
mer, 28 March 1754 or 1764 (hard to read - HJ) (Albany Co.
Deeds: Vol. 7, p. 314). Jacob Jegenaer was a freeholder
of West Camp in 1763 (Albany Co. Freeholders). He was registered in Capt. Cornelus Dubois's Co. at Caskill in
1767 (Report of the State Historian, Vol. II, p. 876). Ch.:
    i) Petrus[3], b. 13 Oct 1734 and bpt. at Newtown in Pieter
    Eigener's house - sp.: Susanna Eigern and Hannes Mau-
    rer (Loonenburg Luth. Chbk.). He was probably the
    Petrus Eygenaer mentioned with Jacob Eygenaer in 1767
    in Capt. Dubois's Co. (HJ). Petrus[3] md. 6 Jan 1756
    Neeltje Laux (Loonenburg Luth. Chbk.); they had ch.
    bpt. at Loonenburg Luth., Germantown Ref., and West
    Camp Luth. Churches.
    ii) Jacob[3], b. 23 Oct 1740 and bpt. Newton - sp.: Pieter
    Eigener and An. Margr., grandparents (Loonenburg Luth.
    Chbk.).
    iii) Johannes[3], b. 24 Sept 1745 and bpt. Newton - sp.:
    Peter Maurer and Catharina, grandparents (Loonenburg
    Luth. Chbk.).
2) Susanna Margaretha[2], b. 9 Feb 1714 - sp.: Margretha Schramm,
Susanna Kuester, Mattheus Schlemmer, and Jorg Wilhelm Kaehl
(West Camp Luth. Chbk.). Susanna Eigenern was conf. 24 Feb
1731 at Newton, aged 25 yrs. (N.Y. City Luth. Chbk.). She
md. Johannes Maurer 19 Jan 1739 (Loonenburg Luth. Chbk.).
3) Johann Friederich[2], b. 29 March 1716 - sp.: Valentin

Fuehrer, Fridrich Schramm, and Anna Maria Kuester (West
Camp Luth. Chbk.). Joh. Frid. Eigener was conf. 1 April
1733, aged 16 at Newton (Loonenburg Luth. Chbk.). He md.
Christina Maurer 2 Dec 1739 (Loonenburg Luth. Chbk.). Ch.:

    i) Catharina[3], b. 15 Dec 1741 and bpt. Newton - sp.:
    Hannes Maurers and wife Susanna (Loonenburg Luth.
    Chbk.). She md. Adam Mattestock (HJ).

    ii) Petrus[3], b. 19 Feb 1745 and bpt. Newton - sp.: Jo:
    Jac: Eigener and Hanna Margr. (Loonenburg Luth.
    Chbk.). He md. Elisabetha Mattestock (HJ).

   iii) Andreas[3], bpt. 11 April 1748 - sp.: Pieter Eigenaar
    and Catharina Maurer (Katsbaan Ref. Chbk.).

    iv) Maria[3], b. 1 March 1753 - sp.: Lenert Lucas and Anna
    Maria (Loonenburg Luth. Chbk.).

    v) Cornelius[3], b. 20 Oct 1756 - sp.: Petrus Laux and
    Catharina Maurer (Loonenburg Luth. Chbk.).

    vi) Friederich[3], b. 28 May 1760 - sp.: Dieterich Mates-
    tok and Eva Maria (Loonenburg Luth. Chbk.).

   vii) Johannes[3], b. 25 Feb 1764 - sp.: Hans Eigener and
    Greetje Dieterich (Loonenburg Luth. Chbk.).

4) Johann Balthasar[2], b. 26 Aug 1718 - sp.: J. Balthasar Kuester, and the w/o Veltin Falckenburg (West Camp Luth. Chbk.).
He d. 26 Aug 1718, aged 1 day (West Camp Luth. Chbk.).

PETER EYGNER'S WIDDOW (Hunter Lists #182)

Peter Eygner's wid[W] made her only appearance on the Hunter
Lists 1 July 1710. By closely studying the juxtaposition of names
surrounding her on these rolls, I believe she actually was #183
Jeremia Eygnerin's wid[W], and that the incorrect name was entered
(HJ).

JEREMIA EYGNERIN (Hunter Lists #183)

Jeremia Eygner's wid[W] was noted on the Hunter Lists 4 Aug
1710 in the same location in the journal as #182 above; she also
had but 1 pers. over 10 yrs. in her family.

PETER FAEG (Hunter Lists #184)

The German origins of the Faeg family were 6580 Idar-Oberstein
(14 km. s.w. of Kirn; Chbks. begin 1669, Luth.). The earliest known
ancestor of the Tulpehocken pioneer was Johannes Schneider . His
son Nicolaus Schneider md. 28 Sept 1671 Anna Margaretha, d/o Wilhelm Koch. Wilhelm Koch d. Sept 1674, aged 59 yrs. and his wife
Lucia d. 29 Sept 1679. Nicolaus Schneider was bur. as Nicolaus Feg

27 April 1724, aged 76 yrs., 1 month, 3 weeks, and 1 day; Anna
Margaretha, his wife, d. Nov 1697, aged 45 yrs. Johann Peter, s/o
Nicolaus and Anna Margaretha Schneider, was bpt. 17 Nov 1672.
Johann Peter Feg md. Anna Maria, d/o Johannes Risch, 26 Nov 1697.
Anna Maria, d/o Johannes Risch and Anna Margaretha, was bpt. 1 May
1681. The N.Y. 1709er Jacob Risch md. Margaretha Petri the same
day at Idar, and a notation after this double wedding mentioned
the both these couples have left here and moved to Pennsylvania.

Peter Faeg made his first appearance on the Hunter Lists,
next to Johannes Faeg, 4 July 1710 with 2 pers. over 10 yrs. of
age and 3 pers. under 10 yrs. in the family; the size increased
to 3 pers. over 10 yrs. and 3 pers. under 10 on 24 June 1711.
The entry for 24 June 1712 read 4 pers. over 10 yrs. and 2 pers.
under 10 yrs., and the notation for 13 Sept 1712 recorded 3 pers.
over 10 yrs. and 2 pers. under 10. Peter Feeck was nat. 11 Oct
1715 (Albany Nats.). Peter Feck and Anna Maria with 4 ch. were
at Neu-Stuttgardt ca. 1716/17 (Simmendinger Register). Peter Feg
d. 5 Dec 1744, aged 72 yrs. (Reed's Chbk., Tulpehocken). The will
of Peter Feck was probated in 1748 (Philadelphia Co. Will Bk. I,
p. 68). The ch. of Peter¹ Feg and Anna Maria were:
1) Anna Catharina², md. Peter Reed (Will).
2) Anna Eva², md. Johann Conrad Weiser (Will).
3) Eva Elisabetha², conf. as Eva Elisabeth Fetzin in 1720
   at Tschoghari at the so-called Fuchsen-Dorp (N.Y. City
   Luth. Chbk.).
4) Elisabetha², b. 14 Feb 1713 at Norman's Kill, Albany and
   bpt. Albany - sp.: Nickel Ecker and Elisabeth Schmid (N.Y.
   City Luth. Chbk.). She md. Peter Schäffer in 1729 (Reed's
   Chbk., Tulpehocken).
5) Anna Margaretha², b. 18 Dec 1715 and bpt. Schoharie - sp.:
   Johann Georg Kast and his wife, and Anna Maria Feeg (West
   Camp Luth. Chbk.).
6) Johann Leonhardt², md. as s/o Peter Feg 2 Nov 1742 Janige
   Von Huss(en) (Reed's Chbk., Tulpehocken). The Berks Co.
   Orphan's Court (p. 50) noted 16 May 1766 that Leonard Feck
   d. 8 yrs. earlier leaving a widow Johanna, since md. to
   Jno. Roos, and 3 ch.:
   i) Johannes³, the eldest son (Orphan's Court Record).
   ii) Peter³, aged 17 in 1766 (Orphan's Court Record).
   iii) Anna Maria³, aged 14 in 1766 (Orphan's Court Record).
7) Peter², md. as s/o Peter Feg 2 May 1743 Christina Karr
   (Reed's Chbk., Tulpehocken). The will of Peter Faeg of
   Heidelberg was dated 19 July 1790 and probated 29 Oct 1790

(Berks Co. Will Bk. 3, p. 150). Ch. from that will:

    i) Jacob[3].
   ii) Anna Maria[3].
  iii) Elisabetha[3].
   iv) Eva Magdalena[3].
    v) Anna Catharina[3].
   vi) Anna Margaretha[3].
  vii) Christina[3].
 viii) Maria Catharina[3].
   ix) Sophia[3].
    x) Magdalena[3].

JOHANNES FAEG (Hunter Lists #185)

Leonard Feg of Schoharie, s/o the late Johann Feg of Oberstein in the duchy of Nastau-Sig, md. Anna Catharina Schutz, d/o the late Conrad Schutz of Langen Sollwest in the earldom of Isenberg, 1 Nov 1715 (West Camp Luth. Chbk.). As noted in the section on #184 Peter Faeg, the ancestral home of this family was 6580 Idar-Oberstein (14 km. s.w. of Kirn; Chbks. begin 1669, Luth.). The earliest known ancestor of #185 Johannes Faeg was Johannes Schneider of Vollmersbach, the same man who was grandfather to #184 Peter Faeg. Johannes Schneider (Jr.) md. 12 April 1689 Anna Margaretha Becker, d/o Martin Becker. Anna Margaretha, d/o Martin and Elisabetha Becker, was bpt. 28 Oct 1672. Johannes Schneider (Jr.) also changed his name to Faeg: the Idar Chbk. mentioned in 1693 that John Veeck has moved to Pennsylvania with wife and ch. A Johan Faech, his wife, and 4 ch. were listed on Capt. Johan Enrit or Encrist's ship in Holland in 1709 (Rotterdam Lists).

Johannes Faeg made his initial appearance on the Hunter Lists 4 July 1710, next to Peter Faeg, with 7 pers. over 10 yrs. in his family. The size increased to 7 pers. over 10 yrs. and 1 pers. under 10 yrs. 31 Dec 1710, after a separate entry had been recorded for his child under 10 yrs. on 4 Oct 1710. Johannis Feeg of Queensbury was a soldier in 1711 (Palatine Volunteers To Canada). Johannes Feeck was nat. 11 Oct 1715 (Albany Nats.). Joh. Feck, Anna Maria Margretha with 5 ch. were at Neu-Stuttgardt ca. 1716/17 (Simmendinger Register). Widow Anna Margaretha Feg was living in Pa. in April 1745 (Reed's Chbk., Tulpehocken). The ch. of Johannes[1] Feg and wife Anna Margaretha were:

  1) Elisabetha Barbara[2], bpt. 25 Dec 1693 (Idar Chbk.). She md. as d/o Johannes Feg 31 March 1714 Frantz Finck (West Camp Luth. Chbk.).

  2) Leonhardt[2], md. as s/o Johannes Feeg 1 Nov 1715 Anna

Catharina Schutz (West Camp Luth. Chbk.). Leonhard Feck and his wife Catharina were at Neu-Stuttgardt ca. 1716/17 (Simmendinger Register). The will of Leonhard Fech was dated 23 May 1743 and probated 2 Sept 1743 (Philadelphia Co. Admin. Bk. E, p. 5). Issue:

    i) Elisabetha Magdalena[3], md. as d/o Leonhard Feg Dom. 17, p. Trin: 1745 Leonhard Noef (Tulpehocken Chbk.).

    ii) Johannes[3] (Will).

    iii) Anna[3] (Will).

    iv) Anna Margaretha[3] (Will).

    v) Maria Barbara[3] (Will).

3) Catharina[2] (HJ), perhaps the Catharina Feg conf. 23 March 1712 at Queensberg (West Camp Luth. Chbk.), unless she was the d/o #184 Peter Faeg (HJ).

4) Maria Barbara[2], md. 15 May 1717 Michael Rieth (Reed's Chbk., Tulpehocken).

5) Maria Margaretha[2], bpt. 24 Sept 1710 at N.Y. - sp.: J. Jacob Risch, Anna Maria Feeg, and Margretha Kuntz (West Camp Luth. Chbk.). She md. Hermannus Walborn (HJ).

6) Jacob[2] (HJ), md. Anna Maria Dausweber (HJ). Jacob Feeck was nat. 11 Oct 1715 (Albany Nats.). He sp. Michael Rieth and his wife Maria Barbara Feg in 1723 (Reed's Chbk., Tulpehocken). The wid/o Jacob[2] md. Zacharias Oenmaest 7 Nov 1724 (Tappan Ref. Chbk.). The ch. of Jacob[2] Feeck were:

    i) Jacob[3], b. 11 April 1716 at Packquee - bpt. in Highland - sp.: Theobald Sherer and wife Justina, in their absence Hannes Mittler and wife Eliz. (N.Y. City Luth. Chbk.).

    ii) Christina[3], b. 5 Dec 1718 in Highland - sp.: Andreas Volck and Christina Tansweber (N.Y. City Luth. Chbk.).

    iii) Nicolaus[3], b. 3 March 1721 at Tapan and bpt. Hackinsack - sp.: Niclaes Neiddebber and Elisabeth Finck (N.Y. City Luth. Chbk.).

    iv) Margaretha[3], b. 1 Feb 1723 - sp.: Pieter Haringh and wife Grietie Bogaart (Tappan Ref. Chbk.).

7) Nicolaus[2] (HJ), a sp. to Michael Rieth and wife Maria Barbara Feg in 1718 (Reed's Chbk., Tulpehocken). Nicolas Fege was noted on Pastor Sommer's list of Luth. families at Schoharie ca. 1744/45 (Schoharie Luth. Chbk.). He d. 25 June 1746, aged 47 yrs. (Schoharie Luth. Chbk.). His wife was Margaretha Miller, and she may have been the Old Mrs. Feeg who d. 1 Nov 1772 (Schoharie Luth. Chbk.). The ch. of Nicolaus[2] and his wife Margaretha were:

    i) Jacob[3] (HJ), md. 31 Oct 1749 Anna Maria Vroman

(Schoharie Luth. Chbk.). Jacob Feek was a freeholder at Schoharrie in 1763 (Albany Co. Freeholders). Jacob Feake was in Capt. Thomas Ackeson's Co. in 1767 (Report of the State Historian, Vol. II, p. 845). The will of a Jacob Fack, deceased yeoman of Middleburgh was dated 17 Sept 1797 and probated 12 March 1798 (Schoharie Co. Will Bk. A).

ii) Johannes[3] (Schoharie Luth. 1744/45 List). A Johannes Veeg md. Jannetje Last 2 Feb 1758 (Schoharie Luth. Chbk.). Johannes Feek was a freeholder at Schoharrie in 1763 (Albany Co. Freeholders). Johannis Feake was a soldier in Capt. Thomas Ackeson's Co. in 1767 (Report of the State Historian, Vol. II, p. 845).

iii) Magdalena[3] (Schoharie Luth. 1744/45 List), d. 24 June 1746, aged 19 yrs. and 6 months (Schoharie Luth. Chbk.).

iv) Margaretha[3] (Schoharie Luth. 1744/45 List), d. 24 June 1746, aged 14 yrs. and 5 months (Schoharie Luth. Chbk.).

v) Cornelius[3], bpt. Nov 1735 - sp.: Cornelis Vroman and Maria Catje Snell (Schoharie Ref. Chbk.).

vi) Maria[3], bpt. 25 June 1738 - sp.: Michel Vrymayer and Anna Maria Bauch (Schoharie Ref. Chbk.).

vii) Elisabetha[3], bpt. 23 May 1740 - sp.: Jacob Schnyder and Elisabeth Schnyder (Schoharie Ref. Chbk.).

viii) Peter[3], bpt. 6 March 1741/42 - sp.: Pieter Sneider and Mary Cathrin, his wife (Schoharie Ref. Chbk.). Pieter Feake was in Capt. Thomas Ackeson's Co. in 1767 (Report of the State Historian, Vol. II, p. 847).

HENRICH FÄHLING (Hunter Lists #186)

There were Fahlings found at 6331 Kröffelbach in an area where several Mohawk Valley 1709ers originated: Henrich Fahling d. 1696, aged 55 yrs.; however, no firm connective to the N.Y. family of Failings has been found. Henrik Schling and his wife were listed next to the N.Y. Palatine Koenraat Krants in the 4th party in Holland on Capt. Robbert Bulman's ship (Rotterdam Lists). Henry Fehling aged 24, and his wife, Ref., husbandman and vinedresser, were in England (recorded next to Conrad Krantz) in the 4th arrivals in 1709 (London Lists).

Henrich Fähling made his first appearance on the Hunter Lists 1 July 1710 with 2 pers. over 10 yrs. of age and 1 pers. under 10; the size of the family diminished 25 March 1711 to 2 pers. over

10 yrs. of age, and then increased again 24 June 1712 to 2 pers.
over 10 yrs. of age and 1 pers. under 10 yrs. of age in the family. Hendrick Fehling of Annsberg was a soldier in 1711 (Palatine
Volunteers To Canada). Heinrich Fallinger, his wife and 3 ch. were
noted at Neu-Ansberg ca. 1716/17 (Simmendinger Register). In May
of 1762 Henrich Failing agreed with his six sons to transfer his
real estate to them in return for their support for himself and
his wife; this document is a wonderful source for genealogists
studying the family, as it names all six sons. Hendrick Feeling
was a freeholder of Canajoharrie in 1763 (Albany Co. Freeholders).
An endorsement on the back of the 1762 document implies that Hendrick Failing and his wife Mary spent their last days with their
son Jacob on Lot #15 of the Harrison Patent in St. Johnsville, and
that Henrich d. 1768/9 and Mary in 1767/8. The ch. of Henrich[1]
Failing and his wife Anna Maria Kunigunda (probably the Mary named
in the 1762 mss.) were:

1) Johannes[2] (1762 mss.), md. Maria Magdalena Wagner, the
   Widow Failing who d. 7 March 1817, aged 97-1-5 (Fort Plain
   Ref. Chbk.). Johannes signed the acceptance of Pastor Wer-
   ner in 1751, and was d. by Dec 1765.

2) Johann Jacob[2], b. 9 Oct 1713 - sp.: Jacob Best, and the w/o
   Martin Zerb (West Camp Luth. Chbk.). He md. 4 April 1756
   Anna Maria Catharina Gerlach. He signed the 1762 document
   granting support to his parents. He wrote his will 21 Dec
   1791, and d. between Feb 1797 and May 1799.

3) Nicolaus[2], b. 7 Jan 1716 and bpt. at Schoharie - sp.: Niclaus Ruhl and wife (West Camp Luth. Chbk.). He md. Elizabeth Snell. Nicklus Fely signed the 1762 mss. supporting
   his parents and built a stone dwelling near Canajoharie
   called Fort Failing. Letters of Administration on the estate of Nicholas Failing were granted to Lawrence Gross and
   Jacob Timmerman 14 May 1791 (Montgomery Co. Surrogate's
   Records).

4) Henrich[2] (1762 mss.), md. 17 July 1764 Elisabetha, d/o
   Conrad Zimmerman (Stone Arabia Ref. Chbk.). He signed the
   document promising support for his parents in 1762 and d.
   in Canajoharie 9 April 1790; his obituary in the Fort Plain
   Ref. Chbk. recorded that he was b. in 1718.

5) Dieterich[2] (1762 mss.), md. Anna Eva (--). He signed the
   1762 bond with his brothers. He also was known as Richard.

6) Georg[2] (1762 mss.), md. 4 Dec 1770 Catharina Walrath (Stone
   Arabia Ref. Chbk.). He also signed the 1762 bond.

7?) Anna[2], md. Peter Wormwood and d. 6 Oct 1797.

226

David Kendall Martin, a dear friend and an extremely fine genealogist, has written <u>The Eighteenth Century Failing Family of the Mohawk Valley</u>; I recommend it highly, as it recounts the family history with detailed documentation, clarity, and style (HJ).

<h2 style="text-align:center"><u>ARNOLD FALCK</u> (Hunter Lists #187)</h2>

The German home of Arnold Falck was 6509 <u>Spiesheim</u> (18 km. e. of Bad Kreuznach; Chbks. begin 1698, Cath.). The earliest known ancestor of the emigrant was his father <u>Johannes Falk</u>. Johannes Falck, a Cath., was listed on the 1698 Census at Spiesheim (Alzey Census of 1698) and d. 13 Aug 1724, aged 79 yrs. Arnoldus Falk, s/o Joannis Falk at Spiesheim, md. Anna Elisabetha, d/o Reinhard Burchardt of Hilmshan (?) in Hessia, 25 Sept 1704. Arnold Falig, his wife, and 2 ch. were registered on Capt. Frans Waerde's ship in Holland in 1709 (Rotterdam Lists). Arnold Falck aged 32, his wife, and sons aged 6 and 2, Cath., husbandman and vinedresser, were in England later that year (London Lists).

Arnold Falck made his first appearance on the Hunter Lists 1 July 1710 with 2 pers. over 10 yrs. and 1 pers. under 10 in the family. Arnold Falck aged 36, Anna Eliz. Falck aged 35, and Johannes Falck aged 6 were in N.Y. City in 1710/11 (Palatines In N.Y. City). Arnelt Falck was nat. next to Johannis Falck 8 and 9 Sept 1715 (Kingston Nats.). Arnold Falck and Anna Elisabetha with 1 child were at Beckmansland ca. 1716/17 (Simmendinger Register). He was involved in a court case versus Hans Ju^r Elich in 1728-30 (Kingston Town Court Records). The ch. of Arnold[1] Falck were:

1) <u>Johannes[2]</u> (Palatines In N.Y. City), nat. 8 and 9 Sept 1715 next to Arnelt Falck (Kingston Nats.). Banns for his marriage to Maria Henrichs were issued 9 Feb 1729 (Kingston Ref. Chbk.), and from this 1st marriage he had issue:
   - i) <u>Regina[3]</u>, bpt. 18 Jan 1730 - sp.: Arenhout Valk and Reyina Hendriks (Kingston Ref. Chbk.).
   - ii) <u>Elisabetha[3]</u>, bpt. 21 March 1731 - sp.: Arnold Falk and Elisabeth Falk (Katsbaan Ref. Chbk.).
   - iii) <u>Wilhelmus[3]</u>, b. 21 May 1733 and bpt. at Kisket - sp.: Jurge Wilhelm Dieterich and Gertruyd Volk (Loonenburg Luth. Chbk.). He md. Anna Maria Engel (HJ).
   - iv) <u>Lorentz[3]</u>, b. 13 Oct 1735 and bpt. Newton - sp.: Lorenz Henrichs and Regina, grandparents (Loonenburg Luth. Chbk.).
   - v) <u>Margaretha[3]</u>, b. 29 Nov 1737 and bpt. at Newton - sp.: Hendryk Brouwer and wife Margreta (Loonenburg Luth. Chbk.).

vi) <u>Johannes</u>[3], bpt. 27 Jan 1740 - sp.: Johannes Velter
and Margriet Hendrik (Kingston Ref. Chbk.). He d.
2 Nov 1822, and his wife Maria Mauterstock d. 7 March
1815 (Old Falck Cem. near Katsbaan).

vii) <u>Maria</u>[3], bpt. 4 July 1742 - sp.: Frans Hendrik and
Elisabeth Valk (Kingston Ref. Chbk.). She md. Thomas
Bexter (Will of Johannis Folk of Churchland dated
23 June 1775 and probated 8 Aug 1784, <u>Fernow Wills</u>
#641).

Johannes[2] md. 2nd. Anna Maria Speichermann 6 June 1743
(Kingston Ref. Chbk.). She may have been the Maria Falck
who d. 18 Aug 1795 (Old Falck Cem. near Katsbaan); her
grave was near a stone carved with "I.F., 21 Aug 1776."
The ch. of Johannes[2] and Anna Maria Speichermann Falck:

viii) <u>Arnold</u>[3], bpt. 27 Sept 1744 - sp.: Hiskis Wyn-oop and
wife Mareitje Deffenpoort (Katsbaan Ref. Chbk.).

ix) <u>Christina</u>[3], bpt. 1 April 1746 - sp.: Johannes Tromboor and wife Christina Fierer (Katsbaan Ref. Chbk.).
She md. James Jones (Will).

x) <u>Jacob</u>[3], bpt. 9 June 1747 - sp.: Jacob Eiler with his
wife (Katsbaan Ref. Chbk.).

xi) <u>Elisabetha</u>[3], bpt. 8 Oct 1750 - sp.: Pieter Jonk and
wife Elisabeth Moschier (Katsbaan Ref. Chbk.).

xii) <u>Lea</u>[3], bpt. 2 Jan 1754 - sp.: Tobyas Wynkoop and wife
Lea Leg (Katsbaan Ref. Chbk.).

2) <u>Johann Jacob</u>[2], bpt. 28 Oct 1707 - sp.: Joannes Jacobus
Falk (Spiesheim Chbk.).

3) <u>Elisabetha</u>[2] (HJ), md. Frans Henrich 16 Sept 1735 (Kingston
Ref. Chbk.).

4) <u>Johann Peter</u>[2], b. 10 Dec 1713 - sp.: Johann Peter Sutz
and Anna Maria Burckhard (West Camp Luth. Chbk.). "The
child of Arnold Falck d. 1713" (West Camp Luth. Chbk.).

5) <u>Gertraud</u>[2], b. 18 Feb 1715 - sp.: Niclaus Rau and wife
Gerdraut (West Camp Luth. Chbk.). Perhaps this child was
named for the mother of Arnold[1] Falck, Gertrud Falck who
d. at Speisheim 11 April 1708, aged 61 yrs. (HJ). Gertraud[2] md. Henrich Schenckel (HJ).

<u>JOHANN WILHELM FALCKENBURG</u> (Hunter Lists #188)

The European home of Johann Valentin (sometimes Wilhelm)
Falckenburg was 5450 <u>Niederbieber</u> (2 km. n. of Neuwied; Chbks.
begin 1655). The earliest known forefather of the American line
was <u>Peter Falckenberg</u> of Oberbieber, who was bur. 29 May 1682,

aged 75 yrs. Johannes Falckenberg, s/o Petter Falckenberg, md.
17 Jan 1667 Margaretha Daufenbach, d/o Wilhelm Daufenbach. Issue
of <u>Johannes Falckenberg</u>, who was bur. 31 Dec 1694, and Margaretha:

+ <u>Valentin</u>, bpt. 10 Dec 1671 - sp.: Johannes Moritz, Valentin
Friedrich, and Juliana - d/o Herbert Neitzert at O.B.
<u>Johann Christian</u>, bpt. 16 Jan 1676 - sp.: Christian Mäurer,
Johannes Dauffenbach - brother of the child's father, and
Barbara - d/o the late Herbert Neitzert there.
<u>Anna Gertraud</u>, bpt. 16 Jan 1681 - sp.: Gerdraudt - d/o Christ
Stertz, Agnes - surviving d/o Johannis Krafft at Rengsdorf,
and Caspar - brother of the child's mother.

Valentin, s/o the late Johannis Falkenberger at Oberbieber, md.
7 Feb 1702 Maria Elisabetha, d/o the late Johannis Becker at Wiedt.
Johan Felden Valkenburg, his wife, and 2 ch. were listed on Capt.
Robbert Lourens's ship in Holland in 1709 (Rotterdam Lists); they
were recorded near their relatives Johan Peter Bekker and Paulus
Preker (sic), as well as other 1709ers from the Neuwied area such
as Paulus Dentger, Nicolaus Heistrebath, and Jacob Wolpret. Valentin Falckenburg aged 38, his wife, and sons aged 7 and 2, Ref.,
husbandman and vinedresser, were in the 3rd arrivals in England
in 1709 (London Lists).

Johann Wilhelm Falckenburg made his first appearance on the
Hunter Lists 4 July 1710 with 1 pers. over 10 yrs. of age and 1
pers. under 10 yrs. in the household; on 4 July 1710 and thereafter, the family was recorded with 2 pers. over 10 yrs. of age
and 1 pers. under 10 yrs. The Hunter entries on this emigrant
called him both Johann Wilhelm and Valentin. Valin Ffauldkinberg:
1 man, 1 boy aged 8 and under, and 1 woman were in Ulster Co. in
1710/11 (West Camp Census). Valentin Falckenburg and Elisabetha,
with 2 ch. were at Beckmansland ca. 1716/17 (Simmendinger Register). The ch. of Valentin[1] Falckenburg and Maria Elisabetha were:

1) <u>Johann Ernst[2]</u>, bpt. 9 April 1703 - sp.: H. Ludewig Ernst
Lysemann, Johannes Remagen at Seg., and Anna Maria - w/o
Jacob Becker at Wiedt (Niederbieber Chbk.).

2) <u>Anna Gertraud[2]</u>, bpt. 29 March 1705 - sp.: Anna Gertraudt
- sister of the child's father, Johanna Magdalena - d/o
the late Peter Michel, and Henrich - s/o the late Conradt
Brün at O.B. (Niederbieber Chbk.).

3) <u>Johann Peter[2]</u>, bpt. 5 Feb 1708 - sp.: Peter - s/o the late
Johannis Becker at Wiedt, Johann Henrich - s/o the late
Johannis Falckenberg, and Magdalena - d/o Georg Hümmer-
ich at O.B. (Niederbieber Chbk.).

The mother of Valentin's[1] later ch. bpt. by Pastor Kocherthal was

called Elisabetha Maria - and not Maria Elisabetha, as was the
wife in Germany. Even though Valentin's initial entry on the Hunter Lists shows only 1 pers. over 10 yrs. of age and 1 pers. under 10, it is possible that Kocherthal transposed Valentin's
wife's name from Maria Elisabetha to Elisabetha Maria, as the
1st wife's brother Johann Peter Becker continues to sp. the family in America; thus it is difficult to determine with certainty
if Valentin[1] md. twice (HJ). With wife Elisabetha Maria he had:

4) <u>Anna Gertraut</u>[2], b. 1 Aug 1711 - sp.: Jacob Manck, Ger-
truda Kohl, and Anna Margretha Herdel (West Camp Luth.
Chbk.). She md. Henrich Kuhn (HJ).

5) <u>Johann Hieronymus</u>[2], b. 24 Nov 1714 - sp.: Hieronymus Klein,
J. Wilhelm Kuester, and Catharina Schreib (West Camp Luth.
Chbk.). He md. 1st in May 1736 Maria Elisabetha Meyer
(Katsbaan Ref. Chbk.); the dates on her tombstone read
8 Aug 1711 - 17 March 1769 (Old Meyer Farm Cem., Churchland, Saugerties, N.Y.). He md. 2nd as a widower in Oct
1771 Sophia Beckker (Red Hook Luth. Chbk.). His ch. with
his 1st wife were:

i) <u>Anna</u>[3], b. 7 March 1737 and bpt. Newton - sp.: Christian Meyer and Gertr. (Loonenburg Luth. Chbk.).

ii) <u>Maria</u>[3], b. 18 Jan 1739 - sp.: Peter Becker and wife
(Loonenburg Luth. Chbk.).

iii) <u>Catharina</u>[3], bpt. 5 Jan 1741 - sp.: Johannes Mejer and
Catharina Mejer (Katsbaan Ref. Chbk.). She md. Petrus
Langendyk 6 Nov 1765 (Germantown Ref. Chbk.).

iv) <u>Lydia</u>[3], bpt. 26 Dec 1742 - sp.: Beck De Wit and wife
Mareitje Theunjes (Katsbaan Ref. Chbk.). She md.
Bastian Straub (HJ).

v) <u>Sarah</u>[3], bpt. 7 May 1745 - sp.: Willem Mejer and wife
Sara Nieuwkerk (Katsbaan Ref. Chbk.). She md. Ephraim Van Keuren 21 June 1765 (Germantown Ref. Chbk.).

vi) <u>Johannes</u>[3], bpt. 10 Aug 1746 - sp.: Chritiaan Meyer
and Maria Snyder (Kingston Ref. Chbk.). He d. 24 Sept
1827, aged 82-2-20, and his wife Eva Dieterich d. 31
July 1841, aged 84-3-9 (Unionville Cem, Saugerties).

vii) <u>Christian</u>[3], bpt. 26 Dec 1749 - sp.: Christian Mejer
and wife Anna Geerrtrouwt Theunges (Katsbaan Chbk.).

viii) <u>Margaretha</u>[3], bpt. 26 Dec 1752 - sp.: Jurg Koolman and
wife Margriet Falkenburg (Katsbaan Ref. Chbk.). She
md. Abraham Post (HJ).

6) <u>Agnes</u>[2], b. 24 Nov 1714 - sp.: Christian Dietrich, Anna
Elisabeth Becker, and Agnes Dieterich (West Camp Luth.
Chbk.). She md. Adam Reiffenberger (HJ).

7) <u>Anna Margaretha</u>[2] (HJ), md. 20 April 1738 Georg Kilmer
   (Loonenburg Luth. Chbk.).

VALENTIN FASIUS (Hunter Lists #189)

Valentin Fasius made his first appearance on the Hunter Lists
with Johannes Fasius 1 July 1710 with 1 pers. over 10 yrs. of age
in the household; he was also listed next to Johannes Fasius on
4 Aug 1710. William Vesi, Valentin Vesi, and Anna Vesin were at
Hackensack ca. 1716/17 (Simmendinger Register). The ch. of Valentin[1] Fasius (written Fasigk, Fasi, and Fasie at Freehold, N.J.)
and his wife Anna Catharina Hausmann (written Hosman and Harsman)
were:
   1) <u>Henrich</u>[2], bpt. 9 April 1732 - sp.: Kristiaan Hosman and
      wife Hanna (Freehold/Middletown Ref. Chbk.).
   2) <u>Johannes</u>[2], bpt. 20 June 1736 - sp.: Joh: Wert and Eliana
      (Freehold/Middletown Ref. Chbk.).
   3) <u>Hermann</u>[2], bpt. 4 June 1738 - sp.: Johannes Wert and Eliana
      (Freehold/Middletown Ref. Chbk.).

JOHANNES FASIUS (Hunter Lists #190)

Johannes Fasius made his first appearance with Valentin Fasius 1 July 1710 with 1 pers. under 10 yrs. of age; he was recorded
next to Valentin Fasius again 4 Aug 1710 with 1 pers. over 10 yrs.
of age. He may have been the William Vesi registered with Valentin
Vesi and Anna Vesin at Hackensack ca. 1716/17 (Simmendinger Register). The wife of Johannes[1] Fasius was named Rosina (possibly
related to the Georg Sponheimer or Robert Bolmer families - HJ),
and they had ch.:
   1) <u>Jan</u>[2], bpt. 2 March 1735 (Somerville Ref. Chbk.).
   2) <u>Wilhelm</u>[2], bpt. 28 May 1738 (Somerville Ref. Chbk.).
   3) <u>Rosina</u>[2], bpt. 28 Feb 1742 (Somerville Ref. Chbk.).
   4) <u>Robert</u>[2], bpt. 19 May 1745 (Somerville Ref. Chbk.).

NICLAUS FELLER (Hunter Lists #191)

Johann Philipp Feller, s/o Niclaus Feller of Guntersblum in
the earldom of Leinnig-Hartenburg, md. Catharina Elisabetha Rauh,
d/o Niclaus Rauh of Oppenheim in the Pfaltz, 18 Sept 1716 (West
Camp Luth. Chbk.). The town of origin was 6524 <u>Guntersblum</u> (7 km.
s. of Oppenheim; Chbks. begin 1651, Luth.). A possible ancestor
of the American line was Dalwig Fehler, d. 12 Jan 1674; he had a
son Jacob Feller, who d. 23 May 1682, aged 29 yrs. Sp. at Guntersblum show that the w/o Nicolaus[1] Feller was Magdalena Elisabetha,

d/o Benedict Braun of Udenheim.

Niclaus Feller made his first appearance on the Hunter Lists 1 July 1710 with 2 pers. over 10 yrs. and 2 pers. under 10; the entry changed 4 Oct 1710 to 3 pers. over 10 and 1 pers. under 10 yrs. On 31 Dec 1710 the family was recorded with 4 pers. over 10 yrs. and 2 pers. under 10 yrs. of age, on 29 Sept 1711 there were 5 pers. over 10 and 1 under 10 yrs, on 25 March 1712 the entry read 4 pers. over 10 yrs. and 1 under 10, and finally on 13 Sept 1712 the household had 4 pers. over 10 yrs. and 2 pers. under 10. Niclaus Feller of Queensbury was a soldier in 1711 (Palatine Volunteers To Canada). Nicolaus Feller and his wife Elisabetha with 6 ch. were at Neu-Quunsberg ca. 1716/17 (Simmendinger Register). Nicholas Ffeller and Mary Ffeller (wife of Nicholas Ffeller) were each patentees 30 April 1725: he was on the n. side of the Mohawk, and she on the s. side (Burnetsfield Patent). The will of Nicholas Feller of Burnetsfield, husbandman, was dated 28 May 1734 and proved 9 Feb 1763 (History of the Ref. Church of Herkimer, N.Y., by Rev. H. M. Cox, p. 71). The ch. of Nicolaus[1] Feller and Magdalena Elisabetha Braun (called Maria Elisabetha in American records, hinting at a 2nd marriage - HJ) were:

1) Johann Philip[2], md. 18 Sept 1716 as s/o Nicolaus Feller to Catharina Elisabetha Rau (West Camp Luth. Chbk.). Flip Veller was nat. 8 and 9 Sept 1715 (Kingston Nats.). He made his first appearance on tax rolls in 1717/18 and continued until Feb 1761 (Dutchess Co. Tax Lists). A bond survives for him dated 1760 (Dutchess Co. Ancient Docs. #3847). The will of Philipp Veller of Rynebeek was dated 1763 and probated 1 Feb 1768 (Fernow Wills #1869). Ch.:

   i) Johann Nicolaus[3], b. 21 July 1717 - sp.: Johann Niclaus Rau (West Camp Luth. Chbk.). He was conf. at Theerbos 13 April 1740 (Loonenburg Luth. Chbk.). He md. Anna Maria Neher (HJ) and moved to Rensselaer Co. Nicholas Vellar was a deserter from Capt. Arnout Viele's Co. at Fort Edward in 1757, and in Capt. Abraham Van Aernam's Co. in 1767 from Poest's Creek to Tjerk's Creek (Report of the State Historian, Vol. II, pp. 785 & 811).

   ii) Johannes[3] (HJ), conf. with Niclas Feller at Theerbos 13 April 1740 (Loonenburg Luth. Chbk.). He md. Anna Barbara Dater (HJ) and d. 28 Sept 1791, aged 72 yrs. and 6 months (Rhinebeck Luth. Cem.).

   iii) Gertraud[3], b. 21 Dec 1720 at Rheinbeeck - sp.: Niclaes Rau and wife Gertrude (N.Y. City Luth. Chbk.).

She md. Adam Schäffer (HJ).

  iv) <u>Philip</u>[3], bpt. 14 July 1723 - sp.: Philippus Meller
and Margriet Oel (Kingston Ref. Chbk.). He md. 29
Nov 1748 Susanna Elisabetha Schäffer, d/o Johann Valentin Schäffer (Rhinebeck Luth. Chbk.).

  v) <u>Catharina</u>[3], bpt. 14 July 1723 - sp.: Johannes Rystor
and Margriet Rystor (Kingston Ref. Chbk.).

  vi) <u>Elisabetha</u>[3], bpt. 24 Sept 1727 - sp.: Jurrie 'Tzoe-
velt and Elizabeth (Kinderhook Ref. Chbk.). Lisabeth
Veller was conf. 21 Oct 1744 at Rhynb. (Loonenburg
Luth. Chbk.). She md. Friederich Schäffer (HJ).

  vii) <u>Zacharias</u>[3], b. 12 April 1732 at Rhynbek - sp.: Zacharias Smid and wife Matje (Loonenburg Luth. Chbk.).

  viii) <u>Jacob</u>[3], b. 17 Feb 1734 - sp.: Georg Adam Zufeld and
wife (Rhinebeck Luth. Chbk.).

  ix) <u>Johann Wilhelmus</u>[3], b. 9 April 1736 and bpt. at Rhinebeck in Jurge Deter's barn - sp.: Nicolas Rauw and
Gertruyd, grandparents (Loonenburg Luth. Chbk.). He
md. Catharina Reichart (HJ).

  x) <u>Rebecca</u>[3], b. 7 Feb 1738 and bpt. at Rhinebeck - sp.:
Frans Neher and wife Rebecca (Loonenburg Luth. Chbk.).
She md. 21 May 1754 Samuel Häner (Kingston Ref.
Chbk.).

2) <u>Anna Catharina</u>[2], bpt. 31 May 1700 - sp.: Anna Catharina -
the sister of the mother and d/o Benedict Braun from Udenheim (Guntersblum Chbk.). She may have been the d/o Nic.
Veller who sp. Johann Greussler's daughter Anna Catharina
at Guntersblum in 1708 (HJ). She md. Lambert Sternberger
(Will).

3) <u>Johannes</u>[2], bpt. 7 July 1705 - sp.: Joh. Eyerich - cooper
and Gemeinsmann here (Guntersblum Chbk.). A s/o Nicolaus
Veller was bur. 7 May 1708, aged 3 yrs. (Guntersblum
Chbk.).

4) <u>"A Son"</u>[2], bpt. 19 Oct 1708 - sp.: the s/o Conrad Stiel
(Riel?) (Guntersblum Chbk.).

5) <u>Maria Elisabetha</u>[2], b. 26 July 1712 - sp.: Maria Elisabetha
Schall (West Camp Luth. Chbk.). She md. Georg Helts (Will).

6) <u>Catharina</u>[2] (Will), md. Nicolaus Wohlleben (Will). As Nicolaus[1] had two daughters named Catharina, perhaps one was
bpt. Maria Catharina (HJ); other references to the w/o
Nicolaus Wohlleben give her name as Maria Elisabetha, com-
pounding the confusion (HJ).

7) <u>Margaretha</u>[2] (Will), md. Johannes Christmann (Will).

A Jacob Fehler, who may have been related to Nicolaus[1], was quite prominent in the Tulpehocken, Pa. region 1740-50 (HJ).

DIETRICH FEWERSBACH (Hunter Lists #192)

Diderig Fischbag was recorded on the 6th party rolls at Rotterdam in 1709 (Rotterdam Lists). The family was an old one in the Westerwald-Siegen area (HJ).

Dietrich Fewersbach made his initial appearance on the Hunter Lists 4 Aug 1710. Deitrich Feversback aged 21A (sic) was in N.Y. City in 1710/11 (Palatines In N.Y. City). He md. Magdalena (--) and had issue:

    1) Volckart[2], bpt. 30 April 1721 (New Brunswick Ref. Chbk.). The father's surname was spelled Veyerschbach in this entry.

GOTTFRID FIDLER (Hunter Lists #193)

The roots of the Tulpehocken Fidler family were at 6104 Jugenheim (14 km. s.w. of Darmstadt; Chbks. begin 1669, but gaps) and 6450 Hanau (15 km. e. of Frankfurt; Chbks. begin 1643, Johanniskirche Luth.). The probable father of the emigrant Gottfried[1] was the "Erbach'schen Hunter" Johann Georg Fiedler who, with his wife Anna Barbara, bur. two stillborn ch. in 1676 and 1678 at Jugenheim. Gottfried Fideler, joiner-fellow in the old town, md. 17 April 1704 Anna Elisabetha Solomon from Lämmerspiel near Offenbach (Hanau Luth. Chbk.).

Gottfrid Fidler made his first appearance on the Hunter Lists 4 Oct 1710 with 2 pers. over 10 yrs. of age; on one of the two entries for 24 Dec 1711 the family was noted with only 1 pers. over 10 yrs. Godfrey Fidler: 1 man and 1 woman were in Ulster Co. in 1710/11 (West Camp Census). Jan Godfried Vytelar sp. Antoni Schayt in 1712 and Jacob Warnouwff in 1713 (Schenectady Ref. Chbk.). Gottfrid Viebler and his wife Anna Elisatha with 2 ch. were at Neu-Heidelberg ca. 1716/17 (Simmendinger Register). His last mention in a N.Y. record was in Jan 1722 when he sp. Peter Wagener (Stone Arabia Luth. Family Book). He purchased a farm in Plumpton Manor 5 June 1745 from John Page (Die Shilgrut, Vol. VI, No. 1). The ch. of Gottfried[1] Fidler and his wife Anna Elisabetha were:

    1) Elisabetha[2], bpt. 21 Dec 1704 - sp.: the w/o Henrich Nickel List (Jugenheim Chbk.). She was bur. 7 Jan 1705, aged 3 weeks (Jugenheim Chbk.).

    2) Eva Elisabetha[2], bpt. 21 May 1706 - sp.: the w/o Johan

Adam Munck (?) (Jugenheim Chbk.).

3) <u>Conrad</u>², bpt. 4 March 1709 - sp.: Conrad Genner - Erbach Fürstenauischer Hunter (Jugenheim Chbk.).

4) <u>Johann Gottfried</u>² (HJ), md. Elisabetha Schauer, d/o Michael Schauer. Administration Papers in the estate of Godfrey Fidler of Tulpehocken were issued to the wid. Elisabetha 6 Feb 1754 (Berks Co. Admin. Bk. I, p. 16). The ch. of Gottfried² Fidler Jr. and his wife Elisabetha were:

   i) <u>Stephen</u>³, aged 17 in 1755 (Berks Co. Orphan's Court, Vol. I, p. 4).

  ii) <u>Elisabetha</u>³, aged 16 in 1755 (Berks Co. Orphan's Court, Vol. I, p. 4).

 iii) <u>Catharina</u>³, b. 18 Dec 1740 and bpt. Northkill - sp.: Michael Schauer and wife (Stoever Chbk.).

  iv) <u>Andreas</u>³, b. 6 Nov 1742 and bpt. Northkill - sp.: Andreas Krafft and wife (Stoever Chbk.).

   v) <u>Maria Catharina</u>³, b. 5 Aug 1745 and bpt. Northkill - sp.: Heinrich Frey and wife Catarina (Stoever Chbk.).

  vi) <u>Margaretha</u>³, b. 10 Dec 1747 and bpt. Northkill - sp.: Albrecht Strauss and wife (Stoever Chbk.).

 vii) <u>Johann Peter</u>³, b. 23 Feb 1750 and bpt. Northkill - sp.: Heinrich Fiedler and wife (Stoever Chbk.).

viii) <u>Engel</u>³, aged 3 in 1755 (Berks Co. Orphan's Court, Vol. I, p. 5).

  ix) <u>Gottfried</u>³, aged 1 in 1755 (Berks Co. Orphan's Court, Vol. I, p. 5).

5) <u>Johann Henrich</u>², md. as s/o Gottfried Fitteler 13 June 1744 Magdalena, d/o Johann Michael Schauer (Tulpehocken Chbk.). John W. Harper gives him dates 14 Feb 1723 - 2 Nov 1777. Papers in the estate of Henry Fidler of Heidelberg were issued to his eldest son John Adam 18 Nov 1777 (Berks Co. Admin. Bk. III, p. 209). Ch. from Orphan's Court Records, Vol. II, p. 118:

   i) <u>Johann Adam</u>³.

  ii) <u>Catharina</u>³, md. Henry Knob.

 iii) <u>Magdalena</u>³, md. John Benitch.

  iv) <u>Henrich</u>³, 21 March 1752 - 3 June 1831, md. Eve Lenig 27 Feb 1776 (dates per John W. Harper).

   v) <u>Eva</u>³.

  vi) <u>Rosina</u>³.

 vii) <u>John</u>³.

viii) <u>Catharina Elisabetha</u>³.

  ix) <u>Johann Jacob</u>³, 1 Oct 1766 - 30 May 1858, md. 30 March 1790 Anna Maria Rieth (dates per John W. Harper).

6) Anna Margaretha[2], conf. 9 Oct 1748, aged 23 yrs. and 2
   months (Tulpehocken Chbk.). An Anna Margaretha Fiedler
   md. Johann Lewis Rosser 6 Nov 1749 (Tulpehocken Chbk.).

There also were other early Fidlers near Tulpehocken who may
have been ch. of Gottfried[1]: Jacob, Johannes, and Anna Juliana
(HJ). "The Saga of Godfrey Fidler" by John W. Harper in Die Shilgrut, Vol. V, No. 1 is an excellent study of this Pa. pioneer.

WILHELM PHILIPP FILS (Hunter Lists #194)

Wilhelm Philipp Fils was entered on the Hunter Lists 4 Oct
1710 with 1 pers. over 10 yrs. of age.

PHILIPP FILLS (Hunter Lists #195)

Philipp Fils was noted on the Hunter Lists 4 Aug 1710 with
2 pers. over 10 yrs. of age in the household. There was a Viele
family in colonial N.Y., but they were in Ulster Co. pre-1710
(HJ).

JOHANN WILHELM FINCK (Hunter Lists #196)

Johan Willem Fink, his wife and 6 ch. were in the 5th party
in Holland (Rotterdam Lists); the family was surrounded on the
list by emigrants mainly from the Nassau region (i.e. Philippus
Wagner and Johan Willem Klopper). In the heart of this locale,
a Johann Wilhelm Finck md. 25 Nov 1681 Johannata (--) at 6251
Runkel, and this entry may be a clue to the origins of the family
(HJ).

Johann Wilhelm Finck made his appearance on the Hunter Lists
4 July 1710 with 2 pers. over 10 yrs. of age and 2 pers. under
10 yrs. After studying the juxtaposition of names on the Hunter
Lists, it appears that his entries were continued by #199 Magdalena Finckin (HJ). Probable ch. of Johann Wilhelm[1] and Magdalena[1]
Finck were:

1) Anna Margaretha[2] (HJ), noted at Quunsberg as single with
   Maria Finckin, single, in 1716/17 (Simmendinger Register).
   These two girls were listed next to Michael Haug (Hönig)
   and Magdalena and Heinrich Brugler and Magdalena with
   their respective families; this might tend to show that
   Magdalena Finck md. either Brugler or Hönig after the
   death of Johann Wilhelm[1] Finck (HJ). Margaretha[2] md. Peter
   Wohlleben (HJ).
2) Maria[2], also mentioned as single and at Quunsberg in 1716/
   17 with Anna Margaretha Finckin (Simmendinger Register).

FRANTZ FINCK (Hunter Lists #197)

Frantz Finck made his initial appearance on the Hunter Lists 4 July 1710 with 2 pers. over 10 yrs. of age in the family; the size diminished to 1 pers. over 10 yrs. on 31 Dec 1710, when he was recorded next to Elizabeth Finckin md. Anan: Thiel. Frantz Finck of Queensbury was a soldier in 1711 (Palatine Volunteers To Canada). Frantz Finck and his wife Anna Elisabetha with 1 ch. were at Hackensack ca. 1716/17 (Simmendinger Register). Frantz Funk, s/o the late Joh. Adam Funk of Trarbach in the commune of Burckenfeld, md. 31 March 1714 Elisabetha Barbara Feeg, d/o Johann of the commune of Oberstein in the Pfaltz (West Camp Luth. Chbk.). The issue of Frantz[1] Finck and his wife was:

1) <u>Johannes</u>[2], b. 29 Nov 1717 (?) - sp.: Johannes Moets and Zusanna Klaeging (Tappan Ref. Chbk.).

ANDREAS FINCK (Hunter Lists #198)

An Andreas Finck of the Amt. Bobenhausen md. 19 Feb 1689 Apollonia Fiescher, d/o Hans Fiescher here at 6237 <u>Oberlieder-bach/Taunus</u>. Apollonia, d/o Johann Fischer, was conf. 1672, aged 14 yrs. there; however, no firm connective to the Mohawk Valley family has been found with this Oberliederbach group (HJ). Andreas Ving, his wife and 1 child were in the 2nd party of Palatines in Holland in 1709 (Rotterdam Lists). Andreas Fink aged 34, his wife, and a son aged 9, Ref., husbandman and vinedresser, were in the 2nd arrivals in England that year (London Lists).

Andreas Finck made his first appearance on the Hunter Lists 4 Aug 1710 with 3 pers. over 10 yrs. of age; the size increased to 3 pers. over 10 and 1 pers. under 10 yrs. on 13 Sept 1712. Andreas Vink was nat. 22 Nov 1715 (Albany Nats.). Andreas Finck and Anna Maria with 2 ch. were at Neu-Ansberg ca. 1716/17 (Simmendinger Register). Andreas Finck was a patentee at Stone Arabia in 1723 (Stone Arabia Patent). The ch. of Andreas[1] and Anna Maria Finck were:

1) <u>Christian</u>[2] (HJ), nat. 3 Jan 1715/16 (Albany Nats.). Christian Finck also was a patentee in 1723 (Stone Arabia Patent). Catharina, wid/o Christian Finck of Stone Arabia md. 2 Oct 1744 Michael Franck (Schoharie Luth. Chbk.). A s/o Christian[2] Finck was:

   i) <u>Andreas</u>[3], who called Michael Franck his step-father in his will dated 15 July 1786 and probated 13 Nov 1793 (Montgomery Co. Will Bk. I). He d. 22 Aug 1786, aged 64-11-20, and his wife Catharina Laux's dates were 11 March 1720 - 31 March 1790 (Stone Arabia

Ref. Chbk. and Cem.). Andreas Finck was in Capt. Soffrines Deychert's Co. in 1757 and in 1763 at German
Flatts (Report of the State Historian, Vol. II, pp.
783 & 792) Andries Finck was a freeholder at Stonrabie in 1763 (Albany Co. Freeholders).

    2) Jacob[2], b. 28 July 1712 - sp.: Jacob Kobel (West Camp
    Luth. Chbk.).

There were other early Fincks in the Schoharie-Mohawk region
who probably were either ch. or grandch. of Andreas[1] Finck: 1) Jo-
hannes Finck md. Maria Eva Hiltz and had ch. at the Schoharie Ref.
Church 1745-60; 2) Wilhelm Finck md. Anna Margaretha, d/o Johannes
Schnell and had ch. at Stone Arabia Ref. Church; 3) Margaretha
Finck md. Johannes Schnell; and 4) Elisabetha Finck md. Philip
Bellinger 26 June 1749 (Schoharie Luth. Chbk., Sommer's Journal).

MAGDALENA FINCKIN (Hunter Lists #199)

Magdalena Finckin made her initial appearance on the Hunter
Lists 4 Aug 1710 with 2 pers. over 10 yrs. of age and 2 pers. under 10 yrs; her 2nd entry for 24 Dec 1711 (cumulative) read 1 pers.
over 10 yrs. and 1 pers. under 10. Juxtaposition of names surrounding her family on the Hunter Lists suggests she was continuing the entries of #196 Johann Wilhelm Finck (HJ).

MELCHIOR FITTZ alias FOLTZ (Hunter Lists #200)

Melchior Foltz made his first appearance on the Hunter Lists
1 July 1710 with 2 pers. over 10 yrs. of age in the household; on
25 March 1712 the size of the family increased to 2 pers. over 10
yrs. and 1 pers. under 10 yrs. Melch. Foltz of Haysbury was a
soldier in 1711 (Palatine Volunteers To Canada). Melgert Volts was
nat. 3 Jan 1715/16 (Albany Nats.). Melchior Foltz and wife Margretha with 3 ch. were at Neu-Heessberg ca. 1716/17 (Simmendinger
Register). Melgert Ffols was a patentee on the n. side of the Mohawk 30 April 1725 (Burnetsfield Patent). He may have been md.
three times, as he and wife Anna Eva sp. Johann Michael Freymeyer
in 1711 (West Camp Luth.), his wife was called Margaretha ca.
1716/17 in Simmendinger, and noted as Anna Catrina in his will
(HJ). The will of Melchert Folts was dated 29 Jan 1724/25 or 1734/
35 (History of Herkimer Co., N.Y., pp. 246-8). The ch. of the emigrant Melchior[1] Foltz were:

    1) Johann Jacob[2], called eldest son in his father's will.
    Jacob Ffols was a patentee on the s. side of the Mohawk
    River 30 April 1725 (Burnetsfield Patent). He was a free-
    holder at the Falls in 1763 (Albany Co. Freeholders).

Jacob Fols was a Lieut. under Col. John Jost Herekheimer
in 1767 (Report of the State Historian, Vol. II, p. 848).
The will of Jacob Vols of German Flatts was written 16
Oct 1793 and probated 9 June 1808 (Herkimer Co. Will Bk.
B). His tombstone recorded his dates as 11 Nov 1711 - 30
Jan 1808; his wife Catharina lived 14 July 1714 - 11 June
1799 (Oak View Cem., Frankfort). Ch. in the will of Jacob²
were:

  i) Elisabetha³ (Will).
  ii) Catharina³ (Will).
 iii) Anna Maria³ (Will).
  iv) Anna Delia³ (Will).
   v) Anna³, md. Jacob Bauman (Will).
  vi) Conrad³ (History of Herkimer Co., N.Y., p. 247)
      10 Dec 1747 - 7 June 1793 (Oak View Cem., Frankfort).

2) Johann Peter² (Will), a Lieut. in Col. John Jost Herekheimer's Co. in 1767 (Report of the State Historian, Vol.
II, p. 848).

3) Johann Conrad² (Will), a freeholder at the Falls in 1763
(Albany Co. Freeholders). Conrad Vols was a Sergeant in
Capt. Marx Petry's Co. at Bornets Field in 1767 (Report
of the State Historian, Vol. II, p. 854).

4) Anna Margaretha² (Will).

5) Elisabetha Catharina² (Will).

JOHANN PHILIPP. FINCKEL (Hunter Lists #201)

Johann Philipp Finckel made his initial appearance on the
Hunter Lists 1 July 1710 with 2 pers. over 10 yrs. of age and 2
pers. under 10; on 4 Oct 1710 the entry read 3 pers. over 10 and
1 pers. under 10, and on 31 Dec 1710 the notation recorded 3 pers.
over 10 and 2 under 10. The size of the Finckel family then fluctuated: 3 pers. over 10 and 1 under 10 on 24 June 1711, 3 pers.
over 10 29 Sept 1711, 2 pers. over 10 24 Dec 1711, and 2 pers.
over 10 and 1 pers. under 10 on the last entry 13 Sept 1712. An
old mss. for Philipp Finckel the tailor survives dated 1712 (N.Y.
Col. Mss., Vol. 57, p. 124b). Philips Vingler was nat. 17 Jan
1715/16 (Albany Nats.). Philipp Finckel and Anna Catharina with
3 ch. were at Wormsdorff ca. 1716/17 (Simmendinger Register).
Philip Vinkel was recorded on Palatine Debt Lists in 1718, 1719
(of Annsberry), 1721 and 1726 (Livingston Debt Lists). Pfilibs
Finikel was a Palatine willing to remain at Livingston Manor 26
Aug 1724 (Doc. Hist. of N.Y., Vol. III, p. 724). His ch. were mentioned in the St. Peter's Luth. list of 1734 (Rhinebeck Luth.

Chbk.). The issue of Philipp[1] Finckel and Anna Catharina were:

1) <u>Elisabetha[2]</u>, called sister of Joh. Philipp Finckel (Jr.) on the 1734 St. Peter's List. She md. Bernhardt Häner (HJ).

2) <u>Johann Philipp[2]</u>, b. 26 July 1712 - sp.: Johann Philipp Zerb and Anna Maria Schneider (West Camp Luth. Chbk.). He was on the 1734 Rhinebeck Luth. list with his brother and sisters. He md. Anna Gertraud Linck (HJ). Philip Finkel and Anna Geertruy of 2nd 9 Partners in Dutchess Co. deeded land to Tiel Rockevelt of Camp (Albany Co. Deeds, Vol. 7, p. 3). A Philip Finkle had land in Northeast 1753-June 1763 (Dutchess Co. Tax Lists). His ch. were:

   i) <u>Philip[3]</u>, b. 14 Feb 1736 - sp.: Wilhelm Link, and Anna Christina Dik - w/o Paul (Rhinebeck Luth. Chbk.).

   ii) <u>Johannes[3]</u>, bpt. 19 Oct 1742 - sp.: Johannes Hener and wife Anna Maria Schever (Germantown Ref. Chbk.). There were two Johannes Finkels who had ch. at Red Hook Luth. Church in 1768: one md. Catharina Hoffman and the other md. Anna Maria Meyer (HJ).

   iii) <u>Wilhelm[3]</u>, bpt. 15 May 1744 - sp.: J. Wilhel. Link and Anna Eva Linck (Germantown Ref. Chbk.). A Wilhelm Finckel md. Lois (--) and had ch. at Pine Plains Church (HJ).

   iv) <u>Johann Jost[3]</u>, b. 4 March 1748 - sp.: Johan J. Proper and Maria Herter (Germantown Luth. Chbk.). A Johann Jost Finckel md. Catharina (--) and had ch. at Manorton Luth. Church.

   v) <u>Georg[3]</u>, b. 22 March 1750 and bpt. Ancram - sp.: Georg Junghans and Catharina Rhaw (Rhinebeck Luth. Chbk.).

   vi) <u>Anna Margaretha[3]</u>, b. 12 July 1752 - sp.: Matheus Junghanns and wife Anna Margaretha (Rhinebeck Luth. Chbk.).

   vii) <u>Johann Nicolaus[3]</u>, b. 2 Oct 1756 - sp.: Ernst Beeker and Regina Junghanns (Rhinebeck Luth. Chbk.).

3) <u>Johann Georg[2]</u>, on the 1734 Rhinebeck Luth. list. He md. Elisabetha Henn (HJ). Jury Finkle was on the Dutchess Co. rolls at Northeast Feb 1745/46 - June 1759 (Dutchess Co. Tax Lists). Jurrie Finkel was in Capt. Jeremiah Hogeboom's Co. in 1767 (<u>Report of the State Historian</u>, Vol. II, p. 864). The ch. of Johann Georg[2] Finckel and Elisabetha were:

   i) <u>Eva[3]</u>, bpt. 28 May 1740 - sp.: Johannes Wilhelm Herder and Eva Hen (Germantown Ref. Chbk.).

   ii) <u>Philip[3]</u>, b. 6 March 1742 and bpt. at Goghkameko, Ankrom - sp.: Philip Finkel and wife Anna Gertrud (Loonenburg Luth. Chbk.).

   iii) <u>Anna Margaretha</u>³, bpt. 29 Jan 1744 - sp.: Johannes
Konradt and Margredt Konradts (Germantown Ref.
Chbk.).

   iv) <u>Georg</u>³ (HJ), md. Margaretha Simon and had ch. at
Claverack Ref. Church (HJ).

    v) <u>Elisabetha</u>³, b. 25 Feb 1747 - sp.: Bernhard Heiner
and Elisabeth (Germantown Luth. Chbk.).

   vi) <u>Catharina</u>³, b. 23 Feb 1752 and bpt. at Peter Silbernagel's - sp.: Conrad Silbernagel and wife Elisabetha, ... (Rhinebeck Luth. Chbk.).

  vii) <u>Johannes</u>³, bpt. 20 July 1755 - sp.: Johannes Bettch-
er and wife (Gallatin Ref. Chbk.).

4) <u>Anna Margaretha</u>², b. 24 Nov 1720 at Annsberg - sp.: Kilian
Minckler and wife Anna Margareta (N.Y. City Luth. Chbk.).
She was also on the 1734 St. Peter's List (Rhinebeck Luth.
Chbk.). She md. Martin Leick (HJ).

There was a Gertraut Finckel who md. 15 Aug 1767 Petrus
Funck (Linlithgo Ref. Chbk.); she was either a d/o Philip² or
Georg² Finckel (HJ).

<u>PETER FISCHER</u> (Hunter Lists #202)

Pieter Visser, his wife and 2 ch. were on Capt. Duk's ship
in Holland in the 4th party of 1709 (Rotterdam Lists). Peter
Fischer aged 36, his wife, daughters aged 5 and 2, Ref., husbandman and vinedresser, were in the 4th arrivals in England later
that year (London Lists).

Peter Fischer made only one appearance on the Hunter Lists,
on 4 Oct 1710 with 1 pers. over 10 yrs. of age in the family.
A Pieter Visser, single man from Wurtemberg in Germany, had banns
18 Aug 1722 to marry Catrÿna Van Deuse, single woman b. Acquig-
genonck (Hackensack Ref. Chbk.).

<u>SEBASTIAN FISCHER</u> (Hunter Lists #203)

Johanna, w/o Sebastian Fischer, d. in Jan 1696 in childbed,
aged 30 yrs. at 6753 <u>Alsenborn</u>; this village is in the heart of
the region where several Tulpehocken 1709ers originated (Nicolaus
Schäffer and Johann Georg Riedt, for example), so perhaps the Alsenborn man may have been our emigrant (HJ). A Sebastian Fischer
was also documented at 6525 <u>Westhofen</u>. Sebastiaan Vischer, his
wife and 2 ch. were in the 6th party in Holland in 1709 (Rotterdam Lists).

Sebastian Fischer made his initial appearance on the Hunter

Lists 4 July 1710 with 2 pers. over 10 yrs. of age and 1 pers.
under 10 yrs. in the household; this number continued through 13
Sept 1712, except for one entry 29 Sept 1711 with 4 pers. over
10 yrs. and 1 pers. under 10 (which may be an error - HJ). Sebastian Fischer of Annsberg was a soldier in 1711 (Palatine Volunteers To Canada). Sebastian Fischer and Susanna, with 3 ch. were
at Neu-Cassel ca. 1716/17 (Simmendinger Register). He came to
the Tulpehocken region in 1723 and signed the petition to Gov.
William Keith as Sebastian Pisas (Colonial Records Of Pa., Vol.
III, p. 323). He was on a 1743 roll of families at Tulpehocken
(Tulpehocken Chbk.). The ch. of Sebastian[1] Fischer were:

1) Lorentz[2] (HJ), conf. at Tschoghari in the so-called Weisert's Dorp in 1720 (N.Y. City Luth. Chbk.).
2) Johann Jacob[2] (HJ), md. Maria (Margaretha) Elisabetha
   Frederich 9 Dec 1743 at Tulpehocken (Stoever Chbk.). They
   sp. Johann Anspach and Elisabeth Fischer in 1745 (Tulpehocken Chbk.).
3) Johann Adam[2] (HJ), a sp. to Johann Jacob[2] Fischer in 1747
   (Tulpehocken Chbk.).
4) Anna Elisabetha[2], md. as d/o Sebastian[1] Fischer Pentacostal Tues.: 1744 Johannes Anspach (Tulpehocken Chbk.).

There were many other early Fischers near Tulpehocken in the
mid-18th century: 1) Elisabetha Fischer md. Johann Georg Glass-
brenner 7 Feb 1738 at Tulpehocken (Stoever Chbk.); 2) Catharina
Fischer md. 11 Dec 1748 at Tulpehocken Johann Leonhardt Förster;
and 3) a Georg Ulrich Fischer was in the region. Perhaps some of
these individuals were related to Sebastian[1] (HJ).

ZACHARIAS FLUGLER (Hunter Lists #204)

Zacharias Flagler was a traveler well before 1709: he was
documented at 6980 Urphar (5 km. e. of Wertheim; Chbks. begin
1666), at 6761 Dannenfels (9 km. e. of Rockenhausen; Chbks. begin
1698), and at 6791 Glan-Münchweiler (8 km. s. of Kusel; Chbks. begin 1664). The father of the emigrant was Hans Flegler. His ch.
were:

Zacharias, bpt. 1 Feb 1674 - sp.: Zacharias Collmar (Urphar
Chbk.). The child d. 2 April 1675, aged 1 yr. and 8 weeks.
+ Zacharias, bpt. 8 Oct 1676 - sp.: Zacharius Collmar (Urphar
Chbk.).

Zacharias was a teacher in Germany (Glan-Münchweiler Chbk.). Zacharias Flegeler aged 36, with his wife, sons aged 8 and 4, a daughter aged 1, Luth., carpenter, were in the 2nd arrivals in England
(London Lists).

Zacharias Flügler made his first appearance on the Hunter
Lists 30 June 1710 with 1 pers. over 10 yrs. of age and 1 pers.
under 10 yrs.; the family increased to 3 pers. over 10 yrs. on
4 Oct 1710. The entries diminished to 2 pers. over 10 yrs. 25
March 1712 and then increased again to 3 pers. over 10 yrs. on
24 June 1712; there was a special notation for his wife Gertrude
Hahmin 4 Aug 1710 with 1 pers. over 10 yrs. of age. Zacharias
Fliegler and Elisabetha with 2 ch. were at Heessberg ca. 1716/17
(Simmendinger Register). Zacharias Flegelar made his initial appearance on the rolls of the Middle Ward in 1717/18 (Dutchess Co.
Tax Lists). With his 1st wife Anna Elisabetha the ch. of Zachar-
ias[1] Flagler were:

1) <u>Philipp Salomon</u>[2], b. 21 Aug 1701 - sp.: Philipp Salomon
   Ess from Wahlheim and the Pastor's servant Anna Magdalena
   Heck from Marnheim (Dannenfels Chbk.). He made his first
   appearance on tax rolls in 1724/25 (Dutchess Co. Tax Lists)
   and was an overseer of the common ways back out of ye woods
   to the neighborhood in the South Ward in 1728 (Dutchess Co.
   Supervisor's Records). The dates on his tombstone read
   15 Aug 1701 - 14 April 1766, aged 65 yrs. and 5 months;
   his wife was Anna Margaretha Dopp, and her stone stated
   she d. 6 July 1764, aged 72 yrs. (Beekman Cem., Pough-
   quag). Their issue were:

   i) <u>Zacharias</u>[3], bpt. 30 May 1726 - sp.: Johannes Dop and
      Catrina Everts (Kingston Ref. Chbk.). He was conf.
      11 April 1745 (Rhinebeck Flats Ref. Chbk.).

   ii) <u>Catharina</u>[3], bpt. 6 months old 20 Aug 1727 at Pieter
       Lassing's - sp.: Sara and Ysaak Lassing (N.Y. City
       Luth. Chbk.).

   iii) <u>Anna</u>[3] (HJ), conf. with Zacharias and Sara 11 April
        1745 (Rhinebeck Flats Ref. Chbk.).

   iv) <u>Sarah</u>[3], b. 7 weeks before Easter 1730 and bpt. at
       Pieter Lassing's - sp.: Philip Miller and wife Mar-
       grete (N.Y. City Luth. Chbk.). She was conf. 11 April
       1745 (Rhinebeck Flats Ref. Chbk.).

   v) <u>Philip</u>[3], bpt. 24 Oct 1731 - sp.: Philip Amigh and
      Maria Amigh (Fishkill Ref. Chbk.). He d. 7 April 1804
      aged 72-5-26, and his wife Sarah d. 3 April 1802, aged
      68-7-5 (Flagler Cem., Beekman).

   vi) <u>Helena</u>[3], bpt. 2 Dec 1733 - sp.: David Bryl and Kat-
       rinen Pyck (Fishkill Ref. Chbk.).

2) <u>Anna Maria</u>[2], b. 26 Aug 1708 - sp.: Mathes Anthes the cowherd and Anna Maria - w/o Debold Jung (Glan-Münchweiler
   Chbk.).

Zacharias Flegler, widower of Wertheim in Franckeland, md. Anna
Gertrauda Hun, d/o the late Dietrich Hun of Wallbruhl in the commune of Berg, 15 Aug 1710 (West Camp Luth. Chbk.). Zacharias Flegler of Wertheim in Franckenland md. 12 March 1711 Anna Elisabetha,
wid/o Georg Schultz of Darmstatt (West Camp Luth. Chbk.); the marriage was also entered in the N.Y. City Ref. Chbk., and the bride
was recorded as Anna Elisabetha Hobin, wid/o J. Jürrie Schout of
Darmstaderland, at their wedding 11 March 1711. The ch. of Zacharias[1] Flagler and his 3rd wife Anna Elisabetha were:

3) Anna Magdalena Elisabetha[2], b. 19 Sept 1712 - sp.: Magdalena - w/o Niclaus Jung (West Camp Luth. Chbk.). She md.
Johann Jost Schneider Jr. (HJ).

4) Simon[2], b. 16 Feb 1714 - sp.: Simon Haas (West Camp Luth.
Chbk.). Simon Vlegelar made his first appearance on tax
rolls in 1739/40 at Crum Elbow (Dutchess Co. Tax Lists).
The will of Simon Flagler of Charlotte Precinct was dated
29 Nov 1774 and probated 3 Jan 1775 (Fernow Wills #640).
He md. 1st Jannet Vielen (HJ) and 2nd Hester (--) (Will).
The ch. of Simon[2] Flagler were:

i) Zacharias[3], bpt. 23 Aug 1741 - sp.: Zacharias Vleg-
elaar and Elisabeth Ellen (Rhinebeck Flats Ref.
Chbk.).

ii) Petrus[3], bpt. 7 Feb 1743 (?) - sp.: Jeremia Du Boys
and Rachel Viele (Poughkeepsie Ref. Chbk.).

iii) Petrus[3], bpt. Feb 1745 - sp.: Minardt Viele and Re-
becca Parmentier (Poughkeepsie Ref. Chbk.). Peter
Flagler d. 17 Dec 1823, aged 79-3-11 (Presbyterian
Church Cem., Pleasant Valley).

iv) Simon[3] (Will).

v) John[3] (Will).

vi) Johanna[3], md. Henry Van Voorhis (Will).

vii) Elisabetha[3], md. Jacob Lester (Will).

viii) Sarah[3] (Will).

ix) Jane[3] (Will).

x) Helena[3] (Will).

5) Gertraud[2], b. 18 March 1716 at Pachque and bpt. in the
Highland - sp.: Jacob Feek and wife Anna Maria (N.Y. City
Luth. Chbk.).

6) Margaretha[2], bpt. 12 Feb 1719 - sp.: Abraham De Jong
(Poughkeepsie Ref. Chbk.). She md. Peter Frölich 30 Oct
1741 (Kingston Ref. Chbk.).

7) Zacharias[2], bpt. 12 Oct 1720 - sp.: Elias Van Bunschouten
and Cat Keyser (?) (Poughkeepsie Ref. Chbk.). He md. 1st
Elisabetha Heegeman and 2nd Sarah Barter or Barton (HJ).

JOHANN GEORG FÖRSTER (Hunter Lists #205)

The ancestral origins of Johann Georg Förster may have been 6926 <u>Berwangen</u> (10 km. s.e. of Sinsheim; Chbks. begin 1650): a Jacob Förster, s/o Martin Förster - formerly citizen and shoe-maker here, md. 21 Jan 1668 Elisabetha, d/o Wolff Müller - citizen at Nügheim (?); this couple had a son Georg b. 6 Dec 1669 - sp.: Johann Georg Zoller from Eßlingen, Catharina Geiger, and Anna Kober from Berwangen. The age of this child Georg agrees with the age on the London Lists (HJ). A Hanß Görg Forster and wife Maria Catharina had a daughter Anna Maria bpt. 4 March 1705 - sp.: Hans Görg Streithoff - citizen and smith at Freckenfelht, and Anna Maria - w/o Ludwig Bauers at 6741 <u>Minfeld</u>, but no proof has been found that he was the emigrant (HJ). Jürg Vorster, his wife, and 4 ch. were on Capt. John Sewel's ship in Holland in 1709 (Rotterdam Lists). Georg Forster aged 39, his wife, daughters aged 14, 10, 7, and 5, Luth., linnen and cloth weaver, were at London later that year (London Lists).

Johann Georg Förster made his first appearance on the Hunter Lists 4 Oct 1710 with 3 pers. over 10 yrs. of age and 1 pers. under 10 yrs.; the family increased to 3 pers. over 10 yrs. and 2 under 10 yrs. of age on 31 Dec 1710. Georg Forster and Maria Margar. with 3 ch. were at Quunsberg ca. 1716/17 (Simmendinger Register). Jury Foster was noted on Palatine Debt Lists in 1718, 1719 (on our land), 1721, 1722, and 1726 (Livingston Debt Lists). Joh. Georg Forster and Maria Margretha, his wife, were on the St. Peter's Luth. List of 1734 (Rhinebeck Luth. Chbk.). The ch. of Johann Georg[1] Förster and his wife were:

1) <u>Anna Rosina</u>[2] (HJ), md. Peter Wohlleben (HJ).
2) <u>Susanna Margaretha</u>[2] (HJ), conf. Easter 1714 at Queensberg (West Camp Luth. Chbk.). She md. Friederich Proppert (HJ).

There was a Jürgen Förster who md. 14 July 1747 Maria Catharina Freymeyer (Schoharie Luth. Chbk.), but no known connective to the 1709er Johann Georg[1] Förster has been established (HJ). A Peter Forster was mentioned at Hackensack ca. 1716/17 on the Simmendinger Register, but probably this man was #202 Peter Fischer (HJ).

JOHANNES FRANCK (Hunter Lists #206)

Johannes Franck, widower of Altzheim on the lower Rhine in the Pfaltz, md. 10 July 1711 Magdalena, wid/o Ludwig Streit of Westhofen in the commune Altzey in the Pfaltz (West Camp Luth.

Chbk.). The ancestral origins were at 6526 <u>Alsheim</u> (10 km. s. of
Oppenheim; Chbks. begin 1688, Ref., but gaps). The father of the
emigrant was <u>Wilhelm Franck</u> the Allmoßenpfleger, d. 1 July 1678,
aged 40 yrs. He md. Margaretha Jansen and had issue:

+ <u>Johannes</u>, conf. as s/o the late Wilhelm Franck in 1690, aged
15 yrs.
<u>Anna Margaretha</u>, bpt. 19 Sept 1675 - sp.: Anna Marg. - w/o
Hans Baur here.
<u>Anna Maria</u>, b. 25 Nov 1678 - sp.: Anna Maria - w/o the fath-
er's brother Hans Görg Franck at Weinolsheim.

Johannes Franck made his initial appearance on the Hunter
Lists 30 June 1710 with 1 pers. over 10 yrs. of age in the family. The entry increased to 2 pers. over 10 yrs. 25 March 1711
and then 3 pers. over 10 yrs. and 2 under 10 yrs. 29 Sept 1711.
Jno. Franck: 1 man and 1 girl 8 yrs. and under were in Ulster Co.
in 1710/11 (West Camp Census). Johannis Franck was nat. 8 and 9
Sept 1715 (Kingston Nats.). Johannes Frantz and Magdalena with 2
ch. were at Heessberg in 1716/17 (Simmendinger Register).

JOHANN GEORG FRED (Hunter Lists #207)

Johann Georg Fred made his initial appearance on the Hunter
Lists 1 July 1710 with 2 pers. over 10 yrs. of age in the house-
hold; the last entry was 4 Oct 1710 with 2 pers. over 10 yrs.
A Maria Margretha Frehd sp. Martin Zerb in 1715 (West Camp Luth.
Chbk.).

CHRISTOPH FREIL (Hunter Lists #208)

Christoph Freil made his only appearance on the Hunter Lists
4 Aug 1710 with 1 pers. over 10 yrs. of age.

HENRICH FREY (Hunter Lists #209)

In his article "New Light on Frey Family History" in the
N.Y. Genealogical & Biographical <u>Record</u> (Vol. 108, No. 3), Wayne
Lenig corrects the long-held tradition of Henrich Frey arriving
in America in 1688 by means of a document dated 14 Dec 1708 which
Frey probably brought with him to America in 1710. It stated that
Johann Henderick Frey was b. 14 Oct 1680 in the village of Ermel-
stadt, district of Regensdorf, Canton Zurich, Switzerland; he con-
tinued to live in the vicinity of Zurich during his youth and was
trained as a carpenter. Sometime previous to 1708 he moved to
Gruenstadt in the Dukedom of Dormstadt, part of the Rheinish
Palatinate. The actual origins of the American settler were at

6718 Grünstadt (25 km. w. of Mannheim; Chbks. begin 1588, Luth.)
and 6741 Essingen (30 km. sw. of Mannheim; Chbks. begin 1704,
Luth.). Joh. Hendrik Frei, his wife, and 2 ch. were in the 2nd
party in Holland in 1709 (Rotterdam Lists). Henrich Frey aged 27,
his wife, a daughter aged ½, Ref., carpenter, were in the 2nd arrivals in England in 1709 (London Lists).

Henrich Frey made his initial appearance on the Hunter Lists
4 Aug 1710 with 2 pers. over 10 yrs. of age and 1 pers. under 10;
the family increased to 3 pers. over 10 yrs. and 1 pers. under 10
on 4 Oct 1710. The family size diminished to 2 pers. over 10 yrs.
31 Dec 1710. Henrich Fry was among other Palatine carpenters on
a list dated 1712 (N.Y. Colonial Mss., Vol. 57, p. 27a). Heinrich
Frey and his wife Maria Margaretha with 1 child were at Neu-Quunsberg ca. 1716/17 (Simmendinger Register). Hendrick Frey was a
patentee in 1723 (Stone Arabia Patent). Harme Van Slyck of Schenectady deeded land to Hendrick Fry of Stone Arabia in 1728 (Albany Co. Deeds: Vol. 6, p. 169). The ch. of Henrich[1] Frey were:

1) Johann Conrad[2], b. 2 Nov 1701 to "H... Frey, vormahlen
Lieutnandt zu Pferd in Frankreich, and Maria Elisabeth"
(Grünstadt Chbk.).

2) Maria Margaretha[2], bpt. 29 June 1708 to Henrich Frey, a
Ref. merchant of Switzerland passing through Essingen,
and his wife Elisabetha - sp.: Maria Margaretha - d/o the
late Philipp Jacob Frankenstein (Essingen Chbk.).

3) Henrich[2] (History of Montgomery Co., p. 151). He md. Anna
Margaretha Keyser (Mohawk Valley in the Revolution, p.
253). Hendrick Fry was a freeholder of Canajoharrie in
1763 (Albany Co. Freeholders). Pastor Sommer wrote 15
Sept 1763 that "I have bur. my brother-in-law Henrich Fry
at Canischogary" (Schoharie Luth. Chbk., Sommer's Journal). Papers in the estate of Hendrick Frey of Canagorie
were issued to his son Henry Hendrick Frey of Canajory
14 April 1764 (Genealogical Data from Administration Papers, by Dr. Kenneth Scott, p. 119). Issue:

   i) Henrich[3] (Administration Papers of Henrich[2]). He was
an officer in several military regiments in the Mohawk Valley (see Report of the State Historian, Vols.
I & II) and was a Loyalist in the revolution (Simm's
History of Schoharie, p. 261). He d. 13 Sept 1827,
aged 93 yrs. in Canajoharie, and his wife Elisabetha
Herkimer d. 10 Dec 1825, aged 92 yrs. (Albany Gazette, 21 Sept 1827 and 3 Feb 1826).

   ii) Johannes[3] (Simm's History of Schoharie, p. 261), a

member of the Tryon Co. Committee of Safety (<u>Mohawk</u>
<u>Valley in the Revolution</u>, p. 253).

iii) <u>Catharina</u>[3], called sister of Col. Hendrick and Major
John Frey in her obituary. She d. 18 July 1817, aged
72 at Canajoharie, and md. John Loucks (Albany Gazette, 31 July 1817).

iv) <u>Barend</u>[3], bpt. 26 Feb 1749 at Cani-Scohare (Schoharie
Luth. Chbk.). He was a Loyalist and went to Canada.
A fascinating letter from this Bernhard Frey is in
<u>Mohawk Valley in the Revolution</u>, pp. 251-52.

v) <u>A daughter</u>[3], md. Christopher P. Yates (Simm's <u>His-</u>
<u>tory of Schoharie</u>, p. 499).

BARBARA FREYIN (Hunter Lists #210)

Barbara Freyin made her first appearance on the Hunter Lists
1 July 1710 with 1 pers. over 10 yrs. of age and 1 pers. under
10 yrs. The size of the family increased to 2 pers. over 10 yrs.
and 1 pers. under 10 4 Aug 1710 and then to 3 pers. over 10 yrs.
and 1 pers. under 10 yrs. 25 March 1711. The entry for 24 Dec
1711 read Paul Duntzer's wife with 2 pers. over 10 yrs. of age.
Anna Barbara Freyin, a widow with 2 ch., was at Neu-Heessberg ca.
1716/17 (Simmendinger Register).

MICHAEL FREYMEYER (Hunter Lists #211)

Michel Freÿmeier, his wife, and 5 ch. were on Capt. Jno. Untank's ship in Holland in 1709 (Rotterdam Lists).

Michael Freymeyer made his initial appearance on the Hunter
Lists 4 July 1710 with 3 pers. over 10 yrs. of age and 2 pers.
under 10 yrs. The household changed to 2 pers. over 10 yrs. and
3 pers. under 10 on 4 Aug 1710, then to 2 pers. over 10 and 2
pers. under 10 yrs. 4 Oct 1710, increased to 3 pers. over 10 yrs.
and 3 pers. under 10 25 March 1711, and finally was noted with 3
pers. over 10 yrs. and 4 pers. under 10 24 Dec 1711. Michiel Frymeyer was nat. next to Jacob <u>P</u>rymeyer 13 March 1715/16 (Albany
Nats.). Michael Freymayer and Anna Elisabetha with 6 ch. were at
Neu-Stuttgardt ca. 1716/17 (Simmendinger Register). His name appears to have been on Pastor Sommer's 1744 list of Schoharie Luth.
families with wife Anna Elisabetha and daughter Margaretha, but
the entry now is torn and/or blotted (Schoharie Luth. Chbk.). Old
Michel Freymäuer d. 26 Oct 1757, and his wife Anna Elisabetha was
probably The Old Mrs. Freymauer who d. 1 April 1766 (Schoharie
Luth. Chbk.). The ch. of Michael[1] Freymeyer were:

1) <u>Jacob</u>[2] (HJ), nat. alongside Michiel Frymeyer as Jacob Prymeyer 13 March 1715/16 (Albany Nats.). Papers in the estate of a Jacob Freymeyer of Heidelberg were issued to the widow Anna Sibilla Freymeyer 19 Feb 1778 (Berks Co. Administrations Bk. 3, p. 223); Papers in the estate of Sibilla Fremeyer of Berks Co. were issued to her eldest son Christian Freymeyer 6 June 1785 (Berks Co. Administrations Bk. 4, p. 18).

2) <u>Anna Margaretha</u>[2] (Schoharie Luth. 1744 List). Anna Maragareta Freymeyern was conf. in 1720 at Tschoghari in the so-called Weiserts Dorp (N.Y. City Luth. Chbk.). She probably md. Peter Jung 2 Aug 1748 (Schoharie Luth. Chbk.).

3) <u>Maria Elisabetha</u>[2] (HJ), md. Johannes Braun (HJ).

4) <u>Anna Eva</u>[2], bpt. 6 Nov 1711 - sp.: Melchior Voltz and wife Anna Eva (West Camp Luth. Chbk.). She md. Adam Braun (HJ).

5) <u>Conrad</u>[2] (HJ), near others in Michael[1] Freymeyer's family on the 1744 list (Schoharie Luth. Chbk.). He had banns 20 Oct 1739 to marry Anna Maria Berg (Schoharie Ref. Chbk.). Counrate Frymier was in Capt. Thomas Ackeson's Co. in 1767 (<u>Report of the State Historian</u>, Vol. II, p. 846). He had issue with Anna Maria Berg:

   i) <u>Johann Philip</u>[3], bpt. as John Lips 24 Nov 1740 - sp.: Johan Lips Berg and Mary Catharin Vreymeyir (Schoharie Ref. Chbk.). He was listed next to Counrate Frymier in Capt. Ackeson's Co. in 1767. Catharina, w/o Philip Freymäuer d. 18 July 1773 (Schoharie Luth. Chbk.).

   ii) <u>Elisabetha</u>[3], bpt. 17 April 1742 - sp.: C. Vreymeyer and wife Elisabeth (Schoharie Ref. Chbk.).

   iii) <u>Johannes</u>[3], b. 8 Dec 1743 - sp.: Johannes Freymäuer and Anna Elisabet Berg (Schoharie Luth. Chbk.). Johannis Frymier was in Capt. Ackeson's Co. in 1767 also. Johannes Freymauer md. Dorothea Bauch 13 Feb 1770 (Schoharie Luth. Chbk.).

   iv) <u>Nicolaus</u>[3] (HJ), md. 18 Oct 1775 Elisabetha Borst (Schoharie Luth. Chbk.). He was a Loyalist, a soldier in the 1st Batt., K.R.R.N.Y., and went to Williamsburgh, Canada (<u>Loyalists in Ontario</u>, p. 121).

   v) <u>Catharina</u>[2], b. 11 Nov 1763 - sp.: Philip Kayser and Catharina - d/o Lorentz Lawyer (Schoharie Luth. Chbk.).

6) <u>Johannes</u>[2] (HJ), near Michael[1] on the 1744 Sommer's List. He md. 14 July 1747 Anna Matheus (Schoharie Luth. & Ref. Chbks.). Johannis Frymier (one of two of that name) was

in Capt. Thomas Ackeson's Co. in 1767 (<u>Report of the
State Historian</u>, Vol. II, p. 847). Johannes Freemye was
a freeholder of Schoharrie in 1763 (Albany Co. Freeholders). The will of a John Frymier was proved 19 Nov 1790
(Albany Co. Will Bk. I, p. 311). Their ch. were:

    i) <u>Johannes</u>[3], b. 13 Nov 1748 - sp.: Johannes Braun and
       his wife. The child d. 25 Dec 1748, aged 4 weeks
       and 11 days (Schoharie Luth. Chbk.).

   ii) <u>Catharina</u>[3], b. 14 Nov 1749 - sp.: Michel Freimäuer
       and Catharina Matthes (Schoharie Luth. Chbk.). A
       Catharina Freymeyer md. Peter Schuyler 23 July 1776
       (Schoharie Luth. Chbk.).

  iii) <u>Jacob</u>[3], b. 30 Sept 1751 - sp.: Nickel Matthes and
       wife (Schoharie Luth. Chbk.).

   iv) <u>Jeremias</u>[3], b. 15 July 1753 - sp.: Jürgen Werner and
       wife (Schoharie Luth. Chbk.).

    v) <u>Michael</u>[3], b. 21 June 1755 - sp.: Michel Freymauer
       and wife (Schoharie Luth. Chbk.). He d. in 1829, aged
       73 at Penfield (Rochester Anti-Masonic Inquirer, 4
       Aug 1829).

   vi) <u>Sarah</u>[3], b. 17 Nov 1756 - sp.: Adam Braun, Jr. and
       Sara Matthes (Schoharie Luth. Chbk.). She md. Lam-
       bert Schaffer 8 Oct 1775 (Schoharie Luth. Chbk.).

  vii) <u>Elisabetha</u>[3], b. 1 Aug 1758 - sp.: Nickel Matthes and
       wife (Schoharie Luth. Chbk.).

 viii) <u>Anna</u>[3], b. 31 March 1760 - sp.: Jürgen Förster and
       wife (Schoharie Luth. Chbk.). She md. Martinus Fors-
       ter 24 Feb 1778 (Schoharie Luth. Chbk.).

   ix) <u>Johannes</u>[3], b. 17 Feb 1762 - sp.: Johannes Braun and
       Magdalena Braun (Schoharie Luth. Chbk.).

    x) <u>Abraham</u>[3], b. 24 Jan 1764 - sp.: Johannes Bauch and
       wife (Schoharie Luth. Chbk.).

   xi) <u>David</u>[3], b. 28 Jan 1765 - sp.: Friederich Matthes
       and wife (Schoharie Luth. Chbk.).

   xii) <u>Gertraut</u>[3], b. 17 March 1767 - sp.: David Becker and
       wife (Schoharie Luth. Chbk.).

  xiii) <u>Margaretha</u>[3], b. 26 April 1770 - sp.: Johannes Bellin-
       ger Jr. and wife Margaretha (Schoharie Luth. Chbk.).

   xiv) <u>Magdalena</u>[3], b. 20 Dec 1772 - sp.: Jurgen Werner and
       Lena Forster (Schoharie Luth. Chbk.).

7) <u>Maria Catharina</u>[2], on 1744 list with Michael's family
   group. She md. Jürgen Förster 14 July 1747 (Schoharie
   Luth. Chbk.).

8) <u>Michael</u>[2], in the group with Michael[1] on Sommer's List of

1744. Michael Frymer was a freeholder in 1763 at Schoharrie (Albany Co. Freeholders). He md. Magdalena Neuberg
30 Aug 1761 (Schoharie Luth. Chbk.) and had issue:

  i) Michael[3], b. 29 Dec 1762 - sp.: Michel Merckel and
     wife (Schoharie Luth. Chbk.).

 ii) Eva[3], b. 29 Sept 1764 - sp.: Henrich Werner and Eva
     Zahe (Schoharie Luth. Chbk.).

iii) Johannes[3], b. 7 Feb 1767 - sp.: Johannes Becker Jr.
     and wife Anna Maria (Schoharie Luth. Chbk.).

CONRAD FRIDERICH (Hunter Lists #212)

Koenraat Fredrik, his wife, and 2 ch. were recorded on Capt.
Lionel Allan's ship in Holland in the 5th party of 1709 (Rotterdam Lists); on that same vessel were Palatines from the Nassau-
Darmstadt region who also eventually settled in colonial N.J.
(i.e. Koenraat and Bastiaan Meinsinger, Peter Wannemager and Adam Labag) (HJ).

Conrad Friderich made his initial appearance on the Hunter
Lists 1 July 1710 with 4 pers. over 10 yrs. of age in the household. Conrad Frederick aged 52, Anna Maria Frederick aged 45,
John Peter Frederick aged 14, and John Conrad Frederick aged 13,
remained in N.Y. City in 1710/11 (Palatines In N.Y. City). Certain provisions were advanced to him as a settler on the Ramapo
Tract: a bushel of wheat and 1 skipel of peas 9 April 1713, 6
fathoms of white roap 17 April 1713, 2 bushels of wheat 10 May
1713, and 2 bushels indian corne 26 May 1713 (Ramapo Tract Mss.).
Conrad Feiederich and his wife Anna Maria with 2 ch. were at
Hackensack ca. 1716/17 (Simmendinger Register). A sp. in 1711
gave the maiden name of his wife Anna Maria as Wysing (N.Y. City
Ref. Chbk.). The ch. of Johann Conrad[1] and Anna Maria were:

1) Peter[2] (Palatines In N.Y. City), md. 15 or 19 June 1717
   at Campua near Remobuch, N.J. at Jacob Demuth's to Anna
   Dorothea Demuth (N.Y. City Luth. Chbk.). Mr. Pieter Friederich was a delegate to a Luth. assembly in 1735 (Albany
   Protocol, p. 147). Issue:

     i) Anna Maria[3], bpt. 9 June 1718 at Remobuch and b. at
        Mauwe - sp.: Joh: Cunrad Friedrich and Anna Maria
        Friedericks (N.Y. City Luth. Chbk.). She was conf.
        in 1734 (N.Y. City Luth. Chbk.).

    ii) Anna Elisabetha[3], b. 19 June 1720 at Mauwee and bpt.
        at Remobuch - sp.: Jacob Demuth and Anna Elisabeth;
        J.D. absent so Cunrad Friedrich stood (N.Y. City
        Luth. Chbk.).

iii) <u>Conrad</u>³, bpt. 17 Feb 1723 - sp.: Coenraet Vrerikse
and wife Maritie (Hackensack Ref. Chbk.). He may
have been the Conrad Frederick who md. Sarah (--)
and had a child at Pompton Plains Ref. Church in
1746 (HJ).

iv) <u>Maria</u>³, b. 11 June 1731 at Wagha and bpt. Hackinsak
- sp.: Friderich Demuth and wife Annatje (N.Y. City
Luth. Chbk.).

2) <u>Conrad</u>² (Palatines In N.Y. City). He was conf. at N.Y.
19 July 1710 (West Camp Luth. Chbk.) and sp. Cunrad Meyssinger at Hackinsack in 1720 (N.Y. City Luth. Chbk.).

HANNS ADAM FRIDERICH (Hunter Lists #213)

Hans Adam Fredrig, his wife, and 1 child were on Capt. William Newton's ship in Holland in the 5th party of 1709 (Rotterdam Lists); he was surrounded on this roll by other emigrants
from the Kraichgau region of Germany (i.e. Hans Michel Wechel,
Joost Heÿt, and Hans Georg Müller) (HJ).

Johann Adam Friderich made his initial appearance on the
Hunter Lists 4 July 1710 with 1 pers. over 10 yrs. of age. The
family increased to 2 pers. over 10 yrs. of age on 4 Aug 1710;
entries in the year 1712 showed 1 pers. over 10, 3 pers. over 10,
and 2 pers. over 10 yrs. of age. Jno. Adam Friedrich: 1 man and
1 woman were in Ulster Co. in 1710/11 (West Camp Census). Johan
Adam Frierich was nat. 8 and 9 Sept 1715 (Kingston Nats.). Johann
Adam Friedrich and Regina Maria were at Beckmansland ca. 1716/17
(Simmendinger Register). Hans Adam Frederick made his initial appearance on tax rolls in the North Ward in 1717/18 and continued
until 1725/26 (Dutchess Co. Tax Lists).

There were other Friederichs in the early part of the 18th
century in colonial N.Y. A Michael Frederick md. Gertraud Livingston and resided in the Schoharie area as early as 1738/39. A Johann Peter Friederich md. Anna Veronica (--) and had several ch.
bpt. at Fort Hunter beginning in 1739.

MARIA ELIZABETH FRILLIN (Hunter Lists #214)

Maria Elizabetha Frillin made her first appearance on the
Hunter Lists 4 Aug 1710 with 1 pers. over 10 yrs.; she was called
Anna Maria Frillin on 4 Oct 1710, her last entry on the Hunter
Lists.

Perhaps she may have been originally in the family of either
William Friel or John Nicol Vreel in the 2nd London arrivals (HJ).

JOHN WILHELM FRITZ (Hunter Lists #215)

Jurg Willem Frits, his wife, and 3 ch. were in the 6th party of Palatines in Holland in 1709 (Rotterdam Lists). The family often appeared in various American records near other 1709ers who originated near Neuwied, and a Johann Wilhelm Fritz and wife Reiesmund (?) had a daughter Mariana bpt. 10 Nov 1692 at 5451 Anhausen near Neuwied (HJ).

John Wilhelm Fritz made his first appearance on the Hunter Lists 1 July 1710 with 3 pers. over 10 yrs. of age in the family. Georg Wilhelm Fritz with wife and ch. were at Hunderston ca. 1716/ 17 (Simmendinger Register). Jury Wm. Fretts was on Palatine Debtors Lists dated 1718, 1719, 1722, and 1726 (Livingston Debt Lists). The ch. of Georg Wilhelm[1] (or John Wilhelm) Fritz were:

1) Maria Elisabetha[2] (HJ), md. Adam Schauer 3 April 1720 (N.Y. City Luth. Chbk.).

2) Johann Christophel[2] (HJ). Christ. Fretts was a Palatine Debtor 23 Feb 1726 (Livingston Debt Lists). He md. Agnes (--), whom sp. and German bpt. records strongly suggest was a Dieterich (HJ). They had issue:

   i) Christian[3] (HJ), md. Elisabetha Waldorff (HJ). They had ch. bpt. at Germantown Ref. and Luth., Katsbaan Ref., and Linlithgo Ref. Churches.

  ii) Anna Maria[3], bpt. 11 Aug 1726 at Haneman Saalbach's at Kamp - sp.: Anna Maria Dieterich and Adam Hof (N.Y. City Luth. Chbk.). She md. 11 Dec 1750 Johann Wilhelm Waldorff (Germantown Ref. Chbk.).

 iii) Johann Peter[3], b. 1 April 1728 and bpt. Kamp - sp.: Pieter Althuiser and Maria Cathr. Dieterichs (N.Y. City Luth. Chbk.). He md. Catharina Holzapfel (HJ), and they had ch. bpt. at Germantown Ref., Linlithgo Ref., and Gallatin Ref. Churches.

  iv) Hermann[3] (HJ), md. 16 April 1754 Christina Mustiir (Mosier et var.) (Katsbaan Ref. Chbk.). They had ch. bpt. at Germantown Ref. and Luth., and Gallatin Ref. Churches.

   v) Anna Magdalena[3], b. 1 Feb 1734 - sp.: Artonius Schneider and wife Margret (Rhinebeck Luth. Chbk.). She md. Jacobus Mustiir (Musier) (HJ).

  vi) Catharina[3], md. as d/o the late Christoffel Fritz 19 Nov 1765 Adam Klum (Germantown Ref. Chbk.). She joined the Germantown Ref. Church 17 April 1747 (Germantown Ref. Chbk.).

STEPHAN FRÖLICH (Hunter Lists #216)

Stephan Frölich made his initial appearance on the Hunter Lists 1 July 1710 with 2 pers. over 10 yrs. of age and 3 pers. under 10 yrs. in the family. On 4 Oct 1710 the entry read 3 pers. over 10 yrs. and 2 pers. under 10; on 24 June 1711 the household had 3 pers. over 10 yrs. and 1 pers. under 10 yrs. Stephan Frolich: 1 man, 1 woman, 2 maids aged 9-15, and 1 girl 8 yrs. and under were in Ulster Co. in 1710/11 (West Camp Census). Stephen Frilich was nat. 8 and 9 Sept 1715 (Kingston Nats.). Stephan Frölich and Anna Elisabetha with 2 ch. were at Beckmansland ca. 1716/17 (Simmendinger Register). Stephen Frylygh was an overseer of ye King's Highway in the North Ward in 1726 (Dutchess Co. Supervisor's Records). His wife was Anna Elisabetha (most probably Wohlleben - HJ). Elizabeth Freelich "still alive" joined the Rhinebeck Flats Ref. Church 14 Aug 1761 (HJ). They had ch.:

1) <u>Ursula²</u> (HJ), md. Martin Burckhardt 16 May 1721 (Kingston Ref. Chbk.).

2) <u>Elisabetha²</u> (HJ), md. Georg Jacob Sorenberger 8 or 18 Aug 1726 (Kingston Ref. Chbk.).

3) <u>Anna Catharina²</u>, b. 14 Dec 1712 - sp.: Anna Catharina Krantz (West Camp Luth. Chbk.). She was conf. 22 June 1731 at Beekman's Mill (N.Y. City Luth. Chbk.). Anna Catharina md. Johannes Wust (HJ).

4) <u>Anna Eva²</u>, bpt. 13 March 1715 - sp.: Marten Boek and Anna Catryn (Kingston Ref. Chbk.). She also was conf. at Beekman's Mill 22 June 1731 (N.Y. City Luth. Chbk.). She md. David Eckhardt (HJ).

5) <u>Johann Peter²</u>, a s/o Stephan¹ on the 1734 St. Peter's Luth. List. Joh. Pieter Frolich, s/o Steffen Frölich, was conf. in 1737 (N.Y. City Luth. Chbk.). He md. 30 Oct 1741 Margaretha Flegeler (Kingston Ref. Chbk.). Peter made his initial appearance on tax rolls in 1742 (Dutchess Co. Tax Lists). The will of Peter Freligh of Rhynbeck Precinct was dated 6 March 1788 and probated 12 July 1792 (Dutchess Co. Will Bk. A). He had issue:

    i) <u>Stephanus³</u> (Will), md. 23 Oct 1764 Maria Van Binschoten (Red Hook Luth. Chbk.). They had ch. at Red Hook Luth. and Rhinebeck Flats Ref. Churches.

    ii) <u>Elisabetha³</u>, bpt. 26 Feb 1744 - sp.: Elisabet Demoot and Johannis Reysdorp (Rhinebeck Flats Ref. Chbk.). She md. Petrus Eckert 23 July 1762 (Rhinebeck Flats Ref. Chbk.).

    iii) <u>Maria³</u>, bpt. 16 Feb 1746 - sp.: Pieter Dumoet and

Marya Burrger (Rhinebeck Flats Ref. Chbk.). She md.
Garret Dedrick (Will).

iv) Petrus³, bpt. 26 Sept 1748 - sp.: Pieter Top and
Catharina Schryver (Rhinebeck Flats Ref. Chbk.).
He md. Elisabetha Feller (HJ).

v) Margaretha³, bpt. 30 Jan 1751 - sp.: Stephanus Burger and Margriet Burger (Rhinebeck Flats Ref. Chbk.).
She md. Albertus Schryver (Will).

vi) Catharina³, b. 24 June 1753 - sp.: Johannes Creemer
and his wife (Rhinebeck Flats Ref. Chbk.). She md.
Peter Trever Jr. (Will).

vii) Anna³, b. 6 Jan 1756 - sp.: Pieter Schryver and Anna
Barbera Scheever (Rhinebeck Flats Ref. Chbk.). She
md. Georg Eckhardt (Will).

viii) Magdalena³, b. 5 Feb 1759 - sp.: Marten Schryver
and his wife (Rhinebeck Flats Ref. Chbk.). She md.
Sebastian Trever (Will).

ix) Philip³, b. 19 Feb 1761 - sp.: David Marquadt and
wife (Rhinebeck Flats Ref. Chbk.).

x) Rebecca³, b. 1 Sept 1763 - sp.: Martinus Borgart
and Rebecca Dippel (Rhinebeck Luth. Chbk.). She md.
David Ring (Will).

xi) Sarah³, bpt. 15 June 1766 - sp.: Georg Reisdorf and
Margaretha Van Aken (Red Hook Luth. Chbk.). She md.
Baunt Van Etten (Will).

xii) Rachel³, bpt. 11 June 1769 - sp.: Johannes Cremer
and Catharina Cremer (Rhinebeck Flats Ref. Chbk.).

xiii) Christina³, bpt. 15 March 1772 - sp.: Tones V: Bin-
schooten and wife Elsjen Dumon (Red Hook Luth.
Chbk.).

VALENTIN FRÖLICH (Hunter Lists #217)

The ancestral origins of the Valentin Frölich family were
at 6761 Mannweiler (10 km. e. of Meisenheim), entries for this
village at 6762 Oberndorf (1 km. n. of Mannweiler; Chbks. begin
1652, Ref.), at 6761 Dielkirchen (3 km. s. of Mannweiler; Chbks.
begin 1697, Luth.), and at 6762 Alsenz (3 km. n. of Mannweiler;
Chbks. begin 1561, but severe gaps). The earliest known ancestor
of the American line was the emigrant's father Hans Henrich Frölich of Mannweiler, bur. 24 March 1721, aged 70 yrs. and 3 weeks;
his wife Anna Margaretha was bur. 12 April 1723, aged 64 yrs.
(Dielkirchen Chbk.). A fascinating document survives at Speyer
Archives dated 22 May 1723 at Mannweiler on this couple:

"After Johann Henrich Fröllich d. already two yrs. ago,
and after his wife Anna Margaretha followed him five
weeks ago, therefore this deceased couple left behind
them as survivors:
   Valentin, who is absent and went with his wife
   Apolonia born Rappin also two ch. in the New
   Country,
   Bernhard Fröllich, md. to Anna Elisabeth Fröl-
   ichen,
   Jacob Fröllich, md. Maria Margaretha born Hoffmann, born at Nieder-Moschel,
   Johannes Fröllich in St. Alban, md. to Hanß Valentin Stegen's daughter Anna Barbara,
   Johann Hinrich Fröllich, single,
   Maria Margaretha, md. to Philipp Ludwig Luth in
   the Rüben (?) Mill...district living...
   Philipp Fröllich, single;
therefore the inheritance was distributed among the aforementioned heirs, as per Churpfälz. Landordnung, which
was used in the presence of Erasmi Kumers, the Churpfälz Amts-Keller at Rockenhausen, and Friedrich Wein-
kauf, the community Schultheiß, and furthermore all
of the Gerichts and all of the heirs, without Valentin,
of whom one does not know if he is (still) alive.
       19 May 1723   Hauß. and Hoff zu Mannweiler
Johannes Fröllich zum Loß

Johann Valentin Frölich, s/o Hans Henrich Frölich of Mannweiler, md. 29 Jan 1704 Anna Apollonia Rapp, d/o Peter Rapp of
Mannweiler (Dielkirchen Chbk.). Appollonia, d/o Hans Peter Rapp
and Anna Margaretha from Mannweiler, was bpt. 22 Jan 1682 (Oberndorf Chbk.). Hans Peter Rapp, s/o Herr Aßmus Rapp - Pfaltz-
zweybrück. Oberschultheissen here, md. 3 June 1673 Anna Margaretha, d/o Claus Sontag at Mannweiler (Alsenz Chbk.); Herr Asmus
Rapp md. 23 Nov 1652 Appolonia Wenz (Alsenz Chbk.). Valentÿn
Frölüg, his wife, and 2 ch., were recorded next to Philippus
Müller - also from Mannweiler - on Capt. John Encrist's ship
in Holland in 1709 (Rotterdam Lists).

Valentin Frölich made his first appearance on the Hunter
Lists 30 June 1710 with 2 pers. over 10 yrs. of age and 2 pers.
under 10 yrs. in the family. Vallindin Frollig was nat. 8 and 9
Sept 1715 (Kingston Nats.). He undoubtedly was the Johan Valentin Felten and Apollonia with 3 ch. on the Simmendinger Register,
which placed him ca. 1716/17 at Beckmansland (HJ). His widow
Apollonia probably md. Johannes Straub (HJ). The ch. of the emigrant Valentin[1] Frölich and his wife Apollonia were:

   1) Charlotta Amalia[2], bpt. 14 Dec 1704 and b. at Mannweiler
      (Dielkirchen Chbk.). She md. Michael Krans 12 Sept 1726
      (Kingston Ref. Chbk.).

   2) Johann Henrich[2], bpt. 15 April 1708 and b. at Mannweiler
      (Dielkirchen Chbk.). Hend[k] Frollig was nat. 8 and 9 Sept
      1715 (Kingston Nats.). Hendrick Frelingh was a freeholder

of Kingston in 1728 (Ulster Co. Freeholders). Hendrick
Vreligh was in the foot company of the Kingston, Ulster
Co. militia in 1738 (Report of the State Historian, Vol.
I, p. 604). A law suit relating to Hendrick Frelig vs.
Juryan Tappan in 1743 was found in the Kingston Court of
Common Pleas. Kingston Trustees Records noted him in Bk.
I, part C, pp. 119 & 120, and Bk. II, pp. 37 & 38. He md.
Elisabetha Catharina Schneider 12 Dec 1726 (as Hendrik
Frederik and Elsjen Snyder) (Kingston Ref. Chbk.). Issue:

   i) Johannes[3], bpt. 3 March 1728 - sp.: Joh: Willem Sny-
      der and Apolona Vreelig (Kingston Ref. Chbk.). He
      md. Elisabetha Fuhrer and had ch. at Katsbaan Ref.
      and Catskill Ref. Churches (HJ).

  ii) Petrus[3], bpt. 7 Sept 1729 - sp.: Johannes Freelig
      and Catrina Hommel (Kingston Ref. Chbk.). He md. 20
      Dec 1748 Mary Wood (Kingston Ref. Chbk.); they had
      ch. at Kingston Ref., Katsbaan Ref., and Marbletown
      Ref. Churches.

 iii) Henrich[3], b. 11 Oct 1732 and bpt. at Newton - sp.:
      Friderich Rauw and wife Catharina (Loonenburg Luth.
      Chbk.). He md. 7 June 1754 Margaretha Van Leeuwen
      (Kingston Ref. Chbk.). They had issue at Katsbaan
      Ref., West Camp Luth., and Red Hook Luth. Churches.

  iv) Wilhelm[3], bpt. 7 April 1735 - sp.: Johannes Hommel
      and Catharina Lisjong (Katsbaan Ref. Chbk.). He md.
      14 April 1754 Anna Wells (Katsbaan Ref. Chbk.) and
      2nd on 19 Aug 1757 Tanneke, wid/o John West (Kings-
      ton Ref. Chbk.).

   v) Margaretha[3], bpt. 10 Oct 1736 - sp.: Hermanus Homel
      and Margrietje Hommel (Kingston Ref. Chbk.). She md.
      David Fuhrer 31 Oct 1751 (Kingston Ref. Chbk.).

  vi) Georg[3], bpt. 20 April 1739 - sp.: Jurg Schneider and
      Johanna Swart (Katsbaan Ref. Chbk.).

 vii) Benjamin[3], bpt. 26 July 1741 - sp.: Johannes Trom-
      boor and Christina Fierer (Kingston Ref. Chbk.).

viii) Anna[3], bpt. 1 Aug 1742 - sp.: Johannes Schneider and
      Antje Theunges (Kingston Ref. Chbk.).

  ix) Georg[3], bpt. 31 Oct 1743 - sp.: Jury Willem Right-
      meyer and Antje Hommel (Katsbaan Ref. Chbk.).

   x) Valentin[3], bpt. 7 May 1745 - sp.: Valetin Fierer and
      wife Catharina Schram (Katsbaan Ref. Chbk.).

  xi) Catharina[3], bpt. 9 June 1747 - sp.: Andreas Tromber
      and Catharina Rau (Katsbaan Ref. Chbk.).

 xii) Maria[3], bpt. 28 March 1749 - sp.: Nicolass Brits and

wife Maria Rau (Katsbaan Ref. Chbk.).

xiii) Benjamin³, bpt. 31 Oct 1751 - sp.: Jurg Hommel and
wife Margriet Fierer (Katsbaan Ref. Chbk.).

3) Johannes², b. 26 Feb 1713 - sp.: Johann Emmerich and wife
Anna Margretha (West Camp Luth. Chbk.). Johannes Frölich,
aged 16 yrs., was conf. at Newtown in Andr. Elig's house
14 Jan 1730 (N.Y. City Luth. Chbk.). The Church Council
asked Pastor Berkenmeyer to examine Hannes Vrolich, as
to whether he was capable of being a lay reader 27 May
1733 (Albany Protocol, p. 64). Johannis Frelegh was mentioned in the Kingston Trustees Records, Bk. II, pp. 328-
330. He md. as surviving s/o Valentin Frolich on 1 April
1734 Maria Margaretha Lehmann, d/o Clement Lehmann (Loonenburg Luth. Chbk.). They had ch.:

i) Valentin³, bpt. in house of H. Frolich 6 Jan 1735 -
sp.: Clement and Gertruyd, the grandparents (Loonenburg Luth. Chbk.).

ii) Anna³, b. 3 Jan 1736 and bpt. at Kisket. - sp.: Johannes Stroub and wife Anna Apollonia (Loonenburg
Luth. Chbk.).

iii) Elisabetha³, b. 17 Dec 1736 and bpt. at Kisket - sp.:
Jacob Straub and Lisabeth Lehmann (Loonenburg Luth.
Chbk.).

iv) Catharina³, b. 4 Dec 1737 and bpt. Kisket. - sp.:
Henrich Frolich and Liese Catharine (Loonenburg
Luth. Chbk.). She md. 19 Trin.: 1755 Georg Fried.
Rheinhard (Loonenburg Luth. Chbk.).

v) Johannes³, b. 13 Feb 1739 and bpt. Kisket. - sp.:
Bernhard Frolich and Catharina Lehman (Loonenburg
Luth. Chbk.). A Johannis Freliegh, with (his bro-
thers - HJ) Clement and Jacob Freliegh, was noted in
Capt. Jacob Halenbeck's Co. in 1767 (Report of the
State Historian, Vol. II, p. 828).

vi) Christina³, b. 19 April 1740 and bpt. Newton - sp.:
Jurge Kreisler and wife Christina (Loonenburg Luth.
Chbk.).

vii) Jacob³, b. 2 May 1741 and bpt. Newton - sp.: Jan
Laux and Lisabeth - wid/o Jan Straub. A Jacob Fra-
lick d. in 1829, aged 89 yrs. in Canajoharie (Albany Gazette, 22 Jan 1829).

viii) Agnes³, b. 14 Aug 1742 and bpt. Newton - sp.: Jury
Lehman and Agneta Borter (Loonenburg Luth. Chbk.).

ix) Maria³, b. 7 Dec 1743 and bpt. Newton - sp.: Frid.
Rauw and wife Catharina (Loonenburg Luth. Chbk.).

    x) <u>Gertraud</u>[3], b. 21 March 1745 and bpt. Hosek - sp.: Peter Lampman Sen. and wife Johanna Elis. (Loonenburg Luth. Chbk.).

   xi) <u>Benjamin</u>[3], b. 19 April 1747 and bpt. Kisket. - sp.: Frider Rauw Jr. and Cathar. Rauw (Loonenburg Luth. Chbk.). Cpl. Benjamin Frelick of Butler's Rangers was at Niagara in 1783, aged 36 (<u>Loyalists In Ontario</u>, p. 113).

  xii) <u>Clement</u>[3], b. 18 Dec 1748 and bpt. Kisket. - sp.: Wilhelm Lehman and Gertrud Lehman (Loonenburg Luth. Chbk.).

 xiii) <u>Wilhelmus</u>[3], b. 8 July 1750 and bpt. Kisket., a twin, other being dead - sp.: Jo: Wilh. Schram and wife Cath. (Loonenburg Luth. Chbk.).

  xiv) <u>Petrus</u>[3], b. 27 March 1752 - sp.: Pieter Laux and Neeltje (Loonenburg Luth. Chbk.).

   xv) <u>Abraham</u>[3], b. 14 Feb 1754 - sp.: Hans Frolich, Jr. and Liesabeth (Loonenburg Luth. Chbk.).

  xvi) <u>Maria</u>[3], b. 10 Jan 1756 - sp.: Philip Spaun and Mareitje (Loonenburg Luth. Chbk.).

 xvii) <u>Elisabetha</u>[3], b. 9 Nov 1758 - sp.: Niclaas Bronck and Catharina (Loonenburg Luth. Chbk.).

4) <u>Johann Bernhard</u>[2], b. 3 Jan 1717 - sp.: Bernhard Lueckhard and wife Justina (West Camp Luth. Chbk.). He md. 13 Feb 1743 Lydia De Lange (Fishkill Ref. Chbk.). They sp. Michael Krans and Charlotta Frolich in 1744 at the Montgomery Ref. Church, and Barent Frielick made his first appearance on Poughkeepsie tax rolls in 1739/40 (Dutchess Co. Tax Lists). They had ch.:

    i) <u>Anna</u>[3], b. 27 Oct 1743 and bpt. Bachway - sp.: Barend Lickhard and Justina (N.Y. City Luth. Chbk.).

   ii) <u>Benjamin</u>[3], b. 24 June 1745 and bpt. Bachway - sp.: Pieter/: Pietersen/Lassing and Anna Maria (sic) (N.Y. City Luth. Chbk.). He md. April 1775 Margaretha Schmid (Loonenburg Luth. Chbk.).

  iii) <u>Elisabetha</u>[3], bpt. 13 Oct 1751 - sp.: Jurian Overpach and Elisabeth Overpach (Catskill Ref. Chbk.).

  iv) <u>Margaretha</u>[3], bpt. Jan 1754 - sp.: Henderik Valentyn and Marejtye Eykelaer (Catskill Ref. Chbk.).

   v) <u>Catharina</u>[3], bpt. 3 Oct 1756 - sp.: H. Jurrian Overpagh and Catrina Smith (Catskill Ref. Chbk.).

  vi) <u>Lydia</u>[3], bpt. 9 June 1758 (Catskill Ref. Chbk.). (?)

 vii) <u>Jan</u>[3], bpt. 29 Nov 1760 - sp.: Jan Schermerhorn and Elizabeth Diderik (Catskill Ref. Chbk.).

JOHANN CHRISTOPH FUCHS (Hunter Lists #218)
JOHANN PHILIPP FUCHS (Hunter Lists #219)

The ancestral home of the Schoharie-Mohawk Fox family was
at 5450 Niederbieber (2 km. n. of Neuwied; Chbks. begin 1655).
The earliest known ancestor of the American line was the father
of Philip[1] Fuchs, Christoffel Fuchs, who was bur. 27 Nov 1698,
aged ca. 90 yrs. Christoffel Fuchs at Wiedt had banns to marry
Dom. 10 p. Trin.: 1683 Anna, wid/o the late Daniel Linckenbach
(Rengsdorf Chbk.); this was a 2nd marriage (HJ). The ch. of
Christoffel Fuchs and his 1st wife Maria were:

"A Son", bpt. 17 March 1661 - sp.: Werner ..., Anastina ...
- Johan von Grevenwied, and Hansenstien from Ölsched.

+ Johann Philip.

Johann Philips, s/o Christoffel Fuchs at Grawenwiedt, md. 22 March
1683 Catharina, d/o the late Herr Johann Wilhelm Neitzert at N.B.
Catharina, w/o Philipp Fuchs the miller here, d. 6 March 1707,
aged 49 yrs. Johann Philips Fuchs, widower, miller, and Gerichtsschöffe at N.B., md. 7 July 1707 Eulalia, wid/o the late Sebastian Berner, citizen at N. wiedt. Johann Philip[1] sp. several future N.Y. Palatine settlers in the Neuwied area prior to 1709,
including Görg Friderich Neeff - a relative via his wife's Neitzert family - at Neuwied in 1699 and Hans Wilhelm Dieterich at
Niederbieber in 1704.

Johann Philipp Fuchs made his initial appearance on the Hunter Lists 1 July 1710 with 8 pers. over 10 yrs. of age; the family was noted with 7 pers. over 10 yrs. 4 Aug 1710, followed by
somewhat erratic entries until 13 Sept 1712 again with 7 pers.
over 10 yrs. On the 4 Oct 1710 registration, Philip[1] Fuchs was
recorded next to his relative Georg Friederich Neff from Neuwied
(HJ). Both Philip[1] and his son Christophel[2] were millers in N.Y.,
as in Germany, as evidenced by repeated notations concerning them
in the letters of Jean Cast to Robert Livingston in April 1711:

"Capt. (Christophel) Fox left his work in a huff, and
has not returned, as promised by his father..."
"Old Fuchs is willing to work for fifteen days on trial
without pay to show his worth, but then wanted £25 a
year..." (Genealogy of the Mohawk Valley Bellingers and
Allied Families, by Lyle Frederick Bellinger, p. 14).

Philipp Fuchs and his wife Anna Eva, with their 4 ch. were at Neu-
Heessberg ca. 1716/17 (Simmendinger Register). Jan Ph: Faux was
a Palatine Debtor in one of the four villages 26 Dec 1718 (Livingston Debt Lists). He and his wife Anna Eva sp. Henrich Schäffer in 1738/39 (Schoharie Ref. Chbk.). The ch. of the emigrant
Johann Philip[1] Fuchs and his 1st wife Catharina Neitzert were:

1) <u>Johann Christophel</u>[2], bpt. 6 Jan 1684 - sp.: Johann Christophel - brother of the child's mother, and Anna Margaretha - d/o Joh. Ludwig Alstorff (Niederbieber Chbk.).
Johann Christoph Fuchs made his initial appearance as
#218 on the Hunter Lists 4 Oct 1710 with 2 pers. over 10
yrs. of age; the size of the family increased to 3 pers.
over 10 yrs. 24 June 1711, when the household was noted
next to Philip[1] Fuch's family. Johanna Eliz Fucks Frau
aged 22 was in N.Y. City in 1710/11 (Palatines In N.Y.
City); she was entered in the family of Ludolf Korning
(thus her father was #108 Ludolff Coring - HJ). John
Christopher Ffucks was a Capt. in the Canadian expedition
of 1711 (Palatine Volunteers To Canada); he was called
of Haysbury in that document. Christoffel Foux was on a
list of Palatines in March 1712/13 in the Livingston
Debt Lists (<u>Settlers & Residents</u>, Vol. I, p. 16). Christopher Fox was a patentee on the s. side of the Mohawk
River 30 April 1725 (Burnetsfield Patent). The will of
Christophel Fox of Burnett's Field was dated 28 Aug 1766
and proved at Albany 13 Feb 1767 (<u>N.Y. Historical Society
Collections</u>, Vol. VII, p. 334). One of his later wives
may have been the Anna Elisabetha, wid/o Christoph Fuchs,
who was b. 15 July 1715 and d. 7 Sept 1793 (Fort Plain
Ref. Chbk.). The ch. of Christophel[2] Fuchs included:

   i) <u>Johann Philip</u>[3], b. 31 July 1712 - sp.: Johann Ludolph Curring and Johann Philipp Fuchs (West Camp
Luth. Chbk.).

  ii) <u>Friederich</u>[3], called eldest son in his father's will;
however, as I have not seen the original will, this
name may have actually read "Philip", who was indeed
the eldest son of Christophel[2] (HJ).

 iii) <u>Johannes</u>[3] (Will).

  iv) <u>Elisabetha</u>[3] (Will).

   v) <u>Maria</u>[3] (Will).

2) <u>Anna Elisabetha</u>[2], bpt. 16 Aug 1685 - sp.: Anna Elsa - w/o
Wilhelm Anhausen, and Marcus Engel - "Küchenschreiber bei
Ihro hochgr. Gn. Graf Georg Hermann " (Niederbieber Chbk.).
The child d. in 1691 (Niederbieber Chbk.).

3) <u>Johann Matthias</u>[2], bpt. 19 June 1687 - sp.: Johann Matthias - brother of the child's father, and Gerdrauth - d/o
Henrich Wagner from Pleet (Niederbieber Chbk.). The child
d. in 1689.

4) <u>Christina</u>[2], bpt. 21 April 1689 - sp.: Hans Thönges Bell
and Christina - sister of the child's mother (Niederbieber

Chbk.). She sp. Henrich Sixt at Schoharie in 1716 (West
Camp. Luth. Chbk.).

5) Johann Nicolaus[2], bpt. 15 March 1691 - sp.: Johan Henrich
Peusser - at the time teacher here, Nicol. Müller, and
Johanna Magdalena - d/o the Pastor (Niederbieber Chbk.).
The child d. in 1692 (Niederbieber Chbk.).

6) Anna Margaretha[2], bpt. 25 Sept 1692 - sp.: Hans Wilhelm
Nöll - miller at Fahr, and Anna Margaretha - d/o the late
Peter Nef. (Niederbieber Chbk.). The child d. in 1693
(Niederbieber Chbk.).

7) Anna Margaretha[2], bpt. 4 March 1694 - sp.: Anna - w/o
Georg Schenckelberg at Rengsd., Margaretha - w/o Hupert
Bösch at N.B., and Johann Henrich Becker at Gräfenwies
(Niederbieber Chbk.).

8) Anna Elisabetha[2], bpt. 22 Dec 1695 - sp.: Anna Elisabeth -
surviving d/o Joh. Christoffel Wagner, Anna Marg. - w/o
Johann Daniel Nöll at N.B., and Simon Mittler - miller in
the Tonnerey (?) (Niederbieber Chbk.). She md. Johann
Peter Deichert (HJ).

9) Johann Wilhelm[2] (HJ), probably bpt. at Feldkirchen near
Neuwied 1696-1699, the registers of which are missing (HJ).
Johan Willem Foex was nat 31 Jan 1715/16 (Albany Nats.).
William Fox was a patentee in 1723 (Stone Arabia Patent).
He md. Anna Margaretha, d/o Georg Kast (Will of Jurreije
Kast, Fernow Wills #971). She probably was the Anna Margaretha Fuchs on Pastor Sommer's 1744 list (Schoharie Luth.
Chbk.). William Fox was a freeholder of Canajoharrie in
1763 (Albany Co. Freeholders). The will of Margaret Fox,
a widow of advanced aged of Palatine, was dated 29 Nov
1784 and probated 29 April 1791 (Montgomery Co. Will Bk.
I). They had ch.:
   i) Anna Eva[3], md. as eldest d/o Wilhelm 25 Oct 1743
      Jacob Sternberg (Schoharie Luth. Chbk.).
  ii) Christina[3] (HJ), md. 25 Oct 1748 Johann Philip Berg
      (Schoharie Luth. Chbk.).
 iii) Wilhelm[3] (Mohawk Valley in the Revolution, p. 249).
  iv) Johann Georg[3], bpt. 20 March 1733 - sp.: Georg Kass
      and Anna Kass (Schoharie Ref. Chbk.).
   v) Maria[3], bpt. Feb 1735/36 - sp.: Jurr. Zybel and Engel
      Zybel (Schoharie Ref. Chbk.).
  vi) Philip W.[3] (Will of Margaret Fox).
 vii) Anna[3], probably the daughter who md. John Hess men-
      tioned in the will of Margaret Fox (HJ).
viii) Christopher W.[3] (Mohawk Valley in the Revolution, p.

249).

10) <u>Anna Catharina</u>[2], bpt. 31 Oct 1700 - sp.: Anna - w/o Joh.
Hupert Eckard, Agnes - w/o Hans Georg Schneider at Neuwied, and Hermann Alsdorf at N.B. (Niederbieber Chbk.).

11) <u>Johann Andreas</u>[2], b. in the mill at N.B. and bpt. 10 Sept
1702 - sp.: Andreas Runckel - Gerichtsschöffe at O.B.,
Hans Wilhelm Neitzert - Landreuter at N. Wiedt, and Maria
- w/o Johannes Mäurer in Fahr (Niederbieber Chbk.).

There are several unplaced Fuchs-Fox family members in the
Mohawk-Schoharie region: 1) Catharina Fuchs md. Jost Borst 10
Oct 1758 (Schoharie Luth. Chbk.), 2) Anna Margaretha Fuchs md.
Johannes Klock, and 3) Magdalena Fuchs, whom descendants say md.
Jacob W. Walrath (HJ).

JOHANN PETER FUCHS (Hunter Lists #220)

The ancestral origins of this emigrant 1709er were at 5249
<u>Öttershagen</u> (2 km. s. of Wissen; entries at <u>Roßbach/Sieg</u> begin
1689, Luth.) and 6200 <u>Wiesbaden/Erbenheim</u> (6 km. e. of Mainz;
Chbks. begin ca. 1660). Johann Peter Fuchs, widower from Eders-
hagen (?) aus dem Newburgschen Ambt Windeck, md. 21 Feb 1702
Anna Maria, d/o Johannis Salbach (Erbenheim Chbk.). The birth-
place of Johann Peter Fuchs was actually Öttershagen; registers
were investigated for this village at Roßbach/Sieg, but only two
marriages for a Christian Fuchs in 1696 and 1699 were found
there. Johan Peter Focks, his wife and 2 ch. were listed next to
Johan and Johan Emend Salbach, Peter Sagedorn (sic), and Ananias
Tiell - all documented at Erbenheim - on Capt. Robbert Bulman's
ship in Holland in 1709 (Rotterdam Lists). John Fuchs aged 30,
his wife, and sons aged 4 and 1, Luth., husbandman and vinedresser, were in the 4th arrivals in England later that year (London
Lists); as is so often the case, he was noted near his same
neighbors from Erbenheim at London also (HJ).

Johann Peter Fuchs made his first appearance on the Hunter
Lists 4 July 1710 with 2 pers. over 10 yrs. of age and 1 pers.
under 10; on 24 June 1711, the entry read 3 pers. over 10 yrs.
of age. John Peter Ffucks aged 31 and Anna Margt. Ffucks aged
24 were in N.Y. City in 1710/11 (Palatines In N.Y. City). John
Peter Fuchs subscribed 14 shillings N.J. money in 1727 (<u>N.Y.
City Luth. Protocol</u>, p. 89). The ch. of Johann Peter[1] Fuchs
(Fox, Voss) and his wife Anna Maria were:

1) <u>Johann Nicolas</u>[2], bpt. 18 April 1703 - sp.: Joh. Nicol.
Kneip and Joh. Nicol. Friederich (Erbenheim Chbk.).

2) <u>Johann Jacob</u>[2], bpt. 7 March 1706 - sp.: Johann Jacob

- s/o Catharina Rossel, and Johann Nicol - s/o Erasmi
Merthen Sr. (Erbenheim Chbk.).

3) <u>Anna Elisabetha[2]</u>, bpt. 29 June 1712 - sp.: Anna Christina
... (Kingston Ref. Chbk.).

4) <u>Anna Catharina[2]</u>, b. 28 Aug 1714 at Dans Kaamer and bpt.
in Highlands - sp.: Jurgen Loocksteed and Anna Catharina
Volck (N.Y. City Luth. Chbk.).

5) <u>Johann Georg[2]</u>, b. 12 July 1717 at Middle Bosch and bpt.
at Raritons - sp.: Jacob Risch and wife, and Jurgen Rie-
mer (N.Y. City Luth. Chbk.). Jerry Fox, a son to Peter
Fox, was mentioned in the Janeway Account Books 1735-45,
as was Peter[1] who lived at No. Rockaway, alias Fox Hill
(Janeway Account Books).

6) <u>Johann Peter[2]</u>, b. 4 March 1720 and bpt. at Raritons at
the house of Baldus Pickel - sp.: Pieter Kastner and
Margareta Suet (N.Y. City Luth. Chbk.).

There were other Fuchs-Fox-Voss families in N.Y. City and
N.J. in the early part of the 18th century: 1) Henrich Voss and
wife Anna Margaretha had a child bpt. at Remmerbuch 11 Feb 1747
(N.Y. City Luth. Chbk.); 2) A Jacob Voss Sr. had sons Jacob Jr.
and Johannes in the Somerset/Raritan area 1735-45 (Janeway Account Books); 3) Johannes Vos and wife Maria (Fitsch) had ch.
bpt. at Hackensack Ref. and Pompton Plains Ref. Churches in 1735
and 1738; and 4) a Johannes Vos and wife Lena Catharina had ch.
bpt. in the N.Y. City Ref. and Luth. Churches 1728-43.

JOHANNES FUHRER (Hunter Lists #221)

John Fuhrer aged 40, his wife, sons aged 13 and 6, daughters
aged 8 and 1, Roman Catholic, husbandman and vinedresser, were
in the 2nd arrivals at London in 1709 (London Lists); another of
that name was John Fohrer aged 60, his wife, sons aged 20 and 18,
Cath., husbandman and vinedresser also a tanner, in the 3rd arrivals at London (London Lists).

Johannes Fuhrer made his initial appearance on the Hunter
Lists 4 Aug 1710 with 3 pers. over 10 yrs. of age and 1 pers. under 10 yrs.; the size of the family increased to 4 pers. over 10
yrs. of age and 1 pers. under 10 on 4 Oct 1710. Johann Fuhrer,
widower of Newtown, md. Anna Maria, wid/o Andreas Richter of Newtown 7 April 1713 (West Camp Luth. Chbk.). Johannis Führer was
nat. (next to Valedien Führer) 8 and 9 Sept 1715 (Kingston Nats.).
Johannes Fferher was taxed £3 at Kingston in 1718/19, and Johannis
Ferber was taxed £12 at Kingston in 1720/21 (Ulster Co. Tax
Lists). The ch. of Johannes[1] Fuhrer were:

1) <u>Valentin</u>[2] (HJ), nat. next to Johannis Führer 8 and 9 Sept
   1715 (Kingston Nats.). Felter Fier was a freeholder of
   Kingston in 1728 (Ulster Co. Freeholders). In the case of
   Falentyn Fiere vs. Wm. Smith in 1730, Fiere wanted 14
   shillings for his share of a bill (Kingston Town Court
   Records). Another case was Martinus Hofman v. Velte Fiero
   in 1745 (Kingston Court of Common Pleas). Valledeyn Fir-
   her was a Justice of the Peace in Ulster Co. (Albany Co.
   Deeds, Vol. 6, p. 391). The will of Vallentyn Fierer of
   the Catsbaen was dated 14 July 1764 and probated 10 Feb
   1770 (<u>Fernow Wills</u> #629); it was also probated 21 June
   1765 in Albany Co. (Albany Co. Deeds, Vol. 7, p. 376).
   The ch. of Valentin[2] Fuhrer (Fiero) and wife Catharina
   Schramm were:

   i) <u>Johannes</u>[3], md. as s/o Valentin 13 Jan 1741 Anna
      Margaretha Elig (Loonenburg Luth. Chbk.). They had
      ch. at Loonenburg Luth. and Katsbaan Ref. Churches.

   ii) <u>Christina</u>[3], bpt. 25 Dec 1721 - sp.: Hans Nieuwkerk
       and Christina Muller (Kingston Ref. Chbk.). She md.
       Johannes Trombauer (HJ).

   iii) <u>Christian</u>[3], bpt. 28 June 1724 - sp.: Christian Fier
        and Elisabeth Mulder (Kingston Ref. Chbk.). He md.
        Christina Schneider 22 May 1745 (Kingston Ref.
        Chbk.), and they had issue at Kingston Ref. and
        Katsbaan Ref. Churches.

   iv) <u>Anna Maria</u>[3], bpt. 1½ months old 12 Oct 1726 at New-
       ton - sp.: Friderich Schram and wife Anna Maria
       (Loonenburg Luth. Chbk.).

   v) <u>Henrich</u>[3], b. 18 Feb 1728 - sp.: Henrich Schram and
      wife Margareta (Loonenburg Luth. Chbk.). Hendrick
      Fiero was in Capt. Cornelus Dubois's Co. at Caskill
      in 1767 (<u>Report of the State Historian</u>, Vol. II, p.
      877). He md. Gertraud Meyer (HJ) and had ch. at
      Katsbaan Ref. Church.

   vi) <u>Friederich</u>[3] (HJ), a sp. in 1753 and 1754 at Kats-
       baan Ref. and Loonenburg Luth. Churches.

   vii) <u>Johann Valentin</u>[3], b. 8 March 1733 and bpt. Newton -
        sp.: Hannes Frolich and Catharina Liese Jung (Loon-
        enburg Luth. Chbk.).

   viii) <u>Harmanus</u>[3], bpt. 4 weeks old ... 1737 - sp.: Herman-
         nus Beehr and Marlentje (Loonenburg Luth. Chbk.).

   ix) <u>Anna Margaretha</u>[3], b. 1 Feb 1740 and bpt. Newton -
       sp.: Veltin - s/o Christian Fuhrer, and Anna Mar-
       greta Eligs (Loonenburg Luth. Chbk.). She md.

Zacharias Schneider (Will).

2) <u>Christian²</u> (HJ), who may have been the Christian Former nat. 3 Jan 1715/16 (Albany Nats.). He md. 8 Sept 1722 Maria Elisabetha Müller (Kingston Ref. Chbk.). Christian Fier made his first appearance on Dutchess Co. tax rolls in 1753 (Dutchess Co. Tax Lists). The will of Johann Christian Fiero of Kingston Corporation was dated 16 Nov 1786 and probated 26 Feb 1787 (Fernow Wills #653). By his 1st wife Maria Elisabetha the ch. of Christian² were:

   i) <u>Valentin³</u>, bpt. 11 Aug 1723 - sp.: Valentyn Viele and Cath. Schram (Linlithgo Ref. Chbk.). He md. Margaret Loesch, and his dates given in Moravian Church records at Bethlehem, Pa. are b. 1724 at Esopus, N.Y. and d. 1808.

   ii) <u>Margaretha³</u> (HJ), md. Georg Hommel 6 Oct 1742 (Katsbaan Ref. Chbk.).

   iii) <u>Elisabetha³</u>, bpt. 5 Feb 1727 - sp.: Freederik Mouwel and Orseltjen Mouwel (Kingston Ref. Chbk.). She md. Johannes Frölich (HJ).

   iv) <u>David³</u>, bpt. 30 Sept 1728 - sp.: David Miller and Margriet Miller (Kingston Ref. Chbk.). He joined the Red Hook Luth. Church 2 April 1758, and md. 31 Oct 1751 Margaretha Frölich (Kingston Ref. Chbk.). They had ch. at Katsbaan Ref., Rhinebeck Luth., and Red Hook Luth. Churches.

   v) <u>Anna³</u>, bpt. 25 Aug 1734 - sp.: Hennerich Fehr and Juliana Becker (Catskill Ref. Chbk.). She md. Hieronymus Gernreich (Will).

   vi) <u>Peter³</u>, md. as s/o Christian 30 Jan 1759 Anna Margaretha Stickel (Red Hook Luth. Chbk.). Ch. at Red Hook Luth. and Rhinebeck Luth. Churches.

   vii) <u>Christian³</u>, b. 3 Aug 1736 and bpt. Kisket. - sp.: Christian Decker and wife Anna (Loonenburg Luth. Chbk.).

   viii) <u>Philip³</u>, bpt. 5 weeks old at Kisket. 29 Oct 1738 - sp.: Philip Spahn and Margreta Eligs (Loonenburg Luth. Chbk.).

Christian Fuhrer, widower, md. Catharina Elisabetha Marten, wid/o Hannes Emmerich 16 Feb 1740 (Loonenburg Luth. Chbk.). Some firm ch./o Christian, possibly from this marriage were:

   ix) <u>Lydia³</u> (Will), md. Conrad Löscher 24 Nov 1767 (Germantown Ref. Chbk.).

   x) <u>Esther³</u> (Will), md. Lorentz Falk (Will).

Christian Fuhrer, widower living Saag Kill in Reinbech
Precinct, md. 1 Sept 1756 Maria Breidenbach (Red Hook
Luth. Chbk.). They had issue:

xi) Rosina[3], b. 10 Nov 1756 - sp.: Johannes Laun and
wife Rosina (Rhinebeck Luth. Chbk.). She md. Johannes Fitzel (Will).

xii) Catharina[3], b. 18 Aug 1761 - sp.: Michael Schuhmacher and wife Catharina (Rhinebeck Luth. Chbk.).

3?) Anna Maria[2]. An Anna Maria Veererin md. Henrich Winter
25 April 1726 (N.Y. City Luth. Chbk.).

PETER FUNCK (Hunter Lists #222)

The ancestral home of the N.Y. Funck family was 6349 Medenbach. Records of the family were found at 6349 Breitscheid (8 km.
w. of Herborn; Chbks. begin 1636) and 6340 Dillenburg (7 km. n. of
Herborn; Chbks. begin 1646). The father of the emigrant 1709er
was Johann Henrich Funck of Donsbach, d. 10 March 1703. He md.
Katharina (--) and had issue:

Gela, b. 4 April 1666 - sp.: Johannes Herr (?) from Medenbach and Frila (?) - w/o Johannes Sommer at Donsbach (Dillenburg Chbk.).

Anna Catharina, b. 24 Sept 1668 - sp.: Anna Katharina - d/o
the late Johannes Funck at Medenbach, and Hannes - s/o Johannes Lang (?) from Donsbach (Dillenburg Chbk.).

+ Peter, b. 4 June 1675 - sp.: Peter Lang at Breidscheidt, and
Julia - w/o Stein (?) Nicodemi from Medenbach (Dillenburg
Chbk.).

Johann Velten, b. 29 Feb 1679 at Donsbach - sp.: Velten
Sohns and Gertraut - w/o Johannes Wagener (Dillenburg Chbk.).

Anna Margaretha, b. 2 Nov 1682 - sp.: Jost Henrich Schneider
at Heyger and Anna Margreth - d/o Johannes Schäfer at Donsbach (Dillenburg Chbk.).

Anna Elisabetha, b. 20 May 1687 - sp.: Johannes Theiss -
smith at Donsbach, and Anna Liesbeth - d/o Johannes Deher (?)
at Sexhelden (Dillenburg Chbk.).

Banns were published 18 Nov 1694 for the marriage of Peter Funck,
s/o Johan Henrich Funck at Donsbach, and Juliana, d/o Hartman
Clemens from Medenbach (Dillenburg Chbk.); the marriage took place
29 Jan 1695 (Breitscheid Chbk.). Peter Funck, his wife and 4 ch.
petitioned to leave Medenbach in 1709 (Nassau-Dillenburg Petitions). Peter Funck, his wife, and 4 ch. were in the 6th party
of Palatine emigrants in 1709 (Rotterdam Lists); also in this
party was an Anna Katrina Funck (alone).

Peter Funck made his first appearance on the Hunter Lists
4 July 1710 with 2 pers. over 10 yrs. of age and 4 pers. under 10
yrs.; the entry changed 4 Oct 1710 to 4 pers. over 10 yrs. and 2
pers. under 10. Pieter Vonk was nat. 22 Nov 1715 (Albany Nats.).
Peter Funck with wife and 4 ch. was a Hunderston ca. 1716/17 (Simmendinger Register). Peter Vonk was a Palatine Debtor in 1718,
1719 ("on our land"), and 1722 (Livingston Debt Lists). With wife
Anna Juliana (sometimes called Gela) the ch. of Peter[1] Funck were:

1) <u>Elisabetha[2]</u>, b. 24 Nov 1697 at Donsbach - sp.: Johan Val-
   entin Funk from Donsbach and Elisabetha - w/o Hartmann
   Clemens, the Hofmann at Hirschberg (Dillenburg Chbk.).
   She md. Simon Kilmer (HJ).

2) <u>"A Daughter"[2]</u>, bpt. 5 Feb 1701 at Medenbach - sp.: Jost
   Funck and Anna - w/o Jost Henrich Scherer, all at Medenbach (Breitscheid Chbk.).

3) <u>"A Daughter"[2]</u>, bpt. 2 March 1704 - sp.: Anna Catharina -
   wid/o the late Johann Henrich Funcke at Donsbach (Breitscheid Chbk.). Sp. show this daughter was named <u>Anna Cath-
   arina</u> (HJ); Catharina Funck md. Adam Bitzer 23 Nov 1725
   (Linlithgo Ref. Chbk.).

4) <u>"A Daughter"[2]</u>, bpt. 19 March 1707 - sp.: Johann Elias
   Merckel and Anna Christina Brinckmänn, both at Medenbach
   (Breitscheid Chbk.). Sp. show that this daughter was named
   <u>Anna Christina</u> (HJ); "Christina Peter Funken" md. 15 Nov
   1726 Johann Nicolas Philips (Linlithgo Ref. Chbk.).

5) <u>Henrich[2]</u> (HJ), on the 1734 list of families at St. Peter's
   Luth. Church in Rhinebeck.

6) <u>Johann Wilhelm[2]</u> (HJ), md. Anna Juliana Becker (HJ) and had:

   i) <u>Anna Margaretha[3]</u> (HJ), md. Henrich Stahl (HJ).

   ii) <u>Elisabetha[3]</u>, b. 5 March 1743 and bpt. at Newton - sp.:
       Peter Becker and wife Lisabeth (Loonenburg Luth.
       Chbk.).

   iii) <u>Petrus[3]</u>, bpt. 19 May 1745 - sp.: Petrus Pecker and
        Marytje Sipperlie (Linlithgo Ref. Chbk.). He md. Ger-
        traud Finckel 15 Aug 1767 (Linlithgo Ref. Chbk.).
        They had ch. at Linlithgo Ref. and Manorton Luth.
        Churches.

   iv) <u>Johann Denus[3]</u>, bpt. 19 Sept 1747 - sp.: Denis Becker
       and Anna Eva Becker (Germantown Ref. Chbk.). He ap-
       pears to have md. twice: 1) Elisabetha Jacobi, and
       2) Catharina (--).

   v) <u>Elisabetha[3]</u>, bpt. 20 Aug 1749 - sp.: Herman Funck
      and Engel (Germantown Ref. Chbk.).

   vi) <u>Wilhelm[3]</u> (HJ), md. Margaretha Finckel (HJ).

vii) <u>Jacobus</u>[3], bpt. 13 Nov 1757 - sp.: Jac: Best and wife Annatgen Taht (Germantown Ref. Chbk.).

7) <u>Hermann</u>[2] (HJ), md. Engel Minckeler (HJ). Hermen Funck was a Sergent (sic) in Capt. Frederick Kortz's Co. at East Camp in 1767 (<u>Report of the State Historian</u>, Vol. II, p. 869). He had issue:

   i) <u>Catharina</u>[3] (HJ), md. Johannes Wagener (HJ).

  ii) <u>Petrus</u>[3], bpt. 11 Jan 1746 - sp.: Petrus Funck and Gertraudt (Germantown Ref. Chbk.).

 iii) <u>Hermann</u>[3], bpt. 11 Sept 1748 - sp.: Herman Minkeler and Gretgen (Germantown Ref. Chbk.).

  iv) <u>Gertraut</u>[3], bpt. 26 Aug 1750 - sp.: Luss Minkler and Gertraut Minkler (Germantown Ref. Chbk.).

   v) <u>Jacob</u>[3], bpt. 12 Nov 1752 - sp.: Bastian Lup (?) and Margarut Minkelaar (Germantown Ref. Chbk.).

  vi) <u>Johannes</u>[3], b. 9 Nov 1754 - sp.: Pieter Harder and Elisabeth Thomas (Rhinebeck Flats Ref. Chbk.).

 vii) <u>Antonius</u>[3], bpt. 9 March 1757 - sp.: Antonius Minckeler and Margaretha Hoch (Germantown Ref. Chbk.).

viii) <u>Christian</u>[3], bpt. 30 Dec 1759 - sp.: Christiaen Philip and Eva Herder (Linlithgo Ref. Chbk.).

  ix) <u>Adam</u>[3], b. 5 March 1762 - sp.: Adam Bitzer and Cath: (Germantown Luth. Chbk.).

   x) <u>Wilhelm</u>[3], bpt. 16 Dec 1764 - sp.: Willem Fonk and wife Annatien Bekker (Germantown Ref. Chbk.).

  xi) <u>Maria</u>[3], bpt. 18 Jan 1767 - sp.: Adam Klum and wife Catharina Fritz (Germantown Ref. Chbk.).

8) <u>Johannes</u>[2], b. Dec 1719 at Camp on the e. bank of (the) Hudson - sp.: Johannes Melhart (N.Y. City Luth. Chbk.). (The mother was called Gertraud on this bpt. entry - HJ). Johannes[2] md. 8 May 1748 Anna Maria Webber, d/o Peter Webber (Weaver)(Germantown Ref. Chbk.) and had ch.:

   i) <u>Catharina</u>[3], bpt. 4 June 1749 - sp.: Hennrich Weber and Catharina Philipp (Gallatin Ref. Chbk.).

  ii) <u>Gertraut</u>[3], bpt. 15 Sept 1750 - sp.: Peter Wever and Gertraut Funck (Germantown Ref. Chbk.).

 iii) <u>Maria</u>[3], bpt. 5 Sept 1756 - sp.: Joh: Jacob Milius and Anna Maria Dings (Gallatin Ref. Chbk.).

  iv) <u>Christina</u>[3] (?), bpt. 18 Aug 1760 - sp.: Johannes Kilmer and Christin Weber (Gallatin Ref. Chbk.).

   v) <u>Elisabetha</u>[3], bpt. April 1763 - sp.: Simon Kilmer and wife Elisabeth (Pine Plains Chbk.).

  vi) <u>Eva</u>[3], bpt. 29 Sept 1765 - sp.: Willem Kilmer and wife Eva Kohler (Gallatin Ref. Chbk.).

JACOB FUHRMAN (Hunter Lists #223)

The German origins of the Fuhrmann family were at 6704 Mutterstadt (10 km. s. of Frankenthal; Chbks. begin 1700, Ref.). Jacob Fuhrman, widower of Mutterstadt, md. Catharina Bähr, d/o Henrich Bähr of Rabsweiller ausem Ober Elsas, 10 Nov 1709 (London Churchbooks and the German Emigration of 1709, by John P. Dern, p. 25). Fuhrman had arrived in May of 1709 and was recorded on the Tribbeko-Ruperti rolls as Jacob Fuhrman aged 34, with daughters aged 7 and 5, Ref., husbandman and vinedresser (London Lists).

Jacob Fuhrman made his initial appearance on the Hunter Lists 4 Aug 1710 with 3 pers. over 10 yrs. of age and 1 pers. under 10 in the household. The last entry in Hunter noted 4 pers. over 10 yrs. of age in the family. Jacob Fuhrmann with wife and ch. were registered at Wormsdorff ca. 1716/17 (Simmendinger Register). Jacob Frayman was on the Tulpehocken tax rolls in 1725 (The Hub of the Tulpehocken, by Earl W. Ibach, p. 12). The will of Jacob Fuhrman was dated 4 April 1748 and probated in 1754 (Philadelphia Co. Will Bk. K, p. 182). The ch. of Jacob[1] Fuhrmann by his two wives were:

1) Anna Apollonia[2], bpt. 14 Sept 1703 - sp.: Peter ... and Anna Apollonia Renner (Mutterstadt Chbk.); the mother in this entry was called Catharina.

2) Maria Catharina[2] (Will).

3) Johannes[2] (Will).

ANNA MARIA GALADEH & BROTHER (Hunter Lists #224)

The ancestral roots of the Pa. Galathé-Colliday family were at 6800 Mannheim (14 km. s.e. of Worms; Chbks. begin 1515) with some references to the family also found at 6729 Bellheim (16 km. s.w. of Speyer; Chbks. begin 1684, Cath.) and at 6730 Neustadt an der Weinstraße (20 km. w. of Speyer; Chbks. begin 1585, Ref.). The earliest known forefather of the emigrant 1709ers was Jacob Galathé, called an assessor in 1669 and a shoemaker in 1672; he md. Anna Maria Berge and had issue:

Jacob, bpt. 16 May 1669 - sp.: Jacob Keller - citizen, and Anna Margaretha - w/o Thomas Sporkel citizen and innkeeper at the Rosebush (Mannheim Ref. Chbk.).

Anna, bpt. 1670 (Mannheim Ref. Chbk.).

+ Jacob, bpt. 26 May 1672 - sp.: Jacob Dinass, citizen and woolen-weaver at this place, and his wife Anna Catharine (Mannheim Ref. Chbk.).

Anna Margaretha, bpt. 8 Sept 1684 - sp.: Jacob Herre and wife Anna Margaretha (Bellheim Cath. Chbk.).

> Anna Maria, bpt. 26 Oct 1687 - sp.: Anna Maria - single d/o
> the late Herr Phil. Peter Kirchner, formerly customs officer
> here (Neustadt Chbk.).

Jacob Galathe, bpt. 1672, md. Anna Maria (--); he was called a master shoemaker like his father in the Mannheim Chbk. John Jacob
Galathe aged 32, his wife, a son aged 2 and a daughter aged 6, Ref.,
shoemaker, were in the 1st arrivals in England in 1709 along with
Jacob Galathe aged 75, carpenter, Ref., and the John William Galathe
family (London Lists); this man was the William Golliday listed
as head of a Palatine family in Ireland in 1715 (The Palatine Families of Ireland, p.26).

Anna Maria Galadeh made her initial appearance on the Hunter
Lists 4 Aug 1710 with 2 pers. over 10 yrs. of age and 1 pers. un-
der 10 yrs.. The Journal section of Hunter recorded Anna Maria and
Jacob Galadeh 4 Oct 1710 with 2 pers. over 10 yrs. and 2 pers. un-
der 10 in the household; the cumulative entry for 24 Dec 1711 read
1 pers. over 10 yrs. and 2 pers. under 10, and the final notation
on 25 March 1712 for N.Y. City was 1 pers. over 10 yrs. of age.
Maria Galete, widow, aged 38, Sarah Margaret Galete aged 7, and
Jacob Galete aged 4, were in N.Y. City in 1710/11 (Palatines In
N.Y. City). The ch. of Anna Maria[1] Galathe and her husband (Johann)
Jacob Galathe were:

1) Sarah Margaretha[2], bpt. 3 Oct 1703 - sp.: Daniel Bentz,
   citizen and boatman at this place, and wife Anna Margar-
   etha (Mannheim Ref. Chbk.). She md. Christianus Kensey
   (Küntzy, Kinsey) on 31 10 mo. (Dec) 1723 (1st Presbyterian
   Church of Philadelphia Chbk.); they lived in Alsace Twp.,
   Berks Co., Pa.

2) Nicolaus[2], bpt. 24 March 1705 - sp.: Nicolaus Frankh, citizen and master shoemaker in Frankenthal, and wife Anna
   Maria (Mannheim Ref. Chbk.).

3) Johann Jacob[2], bpt. 3 Feb 1707 - sp.: Johann Jacob Dietz,
   citizen and master cabinet maker at this place, and wife
   Susanna (Mannheim Ref. Chbk.). He md. Catharina Juliana
   Rübenkam 24 9 mo. (Nov) 1727 (1st Presbyterian Church of
   Philadelphia Chbk.). A list of the names of inhabitants of
   Philadelphia Co. in 1734 mentioned Jacob Colleday owning
   30 acres in Creesom, late part of Germantown (Publications
   of the Genealogical Society of Pa., Vol. I, p. 166-8).
   In the ledger of Benjamin Franklin was noted that he paid
   £2 and 4 d. to Jacob Koliday and charged to the account of
   Wm. Deweese, Jr. 12 Nov 1737. Jacob[2] had many land transactions in the Philadelphia-Montgomery Co. area, and he
   eventually built a paper mill on the n. bank of the Sandy

Run in present-day Montgomery Co.; he appears to have
been a manufacturer of paper, a miner and manufacturer
lime, a farmer, and a cordwainer - all at the same time
(Ancestry of Wayne Van Leer Jones, p. 224-5). Jacob[2] d.
intestate ca. 1750, and letters of administration were
issued to his widow 25 Oct 1750 (Philadelphia Co. Administration Bk. F, p. 334). His widow Catharina Juliana md.
2nd Blasius Daniel Mackinet (Macknet); Macknet wrote a
fascinating memorandum on his wife's family (printed in
"The Rübenkam Family of Hessen" by Milton Rubincam in
the Pennsylvania Genealogical Magazine, Vol. XXII, pp.
107-112):

> Whereas our Daughter Sarah Meng living in German-
> town is desirous of knowing her line of Nativity,
> I therefore, through this make known unto her the
> same, so far as I have Knowledge of it.
> Her father was a Burger's Son of Manheim in Pfaltz
> (a Place so called) and came to this Country with
> his Mother very young; his Name was Jacob Colladay:
> his Father d. crossing the Ocean. Her Mothers Name
> is Catharina Juliana, Father's Name Ribenkam, was
> b. 1703 in Wasinfried in Hessia where her Father
> named Jn° Philip Ribenkam, was Preacher, & preached
> the Gospel 19 yrs. and his Father was Preacher at
> Eschwig (a Place so calld) Her Mothers Name was
> Magretta (sic) Catharine, a Ministers Daughter of
> Saxone in Hessia, her Fathers Name Sattorin, Her
> Mothers Name Anna Juliana of Luninburgh in Hol-
> stein. This may serve as a Memorendom, if perhaps
> sooner or later some of the Relations should come
> to this part of the World. Your Grand Mother, a
> Widow, came over with 6 grown Children in 1726,
> Viz. 3 Sons & 3 Daughters the eldest Daughter she
> left in Germany in Berlinburgh, where her Father
> d. she is marryed to a Merchant of that Place, nam-
> ed Holtzklaus who - with his Wife are, at this time
> dead. They have left Issue, one Daughter, who is
> marryed & lives in the (undecipherable) Mother d.
> Her Husband's name is I believe, Reuschell. Here
> follows a List of your Mothers Children b. in this
> Country Viz -
> ```
>   1st Margaret Catharina, b. 1728 Sept 23 dead
>   2   Anna Maria............ 1731 April 23
>   3   Jacob Colladay........ 1733  d°   15
>   4   Catharine............. 1735 May 30
>   5   Sarah................. 1737  d°  12
>   6   William............... 1738 Sept 16
>   7   Susanna............... 1741 April 17
> ```
> And Whereas I was well acquainted with your Grand
> Mother, I can give her the Testimony that she was
> a pious good Woman, led a Virtuous life, & was an
> Ornament to her Sex. The follies & pleasures of
> this World, she despisd, & took upon her the (unde-
> cipherable) Cross of Christ (rest of this line un-
> decipherable)   Blasius Daniel Macknet

Mr. Wayne V. Jones was generous as always in sharing with
me his wealth of knowledge on this interesting family.

JOHANNES GANTZ (Hunter Lists #225)

Johann Ganns from Romershausen in the commune of Blancken-
stein near Giesen md. 19 July 1710 Gertrauda from Berith, wid/o
Niclaus Schmid of the commune Hachenburg (West Camp Luth. Chbk.).
The origins of the Ganß family then were at 3569 Römershausen, 17
km. e. of Dillenburg; entries at 3568 Gladenbach (5 km. further
e.; Chbks. begin 1651). There were two potential emigrants named
Johannes Ganß found in the Gladenbach registers: 1) The "filius"
b. to Johan Adam Ganß from Römerßhausen 15 April 1685 - sp.: Hanß
Burck from Sinkershausen, Margreth - d/o Tönges Schäfer from Röm-
ersh., and Jacob - s/o the late Möller from Burgeln (?); as the
prime bpt. sp. to this boy was named Hanß, perhaps this was our
emigrant 1709er (HJ); and 2) The "filius" b. to Ludwig Ganß and
wife Margreth Becker 25 Aug 1682 - sp.: Johannes Ganß, also from
Römershausen as were the parents, and Gertrautt - d/o Theiß Keutt;
this boy also may have been the 1709er, again due to the bpt. sp.
(HJ); however, it should be noted that Johannes, s/o Ludwig Ganß,
md. 26 July 1701 Maria, d/o Hanß Georg Thomas, and had four ch.
b. at Römershausen 1703-09, but that the 1709er appeared to have
been single at the time of his marriage in N.Y. in 1710 (HJ).

Johannes Gantz made his first appearance on the Hunter Lists
4 Aug 1710 with 3 pers. over 10 yrs. of age in the family. The entry for 4 Oct 1710 read 2 pers. over 10 yrs. and 1 pers. under 10
in the household; the size increased to 2 pers. over 10 yrs. and
2 pers. under 10 on 24 June 1711, and then it grew again 24 June
1712 to 2 pers. over 10 yrs. and 3 pers. under 10 and finally
read 2 pers. over 10 and 2 pers. under 10 yrs. on 13 Sept 1712.
Johannis Skans was nat. 3 Jan 1715/16, next to Johan Christ. Smit
(Albany Nats.). Johannes Grantz with wife and ch. was at Hunderston ca. 1716/17 (Simmendinger Register). He and his wife sp. Balthasar Aanspach at Taarboss in 1721 (N.Y. City Luth. Chbk.). After
that date, he migrated to Pa.: Johannes Lantz signed a petition
in the Tulpehocken region in May 1723 (Colonial Laws of Pa., Vol.
III, p. 323). The will of John Gantz was probated in Pa. in 1736
and mentioned his wife Gartrud and his daughter's child Anne Mary
Schuckeren (Philadelphia Co. Will Bk. F, p. 18). Issue:

1) Anna Catharina[2], bpt. 10 June 1711 in the Upper German
   Colonies - sp.: Georg Adam Schmid, Anna Catharine Pulfer,
   and Cathar: Fulz (West Camp Luth. Chbk.). She md. Johann
   Henrich Schuchart (Schucker et var.), and they were the
   parents of the child mentioned in the last will and test-
   ament of the emigrant 1709er and N.Y. and Pa. pioneer,
   Johannes[1] Gantz (HJ).

ANNA MARGARETHA GEBELIN-GÖBELIN (Hunter Lists #226)

The origins of this emigrant were at 6526 Alsheim (10 km. s. of Oppenheim; Chbks. begin 1668, Ref., but gaps). The earliest known forefather of Anna (Maria) Margaretha's husband Sebastian Gebel was Michael Göbel, d. 24 Nov 1676, aged 71 yrs. and called a Gerichts-elder at Alsheim in 1668; his wife was Susanna (--), d. 15 March 1684, aged 75 yrs. Sp. show that a s/o Michael Göbel was Lorentz Gebell, d. 24 March 1687, aged 46 yrs. and 6 months. Lorentz md. Anna Maria Kropfin and had ch.:

> Michael, conf. 1683, aged 16 yrs.
>
> Johann Valentin, bpt. 10 Nov 1667 - sp.: H. Valentin Grob, the Churf.pfaltz. Schultheiss at Langen Wahlheim. He was conf. in 1683, aged 14 yrs. (sic), and d. 8 Sept 1687, aged 20 yrs.
>
> + Sebastian, bpt. 14 Nov 1669 - sp.: Sebastian Muth - s/o Sebastian Muth from Gimbsheim. He was conf. Easter 1686, aged 15 yrs. (sic)
>
> Maria Magdalena, conf. 13 Aug 1689, aged 17½ yrs.
>
> Susanna, b. 23 April 1674 - sp.: Susanna, mother of the father.
>
> Anna Catharina, b. 11 Feb 1676 - sp.: Anna Cath. - w/o Hans Conrad Blum at Walheim.
>
> Johannes, b. 3 Aug 1683 - sp.: Johannes Hirsch here.
>
> Valentin, b. 21 April 1686 - sp.: Velten Muth at Gimbsheim.
>
> Hans Henrich, b. 21 March 1680.

Sebastian Gebel was recorded at Alsheim am Altrhein as a member of the Ref. faith in 1698 (Alzey Census of 1698).

Anna Margretha Göbelin made her initial appearance on the Hunter Lists 30 June 1710 with 2 pers. over 10 yrs. of age and 1 pers. under 10 yrs.; Anna Maria Göbelin was noted on 4 Aug 1710 and on 4 Oct 1710 was recorded with 1 pers. over 10 yrs. of age and 1 pers. under 10 in her household. She usually was recorded on Hunter as living near others from Alsheim, such as Magdalena Beckerin, Anthoni Krämer, and Johannes Franck. Her entry for 24 June 1711 read Sebastian Gebel's Wid[W], and on 25 March 1712 the notation recorded Philipp Wolleben and Wid[W] Gebelin. Anna Maria Gablin aged 34 and Anna Maria Gablin aged 7 were in N.Y. City in 1710/11 (Palatines In N.Y. City).

JOHANN ANTHONI GEORG (Hunter Lists #227)
JOHANN WILHELM GEORG (Hunter Lists #228)
ANNA ELISABETHA GEORGIN (Hunter Lists #229)

The European home of the three Georg-Yorck emigrants was 5329
Höchstenbach (7 km. s.w. of Hachenburg; Chbks. begin 1670, Luth.
and family book). The founder of the family was <u>Georg Georg</u> who
md. Gertraut (--) 14 Feb 1678; he d. in 1690, and the Ref. Chbk.
of the village noted that she d. that same yr. They had issue:

> <u>Adam</u>, bpt. 26 Trin.: **16**... sp.: Georg Mert (?), Trien Adam,
> and the mother's sister Maria.
>
> <u>Matthias</u>, bpt. 10 Trin.: 1680 - sp.: the father's brother
> Henrich, the mother's brother Theiß, and the w/o Georg Tongeß.
>
> <u>Maria Gertraut</u>, bpt. 2 Trin.: 1682 - sp.: Gaß's widow, the d/o
> Henrich Spieß, Maria - ... Adam Georg Becker, and Martin Rör-
> ich. She d. 4 Nov 1716.
>
> + <u>Johann Wilhelm</u>, bpt. Dn. Septuag.: 1684 - sp.: Joh. Tönges
> Göbeler, Hans Wilhelm - brother of the mother, the w/o Joh.
> Wilh. Meyer, and Johannata - w/o Hans Henrich Becker. He md.
> Maria (--) 29 April 1704.
>
> <u>Johann Jacob</u>, bpt. 9 Trin.: 1686 - sp.: Johan Schumann, Joh.
> Jacob Rörich, and Michels Gerth (?).
>
> + <u>Johann Anthony</u>, bpt. 11 Jan 1689 - sp.: Johannes Meyer, Georg
> Tönges, and Anna Maria - d/o H. Henrich Becker. He may have
> been the Antonÿ Jorg with wife and 6 ch. who were mentioned
> in the 6th party of Palatines at Rotterdam (Rotterdam Lists);
> however, in actuality, he was not father of all the NY Georg
> families (HJ).

Johann Anthoni Georg made his initial appearance on the Hunter Lists 4 July 1710 (next to Johann Wilhelm Georg) with 2 pers.
over 10 yrs. of age in the family; on 4 Oct 1710 he was noted
(next to Johann Wilhelm and Anna Elisabeth Georgin) with but 1 pers.
over 10 yrs.

Johann Wilhelm Georg made his initial appearance on Hunter
4 July 1710 (next to Anthoni Georg) with 2 pers. over 10 yrs.;
the size increased to 2 pers. over 10 and 1 under 10 yrs. 24 June
1711, decreased to 1 pers. over 10 and 1 under 10 on 25 March 1712,
and then gained again 24 June 1712 to 2 pers. over 10 and 2 pers.
under 10 yrs. The last entry on the Hunter Lists was for 2 pers.
over 10 and 1 under 10 yrs. on 13 Sept 1712. Wm George of Queensbury was a Lieut. in the Canadian expedition of 1711 (Palatine
Volunteers To Canada). Wilhelm Georg and Anna Maria with 3 ch.
were at Neu-Stuttgardt ca. 1716/17 (Simmendinger Register). Wilhelmus York was a Palatine Debtor 26 Dec 1718 (Livingston Debt
Lists). The ch. of #228 Johann Wilhelm[1] Georg and wife Maria were:

> 1) <u>Maria Frey</u>[2], bpt. 4 Epiph.: 1705 and d. 21 March 1705
> (Höchstenbach Luth. Chbk.).

2) <u>Adam²</u>, bpt. 3 Nov 1705 and d. eodem die (Höchstenbach Luth. Chbk.).

3) <u>Anna Gertraut²</u>, bpt. 14 Nov 1706 - sp.: Eyda at Freyrachdorf, Maria Gerth - w/o Johannes Meyer, and Joh. Henrich Schmid at Roßbach. She d. 2 July 1707 (Höchstenbach Luth. Chbk.).

4) <u>Adam²</u>, bpt. 15 Feb 1708 - sp.: Adam Clauß (Hochstenbach Luth. Chbk.).

5) <u>Johann Nicolaus²</u>, bpt. 10 June 1711 in the Upper German Colonies - sp.: Niclaus Hess, Jacob Dings, and Margretha Weishard (West Camp Luth. Chbk.). He md. Maria Elisabetha Berg (HJ) and d. 6 Oct 1755 suddenly while eating his supper. The will of Nicholas York of Schohary was dated 15 Jan 1755 and probated 4 July 1783 (<u>Fernow Wills</u> #2158). Nicolaus² must have been quite a character, as evidenced in some reminiscences of Judge Brown (<u>Simm's History of Schoharie</u>, p. 158):

> The marriage ceremony (of George Henry Stubrach) took place in the early part of the day ... On such occasions, there was generally some "quid-nunc" present, who assumed the responsibilities of a captaincy, to direct the movements of the joyous company. At the time of which we are speaking Nicholas York was the admitted dictator. While all were busily engaged in such occupations as their own taste selected, a circumstance took place which afforded the party an unexpected source of amusement. A woodchuck made its appearance in a fallow near the booth. Captain York instantly ordered the field surrounded, directing a simultaneous march to the centre. The party had not approached to a concussion, before the intruder was slain. It was handed over to the captain - whose word on such occasions was law. He cut a piece of flesh from the warm victim and ate it, requiring all, male and female, to follow his example. Most attempted, but few succeeded in getting down the dainty morsel...

6) <u>Anna Dorothea²</u> (HJ), md. Wilhelm Becker (HJ).

Anna Elizabetha Georgin was recorded (twice) on the Hunter Lists as #229 on 4 Oct 1710 with 1 pers. in the family. On that date, she was registered next to Anthoni Georg. Searches at Höchstenbach failed to firmly establish her identity; however, she may have been the Elisa(betha) Cath., d/o Martin Georg and wife Veronica of Mündersbach, bpt. in 1675 in the Höchstenbach Luth. Chbk. (HJ).

There were other Georges in colonial N.Y., such as Johannes Jurg (Shurrig) who md. Annaetye Outwater in Oct 1730 (Hackensack Ref. Chbk.) and Jan Georg who md. Anna Maria Planck 9 Aug 1752 (Loonenburg Luth. Chbk.).

PETER GERLACH (Hunter Lists #230)

The German homes of the N.J. Gerlach-Garlock family were at
5450 Heddesdorf/Neuwied (10 km. n. of Koblenz; Chbks. begin 1674)
and 5455 Rengsdorf (7 km. n. of Neuwied; Chbks. begin 1677). The
earliest firm ancestor of the 1709er was his father Wilhelm Gerlach, the old and honorable Syndschöff and later hoffmann auff
Rheintal, who d. 9 March 1723, aged 83 yrs. (Heddesdorf Chbk.).
The w/o Wilhelm was probably the Apolonia, w/o The Old Gerlach,
who d. 23 Aug 1712, aged 70 yrs. (Heddesdorf Chbk.). There were
earlier Gerlachs found at Heddesdorf who may have been parents of
Wilhelm (HJ): the old Joes (Johannes) Gerlach, bur. 11 Nov 1686,
and his widow bur. 17 July 1690. The ch. of Wilhelm Gerlach were:

+ Johann Peter, bpt. 16 Feb 1673 - sp.: Peter Wagner from Rodenbach, Johannes Herman from Günnersdorff, and Anna Catharina
  Gerlach from Heddestorf (Heddesdorf Chbk.).

  Anna Barbara, bpt. 17 Oct 1675 - sp.: Sebastian Berner, Barbara - d/o Hans Willem Söhn (?), and Anna Catharina - w/o
  Hans Willem Hartzig (Heddesdorf Chbk.).

  "A Daughter", bpt. 9 June 1678 - sp.: Joh. Görg Schneider,
  the w/o Johannes Mies, and ... (Heddesdorf Chbk.).

  "A Son", bpt. 3 July 1681 - sp.: Hans Adam Backes, Philipp
  Melsbach, and the w/o Hermann Schmid (Heddesdorf Chbk.).

Peter Geerlof, his wife and 4 ch. were on Capt. John Enrit or Encrist's ship in Holland in the 5th party of Palatines in 1709
(Rotterdam Lists); on this same boat were other N.Y. 1709ers from
the Neuwied-Rengsdorf area (i.e. Philippus Herman Lepper, Bertram
Wolft, and Hans Willem tietruy).

Peter Gerlach made his first appearance on the Hunter Lists
on 4 Oct 1710 with 3 pers. over 10 yrs. of age in the household;
the 24 June 1711 entry read 5 pers. over 10 yrs., but thereafter
the notation gave 3 pers. over 10 yrs. of age. Peter Garlack aged
37, Magdalena Garlack aged 39, and Margaretta Garlack aged 12 were
in N.Y. City in 1710/11 (Palatines In N.Y. City). Peter Kerlack
was mentioned in the records of the Ramapo Tract in 1713. Peter
Gerlach, his wife, and 1 child were at Hackensack ca. 1716/17 (Simmendinger Register). The ch. of Peter[1] Gerlach and Magdalena were:

1) Margaretha[2] (Palatines In N.Y. City), md. Adolf Sivert 23
   Oct 1719 (Hackensack Ref. Chbk.).

2) Wilhelm[2], bpt. Dom. 2 p. Trin.: 1702 - sp.: Wilhelm Gerlach from Hedsdorf and Anna Veronica Ruckel from Rengsdorf (Rengsdorf Chbk.).

3) Ludwig[2], bpt. 13 Sept 1705 - sp.: Ludwig Runckel, Marg. -
   w/o Mattheis Mant, and Thönges - s/o the late Wilhelm

Runckel (Rengsdorf Chbk.).

4) Johann Georg², bpt. 28 Oct 1708 - sp.: Georg Krähmer, Johann Wilhelm Jungblut, and Clara - d/o Thönges Christ (Rengsdorf Chbk.). He md. Elsje Lutzenius (seemingly at a very young age - HJ) and had ch.:

    i) Peter³, bpt. 22 Sept 1723 - sp.: Pieter Keerligh and wife (Hackensack Ref. Chbk.).

    ii) Johannes³, bpt. 31 March 1734 - sp.: Joannes Brikker and wife (Hackensack Ref. Chbk.).

JOHANN CHRIST GERLACH (Hunter Lists #231)

The European origins of this branch of the N.Y. Garlock family were at 3432 Laudenbach (5 km. s.e. of Großalmerode; Chbks. begin 1717). Carla Mittelstaedt-Kubaseck, my faithful German researcher, found a crucial reference to the emigrant Christian Gerlach overseas, but unfortunately the chbk. source has been misplaced; the item noted that Christian Gerlach, Neuburg soldier from Laudenbach near Hessen-Cassel, and his wife Margarethe had a son Theobald in 1700. Perhaps this same soldier was the Christoph Gerlach the Artillerie-Knecht who, with wife Anna Margaretha, had a son Johann Balthasar bpt. in 1707 at Darmstadt (HJ). Johan Krist Geerlof, his wife and 3 ch. were on Capt. Thomas Key's ship in Holland in the 5th party of Palatines in 1709 (Rotterdam Lists).

Johann Christ Gerlach made his first appearance on the Hunter Lists 4 July 1710 with 3 pers. over 10 yrs. of age and 2 pers. under 10 yrs.; entries on the family fluctuated until 24 June 1712 when the family was noted with 5 pers. over 10 yrs. of age and 1 pers. under 10 yrs. Jno. Christ Gerlach CTP: 1 man, 2 lads aged 9 to 15, 1 woman, and 1 girl aged 8 and under were in Ulster Co. in 1710/11 (West Camp Census). He was a Palatine Listmaster, and on a mss. signed by all of these officials, his wife Anna Margaretha signed for him in 1712 (N.Y. Colonial Mss., Vol. 57, p. 123). Johann Christian Gerlach and Anna Maria Margretha with 3 ch. were at Neu-Cassel ca. 1716/17 (Simmendinger Register). Jan Chr: Garlagh was a Palatine Debtor 26 Dec 1718 (Livingston Debt Lists). John Christian Garlock was one of the prime, original patentees in the Mohawk in 1723 (Stone Arabia Patent). The ch. of Johann Christian¹ Gerlach and his wife Anna (Maria) Margaretha were:

1) Theobald², bpt. 26 Nov 1700 - sp.: Theobald Acker, citizen at Weinheim (Chbk. source misplaced). Deobald Garlock was also a patentee in 1723 (Stone Arabia Patent). He moved to the Shenandoah Valley of Va. with his fellow-Mohawk-Valley resident Carl Erhardt, s/o the 1709er Simon Erhardt (HJ).

He md. Anna Catharina Volmer (HJ) and had issue:

    i) <u>Anna Catharina</u>[3], b. 22 June 1726 - sp.: Elias Kehr-
      lach and Anna Margrit (Schenectady Ref. Chbk.).

    ii) <u>Johann Georg</u>[3], b. 22 Nov 1737 - sp.: John Georg Bau-
       mann and wife Maria (Stoever Chbk.).

2) <u>Elias</u>[2] (HJ), nat. as Elias Garlof 11 Sept 1761 (<u>Deniza-
tions, Naturalizations, and Oaths of Allegiance in Colonial N.Y.</u>, by Kenneth Scott and Kenn Stryker-Rodda, p.
30). Elias Garlock was a patentee at Stone Arabia in 1723
(Stone Arabia Patent). He sp. Thewalt Kehrlach in 1726
(Schenectady Ref. Chbk.). Simm's <u>History of Schoharie</u>, p.
78, mentioned Elias[2] (or possibly Johann Christian[1]):

> Tradition has preserved but little in the life of
> Justice Garlock, the most noted of the Schoharie
> Germans, who removed to the Mohawk Valley. He is
> said, while there, to have been the only justice
> of the peace in the Schoharie Valley. The name of
> the shrewd constable who aided him in administer-
> ing the few laws by which they were governed, has
> been lost. Only one important decision of this sage
> justice is known to the author. His summons was us-
> ually delivered to the constable "viva voce", and
> thus by him to the transgressor of the law. If the
> justice wished to bring a culprit before him, he
> gave his jack-knife to the constable, who carried
> it to the accused, and required him at the appoint-
> ed time to appear with it before the justice. What
> it meant he well understood. If two were to be sum-
> moned at the same time, to the second he gave the
> tobacco-box of the justice, and as that usually
> contained a liberal supply of the delectable nar-
> cotic, the consequences of a failure to return it
> in person to the justice, in due time, were dang-
> erous in the extreme. The decision of Justice Gar-
> lock alluded to, terminated so happily for those
> most interested, that I cannot withhold it from
> the reader. A complaint having been entered before
> him, the knife was issued, and the parties assem-
> bled forthwith. The plaintiff told his story,
> which appeared simple and true. The defendant,
> with more zeal and eloquence, plead his cause -
> quoting, if I mistake not, some previous decis-
> ions of his honor - and made out, as he thought,
> an equally good case. After giving the parties a
> patient hearing, the justice gave the following
> very important decision. "Der blandif an derfendur
> bote hash reght; zo I dezides, an pe dunder, der
> knonshtopple moosh bay de kosht."

Elias[2] md. Anna Margaretha (--) and had ch.:

    i) <u>Wilhelm</u>[3] (HJ), md. Magdalena Horning (HJ).

    ii) <u>Maria Catharina</u>[3] (Jacob Failing's ornamental family
       record, ca. 1766), md. 4 April 1756 Johann Jacob
       Failing, and d. 3 June 1806, aged 75 yrs. and 3
       months (<u>The Eighteenth Century Failing Family of the
       Mohawk Valley</u>, by David Kendall Martin, p. 13).

iii) Nicolaus[3] (HJ), listed as aged 28 and b. Mohawk River
in Stephan Schuyler's Co. in Albany Co. 3 May 1760
(Report of the State Historian, Vol. II, p. 567).

iv) Johann Adam[3] (HJ), 1732/33 - 1822, md. 1765 Maria
Lena Schill 1743/44 - 1834, both bur. Snells Bush
(Data from David Kendall Martin).

v) Philip[3] (HJ), a sp. to Jacob Failing and Maria Catharina (Gerlach) in 1764 (Stone Arabia Ref. Chbk.).

vi) Simon[3] (HJ), a sp. to Jacob Failing and Maria Catharina (Gerlach) in 1761 (The Eighteenth Century Failing Family of the Mohawk Valley, by David Kendall
Martin, p. 15).

Peter and Charles Gerlagh, along with Adam and Philips Ger-
lagh, were in Capt. Jacob Klock's Co. in 1763 (Report of the State
Historian, Vol. II, p. 794); Peter and Charles may have been sons of
Elias[2] or perhaps of the fourth generation of Mohawk Garlocks (HJ).

OTTILIA GERLACHIN (Hunter Lists #232)

The origins of the Conrad Gerlach family were at 6209 Breithardt (14 km. n.w. of Wiesbaden; Chbks. begin 1644). Johan Koenraat geerlach, his wife and 4 ch., were on Capt. Robbert Bulman's
ship in the 4th party of Palatines in 1709 (Rotterdam Lists); they
were recorded very near Georg Volpert Smit and Henrik Bartel who
also came from this same Taunus region (HJ). Conrad Gerlach aged
49, his wife, sons aged 7 and 5, daughters aged 16 and 11, Ref.,
huntsman, were in the 4th arrivals in England (London Lists).

Ottilia Gerlachin made her initial appearance on the Hunter
Lists 1 July 1710 with 1 pers. over 10 yrs. of age and 2 pers. under 10 yrs. Margrita Ottilia Gerlag and Dorothea Elisabeth Gerlag
joined the N.Y. City Ref. Church 26 Feb 1712. Margrite Ottilia
Stikraad, wid/o Coenraad Gerlag of Germany, md. John Crump of England 27 March 1712 (N.Y. City Ref. Chbk.). Issue of Conrad Gerlach,
called huntsman at Breithardt, and Margaretha Ottilia[1], his wife:

1) Dorothea Elisabetha[2] (HJ), joined N.Y. City Ref. Church 1712.

2) Johannes Ehrhardt[2], b. 3 Feb 1702 - sp.: H. Joh. Ehrhardt
Stickrath - Ref. Prediger at Pfeddersheim near Wormbs, Johannes Banf ..., and Fr. Anna Elisabetha Stein, the Pastor's wife (Breithardt Chbk.). John Conearhart aged 9, s/o
Margt Otteene, was bound to Robt. Walter of N.Y. 18 Oct
1710 (Apprenticeship Lists).

3) Johann Philips[2], bpt. 14 Feb 1704 - sp.: H. Nöll, Frantz
Gerlach from Eschbach, and Anna Veronica Gerhard (Breithardt Chbk.).

4) <u>Johann Lorentz</u>[2], b. 30 March 1707 - sp.: Johannes Grimmel
   - Keller at Gronau, Agnetha Christina Neuber - w/o the
   Ref. Pastor Remellensis, and Joh. Lorentz Rudolph - cup-
   bearer at Idstein. The child d. 4 April 1707 (Breithardt
   Chbk.).

5) <u>Maria Margaretha</u>[2], bpt. 3 June 1708 - sp.: Christoph Schörmer ..., Marg. Catharina Will at Limbach, and Maria Agnesa - w/o Christian Roßger at Neuhoff (Breithardt Chbk.).

JACOB GERMANN (Hunter Lists #233)

The home village of the German family was 7532 <u>Niefern</u> (8 km.
n.e. of Pforzheim (Chbks. begin 1608). Jacob Germann, bricklayer
and s/o Georg Germann - inhabitant at Merishausen Schaffhauser
Gebieth in the Schweiz, md. Anna Catharina, d/o the late Hans
Eichinger - citizen at Entzberg, 4 Christmonat (4 Dec ?): 1703.

Jacob Germann made his first appearance on the Hunter Lists
4 July 1710 with 2 pers. over 10 yrs. of age and 1 pers. under
10 yrs. in the household. Jacob Cerman was nat. 14 Feb 1715/16
(Albany Nats.). Jacob German and Maria Catharina with 1 child were
at Quunsberg ca. 1716/17 (Simmendinger Register). The West Camp
Luth. Chbks. show that Jacob's wife Anna Catharina sp. Johann
Friederich Contermann in 1714, and together they sp. Contermann
in 1716; Hans Friederich Gundermann (Contermann, Countryman) also
was documented at Niefern (HJ). The family appears to leave the
Hudson Valley by 1722 (HJ). The ch. of Jacob[1] Germann were:

1) <u>Hans Jacob</u>[2], bpt. 1 Jan 1706 - sp.: Thomas Falck, Hans
   Jacob - single s/o Hans Georg Neef, and Catharina - single
   d/o the teacher Hans Jacob Kopp at Entzberg (Niefern
   Chbk.). He d. 20 Feb 1709 (Niefern Chbk.).

2) <u>Hans Georg</u>[2], bpt. 5 Aug 1707 - sp.: same as before (Niefern Chbk.). Johan Jurgen German sp. Peter Bernhardis
   Schmidt at Camp Queensberry in 1722 (N.Y. City Luth.
   Chbk.). Perhaps he was the George German whose will was
   proved in Pa. in 1796 (Lancaster Co. Will Bk. F, p. 645).

Other early Germans in Pa. records include Margaretha German,
who md. Roger Evans 19 Oct 1731 (Stoever Chbk.), and John Jacob
German who md. Maria Cath. Gast 8 March 1750 (Tulpehocken Chbk.).

GEORG GERNER (Hunter Lists #234)

Georg Gerner had his own heading in the Hunter Lists, but
had no entries in the Journal Section of these rolls. A Johann
Jörg Gernert and wife Sophia were found at 6251 <u>Runkel</u> pre-1709.

HENRICH GESINGER (Hunter Lists #235)

The home village of N.Y. Gesner family was 6701 Kallstadt
(5 km. n. of Bad Dürkheim; Chbks. begin 1661, Luth.). Johan Henrich Geßinger, s/o the late Mattheus Geßinger formerly miller at
Trarbach on the Mosel - and carpenter fellow here, md. Anna Elisabeth Schmidt, d/o the late Henrich Schmidt citizen-administrator
and landlord at Ritter St. Georg, on 7 Feb 1708. The Kallstadt
registers also show that Johann Henrich Schmit and his wife Elisabeth had other ch. bur. there. Henry Gessienger aged 28, his
wife, and a daughter aged $\frac{1}{4}$, carpenter, Luth. were in the 1st arrivals in England in 1709 (London Lists).

Henrich Gesinger made his initial appearance on the Hunter
Lists 4 Aug 1710 with 3 pers. over 10 yrs. of age; the entry
changed to 2 pers. over 10 yrs. and 1 pers. under 10 yrs. on 4
Oct 1710. This notation remained constant, except for 25 March
1712 where the rolls showed 1 pers. over 10 yrs. and 1 pers. un-
der 10 in the family. Johan Henrich Gossinger aged 31, Anna Eliz
Gossinger aged 27, and Anna Margt. Gossinger aged 2, were in N.Y.
City in 1710/11 (Palatines In N.Y. City). Hendrick Gessiner of
Westchester Co., yeoman, was nat. 10 Jan 1715/16 (Denizations,
Naturalizations, and Oaths of Allegiance in Colonial N.Y., by
Kenneth Scott and Kenn Stryker-Rodda, p. 30). Heinrich Giffener,
and his wife, with 1 child were in Neu Yorck ca. 1716/17 (Simmen-
dinger Register). Henr. Essinger subscribed £1 in 1727 to the
Luth. Church in N.Y. City, and Henr. Kissinger gave 8 sh. for the
Pastor's salary in 1729 (N.Y. City Luth. Protocol, pp. 65 & 155).
The will of Hendrick Gessener of Tappan, Orange Co. was dated 30
Oct 1745 and probated 16 June 1748 (Fernow Wills #676). The ch.
of Johann Henrich[1] Gesinger and Anna Elisabetha were:

1) Anna Margaretha[2], b. 28 Jan 1709 - sp.: Joh. Hartmann Lo-
   melius (?) - cooper and s/o the Erbbeständer in Pfeffin-
   gen, and his wife Anna Margaretha (Kallstadt Chbk.).
   She md. Jacob Valentyn (HJ).
2) Johann Henrich[2] (HJ), md. 5 Sunday after Easter: 1744
   Femmetje Brouwer (N.Y. City Luth. Chbk.). There is a Gesner Family History (author and publication date unknown)
   which details the lives of Johann Henrich[2] (giving him
   dates of 1724 - 1811) and his ch. (HJ).

DANIEL GETEL'S WIDDOW (Hunter Lists #236)

The origins of the N.Y. Kittel family were at several villages near Kaiserslautern: 1) at 6791 Reichenbach (16 km. n.w. of
Kaiserslautern; Chbks. begin 1660, but severe gaps), 2) at 6761

Steinbach am Donnersberg (22 km. n.e. of Kaiserslautern; Chbks. begin 1693, but severe gaps), and 3) at 6759 Rathskirchen (20 km. n. of Kaiserslautern; Chbks. begin 1706, Luth.). There were several Daniel Gödels found in the overall Kaiserslautern region pre-1709 who somewhat confuse the picture, but as of this writing it appears that the emigrant 1709er md. 1st Anna Eva (--) and had ch. bpt. at Reichenbach; Johann Daniel Göddel, a widower and Gemeinsmann at Nußbach, md. (2nd) Maria Elisabetha, surviving d/o Engelbert Doll from Eckenhagen Windecker Ambts im Bergischen on 24 Oct 1702 at Zweikirchen (Steinbach am Donnersberg Chbk.). Nußbach appears to have been the last German home of the emigrant (HJ). Daniel Goettel (or Gettel), his wife, and 7 ch. were documented in the 5th party of Palatines in Holland on Capt. Johan Enrit's (or Encrist's) ship in July 1709 (Rotterdam Lists); they were recorded near Hans Peter Schey and Tennes Prettert who also came from the general Kaiserslautern area (HJ).

Daniel Gettel made his first appearance on the Hunter Lists 4 July 1710 with 6 pers. over 10 yrs. of age and 2 pers. under 10 yrs.; on this roll he was registered near Simon Haas and Friederich Merckel, who also originated near his German home. The family size diminished to 5 pers. over 10 yrs. and 2 under 10 on 29 Sept 1711, when Daniel Göttel's Widd[W] was noted. The family then shrunk even more to 3 pers. over 10 and 2 under 10 on 25 March 1712, and finally read 3 pers. over 10 yrs. of age 24 June 1712. Daniel Goettel's wife, Epis., joined the church at N.Y. City 19 July 1710 (West Camp Luth. Chbk.). The ch. of Johann Daniel[1] Getel were:

1) Johannes[2], bpt. Dom. 1. Advent: 1680 - sp.: Johann Abrahamb Gödtel from Jettenbach, Johann Gödel, the s/o Nickel Rüben from Gimspach, and Margaretha - w/o Wilhelm Junge the miller at Schmesbach (Reichenbach Chbk.).

2) Johann Adam[2], bpt. 30 March - 9 April 1684 - sp.: Hans Adam Heyl the miller there, Fritz Leiß from Alberspach, and Margaretha - w/o Michel Hoffmann (Reichenbach Chbk.).

3) Barbara[2], bpt. 19 Oct - 29 Oct 1685 - sp.: H. Samuel Satzger (?) - Amtsschreiber and Kirchenhafner, Anna Barbara - d/o Nickel Rüben, and Elisabetha - w/o Philipp Kindten (?) from Kusel (Reichenbach Chbk.).

4) Johanna Elisabetha Catharina[2], bpt. 17 Oct - 27 Oct 1686 - sp.: Herr Oberamtmann von Strauch, the d/o Herr Pfarrer Joh. Ludw. Schmidt (Elisab. Marg. Susanna), Anna Cath. - w/o Daniel Pötz, and Herr Joh. Philipp Grapp - Amtskeller (Reichenbach Chbk.).

5) Johann Daniel[2], bpt. 18 March - 28 March 1689 - sp.: Joh.

Philip Würth, Joh. Daniel Potz, Anna Catharina - w/o Nickel Herbert, and Anna Barbara Rübin (Reichenbach Chbk.). He md. Debora (--) (HJ) and had issue:

    i) Margaretha[3], bpt. 24 Jan 1722 - sp.: Jacob V. D. Heyden and Susanna Bratt (Albany Ref. Chbk.).

6) Maria Barbara[2], bpt. 5 Oct 1691 - sp.: Anna Barbara - w/o Johannes Gödel the elder, Anna Barbara - w/o Frantz Winter at Fickelberg, Anna Barbara - w/o Hanß Adam Heyl the miller here, Joh. Philipp Potz here, and Joh. Daniel Apffel (Reichenbach Chbk.).

7) Johann Nicolaus[2] (HJ), conf. 1706 as Johann Nicolaus Gödel from Nußbach (Rathskirchen Chbk.). Niclaus Gottel of Haysbury was a soldier in 1711 (Palatine Volunteers To Canada). Nicolas Kettel was nat. 8 and 9 Sept 1715, noted next to Henrich Kettel (Kingston Nats.). Nicolas Kitle was on Palatine Debt Lists dated 1718, 1721, and 1726 (Livingston Debt Lists). A Nicolaes Ketel was an early settler of Schodack (History of the Seventeen Towns of Rensselaer Co., by A. J. Weise, p. 71). Catharina Drom, w/o Niclaes Kittel, was a member of the Schodack Church in 1770. They had issue:

    i) Elisabetha[3], bpt. 7 Jan 1722 - sp.: Christ and Cath. Schayns (Albany Ref. Chbk.).

    ii) Daniel[3], bpt. 1 March 1724 - sp.: Gerr. and Cath. Lansingh (Albany Ref. Chbk.).

    iii) Margaretha[3], bpt. 6 Nov 1726 - sp.: Bar. and Marr. Sanders (Albany Ref. Chbk.).

    iv) Andreas[3], bpt. 16 March 1729 - sp.: Leendert Conyn and Immetje Conyn (Kinderhook Ref. Chbk.).

    v) Henrich[3], bpt. 9 May 1731 - sp.: Gysberth Clauw and Mareytje Rousus (Kinderhook Ref. Chbk.).

    vi) Johannes[3], bpt. 28 July 1734 - sp.: Hendrik Gardener Jr. and Eva Van Valckenburgh (Kinderhook Ref. Chbk.).

8) Anna Margaretha[2], bpt. 26 Oct 1693 - sp.: Johannes Schumacher from Neunkirchen, Lorentz Gödel - carpenter at Föckelberg, Margaretha - w/o Michel Frieß the cartwright at Schwandten, Elisab. Margaretha - w/o Fritz Leyß at Alberspach, and Margaretha - w/o Daniel ... the cartwright at Eßweiler (Reichenbach Chbk.).

9) Johann Philipp Hermann[2], bpt. 1 Dec 1696 - sp.: Herr Oberamtmann Johann Hermann von Strauch, Philips Herdel from Mackenbach, Philipp Raab, Elisabetha - w/o Joh. Gödel Rüben, Fr. Anna Elisabetha - w/o H. Andreas Merckel the Oberschultheiß, and Anna Magdalena - w/o Benedict Lavau

(?) the Borthenschnitter (Reichenbach Chbk.).

10) Anna Christina[2] (HJ), conf. 23 March 1712 at Queensberg (West Camp Luth. Chbk.). She md. Henrich Fees 22 Aug 1718 (Kingston Ref. Chbk.). They sp. Hendrik Kittel in 1727 (Kingston Ref. Chbk.) and Wm. Van Deuzen and Christina Kittel in 1753 (Rhinebeck Flats Ref. Chbk.).

11) Henrich[2] (HJ), nat. along with Nicolas Kettel 8 and 9 Sept 1715 (Kingston Nats.). The Kingston Town Court Records show a case involving Hendrik Kittel vs. Theunis Ploegh, both absent, in 1726. Hendrik Kittel, single man b. Germany, md. Catharina Deenmarken, single woman b. Germany, 9 Oct 1724 (Kingston Ref. Chbk.); at that time they both resided under the jurisdiction of Hurley. Catharina Deenmarken Kittel md. as wid/o Henrich 9 July 1731 Johannes Wever (Kingston Ref. Chbk.). The ch. of Henrich[2] were:

   i) Christina[3], bpt. 4 June 1727 - sp.: Hendrik Fees and Christina Kittel (Kingston Ref. Chbk.). She joined the church at Rhinebeck Flats 27 June 1746 and md. Wilhelmus Van Deusen (HJ).

   ii) Margaretha[3], bpt. 19 Jan 1729 - sp.: Niclaas Koen and Margriet Denemarken (Kingston Ref. Chbk.).

There were other pre-1709 Kittels in colonial N.Y., such as Jeremias Kittel of Marbletown, whose will was probated 7 Sept 1704 (Fernow Wills #959); this group md. some 1709er women which has added some difficulty in sorting out all the various Kittels in America in the 18th century (HJ).

BARBARA GETTMÄNNIN (Hunter Lists #237)
MARIA BARBARA GETTMÄNNIN (Hunter Lists #238)

Kasper Gettman, his wife, and 8 ch. were of Capt. Georg Gouland's ship in the 4th party in Holland in 1709 (Rotterdam Lists). Caspar Getman aged 36, his wife, sons aged 16, 14, 8, and 5, daughters aged 6, 5, and 2, Luth., husbandman and vinedresser, were in the 4th arrivals in England (London Lists); the family was recorded near other N.Y. 1709ers such as Henry Fehling, Conrad Krantz, and Martin Zerbst on the English list (HJ).

Close scrutiny of the originals of the Journal section of the Hunter Lists show that #237 Barbara Gettmännin and #238 Maria Barbara Gettmännin were the same person, as evidenced by other 1709er names near them (again Fehling, Krantz and Zerbe) (HJ). Maria Barbara Gettmännin with 2 pers. over 10 yrs. of age was listed but one name from Johannes Biermann on 4 Oct 1710; Biermann's entry read 1 pers. over 10 yrs. and 1 under 10 as of that date. An

indenture dated 23 Sept 1771 from Johannes Beerman of German Flats
to his step-son Frederick Gettman of Stoneraby has survived (D.A.R.
Records of N.Y. State, Vol. 146, p. 300). Noting this indenture
and also the fact that Johannes Biermann's entry in Hunter on 31
Dec 1710 increased to 3 pers. over 10 yrs. and 1 under 10, with
(Maria) Barbara Gettmännin disappearing from the Hunter Lists except for the cumulative 24 Dec 1711 entry with 2 pers. over 10
yrs., the evidence strongly shows that (Maria) Barbara[1] Gettmännin
md. 2nd Johannes Biermann. The issue of (Maria) Barbara[1] and her
husband Caspar Gettmann was:

1) Frederich[2] (HJ), nat. as Frederick Kietman, next to Johannis Beerman, 22 Nov 1715 (Albany Nats.). History of Montgomery and Fulton Counties, N.Y., p. 221, mentions Frederick Getman and Johannes Bearman as early settlers of Eph-
   ratah, Fulton Co., buying land from Hendrick Six in 1743;
   the article notes that Frederich[2] had four sons, namely
   Frederich Jr., Georg, John, and Christian. Friderick Kit-
   man was a freeholder at Stonrabie in 1763 (Albany Co.
   Freeholders). Frederich[2] had ch.:

   i) Frederich[3] (HJ). The will of a Frederik Gottman on
      7 April 1788 was mentioned in D.A.R. Records of N.Y.
      State, Vol. 146, p. 313.
   ii) Georg[3] (HJ), b. 23 May 1723 and d. 1 Sept 1789 (Stone
      Arabia Ref. Chbk.). He md. Ottilia Schumacher in June
      1750 at the Falls (Sommers Journal, Schoharie Luth.
      Chbk.). George Gethman (with John and Christian Geth-
      man) was a soldier in Soffrines Deychert's Co. in
      1757 and in 1763 (Report of the State Historian, Vol.
      II, pp. 784 & 792). Yurrie Gitman was a freeholder
      at the Falls in 1763 (Albany Co. Freeholders). The
      will of George Getman of Stone Arabia was dated 2
      Dec 1783 and probated 28 Jan 1790 (Montgomery Co.
      Wills Vol. I).
   iii) Anna Maria[3] (HJ), md. Henrich Mayer and d. 16 Oct
      1811, aged 90 (Herkimer Ref. Chbk.).
   iv) Christian[3], md. as s/o Freiderich to Anna Eva (Zim-
      mermann), wid/o Johannes Merckel 8 July 1760 (Stone
      Arabia Ref. Chbk.). The will of Christian Getman of
      Palatine was written 15 April 1803 and probated 10
      July 1821; his line is well documented in David Ken-
      dall Martin's The Eighteenth Century Zimmerman Fam-
      ily of the Mohawk Valley, p. 53, and in History of
      Montgomery and Fulton Counties, N.Y., p. 126.
   v) Johannes[3], md. as s/o Friederich 10 Aug 1762 Anna

Maria, d/o Johann Henrich Merckel (Stone Arabia Ref. Chbk.).

There may have been other ch. of Friederich[2], such as the Margaretha Goedmänn and the Catterina Gettmann who sp. Georg[3] at Stone Arabia Ref. in 1752 and 1754 (HJ). There also was a Johannes Ketteman (Kedman) with wife Christina in Rhinebeck in the 1760's, and a Johannes Guedeman and wife Eva at New Brunswick, N.J. 1729 - 1734 (HJ).

SIBILLA GIESERIN (Hunter Lists #239)

Sibylla Gieser, d/o the late Johann Gieser of Ober-Moshel-Landsberg in the commune Zweybrucken, md. 24 July 1711 Johann Eberhard, widower of S. Johann near Creutzenach (West Camp Luth. Chbk.). The Gieser origins were at 6763 Obermoschel (7 km. n.e. of Meisenheim; Chbks. begin 1703, Luth.). The only item found on the family so far was the marriage (2nd? - HJ) of one Johannes Giess, burtig in dem stift Fulda itzo shepherd at Dürrmoschel, to Anna Barbara, wid/o Niclass Walther - formerly shepherd at Alsenz, on 17 Nov 1705.

Sibilla Gieserin was entered once on the Hunter Lists 24 June 1711 with 1 pers. over 10 yrs. of age. On 29 Sept 1711 the Journal noted she was with Johannes Eberhardt, and in the 2nd 24 Dec 1711 entry she was filed under Bernhard Lickard for Syb: Gieserin.

PETER GIESLER (Hunter Lists #240)

As with the N.Y. 1709ers Jacob Bär, Henrich Ohrendorf, Hieronymus Weller, and Hermann Hoffmann, the German ancestral town of the Gieslers was at 5905 Oberfischbach (8 km. w. of Siegen; Chbks. begin 1670). The earliest known forefather of the emigrant was his father, the honourable Stephan Gieseler, churchelder, who was bur. 10 Dec 1705, aged ca. 60 yrs. The ch. of Stephan Gieseler and his wife Maria were:

Johann Paulus, md. 1st Anna Lucia Bruder in 1690 and 2nd Anna Maria Wisse in 1709.

Henrich, bpt. 28 Jan 1672 - sp.: Henrich Weisgerber from Niederndorff. He md. Margaretha Bettendorf in 1695.

+ Peter, bpt. 21 Nov 1675 - sp.: Peter Wüste, a Papist.

Johann Peter, bpt. 17 Feb 1680 - sp.: Peter - s/o Johann Fischbach, and Anna Margaretha, d/o the late Johannes Gieseler at Oberholzklau. The child was bur. 26 May 1681.

Peter Giseler, s/o Steffen Giseler here, md. Anna Lucia, d/o

Hermann Hoffmann here, on 7 Oct 1703. An inhabitant list of Oberfischbach dated 7 May 1708 mentioned Peter Gieseler and Anna Loysa, the old mother Maria, and little daughter Anna Catharina.

Peter Giesler made his initial appearance on the Hunter
Lists 1 July 1710 with 3 pers. over 10 yrs. of age and 1 pers.
under 10; the family size diminished to 2 pers. over 10 yrs. and
1 pers. under 10 on 24 Dec 1711, and then increased again to 2
pers. over 10 yrs. and 2 pers. under 10 on 13 Sept 1712. Peter
Keiseler: 1 man, 1 boy aged 8 and under, and 2 women, were in
Ulster Co. in 1710/11 (West Camp Census). Peter Kieselar was nat.
8 and 9 Sept 1715 (Kingston Nats.). Peter Kreussler and Anna Lucia
with 3 ch. were at Beckmansland ca. 1716/17 (Simmendinger Register). Pieter Kieselaer was taxed £10 at Kingston in 1718/19 and
1720/21 (Ulster Co. Tax Lists). The Kingston Trustees Records
noted Pieter Kieslaer in Book I, Part B, pp. 118 & 119. The ch.
of Peter[1] Giesler and wife Anna Lucia were:

1) Anna Catharina[2], bpt. 1 March 1705 - sp.: Anna Cathrin -
   single d/o Hermann Hoffmann here (Oberfischbach Chbk.).
2) Johann Paulus[2], bpt. 1 July 1708 - sp.: Joh. Paulus Gieseler, brother of the child's father (Oberfischbach Chbk.).
   There was a Paulus Gieseler bur. in Oberfischbach 29 May
   1708 or 1709, but he probably was not this child (HJ).
   Paulus Kieselaer md. Lea Hoffman. The will of a Paulus Keselar of Haverstraw Precinct in Orange Co. was dated 30
   May 1774 and probated 11 June 1784 (Fernow Wills #994).
   The ch. of Paulus[2] and wife Lea were:
   i) Anna[3], b. 14 May 1734 - sp.: Pieter Kieselaer and
      wife Annietie (Tappan Ref. Chbk.).
   ii) Harmannus[3], b. 28 Feb 1737 - sp.: Harmanis Hofman
       and wife Gert. (Tappan Ref. Chbk.). Harmanus Kese-
       ler was aged 23 in Col. Abraham Hering's Orange Co.
       Regiment 24 April 1759 (Report of the State Histor-
       ian, Vol. I, p. 917).
   iii) Petrus[3], b. 14 Sept 1739 - sp.: Pieter Kieselaer
        and wife Antie (Tappan Ref. Chbk.).
   iv) Paulus[3], b. 15 Nov 1742 - sp.: Hermanis Kieselaer
       and wife Rachel (Tappan Ref. Chbk.).
   v) Georg[3], b. 3 April 1744 - sp.: Jurrie Kieselaer and
      wife Rachel (Tappan Ref. Chbk.).
   vi) Maria[3], b. 24 July 1746 - sp.: Hermanis Hoffman and
       wife Geertruyt (Tappan Ref. Chbk.).
   The 1774 will for Paulus Keselar, if indeed it is Paulus[2],
   mentioned wife Maria and additional ch. Philipp and Christian (HJ).

3) Johann Hermann², b. 5 Aug 1712 - sp.: J. Hieronymus Weller,
Hermann Hoffmann, and Anna Veronica Schlemmer (West Camp
Luth. Chbk.). He md. Rachel Hoffmann (HJ) and had issue:
    i) Gertraud³, b. 13 April 1738 - sp.: Harmanus Hofman
      and wife Geertruyt (Tappan Ref. Chbk.).
    ii) Petrus³, b. 15 Dec 1739 - sp.: Pieter Kieselaer and
      wife Antye (Tappan Ref. Chbk.).
    iii) Gertraud³, b. 29 March 1742 - sp.: Hermanis Hofman
      and wife Geertruyt (Tappan Ref. Chbk.).
    iv) Johannes³, b. 11 June 1744 - sp.: Johannes Snyder and
      wife Christina (Tappan Ref. Chbk.).
    v) Anna³, b. 24 Nov 1746 - sp.: Paulus Gisselaer and
      wife Lea (Tappan Ref. Chbk.).

4) Johann Georg², b. 9 Nov 1716 - sp.: Johann Menges, Georg
Wilhelm Kehl, and Anna Catharina Scheib (West Camp Luth.
Chbk.). He md. Rachel Huysman and had ch.:
    i) Petrus³, b. 25 June 1742 - sp.: Pieter Kieselaer
      (Tappan Ref. Chbk.).
    ii) Johannes³, b. 7 June 1745 - sp.: Matteues Hoppen and
      wife Aeltye (Tappan Ref. Chbk.).

5) Peter² (HJ), md. Christina Felten (HJ) and had issue:
    i) Paulus³, b. 28 Nov 1743 - sp.: Paulus Kieselaer and
      wife Lea (Tappan Ref. Chbk.).
    ii) Theunis³, b. 6 Nov 1745 - sp.: Klaas Cuyper and wife
      Marytye (Tappan Ref. Chbk.).

The registers at Tappan and vicinity should be checked for
further third-generation children in this family (HJ).

HENRICH GLOCK (Hunter Lists #241)

There was a Henrich Klock (? - hard to read) conf. in 1685
aged 14 yrs. at 6394 Grävenwiesbach; this entry may be a good clue
to the German origins of the N.Y. pioneer, as the roots of the Mohawk Valley Laux and Zimmermann families appear to have been in
this little village (HJ). A Johann Henrich Glock md. 9 Jan 1696
Anna Margaretha, wid/o Joh. Jüngling - Gemeinsmann in Rauheim (?)
at either 6146 Alsbach/Bergstraße or 5411 Alsbach/Unterwesterwald,
but no proof has been found that he was the 1709er (HJ). Johan
Heinrich Glock sp. Joh: Antonius Kexel in Holland in 1709 (Brielle
Ref. Chbk.). A newly-found list of Palatines returned to Holland
in 1710 recorded Henrich Glock with 2 pers. in his family on the
ship Martha sailing 24 Jan 1710 and arriving 27 Feb 1710 (P.R.O.
T 1/125, 203 (#44B), and T 1/125, 230 (#44P); since there were only two pers. in his family and the sailing dates overlap those of

the N.Y. Palatine contingent's embarkation for the new world, it is probable that there were two individuals emigrating in 1709/10 named Henrich Glock (HJ).

Henrich Glock made his initial appearance on the Hunter Lists 30 June 1710 with 1 pers. over 10 yrs. of age and 3 pers. under 10 yrs. in his family. Besides his normal entry on 4 Oct 1710, the Hunter Lists added to his household an allowance for An: Gertr: Bromwasser's subsistence. His notation read 2 pers. over 10 and 2 under 10 on 24 June 1711, 3 pers. over 10 and 1 under 10 on 29 Sept 1711, and 3 pers. over 10 and 2 pers. under 10 on 24 Dec 1711 and thereafter; the 24 Dec 1711 entry read Henrich Glock and Mar: Schopferin. Hendrick Klock was nat. 11 Oct 1715 (Albany Nats.). Heinrich Klock and his wife Maria Margretha were at Neu-Quunsberg ca. 1716/17 with their 4 ch. (Simmendinger Register). His gravestone in the ancient Klock cemetary e. of the village of St. Johnsville reads Here Ley HK 1760, 97 (The Old Palatine Church, p. 33). There is no better example than the Klock family as to how the loss of the chbks. of Pastor Hager and others makes links between the Mohawk Valley Palatine families extremely difficult to make; however, there does appear to have been a will for the 1709er Henrich[1] dated 1742 and an old family Bible, once belonging to Henry Klock of Kansas City (neither of which I have seen) which help to clear up the family structure (see Genealogy of the Mohawk Valley Bellingers and Allied Families, p. 12). Using these sources and some documented references, the family picture seems to be as follows: Henrich[1] Klock had four wives, at least ten ch., and was 15 yrs. a widower when he d. in 1760, aged 97. By his 1st German wife, he had among his ch.:

1) Johann Henrich[2] (HJ), nat. as Hans Hendrick Clock 3 Jan 1715/16 (Albany Nats.). Hendrick Clock Jr. was a freeholder at Canajoharie in 1763 (Albany Co. Freeholders).

2) Barbara Elisabetha[2] (HJ), probably the Barvalis who md. 29 Feb 1718 Christian Nellis (The Old Palatine Church, p. 31).

3) Margaretha[2] (HJ), md. Wilhelm Nellis (HJ).

By his 1st or 2nd wife Henrich[1] had:

4) Jacob[2] (HJ), md. Elisabetha Bellinger (Will of Frederick Bellinger). His will was dated 8 May 1798 (Montgomery Co. Will Bk. I). He was a freeholder at Canajoharrie in 1763 (Albany Co. Freeholders). See also Report of the State Historian, Vols. I & II.

Henrich[1] Klock md. 2nd Maria Margretha (Schopfer - HJ) and had:

5) Johannes[2], b. 30 Oct 1711 - sp.: Johannes Hayner (West Camp Luth. Chbk.). He md. Anna Margaretha Fuchs (HJ) and

was a freeholder at Canajoharrie in 1763 (Albany Co. Freeholders).

6) <u>Georg</u>² (HJ) md. Margaretha Walrath (Will of Henrich Conrad
Walrath). He was a freeholder in 1763 at Canajoharrie also.

By his 3rd wife Jacomyntie, a child of Henrich¹ Klock was:

7) <u>Magdalena</u>², bpt. 9 June 1728 - sp.: Ph. and Magdal. Louk
(Albany Ref. Chbk.). She md. Johannes Bellinger (HJ).

By his 4th wife, ch. of the emigrant Henrich¹ were:

8) <u>Conrad</u>² (HJ), a minor in 1742 (Will).

9) <u>Johann Adam</u>² (HJ), probably the Han. Arum in the will,
a minor in 1742 (Will).

10) <u>Johann Jost</u>² (HJ), a minor in 1742 (Will).

<u>PHILIPP GLUMP</u> (Hunter Lists #242)

Sponsorships and juxtaposition of names on the Hunter Lists
strongly suggest that the Hudson Valley Clum family had its roots
somewhere in the Nassau or Darmstadt region (HJ). A Johann Peter
Klamp md. Anna Elisabetha Geissig, a relative of the N.Y. 1709er
Peter Wagener, 17 Feb 1685 at 5421 <u>Dachsenhausen</u>; this family then
appears to have moved to 5429 <u>Niederwallmenach</u>, home of the N.Y.
settlers Georg Volpert and Henrich Schmidt. Klumpps were found at
6239 <u>Eppstein/Taunus</u> and 5409 <u>Singhofen</u>. But the best potential
clue to the origins of the family were found at 6101 <u>Roßdorf</u> (3
km. s. of Darmstadt; Chbks. begin 1657) when Johan Philip Klumpf
from Darmstadt, citizen and tailor at Darmstadt, md. 4 Oct 1703
Anna Clara Ruhel, the d/o the Pastor. A civil record in the Darmstadt Archives (E8 B - 141/11) listed Joh. Philipp Klumb of Nied
- Ramstadt, aged 22 yrs., married, tailor. As our emigrant Glump
was enrolled only one name from Conrad Schawerman of Arheilgen
next to Darmstadt in Oct 1710 on the Hunter Lists, perhaps this
Roßdorf marriage was the first one for Philip¹ Glump (HJ).

Philipp Glump made his first appearance on the Hunter Lists
4 Oct 1710 with 2 pers. over 10 yrs. of age; the size of the family increased 31 Dec 1710 to 2 pers. over 10 yrs. and 1 pers. under 10, and then decreased to 2 pers. over 10 yrs. 24 June 1711.
The household grew again to 2 pers. over 10 and 1 under 10 yrs.
29 Sept 1711. Philip Clom was nat. 31 Jan 1715/16 (Albany Nats.).
Philipp Glump with wife and ch. was at Hessberg ca. 1716/17 (Simmendinger Register). Philip Klomp was recorded on Palatine Debt
Lists in 1718, 1719 (on our land), 1721, 1722 and 1726 (Livingston Debt Lists). He md. Anna Margaretha Veronica (--); a Grietje
Schyveringh sp. with a Peter Clomp (I think this man was Philip¹)
at Linlithgo in 1725, and Philip¹ Glump was but one name from the

large Johannes Schäffer family on the 31 Dec 1710 Hunter Lists, so perhaps Anna Margaretha Veronica's surname may have been Schäffer (HJ). The ch. of Philip[1] Glump and Anna Margaretha Veronica were:

1) <u>Johann Georg</u>[2], b. 23 Aug 1711 - sp.: Anna Maria Peter and Johann Georg Schultheiss (West Camp Luth. Chbk.). He md. Anna Maria Schneider 3 Aug 1734 (Catskill Ref. Chbk.) and had ch.:

    i) <u>Johannes</u>[3], b. 26 Nov 1734 - sp.: Joh: Schneider - young s/o Wilhelm, and Anna Maria Klum (Rhinebeck Luth. Chbk.). He md. Anna Maria Bernhardt 19 Dec 1758 (Germantown Ref. Chbk.).

    ii) <u>Johann Philip</u>[3], bpt. 1 Nov 1736 - sp.: Philip Klom and Gertraut Sneider (Red Hook Luth. Chbk.). He md. Christina Pulver (HJ).

    iii) <u>Wilhelm</u>[3], bpt. 6 Nov 1738 - sp.: Willem Snyder and Maria Frona (Red Hook Luth. Chbk.). He md. in March 1765 Margaretha Maul (Red Hook Luth. Chbk.).

    iv) <u>Gertraud</u>[3], bpt. 28 May 1740 - sp.: Jacob Berringer and Gertraut Sneider (Germantown Ref. Chbk.). She md. Jacob Betzer (HJ).

    v) <u>Catharina</u>[3], bpt. 20 Oct 1742 - sp.: Antonius Klom and Catharina Schneider (Germantown Ref. Chbk.). She md. Michael Mohr (HJ).

    vi) <u>Engel</u>[3], bpt. 23 June 1745 - sp.: Wilm Schneider Jr. and Engel Klom (Red Hook Luth. Chbk.). She md. Wendel Pulver 21 March 1769 (Germantown Ref. Chbk.).

    vii) <u>Christina</u>[3], bpt. 22 Feb 1747 - sp.: Henrich Schneider and Christin Betzer (Germantown Ref. Chbk.). She md. Wilhelm Pulver 29 April 1770 (Germantown Ref. Chbk.).

    viii) <u>Henrich</u>[3], bpt. 26 Aug 1750 - sp.: Henrich Klum and Elske Schneider (Germantown Ref. Chbk.).

    ix) <u>Anna Maria</u>[3], bpt. 12 Nov 1752 - sp.: Willem Klom and Anna Maria Scherp (Germantown Ref. Chbk.)

2) <u>Anna Maria</u>[2] (HJ), md. Johannes Lescher (HJ).

3) <u>Anna Margaretha</u>[2], b. 1 Feb 1717 - sp.: Philipp Mohr, Anna Catharine Lutt, and Anna Margretha Dolest (West Camp Luth. Chbk.). As she was called Frony at Albany Ref. in 1766, her full bpt. name was probably like her mother's: Anna Margaretha Veronica (HJ). She md. Johann Philip Conradt (HJ).

4) <u>Anthonius</u>[2], b. June 1721 at Camp Queensberry - sp.: Denis Schneider and Anna Cath: Huff (N.Y. City Luth. Chbk.). He md. 13 Jan 1747 Catharina, d/o Wilhelm Schneider (Germantown Ref. Chbk.) and had ch.:

    i) <u>Philip</u>[3], bpt. 5 Feb 1747 - sp.: Philipp Klum and Ver-
onica (Germantown Ref. Chbk.).

   ii) <u>Anna Gertraud</u>[3], bpt. 1 Oct 1749 - sp.: Wilhelm Schneider and Anna Gertgen Schneider (Germantown Ref.
Chbk.).

  iii) <u>Wilhelm</u>[3], bpt. 24 April 1753 - sp.: William Klom and
Magdalena Botzer (Red Hook Luth. Chbk.).

5) <u>Johann Henrich</u>[2], bpt. 10 Aug 1723 - sp.: Jo: Henrich Moor
and Elisabeth Hymer (Linlithgo Ref. Chbk.). He md. 20 Nov
1750 Elisabetha Schneider, d/o Wilhelm (Germantown Ref.
Chbk.). Hendrick Kloom was listed above Poesten Kill in
1767 (<u>Report of the State Historian</u>, Vol. II, p. 814), and
one of that name had ch. bpt. at Centre Brunswick (HJ).
His issue were:

    i) <u>Catharina</u>[3], b. 15 May 1752 - sp.: Adam Schneider and
Catrina Colom (Rhinebeck Flats Ref. Chbk.).

   ii) <u>Philip</u>[3], b. 28 July 1762 - sp.: Philip Klum and C:
(Germantown Luth. Chbk.). He d. 20 Sept 1837, aged
75-1-23 (Germantown Ref. Cem.).

6) <u>Engel</u>[2], bpt. 22 May 1725 - sp.: Christoffel Fritz and Engel
Lisser (?) (Linlithgo Ref. Chbk.). She md. Wilhelm Schneider (HJ).

7) <u>Philip</u>[2], md. as s/o Philip Klum 5 Nov 1751 Margaretha, d/o
Lutwig Batz (Germantown Ref. Chbk.). The will of Philip
Klum of Germantown was dated 6 Feb 1809 and probated 29
Aug 1809 (Columbia Co. Will Bk. C). Issue:

    i) <u>Catharina</u>[3] (Will), md. Conrad Lescher (HJ).

   ii) <u>Philip</u>[3], bpt. 7 Aug 1754 - sp.: Philip Clom and Fran-
ica Clom (Linlithgo Ref. Chbk.). He was d. by 1809.

  iii) <u>Adam</u>[3], bpt. 31 Oct 1756 - sp.: Adam Klumm and Phron-
ica Lescher (Germantown Ref. Chbk.). He d. 9 Feb 1840
aged 84 yrs. and was a member of the Ref. Church
(Germantown Luth. Chbk.), bur. Cheviot Cem.

   iv) <u>Christina</u>[3], bpt. 18 Feb 1759 - sp.: Conradt Lescher
and wife Christina Batz (Germantown Ref. Chbk.).

    v) <u>Wilhelm</u>[3], bpt. 25 Jan 1762 - sp.: Willem Klumm and
Barbara Tatts (Germantown Ref. Chbk.).

   vi) <u>Anna Maria</u>[3], bpt. 2 Dec 1764 - sp.: Georg Klum and Anna Maria Schneider (Germantown Ref. Chbk.).

  vii) <u>Margaretha</u>[3], bpt. 14 March 1767 - sp.: Johannes Batz
and wife (Elsien) Schneider (Germantown Ref. Chbk.).

 viii) <u>Johannes</u>[3], bpt. 20 Jan 1770 - sp.: Johannes Klum and
wife Marytjen Bernhard (Germantown Ref. Chbk.).

   ix) <u>Gertraud</u>[3], bpt. 22 Aug 1772 - sp.: Henrich Schneider and Gertjen Klum (Germantown Ref. Chbk.).

Philip[2] probably md. 2nd Elisabetha Tenderle and had:

   ix) Veronica[3], bpt. 19 March 1776 at home - sp.: Charles
      Tenderle and Hilatjen Hamm (Germantown Ref. Chbk.).

   x) Georg[3] (Will), although this child may have been b.
     to his 1st wife (HJ).

8) Wilhelm[2] (HJ), md. Magdalena Betzer (HJ). Wilhelm, Catharina, and Lisabeth Klum joined the Germantown Ref. Church
   in 1748. The ch. of Wilhelm[2] and Magdalena were:

    i) Petrus[3], bpt. 27 Oct 1754 - sp.: Pieter Bötzer and
      wife Catharina Philip (Germantown Ref. Chbk.).

    ii) Philip[3], bpt. 28 Nov 1756 - sp.: Philip Klumm and
      wife Phronica (Germantown Ref. Chbk.).

    iii) Catharina[3], bpt. 24 June 1759 - sp.: Adam Petzer and
      Catharina Benner (Red Hook Luth. Chbk.).

    iv) Elisabetha[3], b. 9 March 1761 - sp.: Henrich Glum and
      wife Elsie (Rhinebeck Luth. Chbk.).

    v) Adam[3], bpt. 8 July 1764 - sp.: Adam Klum and Anna
     Link (Red Hook Luth. Chbk.).

    vi) Christina[3], bpt. 5 April 1767 - sp.: Nicolas Phillip
      and Christina Kulmer (Red Hook Luth. Chbk.).

    vii) Margaretha[3], bpt. as Gritjen 15 April 1770 - sp.:
      Phillip Klum and wife Gertjen Batz (Germantown Ref.
      Chbk.).

9) Catharina[2], bpt. 23 Feb 1732 - sp.: Hans Jurich Louder
   and Catharina (Germantown Ref. Chbk.). She joined the
   Germantown Ref. Church in 1748 and md. Adam Schneider
   (HJ).

10) Elisabetha[2] (HJ), joined the Germantown Ref. Church in
    1748 with Wilhelm[2] and Catharina[2] Klum.

11) Adam[2], md. as s/o Phillip Klum 19 Nov 1765 Catharina, d/o
    the late Christoffel Fritz (Germantown Ref. Chbk.). Adam
    Clumb was a deserter from Capt. Arnout Viele's Co. at
    Fort Edward in 1757, and in Capt. Frederick Kortz's Co.
    at East Camp in 1767 (Report of the State Historian, Vol.
    II, pp. 785 & 870). There was a will for an Adam Clumb
    dated 23 May 1788 in Albany Co. Wills Bk. I, p. 99.

Mrs. Virginia F. W. Reichelt of Tallahassee, Florida has
been researching this interesting family for years and soon will
be publishing her findings. In her correspondence with me in the
early stages of my project, she mentioned knowledge of a private
source which gave the maiden name of Anna Margaretha Veronica,
w/o Philip[1] Klum, as Lasher (Löscher). It will be intriguing to
see if documentation bears this out (HJ).

CONRAD GOLDMANN (Hunter Lists #243)

The origins of the Tulpehocken Goldmann family probably were at 6521 Gundheim (12 km. s.e. of Alzey), entries found at 6521 Dalsheim (2 km. further s.; Chbks. begin 1692, Ref.). Joh. Conrad Goldtmann, along with an Anton Goldtmann, was a Luth. at Gundheim in 1698 (Alzey Census of 1698). Koenraat Koltman, his wife and 5 ch. were in the 6th party in Holland in 1709 (listed twice) (Rotterdam Lists).

Conrad Goldmann made his first appearance on the Hunter Lists 4 July 1710 with 2 pers. over 10 yrs. of age and 3 pers. under 10 in the household; the entry for 4 Oct 1710 read 3 pers. over 10 and 1 under 10, and the notation for 31 Dec 1710 recorded 3 pers. over 10 and 2 under 10 yrs. The entries continued to fluctuate through 1711 with 3 - 1 on 25 March, 3 - 3 on 29 Sept, and 3 - 2 on 24 Dec 1711. The last notation in Hunter read 4 pers. over 10 yrs. of age and 1 pers. under 10 on 13 Sept 1712. Cond. Goldman of Hunterstown was a soldier in 1711 (Palatine Volunteers To Canada). Conrad Goldman's Widow with 3 ch. were at Neu-Ansberg ca. 1716/17 (Simmendinger Register). The ch. of Conrad[1] Goldmann were:

1) Johanna Catharina[2], bpt. 26 Dec 1704 - sp.: Johanna Catharina - w/o H. Johannes Wagner at Gundheim (Dalsheim Chbk.).

2) Conrad[2] (HJ), whose will was dated 9 Sept 1744 (Philadelphia Co. Will Bk. G, p. 150). He md. Maria Clara (--) (Will). She may have been the Old Mrs. Goldman bur. 10 May 1748 (Tulpehocken Chbk.), but probably she was the w/o Conrad[1] (HJ). Ch. of Conrad[2] were:

  i) Maria Catharina[3] (Will).

  ii) Maria Margaretha[3], md. as orphan d/o Conrad Goldmann 12 April 1748 John Kohl (Tulpehocken Chbk.).

  iii) Jacob[3] (HJ), bur. April 1803, aged 80 yrs. less 2 months; obituary stated he was b. in Tulpehocken in June 1723 and bpt. in Ref. Church, and that he lived with his 1st wife 36 yrs. and had 6 ch. (Salem Ev. Luth. Chbk., Lebanon, Lebanon Co., Pa.).

  iv) Johann Georg[3] (HJ), on a membership list in 1743 (Tulpehocken Chbk.).

  v) Conrad[3] (HJ), whose estate was probated in 1765 (Lancaster Co., Pa. Administration Bk.).

JOHANN FRIDERICH GONDERMANN (Hunter Lists #244)

Andreas Frantz Coutermann, s/o Johann Fridrich of Eutzberg in the commune of Maulbrunner in the duchy of Wurtemberg, md. 19

Sept 1715 Sibylla Scharrmann, d/o Johann Henrich of Fishborn in the commune of Isenburg (West Camp Luth. Chbk.). The village of origin was 7130 <u>Enzberg</u> (6 km. s. of Maulbronn), entries in the registers of 7532 <u>Niefern</u> (2 km. further s.; Chbks. begin 1608). Hans Friedrich Gundermann was called a Hindersaß at Entzberg in 1698.

Johann Friderich Gondermann made his first appearance on the Hunter Lists 30 June 1710 with 3 pers. over 10 yrs. and 2 pers. under 10 in the family. The registration changed to 5 pers. over 10 4 Oct 1710, to 4 pers. over 10 on 24 Dec 1711, to 5 over 10 on 24 June 1712, and finally to 6 pers. over 10 yrs. of age on 13 Sept 1712. Jno. Ffred Conterman: 1 man, 3 lads aged 9 to 15, and 1 woman, were in Ulster Co. in 1710/11 (West Camp Census). John Fredk Conterman was nat. (next to John Gorg and John Coenr. Conterman) 8 and 9 Sept 1715 (Kingston Nats.). Friederich Cunterman and Mar. Barbara with 3 ch. were at Heessberg ca. 1716/17 (Simmendinger Register). Their ch. were:

1) <u>Andreas Frantz</u>[2], md. as s/o Johann Friederich 19 Sept 1715 (1st) Anna Sibylla Scharrmann (West Camp Luth. Chbk.). Andries Contryman was nat. 8 and 9 Sept 1715 (Kingston Nats.). Andris Contreman made his initial appearance on Dutchess Co. rolls in the North Ward in 1718/19 (Dutchess Co. Tax Lists); he continued on the lists until 1725/26, when it appears that Counrate Hooffmann took control of his land (HJ). Andreas Conterman was in the foot company of the Marbletown, Ulster Co., militia in 1738 (<u>Report of the State Historian</u>, Vol. I, p. 606). A case dated 1743 between Andries Contreman vs. Edward Whitacker was found in the Kingston Court of Common Pleas. By his 1st wife Sibylla he had issue:

   i) <u>Elisabetha</u>[3], b. 20 Sept 1716 - sp.: Gerdaut Kraemer (West Camp Luth. Chbk.). She md. Jacob Keyser Jr. 30 Dec 1737 (Kingston Ref. Chbk.).

   ii) <u>Johann Henrich</u>[3], b. 6 Sept 1719 at Rheinbeck - sp.: Henrich Scharman and wife Anna Catharina (N.Y. City Luth. Chbk.). He also was in the Marbletown militia in 1738; with wife Arriaentje Keyser, he had ch. at the Walpeck Ref. Church (HJ). The estate of a Henry Cuntryman, late of Marbletown, was probated 7 Oct 1806 (Ulster Co. Administration Bk. B).

   iii) <u>Anna Barbara</u>[3], b. March 1722 at Rheinbeeck - sp.: Friedrich Meyer and wife Anna Barbara (N.Y. City Luth. Chbk.).

Anderies Konterman, b. Germany and a widower of Sewine

Scheerman, md. 6 Sept 1728 Cornelia Keyser, single woman
b. Marbletown (Kingston Ref. Chbk.). They had ch.:

 iv) Samuel[3], bpt. 5 Oct 1729, father called Andries
   France in the entry - sp.: Andries Kermer and Apolonia Keyser (Kingston Ref. Chbk.).

 v) Friederich[3] (HJ), who had a son Andreas bpt. in 1754
   with his wife Elizabeth Scheef (Marbletown Ref.
   Chbk.).

 vi) Andreas[3], bpt. 30 April 1732 (Kingston Ref. Chbk.).

 vii) "A Child, name torn out"[3], bpt. 25 March 1733 - sp.:
   Tjerk De Wit and Nenny Paaling (Kingston Ref. Chbk.).

 viii) Peter[3] (HJ), a sp. in 1753 (Walpeck Ref. Chbk.).

2) Johann Georg[2], bpt. 28 July 1698 - sp.: Hans Georg Hiltler the baker, Conrad Schrode, and Rosina - single d/o
Georg Dieffenbacher (Niefern Chbk.). Joh[n] Gorg Conterman
was nat. 8 and 9 Sept 1715 (Kingston Nats.). He md. Anna
Elisabeth Melchior 12 Sept 1718 (Albany Ref. Chbk.); she
may have been the d/o the 1709er Melchior[1] Wiess (HJ).
They sp. Joseph Bestede in 1741 (Schoharie Ref. Chbk.).

3) Johann Conrad[2], bpt. as Georg Cunradt 30 Jan 1701 - sp.:
Melchior Zuflühe - meadow servant in Nieffern, Hans Georg
Hiltler the baker, Cunrad Schrode, and Rosina - d/o Georg
Dieffenbacher - all at Entzberg (Niefern Chbk.). Joh[n]
Coenr. Conterman was nat. 8 and 9 Sept 1715 (Kingston
Nats.). Conrad Cunterman, with Hartman Windecker and Casper Leyp, was granted 2000 acres 3 miles s. of the Mohawk
in 1730 (N.Y. Land Papers, Vol. X & XI). A tract of 905
acres was granted to Coenradt Gunterman 13 Oct 1753 in the
present town of Minden (History of Montgomery & Fulton
Counties, N.Y., p. 73). Elizabeth T. Dehn kindly alerted
me to the existence of the will of Johann Conrad[2], dated
19 Aug 1768, now in N.Y. State Library Mss. Room (Acc.
#9550-9567). The ch. of Johann Conrad[2] were:

 i) Adam[3] (Will), 21 June 1719 - 22 Dec 1804 (Fort Plain
   Ref. Chbk.). The will of Adam Conderman of Minden was
   dated 6 Sept 1802 and probated 25 Feb 1805 (Montgomery
   Co. Wills Vol. I). He md. Anna Margaretha Leyp (HJ).

 ii) Georg[3] (Will), listed next to Jacob, Johannis, and
   Frederick Countrieman in Capt. Jacob Klock's Co. in
   1763 (Report of the State Historian, Vol. II, p. 795).
   Georg[3] md. Christina Diefendorf (HJ, per E. T. Dehn).

 iii) Johannes[3] (Will), md. Rachel Pickert (HJ, per E. T.
   Dehn and research by the Herbert A. Schraders).

 iv) Jacob[3] (Will).

    v) <u>Conrad</u>³ (Will).

   vi) <u>Anna Margaretha</u>³ (Will), md. (John) Plance (Will).

 vii) <u>Anna Rosina</u>³ (Will), md. (Johannes) Pickert (Will).

viii) <u>Barbara</u>³ (Will), md. (--) Mattys (Will).

  ix) <u>Eva</u>³ (Will), md. (--) Dillenbach (Will).

It is fascinating to note that <u>Marcus</u>³ (21 Oct 1720 - 13 Jan 1793, who md. Catharina Bellinger 22 May 1726 - 21 Jan 1812, both per Fort Plain Ref. Chbk.) and <u>Friederich</u>³ are not mentioned in the will of Johann Conrad², although they lived in geographic proximity to his ch.; I believe there is a <u>slight</u> chance these two both may have been sons of the mysterious Johann Georg² (HJ).

4) <u>Margaretha Barbara</u>², bpt. 24 Vine-month (October ?) 1703 - sp.: Melchior Zuflühe - the meadow servant in Nieffern, Hans Georg Hiltler the baker, Rosina - w/o Hans Georg Binder, and Margaretha - single d/o Cunrad Schrode, all at Entzberg (Niefern Chbk.). Barbara, d/o Friedrich Gunderman d. 30 Sept 1707, aged 4 yrs. (Niefern Chbk.).

5) <u>Anna Catharina</u>², bpt. 22 April 1706 - sp.: Melchior Zuflühe - meadow servant at Nieffernburg, Hans Georg Binder, for him his Schwieger Rosina, Margaretha - w/o Hans Wendel Feyler at Entzberg, and Anna Cath. - w/o Andreas Münderer the vine-dresser at Steinbacher Hof in the Württembergische (Niefern Chbk.).

6) <u>Hans Friederich</u>², bpt. 13 Oct 1708 - sp.: as before (Niefern Chbk.).

7) <u>Anna Eva</u>², b. 12 April 1714 - sp.: Anna Catharina German (West Camp Luth. Chbk.). An Eva Contermann was w/o John Wald or Wood at Germantown Ref. Church in 1740 (HJ).

8) <u>Jacob</u>², b. 12 Aug 1716 - sp.: Jacob Gormann and his wife Anna Catharina (West Camp Luth. Chbk.). The Tulpehocken Chbk. notes a Jacob Conterman there in the 1740's (HJ).

There were other Countrymans in colonial N.Y.: 1) a Catharina Countryman md. Austin Schoolkraft and was in the Schoharie area in 1743; and 2) a Maria Elisabetha Contermann md. Johann Christ: Jong and had issue in Montgomery, Orange Co., N.Y. in the 1750's (HJ). Mrs. Elizabeth T. Dehn of Schenectady, N.Y. and Mr. Wesley Contryman of Grand Island, N.Y. have helped me on this family (HJ).

JOHANNES GRAD (Hunter Lists #245)

Johannes¹ Grad was documented at 5419 <u>Dierdorf</u> (18 km. n.e. of Neuwied; Chbks. begin 1676); in 1704 he was called a shepherd at Brückrachdorf (Dierdorf Chbk.). The family was an old one in the Neuwied - Westerwald area, some residing at 5905 <u>Oberfischbach</u>.

Johannes Gradt made his initial appearance on the Hunter
Lists 1 July 1710 with 3 pers. over 10 yrs. and 2 pers. under 10.
The reading changed to 2 pers. over 10 yrs. and 3 under 10 on 29
Sept 1711, and then again to 3 pers. over 10 yrs. and 3 pers. un-
der 10 on 24 Dec 1711. Johan Kradt was a soldier from Annsberg
in 1711 (Palatine Volunteers To Canada). Johannis Graet was nat.
14 Feb 1715/16 (Albany Nats.). Johannes Kroth and Walburgis with
5 ch. were at Wormsdorff ca. 1716/17 (Simmendinger Register).
Johanes Craat was on Palatine Debt Lists in 1718, 1721, and 1726
(Livingston Debt Lists). He md. Johanna Walpurga (--) and had:

1) Gabriel², called s/o Joh's of Katteway in Banns 22 Nov
   1733 for his marriage to Catharina Kreisseler, only d/o
   Joh: Phil. Kreisseler of Kisk. (Loonenburg Luth. Chbk.).
   They were md. 11 Dec 1733 (Catskill Ref. Chbk.). Gabriel²
   was listed as a farmer at Claverack, aged 59, in 1762
   (Settlers & Residents, Vol. III, Part I, p. 19). He ap-
   peared on Rhinebeck tax rolls 1737/8 - 1741/42 (Dutchess
   Co. Tax Lists). The ch. of Gabriel² and Catharina were:

   i) Anna³, b. 28 April 1736 and bpt. Kisket. - sp.: Jacob
      Philip and Barbara Graad (Loonenburg Luth. Chbk.).
      She probably md. George Charters (HJ).

   ii) Johannes³, bpt. 24 April 1737 - sp.: Johannes Veller
       and Lisabeth Graad (Rhinebeck Flats Ref. Chbk.).

   iii) Nicolaus³, bpt. 29 April 1739 - sp.: Niclaas Link
        and Catrina Smit (Rhinebeck Flats Ref. Chbk.). Nich-
        laes and Hendrick Graet were listed together in
        Capt. Johannis Hogeboom's Co. in 1767 (Report of the
        State Historian, Vol. II, p. 875).

   iv) Catharina³, bpt. 14 April 1740 - sp.: Johan Jurge
       Streit and Catharina Hagedorn (Red Hook Luth. Chbk.).

   v) Henrich³, bpt. 14 Sept 1741 - sp.: Heinrich Great
      and Catharina Dietrich (Red Hook Luth. Chbk.).

   vi) Philip³, b. 11 March 1743 and bpt. Newton - sp.:
       Hans Jurge Kreisler and wife Christina (Loonenburg
       Luth. Chbk.).

   vii) Christina³, bpt. 26 March 1744 - sp.: Johan Jurge
        Kreiselaar and Christina Reid (Katsbaan Ref. Chbk.).

   viii) Philip³, b. 15 June 1745 and bpt. at Kisket. - sp.:
         Philip Kreisler and Lisabeth Spon (Loonenburg Luth.
         Chbk.).

   ix) Maria³, b. 20 Sept 1746 and bpt. Kisket. - sp.: God-
       fried Brandauw and wife Maria (Loonenburg Luth.
       Chbk.).

   x) Elisabetha³, b. 26 March 1749 and bpt. Kisket. -

sp.: Andreas Eigler and Cathar. Kreislers (Loonenburg Luth. Chbk.).

   xi) <u>Maria</u>[3], bpt. 14 April 1751 - sp.: Casparus Lodewyck
and Maria Schever (Kinderhook Ref. Chbk.).

  xii) <u>Hieronymus</u>[3], bpt. 14 April 1751, twin to Maria[3] -
sp.: same as above (Kinderhook Ref. Chbk.).

 xiii) <u>Elisabetha</u>[3], bpt. 23 April 1755 - sp.: Adam Van Alen
and Maria Roseboom (Kinderhook Ref. Chbk.).

2) <u>Eva Margaretha</u>[2], b. 9 July 1704 - sp.: Godhard - shepherd
from Marchrachdorf, Margaretha - d/o Thönges Müller from
Krummel, and Eva - w/o Johann Henrich from Brüchrachdorf
(Dierdorf Chbk.). She md. Friederich Dieterich (HJ).

3) <u>Henrich</u>[2], called s/o Johannes 1738 in sp. Hendrick Gratt
was a freeholder at Claverack in 1763 (Albany Co. Freeholders). Hendrick Grat, along with John, Wilhelmus, and
Hendrick Graat Jr., was in Capt. Jeremiah Hogeboom's Co.
in 1767 (<u>Report of the State Historian</u>, Vol. II, p. 865).
The will of Hendrick Groat of Claverack, yeoman, was dated
16 May 1780 and probated 28 March 1801 (Columbia Co. Will
Bk. B). He md. Maria Catharina Dieterich in 1734 (Catskill
Ref. Chbk.) and had issue:

    i) <u>Anna Maria</u>[3], bpt. 2 March 1735 - sp.: Georg Wilhelm
Diederich and Marytche Gradt (Catskill Ref. Chbk.).
She probably md. Peter Wiesmer (HJ).

   ii) <u>Anna</u>[3], b. 8 Oct 1736 and bpt. Newton - sp.: Jo: Wilhelm Dieterich and Anna Marg. (Loonenburg Luth.
Chbk.).

  iii) <u>Johannes</u>[3], b. 5 Sept 1738 and bpt. Newton - sp.: Hannes Graad the grandfather, and Catharina - w/o Jo.
Math. Jurg (Loonenburg Luth. Chbk.). He md. 29 Oct
1768 Sarah Bouwman (Linlithgo Ref. Chbk.), and they
had ch. bpt. at Kinderhook Ref. and Claverack Ref.
Churches (HJ).

   iv) <u>Catharina</u>[3] (Will), md. Hendrick Shutt (Will).

    v) <u>Anna</u>[3], bpt. 26 March 1744 - sp.: Frederich Dederich
and wife Eva Graat (Katsbaan Ref. Chbk.). She md.
Petrus Philip (Will).

   vi) <u>Henrich</u>[3], bpt. 2 Oct 1748 at Newton - sp.: Gabriel
Grad and wife Cathar. (Loonenburg Luth. Chbk.). He
d. in 1832, aged 85 yrs. (Leggett Farm Cem., Columbia Co.).

  vii) <u>Wilhelmus</u>[3], twin to the above, bpt. 2 Oct 1748 - sp.:
Jurge Wilh. Dieterich and wife Catharina (Loonenburg
Luth. Chbk.). He md. Christina Heiser (HJ).

viii) <u>Elisabetha</u>³, bpt. 26 Dec 1750 - sp.: Henricus Diederich and Mareitje Brando (Katsbaan Ref. Chbk.). She
md. Wilhelmus Ostrander (Will).

ix) <u>Petrus</u>³, b. 21 Feb 1753 - sp.: Jacob Philip and Barbara Krad (Schoharie Luth. Chbk.).

x) <u>Margaretha</u>³, bpt. 23 Aug 1755 - sp.: Helmus Diederik
and Elizabeth Diederik (Catskill Ref. Chbk.).

xi) <u>Jannet</u>³, bpt. 4 Aug 1757 - sp.: Gabriel Esselsteyn
and Jannetje Esselsteyn (Claverack Ref. Chbk.). She
md. William Pike (Will).

xii) <u>Friederich</u>³, bpt. 30 June 1760 - sp.: Petrus Philip
and Marytje Philip (Claverack Ref. Chbk.).

4) <u>Barbara</u>² (HJ), md. Jacob Philip (HJ).

5) <u>Anna Elisabetha</u>², b. 9 July 1714 - sp.: Balthas Steuber
and Anna Elisabeth Duntzbach (West Camp Luth. Chbk.).
She md. Henrich Mesick 24 Nov 1739 (Katsbaan Ref. Chbk.).

6) <u>Margaretha</u>², a sp. with brother Gabriel² in 1729 (Loonenburg Luth. Chbk.).

7) <u>Maria</u>² (HJ), md. Friederich Brandau 5 Dec 1737 (Loonenburg Luth. Chbk.).

<u>PHILIPP PETER GRAUBERGER</u> (Hunter Lists #246)

Peter Crabbecher aged 28, his wife, and a son aged 2, Luth.
husbandman and vinedresser, were noted between Friederik Batz and
Georg Tachstetter in the 4th arrivals at London in 1709 (London
Lists).

Philipp Peter Grauberger made his first appearance on the
Hunter Lists 4 July 1710 with 2 pers. over 10 yrs. in the house-
hold; the entry changed to 2 pers. over 10 and 1 under 10 on 25
March 1712, and then grew to 3 pers. over 10 yrs. and 1 under 10
on 24 June 1712. Philip Peter Grauberger aged 29 and Anna Barbara
Grauberger aged 33 were in N.Y. City in 1710/11 (Palatines In N.Y.
City). Peter Groberger and his wife Barbara with 2 ch. were at
Hackensack ca. 1716/17 (Simmendinger Register). They had ch.:

1) <u>Johann Friederich</u>², b. 1 Jan 1712 - sp.: Fridrich Maul
and Johann Fuehrer (West Camp Luth. Chbk.).

2) <u>Anna Margaretha</u>², b. 23 Aug 1714 and bpt. at Jan Loot's
at Greenneck, Hackensack - sp.: Johann Philipp Ruger and
wife Anna Margareta (N.Y. City Luth. Chbk.).

3) <u>Henrich</u>², conf. as s/o Pieter Graubinger with his sister
Margareetje 30 April 1738 (N.Y. City Luth. Chbk.). He md.
Maria Margaretha Hoffmann at Hackensack 10 Dec 1741 (N.Y.
City Luth. Chbk.). They had issue:

       i) <u>Anna</u>³, b. 2 Dec 1742 and bpt. at Pieter Lassings in
          Highland - sp.: Pieter Grauberger and Anna (N.Y. City
          Luth. Chbk.). She may have been the Hannah Graghburgh-
          er who had a licence to marry Johan Bastian Kuysrock
          3 Dec 1761 (HJ).
      ii) <u>Johannes</u>³, b. 8 May 1749 and bpt. at Pieter Lassings
          in Highland - sp.: William Eduard and Anna (N.Y. City
          Luth. Chbk.). A Hannes Grauberger sp. Jurriaan Hof-
          man in 1771 (New Hackensack Ref. Chbk.).
   4) <u>Anna</u>², b. 20 April 1718 at Hackinsack - sp.: Cornelis Van
     Hoorn and wife Margareta (N.Y. City Luth. Chbk.). Anna,
     d/o Peter Graubinger, was conf. 26 April 1738 in the house
     of Pieter Grauberger (sic) (N.Y. City Luth. Chbk.). She
     md. the Friday after the 10th Trinity: 1737 William Eduard
     at Hackensack (N.Y. City Luth. Chbk.).

<u>GERLACH GRAW'S WIDDOW</u> (Hunter Lists #247)

At the marriage of Michiel Moor to Elisabeth Grauw 6 May
1719, the origins of both participants were recorded as Nassouw
(N.Y. City Ref. Chbk.). The marriage of one Johann Gerlach Graa,
widower of Bach in the Kirchspiel Marienberg, to Anna Elisabeth
Pfau, d/o Jost Pfau and wid/o Engelberth Sauer, was found in the
ancient registers of 5909 <u>Burbach</u> on Dom. 1 Trin: 1703; however,
it appears that this family stayed in Germany post 1709 (HJ).

Gerlach Graw made his initial appearance on the Hunter Lists
1 July 1710 with 4 pers. over 10 yrs. and 3 pers. under 10 in the
family; the entry read 5 pers. over 10 and 2 under 10 on 4 Oct
1710. On 29 Sept 1711 the head of the family changed to Catharina
Grawin with 2 pers. over 10 yrs. in the household. Anna Cath.
Grauin aged 40, Anna Eliz Grauin aged 18, Anna Sophia Grauin aged
10, and Johannes Grauin aged 11, were in N.Y. City in one family
in 1710/11 (Palatines In N.Y. City). Anna Catharina and Elisabeth
Grauin joined the N.Y. City Ref. Church 26 Feb 1712. Catharina
Kroin, widow with 3 ch., was at Hackensack in 1716/17 (Simmendin-
<u>ger</u> Register). Anne Catriena Grau d. 19 April 1734 (N.Y. City Ref.
Chbk.). The issue of Gerlach¹ Graw and Anna Catharina were:
   1) <u>Anna Elisabetha</u>² (Palatines In N.Y. City), md. 6 May 1719
     Michael Mohr (N.Y. City Ref. Chbk.).
   2) <u>Johannes</u>² (Palatines In N.Y. City), md. Anna (--). Johan-
     nes Graw (Gray and Grey) was noted in the Janeway Accounts
     1736-1747. He had issue:
       i) <u>Garret</u>³, probably bpt. as Gerritje 25 Dec 1722 - sp.:
          Robbert Bolmer and wife Rosina (Somerville Ref. Chbk.).

Garret Gray posted security for his son Robert's
fine for stealing watermelons 7 Sept 1769 (<u>Geneal-
ogical Magazine of N.J.</u>, Vol. 43, p. 58). Garret[3]
md. Lydia or Elidea (--), moved from Somerset Co.,
N.J., bought land in 1779 in Faquier Co., Va., and
then moved on to Newberry Co. S. C. (Research by
Mr. and Mrs. Shaler Gordon Smith Jr. of Claymont,
Del.).

ii) <u>Catharina</u>[3], bpt. 20 Dec 1724 (Somerville Ref. Chbk.).

iii) <u>Maria</u>[3], bpt. 25 June 1727 - sp.: Hans Jurgen and
... Spoeneman (Somerville Ref. Chbk.).

iv) <u>Elisabetha</u>[3], bpt. 18 May 1729 (New Brunswick Ref.
Chbk.).

v) <u>Johannes</u>[3], bpt. 17 Oct 1731 (New Brunswick Ref.
Chbk.).

vi) <u>Petrus</u>[3], bpt. 21 April 1734 (New Brunswick Ref.
Chbk.).

vii) <u>Sophia</u>[3], bpt. 14 Nov 1736 (Somerville Ref. Chbk.).

viii) <u>Wilhelm</u>[3], bpt. 13 May 1739 (Somerville Ref. Chbk.).

ix) <u>Anna</u>[3], bpt. 6 June 1742 (Somerville Ref. Chbk.).

3) <u>Anna Sophia</u>[2] (Palatines In N.Y. City), md. Johannes
Rohrbagh 25 March 1727 (N.Y. City Ref. Chbk.). She joined
the N.Y. City Ref. Church 26 Aug 1729.

ANNA MARIA GRAWSIN (Hunter Lists #248)

A possible husband to Anna Maria[1] Graw was the Johan Jeorg
Kro listed with his wife and 3 ch. next to Johan Philips Kro on
Capt. Robbert Bulman's ship in the 4th party in Holland in 1709
(Rotterdam Lists). Georg Gro aged 40, his wife, a son aged 2,
daughters aged 7 and 5, Luth., husbandman and vinedresser, were
in the 4th arrivals in England later that year. The Philip Crow
noted on the ship with Johann Georg eventually settled with Mr.
Edward Browne at Evelary in Co. Cork (<u>The Palatine Families of
Ireland</u>, p. 16). However, in my opinion, as no one named Kraus
was enrolled on the Hunter Lists and as there were prominent
Palatines of that name in the Mohawk Valley at an early date, I
believe that #248 Anna Maria Grawsin, called Grausin on her first
notation in Hunter, was not a Graw, but a Kraus (HJ). A Jacob
Kruis, his wife, and 2 ch. were on Capt. Jno. Blouwer's ship in
the 5th party in Holland in 1709; also in the 5th party were Jacob Grausch's Widow with 3 ch. on Capt. Jno. Untank's vessel
(Rotterdam Lists).

Anna Maria Grausin made her first appearance on the Hunter

Lists 1 July 1710 with 1 pers. over 10 yrs. of age and 2 pers. under 10 yrs.; her last entry with this figure was 4 Oct 1710, again as Grausin. Anna Maria, wid/o Johann Jacob Kraus of Simmern in Pfaltz, md. 22 Aug 1710 Johann Paul Reitshaft of Duhren in the district of Pfortzheim in the commune Durlach (West Camp Luth. Chbk.). The ch. of Anna Maria[1] Grausin were:

1) Johann Jacob[2] (HJ), nat. 14 Feb 1715/16 (Albany Nats.).
   A Jacob Crous was a freeholder of Canajoharrie in 1763
   (Albany Co. Freeholders). Probable issue:

   i) Jacob[3] (HJ), md. Gertraud Helmer (HJ).
   ii) Maria Elisabetha[3] (HJ), md. Henrich Laux 10 Oct 1749
       (Stone Arabia Ref. Chbk.).
   iii) Maria Margaretha[3] (HJ), md. Dieterich Horning (HJ).
   iv) Anna[3], called his single daughter in 1760 (Stone Arabia Ref. Chbk.).
   v) Georg[3] (HJ), soldier in Capt. Robert Mc Ginnis's Co.
      in 1756 with others from the Mohawk region (Report of the State Historian, Vol. I, p. 827).

2) Maria Elisabetha[2] (HJ), conf. at Tschoghari at the so-called Fuchsen-dorp in 1720 (N.Y. City Luth. Chbk.). She md. Georg Zimmer (HJ).

There was a Johannis Krous in Capt. Thomas Ackeson's Co. in the Schoharie area in 1767 (Report of the State Historian, Vol. II, p. 847); he may have been connected to the Mohawk group (HJ).

JOHANN PHILIPP GREISLER (Hunter Lists #249)

The German origins of the Chrysler family were at 6524 Guntersblum (6 km. s. of Oppenheim; Chbks. begin 1651, Luth.). The earliest known ancestor of the American line was Leonard Kreußler, a Gemeinsmann at Herrnsheim. On 23 Nov 1658, Johannes Kreußler, single s/o Leonhard Kreußler - formerly Gemeinsmann at Herrnsheim, md. Elisabetha, d/o the late Adam Schmidt - Gemeinsmann here. Elisabetha, w/o Johan Kreußler - Gemeinsmann and tailor here, d. 23 Aug 1660, after the birth of a dead son a few days before. Johannes Kreußler, tailor here, md. Elisabeth Seyfried 21 April 1661. A child of Johannes Kreußler and Elisabeth was:

Paulus, bpt. at home 7 Jan 1666 - sp.: Paulus Kreußler from Bechtheim.

Johannes Kreußler md. (3rd) Anna Maria, d/o Conrad Sylwy from Alsheim am Altrhein on 13 July 1669. Johannes Kreußler, tailor and Gemeinsmann here was bur. 15/25 Oct 1686, aged 51 yrs. His ch. by his 3rd wife Anna Maria were:

Henrich, bpt. 2 April 1671 - sp.: Heinrich Becker, Gemeinsmann here.

+ <u>Johann Philipp</u>, bpt. 26 Aug 1672 - sp.: Philipp Weynath, Gemeinsmann here.

"A Daughter", bpt. 31 Oct 1675 - sp.: his mother Elisabetha
(This probably refers to Johannes's mother, w/o Leonhard -
HJ).

<u>Anna Margaretha</u>, bpt. 17 Nov 1678 - sp.: Anna Margaretha -
w/o Andreas Obrecht.

Johann Philipp Kreussler, s/o the late Johan Graussler - Gemeins-
man here, md. Anna Catharina, d/o the late Benedict Braun - formerly teacher at Udenheim, 26 April 1701. (Note two different
spellings of the same surname in one entry! - HJ).

Johann Philipp Greisler made his initial appearance on the
Hunter Lists 1 July 1710 with 2 pers. over 10 yrs. of age and 2
pers. under 10 in the family. The entries changed to 3 pers. over
10 yrs. and 1 under 10 on 24 June 1711 and then to 4 pers. over
10 25 March 1712. Johan Phillip Greisler aged 40, Catharine Greisler aged 40, John George Greisler aged 11, and Johannes Greisler
aged 7, were in N.Y. City in 1710/11 (Palatines In N.Y. City).
John Phil. Chryselar was nat., next to Gorg Chryselar, 8 and 9
Sept 1715 (Kingston Nats.). Joh. Philipp Kreussler and Anna Catharina with 3 ch. were at Beckmansland ca. 1716/17 (Simmendinger
Register). Joh: Phil: Kryselaer was a Palatine Debtor in 1718 and
1721 (Livingston Debt Lists). (--) Kräusler, the father, was mentioned as living in the family of Hieronymus Kräusler ca. 1744
in the Schoharie Valley (Schoharie Luth. Chbk.). The ch. of Johann Philip[1] Greisler and his wife Anna Catharina were:

1) <u>Johann Georg[2]</u>, bpt. 30 April 1702 - sp.: Joh. George -
   eldest s/o the Unterschultheiss Joh. Jacob Loosens (Guntersblum Chbk.). Johann Georg Kreystler was conf. at Easter 1714 at Newtown (West Camp Luth. Chbk.). Gorg Chryselar was nat. 8 and 9 Sept 1715 (Kingston Nats.). Jurie
   Cryselaar was a freeholder at Caters Kill and Cats Kill
   in 1763 (Albany Co. Freeholders). He md. Christina Streit
   (HJ) and had ch.:

   i) <u>Philip[3]</u>, bpt. 27 Dec 1724 - sp.: Johannes Gryselaar
      and Catrina Ham (Kingston Ref. Chbk.). He md. Sarah
      Boorhans and had ch. at Katsbaan Ref. and Loonenburg
      Luth. Churches (HJ).

   ii) <u>Johann Friederich[3]</u>, md. as s/o Hannes Jurge 13 Aug
       1751 Catharina, d/o Pieter May (Loonenburg Luth.
       Chbk.). Frid. Kreisler was conf. at Newton 3 June
       1744 (Loonenburg Luth. Chbk.). Fredrick and Sgt.
       Nickolaes Chruyselaer were in Capt. Cornelus Dubois's

Co. in 1767 (<u>Report of the State Historian</u>, Vol. II,
pp. 876 & 878).

iii) <u>Magdalena</u>[3], bpt. as Marlene 13 days before her time
26 Jan 1729 - sp.: Friderich Streit and wife Catharina (Loonenburg Luth. Chbk.).

iv) <u>Nicolaus</u>[3], b. 8 Feb 1731 and bpt. Newton - sp.: Niclas Schmid and Anna Elisabeth (Loonenburg Luth.
Chbk.). He was conf. 17 April 1748 at Kisket. (Loonenburg Luth. Chbk.). He md. Anna Maria May M'Dagnaa
2 Adv.: 1757 (Loonenburg Luth. Chbk.).

v) <u>Catharina</u>[3], b. that morning and bpt. in Kreisler's
house 5 March 1733 - sp.: Daniel Lickhard and Cath.
Kreistern (Loonenburg Luth. Chbk.). She was conf. in
April of 1746 and md. Hannes Schram 17 Dec 1749 (Loonenburg Luth. Chbk.).

vi) <u>Christina</u>[3], b. 24 May 1735 and bpt. at Kisket. - sp.:
Christina Brandauw and Philip Spoh, being absent his
father and mother (Loonenburg Luth. Chbk.). She md.
William Welsch (HJ).

vii) <u>Maria</u>[3], b. 26 July 1737 and bpt. Kisket. - sp.: Friderich Martin and wife Eva Maria (Loonenburg Luth.
Chbk.).

viii) <u>Gertraud</u>[3], b. 27 Nov 1739 and bpt. Newton - sp.:
Clemens Lehman and wife Gertrude (Loonenburg Luth.
Chbk.). She md. Hans König 18 July 1763 (Loonenburg
Luth. Chbk.).

ix) <u>Petrus</u>[3] (HJ), a sp. to Wilhelmus Welsch and Christina
Kreiselaer in 1774 (Katsbaan Ref. Chbk.).

x) <u>Elisabetha</u>[3], b. 6 Jan 1743 and bpt. Newton - sp.:
Hannes Hertel, Nic. Schmid, and Lisabeth Schmid
(Loonenburg Luth. Chbk.).

2) <u>Johannes</u>[2], bpt. 2 Dec 1703 - sp.: Johannes Eyrich - sexton
or cooper here (Guntersblum Chbk.). Johannes Greysler was
conf. Easter 1717 at Newtown (West Camp Luth. Chbk.). Johannis Krissalaer was on a list of Palatine Debtors 13
Dec 1747 (<u>Settlers & Residents</u>, Vol. I, p. 33). Johannes,
Antje, Elisabeth, Margriet and Catharina Kreiseler joined
the Red Hook Luth. Church 5 April 1749. Johannis Cryselaer
was recorded on tax rolls for Rhinebeck from 1738/39 -
Feb 1753, when his estate was listed (Dutchess Co. Tax
Lists). He md. Eva Catharina Manck (HJ) and had ch.:

i) <u>Anna Margaretha</u>[3], bpt. 7 weeks old 15 Sept 1726 -
sp.: Philip Kreisler and Anna Margareta Mank (Loonenburg Luth. Chbk.).

ii) <u>Wilhelmus</u>[3], b. 26 July 1727 and bpt. at East Camp -
sp.: Wilhelm Lehman and wife Maria Eva (Loonenburg
Luth. Chbk.). He md. Catharina Schauer (HJ) and had
ch. bpt. at Rhinebeck Luth., Rhinebeck Flats Ref.,
and Churchtown Luth. Churches.

iii) <u>Johannes</u>[3], b. 1 Dec 1728 and bpt. at Loonenburg - sp.:
Johannes Maul and Catharina Kreislers (Loonenburg
Luth. Chbk.). Johanis Cryslar was a deserter from
Capt. Arnout Viele's Co. in 1757 (<u>Report of the State
Historian</u>, Vol. II, p. 785). He md. Susanna Stickel
and had ch. bpt. at Rhinebeck Flats Ref., Red Hook
Luth., Rhinebeck Luth., and Gallatin Ref. Churches
(HJ).

iv) <u>Elisabetha</u>[3], bpt. 9 March 1732 - sp.: Nicolass Schmid
and Anna Elisabetha (Catskill Ref. Chbk.). She may
have been the Elisabetha Kreuseler who joined the
Red Hook Luth. Church with Mathias Kreuseler 4 June
1756 (HJ). She md. Johannes Tromm (HJ).

v) <u>Margaretha</u>[3], b. 2 Aug 1733 and bpt. at Kisket. - sp.:
Daniel Lickhard and Gritje Lehmans (Loonenburg Luth.
Chbk.). She md. Wilhelm Schauer (HJ).

vi) <u>Catharina</u>[3], b. 23 March 1735 and bpt. at Kisket. -
sp.: Judge Wilhelm Dieterich and Cath. Elisabeth Jung
(Loonenburg Luth. Chbk.). She md. Hermann Kuhn (HJ).

vii) <u>Maria</u>[3], b. 16 May 1736 and bpt. at Kisket. in Hannes
Kreisler's house - sp.: Friderich Eigener and Maria
Jung (Loonenburg Luth. Chbk.).

viii) <u>Matthias</u>[3], b. 13 Aug 1737 and bpt. at Kisket. - sp.:
Matthys Junge and wife Catharina (Loonenburg Luth.
Chbk.). He md. as a single man b. Blauwe Bergen 15
Aug 1759 Carolina Beys (Rhinebeck Flats Ref. Chbk.),
and they had issue bpt. at Gallatin Ref., Rhinebeck
Luth., and Red Hook Luth. Churches (HJ).

ix) <u>Henrich</u>[3], b. 24 Sept 1739 and bpt. Teerbosch - sp.:
Henrich Michel and Marytje Brasy (Loonenburg Luth.
Chbk.). Henricus Kreuseler joined the Red Hook Luth.
Church 4 June 1757. He md. Anna Dorothea Klom (or
perhaps Klein - HJ) and had issue at Rhinebeck Flats
Ref., Rhinebeck Luth., and Churchtown Luth. Churches
(HJ).

x) <u>Anna</u>[3], bpt. 2 March 1742 - sp.: Heinrich Major and
Lisabeth Major (Red Hook Luth. Chbk.).

xi) <u>Eleonora Catharina</u>[3], bpt. 24 Dec 1743 - sp.: David
Krisler and Leonora Cattarina, his wife (Red Hook

Luth. Chbk.).

3) <u>Beata Maria</u>², bpt. 19 Sept 1706 - sp.: the d/o the cooper Johannes Eyrich (Guntersblum Chbk.).

4) <u>Johann Henrich Valentin</u>², bpt. 13 Sept 1710 at N.Y. - sp.: Henrich Mehs and Valentin Presler (West Camp Luth. Chbk.).

5) <u>Johann Hieronymus</u>², b. 6 March 1713 - sp.: Hieronymus Klein and Johann Planck (West Camp Luth. Chbk.). Hierony- mus Kreisler was conf. 15 April 1729, aged 17 yrs. at New- ton (N.Y. City Luth. Chbk.). He d. 21 Sept 1751 (Schoharie Luth. Chbk.). His widow Maria Margaretha (Bauch? - HJ) md. 7 Nov 1752 Michel Hilsinger and then d. 20 June 1753 (Scho- harie Luth. Chbk.). Administration papers in the estate of Jeronemus Cryselaer of Schohary Co. were recorded 24 Jan 1752 (<u>Genealogical Data from Administration Papers</u>, p. 79). The ch. of Hieronymus² Greisler were:

  i) <u>Adam</u>³ (Schoharie Luth. Chbk. List, ca. 1744), called eldest s/o Hieronymus 1 March 1763 at estate settle- ment cited above. He md. Anna Maria Braun 10 July 1760 (Schoharie Luth. Chbk.). He was a very active tory, known as the notorious Adam Crislar (see Simm's <u>History of Schoharie</u>, pp. 156, 365, 393, and 434).

  ii) <u>Balthasar</u>³ (Schoharie Luth. Chbk. List, ca. 1744), md. 12 Feb 1767 Elisabetha Baxter (Stone Arabia Ref. Chbk.).

  iii) <u>Philip</u>³ (Schoharie Luth. Chbk. List, ca. 1744), md. Elisabetha Braun 19 Nov 1762 (Schoharie Luth. Chbk.). William, Adam, Baltus, and Phillip Cryslar were in Capt. Thomas Ackeson's Co. in 1767 (<u>Report of the State Historian</u>, Vol. II, pp. 846 & 847). Philip Cris- lor, late of Tryon Co., filed a claim 30 Oct 1787 for compensation in Ontario as a U.E.L. (2nd Report, Ontario Provincial Archivist, 1904, p. 1056).

  iv) <u>Elisabetha</u>³, bpt. 5 June 1737 at Schohari - sp.: Mich Treymeyer and Lisabeth Berniger (Loonenburg Luth. Chbk.).

  v) <u>Catharina</u>³ (Schoharie Luth. Chbk. List, ca. 1744).

  vi) <u>Margaretha</u>³, bpt. 8 March 1743 - sp.: Jacob Frederick Lawyer and Elisabeth Staarnberger (Schoharie Ref. Chbk.).

  vii) <u>Johannes</u>³, b. 18 Dec 1744 - sp.: Johannes Braun and his wife (Schoharie Luth. Chbk.). Hannes Kreysseller was in Capt. Jacob Sternberger's Co. at Schohare in 1767 (<u>Report of the State Historian</u>, Vol II, p. 843). Johannes Crysler, late of Tryon Co., also filed a

308

U.E.L. claim 8 March 1788.

    viii) <u>Wilhelm³</u>, b. 10 Nov 1746 - sp.: Johan Wilhelm Bauch and his wife (Schoharie Luth. Chbk.).

    ix) <u>Maria³</u>, b. Oct 1748 - sp.: Jacob Veeg and Margaretha Braun (Schoharie Luth. Chbk.). She md. Johannes Bauch 15 July 1772 (Schoharie Luth. Chbk.).

    x) <u>Georg³</u>, b. 19 Oct 1750 - sp.: Jürgen Henrich Stubrach and Elisabeth Becker (Schoharie Luth. Chbk.).

6) <u>Anna Catharina²</u>, b. 13 Oct 1714 - sp.: Catharina Elisabetha Rau, Apolonia Froehlich, and Johann Philipp Feller (West Camp Luth. Chbk.). She md. as the only d/o Philip of Kisk. 22 Nov 1733 Gabriel Graad (Loonenburg Luth. Chbk.).

Mr. Theodore L. Brownyard has written "Descendants of Johan Philip Kreisler" in the <u>N.Y. Genealogical & Biographical Record</u>, Vol. 105, No. 1, which I recommend highly.

MARIA ELIZABETH GRESSERIN (Hunter Lists #250)

Hans Müsel Crisser, his wife, Hans Miüsel, Katrina, and 2 (other) ch. were in the 2nd party of Palatines in Holland in 1709 (Rotterdam Lists).

Maria Elizabeth Gresserin made her initial appearance on the Hunter Lists 4 Aug 1710 with 3 pers. over 10 yrs. of age and 1 pers. under 10 in the household. The last entry for the family was with the same number on 31 Dec 1710, where she was recorded as Elizabetha Gresserin.

MARIE GRIFFON (Hunter Lists #251)

The probable origins of this family were at 6749 <u>Barbelroth</u> (7 km. e. of Bad Bergzabern; Chbks. begin 1678, Ref.). Frantz Griffon auß der Schweitz md. 3 July 1704 Jane Marie Dumottier, b. in Lausanne and d/o the late Moos (?) Dumottier.

Marie Griffon made her first appearance on the Hunter Lists 4 Aug 1710 with 1 pers. over 10 yrs. and 1 under 10 yrs.; she was near Anna Maria Stambuchin and Rudolph Stähl who also came from villages near Barbelroth (HJ). Anna Maria Griffon was entered for the last time on the Hunter Lists on 4 Oct 1710 with 1 pers. over 10 and 1 under 10 yrs. in the household.

JEAN GRIOT (Hunter Lists #252)

Jean Griot was one of the several Huguenot 1709ers who migrated with the German emigrants and settled in colonial N.Y.

A Jean Griot, s/o Thomas Griot de Toussant en la Gallée (Ballé)
de Prajela, md: Marguiritte Girard, d/o Anthoine Girard, on 27
Sept 1688 at the Hanau Wallonische Church. However, a more likely
candidate for the N.Y. 1709er would be one of the two Jean Griots
who sp. Pierre Michelot and Susanne Bruere's child 19 June 1707
at 6331 Daubhausen (HJ); the Brueres and Jean Griot were listed
near each other on the Hunter Lists 1 July 1710. There was a John
Carat aged 16, Ref., mason, in the 4th arrivals in England in
1709 (London Lists); he may have been the N.Y. settler (HJ).

Jean Griot had two listings on the Hunter Rolls: on 1 July
and 4 Aug 1710 with 1 pers. in the family.

ARNOLD GRUCKO (Hunter Lists #253)

The ancestral origins of this family were at 6509 Gau-Odernheim (7 km. n.e. of Alzey; Chbks. begin 1690, Ref.). Arnoldt Kru-
got was called a citizen and joiner there in 1701. Arnold Kriget,
his wife, and 2 ch. were in the 2nd party of Palatines in Holland
in 1709 (Rotterdam Lists). Arnold Crukot aged 42, his wife, a son
aged 2 and a daughter aged 8, Ref., joiner, were in England later
that year (London Lists).

Arnold Grucko made his initial appearance on the Hunter Lists
4 Oct 1710 with 1 pers. over 10 yrs. of age and 2 pers. under 10
yrs. in the household; his last entry with the same numbers was
on 4 Oct 1710. His wife in Germany was called Agnetha, and they
had issue:

1) Apollonia[2], bpt. 18 July 1701 - sp.: Apollonia Hedderich
   - d/o the late Andres Heddrich, formerly miller and Gemeinsmann at Fremersheim under Altzey (Gau-Odernheim
   Chbk.).

JOHANN PETER GRUCKO Orphan (Hunter Lists #254)

Johann Peter Grucko had but one entry on the Hunter Lists on
4 Oct 1710 with 1 pers. over 10 yrs. of age. He may have been related to #253 Arnold Grucko (HJ).

SIMON HAAS (Hunter Lists #255)

The European roots of the Simon Haas family were at 6791
Steinwenden (16 km. w. of Kaiserslautern; Chbks. begin 1684, Ref.),
6791 Neunkirchen a/Potzbach (6 km. further n.; Chbks. begin 1695,
Luth.) and 6751 Sippersfeld (17 km. n.e. of Kaiserslautern; Chbks.
begin 1702, Luth.). Hans Simon Haß, widower from Albsheim auf der
Eys, Linniger (?) Westerb. Herrschaft, md. 15 Aug 1697 Anna Rosina

- d/o Franz Zöller from Makenbach (Mackenbach), both Luth. (Steinwenden Chbk.). Rosina was a sp. from Etschberg at Neunkirchen, 1706.

Simon Haas made his first appearance on the Hunter Lists 4
July 1710 with 2 pers. over 10 yrs. of age and 1 pers. under 10;
the size of the household increased to 2 pers. over 10 yrs. and
2 under 10 on 31 Dec 1710. Symon Haes was in Capt. Van Alstyn's
Co. at Albany in 1715 (Report of the State Historian, Vol. I, p.
464). Symon Hawse was nat. 27 April 1716 (Albany Nats.). Simon
Hass with wife and ch. was at Wormsdorff ca. 1716/17 (Simmendinger
Register). Syms P'r Hees was a Palatine Debtor in 1726 (Livingston
Debt Lists). The ch. of Simon[1] Haas and Anna Rosina were:

1) "A Child"[2], bpt. 20 Sept 1705 - sp.: Philip Dil here,
   Margaretha Catharina - Theobald's ..., and Anna - w/o
   Baltes from Mackenbach (Neunkirchen a/Potzbach Chbk.).
2) Johann Nicolaus[2], born at Breunigweiler and bpt. 25 April
   1707; mother not named in this entry (Sippersfeld Chbk.).
3) Anna Barbara[2], bpt. 10 June 1711 in the upper German colonies - sp.: Anna Barbara Schumacher (West Camp Luth.
   Chbk.). Anna Berbel Simon Haase was conf. Dom. Quasim:
   1726 at Loonenburg (N.Y. City Luth. Chbk.).
4) Zacharias[2], b. 12 Dec 1713 - sp.: Zacharias Flegler and
   wife Eve Anna Elisabetha (West Camp Luth. Chbk.). Zacrias
   Haas was enrolled in Capt. Jeremiah Hogeboom's Co. in 1767
   (Report of the State Historian, Vol. II, p. 864). He md.
   28 Sept 1737 Geesje Witbeek (Albany Ref. Chbk.) and had:
   i) Simon[3], bpt. 18 June 1738 - sp.: Thomas Vlyd and Antje
      Vlydt (Albany Ref. Chbk.). Seyma Haas was in Capt.
      Fraens Claevw Jr.'s Co. in 1767 at Kinderhoeck (Re-
      port of the State Historian, Vol. II, p. 868). He md.
      Jannet Kohl and had issue at Germantown Ref., Linlith-
      go Ref., Kinderhook Ref., and Claverack Ref. Churches.
   ii) Lena[3], bpt. 31 Aug 1740 - sp.: Johannes and Jannetje
       Goewyck (Albany Ref. Chbk.).
   iii) Anna[3], bpt. 1 Aug 1742 - sp.: Lambert Kool and Willem-
        tje Bradt (Albany Ref. Chbk.).
   iv) Anna[3], bpt. 21 Oct 1744 - sp.: Anthony and Willempje
       Brat (Albany Ref. Chbk.).
   v) Catharina[3], bpt. 23 Aug 1747 - sp.: Daniel and Alida
      Marrh (Albany Ref. Chbk.).
   vi) Johannes[3], bpt. 6 Aug 1758 - sp.: Andries Witbeek and
       Maria Herder (Claverack Ref. Chbk.).
   vii) Anna[3], bpt. 12 Aug 1761 - sp.: Jan de la Mettre and
        wife Heyltje Muller (Claverack Ref. Chbk.).
   This couple probably had other ch. 1748-57 (HJ).

5) <u>Johannes</u>[2], b. or bpt. 5 Aug 1716 at Nootenhoeck, Albany;
   bpt. at Klinckenberg - sp.: Justus Falckner the Pastor and
   Anna Catharina Stubber (N.Y. City Luth. Chbk.).

6) <u>Anna Catharina</u>[2], b. 2 Dec 1718 at Nootenhoeck and bpt. at
   Lonenburg - sp.: Jan Jurgen Rau and wife Anna Catharina
   (N.Y. City Luth. Chbk.).

<u>NICLAUS HAAS</u> (Hunter Lists #256)

On most Palatine mss. in their original state, Nicolaus Haas
was surrounded by N.Y. 1709ers, such as Johannes Zeh, Johann Jost
Braun, and Henrich Mattheus, who originated in the Alzey-Oppenheim
region of Germany (HJ). A Johann Nicolaus, s/o Abraham Haass -
soldier 'uff Landskron - and his wife Christina, was bpt. 19 Sept
1677 at St. Katharinen's Ref. Church in Oppenheim; however, his
age is far from the 1664/65 date given on the London Lists (HJ).
There was a Nicolaus Haas and wife Anna Elisabeth who had a son
Johann Conrad b. 29 Dec 1707 at 6763 <u>Obermoschel</u> who bears investigation also (HJ). Nicolaes Hasch, his wife, and 4 ch. were on
Capt. Tomas Wilken's ship in the 3rd party in Holland in 1709 (Rotterdam Lists). Nicol Haas aged 44, his wife, sons aged 7, 4, and
1, a daughter aged 10, Luth., husbandman and vinedresser, were in
the 3rd arrivals in England (London Lists).

Niclaus Haas made his initial appearance on the Hunter Lists
1 July 1710 with 3 pers. over 10 yrs. of age and 3 pers. under 10;
the entry read 3 pers. over 10 and 4 pers. under 10 on 25 March
1712, and then 4 pers. over 10 and 3 under 10 on 24 June 1712.
His wife was named Maria Sabina (--). Maria Sophia Hassin, a
widow with 5 ch., was at Hessberg ca. 1716/17 (Simmendinger Register). A note from Maria Sawena Haas dated 1718 survives in the
Livingston Papers (Reel #3). She was a Palatine Debtor in 1718,
1719 (at Haysberry), and 1721 (Livingston Debt Lists). The ch. of
Nicolaus[1] Haas and Maria Sabina were:

1) <u>Catharina</u>[2] (HJ), md. Georg Schmidt and Philip Launhardt (HJ).

2) <u>Johann Georg</u>[2] (HJ), probably the Hans Georg, s/o Nicolaus
   Haas (mother not named), b. 14 May 1703 - sp.: Hans Georg
   Hoffmann, Gemeinsmann at Eppelsheim (Alzey Chbk.). Hans
   Jury Haas was nat. 16 Dec 1737 (<u>Denizations, Naturaliza-
   tions, and Oaths of Allegiance in Colonial N.Y.</u>, p. 32).
   He first appeared on Rhinebeck tax rolls in 1738/39 (Dutch-
   ess Co. Tax Lists). The administration papers of Hans Jury
   Haas of Rhinebeck Precinct were dated 8 July 1763 (Dutch-
   ess Co. Administration Bk. A). He md. Elisabeth Oliver
   (HJ), and they had issue:

      i) <u>Elisabetha³</u>, b. 15 Jan 1752 - sp.: Colonell Henry
         Beekman and Alida Rutske (Rhinebeck Flats Ref. Chbk.).
     ii) <u>Margaretha³</u>, b. 10 June 1754 - sp.: Thomas Oliver and
         Peggy Oliver (Rhinebeck Flats Ref. Chbk.).
   iii) <u>Johannes³</u>, b. 28 Jan 1757 - sp.: Philip Laundert and
         Catrina Haas (Rhinebeck Flats Ref. Chbk.).

There were other members of the Haas family in colonial N.Y.,
probably later arrivals, such as Georg, Peter, and Caspar Haas
at the Hebron Church in Orange Co., Jacob Haas and wife Maria in
Albany in 1753, and Daniel Haes at Kinderhook in 1770 (HJ).

<u>CHRISTIAN HABER</u> (Hunter Lists #257)
<u>CHRISTIAN HABER'S SISTER ELIZABETH</u> (Hunter Lists #257)

    Christian Haber of Saltzberg in the commune Homburg in Hes-
ten-Castel md. Anna Gertraud, d/o Michael Werner of Rheinfels on
Rhine on 21 Dec 1711 (West Camp Luth. Chbk.). The village of origin was 6431 <u>Salzberg</u> (24 km. n.e. of Alsfeld), records in the
registers of 6431 <u>Raboldshausen</u> (3 km. further n.e.; Chbks. begin
1692). The probable grandfather of the emigrants was <u>Engelhard
Habber</u> who d. 9 April 1699, aged 81 yrs. and nearly 5 months (HJ).
The bpt. of the emigrant Christian Haber took place prior to 1692,
but he probably was the s/o <u>Didymus Haber</u>, as Ditmut Haber, his
wife, and 6 ch. were on Capt. Jno. Untank's ship in Holland in
1709 in the 5th party of Palatines (Rotterdam Lists). The ch. of
Didymus Habber were:
  + <u>Christian</u> (HJ).
    <u>Magdalena</u> (HJ), conf. in 1697, aged 15 yrs., but no parents
    mentioned.
  + <u>Elisabetha</u> (HJ), conf. in 1699, aged 15 yrs., but no parents
    mentioned.
  + <u>Catharina</u> (HJ).
    <u>Johann Henrich</u>, b. at Salzberg and bpt. 26 Jan 1693 - sp.:
    Henrich Schmitt.
    <u>Anna Barbara</u>, b. 21 March 1696 - sp.: Anna Barbara - d/o Hans
    Herman Hönig.
    <u>Johann Adam</u>, bpt. 22 March 1699 - sp.: his cousin Johann Adam
    - s/o ... Mendel.
A Krist Hober was a passenger on Capt. Jno Bouwel's vessel in the
5th party in Holland in 1709 (Rotterdam Lists).

    Christian Haber made his initial appearance on the Hunter
Lists 4 July 1710 with 3 pers. over 10 yrs.; the entry for 24 Dec
1711 read Christian Haber and Sisters. His sister Elizabeth had a
special notation correcting an error in bookkeeping throughout

1712. Christian Haber of Queensbury was a soldier in 1711 (Palatine Volunteers To Canada). Christiaen Haver was nat. 17 Jan 1715/16 (Albany Nats.). Ensign Christeian Haber was an officer in ye Palatin villages in the Albany Co. Militia in ye Mannor of Livingston in 1733 (Report of the State Historian, Vol. I, p. 573). Christian Haver was on tax rolls in the Rhinebeck region 1739/40 to 1741/42 (Dutchess Co. Tax Lists). He was a freeholder in 1763 at East Camp (Albany Co. Freeholders). Administration Papers in the estate of Christian Haver of the Manor of Livingston were issued 5 June 1775 (Genealogical Data from Administration Papers, p. 146). The ch. of Christian[1] Haber and Anna Gertraud were:

1) Peter[2], md. 14 April 1735 Anna Maria Minckeler (Catskill Ref. Chbk.). Papers in the estate of Peter Hawver (Haver?) were issued 1 April 1779 (Genealogical Data from Administration Papers, p. 147). His ch. were:

   i) Christian[3], b. 27 Dec 1737 and bpt. at Teerbosch - sp.: Christian Haber and Gertrud, the grandparents (Loonenburg Luth. Chbk.). He md. Ursula Richter and had ch. bpt. at Linlithgo Ref. and Manorton Luth. Churches (HJ).

   ii) Jacob[3], b. 25 Feb 1740 - sp.: Jacob Scheffer and wife Anna Dorothea (Loonenburg Luth. Chbk.). He md. 14 March 1764 Susanna Richter (Linlithgo Ref. Chbk.) and had ch. bpt. at Linlithgo Ref. and Manorton Luth. Churches (HJ).

   iii) Margaretha[3], b. 3 Feb 1742 and bpt. at Teerbosch - sp.: Kilian Minckler and Margreta (Loonenburg Luth. Chbk.).

   iv) Henrich[3], b. 28 June 1744 - sp.: Henr. Plass and wife Lies. Cath. (Loonenburg Luth. Chbk.). He md. Elsje Kohl and had ch. bpt. at Linlithgo Ref. and Manorton Luth. Churches (HJ). The will of a Hendrick Haver of the Manor of Livingston was dated 10 Dec 1788 and probated 9 March 1789 (Columbia Co. Will Bk. A).

   v) Peter[3], bpt. 5 Oct 1746 - sp.: Peter Philipp and Magdalena Haver (Germantown Ref. Chbk.). He md. Margaretha Reiffenberger and had ch. bpt. at Linlithgo Ref. and Germantown Ref. Churches (HJ).

   vi) Johannes[3], bpt. 11 Oct 1748 - sp.: Johannes Vinger and wife Catharina Hes (Linlithgo Ref. Chbk.). He md. Gertraud Stahl, who d. 18 June 1832, aged 86 (Germantown Ref. Cem.). There were papers issued in the estate of John P. Haver of German Camp District 12 March 1787 (Genealogical Data from Administration Papers,

p. 146).

vii) <u>Hermann</u>[3], bpt. 14 Jan 1752 - sp.: Harmanus Vonk and
Engeltje Minklaer (Linlithgo Ref. Chbk.). He md.
Margaretha Mohr (HJ).

viii) <u>Georg</u>[3], bpt. 24 June 1759 - sp.: Jurry Smidt and
wife Barbara Minkelaer (Linlithgo Ref. Chbk.).

2) <u>Friederich</u>[2], called s/o Christian Haber of Queenbury in
the Camp in Albany Co. when he ran away from his father
17 July 1732, aged 16 yrs. (New York Gazette, 7 Aug 1732).
He was on Rhinebeck tax rolls 1743/44 - June 1748, and
on Northeast rolls Feb 1753 to Feb 1759, when his widow
was listed (Dutchess Co. Tax Lists). F. Haber was indicted
for forceable entry in 1750, and noted again at Rhinebeck
in 1755/56 (Dutchess Co. Ancient Docs. #569, 764, and
3570). He md. Catharina Leick (HJ) and had ch.:

i) <u>Johannes</u>[3], bpt. 26 Jan 1739/40 - sp.: Johannis Luyck
and Anna Barbel Haver (Claverack Ref. Chbk.). He md.
Christina Buys and had ch. bpt. at Red Hook Luth.
and Linlithgo Ref. Churches (HJ).

ii) <u>Friederich</u>[3], bpt. 7 Oct 1741 - sp.: Frederick Propper
and wife Susanna Vorster (Germantown Ref. Chbk.).
He md. Magdalena Buys and had issue at St. Paul's
of Wurtemburg and Rhinebeck Flats Ref. Churches (HJ).

iii) <u>Jacob</u>[3], bpt. 30 Oct 1743 - sp.: Jacob Drom and wife
Margrid (Red Hook Luth. Chbk.). He md. Elisabetha
Reiffenburg and had issue at Gallatin Ref. and Red
Hook Luth. Churches (HJ).

iv) <u>Christian</u>[3], bpt. 22 Feb 1749 - sp.: Christian Haver
Sr. and Gertraut Haver (Germantown Ref. Chbk.). He
md. Elisabeth Lewys (HJ).

v) <u>Abraham</u>[3], bpt. 18 June 1752 - sp.: Arie Buis and wife
Margaret Haber, and Orgel Huiser and wife Catharina
Haber (Germantown Ref. Chbk.). He md. Gertraud Ost-
rander and had ch. bpt. at Red Hook Luth. Church (HJ).

vi) <u>Catharina</u>[3], twin to the above bpt. 18 June 1752 -
sp. same as above (Germantown Ref. Chbk.).

vii) <u>Christina</u>[3], b. 22 Feb 1755 - sp.: Jurrian Hyter and
Christina Haver (Rhinebeck Flats Ref. Chbk.).

viii) <u>Zacharias</u>[3], bpt. 11 Dec 1757 - sp.: Fried: Fees and
wife Cath: Hoff (Germantown Ref. Chbk.).

3) <u>Anna Catharina</u>[2] (HJ), md. Orgel Heiser (HJ). She d. 2 Dec
1804, aged 86 yrs. and 7 months (Germantown Ref. Chbk.).

4) <u>Margaretha</u>[2] (HJ), md. Arie Buys (HJ).

5) <u>Christina</u>[2], b. 12 Jan 1721 at Camp - sp.: Michel Werner

and Christina Moor (N.Y. City Luth. Chbk.). She md. Georg
Peter Heiser (HJ).

6) Magdalena², b. 15 Oct 1722 and bpt. at Camp Queensberry
- sp.: Peter Philipp and wife Magdalena (N.Y. City Luth.
Chbk.).

7) Christian², b. 29 Sept 1726 (and bpt.? - HJ) at Jacob
Schumacher's at Kamp - sp.: Christian Dietericks and wife
Anna Marie (N.Y. City Luth. Chbk.). He md. Engel Reuter
or Van De Werken 16 Feb 1748 (Germantown Ref. Chbk.). They
had ch.:

   i) Christian³, bpt. 1 Jan 1749 - sp.: Christian Haver Sr.
and Gertraut Haver (Germantown Ref. Chbk.).

   ii) Gertraud³, bpt. 2 June 1751 - sp.: Jacob Van De Werken and Maria Ouderkerk (Albany Ref. Chbk.).

   iii) Christian³, bpt. 3 June 1753 - sp.: Joh: Jurry and
Anna Primer (Albany Ref. Chbk.). He may have md.
Margaretha Jacobi (HJ).

8) Barbara², md. as d/o Christian 21 Nov 1749 Henrich Henner
(Heuser? - HJ) (Germantown Ref. Chbk.).

9) Elisabetha², bpt. 3 May 1733 - sp.: Henrich Stoppelbein
and Maria Eliza. Myer (Germantown Ref. Chbk.). She md.
5 Feb 1756 Henrich Seeger (Germantown Ref. Chbk.).

10) Zacharias², b. 30 Jan 1735 - sp.: Zachar: Haber and wife
Anna Constantia (Rhinebeck Luth. Chbk.).

11) Johannes², md. as s/o Christian 29 Nov 1757 Barbara Laurie
(Germantown Ref. Chbk.). They had issue:

   i) Maria³, bpt. 23 Dec 1757 - sp.: ... Lauer (Germantown
Ref. Chbk.).

   ii) Gertraud³, bpt. 4 March 1759 - sp.: Christian Hafer
and Gerdraut Werner (Germantown Ref. Chbk.).

   iii) Christian³, b. 27 March 1761 - sp.: Christ Haber and
E: (Germantown Luth. Chbk.).

   iv) Maria³, bpt. 28 Nov 1762 - sp.: Christoffel Hover and
wife Marytje Lauwries (Germantown Ref. Chbk.).

   v) Elisabetha³, bpt. 10 Feb 1765 - sp.: Henrich Philip
and wife Eva Caspar (Germantown Ref. Chbk.).

   vi) Johannes³, bpt. 1 March 1767 - sp.: Urgel Heiser and
wife Catharina Haber (Germantown Ref. Chbk.).

   vii) Catharina³, bpt. 17 Sept 1769 - sp.: Pieter Phillip
and wife Catharina Heiser (Germantown Ref. Chbk.).

   viii) Christina³, bpt. 20 Oct 1771 - sp.: Georg Pieter Heiser and wife Christina Haber (Germantown Ref. Chbk.).

   ix) Petrus³, bpt. 6 Feb 1773 - sp.: Georg Peter Heiser
and wife Christina Haber (Germantown Ref. Chbk.).

The entry for 24 Dec 1711 mentioned Christian Haber and his sisters; two of the sisters were Elisabetha and Catharina (HJ). Elisabeth Haber joined the N.Y. City Ref. Church 1 Sept 1712 with a certificate from the German preacher stating that her countrymen testified that she had taken part in the Lord's Supper in their country as a member of the Ref. Church. Anna Catrina Haver aged 10, was an orphan bound to Jacob Goelet of N.Y. 18 Oct 1710 (Apprenticeship Lists). Chat Haver md. Thomas Wyllaer 26 June 1722 (Albany Ref. Chbk.); she may have md. again, as Catharina Haver, w/o Jan Pieterssen of N. Albanie, joined the N.Y. City Ref. Church 20 Nov 1733 (HJ).

A Zacharias Haber was a later arrival to colonial N.Y. and related to Christian[1] Haber, as Zacharias sp. Christian in 1735 (Rhinebeck Luth. Chbk.). Zacharias Haber was nat. 22 June 1734 (Denizations, Naturalizations, and Oaths of Allegiance in Colonial N.Y., p. 33). Zacharias md. Anna (Constantia) (Reichardt? - HJ), and he d. 15 Feb 1757 (Germantown Ref. Chbk.).

JOHANN GEORG HÄHN (Hunter Lists #258)

Johann Georg Hähn often was listed near Balthasar Anspach on the Hunter Lists, so Hähn also may have originated like Anspach in the Taunus region near Wiesbaden (HJ). A Georg Hön or Henn was found at 5455 Rengsdorf, home of many other N.Y. 1709ers: Georg Henn, s/o the late Thönges Henn from Wiedt, md. Maria Barbara, d/o Daniel Busch at Wiedt, on Dom. Canate: 1691 (Rengsdorf Chbk.). They had a daughter Maria Gertraut bpt. 1694 (Neuwied Chbk.); however no firm proof exists to show this was the emigrant (HJ). Johan Jürg Haan, his wife and 7 ch. were in the 6th party of Palatines in Holland in 1709 (Rotterdam Lists); however Hans George Hahn with 9 pers. in his family were shipped back to Rotterdam on the ship Martha, Nehemiah Wotton - Commander, 24 Jan 1709/10 (P.R.O. T 1/125, 203, #44B).

Johann Georg Hähn made his initial appearance on the Hunter Lists 4 Oct 1710 with 2 pers. over 10 yrs. of age and 1 pers. under 10 in the household; the family was recorded with 3 pers. over 10 yrs. 29 Sept 1711, and the notation read 3 pers. over 10 yrs. and 1 pers. under 10 yrs. 25 March 1712. Georg Helen: 2 men, 1 woman, and 1 maid 9-15 yrs. were in Ulster Co. in 1710/11 (West Camp Census). Johannis Jury Heyn was nat. 3 Jan 1715/16 (Albany Nats.). Hanss Jurg Kern and Veronica with 5 ch. were at Neu-Cassel ca. 1716/17 (Simmendinger Register). A deposition of Godfrey Fidler dated 6 Oct 1726 mentioned that George Haine met with Sir Wm. Keith and then encouraged his fellow Germans to move to Pa. The

will of George Hen of Lancaster Co. was written in 1743 and proved
8 April 1746 (Philadelphia Co. Will Bk. H, p. 110). Administration
papers in the estate of Fronica Hains, wid. of Heidelberg, were issued 16 July 1756 to her second son Peter Hains and Wilhelm Fischer,
husband of her daughter Elisabetha (Berks Co. Administration Bk.).
The ch. of Johann Georg[1] Hähn and his wife Veronica were:

1) <u>Anna Sibilla[2]</u> (Will).

2) <u>Elisabetha[2]</u> (Will), md. Wilhelm Fischer (Will).

3) <u>Johann Christ[2]</u>, b. 6 April 1713 and bpt. at Albany at the
   house of Evert Jansen - sp.: Johan Christ Gerlach, Joh.
   Jacob Becker, and Maria Margareta Man (N.Y. City Luth.
   Chbk.). Papers in the estate of John Christian Hehn of
   Heidelberg were issued 30 Oct 1772 to his eldest son
   George, the widow Maria Barbara renouncing (Berks Co. Administration Bk.). Berks Co. Orphan's Court records, p.
   96, show the following ch. of Johann Christ(ian)[2]:
     i) <u>Georg[3]</u>.
    ii) <u>Samson[3]</u>.
   iii) <u>Abraham[3]</u>.
    iv) <u>Rosina[3]</u>.
     v) <u>Elisabetha[3]</u>.
    vi) <u>Margaretha[3]</u>.

4) <u>Peter[2]</u> (Will). Berks Co. Orphan's Court records, p. 8,
   noted 10 Aug 1758 that Peter Haine, recently deceased miller of Heidelberg Twp., left the following ch. with his
   widow Barbara:
     i) <u>Johannes[3]</u>, aged 16 yrs.
    ii) <u>Henrich[3]</u>, aged 14 yrs.
   iii) <u>Mark[3]</u>, aged 12 yrs.
    iv) <u>Margaretha[3]</u>, aged 9 yrs.
     v) <u>Susannah[3]</u>, aged 7 yrs.
    vi) <u>Sarah[3]</u>, aged 5 yrs.
   vii) <u>Peter[3]</u>, aged 2 yrs.
  viii) <u>Georg[3]</u>, aged 9 months.

5) <u>Johann[2]</u>, b. 8 Feb 1717 - sp.: Johann Cast, the commissioner (West Camp Luth. Chbk.).

6) <u>Johann Georg[2]</u> (Will).

7) <u>Johann Adam[2]</u> (Will). The will of Adam Haehn of Heidelberg
   was dated 1 July 1773 and probated 5 Oct 1773 (Berks Co.
   Will Bk. II, p. 133). He mentioned wife Magdalena and ch.:
     i) <u>Johannes[3]</u> (Will).
    ii) <u>Anna Maria[3]</u> (Will), w/o Philip Heckert (Will).
   iii) <u>Rosina[3]</u> (Will).
    iv) <u>Elisabetha[3]</u> (Will), w/o Peter Klopp (Will).

      v) <u>Catharina</u>[3] (Will).

     vi) <u>Anna</u>[3] (Will).

    vii) <u>Eva</u>[3] (Will).

  8) <u>Johann Friederich</u>[2] (Will). Papers in the estate of a Frederick Hain were issued to Daniel Hahn in 1812 (Berks Co.
Administration Bk. 7, p. 224).

  9) <u>Johann Henrich</u>[2] (Will).

10) <u>Johann Caspar</u>[2] (Will). Casper Hohn d. 2 Oct 1762, aged 38
yrs. (Hain's Ref. Church Cem., Lower Heidelberg Twp.). The
will of Casper Hains of Heidelberg was dated 21 Aug 1762
and probated 29 Oct 1762 (Berks Co. Will Bk. I, p. 127).
In this old mss. he mentioned his wife Catharina and ch.:

     i) <u>Johannes</u>[3], eldest son (Will).

    ii) <u>Elisabetha</u>[3] (Will).

  iii) <u>Friederich</u>[3] (Will).

   iv) <u>David</u>[3] (Will).

There were other Palatines with names similar to #258 Johann
Georg[1] Hähn. Anna Gertrauda, d/o the late Dietrich Hun of Wallbruhl
in the commune Berg, md. Zacharias Flegler, widower of Wertheim in
Franckeland, 15 Aug 1710 (West Camp Luth. Chbk.). The Hun town of
origin was 5220 <u>Waldbröl</u> (13 km. n. of Wissen; Chbks. begin 1660,
but bad gaps, Cath.). Diederich Hohn was bur. 13 April 1691 there;
he had been md. as Diederich Luther on 'uff St. Johannis' 1684 to
Maria Noiß, and they had a daughter Anna Margaretha bpt. Dom. IV:
1688.

PETER HAGEDORN (Hunter Lists #259)

<u>JOHANN PETER HAGEDORN</u> (Hunter Lists #260)

The German origins of the Hudson Valley Hagedorn family were
at 6200 <u>Wiesbaden/Erbenheim</u> (4 km. e. of Mainz; Chbks. begin 1625,
but large gaps). The earliest known ancestor of the emigrant Peter[1]
was his father <u>Jacob Hagedorn</u>, a wheelwright. He md. Christina (--)
and had issue:

  <u>Maria</u>, bpt. 1638.

+ <u>Peter</u>, bpt. 'uff Pfingsten': 1648.

Peter Hagedorn md. Elisabetha, d/o Christoph Job from Eppstein
(1687 sp.). Elisabetha, w/o Peter Hagedorn, was conf. 22 Nov 1689
and noted as being formerly a Cath. The family had to flee from
Erbenheim to Wiesbaden in 1689 to bpt. a child (Wiesbaden Chbk.).
Peter Sagedoren, his wife, and 5 ch. were on Capt. Robbert Bulman's
ship in Holland in 1709; they were registered near Ananias Tiell
and Johan Salbach, who also were documented at Erbenheim (Rotterdam Lists). Peter Hagedorn aged 60, his wife, sons aged 24, 22,

and 15, daughters aged 17 and 11, Luth., husbandman and vinedresser, were near these same other Erbenheim families in England in 1709 (London Lists).

#259 Peter Hagedorn made his first appearance on the Hunter Lists 1 July 1710 with 7 pers. over 10 yrs. of age in the family. The size changed to 6 pers. over 10 yrs. 4 Oct 1710. Peter Hagedorn was a soldier in 1711 (Palatine Volunteers To Canada). Peter Hagendorn with his wife Elisabetha Catharina and 4 ch. were at Quunsberg ca. 1716/17 (Simmendinger Register). Peter Hagedoorn was a Palatine Debtor in 1718, 1719 (at Kingsberry), 1721 and 1726 (Livingston Debt Lists). Peter Hagendorn was a Palatine willing to remain at Livingston Manor in 1724 (Doc. Hist. of N.Y., Vol. III, p. 724). (Some of the aforementioned data may refer to Johann Peter² Hagedorn - HJ). The ch. of Peter¹ Hagedorn and Elisabetha were:

1) Johann Peter², bpt. 4 Sept 1684 - sp.: Asmus Merthen and Hans Peter Steiger (Erbenheim Chbk.). #260 Johann Peter Hagedorn made his initial appearance on the Hunter Rolls 4 Oct 1710 with 1 pers. over 10 yrs. of age; however, the notation read Johann Peter Hagedorn's wid^W in the Journal and then on 31 Dec 1710 Johann Georg Hagedorn's wid^W, suggesting several potential errors by Hunter's secretary (HJ). Peter Hagadorn was recorded on Dutchess Co. rolls in the Rhinebeck area from 1728/29 to June of 1761 (Dutchess Co. Tax Lists). His signature survives in Reel #4 of the Livingston Papers. A complete list of his ch. was entered in the family book at St. Peter's Luth. Church, Rhinebeck ca. 1734. Johann Peter² md. Anna Barbara (probably the d/o Ferdinand Maenti or Mentgen, as reflected in a 1740 sp. at Rhinebeck Flats Ref. Church - HJ). They had issue:

i) Gertraud³ (St. Peter's Family List), md. Georg Bennet (HJ).

ii) Catharina³ (St. Peter's Family List). Catharina Hagedorn was conf. Dom. 6 Trin: 1737 at Theerbosch (Loonenburg Luth. Chbk.). She md. David Kuhns (HJ).

iii) Anna Barbara³, b. 20 March 1726 and bpt. at Camp - sp.: Christoph Hagedorn and wife Anna Berbel (N.Y. City Luth. Chbk.). She was conf. at Rhynbek 17 June 1744 (Loonenburg Luth. Chbk.) and md. Johann David Bohnenstiel 1 April 1749 (Rhinebeck Luth. Chbk.).

iv) Wilhelm³ (St. Peter's Family List), conf. as Joh. Wilhelm 6 Nov 1743 at Rhynbek (Loonenburg Luth. Chbk.). He md. 24 Nov 1747 Anna Maria, d/o Peter

Treber (Rhinebeck Luth. Chbk.) and d. prior to 8 Feb 1767 when his wid. md. Friederich Schafer (Red Hook Luth. Chbk.).

   v) <u>Elisabetha</u>[3] (St. Peter's Family List).

  vi) <u>Johann Jacob</u>[3], bpt. 1731 - sp.: Johannes Richter, Jacob Pulver, and Anna Elizabeth Simon (Red Hook Luth. Chbk.). He was conf. 15 April 1749, aged 18 yrs. (Rhinebeck Luth. Chbk.). He md. Maria (--). The will of Jacob Hagedorn of Rhinebeck Precinct was dated 22 June 1784 and probated 5 Oct 1784 (<u>Fernow Wills</u>, #869). Jacob Hangadorn d. 23 July 1784, aged 53 yrs. (Rhinebeck Luth. Church Cem.).

 vii) <u>Anna Maria</u>[3] (St. Peter's Family List). She md. Martin Frölich (HJ).

2) <u>Johann Christopher</u>[2], bpt. 6 Feb 1687 - sp.: Johann Nicolaus Gottschalk, single, and Christoph Job from Eppstein - the grandfather of the child (Erbenheim Chbk.). Johann Christoph Hagendorn, s/o Peter Hagendorn, was conf. in 1701, aged 14 yrs. (Erbenheim Chbk.). Cristo Hagedorn of Queensbury was a soldier in 1711 (Palatine Volunteers To Canada). Christophel Hagedorn was nat. 22 Nov 1715 (Albany Nats.). Christoph Hagendorn and Anna Barbara with 1 child were at Quunsberg ca. 1716/17 (Simmendinger Register). Stoffel Hagedorn was a Palatine Debtor in 1718, 1719 (at Kingsberry), 1721, and 1726 (Livingston Debt Lists). He was one of the prime leaders of the Palatines along the Hudson in obtaining their 1724 Patent at Germantown, and was a Palatine willing to remain at Livingston Manor 26 Aug 1724 (<u>Doc. Hist. of N.Y.</u>, Vol. III, p. 724). He was often mentioned by Berkenmeyer in his <u>Albany Protocol</u> (see pp. 41-2, 47, 75, 83, 101, and 162). Jacob and Pieter Hagedorn of Albany Co were called heirs of the late Christophell Hagedorn, late of the Camp, who had a Patent of 6000 acres, on 8 March 1749 (Albany Co. Deeds, Vol. 6, p. 512). The ch. of Johann Christopher[2] and Anna Barbara were:

   i) <u>Johann Jacob</u>[3], md. as s/o Christopher 20 April 1738 at Camp to Maria Barbara Miller (Loonenburg Luth. Chbk.). They had ch. bpt. at Loonenburg Luth., Germantown Luth. and Ref., and Claverack Ref. Churches (HJ).

  ii) <u>Johann Peter</u>[3], md. as s/o Christopher 5 May 1743 Anna, d/o Samuel Miller (Loonenburg Luth. Chbk.). They had ch. bpt. at Schoharie Luth., Germantown

Luth. and Ref., Loonenburg Luth., and Rhinebeck Luth. Churches (HJ).

    iii) Anna Catharina³ (HJ), md. Georg Häner (HJ).

3) Johann Mattheus², bpt. 15 June 1689 after the family fled to Wiesbaden - sp.: Mattheus Birck (Erbenheim Chbk., also in Wiesbaden Chbk.). He was bur. 16 Aug 1689 (Erbenheim Chbk.).

4) Anna Catharina², bpt. 29 Nov 1691 - sp.: Anna Christina Lotz from Dotzheim, and Catharina - w/o the miller from Sperschen (?) (Erbenheim Chbk.). She was conf. at Erbenheim in 1705. She probably md. Johannes Plass (HJ).

5) "A Son"², bur. 1 May 1692 (Erbenheim Chbk.).

6) Johann Wilhelm², bpt. 3 March 1695 - sp.: Wilhelm Gromann (Erbenheim Chbk.). He was nat. 14 Feb 1715/16 (Albany Nats.) and was a Palatine Debtor in 1718/1719 (at Hunterstown) and 1721 (Livingston Debt Lists). He also was willing to continue at Livingston Manor in 1724 (Doc. Hist. of N.Y., Vol. III, p. 724). Reel #4 of the Livingston Papers contains a letter from Wm. Hagedorn dated 1723. Will: Hagedoren was an officer in the Albany Co. Militia of ye Palatin's Villages in ye Mannor of Livingston in 1733 (Report of the State Historian, Vol. I p. 573). He md. Maria Barbara (Dieterich - HJ), who may have been the mother of Christopher Hagedorn who d. 8 Oct 1802 (Churchtown Luth. Chbk.). William Hagedorn was a freeholder at East Camp in 1763 (Albany Co. Freeholders). Issue:

    i) Anna Margaretha³ (St. Peter's Family List), md. 9 Oct 1745 Andreas Müller (Loonenburg Luth. Chbk.).

    ii) Johann Christopher³, b. 25 8br 1728 and bpt. Kamp - sp.: Johan Christopher Hagedorn and wife Anna Barbel (N.Y. City Luth. Chbk.). He md. Anna Maria Louwrie 13 Nov 1752 (Germantown Ref. Chbk.). The will of Christopher Hagadorn of Livingston was dated 11 Sept 1800 and probated 10 May 1803 (Columbia Co. Will Bk. B), and mentioned ch. of his sisters.

    iii) Anna Catharina³ (St. Peter's Family List), conf. with Christ. in 1748 (Loonenburg Luth. Chbk.). She md. Friederich Batz 18 June 1752 (Germantown Ref. Chbk.).

    iv) Johann Jacob³, b. 21 Nov 1734 - sp.: Jacob Beyer and wife Anna Margreta (Rhinebeck Luth. Chbk.).

    v) Anna Barbara³, b. 21 Oct 1738 and bpt. at Teerbosch at Jacob Scheffer's - sp.: Christoffer Hagedorn and wife Anna Barbel (Loonenburg Luth. Chbk.).

    vi) Johann Jacob³, b. 16 Dec 1741 (?) and bpt. 22 March

1742 at Teerbosch (Loonenburg Luth. Chbk.).
7) Maria Gertraud[2], bpt. 30 Nov 1697 - sp.: Maria Agnesa -
w/o Joh. Nicol Merthens, and Gertraut - d/o the former
shepherd Henrich Morbeck (Erbenheim Chbk.). Maria Gerdraut
Hagendorn was conf. 23 March 1712 at Queensberg (West Camp
Luth. Chbk.). She md. Christian Dieterich (HJ).

A Hermann, Dirck, and Samuel Hagedoorn were in the Schenec-
tady/Schoharie area at an early date, but Albany Co. Deeds Vol.
7, p. 449 suggests they were here prior to 1709 (HJ).

JOHANN FRIDERICH HÄGER (Hunter Lists #261)

I have great affection, empathy, and respect for Pastor Jo-
hann Friederich Häger, the Ref. minister of the N.Y. Palatines.
His European origins were at 5902 Netphen (7 km. n.e. of Siegen;
Chbks. begin 1624 or earlier). The father of Pastor Häger was Pfr.
Johann Henrich Häger, who md. Anna Catharina, d/o the late Jacob
Friesenhagen - formerly Burgomaster at Freudenberg 3 Dec 1678
(Siegen Chbk.). Pfr. Johann Henrich Häger eventually came to the
new world himself, leaving from Oberfischbach in the summer of
1713; he d. in Prince William Co., Va. in 1737. (For a scholarly
treatment of the ancestry and descendants of Pfr. Johann Henrich
Häger, I suggest the Ancestry and Descendants of the Nassau-Siegen
Immigrants to Virginia 1714-1750, by B. C. Holtzclaw, Harrisonburg,
Va., 1964). Johann Friederich Häger, s/o Pfr. Johann Henrich Häger
and Anna Catharina, was bpt. 18th Sunday after Trinity: 1684 - sp.:
Monsieur Johann Friedrich Prume, single (Netphen Chbk.). He mat-
riculated 5 July 1703 at the Herborn Paedagogium (Hohe Schule Mss.
#3692, Herborn). Holtzclaw notes that he was examined by the Con-
sistory in Siegen and licensed as a preacher 14 Feb 1708. Upon
agreeing to Anglican ordination by the Bishop of London, he was
appointed by the Society for the Propagation of the Gospel in Foreign Parts to minister to the Palatines (Knittle, p. 143). An
endorsement signed by several Palatine leaders quartered at
the Red House 5 Dec 1709 survives which helped Pastor Hager obtain his position; among the signatories who eventually found their
way to colonial N.Y. were Johann Christ: Gerlach, Hans Jacob Bosch-
aar, Philippus Hermann Lepper, Henrich Bass, Christ: Wormbs, Henrich Charman, and Johan Adolph Artopaeus. Johan Fredrik Heger
headed the list of Palatines in the 6th party at Rotterdam in
1709 (Rotterdam Lists).

Johann Friderich Häger made his initial entry in the Hunter
Lists 29 Sept 1711 with 1 pers. in the household. His letters back
to the Society for the Propagation of the Gospel are so moving, as

they detail Häger's trials and tribulations ministering to his im-
poverished flock (see Ecclesiastical Records of the State of N.Y.,
edited by Hugh Hastings et al., 8 vols., Albany, 1901-1916, for
some of his letters). N.Y. Col. Mss. Vol. 55, p. 29b and 29c, and
Vol. 58, p. 57a contain brief notes from Pastor Häger; the former
deals with the building of a schoolhouse at Queensbury early in
June 1711. Society for the Preservation of the Gospel records show
that Häger bpt. 61 children and md. 101 couples from July 1710 to
July 1712; my dream in life would be to recover Pastor Häger's
long-missing churchbook, which would help clarify certain Palatine
family structures and cement some lines now bound only by strong
circumstantial evidence. The Reverend John Fredrick Hager, Palatine Minister, was nat. 4 Oct 1715 at N.Y. City (Denizations, Naturalizations, and Oaths of Allegiance in Colonial N.Y., p. 33).
Rev. Johann Fridrich Hager, High-German Pastor at Kingsberg, md.
Anna Catharina Rohrbach 13 Nov 1716 (West Camp Luth. Chbk.); she
was the d/o the 1709er Johannes Rohrbach, who perhaps was the Mr.
Rohrbach who bpt. a child of Caspar Brendel on the ship Leon 2
May 1710 according to Kocherthal (HJ). On 26 Sept 1717, Pastor
Häger wrote a letter stating "myn wife is delivert, but the child
is death." (Livingston Papers Reel #3). Dom. Hager was a Palatine
Debtor at Kingsberry in 1719 (Livingston Debt Lists). Johann Fried-
erich Häger d. in 1721 (Luth. Church in N.Y. and N.J. 1722-1760,
p. 9). His widow remarried to Rev. Ogilvie (HJ).

MARIA HÄGERIN (Hunter Lists #262)

The origins of #287 Henrich Häyer and his wife #262 Maria
Hägerin were also at 5902 Netphen. Johann Henrich Häger, s/o Johannes Häger, md. Anna, d/o the late Johann Sibel, 4 Feb 1700;
Anna, w/o Henrich Häger, was bur. 11 Dec 1701. Johann Henrich Häger, a widower at Anzhausen, md. Maria, d/o the late Johannis Jacobi - also from Anzhausen, 19 June 1702.

#287 Henrich Häyer made his initial appearance on the Hunter
Lists 4 July 1710 with 2 pers. over 10 yrs. of age and 1 pers. under 10 yrs.; his last entry was 4 Aug 1710. #262 Maria Hägerin
was noted 4 Oct 1710 with 1 pers. over 10 yrs. and 1 pers. under
10, and her last notations were with 2 pers. over 10 yrs., ending
24 June 1711. The Hunter Ledger recorded that she md. John Muller,
reflected in the Journal entry of 29 Sept 1711. A letter back to
Germany dated 10 July 1749 and written jointly by Anna Maria (Jacobi) Häger and her 2nd husband Johannes Müller mentioned:

> "...we arrived in 1710 in N.Y. after a long and trouble-
> some journey, and then during harvest time my husband d.
> after a short illness, being well at noon and dead in

the eveuing. The infant boy, b. to us in Germany, Henr.
Heger by name, has md. here and has 11 living ch. I
have remarried in 1711. My husband, Johannes Müller by
name, still living in the grace of God, comes from Rüt-
ershausen, district office of Ebersbach, by whom in
peaceful matrimony together we had 5 sons and 3 daughters which the Lord up to this time has kept alive; of
them 4 sons and 2 daughters are md."

Maria Highrin: 1 boy 8 yrs. and under, and 1 woman were in Ulster
Co. in 1710/11 (West Camp Census). The ch. of Johann Henrich[1]
Häger and his wife Anna Maria[1] were:

1) Henrich[2] (1749 letter of Anna Maria[1] Jacobi Häger Müller).
   He probably was the "son", b. to Johann Henrich Häger and
   Maria at Anzhausen and bpt. 23 Dec 1703 - sp.: Johannes
   Jacobi from Anzhausen (Netphen Chbk.). Hendrick Heger was
   nat. 3 May 1755 (Denizations, Naturalizations, and Oaths
   of Allegiance in Colonial N.Y., p. 34). Hendrick Heeger
   was a freeholder at Schoharrie in 1763 (Albany Co. Freeholders). Jeptha R. Simms mentioned him often in his History of Schoharie Co. and Border Wars (pp. 237, 294, 381-
   387), calling him an aged patriot over 70 yrs. in 1777,
   who warned the Schoharie Valley of the Tory menace; he
   eventually was made a prisoner and was cruelly treated
   with tomahawk blows on a forced march. The will of Handrick Hager of Schohary in Albany Co. was dated 13 Sept
   1793 (Schoharie Co. Will Bk. A). He md. Dorothea Kast 1st
   (HJ) and lived with her in the Mohawk region in the early
   yrs. of their marriage (Henry Heger was a Patentee at Burnetsfield on the n. side of the Mohawk 30 April 1725). The
   child of Henrich[2] and his 1st wife Dorothea Kast was:

   i) Anna Maria[3] (Will of Georg Kast, Fernow Wills #971).
      She was conf. 4 Oct 1747 (Schoharie Ref. Chbk.). She
      md. Johann Jacob Meyer (HJ).

   Henrich[2] md. 2nd Gertraud Petri, and they had issue:

   ii) Anna[3], b. Burnetsfield, who had Banns 14 Jan 1756 to
       marry Friederich Becker (Schoharie Ref. Chbk.).

   iii) Jacob[3] (Will), md. 8 July 1764 Cornelia Vroman (Al-
        bany Ref. Chbk.). He d. 21 May 1819, aged 85 yrs.,
        and she d. 29 May 1826, aged 85 (both Hager Cem.,
        N. Blenheim). His obituary in the Albany Gazette
        6 Sept 1819 stated that he served in the French War
        in 1756 and was a Capt. in the revolution (see Simms).

   iv) Johann Jost[3] (Will). Perhaps he was the Johannis Ha-
       ger who served with Jacob Hager in Capt. Thomas Ack-
       eson's Co. in 1767 (Report of the State Historian,
       Vol. II, pp. 845 & 847). A Johannes Heeger, s/o

Henrich, md. 15 Jan 1769 Maria Swart (Schoharie Ref. Chbk.).

  v) Elisabetha[3], b. Burnetsfield, who had Banns to marry Christian Braun 25 March 1760 (Schoharie Ref. Chbk.).

 vi) Peter[3], bpt. 7 March 1746 - sp.: Piter Snyder and Catarin Broekert (Schoharie Ref. Chbk.).

vii) Gertraud[3], bpt. 10 Jan 1747/48 - sp.: Hendrick Coenraad and wife Margarith (Schoharie Ref. Chbk.). She md. Mattheus Braun in Jan 1771 (Schoharie Ref. Chbk.).

viii) Sarah[3], b. 5 Nov 1749 - sp.: Johannes Finck and wife Maria Eva (Schoharie Ref. Chbk.). She md. Jost Borst 7 July 1776 (Schoharie Luth. Chbk.).

  ix) Henrich[3], perhaps the un-named child bpt. 3 May 1751 (Schoharie Ref. Chbk.). He md. Maria Larroway (HJ).

   x) David[3], b. 14 Oct 1753 - sp.: Jeorg Henderch Snyder and Maria Snyder (Schoharie Ref. Chbk.).

  xi) Dorothea[3], b. 27 July 1756 - sp.: Philip Freymäuer and Maria Elisabeth Yorck (Schoharie Luth. Chbk.). She md. Johannes Mattheus in March 1775 (Schoharie Ref. Chbk.).

 xii) Eva[3] (Will), md. Conrad Mattheus (HJ).

xiii) Delia[3] (Will) md. Jonas Vroman (HJ).

 xiv) Catharina[3] (Will), md. (--) Vennes (Will).

Due to gaps in the Mohawk Valley registers, the order of birth of the ch. of Henrich[2] may be different than written above (HJ).

2) "A Daughter"[2], b. at Anzhausen and bpt. 17 Jan 1706 - sp.: Maria Elisabeth - d/o Henrich Jung at Anzhausen (Netphen Chbk.).

There were several unplaced Hägers in colonial N.Y. A Dorothea Heegerin joined the Schoharie Ref. Church 4 Oct 1747 with Anna Maria Heegerin. Petrus Heger or Hoger md. Anna Maria Helmer at the Falls in June 1750 (Sommer's Journal in the Schoharie Luth. Chbk.).

URBANUS HAINTZ (Hunter Lists #263)

The ancestral roots of the Haintz family were at 6719 Ilbesheim near Kirchheimbolanden (6 km. s. of Alzey; Chbks. begin 1682, but gaps, Luth.). Urban Heintz was a Luth. resident there in 1698 (Alzey Census of 1698). Anna Eva, w/o Urban Heinz, was bur. 17 Dec 1706, aged 37 yrs.

Urbanus Haintz made his initial appearance on the Hunter Lists 4 Aug 1710 with 3 pers. over 10 yrs. of age. The size of the family increased to 3 pers. over 10 yrs. and 1 pers. under 10 yrs. on 24 June 1711. Urban Heintz and his son were at Hackensack ca. 1716/17 (Simmendinger Register). Maria Apollonia, wid/o Urbanus Hents md. Paulus Tenkelbag (Dinckelbach) 2 Sept 1723 (N.Y. City Ref. Chbk.). By his 1st wife, Urbanus[1] Haintz had issue:

1) Maria Margaretha[2], d. 24 April 1701, aged 8 yrs. (Ilbesheim Chbk.).

2) Johann Peter[2], conf. as s/o Urban Heinz 1708 (Ilbesheim Chbk.). Johann Peter Hents md. 14 Sept or Oct 1718 Maria Apollonia Berger (N.Y. City Luth. Chbk.). Issue:

   i) Maria[3], b. Fall of 1720 in the Highland and bpt. in N.Y. - sp.: Andreas Birger and wife Maria Agatha (N.Y. City Luth. Chbk.).

   ii) Johann Peter[3], b. in middle June and bpt. 4 Sept 1723 at Philippsburg near the farthest mill at the house of David Sturm (N.Y. City Luth. Chbk.).

   iii) Andreas[3], bpt. 24 June 1727 - sp.: Andries Berger and wife Barber (Tarrytown Ref. Chbk.).

   iv) Petrus[3], b. Dec 1730 and bpt. N.Y. - sp.: Herman Wagener and sister Dina Wagener, and in the father's place Caspar Hartwig (N.Y. City Luth. Chbk.).

On some entries above, the w/o Johann Peter[2] was called Clara.

3) Johann Nicolaus[2], d. 7 June 1707, aged 6 yrs., 6 months, 2 weeks, and 2 days (Ilbesheim Chbk.).

4) Johann Adam[2], bpt. as twin 25 Dec 1703 - sp.: Johan Adam Prem (Ilbesheim Chbk.). He d. 28 June 1704, aged 6 months, 3 days (Ilbesheim Chbk.).

5) Maria Susanna[2], bpt. as twin 25 Dec 1703 - sp.: Maria Susanna Geier of Ilbesheim (Ilbesheim Chbk.). She d. 1 Jan 1704, aged 6 days old (Ilbesheim Chbk.).

By his wife Maria Apollonia he had issue:

5) Maria Elisabetha[2], b. the later part of Aug 1714 at Philippsburg, N.Y. - sp.: Quirinus Nidhebber and wife (N.Y. City Luth. Chbk.). Maria Elisabeth Heins was conf. 24 May 1735 (N.Y. City Luth. Chbk.).

6) Johann Henrich[2], b. 31 Oct 1716 in Westchester Co. - sp.: Joh: Henrich Gessinger and wife Anna Elisabeth (N.Y. City Luth. Chbk.). Henrich, Reinhard and Jacob Häns were on Pastor Sommer's List of Schoharie Luth. families ca. 1744. Hendrick Heins was a freeholder at Schoharrie in 1763 (Albany Co. Freeholders). The will of Hendrick Hens of New Dorlough, Co. of Montgomery, was dated 10 Sept 1789 (Schoharie Co. Will Bk. A). He md. Elisabeth Rickert 8 March

1748 (Schoharie Luth. Chbk.). They had ch.:

   i) Jacob[3], b. 7 Dec 1748 - sp.: Jacob Häns and his wife (Schoharie Luth. Chbk.). He d. 4 March 1832, aged 83 yrs. (Haynes Farm Cem., Fulton, Schoharie Co.).

   ii) Eva[3], b. 24 March 1750 - sp.: Lorentz Lawyer and his wife (Schoharie Luth. Chbk.). She md. Georg Thompson 12 Nov 1769 (Schoharie Luth. Chbk.).

   iii) Rebecca[3], b. 3 May 1752 - sp.: Johannes Braun and his wife (Schoharie Luth. Chbk.). She md. Johannes Schäffer 24 Jan 1773 (Schoharie Luth. Chbk.).

   iv) Henrich[3], b. 18 May 1754 - sp.: Henrich Schäfer and his wife (Schoharie Luth. Chbk.). He md. Sophia Borst 24 May 1774 (Schoharie Luth. Chbk.).

   v) Marcus[3], b. 26 May 1756 - sp.: Marx Rickert and Elisabeth Bellinger (Schoharie Luth. Chbk.).

7) Johann Reinhardt[2], b. 25 Sept 1718 at Philippsburg and bpt. N.Y. - sp.: Johann Reinhard Haus and wife Anna Elisabeth (N.Y. City Luth. Chbk.). He md. Anna Mercki 11 Feb 1752 (Schoharie Luth. Chbk.) and had issue:

   i) Elisabetha[3], b. 27 Aug 1753 - sp.: Henrich Merki and his wife (Schoharie Luth. Chbk.). She may have been the Elisabeth Heens who md. John Berry 8 Feb 1774 (Schoharie Luth. Chbk.).

   ii) Jacob[3], b. 21 Nov 1755 - sp.: Jacob Merckel and Cath: Ingold (Schoharie Luth. Chbk.). He md. Christina Merckle 10 Nov 1776 (Schoharie Luth. Chbk.).

Anna Merki, wid/o Reinhard Heens, md. John Gerner 20 Nov 1766 (Schoharie Ref. Chbk.).

8) Johann Jacob[2], b. 17 Nov 1721 at Philippsburg and bpt. N.Y. - sp.: Johan Jacob ... and wife Magdalena (N.Y. City Luth. Chbk.). He md. 28 Oct 1746 Anna, d/o Ludwig Rickert (Schoharie Luth. Chbk.) and had ch.:

   i) Maria[3], b. 2 March 1748 - sp.: Henrich Häns and wife (Schoharie Luth. Chbk.). She d. 9 July 1748, aged 3 months, 6 days (Schoharie Luth. Chbk.).

   ii) Adam[3], b. 5 Aug 1749 - sp.: Ludwig Rickert and wife (Schoharie Luth. Chbk.).

   iii) Catharina[3], b. 6 July 1751 - sp.: Marx Rickert and Catharina Ingold (Schoharie Luth. Chbk.). A little girl of Jacob Häns d. 1 Aug 1753 (Schoharie Luth. Chbk.).

   iv) Eva[3], b. 17 Feb 1753 - sp.: Johannes Becker and Anna Maria Rickert (Schoharie Luth. Chbk.). A little girl of Jacob Häns d. 7 July 1754 (Schoharie Luth. Chbk.).

v) <u>Urbanus</u>[3], b. 5 Dec 1754 - sp.: Christian Bauch and his wife (Schoharie Luth. Chbk.).

vi) <u>Elisabetha</u>[3], b. 16 Feb 1757 - sp.: Michel Freymauer and Elisabeth Rickert (Schoharie Luth. Chbk.).

vii) <u>Ludwig</u>[3], b. 18 March 1759 - sp.: Ludwig Schneider and Catharina Rickert (Schoharie Luth. Chbk.). He md. Margaretha Vroman 17 Oct 1784 (Schoharie Luth. Chbk.).

viii) <u>Anna</u>[3], b. 15 Nov 1762 - sp.: Conrad Rickert and wife (Schoharie Luth. Chbk.).

A Peter Heen and wife Anna Elisabetha Luckenbach were in the Schoharie area from 1753; as I can find no family connective between this Peter Heen and the Urbanus Haintz family, he was probably the Peter Heen nat. 20 March 1762, thus a later arrival (HJ). I also see no connection between Urbanus Haintz's family and the William Hains of Cobleskill, whose administration papers were probated 20 Feb 1781 (<u>Genealogical Data from Administration Papers</u>, p. 138).

JOHN WILHELM HAMBUCH (Hunter Lists #264)

Johann Wilhelm Hanbuch, widower of Nider Biber in the commune of Neuwid, md. Anna Catharina, wid/o Johann Peter Lutt of Wald-Lebersheim near Bingen in the earldom of Schomburg, 2 July 1717 (West Camp Luth. Chbk.). The village of origin was actually 5450 <u>Niederbieber</u> (3 km. n. of Neuwied; Chbks. begin 1655). The father of the emigrant 1709er was <u>Bernhard Hambuch</u>, who d. 1 April 1701; his wid. Elsa (Elisabetha) d. 10 Jan 1704, aged 70 yrs. and more. They had two sons:

<u>Johann Christophorus</u>, bpt. 17 June 1660 - sp.: Christopf Stürtz - new citizen at Oberbieber, Johannes Antonius - s/o Johannis Bell the sexton at N.B., and Vraigen - d/o Theiss ...

+ <u>Johann Wilhelm</u>, bpt. 27 Oct 1662 - sp.: Johann Christoffel Wagner, Eva - d/o Michel Theis from N.B., Joh. Wilhelm Schleumer from Bunnesfeldt, and Ursula - w/o Peter from ...

Johan Wilhelm Hambuch, soldier of Rheinfels from Nider biber in the Grafschaft Neuen Wiedt, and Elisabeth, wid/o the master-bricklayer Matthias Perlett, had their marriage proclaimed 1 July 1683 (St. Goar Ref. Chbk.).

John Wilhelm Hambuch made his initial appearance on the Hunter Lists 1 July 1710 with 2 pers. over 10 yrs.; on 31 Dec 1710 the entry read 2 pers. over 10 and 1 under 10, and on 24 Dec 1711 the notation added 3 over 10 yrs. before going back to 2 over 10 on 25 March 1712. Jno Wm. Hambuch was a soldier in 1711 from Haysbury (Palatine Volunteers To Canada). Johan Wm. Hambough was nat.

17 Jan 1715/16 (Albany Nats.). Wilhelm Hanbruch a widower was at
Hessberg ca. 1716/17 (Simmendinger Register). Wm. Hombugh was a
Palatine Debtor in 1718 and 1719 (at Haysberry) (Livingston Debt
Lists). Willm Hanbuch was a Palatine willing to remain at Livings-
ton Manor 26 Aug 1724 (Doc. Hist. of N.Y., Vol. III, p. 724).
Catharina Hanbuch was called the wife's mother in the family of
Carl and Maria Ottilia Danerly ca. 1734 (St. Peter's Luth. Family
List, Rhinebeck).

JOHANN HENRICH HÄMER (Hunter Lists #265)

Johann Henrich Hämer was noted near other 1709ers who originated in the Neuwied/Westerwald region on originals of the Hunter
Lists, such as Ferdinand Mentgen, Christian Dietrich, Johann Wilhelm Dahles, and Andreas Hoff (HJ). The marriage of one Joh: Henrich Hömmer and Maria Magdalena (--) was found at 5419 Dierdorf
in the year 1691, and he may have been the emigrant (HJ).

Johann Henrich Hämer made his initial appearance on the Hunter Lists 1 July 1710 with 4 pers. over 10 yrs. of age in his family; the entry decreased to 3 over 10 4 Aug 1710, increased to 4
again 4 Oct 1710, and then to 4 over 10 and 1 under 10 24 June
1711. The 1st 24 Dec 1711 notation recorded 5 pers. over 10 yrs.
of age, while the 2nd 24 Dec 1711 cumulative entry read 4 pers.
over 10 yrs.; all the 1712 entries read 4 pers. over 10 yrs. and
1 pers. under 10 yrs. Henr. Hammer of Haysberry was a soldier in
1711 (Palatine Volunteers To Canada). The ch. of Johann Henrich[1]
Hämer were:

1) Anna Catharina[2] (HJ), md. Adam Hoff (HJ).
2) Elisabetha Catharina[2] (HJ), the Elisabetha Catharina Semerin next to Maria Christina Semerin and near Johann Adam
   Hoff and wife Anna Catharina ca. 1716/17 at Hessberg (Simmendinger Register). She md. Georg Löscher 2 Feb 1726
   (N.Y. City Luth. Chbk.).
3) Maria Christina[2] (HJ), md. Jost Bernhardt (HJ).

PETER HAMM (Hunter Lists #266)

The Simmendinger Register ca. 1716/17 listed Peter Hamen,
Conrad Hamen, and Caspar Hamen next to each other, followed a few
names later by Martin Buch with the wid/o Nicolaus Hamen; thus a
relationship between all these Hudson Valley Hamms seems most probable (HJ). So far, their European origins have escaped firm detec-
tion. Hans Peter Hamm, with a Volpert and Hans Velten Hamm, were
recorded at 6509 Schornsheim (Alzey Census of 1698); this family
probably was at 6524 Guntersblum also, as Volpert Hamm's brother

Johann Peter Hamm was a sp. there (no date). A Hans Niclas Hamm,
s/o Hans Peter Hamm from Baumholder, md. Anna Maria Rauschkolben
14 Feb 1699 at 6719 (?) Großbockenheim.

Peter Hamm made his first appearance on the Hunter Lists 30
June 1710 with 2 pers. over 10 yrs. and 1 pers. under 10; the size
diminished to 1 pers. over 10 yrs. and 1 pers. under 10 on 29 Sept
1711, then increased to 2 pers. over 10 yrs. and 1 under 10 on 25
March 1712. The 24 June 1712 notation read 2 pers. over 10 yrs.
and 2 pers. under 10 yrs. Peter was often near Conrad and Caspar
Hamm on the Hunter Lists; the entry on 25 March 1712 added Peter
Hamm and Andr: Bergman's Wid[W]. Peter Ham was nat. 28 Feb 1715/16
(Albany Nats.). Peter Hamen and Anna Maria Christina Sibylla with
3 ch. were at Quunsberg ca. 1716/17 (Simmendinger Register). Peter
Ham was a Palatine Debtor in 1718, 1721, and 1726 (Livingston
Debt Lists). He was a Palatine willing to continue at Livingston
Manor 26 Aug 1724 (Doc. Hist. of N.Y., Vol. III, p. 724). The ch.
of Peter[1] Hamm and Anna Catharina Sibylla were:

1) Anna Catharina[2], b. 1 Sept 1714 - sp.: Niclaus Schmid and
   Anna Catharina Rohrbach (West Camp Luth. Chbk.).

2) Caspar[2] (HJ), md. Anna Barbara Richter (HJ). Caspar Ham
   was assessed in Rhinebeck from 1744 through June 1748
   (Dutchess Co. Tax Lists). He had issue:

   i) Anna Catharina[3], bpt. 17 Aug 1740 - sp.: Pieter Ham
      and Anna Catharina (Linlithgo Ref. Chbk.).

   ii) Andreas[3], bpt. 12 Dec 1742 - sp.: Andries Richter and
       Elizabeth Stahl (Red Hook Luth. Chbk.).

   iii) Anna[3], bpt. 25 Aug 1745 - sp.: Pitter Ham and Anna
        Magdalena Richter (Red Hook Luth. Chbk.). She md.
        Arie Boys (HJ).

   iv) Johannes[3], bpt. 6 March 1748 - sp.: Johannes Richter
       and Lisabeth (Germantown Ref. Chbk.).

   v) Elsgen[3], bpt. 25 Dec 1750 - sp.: Andreas Richter and
      wife An Els (Red Hook Luth. Chbk.).

   vi) Petrus[3], bpt. 24 April 1753 - sp.: Petrus Jager and
       Elisabeth Michel (Red Hook Luth. Chbk.). He md. Cath-
       arina Stahl (HJ).

   vii) Henrich[3], bpt. 23 Nov 1755 - sp.: Henrich Stahl and
        Anna Margretha Jager (Red Hook Luth. Chbk.). He md.
        Eva Bitzer (HJ).

   viii) Elisabetha[3], bpt. 11 March 1759 - sp.: Andreas Rich-
         ter and Maria Elies: Richter (Red Hook Luth. Chbk.).

   ix) Jacob[3], b. 25 May 1761 - sp.: Jacob Fries and Cath-
       arina (Rhinebeck Luth. Chbk.).

     x) <u>Anna Maria</u>³, a twin bpt. 27 May 1764 - sp.: Adam Bizer
and Anna Maria Richter (Red Hook Luth. Chbk.).

    xi) <u>Anna Margaretha</u>³, a twin bpt. 27 May 1764 - sp.: Han-
nes Richter and Lisabeth Simon (Red Hook Luth. Chbk.).

3) <u>Anna Maria</u>², b. 11 April 1720 at Queensberry and bpt. East
Camp - sp.: Jacob Scherp and Anna Maria Scherp (N.Y. City
Luth. Chbk.). She probably md. Samuel Taylor (HJ).

4) <u>Anna Barbara</u>², b. 18 Nov 1722 at Queensberry and bpt. Camp
- sp.: Jacob Schumacher and wife Barbara (N.Y. City Luth.
Chbk.). She md. Andreas Mohr (HJ).

5) <u>Johann Peter</u>², b. 18 Jan 1726 - sp.: Johann Peter Philip
and his wife Catharina (West Camp Luth. Chbk.). The will
of Peter Ham Sr. of Livingston Manor was dated 2 July 1791
and probated 3 Jan 1795 (Columbia Co. Will Bk. A). He md.
1st Maria Deickmann and had issue:

     i) <u>Casparus</u>³, bpt. 14 Jan 1752 - sp.: Casparus Ham and
Barbara Rechter (Linlithgo Ref. Chbk.).

    ii) <u>Helletje</u>³, bpt. 31 May 1753 - sp.: Pieter Kreim and
Helletje Diekman (Germantown Ref. Chbk.).

   iii) <u>Johannes</u>³, bpt. 7 Aug 1754 - sp.: Coenraet Ham, Jr.
and Debora Beeckman (Linlithgo Ref. Chbk.).

    iv) <u>Catharina</u>³, bpt. 4 April 1756 - sp.: Samuel Deeler
and wife Maria Hamm (Germantown Ref. Chbk.).

     v) <u>Maria Christina</u>³, bpt. 26 June 1757 - sp.: Jac. Pul-
ver and wife Maria Christina Bernhardt (Germantown
Ref. Chbk.).

Peter Ham, widower of the Camp, md. 27 March 1758 Catharina
Laurie, wid/o the late Johannes Leik of the Camp (Germantown Ref. Chbk.). They had ch.:

    vi) <u>Petrus</u>³, bpt. 11 Jan 1761 - sp.: Pieter Vosberg and
wife Dorothe Knickerbacker (Linlithgo Ref. Chbk.).

   vii) <u>Georg</u>³, bpt. 24 July 1763 - sp.: Jurry Best and Maria
Madlena Hooft (Linlithgo Ref. Chbk.).

  viii) <u>Jeremiah</u>³ (Will).

    ix) <u>Maria</u>³ (Will), may be Maria Christina above (HJ).

CONRAD HAMM (Hunter Lists #267)

Conrad Hamm made his initial appearance on the Hunter Lists
30 June 1710 with 2 pers. over 10 yrs. of age in the household.
The family increased to 3 pers. over 10 yrs. 4 Aug 1710, and then
to 3 pers. over 10 yrs. and 1 under 10 yrs. 31 Dec 1710. The reading was 3 pers. over 10 yrs. 24 June 1711 and 29 Sept 1711, when
Conrad and Caspar Hamm were listed together in one entry. On 24
Dec 1711, the family size was reduced to 2 over 10 yrs, and on

24 June 1712 the roll noted 2 pers. over 10 yrs. and 1 pers. under
10 in the household. Coenraet Ham was on the roll of the independent companie of the Mannor of Livingston 30 Nov 1715 (Report of
the State Historian, Vol. I, p. 522). Coenraet Ham was nat. 17
Jan 1715/16 (Albany Nats.). Conrad Hamen and Rahel with 3 ch. were
at Quunsberg ca. 1716/17 (Simmendinger Register). Coonrodt Ham
was a freeholder in Northpart Livingston in 1720 (Albany Co. Freeholders). Coenradt Ham was a Palatine Debtor in 1718, 1719, 1722,
and 1726 (Livingston Debt Lists). Conrad[1] md. Rachel Rohrbach (HJ)
and had issue:

1) Martin[2], md. as s/o Conrad 8 June 1736 Margaretha, d/o
Friederich Maul (Loonenburg Luth. Chbk.). They had ch.:

   i) Johannes[3], bpt. 6 March 1737 - sp.: Johannes Maul and
   Geertje Snyder (Kingston Ref. Chbk.). He md. 1st
   Catharina Bender, who d. 1770, aged 27 yrs. (Gallatin
   Ref. Cem.). Johannes[3] md. 2nd Catharina Schneider,
   who d. 1815, aged 68 yrs.; Johannes[3] d. in 1810, aged
   74 yrs. (both Gallatin Ref. Cem.). He had ch. bpt.
   at Gallatin Ref., Manorton Luth., Red Hook Luth.,
   Rhinebeck Luth., and Linlithgo Ref. Churches (HJ).

   ii) Anna Catharina[3], bpt. 21 May 1739 - sp.: James Ochelbie and Catharina Ochelbie (Red Hook Luth. Chbk.).

   iii) Rachel[3], b. 28 May 1741 and bpt. Teerbosch - sp.:
   Conrad Ham and Rahel, grandparents (Loonenburg Luth.
   Chbk.). She md. Johannes Kupper (HJ).

   iv) Friederich[3], bpt. 12 Feb 1744 - sp.: Frederick Ham
   and Cattarina Ham (Rhinebeck Flats Ref. Chbk.). He
   md. Maria Schmidt (HJ); he d. 1825, aged 83 yrs., and
   she d. 1825, aged 77 yrs. (Gallatin Ref. Cem.). They
   had ch. at Gallatin Ref. and Catskill Ref. Churches
   (HJ).

   v) Anna[3], bpt. 19 Jan 1746 - sp.: Jan Hoogteeling and
   Jannietie Kool (Rhinebeck Flats Ref. Chbk.). She
   possibly md. Veit Roschmann (HJ).

   vi) Elisabetha[3], bpt. 26 Sept 1748 - sp.: Frederich Streid
   and Catharina Maul (Rhinebeck Flats Ref. Chbk.). She
   md. Jacob Roschmann (HJ) and d. 23 Dec 1849, aged 100
   yrs. (Hudson Rural Repository, 5 Jan 1850).

   vii) Jacob[3], bpt. 7 Aug 1754 - sp.: Jacob Ham and Christina Ham (Linlithgo Ref. Chbk.).

   viii) Maria[3], bpt. 19 June 1757 - sp.: Hendrick Miesick and
   Catharina Diderich (Linlithgo Ref. Chbk.).

   ix) Christina[3], bpt. 14 Nov 1761 - sp.: Coenrad Ham and
   Christina Strydt (Claverack Ref. Chbk.).

x) Petrus³, bpt. 20 March 1763 - sp.: James Van Deusen
and wife Lisabeth Smidt (Linlithgo Ref. Chbk.). Peter
M. Ham d. 1844, aged 81 yrs. (Gallatin Ref. Cem.).

2) Wendel² (HJ), joined the N.Y. City Ref. Church 20 Aug 1744.
He md. 5 May 1741 Maria Romer (N.Y. City Ref. Chbk.) and
was made a freeman of N.Y. City 6 Dec 1741, called a baker
(N.Y. Hist. Soc. Collections, Vol. 18). The will of Wandle
Ham, baker - formerly of N.Y. City but at present Manor
of Livingston, was dated 6 Sept 1790 and probated 9 Dec
1800 (Columbia Co. Will Bk. B). Issue:
   i) Conrad³ (Will), a resident of N.Y. City in 1790 Will).

3) Henrich² (HJ) md. Eva Henn (HJ). They had issue:
   i) Conrad³, bpt. 19 May 1745 - sp.: Coenraet Ham and
   Rachel (Linlithgo Ref. Chbk.).
   ii) Jacob³, bpt. 19 Feb 1747 - sp.: Jacob Hamm and Catharina Ham (Germantown Ref. Chbk.).
   iii) Wendel³, bpt. 30 July 1749 - sp.: Daniel Reiffenberger
   and Elizabeth (Germantown Ref. Chbk.).
   iv) Henrich³, bpt. 6 Jan 1751 - sp.: Hendrick Smith and
   Elisabeth Millers (Linlithgo Ref. Chbk.).
   v) Tiel³, bpt. 20 March 1753 - sp.: Tiel Rockvel and
   wife (Germantown Ref. Chbk.). He d. 6 Dec 1830, aged
   77-8-8 (Livingston Cem.).
   vi) Anna Margaretha³, bpt. 8 Oct 1755 - sp.: Marthen Hamm
   and Margareth Maul (Germantown Ref. Chbk.).
   vii) Christina³, bpt. 6 July 1757 - sp.: Coenraed Ham and
   Christina Ham (Linlithgo Ref. Chbk.).
   viii) Catharina³, bpt. 20 Jan 1760 - sp.: Philip Bartel and
   wife Cathrina Ham (Linlithgo Ref. Chbk.).
   ix) Friederich³, bpt. 15 July 1764 - sp.: Frederick Ham
   and Eva Finkel (Linlithgo Ref. Chbk.). He d. 7 May
   1842, aged 77-10-27 (Lawyersville Cem., Schoharie
   Co.).

4) Friederich² (HJ), d. 24 November 1785 at Washington Hollow
near Millbrook in the town of Washington, Dutchess Co.
(letter from Ralph E. Boyce to David K. Martin). He md.
Catharina Streit (Straight), who d. 22 May 1805, bur. with
her husband. They had issue:
   i) Rachel³, bpt. 1 Aug 1749 - sp.: Casper Ham and Greit
   Streid (Rhinebeck Flats Ref. Chbk.).
   ii) Friederich³, bpt. 30 Jan 1751 - sp.: Frederik Stryt
   and Cathrina Stryt (Rhinebeck Flats Ref. Chbk.).
   iii) Catharina³, b. 13 March 1753 - sp.: Frederik Stryt
   and wife (Rhinebeck Flats Ref. Chbk.).

    iv) Anna Maria³, b. 13 Aug 1755 - sp.: Johannes Akkert and Anna Maria Stryt (Rhinebeck Flats Ref. Chbk.).

    v) Conrad³, bpt. 20 Nov 1757 - sp.: Conradt Hamm and Christina Streit (Red Hook Luth. Chbk.).

    vi) Caspar³, b. 16 Oct 1762 (Rhinebeck Flats Ref. Chbk.).

    vii) Elisabetha³, bpt. 19 May 1765 - sp.: Ludewig Streit and Rahel Ham (Red Hook Luth. Chbk.).

5) Caspar² (HJ), md. 1750 Margaretha Streit (Linlithgo Ref. Chbk.). Ralph E. Boyce mentioned that Caspar Ham was a surveyor for Robert Livingston and was killed in a boundary dispute in 1757 (Letter from David K. Martin). Issue:

    i) Catharina³, bpt. July 1751 - sp.: Frederick Strydt and Catharina Strydt (Linlithgo Ref. Chbk.).

    ii) Rachel³, b. 22 Sept 1753 - sp.: Conrad Ham and his wife (Schoharie Luth. Chbk.).

    iii) Christina³, bpt. 27 Nov 1755 - sp.: Conradt Hamm and Christina Hamm (Germantown Ref. Chbk.).

    iv) Magdalena³, bpt. 11 Sept 1757 - sp.: Friderik Strydt and wife Catharina Maul (Linlithgo Ref. Chbk.).

6) Johann Conrad², bpt. 13 Feb 1726 - sp.: Coenrad Petri and Maria Kette (Linlithgo Ref. Chbk.). The will of Conrad Ham of Schodack was dated 14 March 1806 and proved 25 Feb 1808 (Rensselaer Co. Will Bk. 3). He md. Christina Streit (HJ) and had issue:

    i) Friederich³, bpt. 16 Sept 1759 - sp.: Frederik Stryt and wife Catharina Maul (Linlithgo Ref. Chbk.). He d. 10 Feb 1845, aged 85 yrs. and 5 months (Nassau-Schodack Cem.).

    ii) Catharina³, bpt. 6 Oct 1763 - sp.: Jacob Ham and Cathrina Smidt (Linlithgo Ref. Chbk.).

    iii) Conrad³, bpt. 1766 - sp.: Marten Ham and wife Grietje Maul (Linlithgo Ref. Chbk.).

    iv) Anna³, bpt. 10 April 1768 - sp.: Fyt Rosman and wife Annatje Ham (Linlithgo Ref. Chbk.).

    v) Christina³, bpt. 17 June 1770 - sp.: Niclaes Smith and wife Christina Ham (Linlithgo Ref. Chbk.).

    vi) Magdalena³, b. 3 May 1773 - sp.: Denus Schmidt and Debeita (Manorton Luth. Chbk.).

    vii) Anna Maria³, bpt. 14 June 1775 - sp.: Ludwig Strd: and wife Anna Maria Felder (Linlithgo Ref. Chbk.).

    viii) Caspar³, bpt. 29 April 1781 (Linlithgo Ref. Chbk.).

    ix) Elisabetha³ (Will).

7) Jacob², md. as s/o Conrad 27 Nov 1755 Catharina Schmidt (Germantown Ref. Chbk.). They had ch.:

   i) Margaretha³, bpt. 19 Sept 1756 - sp.: Michel Smith
      and wife Grietje Heyser (Linlithgo Ref. Chbk.).

  ii) Conrad³, bpt. 15 July 1759 - sp.: Coenraed Ham and
      wife Christina Strydt (Linlithgo Ref. Chbk.).

 iii) Magdalena³, bpt. 1 Jan 1762 - sp.: Niclaes Smith and
      Magdalena Smith (Linlithgo Ref. Chbk.).

  iv) Rachel³, bpt. 1 April 1764 - sp.: Fredrick Ham and
      Rachel Ham (Linlithgo Ref. Chbk.).

   v) Christina³, bpt. 25 Jan 1767 - sp.: Niclaes Smit and
      wife Christina Ham (Linlithgo Ref. Chbk.).

  vi) Elisabetha³, bpt. 15 April 1769 - sp.: James Van Deu-
      sen and wife Lisabet Smit (Linlithgo Ref. Chbk.).

 vii) Anna³, also bpt. 15 April 1769 - sp.: Fyt Rosman and
      wife Annatje Ham (Linlithgo Ref. Chbk.).

viii) Michael³, bpt. 3 May 1772 - sp.: Michel Schmit and
      Marytjen Schmidt (Germantown Ref. Chbk.).

8) Tabitha², bpt. as Davida 25 April 1731 - sp.: Georg Ror-
   bach and Davida Rorbach (Katsbaan Ref. Chbk.). She d. 27
   June 1810 and her husband Augustinus Smith d. 27 Aug 1810
   (Nassau Cem.).

9) Catharina² (HJ), joined the Germantown Ref. Church with
   Jacob and Conrad Ham 17 April 1747. She md. Robert Van
   Deusen (HJ).

10) Christina², b. 14 Dec 1733 - sp.: Rupert Von Di(se) and
    wife Christina (Rhinebeck Luth. Chbk.), md. Nic: Smit (HJ).

11?) Elisabetha², md. Henrich Reiffenberger on 21 May 1765
    (Linlithgo Ref. Chbk.). She either belongs here, or as a
    d/o Henrich² and Eva Henn (HJ).

Caspar Ham, nat. at Albany 14 Feb 1715/16, probably was a
brother to Conrad¹, since he appears with Conrad on the Hunter List
29 Sept 1711 (HJ). Caspar Hamen, unmd., was at Quunsberg ca. 1716/
17 (Simmendinger Register). A map of the Manor of Renselaerwick
made in 1767 noted the dwelling of Casper Ham in what is now East
Schodack (Doc. Hist. of N.Y., Vol. III). He md. Anna Leip (sometimes written Leych or Leyb) 21 Oct 1721 (Albany Ref. Chbk.). Issue:

1) Johannes², bpt. 20 Feb 1723 - sp.: Jan and Rebecka Maassen
   (Albany Ref. Chbk.).

2) Catharina², bpt. 29 Nov 1724 - sp.: Casp. Leyb and Sara
   Gardenier (Albany Ref. Chbk.). She md. Henrich Schans (HJ).

3) Gertraud², bpt. 23 Feb 1726 - sp.: Jan and Agnietie Witbeek (Albany Ref. Chbk.). She joined the Kinderhook Ref.
   Church as w/o Albert Dingmanse 7 Oct 1757.

4) Petrus², bpt. 16 March 1729 - sp.: Petrus Ham and Cath.
   Leyth (Albany Ref. Chbk.). On 27 May 1768, a marriage

license was issued to Petrus Ham and Maria Mitchel, both
of the Colonie (Albany Ref. Chbk.). The will of Peter Ham
of Schodack was proved 24 Feb 1808 (Rensselaer Co. Will Bk.
3).

5) <u>Maria²</u>, bpt. 10 Sept 1732 - sp.: L. Schreydel and H. Schey-
ldel (Albany Ref. Chbk.).

As always, David Kendall Martin of Mouse Hill, West Chazy,
N.Y. was helpful by sharing his data on this complicated family.

GERTRUDE HAMMIN, ZACHAR: FLUGLER'S WIFE (Hunter Lists #268)

Even the secretaries who wrote the Hunter Lists appear to
have confused Gertraud Höhn (Huen, Hahn) who md. Zacharias Flegeler
with Maria Gertraud Hammin who md. Martin Buck (HJ). Although
#268 was called Zachar: Flugler's wife in the Ledger section of
the Hunter Lists, she firmly was noted as Maria Gertrud Hamin
and Martin Buck 4 Oct 1710, both next to Conrad Hamm and Peter
Hamm, in the Journal section. Martin Buch with Nicolaus Hamen's
widow and 2 ch. were at Quunsberg ca. 1716/17 (Simmendinger Register); they were recorded but four names from Peter, Conrad, and
Caspar Hamen on this list (HJ).

See pg. 318 for more on the German background of Gertraud
Höhn Flegeler.

JOHANN NICLAUS HÄRTER (Hunter Lists #269)

An un-named child was bpt. 4 Dec 1681 to Johannes Hürter
from Dreyfelden at 5419 <u>Rückeroth</u>. The prime bpt. sp. to this event
was Nicolaus Weserdt; however no firm proof exists which shows this
child was the emigrant 1709er, even though later-arriving Härters
originated in this lovely area of the Westerwald (HJ). Friedrich
R. Wollmershäuser discovered a Pfalz Generalia Huldigung dated
1690; one Nicklaus Hörter was enrolled that year at 6906 <u>Leimen</u>,
home of Georg Kast, a 1709er who also went to the Mohawk Valley,
and he merits future study (HJ).

Johann Niclaus Härter made his initial appearance on the Hunter Subsistence Lists 1 July 1710 with 3 pers. over 10 yrs. of age
and 2 pers. under 10 yrs. in the family; he was noted just one
name (Peter Philipp) away from Johann Michael Härter on that date.
The family size increased to 4 pers. over 10 yrs. and 2 under 10
4 Aug 1710. The household dwindled to 2 pers. over 10 yrs. 24 June
1711. On 29 Sept 1711 Niclaus Härter's widow was recorded with 1
pers. over 10 yrs. and 1 under 10 yrs. Anna Härterin was listed
on the cumulative 24 Dec 1711 entry. Their son was:

1) <u>Lorentz²</u> (HJ), nat. as Lawrence Herder 28 Feb 1715/16 (Albany Nats.). Lawrence Herter and Appolone Herter were each
   Patentees on the s. side of the Mohawk River 30 April 1725
   (Burnetsfield Patent). The will of Lorentz Herther of Burnetsfield in Tryon Co. was dated 1 July 1776 and recorded
   28 May 1792 (Herkimer Co. Will Bk. A). The old Herrther
   family Bible survived and noted that Lorentz Herrther was
   b. 14 Oct 1698 and his wife Abolinia (Apollonia) was b.
   30 (--) 1702; because of Härter - Helmer associations in
   later generations and because the name Philip has come down
   in the Härter family, I believe that Apollonia Härter, w/o
   Lorentz², may have been the Anna Apolonia, d/o Philip Helmer and wife Elisabetha Möckler, bpt. 30 March 1703 at
   6730 <u>Neustadt an der Weinstraße</u> (HJ). The ch. of Lorentz²
   and Apollonia Härter were:

     i) <u>Johann Nicolaus³</u>, b. 25 Aug 1723 (Bible).
    ii) <u>Johann Friederich³</u>, b. 8 Nov 1726 (Bible).
   iii) <u>Philip³</u>, b. 13 Nov 1729 (Bible).
    iv) <u>Henrich³</u>, b. 17 Feb 1731 (Bible).
     v) <u>Catharina³</u>, b. 2 April 1733 (Bible).
    vi) <u>Anna Margaretha³</u>, b. 13 (--) 1735 (Bible).
   vii) <u>Elisabetha³</u>, b. 29 July 1737 (Bible).
  viii) <u>Maria Barbara³</u>, b. 9 Oct 1740 (Bible).
    ix) <u>Lorentz³</u>, b. 26 Dec 1742 (Bible).

<u>The Mohawk Valley Harters and Allied Families</u>, by Marion Kof-
mehl and Hazel Patrick is a fine addition to Palatine genealogy
and recommended.

JOHANN MICHAEL HÄRTER (Hunter Lists #270)

Johann Michael Härter was recorded first on the Hunter Lists
on 1 July 1710 with 3 pers. over 10 yrs. of age and 3 pers. under
10 yrs. in the household; he was listed next to Johann Niclaus
Härter 4 Oct 1710. The family was noted with 2 pers. over 10 yrs.
and 3 pers. under 10 on 31 Dec 1710, with 3 pers. over 10 and 2
under 10 on 25 March 1711, with 4 pers. over 10 and 1 pers. under
10 on 24 June 1711, and with 4 pers. over 10 yrs. and 2 pers. under 10 yrs. on 24 Dec 1711. Michel Herder was nat. 17 Jan 1715/16
(Albany Nats.). Michael Harter's widow with 4 ch. was listed (next
to Peter Philipp once again) at Quunsberg ca. 1716/17 (Simmendinger Register). Jacob Eschwyn, widower at Claverack, md. 27 Nov
1720 Maria Herderin, wid. at Queensberry (N.Y. City Luth. Chbk.).
The ch. of Johann Michael¹ Härter and his wife were:

1) <u>Johann Peter²</u> (HJ), md. Elisabetha Thomas (HJ), perhaps

a relative of the Anna Eva Thomas who sp. a child of Johann Fridrich Bell with Johann Michael[1] Herder in 1712
(West Camp Luth. Chbk.). The ch. of Johann Peter[2] were:

   i) Michael[3] (HJ), who's wife Agnes Dieterich joined the
      Germantown Ref. Church in 1755. The will of Michael
      Harder of German town was dated 28 Jan 1796 and pro-
      bated 6 Aug 1801 (Columbia Co. Will Bk. B).

  ii) Maria[3], b. 5 Nov 1734 - sp.: Jacob Escherman and wife
      Maria (Rhinebeck Luth. Chbk.).

 iii) Jacob[3], bpt. 14 Nov 1736 - sp.: Jacob Philip and Antje
      Schans (Germantown Ref. Chbk.).

  iv) Christina[3], bpt. 24 Jan 1739 - sp.: Pieter Fonk and
      Elisabeth Thomas (Linlithgo Ref. Chbk.).

   v) Adam[3], bpt. 17 Aug 1740 - sp.: Machiel Herder and
      Hilletje Hardick (Linlithgo Ref. Chbk.). He md. Engel
      Kuper 6 Dec 1768 (Germantown Ref. Chbk.).

  vi) Eva[3], b. 23 March 1743 and bpt. Camp - sp.: Jacob
      Best and wife Catharina (Loonenburg Luth. Chbk.).
      She md. Nicolaus Schuch or Shaver 19 Feb 1767 (Ger-
      mantown Ref. Chbk.).

 vii) Elisabetha[3], bpt. 14 June 1746 - sp.: Elisabeth Bauer
      (Germantown Ref. Chbk.). She md. Adam Rath (HJ).

viii) Jacob[3], bpt. 8 April 1748 - sp.: Jacob Harter and
      Maria (Germantown Ref. Chbk.). He md. Catharina Thomas
      1 Dec 1767 (Germantown Ref. Chbk.).

  ix) Johannes[3], mentioned in will of Michael[3] above.

   x) Peter[3], bpt. 1 Feb 1755 - sp.: Pieter Syperli and
      Antje Schans (Linlithgo Ref. Chbk.).

2) Jacob[2], md. as s/o Michael 3 Aug 1738 Maria Van Hoesen
(Loonenburg Luth. Chbk.). He md. 2nd Catalyna De Lamater
27 June 1777, who was probably the Catlina Herder of Claverack who's will was probated 9 Nov 1801 (Columbia Co.
Will Bk. B). The will of Jacob Herder of Hudson, yeoman,
was probated 8 Aug 1799 (Columbia Co. Will Bk. B). Issue
of Jacob[2] and 1st wife Maria were:

   i) Maria[3], b. 18 Dec 1738 - sp.: Francis Herdyk and wife
      Anna Maria (Loonenburg Luth. Chbk.). She md. Joris
      Decker (Will).

  ii) Jan[3], b. 20 Oct 1740 - sp.: Arend Becker and wife
      Catharina (Loonenburg Luth. Chbk.). He md. Magdalena
      Maul 11 Sept 1768 (Linlithgo Ref. Chbk.). Jan, Michel,
      and Peter Herder were in Capt. Jeremiah Hogeboom's
      Co. in 1767 (Report of the State Historian, Vol. II,
      p. 864).

iii) Michael³ (Will).

  iv) Peter³, bpt. 7 July 1745 - sp. Pitter Herder and Elisa Kattrina Herder (Red Hook Luth. Chbk.). He md. Margaretha Everts (HJ).

   v) Jannetje³, b. 5 Aug 1747 - sp.: Niclas Van Hoesen, in his place Casper Willemse Halenbek and wife Sara (Loonenburg Luth. Chbk.). She md. Cornelius Müller 22 April 1768 (Linlithgo Ref. Chbk.).

  vi) Jacob³, bpt. 25 March 1750 - sp.: Jan Lammatere and Heyltje Muller (Claverack Ref. Chbk.).

 vii) Nicolaus³, bpt. 18 June 1752 - sp.: Willem Philip and wife Eva Schertz (Germantown Ref. Chbk.).

viii) Jacob³, bpt. 23 Nov 1754 - sp.: Jan De Lamater and Hillitje Muller (Claverack Ref. Chbk.).

  ix) Elisabetha³, bpt. 11 April 1757 - sp.: Samuel Halenbeek and wife Jannetje Van Hoesen (Claverack Ref. Chbk.). She md. Glaudey D'Lmater (Will).

   x) Nicolaus³, bpt. 26 April 1760 - sp.: Zacharias Haes and Sara Valkenaer (Claverack Ref. Chbk.).

3) Michael² (HJ), md. as s/o Joh: Herder 28 June 1740 Hilletje Hardick, d/o Jan Herdyk (Loonenburg Luth. Chbk.). Issue:

   i) Maria³, b. 14 June 1741 - sp.: Jacob Herder and wife Maria (Loonenburg Luth. Chbk.).

  ii) Jan³, b. 3 Aug 1743 - sp.: Francis Jans Herdyk and wife Marytje (Loonenburg Luth. Chbk.). John M. Herder d. 11 Sept 1835, aged 92-1-8, and his wife Commerche (Hoes) d. 1 Nov 1828, aged 78-4-23 (Claverack Ref. Cem)

 iii) Michael³, bpt. 1746 - sp.: Wendel E and Grettie Herdigh (Claverack Ref. Chbk.). He d. 18 June 1828, aged 83 yrs. (Claverack Ref. Cem.). He md. Cath: Schmidt.

  iv) Hilletje² , b. 24 Sept 1748 - sp.: Leysnaar Van Hoesen and Antje (Loonenburg Luth. Chbk.).

Hilletje Herdik Herder d. 24 Sept 1748 (Loonenburg Luth. Chbk.). Michael² then md. Maria Rees (HJ). The will of Michael Herder of Claverack was dated 15 Jan 1794 and probated 10 Oct 1795 (Columbia Co. Will Bk. A). Issue from 2nd marriage:

   v) Benjamin³, bpt. 26 Aug 1752 - sp.: Benjamin Rees and Geertruy Witbeek (Albany Ref. Chbk.). He d. 5 March 1833, aged 81, formerly of Claverack - now of Delhi, Delaware Co. (Hudson Rural Repository 6 April 1833).

  vi) Maria³, bpt. 5 April 1756 - sp.: Benjamin B. Rees and Maria Herder (Albany Ref. Chbk.).

 vii) Gertraud³, bpt. 16 July 1758 - sp.: Willem Bartel and

wife Geertruy Rees (Claverack Ref. Chbk.).

   viii) <u>Hilletje</u>[3], bpt. 23 Nov 1760 - sp.: Hendrick Bresie
and wife Cathrina Rees (Claverack Ref. Chbk.).

    ix) <u>Lyntje</u>[3], bpt. 13 March 1763 - sp.: Charles Smith and
wife Margriet Essewyn (Claverack Ref. Chbk.).

     x) <u>Sophia</u>[3], bpt. 20 Oct 1765 - sp.: David Brouwer and
Tanneke Rees (Linlithgo Ref. Chbk.).

    xi) <u>Lydia</u>[3], bpt. May 1768 - sp.: Dirk Muller and Margriet
Hardick (Claverack Ref. Chbk.).

   xii) <u>Georg</u>[3] (Will).

  xiii) <u>Peter</u>[3] (Will).

  4) <u>Wilhelm</u>[2] (HJ), d. 5 Sept 1750 (Germantown Ref. Chbk.).

There were later-arriving Härters from the Westerwald, such
as Johann Philip Härter and wife Elisabetha Gertraud (HJ).

JOHANN HERMANN HARTMAN (Hunter Lists #271)

The German home of this Hartmann family was 6344 <u>Ewersbach</u>
(11 km. n. of Dillenburg; Chbks. begin 1635). The earliest known
forefather of the emigrant was <u>Hermann Hartmann Sr.</u> He md. a Margaretha (--) and had issue:

+ <u>Johann Hermann</u>.

"A Daughter", bpt. 19 Oct 1673 - sp.: Jost Hartmann at Ebersb.
and Magdalen - d/o the late Johan Henrich at Rütt.

<u>Jost</u>, b. 10 May 1677 - sp.: Jost Schäfer and Catharina - d/o
Johannis Ebert at Rütt.

"A Son", b. 4 Sept 1680 - sp.: Johs. Schäfer, and Elsbeth -
w/o Daniel Eckert, both at Rütt.

Hans Hermann, s/o Hermann Hartmann and Anna Margaretha, md. Ann,
d/o Hans Georg Eckert and Magdalena, 24 Nov 1689; both families
were from Rüttershausen. Hans Hermann Hartmann, his wife, and 2
ch. petitioned to leave Rittershausen in 1709 (Nassau-Dillenburg
Petitions).

Johann Hermann Hartman made his initial appearance on the
Hunter Lists 1 July 1710 with 2 pers. over 10 yrs.; the size increased to 2 pers. over 10 and 1 pers. under 10 24 June 1711. Huns
Harmen Hartmän was nat. 8 and 9 Sept 1715 (Kingston Nats.). Hanss
Hermann Hartmann and Anna with 1 child were at Beckmansland ca.
1716/17 (Simmendinger Register). A letter back to Germany dated
1749 from Johannes Müller of Ewersbach mentioned that (--) Hartmann was deceased. Pastor Stoever bpt. a child of a Herman Hartman at Monocacy in 1740, but no known connection to the N.Y. family has been established (HJ). The ch. of Johann Hermann[1] Hartmann and his wife Anna were:

1) "A Daughter"², b. 29 Dec 1690 - sp.: the d/o Johannes Eckert and Magdalen - d/o Hermann Hardtmann, all at Rüttersh.
   (Ewersbach Chbk.).

2) "A Daughter"², b. 16 Dec 1692 - sp.: Andreas - s/o Hans
   Georg Eckert, Anna Maria - d/o Johann Eckert, and Elsche
   - d/o Hans Georg Kun..., all there (Ewersbach Chbk.).

3) "A Son"², b. 21 June 1694 - sp.: Hans Georg - s/o Daniel
   Giese, Thomas - s/o Hans Gorg Möller, and Immel - d/o Conrad Christ, all at Rüttersh. (Ewersbach Chbk.). Due to the
   prime bpt. sp., this child may have been the Hans Jurie
   Hortman who sp. Joh. Conrad Miller and Anna Maria Ekkert
   (both of Ewersbach) in 1710 at N.Y. City Ref. Church (HJ).

4) "A Son"², b. 24 Oct 1696 - sp.: Daniel Eckers, Johann Jost
   Hartmann, and Elsche - d/o Johannis Eckert (Ewersbach
   Chbk.).

5) "A Son"², b. 8 July 1699 - sp.: Johann Conrad Möller and
   Anna Maria - w/o Jacob Orth (Ewersbach Chbk.).

6) "A Son"², b. 21 Jan 1704 - sp.: Johannes - s/o Johannes
   Henrich, Hans Hinrich - s/o Johannis Möller, and Agnes -
   d/o Hans Georg Eckert (Ewersbach Chbk.).

PETER HARTTMANN (Hunter Lists #272)

As Peter Hartmann was recorded often on the Hunter Lists near
other 1709ers (i.e. Christian Streith and Georg Volbert Schmidt)
who originated in the Nassau - Kirberg region, perhaps he was the
Hans Peter, s/o Henrich Hartmann, bpt. 14 Sept 1662 - sp.: Hans
Martin Keyser, Hans Peter Hartmann, and Maria Lyss - w/o Johannes
Röder from Nastätten, at 5429 Holzhausen a/d Haide in the heart
of this area (HJ).

Peter Harttmann made his initial appearance on the Hunter Lists
30 June 1710 with 2 pers. over 10 yrs. and 1 under 10; the entry
read 2 pers. over 10 on 25 March 1711 and then 1 pers. over 10 yrs.
on 24 June 1711.

ANNA MARIA HARTTMÄNNIN (Hunter Lists #273)

Anna Maria, wid/o Conrad Hartman, md. Johann Michael Wagelin
of Bohnfeld in Craichgau 26 July 1710 (West Camp Luth. Chbk.).
There were two different Conrad Hartmanns in the 3rd party at Rotterdam and the 3rd arrivals at London; one of these families was
returned to Holland in 1709 (HJ).

Anna Maria Harttmännin first was enrolled on the Hunter Lists
30 June 1710 with 1 pers. over 10 yrs.; her last entry was 4 Aug
1710 with 1 pers. over 10 yrs. of age.

342

CASPAR HARTWIG (Hunter Lists #274)

Kasper Hartwig, his wife, and 3 ch. were in the 2nd party in Holland in 1709 (Rotterdam Lists). Caspar Hartwig aged 38, his wife, sons aged 5 and 4, a daughter aged 7, Ref., baker, were in the 2nd arrivals in England later that year (London Lists).

Caspar Hartwig made his initial appearance on the Hunter Rolls 4 Aug 1710 with 2 pers. over 10 yrs. and 3 under 10 yrs. The entry changed to 3 pers. over 10 yrs. and 2 under 10 yrs. 24 June 1711, showed 2 over 10 and 2 under 10 on 25 March 1712, and then went back to 3 pers. over 10 yrs. and 2 under 10 yrs. on 24 June 1712. Caspar Hartwig aged 39, Anna Eliz Hartwig aged 39, Johan Bernhard Hartwig aged 8, Johan Lorentz Hartwig aged 6, and Magdalena Hartwig aged 10, were in N.Y. City in 1710/11 (Palatines In N.Y. City). They sp. Nicolaus Passen (Bason) in 1716 (Somerville Ref. Chbk.). Caspar Hartwig and his wife with 3 ch. were auf dem Rarendantz ca. 1716/17 (Simmendinger Register). He was called a kinsman to Henry and Jacob Millbagh in 1724 (Indentures of Apprentices 1718-27, p. 165). Caspar Hartwich, widower, md. Catharina Folpert, wid/o Pauly Wagenaar, 18 May 1726 (N.Y. City Ref. Chbk.). Issue from 1st wife:

1) Magdalena² (Palatines In N.Y. City).
2) Johann Bernhard² (Palatines In N.Y. City). He sp. Michael Moor in 1729 (Harlingen Ref. Chbk.). Bernhard (Barend)² md. a Maria (--) and had ch.:
   i) Elisabetha³, bpt. 24 Feb 1734 (New Brunswick Ref. Chbk.).
   ii) Johannes³, bpt. 16 Feb 1735 (New Brunswick Ref. Chbk.).
   iii) James³, bpt. 20 March 1738 (New Brunswick Ref. Chbk.).
   iv) Joanna³, bpt. 15 June 1741 (New Brunswick Ref. Chbk.).
   v) Tice³, bpt. 26 June 1743 - sp.: Tice and Debera Sollom (New Brunswick Ref. Chbk.).
3) Johann Lorentz² (Palatines In N.Y. City). Lawrance Hartwick was mentioned in the ledgers of a colonial store in N.J. in 1736 (Janeway Account Books).

ADAM HARTTWELL - HÄRTTEL (Hunter Lists #275)

Adam Hertel, widower of Georg Town of Liferspach near Heppenheim, md. Gertraud, wid/o Johann Waiden of Wallwig in the duchy of Nastau-Dillenburg, 26 June 1716 (West Camp Luth. Chbk.). The Hertel home was actually Nieder-Liebersbach (15 km. n.e. of Mannheim), entries for this village in registers of 6943 Birkenau (3 km. further s.; Chbks. begin 1690). Adam Härtel md. Eva, wid/o Wendel Kopp, 13 Nov 1694; Hans Wendel Kopp had d. 29 Jan 1693, aged 31 yrs. Eva, w/o Adam Hartel at Unter Liebersbach, d. 27 April

1708, aged 54 yrs. and 9 weeks. Adam Härtel, widower from Unter Liebersbach, md. Anna Margaretha, d/o the late Hans Dußler (?) from Rimbach, 18 Sept 1708. Adam Herdel, his wife and 1 child were on Capt. John Sewell's ship in the 4th party of Palatines in Holland in 1709 (Rotterdam Lists). Adam Hertel aged 44, his wife, a daughter aged 14, Luth., husbandman and vinedresser, were in the 4th arrivals in England in 1709 (London Lists).

Adam Harttel made his initial appearance on the Hunter Lists 30 June 1710 with 3 pers. over 10 yrs. of age in the family; the household increased to 3 pers. over 10 yrs. and 1 under 10 yrs. on 25 March 1711. Adam Hardel: 1 man, 1 boy aged 8 and under, 1 woman, and 1 maid aged 9 to 15 were in Ulster Co. in 1710/11 (West Camp Census). Adam Hertile was nat. 8 and 9 Sept 1715 (Kingston Nats.). He was a member of Berkenmeyer's church council in 1735 (Albany Protocol, p. 115). Issue from 1st wife Eva:

1) Elisabetha², b. 25 Nov 1695 at Liebersbach - sp.: Elisabeth auf dem Kerschhäuser Hoff (Birkenau Chbk.). She was conf. as a d/o Adam Härtel at Liebersbach Dom. Quasimodogeniti: 1708, aged 13 yrs. (Birkenau Chbk.). She md. Georg Beem 14 Nov 1719 (Kingston Ref. Chbk.).

His 2nd wife Anna Margaretha donated a white cloth for use at church services in Dec 1715 (West Camp Luth. Chbk.). With her, he had ch.:

2) Maria Elisabetha², b. 31 Aug 1712 - sp.: Elisabetha Catharina Backus and Maria Elisabeth (--) (West Camp Luth. Chbk.). A child of Adam Hertel d. in 1713 (West Camp Luth. Chbk.).

3) Eva Maria², b. 9 Jan 1715 - sp.: Hieronymus Weller and Maria Klein (West Camp Luth. Chbk.). Eva Maria Herteln was conf. 24 Feb 1731 at Newton (N.Y. City Luth. Chbk.). She md. Johann Dieterich Matestock 4 Jan 1736 (Loonenburg Luth. Chbk.).

4) Johannes² (HJ), conf. 1 April 1733, aged 15 yrs. (Loonenburg Luth. Chbk.). The Kingston Trustees Records mentioned Johannis Hertel in Bk. 2, pp. 194 & 195. Joh: Herdel of West Camp deeded land to Harmanus Beer in 1749/50 (Albany Co. Deeds, Vol. 7, p. 336). He md. Regina (--) (HJ) and had ch.:

   i) Petrus³, b. 21 Jan 1754 - sp.: Dieterich Matestock and Eva Maria (Loonenburg Luth. Chbk.).

   ii) Johannes³, b. 3 Dec 1755 - sp.: Johannes Falk and Gertruyd Hertel (Loonenburg Luth. Chbk.). A John Hartle Sr. was a U.E.L. who lived in Cornwall, Ontario (Loyalists of Ontario, p. 142).

iii) Adam[3], b. 20 Dec 1757 - sp.: Adam Matestok, Catharina
Maurer, in their place Wilhelmus Rau and the child's
mother (Loonenburg Luth. Chbk.). An Adam Hartle of
Cornwall, Canada was a U.E.L. (Loyalists Of Ontario,
p. 141).

iv) Elisabetha[3], b. 4 Feb 1760 - sp.: Wilhelmus Falk and
Greetje (Loonenburg Luth. Chbk.).

WILHELM HÄSEL (Hunter Lists #276)

William Hessel aged 22, Ref., husbandman and vinedresser, was
in the 3rd arrivals in England in 1709 (London Lists).

Wilhelm Häsel made his first appearance on the Hunter Rolls
4 Aug 1710 with 1 pers. over 10 yrs. of age in his family. Wilhelm Hess and his wife were at Hackensack ca. 1716/17 (Simmendinger
Register). Willem Hessel, single man b. Germany, had banns to marry
Angenitie Kammegaer (Kammega), single woman b. N. Utrecht, 17 March
1716 (Hackensack Ref. Chbk.). Wilm Hese md. 2nd 9 Sept 1727 Geert-
jen Pietersen, single woman (Hackensack Ref. Chbk.). Issue from
his 1st marriage:

1) Anna Maria[2], bpt. 6 Jan 1719 - sp.: Hendrik Kammega and
wife Margrita (Hackensack Ref. Chbk.).

2) Henrich[2], bpt. 20 May 1722 - sp.: Barnardus Verveele and
wife Titie (Hackensack Ref. Chbk.).

JOHN HENRICH HÄSELIN (Hunter Lists #277)

Johann Henrich Häselin made his initial appearance on the
Hunter Lists 1 July 1710 with 1 pers. over 10 yrs. of age in the
household; his last entry was dated 4 Oct 1710 with the same recordation.

DIETRICH HASSMANN (Hunter Lists #278)

Dietrich Hassmann made his initial appearance on the Hunter
Lists 4 July 1710 with 2 pers. over 10 yrs. of age. The family
size increased to 2 pers. over 10 yrs. and 1 under 10 on 4 Oct
1710, then diminished to 2 pers. over 10 yrs. on 31 Dec 1710. The
family increased yet again 29 Sept 1711 when 2 pers. over 10 yrs.
and 1 pers. under 10 yrs. were registered. Theodoric Hassman of
Haysbury was noted in an old mss. dated 1712 (N.Y. Colonial Mss.,
Vol. 58, p. 48j or 48k). His wife was named Anna Eulalia, and sp.
strongly suggest she md. Johannes Bernhardt after Dieterich[1] Hassmann's death (HJ). The child of Dieterich[1] Hassmann was:

1) Anna Maria[2], bpt. Aug 1710 at N.Y. - sp.: Anna Maria Hausmann (West Camp Luth. Chbk.).

PHILIPP HAÜPT (Hunter Lists #279)

The European origins of the Haupt family were at 6348 <u>Herborn</u>
(8 km. s. of Dillenburg; Chbks. begin 1638) and at 6349 <u>Fleisbach</u>
(4 km. further s.; Chbks. begin 1647). The earliest known antecedent of the emigrant was also a <u>Philipp Haupt</u>. Henrich Haupt, s/o
Philipp Haupt from Atzbach im Ampt Gleiberg (near Wetzlar), md.
Anna Catharina, d/o Hans Enders of this village, 21 Nov 1654 (Fleisbach Chbk.). Anna Catarina, w/o the smith Henrich Haupt, was bur.
4 Advent: 1658 (Fleisbach Chbk.). Henrich Haupt, widower here, md.
Sophia, d/o Philips Peter from Fleisbach, 15 Nov 1659; Henrich
Haupt d. 10 March 1672, and Sophia, wid/o the late Hinrich Haupt,
d. 2 Feb 1681 (all from Fleisbach Chbk.). Ch. of <u>Henrich Haupt</u> by
his 2nd wife were:

+ "A Son", bpt. Friday after 22 Trin: 1660 - sp.: Philips Cuntz
  and Anna - w/o Hermannus Teis (Fleisbach Chbk.).
  "A Son", bpt. ... Trin: 1664 - sp.: Johann Henrich Wissenbach
  - son of the Pfarrer, Johann Hermannus, and Gein - d/o the
  late Philip Peters (Fleisbach Chbk.).
  "A Son", bpt. XIX Trin: 1666 - sp.: Hermannus Hermanni, Jost
  - s/o Ludwig Benner at Fleisbach, and Susanna- w/o Enners
  Hansen there (Fleisbach Chbk.). Hermannus Haupt, s/o the late
  Henrich Haup from Fleisbach, md. 29 Dec 1699 Anna Elisabeth,
  d/o Matthias Haar from Herborn (Herborn Chbk.).

Philippus Haupt, s/o the late Henrich Haupt at Fleisbach, md. Anna
Catharina Dresden (Dörsch), d/o the late Christ Dörsch at Herbach
(Fleisbach Chbk.). Christ (Jacob?) Dörsch, widower and Hoffmann at
Hirschberg, md. Anna Maria, d/o Ludwig Kolb at Herbach, 3 Trin:
1650 (Fleisbach Chbk.); their daughter Anna Catharina was bpt. uff
Estomihi: 1661 (Fleisbach Chbk.). Philippus Heipt, his wife and 3
ch. were on Capt. Francois Waren's ship in Holland in the 5th party
of 1709 Palatines (Rotterdam Lists).

Philipp Haüpt first was entered on the Hunter Lists 1 July
1710 with 3 pers. over 10 yrs. of age; the entry for 13 Sept 1712
read 2 pers. over 10 and 1 under 10 yrs. Philips Heypt was nat.
17 Jan 1715/16 (Albany Nats.). Philipp Heupt and his wife named
Gertrud with 3 ch. were at Quunsberg ca. 1716/17 (Simmendinger Register). Philip Heyt was a Palatine Debtor in 1718, 1719 (at Kingsberry) and 1721 (Livingston Debt Lists). Phillip Haupt, Gertraut
his wife, and (daughter) Catharina were on the St. Peter's Luth.
family list ca. 1734 (Rhinebeck Luth. Chbk.). The ch. of Philip[1]
Haüpt and his 1st wife Anna Catharina were:

1) "A Daughter"[2], bpt. 20 Feb 1685 and b. Hörbach (Herborn
   Chbk.).

2) <u>Johann Jost²</u>, bpt. 19 Oct 1688 - sp.: Joost Peters and Anna
Elisabet Ruperts (Herborn Chbk.).

3) <u>Anna Margaretha²</u>, bpt. 6 Nov 1692 - sp.: Hermannis Haupt -
s/o the late Henrich Haab from Fleisbach, and Anna Margareta - w/o Joh. Petri (Herborn Chbk.).

4) <u>Hermannus²</u>, bpt. 29 April 1694 - sp.: Hermannus Haub and
Anna Margareta - w/o Joh. Jacob Peter (Herborn Chbk.).

5) <u>Anna Catharina²</u>, bpt. 28 Sept 1695 - sp.: Theiss Peter at
Hirschberg and Anna Catharina - d/o Jürgen Müller at Hirsch-
berg (Herborn Chbk.). Anna Catharina Haupt was conf. 23
March 1712 at Queensberg (West Camp Luth. Chbk.).

With his 2nd wife Gertraud he had issue:

6) <u>Catharina²</u>, b. 18 Feb 1715 - sp.: Bernhard Noll and Bernhard Schmid (West Camp Luth. Chbk.). A Catharina Basin (?)
born Heuptin joined the church at Camp in 1732 (Loonenburg
Luth. Chbk.).

LUCAS HAUG[S] WIDDOW MARGARETHA (Hunter Lists #280)

Magdalena, wid/o Lucas Haug of Lichtenberg in the commune of
Zweybrucken, md. Johann Beer, widower of Dicksener in the commune
of Oppenheimer in the Pfaltz, 4 Dec 1711 (West Camp Luth. Chbk.).
The family Hauch was found near Lichtenberg at 6587 <u>Baumholder</u> (10
km. n. of Kusel; Chbks. begin 1675, Ref., but gaps). Laux Hauch,
s/o the late Wilhelm Hauch at Langenbach, md. Elisabeth, d/o the
late Hanß Bierr (Birr) at Fohren 29 May 1687. Hanß Birr at Fohren
was bur. 20 Feb 1687 and Nopre, wid/o the late Hanß Birr at Fohren,
was bur. 1 May 1687. Elisabeth, w/o Laux Hauch at Fohren, was bur.
12 March 1704; by 1706, Lucas had md. 2nd to Magdalena (--). Lucas
Houg, his wife, and 9 ch. were in the 4th party of Palatines on
Capt. Robbert Bůlman's ship in 1709 (Rotterdam Lists). Lucas Hauch
aged 31 (sic), his wife, sons aged 22, 16, 13, 9, 3, and 8 days,
and daughters aged 13, 12, and 9, Ref., husbandman and vinedresser,
were in England later that summer (London Lists).

Lucas Haug made his initial appearance on the Hunter Lists 1
July 1710 with 4 pers. over 10 yrs. and 2 pers. under 10; the entry
for 4 Oct 1710 read 6 pers. over 10 yrs. and 1 pers.under 10. Lucas
Haug's wid[W] was noted 24 June 1711 with 3 pers. over 10 yrs. and
2 under 10 yrs. Margaretha Haugin was noted 29 Sept 1711 with 4
pers. over 10 and 1 under 10 yrs. Johannes Bähr and Mag[d] Haukin
were recorded 24 Dec 1711. Lucas Hauch dead aged 44, Anna Magda
Hauch aged 45, Maria Cathar Hauch aged 16, Maria Margt. Hauch aged
18, John Jacob Hauch aged 13, John George Hauch x aged 12, Maria
Eliz Hauch x aged 11, and Johannes Hauch aged 4, were in N.Y. City

in 1710/11 (Palatines In N.Y. City). The Johannes Bär family with Hauch's ch. moved to N.J., according to Simmendinger. The ch. of Lucas[1] Hauch and his 1st wife Elisabetha were:

1) Johann Nicolaus[2], bpt. 14 March 1688 and b. Langenbach - sp.: H. Nickel Albert - Schultheiß at Berschweiler, Johannes Hauch from Wollfertsweiler, Johannes Kohl from Berschweiler, Maria Catharina - w/o Matheß Hauch at Langenb., and Cathrina - ... of Niclaß Welsch there (Baumholder Chbk.).

2) Anna Maria[2], bpt. 30 May 1689 and b. Langenbach - sp.: Hans Nickel Braun at Fohren, Nickel Meyer from Heimbach, Anna Eva - w/o Laux Bier at Fohren, and Maria - d/o the late Wilhelm Hauch (Baumholder Chbk.).

3) Maria[2], bpt. 6 Nov 1690 and b. Langenbach - sp.: Jacob Albert at Mettweiler, Hans Velten Pfeifer ..., Anna Greth - d/o Laux Birr, and Hans Welch ... (Baumholder Chbk.). She was bur. 25 March 1704, aged 13 yrs. (Baumholder Chbk.).

4) Johann Laux[2], bpt. 21 Dec 1692 and b. at Fohren - sp.: Laux Rothfuchs at Fohren, Nickel Kohl there, Hans Nickel Meyß from Hinten (?), Anna Catharina - w/o Hanß Nickel Albert at Berschweiler, and Anna Margreth - d/o Johannes Birr (Baumholder Chbk.).

5) Maria Margaretha[2] (Palatines In N.Y. City).

6) Johann Jacob[2] (Palatines In N.Y. City). The will of a Jacob Hauck of Oxforth in Essex Co., N.J. was probated in Hunterdon Co. 14 March 1757 (N.J. Wills, Lib. 8, p. 406).

7) Maria Catharina[2], bpt. 20 Jan 1696 and b. Fohren - sp.: Hanß Conrad Schäfer from Mettweiler, Johannes - s/o Phil. Welsch from Berschw., Maria - w/o H. Nickel Albert the Schultheiß. and Anna Catharina - w/o Wilhelm Dickeß at Fohren (Baumholder Chbk.).

8) Johann Georg[2], bpt. 23 May 1698 and b. at Fohren - sp.: Hans Peter Meyer the teacher at Berschw., Hanß Jörg Birr - s/o Laux Birr there, Margreth - w/o Hans Nickel Hauch at Langenbach, Johann Wilhelm Beuck - shepherd at Fohren, and Appollonia - w/o Nickel Schäfer at Mettweiler (Baumholder Chbk.). A Georg Hauch and wife Anna Hausmann appeared on Rhinebeck tax rolls 1734/35 to Feb 1754 (Dutchess Co. Tax Lists). Hausmanns were in N.J. at one time, and this Georg who appeared in Red Hook Luth. Church records may have been Georg[2], s/o Lucas[1], as the Red Hook family often were sp. by Drums, who also originated near Kusel (HJ); however, the John George[2] listed in 1710/11 in N.Y. City had an "x" after his name, usually denoting that the person died (HJ). Thus a firm connective between Georg[2] and the Red Hook man

is difficult to make with absolute certainty (HJ).

9) <u>Maria Elisabetha</u>[2] (Palatines In N.Y. City).

10) <u>Johann Philip</u>[2], bpt. 31 July 1701 - sp.: Phil. Welsch at Berschw., Johannes Albert the younger there, Maria Barbel - w/o Wilhelm Kohler at Mettweiler, Johannes Finck the miller at Hirsenhaus (?) Mill, and Margreth - d/o the shepherd at Fohren (Baumholder Chbk.). Johann Philips, s/o Laux Hauch at Fohren, was bur. 22 Oct 1708, aged 7 yrs. (Baumholder Chbk.).

Lucas Hauch and his 2nd wife Magdalena had issue:

11) <u>Johannes</u>[2], bpt. 15 Sept 1706 - sp.: Johann Kohl - tailor at Mettweiler, Johannes Finck the miller, Appolonia - w/o Nickel Schäfer at Mettweiler, and Anna Margreth - d/o Hans Nickel Hauch at Langenbach (Baumholder Chbk.).

PLAICHARD HAUG (Hunter Lists #281)

The origins of this Hauch family were at 6908 <u>Wiesloch</u> (10 km. s. of Heidelberg; Chbks. begin 1698). Georg Bleichardt Hauck md. Anna Elisabeth Schieler 13 Dec 1699. A note in the Wiesloch registers reported that Georg Bleichardt Hauck, his wife and 2 ch. left 15 May 1709 with the family of Hans Conradt Dieffenbach for the Island of Carolina. Leickert Haub, his wife and 2 ch. were near Hans Koenraad Thirffenbach's family on the roll of passengers on Capt. John Sewell's ship in Holland in 1709 (Rotterdam Lists).

Plaichard Haug made his initial appearance on the Hunter Lists 1 July 1710 with 2 pers. over 10 yrs. of age and 1 pers. under 10 in the household; the size increased to 2 pers. over 10 and 2 under 10 yrs. 24 June 1711, and then rose again to 2 pers. over 10 and 3 under 10 24 Dec 1711. The last entries on the family in 1712 read 2 pers. over 10 yrs. and 2 pers. under 10 yrs. of age. The latter entries in Hunter recorded Georg Haug rather than Pleikhard Haug. Jury Houck was nat. 17 Jan 1715/16 (Albany Nats.). Georg Haug, his wife Anna Elisabetha with 2 ch. were at Neu-Heidelberg ca. 1716/17 (Simmendinger Register). Their ch. were:

1) <u>Johann Georg</u>[2], bpt. 10 Oct 1700 - sp.: Hans Georg Schlosser the cartwright. The father was called a sadler in this entry (Wiesloch Chbk.).

2) <u>Johann Henrich</u>[2], bpt. 28 March 1703 - sp.: Hans Henrich Lamete at Altwißloch (Wiesloch Chbk.). Hans Hendrick Hock was nat. 17 Jan 1715/16 (Albany Nats.). Hendrick Honck was a freeholder at Schoharrie in 1763 (Albany Co. Freeholders). The will of Hendrick Houck of Schoharie in Albany Co. was dated 25 July 1778 and probated 18 Nov 1782 (<u>Fernow Wills</u>

#853). He md. Anna Veronica (Enders - HJ) and had ch.:

   i) <u>Catharina Elisabetha</u>[3], conf. 14 May 1740 and md. 12
Oct 1749 Henrich Dietz (both Schoharie Ref. Chbk.).
She then md. 2nd Harme Sidnigh (Will).

  ii) <u>Anna Maria</u>[3], md. 22 June 1752 Henrich Merkel, Jr.
(Schoharie Ref. Chbk.).

 iii) <u>Peter</u>[3], eldest s/o Henrich named in will. He was conf.
6 April 1748 (Schoharie Ref. Chbk.). Pitter Hauck
and Henrich Hauck Jr. were both in Capt. Jacob Sternberger's Co. at Schohare in 1767 (<u>Report of the State
Historian</u>, Vol. II, p. 842). He md. 1st Elisabetha
Barbara (--) and then md. 2nd Christina (--) (Will).
The will of Peter Hauck of Knieskern Dorph in Albany
Co. was dated 6 Jan 1777 and probated 23 July 1783
(<u>Fernow Wills</u> #846).

  iv) <u>Maria Elisabetha</u>[3] (Will), conf. in 1743 and md. Joh:
Jacob Werth 31 May 1747 (both Schoharie Ref. Chbk.).

   v) <u>Maria Hester</u>[3] (Will).

  vi) <u>Catharina</u>[3] (Will), md. Johannes Rickert 22 Nov 1757
(Schoharie Luth. Chbk.).

 vii) <u>Margaretha</u>[3] (Will). An Elisabeth Margareth Hauck md.
Jost Kniskern 18 Oct 1763 (Schoharie Luth. Chbk.)
and this may have been Margaretha's[3] marriage (HJ).

viii) <u>Henrich</u>[3] (Will), md. 29 March 1767 Catharina Knieskern (Schoharie Ref. Chbk.).

  ix) <u>Christina</u>[3], b. 20 May 1740 - sp.: Bartram Enters and
Mary Christina - w/o Bartram Enders (Schoharie Ref.
Chbk.). She md. Georg Henrich Mann 11 April 1760
(Schoharie Luth. Chbk.).

   x) <u>Lambert</u>[3], bpt. 4 Oct 1743 - sp.: Lambert Starenberg
his wife (Schoharie Ref. Chbk.).

3) <u>Apollonia</u>[2], bpt. 24 Jan 1707 - sp.: Appolonia Schlosser
(Wiesloch Chbk.).

4) <u>Anna Margaretha</u>[2], b. 17 March 1717 and bpt. at Schoharie
- sp.: Johann Kraemer and his wife (West Camp Luth. Chbk.).

JOHN CHRISTIAN HAUS (Hunter Lists #282)

Christian Hauss, widower and carpenter of Alten Staeden near
Wetzler in the duchy of Solm, md. Anna Catharina, wid/o Johann
Becker of Durnberg near Dietz in the commune Schemburg, 27 Sept
1710 (West Camp Luth. Chbk.). The actual home of origin for the
Haus family was <u>Klein Altenstadten</u> near 6300 <u>Wetzlar</u> (15 km. w.
of Giessen). The Marburg Archives contain some old lists of Shrove
Tuesday hens, garden taxes, and subject money (110 Acc. 1939/31,

No. 167) for Amt König̈sberg and Hohensolms. A Peter Hauß was noted
at Altenstedten there in 1558, 1559, and 1565; a Jorg Haus and a
Jacob Hauß were recorded at Altenstedten in 1579, and a Johannchen
and Jürgen Hauß were registered there in 1586. A later list dated
1694 mentioned one Daniel Hauß of Königsberg. Johan Kristhaus, his
wife, and 6 ch. were listed next to Görg Zufungs and Johan Peter
Diepel in the 6th party at Rotterdam in 1709 (Rotterdam Lists).

Johann Christian Haus made his initial appearance on the Hunter Lists 4 July 1710 with 4 pers. over 10 yrs. of age and 3 pers.
under 10 yrs.; the family was recorded with 2 pers. over 10 yrs.
and 4 under 10 on 4 Aug 1710, 3 pers. over 10 and 2 under 10 on
4 Oct 1710, and 3 pers. over 10 and 1 under 10 on 31 Dec 1710.
The household had 6 pers. over 10 yrs. and 2 under 10 yrs. on 25
March 1711, 4 pers. over 10 and 4 under 10 on 24 June 1711, 5 pers.
over 10 and 5 under 10 on the cumulative 24 Dec 1711 entry, 4 pers.
over 10 and 5 under 10 on 25 March 1712, and 5 pers. over 10 and 4
under 10 on the 24 June 1712 notation. Christian Houys was nat. 11
Oct 1715 (Albany Nats.). Christian Hauss and his wife Maria Catharina, with 8 ch. were at Neu-Heessberg ca. 1716/17 (Simmendinger
Register). Harmonas Wendell transfered a parcel of land in the
Harrison Patent to Christian Haus and Hendrick Klock on 26 Aug 1725
(Albany Co. Deeds, Vol. 7, p. 87). The missing Mohawk Valley church
registers make a full list of Christian[1] Haus's ch. difficult to
establish, however, they appear to have been:

1) Rheinhardt[2] (HJ), nat. as Rynier Hous of Phillipsburg, yeoman, at N.Y. City 10 Jan 1715/16 (Denizations, Naturalizations, and Oaths of Allegiance in Colonial N.Y., p. 37).
   Hanss Reinhard Huss and Anna Elisabetha with 1 child were
   at Hackensack ca. 1716/17 (Simmendinger Register). Reind-
   ert Haus subscribed £1 in 1727 (N.Y. City Luth. Protocol).
   The ch. of Rheinhardt[2] and Anna Elis. (Neidhofer? - HJ) were:
   i) Johann Henrich[3], b. 5 Nov 1715 at Yonckers Fall and
      bpt. N.Y. - sp.: Johann Marcus Koning, and Johann Hen-
      rich Gessinger and wife Anna Elisabeth (N.Y. City Luth.
      Chbk.). He md. 11 July 1736 at P. Lassing's Anna Cath-
      arina, d/o Joh. Eberhard and Gertruyd Jong (N.Y. City
      Luth. Chbk.), and they had ch. bpt. at Fishkill Ref.,
      Loonenburg Luth., and Tappan Ref. Churches (HJ).
   ii) Anna Juliana[3], b. 5 Feb 1718 at Philipsburg and bpt.
       at N.Y. - sp.: Johannes Reitelsdorffer and Anna Jul-
       ianna Mutsch (N.Y. City Luth. Chbk.). She was conf.
       16 Oct 1734 (N.Y. City Luth. Chbk.).
   iii) Susanna[3], b. 9 April 1720 at Tappan and bpt. at Hack-
        insack - sp.: Johann Niclaes Neiddebber and Susanna

Klug (N.Y. City Luth. Chbk.).

iv) Jannet[3] (HJ), md. 1737 Thomas Meredic (HJ).

v) Christian[3], b. 2 Aug 1722 at Tappan and bpt. Hackinsack - sp.: Philipp Zerbe and Christina Velden (N.Y.
City Luth. Chbk.). He md. an Elisabetha (--) (HJ).

vi) Johannes[3], bpt. 9 weeks old 29 May 1726 - sp.: Hannes
Moots and Anna Marie Veltin (N.Y. City Luth. Chbk.).
He md. Sarah Wheeler (HJ) and had ch. bpt. at Tappan
Ref., Clarkstown Ref., Ramapo Luth., Linlithgo Ref.
and Churchtown Luth. (HJ).

vii) Maria[3], bpt. 6 weeks old 27 8br 1728 - sp.: Martinus
May and wife Maria (N.Y. City Luth. Chbk.).

viii) Maria Elisabetha[3], bpt. 2 months and 14 days old on
5 June 1731 - sp.: Qvirynus Neidhebber and wife Maria
Elisabeth (N.Y. City Luth. Chbk.).

ix) Rheinhardt[3], bpt. 21 Aug 1733 - sp.: Johannis Clemens
and wife Maritie (Tarrytown Ref. Chbk.).

2) Conrad[2] (HJ), a sp. to Lambert Starenberger in 1732 (Schoharie Ref. Chbk.). A Conrad Haus and wife Englige sp. in
1756, and Conrad Haus and wife Margaretha sp. 1755 at Stone
Arabia.

3) Georg[2] (HJ), a communicant of Berkenmeyer at Fontyndorp in
1736 (Albany Protocol, p. 189). He md. Maria Catharina
Ehrhardt (HJ) and had ch.:

i) Maria Elisabetha[3], bpt. 30 Oct 1734 - sp.: Hermann
Hauss and Maria Elisabeth (Schoharie Ref. Chbk.).

ii) Maria Dorothea[3], bpt. 7 Jan 1736 - sp.: Hendrik Knÿs-
kerl and Maria Dorothea Wanner (Schoharie Ref. Chbk.).

iii) Johann Georg[3], bpt. 18 Nov 1737 - sp.: John Jurrie Ecker and Elisa Margareth Wanner (Schoharie Ref. Chbk.).

iv) "A Little Boy"[3], bpt. 9 Oct 1749 at Cani-Scohare and
Stone Arabia (Schoharie Luth. Chbk.).

4) Hermannus[2] (HJ), md. Maria Margaretha Wallrad (HJ) and had:

i) "A Little Girl"[3], bpt. 1 Oct 1749 and Caniscohare and
Stone Arabia (Schoharie Luth. Chbk.).

ii) Anna Barbara[3], bpt. 20 June 1751 - sp.: Adam Wallrad
and Anna Barbara, his wife (Stone Arabia Ref. Chbk.).

iii) Johann Jacob[3], b. or bpt. 28 Jan 1753 - sp.: Jacob
Wallrath and wife Eleanora (Stone Arabia Luth. Chbk.).

5) Anna Elisabetha[2] (HJ), conf. at Tschoghari in the so-called
Fuchsen-Dorp in 1720 (N.Y. City Luth. Chbk.). She md.
Conrad Rickert (HJ).

Possible relatives of Christian[1] include: 1) Johannes Hausz
nat. 27 July 1721 (Denizations, Naturalizations, and Oaths of

Allegiance in Colonial N.Y., p. 33); 2) Elisabeth Hous joined the
Schoharie Ref. Church in 1733; 3) Peter Haus, who was in the Mohawk
at an early date; and 4) possibly the Elias Haus #23 in the list
of the Van Slyke Patent in 1716, noted in Shaver's House Family (HJ).
Perhaps private sources will reveal more 3rd generation Hauses (HJ).

NICLAUS HAYD (Hunter Lists #283)

Nickel Heyd, who d. ca. 1699/1700 and was father of the emigrants Peter Heyd and Catharina Barbara - w/o Lazarus Dorn, had a
son Hans Niklaus bpt. 1 March 1678 at 6799 Pfeffelbach; a Johann
Nickel Hayd, s/o Johannes Heyd at Fronhaussen, md. Susan (?) Elisabeth Peess 2 Nov 1700 at nearby 6587 Baumholder. Johann Ulrich
Heid and wife Catharina Maria had a son Johan Niklass bpt. 9 Aug
1689 at 6200 Wiesbaden. However, no firm connective to the emigrant Nicolaus Hayd has been established (HJ). Nicol Heyd aged 24,
Catholic, linnenweaver, was in the 3rd arrivals in England in 1709
(London Lists).

Niclaus Hayd made his first appearance on the Hunter Lists
4 July 1710 with 2 pers. over 10 yrs. of age; the size of the family increased 4 Oct 1710 to 2 pers. over 10 yrs. and 1 pers. under
10 yrs. and then to 2 pers. over 10 and 2 under 10 yrs. 25 March
1711. The household dwindled down to 2 pers. over 10 and 1 under
10 on 24 June 1711 and then to 1 pers. over 10 yrs. and 1 under
10 on 25 March 1712. The entry for 24 June 1712 read 2 pers. over
10 yrs. of age and 1 under 10 yrs. Niclaus Hayd of Annsberg was a
soldier in 1711 (Palatine Volunteers To Canada). Nich: Heyt was
in Col. Thomas Ffarmar's Regt. in the 6th Co. in N.J. in 1715 (Report of the State Historian, Vol. I, p. 536). Nicolaus Heyd and
his wife with 2 ch. were auf dem Rarendantz ca. 1716/17 (Simmendinger Register). The w/o Nicolaus[1] Hayd was Susanna (--). Issue:
1) Henrich[2], bpt. 12 April 1716 - sp.: Hendrick Vechte and
   wife (Somerville Ref. Chbk.). (Mother not named on entry).
2) Cataleyn[2], bpt. 15 Oct 1717 - sp.: Hendrick Wever and wife
   Wevers (Somerville Ref. Chbk.). (Mother not named on entry).
3) Susanna[2], bpt. 5 March 1721 - sp.: Baerent Veter and wife
   Elisabeth (Somerville Ref. Chbk.).

There were later N.J. Hayts who may have been related to Nicolaus[1]: a Lucas Hoed and wife Joanna had a son Aaron bpt. 31 Oct
1742 (Readington Ref. Chbk.); a John Hite was a freeholder at Amwell, Hunterdon Co. in 1741 (Hunterdon Co. Freeholders); and a
James Hude family was found in the old church registers of New
Brunswick, N.J. (HJ).

JOHANN JOST HAYD (Hunter Lists #284)

The methods which I used to find this Va. family overseas, and the data found are set forth in the booklet German Origins of Jost Hite - Va. Pioneer 1685-1761, by Henry Z Jones, Jr., Ralph Connor, and Klaus Wust. The ancestral home of this prominent settler was at 6927 Bonfeld (5 km. w. of Bad Wimpfen; Chbks. begin 1607). The earliest known ancestor of Jost[1] was his father Johannes Heydt, a Heiligen-Fleger and butcher at Bonfeld. Johannes Heydt was noted on a 1687 Assessment Receipt of Bonfeld as follows: house - 1 two-story incl. barn, fields - 2 morgens, meadows - 2 viertels, vineyard - 1 viertel, and garden - ½ viertel (Generallandesarchiv Karlsruhe 125/3094). Johannes Heydt md. 1st Anna Magdalena (--), who d. 6 April 1695, aged 42 yrs. The ch. of Johannes and Anna Magdalena were:

?Johannes (possibly), who might be the husband of a mysterious Margret, nee Ebald, w/o Johann Heyd the butcher and civic warden here, who d. 15 Dec 1697, aged 49 yrs.; this Johannes[2] may have moved away from Bonfeld at an early date (HJ). It is also possible that this Margaretha Ebald - w/o Johannes Heyd a butcher - may have been the 2nd w/o Johannes Heyd Sr., and that the date of her death was wrongly entered in the Bonfeld Chbks. (HJ).

Anna Maria, md. as d/o Johannes Hayd the butcher 17 April 1697 Ernst Kleemann, drummer in Col. Hallstein's Regt.

Maria Dorothea, md. as d/o Johann Heyd the butcher 16 Jan 1703 Johannes Welck, s/o Jerg Welck the Schultheiß at Unter-Steppach (?) in the territory of Hall.

Anna Catharina, b. 18 Oct 1683 - sp.: Anna König - d/o Anwald, Anna Maria - d/o Simon Muth, and ... - d/o Michael.

+ Johann Jost, b. 5 Dec 1685 and bpt. as Hans Justus - sp.: Hans ..., Jeremias Bengel, and Anna König.

Johann Jeremias, b. 18 Jan 1688 - sp.: Hans Jost Klempp - citizen and innkeeper at Rappenau, Jeremias Bengel - single, and Anna Catharina - single d/o Michael Braun. The child d. 21 March 1688, aged 9 weeks old.

Anna Barbara, bpt. 24 Jan 1689 - sp.: the w/o Hans Jost Klemp - citizen and landlord at Rappenau, Anna Catharina Braun - single, and Jeremias Bengel.

Anna Rosina, bpt. 1 Nov 1691 - sp.: Anna Catharina Braun - single, Rosina - d/o the teacher here, and Hans Jeremias Bengel - citizen son here. Anna Rosina, d/o Joh. Heyd - formerly citizen and butcher here, md. Joh. Jacob Rudolff, s/o the late Joh. Balthasar Rudolf - miller in the Herrenbach, 18 Nov 1710.

Johannes Heyd, citizen and Gerichtsmann here, md. Anna Maria,
wid/o the late Caspar Schultze - citizen at Aglasterhausen, 6
March 1697. She was b. 4 Sept 1667 as Anna Maria, d/o Andreas and
Maria Agatha Nothwang at 6954 Hochhausen/Neckar. By his wife Anna
Maria, the ch. of Johannes Heydt were:

> Anna Eva Catharina, bpt. 19 June 1699 - sp.: Eva Magdalena
> Schüßler, Anna Barbara Frey, and Rosina Catharina Reinsmund.
> Anna Maria, b. 23 Oct 1701 - sp.: Anna Cath. Epp - the cooper's
> here ..., Eva Magdalena Schüßler, Anna Barbara Frey, and Ros-
> ina Catharina Reinsmund, all single.
> Anna Barbara, b. 4 Jan 1705 - sp.: Anna Catharina Epp - d/o
> the cooper, Eva Magdalena Schüßler, both single.
> Johann Martinus, b. 3 Aug 1707.

Johan Justus Heyd, linenweaver and s/o Johannis Heyd the butcher
and Gerichtsverwandten here, md. Anna Maria, d/o Abraham Merckle
- citizen here, 11 Nov 1704. Anna Maria, d/o Abraham and Anna Veronica Merckle, was b. 16 Jan 1687 - sp.: Veronica Maria Landvatter
- d/o David Landvatter. Abraham, s/o Jörg Merckle and his wife Eva,
was bpt. 2 March 1664. Jörg Merckle was bur. 16 Dec 1686, aged 83
yrs., and Eva, his widow, d. 13 March 1690, aged 73 yrs. On the
last page of the Bonfeld Chbk. is a Pastor's list of Emigrants
From This Village; on this ancient roll under the date of 1710
are Johannes Heyd with his family, and Justus Heyd, his son, with
his family, and under the date 1717 are Abraham Merckle, his wife,
with 5 ch. and his son in law, among others. Joost Heÿt, his wife,
and 1 child were on Capt. William Newton's ship in the 5th party
of Palatines in Holland in 1709 (Rotterdam Lists); they were listed
next to Simon Vegt and Hans Michel Wechel, both citizens of Bonfeld (HJ).

Johann Jost Hayd was enrolled on the Hunter Lists 30 June 1710
with 2 pers. over 10 yrs. of age; on the 4 Aug 1710 list he was
noted next to Maria Haydin. The 4 Oct 1710 entry read 2 pers. over
10 yrs. of age and 1 pers. under 10 yrs. in the household. In May
1714, he purchased 150 acres of land on the Skippack from Johannes
Kolb (Philadelphia Co. Deed Bk. F, Vol. II, p. 48, per Ralph Connor). Hans Joest Heyt and Anna Maria sold land in Pa. to her brother Jacob Merckley in 1728, and then on 5 Aug 1731 he acquired
from John and Isaac Vanmeter the rights to a conditional grant of
40,000 acres in the Shenandoah Valley (see our German Origins of
Jost Hite for more transactions and complete sources on his Pa.
and Va. activities). The will of Jost Heid of Frederick Co. in Va.
was dated 25 April 1758 and probated 7 May 1761 (Frederick Co.
Will Bk. II, pp. 487-88). The ch. of Johann Jost[1] Hite were:

1) <u>Anna Maria²</u>, b. 22 Feb 1706 - sp.: Maria Felicitas Hahn-
stätter and Anna Barbara Walter, single (Bonfeld Chbk.).
She d. 24 Feb 1706, aged 2 days (Bonfeld Chbk.).

2) <u>Maria Barbara²</u>, b. 28 Jan 1707 - sp.: Maria Felicitas Hahn-
stätter and Anna Barbara Walter - both single, and Maria
Agatha - w/o Joh. Andreae (Bonfeld Chbk.). She d. 1 March
1707, aged 1 month (Bonfeld Chbk.).

3) <u>Maria²</u> (HJ), md. George Bowman (HJ).

4) <u>Elisabetha²</u>, bpt. 4 Nov 1711 - sp.: Corn. Elten and Rebekka Elten (Kingston Ref. Chbk.). She md. Paul Froman (HJ).

5) <u>Magdalena²</u>, bpt. 6 Sept 1713 - sp.: Jacob Capoesjen and
Madalena (Kingston Ref. Chbk.). She md. Jacob Chrisman
(HJ).

6) <u>Johannes²</u> (Will).

7) <u>Jacob²</u> (Will).

8) <u>Isaac²</u> (Will).

9) <u>Abraham²</u> (Will).

10) <u>Joseph²</u> (Will).

<u>PETER HAYD</u> (Hunter Lists #285)

The origins of this Hayd family were at 6587 <u>Baumholder</u> (21
km. n.e. of St. Wendel; Chbks. begin 1675, but gaps). The father
of the emigrant Peter¹ was <u>Nickel Heyd</u>, d. between Oct 1699 and
April 1700; his widow Anna Catharina d. Dennweiler and was bur.
11 Feb 1728, aged 75 yrs. and 3 months. Nickel Heyd md. 17 Dec
1672 Catharina Barbara - d/o Stephan Burckhard (Pfeffelbach Chbk.);
this may have been his marriage to the mother of his children,
known as Anna Catharina in bpt. records (HJ). Their ch. were:

+ <u>Peter</u>, md. as s/o the late Nickel Heyd from Dennweiler 17
July 1700 Anna Catharina, d/o the late Philip Nickel Schlosser - the little ploughman.

+ <u>Catharina Barbara</u>, md. as d/o the late Nickel Heyd from Dennweiler 3 April 1700 Lazarus Dorn from Oberalben, also a N.Y.
1709er (HJ). She had an illegitimate child Christoffel bpt.
15 Sept 1697, fathered by Hans Nickel Aulenbach at Frohnbach.
<u>Hans Nicolaus</u>, bpt. 1 March 1678 (Pfeffelbach Chbk.).
<u>Hanß Bernhard</u>, bpt. in Lichtenberg 1682 - sp.: Hans Conrad
Mack at Ober Alben, Bernd Faust at Grünebach, and Rosin - d/o
Hans Ebert at Mesbach (?).
<u>Hanß Nicolaus</u>, bpt. 29 Nov 1683 - sp.: Nickel Schultheiß -
s/o Johann Schultheiß at Dennweiler, Hans Jörg Dick - s/o
the Schultheiß at Ulmet, and Catharina - w/o Christoffel Doll
at Dennweiler.
<u>Anna Elisabetha</u>, bpt. 5 April 1686 - sp.: Peter Kayser at

Fronbach, Rosina - wid/o Abraham Jung, and the shepherd Elß
at Dennweiler.

Anna Margaretha, bpt. between 30 Jan and 15 Feb 1688 - sp.:
Johannes Schultheiß the younger at Dennweiler, Jacob Neubauer
at Irtzweiler, Anna Maria - w/o Hans Nickel Doll there, and
Anna Margaretha - w/o Hans Nickel Hemmer (?) at Malbachel (?).
She md. Johannes Esco from Hesse 18 May 1706.

Anna Magdalena, bpt. 19 May 1689 - sp.: Johannes Hemmer at
Mahbechel, Anna Magdalena - w/o H. Joh. Albert the Schultheiß,
and Catharina - w/o Fritz Gerhard at Oberalben.

Johann Christophel, bpt. 3 Dec 1691 - sp.: Christoffel Doll
at Dennweiler, Johannes Getzge - miller in Lockersmill, Johannes Klee from Heimbuch, and Maria Elisabeth - w/o Hans
Arnd Heyd from Blaubach. He d. in 1694, aged 3 yrs.

Hanß Jacob, bpt. 10 April 1693 - sp.: Hanß Jacob Mack - s/o
Conrad Mack at Oberalben, Abraham Heyderick - shepherd at Ober-
alben, Agneß - d/o Peter Mack there, and Anna Margreth - d/o
Jonas Koch at Fronbach.

Hanß Melchior, bpt. 24 April 1695 - sp.: Hans Melchior Faust
from Grünbach, Hans Christoffel Doll from Irtzweiler, Elisabeth - w/o Hans Adam Heyderich, and Salome - w/o Henrich Loch
the shepherd at Dennweiler.

Hanß Adam, bpt. 3 Nov 1697 - sp.: Hanß Adam Heyderich at Oberalben, Friedrich Mack from Oberalben, the w/o Jost Müller, ...
Peter Heyde aged 28, his wife, and a son aged 1½, Ref., Joyner, were
in the 1st arrivals in England in May 1709 (London Lists); however,
he probably was not the N.Y. emigrant, but another of that name (HJ).

Peter Hayd made his initial appearance on the Hunter Lists 4
July 1710 with 2 pers. over 10 yrs. of age and 2 pers. under 10;
the entry for 4 Oct 1710 read 2 pers. over 10 and 1 under 10 yrs.,
and the reading for 25 March 1711 noted 2 pers. over 10 yrs. The
lists recorded 2 over 10 and 1 under 10 yrs. 24 June 1712. Peter
Hayd was recorded next to (his brother in law) Lazarus Dorn 4 Oct
1710 on the unalphabetised list, helping cement the fact that the
Baumholder man was indeed the 1709er (HJ). Peter Hayd of Haysbury
was a soldier in 1711 (Palatine Volunteers To Canada). Peter Heyd
and Maria Elisabetha with 1 child were at Hessberg ca. 1716/17 (Simmendinger Register). He was a Palatine Debtor in 1718, 1719 (at
Haysberry) and 1721 (Livingston Debt Lists). He then seems to dis-
appear from N.Y. Palatine records (HJ). As Rheinhardt Hëyd, s/o
Peter Heÿd - hunter at Dennweiler, md. 22 June 1723 Anna Elisabetha
Müller of Fronbach at Baumholder, it is quite possible that Peter[1]
may have returned to Germany!; he was not found at Baumholder 1710-
1721 when he was known to be in colonial N.Y. (HJ). The ch. of

Peter[1] Hayd and his 1st wife Anna Catharina were:

1) <u>Elisabetha Catharina</u>[2], bpt. 10 July 1701 - sp.: Johannes
   Most of Frohnbach, Joh. Nickel Doll of Dennweiler, Elisa-
   betha - w/o (?) Hans Adam Heydrich from Oberalben, and Anna
   Catharina - d/o Jacob Aulenbach (Baumholder Chbk.).

2) <u>Johann Rheinhardt</u>[2], bpt. 30 Dec 1702 - sp.: Nickel Heyd,
   Rheinhard Ameshot (?) - schoolmaster at ..., Elisabetha -
   w/o Johannes Schulteis of Dennweiler, and Salome - s/o Hennrich Loch the cowherd (Baumholder Chbk.). He md. 22 June
   1723 Anna Elisabetha, d/o Jost Müller of Frohnbach (Baumholder Chbk.).

3) <u>Johannes</u>[2], md. as s/o Peter of Dennweiler 21 July 1729 Anna Elisabetha, d/o Johannes Schneider of Blaubach (Baumholder Chbk.).

MARIA CUNIGUNDA HAYDIN (Hunter Lists #286)

This woman was listed but a few names from #284 Johann Jost
Hayd on 30 June 1710 in the Hunter Lists; the entry read 1 pers.
over 10 yrs. of age and 1 pers. under 10 yrs. I believe that the
Hunter secretaries confused #286 Maria Cunigunda Haydin with #307
Anna Maria Heydin, as entries for both ladies never overlap on the
Hunter rolls (HJ). #307 Maria Haydin was next to Johann Jost Hayd
on 4 Aug 1710 with but 1 pers. in the household; this strongly suggests that she was the wid/o Johannes Heydt, butcher of Bonfeld and
father of Johann Jost Hayd (HJ). Anna Maria Heidin aged 50, a widow,
was in N.Y. City in 1710/11 (Palatines In N.Y. City).

HENRICH HAYER (Hunter Lists #287)

This 1709er was called Henrich Häger on 4 July 1710 on the
Hunter Lists, and Johann Henrich Hager on his last entry 4 Aug 1710
with 2 pers. over 10 yrs. and 1 under 10; his history is discussed
in the section dealing with #262, his wife Maria Hägerin (HJ).

MICHAEL HEBMANN (Hunter Lists #288)

Maria Catharina Vogelezang, wid/o Michiel Hupman of the Graafschap Hardenberg, md. Joh[S] Coens 23 Jan 1711 (N.Y. City Ref. Chbk.).
The entries for Hardenburg are at 6702 <u>Bad Dürkheim</u> (19 km. w. of
Mannheim; Chbks. begin 1645, but gaps, Luth.). In the 17th and 18th
centuries, the Christian names Michael and Melchior often interchanged (HJ): Melchior Heppmann, master-miller auf der Herrschaft-
lichen Schn... and ... at Harttenb. - s/o the late Georg Heppmann
formerly master-miller at Rodenburg an der Tauber, md. Anna Barbara,
d/o Clemens Löscher at Weilersbach 20 Jan 1680. The registers of

8803 <u>Rothenburg ob der Tauber</u>, the correct name of the town, begin early in 1579 and show several marriages for a Georg Heppmann: 1) Georg Heppmann, baker here, md. 3 Dec 1616 Apollonia Gering; 2) Georg Hepmann, widower, md. Apollonia Holzmann, widow, 7 May 1622; 3) Georg Heppmann, Brunnen-miller, md. Susanna Schuster - wid/o the baker, 2 April 1638; and 4) Jörg Hepmann, widower and Brunnen-miller, md. Barbara Baůr - d/o the late Michel Baůr from Oberdach-stetten, 11 Aug 1640 (Rothenburg Chbk.). Williger Hepman, his wife, and (ch.) Haningel, Maria Geertůit, and 1 (additional) child, were in the 2nd party of Palatines in Holland in 1709 (Rotterdam Lists). Melchior Hepman aged 53, his wife, and daughters aged 17, 12, and 8, Luth., husbandman and vinedresser, were in the 2nd arrivals in England later that year (London Lists).

Michael Hebmann first made his appearance on the Hunter Rolls 4 Aug 1710 with 4 pers. over 10 yrs. of age and 2 pers. under 10 yrs.; the notation read 6 pers. over 10 yrs. on 4 Oct 1710. Maria Cath Hebmannin aged 40 - a widow, Anna Engel Hebmannin aged 21A (sic), Gertrude Hebmannin aged 14, and Anna Magdalena Hebmannin aged 11, were in N.Y. City in 1710/11 (Palatines In N.Y. City). The ch. of Melchior (Michael) Hebmann by his various wives were:

1) <u>Maria Charlotta²</u>, bpt. at Hartenb. 6 Jan 1681 - sp.: Hans Geyer - master carpenter at Hartenb., Apollonia - single d/o the late Joh. Hickfußen, the Landlord at Hartenb., and Charlotta Maria - single d/o Hans Schwartz ... (Bad Dürkheim Chbk.). In this entry, the father was called a miller at Harttenb., and the mother's name was Anna Barbara (HJ).

2) <u>Anna Engel²</u> (Palatines In N.Y. City).

3) <u>Maria Gertraud²</u> (Palatines In N.Y. City).

4) <u>Anna Magdalena²</u> (Palatines In N.Y. City). Perhaps she was the Anna Hepmann who md. Jurg Wm. Morig 6 Oct 1723 at the N.Y. City Ref. Church (HJ).

A Michiel Hopma sp. Hen: Beer in 1724 at Hackensack Ref. Church, and The Old Mr. Hobman d. 31 Nov 1772 at the Schoharie Luth. Church; however, both these men probably were not related to the 1709er (HJ).

JACOB HEEL (Hunter Lists #289)

Hans Jacob Heil (alone) was in the 6th party of Palatines in Holland in 1709 (Rotterdam Lists).

Jacob Hähl made his first appearance on the Hunter Lists 4 July 1710 with 2 pers. over 10 and 1 under 10; the entry for Jacob Heel dated 4 Oct 1710 read 2 pers. over 10 yrs. Jacob Heal (Hell) appeared in the records of the Ramapo Tract in 1712/13. He md.

Anna Maria (--) (HJ) and had issue:

1) Elisabetha², bpt. 8 April 1711 - sp.: Abram Housman and Gerrebreght Terhuyne (Hackensack Ref. Chbk.).

2) Nicolaus², bpt. 4 Oct 1712 - sp.: Nicasie Kip and wife An-tie (Hackensack Ref. Chbk.). Nicolaus Heyle, single man of Hanover Co., md. Rachel Defvenport, single woman of Hanover Co., 14 June 1733 (Acquackanonk Ref. Chbk.). He may have been the Nicolaus Hale who sp. Hannes Cleyn in 1738/39 at Fort Hunter in the Mohawk Valley (HJ). Issue:

    i) Johannes³, bpt. 1740 - sp.: Joh^S Snyder and Cath. (Pompton Plains Ref. Chbk.).

3) Margaretha², bpt. 8 Aug 1714 - sp.: Coenrades De Maier and wife (Hackensack Ref. Chbk.).

4) Maria², bpt. 19 Feb 1716 - sp.: Jan Everse and wife Maritie Barber (Hackensack Ref. Chbk.).

5) Catharina², bpt. 27 Oct 1717 - sp.: Jan Verwey and wife Catrÿn (Hackensack Ref. Chbk.). She md. Johannes Schneider (HJ).

6) Petrus², bpt. 14 Aug 1720 - sp.: Pieter Kerligh and wife (Hackensack Ref. Chbk.).

On several of the aforementioned bpt. entries, the father was called simply Jacob the German (HJ).

Catharina, d/o Joh. Wilhelm Heyl late of Williamsdorst in the Duchy of Nastau-Sig, md. Robert, s/o Edwart Wihler of Kinderhook, 27 Oct 1715 (West Camp Luth. Chbk.). She may have been related to #289 Jacob Heel, but no connection has been found as yet (HJ). Her home overseas was 5901 Wilnsdorf (8 km. s.e. of Siegen). Johann Wilhelm Heyl, s/o Herr Friedrich Heyl, md. Ehl Becker, d/o Jacob Becker of Salchendorf, 28 Jan 1687 (Obersdorf-Rödgen Chbks.); their daughter Anna Catharina was bpt. 1692 (Burbach Chbk.). The Heyl family is an old one in the Siegen area: Friedrich Heyl, Pastor at Rödgen and Wilnsdorf and s/o the late Martin Heyl of Wiljungen aus dem Fürstenthumb Hessen, md. Catharina, d/o Tilmann Schütz, 16 Oct 1655 (Obersdorf-Rödgen Chbk.); their son Johann Wilhelm was bpt. 13 Jan 1660 (Obersdorf-Rödgen Chbk.), and he was father to Cathar-ina, w/o Robert Wihler (HJ).

GEORG JACOB HEYDELBERG (Hunter Lists #290)

Georg Jacob Heydelberg made his first appearance on the Hunter Lists 4 July 1710 with 2 pers. over 10 yrs. of age and 3 pers. un-der 10; his last entry was 4 Aug 1710. He was recorded on Hunter near passengers from the Westerwald-Siegen area who were also noted at Rotterdam in 1709 near one Hirchel Heidelberger, his wife, and

2 ch., so perhaps a relationship existed between Georg Jacob and Hirschel (HJ). Jacob Heydelburgh and his wife Anna Heydelburgh were received into the Neshaminy congregation 6 Sept 1711 (Records of Rev. Paulus Van Vlecq at Neshaminy or Southhampton, Bucks Co., Pa.).

JOHANNES HEYNER (Hunter Lists #291)

Johann Henor, widower of Birsen in the commune of Oftenbach, md. Catharina, d/o Johann Jacob Mustier of Steinfort in Creichgau, 27 July 1710 (West Camp Luth. Chbk.). The town mentioned in the Kocherthal records actually was 6484 Birstein (12 km. n. of Wächtersbach), entries in registers at 6484 Unterreichenbach (2 km. further n.; Chbks. begin 1599, but gaps). The Unterreichenbach Chbks. show that Johannes Häner, s/o Conrad Häner - miller at Sturendorf, md. 17 Jan 1703 Anna Catharina, d/o the late Johann Schneider of Fischborn. The Häners' home then was 6323 Storndorf (10 km. w. of Lauterbach). The Chbks. at Storndorf noted that Curdt Hayner was bur. 18 Feb 1713. The ch. of Conrad (Curt) Häner (Hüner, Hahner) bpt. at Storndorf (no wife mentioned) were:

Johannes, bpt. Dom. 1. Trin.: 1673 - sp.: Johannes ... from Vadenrod. He md. 22 Nov 1703 Juliana, d/o Casper Jost, and d. at Storndorf 16 April 1738, aged 65 yrs. minus 2 months.

+ Johannes, bpt. 22 Jan 1675 - sp.: Johannes - s/o Hans Matthes.

Sophia Catharina, bpt. 27 Dec 1677 - sp.: Debora Sophia from Seebach, Sophia Maria Eleonora from Bobenhausen, and ...

Margaretha, bpt. 2 May 1680 - sp.: Margretha - w/o Johannes Möller from Netzloss/Mossergrund.

Anna Margaretha, bpt. 5 Feb 1682 - sp.: Margretha - w/o Johann Decher.

Ottilia, bpt. 28 March 1684 - sp.: sein schwieger Hans Scheuben's wife.

Anna Gela, bpt. 26 Sept 1686 - sp.: sein Schwester Gela zu Metzloss.

Anna Maria, bpt. 3 Nov 1688 - sp.: Anna Maria - w/o Anthoni Riehl.

Johann Walther, bpt. 22 Feb 1691 - sp.: Walther Schmid here.

Anna Sophia, bpt. 5 March 1693 - sp.: ... Herr Hans Reinhart from Utteroth ...

It is fascinating to note that Conrad Häner had two sons named Johannes who both survived, as did Johannes[1] Häner, the 1709er; although a strange custom to our modern eyes, naming two children with the same Christian names was not uncommon in Germany in the 17th and 18th centuries (HJ).

Johannes Heyner made his initial appearance on the Hunter

Rolls 30 June 1710 with 1 pers. over 10 yrs. of age; the family
increased 4 Oct 1710 to 2 pers. over 10 yrs., and then rose again
to 2 pers. over 10 yrs. and 1 pers. under 10 yrs. 24 Dec 1711.
The 25 March 1712 listing read 3 pers. over 10 and 1 under 10 yrs.
and then diminished to 2 pers. over 10 and 1 under 10 on 24 June
1712. Johannis Heiner was nat. 3 Jan 1715/16 (Albany Nats.). Johannes Honner with wife and ch. was at Quunsberg ca. 1716/17 (Simmendinger Register). Johanes Hener was a Palatine Debtor in 1718
and 1721 (Livingston Debt Lists). Johannes Hoe Mier was a Palatine
willing to remain at Livingston Manor 26 Aug 1724 (Doc. Hist. of
N.Y., Vol. III, p. 724). He was the surviving trustee of the 6000
acre tract which became Germantown when he deeded 40 acres for
church purposes to the Luth. church 5 Aug 1758 (Settlers & Residents, Vol. I, p. 1). Berkenmeyer mentioned a visit with Johannes[1]
on 3 Sept 1732 in his Albany Protocol, p. 41:

> Before the service began, Schumacher and Scheffer came
> to me, much upset, saying what a mishap it was that H.
> Heiner had come to the village. As I went to the church,
> Capt. Hagedorn came to meet me, saying that I should say
> nothing today about an election, because there was not
> enough time. I replied: That is a matter for the congre-
> gation, since the congregation must decide, not I.
> After the prayer I began a hymn, but Heiner immediately
> took it up. So I turned the singing over to him. After
> the sermon, the Lord's Supper, the baptism, and the
> marriage were ended and as Heiner passed the table, I
> grasped him by the sleeve. "Friend Heiner, " I said,
> "No one must leave here unreconciled. Since the whole
> congregation has been reconciled with God, come, I for-
> give." He was so saddened by this that he did not speak
> two words. Therefore I gave him the chalice to bring
> peace to the whole congregation. On the way home, I
> called at Capt. Hagedorn's to ask if Heiner would not
> eat with me or smoke with me after dinner. After some
> exchange of words with him about Saalbach's house and
> people, he said, "What will people say about my run-
> ning after the Pastor this way?" Laughing, I said to
> that, "What will people say about my running after H.
> Heiner this way? Fiddle-faddle to that. Come and be
> at ease." So he promised to come, and he did come, too.
> He seemed to be vexed over Scheffer's (approaching)
> marriage here (at the Camp) and the fact that it would
> take place secretly. He said that J(ohann Michael)
> Schut was going to bring a pastor, but that he did not
> have enough in his collection. Finally he left, since
> his wife wanted to go to bed. Such an excuse being
> unacceptable to the others, he added, "We shall cer-
> tainly not make one another any wiser this evening."

Later, Johannes[1] Häner and Pastor Berkenmeyer became enemies, as
Berkenmeyer noted 17 Sept 1734 in a letter to the Luth. Ministerium of Hamburg that H. Heiner was an evil man who by force wanted
to have a pastor from England; Berkenmeyer added that Heiner had
said that hanging was too mild (for Berkenmeyer), and that he wanted to cut strips of flesh off him! (Luth. Church in N.Y. and N.J.,
p. 64). The issue of Johannes[1] Häner and Catharina were:

1) <u>Bernhardt²</u> (HJ). Bernhart Hener and his wife Catharina were on the St. Peter's Church Family List ca. 1734 (Rhinebeck Luth. Chbk.). He md. Elisabetha Finckel (HJ) and had ch.:

    i) <u>Johannes³</u>, b. 22 April 1736 - sp.: Joh: Hener and wife Catharina (Rhinebeck Luth. Chbk.).

    ii) <u>Elisabetha³</u>, b. 9 Jan 1742 and bpt. at Camp - sp.: Lisabeth Heiner and Werner Heiner (Loonenburg Luth. Chbk.).

    iii) <u>Catharina³</u>, bpt. 28 Oct 1743 - sp.: Johan Mussier and Catharina (Germantown Ref. Chbk.).

    iv) <u>Anna Maria³</u>, bpt. 11 Jan 1746 - sp.: J. Hener and Anna Maria Hener (Germantown Ref. Chbk.). She md. Johannes Hopp (Hap) (HJ).

    v) <u>Bernhardt³</u>, b. 30 March 1747 - sp.: Georg Finckel and Elisabeth (Germantown Luth. Chbk.). He md. Anna Hop 5 Aug 1770 (Germantown Ref. Chbk.). They had ch. at Germantown Ref. and Gilead Luth. Churches.

    vi) <u>Catharina³</u>, bpt. 8 Oct 1749 - sp.: Philip Hener and Catharina Muschier (Germantown Ref. Chbk.).

    vii) <u>Conrad³</u>, b. 28 June 1751 - sp.: Conraad Loscher and Engeltje (Loonenburg Luth. Chbk.).

    viii) <u>Martinus³</u>, bpt. 20 March 1753 - sp.: Martin Linck and wife (Germantown Ref. Chbk.). He was a sp. at Schaghticoke Ref. Church in 1773.

2) <u>Rebecca²</u> (HJ), md. 5 July 1734 Mathys Van den Burg (Catskill Ref. Chbk.).

3) <u>Johannes²</u> (HJ), md. Anna Maria Schäffer (HJ). Issue:

    i) <u>Catharina³</u>, bpt. 7 Oct 1741 - sp.: Johannes Hener and Catharina (Germantown Ref. Chbk.).

    ii) <u>Johannes³</u>, bpt. 28 Oct 1743 - sp.: J. Valentin Schaster and Maria Barbara Schaster (Germantown Ref. Chbk.).

    iii) <u>Jacob³</u>, b. 26 Sept 1745 and bpt. at the Camp - sp.: Jurge Heiner and wife Cathar. (Loonenburg Luth. Chbk.).

    iv) <u>Petrus³</u>, b. 18 Jan 1746 - sp.: Petrus Hagedorn and Anna (Germantown Luth. Chbk.).

    v) <u>David³</u>, b. 16 Jan 1749 - sp.: Bernh: Heiner and Elisabeth (Germantown Luth. Chbk.).

    vi) <u>Elisabetha³</u>, bpt. 22 Sept 1751 - sp.: Friderich Shöster and Lisabeth (Germantown Ref. Chbk.).

    vii) <u>Friederich³</u>, bpt. 21 Jan 1754 - sp.: Frederick Bats and Catharina Hogeborn (Germantown Ref. Chbk.).

    viii) <u>Catharina³</u>, bpt. 4 Feb 1756 - sp.: Orgel Hauser and wife Anna Cath: Haver (Germantown Ref. Chbk.).

4) <u>Georg²</u> (HJ), taxed in Rhinebeck in 1743/44 (Dutchess Co.

Tax Lists). He md. Catharina Hagedorn (HJ) and had ch.:

    i) Johannes³, b. 7 Aug 1744 and bpt. Teerbosch - sp.: Hannes Hener and wife Maria (Loonenburg Luth. Chbk.).

    ii) Anna³, b. 9 Nov 1746 and bpt. in Camp - sp.: Petris Hagedorn and wife Anna (Rhinebeck Luth. Chbk.).

    iii) Elisabetha³, b. 31 Dec 1748 or 1749 - sp.: Bernh: Heiner and Elisabeth (Germantown Luth. Chbk.).

    iv) Margaretha³, b. 11 April 1751 - sp.: Andreas Loew and wife Margaretha (Rhinebeck Luth. Chbk.).

    v) Thomas³, bpt. 6 Nov 1757 - sp.: Thomas Bechtel and wife Catharina Hagendoorn (Claverack Ref. Chbk.).

    vi) Jacob³, b. 13 May 1761 - sp.: Jacob Hagedorn and Barbara (Churchtown Luth. Chbk.).

5) Eva² (HJ), md. Johannes Conrad (HJ).

6) Anna Maria² (HJ), md. Johannes Hunsinger (HJ).

7) Johannes² (HJ), md. 20 April 1746 as a single man b. Livingston Manor Eva Van Etten (Rhinebeck Flats Ref. Chbk.). Johannes Hoener was conf. 12 April 1748 (with Samuel, Philip, and Jacob Hoener - firm sons of Johannes¹) and noted then as aged 24 yrs., having been bpt. by the N.Y. minister Johann van Driesen, sp. at his bpt. being Joh: Blass and his wife (Rhinebeck Luth. Chbk.). Thus, his bpt. and conf. records prove his N.Y. birth, cementing then that he had to be s/o Johannes¹, who like his father in Germany Conrad Häner, had two surviving sons named Johannes! (HJ). The ch. of this Johannes² Häner and Eva were:

    i) Johannes³, bpt. 12 Oct 1746 - sp.: Joannes Heiner and Catharina Mussier (Red Hook Luth. Chbk.).

    ii) Catharina³, bpt. 13 Jan 1748 - sp.: Waner Hener and Catharina Mussy (Red Hook Luth. Chbk.).

    iii) Samuel³, bpt. 29 Aug 1756 - sp.: Samuel Hohner and Rebecca Veller (Red Hook Luth. Chbk.).

    iv) Joseph³, bpt. 11 May 1759 - sp.: Joseph Reichard and Anna Nier (Red Hook Luth. Chbk.).

    v) Zacharias³, b. 22 July 1761 - sp.: Lodewyk Elschever and Susanna Rukhart (Rhinebeck Flats Ref. Chbk.).

    vi) Margaretha³, b. 1 May 1764 - sp.: Stephanus Borgard and wife Rebecca (Rhinebeck Luth. Chbk.).

8) Samuel², bpt. 23 Oct 1726 at Jacob Schumacher's at Kamp, one of twins - the other dead - sp.: Samuel Miller and wife Anna Catharina (N.Y. City Luth. Chbk.). Samuel Hoener was conf. 12 April 1748 aged 21 yrs. (Rhinebeck Luth. Chbk.). He md. 21 May 1754 at Rhinebeck Rebecca Feller (Kingston Ref. Chbk.) and had issue:

    i) <u>Rebecca</u>[3], bpt. 9 July 1754 - sp.: Pieter Reller and
       Anna Maria Kreller (Red Hook Luth. Chbk.).

   ii) <u>Phillipus</u>[3], bpt. 28 Jan 1759 - sp.: Phillip Veller
       and Catharina Rauh (Red Hook Luth. Chbk.).

  iii) <u>Wilhelm</u>[3], b. 24 Dec 1760 - sp.: Helmus Feller and
       Catharina Reichert (Rhinebeck Luth. Chbk.).

   iv) <u>Catharina</u>[3], bpt. 4 weeks old in 1763 - sp.: Fred. and
       Elisabet Schefer (Albany Ref. Chbk.).

9) <u>Henrich</u>[2], b. 30 April 1728 and bpt. Kamp - sp.: Henr. Hay-
dorn and wife Anna Maria (N.Y. City Luth. Chbk.). He md.
as s/o Hannes Henner 21 Nov 1749 Barbara, d/o Christian
Haver (Germantown Ref. Chbk.) and had issue:

    i) <u>Petrus</u>[3], bpt. 12 March 1751 - sp.: Jurgin Pieter and
       Christina Heuber (Germantown Ref. Chbk.).

   ii) <u>Henrich</u>[3], bpt. 22 Nov 1761 - sp.: Hendrick Philip and
       wife Lisabeth Caspar (Linlithgo Ref. Chbk.).

  iii) <u>Abraham</u>[3], bpt. 6 Oct 1763 - sp.: Pieter Huyser and Eva
       Plas (Linlithgo Ref. Chbk.).

10) <u>Werner</u>[2] (HJ), a sp. to Bernhardt[2] Häner at Camp in 1742
(Loonenburg Luth. Chbk.), to Johannes[2] Häner Jr. in 1748
(Red Hook Luth. Chbk.), and to Jacob[2] Häner in 1754 (Rhine-
beck Flats Ref. Chbk.).

11) <u>Philip</u>[2], md. as s/o Johannes[1] 15 Oct 1751 Eva, d/o Peter
Treber (Rhinebeck Luth. Chbk.). Philip Hoener was conf. 12
April 1748 aged 18 yrs. (Rhinebeck Luth. Chbk.). Issue:

    i) <u>Rebecca</u>[3], b. 1 June 1754 - sp.: Samuel Huener and Re-
       bekka Feller (Rhinebeck Flats Ref. Chbk.).

   ii) <u>Johannes</u>[3], bpt. 19 June 1757 - sp.: Joh: Hohner and
       Eva Van Etten (Red Hook Luth. Chbk.).

  iii) <u>Anna Maria</u>[3], b. 5 Feb 1762 - sp.: Niclas Feller and
       wife Anna Maria (Rhinebeck Luth. Chbk.).

   iv) <u>Anna</u>[3], b. 18 Nov 1764 - sp.: Frerik Concher and Anna
       Concher (Albany Ref. Chbk.).

    v) <u>Philip</u>[3], b. 5 Feb 1767 - sp.: Johs Eedel and Grietje
       Heiner (Albany Ref. Chbk.).

   vi) <u>Petrus</u>[3], b. 25 March 1770 - sp.: Frerik and Johanna
       Canker (Albany Ref. Chbk.).

12) <u>Jacob</u>[2], bpt. 16 Dec 1732 - sp.: Jacob Beyer and Margaretha
Beyer (Germantown Ref. Chbk.). He was conf. 12 April 1748
aged 15 yrs. (Rhinebeck Luth. Chbk.). Jacob[2] md. Magdalena
Kreller (HJ) and had issue:

    i) <u>Maria</u>[3], bpt. 27 March 1754 - sp.: Warner Hener and
       Maria Kreller (Rhinebeck Flats Ref. Chbk.).

   ii) <u>Margaretha</u>[3], b. 25 March 1756 - sp.: Johannes

Hondtsicker and Margriet Keller (Rhinebeck Flats Ref.
Chbk.).

  iii) <u>Catharina</u>[3], bpt. 27 Jan 1765 at Hoseck - sp.: Sebastian Diel and wife (Schoharie Luth. Chbk.).

   iv) <u>Wilhelm</u>[3], b. 24 April 1767 - sp.: Hanne Hheene and
Marg. Davenp(oort) (Schaghticoke Ref. Chbk.).

    v) <u>Cornelius</u>[3], b. 15 March 1770 - sp.: Cornelis V. Esch
and Alida V. Woert (Albany Ref. Chbk.).

   vi) <u>Johannes</u>[3], b. 20 May 1775 (Schaghticoke Ref. Chbk.).

The very active Hayner Family Association has been most supportive of my project over the years. Major Donald C. Holmes, U.E.,
of Kanata, Ontario, was generous in sharing data on the Loyalist
branch of the family, descending from Johannes[3], s/o Georg[2] Häner.

NICOLAUS HEITERSBACH (Hunter Lists #292)

The origins of the Palatine Heisterbach family were at 5450
<u>Niederbieber</u> (2 km. n. of Neuwied; Chbks. begin 1655) and at 6533
<u>Bacharach</u> (9 km. s. of St. Goar; Chbks. begin 1577). The father
of the emigrant was <u>Melchior Heisterbach</u>, who had sons:

+ Johann Nicolaus.

  <u>Hans Jacob</u>, md. as s/o the late Melchior Heisterbach 18 Feb
  1673 Anna Margaretha, d/o Merten Michael (Bacharach Chbk.).
Johan Niclas Heisterbach, s/o the late Melchior Heisterbach - citizen at Bacherach, md. 9 Feb 1702 Gertraudt, d/o the late Hans
Wilhelm Gladbach at O. Bieber (Niederbieber Chbk.). Nicolaues
Heistrebach, his wife, and 4 ch. were in the 3rd party of Palatines
on Capt. Robbert Lourens's ship in Holland in 1709 (Rotterdam
Lists). Nicol Heisterbach aged 52, his wife, a son aged 3, and
daughters aged 7 and 5, Ref., shoemaker, were in the 3rd arrivals
in England later that year (London Lists).

Nicolaus Heitersbach made his initial appearance on the Hunter Lists 1 July 1710 with 1 pers. over 10 yrs. and 2 pers. under
10 in the household; the last entry for the family was 4 Oct 1710,
other than the cumulative 24 Dec 1711 notation. Niclaus Heisterbach
aged 53, Johan Jacob Heisterbach aged 4, and Christina Cath Heisterbach aged 10 were in N.Y. City in 1710/11 (Palatines In N.Y.
City). The ch. of Nicolaus[1] Heisterbach and Gertraut were:

  1) <u>Christina Catharina</u>[2], bpt. 5 Nov 1702 - sp.: Christina
Cath. - d/o Andreas Runckel at O.B., Christine - d/o the
cowherd Johannis Dauffenbach at Dierdorf, and Johann Wilhelm - s/o Paulus Linen at Melsbach (Niederbieber Chbk.).

  2) <u>Maria Catharina</u>[2], bpt. 2 Aug 1704 - sp.: Maria Cath. - d/o
the late Michel Neutzert (?) at Rengsdorf, and Johannes

Gladebach at N.B. (Niederbieber Chbk.). She probably was
the Margaret Oysterberk aged 7, an orphan bound to Hugh
Nesbitt of Stratford, Conn. 12 Jan 1711 (Apprenticeship
Lists).

3) <u>Johann Jacob</u>[2], bpt. 11 April 1706 - sp.: Johann Henrich
   Hoffmann, Jacob Manck at Oberbieber, and Elisabetha - d/o
   the late Thomas Stein im Ampt Marburg (Niederbieber Chbk.).
   Jacob Oysterberk aged 3 was an orphan bound to John Will-
   iams of Fairfield, Conn. 12 Jan 1711 (Apprenticeship
   Lists). In Conn., he was known as Oysterbanks (HJ).

<u>PHILIPP HELMER</u> (Hunter Lists #293)

The origins of the Mohawk Valley Helmer family were at 6730
<u>Neustadt an der Weinstraße</u> (28 km. s.e. of Kaiserslautern; Chbks.
begin 1622). The earliest known antecedent of the emigrant was
his grandfather <u>Georg Helmer</u>. Leonhardt Helmer, s/o the late Görg
Helmer - citizen here, md. Apollonia, wid/o Hans Holder, 25 Oct
1654; Hans Holder, citizen and furrier, had md. Apollonia Maria,
d/o the late Andres Rippel, 10 Jan 1644. The ch. of Leonhard Helmer and his 1st wife Apollonia Maria were:

  <u>Elisabetha</u>, bpt. 9 July 1656 - sp.: Elisabetha - wid/o Jacob
  Müller.

+ <u>Hans Philipp</u>, bpt. 20 March 1659 - sp.: Philipps Plaum the
  Haffner.

The w/o Leonhard Helmer was bur. 2 Nov 1663. Leonhard Helmer, citizen here, md. Catharina Elisabetha, d/o Conrad Sengeiß, 13 June
1665. Conrad Sengeiß was bur. 8 Dec 1675. By his 2nd wife Leonhard Helmer had issue:

  <u>Christian</u>, bpt. 29 Sept 1666 - sp.: Christian - s/o Conrad
  Sengeiß.

  <u>Johann Mattheus</u>, bpt. 26 Aug 1668 - sp.: Joh. Mattheus Sengeiß
  - citizen and shoemaker here. He md. Anna Barbara (--) from
  Mußbach 23 June 1694.

  <u>Anna Catharina</u>, bpt. 20 July 1671 - sp.: Anna Catharina - d/o
  Conrad Sengeiß. She d. 1747.

  <u>Johann Jacob</u>, bpt. 7 July 1674 - sp.: Hans Jacob - s/o Christian Schönig.

  <u>Christian</u>, bpt. 19 Oct 1675 - sp.: Christian Sengeiß - citizen
  and Haffner here. He md. as s/o the late Leonhard Helmer 16
  Feb 1707 Anna Maria Kölsch.

  <u>Georg</u>, bpt. 19 Oct 1675 as twin to the above - sp.: Hans Görg
  Sengeiß - Barbierer at Düseldorf. He md. as s/o the late Leonhard Helmer 14 April 1700 Anna Maria Bury.

  <u>Catharina Elisabetha</u>, bpt. 8 Nov 1678 - sp.: Anna Catharina

d/o the citizen and baker Georg Kuhn.

Anna Elisabetha, bpt. 23 Jan 1682 - sp.: Anna Elisabetha - w/o the citizen and baker Peter Schneider here.

Leonhard Helmer was bur. 24 Sept 1691, aged 74 yrs. Philipp Helmer, s/o Leonhard Helmer - citizen here, md. Elisabetha, d/o Johann Wilhelm Möckler - citizen here, 15 June 1685. Philips Helmer, his wife, and 6 ch. were on Capt. Johan Facit's ship in the 5th party in Holland in 1709 (Rotterdam Lists).

Philipp Helmer made his initial appearance on the Hunter Lists 4 July 1710 with 5 pers. over 10 yrs. of age and 3 pers. under 10. The entry read 7 pers. over 10 and 1 pers. under 10 on 24 June 1711, 6 pers. over 10 yrs. and 2 under 10 on 29 Sept 1711, 6 over 10 and 1 under 10 on 24 Dec 1711, and 7 over 10 yrs. of age and 1 under 10 on 24 June 1712. Philip Kelmer: 2 men, 2 lads aged 9 to 15, 1 boy 8 yrs. and under, 1 woman, and 2 maids aged 9 to 15 yrs. were in Ulster Co. in 1710/11 (West Camp Census). Philips Helmer was nat. 11 Oct 1715 (Albany Nats.). Philipp Helmer and Elisabetha with 5 ch. were at Neu-Cassel ca. 1716/17 (Simmendinger Register). Philip Helmer was a patentee on the n. side of the Mohawk 30 April 1725 (Burnetsfield Patent). The ch. of Philip[1] and Elisabetha Helmer were:

1) Maria Barbara[2], bpt. 14 March 1688 - sp.: Maria Barbara - d/o Henrich Kauß - Kopfwirth here (Neustadt an der Weinstraße Chbk.).

2) Leonhard[2], bpt. 5 Feb 1690 - sp.: Leonhard Florcking - citizen and cooper here (Neustadt an der Weinstraße Chbk.). Leendert Helmer was nat. 11 Oct 1715 (Albany Nats.). Leonhard Kollmer and Elisabetha with 2 ch. were at Neu-Cassel ca. 1716/17 (Simmendinger Register). Lendert Helmer and his wife Elisabeth were each patentees on the n. side of the Mohawk 30 April 1725 (Burnetsfield Patent). Lendert Helmer was a freeholder of Canajoharrie in 1763 (Albany Co. Freeholders). The will of Lenard Helmer of Palatine was dated 27 June 1781 and probated 28 April 1791 (Montgomery Co. Will Bk. I). Issue:

   i) Johann Gotfried[3], b. 27 Dec 1715 and bpt. at Schoharie - sp.: Gottfrid Ruehl and his wife (West Camp Luth. Chbk.). The will of Gottfried Helmer of Canajoharie in Albany Co. was dated 14 March 1765 and probated 1 Dec 1783 (Fernow Wills #807).

   ii) Philip[3] (Will).

   iii) Johannes[3] (Will). The estate of John Helmer of Canijohary, Montgomery Co., yeoman, was probated 1 Jan 1787 (Genealogical Data from Administration Papers,

p. 150).

- iv) Maria Margaretha[3] (Will), md. John Headcock (Will).
- v) Gertraud[3] (Will), md. Jacob Kraus (Will).
- vi) Anna Magdalena[3] (Will), md. Philip Peer (Will).
- vii) Elisabetha[3] (Will), md. Peter Eygenbrodt (Will).
- viii) Johann Leonhard[3] (HJ), mentioned in The Helmer Family, p. 3 as signing a paper dealing with Stone Arabia churches in 1751.

3) Catharina Elisabetha[2], bpt. 27 April 1692 - sp.: Catharina - w/o Melchior Schard (Neustadt an der Weinstraße Chbk.).

4) Johannes[2], bpt. 25 July 1694 - sp.: Johannes Schimpf - citizen here (Neustadt an der Weinstraße Chbk.).

5) Melchior[2], bpt. 5 April 1696 - sp.: Melchior Schardt - citizen and joiner here (Neustadt an der Weinstraße Chbk.).

6) Johann Adam[2], bpt. 24 Aug 1698 - sp.: Hans Adam Matern - citizen here - and wife Anna Barbara (Neustadt an der Weinstraße Chbk.). John Adam Helmer and his wife Anna Margaret were both patentees 30 April 1725; he was on the n. side of the river and she on the s. side (Burnetsfield Patent). Adam Halmer was a freeholder in 1763 at the Falls (Albany Co. Freeholders). The ch. of Adam[2] Helmer probably were:

- i) Henrich[3], mentioned in the will of Leonhard[2]. Henry, Phillip, Adam, and John Hellmer were listed next to each other on the roll of Capt. Marx Petry's Co. in 1767 at Bornets Field (Report of the State Historian, Vol. II, p. 855).
- ii) Adam[3] (HJ), called Jr. in Capt. Petry's Co. in 1757 (Report of the State Historian, Vol. II, p. 781).
- iii) Friederich[3] (HJ), called Friederik Adam Helmer, Corp'l in Petry's 1767 Co.
- iv) Philip[3] (HJ).
- v) Johannes[3] (HJ).
- vi) Margaretha[3], a sp. in 1760 (Stone Arabia Ref. Chbk.).
- vii) Catharina[3], md. as d/o Adam 26 Dec 1759 Friederich Riegel (Stone Arabia Ref. Chbk.).
- viii) Elisabetha Margaretha[3], md. as d/o Adam 30 Sept 1760 Ekabod Baant (Stone Arabia Ref. Chbk.).

7) Maria Margaretha[2], bpt. 31 Oct 1700 - sp.: Maria Margretha - d/o Johannes Helmstätter (Neustadt an der Weinstraße Chbk.).

8) Anna Apollonia[2], bpt. 30 March 1703 - sp.: Apolonia - w/o Johannes Böckel - citizen and vinedresser (Neustadt an der Weinstraße Chbk.). She most probably md. Lorentz Herter (HJ).

9) Georg Friederich[2], bpt. 9 June 1706 - sp.: Georg Friedrich

Fischer and Anna Margaretha Caus - d/o the landlord (Neustadt an der Weinstraße Chbk.). Frederick Helmer was a patentee on the n. side of the Mohawk 30 April 1725 (Burnetsfield Patent). Frederick Helmer was a freeholder at the
Falls in 1763 (Albany Co. Freeholders). The probable ch.
of Friederich² were:

  i) Friederich³ (HJ), perhaps the Fridrich Helmer Jr.
     noted on Capt. Mark Petry's Co. in 1757 (Report of the
     State Historian, Vol. II, p. 781).

 ii) Adam³ (HJ). Adam Friederik, Georg, and Phillip Helmer
     Jr. were listed next to each other on Petry's rolls
     at Bornets Field in 1767 (Report of the State Histor-
     ian, Vol. II, p. 855).

iii) Philip³ (HJ).

 iv) Georg³ (HJ).

There are many unplaced Helmers of the 3rd generation from
Philip¹: 1) Gertrud, wid/o Leonard Helmer d. 23 May 1808, aged 83
yrs. (Herkimer Ref. Chbk.); 2) Johann Friederich Helmer and wife
Sabina had a son Johann Georg b. 13 Nov 1760 at Stone Arabia Ref.
Church; 3) the w/o Philip Helmer d. Aug 1829, aged 84 yrs. in Herkimer (Albany Gazette 28 Aug 1829); 4) The will of Phillip Helmer
of Otsego Town was probated 29 June 1797 (Otsego Co. Will Bk. I);
5) Will. Helmer sp. Dan. Yorck in 1737 at Albany Ref. Church; and
6) a Magdalena Helmer md. Marcus Rees in the Mohawk region at an
early date. Students of this difficult group should be able to
add more 3rd generation Helmers to this sketch by further study in
Mohawk Valley Chbks. and private sources (HJ).

PETER HELMER (Hunter Lists #294)

Although called Helmer in the ledger of the Hunter Lists, this
emigrant really was Peter¹ Helm. The roots of this Palatine family
were at 6752 Winnweiler (17 km. n.e. of Kaiserslautern; Chbks. begin 1700, Luth.) and at 6753 Alsenborn (12 km. n.e. of Kaiserslautern; Chbks. begin 1663). A Peter Helm, miller, sp. the emigrant
1709er Georg Riedt at Otterberg in 1682. Peter Helm was called a
resin-burner at the smelter pool in 1704, and a shepherd at Horin-
gen (?) in 1706 (Winnweiler Chbk.). His wife was Anna Engel (or
sometimes written Angelica) Jung (Alsenborn Chbk.). Pr Helm, his
wife, (sons) Simon, Leenhart, and 5 (more) ch., were on Capt. Bouwel's ship in the 2nd party in Holland in 1709 (Rotterdam Lists).
Peter Helm aged 30, with his wife, sons aged 15, 11, 9, 6, 4, and
¼, Ref., labourer, were in the 2nd arrivals in England later that
year (London Lists).

Peter Helmer made his initial appearance on the Hunter Lists
4 Aug 1710 with 2 pers. over 10 yrs. and 2 pers. under 10; the entry changed to 3 pers. over 10 and 1 under 10 on 4 Oct 1710, and
then rose to 3 over 10 and 2 under 10 yrs. on 31 Dec 1710. The family showed 4 pers. over 10 yrs. and 1 pers. under 10 on 24 June
1711, 2 pers. over 10 and 1 under 10 on 25 March 1712, and 2 pers.
over 10 and 2 pers. under 10 yrs. on 24 June 1712. The ch. of
Peter[1] Helm and Anna Engel were:

1) Simon[2] (Rotterdam Lists). Simon Helm, s/o Peter Helm, was
   bound to John Rutsen of Kingston 2 June 1711 at the age
   of 12 yrs. (Apprenticeship Lists). Symon Helm was nat. 8
   and 9 Sept 1715 (Kingston Nats.). Symen Helen was in a
   foot Co. of mallitia for the town of Shawangunk under the
   command of Capt. Nicolas Hoffman in Jacob Rutsen's Regt.
   in Ulster Co. in 1715 (Report of the State Historian, Vol.
   I, p. 564). Simon Helm was listed with Peter Helm and next
   to Johann Michael Helm in Neu Yorck ca. 1716/17 (Simmendinger Register). He was taxed £2 at Kingston in 1720/21
   (Ulster Co. Tax Lists). Simon Helm was in the foot Co. of
   Hurly in the Ulster Co. Militia in 1738 (Report of the
   State Historian, Vol. I, p. 610). He md. Johanna Schäfer
   (HJ) and had issue:

   i) Catharina[3], bpt. 4 June 1721 - sp.: Johannes Rutsz and
      Catrina Beekman (Kingston Ref. Chbk.).

   ii) Peter[3], bpt. 9 Dec 1722 - sp.: Pieter Van der Helm
      and Elisabeth Krans (Kingston Ref. Chbk.).

   iii) Elisabetha[3], bpt. Nov 1724 - sp.: Machiel Helm and
      Elisabeth Schever (Kingston Ref. Chbk.). She md. Peter
      Dijo Jr. 25 Jan 1745 (Kingston Ref. Chbk.).

   iv) Engel[3], bpt. 7 Aug 1726 - sp.: Adam Schrever and El-
      isabeth Schinkel (Kingston Ref. Chbk.). She had Banns
      to marry David Windviel 3 Sept 1749 (Kingston Ref.
      Chbk.).

   v) Jacob[3], bpt. 13 Oct 1728 - sp.: Adam Scheever and El-
      isabeth Scheever (Kingston Ref. Chbk.). He md. as a
      single man b. Rosendale 14 Oct 1748 Margaretha Schmidt
      (Kingston Ref. Chbk.).

   vi) Johannes[3], bpt. 15 March 1730 - sp.: Jacob Rutsz and
      Lea Nieuwkerk (Kingston Ref. Chbk.).

   vii) Catharina[3], bpt. 2 April 1732 - sp.: Niclaas Blansjan
      and Catrina Eswyn (Kingston Ref. Chbk.).

   viii) Abraham[3], bpt. 24 March 1734 - sp.: Nicolaas and Sarah
      Roos (New Paltz Ref. Chbk.). He md. Catharina Smedes
      10 July 1761 (Kingston Ref. Chbk.). He and Simon Helm

sp. John Hadkins in 1752 at Rhinebeck Luth. Church. Abraham[3] had ch. bpt. at Kingston Ref. and Marbletown Ref. Churches (HJ).

  ix) Sarah[3], bpt. same day 24 March 1734 - sp.: Gerrit and Anna Neuwkerk (New Paltz Ref. Chbk.).

   x) Johanna[3], bpt. 17 Oct 1736 - sp.: Michael Helm and Johanna Louw (Kingston Ref. Chbk.). She md. William Krom (HJ).

  xi) Johannes[3], bpt. 8 April 1739 - sp.: Christiaan De Zoo and Marytjen De Graav (Kingston Ref. Chbk.).

2) Leonhardt[2] (Rotterdam Lists).

3) Peter[2] (HJ), md. as single man b. Germany 5 Nov 1725 Elisabetha Schinckel (Kingston Ref. Chbk.). He may have md. Maria Rous as a 2nd wife (HJ). By his 1st wife Peter[2] had:

   i) Petrus[3], bpt. 20 Nov 1726 - sp.: Zymen Helm and Annaatjen Schever (Kingston Ref. Chbk.). Pieter Helm Jr. was in Capt. Johannis Van Hoesen's Co. at Claverack in 1767 (Report of the State Historian, Vol. II, p. 857). He md. Christina Schäfer (HJ) and had ch. bpt. at Claverack Ref. and Kinderhook Ref. Churches (HJ).

  ii) Margaretha[3], bpt. 7 April 1728 - sp.: Michael Helm and Margriet Schenkel (Kingston Ref. Chbk.). She md. 9 Nov 1748 Francis Herdyk (Loonenburg Luth. Chbk.).

 iii) Jonas[3], bpt. 25 Dec 1733 - sp.: Jonas, Geertruy and Maria Schinckel (Kinderhook Ref. Chbk.).

  iv) Anna[3], bpt. 28 Feb 1736 - sp.: Claes V. D. Karre and Anna (Kinderhook Ref. Chbk.).

   v) Jacob[3], bpt. 23 Jan 1739 - sp.: Henrich Schinckel and Geertruy Valk (Linlithgo Ref. Chbk.).

4) Michael[2] (HJ), md. as single man b. Germany 28 June 1728 Johanna Louw (Kingston Ref. Chbk.). Michael Helme was nat. 8 and 9 Sept 1715 (Kingston Nats.) and was in the foot Co. at Rocester, Ulster Co. in 1738 (Report of the State Historian, Vol. I, p. 611). Issue:

   i) Peter[3], bpt. 27 April 1729 - sp.: Pieter Helm and Elisabeth Sinkel (Kingston Ref. Chbk.). He md. Elisabetha Consalis (HJ).

  ii) Jacob[3], bpt. 1 Jan 1738 - sp.: Jacob Rutsz, Jr. and Alida Lievengstond (Kingston Ref. Chbk.).

5) "A Daughter"[2], b. 21 May 1704 - sp.: Hans Henrich - s/o Peter Hager, ... from Wartenberg, and Barbara - d/o Hans Bally (?) from Wartenberg (Winnweiler Chbk.).

6) "A Son"[2], b. 4 Dec 1706 - sp.: Velten Weber from Enkenbach and Anna Cath. - w/o Peter Kuhn at Heringen (Winnweiler

Chbk.).

7) <u>Jacob</u>[2], bpt. 5 May 1709 - sp.: Jacob Gejer and his wife, and also J. Bocke the nailsmith from Enkenbach (Alsenborn Chbk.).

8) <u>Margaretha</u>[2] (HJ), md. Jacob Hoornbeek as a single woman b. Dutchess Co. 16 Sept 1733 (Kingston Ref. Chbk.).

ANNA BARBARA HEMMERLE (Hunter Lists #295)

Johan Jacob Heymerleÿ, his wife, and 4 ch. were on Capt. Frans Robbenson's ship in the 3rd party of Palatines in Holland in 1709 (Rotterdam Lists). John Jacob Hammerlein aged 45, his wife, a son aged 13, daughters aged 11, 7, and 2, Ref., husbandman and vine-dresser, were in the 3rd arrivals at London in 1709 (London Lists).

Anna Barbara Hemmerle made her first appearance on the Hunter Lists 1 July 1710 with 1 pers. over 10 yrs. of age and 1 pers. under 10 yrs.; her last entry with the same numbers was 4 Aug 1710.

MICHAEL HENNESCHIEDT (Hunter Lists #296)

Anna Catharina Snyder, wife of Michiel Himmeschied of Honellen, joined the N.Y. City Ref. Church 28 Aug 1711. This village was 6759 <u>Hohenöllen</u> (5 km. n.e. of Wolfstein), and records pertaining to this fascinating family were found at nearby 6759 <u>Reipoltskirchen</u> (3 km. further n.; Chbks. begin 1680, Cath.). The father of the emigrant was <u>Wilhelm Hüneschied</u> (or Hinterschied), who was granted a hereditary lease to Naumburger Hof by Duke Friedrich Ludwig 19 July 1673, along with his brother-in-law Matthes Krebs of Bübelsheim in Bergischen. To obtain the lease, Hüneschied and Krebs put forward the following conditions:

1) If the lord provided a free allowance of wood from his forests, they would build house, barn and stable at their own expense.
2) They should be free from rent for two to three yrs.
3) To pay interest on loans they incurred, the Duke should pay them a subsidy of 100 Rt.
4) The free wood for construction was to be delivered without charge as an obligatory feudal service.
5) For rent later the annual payment should be 24 bushels of two kinds of grain.
6) During the period of construction they were to receive a supplement of ten to twelve bushels of rye for expenses.

Life at Naumburger Hof was not easy, with an army plundering the land in 1675, a conflict between Hüneschied and Krebs in 1676, and small harvests for many yrs. Wilhelm Hüneschied d. in 1688, and his widow Anna Maria Baltes ran the farm thereafter. In 1709, she proposed that the farm be divided between herself and her son Anton; she d. ca. 1724. The ch. of Wilhelm and Anna Maria were:

Anna Maria, md. Theobald Hack (Haak, Hart).

Anna Magdalena, md. Daniel Lammericks 7 Dec 1690 (Meisenheim
Luth. Chbk.).

+ Johann Michael.

Johann Peter, md. Maria Cohnß.

Maria Catharina, md. Adolph Schuhmacher.

Johann Christoph, bpt. 1682 - sp.: Joes Christ. Merck, Christ.
Lonn (?), and Elisabetha Reusch (?). He md. Maria Margaretha
(--).

Johann Antonius, bpt. 1 April 1684 - sp.: Antonius Schmidt,
Joes Petrus Hünescheidt, and Anna Odilia Yong (Jung?). He md.
17 July 1708 Anna Elisabetha Weigand (Meisenheim Luth. Chbk.).

Maria Elisabetha, bpt. 2 March 1686. She md. Meinrad Köhlmeier.
Michael Hünneschied had left Naumburger Hof and was living in Hohenöllen, according to his mother's petition dated 16 April 1709
(Landesarchiv Speyer, B. 2, Nr. 904, fol. 85). Michel Hindterschit,
his wife, and 3 ch. were in Holland in the 6th party of Palatines
in 1709 (Rotterdam Lists).

Michael Henneschiedt made his initial appearance on the Hunter Lists 4 July 1710 with 2 pers. over 10 yrs. of age and 3 pers.
under 10 yrs.; a special notation for a young child was added 4
Aug 1710 with 1 other pers. over 10 yrs. The entry for 29 Sept 1711
read 3 pers. over 10 yrs. and 2 pers. under 10, while the family
was recorded with 4 pers. over 10 yrs. and 1 under 10 13 Sept 1712.
An extra entry for 23 Sept 1713 showed 3 pers. over 10 yrs. and 2
pers. under 10. Michael Henneschid aged 36, Anna Catharina Henneschid aged 30, Casper Henneschid aged 11, John Peter Henneschid
aged 1, and Maria Sophia Henneschid aged 6, were in N.Y. City in
1710/11 (Palatines In N.Y. City). Michael Hinterschied and Anna
Catharina, with 4 ch. were auf dem Rarendantz ca. 1716/17 (Simmendinger Register). Michel Hunerschut was an elder in the N.J. German
Luth. congregations 13 Sept 1731 (Letter to the Luth. Ministerium
of Hamburg on that date). The Luth. Church in N.Y. and N.J. 1722-
1760 is filled with interesting references to this 1709er, particularly in regard to internal squabbles between the Luth. laymen
and Pastors. Michael Hendeshott was a freeholder of Lebanon Twp.
in 1741 (Hunterdon Co. Freeholders). One source, Weygand's diary
which I have not seen firsthand, noted that he d. 19 Jan 1749.
The issue of Johann Michael[1] Henneschied and Anna Catharina were:

   1) Caspar[2] (Palatines In N.Y. City). Casp. Hamersmid subscri-
      bed 5 sh. in 1727 (N.Y. City Luth. Protocol). He was noted
      with his father in 1735 in the Janeway Accounts. Gaspar
      Hendeshott was a freeholder of Lebanon Twp. in 1741 (Hunt-
      erdon Co. Freeholders). He signed the call to Rev. John

Albert Weygand in 1749 (<u>Chambers</u>, p. 401).

2) <u>Johann Peter²</u>, b. in Hohenöllen and bpt. 15 Feb 1702 - sp.:
Joes Petrus Hünescheidt from Premerhof (?) and the widow
from Stolzenberger (?) (Reipoltskirchen Chbk.).

3) <u>Maria Rosina Catharina²</u>, b. in Hohenöllen and bpt. 18 Feb
1704 - sp.: Julius Hess, Joes Christoph Hinneschet, Joan
Jacob Klein, Catharina Barens (?), Rosina Schneider, and
Anna Maria Simons (Reipoltskirchen Chbk.).

4) <u>Johann Henrich²</u>, bpt. 19 April 1706 - sp.: Joes Petrus
Cranerius (?), Petrus Mattheis, Joes Henricus Baltes, Elisab. Marg. Klein, Anna Maria Hindescheid, and Anna Elisabetha Müller (Reipoltskirchen Chbk.).

5) <u>Michael²</u> (N.Y. Luth. Chbk. sp. 1733/34). The will of Michael Hendershot of Sussex Co. was dated 14 June 1786 and
proved 11 Nov 1786 (N.J. Wills, Lib. 28, p. 464). He was
listed in the Janeway Accounts in 1736. Issue:

   i) <u>Michael³</u>, b. 5 April 1733/34 and bpt. at Rareton at
      Rachewaij - sp.: Michel Henneschutt the child's grand-
      father and wife Catharina (N.Y. City Luth. Chbk.).

  ii) <u>Johannes³</u> (Will).

 iii) <u>Elisabetha³</u> (Will), md. a Bemer (Will).

  iv) <u>Catharina³</u> (Will).

   v) <u>Anthonius³</u> (Will) (this entry somewhat confusing -HJ).

  vi) <u>Caspar³</u> (Will).

 vii) <u>Jacob³</u> (Will).

viii) <u>Wilhelm³</u> (Will).

  ix) <u>Sarah³</u> (Will), md. a Roof (Will).

   x) <u>Sophia³</u> (Will), md. a Roof (Will).

6) <u>Elisabetha²</u>, b. 17 Jan 1716 at Millstone River and bpt. at
Raritons - sp.: Johann Tittel and wife Elisabeth (N.Y. City
Luth. Chbk.).

7) <u>Eva²</u>, b. 27 Dec 1717 at Millstone River and bpt. at Raritons at Middlebosch - sp.: Daniel Schoemacher and Eva
Weber (N.Y. City Luth. Chbk.). She md. Wm. Pettinger (HJ).

8) <u>Johannes²</u>, b. 23 Jan 1720 and bpt. at Raritons at Baldus
Pickel's - sp.: Baldus Pickel and wife Gertrud (N.Y. City
Luth. Chbk.). He was registered in the Janeway Accounts
as s/o Michael in 1740-42.

Mr. John E. Ruch of Montreal, Canada has assembled a tremend-
ous amount of documented data on this family, especially in regard
to the history of Naumburger Hof. His in-depth research in the civil documents and land records of the Henneschiedt region has been
most helpful to my project.

LORENTZ HENRICH (Hunter Lists #297)

Lorentz Henrich aged 28, his wife, a son aged 2½, a daughter aged 1¼, Ref., cooper, were in the 1st arrivals in England in May 1709 (London Lists).

Lorentz Henrich made his first appearance on the Hunter Rolls 4 Aug 1710 with 1 pers. over 10 yrs. and 1 pers. under 10 yrs. The family increased to 2 pers. over 10 yrs. and 3 under 10 yrs. on 4 Oct 1710 and rose again to 3 pers. over 10 and 3 under 10 on 31 Dec 1710. The entry for 25 March 1711 read 3 over 10 and 2 under 10, for 24 June 1711 the notation recorded 2 over 10 yrs. and 3 under 10, and finally the entry stated 2 pers. over 10 yrs. and 4 under 10 13 Sept 1712. Many of these fluctuations on the Hunter Lists were due to the fact that the widower Lorentz Henrich md. in ca. Sept 1710 Anna Regina, d/o Weil Halm and wid/o Johann Wilhelm Voland (HJ); her son Johann Philip Voland was called s/o L. Hendrick in 1728/29 (Dutchess Co. Tax Lists). Lourens Henrich was nat. 8 and 9 Sept 1715 (Kingston Nats.). Lorentz Henrich and Regina with 5 ch. were at Heessberg ca. 1716/17 (Simmendinger Register). Lowerence Hendereik made his initial appearance on North Ward rolls in 1717/18 and continued until 1725/26 (Dutchess Co. Tax Lists). The ch. of Lorentz[1] Henrich were:

1) Maria[2] (HJ), md. 9 Feb 1729 Johannes Falck (Kingston Ref. Chbk.).

2) Peter[2] (HJ), md. 24 June 1729 Anna Schmidt (Kingston Ref. Chbk.). He made his first appearance on North Ward rolls in 1733/34 and continued until June 1748 (Dutchess Co. Tax Lists). Issue from 1st wife:

   i) Georg Adam[3], b. 27 Feb 1736 - sp.: Georg Adam Zufeldt and wife Elisabet (Rhinebeck Luth. Chbk.).

   ii) Philip[3], bpt. 31 Dec 1738 - sp.: Philip Voland and Eva Switseler (Kingston Ref. Chbk.).

He md. 2nd Anna Margaretha Erckenbreght and had ch.:

   iii) Eva[3], bpt. 26 Oct 1742 - sp.: Joh: Philip Voland and Eva Schwitzer (Red Hook Luth. Chbk.). She joined the Red Hook Luth.Church 4 June 1757.

   iv) Elisabetha[3], bpt. 15 April 1745 - sp.: Elisabeth Kreller and Petterus Krans (Red Hook Luth. Chbk.).

   v) Johannes[3], b. 26 Oct 1746 - sp.: Peter Joh: Reisdorf and wife Elisabeth (Rhinebeck Luth. Chbk.).

   vi) Lorentz[3], bpt. 24 Oct 1748 - sp.: Laurentz Reisdorf and Margriet Sarenberger (Red Hook Luth. Chbk.).

3) Margaretha[2] (HJ), md. 12 Aug 1732 Johann Max Velde (Kingston Ref. Chbk.).

4) <u>Frantz²</u>, b. 4 Sept 1715 - sp.: Frantz Keller and wife Barbara (West Camp Luth. Chbk.). Frans Hendrick was in the
   foot Co. of the Kingston, Ulster Co. militia in 1738 (<u>Re-
   port of the State Historian</u>, Vol. I, p. 602). Frans Henderick was recorded in Bk. 2, pp. 280 & 287 of the Kingston
   Trustees Records. He md. 16 Sept 1735 Elisabetha Falck
   (Kingston Ref. Chbk.). They had issue:

   i) <u>Lorentz³</u>, bpt. 27 June 1736 - sp.: Louwerens Hendrik
      and Regina Weyl (Kingston Ref. Chbk.). He md. Elisa-
      betha Ploeg 6 May 1763 (Kingston Ref. Chbk.).

   ii) <u>Johannes³</u>, bpt. 2 Dec 1739 - sp.: Johannes Valk and
       Mareitje Henrich (Kingston Ref. Chbk.).

   iii) <u>Jacob³</u>, bpt. 27 Sept 1741 - sp.: Jacob Henrich and
        Catharina Zuvelt (Kingston Ref. Chbk.). He md. 24 Aug
        1771 Ariaantje Louw (Kingston Ref. Chbk.).

   iv) <u>Elisabetha³</u>, bpt. 29 April 1744 - sp.: Johannes Velde
       and his wife Margrietje Henrich (Kingston Ref. Chbk.).

   v) <u>Philip³</u>, bpt. 17 July 1748 - sp.: Philippus Voland and
      wife Eva Switselaar (Kingston Ref. Chbk.). He md. 27
      Dec 1775 Catharina Van Stynberg (Kingston Ref. Chbk.).

   vi) <u>Petrus³</u>, twin to the above, bpt. 17 July 1748 - sp.:
       Pieter Henrich and wife Margriet Argebreeh (Kingston
       Ref. Chbk.).

   vii) <u>Catharina³</u>, bpt. 16 Feb 1752 - sp.: Henricus Van Keur-
        en and wife Catharina Swart (Kingston Ref. Chbk.). She
        md. Petrus Osterhout in 1773 (Kingston Ref. Chbk.).

5) <u>Jacob²</u> (HJ), mentioned in Kingston Trustees Records Bk. 3,
   pp. 169 -170. He md. Catharina Koch, who joined the Red Hook
   Luth. Church in Dec 1744. He appeared on Rhinebeck rolls
   beginning in 1740/41 (Dutchess Co. Tax Lists). Issue:

   i) <u>Catharina³</u>, bpt. 13 Jan 1748 - sp.: Henrich Coultmann
      and Klabeck Hock (Red Hook Luth. Chbk.). A Catharina
      Henrich md. Johannes Dippel by 1770 (HJ).

   ii) <u>Frantz³</u>, bpt. 1 Aug 1749 - sp.: Frans Henrich and El-
       isabeth Valk (Rhinebeck Flats Ref. Chbk.).

   iii) <u>Johannes³</u>, b. 22 Nov 1751 - sp.: Johannes Lambert and
        Anna Lambert (Rhinebeck Flats Ref. Chbk.).

   iv) <u>Jacobus³</u>, bpt. 26 Sept 1756 - sp.: Jac. Voolandt and
       Anna Zufeldt (Red Hook Luth. Chbk.). He d. 19 Dec
       1835, aged 79 yrs. (Rhinebeck Ref. Cem.).

A Johann Henrich sp. Henrich Schneider at Lonenburg in 1720
(N.Y. City Luth. Chbk.); he may have been the same Johannes Hend-
riksz who md. Aaltjen Van Garden and had a daughter Elisabeth bpt.
17 June 1733 at Kingston Ref. Church - the same day Lorentz Henrich

JOST HERMANN (Hunter Lists #298)

The European origins of this family were at 6209 Kettenbach
(19 km. n.w. of Wiesbaden; Chbks. begin 1645). The father of the
1709er was Jacob Hermann of Daisbach, who d. 4 May 1710, aged 77
yrs. Johann Jost, s/o Jacob Hermann at Daisbach, was bpt. 12 May
1669 - sp.: Johannes Reinhard, Jost Zisen, and Anna Margaretha -
his step-sister. Joh. Just Hermann md. 30 Aug 1696 Maria Catharina,
d/o Johannes Reinhard at Daissbach. Maria Catharina, d/o Johann
Reinhard, was b. at Daisbach and bpt. 15 Oct 1671. Johannes Reinhard md. Emilie Bodenheimer 15 Feb 1659; Johannes Reinhard was bur.
7 Dec 1702, and Emilia, w/o Johannes Reinhard, was bur. 3 Jan 1694.
Johan Joost Herman, his wife, and 2 ch. were on Capt. John Sewell's
ship in Holland in 1709 (Rotterdam Lists). Justus Herman aged 41,
his wife, and daughters aged 14 and 7, Luth., husbandman and vinedresser, were in the 4th arrivals in London later that yr. (London
Lists).

Jost Hermann made his initial appearance on the Hunter Lists
1 July 1710 with 3 pers. over 10 yrs. of age and 1 pers. under 10
yrs.; his last entry with the same numbers was 4 Aug 1710. The ch.
of Jost[1] Hermann were:

1) Anna Maria[2] (HJ). Anna Maria Harmin aged 14, an orphan, was
   bound to Laurce Van Hook of N.Y. 26 Sept 1710 (Apprenticeship Lists).

2) Johann Nicolaus[2], b. Daisbach and bpt. 18 Feb 1700 - sp.:
   Johann Georg Wilhelm's son from Mudershausen, Johann Clos
   Kirperger, Anna Dorothea Hermann, and Anna Dorothea - w/o
   Joh. Reinhard. He was bur. 21 May 1700 (both Kettenbach
   Chbk.).

3) Rosina Maria[2], b. at Daisbach and bpt. 19 Feb 1702 - sp.:
   Rosina Maria Hermann, Maria Catharina - d/o Baltzer Weber
   from Oberhäuser Hof, Georg - a carpenter, and Johannes Dau-
   binger (Kettenbach Chbk.). Susan Maria Harmin aged 7, an
   orphan, was bound to Jasper Hood of N.Y. 26 Sept 1710 (Apprenticeship Lists).

4) "A Daughter"[2], bur. 1 March 1707 aged 7 weeks old, who was
   b. at Hohlenfels near Hahnstätten and d. Daisbach (Kettenbach Chbk.).

5) Maria Elisabetha[2], b. at Daisbach and bpt. 11 Sept 1708 -
   sp.: Anna Elisabeth Buff from Daisbach, Maria Eva Weidebach
   from Rückershausen, Johann Japhet Kettenbach, and Joh. Gottfried Hermann (Kettenbach Chbk.). Maria Elisab., d/o Joh.
   Just Hermann, d. at Daisbach and was bur. 14 Sept 1708
   (Kettenbach Chbk.).

LUDWIG ERNST HERNER (Hunter Lists #299)

Margaretha, d/o the late Ludwig Ernst Horner of Unter-Owissheim in Wurtemberg, md. 5 Sept 1710 Johann Keyser of the same
place (West Camp Luth. Chbk.). The village of origin was 7527 Unter-
Öwisheim (2 km. e. of Bruchsal; Chbks. begin 1594). Although some
descendants of the family claim to have documented the family there
as Krafft-Hörner, my researcher was unable to find them in the old
chbks. (HJ). A Ludwig Wagener with 6 ch. in the family were in the
3rd party in Holland (Rotterdam Lists), and an Ernst Ludwig Wagner
aged 40, his wife, sons aged 16, 13, 10, 6, and 3, and a daughter
aged 10, Luth., husbandman and vinedresser, arrived later that yr.
in England (London Lists); probably this family were indeed Wage-
ners and had no relationship to the emigrant Horners, but the sim-
ilarity of names is intriguing (HJ).

Ernst Ludwig Herner made his initial appearance on the Hunter
Rolls 1 July 1710 with 4 pers. over 10 yrs. of age and 1 pers. under 10 yrs.; Ludwig Ernst Herner was listed 4 Aug 1710 with the
same numbers. The family size diminished 4 Oct 1710 to 3 pers. o-
ver 10 yrs. of age and 1 pers. under 10 yrs., and the family was
recorded under Conrad Matheus Herner's name. The ch. of Ludwig
Ernst[1] Herner were:

1) Anna Margaretha[2], md. as d/o Ludwig Ernst Horner 5 Sept
   1710 Johannes Keyser (West Camp Luth. Chbk.).
2) Johann Conrad Mattheus[2] (HJ), as Johs Coenrt Mat. Horner, 15,
   bound as an orphan to Enoch Ffreeland of N.Y. 23 Nov 1710
   (Apprenticeship Lists)
3) Johann Michael Ernst[2] (HJ), an early settler in the Tulpehocken region. Pastor Stoever bpt. his child at South
   Branch in 1743 (Stoever Chbks.).

JACOB HERTZEL (Hunter Lists #300)

Jacob Hertzell, his wife and 1 child were on Capt. Wm. Newton's
ship in Holland in 1709 (Rotterdam Lists). A Jacob Hertzel md. 1st
Anna Elisabetha, wid/o Peter Eisenhauer, 23 Aug 1682, and md. 2nd
Apollonia Bicke-hauer 11 Jan 1687 at 6120 Erbach/Odenwald; however,
no known relationship between this man and the 1709er has been
found (HJ).

Johann Jacob Hertzel made his first appearance on the Hunter
Lists 4 Aug 1710 with 3 pers. over 10 yrs. of age and 1 pers. under 10 yrs. The family showed 3 over 10 yrs. 31 Dec 1710, 3 pers.
over 10 and 1 under 10 29 Sept 1711, 4 pers. over 10 and 1 under 10
24 Dec 1711 (cumulative), and finally 3 pers. over 10 yrs. in 1712.

HENRICH HERTZOGS WIDDOW (Hunter Lists #301)

A Johan Henrich Hertzog, s/o H. Hans Jörg Hertzog - innkeeper in Mosbach, md. 21 Feb 1688 Margaretha, d/o H. Hans Jörg Lenich - innkeeper here, at 6962 Adelsheim; however, no known connection between this man and the emigrant 1709er has been found (HJ).

Henrich Hertzog made his initial appearance on the Hunter Lists 1 July 1710 with 1 pers. over 10 yrs. of age; on 4 Oct 1710 the entry read Elizabeth Hertzogin with 1 pers. over 10 yrs. of age.

There were other members of the Hertzog family in colonial N.Y. and N.J.: 1) Heronimus Hartshook was noted in N.J. in the Janeway Accounts in 1735 and then, with wife Anna Margaretha Winther, had a child bpt. 8 Dec 1738 at the Schoharie Ref. Church in N.Y.; 2) Peter Hertsogh and wife Anna Margaretha had ch. bpt. 1733/34 - 1745 at the Somerville Ref. Church in N.J.; and 3) Henrich Wilhelm Hartshook/Herzog was recorded in the Janeway Accts. in 1735 - 44, and sp. in Montgomery, Orange Co., N.Y. in 1738.

JOHANNES HESS (Hunter Lists #302)

Johannes Hess, blacksmith of Bleichenbach in the earldom of Hanau, md. 29 Aug 1711 Anna Catharina, d/o Ludolst Curring of Hellstein in the earldom of Isenburg (West Camp Luth. Chbk.). The roots of this Mohawk Valley family were then at 6474 Bleichenbach (5 km. n.w. of Budingen; Chbks. begin 1650, Ref.); entries on the group were also found at 6474 Selters (1 km. further n.w.; Chbks. begin 1672, but gaps, Luth.). The earliest known antecedent of the American family was Henrich Hess, called a wagner in Bleichenbach on an inhabitant list of 1694 (Selters Chbk.). He md. an Anna Maria (--) and had issue:

Johannes, a wagner in Bergheim in 1692 (Selters Chbk.).

Henrich, d. 20 April 1699, aged 51 yrs. (Bleichenbach Chbk.).

+ Augustinus.

Augustinus Hess, a blacksmith and s/o Henrich Hess the Wagner, md. Kunigunda, d/o Johann Emmerich of Bleichenbach, 20 Oct 1680 (Selters Chbk.); for more on Kunigunda Emmerich's ancestry, see the section on #164 Johannes Emmerich, her brother. Augustinus Hess d. 17 April 1731, aged 74½ yrs. old (Bleichenbach Chbk.); Kunigunda Hess, his wife, d. 10 March 1725, aged 65 yrs. and 9 months (Bleichenbach Chbk.). Their ch. were:

Johann Henrich, b. 24 Nov 1681 - sp.: Johann Emmerich (Selters Chbk.). The child was bur. 28 March 1682 (Selters Chbk.).

Anna Catharina, d. 4 July 1686, aged 2 yrs. and 5 months (Selters Chbk.).

380

+ <u>Johannes</u>, b. 2 April 1687 - sp.: Johannes - s/o Weigel Schütz
(Selters Chbk.). He was conf. 29 May 1699 (Bleichenbach Chbk.).
<u>Anna Eva</u>, b. 16 Aug 1689 - sp.: Anna Maria - wid/o Henrich Hess
the wagner (Selters Chbk.).
<u>Johann Henrich</u>, b. 17 April 1692 - sp.: Johann Hess - wagner
from Bergheim and the father's brother (Selters Chbk.). He
was conf. 23 May 1706 (Selters Chbk.).
<u>Augustinus</u>, b. 22 Jan 1696 - sp.: Augustinus Glas ... (Selters
Chbk.). He was conf. in 1709 (Selters Chbk.).
<u>Anna Maria</u>, b. 31 Jan 1700 - sp.: Maria - wid/o Johan Wendel
Dippel the Bürger in Ortenberg (Bleichenbach Chbk.).

A Johan Hes was listed alone on Capt. Francois Warens' ship in Holland in 1709 in the 5th party of Palatines (Rotterdam Lists).

Johannes Hess made his initial appearance on the Hunter Lists 30 June 1710 with 1 pers. over 10 yrs. of age in the family; the household increased to 2 pers. over 10 yrs. 29 Sept 1711. Johannis Hes was nat. 17 Jan 1715/16 (Albany Nats.). Joseph Hess and his wife Catharina with 1 child were at Neu-Heessberg ca. 1716/17 (Simmendinger Register). Johannes Hess was a patentee on the s. side of the Mohawk River 30 April 1725 (Burnetsfield Patent). Johannis Hess and Fredrich Pillenger received land from Lewis Morris Jr. in 1732 (Albany Co. Deeds, Vol. 6, p. 348). Berkenmeyer mentioned that he started for the Falls 12 Aug 1734 and arrived late in the evening at the home of Hannes Hess, who treated him kindly; later Hess and his wife were so gracious that he stayed longer than expected (<u>Albany Protocol</u>, pp. 91 & 94). (Johannes) Hess was noted with Johannes (Jr.) on Pastor Sommer's List of families ca. 1744 (Schoharie Luth. Chbk.). A Johannes Hess was recorded at Canajoharrie in 1763 (Albany Co. Freeholders). The ch. of Johannes[1] Hess and his wife Anna Catharina were:

1) <u>Jannicke[2]</u>, b. 20 May 1712 - sp.: Andreas Baggs and Anna
Persch (West Camp Luth. Chbk.).
2) <u>Anna Eva[2]</u> (some doubt as to name of child), b. or bpt. 24
Sept 1713 - sp.: Joh. Emerich and wife Margaretha (Stone
Arabia Luth. Family List in Chbk.).
3) <u>Anna Maria[2]</u>, b. or bpt. 25 March 1715 - sp.: Anna Margreth
Burckhard or Borkis (West Camp Luth. Chbk. & Stone Arabia
Luth. Family List in Chbk.). West Camp Luth. gives b. 19
April 1715.
4) <u>Anna Catharina[2]</u>, b. 25 March 1717 - sp.: Anna Catharina Conrad (West Camp Luth. Chbk.); the sp. were Marx Bellinger and
wife Anna in the Stone Arabia Luth. Family List in Chbk.
5) <u>Augustinus[2]</u>, b. or bpt. 21 Dec 1718 - sp.: Joh. Ludolff Coring and wife Utilia (Stone Arabia Luth. Family List in

Chbk. Augustines Hess was a patentee on the n. side of the
Mohawk River 30 April 1725 (Burnetsfield Patent). Achis-
tenes Hess was a freeholder at the Falls in 1763 (Albany
Co. Freeholders). He md. an Anna (--) and had issue:

    i) Johann Nicolaus[3], bpt. 7 Aug 1760 - sp.: Johann Nico-
        las Weber and Margretha (Stone Arabia Ref. Chbk.).

    Maryly B. Penrose's excellent Mohawk Valley in the Rev-
    olution lists additional ch. for Augustinus[2] Hess:

    ii) Johann Conrad[3], bpt. 3 April 1762.

  iii) Johannes[3], b. 25 April 1764.

   iv) Daniel[3], b. 19 April 1766.

    v) Anna Eva[3], b. 27 May 1768.

6) Johannes[2], b. or bpt. 5 May 1721 - sp.: Thomas Schumacher and
   wife Dorothea (Stone Arabia Luth. Family List in Chbk.).
   The will of Johannes Hess of Canajohary in Albany Co., farmer, was dated 28 Oct 1760 and probated 30 April 1771 (Fernow Wills #798). He md. Anna Margaretha Jung 10 Nov 1743
   (Stone Arabia Luth. Chbk.) and had issue:

    i) Catharina[3], b. or bpt. 16 July 1744 - sp.: Johannes
       Hess Sr. and wife Catharina (Stone Arabia Luth Chbk.).

    ii) Johannes[3], b. or bpt. 27 Oct 1745 - sp.: Johann Frid-
       erich Hess and Elisabetha Jung (Stone Arabia Luth.
       Chbk.).

  iii) Elisabetha[3], b. or bpt. 12 Aug 1747 - sp.: Jacob Star-
       ing and Dorothea Elisabetha Jung (Stone Arabia Luth.
       Chbk.).

   iv) Anna[3], b. or bpt. 25 March 1749 - sp.: Augustinus Hess
      and wife Catharina (Stone Arabia Luth. Chbk.).

    v) Johann[3], b. or bpt. 10 May 1751 - sp.: Joh. Friderich
      Jung and Anna Margaretha Nellis (Stone Arabia Luth.
      Chbk.).

   vi) Theobald[3], b. or bpt. as Debalt 22 Sept 1753 - sp.:
      Debalt Jung and wife Catharina (Stone Arabia Luth.
      Chbk.).

  vii) Daniel[3] (Will).

 viii) Friederich[3] (Will).

7) Johann Friderich[2], b. or bpt. 5 Sept 1722 - sp.: Friderich
   Bellinger and wife Elisabetha (Stone Arabia Luth. Family
   List in Chbk.). The will of Frederick Hess of German Flats
   was dated 25 Aug 1795 and recorded 12 Feb 1796 (Herkimer
   Co. Will Bk. A). He md. Mary (Will) and had ch.:

    i) Friderich[3] (Will).

    ii) Henrich[3] (Will).

  iii) Conrad[3] (Will).

    iv) <u>Elisabetha</u>³ (Will).

    v) <u>Catharina</u>³ (Will).

    vi) <u>Magdalena</u>³ (Will, as Lana).

8) <u>Anna Dorothea</u>², b. or bpt. 25 March 1724 - sp.: Thomas Schumacher and wife Dorothea (Stone Arabia Luth. Family List in Chbk.). She md. Adolph Wallrath (HJ).

There were several others members of the Hess family in the Mohawk Valley: 1) An Augustinus Hess d. 31 March 1838, aged 85 yrs. (Columbia Cem., Ref. Church, Herkimer Co.); 2) A Johann Jost Hess d. 22 July 1841, aged 85 yrs. and 7 months (Columbia Cem., Ref. Church, Herkimer Co.); and 3) a Hendrick Hess of Canajoharry wrote his will 26 Aug 1801, and it was probated 13 June 1810 (Montgomery Co. Will Bk. I).

NICLAUS HESS (Hunter Lists #303)

The German home of this Palatine family was at 5419 <u>Freirachdorf</u> (22 km. n.e. of Neuwied; Chbks. begin 1689). Nicolaus Hess md. Veronica Catharina (--) 30 July 1702; a notation in the chbk. mentioned that the couple had lived together a long time previous to their marriage in whoring and had an illegitimate child. Niklaas Hesche, his wife and 1 child were listed in the 6th party of Palatines in Holland in 1709 (Rotterdam Lists); they were recorded near Johan Herman Bötser, Johan diderig Schniter, Johan Wilhellem Sneiter, and Hans Jacob dinges - all of whom came from villages bordering Freirachdorf (HJ).

Niclaus Hess made his initial appearance on the Hunter Lists 4 July 1710 with 2 pers. over 10 yrs. and 3 pers. under 10; the entry changed 4 Aug 1710 to 3 pers. over 10 and 2 under 10. In most all of his entries on the Hunter Rolls, Nicolaus Hess was recorded near other 1709ers from the Neuwied-Westerwald region (HJ). Niccolas Hes was nat. 17 Jan 1715/16 (Albany Nats.). He was a Palatine Debtor in 1718, 1719 (at Kingsberry), and 1721. Nicklas Hes was a Palatine willing to remain at Livingston Manor 26 Aug 1724 (<u>Doc. History of N.Y.</u>, Vol. III, p. 724). He had ch.:

1) <u>Peter</u>², bpt. 25 June 1702 - sp.: Peter Kaus, Peter Schumacher, and Anna Maria Hess (Freirachdorf Chbk.).

2) <u>Maria Catharina</u>², bpt. 5 Aug 1703 - sp.: Petrus Hess, and Catharina - d/o Jacob Hess. The child d. 2 Sept 1703 (both Freirachdorf Chbk.).

3) <u>Anna Maria</u>², bpt. 2 Sept 1704 - sp.: Anna Maria - d/o Jacob Schumacher, and Anna Margaretha - d/o Antoni Hachenburg (Freirachdorf Chbk.). She md. Johann Dieterich Dick (HJ).

4) <u>Elisabetha Catharina</u>², bpt. 28 March 1706 - sp.: Jacob

Schmidt, Eva Catharina - d/o Frederic Hümeric, and Elisabeth - w/o Matthaeus Schumacher (Freirachdorf Chbk.). Catharina Hess md. Johannes Finger in 1725/26 (Linlithgo Ref.
Chbk.).

Peter², s/o Nicolaus Hess, probably d. young (HJ). A later-
arriving Johann Pieter Hes joined the Germantown Ref. Church 19
Oct 1751 with papers from the church at Rhosbach; Roßbach is the
parish seat for Freirachdorf in Germany (HJ).

JOHANNES HETTERICH (Hunter Lists #304)

Several potential Johannes Hetterichs were documented in Germany: 1) Johannes, s/o Michael and Anna Margaretha Hedderich, was
bpt. 20 Feb 1681 at 6501 Hahnheim; 2) Johannes Hedderich, b. 8 June
1684, md. 28 Jan 1705 Anna Elisabetha, d/o Jacob Schütz, at 6316
Burg-Gemünden; and 3) Johannes Hetterich, a carpenter from near
Homburg an der Ohm, md. 19 Sept 1699 Catharina, d/o Georg Osterling,
at 6200 Nordenstadt.

Johannes Hetterich made his initial appearance on the Hunter
Lists 30 June 1710 with 2 pers. over 10 and 1 under 10 yrs.; the
family was recorded with 2 pers. over 10 on 4 Aug 1710 and then 3
pers. over 10 yrs. on 4 Oct 1710. The cumulative entry for 24 Dec
1711 gave 2 pers. over 10 yrs. for Johann Hetterich's Wid^W. A probable d/o Johannes¹ Hetterich was:

1) Maria Catharina² (HJ), who as Mary Catharina Hendrick aged
   15, orphan, was bound to Daniel Ebbetts of N.Y. 16 Jan
   1711 (Apprenticeship Lists).

There were many Hedderichs noted by Pastor Stoever including
Peter of Lebanon in 1743, Wilhelm of Northkill in 1744, Georg of
Lebanon in 1743, and Jost of Northkill in 1744 (HJ).

JOHANES CONRAD HETTICH (Hunter Lists #305)

Possible emigrants of this name found in Europe include: 1)
Johann Conrad, s/o Henrich Hedderich from Eyches, md. 14 Nov 1708
Anna Catharina, d/o H. Johann Appel at Bobenhausen, at 6314 Ulrich-
stein; 2) Conrad Hedderich, md. 1st 19 Sept 1676 Maria Bechtolf
and md. 2nd 8 Feb 1698 Anna Ursula, wid/o Joh. Steiffenberger, at
6081 Biebesheim; and 3) the Dragoon Conrad Hedderich who with wife
Maria Judith had a son bpt. 9 April 1690 at 6086 Crumstadt. Koenraat Hetirug, his wife, and 1 child were on Capt. John Howlentzen's
ship in Holland in 1709 (Rotterdam Lists). Conrad Hedgen aged 42,
his wife, a son aged 17 and a daughter aged 1, Ref., husbandman
and vinedresser, were in the 4th arrivals in England (London Lists).

Johañes Conrad Hettich made his first appearance on the Hunter Lists 4 Aug 1710 with 2 pers. over 10 yrs. of age; the cumulative entry for 24 Dec 1711 read 2 over 10 yrs. and 1 under 10 yrs. Conrad Hellich aged 30, Anna Marie Hellich aged 26, and Johannes Hellich aged 1, dead, were in N.Y. City in 1710/11 (Palatines In N.Y. City). Conrad Heding's surviving widow and Meisingerin were at Hackensack ca. 1716/17 (Simmendinger Register). A child of Conrad[1] Hettich and wife Anna Maria was:

1) Johannes[2], b. or bpt. 3 Sept 1710 at N.Y. - sp.: Johann Wihs (West Camp Luth. Chbk.).

JOHANN PETER HEUSER (Hunter Lists #306)

The German origins of this 1709er most probably were at 6109 Nieder-Ramstadt (5 km. s.e. of Darmstadt; Chbks. begin 1636). Johann Peter, s/o Johannes Heußer, was b. 30 Jan 1670 - sp.: Hans Paul at Waschbach and Peter Nungesser. Johann Peter Heuser was conf. at Nieder-Ramstadt in 1683 and md. 25 Oct 1692 Ottilia, d/o the late Master Lorentz Schneider - miller and Gemeinsmann at Pfungstadt. It is difficult to firmly identify the N.Y. settler on extant 1709 Palatine lists, but a Pieter Heisen and wife Eva Jacops had a daughter Catharina bpt. 18 July 1709 - sp.: Magriet Van Leubben for Elisabeth Jacops, absent, at the Brielle Cath. Church in Holland; also a Johannes Haiser, his wife and 3 ch. were in the 2nd party in Holland (Rotterdam Lists), and John Heischer aged 30, his wife, sons aged 5 and ¼, and a daughter aged 6, Luth., husbandman and vinedresser and a linenweaver, were in the 2nd arrivals at London later in 1709 (London Lists).

Johann Peter Heuser made his initial appearance on the Hunter Lists 1 July 1710 with 3 pers. over 10 yrs. of age. On the 4 Aug 1710 roll, he was recorded near Niclaus Ruhl (who came from Nieder-Ramstadt) and Johannes Planck (probably b. near there); on the 4 Oct 1710 list, Johann Peter Heuser was enrolled one name from Johann Peter Abelmann (of Nieder-Ramstadt) and showed 2 pers. over 10 yrs. in the household. The 24 June 1711 entry read Johann Peter Heuser and Eliz: Christmann with 3 pers., and the 24 Dec 1711 notation showed 2 pers. over 10 yrs. and 2 pers. under 10. The 24 June 1712 entry registered 3 pers. over 10 yrs. and 2 under 10, while the 13 Sept 1712 entry recorded 2 over 10 and 2 under 10 yrs. Hans Peter Heyser was nat. 22 Nov 1715 (Albany Nats.). Peter Heusser and Anna Elisabetha with 5 ch. were at Hunderston ca. 1716/17 (Simmendinger Register). Hans Peter Heser was a Palatine Debtor in 1718, 1719 (at Hunterstown), and 1721 (Livingston Debt Lists). Peter Heusser was a Palatine not willing to continue 26 Aug 1724 (Doc. Hist. of N.Y., Vol. III, p. 724). He had issue with his 1st wife:

1) Johann Peter[2], bpt. 21 Sept 1693 - sp.: Peter Luckhaupt (Nieder-Ramstadt Chbk.).

By his 2nd wife Widow Elisabetha Christmann he had issue:

2) Urgel[2] (HJ), who md. Anna Catharina Haber (HJ); she d. 2 Dec 1804, aged 86 yrs. and 7 months (?) (Germantown Ref. Chbk.). Orgel Heiser was a Sgt. in Capt. Frederick Kortz's Co. at East Camp in 1767 (Report of the State Historian, Vol. II, p. 869). The will of Uriel Heyser of Camp was dated 16 Nov 1768 and probated 2 March 1789 (Columbia Co. Will Bk. A). The ch. of Urgel[2] and Anna Catharina were:

    i) Peter[3], bpt. 12 Jan 1737 - sp.: Peter Haber and Maria Haber (Germantown Ref. Chbk.). He md. Eva Plass (HJ).

    ii) Simon[3] (Will).

    iii) Johannes[3], b. 28 Feb 1742 and bpt. Teerbosch - sp.: Jo: Peter Heuser and Barbel Haber (Loonenburg Luth. Chbk.).

    iv) Catharina[3], bpt. 18 Nov 1744 - sp.: David Kisselaer and Cath. (Germantown Ref. Chbk.). She md. Peter Philip (Will).

    v) Jacob[3] (Will), md. Catharina Schieffer (HJ).

    vi) Christina[3] (Will).

    vii) Eva[3] (Will).

3) Georg Peter[2], b. Oct 1719 and bpt. as Hans Peter 13 Jan 1720 at East Camp - sp.: Peter Lauer and wife Catharina (N.Y. City Luth. Chbk.). He joined the Germantown Ref. Church in 1746. Peter Hesser was a freeholder at East Camp in 1763 (Albany Co. Freeholders). Lt. George P. Heiser was also in Capt. Kortz's East Camp Co. in 1767. The will of George Peter Heiser of East Camp was dated 28 Sept 1786 and probated 12 April 1787 (Columbia Co. Will Bk. A). He md. Christina Haber (HJ) and had issue:

    i) Anna[3], bpt. 13 Jan 1741 - sp.: Arie Buist and Grietje Haver (Red Hook Luth. Chbk.). She md. Simon Neu (HJ).

    ii) Gertraud[3], bpt. 5 weeks old 23 Aug 1742 at Camp - sp.: Christina Haber and Gertraud, grandparents (Loonenburg Luth. Chbk.). She md. 22 Oct 1765 Henrich Schneider (Germantown Ref. Chbk.).

    iii) Catharina[3], bpt. 8 weeks old 15 July 1744 at Camp - sp.: Uriel Heuser and Catharina, his wife (Loonenburg Luth. Chbk.). She md. Jacob Scherp 30 Nov 1763 (Germantown Ref. Chbk.).

    iv) Peter[3], bpt. 8 Sept 1746 - sp.: Peter Jager and Barbara Jager (Germantown Ref. Chbk.). He md. 26 April 1768 Elisabetha Jacobi (Germantown Ref. Chbk.).

    v) Christina[3], bpt. 16 July 1751 - sp.: Nicolass Philip

and Christina Funck (Germantown Ref. Chbk.).She md.
Wilhelm Graat (HJ), probably on 30 Sept 1770 (Germantown Ref. Chbk. - some confusion as to groom's name).

vi) Jacob³, bpt. 21 Aug 1755 - sp.: Jacob Best and Anna
Best (Germantown Ref. Chbk.).

vii) Magdalena³, bpt. 26 June 1757 - sp.: Johan Caspar Ru-
bel and Maria Magdalena Jacobina Engels (Germantown
Ref. Chbk.).

There is a slight possibility that the Johann Peter² Heuser
bpt. at Nieder-Ramstadt in 1693 may have been the father of Urgel²
and Georg Peter² Heuser, rather than an elder brother (HJ).

ANNA MARIA HEYDIN (Hunter Lists #307)

For data on this emigrant, see #286 Maria Cunigunda Haydin.

HENRICH HEYDORN (Hunter Lists #308)

Henrich Heidorn, widower of Gelhausen near Hanau, md. 10 Sept
1711 Elisabetha, wid/o Jerg Humbel of Mossbach in the Pfaltz (West
Camp Luth. Chbk.). The origins of this family were at 6460 Gelnhausen, records of the emigrant found nearby at 6464 Altenhaßlau
(11 km. e. of Langenselbold; Chbks. begin 1653, Ref.). An entry in
the Altenhaßlau registers in 1693 noted that Henrich Heydorn was
a saltpetre refiner in the village.

Henrich Heydorn made his first appearance on the Hunter Rolls
4 Aug 1711 with 3 pers. over 10 yrs. and 1 pers. under 10; the entry for 31 Dec 1710 noted 2 over 10 and 1 under 10 yrs., while the
24 June 1711 notation recorded 2 pers. over 10 yrs. of age. The
Hunter Lists dated 24 Dec 1711 registered Henrich Heydorn and Georg
Hummel's Wid^W with 4 pers. over 10 yrs. The last entry on 13 Sept
1712 showed 4 pers. over 10 and 1 under 10 in the family. Hendrick
Heydorn was nat. 17 Jan 1715/16 (Albany Nats.). Heinrich Heudohrn
and Elisabetha with 2 ch. were at Hunderston ca. 1716/17 (Simmendinger Register). Hend: Heedoorn was a Palatine Debtor in 1718,
1719 (at Hunterstown), 1721, and 1726 (Livingston Debt Lists). Henrig Haeudorn was a Palatine willing to continue at Livingston Manor
26 Aug 1724 (Doc. Hist. of N.Y., Vol. III, p. 724). The ch. of Henrich¹ Heydorn were:

1) Anna Margaretha², b. 16 July 1693 - sp.: his mother-in-law
in Gelnhausen (Altenhaßlau Chbk.).

2) Henrich² (HJ), on the St. Peter's Luth. Family List ca.
1734 (Rhinebeck Luth. Chbk.). He md. Elisabetha Barbara
Schauermann (HJ) and had ch.:

i) Conrad³ (St. Peter's Family List), a sp. in 1753 to

Peter Schauerman (Schoharie Luth. Chbk.) and at Churchtown Luth. in the 1760's. The will of Conrad Hydorn,
late of Brunswick, was dated 2 May 1806 and recorded
2 April 1812 (Rensselaer Co. Will Bk. 4).

- ii) Johannes[3], b. 2 Feb 1732 and bpt. at Loon - sp.: Johannes Smid and Cathar. Schauer (Loonenburg Luth.
Chbk.). He sp. at Loonenburg Luth. in 1751.

- iii) Johann Henrich[3], b. 22 Aug 1735 - sp.: Hendrich Schmid
and wife Anna (Rhinebeck Luth. Chbk.).

- iv) Petrus[3], b. 25 Jan 1738 and bpt. at the Manor - sp.:
Peter Schauer and Catharina Berteln (Loonenburg Luth.
Chbk.). He md. Hannah (Aalswort? - HJ), and they had
ch. bpt. at Manorton Luth. and Churchtown Luth.
Churches (HJ). He was also noted in the Gilead Luth.
and Linlithgo Ref. registers (HJ).

- v) Maria[3], b. 19 April 1740 and bpt. at Loon. - sp.: Jacob Van Hoesen and wife Gertrude (Loonenburg Luth.
Chbk.).

- vi) Catharina[3], bpt. 10 Oct 1742 - sp.: Emmerich Schouw-
erman and Catharina (Linlithgo Ref. Chbk.).

- vii) Elisabetha[3], b. 10 July 1744 and bpt. Teerbosch - sp.:
Wilh. Bartel and Lysabeth Barteln (Loonenburg Luth.
Chbk.).

- viii) Gertraud[3], bpt. 1 June 1746 - sp.: Jacob Schmid and
wife Gertraut (Germantown Ref. Chbk.).

- ix) Adam[3], b. 12 April 1749 and bpt. Loon. - sp.: Hendr.
Rees and wife Elsje (Loonenburg Luth. Chbk.).

- x) Christoph[3] (HJ), d. 21 March 1807 (Churchtown Luth.
Chbk.). The will of Christopher Heydorn of the Corp.
of Hudson was dated 5 Feb 1807 and probated 11 July
1807; it mentioned his brother Adam Heydorn and his
sister's son Hendrick Nukel, as well as his brother's
son Thomas Heydorn (Columbia Co. Will Bk. C).

- xi) Susanna[3], bpt. 19 Jan 1754 - sp.: Johannes Saurman and
Elisabeth Smith (Linlithgo Ref. Chbk.).

ANNA CATHARINA HILDEBRANDT (Hunter Lists #309)

There were Hildebrandts documented at 6140 Schwanheim, and it
was also noted that Johan Hildebrand from Friedberg md. Anna Catharina, wid/o Paul Neumann, in 1691 at 6450 Hanau. Johan Hildebrand
aged 50, his wife, a son aged 11, a daughter aged 15, Luth., husbandman and vinedresser, were in England in 1709 (London Lists).

Anna Catharina Hildebrandt was listed once on the Hunter Lists
4 Oct 1710 with 1 pers. over 10 together with Gertrud Meisenheim.

GEORG HIRCHEMER (Hunter Lists #310)

The origins of the Herkimer family of the Mohawk Valley were at 6902 Sandhausen (5 km. s. of Heidelberg), records in the registers of 6906 Leimen (1 km further s.e.; Chbks. begin 1694, Ref., but gaps). The probable father of the emigrant Georg[1] was one Christoph Herchheimer: Heinrich Hörchheimer, s/o the late Christoph Herchheimer - formerly citizen at Sandhausen, md. Anna Maria Schneider 13 Jan 1711 at Leimen. A Stoffel Heschemer was a resident at Sandhausen in 1690 (Generallandesarchiv Karlsruhe, GLAK 77/4146).

Georg Hirchemer made his initial appearance on the Hunter Lists 4 Oct 1710 with 2 pers. over 10 yrs. of age and 1 pers. under 10 yrs. The entry for 31 Dec 1710 read 4 pers. over 10 and 1 under 10, while the notation for 24 June 1711 showed 5 pers. over 10 yrs. of age; the 24 Dec 1711 entry read 4 pers. over 10 yrs. An old mss. survives mentioning Georg Hirchemer and Nicolaus Horning dated June 1711 (N.Y. Col. Mss., Vol. 55, pp. 21 a-c); Horning also was documented at Leimen (HJ). Gro. Kerchmer of Hunterstown was a soldier in 1711 (Palatine Volunteers To Canada). Juryh Herck Heemmer was nat. 11 Oct 1715 (Albany Nats.). Georg Hirchmer and his wife Magdalena with 1 child were at Neu-Heidelberg ca. 1716/17 (Simmendinger Register). Madalana Erghemar and Jurgh Erghemar were patentees in 1725 (Burnetsfield Patent). By his 1st wife Eva Barbara, a child of Georg[1] Hirchemer was:

1) Friederich Michael[2], bpt. 8 Aug 1695 - sp.: Friedrich Michael, s/o the late Bernhard Scheid - hunter at Sandhausen (Leimen Chbk.).

By his 2nd wife Magdalena (--), Georg[1] Hirchemer (spelled Herxemer, Hörchemer, and Hörchheimer in the Leimen registers) had issue:

2) Georg Lorentz[2], bpt. 1 Dec 1697 - sp.: Lorentz Hersemer - citizen and fisherman at Necker Gemünd (Leimen Chbk.).

3) Johann Jost[2], bpt. 20 June 1700 - sp.: H. Johann Jost Schwab - Gerichts at Sandhausen (Leimen Chbk.). Johann Jost Erghemar was a patentee also in 1723-25 (Burnetsfield Patent). Lt. Johann Jost Herkemer was an officer in the Albany Co. Militia in 1733 above ye falls on ye Maquas River; he also was a Col. at Burnets Field in 1767 (Report of the State Historian, Vol. I, p. 572 & Vol. II, p. 848). The will of Johan Jost Herchheimer of Burnetsfield in Albany Co. was dated 5 April 1771 and probated 4 Oct 1783 (Fernow Wills # 818). The Mohawk Valley Petries And Allied Families, edited by Hazel Patrick, quotes private family sources stating that the w/o Johann Jost[2] Hirchemer was Catharina

Petri, and also notes biographical material on some of Johann Jost² Hirchemer's ch., who were:

    i) <u>Gertraud³</u> (Will of Nicolaus³), md. Rudolph Schumacher (Petrie Book).

    ii) <u>Magdalena³</u> (Will of Nicolaus³), md. 1st Warner Dygert, 2nd Nicholas Snell, and 3rd John Roorbach (Petrie Book).

    iii) <u>Elisabetha Barbara³</u> (Will of Nicolaus³), md. 9 June 1743 Peter David Schuyler (Petrie Book).

    iv) <u>Nicolaus³</u> (Will of Johann Jost²), the famous General Herkimer of the revolution. His biography has been well chronicled in <u>History of Herkimer Co., N.Y.</u>, by F. W. Beers & Co., 1879, pp. 55 & 123, as well as many other Mohawk Valley sources. The will of Nicholas Herchheimer of Canajoharie, Tryon Co. was dated 7 Feb 1777 and probated 4 Oct 1783 (<u>Fernow Wills</u> #849).

    v) <u>Ottilia³</u> (Will of Nicolaus³), md. Jan 1750 Peter Bellinger (Petrie Book).

    vi) <u>Catharina³</u> (Will of Nicolaus³), md. Georg Henrich Bell (Petrie Book).

    vii) <u>Henrich³</u> (Will of Jost²). A list of the ch. of Henrich³ appears in the will of Nicolaus³ (HJ). The will of Henrich Herchheimer, s/o Hon Yost of Burnettsfield, German Flats Distr., Tryon Co., was dated 17 Aug 1778 and probated 9 Sept 1783 (<u>Fernow Wills</u> #851). He md. Catharina Dygert (Petrie Book).

    viii) <u>Elisabetha³</u> (Will of Nicolaus³), md. Henrich Frey (HJ).

    ix) <u>Johann Jost³</u> (Will of Johann Jost²), md. Maria Van Alen (Katsbaan Ref. Church sp. 1759). He was a Capt. under his father in 1767 at Burnets Field (<u>Report of the State Historian</u>, Vol. II, p. 848). His family is noted in Reid's <u>Loyalists of Ontario</u>, p. 147.

    x) <u>Anna³</u> (Will of Nicolaus³).

    xi) <u>Georg³</u> (Will of Johann Jost²), also in his father's Co. in 1767 as a Capt. He md. Aug 1775 Aleta Schuyler (Petrie Book).

    xii) <u>Anna Maria³</u> (Will of Nicolaus³), md. Rev. Abraham Rosencranz 27 April 1758 (Petrie Book).

    xiii) <u>Johannes³</u> (Will of Johann Jost²).

4) <u>Philip²</u>, bpt. 26 Dec 1702 - sp.: Philipp Rohrmann - citizen and joiner at Heydelberg (Leimen Chbk.).

5) <u>Friederich Michael²</u>, bpt. 30 Aug 1705 - sp.: Friedrich Michael Scheid, citizen at Sandhausen (Leimen Chbk.).

6) <u>Johann Georg²</u>, bpt. 19 Sept 1706 - sp.: Johan Georg Bott

- s/o the late Hans Bernhard Bott, citizen at Sandhausen
(Leimen Chbk.). A Hans Jury Herckhemer was nat. 31 Jan
1715/16 (Albany Nats.).

JOHANN ADAM HOFF (Hunter Lists #311)

The German origins of this 1709er family were at 5450 Heddesdorf (8 km. n. of Koblenz and near Neuwied; Chbks. begin 1674).
Sp. strongly suggest that both N.Y. Palatine Hoffs, Johann Adam[1]
and Andreas[1], had a common grandfather in Anthonius Hoff, bur. 4
March 1677. A probable list of his ch. included:

Adam, a sp. in 1677.

Gertraud, sp. as d/o Tönges to the Ernst family in 1674.

+ Anthonius or Tönges Hoff.

Bartolomaeus, md. a Christina (--).

Johann Peter, md. a Magdalena (--).

Christina, a sp. in 1674.

Elisabetha Maria, a sp. in 1677.

Andreas, md. in 1695 at the Neuwied Church.

Henrich, sp. in 1686.

+ Johann Daniel.

Johann Daniel Hoff had an illegitimate son with Anna Catharina
Fischer from Segendorf named Johann Adam bpt. 24 Nov 1678 - sp.:
Anna Elisab. - d/o Christ Ernst, Johs. Süttenig, and Joh. Adam Segendorff; all of these sp. had connections with other 1709er families (HJ). Later, Johann Daniel Hoff md. a Maria Veronica (--) and
had issue sp. by members of the Tönges Hoff family (HJ).

Johann Adam Hoff made his initial appearance on the Hunter
Lists 4 Aug 1710 with 3 pers. over 10 yrs.; the entry read 2 over
10 and 1 under 10 yrs. 31 Dec 1710, and then 3 over 10 24 June 1711.
On 29 Sept 1711 he was listed next to Andreas Hoff. He was recorded
with 2 pers. over 10 yrs. 25 March 1712 and with 3 pers. over 10
24 June 1712. Adam Hoft was nat. (next to Andries Hoft) 31 Jan
1715/16 (Albany Nats.). Johann Adam Hoff and Anna Catharina were
at Hessberg ca. 1716/17 (Simmendinger Register). Adam Hooff was a
Palatine Debtor in 1718, in 1719 (at Haysberry), 1721, and 1726
(Livingston Debt Lists). Adam Hoff was a Palatine willing to remain
on the Manor 26 Aug 1724 (Doc. Hist. of N.Y., Vol. III, p. 724).
Adam Hoof was a freeholder in 1763 (Albany Co. Freeholders). He md.
Anna Catharina Hämer (Hemmer) (HJ) and had ch.:

1) Wilhelm[2] (HJ), md. as single man b. Manor of Livingston
8 Dec 1741 Maria Magdalena Michel (Germantown Ref. Chbk.).
They had issue:

i) Maria Magdalena[3], bpt. 17 April 1743 - sp.: Jorg Best

and Maria Magdalene Hoff (Red Hook Luth. Chbk.).

  ii) <u>Elisabetha</u>³, bpt. 10 June 1744 - sp.: Johannes Maul
and Elisabeth Trumbur (Red Hook Luth. Chbk.). She md.
Philip Schmidt 29 Nov 1762 (Red Hook Luth. Chbk.).

  iii) <u>Anna Catharina</u>³, bpt. 1 Sept 1746 - sp.: Henrich Hoff
and Anna Catharina Menkeler (Germantown Ref. Chbk.).

  iv) <u>Adam</u>³, bpt. 5 March 1749 - sp.: Adam Segendorff and
Catharina Hoff (Germantown Ref. Chbk.).

  v) <u>Magdalena</u>³, bpt. 13 Jan 1751 - sp.: Philip Klum and
Magdalena Fritz (Germantown Ref. Chbk.). She md. Johannes Schult 14 March 1769 (Germantown Ref. Chbk.).

  vi) <u>Wilhelm</u>³, bpt. 4 Nov 1753 - sp.: Willem Schult and
Catharina Fritz (Germantown Ref. Chbk.).

  vii) <u>Maria</u>³, bpt. 8 Aug 1756 - sp.: Georg Best and wife
Magdalena Hoff (Germantown Ref. Chbk.).

  viii) <u>Johannes</u>³, bpt. 10 March 1759 - sp.: Joh: Michael and
Cath: Schuldt (Germantown Ref. Chbk.).

  ix) <u>Gertraud</u>³, bpt. 23 May 1763 - sp.: Fredrick Maul and
wife Geertje Sherp (Linlithgo Ref. Chbk.).

2) <u>Johann Philip</u>², b. 26 June 1717 - sp.: Philipp Wilhelm Moor,
Johann Balthas Lutt, and Elisabeth Hemer (West Camp Luth.
Chbk.). He md. 8 Dec 1741, the same day as Wilhelm² Hoff
md., Christina (Crollius), wid/o Albertus Fels (Germantown
Ref. Chbk.). They had ch.:

  i) <u>Catharina</u>³, bpt. 2 March 1742 - sp.: Adam Hoff and
Catharina Heiner (Red Hook Luth. Chbk.).

  ii) <u>Johann Henrich</u>³, bpt. 10 March 1745 - sp.: Hennerich
Hoff and Anna Magdalena Muller (Red Hook Luth. Chbk.).

3) <u>Maria Magdalena</u>², b. 20 March 1722 at Camp Queensberry -
sp.: Michel Rau and Maria Magdalena Hoff (N.Y. City Luth.
Chbk.). She md. Georg Best 11 May 1743 (Germantown Ref.
Chbk.).

4) <u>Johann Henrich</u>², md. as s/o Adam¹ Hoff 10 March 1747 Anna
Catharina Minckler (Germantown Ref. Chbk.). They had ch.:

  i) <u>Maria Magdalena</u>³, bpt. 13 Dec 1747 - sp.: Wilhelm Hoff
and Mari Magdalen Hoff (Germantown Ref. Chbk.).

  ii) <u>Adam</u>³, bpt. 17 June 1750 - sp.: Adam Hoff and Catharina Hoff (Germantown Ref. Chbk.).

  iii) <u>Anna Maria</u>³, b. 8 March 1753 in Col. Co. - sp.: Marjta
Loscher and David Minckler (Schoharie Luth. Chbk.).
She md. Petrus Blass (HJ).

  iv) <u>Wilhelm</u>³, bpt. 23 March 1755 - sp.: Willem Hoff and
Magdalena Michel (Germantown Ref. Chbk.).

  v) <u>Sebastian</u>³, bpt. 17 April 1759 - sp.: Bastian Lescher and Lisabeth Livingston (Gallatin Ref. Chbk.).

    5) Catharina[2], bpt. 19 March 1727 - sp.: Christeffer Friess
and Catrina Keetel (Kingston Ref. Chbk.). She md. Friederich Fees 17 June 1752 (Germantown Ref. Chbk.).

    6) Maria Catharina[2], b. 26 June 1735 - sp.: Herman Segendorf
and wife Maria Cath. (Rhinebeck Luth. Chbk.).

ANDREAS HOFF (Hunter Lists #312)

The father of Andreas[1] Hoff was Anthonius or Tönges Hoff, most
probably s/o the aforementioned Anthonius Hoff, bur. 1677 at Heddesdorf (HJ); see #311 Johann Adam[1] Hoff for data on him. Tönges
Hoff d. 29 Jan 1698; his wife was named Johanna Margaretha, and she
sp. the bpt. of Johanna Margaretha Schmid, future w/o the 1709er
Johann Wilhelm Dales, in 1675 at Heddesdorf. The ch. of Tönges and
Johanna Margaretha Hoff were:

Tönges, md. Anna Catharina (--).

Johann Peter, bpt. 8 Nov 1674 - sp.: Hans Peter Schneider, Hermann Schmid, and Christina Hoff - all from Hedd.

Adam, bpt. Dom. Lätare: 1677 - sp.: Adam Süttenich, Adam Schmid,
and Elisabetha Maria Hoff. This child d. Dom. palmarum.

+ Johann Andreas, bpt. Dom. 11. Epiph: 1679 - sp.: Insp. Dathusius,
Andreas Söhns, and Philippina Margarethe Attendorn.

Johann Caspar, bpt. 9 July 1682 - sp.: Caspar Schmid, Joes
Wirtgen, Anna Catharin - w/o Theis Gollighofer, and Magdalena
Schmid.

Philipp Henrich, bpt. 3 Jan 1686 - sp.: Philipp Melsbach, Henrich Pross, Maria Magdalena Schmidt, and the w/o Master Johann
the bricklayer from Neuwied.

Johann Adolf, bpt. 9 Dec 1688 - sp.: Adam Konigsfeld, Adolf
Ernst, and Christina - w/o Mies Hoff.

Leonhard Friedrich, bpt. 31 Jan 1692 - sp.: Leonhard Voss the
schoolmaster, Thomas Annefeld, Elisabeth - w/o Adam Konigsfeld,
and Margaretha - w/o Joh. Adam Segendorff. He d. July 1692.

Maria Magdalena, b. 9 March 1694 - sp.: Magdalena - wid/o Adolf Bieber, the w/o Thiel Sibert, and Tobias Werth.

Johann Andreas, s/o the late Tönges Hoff, md. 21 July 1706 Catharina Margaretha, d/o the late Christ Ernst, at Heddesdorf. Christ
Ernst d. 6 Feb 1683 and his wife Anna was bur. 10 Feb 1690.

Andreas Hoff made his first appearance on the Hunter Lists 1
July 1710 with 2 pers. over 10 yrs. of age; the entry for 4 Aug 1710
read 1 pers. over 10 yrs., and the notation for 4 Oct 1710 showed
2 over 10 and 1 under 10. The 24 June 1711 recordation was 2 pers.
over 10 yrs. of age. Andries Hoft was nat. 31 Jan 1715/16, the
next name being Adam Hoft (Albany Nats.). Andreas Hoff and Catharina

Margret with 2 ch. were at Heesberg ca. 1716/17 (Simmendinger Register). And's Hooft was a Palatine Debtor in 1718, 1719 (at Haysberry), 1721, and 1726 (Livingston Debt Lists). He was a freeholder of Kingston in 1728 (Ulster Co. Freeholders) and noted in the Kingston Trustees Records (Bk. 2, pp. 102 & 103). Andris Hoof was in the foot company of the Kingston, Ulster Co. Militia in 1738 (Report of the State Historian, Vol. I, p. 600). The ch. of Andreas[1] Hoff and Catharina Margaretha Ernst were:

1) Gerdraut Christina[2], b. 22 Feb 1707 - sp.: Christina - w/o Mies Hoff, Johan Wilhelm Dales - the shepherd here, and Gertraut - w/o Caspar Schmidt, all here (Heddesdorf Chbk.).

2) "A Son"[2], bpt. 11 Nov 1708 - sp.: Johan Philipp - s/o Henrich Hoff, Georg Henrich - s/o Joh. Peter Hoff, and Gerdraut - d/o Adolf Bieber (Heddesdorf Chbk.).

3) Philip[2] (HJ), noted in the Kingston Trustees Records (Bk. 2, pp. 124 & 125). Phillip Hoof was in the foot company of the Kingston, Ulster Co., Militia in 1738 (Report of the State Historian, Vol. I, p. 601). Philip Hoof, single man b. Dutchess Co., had banns to marry Cornelia Nieuwkerk 17 Sept 1738 (Kingston Ref. Chbk.). She md. 2nd Cornelis Van Keuren 14 Oct 1748 (Kingston Ref. Chbk.). Issue:

   i) Catharina[3], bpt. 7 Oct 1739 - sp.: Cornelis Nieuwkerk and Grietjen Hof (Kingston Ref. Chbk.). A Catharina Hoff md. Matheus Dubois 14 April 1760 (Kingston Ref. Chbk.).

   ii) Johannes[3], bpt. 6 Sept 1741 - sp.: John Kendel and Sophia Hof (Kingston Ref. Chbk.).

   iii) Andreas[3], bpt. 31 July 1743 - sp.: Jan Heermanse and Jannitie Nu kerk (Rhinebeck Flats Ref. Chbk.).

   iv) Wilhelmus[3], bpt. 6 weeks old 23 Sept 1744 at Kisket. - sp.: Catharina Lehman and Wilhelmus Lehman (Loonenburg Luth. Chbk.).

   v) Jannet[3], b. 23 Aug 1746 and bpt. Kisket. - sp.: Hannes Frolich and Christina Lehmann (Loonenburg Luth. Chbk.). She md. James Wittaker 14 April 1764 (Kingston Ref. Chbk.).

   Daniel Hoff, Fernow Wills #826, possibly may connect with the family of Philip[2] (HJ).

4) Sophia[2] (HJ), banns to marry John Kendel 16 Aug 1741 (Kingston Ref. Chbk.).

5) Margaretha[2], bpt. 12 March 1721 - sp.: Margriet Welleven (Kingston Ref. Chbk.). She md. as d/o the dec'd Andrew Hoff 28 Nov 1747 Hermann Minkler (Germantown Ref. Chbk.).

6) Maria[2] (HJ), banns to marry Samuel Rossel 18 Aug 1745 (Kingston Ref. Chbk.).

ANNA MARIA HOFFERTIN (Hunter Lists #313)

John Adam Hoffart aged 27 and his wife, Luth., husbandman and vinedresser, were in the 1st arrivals in England in May of 1709 (London Lists).

Anna Maria Hoffertin made her first appearance on the Hunter Lists 4 Aug 1710 with 1 pers. over 10 yrs. of age; her last entry (cumulative) on 24 Dec 1711 read Anna Hoffartin with 1 pers. over 10 yrs.

There was a John George Hoffert who sp. at the Oley Mountains in 1734 (Stoever Chbks.), however, no known relationship has been established between him and the N.Y. family (HJ).

MARGRETHA HOFFIN (Hunter Lists #314)

Margretha Hoffin made her only appearance on the Hunter Lists 1 July 1710 with 3 pers. over 10 yrs. of age in the household. Anna Margaretha Hoffin, widow, with 1 child, was listed next to Johann Adam Hoff ca. 1716/17 at Hessberg (Simmendinger Register). Magdalen Hoff was a Palatine Debtor in 1718, and Widow Houston was a Palatine Debtor in 1719 (at Haysberry) (Livingston Debt Lists). A Maria Magdalena Hoff sp. Adam Hoff at Camp Queensberry in 1722 (N.Y. City Luth. Chbk.).

It seems very probable that, as the burial of Johanna Margaretha - w/o Tönges Hoff of Heddesdorf, was not found in Germany, #314 Margretha Hoffin may have been this woman; also, the Maria Magdalena Hoff who sp. in 1722 may have been the d/o Tönges and Johanna Margaretha bpt. 18 March 1694 at Heddesdorf (HJ).

GABRIEL HOFFMANN (Hunter Lists #315)

Gabriel Hostmann, widower of Wollstein near Creutzenach in the Pfaltz, md. 11 Sept 1711 Anna Catharina, wid/o Fridrich Batz of Aurbach in Hesten-Darmstadt (West Camp Luth. Chbk.). His village of origin then was 6556 Wöllstein (6 km. s.e. of Bad Kreuznach; Chbks. begin 1608, Ref.). Anna Maria, d/o David Hoffmann and wife Agnes of Wöllstein, md. the emigrant Nicolaus Treber there 2 July 1693, and Anna Maria often was listed next to Gabriel Hoffmann on extant Palatine mss. in colonial N.Y. (HJ); therefore, some relationship probably existed between Gabriel Hoffmann and Anna Maria Hoffmann Treber, but, so far, Gabriel Hoffmann has not been documented at Wöllstein (HJ). Gabriel Hofman was listed next to Arnold Kriget in the 2nd party in Holland in 1709 (Rotterdam Lists). Gabriel Hofman aged 40, Ref., a turner, was in the 2nd arrivals in England later that yr. (London Lists).

Gabriel Hoffmann made his first appearance on the Hunter Lists
4 Oct 1710 with 2 pers. over 10 yrs. of age in the household. The
entry for 29 Sept 1711 read Gabriel Hoffman and Cath: Batzin with
3 pers. over 10 and 1 pers. under 10 yrs. The family was recorded
with 2 pers. over 10 and 2 pers. under 10 throughout 1712. (--)
Hofman was listed next to Ana Maria Draberin in 1710/11 with 1 man
and 1 woman in Ulster Co. (West Camp Census). Gabriel Hofmann and
Anna Catharina with 2 ch. were at Neu-Stuttgardt ca. 1716/17 (Simmendinger Register). He was mentioned on tax rolls in the Rhinebeck
area 1727/28 - 1739/40 (Dutchess Co. Tax Lists). With his 1st wife
Susanna he had a child:

1) Joseph[2], bpt. 8 July 1711 - sp.: Joseph Reichard and wife
   Anna Maria (West Camp Luth. Chbk.).

By his 2nd wife Anna Catharina he had issue:

2) Sebastian[2], b. 2 Feb 1713 - sp.: Sebastian Treber and Magdalena Eckhard (West Camp Luth. Chbk.). Bastian Hoffmann
   was conf. among the Germans at Beekman's Land in 1731, aged
   18 yrs. (N.Y. City Luth. Chbk.).

HERMANN HOFFMANN (Hunter Lists #316)

The roots of this family were with so many other 1709ers at
5905 Oberfischbach (5 km. w. of Siegen; Chbks. begin 1670). The
earliest known direct ancestor of the N.Y. family was Johannes Hoffmann of Oberfischbach. Hermann Hoffmann, s/o the late Johannes Hoffmann of Oberfischbach, md. Catharina, d/o Michael Dudenhenn at Ober-
scheld, 28 Feb 1679. The w/o Michael Dudenhanß d. 23 Nov 1679 at
Oberschelt. The ch. of Hermann Hoffmann and Catharina were:

Anna Lucia, md. as d/o Hermann Hoffmann 7 Oct 1703 the emigrant
1709er Peter Giseler.

+ Hermann, b. 1679 at Oberschelden - sp.: Hermann Hoffmann at
  Oberschelt.

Jacob, b. 1687 and md. Anna Marg. Übach in 1715.

Anna Catharina (a twin), b. 1687.

Christopher, b. 1692 and md. Maria Elisab. Starcke in 1717.
Hermann Hoffmann d. 25 May 1719; his obituary stated he was a widower, about 50 yrs. (?), had 5 ch. with his late wife Catharin: 3
sons (2 alive) and 2 daughters, one died, and if the other is alive
is not known, because she went to the Insel Carolina. Catharina, w/o
Hermann Hoffmann d. 20 May 1717, aged in her 60's. Hermannus Hoffmann, s/o Hermann Hoffmann from Oberfischbach, md. Maria Gertrud,
d/o Gerlach Schmid from Asdorff, 5 Aug 1703. Hermannus Hoffmann,
his wife Maria Gertraudt, daughters Anna Loysia, Anna Catharina,
and Catharina, were noted as out of the country on a 1708 Inhabitant List of Oberfischbach.

Hermann Hoffmann made his initial appearance on the Hunter Lists 1 July 1710 with 2 pers. over 10 yrs. and 1 under 10 in the family; the entry changed to 2 pers. over 10 on 4 Oct 1710. Hermanus Hoffman aged 30 and Maria Gertrude Hoffman aged 30 were recorded at Hackensack at John Lotz's in 1710/11 (Palatines In N.Y. City). In some chbk. entries at Hackensack, he was noted as Hermann the German (de Hoogduitscher) during the period 1711-18. The will of Haramanus Hofman of Orange Co. was dated 15 Feb 1752 and probated the last Tuesday in April 1754 (Fernow Wills #778c). Ch.:

1) Anna Lucia², bpt. 13 April 1704 - sp.: Anna Lucia - w/o Peter Gisler (Oberfischbach Chbk.).

2) Anna Catharina², bpt. 20 June 1706 - sp.: Anna Catrin - w/o Johannes Schmid from Heisberg (Oberfischbach Chbk.).

3) Catharina², bpt. 11 March 1708 - sp.: Catharina - w/o Hermann Hoffmann, grandmother of the child (Oberfischbach Chbk.).

4) Catharina², bpt. 23 Sept 1711 - sp.: Willem ... and Hilla Loots (Hackensack Ref. Chbk.). She md. Henrich Schneider (HJ).

5) Christina², bpt. 12 March 1713 - sp.: Johannes Pieterse Engelberts and Cristin Smidt (Hackensack Ref. Chbk.). She md. Johannes Schneider (HJ).

6) Lea², bpt. 20 Feb 1715 - sp.: Jan Loots and Trintie Loots (Hackensack Ref. Chbk.). She md. Paulus Giseler (HJ).

7) Rachel², bpt. 20 Feb 1715 (same day as above) - sp.: Pieter Wannemaker and Cornelia Leydecker (Hackensack Ref. Chbk.). She md. Harmannus Giseler (HJ).

8) Elisabetha², bpt. 25 Nov 1716 - sp.: Jan Everse and wife Maria Berbera (Hackensack Ref. Chbk.).

9) Hermannus², bpt. 14 April 1718 - sp.: Fransoes Moor, and Margritie - wid/o Johannes Pieterse (Hackensack Ref. Chbk.). He md. Sarah Wood (HJ).

10) Johann Georg², b. 16 March 1720 - sp.: Jurrien Kloegh and Juliana Lisabet ... (Tappan Ref. Chbk.). He md. Elisabetha Westervelt (HJ).

11) Wilhelm², b. 24 Nov 1721 - sp.: Willem Felten and wife Christina Smitt (Tappan Ref. Chbk.).

JACOB HOFFMANN (Hunter Lists #317)

Jacob Hofman, his wife and 3 ch. were on Capt. Duk's ship in Holland in the 4th party of 1709 (Rotterdam Lists).

Jacob Hoffmann made his appearance on the Hunter Lists 4 July 1710 with 2 pers. over 10 yrs.; the 29 Sept 1711 entry read 2 over

10 yrs. and 1 under 10. Jacob Hoffmann was a Palatine carpenter, as noted from his signature on a 1712 mss. (N.Y. Col. Mss., Vol. 55, p. 27a). The issue of Jacob[1] Hoffmann and wife Maria Elisabetha:

1) Mattheus[2], b. 22 Aug 1711 - sp.: Mattheus Cuntz (West Camp Luth. Chbk.).

CONRAD HOFFMANN (Hunter Lists #318)

A Johann Conrad Hoffmann, citizen and linenweaver, md. 9 Aug 1705 Margaretha Eleonora Elisabeth, d/o the linenweaver Henrich Kolback, at 6360 Friedberg; however, no proof has been found that this was the N.Y. pioneer (HJ). Koenraat Hoffman, his wife, and 3 ch. were in the 4th party of Palatines in Holland (Rotterdam Lists).

Conrad Hoffmann made his initial appearance on the Hunter Lists 1 July 1710 with 3 pers. over 10 yrs. and 3 pers. under 10 in the family. The rolls noted 4 over 10 and 2 under 10 yrs. on 4 Oct 1710, and then 4 over 10 and 3 under 10 31 Dec 1710. The family diminished to 4 over 10 and 2 under 10 25 March 1711, and then grew again to 4 over 10 and 3 under 10 yrs. 29 Sept 1711. Coenrat Hofman was nat. 8 and 9 Sept 1715 (Kingston Nats.). Conrad Hofmann and Anna Maria Margretha with 5 ch. were at Hunderston ca. 1716/17 (Simmendinger Register). His signature dated 1719 survives in the Livingston Papers, Reel #4. Coenradt Hoffman was a Palatine Debtor in 1718, 1719, 1721, 1722, and 1726 (Livingston Debt Lists). He appeared on tax rolls in the Rhinebeck area 1726/27 to 1740/41, when his widow was registered (Dutchess Co. Tax Lists). With his wife Eva Margaretha, he had issue:

1) Johann Peter[2], b. 11 Sept 1711 - sp.: Johann Peter Glopp (West Camp Luth. Chbk.). Peter appeared on Dutchess rolls 1736/37 through 1778 (Dutchess Co. Tax Lists). He md. Maria Margaretha Schäffer (HJ) and had ch.:

   i) Maria[3], bpt. 1 Nov 1736 - sp.: Hendrick Godfried and Mareitje Godfried (Red Hook Luth. Chbk.).

   ii) Conrad[3], bpt. 11 May 1738 - sp.: Conrad Pulver and Magdalena Schever (Red Hook Luth. Chbk.). He joined the Red Hook Luth. Church 12 May 1758. Conrad[3] md. Catharina Pulver (HJ) and had ch. bpt. at Rhinebeck Luth., Linlithgo Ref., Red Hook Luth., and Manorton Luth. Churches.

   iii) Susanna[3], bpt. 28 May 1740 - sp.: Henrich Koen and Susanna Hofman (Germantown Ref. Chbk.).

   iv) Anna[3], bpt. 19 June 1741 - sp.: Jacob Simon and Anna Schever (Kingston Ref. Chbk.). She joined the Red Hook Luth. Church 9 June 1759, and md. Nicolas Lenhard (HJ).

v) <u>Jacob</u>[3], bpt. as Georg Jacob 7 July 1745 - sp.: Jacob Marden and Barbal Stickel (Red Hook Luth. Chbk.). He md. Catharina Mohr (HJ) and had ch. bpt. at Manorton Luth., Germantown Ref., Gallatin Ref., and Red Hook Luth. Churches (HJ).

vi) <u>Nicolas</u>[3], bpt. 2 Aug 1747 - sp.: Nicolaas Rauw and Lisabeth Hoffman (Germantown Ref. Chbk.). He probably md. Lena Schott (HJ); he d. 22 July 1824, aged 76 yrs. (Dutch Church Cem., Madalin)

vii) <u>Maria</u>[3], bpt. 5 April 1749 - sp.: Jurg Hofman and Mareitje Scheffer (Red Hook Luth. Chbk.). She md. Henrich Mohr (HJ).

viii) <u>Susanna</u>[3], bpt. 11 March 1753 - sp.: Zacharie Philip and Susanna Stickel (Rhinebeck Flats Ref. Chbk.).

ix) <u>Christina</u>[3], b. 10 Feb 1755 - sp.: Zacharias Feller and Christina Loe (Rhinebeck Flats Ref. Chbk.).

x) <u>Magdalena</u>[3], bpt. 1 Sept 1756 - sp.: Wilhelm Petzer and Magdalena Dunsbach (Red Hook Luth. Chbk.).

xi) <u>Petrus</u>[3], bpt. 10 Sept 1758 - sp.: Peter Horter and Maria Schafer (Red Hook Luth. Chbk.).

xii) <u>Adam</u>[3], b. 29 Sept 1760 - sp.: Adam Bitzer and Margaretha Dider (Rhinebeck Luth. Chbk.).

The 2nd wife of Conrad[1] Hoffmann was named Barbara Elisabetha (HJ). She was recorded in the St. Peter's Luth. Family List ca. 1734 as Barbara Elisabetha Hoffmannin with (ch.) Anna Margretha and Anna Maria (Rhinebeck Luth. Chbk.). A child of the marriage to Barbara Elisabetha was:

2) <u>Maria Susanna</u>[2], b. the beginning of Nov 1720 at Ruloff Jansen Kill and bpt. in Taarboss - sp.: Andreas Widderwax and Maria Susanna Forstein (N.Y. City Luth. Chbk.). She md. Henrich Kuhn (HJ).

Additional ch. by either his 1st or 2nd wife were:

3) <u>Catharina</u>[2] (HJ), who as Cathar. Wielerin born Hofmannin joined the church at Rhynbek 21 Oct 1744 (Loonenburg Luth. Chbk.). She md. Bastian Wiehler (HJ).

4) <u>Anna Margaretha</u>[2] (St. Peter's Luth. Family List).

5) <u>Anna Maria</u>[2] (St. Peter's Luth. Family List).

6) <u>Elisabetha</u>[2] (HJ), a sp. in 1747 at Germantown Ref.

7) <u>Georg</u>[2] (HJ), on Dutchess tax rolls beginning 1753. He md. Elisabetha Kilmer (HJ) and had ch.:

i) <u>Conrad</u>[3], bpt. 27 Feb 1757 - sp.: Peter Hoffmann and Margaretha Schafer (Red Hook Luth. Chbk.).

ii) <u>Simon</u>[3], b. 1 Aug 1763 - sp.: Simon Killmer and wife Elisabeth (Rhinebeck Luth. Chbk.). He d. 3 Nov 1838, aged 75-3-5 (Red Hook Luth. Cem.).

    iii) <u>Georg</u>[3], bpt. 5 Oct 1766 - sp.: Georg Hofman and Christina Kulmer (Red Hook Luth. Chbk.).

There was a Georg Hoffmann who md. 28 March 1769 Margaretha Mohr (Red Hook Luth. Chbk.) and had issue bpt. at Gallatin Ref. and Kinderhook Ref.; he may belong in the family of Conrad[1] also (HJ).

HENRICH HOFFMANN (Hunter Lists #319)

There were many Henrich Hoffmanns found in Germany during the course of this project, but, since the name is so common, a match with the meager data known about the N.Y. settler is difficult to make (HJ). Henry Hofman, his wife and 3 ch. were on Capt. Jan Fouler's ship in the 3rd party in Holland; Henrig Hoffman, his wife, and 1 child were on Capt. Jno Untank's ship in the 5th party in Holland; and Henrig Hoffman, his wife, and 2 ch. were in the 6th party of Palatines in Holland (all Rotterdam Lists). Henry Hofman aged 33, his wife, daughters aged 6, 3, and 1, Luth., miller, were in the 3rd arrivals in England (London Lists).

Henrich Hoffmann was recorded with 1 pers. over 10 yrs. and 2 pers. under 10 on 30 June 1710 on the Hunter Lists; he often was listed near Gabriel Hoffmann in Hunter (HJ). The 24 June 1711 entry read 4 over 10 and 2 under 10, the 29 Sept 1711 notation recorded 5 over 10 yrs. and 1 under 10, and the 24 Dec 1711 entry noted 4 over 10 and 1 under 10 yrs. The 25 March 1712 entry read 3 pers. over 10 and 1 under 10, and the notation for 24 June 1712 mentioned 5 over 10 and 1 under 10 for Henrich Hoffmann and Gr Demuth. Hen. Hoffman of Queensbury was a soldier in 1711 (Palatine Volunteers To Canada). Hendrick Hofman was nat. 8 and 9 Sept 1715 (Kingston Nats.). Heinrich Hofmann and his wife with 3 ch. were recorded at Quunsberg ca. 1716/17 (Simmendinger Register). Hend: Hoffman was a Palatine Debtor in 1718, 1721, and 1726 (Livingston Debt Lists) and a Palatine willing to remain on the Manor 26 Aug 1724 (<u>Doc. Hist. of N.Y.</u>, Vol. III, p. 724). His probable daughter was:

    1) <u>Rebecca</u>[2] (HJ), md. Ludwig Batz (HJ). Henrich[2] Hoffmann sp. Bernhard Schmidt in 1726, Rebecca[2] Hoffmann sp. this same Schmidt in 1720, and a Margareta Hoffman sp. Schmidt in 1722 (all at N.Y. City Luth. Church); these connectives are the reasons for my use of the word "probable" in placing Rebecca in the family structure (HJ).

ANNA EVA HOFFMÄNNIN (Hunter Lists #320)

An Anna Eva, d/o the late Johannes Berckhanns from Westernach (?) in Hadamarischen Gebiets, md. Dönges Hoffmann, widower at Langenbach, Dom. 26 p. Trin: 1692 at 5439 Bad Marienberg; however, no firm connective has been found between this woman and the N.Y. 1709er (HJ).

Anna Eva Hoffmännin made her initial appearance on the Hunter Lists 4 Aug 1710 with 1 pers. over 10 yrs. of age; her last entry was 4 Oct 1710 with 1 pers. over 10.

ANNA CATHARINA HOFFMÄNNIN (Hunter Lists #321)

Katarina Hofmenin was on Capt. Robbert Lourens ship in Holland 5 June 1709 (Rotterdam Lists). Catherine Hoffmanin aged 24, Cath., unmd., was in the 3rd arrivals in England later that yr. (London Lists).

Anna Catharina Hoffmännin made her only appearance on the Hunter rolls 4 Oct 1710 with 1 pers. over 10 yrs. of age in the household. Anna Catharina Hostmann joined the church in June 1710; she was called Epis. and admitted by Rev. Dan. Falckner (West Camp Luth. Chbk.).

THOMAS HOMBURGER (Hunter Lists #322)

The obituary of the 1709er Abraham Berg mentioned that he was b. at Langen Hahn under the Electorate of Hessen-Darmstadt and md. Catharina Homberg, d/o Thomas Homberg (Schoharie Luth. Chbk.). The records of Langenhain are found in the registers of 6238 Lorsbach (13 km. e. of Wiesbaden; Chbks. begin 1639, Luth.). Thomas Homberger was called a cowherd at Langenhain in 1699 and 1706.

Thomas Homburger made his initial appearance on the Hunter Lists 30 June 1710 with 2 pers. over 10 yrs. of age in the family; on 4 Aug 1710 the entry noted 1 pers. over 10 yrs. Thomas Hambuch was at Neu-Heidelberg ca. 1716/17 (Simmendinger Register). The ch. of Thomas[1] Homburger were:

1) Johann Philip[2], md. as single s/o the cowherd Thomas Homberger in Langenhain 8 Aug 1699 Anna Margaretha, d/o the late Johann Henrich Berg - Gerichtsmann, bender and inhabitant in Langenhayn (Lorsbach Chbk.).
2) Johannes[2], a sp. in 1702 as youngest brother of Johann Philip[2] (Lorsbach Chbk.).
3) Anna Catharina[2], md. as youngest d/o Thomas Homberger 19 Jan 1706 Johan Abraham Berg (Lorsbach Chbk.).

MICHAEL HÖNIGEN (Hunter Lists #323)

Michael Hönigen made his first appearance on the Hunter Lists 4 July 1710 with 2 pers. over 10 yrs. of age in the family. The surname was spelled Hönnichen, Hennichen, and Hennigen in these rolls. Michiel Heyntie was nat. 17 Jan 1715/16 (Albany Nats.). Michael Haug and Magdalena with 2 ch. were at Quunsberg ca. 1716/17 (Simmendinger Register). Michiel Heyntie was a Palatine Debtor in 1718, 1719, 1721, and 1726 (Livingston Debt Lists). The ch. of Michael[1] Hönigen and wife Magdalena were:

1) Maria Barbara[2] (HJ), md. Johannes Simon (HJ).
2) Anna Elisabetha[2], b. 10 Aug 1717 - sp.: Johann Stahl and Elisabeth Duntzbach (West Camp Luth. Chbk.). It is difficult to establish if she was the Anna Elisabetha Heyntje who md. 1st Paul Kammer and 2nd Wilhelm Klapper, as no sp. seem to connect this latter woman to the family of Michael[1] (HJ).
3) Margaretha[2] (HJ), md. John Losch or Lusk (HJ).
4) Susanna Margaretha[2], b. late Oct 1720 and bpt. at Camp - sp.: Nicolaus Philipp and Susanna Margareta Philipps (N.Y. City Luth. Chbk.).

There were other early Hönigs in the colonies: 1) A Nicolaus and a Joh: Georg Honig both were md. in 1739 in Lancaster, Pa. by Pastor Stoever; and 2) A Johannes and an Elias Henjan were noted in the Red Hook Luth. Chbk. 1762-1776 (HJ).

JOHN HORNE (Hunter Lists #324)

John Hern aged 37, his wife, sons aged 7 and 5, and a daughter aged 2, Ref., husbandman and vinedresser, were in the 4th arrivals in England in 1709 (London Lists).

Johannes Horn was mentioned on the Hunter Lists 30 June 1710 with 2 pers. over 10 yrs. of age; the cumulative entry for 24 Dec 1711 read 3 over 10 yrs. Geertruy Nikkels, w/o Joh[S] Horn of Nywitties Land joined the N.Y. City Ref. Church 29 May 1711, and then was noted as departed. John Horn was recorded in Capt. Cornelis Haring's Co. of the Orange Co. Militia 25 Oct 1715 (Report of the State Historian, Vol. I, p. 481). A child of Johannes[1] and his wife Gertraud was:

1) Anna Elisabetha[2], bpt. as Nanelesbet 10 April 1716 - sp.: Juerreye Kloeck and Ante Katreyn Jace (?) (Tappan Ref. Chbk.).

An unplaced Hieronymus Hoorn had a child bpt. in 1725 at Somerville and was a miller in the Amwell, N.J. area (HJ).

CASPAR HORNE (Hunter Lists #325)

Kasper Horn, his wife, and 3 ch. were on Capt. Johan Enrit's ship 3 July 1709 in the 5th party of Palatines (Rotterdam Lists).

Caspar Horn was enrolled only once on the Hunter Lists on 4 Oct 1710 with 2 pers. over 10 yrs. of age in the family.

A Maria Magdalena Horn md. Nicolaus Eckert in the Schoharie area by 1738, but it is hard to establish the correct Horn (or Horning) family to which she belongs (HJ).

NICLAUS HORNICH (Hunter Lists #326)

The roots of this Mohawk Valley family were at 6906 Leimen (6 km. s.e. of Heidelberg; Chbks. begin 1694, Ref., but gaps). Joh. Nicolaus Hornig, single s/o the late Velten Hornig - Gerichtsverwandten here, md. Anna Maria, single d/o the late Hans Jörg Hoffmann - citizen at Rohrbach, 27 Jan 1705.

Niclaus Hornich made his initial appearance on the Hunter Lists 4 Oct 1710 with 2 pers. over 10 yrs. of age; the family size increased to 2 pers. over 10 and 1 under 10 yrs. 24 June 1711. N.Y. Col. Mss., Vol. 55, pp. 21 a-c, show a surviving document mentioning Nic. Horning and Georg Hirchemer (who also originated at Leimen - HJ). Nicolas Korning was nat. 11 Oct 1715 (Albany Nats.). Nicolaus Hornig and his wife (Anna Maria with 4 ch., adds Mac Wethy) were at Neu-Heidelberg ca. 1716/17 (Simmendinger Register). He represented the Ref. church in a 1744 deed to the Luth. church at Stone Arabia (History of Montgomery & Fulton Counties, p. 155). Nicholas Horning was a freeholder in 1763 at Canajoharrie (Albany Co. Freeholders). Issue with wife Anna Maria:

1) Johann Adam², bpt. 6 Dec 1705 - sp.: H. Johan Adam Lill - Schultheiss at Kirchheim (Leimen Chbk.).
2) Johann Daniel², bpt. 21 Nov 1706 - sp.: Johan Daniel - s/o Hanß Adam Lill - Schultheiß at Kirchheim, and Anna Eva Lill, d/o the late ... (Leimen Chbk.).
3) Anna Catharina², bpt. 28 May 1708 - sp.: Anna Catharina - w/o H. Jacob Schneider (Leimen Chbk.).
4) Magdalena² (HJ), md. Wilhelm Gerlach (HJ).
5) Dieterich² (HJ), md. Maria Margaretha Kraus (HJ). See Penrose's Mohawk Valley in the Revolution, p. 265, for more on this man.

GERHARD HORNING (Hunter Lists #327)

Gerhart Horning, his wife, and 2 ch. were on Capt. John Howlentzen's ship in Holland in the 4th party (Rotterdam Lists).

Gerhard Horning aged 40, his wife, daughters aged 6 and 2, Ref., bricklayer, were in the 4th arrivals in England (London Lists).

Gerhard Horning made his first appearance on the Hunter Lists 24 June 1711 with 2 pers. over 10 yrs. of age in the family. He and his wife sp. David Hupfer, a fellow-passenger on Capt. Howlentzen's ship, in 1714 (West Camp Luth. Chbk.). Gerhard Hornung d. 9 April 1715; Anna Sophia, wid/o Gerhard Hornung of Newtown, md. Andreas Ellich, widower of Necke-Burcken in the commune of Mossbach in the Pfaltz, 9 May 1715 (both West Camp Luth. Chbk.).

VERONICA HOTHENROTHIN (Hunter Lists #328)

Veronica Hottenrothin made her only appearance on the Hunter Lists 4 Oct 1710 with 2 pers. over 10 yrs. of age. The two spellings of her name in the same mss. (the Hunter Lists) are just additional examples of the many spelling variants that may be found when studying the 1709ers (HJ).

BARBARA HUCKIN (Hunter Lists #329)

Barbara Huckin made her initial appearance on the Hunter Lists 30 June 1710 with 1 pers. over 10 yrs. of age; her last entry was 4 Aug 1710 with 1 pers. over 10. Maria Barbra Hoebacke, wid/o Johannes Hoeck, md. 6 Oct 1711 Joh: Evert Moleg (Hackensack Ref. Chbk.).

CHRISTOPH HÜLS (Hunter Lists #330)

The German home of this complex N.Y. family was 6690 Marth (6 km. e. of St. Wendel; records in registers of 6690 Niederkirchen i/Ostertal (1 km. further w.; Chbks. begin 1666, but gaps) and 6799 Konken (10 km. n.e. of Marth; Chbks. begin 1653). Christopfell Hülls was an emigrant from Marth (Sarre) in the Duchy of Zweibrücken in 1709 (Emigrants from the Palatinate to the American Colonies in the 18th Century, by Krebs and Rubincam, p. 31). Kristoffel Hilsch and wife were listed next to Andries Drom, his wife, and 5 ch. on Capt. Jan Coate's ship in Holland in 1709 in the 5th party of Palatines (Rotterdam Lists); perhaps some of Drom's 5 ch. actually belonged to Hilsch (HJ).

Christoph Hüls was first entered on the Hunter Lists 1 July 1710 with 4 pers. over 10 yrs. and 1 pers. under 10. The notation for 4 Oct 1710 read 5 over 10, for 25 March 1711 showed 5 over 10 and 1 under 10, and for 24 June 1711 the entry was 4 pers. over 10 yrs. and 1 under 10. The 25 March 1712 entry showed 3 over 10 and 1 under 10, the 24 June 1712 reading was 4 over 10 and 1 under 10,

and the 13 Sept 1712 notation was 4 pers. over 10 yrs. and 2 under
10 yrs. Christ. Hills was a soldier from Hunterstown in 1711 (Palatine Volunteers To Canada). Christoph Huitz and his wife Eva Catharina with 5 ch. were at Neu-Heidelberg ca. 1716/17 (Simmendinger
Register). This family has been one of the most difficult of all
the 800+ N.Y. Palatine families to put in a genealogical structure,
due to the several missing Mohawk Valley registers (HJ); however,
the descendants of Christoph[1] Hüls (Hils, Hultz, Hieltz, et var)
and Eva Catharina appear to have been:

1) Johann Theobald[2], bpt. 10/20 July 1698 to Stoffel Hiltz
   from Mahrt and Eva Catharina - sp.: Margaretha - w/o Hans
   Jacob Wagner, Hans Theobolt Müller, Hanß Adam Morgenstern,
   and Anna Lovisa - surviving d/o Melchior Ygel (Konken
   Chbk.). He md. Anna Eva Nerbel or Merkelse (HJ) and had
   issue:

   i) Maria Eva[3] (HJ), md. Johannes Finck (HJ).

   ii) Maria Magdalena[3], joined the Schoharie Ref. Church
   14 May 1740. She had banns to marry Adam Schäffer
   (as a d/o Deobald) 16 March 1749 (Schoharie Ref.
   Chbk.).

   iii) Anna Margaretha[3] (HJ), a sp. in 1752 to Johannes
   Finck and Maria Eva Hiltz at Schoharie Ref. Church.

   iv) Anna Dorothea[3], bpt. 1 Feb 1734/35 - sp.: Thom. Schoemaker and Anna Dor. Schoemaker (Schoharie Ref. or Luth.
   Chbk.). Dorothea Hils joined the Schoharie Ref. Church
   15 April 1750. She md. Johannes Werner 26 Sept 1758
   (Schoharie Luth. Chbk.).

   v) Johann Georg[3], bpt. 13 March 1736/37 - sp.: Jurr. Timmer and Mar. Elys Timmer (Schoharie Ref. or Luth.
   Chbk.). He md. 23 Jan 1759 Elisabetha Bellinger (Schoharie Luth. Chbk.).

   vi) Christophel[3], bpt. 25 Nov 1738 - sp.: Jerri Sybel and
   wife Maria Engel Hils (Schoharie Ref. Chbk.). He md.
   as s/o the late Deobald Hils 10 Oct 1773 Maria Borst
   (Schoharie Ref. Chbk.).

   vii) Catharina Elisabetha[3], bpt. 24 Nov 1740 - sp.: Johannes Finck and Catharina Elisabet Ballin (Schoharie
   Ref. Chbk.).

   viii) Elisabetha[3], bpt. 17 April 1742 - sp.: Jacob Sneider
   and wife Elisabeth (Schoharie Ref. Chbk.). She md. as
   d/o the late Deobald Hils of Schoharie 29 Oct 1769
   Johannes Schneider (Schoharie Ref. Chbk.).

2?) Mattheus[2] (HJ), md. Anna Eva Tantelaar (Danler? - HJ). As
   he only appears once in the Schoharie Ref. registers, and

like Johann Theobald² md. an Anna Eva, I believe there is
a good chance this so-called Mattheus may have been really
Johann Theobald² and entered erroneously in the chbk. (HJ).
The Schoharie Ref. Chbks. show that Mattheus Hilts and Anna
Eva Tantelaar had issue:

    i) Maria Engel³, bpt. 28 April 1731 - sp.: Jurrian Sibel
       and Maria Engel Hilts (Schoharie Ref. Chbk.).

3) Maria Engel² (HJ), md. Georg Seybold (HJ).

4) Johann Georg² (HJ), called inhabitant at the Falls at his
   son's marriage 15 April 1760 (Stone Arabia Ref. Chbk.).
   Jurry Hitts was a freeholder at the Falls in 1763 (Albany
   Co. Freeholders). Georg Hielts Sr. and Maria Elisabetha
   sp. Friederich Dornberger and wife Elisabetha Hielts in
   1765 (German Flats Ref. Chbk.). Georg Hils Sr. and Jr. were
   in Capt. Marx Petry's Co. at Bornets Field in 1767 (Report
   of the State Historian, Vol. II, p. 855). Issue:

    i) Johann Nicolaus³, md. as s/o Georg Hültz 15 April 1760
       Elisabetha, d/o Phillip Fox (Stone Arabia Ref. Chbk.).
       He d. 15 Dec 1809, aged 76 yrs. and 8 months (Herki-
       mer Ref. Chbk.). Penrose's Mohawk Valley in the Rev-
       olution, p. 265, notes his family.

    ii) Georg³ (HJ), whose will was dated 26 May 1809 and pro-
       bated 23 April 1814 (Herkimer Co. Will Bk. B).

5?) Christophel² (HJ), called inhabitant at the Fall in 1760
   (Stone Arabia Ref. Chbk.); there is a slight possibility
   that Christophel² may have been Christophel¹, the emigrant,
   but, if so, he would have had to father additional ch. very
   late in life (HJ). Issue:

    i) Maria Catharina³, a sp. in 1760 (Stone Arabia Ref.
       Chbk.).

    ii) Catharina³, md. as d/o Stophel Hültz at the Fall 2
       Sept 1760 Nicolaus Kültz (Stone Arabia Ref. Chbk.).

    iii) Elisabetha³, md. as d/o Stophel Hültz 7 April 1760
       Friederich Dornberger (Stone Arabia Ref. Chbk.).

    iv) Christophel³, md. as s/o the late Stoffel Hiltz in
       Jan 1769 Dorothea Schneider (Schoharie Ref. Chbk.).
   There is also the possibility that Christophel² was actually Christophel³, an elder s/o Johann Georg² Hiltz (HJ).

6) Maria Margaretha², bpt. 21 Dec 1708 - sp.: Andreas Tromb,
   Martin - s/o Marten Maurer, Maria Margreth - w/o Hans Adam
   Müller at Marth, and Margaretha - w/o Hans Georg Schnur
   (Schuer?) (Niederikirchen i/Ostertal Chbk.).

There were several unplaced Hiltzes who may have been kin
of the emigrant Christoph¹: 1) a Jacob Simon Hitts was a freeholder

at the Falls in 1763 (Albany Co. Freeholders); 2) Adam, Stofel,
Jacob, Jacob Jr., and Stofel Hiltz Jr. were in Capt. Mark Petry's
Co. in 1757; and 3) Georg Jacob Hils was in Petry's Co. in 1767
(Report of the State Historian, Vol. II, pp. 781 & 855).

GEORG HUMMEL dead (Hunter Lists #331)

Elisabetha, wid/o Jerg Humbel of Mossbach in the Pfaltz, md.
Henrich Heidorn, widower of Gelnhausen near Hanau, 10 Sept 1711
(West Camp Luth. Chbk.). The ancestral roots of this family then
were at 6950 Mosbach/Baden (17 km. s.e. of Eberbach; Chbks. begin
1626, Ref.). The father of the emigrant was Philip Hummel. Hans
Philip Hummel, citizen and cooper here, d. 27 Dec 1694,aged 80 yrs.,
and his widow Anna was bur. 21 June 1701, aged 83 yrs. Jörg Hummel,
carpenter-fellow and s/o the former citizen Philipp Hummel, md.
22 April 1692 Elisabeth, d/o the late Jacob Toni - formerly a citizen at Bigle in Suisse Berner Gebieths.

Georg Hummel made his initial appearance on the Hunter Lists
1 July 1710 with 3 pers. over 10 yrs. of age in the family; the
entry for 24 June 1711 read Georg Hummel's Wid^W with 3 over 10.
On 29 Sept 1711 the family showed 2 over 10 yrs. of age, and on
24 Dec 1711 the entry read Henrich Heydorn and Georg Hummel's Wid^W.
Two planks for the coffin of Georg Humel were ordered 9 March 1711
(N.Y. Col. Mss., Vol. 55, p. 20a-h). The ch. of Georg[1] Hummel (called a vinedresser at Mosbach 1693 - 1705) were:
1) Maria Barbara[2], bpt. 13 Feb 1693 - sp.: Maria Barbara - d/o
   Maria Cath. Neder here (Mosbach Chbk.). She md. 25 April
   1726 Johann Henrich Conrad (N.Y. City Luth. Chbk.).
2) Maria Margaretha[2], bpt. 30 April 1696 - sp.: Maria Margretha,
   the Nederin (Mosbach Chbk.). She was bur. 26 Sept 1701
   (Mosbach Chbk.).
3) Johann Henrich[2], bpt. 10 Oct 1698 - sp.: Joh. Henrich Jung-
   meister, citizen and brewer here (Mosbach Chbk.).
4) Philip Georg[2], bpt. 30 Oct 1701 - sp.: the bachelor Philipp
   Jerg Hummel (Mosbach Chbk.).
5) Christian[2], bpt. 18 March 1704 - sp.: Christian Minner, citizen and shoemaker here (Mosbach Chbk.). He was bur. 20 Aug
   1704, aged more than 5 months (Mosbach Chbk.).
6) Johann Georg[2], bpt. 21 Aug 1705 - sp.: Hans Jörg Oberleder
   - young s/o M. Hans Jörg Oberle the cutler (Mosbach Chbk.).

HERMANN HUMMEL (Hunter Lists #332)

As Hermann Hummel md. Anna Margaretha, d/o Johann Wilhelm
Schneider prior to emigration in 1709, his origins probably were

near Schneider's ancestral village of 5231 Birnbach in the Westerwald (HJ). Herman Hümmel, his wife, and 1 child were listed near
Hans Willem Sneider in the 6th party of Palatines (Rotterdam Lists).

Herman Hummel first was entered on the Hunter Lists 4 July
1710 with 3 pers. over 10 yrs. of age. The entry for 4 Aug 1710
read 4 over 10 yrs., and the notation for 4 Oct 1710 showed 2 pers.
over 10 yrs. in the household. Harmanus Hommel was nat. (next to
Gorg and Wm: Snider) 8 and 9 Sept 1715 (Kingston Nats.). He was recorded in a list of the Ffoot Co. of Mallitia for the town of Shawangunk under the command of Capt. Nicolas Hoffman in the regt. of
Ulster Co. under Collo. Jacob Rutsen in 1715 (Report of the State
Historian, Vol. I, p. 564). Harmanus Hommell was taxed at Kingston
1718 - 1721 (Ulster Co. Tax Lists) and was a freeholder there in
1728 (Ulster Co. Freeholders). The Kingston Trustees Records mention him in Book I, part C, pp. 116 & 117, Book V, p. 205, and
Book VI, p. 92. The ch. of Hermann[1] Hummel and Anna Margaretha were:
1) Catharina[2], bpt. 30 Dec 1711 - sp.: Johannes Kleyn and
   Catrina Snider (Kingston Ref. Chbk.). She md. Zacharias
   Becker in May 1732 (Kingston Ref. Chbk.).
2) Johannes[2], bpt. 18 July 1714 - sp.: Johannes Blas and Anna
   Joel (Kingston Ref. Chbk.). He md. 1st Maria Teel/Kähl
   (HJ) and had issue:
   i) Margaretha[3], bpt. 17 June 1739 - sp.: Harmanus Hommel
      and Margriet Snyder (Kingston Ref. Chbk.).
   ii) Hermanus[3], bpt. 16 Oct 1740 - sp.: Zacharias Bekker
       and Catharina Hommel (Katsbaan Ref. Chbk.).
   iii) Georg[3], bpt. 1 Aug 1742 - sp.: Johan Jurg Hommel and
        Antje Hommel (Kingston Ref. Chbk.). He d. 27 May 1836,
        aged 93-11-22 (Blue Mt. Cem., Saugerties). Jurry Hum-
        ble aged 18, b. Ulster Co., labourer, 5 foot 6 inches
        tall, dark complexion, brown hair, was in Capt. Rich-
        ard Rea's Co. in 1761 (Report of the State Historian,
        Vol. II, p. 649).
   iv) Anna[3], bpt. 10 Sept 1744 - sp.: Henrich Frölich and
       wife Elsje Schneider (Katsbaan Ref. Chbk.).
   v) Hermanus[3], bpt. 6 Oct 1746 - sp.: Petrus Hommel and
      Catharina Rauw (Katsbaan Ref. Chbk.). He d. 1 April
      1828, aged 82 (Hommel Farm Cem. near Katsbaan).
   By his 2nd wife Anna Maria Schneider, whom he md. as a
   widower 4 Sept 1748 (Katsbaan Ref. Chbk.), he had ch.:
   vi) Martin[3], bpt. 26 June 1749 - sp.: Martinus Schneider
       and wife Antje Bekker (Katsbaan Ref. Chbk.).
   vii) Petrus[3], bpt. 26 Dec 1750 - sp.: Petrus Hommel and
        wife Grietje Schneider (Katsbaan Ref. Chbk.).

viii) Anna³, bpt. 30 March 1752 - sp.: Martinus Schneider
and wife Antje Bekker (Katsbaan Ref. Chbk.).

ix) Maria³, bpt. 6 Oct 1753 - sp.: Zacharias Schneider and
Annaatje Bekker (Katsbaan Ref. Chbk.).

x) Friederich³, bpt. 4 Oct 1755 - sp.: Frederich Rau and
wife Catharina Schneider (Katsbaan Ref. Chbk.).

xi) Johannes³, bpt. 2 Oct 1757 - sp.: Johannes M. Schneider
and Catharina Hommel (Katsbaan Ref. Chbk.).

xii) Catharina³, bpt. 16 April 1759 - sp.: Wilhelmus Hommel
and Catharina Hommel (Katsbaan Ref. Chbk.).

3) Johann Georg², b. 4 Sept 1716 - sp.: Richart Ormen, Johann
Georg Schneider, and Anna Maria Demuth (West Camp Luth.
Chbk.). He md. Margaretha Fierer (HJ) and had issue:

i) Catharina³, b. 18 Aug 1743 and bpt. Newton - sp.:
Christian Fuhrer and wife Cath. Liese (Loonenburg Luth.
Chbk.).

ii) Petrus³, bpt. 7 May 1745 - sp.: Jurg Willem Rigtmeyer
and Antje Hommel (Katsbaan Ref. Chbk.).

iii) Elisabetha³, bpt. 21 April 1747 - sp.: Johannes Frolich
and Lisabeth Fierer (Katsbaan Ref. Chbk.).

iv) Johannes³, bpt. 25 Sept 1749 - sp.: Johannes Hommel and
wife Antje Schneider (Katsbaan Ref. Chbk.).

v) Anna³, twin to above bpt. 25 Sept 1749 - sp.: Hermanus
Hommel and wife Grietje Schneider (Katsbaan Ref. Chbk.).

vi) Maria³, bpt. 5 Oct 1751 - sp.: David Fierer and Grietje
Vrölich (Katsbaan Ref. Chbk.).

vii) Lea³, bpt. 2 Jan 1754 - sp.: Johannes Bakker and Annaatje Bakker (Katsbaan Ref. Chbk.).

viii) Abraham³, bpt. 23 Feb 1757 - sp.: Wilhelmus Hommel and
Margrieta Hommel (Katsbaan Ref. Chbk.).

ix) Rachel³, bpt. 27 Dec 1760 - sp.: Johannes Tromboor and
wife Christina Fierer (Katsbaan Ref. Chbk.).

x) Margaretha³, bpt. 7 Feb 1763 - sp.: Frederick Rouw and
Catharina Rouw (Katsbaan Ref. Chbk.).

4) Peter², b. 8 March 1719 - sp.: Johannes Schneider and Eva
Schuh (West Camp Luth. Chbk.). He md. 17 June 1748 Margaretha Schneider (Kingston Ref. Chbk.) and had ch.:

i) Hermanus³, bpt. 26 Dec 1749 - sp.: Hermanus Hommel and
wife Grietje Schneider (Katsbaan Ref. Chbk.).

ii) Martin³, bpt. 1 July 1751 - sp.: Martinus Schneider and
wife Antje Bakker (Katsbaan Ref. Chbk.).

iii) Maria³, bpt. 23 April 1753 - sp.: Zacharias Schneider
and Catharina Hommel (Katsbaan Ref. Chbk.).

iv) Anna³, bpt. 31 March 1755 - sp.: Johannes Hommel and

wife Antje Schneider (Katsbaan Ref. Chbk.).

5) Wilhelm[2], bpt. 15 Oct 1721 - sp.: Hans Willem Snyder and
   Christyn Tunnjus (Kingston Ref. Chbk.).

6) Anna[2], bpt. 5 April 1724 - sp.: Frederik Rouw and Antjen
   Snyder (Kingston Ref. Chbk.). She md. Georg Wilhelm Regtmeyer 29 Dec 1744 (Kingston Ref. Chbk.).

BENEDICT HUNER (Hunter Lists #333)

A close study of the juxtaposition of names on the Hunter
Lists reveals that #333 Benedict Huner really was #415 Benedict
Kuhner. Benedict Huner made his initial appearance 30 June 1710
with 2 pers. over 10 yrs. and 2 under 10; his last entry as Huner
was 4 Aug 1710, whereupon his family was noted under #415 (HJ).

DAVID HUPPERT (Hunter Lists #334)

David Hupter, his wife and 2 ch. were on Capt. John Howlentzen's ship in the 4th party in Holland in 1709 (Rotterdam Lists).
David Hupfer aged 30, his wife, and daughters aged 12 and 9, Ref.,
husbandman and vinedresser, were in the 4th arrivals later that
yr. (London Lists).

David Huppert made his first appearance on the Hunter Rolls
30 June 1710 with 3 pers. over 10 and 1 under 10 yrs. On 4 Oct
1710 the family listing showed 4 pers. over 10 yrs. of age. The
entry for 25 March 1712 noted 3 over 10, and then 4 over 10 yrs.
24 June 1712. David Huppert of Hunterstown was a soldier in 1711
(Palatine Volunteers To Canada). David Hoefler was nat. 22 Nov
1715 (Albany Nats). David Hubert with wife and ch. was at Hunderston ca. 1716/17 (Simmendinger Register). David Hooper was a freeholder in the North Part Livingston in 1720 (Albany Co. Freeholders). David Hooper (Harper) was a Palatine Debtor in 1718 and
1726 (Livingston Debt Lists). Domine Berkenmeyer noted 23 March
1726 in the N.Y. City Luth. Chbk.:

> David Hupper, the notorious very bad (or foolish) Ger-
> man, residing at Kokshagky, died. Nevertheless, in or-
> der not to seem to despise him because of his poverty,
> I gave him a funeral sermon, setting forth the judge-
> ment of the spirit of God, of the salvation or bless-
> ing of the dead.

The ch. of David[1] Huppert and wife Anna Catharina were:

1) Anna Elisabetha[2] (HJ), conf. at N.Y. 19 July 1710 (West
   Camp Luth. Chbk.).

2) Maria Jacobina[2] (HJ), conf. 30 April 1711 at the new German colony (West Camp Luth. Chbk.).

3) Sophia[2], b. 28 Aug 1714 - sp.: Gerhard Horning and wife
   Sophia (West Camp Luth. Chbk.).

410

JOHANN ADAM HUSSMANN (Hunter Lists #335)

Johann Adam Hussmann appeared but once on the Hunter Lists
4 Aug 1710 with 1 pers. over 10 yrs. of age.

HERMANN HUSSMANN (Hunter Lists #336)

A Johannes Husmann, his wife, and 5 ch. were on Capt. Georg
Brouwell's ship in Holland in June 1709 (Rotterdam Lists).

Hermann Hussmann made his initial appearance on the Hunter
Lists 4 July 1710 with 3 pers. over 10 yrs. and 5 under 10. The
reading for 4 Oct 1710 was 4 over 10 yrs. and 4 under 10, and the
entry for 24 June 1711 read 6 pers. over 10 and 2 under 10 yrs.
The 29 Sept 1711 notation showed 5 over 10 and 3 under 10, the
24 Dec 1711 entry read 6 over 10 and 3 under 10, and the entries
throughout 1712 noted 6 pers. over 10 yrs. and 2 under 10 yrs.
Herman Hastman: 1 man, 2 lads aged 9 - 15, 1 woman, 3 maids aged
9 - 15, and 1 girl aged 8 yrs. and under, were in Ulster Co. in
1710/11 (West Camp Census). Herman Hosman was nat. but one name
away from John Christian Hosman and Johan Lourens Hosman 8 and 9
Sept 1715 (Kingston Nats.). Hermann Hossmann and Anna Maria with
6 ch. were at Hessberg ca. 1716/17 (Simmendinger Register). Herman
Haveman was a Palatine Debtor in 1718 and Harme Horsman was a Palatine Debtor in 1719 at Haysberry (Livingston Debt Lists). Issue:
- 1?) Dieterich² (HJ), #278 on the Hunter Lists. As Anna Maria
  Hausmann sp. him in 1710 - and Anna Maria was w/o #336 Hermann Hussmann - perhaps Dieterich was an elder s/o Hermann (HJ). The ch. of Dieterich and wife Anna Eulalia were:
    - i) Anna Maria³, bpt. 20 Aug 1710 - sp.: Anna Maria Haus-
      mann (West Camp Luth. Chbk.).
    - ii) Anna Eva³, called step-d/o Hans Bernhart (who md.
      Anna Eulalia Hausmann - HJ) at her marriage to Joh.
      Peter Bauer 26 Nov 1727 (N.Y. City Luth. Chbk.). She
      had joined the N.Y. City Luth. Church Misericordia
      Sunday 1726 at Kamp as Eva Hasman.
- 2) Johann Christian² (HJ), nat. but one name away from Herman¹
  8 and 9 Sept 1715 (Kingston Nats.). He and wife Anna or
  Hannah Brouwer sp. Valentyn Fasigk and Katryntie Hosman
  in 1732 in N.J. (Freehold and Middletown Chbks.). They were
  adoptive parents of Elisabetha, d/o Caleb Jones, there in
  1734 (Freehold and Middletown Chbks.).
- 3) Elisabetha² (HJ), conf. Easter 1714 at Queensberg and a
  sp. to Johannes Bernhard and Anna Eulalia in 1715 (West
  Camp Luth. Chbk.).
- 4) Johann Lorentz² (HJ), also nat. but one name away from

Hermann[1] 8 and 9 Sept 1715 (Kingston Nats.). Lowerence
Hausman made his first appearance on tax rolls in the Middle Ward in 1733/34 (Dutchess Co. Tax Lists). Laurens Hosman and wife Mareitje joined the church on the w. side in
1738 (N.Y. City Luth. Chbk.). He md. Anna Maria Rescherret
(HJ) and had ch.:

    i) Anna Eulalia[3], bpt. 4 months old 23 April 1731 - sp.:
      Hannes Bernhard and Anna Eulalia (Loonenburg Luth.
      Chbk.).

    ii) Girje[3], so bpt. 17 March 1734 - sp.: Georg Jacob Sar-
      enberger and Lisabeth Frolich (Rhinebeck Flats Ref.
      Chbk.).

    iii) Barbara[3], b. or bpt. 19 April 1739 and bpt. at P. Las-
      sing's - sp.: Niclaas Neidebber and wife Christina
      (N.Y. City Luth. Chbk.).

    iv) Catharina[3], b. 16 June 1741 and bpt. at Nicolaus Neid-
      ebber's house - sp.: Nicolaus Neidebber and his daugh-
      ter Catharina, with Nich's wife Christina (N.Y. City
      Luth. Chbk.).

    v) Nicolaus[3], b. 3 Aug 1743 and bpt. at Berger Mynder's
      - sp.: Niclaas Neidebber and his daughter Christina
      (N.Y. City Luth. Chbk.).

    vi) Lorentz[3], b. 1 April 1746 and bpt. at the Lassing's
      - sp.: Pieter Janssen and Eva (N.Y. City Luth. Chbk.).

There were several unplaced Hausmanns in colonial N.Y.: 1)
Anna Hausmann md. Georg Hauch by 1741; 2) Martha Hausmann md. Georg
Müller 3 Jan 1749 (Germantown Ref. Chbk.); 3) Zacharias Hosman and
wife Marija had a daughter Hester b. 20 Aug 1741 and bpt. in the
Highland (N.Y. City Luth. Chbk.); and 4) Johann Albert Hausman md.
Catharina Schoeler 18 Sept 1758 (Loonenburg Luth. Chbk.) and was
a soldier in Capt. Jacob Halenbeck's Co. in 1767 (Report of the
State Historian, Vol. II, p. 828).

ULRICH JACOBI (Hunter Lists #337)

An Ulrich Jacky aged 31, Ref., linnenweaver, was in the 2nd
arrivals in England in 1709 (London Lists); however, it is not
known if he was the emigrant who went to colonial N.Y. (HJ).

Ulrich Jacobi made his first appearance on the Hunter Lists
4 Aug 1710 with 2 pers. over 10 yrs. of age in the family; the entry read 2 over 10 and 1 under 10 29 Sept 1711, and then diminished
once again to 2 over 10 yrs. on 24 Dec 1711. Ulrigh Jacobi was nat.
17 Jan 1715 (Albany Nats.). Uldrigh Jacobi was a Palatine Debtor
in 1718, 1719 (at Annsberry), 1721, and 1726 (Livingston Debt

Lists). Olrig Jacobi was a Palatine willing to remain on the Manor 26 Aug 1724 (Doc. Hist. of N.Y., Vol. III, p. 724). His wife undoubtedly was the Gertrude Jacobi who d. 23 Jan 1747, aged 70 yrs. (Germantown Ref. Chbk.). Their ch. were:

1) Wilhelm[2] (HJ), on the Rhinebeck area tax rolls 1738/39 - Feb. 1747/48 (Dutchess Co. Tax Lists). Bastian and William Jacoby were in Capt. Frederick Kortz's Co. in 1767 at East Camp (Report of the State Historian, Vol. II, p. 870). A 1764 reference to him is found in Dutchess Co. Ancient Docs. #5783. He md. Anna Eva Schuh (HJ) and had issue:

    i) Gertraud[3], b. 21 Nov 1734 - sp.: Joh: Milius, and the w/o Peter Jonk (Rhinebeck Luth. Chbk.). She md. James Butler (HJ).

    ii) Johann Sebastian[3], b. 22 Feb 1736 - sp.: Joh. Bastian Jacoby and Anna Maria Til (Rhinebeck Luth. Chbk.). He md. Catharina Schmidt (HJ) and had ch. at Linlithgo Ref. Church (HJ).

    iii) Hermann[3] (HJ), md. Catharina Simon (HJ) and had issue bpt. at Loonenburg Luth., Manorton Luth., Churchtown Luth. and Red Hook Luth. Churches (HJ).

    iv) Anna Catharina[3], b. 23 Oct 1739 and bpt. the Camp - sp.: Henrich Klopper and Gertrude Jacobi (Loonenburg Luth. Chbk.). She md. Balthasar Simon (HJ).

    v) Johann Wilhelm[3], bpt. 6 May 1741 - sp.: Johan Willem Coen and Lisabeth Kilmer (Red Hook Luth. Chbk.). He md. Anna Simon (HJ) and had ch. bpt. at Churchtown Luth. Schoharie Luth., Linlithgo Ref., and Claverack Ref. Churches (HJ).

    vi) Anna[3], bpt. 18 Sept 1743 - sp.: Johan Wilm Funck and Anna Juliana Becker (Red Hook Luth. Chbk.).

    vii) Magdalena[3], bpt. 21 July 1745 - sp.: Christian Jacobi and Anna Magdalena Richter (Red Hook Luth. Chbk.).

    viii) Anna Elisabetha[3], bpt. 30 Aug 1747 - sp.: Adam Reiffenberger and Agnes (Germantown Ref. Chbk.). An Elisabetha Jacobi md. a Teunis Funck (HJ), and another of that name md. 29 Aug 1769 Georg Müller (Linlithgo Ref. Chbk.).

    ix) Anna[3], b. 25 May 1751 - sp.: Wil... (Claverack Ref. Chbk.). She md. Michael Lass (HJ).

    x) Magdalena[3], bpt. 17 Jan 1752 - sp.: Georg Best and wife Maria Hoof (Germantown Ref. Chbk.). She md. Petrus Moon (HJ).

    xi) Eva[3], bpt. 2 May 1756 - sp.: Fried: Doll and Catharina Schmidt (Germantown Ref. Chbk.).

2) <u>Johann Sebastian²</u>, called s/o Olrig Jacobi in his surviving family Bible (found in N.Y. State D.A.R. Records, Vol.
   269, p. 68). Bastian Jacobie was a freeholder of East Camp
   1763 (Albany Co. Freeholders). The will of Bastian Jacobi
   of Camp in the Co. of Albany was dated 28 May 1783 and probated 13 March 1813 (Columbia Co. Will Bk. D). The old Bible notes Johann Bastian² d. 8 April 1785, aged ca. 66 yrs.
   He md. 8 Dec 1741 as a single man b. in Camp Catharina
   Schultes, single woman b. in Germany (Germantown Ref. Chbk.
   and family Bible). Their issue as found in chbks. and in
   the family Bible were:
   i) <u>Anna Maria³</u>, b. 1 Dec 1742 (Bible) and bpt. 12 Jan
      1743 - sp.: Phillip Schultes and wife Anna Maria (Red
      Hook Luth. Chbk.). She md. Carl Laubach (HJ).
   ii) <u>Elisabetha³</u>, b. 19 Sept 1744 (Bible) and bpt. 15 May
      1744 - sp.: J. Daedt and Elizabetha Daedt (Germantown
      Ref. Chbk.) (note conflict in dates - HJ). She md.
      26 April 1768 Peter Heiser (Germantown Ref. Chbk.)
      and d. 30 April 1806 (Bible).
   iii) <u>Johann Wilhelm³</u>, b. 11 May 1746 (Bible) and bpt. 24
      May 1746 - sp.: J. Wilhelm Jacobs and Anna Eva (Ger-
      mantown Ref. Chbk.). He d. 1 Aug 1773 (Bible).
   iv) <u>Philip³</u>, b. 23 July 1748 (Bible) and bpt. 14 Aug 1748
      - sp.: Philip Schultes and wife Anna Maria (Germantown
      Ref. Chbk.). He d. 28 March ... (Bible).
   v) <u>Johannes³</u>, b. 22 Jan 1750 (Bible) and bpt. 11 Feb 1750
      - sp.: Hans Holtzappel and Anna Maria (Germantown Ref.
      Chbk.). He md. Catharina Fritz 6 Dec 1774 (Bible). A
      John Jacobia d. 29 March 1834 at Claverack aged 84
      yrs. (Hudson Rural Repository 12 April 1834).
   vi) <u>Catharina³</u>, b. 19 Feb 1752 (Bible) and bpt. 17 Jan
      1752 - sp.: Henrich Schultes and Catharena Worms (Ger-
      mantown Ref. Chbk.). She md. Philip Schneider (Will).
   vii) <u>Henrich³</u>, b. 28 Sept 1753 (Bible) and bpt. 21 Jan 1754
      - sp.: Hendrick Scholtes and Maria Lesser (Germantown
      Ref. Chbk.). He d. 29 Dec 1807 (Bible). The estate of
      Hendrick Jacobi, dec., was probated 16 Sept 1808 (Col-
      umbia Co. Administration Bk. B).
   viii) <u>Margaretha³</u>, b. 11 April 1756 (Bible) and bpt. 2 May
      1756 - sp.: Philip Klumm and wife Margaretha Batz
      (Germantown Ref. Chbk.). She md. Christian Haber (Will).
   ix) <u>Gertraud³</u>, b. 5 Aug 1758 (Bible) and bpt. 3 Sept 1758
      - sp.: Bastian Lescher and wife Gertraut Schultheis
      (Germantown Ref. Chbk.). She d. 17 May 1779 (Bible).

414

  x) Christina³, b. 25 Nov 1760 (Bible) and noted as b.
     29 Nov 1760 - sp.: Joh: Schultes and C. Loesch...
     (Germantown Luth. Chbk.). She md. John Cammel (Will).

  xi) Sebastian³, b. 14 Sept 1763 (Bible) - sp.: Bastian
     Loescher and G: (Germantown Luth. Chbk.). He d. 25
     Feb 1793 (Bible).

  xii) Rebecca³, b. 27 April 1766 (Bible) and bpt. 12 Oct
     1766 - sp.: David Schultes and wife Rebena Kuper (Ger-
     mantown Ref. Chbk.). She d. 19 Oct 1819 (Bible).

3) Christian², called s/o Ulrich Jacobi at his marriage 17
   Sept 1747 to Margaretha, d/o Francisscus Googen (Hogan? -HJ)
   (Germantown Ref. Chbk.). Margaretha Jacobi joined the Ger-
   mantown Ref. Church um Ostern 1748. The had ch.:

  i) Ulrich³, bpt. 5 Nov 1753 - sp.: Bastian Jacobie and
     wife Catharina Scholdes (Germantown Ref. Chbk.).

  ii) Elisabetha³, bpt. 21 Aug 1755 - sp.: David Schulthes
     and Lisabeth Daadt (Germantown Ref. Chbk.).

  iii) Gertraud³, bpt. 18 Dec 1757 - sp.: Johannis and Cat-
     arina Cuyler (Albany Ref. Chbk.).

  iv) Magdalena³, b. 19 March 1760 - sp.: Will Soul and
     Margrita Wyngaart (Albany Ref. Chbk.).

  v) Frans³, b. 31 July 1762 - sp.: Jacob and Syntje Couper
     (Albany Ref. Chbk.).

  vi) Magdalena³, b. 28 Jan 1766 - sp.: William and Lena
     Brommely (Albany Ref. Chbk.).

  vii) Maria³, b. 13 May 1768 - sp.: Jacob and Annatje Hogh-
     ing (Albany Ref. Chbk.).

  viii) Frans³, b. 13 Aug 1770 - sp.: Abraham and Marg Cuy-
     ler (Albany Ref. Chbk.).

WENDEL JÄGER (Hunter Lists #338)

A Hans Wendel, s/o Hans Velten Jager and wife Apolonia, was
bpt. 25 March 1683 - sp.: Hans Jacob Jäger from Horweiler, and Hans
Wendel Reitzer, at 6531 Oberdiebach. The N.Y. Wendel Jager sometimes was surrounded on the Hunter Lists by fellow-1709ers who
originated near this region (such as Johannes Eberhard, Johannes
Schultheis, and the various Wohlebens), so perhaps the Oberdiebach
family connects with the American Jäger-Yeager group (HJ).

Wendel Jäger made his initial appearance on the Hunter Lists
4 July 1710 with 3 pers. over 10 yrs. and 1 under 10; the family
diminished to 3 pers. over 10 yrs. 25 March 1711. Wendel Jager
and Christina Elisabetha with 2 ch. were at Quunsberg ca. 1716/17
(Simmendinger Register). He was a Palatine Debtor in 1718, 1719
(at Kingsberry), 1721, 1726 and 1747 (Livingston Debt Lists). Wendel

Jager made his first appearance on tax rolls in the Rhinebeck area
in 1739/40 (Dutchess Co. Tax Lists). He md. Christina Elisabeth
(Keutzer? - HJ) and had ch.:

1) Margaretha² (HJ), md. Henrich Stahl (HJ).
2) Johann Jacob² (HJ), md. Elisabetha Wihler who joined the
   Red Hook Luth. Church 20 May 1743. They had issue:
   i?) Nicolaus³ , md. 14 Aug 1764 Maria Livingston (Lin-
       lithgo Ref. Chbk.). Nicolaus³ is difficult to place
       in the family structure with absolute certainty, how-
       ever, he did have several Wihlers sp. his children (HJ).
   ii) Elisabetha³, bpt. 9 July 1754 - sp.: Jurri Jager and
       Geertruy Jager (Red Hook Luth. Chbk.).
3) Johannes², b. 19 Oct 1715 - sp.: Johann Berurer and Johann
   Werner Scaester (West Camp Luth. Chbk.). He md. Elisabetha
   Kuhn (HJ) and had issue:
   i) Christina Elisabetha³, bpt. 2 Oct 1743 - sp.: Wilm Kun
      and Christina Jager (Red Hook Luth. Chbk.).
   ii) Elisabetha³ (HJ), md. Henrich Heiseroth (HJ).
   iii) Catharina³, bpt. 8 Jan 1749 - sp.: David Steiver and
        Catharina Steiver (Germantown Ref. Chbk.).
   iv) Johann Henrich³, bpt. 14 Jan 1752 - sp.: Henrick Stael
       and Grietje Stael (Linlithgo Ref. Chbk.). He may have
       been the Henrich³ who md. Elisabetha Schmidt (HJ).
   v) Margaretha³, bpt. 17 April 1755 - sp.: Hans Michel and
      Grietje Koen (Linlithgo Ref. Chbk.).
   vi) Anna³, bpt. 11 June 1758 - sp.: Hendrik Koen and Anna-
       tje Koen (Linlithgo Ref. Chbk.).
   vii) Margaretha³, bpt. 26 April 1761 - sp.: Jurry Kilmer and
        wife Grietje Valkenburg (Linlithgo Ref. Chbk.).
   viii) Maria³, bpt. 22 Dec 1763 - sp.: Emmerick Shouwerman and
         wife Cathrina Shoerz (Linlithgo Ref. Chbk.).
   ix) Johannes³, bpt. 6 Nov 1768 - sp.: Dirk Jansen and Lis-
       abeth Michel (Linlithgo Ref. Chbk.).
4) Johann Georg², b. 23 April 1720 at Central Camp on East Bank
   - sp.: Jacob Schaffer and Jurgen Sherts (N.Y. City Luth.
   Chbk.). He md. Gertraud Pulver (HJ) and had issue:
   i) Johann Wendel³, bpt. 13 Nov 1743 - sp.: Johan Wendel
      Jager and Christina Keutzer (Red Hook Luth. Chbk.).
      He md. Anna Maria Simon (HJ) and had ch. bpt. at Manor-
      ton Luth., Rhinebeck Luth., and Churchtown Luth.
      Churches (HJ).
   ii) Anna Catharina³, bpt. 29 June 1746 - sp.: Johan Wendel
       Polfer and Anna Cattarina Boes (Rhinebeck Flats Ref.
       Chbk.). She md. Henrich Simon (HJ).

iii) <u>Christina</u>[3], bpt. 22 Nov 1748 - sp.: Jacob Pulver and
Mari Christina Bernhard (Germantown Ref. Chbk.). She
md. Johannes Simon 13 March 1769 (Red Hook Luth. Chbk.).

iv) <u>Conrad</u>[3], b. 3 Oct 1751 - sp.: Peter Jager and Elisabeth Michel (Rhinebeck Flats Ref. Chbk.). He md. Rachel
Kohl (HJ) and had ch. bpt. at Churchtown Luth. and Manorton Luth. Churches (HJ).

v) <u>Elisabetha</u>[3] (HJ), md. Philip Simon (HJ).

vi) <u>Wilhelm</u>[3], bpt. 30 Jan 1757 - sp.: Wilhelmus Petzer
and Magdalena Dunsbach (Red Hook Luth. Chbk.).

vii) <u>Gertraud</u>[3] (HJ), md. Robert Van Duesen (HJ).

viii) <u>Salomon</u>[3], b. 20 Sept 1761 - sp.: Michael Simmon and
wife Barbara (Rhinebeck Luth. Chbk.). He md. Sarah
Preiss (HJ).

5) <u>Johann Peter</u>[2], md. as s/o Wendel Jager 22 Nov 1748 Elisabetha Michel, d/o Henrich (Germantown Ref. Chbk.). Issue:

i) <u>Christina</u>[3], bpt. 13 Aug 1749 - sp.: Wendel Jager and
Christin (Germantown Ref. Chbk.).

ii) <u>Henrich</u>[3], b. 29 July 1751 - sp.: Henrik Michel and
Marytje Michel (Rhinebeck Flats Ref. Chbk.). He may
have been the Henrich[3] who md. Maria Donsbach (HJ).
Henry P. Jager d. 4 May 1827, aged 75 yrs. (Hudson
Rural Repository 12 May 1827).

iii) <u>Philip</u>[3], b. 8 Sept 1753 - sp.: Philip Kulman and his
wife (Schoharie Luth. Chbk.).

iv) <u>Maria</u>[3], bpt. 12 May 1756 - sp.: Samuel Sherts and Marytjen Michel (Linlithgo Ref. Chbk.).

v) <u>Wendel</u>[3], bpt. 18 Nov 1759 - sp.: Johannes Jager and
wife Lisabeth Koen (Linlithgo Ref. Chbk.).

<u>CHRISTIAN JÄGER</u> (Hunter Lists #339)

A Johan Christian Jager from Selters had a son Johann Caspar
bpt. 17 July 1707 - sp.: Caspar Shut, Joh: Peter Staadt, and Anna
Catarin - d/o Johannes Jager, at 5418 <u>Nordhofen</u>, home of so many
N.Y. Palatines (HJ). Kristiaan jeger, his wife, and 1 child, were
noted next to the N.Y. Schoharie settler Geerard Scheefer on Capt.
William Koby's ship in the 5th party in Holland (Rotterdam Lists).

Christian Jäger made his initial appearance on the Hunter Rolls
1 July 1710 with 1 pers. over 10; the entry for 31 Dec 1710 read
2 pers. over 10 yrs., and the notation for 24 June 1711 showed 2
over 10 and 1 under 10 yrs. His wife received a special allowance
on 4 Aug 1710. On most all of his registrations on the Hunter Lists
he was surrounded by fellow 1709ers from near Nordhofen (such as
Johann Christian Wagner, Johann Wilhelm Milges and Johann Adam

Segendorff) (HJ).

PETER JAMM (Hunter Lists #340)

Peter Jamm made his first appearance on the Hunter Rolls 30 June 1710 with 1 pers. over 10 yrs. and 1 pers. under 10. The entry for 31 Dec 1710 read 2 pers. over 10, and for 25 March 1711 the notation showed 1 pers. over 10 yrs. of age for Peter Jamm's Wid^W. A Catharina Jamm md. Jan Salberg by 1731 (HJ).

JOHANN DAVID IFFLANDT (Hunter Lists #341)

David yslant, his wife, and 1 child were on Capt. Jno. Untank'{ ship in Holland in the 5th party of Palatines in 1709 (Rotterdam Lists).

Johann David Ifflandt made his first appearance on the Hunter Lists 1 July 1710 with 2 pers. over 10 yrs. and 1 pers. under 10. The notation showed 2 over 10 and 2 under 10 25 March 1711, 3 over 10 yrs. and 2 under 10 on 24 June 1712, and 2 over 10 and 3 under 10 yrs. on 13 Sept 1712. Johann David Lieffland and his wife Anna Maria with 4 ch. were at Neu-Quunsberg ca. 1716/17 (Simmendinger Register). David Eveland settled on the Proprietor's land near John Reading's on the Rariton and desired a grant of ca. 200 acres, according to a notation dated 6 mo. 15th 1733 in Minute Bk. K of the Board of Property of the Province of Pa. On 28 May 1737 he was deeded a tract of land by the Penn family (Letter from Wayne V. Jones). David Eveline was a freeholder of Amwell in 1741 (Hunterdon Co. Freeholders). The will of David Eveland of Amwell Twp. was dated 28 May 1753 and proved 9 Nov 1761 (N.J. Wills: Lib. 11, p. 147). The ch. of Johann David[1] Ifflandt were:

1) Margaretha[2] (Will).
2) Johannes[2] (Will), md. a d/o Hannis Lowrance (Janeway Accts.) He d. intestate ca. Oct 1765, late of Newtown in the Co. of Sussex. Issue:
    i) Friederich[3], at Walpack, Sussex Co., N.J. by 1766.
    ii) Anna[3], md. William Lee.
3) Peter[2] (Will), a tenant on Monocacy Manor in Md. in 1743. He went to N.C. where he was known as Peter Efland. Ch.:
    i) Catharina[3], md. John Noe.
    ii) Maria[3], md. Nicholas Gibbs.
    iii) Elisabetha[3], md. Hance or Nance.
    iv) David[3], in revolution from N.C., thence to Ind.
    v) Sarah[3], md. Boston Graves.
    vi) Phillis[3], md. John Sharp Sr.
    vii) Johannes[3], b. 13 Feb 1762, md. Margaret May.

4) Friederich[2] (Will), md. Anna Rosina Wohleben and lived in a farm across the Musconetcong River from the present town of New Hampton. Known ch.:

   i) Friederich[3], a Loyalist who md. Sarah De Cou 6 Sept 1806 and then moved to Canada.

   ii) Peter[3], moved at close of revolution to Columbia Co., Pa.

   iii) Johannes[3], b. 3 Jan 1753 in Sussex Co., N.J., md. Esther Van Buskirk, and d. 31 March 1837.

   iv) Daniel[3], b. 17 July 1759 in Sussex Co., N.J. and moved to Columbia Co., Pa.

   v) Sarah[3].

   vi) Maria[3], md. Peter Petty.

   vii) Jacob[3].

   viii) Samuel[3] b. 30 Nov 1768 in Sussex Co., N.J., md. 14 Dec 1790 Jane Colsher, moved to Philadelphia, Pa. and d. 21 Dec 1831.

5) Magdalena[2] (Will).

6) Catharina[2] (Will).

7) Maria[2] (Will).

Much of the 2nd and 3rd generation material on this interesting family was supplied by Wayne V. Jones of Houston, Texas; Mr. Jones has spent years collecting data on the family from old Bibles and private sources and his contribution to this chapter is much appreciated (HJ).

ULRICH INGOLD (Hunter Lists #342)

A Hans ingold, his wife and 5 ch. were in the 6th party of Palatines in Holland in 1709 (Rotterdam Lists).

Ulrich Ingold made his first appearance on the Hunter Lists 30 June 1710 with 2 pers. over 10 yrs.; his last entry was 4 Aug 1710. Issue:

1) Johannes[2] (HJ), a patentee in 1723 (Stone Arabia Patent), unless this actually refers to his father (HJ). Johannes[2] md. Anna Margaretha Becker (HJ); he d. 31 Jan 1743, struck down by a tree (Schoharie Luth. Chbk.). Margaretha Ingold and (son) Elias were on Pastor Sommer's Luth. Family List there ca. 1744; Margaretha Becker Ingold md. 2nd 23 Jan 1753 Anthony Widmer (Schoharie Ref. Chbk.). Ch. of Johannes[2] and Anna Margaretha were:

   i) Sophia[3], banns to marry Johann Nicolaus Mathees 29 Sept 1753 (Schoharie Ref. Chbk.).

   ii) Anna Catharina[3], bpt. 1 Feb 1734/35 - sp.: Johan B.

Borst and Cathrina Layer (Schoharie Luth. or Ref.
Chbk.). She md. Johann Friederich Bauch Jr. 7 April
1761 (Schoharie Luth. Chbk.).

   iii) Johannes[3], bpt. 13 March 1736/37 - sp.: Joh[S] Layer and
Elys. Layer (Schoharie Luth. or Ref. Chbk.). Hannes
Ingold was in Capt. Jacob Sternberger's Co. at Schohare in 1767 (Report of the State Historian, Vol. II,
p. 843). He d. 3 Dec 1809, aged 74 yrs., and his wife
Elisabetha d. 11 June 1806, aged 67 yrs. (both Old
Stone Fort Cem., Schoharie, N.Y.). The will of Johannis Ingold of Schoharie was dated 28 Aug 1809 and probated 18 Jan 1810 (Schoharie Co. Will Bk. A). (See
also Simm's History of Schoharie, p. 413).

   iv) Anna Maria[3], bpt. 9 Nov 1740 - sp.: Henrich Bellinger
and his wife (Schoharie Ref. Chbk.).

   v) Elias[3], b. after his father's death 20 July 1743 - sp.:
Mr. Johannes Lawyer and his wife Elisabeth Lawyer
(Schoharie Luth. Chbk.). On Pastor Sommer's Family
List is an "x" after Elias's name (Schoharie Luth.
Chbk.).

2) Maria Magdalena[2] (HJ), joined the Schoharie Ref. Church 14
May 1740. She md. Henrich Mattheus (HJ).

JOHANN MICHAEL ITTICH (Hunter Lists #343)

Johann Michael Ittich made his initial appearance on the Hunter Rolls 1 July 1710 with 1 pers. over 10 yrs. and 2 under 10. The
entry for 4 Oct 1710 read 3 pers. over 10 yrs. and 1 under 10, while
the notation for 24 June 1711 showed 3 over 10 and 2 under 10 yrs.
Mich Ittich of Haysbury was a soldier in 1711 (Palatine Volunteers
To Canada). Hans Michiel Edich and Hans Michiel Edich Jr. were nat.
together 14 Feb 1715/16 (Albany Nats.). Michael Editch and John
Michall Edigh were each patentees on the s. side of the Mohawk River 30 April 1725 (Burnetsfield Patent); an Elisabeth Edigh was a
patentee on the n. side of the Mohawk River 30 April 1725 (Burnetsfield Patent). It is possible that Elisabetha Edigh was the wife
of Michael[1], as several wives of 1st generation Palatines received
land (HJ). If this indeed is true, then the w/o Michael[2] was named
Eva, noted by Pastor Sommer in the congregation at the Fall ca.
1744 in the Schoharie Luth. Chbk. as Eva Ittichs (HJ). Two sons of
Michael[1] were:

1) Johann Michael[2] (HJ), nat. with his father 1715/16 (Albany
Nats.) and a patentee 30 April 1725 (Burnetsfield Patent).
Hans Michael Eadick was a freeholder at the Falls in 1763
(Albany Co. Freeholders). He probably md. Eva (--) (HJ).

The ch. of Michael² and Eva were:

    i) Margaretha³, bpt. 1713 - sp.: Adam and Margarit Bou-
man (Schenectady Ref. Chbk.).

   ii) Johann Michael³, called s/o Hans Michael Ittig at his
marriage 20 Nov 1760 to Catharina, d/o Friedrich Ohrn-
dorff (Stone Arabia Ref. Chbk.). He d. 9 March 1806,
aged 71-9-5 (Herkimer Ref. Chbk.) or aged 71-8-25
(Fort Herkimer Cem.). The will of Michael Ittig of
German Flats was dated 28 Nov 1805 and probated 30
April 1806 (Herkimer Co. Will Bk. B).

  iii) Marcus³ (HJ), md. 1st Maria Margaretha (--) (HJ) and
md. 2nd Barbara Weber 14 Sept 1762 (Stone Arabia Ref.
Chbk.).

2) Jacob², called Jacob Michel Idigh at his marriage in 1725
to Margaretha (?) Van Slyck (Schenectady Ref. Chbk.). Jacob
Edich was a patentee on the s. side of the Mohawk River 30
April 1725 (Burnetsfield Patent). There was a Jacob Ealick
who was a freeholder at the Falls in 1763 (Albany Co. Freeholders).

There were other members of this family in the Mohawk who undoubtedly were descendants of Johann Michael¹: 1) Christian Ittig
was a Corporal in the same Co. as Mich'l Ittig, Jacob Ettige, and
Markes Ittig in 1767 (Report of the State Historian, Vol. II, p.
849). A notice of the administration of the estate of Christian
Ittick, deceased, of German Flats was dated 7 Nov 1793 (Albany Gazette 9 Jan 1794); and 2) a Jacob Ittig and wife Sarah had ch. at
the German Flats Ref. Church in the 1760's (HJ).

JOHANN EBERHARD JUNG (Hunter Lists #344)

Johan Eberhard jung, his wife, and 1 child were listed 12
names from Joh: junge's Wid^W and her family in the 6th party of
Palatines in Holland in 1709 (Rotterdam Lists). The juxtaposition
of names on this roll strongly suggests that the family originated
somewhere near 5900 Siegen (HJ).

Johann Eberhard Jung made his initial appearance on the Hunter
Lists 4 July 1710 with 2 pers. over 10 yrs. and 1 pers. under 10
yrs. of age. The entry for 4 Aug 1710 read 1 pers. over 10 yrs.
and 1 pers. under 10; he was enrolled next to Maria Jungin on this
Aug notation. Eberhard Jung with his wife and ch. were at Heessberg
ca. 1716/17 (Simmendinger Register). Everhert Jonge made his initial appearance in the South Ward in 1717/18 and continued to 1720/
21; De Weddow of Everhert Jonge was recorded 9 Aug 1722 until 1726/
27 (Dutchess Co. Tax Lists). By his 1st wife, a child of Johann

Eberhard¹ Jung was:
1) Johannes² (HJ), on tax rolls in the South Ward area beginning in 1727/28 and noted there until 1761 (Dutchess Co.
   Tax Lists). The will of Catharine Brett of Rumbout mentioned
   the wid/o Hans Yung as living on the leasehold of the Brett
   estate at that time (1763) ("The Young Family of Fishkill
   and Babylon, N.Y." in the N.Y. Genealogical & Biographical
   Record, April 1966). He md. Eva Brill (HJ) and had issue:
   i) Elisabetha³, bpt. 19 Dec 1731 - sp.: David Bril and
      Elizabeth Yong (Fishkill Ref. Chbk.).
   ii) Johannes³, bpt. 12 May 1733 - sp.: Johannes Bos and
      Lena Bos (Fishkill Ref. Chbk.).
   iii) David³, bpt. 5 April 1735 - sp.: Jacobus Swartwoud
      and Geelitje Nieuwkirk (Fishkill Ref. Chbk.).
   iv) Abraham³, bpt. 26 May 1739 - sp.: Joseph Bosch and
      Maria De Moet (Poughkeepsie Ref. Chbk.).
   v) Isaac³, bpt. 10 Sept 1740 - sp.: Jurri Moesjer and
      Christina Asswyn (Fishkill Ref. Chbk.).
   vi) Jacob³, bpt. 29 Aug 1742 - sp.: Hendrick Philip and
      Marritje Oostrum (Fishkill Ref. Chbk.).
   vii) Jannetje³, bpt. 1 June 1746 - sp.: Maas (?) Ostrander
      and Jannetje Swartwont (Fishkill Ref. Chbk.).
The ch. of Johann Eberhard¹ Jung and his 2nd wife Anna Gertraud
Schmidt (HJ) were:
2) Maria² (HJ), md. Johannes Storm (HJ).
3) Nicolaus², b. 16 Jan 1714 and bpt. at Fishkill in the Highland - sp.: the parents and Isaac Henrickse (N.Y. City
   Luth. Chbk.). He md. Martha Hedden (HJ) and had ch.:
   i) Ephraim³, bpt. 15 May 1737 - sp.: Efrim Schut and Tryn-
      tje Buys (Fishkill Ref. Chbk.).
   ii) Abraham³, bpt. 1 July (?) 1739 (Fishkill Ref. Chbk.).
   iii) Elisabetha³, bpt. 24 Aug 1740 (Fishkill Ref. Chbk.).
   iv) Maria³, bpt. 29 Aug 1742 - sp.: Elisabeth Hedde (Fish-
      kill Ref. Chbk.).
   v) Martha³, bpt. 2 Sept 1744 - sp.: Rodulvers Swartworst
      and Jacomyntje (Fishkill Ref. Chbk.).
   vi) Jannetje³, bpt. 6 Oct 1745 - sp.: Hendrick Phillips and
      Marytie Oostro(m) (Fishkill Ref. Chbk.).
4) Elisabetha² (HJ), md. Edward Walker (HJ).
5) Anna Catharina², md. as d/o Eberhard 11 July 1736 Johann
   Henrich Haus, s/o Rheinhard Haus (N.Y. City Luth. Chbk.).
   She md. 2nd Wilhelm Tytzort 3 Jan 1748 (Fishkill Ref. Chbk.).
6) Johann Eberhard², bpt. 21 Nov 1722 - sp.: Barent Van Kleck
   and Anthonetta Parmentier (Poughkeepsie Ref. Chbk.).

PETER JUNG (Hunter Lists #345)

Johan Peter Jung was on Capt. William Newton's ship in the 5th party in Holland in 1709 (Rotterdam Lists).

Peter Jung was recorded once on the Hunter Rolls on 1 July 1710 with 2 pers. over 10 yrs. of age.

HENRICH JUNG (Hunter Lists #346)

Johan Henrig Jungst, his wife and 3 ch. were recorded next to Mr. Timmerman and Johan Regebag on Capt. William Newton's ship in the 5th party of Palatines in Holland in 1709 (Rotterdam Lists).

Henrich Jung made his first appearance on the Hunter Lists 4 Aug 1710 with 2 pers. over 10 yrs. of age in the household. The family dwindled down to 1 pers. over 10 yrs. 4 Oct 1710, then back up to 2 over 10 yrs. on 31 Dec 1710, 2 over 10 and 1 under 10 yrs. on 24 June 1711, 2 over 10 yrs. on 29 Sept 1711, and finally 2 over 10 and 1 under 10 24 Dec 1711. Henrich Jung of Queensbury was a soldier in 1711 (Palatine Volunteers To Canada). Hendrick Jong was nat. next to Tebald Young 3 Jan 1715/16 (Albany Nats.). Heinrich Jung and his wife Anna Margretha with 4 ch. were listed next to Dewalt Jung and his family at Neu-Heessberg ca. 1716/17 (Simmendinger Register). Hendrick Young and Jacob Timmerman bought lot 14 of the Harrison Patent from Col. Philip Schuyler, 703 acres in what is now St. Johnsville, 13 July 1730; Hendrick Young of the Moakes Country, planter, sold ½ of the land to Stephanies Grooesbeck of the City of Albany 4 April 1732 (Albany Co. Deeds: Vol. 6, p. 244). The ch. of Henrich[1] Jung and his wife Anna Margaretha were:

1) Maria Catharina[2], b. 28 Oct 1711 - sp.: Jacob Zimmerman, the w/o Jorg Mattheson, and Maria - w/o Jacob Porster (West Camp Luth. Chbk.).

2) Jacob[2] (HJ), d. 12 June 1794, aged 84 yrs. (Fort Plain Ref. Chbk.). The will of Jacob Young of Canajohary was dated 22 March 1790 and probated 17 March 1795 (Montgomery Co. Will Bk. I). He md. Dorothea (--) (Will) and had issue:

  i) Jacob[3] (Will).

  ii) Peter[3] (Will).

  iii) Henrich[3] (Will).

  iv) Catharina[3] (Will).

  v) Margaretha[3] (Will).

  vi) Elisabetha[3] (Will).

3) Anna Margaretha[2], b. 24 Jan 1716 and bpt. Schoharie - sp.: Jacob Weber and Anna Margretha Zimmerman (West Camp Luth. Chbk.). She probably md. Johannes Hess Jr. (HJ).

4) <u>Johann Henrich²</u>, twin to above, b. 24 Jan 1716 and bpt.
Schoharie - sp.: Conrad Schuetz and Ottilia Weber (West
Camp Luth. Chbk.). He md. Catharina Landtman 24 Jan 1744
(Albany Ref. Chbk.) and had ch.:

    i) <u>Peter³</u>, bpt. 23 Nov 1746 - sp.: Pieter Hogel and Cat-
rina Vos (Albany Ref. Chbk.).

    ii) <u>Peter³</u>, bpt. 4 Dec 1748 - sp.: Pieter Schuyler and El-
izabeth Renselaar (Albany Ref. Chbk.).

    iii) <u>Elisabetha³</u>, bpt. 28 April 1751 - sp.: Lucas Van Vegten
and Maria Lantman (Albany Ref. Chbk.).

    iv) <u>Johannes³</u>, bpt. 20 May 1753 - sp.: Johannes Lantman
and Susanna Litcher (Albany Ref. Chbk.).

    v) <u>Catharina³</u>, bpt. 6 April 1755 - sp.: Benjamin Goewey
and Engeltje Van Veghten (Albany Ref. Chbk.).

    vi) <u>Stephen³</u>, bpt. 23 Oct 1757 (Trinity Church, N.Y. City).

    vii) <u>Jacob³</u>, bpt. 17 Feb 1760 (Trinity Church, N.Y. City).

    viii) <u>Abraham³</u>, bpt. 7 weeks old 31 Oct 1762 - sp.: Waldraat
and Marytje Kryger (Albany Ref. Chbk.).

    ix) <u>Friederich³</u>, b. 15 Nov 1764 - sp.: Johannes Rickert
and wife (Schoharie Luth. Chbk.).

    x) <u>Isaac³</u>, b. 14 March 1767 - sp.: Yzaac Vosburg and Cath-
arina Staats (Albany Ref. Chbk.).

5) <u>Peter²</u>, called s/o Henrich Jung and b. at Schoharie when
Banns registered 14 June 1748 to marry Maria Anderson (Schoharie Ref. Chbk.); this marriage probably never took place
(HJ). Peter Jung md. Margaretha Freymäuer 2 Aug 1748 (Schoharie Luth. Chbk.). Peter Jung and a Margaretha Jung (his
mother? - HJ) were on Pastor Sommer's List of Families
ca. 1744 (Schoharie Luth. Chbk.). Peter Young was a freeholder of Schoharrie in 1763 (Albany Co. Freeholders). The
ch. of Peter² and Margaretha Jung were:

    i) <u>Elisabetha³</u>, b. 5 May 1749 - sp.: Michel Freymäurer
and his wife (Schoharie Luth. Chbk.). She md. as d/o
Piter Jung 10 Aug 1771 Johannes Loeb (Schoharie Ref.
Chbk.).

    ii) <u>Johannes³</u>, b. 28 May 1754 - sp.: Johannes Freymäuer and
his wife (Schoharie Luth. Chbk.).

    iii) <u>Eva³</u>, b. 11 Oct 1756 - sp.: Henrich Schäfer and his
wife (Schoharie Luth. Chbk.).

    iv) <u>Catharina³</u>, b. 19 Nov 1758 - sp.: Adam Braun and Cath-
arina Ingold (Schoharie Luth. Chbk.).

    v) <u>Peter³</u>, b. 8 Aug 1761 - sp.: Johannes Ingold and Mag-
dalena Braun (Schoharie Luth. Chbk.).

    vi) <u>Anna³</u>, b. 28 Oct 1764 - sp.: Henrich Borst and Anna

Werner (Schoharie Luth. Chbk.).

vii) Johannes³, b. 9 Aug 1767 - sp.: Peter Nicolas Sommer
and wife (Schoharie Luth. Chbk.).

6) Margaretha Catharina², md. as d/o Henrich Jung 14 June 1748
Johannes Rickert (Schoharie Ref. Chbk.).

7) Gertraud² (HJ), md. Nicolaus Eckert (HJ).

8?) Dorothea Elisabetha² , a sp. to Johannes Hess Jr. and to
Anna Margaretha Jung in 1747 (Stone Arabia Luth. Family
Book). She md. Michael Kaiser (HJ).

9?) Elisabetha² , also a sp. to Johannes Hess Jr. and Anna Margaretha Jung

10) Johann Friderich² (HJ), md. Catharina Schumacher, wid/o
Melchior Bell 18 March 1762 (Stone Arabia Ref. Chbk.).

As members of the Goewey and Hoghill families sp. both Hen-
rich² Jung and Georg Young and wife Catharina Litcher, and Hannes
Hoghill and wife Sarah Young, there is a possibility that Georg
and Sarah Young Hoghill belong in the family of Henrich¹ Jung (HJ).
If Henrich¹ Jung's daughter Anna Margaretha did not marry Johannes
Hess Jr., then the Anna Margaretha Jung who did marry Hess was a
d/o #350 Theobald Jung; if so, then #s 8 and 9 above (Dorothea
Elisabetha and Elisabetha) should be put into the family of #350
Theobald¹ Jung (HJ).

MARIA JUNGIN (Hunter Lists #347)

Johannes junge's wed. with 5 ch. were in the 6th party of Palatines in Holland in 1709 (Rotterdam Lists); they were enrolled
12 names from Johan Eberhard jung and his family (HJ).

Maria Jungin made her initial appearance on the Hunter Lists
4 July 1710 with 3 pers. over 10 yrs. of age. On the unalphabetised
list of 4 Aug 1710 she was registered next to Johann Eberhard Jung.
Her last entry was 4 Oct 1710 with 3 pers. over 10 yrs. of age.

JOHANNES JUNG (Hunter Lists #348)

There were several Johannes Jungs in Rotterdam and London
in 1709 who could have been the N.Y. resident, however, the family
who best matches known U.S. data were Johan Jung aged 32, his wife,
a son aged 9, and a daughter aged 1, Cath., husbandman and vinedresser, in the 3rd arrivals in England in 1709 (London Lists).

Johannes Jung made his first appearance on the Hunter Lists
4 July 1710 with 2 over 10 yrs.; the entry for 24 June 1711 read
2 over 10 and 1 under 10 yrs., and then returned to 2 over 10 yrs.
29 Sept 1711. Johannes Jung aged 32 and Anna Jung aged 35 were in
N.Y. City in 1710/11 (Palatines in N.Y. City).

ANNA ELIZABETH JUNGIN (Hunter Lists #349)

Johann Mattheus Jung, s/o Jerg Hans Jung - deceased of Gernheim in the commune Stromberg in the Pfaltz, md. 28 Sept 1714 Anna Veronica, d/o Master Jacob Mancken of Urbach in the commune of Neuwied (West Camp Luth. Chbk.). The village of origin for this Jung family was 6531 Genheim (11 km. n. of Bad Kreuznach; Chbks. begin 1673, but gaps) with some records of the family at 6534 Stromberg (3 km. further n.w.; Chbks. begin 1646, Ref.). The earliest known ancestor of the American line was Daniel Jung, who md. Anna Barbara (--) and had issue:

+ Johann Georg, bpt. 5 Feb 1665 - sp.: H. Görg - the Captain from Ausschuß (?) and his wife Martha, and Johs. Metzler - the Rheingräfl. Und-Schultheiß there and his wife Martha (Genheim and Stromberg Chbks.).

    Johann Querin, bpt. 16 Feb 1673 - sp.: Johannes Müller and Querin Hanau (Genheim Chbk.).

    Johann Nicolaus, bpt. 16 Feb 1687 - sp.: Jörg Hanß Jung and Nickel Ohlweiler (Genheim and Stromberg Chbks.).

Johann Georg Jung md. 1 Sept 1693 Anna Elisabetha Rißwick (Genheim Chbk.). The Genheim Chbks. call the 1709er Johann Georg and Georg Hanß Jung at different times (HJ). Anna Elisabetha, d/o Johannes von Rißwich and his wife Ahl or Alheit, was bpt. 15 April 1671 - sp.: Mathes Glock and his wife Anna Barbara, and Elisabeth - single d/o Hans Philipp Weber (Stromberg Chbk.). Anna Elisabetha, d/o Joh. Ryßwig from Gehnheim, was conf. in 1686 (Stromberg Chbk.). Johannes Rieswyck, formerly Gemeinsmann and Elder at Gehnheim, d. there in 1701, aged 60 yrs.; Adelheida, w/o Jean Ryswich - churchwarden and Gemeinsmann at Gehnheim, d. 20 Jan 1699, aged 55 yrs. (both Stromberg Chbk.). An Elizabeth Jung family was at Rotterdam and London in the 2nd party, but the names and ages of this group do not match known U.S. and German data (HJ).

Anna Elizabeth Jungin made her initial appearance on the Hunter Lists 4 Oct 1710 with 3 pers. over 10 yrs. of age and 1 pers. under 10 yrs. in the family. The notation read 2 over 10 and 1 under 10 yrs. on 29 Sept 1711, 3 over 10 on 24 Dec 1711, and 4 over 10 yrs. on 13 Sept 1712. Elisab. Jungin: 1 man, 1 lad aged 9 - 15, 1 woman, and 1 girl 8 and under, were in Ulster Co. in 1710/11 (West Camp Census). Elisabetha Jungin was at Beckmansland ca. 1716/17 (Simmendinger Register). The ch. of Georg Hanß[1] Jung and his wife Anna Elisabetha[1] were:

1) Johann Mattheus[2], bpt. 11 July 1694 - sp.: Joh. Mattheus Müller and Joh. Wißwycks (probably Rißwycks - HJ) (Genheim Chbk.). Johan Mathis Junck was nat. 8 and 9 Sept 1715

(Kingston Nats.). Albany Co. Deeds Vol. 7, p. 318 mentions
all the heirs of Johann Mattheus Young 11 Jan 1762. He md.
2nd as a widower of West Camp Catharina Dederik on 14 Nov
1731 (N.Y. City Ref. Chbk.). By his 1st wife Anna Veronica
Manck, the ch. of Johann Mattheus[2] Jung were:

i) Catharina Elisabetha[3], b. 2 Sept 1715 - sp.: Christoph Maul, Elisabetha Jung, and Eva Catharine Manck
(West Camp Luth. Chbk.). She md. Georg Wilhelm Dieterich 20 May 1735 (Catskill Ref. Chbk.).

ii) Eva Maria[3], b. 8 April 1718 - sp.: Andreas Ellich,
Anna Maria Demuth, and Maria Christina Oberbach (West
Camp Luth. Chbk.). She md. Conrad Engel 21 June 1745
(Kingston Ref. Chbk.).

iii) Anna Margaretha[3], b. 15 March 1721 at Newtown, Albany
Co. - sp.: Hieronymus Kleyn and Anna Margareta Manck
(N.Y. City Luth. Chbk.).

iv) Elisabetha[3], bpt. 15 July 1722 - sp.: David Kieselaar
and Elisabeth Jong (Kingston Ref. Chbk.). She md.
Wilhelm Brown 10 Sept 1744 (Katsbaan Ref. Chbk.).

v) Georg Johann[3] (HJ), md. 26 March 1744 Maria Emmerich
(Katsbaan Ref. Chbk.). Yuryan and Mathys Yongh were
in Capt. Cornelus Dubois's Co. at Caskill in 1767 (Report of the State Historian, Vol. II, p. 877).

vi) Peter[3], bpt. 14 Feb 1725 - sp.: Joh: Pieter Overpag
and Annetjen Zarrejis (Kingston Ref. Chbk.). He md.
Elisabetha Moschier 20 Dec 1745 (Kingston Ref. Chbk.).
They had issue at Loonenburg Luth., Katsbaan Ref.,
and Schoharie Luth. Churches (HJ).

vii) Gertraud[3], b. 23 Feb 1726 at Newtown - sp.: Wilhelm
Schmidt, Gertrud Falkenburg, and Elisabetha Klein
(Loonenburg Luth. Chbk.). She md. 2 May 1749 Johan-
nes, s/o Georg Muschier (Germantown Ref. Chbk.).

viii) Jacob[3], b. 7 July 1727 and bpt. Kisket. - sp.: Johan
Jacob Eigener (not present), his father Pieter Eig-
ener, proxy, and Anna Marg. Mank (Loonenburg Luth.
Chbk.).

ix) Johannes[3], b. 13 Jan 1729 and bpt. at Kisket. - sp.:
Johan Scheffer and Maria Elisabeth Schmid (Loonenburg
Luth. Chbk.). He md. 4 Oct 1754 Anna Dieterich (Kats-
baan Ref. Chbk.). They had issue bpt. at Katsbaan
Ref., Red Hook Luth., Linlithgo Ref., and Germantown
Ref. Churches (HJ).

2) Johann Querin[2], bpt. 20 May 1696 - sp.: Joh. Jacob Rißwick
and his wife Anna Ottilia, and Joh. Querin Jung (Genheim

Chbk.). Johann Quirinius Jung d. 17 March 1715 (West Camp
Luth. Chbk.).

3) <u>Maria Catharina</u> , bpt. 2 Oct 1700 - sp.: Hanß Culmann from
Oberhausen, and Anna Maria Meier from Genheim (Genheim
Chbk.).

4) <u>Anna Catharina</u> , twin to the above, bpt. 2 Oct 1700 - sp.:
Mattheus Riswick and his wife from Langlosheim (Genheim
Chbk.).

5) <u>"A Daughter"</u> , bpt. 4 May 1702 - sp.: Elisabetha Glock -
single woman at Genheim, and ... (Genheim Chbk.). Sp.
strongly suggest that this girl was named <u>Elisabetha</u> (HJ).
Elisabetha Jung md. 18 Nov 1721 Johannes Schäffer (Kingston Ref. Chbk.). (Her husband was called Scherer in error
in one entry - HJ).

THEOBALD JUNG (Hunter Lists #350)

Several potential Theobald Jungs were documented in Germany:
1) Theobald Jung md. Gretha Katharina (--) in 1708 and had a child
Theobald Jr. later that yr. at 6799 <u>Theisbergstegen</u>; 2) Johan Theobaldt Jung md. Anna Apollonia Traut in 1707 at 6741 <u>Impflingen</u>; and
3) Theobald, s/o Johannes Jung, md. Anna Maria, d/o Johannes Kieffer
at Reichenbach, 20 April 1694 at 6791 <u>Steinwenden</u>; they may be the
Debald and Anna Maria Jung who were parents of Anna Ottilia, b.
1705, and Johann Henrich, bpt. 1707, at 6791 <u>Glan-Münchweiler</u>. However, I believe that Theobald (and #346 Henrich[1] Jung, his relative)
eventually will be documented somewhere in the Nassau-Weilburg-
Wetzlar overall region (HJ).

Theobald Jung made his first appearance on the Hunter Lists
4 Oct 1710 with 1 pers. over 10 yrs. of age; he was recorded next
to Henrich Jung. His last entry on Hunter was 13 Sept 1712, still
with but 1 pers. over 10 yrs. of age. Tebald Young was nat. 3 Jan
1715/16 next to Hendrick Jong (Albany Nats.). Dewalt Jung and his
wife Maria Catharina were at Neu-Heessberg ca. 1716/17 (Simmendinger Register). He witnessed a deed signed by Hendrick Jung 4 April
1732 (Albany Co. Deeds: Vol. 6, p. 244). Albany Co. Deeds: Vol. 6,
p. 515 show that on 18 April 1732 John Haskell et al sold the s. $\frac{1}{2}$
of lots 15 and 18 of the Harrison Patent to Teobald Young, who on
10 July 1754 deeded them to Jacob Timmerman of Canaioharie. In
1751 and 1752 Theobald Young and others attempted to acquire the
14,000 acre Young Patent at what is now the Kyle and Little Lakes
section of Herkimer Co. (<u>The 18th Century Zimmerman Family of the
Mohawk Valley</u>, by David Kendall Martin, p. 8). David Young was a
freeholder at Canajoharrie in 1763 (Albany Co. Freeholders). Papers

in the estate of Teobalt Young of Canagore were issued 9 Oct 1771 (<u>Genealogical Data from Administration Papers</u>, p. 375). The ch. of Theobald[1] Jung and wife Maria Catharina were:

1) <u>Johann Adam[2]</u>, b. 17 May 1717 and bpt. at Schoharie - sp.: Johann Just Laux, Johann Adam Kopp, and Catharina Frey (West Camp Luth. Chbk.). Adam Young was a freeholder at Canajoharrie in 1763 (Albany Co. Freeholders). He was a Loyalist and settled at Grand River, Ontario; his will was dated 22 Jan 1790 (for further information see "The Papers and Records of a Family of Youngs of the Grand River", by George A. Nunamaker in <u>The Ontario Register</u>, Vol. 4, #2). Johann Adam[2] md. Catharina Elisabetha Schrembling (HJ) and had issue:

    i) <u>Johannes[3]</u>, bpt. 1742 - sp.: Fridrich Jung and Thoredea Hes (Stone Arabia Ref. Chbk.).

    ii) <u>David[3]</u> (Statement of Col. John Butler, 17 July 1795).

    iii) <u>Johann Nicolaus[3]</u>, bpt. 17 June 1750 (?) at Cani-Scohare and Stone Arabia (Schoharie Luth. Chbk.).

    iv) <u>Daniel[3]</u> (Will).

    v) <u>Elisabetha[3]</u> (HJ), md. Joseph House (HJ).

    vi) <u>Henrich[3]</u>, bpt. 17 Aug 1762 (Stone Arabia Ref. Chbk.).

    vii) <u>Abraham[3]</u>, bpt. 17 Aug 1762 (Stone Arabia Ref. Chbk.).

2) <u>Friederich[2]</u>, in 1763 a freeholder of Canjoharrie who was listed next to Adam Young (Albany Co. Freeholders). He was mentioned in the adminstration proceedings of Theobald[1] in 1771. He was recommended for a commission as First Lieutenant in 1768, along with Adam Yung (<u>Report of the State Historian</u>, Vol. II, p. 891).

3) <u>Andreas[2]</u>, called brother to Adam and Frederick Young in a document dated 17 Feb 1776 (<u>Mohawk Valley in the Revolution</u>, p. 71). He md. Elisabetha (--) (HJ).

4) <u>Theobald[2]</u> (HJ), md. 14 June 1763 Margaretha Hauss (Stone Arabia Ref. Chbk.).

See the section on #346 Henrich[1] Jung for other possible ch. of Theobald[1]. Among other unplaced Mohawk Jungs were Margaretha, w/o the late Johannes Jung, who was b. in 1727 and d. 1 Aug 1789 (Fort Plain Ref. Chbk.), and the Anna Jung who md. Henrich Klock 7 Jan 1762 (Stone Arabia Ref. Chbk.). There was a Peter Young who md. Anna Eva (--) and had ch. bpt. at Fort Hunter in the early 1740's (HJ)

<u>JULIANA JUNGIN</u> (Hunter Lists #351)

Juliana Jung made her initial appearance on the Hunter Lists

1 July 1710 with 1 pers. over 10 yrs. of age. Juliana, wid/o Jacob
Jung, had an illegitimate child with Kilian Planck, a Hollander of
Albany, in 1712 (West Camp Luth. Chbk.).

NICLAUS JUNGENS (Hunter Lists #352)

The European home of this family was at 5551 Veldenz (8 km.
s. of Traben-Trarbach; Chbks. begin 1646, but defective). The father
of the emigrant was Cornelius Jungens, bur. 10 May 1703, aged 58
yrs.; his wife Anna Magdalena was bur. 4 May 1703, aged 57 yrs.
Cornelius Jungens md. Anna Magdalena Weimets 9 Feb 1669. Issue:

Johann Michael, bpt. 20 April 1673 - sp.: Hans Adam Pulb,
Michael Aulen, and Anna Maria Jungin. He d. 19 Aug 1705.

Johann Jacobus, bpt. 29 April 1677 - sp.: Jacob Spross, Hans
Rupert Thiel, and Anna Maria Hausdorff - d/o the Pastor.

Anna Elisabetha, bpt. 31 Aug 1679 - sp.: Matthias Todtenburger,
Barbara Elisabeth Auler, and Anna Maria Jungens.

Johann Adam, bpt. 5 Aug 1682 - sp.: Andreas Becker, Adam Todtenburger, and Anna Cath. Weinets. The child d. 15 Oct 1691,
aged 9 yrs.

+ Johann Nicolaus.

Joh. Nicol. Jungens, s/o the late Cornelius Jungens, md. 2 Feb 1706
Anna Magdalen, d/o Johannes Hass. Johannes, s/o Hans Peter Haas,
md. Anna Margaretha, d/o the late Otto Jacob Platz at Burgen, 11
May 1683. Anna Margaretha, d/o Otto Jacob Blatz and wife Barbara
Stephan, was bpt. 28 Sept 1662. Johannes, s/o Hans Peter Haas and
wife Margaretha, was bpt. 16 Feb 1660; Johannes Hass, citizen at
Burgen, was bur. 18 Feb 1707, aged 47 yrs. Margaretha, w/o Hans Pe-
ter Haas at Veldenz was bur. 8 Nov 1689, aged 71 yrs. Johan Nikel
jung and his wife were enrolled in the 6th party of Palatines in
Holland in 1709 (Rotterdam Lists); they were listed next to Mattȳs
Bron and his family who also originated at Veldenz (HJ).

Niclaus Jungens first was entered on the Hunter Lists 4 July
1710 with 2 pers. over 10 yrs. of age in the household. Niclaus
Jungens aged 38, works in ye Govr Gard, and Anna Magdalena Jungens
aged 25, were in N.Y. City in 1710/11 (Palatines In N.Y. City).
He sp. Mattheus Brunck in 1713 (West Camp Luth. Chbk.). Niclaus
Jung drowned 23 Dec 1715 (West Camp Luth. Chbk.).

ANNA SIBILLA KABSIN (Hunter Lists #353)

Anna Sibilla Kabsin vid Kopff was noted in the Journal of the
Hunter Lists 4 Oct 1710 with 1 pers. over 10 yrs. of age. The cumulative entry for 24 Dec 1711 recorded Anna Sybilla Kabin with
1 pers. over 10 yrs. of age in the family.

JOHANN WILHELM KÄHL (Hunter Lists #354)

The ancestral origins of this Ulster Co. group were at 5455 Rengsdorf (7 km. n. of Neuwied; Chbks. begin 1677). The earliest known ancestor of the emigrant 1709er was his father Hans Peter Kell. Anna, wid/o Hans Peter Kell at Melsbach d. 15 June 1719. The ch. of Hans Peter and Anna Kell at Melsbach were:

Georg, md. Dom. Rogate et Seg: 1698 Amelia Christina, d/o Theiss Fritz of Niederbieber.

+ Georg Wilhelm, bpt. 9 April 1681 - sp.: Georg Eisenhart, Margaretha Gerlach, and Wilhelm Lumbard - all from Melsbach.

Johann Wilhelm, d. 8 Dec 1708, aged 22 yrs.

Georg Wilhelm, s/o Hans Peter Kell at Melsbach, md. 26 June 1704 Gertraut, d/o Johannes Winnen at Rockenfeldt. Jörg Willem Roll, his wife, and 3 ch. were listed among others from the Neuwied region (Bertram Wolff, Johan Willem Remmer, Peeter Geerlof, and Hans Willem tietruy) on Capt. Johan Enrit's ship in Holland in the 5th party of 1709 (Rotterdam Lists).

Johann Wilhelm Kähl made his initial appearance on the Hunter Lists 4 Oct 1710 with 2 pers. over 10 yrs. and 1 under 10. George Wm. Kiel: 1 man, 1 woman, and 1 girl aged 8 and under were in Ulster Co. in 1710/11 (West Camp Census). Georg Wilh^m Keal was nat. 8 and 9 Sept 1715 (Kingston Nats.). Georg Wilhelm Kell and Anna Gertraud with 2 ch. were at Beckmansland ca. 1716/17 (Simmendinger Register). Wm. Keale was taxed at Kingston in 1718/19 and 1720/21 (Ulster Co. Tax Lists). He was a freeholder at Kingston in 1728 (Ulster Co. Freeholders). William Keils was an ensign in the Wall a Kill Co. of the Ulster Co. Militia in 1738 (Report of the State Historian, Vol. I, p. 607). The ch. of Georg Wilhelm[1] Kähl and Gertraud were:

1) Sybilla Catharina[2] (HJ) md. 6 April 1724 Lorentz Merckel (Kingston Ref. Chbk.).
2) Margaretha[2] (HJ), md. Mattheus Merckel (HJ).
3) Georg Wilhelm[2], bpt. 23 Sept 1722 - sp.: Jury Overpag and Magdalena Stier (Kingston Ref. Chbk.).

JOHANN WILHELM KÄMER (Hunter Lists #355)

The German roots of the Schoharie Valley Kämer family were at 5450 Niederbieber (2 km. n. of Neuwied; Chbks. begin 1655). The earliest known ancestor of the emigrant was Thonges Kämmer, Landfrohn at Niederbieber. Hans Wilhelm, s/o Thönges Kämmer - Landfrohn at N. Bieber, md. Catharina, wid/o Johannes Ersfeldt at Segendorf, 9 Nov 1699. Johannes, s/o the late Christ Ersfeldt at Seg., had md. Catharina, d/o Johannes Mees there, 14 May 1691;

Johannes Ersfeld at Segendorf was bur. 26 Dec 1698. The Niederbieber
registers show the parents of Catharina Mees Kämer were Johannes
and Gertraud Mees, parents of the 1709er Johann Henrich Mees. Johan
Willem Remmer, his wife, and 5 ch., were listed among other 1709ers
from Neuwied on Capt. Johan Enrit's ship in the 5th party in Holl-
and in 1709 (Rotterdam Lists).

Johann Wilhelm Kämer made his first appearance on the Hunter
Lists 1 July 1710 with 3 pers. over 10 yrs. and 2 pers. under 10.
The entry for 31 Dec 1710 read 4 over 10 yrs., for 24 June 1711
noted 3 over 10 and 1 under 10, for 24 Dec 1711 was 2 over 10 and
1 under 10, and for 24 June 1712 showed 3 pers. over 10 yrs. and
1 under 10 yrs. Johan Wm Kammer of Annsberg was a soldier in 1711
(Palatine Volunteers To Canada). Johan Wilhelm Kramer and Anna
Maria with 1 child were at Neu-Ansberg ca. 1716/17 (Simmendinger
Register). Jan Wm. K(emner) was a Palatine Debtor in 1718 (Liv-
ingston Debt Lists). Wilhelm Cämmer d. 14 Oct 1749 in the 70th yr.
(Schoharie Luth. Chbk.). He appears to have md. 3 times (HJ): 1)
Catharina Mees; 2) Anna Maria (--), noted on Simmendinger; and 3)
Anna Apollonia Warnar, a communicant in the Schoharie settlements
in 1736 (Albany Protocol, p. 189). His ch. by his 1st wife were:

1) Anna Maria[2], bpt. 6 June 1700 - sp.: Johann Hupert Eckhardt
   at N. Bieber, Anna Margaretha - d/o Johannis Breydebach at
   Seg., and Anna Maria - w/o Anthonis Kämmer at Hedestorf
   (Niederbieber Chbk.).

2) Johann Wilhelm[2], bpt. 14 Aug 1701 - sp.: Wilhelm Wirtgen,
   Johannes Remagen, and Anna Margaretha - sister of the child's
   mother, all at Segendorf (Niederbieber Chbk.).

3) Johann Peter[2], bpt. 25 March 1703 - sp.: Dietrich, s/o Hans
   Adam Eckardt auf Heulenberg, Johann Peter - s/o Johannis
   Breydebach at Seg., and Catharina - d/o Hans Jacob Mees
   (Niederbieber Chbk.).

4) Anna Christina[2], bpt. June of 1704 - sp.: Johan Wilh. Kämmer, Elsa Christina - d/o Christian Diederich there, Anna
   Gertraudt - servant at Johannes Mees's from the Neuburgische
   country, and Johann Daniel - s/o Weyandt Wirttges at Seg.
   (Niederbieber Chbk.). She md. James Schoolkraft (HJ); the
   will of William Schoolcraft of Schoharie 22 Sept 1760 mentioned property left by his grandfather William Cammer
   (Fernow Wills #1551).

5) Lorentz[2], bpt. 5 April 1706 - sp.: Johannes Meess, Lorentz
   ..., and Anna Catharina Prüsser (Niederbieber Chbk.).

6) Anna Ottilia[2], bpt. 27 Nov 1707 - sp.: Ottilia - d/o Peter
   Remagen, Anna Magdalena - d/o the late Christian Gerlach at
   Rodenbach, and Christian - brother of the child's father
   now a Union soldier (Niederbieber Chbk.).

JOHANN PETER KÄMG (Hunter Lists #356)

Martin Peter Kamig made his initial appearance on the Hunter
Lists 1 July 1710 with 3 pers. over 10 yrs. of age. The family
size remained constant with 3 over 10 yrs. until 24 June 1711,
their last regular entry; Johann Martin Kämg was noted 4 Oct 1710,
and Johann Martin Kämich was recorded 31 Dec 1710. Johann Wilhelm
Kamich was registered on the cumulative entry 24 Dec 1711. Joh's
Marten Keem and Joh's Nicholas Keem were listed next to each other
on the roll of Capt. James Pollion's Company in the Richmond Co.
Militia in 1715 (Report of the State Historian, Vol. I, p. 549).

ANNA MARGRETHA KÄSCHELIN (Hunter Lists #357)

A Hans Jacob Keusel, his wife, and 5 ch. were on Capt. Georg
Gouland's ship in the 4th party in Holland in 1709 (Rotterdam
Lists). Jacob Kensel aged 44, his wife, sons aged 7 and 1½, daugh-
ters aged 13 and 11, Luth., husbandman and vinedresser, were in
England later that year (London Lists).

Anna Margretha Käschelin was entered first on the Hunter Lists
4 Oct 1710 with 1 pers. over 10 yrs. of age; her cumulative entry
24 Dec 1711 called her Anna Käschelin.

CHRISTIAN KASSELMANN (Hunter Lists #358)

The roots of this family in Europe were at 7519 Adelshofen
(10 km. s. of Sinsheim; Chbks. begin 1655). The earliest known direct ancestor of both Christian[1] and Dieterich[1] Kasselmann was Hanß
Caßellmann. Johannes (Hanß) Caßelman d. 27 April 1680; his widow
Anna was bur. 26 Dec 1693. An earlier Anna Caßelmann (perhaps mother
of Hanß - HJ) d. 10 Oct 1699, aged 84 yrs. The ch. of Hanß Caßelmann and Anna were:

Anna Barbara, md. as d/o Hanß Caßelman 14 Nov 1671 Nicolaus
Peters.

+ Hanß Frantz, md. as s/o Hanß Caßelmann 2 Feb 1674 Margaretha
Walter from Gochsheim.

Hanß Jacob, bpt. 6 Feb 1659 - sp.: Hans Gerich and Jacob Ammon, both citizens here. He d. in 1718.

Hanß Matthias, b. 5 Feb 1661 - sp.: Hans Dietrich Sommer, Jacob
Ammon, and Hans Matthieß - s/o Daniel Stupen. He d. 2 April
1661, aged 7 weeks, 3 days.

+ Hanß Dieterich, b. 13 Nov 1662 - sp.: Hans Dietrich Sommer,
Johann Adrian Donnhoffer, and Hans Matthiß Stup.

Georg, md. as s/o the late Johan Kasselman 9 Nov 1686 Elisabetha Krautter, wid/o Johan Krautter.

Anna Catharina, b. 5 July 1668 - sp.: Anna Cathrina Sommer.

Margaretha, w/o Hanß Frantz Cassellmann, d. 15 March 1676. Hanß
Frantz md. 2nd 4 June 1677 Anna Huber. By his 1st marriage to Mar-
garetha Walter a s/o Hanß Frantz Caßelmann was the emigrant Christ-
ian, b. 3 Oct 1674 - sp.: Christian Plitsch (?) from Hilsbach.
Christianus Casselmann, s/o Hanß Frantz Casselmann, md. 10 Oct 1702
Maria Judith, d/o the late Bernhard Friedrich Hirtz - citizen here.
Bernhardt Friedrich Hirz, citizen and widower here, md 24 Nov 1679
Elisabetha, d/o Hans Georg Steinecker - formerly citizen at Bley-
erbuch (?) Berner Gebieth ...; their daughter Maria Judith was bpt.
in May 1682 - sp.: Fr. Schopf ..., Judith Elard ... Bernhardt
Friedrich Hirtz d. 24 Aug 1693, aged 50 yrs. Christian Caselman
aged 37, his wife, and a son aged 2, Luth., husbandman and vinedresser, were at London in the 2nd arrivals in 1709 (London Lists).

Christian Kasselmann made his initial appearance on the Hunter
Lists 4 Aug 1710 with 2 pers. over 10 yrs. of age; on the 4 Oct
1710 list he was noted next to Dietrich Kasselmann. The family was
recorded with 2 pers. over 10 yrs. and 1 pers. under 10 on 24 June
1711. Christian Castleman aged 36, Anna Judeth Castleman aged 27,
and Eva Maria Cath Castleman aged 12, were registered at N.Y. City
in 1710/11 (Palatines In N.Y. City). Christ[n] Caselman was nat. 8
and 9 Sept 1715 (Kingston Nats). Christian Kasselmann and Maria
Judith with 2 ch. were at Beckmansland ca. 1716/17 (Simmendinger
Register). Christian Casselman and Anna Maria, his wife, were com-
municants in 1736 in the Schoharie Valley (Albany Protocol, p. 189).
Christian Casselmann and (sons) Johan Peter and Johannes were mentioned in Pastor Sommer's Family List ca. 1744 (Schoharie Luth.
Chbk.). The ch. of Christian[1] Kasselmann and Maria Judith were:

1) Anna Maria[2], b. 24 Nov 1703 - sp.: Anna Caßelmann and Anna
   Maria Seitz (Adelshofen Chbk.). She d. 13 March 1705, aged
   1 yr. and 3 months (Adelshofen Chbk.).

2) Hans Dieterich[2], b. 4 March 1705 - sp.: Hans Dietrich Weidknecht, Hans Michel Seitz, and Elisab. Veronica Bauder
   (Adelshofen Chbk.). The child's name was marked "+".

3) Johann Michael[2], b. 20 July 1707 - sp.: Hans Mich. Seitz,
   Hans Jerg ..., the young smith (Adelshofen Chbk.).

4) Eva Catharina[2], bpt. 20 Oct 1710 - sp.: J. Michael Waid-
   knecht and Elisabetha Mueller (West Camp Luth. Chbk.).

5) Maria Justina[2], b. 23 Aug 1713 - sp.: Justina Lueckhard
   (West Camp Luth. Chbk.).

6) Johann Peter[2], b. 3 April 1715 - sp.: Johann Peter Burckhard and Andreas Ellich (West Camp Luth. Chbk.). He was
   mentioned with his father on Sommer's 1744 list at Schoharie. He md. Elisabetha Weas or Weaver (HJ). They had
   issue:

i) <u>Christian</u>[3], bpt. 27 Oct 1751 - sp.: Henderick and
Sophia Magdalena Paschase (Albany Ref. Chbk.).

ii) <u>Margaretha</u>[3], bpt. 3 Feb 1754 (Trinity Church, N.Y.
City).

iii) <u>Maria</u>[3], b. 3 Jan 1760 - sp.: Maria Dillebach and Christian Dillebech, both unmarried (Stone Arabia Ref. Chbk.).

7) <u>Sophia Magdalena</u>[2], b. 22 March 1718 - sp.: Andreas Ellich
and wife Sophia, and Magdalena Sutz (West Camp Luth. Chbk.).
She md. Henrich Passage (HJ).

8) <u>Johannes</u>[2] (Family List, Schoharie Luth. Chbk.). Hannis and
Hans Kaselman were in Lt. Veeder's Company in the Colony
of Rencelarswick in 1767 (<u>Report of the State Historian</u>,
Vol. II, p. 818). He md. Maria Eva Seibel 21 Jan 1747
(Schoharie Luth. and Ref. Chbks.) and had ch.:

i) <u>Johannes</u>[3], b. 15 Oct 1747 - sp.: Jürgen Seibel and his
wife (Schoharie Luth. Chbk.).

ii) <u>Maria Engel</u>[3], b. 23 May 1750 - sp.: Margareta Seibel
and Jürgen Rickert (Schoharie Luth. Chbk.).

iii) <u>Elisabetha</u>[3], md. as d/o Johannes Casselman 17 Nov 1770
Peter Zimmer (Schoharie Ref. Chbk.).

iv) <u>Dorothea</u>[3], b. 14 July 1756 - sp.: Jost Matthes, Jr.
and Dorothea Seibel (Schoharie Luth. Chbk.). She md.
John Philip Wagener 10 Dec 1772 (Schoharie Ref. Chbk.).

v) <u>Maria</u>[3], b. 1 Jan 1759 - sp.: Jürgen Seibel and his
wife (Schoharie Luth. Chbk.). She md. Michel Wielemann
15 July 1781 (Schoharie Luth. Chbk.).

vi) <u>"A Daughter"</u>[3], b. 17 Dec 1761 - sp.: Jeremias Marinus
and wife (Schoharie Luth. Chbk.).

vii) <u>Christina</u>[3], b. 6 Aug 1764 - sp.: Jeremi Marinus and
wife (Schoharie Luth. Chbk.). She md. Alexander Thom-
son 17 July 1783 (Schoharie Luth. Chbk.).

viii?) <u>Sophia</u>[3] (HJ), md. Jacob Weisgerber 16 Sept 1783 (Schoharie Luth. Chbk.).

<u>DIETRICH KASSELMANN</u> (Hunter Lists #359)

For the documented ancestry of this 1709er, see #358 Christian[1]
Kasselmann. Johan Dietrich Kasselman, s/o the late Joh. Kasselman
- inhabitant here, md. Anna, d/o the late Joh. Peter Rinder from
Glottfelden Zürcher Gebieth in Switzerland, 15 Nov 1687 (Adelshofen
Chbk.).

Dietrich Kasselmann made his initial appearance on the Hunter
Lists 4 Aug 1710 with 4 pers. over 10 yrs. and 1 pers. under 10;
the 4 Oct 1710 entry read 4 pers. over 10 yrs., and the 31 Dec 1710
listing noted 3 over 10 and 1 under 10 yrs. The 24 June 1711 entry

showed 4 over 10 yrs., and the 29 Sept 1711 notation read 4 over
10 yrs. and 1 under 10 yrs. Jno Ffrid Caselman: 1 man, 1 lad aged
9 to 15 yrs., 2 women, were in Ulster Co. in 1710/11 (West Camp
Census). Dieterich Casselmann and Anna with 2 ch. were at Neu-
Stuttgardt ca. 1716/17 (Simmendinger Register). Hans Dederick Casselman was a patentee in 1723 (Stone Arabia Patent). The ch. of
Dieterich[1] Kasselmann and wife Anna were:

1) Anna Barbara[2], b. 20 Oct 1688 and bpt. at Eppingen - sp.:
   Joh. Lorentz Sommer, Joh. Andreas Hüger, and Anna Barbara
   Joß from Eppingen (Adelshofen Chbk.).

2) Anna Elisabetha[2], b. 19 June 1690 - sp.: Elisabetha Weid-
   knecht, Anna Wähl, and Andreas Hüger (Adelshofen Chbk.).
   She md. 24 Feb 1713 Georg Martin Dillenbach (West Camp
   Luth. Chbk.).

3) Elisabetha[2], b. 7 April 1696 - sp.: Anna Elisabetha Weydknecht, Anna Gretha Schlauch - single, and Fried. Paulus
   Sitzler (Adelshofen Chbk.).

4) Andreas Ludwig[2], b. 6 Nov 1698 - sp.: Andreas Weydknecht
   - Schultheiß here, Andreas Hüger, and Ludwig Paulus Sitzler,
   single (Adelshofen Chbk.). Johann Ludwig Castelmann was
   conf. at Schoharie 7 Feb 1714 (West Camp Luth. Chbk.).
   And. Lod'k Casselman was nat. 17 Jan 1715/16 (Albany Nats.).
   Lodowick Casselman was a patentee in 1723 (Stone Arabia
   Patent). Ludwig Casselmann and (wife) Margaretha Elisabet
   Casselman were on Pastor Sommer's Family List ca. 1744
   in the Stone Arabia and Cani-schohare congregation (Schoharie Luth. Chbk.). The ch. listed on this Family List
   were:
     i) Johann Dieterich[3].
    ii) Johannes[3]. Perhaps he was the Johannes Casselman,
        single man b. at Schoharie, who md. Margriet Snyder,
        single woman b. Palinskill, 10 Jan 1748 (Smithfield,
        Pa. Chbk.) (HJ).
   iii) Conrad[3].
    iv) Johann Jacob[3].
     v) Anna[3].
    vi) David[3].
   vii) Elisabetha[3].
  viii) Sophia[3].

5) Anna[2], b. 19 Aug 1702 - sp.: Anna Elis. Weydknecht ...,
   Margaretha Schlauch, and Georg Ludwig Paulus Sitzler (Adelshofen Chbk.). She has a mark "+" after her name in the
   chbk.

6) Johann Dieterich[2], b. 23 July 1706 - sp.: Andreas

Weydknect - Schultheiß, Joh. Dietrich Weidknecht, and Andreas Füger (Adelshofen Chbk.).

7) <u>Anna²</u>, b. 2 Nov 1708 - sp.: Anna Füger - the innkeeper here,
   Anna Elisabetha Weidknecht - wid/o the Schultheiß, and Johannes Wied - citizen at Hilspach (Adelshofen Chbk.).

8) <u>Wilhelm²</u>, b. 19 July 1711 - sp.: Philipp Müller the sexton
   (West Camp Luth. Chbk.). Johan Wilhelm Casselmann appeared
   on Pastor Sommer's 1744 Family List also (Schoharie Luth.
   Chbk.). Wilhelmus Kesselman aged 50, b. Albany, Labourer,
   5' 7", fair complexion, brown eyes, sandy hair, was in Capt.
   Christopher Yates Company 5 May 1760 (<u>Report of the State
   Historian</u>, Vol. II, p. 587). He md. 1st Margaretha Saltz-
   mann (HJ) and had issue:

   i) <u>Anna Margaretha³</u> (Sommer's Family List).

   ii) <u>Anna Maria³</u> (Sommer's Family List).

   iii) <u>Elisabetha³</u>, bpt. 1741 - sp.: Henrich Salsman and Lisabet Dillebach (Stone Arabia Ref. Chbk.).

   iv) <u>Anna Magdalena³</u>, b. 20 Jan 1744 at Stone Arabia - sp.:
   Miss Anna Magdalena ..., Miss Anna Elisabeth Walrath,
   and Johannes Casselman (Schoharie Luth. Chbk.).

   v) <u>Suphrenius³</u>, called s/o Wilhelm in 1759 (Stone Arabia
   Ref. Chbk.). Severin's, Peter, John, and William Caselman were all in Lt. Van Alstein's Co. in 1763 (<u>Report
   of the State Historian</u>, Vol. II, p. 798). Suffrenus
   Cassleman was a Loyalist and went to Canada (see <u>Ad-
   vanced Genealogical Research</u>, by Archibald F. Bennett,
   pp. 117 - 127, and <u>The Loyalists In Ontario</u>, pp. 56
   - 58, for data on Loyalist Kasselmanns).

   vi) <u>Wilhelm³</u>, called brother of Severinus 23 April 1777
   (<u>Mohawk Valley in the Revolution</u>, p. 111).

   vii) <u>Werner³</u>, called brother of Wilhelm in his Loyalist
   Claim dated 27 Feb 1788 at Montreal (<u>Second Report of
   the Bureau of Archives for the Province of Ontario</u>,
   1904, p. 454).

   Wilhelm Casselmann md. 2nd Anna Margaretha Emigin (HJ); ch.:

   viii) <u>Dieterich³</u>, b. or bpt. 13 March 1753 - sp.: Dieterich
   Tillenbach and Maria Margaretha Merckle (Stone Arabia
   Luth. Chbk.).

   ix) <u>Christian³</u>, b. or bpt. 6 March 1755 - sp.: Christian
   Nellis and Margaretha Crims (Stone Arabia Luth. Chbk.).

   x) <u>Dorothea³</u>, b. or bpt. 14 May 1759 - sp.: Johannes Kaiser and Dorodea Crims (Stone Arabia Luth. Chbk.).

9?) <u>Johannes²</u> (HJ). I put him as brother of Wilhelm², rather
   than his son, as Johannes² does not appear on Sommer's

Family List ca. 1744 in Wilhelm's family (HJ). Johannes md.
Anna Eva (--) and had ch.:

- i) Johannes³, b. 5 Oct 1760 - sp.: Deobald Nelles and wife
  Anna (Stone Arabia Ref. Chbk.).
- ii) Gertraud³, b. 22 Feb 1764 - sp.: Gertraud Bäyer and
  Wilhelm Kasselman (Stone Arabia Ref. Chbk.).
- iii) Suphrenius³, b. 27 April 1766 - sp.: Severinus Koch
  and Elisabeth Emgie (Stone Arabia Ref. Chbk.).
- iv) Adam³, b. 17 Nov 1768 - sp.: Adam Vorror and Regina
  Sprecher (Stone Arabia Luth. Chbk.).
- v) Anna Eva³, b. 5 Jan 1771 - sp.: Johan Devis and Anna
  Eva Emgin (Stone Arabia Luth. Chbk.).

JOHANN GEORG KAST (Hunter Lists #360)

The European origins of the Mohawk Valley Kast family were at
6906 Leimen (5 km. n. of Wiesloch; Chbks. begin 1700, Luth.). Georg
Kast was called a citizen from Rohrbach in the Leimen registers in
1703. Johan Jürg Kast, his wife and 4 ch. were listed next to Johan
Paul Kloter on Capt. Frans Robbenson's ship in the 3rd party of
Palatines in Holland in 1709 (Rotterdam Lists). John Georg Kast
aged 30, his wife, a son aged 8, and daughters aged 6, 4, and 2,
Luth., husbandman and vinedresser, were in England later that
year (London Lists).

Johann Georg Kast made his first appearance on the Hunter Lists
1 July 1710 with 2 pers. over 10 yrs. of age and 3 pers. under 10.
The entry for 25 March 1711 read 2 over 10 yrs. and 4 under 10, the
notation for 24 June 1711 showed 4 over 10 and 2 under 10, and the
reading for 24 Dec 1711 was 3 over 10 and 3 under 10 yrs. The Hunter Lists noted 2 over 10 and 3 under 10 25 March 1712 and 3 over
10 and 3 under 10 yrs. 24 June 1712. A document dated 1712 survives
for Georg Kast in N.Y. Col. Mss., Vol. 58, p. 48-L. Hans Jury Kast
was nat. 11 Oct 1715 (Albany Nats.). Johann Georg Last and Anna
with 7 ch. were at Neu-Stuttgardt ca. 1716/17 (Simmendinger Register). Johan Jurgh Kast was a patentee on the n. side of the Mohawk
River 30 April 1725 (Burnetsfield Patent). Johan Jurgh Kass and his
ch. received 1100 acres of land in the Herkimer Co. area in 1724
(History of Herkimer Co., by Benton, p. 200). Capt. Johan Jurgh Kast
was an officer in the Albany Co. Militia above ye falls on ye Maquas
River in 1733 (Report of the State Historian, Vol. I, p. 572). Johan Jürgen Cast, Sr. was recorded on Pastor Sommer's Family List in
the Congregation at the Fall ca. 1744 (Schoharie Luth. Chbk.). The
will of Jurreje Kast of Albany Co. was dated 30 April 1755 and probated 18 Oct 1757 (Fernow Wills #971). The 14 March 1768 issue of
the N.Y. Gazette-Mercury mentioned the division of his land and

all of his ch. The issue of Johann Georg[1] Kast and Anna were:

1) Anna Catharina[2], bpt. 2 Sept 1703 - sp.: Hans Jacob Neidig and his wife Veronica ... (Leimen Chbk.).

2) Anna Elisabetha[2] (Will), conf. at Tschoghari in the so-called Weiserts Dorp in 1720 (N.Y. City Luth. Chbk.). She md. Nicolaus Mattice (Will).

3) Regina[2], bpt. 25 Sept 1707 - sp.: Regina Gnenberg (?) (Leimen Chbk.).

4) Margaretha[2] (Will), md. Johann Wilhelm Fuchs (Will).

5) Ludwig[2] (N.Y. Gazette-Mercury, 1768). The will of Lodewick Kass of Albany Co. was dated 11 Aug 1753 and probated 29 March 1760 (Fernow Wills #1014).

6) Johann Georg[2] (Will). Johan Jurgh Kast Jr. was a patentee on the n. side of the Mohawk River 30 April 1725 (Burnetsfield Patent). He and his wife sp. Jacob Timmerman in 1734 (Schenectady Ref. Chbk.). Johan Jürgen Jr. and his father were visited by Pastor Berkenmeyer in 1734 (Albany Protocol, p. 92 & 94). Johan Jürgen Cast Jr. and his wife Gertraud were noted with their ch. on Pastor Sommer's Family List at the Fall ca. 1744 (Schoharie Luth. Chbk.). Issue:

  i) Elisabetha[3] (Sommer's Family List).

  ii) Conrad[3] (Sommer's Family List).

  iii) Friederich[3] (Sommer's Family List). He sp. Reykert Bovie in 1750 (Albany Ref. Chbk.). His wife was named Elisabetha (--) (HJ). Friederik Kast was a soldier in Capt. Marx Petry's Company at Bornets Field in 1767 (Report of the State Historian, Vol. II, p. 856).

  iv) Sarah[3] (N.Y. Gazette-Mercury, 1768).

  v) Dorothea[3] (N.Y. Gazette-Mercury, 1768).

7) Sarah[2] (Will), md. Teady Maginnes (Will of Georg[1] Kast and Ludwig[2] Kast).

8) Anna Dorothea[2], b. 13 Nov 1715 and bpt. at Schoharie - sp.: Christian Bauch and his wife (West Camp Luth. Chbk.). She md. Henrich Hager (Will).

9) Anna Maria[2] (Will).

10) Maria[2] (N.Y. Gazette-Mercury, 1768). Either Maria[2] or Anna Maria[2] md. Georg Rechtmeyer (Will) (HJ).

11) Maria Barbara[2] (Will), possibly #10 above (HJ). She md. Friederich Kelmer (Will) (Helmer? - HJ).

JOHANN WILHELM KAYSSER (Hunter Lists #361)

The Hunter secretaries seem to have confused the several Kayser families (HJ). See section #363 Maria Kayserin - her son Jon. Kayser for data on this family.

JOHANN MATHEUS KAYSER (Hunter Lists #362)

A Matthias Kaysser, s/o Godhard Keyser - Gemeinsmann and Gerichtsmann at Gudenberg, md. 25 Aug 1693 Anna Catharina, d/o the
late Niclas Kuch (?), at 6551 Roxheim. Another Matheus Keyser, s/o
the late Hans Jerg Kaiser, md. 1 Oct 1696 Anna Regina, d/o the
smith Michel Schumann, at 7105 Großgartach; however, no proof has
been found that either of these men was the N.Y. 1709er. Mattheus
Keizer, his wife, and (daughter) Anna Elisabet were in the 2nd party in Holland in 1709 (Rotterdam Lists). Matthew Keyser aged 38,
his wife, and a daughter aged 12, Ref., husbandman and vinedresser,
were in the 2nd arrivals in England later that year (London Lists).

Johann Matheus Kayser made his initial appearance on the Hunter Lists 4 Oct 1710 with 1 pers. over 10 yrs. of age in the family; the last entry on Hunter was 24 June 1711 with 1 pers. over
10 yrs and written as Mathias Kayser. John Matheus Keiser aged 23
was in N.Y. City in 1710/11 (Palatines In N.Y. City). Johan Marte
Keiser of the Pals joined the N.Y. City Ref. Church 2 June 1713.
Martin Kayser was auf dem Rarendantz ca. 1716/17 (Simmendinger
Register). The will of a Matthew Keyser was probated in 1766 in
Pa. (Philadelphia Co. Will Bk. O, p. 43).

MARIA KAYSERIN her son Jn̊: KAYSER (Hunter Lists #363)

Maria Kayserin was entered first on the Hunter Rolls 1 July
1710 with 3 pers. over 10 yrs. of age in the household. The entry
for 4 Oct 1710 read Johannes Kayser with 2 pers. over 10 yrs. I
believe the Hunter secretaries then confused this family with #361
Johann Wilhelm Kaÿsser, who may never have existed (HJ). Johann
Wilhelm Kayser with 3 pers. over 10 yrs. and 1 pers. under 10 was
noted 31 Dec 1710. From 24 June 1711 on, this family was recorded
under the title of Johannes Kayser, except for the cumulative entry
24 Dec 1711 with 5 pers. over 10 and 1 under 10 which read Johannes
Kayser and his mother. The entries for 24 June and 13 Sept 1712
registered 4 pers. over 10 and 1 under 10 yrs. for Johannes Kayser.
The son of Maria[1] Kayser was:

1) Johannes[2] (Hunter Lists). Johan Kyser of Haysbury was a
   soldier in 1711 (Palatine Volunteers To Canada). Johannis
   Keyser was nat. 11 Oct 1715 (Albany Nats.). Johannes Kayser
   and his wife Margretha with 2 ch. were at Neu-Heessberg ca.
   1716/17 (Simmendinger Register). The Frontiersmen of N.Y.,
   by Simms, p. 163 mentions Johannes Keyser on a map of the
   Stone Arabia Patent, although not one of the original patentees. Berkenmeyer noted a message delivered by Hannes
   Kaiser in 1734 (Albany Protocol, p. 96). He was a trustee

of the Luth. Church of Stone Arabia (History of Montgomery Co., p. 156). The family of Johannes Kayser was listed on Pastor Sommer's Family List ca. 1744 (Schoharie Luth. Chbk.). Johannes Kesser was a freeholder at Stonrabie in 1763 (Albany Co. Freeholders). Johannes Keyser of Unter-Owissheim in Wurtemberg md. 5 Sept 1710 Margretha, d/o the late Ludwig Ernst Horner of the same place (West Camp Luth. Chbk.). The ch. of Johannes[2] and Anna Margaretha Kayser were:

   i) Bernhard[3] (Barend), called brother-in-law by Pastor Sommer, who md. a proven d/o Johannes[2] (Schoharie Luth. Chbk.). Barend Keyser's barn burned down in 1751 (Sommer's Journal). He d. 8 Dec 1777, aged 65 yrs. (Schoharie Luth. Chbk.). With his wife Maria Barbara (Berg - HJ), he had 11 ch.; bpts. for 9 ch. survive in the Schoharie Luth. and Ref. Chbks. (HJ).

  ii) Anna Margaretha[3], b. 13 Nov 1716 and bpt. by P. Van Driesen, the Low-German Pastor of Albany - sp.: Henrich Jung and his wife (West Camp Luth. Chbk.).

 iii) Christina[3], called sister of Barend[3] in a crossed-out section of the 1744 Sommer's Family List (Schoharie Luth. Chbk.).

  iv) Maria[3], called 3rd legt. unmd. d/o Johannes at her marriage 16 May 1744 to Pastor Peter Nicolaus Sommer (Schoharie Luth. Chbk.).

   v) A Child[3], whose name ended with ..us (?), found on a torn section of the 1744 Family List (HJ).

  vi) A Daughter[3], whose name ended with ...ab Barbara, found on a torn section of the 1744 Family List. Her name probably was Elisabetha Barbara (HJ).

 vii) Johann Michael[3] (Sommer's Family List), md. Dorothea Elisabetha Jung (HJ). Migell and Johannes Keyser were in Soffrines Deychert's Company in 1757 (Report of the State Historian, Vol. II, p. 783). He later was a Lieutenant in the same Company in 1763 (Report of the State Historian, Vol. II, p. 792).

viii) Elisabetha[3] (Sommer's Family List).

  ix) Johann Georg[3] (Sommer's Family List). He sp. Michael[3] Kaiser in 1755 (Stone Arabia Luth. Chbk.).

   x) Johannes[3] (Sommer's Family List). He sp. Joh: Martin Nestel in 1753 and Wilhelm Casselman in 1759 (Stone Arabia Luth. Chbk.). Johannes Kayser md. Anna Margaretha Crems 6 Nov 1759 at Stone Arabia (Schoharie Luth. Chbk.).

EVA CATHARINA KÄSIN (Hunter Lists #364)

Eva Catharina Käsin made her first appearance on the Hunter
Lists 4 Oct 1710 with 1 pers. over 10 yrs. of age; the cumulative
entry for 24 Dec 1711 read 1 pers. under 10 yrs. of age for Eva
Käsin.

FRANTZ KELLER (Hunter Lists #365)

The Huldigungslisten for the village of Neütsch in Ampt Lichtenberg for the year 1696 listed Johann Frantz Keller as a resident
there (E 9 Konv. 20, Darmstadt Archives). Records for the village
of Neutsch are found at 6101 Neunkirchen/Odw. (12 km. n.e. of Bensheim; Chbks. begin 1635, but gaps). A possible 1st marriage for
the N.Y. settler may have been 20 July 1693 when Johann Frantz
Keller, single fellow from Neutsch, md. Anna Magdalena, d/o the
late Michel Müller - Gemeinsmann at Gergenhausen. This couple had
two ch. bpt. at Neunkirchen, Johann Adam, b. 29 Sept 1695, and
Anna Elisabetha, b. 27 Oct 1697 - sp.: Elisabetha - single d/o
Caspar Keller the sexton at Niederbach. A 1650 mss. at Darmstadt
noted a Matthes Keller and wife Kunigunde with sons Stoffel, Hans
Philipp and Kaspar at Klein-Lieberau. No firm proof yet has emerged
to cement the N.Y. Frantz Keller to this Neunkirchen - Klein Lieb-
erau group; however, it should be noted that the w/o the emigrant
N.Y. Frantz Keller was Barbara Adam, and the Adams were an ancient
family at Klein-Lieberau also (Elisabetha Barbara Adam of this
family md. the N.Y. 1709er Johann Peter Kneskern) (HJ).

Frantz Keller made his initial appearance on the Hunter Lists
4 July 1710 with 2 pers. over 10 yrs. of age in the household.
The family increased to 2 over 10 yrs. and 1 under 10 on 31 Dec
1710, diminished to 2 over 10 yrs. 25 March 1711, and then increased again to 2 over 10 yrs. and 1 under 10 yrs. 29 Sept 1711.
Frank Keller: 1 man, 1 boy aged 8 and under, and 1 woman were in
Ulster Co. in 1710/11 (West Camp Census). Ffrans Kelder was nat.
8 and 9 Sept 1715 (Kingston Nats.). Frans Kelder made his first
appearance on tax rolls in the North Ward in 1717/18 and continued
there until 1732 (Dutchess Co. Tax Lists). He was a surveyor of
fences for the North Ward in 1729 (Dutchess Co. Supervisor's Records). Frans, Felter, William, and Jacob Kelder were in the foot
Company of the Rocester, Ulster Co., Militia in 1738 (Report of
the State Historian, Vol. I, p. 611). The ch. of Frantz[1] Keller
and his wife Barbara Adam (HJ) were:

   1) Joseph[2], b. 21 June 1711 - sp.: Joseph Reichart and wife
      Anna Maria (West Camp Luth. Chbk.).
   2) Jacob[2], bpt. 28 June 1713 - sp.: Jacob Capoesjen and

Maydalena (Kingston Ref. Chbk.). He md. Barbara Hein (HJ) and had ch.:

    i) Maria[3], bpt. 22 April 1739 - sp.: Velde Keller and Margriet Hein (Kingston Ref. Chbk.).

    ii) Lydia[3], bpt. 19 Oct 1740 - sp.: William Hein and Mareitje Tak (Kingston Ref. Chbk.).

    iii) Anna[3], bpt. 10 Feb 1747 - sp.: Hardman Hein and wife Mareitje Sak (Marbletown Ref. Chbk.).

    iv) Frantz[3], bpt. 15 April 1750 - sp.: Frederich Sienich and Catharina Keller (Kingston Ref. Chbk.).

    v) Abraham[3], bpt. 15 Sept 1754 - sp.: Salomon Terwilligen Jr. and Henderickje Terwilligen (Marbletown Ref. Chbk.).

    vi) Petrus[3], bpt. 11 June 1757 - sp.: Petrus Dumon and Maria Van Wagene (Marbletown Ref. Chbk.).

3) Johann Wilhelm[2], b. 31 Jan 1715 - sp.: Johann Jacob Kaputski and his wife (West Camp Luth. Chbk.). He sp. Pouiver Hesil and wife Rachel Kelder in 1741 (Kingston Ref. Chbk.).

4) Rachel[2] (HJ), md. Pouiver Hesil (HJ).

5) Valentin[2] (HJ), md. 4 Oct 1741 Christina Schmidt (Kingston Ref. Chbk.); he resided at Rochester at the time of his marriage. A suit in the Court of Common Pleas at Kingston between Felten Kelder vs. Antony Maxwell was dated 1741. The ch. of Valentin[2] Keller and Christina Schmidt were:

    i) Maria[3], bpt. 6 Nov 1743 - sp.: Henrich Schmidt and Catharina Keller (Kingston Ref. Chbk.).

    ii) Joseph[3], bpt. 25 Nov 1744 - sp.: Henrich Schmid and Catharina Keller (Kingston Ref. Chbk.).

    iii) Isaac[3], bpt. 4 Nov 1746 - sp.: Isaac Schmid and Catharina Schmid (Marbletown Ref. Chbk.).

    iv) Elisabetha[3], bpt. 17 Dec 1749 - sp.: Velde Schmidt and his wife Metge Kermer (Kingston Ref. Chbk.).

    v) Petrus[3], bpt. 8 Sept 1751 - sp.: Petrus Schmid and Elisabeth Schmid (Kingston Ref. Chbk.).

    vi) Wilhelm[3], bpt. 12 March 1757 - sp.: Felte Smith Jr. and Grietje Smith (Marbletown Ref. Chbk.).

    vii) Henrich[3], bpt. 28 Jan 1759 - sp.: Jonas Schmidt and Maria Keller (Kingston Ref. Chbk.).

    viii) Abraham[3], bpt. 6 Jan 1762 - sp.: Johannes Hender(g)ren and Lydia Keller (Marbletown Ref. Chbk.).

6) Catharina[2], b. Sept 1721 at Rheinbeck - sp.: Bernt Null and wife Catharina (N.Y. City Luth. Chbk.). Catharina Keller, wid/o Petrus Osterhout, had banns to marry Frederich Senich of Germany in 1754 (Kingston Ref. Chbk.).

CHRISTIAN KELLER'S WIDDOW AN: MARGR: (Hunter Lists #366)

Christian Keller made his first appearance on the Hunter Lists 1 July 1710 with 5 pers. over 10 yrs. of age and 1 pers. under 10 yrs. The family decreased to 5 pers. over 10 4 Oct 1710 and then to 4 pers. over 10 yrs. and 1 pers. under 10 yrs. 24 June 1711. On the 31 Dec 1710 entry the name changed to Anna Margretha Kellerin and on 25 March 1711 Christian Keller's Wid^W was noted. Margr't Kelder was a Palatine Debtor in 1721 and 1722 (Livingston Debt Lists). The ch. of Christian[1] and Anna Margaretha Keller were:

1) Conrad[2] (HJ), a soldier from Hunterstown in 1711 (Palatine Volunteers To Canada). Conrad Keller and his mother with her ch. were at Hunderston ca. 1716/17 (Simmendinger Register). He was a Palatine Debtor in 1718, 1719, 1721, 1722, and 1726 (Livingston Debt Lists). Coonrod Kelder was a freeholder in the Northpart Livingston in 1720 (Albany Co. Freeholders). His signature survives in Reel #4 of the Livingston Papers. He md. Maria Barbara Proper (HJ); issue:

   i) Anna Elisabetha[3], b. 15 April 1722 in Taarboss and bpt. Gospelhoeck - sp.: Jan Hardick,mv wife Gerritge and my-self (N.Y. City Luth. Chbk.). She md. Isaac Esselstein (HJ).

   ii) Christian[3], bpt. ca. 3 weeks old 11 Aug 1726 in pass-ing from Theerbosch - sp.: Joh. Jost Propper's son and Sam Miller's daughter (N.Y. City Luth. Chbk.). Christiaen Kelder was above Poesten Kill in Capt. Ab-raham Van Aernam's Company in 1767 (Report of the State Historian, Vol. II, p. 813). He md. Elisabetha Backus and had ch. bpt. at Rhinebeck Flats Ref., Ger-mantown Ref., Linlithgo Ref., Albany Ref., and Clav-erack Ref. Churches (HJ).

   iii) Johann Jost[3], md. as a s/o Conrad Keller 18 Oct 1748 Anna Klapper (Germantown Ref. Chbk.). Johan Jost and Hendrick Kelder were in Capt. Jeremiah Hogeboom's Comp-any in 1767 (Report of the State Historian, Vol. II, pp. 864 & 865). Papers in the estate of Johan Jost Keller, deceased, of Livingston, farmer, were issued to Hendrick and William Keller of the City of Hudson 2 Jan 1797 (Columbia Co. Administration Bk. B). He had ch. bpt. at Loonenburg Luth., Linlithgo Ref., and Claverack Ref. Churches (HJ).

   iv) Maria[3], b. 27 March 1729 - sp.: Gerrit Van Hoesen and Marytje (Loonenburg Luth. Chbk.). She md. 1 Feb 1749 Johann Ernst Defuh (Germantown Ref. Chbk.).

v) <u>Anna</u>[3] (HJ), md. Georg Defuh (HJ).

vi) <u>Christina</u>[3] (HJ), md. John Mc Fall (HJ).

vii) <u>Catharina</u>[3] (HJ), md. Daniel Defuh (HJ).

viii) <u>Henrich</u>[3] (HJ), md. Catharina Althauser (HJ). They had
ch. bpt. at Kinderhook Ref., Linlithgo Ref., and
Churchtown Luth. Churches (HJ).

ix) <u>Agnes Flora</u>[3], b. 4 July 1739 and bpt. in my house -
sp.: Emmerich Plass and wife Agnesa Flora (Loonenburg
Luth. Chbk.).

x) <u>Jacob</u>[3], b. 10 Aug 1742 and bpt. Teerbosch - sp.: Jacob
Van Hoesen and wife Gertruyd (Loonenburg Luth. Chbk.).

2) <u>Anna Christina</u>[2] (HJ), md. 1st John Price and 2nd Henrich
Schurtz or Schutz (HJ).

3) <u>Anna Margaretha</u>[2] (HJ), md. Adam (sometimes known as Adolff)
Diel 9 Jan 1722 (N.Y. City Luth. Chbk.).

ANNA MARIA KERCHERIN (Hunter Lists #367)

Anna Maria Kercherin made her initial appearance on the Hunter Lists 1 July 1710 with 3 pers. over 10 yrs. and 1 pers. under
10 yrs. of age. The entry for 4 Aug 1710 read 2 pers. under 10 yrs.
of age.

JOHANNES KESSLER (Hunter Lists #368)
ANNA MARIA KESSLERIN (Hunter Lists #369)

The German origins of the Mohawk Valley Casler-Kessler family
were at 6344 <u>Ewersbach</u> (10 km. n. of Dillenburg; Chbks. begin
1635). The earliest known ancestor of the American line was <u>Hans
Kesseler</u>. Hans Jacob, s/o the late couple Hans Kesseler and wife
Enche from Rüttershausen, md. Magdalehn, wid/o the late Caspar Eickert from Niederrossbach on Dom. Exaudi: 1678. Another child of the
early Hans Kesseler was named Agnes, and she md. Johannes Möller
10 Jan 1675; they were parents of the emigrant 1709er Johannes Müller, b. 19 Nov 1687. The ch. of <u>Hans Jacob</u> and Magdalena Kesseler
were:

+ <u>Anna Maria</u>, b. 12 Nov 1679 at Rittershausen - sp.: Johannes
Kesseler there and Anna Maria ...

+ <u>Johannes</u>, b. 2 July 1686 - sp.: Johannes Henrich and Thomas
Möller, and Els - d/o Velten Kraus, all from there.

Joh. Daniel Busch from Ebersbach, his wife, and 3 ch., and his
wife's sister, Hans Jacob Kesseler's daughter, left Rittershausen
without release in 1709; next of the list was Joh[S] Kesseler, brother-in-law of Busch, unmarried, also without release (Nassau-
Dillenburg Petitions).

Johannes Kessler made his initial appearance on the Hunter
Lists 24 June 1711 with 2 pers. over 10 yrs.; the entry for 24 Dec
1711 read Johannes Kessler and his sister with 3 pers. over 10 yrs.
of age. The last entry for Johannes on 13 Sept 1712 recorded 2 pers.
over 10 yrs. of age. Anna Maria Kessler was registered with 1 pers.
over 10 yrs. of age 25 March 1712; she continued as Margretha Kes-
slerin with 1 pers. over 10 throughout 1712. Johannis Kisler of
Queensbury was a soldier in 1711 (Palatine Volunteers To Canada).
Johannis Kessler was nat. 3 Jan 1715/16 (Albany Nats.). Johannes
Kessler and his wife Maria Margretha with 3 ch. were at Neu-Quunsberg ca. 1716/17 (Simmendinger Register). Johannes Reslaer was
recorded next to Nicolas Kaslaer when both were patentees on the
s. side of the Mohawk River 30 April 1725 (Burnetsfield Patent).
Johannes Kesselaer of Burnetsfield deeded land to John Sanders of
Schenectady 3 Sept 1762 (Albany Co. Deeds: Vol. 7, p. 505). The
ch. of Johann[1] Kessler and Anna (Maria) Margaretha were:

1) Nicolaus[2] (HJ), also a patentee in 1725 on the s. side of
   the Mohawk River (Burnetsfield Patent). Albany Co. Deeds
   (Vol. 7, p. 505) dated 3 Sept 1762 mentioned the house of
   Nicolas Kesselaer, late deceased.

2) Anna Eva[2] (HJ), md. Marcus Petri (HJ). The Mohawk Valley
   Petries & Allied Families, edited and indexed by the dedicated Hazel Patrick, p. 1, details this branch; a private
   family source in the possession of the Petrie descendants
   evidently cements this Kessler-Petrie link (HJ).

3) Anna Catharina[2], b. 21 Nov 1715 and bpt. at Schoharie -
   sp.: Johann Just Schnell and Anna Catharina Groster (West
   Camp Luth. Chbk.).

4) Johannes[2], b. 5 Feb 1717 and bpt. at Schoharie - sp.: Johann Mueller and Gertraut Hettmann (West Camp Luth. Chbk.).
   John, Micheal, Jacob John, and Conrad Kessler were listed
   next to Johanis and Nich'ls Miller in 1767 in Capt. Conrad
   Frank's Company (Report of the State Historian, Vol. II,
   p. 850).

5) Jacob[2] (HJ), d. 31 Dec 1809, aged 88 yrs. (Herkimer Ref.
   Chbk.). Jacob Keslar and Tomas Keslar were enrolled in Capt.
   Mark Petry's Company in 1757 (Report of the State Historian,
   Vol. II, p. 781). Jacob Kesselaer was a freeholder at the
   Falls in 1763 (Albany Co. Freeholders).

There were several 3rd-generation Kesslers in Mohawk Valley
records: 1) Jacob N. Kessler md. Delia, who d. March 1804, aged 61-
4-22 (Herkimer Ref. Chbk.); 2) Johannes Kessler md. Gertraud (--)
and had issue bpt. at Stone Arabia Ref.; 3) Jacob Kessler md. Maria
Dorothea (--) and had ch. bpt. at Stone Arabia Ref.; 4) Johannes

Kessler and wife Anna Maria (--) who had ch. bpt. at Stone Arabia
Ref.; 5) Melchior Kessler and wife Maria Elisabetha (--) who had
issue bpt. at Stone Arabia Ref.; 6) Jacob Kessler and wife Maria
Catharina (--) who had ch. bpt. at Stone Arabia Ref.; 7) Thomas
Kessler and wife Margaretha (--) who had ch. bpt. at Stone Arabia
Ref., and 8) Conrad Casler, whose wid. Catharina d. in April 1828,
aged 72 yrs. - the mother of 16 ch. in German Flats (Albany Gaz-
ette, 9 April 1828).

HENRICH KETTER (Hunter Lists #370)

Henrig Getter, his wife, and 2 ch. were in the 6th party of
Palatines in Holland in 1709 (Rotterdam Lists).

#385 Henrich Klotter probably was the same man as #370 Hen-
rich Ketter on the Hunter Subsistence Rolls (HJ). #385 Henrich
Klotter made his first appearance 4 July 1710 with 2 pers. over
10 yrs. and 2 pers. under 10 in the household; this was Klotter's
only entry on the Hunter Lists. Henrich Ketter made his initial
appearance 4 Aug 1710 with 2 pers. over 10 and 2 under 10 yrs. The
notation for 31 Dec 1710 recorded Henrich Kätter's Wid^W with 2
pers. over 10 and 2 under 10. The entry for 25 March 1711 for
Henrich Kätter's Wid^W noted 1 pers. over 10 yrs. and 2 under 10.
Henrich Ketter's Wid^W & Child were mentioned 24 June 1711, and
Henrich Ketter's Child was recorded 29 Sept 1711 with 1 pers. under 10 yrs. of age. Two boards for Margreth Ketterin's coffin were
ordered 3 May 1711 (N.Y. Colonial Mss., Vol. 55, p. 20a-h). Eleon-
ore Ketterin was mentioned in Vol. 58, p. 48k in the year 1712
in this same series. Probable issue of Henrich[1] Ketter were:

1) Bernhard[2] (HJ), noted as Bernhard Gitter with his wife
   Elisabetha auf dem Rarendantz ca. 1716/17 (Simmendinger
   Register). John Johnston and George Willocks leased land
   in Somerset Co., N.J. to Bernardus Keader 1 March 1721
   (N.J. Historical Society Mss., Folder 4 M 9-16, per the
   kindness of John L. Ely). Bernard Gitter was one of the
   Amwell families who went with Conrad Beissel to the Ephrata Community in Pa. in 1738 (History of East Amwell, p.
   196). He md Elisabetha (Catharina) Lorentz (Will of Johannes Lorentz) and had ch.:
     i) Susanna[3], bpt. 7 Feb 1725 - sp.: Hans Louwrens and
        wife Anna Mary (Somerville Ref. Chbk.).
     ii) Peter[3], bpt. 30 April 1727 (Somerville Ref. Chbk.).
2?) Elisabetha[2] (HJ). An Elisabeth Clater md. Joseph Steppens
    9 Nov 1722 (N.Y. City Luth. Chbk.).

An Augustinus Keeter md. Anna Margaretha Weyd by 1732, but

he probably was connected to Keters who were in the Kingston vicinity prior to 1709 (HJ).

JOHANN WILHELM KIEFFER (Hunter Lists #371)

Anna Maria, d/o Johann Wilhelm Kuster of Langen Gouss Hesten-
Darmstadt, md. Fridrich, s/o Henrich Schramm of Wollensdorst in the
Duchy of Sig, 12 Feb 1717 (West Camp Luth. Chbk.). The family home
was 6306 Lang Göns (8 km. s. of Giessen; Chbks. begin 1684); the
Kieffers were also found at 6308 Griedel (7 km. further s.; Chbks.
begin 1626, Ref.) and 6309 Niederkleen (4 km. s.w. of Lang Göns;
Chbks. begin 1645). The earliest known ancestor of the American
settler was Johann Daniel Kieffer, his father. Joh. Wilhelm Kieffer, s/o Joh. Daniel Kieffer, md. 26 Feb 1691 Catharina, d/o the
late Johannes Plotz (written Klotz at marriage) (Lang Göns Chbk.).
Johann Plitsch was bur. 21 Dec 1688, and his wid. (?) Anna Plitsch
was bur. in 1693 (Lang Göns Chbk.). Johann Wilhelm Kieffer was
called Drund am Rieth miller from Langgöns in 1699 (Griedel Chbk.).

Johann Wilhelm Kieffer made his first appearance on the Hunter
Lists 4 July 1710 with 4 pers. over 10 yrs. and 2 pers. under 10
in the family; the entry for 4 Oct 1710 read 6 pers. over 10 yrs.,
and the notation for 31 Dec 1710 recorded 4 over 10 and 2 under 10.
The registers showed 5 over 10 yrs. 29 Sept 1711. Jno. Wm. Keifer:
1 man, 1 lad aged 9 - 15, 2 women, and 2 maids aged 9 - 15 yrs.
were in Ulster Co. in 1710/11 (West Camp Census). Wilh[m] Koeffer
was nat. next to Baltus Koeffer 8 and 9 Sept 1715 (Kingston Nats.).
Wilhelm Kieffer and Catharina with 3 ch. were at Beckmansland ca.
1716/17 (Simmendinger Register). The ch. of Johann Wilhelm[1] and
Catharina Kieffer were:

1) Anna Maria[2], bpt. 22 Nov 1691 - sp.: Joh. Caspar Schütz's
   wife, Johan Henrich Merckel from Nauwern, Anna Maria - w/o
   Joh. Ludwig Happel from Walnborn, and Antonius Reusch (Lang
   Göns Chbk.). She md. Friederich Schramm 12 Feb 1717 (West
   Camp Luth. Chbk.).
2) Anna Elisabetha[2], b. 2 Jan 1694 - sp.: Elisabetha - w/o
   Thomas Wenzel from Leihgestern, Henrich Käffer - his bro-
   ther, and Elisabetha - wid/o Joh. Jacob Brückel (Lang Göns
   Chbk.). The child was bur. Dom. 3 p. Trin: 1697 (Lang Göns
   Chbk.).
3) Anna Elisabetha[2], b. 3 Jan 1698 - sp.: Anna Elisabetha -
   w/o Joh. Jacob Engel, Conradt - s/o Asmus Laz, and Anna El-
   isabetha - d/o H. Johan Caspar Wagner from Leygestern (Lang
   Göns Chbk.).
4) Balthasar[2], bpt. 22 Oct 1699 - sp.: Balthasar Hoffmann at
   Butzbach (Griedel Chbk.). Baltus Koeffer was nat. with his

father 8 and 9 Sept 1715 (Kingston Nats.). Johann Balthasar
Kuster was conf. at Newtown 12 June 1712 (West Camp Luth.
Chbk.). The Kingston Trustees Records make mention of Bal-
tus Kieffer in Bk. 4, pp. 231 and 232, Bk. 6, p. 394, and
and Bk. 7, pp. 4 and 107. A suit between John Crook vs.
Baltus Kiever was noted in records of the Court of Common
Pleas at Kingston and dated 1740. Balthasar Kiefer was a
member of the Church Council on the w. side of the Hudson
(Albany Protocol, p. 127). Berkenmeyer mentioned him in a
minor dispute in 1736 (Albany Protocol, p. 178):

> I reported that through neglect at the previous time
> for the church service, our worship was interrupted
> in two places (Loonenburg and Newton). I hoped that
> in the future the members would look after this. But
> since Mr. Sam. van Vechten claimed payment for three
> bushels of feed for that trip, it was necessary to
> determine whose fault it was and who should pay this
> bill. Pieter Laux went out of the church and called
> Pieter Borghard. The latter stated that the former
> had ordered Balth(asar) Kiefer and him to get the
> Pastor and take him back. Since both of them argued
> as to who should get him and who should take him
> back, B(althasar) Kieffer had finally promised to
> send his son on Friday morning to P(ieter) Borghard,
> but the son had stayed away. B(althasar) Kieffer,
> who had left the church, was considered to have been
> wrong. The congregation was also of the opinion
> that P(ieter) Laux had not acted wisely, since he
> had not specified who should get the Pastor and
> since Balthasar Kieffer lived at the edge (of the
> village).

A Baltus Kiefor was in Capt. Stephen Nottingham's Company
in the Ulster Co. area in 1758 (Report of the State Historian, Vol. I, pp. 839 & 842). He md. 29 Sept 1723 Anna
Christina Müller (Kingston Ref. Chbk.) and had issue:

    i) Wilhelm[3], bpt. 22 Nov 1724 - sp.: Frerik Schram and
       Marytjen Kiever (Kingston Ref. Chbk.). Wilhelm and
       Henrich Kieffer were conf. 28 Aug 1743 at Newton
       (Loonenburg Luth. Chbk.). He md. 23 June 1749 Elisa-
       betha Swart (Kingston Ref. Chbk.). Papers in the est-
       ate of William Keiffer, late yeoman of Kingston, were
       granted to sons Laurence and Baltus Keiffer of the
       same place 26 June 1794 (Ulster Co. Administration
       Bk. A).

   ii) Henrich[3], b. 5 March 1726 and bpt. at Newtown - sp.:
       Henrich Fees and his wife Christina (West Camp Luth.
       Chbk.). Baltus and Hendrick Kieffer were noted on tax
       rolls in the Rhinebeck area beginning 1747/48 (Dutchess
       Co. Tax Lists). He md. 2 April 1749 Maria Erckenbrecht,
       although the actual marriage entry is somewhat con-
       fusing (HJ), at Rhinebeck Luth. Church; they had issue

bpt. at Red Hook Luth., Rhinebeck Flats Ref., and
Rhinebeck Luth. Churches (HJ).

iii) Catharina³, b. 12 Dec 1727 and bpt. at Kiskatom - sp.:
Catharina Emmerich, the mother of the child acting in
her place, and Hermannus Behr (West Camp Luth. Chbk.).

iv) Anna³, b. 8 Jan 1730 and bpt. at Newtown - sp.: Johan
Jacob Eigener and Anna Maria Eligs (Loonenburg Luth.
Chbk.). She was conf. at Newton 21 March 1747. She
md. Jacob Roos (HJ).

v) Christina³, b. 10 Oct 1732 and bpt. at Newtown - sp.:
Peter May and wife Catharina (Loonenburg Luth. Chbk.).

vi) Catharina³, b. 3 May 1736 and bpt. at Newton - sp.:
Veltin Fuhrer and wife Cath. (Loonenburg Luth. Chbk.).
She md. Nicolaus Stickel (HJ).

vii) Elisabetha³, b. 24 March 1738 and bpt. at Newton -
sp.: Jurge Wilhelm Dieterich and wife Cath. Lis. (Loonenburg Luth. Chbk.).

viii) Johann Balthasar³, b. 10 April 1740 and bpt. at Newton
- sp.: Johannes Schram and Lisabeth Jung (Loonenburg
Luth. Chbk.).

ix) Maria³, b. 3 June 1742 and bpt. at Newton - sp.: Balthasar May and Maria Schramm (Loonenburg Luth. Chbk.).
She md. Arnd Feinhut (HJ).

5) Catharina Susanna², bpt. 1701 (no other date) (Niederkleen
Chbk.). Catharina Susanna Kuster was conf. Easter 1717
(West Camp Luth. Chbk.). She md. Peter May 29 Sept 1723
(Kingston Ref. Chbk.).

DAVID KIESLER (Hunter Lists #372)

David Köselich (alone) was in the 6th party of Palatines in
Holland in 1709 (Rotterdam Lists).

David Kiesler made his initial appearance on the Hunter Lists
1 July 1710 with 1 pers. over 10 yrs. of age; the family rose to
2 pers. over 10 yrs. 31 Dec 1710. A special entry for Eleanore's
subsistence was recorded 4 Oct 1710. David Kesselaer was nat. 17
Jan 1715/16 (Albany Nats.). David Kistlich and Catharina were at
Hunderston ca. 1716/17 (Simmendinger Register). David Kisselaer
was a Palatine Debtor in 1718, 1721, and 1726 (Livingston Debt
Lists); he was a Palatine willing to remain on the Manor 26 Aug
1724 (Doc. Hist. of N.Y., Vol. III, p. 724). He and his wife El-
eonra Catharina sp. many children at many churches along the Hudson 1711-1744 (HJ).

ELIZABETHA KIRTZENBERG (Hunter Lists #373)

Elizabeth Kurtzenberg was noted only once on the Hunter Lists 4 Oct 1710 with 1 pers. over 10 yrs. of age.

ANNA AGATHA KLAPPERIN (Hunter Lists #374)

Johann Wilhelm Klapper, his wife, and 3 ch. were listed twice in the 5th party of Palatines in Holland: once on Capt. Johan Enrit's ship (but a few names from the N.Y. settler Daniel Goettel), and again on Capt. Leonard Allan's vessel (Rotterdam Lists). He most probably was the founder of the N.Y. family (HJ): 1) Henrich[2] Klapper named his firstborn son Johann Wilhem; 2) This firstborn son was sp. at Kingston by Hendrik[2] Kittel, s/o Daniel[1] Goettel - Wilhelm Klapper's fellow-passenger on Capt. Enrit's ship at Rotterdam; and 3) many of the passengers in the 5th party originated in the Nassau-Weilburg-Braunfels region, where the Klapper family was prominent. One Hans Georg Klapper, s/o the late Thomas Klapper at Neunkirchen, md. An Els, d/o the late Philips Heintz at St. Georgen, in 1653 at 6333 Braunfels; this couple had a son Johann Wilhelm bpt. Tuesday Second Christtag of 1654 there - sp.: Joh. Wantil (?) - soldier of the garrison, and Wilhelm - s/o Dietrich Halm ... (Dietrich Halm, father of one of the sp. in 1654, was the grandfather of the N.Y. 1709er Anna Regina Halm Voland Lorentz - HJ). The locale and the date are correct for the 1654 child to be the emigrant Johann Wilhelm Klapper, but more genealogical cement is needed for firm proof (HJ).

Anna Agatha Klapperin made her initial appearance on the Hunter Lists 4 Oct 1710 with 1 pers. over 10 yrs. and 1 pers. under 10 yrs. of age. The cumulative entry for 24 Dec 1711 noted Anna Klapperin with 1 pers. over 10 yrs. of age. Her child was:

1) Henrich[2] (HJ), nat. as Hendr. Clopper 8 and 9 Sept 1715 (Kingston Nats.). He was taxed in the Middle Ward in 1728/29 and continued to be listed in the North Ward - Rhinebeck area until June 1748 (Dutchess Co. Tax Lists). The will of Hendrik Klapper of Claverack in Albany Co. was dated 11 Feb 1772 and probated 29 Jan 1773 (Fernow Wills #987). He md. Anna Margaretha Schmidt 18 Jan 1726 (Linlithgo Ref. Chbk.). The ch. of Henrich[2] and Anna Margaretha Klapper were:

  i) Johann Wilhelm[3], bpt. 19 March 1727 - sp.: Hendrik Kittel and Catrina Deenmarken (Kingston Ref. Chbk.). He md. Anna Elisabetha Heintje (Steentje?), the wid. Kamer, 12 Oct 1756 (Claverack Ref. Chbk.). Jurris, Conrat, Peter, Hendrick, Adam, and William Klapper

(Klaper) served in Capt. Jeremiah Hogeboom's Company in 1767 (Report of the State Historian, Vol. II, pp. 863 - 865).

ii) Anna³, md. as d/o Henrich 18 Oct 1748 Johann (Jost) Keller (Germantown Ref. Chbk.). She joined the Germantown Ref. Church in 1746.

iii) Henrich³ (Will). He md. Eva Holtzapfel (HJ) and had issue bpt. at Germantown Ref., Claverack Ref., and Red Hook Luth. Churches (HJ).

iv) Johannes³, b. 19 Aug 1732 and bpt. at Camp - sp.: Hannes Richter and Anna Maria Glum (Loonenburg Luth. Chbk.).

v) Anna Barbara³, bpt. 16 March 1735 - sp.: Philip Klom and Barbara Shafer (Red Hook Luth. Chbk.). She md. Wilhelm Schneider (HJ).

vi) Adam³ (Will), md. Magdalena Philip (HJ). They had ch. bpt. at Kinderhook Ref., Claverack Ref., and Churchtown Luth. Churches (HJ).

vii) Georg³, b. 17 Oct 1739 and bpt. at Camp at Haneman Saalbach's - sp.: Jurge Glum and wife Anna Maria (Loonenburg Luth. Chbk.). He md. Maria Margaretha (--) (HJ).

viii) Conrad³, bpt. 7 Oct 1741 - sp.: Conrad Lescher and wife Engel Winneker (Germantown Ref. Chbk.). He md. 29 March 1768 Maria Hous (Linlithgo Ref. Chbk.). Conrad Clapper leased a farm of 221 acres in Rensselaerwyck 17 June 1795 (Van Rensselaer Leases, N.Y. State Library, Mss. Room). The will of Coenradt Clopper was dated 6 March 1805 and probated 29 Sept 1805 (Albany Co. Will Bk. 3, p. 252). He had ch. bpt. at Churchtown Luth. Church (HJ).

ix) Peter³, bpt. 2 April 1743 - sp.: Pitter Herder and Eliza Katterina Thomas (Red Hook Luth. Chbk.). He md. Margaretha Hous (HJ) and had ch. bpt. at Claverack Ref., West Sand Lake Luth., Albany Ref., and Churchtown Luth. Churches (HJ). The will of Peter Clapper of Bethlehem was probated 27 Dec 1821 (Albany Co. Will Bk. 5, p. 326); his wife's will was proved 26 Feb 1833 (Albany Co. Will Bk. 7, p. 348).

x) Catharina³, bpt. 1 Jan 1745 - sp.: Jacob Best Jr. and Catharina Berringer (Red Hook Luth. Chbk.).

xi) Gertraut³, bpt. 4 Dec 1746 - sp.: Jacob Beringer with his wife (Red Hook Luth. Chbk.).

xii) Friederich³, bpt. 14 Feb 1748 - sp.: Frederich Muller and Maria Leess (Germantown Ref. Chbk.). He md. 25 Feb

1770 Elisabeth Witmore (Linlithgo Ref. Chbk.). They
had ch. bpt. at Hillsdale Ref., Churchtown Luth., and
Claverack Ref. Churches (HJ).

xiii) <u>Elisabetha³</u> (Will), md. Richard Blameless (Will).

xiv) <u>Gertraud³</u>, bpt. 3 Feb 1751 - sp.: Hendrick Els and
Anna Margriet Els (Linlithgo Ref. Chbk.). She md.
Philip Holzapfel (HJ).

HELENA KLEININ (Hunter Lists #375)

Helena Kleinin made her initial appearance on the Hunter Lists
1 July 1710 with 1 pers. over 10 yrs. and 1 pers. under 10; the
last entry for this family was 4 Aug 1710 with the same numbers.

PETER KLEIN'S WIDDOW (Hunter Lists #376)

Peeter Klein and his wife were on Capt. Thomas Key's ship in
the 5th party of Palatines in Holland in 1709 (Rotterdam Lists).
Another of that name was the Peter Klein aged 42, with his wife,
a son aged 2½ and a daughter aged ¼, Cath., husbandman and vinedresser, in the 1st arrivals in England in May 1709 (London Lists).

Peter Klein made his first appearance on the Hunter Lists 1
July 1710 with 1 pers. over 10 yrs. and 1 pers. under 10. On 4 Oct
1710 the entry read 2 pers. over 10 yrs. of age; on 24 June 1711
Peter Klein's Wid^W with 1 pers. over 10 yrs. and 1 pers. under 10
were recorded. A notation in the Ledger section mentioned that
Peter Klein's Wid^W md. with John Blass. Tree boards for Peter
Klein's coffin were paid for 29 March 1711 (N.Y. Col. Mss., Vol.
55, p. 20a-h). A child of Peter¹ Klein was:

1) <u>Johannes²</u> (HJ), probably the son aged 2½ yrs. noted at London in 1709 (HJ). A Johanes Klein was a Palatine willing
to remain on the Manor 26 Aug 1724 (<u>Doc. Hist. of N.Y.</u>,
Vol. III, p. 724). Joh's Cleyn was a Palatine Debtor in
1726 (Livingston Debt Lists). The Livingston Papers contain a receipt signed by him dated 3 Feb 1726 (Reel #11)
and a deed regarding him dated 1731/32 (Reel #5). Johannes
Klein sp. Henrich Plass in 1730 (Loonenburg Luth. Chbk.);
Henrich Plass was his step-brother, which is my chief reason for placing this Johannes² Klein in the family of Peter¹
Klein (HJ).

HYERONIMUS KLEIN (Hunter Lists #377)

Anna Amalia, d/o Hieronimus Klein of Flommersfeld in the earldom of Sehnish-Hachenburg near Neuwid, md. Johann Peter, s/o Johann
Burckhard - late of Ober-Mockstatt in the earldom of Isenburg, on

5 Nov 1717 (West Camp Luth. Chbk.). The town of origin for the
Kleins was 5232 Flammersfeld (23 km. n. of Neuwied; Chbks. begin
1669, but gaps); the family was documented also at 5455 Rengsdorf
(6 km. n. of Neuwied; Chbks. begin 1677). The parents of the emigrant were Antonius (Thönges) Klein from Hoben (or Hoffen), who d.
13 Sept 1717, aged ca. 80 yrs., and his wife Margaretha, who d. 13
Feb 1713, aged ca. 70 yrs. (both Flammersfeld Chbk.). Hieronymus,
s/o Thünis from Hoffen and Margretha, was bpt. 18 March 1670 - sp.:
Georg Keschett - resident of Flammerschfeldt, the s/o Hieronymus
Kaltschmitt also there, and Anna Cunigunda - w/o Henrich from Orf-
schen (Flammersfeld Chbk.). Hieronimus Klein of Rengsdorf was noted
on a Specification of the Unterthanen, etc. for the parish in 1700,
and Hyronimus Klein was called Bürgermeister of Rengsdorf in 1708
(both from mss. in the Fürstliches Archiv zu Wied). jeronimus klein
with his wife and 3 ch. was on Capt. Richart Waren's ship in Holl-
and in the 5th party of Palatines in 1709 (Rotterdam Lists).

Hyeronimus Klein made his initial appearance on the Hunter
Lists 4 Oct 1710 with 2 pers. over 10 and 2 pers. under 10 yrs.
The entry read 4 over 10 yrs. and 1 under 10 24 June 1711. Hironi-
mus Klein aged 38, Maria Klein aged 38, Amalia Klein aged 12, Anna
Eva Klein aged 14, and Anna Eliz. Klein aged 6, were in N.Y. City
in 1710/11 (Palatines In N.Y. City). Hieronimus Klein was nat. 8
and 9 Sept 1715 (Kingston Nats.). Hieronymus Klein and Maria Margareta with 2 ch. were at Beckmansland ca. 1716/17 (Simmendinger
Register). Hieronimus Klyn was taxed £15 in 1718/19 and £12 in
1720/21 (Ulster Co. Tax Lists); he was a freeholder of Kingston
in 1728 (Ulster Co. Freeholders). He was the plaintiff in a case
vs. Daniel Worms in 1730 and wanted 18 sh. and one pair of shoes;
Klein also was involved in a case as defendant brought by Gere
Van Wagener, but the weather was too poor for Klein to travel to
court (Kingston Town Court Records). The ch. of Hieronymus[1] Klein
and Anna Maria were:
1) Anna Eva[2] (Palatines In N.Y. City).
2) Ludwig[2], bur. 25 May 1698 as the little newborn s/o Hieronimus Klein from Hoben (Flammersfeld Chbk.).
3) Elisabetha Catharina[2], bpt. 9 April 1699 - sp.: Elisab.
   Cath. Hofmann and Johannes Wipper (Rengsdorf Chbk.). She d.
   28 April 1699 (Rengsdorf Chbk.).
4) Anna Amalia[2], bpt. Dom. Quasimod.: 1700 - sp.: Anna Amalia
   Feller, Johannes Mant, and Thönges Runkel (Rengsdorf Chbk.).
   She md. Johann Peter Burckhard 5 Nov 1717 (West Camp Luth.
   Chbk.).
5) Elisabetha Margaretha[2], bpt. 15 March 1703 - sp.: Gerhard
   Reinhart from Oberbieber and Margaretha Mant (Rengsdorf

Chbk.). The child d. in 1703 (Rengsdorf Chbk.).

6) <u>Anna Elisabetha</u>², bpt. 4 Jan 1705 - sp.: Thomas Beith from Melsbach and Anna Marg. - w/o Thiel Licht from Rengsdorf (Rengsdorf Chbk.). She md. Nicolaus Brandau 5 Nov 1726 (Kingston Ref. Chbk.).

7) <u>Johann Maternus</u>², bpt. 15 Jan 1708 - sp.: Joh. Christoph Sensebach from Jahrsfeld, Anna Cath. Licht, and Maternus from Puderbach (Rengsdorf Chbk.).

8) <u>Anna Maria</u>² (HJ), md. Anthonius Schu (HJ).

Pastor Fritsche of Flammersfeld was especially kind and helpful in gathering material on the Klein family; he and his good family even took photos of the ancestral house of Hieronymus Klein for me, and I appreciate their kindness very much.

JOHANNES KLEIN (Hunter Lists #378)

Johan Klein, his wife, and 2 ch. were recorded next to Johan Herman Bötser, Johan diderig Schniter, and Johan Schü (all from the Hachenburg region - HJ) in the 6th party of Palatines in Holland in 1709 (Rotterdam Lists). The family originated at 5238 <u>Hachenburg/Altstadt</u> (14 km. n.w. of Westerburg; Chbks. begin 1661). Johannes Klein, s/o the late Arnold Klein from Neitersen in the parish Schöneberg, md. 16 Oct 1703 Elisabetha Leyendecker, natural d/o Johannes Leyendecker from Oberhatteroth.

Johannes Klein made his initial appearance on the Hunter Lists 4 July 1710 with 2 pers. over 10 yrs. of age. Johannis Klyn was nat. 8 and 9 Sept 1715 (Kingston Nats.). Jan Clyn was on a list of foot Company of Mallitia for the town of Showangung under the command of Cap'n Nicolas Hoffman in the Regt. commanded by Collo. Jacob Rutsen in 1715 (<u>Report of the State Historian</u>, Vol. I, p. 564). Johan Klyn was taxed at Kingston in 1718/19 and 1720/21 (Ulster Co. Tax Lists). Johannes Kleyn, widower of Elsjen Leydekker, had banns to marry Angenietjen Bosch 11 Feb 1728, when both resided at New Marbletown (Kingston Ref. Chbk.). His ch. by his 1st wife were:

1) <u>"A Daughter"</u>², bpt. 3 Aug 1704 - sp.: Wilhelm Klein from Krämges in the parish Schöneberg, Maria Magdalena Leyendecker, and Magdalena Elisabetha Leyendecker from the Altstadt (Hachenburg/Altstadt Chbk.).

2) <u>"A Daughter"</u>², bpt. 10 Sept 1705 - sp.: Görg Wisser, Anna Magdalena Schmid from Altstadt, and Anna Catharina Zepperfeld from Hachenburg (Hachenburg/Altstadt Chbk.).

3&4) <u>"Two Twin Daughters"</u>², one becoming ill, bpt. 15 April 1709 - sp.: (1) Johannes Hahn (?), Magdalena - w/o Joh. Müller,

and Anna Elisabetha Klein from Neiterschen from the Schöne-
bergischen; (2) Hans Bernhard Schmidt and Anna Ottilia -
w/o Johannes Küchermann (Hachenburg/Altstadt Chbk.).

JOHANN JACOB KLEIN (Hunter Lists #379)

A Johan Jacob Klein, s/o Johan Nicolaus Klein of Bährstadt
im Weissbedischen, md. Anna Cath. Jung, d/o Johan Conradt Jung of
Breinchweiller Fürstl. Usingsche Herschaft, 14 Aug 1709 at the Savoy
Luth. Church in London (London Churchbooks and the German Emigration
of 1709, by John P. Dern, p. 24); this Jacob Klein probably was
the man listed as aged 24, alone, Luth., husbandman and vinedresser,
in the 2nd arrivals in 1709 (London Lists). However, a more likely
candidate for our N.Y. settler would be John Jacob Klein aged 25,
with his wife, and a son aged 4, Ref., husbandman and vinedresser
in the 1st arrivals of 1709 (London Lists) (HJ).

Johann Jacob Klein made his first appearance on the Hunter
Lists 4 Aug 1710 with 2 pers. over 10 yrs. and 1 pers. under 10;
the entry for 24 June 1711 noted 2 pers. over 10 and 2 under 10,
and the notation for 29 Sept 1711 recorded 3 pers. over 10 yrs.
and 1 pers. under 10 yrs. in the household. Johan Jacob Klein was
nat. 8 and 9 Sept 1715 (Kingston Nats.). Jacob Klyn was taxed £5
at Hurley in 1718/19 (Ulster Co. Tax Lists). Jacop Clyn was in the
foot Company of Hurly in 1738 (Report of the State Historian, Vol.
I, p. 610). Johann Jacob md. Anna Orsela (she may have been related to Margaretha Ottilia Stuckeroth, w/o the 1709er Conrad Gerlach
and certainly was in the family of the N.Y. Palatine Wilhelm Stuckeroth - HJ); they had a daughter:
1) Anna Margaretha[2], bpt. 1 March 1713 - sp.: Willem Stokker-
   aat and Anna Margriet (Kingston Ref. Chbk.). She had an
   illegitimate child bpt. at Kingston in 1733
Jacob Kleyn, widower of Margriet Stokraad, md. as a resident of
Hurley 2 March 1733 Cornelia Sluyter (Kingston Ref. Chbk.); Cornelia md. 2 Sept 1768 as wid/o Jacob Klein to Johan Rubertus (Kingston Ref. Chbk.). A child of Johann Jacob[1] and Cornelia was:
2) Johannes[2], bpt. 2 June 1734 - sp.: Zalomon Le-Danje and
   Jannetjen Le-danje (Kingston Ref. Chbk.). He may have been
   the Johannes Klein who md. Margriet Sluiter and sp. Jacob
   Sluiter in 1752 at Kingston (HJ).

A Johannes Klein sp. Thomas Brinck and wife Antje Kleyn with
a Catharina Kleyn in 1748 (Walpeck Ref. Chbk.); this Walpeck congregation also had a Thomas Hesson and wife Catharina Kleyn at an
early date (HJ). Perhaps this family belongs with Johann Jacob[1]
Klein and his descendants (HJ).

JOHANN HERMAN KLEIN (Hunter Lists #380)

Johann Herman Klein made his first appearance on the Hunter
Lists 4 Oct 1710 with 1 pers. over 10 yrs. of age; the household
increased to 2 pers. over 10 yrs. 31 Dec 1710. On 24 June 1711
he was recorded with Henrich Klein with 3 pers. over 10 yrs. of
age. The entry for 29 Sept 1711 read 3 pers. over 10 and 1 under
10 yrs., for 24 Dec 1711 noted 2 pers. over 10 and 1 under 10,
and for 25 March 1712 enrolled 2 pers. over 10 yrs. Johann Hermann
Klein and Anna Magdalena with 3 ch. were listed at Neu-Ansberg
ca. 1716/17 (Simmendinger Register); on this census he was recorded
next to Valentin Kuhn, as he was on the Hunter Lists in 1710 (HJ).
The ch. of Johann Hermann[1] Klein and Anna Magdalena were:

1) Gertraud[2] (HJ), md. 27 Nov 1735 Storm Becker Jr. (Schoharie Ref. Chbk.). They had a son Hermannus b. in 1744
   (Schoharie Ref. Chbk.).

2) Anna Maria[2] (HJ), joined the Schoharie Ref. Church in
   1738. She md. Wilhelm Schneider (HJ), and they were sp.
   in 1746 and 1750 at Schoharie Ref. Church by Storm and
   Gertraud Klein Becker (HJ).

HENRICH KLEIN (Hunter Lists #381)

The name Henrich Klein was a common one in 18th century Germany (HJ). Individuals with that name were documented in towns
where other N.Y. Palatines originated, such as 5451 Anhausen, 5419
Dierdorf, and 6251 Runkel (HJ).

Henrich Klein made his initial appearance on the Hunter Lists
4 Oct 1710 next to Johann Hermann Klein; he was given 1 pers. over
10 yrs. of age on the listing. He was recorded with Johann Herman
Klein 24 June 1711. Henrich Klein of Annsberg was a soldier in
1711 (Palatine Volunteers To Canada).

ADAM KLEIN (Hunter Lists #382)

"Eighteenth-Century Emigration From the Duchy of Zweibrücken"
by Friedrich Krebs, as translated and edited by Dr. Don Yoder in
his wonderful book Rhineland Emigrants - Lists of German Settlers
in Colonial America gives 6690 Bubach as the ancestral home of
Adam Klein. The records of this village were found in the registers
of 6690 Niderkirchen i/Ostertal (2 km. e. of St. Wendel; Chbks.
begin 1666, but gaps). The parents of the emigrant were Johannes
Klein and his wife Anna, who had issue:

Catharina Agnes, bpt. 20 June 1675 - sp.: Hans Nicel Müller
at Reich..., Cath. - w/o Matthias Braun at Waldmohr, and Ig-
ness - d/o the late Jacob Balthess at B...

Wendel (1743 Letter).

Jacob (1743 Letter).

+ Hanß Adam, bpt. 7 March 1680 - sp.: Hanß Adam - s/o Hans Jacob
  Seyller at Saahl, Hanß Jacob - s/o Johannes Heylmann at Nied-
  erkirchen, and Maria Salome - w/o Bast Müller at Reichweyller.
Adam Klein aged 28, Ref., wheelwright, was in the 4th arrivals in
England in 1709 (London Lists).

Adam Klein made his first appearance on the Hunter Lists 4
July 1710 with 1 pers. over 10 yrs. of age. Adam Kleyn was nat.
31 Jan 1715/16 (Albany Nats.). Adam Klein and his wife Catharina
with 2 ch. were at Neu-Heidelberg ca. 1716/17 (Simmendinger Register). The aforementioned publication by Krebs and Yoder gives a
fascinating letter from Hans Adam Klein written from Conastocke
(Conestoga) in 1743 to relatives back in Germany:

   The grace of our dear Lord Jesus Christ, which is
better than life, inhabit and preserve, move, enliven and
inspirit all of our hearts, Amen.
   The great joy which I had on receipt of your letter,
which Cousin Ludwig brought over to this country, cannot
sufficiently be expressed, especially since I had had no
word from you in 33 yrs. Now I have found from your letter that you alone of all my brothers and sisters, are
still living. I wish you and your ch. further good health
and good fortune.
   As for me, after I left you in 1709 I finally arrived
in England, and at that time with still more of our countrymen (was sent) by Queen Anne over the sea to America,
and finally arrived in Georgin (York, i.e. New York?),
where I stayed as a single man some three yrs. in the
same neighborhood. Afterwards I was md. according to God's
will to a widow who was without ch. She is a native of
the Hundsrück, from the village of Kellwiler; her maiden
name was Han and she has brothers living in Gettebach and
Oberweiler on the Glan. We then had during our marriage
four ch., i.e., one son and three daughters, of whom two
daughters are still living and are both md. We live in
Albanien (Albany) and my ch. near me. I have worked at
my trade the entire time.
   If otherwise I have been well, yet I have had to
undergo many sicknesses, which also deprived me completely
of my hearing, so that I hear quite laboriously. Yet I
have, thank God, never suffered much want. But now since
I and my wife on account of old age and inconvenience cannot earn much anymore and I now have, through my Cousin
Johann Henrich Klein, heard the first news of you, but
now learn from your letter how my inheritance still stands
among my late brother Wendel's heirs, but in my old age
I am in very great need of what is mine, so along with my
son-in-law I have taken upon myself the far journey of
400 American miles, in order to go to our cousin, from
whom I have learned that he might make a trip to Germany,
so I knew no other way of executing my business than to
give Cousin Henrich full power of attorney, to look up
my properties and to deal with them as if I myself were
present, as you will see from the power of attorney,
which has been prepared by a county judge and justice of
the peace here and which I and my son-in-law have both
signed in our own hand. Now will you, dear Brother Jacob,

do so much for me and be helpful in all parts to Cousin Henrich, so that he can bring over what belongs to me.

When I left, our deceased brother Wendel gave me 70 florins for the journey, for which he was to make use of my properties, on condition, to be sure, that if I should return in three or four yrs., I should give him, Brother Wendel, the 70 florins back. At that time he should place my property in my hands again without attachment. But if I should stay away a longer time, then he should use the property in return for the above-mentioned 70 florins, besides paying the government and give back the property into my hands and minus the 70 florins. Now I believe they will be in accord with this agreement, since they have used it now for 33 yrs., and faithfully and fraternally place in my hand, through Cousin Henrich, what is mine from God and the law. Sontag of Albessen wrote down our agreement, which will surely still be at hand.

Among the 70 florins which the deceased Wendel gave me, were two ducats which were gilded but were of copper, which I had to throw away here in this country. My share of our late father's house I received namely half from Hanß Adam Seyler, the other half from Hanß Müller of Selchenbach, who has written it up, I for my part don't know any more how much it was. Lastly this is my will, that if, after giving for it what it is worth, my property remains among you, then each shall have a share of it like the other, you as as well as Brother Wendel and our late sister Catharina's surviving ch.

Moreover I should wish that before my death I might yet see one of my relationship here in this country, then I would be ready to part from the world more peacefully, since I am now old and weary of life and almost long for death. Sixty-three yrs. have gone by in my lifetime, I don't know how long the dear God may still let me live, yet I hope to see yet another letter from you. I could indeed have wished that one of my sons-in-law had been able to travel to you, but because they are natives of this country and have no knowledge of such a troublesome journey, also can scarcely leave their own properties, since they are both young beginners, also the travel costs on this account would be too heavy, so that they would bring back little of the capital. So I hope Cousin Henrich Klein will be received and recognized in our place.

We have stayed four days at Cousin Henrich's, during which at first I had great joy, but also at times have had to shed tears, since I learned from him and Cousin Ludwig that not only my Brother Wendel and Sister Catharina besides their husband and wife, also many friends have parted from this world. May the Lord give us who are still living, to consider that we must die, so that we become prudent and may prepare ourselves well and in a Christian manner for a blessed hour of death.

It would not really be necessary to write much to you of the state of this country. Cousin Henrich, if God lets him come safe and sound to you, will report everything in detail and with all faithfulness to you.

Also Cousin Henrich will tell you how at the time of my departure Brother Jacob brought me on the road, where then Old Benners who was called Magdalena, went down a piece of the way to the Griesswald, but my brother accompanied me to Duntzweiler, where I had left 200 birchen felloes, which he purchased from me and gave me a doubloon for them, which doubloon I put in his presence between the soles of my shoe, so that I should not lose it. From there we went to Schellweiler, where he

turned back. Also, dear brother, you will still remember
how Schäfer stole your new blue camisole from you, when
we were learning the cartwright trade at Wendel Lang's.
I should have like to report still other memories, but
don't think it necessary.

Lastly, I commend you, dear brother, nephews and
nieces, friends, relations and acquaintances, into the
protection of the Most High and, cordially greeting you
many thousand times, I am and remain till death
Your faithful brother, cousin and friend
Hans Adam Klein from Bubbach
N.B. My family, i.e., my wife and daughters, sons-in-law,
and four grandch., send you hearty greetings. Adieu.
Conastocke (Conestoga), 22 Aug 1743.
(Of the places named in the Hans Adam Klein letter, Dr.
Krebs suggests in his footnotes that Kellweiler is perhaps Gehlweiler (Simmern); Gettebach is Jettenbach (Kusel); Oberweiler is Oberweiler im Tal (Kusel), which
however is not on the Glan but some distance from it;
and Albessen is also in the Kusel area. Conestoga was
of course in Lancaster County, Pa.).

The 1743 letter mentioned that Hanß Adam[1] and Anna Catharina Han
Klein had one son and three daughters, one of whom was:

1) Anna Maria Clara[2], b. 2 Sept 1715 and bpt. at Schoharie -
sp.: J. Peter Thomas, Jerg Herchemer, and Ann Maria Baender (West Camp Luth. Chbk.).

PETER KLOPP (Hunter Lists #383)

Johann Peter Glopp, tailor of Horn in the commune Simmern
in the Pfaltz, md. 12 Sept 1711 Anna Magdalena, wid/o Johann Christoph Lutz of Klingen-Munster in the Pfaltz (West Camp Luth. Chbk.).
The Klopp ancestral village then was 6540 Horn (7 km. n. of Simmern; Chbks. begin 1655). The earliest known ancestor of the American pioneer was Johann Klopp at Horn who had three sons:

Johann Nicolaus, a sp. in 1677. There was a 1709er of that
name in the 5th party of Palatines at Rotterdam who was returned to Holland with his full family in 1711 (HJ).

Hans Veltin, md. as s/o Johann Klopp at Horn 19 Oct 1659 Eva,
d/o Quiten Müller at Bubach; they had 9 ch. bpt. at Horn.

+ Hans Barthel, conf. Christmas 1662 as s/o Johann Klopp at Horn.
Johann Bartel Klopp md. Maria Catharina, d/o the late Niclaus Juncker - formerly Schultheiß at Laubbach, 20 April 1669; it was a triple
marriage, as two of Maria Catharina brothers (Christoffel and Philipp) were md. the same day (HJ). Catharina, d/o Niclaus Juncker
the Schultheiß at Laubbach, was conf. ad Autumn 1661. Niclaus
Juncker, Schultheiß at Laubbach, was bur. 21 July 1656. Johann Barthel Klopp, teacher at Kißelbach, was bur. 13 Nov 1699. The ch.
of Johann Barthel Klopp and Maria Catharina were:

Anna Eva, bpt. 26 Dec 1670 - sp.: Anna Elisabeth - w/o Michel
Schneider at Horn, Eva - w/o Hans Velten Klopp there, and
Michel Schmitt at Chumbt.

Johanna Elisabetha, bpt. 22 Aug 1672 - sp.: Johanna Elisab.
- w/o Joseph Richter the Pfarrer there, and Christoffel Gehl
(?). She was bur. 22 Nov 1707, aged 35 yrs. and 3 months.

Anna Catharina, twin to the above, bpt. 22 Aug 1672 - sp.:
Anna Cath. - w/o Johannes Ulrich at Horn, and Christoffel
Juncker at Laubbach.

Maria Catharina, bpt. 28 March 1675 - sp.: Maria - w/o (?)
Friedrich Strack at Mörßbach, Eulalia Cath. - w/o (?) Anthon-
ius Breydenbach at Horn, and Michael - s/o the late Niclaß
Junckers at Laubbach.

Johannes Niclaß, bpt. 4 Feb 1677 - sp.: Johannes Christophel
- s/o the late Xstophel Benders at Horn, Joh. Niclas - s/o
the late Johs. Klopp there, and Anna Esther - d/o Hans Velten
Klopp at Horn. The child was bur. 11 Sept 1681.

Anna Maria, bpt. 28 Sept 1679 - sp.: Johan Creutz from ...,
Anna Maria - w/o Nicolaus Finck at Horn, and ... She d. 1698.

Johann Philippus, bpt. 5 Feb 1682 - sp.: Johan Wendel Feurer
from Kieselbach, Philippus Juncker from Laubach, and Anna Catarina - w/o Lamberch Demarker from Horn.

Johann Erasamus (bpt. as Erasmum), bpt. 31 Jan 1684 - sp.:
Johs. Erasmus Rumsteig (?) alias Maurius - Pastor Hornensiens,
Georg Mauß the younger from Laubach, and the w/o Hans Jacob
Hoffmann.

+ Johann Peter, bpt. 31/10 Nov 1686 - sp.: Hans Jacob ... at
Argenthal, Peter Landt at Horn, and Catharina - wid/o Niclas
Michel at Mieselbach.

Peter Klopp made his initial appearance on the Hunter Lists
4 Aug 1710 with 1 pers. over 10 yrs. of age. The entry for 24 Dec
1711 read 2 pers. over 10 yrs. of age in the household. Peter Clop
was nat. 17 Jan 1715/16 (Albany Nats.). Peter Klob and his wife
Magdalena with 2 ch. were at Neu-Ansberg ca. 1716/17 (Simmendinger
Register). Their last entry in colonial N.Y. was in 1720 when they
sp. Peter Wagener (Stone Arabia Luth. Family Book). Peter Klopp
came to the Tulpehocken region after 13 May 1723, but before Sept
1727 ("Early Tulpehocken Settlers" by Charles Adam Fisher in 1723-
1973, Anniversary Magazine of the Tulpehocken). The will of Peter
Klopp of Cocalico Twp was dated 11 Sept 1753 and probated 6 Jan
1755 and mentioned his wife and children (un-named) and a brother
Derrick Klopp (who was not found at Horn - HJ) (Lancaster Co. Will
Abstracts in the Genealogical Society of Pa., per Annette K. Burgert). Brother Peter Klop d. 1753 and Sister Magdalena Klop d. 1766
(Ephrata Death Register). The ch. of Peter[1] Klopp and Anna Magdalena were:

1) <u>Susanna</u>[2], b. 1 Jan 1716 and bpt. at Schoharie - sp.: Susanna Schutz (West Camp Luth. Chbk.).

2) <u>A Daughter</u>[2], who d. 6 Oct 1748, aged 30 yrs. and 8 months, and was bur. as Sister Thecla - the faithful d/o old Brother Peter Klopf (Ephrata Death Register).

3) <u>Peter</u>[2] (HJ), an executor of Peter Sr.'s will. He md., as her 3rd husband, Werina Becker (HJ). His dates at the Hain's Church Cem. in Berks Co., Pa. are 22 May 1719 - 22 May 1794, and for her there are 24 June 1713 - 22 Nov 1792.

SUSANNA' KLOTTERIN SON CASPAR (Hunter Lists #384)

Susanna, wid/o Johann Paul Clotter of Berchenheim by Weinheim in the Pfaltz, md. Johann Heinrich Poler of Alt-Zheim on the lower Rhine 24 Aug 1710 (West Camp Luth. Chbk.). The actual ancestral locale of the family was 6943 <u>Birkenau</u> (5 km. e. of Weinheim; Chbks. begin 1690). The registers there mention the death of one Catharina Kloder, wid/o the late Hans Jacob Kloder - formerly an inhabitant of Grießbach (?) in the Grafschaft Henau, on 27 Feb 1699; she probably was the mother of the emigrant Johann Paulus[1] (HJ). Johan Paul Kloter, his wife, and 4 ch. were listed on Capt. Frans Robbenson's ship 5 July 1709 in Holland (Rotterdam Lists). John Paul Clother aged 46, his wife, sons aged 18 and 7, daughters aged 9 and 4, Luth., husbandman and vinedresser, were in the 3rd arrivals in England (London Lists).

Susanna Klotterin with 2 pers. over 10 yrs. and 4 under 10 was noted 30 June 1710 on the Hunter Lists; the 4 Aug 1710 notation read 3 over 10 and 4 under 10 yrs., while the 4 Oct 1710 entry recorded 2 pers. over 10 and 3 under 10 yrs. The 31 Dec 1710 entry noted Susanna Klotterin's son Caspar with 1 pers. over 10 yrs. of age. The ch. of Johann Paulus[1] Klotter and Susanna were:

1) <u>Johann Caspar</u>[2], conf. Fest. Paschatos: 1707 aged 14 yrs. as Hans Caspar Gloter, s/o Paul Gloter (Birkenau Chbk.). Jasper Cladder was in Col. Thomas Ffarmar's Regt. in the 6th Co. in N.J. in 1715 (<u>Report of the State Historian</u>, Vol. I, p. 535). He was noted in the Janeway Accounts 1739/40 - 1742. He was one of several Luth. members of the Rareton, N.J. parish who wanted to go to the Anglican Church 12 Feb 1740 (<u>Luth. Church in N.Y. and N.J.</u>, pp. 151 & 155). Caspar[2] md. Jannet (--) (HJ) and had issue:

    i) <u>Paulus</u>[3], bpt. 3 Dec 1721 - sp.: Daniel ..., and Antje Van Etten (Readington Ref. Chbk.).

    ii) <u>Magdalena</u>[3], bpt. 3 May 1724 (Readington Ref. Chbk.).

2) <u>Anna Catharina</u>[2], b. 4 July 1699 - sp.: Anna Catharina

Schönherr (Birkenau Chbk.).

3) <u>Johannes[2]</u>, b. 30 Sept 1701 - sp.: Johannes Ehrhardt, s/o the smith here (Birkenau Chbk.).

4) <u>Elisabetha[2]</u>, b. 15 Jan 1706 - sp.: Elisabetha, w/o Theobald Schuh the weaver here (Birkenau Chbk.).

5) <u>Susanna Catharina[2]</u>, b. 7 July 1708 - sp.: Anna Catharina - d/o Johann Erhard Sr. the smith here (Birkenau Chbk.).

<u>HENRICH KLOTTER</u> (Hunter Lists #385)

He appeared once on the Hunter Lists as Henrich Klotter with 2 pers. over 10 yrs. of age and 2 under 10 in his household. He probably was the same man as #370 Henrich Ketter (see his section for more details).

<u>JOHANN GEORG KLUG</u> (Hunter Lists #386)

George Klug aged 37, with his wife, a son aged 1½, Ref., husbandman and vinedresser, was in the 1st arrivals in England in May 1709; also on these rolls was Georg Klug's sister's son - a boy of 15 yrs. (London Lists).

Johann Georg Klug made his initial appearance on the Hunter Lists 1 July 1710 with 2 pers. over 10 yrs. and 1 pers. under 10. The entry for 24 Dec 1711 read 3 pers. over 10 and 1 under 10 yrs., for 25 March 1712 noted 1 pers. over 10 and 1 under 10, and for 24 June 1712 recorded 2 pers. over 10 yrs. and 1 under 10 yrs. of age. Georg Klug and his wife Susanna with 2 ch. were in Hackensack ca. 1716/17, as were Hans Georg Gletch and his wife with 2 ch. (both Simmendinger Register). Perhaps Georg[1] mistakenly was entered as the Jeremiah Klooke, freeholder of Amwell, in 1741 (Hunterdon Co. Freeholders) (HJ). The ch. of Johann Georg[1] Klug and his wife Susanna Fisser (Fischer?) (HJ) were:

1) <u>Johannes[2]</u>, bpt. the middle of June 1710 on the ocean - sp.: Johann Mengis and Anna Maria Busch (West Camp Luth. Chbk. and N.Y. City Luth. Chbk.). A John Cluck is mentioned often in <u>A History of East Amwell</u>, pp. 67, 68, 73, 166 & 217.

2) <u>Anna[2]</u>, bpt. 13 Oct 1713 - sp.: Gideon Vervelen and Annatie Verbeelen (Tappan Ref. Chbk.).

<u>LUDWIG KNAB</u> (Hunter Lists #387)

Ludwig Knab was noted with 1 pers. over 10 and 1 under 10 yrs. 30 June 1710; the entry was for 2 over 10 and 2 under 10 on 4 Oct 1710. Catharina Knabin Wid[W] had but 1 pers. over 10 yrs. 31 Dec 1710; she was Ludwig Knab's Wid[W] Catharina 24 Dec 1711.

An Anna Barbara Knoet md. Abram Fort 15 Jan 1716 (Albany Ref. Chbk.), and papers in the estate of Frederick Knab of Tewksbury, Hunterdon Co., N.J. were admitted to probate 13 Aug 1766 (N.J. Wills: Lib. 12, p. 422); however, no connective has been established between them and #387 Ludwig Knab (HJ).

HELENA SOPHIA KNEIBIN (Hunter Lists #388)

Helena Sophia Kneibin made her initial appearance with 1 pers. over 10 yrs. of age on the Hunter Lists dated 1 July 1710; she was listed with Hubert Täschem on this entry. Helena Sophia Knipping md. Elderd Ouderkerk 24 July 1714 (Albany Ref. Chbk.).

HANNS PETER KNESKERN (Hunter Lists #389)

The Genesgern family was one of the most ancient families in the town of 6107 Reinheim (11 km. s.e. of Darmstadt; Chbks. begin 1575, thus yielding one of the oldest, documented pedigrees for any N.Y. 1709er emigrant). Perhaps an ancestor of the N.Y. emigrant was the Hans Genesgern mentioned with an Anna Genesgern and called Honoured in an inhabitant list of Reinheim dated 1575 (list published by Dr. Th. Meisinger, Reinheim). The earliest known firm ancestor of Hanns Peter[1] was his great great grandfather Hans Geneßgern, bur. 8 Aug 1621. He md. Christine Greßer, d/o Leonhard Greßer 31 Dec 1598; Katharina, w/o Lenhart Greser, was bur. 1 May 1609 there. They had issue:

+ Johannes, bpt. 6 Jan 1600 - sp.: Hans Puschmann.

Catharina, bpt. 25 April 1603 - sp.: Catharin, d/o the late Niclaus Remich.

Henrich, bpt. 12 Jan 1606 - sp.: Henrich Ramich. He md. Anna (--) 25 Oct 1635, and they both d. in 1637.

Hans Gnesgern b. in 1600 md. Barbara (--), who md. 2nd after the death of Hans to Hans Jakob Seyfried 25 Oct 1635; Barbara was bur. 20 Nov 1667, aged 68 yrs. as the wid/o Hans Jacob Seyfried. The ch. of Hans Gnesgern Jr. and wife Barbara were:

+ Christophel, bpt. 30 Oct 1625 - sp.: Stoffel Clentze (?) at Ober Ramstadt.

Anna, bpt. 4 May 1628 - sp.: Anna, d/o Hanß Melz.

Christophel Gnesgern at Reinheim was conf. 5 May 1642. Christophel Kneßgern, surviving s/o Hanß Kneßgern at Reinh., md. Anna, d/o the cartwright Peter Seyfried at Bieberau, 17 June 1650. Christoffel Gneßkern d. suddenly when he helped his son in the threshing-floor 11 Dec 1683; his widow Anna d. 22 Aug 1707. The issue of Christophel Knesgern and wife Anna were:

+ Johann Jacob, b. 29 June 1651.

Martin, b. 22 May 1653, md. 8 Aug 1676 Anna Margarete Bopp.

Johann Michael, b. 25 Sept 1655, md. 27 Sept 1688 Anna Kath-
arine Oswald, and 2nd 5 Feb 1691 Anna Dangel von Lichtenberg.
He md. 3rd 21 June 1701 Maria Elisabeth Diel. Joh. Michael
Kneskern d. 2 Dec 1714.

A Stillborn Daughter, b. and d. 19 May 1658.

Elisabetha Barbara, b. 14 June 1659 md. 23 Nov 1682 Hans Caspar
Ment at Erbach.

Johann Daniel, b. 3 Nov 1661, md. 21 Feb 1683 Anna Elisabeth
Neubauer and md. 2nd 8 Jan 1695 Anna Christine Decker. He d.
1 Oct 1707.

Anna Elisabetha, b. May 1664 and d. 11 Sept 1667.

Elisabetha Catharina, b. 24 May 1667 and d. May 1667.

Anna Elisabetha, b. 25 March 1669, md. 15 Sept 1687 Mr. Johan
Georg Schüler, and d. 13 Jan 1740 as a widow.

Anna Margaretha, b. 13 Jan 1672, md. 4 Nov 1697 the tanner
Johann Friedrich Cotte, and d. 26 Aug 1728.

Johann Jacob Knesgern b. in 1651 md. 23 Nov 1676 Veronica Forch.
Vronika, d/o the joiner Christoph Forch and his wife Katharina,
was b. in Jan 1645; Christoph Forch d. 12 July 1670 and his wife
Katharina d. 20 Dec 1680. Hanß Jacob Kneskern d. 17 Jan 1727, aged
76 yrs. less 5 months; Veronica, w/o Joh. Jacob Kneskern, d. 2
April 1711. The ch. of Johann Jacob Kneskern and Veronica were:

Johann Martin, b. 31 Aug 1677.

Maria Elisabetha, b. 13 Feb 1679, md. 19 July 1701 Johann Balthasar Storck, and d. 10 March 1741.

Margaretha, b. 19 March 1681, md. 8 Nov 1703 Johann Philipp
Greifenstein, and d. 11 Feb 1748 and bur. in Ueberau.

+ Johann Peter, b. 25 Oct 1683.

Georg Michael, twin to the emigrant, b. 25 Oct 1683 and d.
28 April 1684.

Elisabetha Margaretha, b. 26 Sept 1686, md. 28 Nov 1709 Joh.
Georg Schuchmann, d. 20 March 1769 as a widow.

Johan Peter Kneskern, s/o Johan Jacob Kneskern, md. 10 May 1708
Elisabetha Barbara, d/o the late Hans Adams at Kleinen Biberau.
Working with files in the Darmstadt Archives dealing with Klein-
Bieberau (a 1650 Seelenregister, and a 1684 Cent Lichtenberg),
data show that Elisabetha Barbara Adam was the d/o one Hans
Adam called the young, s/o Velten Adam b. before 1650, s/o Hans
Adam and wife Margaretha, s/o an early Philip Adam (HJ). Johan
Peter Kneskern and his wife were recorded on Capt. Francois Waren's
ship in Holland 3 July 1709 (Rotterdam Lists).

Hanns Peter Kneskern made his initial appearance on the Hunter Lists 30 June 1710 with 2 pers. over 10 yrs. of age. The family

was registered with 3 pers. over 10 yrs. of age 24 June 1711 and
thereafter. Jno. Peter Kneserkn of Hunterstown was a Captain with
the soldiers to Canada in 1711 (Palatine Volunteers To Canada).
Reel #3 of the Livingston Papers makes reference to Domine Hager's
and Capt. Kniskern's passage to N.Y. 4 Aug 1712. Peter Kneskern
was nat. 11 Oct 1715 (Albany Nats.). Johann Peter Knekkern and his
wife Elisabetha Barbara with 3 ch. were at Neu-Heidelberg ca.
1716/17 (Simmendinger Register). Berkenmeyer noted him often in
his Albany Protocol; for example, he wrote in 1734:

> The sun had gone down when we arrived at Scoghary. I had
> been told that the deacons were Peter Kniskern and Han-
> nes Scheffer. So I went to P[eter] K[niskern], who lived
> nearer by. His wife stood at the door and told me that
> they had no pasture. She persisted in this, even after I
> had told her my name. Finally she said that neither her
> husband nor Scheffer were deacons, but that Abraham Berts
> was. His house I had passed on the left coming into Sco-
> hary. Her husband arrived with a gun on his shoulder, but
> his wife called to him to go over the stream and drive
> the beasts out of the grain. I said I would hold services
> tomorrow (pp. 96-98).

After the services, the Pastor wrote:

> On leaving, I got to thinking about the many tears I had
> shed in my prayers a week ago. My weeping must have oc-
> curred because I saw how far Scoghary was from our Luth-
> eran Jerusalem, since they would neither acknowledge nor
> consider what could serve them for their peace. Coming
> home, H[annes] L[awyer] asked if I would like a dram.
> And when I replied Yes, if he had one, he laughed and
> ordered a cup. After dinner, they went to the pasture.
> When they returned, P[eter] Kniskern stepped up to me
> and said, "You proved your love for us by preaching the
> word of God. We thank you for this love." Here he broke
> down and I replied, "It is enough for me that you ac-
> knowledge it as a proof of love" (pp. 100-101).

Joh. Peter Kneskern was called one of the leaders and elders of
the Luth. congregation at Schoharie in Aug 1741 (Luth. Church in
N.J. and N.J., p. 171). His family appeared on Pastor Sommer's
Luth. Family List of Schoharie ca. 1744. Peter Knieskern was a
freeholder at Schoharrie in 1763 (Albany Co. Freeholders). Old
Jo. Peter Kniskern d. 11 Nov 1759, and his widow d. 31 Oct 1770,
aged 83 yrs. (both Schoharie Luth. Chbk.). (Note that the 1759
death date conflicts with the 1763 Freeholder's record- HJ). The
ch. of Johann Peter[1] and Elisabetha Barbara Kneskern were:

1) Mary[2], bpt. recorded as d/o Peter Snesky, a Palatine, b.
   at sea 5 July 1709 and bpt. London 11 July 1709 (St. Al-
   phege or Alfege Church at Greenwich, found by my friends
   Norman C. Wittwer and John P. Dern). Johann Peter[1] Kneskern
   was indeed at sea at that very time; also, in a few other
   Palatine families, the "n" ending was written "y" (Jacob
   Teshine became Jacob Tesky once the 1709er arrived in Ireland), so I strongly believe this girl was actually d/o

Johann Peter[1] Kneskern, as no other emigrant in the 5th party at Rotterdam seems to fit the Snesky reference (HJ).

2) <u>Johann Henrich[2]</u>, md. as s/o Johann Peter[1] 12 Oct 1736 Elisabetha Schäffer, d/o Johannes (Loonenburg Luth. Chbk.). He appeared on Pastor Sommer's Luth. Family List ca. 1744 (Schoharie Luth. Chbk.). Henrich, Jost, John, and Pitter Kniskern, Jr. were all in Capt. Jacob Sternberger's Company 2 May 1767 at Schohare (<u>Report of the State Historian</u>, Vol. II, pp. 842 & 843). The will of Henrich Knieskern of Shoharry, Albany Co. was dated 8 May 1780 and probated 4 Aug 1784 (<u>Fernow Wills</u> #1001). The ch. of Henrich[2] were:

 i) <u>Johann Peter[3]</u>, b. 17 July 1737 and bpt. at Schohari - sp.: Peter Kniskern and Liese Barbel, gr-parents (Loonenburg Luth. Chbk.). He md. Anna Catharina Kayser 22 Oct 1760 (Schoharie Luth. Chbk.).

 ii) <u>Anna Maria[3]</u>, bpt. 8 Dec 1738 - sp.: Johannes Schefer and Anna Maria Scheiffer (Schoharie Ref. Chbk.).

 iii) <u>Henrich[3]</u>, bpt. 15 May 1740 - sp.: Hendrick Scheffer Jr. and Maria Elisabeth Knieskern (Schoharie Ref. Chbk.). He md. Eva Schafer 19 Aug 1763 (Schoharie Luth. Chbk.).

 iv) <u>Johann Jost[3]</u> (Sommer's List 1744), md. Elisabeth Margareth Hauck 18 Oct 1763 (Schoharie Luth. Chbk.).

 v) <u>Elisabetha[3]</u>, b. 28 June 1743 - sp.: Gotfried Kniskern and his wife Anna Margaretha Kniskern (Schoharie Luth. Chbk.). She md. 24 Oct 1768 Philip Kayser (Schoharie Luth. Chbk.).

 vi) <u>Catharina[3]</u>, b. 21 Feb 1745 - sp.: Jost Kniskern and Catharina Schäfer (Schoharie Luth. Chbk.). She md. Jost Becker (Will).

 vii) <u>Johannes[3]</u>, b. 22 March 1746 - sp.: Johannes Schäfer Jr. and his wife (Schoharie Luth. Chbk.). He md. Margreta Ender 20 Oct 1772 (Schoharie Luth. Chbk.).

 viii) <u>Wilhelm[3]</u>, b. 15 May 1748 - sp.: Wilhelm Enters and his wife (Schoharie Luth. Chbk.).

 ix) <u>Martinus[3]</u>, b. 25 April 1750 - sp.: Martinus Schäfer and Christina Schäfer (Schoharie Luth. Chbk.).

 x) <u>Gotfried[3]</u>, b. 11 June 1752 - sp.: Gotfried Kniskern and wife (Schoharie Luth. Chbk.). A little boy of Henrich Kneskern d. 4 Aug 1752.

 xi) <u>Jacob[3]</u>, b. 21 Nov 1753 - sp.: Jacob Schäfer and his wife Elisabeth (Schoharie Luth. Chbk.). He d. 9 March 1818, aged 64 yrs. (Sloansville Village Cem.).

 xii) <u>Magdalena[3]</u>, b. 24 May 1756 - sp.: Adam Schäfer and

his wife (Schoharie Luth. Chbk.). She d. 25 May 1759
(Schoharie Luth. Chbk.).

xiii?) Anna Maria³, b. 15 July 1760 - sp.: Johannes Schäfer
and his wife Anna Maria (Schoharie Luth. Chbk.).

3) Elisabetha Margaretha², bpt. 14 Aug 1714 - sp.: Hannes
and An. Marg. Gremmer, and Elizabeth Hanghin (Albany Ref.
Chbk.). She md. Wilhelm Enders (HJ).

4) Anna Maria², b. 30 Dec 1715 and bpt. at Schoharie - sp.:
Anna Maria Baender (West Camp Luth. Chbk.). She md. Johannes Becker (HJ).

5) Johann Gottfried², b. 26 April 1717 and bpt. at Schoharie
- sp.: Johann Gottfrid Fidler and his wife (West Camp
Luth. Chbk.). He had banns to marry Anna Margaretha Stubrach 16 June 1739, when both lived Huntersfield (Schoharie
Ref. Chbk.). Gadfrey Knieskern was a freeholder at Schoharrie in 1763 (Albany Co. Freeholders). His ch. were:

   i) Elisabetha³, bpt. 3 Aug 1740 - sp.: Joost Knieskern
    and Elisabeth Berg (Schoharie Ref. Chbk.). She d. 23
    April 1746, aged 5 yrs. and 9 months (Schoharie Luth.
    Chbk.).

  ii) Maria Margaretha³, bpt. July 1742 - sp.: Hendrick
    Stuprach and his wife (Schoharie Ref. Chbk.). She md.
    Johannes Schafer Jr. 5 March 1766 (Schoharie Luth.
    Chbk.).

 iii) Catharina³, b. 9 Aug 1744 - sp.: Jurgen Henrich Stub-
    rach and wife (Schoharie Luth. Chbk.).

  iv) Elisabetha³, b. 11 Nov 1746 - sp.: Henrich Kniskern
    and his wife (Schoharie Luth. Chbk.).

   v) Peter³, b. 8 Oct 1748 - sp.: Johan Peter Kniskern and
    his wife (Schoharie Luth. Chbk.).

  vi) Christina³, b. 22 March 1751 - sp.: Philip Berg and
    his wife (Schoharie Luth. Chbk.).

 vii) Maria³, b. 29 Aug 1753 - sp.: Maria Kniskern and Peter
    Becker (Schoharie Luth. Chbk.).

viii) Eva³, b. 12 June 1756 - sp.: Jost Kniskern and his
    wife (Schoharie Luth. Chbk.).

  ix) Henrich³, b. 20 July 1759 - sp.: Henrich Kniskern Jr.
    and Elisabeth Merckel (Schoharie Luth. Chbk.). He d.
    5 Oct 1845, aged 86 yrs. and 10 months (Cem. on a
    farm near Cobleskill).

   x) Maria Elisabetha³, bpt. 1761 - sp.: Christian Schafer
    and wife (Schoharie Luth. Chbk.).

  xi) Christina³, b. 26 Oct 1763 - sp.: Philip Berg and
    wife (Schoharie Luth. Chbk.).

6) <u>Johann Jost²</u>, md. as s/o Joh. Peter¹ 15 Oct 1745 Catharina
Schäfer, d/o Henrich (Schoharie Luth. Chbk.). He was conf.
Trin: 1737 at Scohare (Loonenburg Luth. Chbk.). Jost d. 13
Feb 1757 of the small-pox (Schoharie Luth. Chbk.). Issue:

    i) <u>Maria³</u>, b. 4 Nov 1746 - sp.: Anna Maria Schäfer and
       Johannes Kniskern (Schoharie Luth. Chbk.).

7) <u>Johannes²</u> (Sommers List 1744), md. 22 March 1748 Sophia
Schäfer (Schoharie Luth. Chbk.). Johannis Kniskerl was in
Capt. Ackeson's Company in 1767 (<u>Report of the State His-
torian</u>, Vol. II, p. 845). The will of Johannes Kniskern of
Bristol was dated 6 June 1803 (Schoharie Co. Will Bk. A).
The ch. of Johannes² and Sophia Kneskern were:

    i) <u>Catharina³</u>, b. 18 June 1748 - sp.: Jost Kniskern and
       his wife (Schoharie Luth. Chbk.).

    ii) <u>Henrich³</u>, b. 17 Aug 1749 - sp.: Captain Henrich Schä-
       fer and his wife (Schoharie Luth. Chbk.).

    iii) <u>Johannes³</u>, b. 9 May 1751 - sp.: Johannes Becker and
       his wife (Schoharie Luth. Chbk.).

    iv) <u>Christian³</u>, b. 5 March 1753 - sp.: Christian Schäfer
       and his wife (Schoharie Luth. Chbk.).

    v) <u>Elisabetha Barbara³</u>, b. 11 March 1755 - sp.: Johan
       Peter Kniskern and wife (Schoharie Luth. Chbk.).

    vi) <u>Nicolaus³</u>, b. 26 Jan 1757 - sp.: Johan Nickel Becker
       and wife (Schoharie Luth. Chbk.). He d. 7 Sept 1766,
       aged 9 yrs. and 8 months (Schoharie Luth. Chbk.).

    vii) <u>Sarah³</u>, b. 3 June 1759 - sp.: Philip Kayser and Sara
       Schäfer (Schoharie Luth. Chbk.).

    viii) <u>Maria Margaretha³</u>, b. 8 March 1761 - sp.: Gotfried
       Kniskern and wife (Schoharie Luth. Chbk.).

    ix) <u>Anna³</u>, b. 18 Sept 1762 - sp.: Jacob Schafer and wife
       (Schoharie Luth. Chbk.).

    x) <u>Peter³</u>, b. 25 June 1764 - sp.: Peter Kniskern and
       wife Catharina (Schoharie Luth. Chbk.).

    xi) <u>Elisabetha³</u>, b. 6 April 1766 - sp.: Lorentz Lawyer
       and wife (Schoharie Luth. Chbk.).

    xii) <u>Christian³</u>, b. 2 Jan 1768 - sp.: Christian Schafer
       and wife (Schoharie Luth. Chbk.).

    xiii) <u>Johann Jost³</u>, b. 24 May 1769 - sp.: Jost Werner and
       wife (Schoharie Luth. Chbk.).

    xiv) <u>Barent³</u>, b. 14 Jan 1771 - sp.: Barent Keiser and wife
       (Schoharie Luth. Chbk.).

8) <u>Maria Elisabetha²</u> (Sommers List 1744), conf. at Scohare
17 June 1739 (Loonenburg Luth. Chbk.). She md. Christian
Schäfer 20 Oct 1747 (Schoharie Luth. Chbk.).

JACOB KOBEL (Hunter Lists #390)

Jacob Cobel aged 27, his wife, a son aged ½, Catholic, miller, were in the 4th arrivals in England in 1709 (London Lists).

Jacob Kobel made his initial appearance on the Hunter Lists 30 June 1710 with 1 pers. over 10 yrs. of age. The family was shown with 2 pers. over 10 yrs. 4 Aug 1710, and then 2 over 10 and 1 under 10 yrs. 13 Sept 1712. Jacob Kobell of Hunterstown was a soldier in 1711 (Palatine Volunteers To Canada). Jacob Kobel and his wife Anna Maria with 2 ch. were at Neu-Heidelberg ca. 1716/17 (Simmendinger Register). Jeptha Simms wrote, "In the course of twenty or thirty yrs. after Weiser and his friends left, several other mills were established in and about Schoharie. One Cobel erected two of those" (Simm's History of Schoharie, p. 80); Cobleskill, N.Y. took its name from this 1709er (HJ). His name appears on Tulpehocken, Pa. tax and road lists beginning in 1726/27 (The Hub of the Tulpehocken, by Earl W. Ibach, p. 12). The will of Jacob Kobel was dated 7 Aug 1731 and filed 16 March 1732/33 (Philadelphia Co. Will Bk. E, p. 184). An especially fine article on Jacob¹ Kobel has been written by Shirley J. Turner, C. G., and published in the National Genealogical Society Quarterly for Sept 1981 and should be studied by all serious students of the family. The ch. of Jacob¹ Kobel and Anna Maria were:

1) Maria Sybilla² (HJ), md. 13 Aug 1734 Johann Adam Diefenbach at Tulpehocken (Stoever Chbks.).

2) Johann Henrich², b. 20 July 1712 - sp.: Johann Henrich Schraemmle (West Camp Luth. Chbk.). He most probably was the (--) Kobel massacred with many of his ch. in Nov 1755. Shirley Turner gives as his ch.:
   i) Johannes³.
   ii) Johann Henrich³.
   iii) Johann Friederich³.
   iv) Johann Jacob³, md. as s/o Henrich² 19 March 1776 Margaretha Elisabetha Emrich (Rehrersburg Chbk.).

3) Maria Barbara² (HJ), md. 10 June 1735 Jacob Schäffer (Reed's Church, Tulpehocken, Chbk.).

4) Johannes², conf. as s/o Jacob¹ on Quasimotogeniti: 1744 (Tulpehocken Chbk.). The will of John Kobel of Heidelberg Twp. was dated 14 Oct 1783 and probated 26 Nov 1783 (Berks Co. Will Bk. A, p. 53). He md. Catharina (--) and had ch.:
   i) Catharina³ (Will), md. Alexander Groh (HJ).
   ii) Elisabetha³ (Will), md. Wendel Weber (HJ).
   iii) Maria Engel³ (Will), md. 29 Nov 1774 John Zeller (HJ).
   iv) Susanna³ (Will, md. 15 Feb 1778 John Keiser (HJ).

5) <u>Maria Engel</u>[2] (Shirley Turner), md. Johann Friederich Rieth (Shirley Turner).

6) <u>Anna Maria Catharina</u>[2] (HJ), md. as orphan d/o the late (--) Kobell 26 June 1744 Johann Simon Binetsch (Tulpehocken Chbk.).

7) <u>Friederich Christian Gottfried</u>[2], conf. as s/o Jacob[1] on Quasimotogeniti: 1744 as just Gottfrid (Tulpehocken Chbk.). He was a carpenter and co-owner with his brother Johannes[2] of their father's grist mill at Plumpton Manor (Shirley Turner). He md. Veronica (--). Papers in the estate of Frederick Kobel of Heidelberg Twp. were granted 2 May 1803 to his relict Francia (Berks Co. Will Bk. 6, p. 107). Ch.:

   i) <u>Elisabetha</u>[3] (Berks Co. Deeds: Vol. 20, p. 22), md. Leonhard Seltzer (HJ).

  ii) <u>Barbara</u>[3] (Berks Co. Deeds: Vol. 20, p. 22), md. Peter Deppen (HJ).

 iii) <u>Johann Jacob</u>[3], conf. as s/o Frederick[2] Whitesunday: 1774, aged 17 yrs. (Christ Luth. Stouchsburg Chbk.). His will was filed 5 Nov 1793 (Berks Co. Will Bk. 4, p. 400).

8) <u>Jacob Nicolaus</u>[2] (Shirley Turner), md. Margaretha (--) (Shirley Turner) and had issue:

   i) <u>Johann Georg</u>[3], b. 2 May 1756 - sp.: Georg Hollstein and Efrosina Brosman (un-named source from Shirley Turner).

GEORG LUDWIG KOCH (Hunter Lists #391)

A Georg Ludwig Koch, barber, and wife Anna Catharina were documented at 7141 <u>Großbottwar</u>. They had ch. Stephan Ludwig bpt. 29 Oct 1686, Johann Georg bpt. 23 Sept 1688, and Rosina Catharina bpt. 1 Jan 1691 there; however, no firm proof has been found linking this family to the N.Y. settler (HJ). Jürg Kogh, his wife, and 4 ch. were in the 6th party sailing from Holland in 1709 (Rotterdam Lists).

Georg Ludwig Koch made his first appearance on the Hunter Lists 1 July 1710 with 2 pers. over 10 yrs.; the entry for 4 Aug 1710 read 1 pers. over 10 yrs., for 31 Dec 1710 showed 2 over 10, and for 29 Sept 1711 recorded 2 pers. over 10 yrs. and 1 under 10. The family had another entry for 4 Oct 1710 with 2 pers. over 10 yrs. in addition to the one showing just 1 pers. over 10. Geo. Lud. Koch of Hunterstown was a soldier in 1711 (Palatine Volunteers To Canada). Anna Maria Kochin, a widow with 3 ch., was at Hunderston ca. 1716/17 (Simmendinger Register). Anna Mar: Koehin was a Palatine

Debtor in 1718 (Livingston Debt Lists). A mss. in Reel #4 of the
Livingston Papers dated 24 April 1721 deals with the disposition
of some movables and land in one of the Palatine villages which
belonged to ye widow woman called Widow Cochin, who was condemned
for murder. The ch. of Georg Ludwig[1] Koch and his wife Anna Maria
were:

1) Anna Margaretha[2] (HJ), md. Johann Friederich Weller (HJ).
   They had a son Jurg Lodewich bpt. in 1748 at Kingston Ref.
2) Maria Idia[2] (HJ), perhaps Maria Ottilia?, a sp. to Joh.
   Friederich Weller and Anna Margaretha[2] Koch in 1743 at
   Montgomery Ref. Church.

There were other Koches-Cooks who were in N.Y. at an early
date: 1) a Rötscher Koek came from N.J. and had sons Adam, Joris,
and Jan who settled near the Hudson (HJ); 2) a Caspar Koch came from
Ober-Steinmur in Switzerland and d. at Stone Arabia 14 Jan 1790,
aged 89 yrs. and 7 months (Stone Arabia Ref. Chbk.), and 3) a Samuel Cock was in the foot Company of the Marbletown, Ulster Co. Militia in 1738 (Report of the State Historian, Vol. I, p. 606).

JOSUA KOCHERTHAL (Hunter Lists #392)

Palatine scholars and descendants owe a great debt to the late
Pastor Heinz Schuchmann: it was he who first discovered that Josua
Harrsch, Pastor at 6925 Eschelbronn, emigrated from Germany to colonial N.Y. in 1708 and became known as Josua Kocherthal, Pastor at
West Camp. Schuchmann's articles, "Der 1708 nach Amerika ausge-
wanderte Pfarrer Josua Kocherthal hieß ursprünglich Josua Harrsch"
and "Sibylla Charlotta Winchenbach - die Ehefrau Josua Kocherthals",
were both published by the dedicated Palatine archivist and scholar Dr. Fritz Braun in his series Mitteilungen zur Wanderungsgesch-
ichte der Pfälzer in 1967 and 1970/1. Schuchmann found that Pastor
Josua[1] Harrsch-Kocherthal's grandfather was Jakob Harrsch, b. in
Leinroden in 1580, md. Maria Merz 7 Nov 1609, and d. 28 Aug 1635.
The father of the emigrant was Hans Jörg Harrsch, b. in Leinroden
in 1610 and d. in Fachsenfeld in 1675. Hans Jörg md. 1st 25 July
1630 Walburga Sattler and had 4 ch.; he md. 2nd 7 May 1639 Katharina Adelmann and had 15 ch.; and Hans Jörg md. 3rd Elisabeth Leonhard 18 Aug 1668 and had 4 ch. (a total of 23 ch.!). Pastor Josua[1]
Harrsch-Kocherthal was b. 30 July 1669 at Fachsenfeld. He was or-
dained at Sindolsheim in 1696. Josua[1] md. Sibylla Charlotta Winchenbach, most probably the d/o Pastor Johann Jakob Winchenbach, b.
at Herborn in 1637 and d. 6 April 1702, aged 64 yrs. at Gericht-
stetten; Pastor Winchenbach md. Charlotta Margaretha, d/o Pastor
Nicolaus Treviranus in Herborn on Whitmonday: 1665. The history

of Pastor Kocherthal is well-chronicled in many books, especially
in Knittle's <u>Early Eighteenth Century Palatine Emigration</u>. Joshua
de Kocherdal, his wife Sibylle Charlotte, and ch. Benigna Sibylle
aged 10, Christian Joshua aged 7, and Susanna Sibylle aged 3, were
in the 1708 immigration to N.Y. (<u>Knittle</u>, p. 243).

Josua Kocherthal made his initial appearance on the Hunter
Lists 31 Dec 1710 with 1 pers. over 10 yrs. of age. The household
increased to 4 pers. over 10 yrs. and 2 pers. under 10 yrs. on 29
Sept 1711. Mr. Kocherthales: 1 man, was in Ulster Co. in 1710/11
(West Camp Census). The Pastor d. St. Johannistage: 1719 (Kocher-
thal Memorial Tablet, West Camp). The ch. of Pastor Josua[1] Harrsch-
Kocherthal and his wife Sibylla Charlotta Winchenbach were:

1) <u>Benigna Sibylla[2]</u>, b. 14/24 Aug 1697 - sp.: Frau Benigna
   von Festenburg of Münchzell - b. Gemmingerin, Frau Sara
   - wid/o H. Friedrich Müller ..., and H. Rudolf Häger -
   Inwohner of Spechbach (Eschelbronn Chbk.). She md. Pastor Wilhelm Christ: Berkenmeyer 25 Oct 1727 (N.Y. City Luth. Chbk.).

2) <u>Johannes[2]</u>, b. 5 July 1700 - sp.: Herr Johannes Sebastian
   Böhlius, Pastor at Reichartshausen (Eschelbronn Chbk.).
   He d. 14 Jan 1701 (Eschelbronn Chbk.).

3) <u>Christian Josua[2]</u>, b. 10 Dec 1701 - sp.: H. Johann David
   Virnhaber ... (Eschelbronn Chbk.). He md. Catlyntje Bensen 26
   Oct 1729 and d. 21 7br 1732 (both N.Y. City Luth. Chbk.).

4) <u>Susanna Sibylla[2]</u>, b. 16 Jan 1705 (Eschelbronn Chbk.). She
   was conf. 27 Oct 1728 in the City of N.Y. as Susanna Sybilla Hurtyn b. Kocherthal (N.Y. City Luth. Chbk.). She md.
   Wm. Heurtin, a Frenchman, 6 May 1727 (N.Y. City Luth. Chbk.).

5) <u>Louisa Abigail[2]</u>, b. 26 Feb 1710 at N.Y. - sp.: Daniel Luet-
   ken, M.D., and Abigail Lispenaer (West Camp Luth. Chbk.).
   She was conf. as Louysa Sybilla Kocherthal 26 Oct 1729 at
   N.Y. (N.Y. City Luth. Chbk.). She md. Johannes Brevoort
   (<u>Albany Protocol</u>, p. 531).

CATHARINA KOHLMEYERIN (Hunter Lists #393)

Catharina Kohlmeyerin made her initial appearance on the Hunter Lists 4 Oct 1710 with 1 pers. over 10 yrs. of age in the family.

ANNA EVA KÖLSCH (Hunter Lists #394)

Anna Eva Kolsch made her only appearance on the Hunter Lists
4 Oct 1710 with 1 pers. over 10 yrs. of age in the family. The Hum-
mer Family Bible notes that Harbert Hommer md. in 1727 in this land
Donges Kolscher's lawful daughter by the name of Eva who came with
her father to this land in 1722, her father having lived in Germany

in the Principality of Nassau in the Office of Beilstein, Parish
of Marienberg, in the village of Nassau ... (transcription by Donald A. Sinclair in the Hunterdon Historical Society Newsletter,
Fall, 1975). If the 1722 arrival date is in error, perhaps this
girl was our #394 Anna Eva Kölsch (HJ).

JOHANN HENRICH KÖLSCH (Hunter Lists #395)

A Henrich, s/o Henrich Kölsch and wife Elss, was bpt. Dom. 2:
1669 - sp.: Henrich, surviving s/o Johann Schmidt, at 5439 Bad
Marienberg, mentioned as a home locale for #394 Anna Eva Kölsch
aforementioned. Also one Joh. Henrich Kölschen md. 26 Aug 1707
Anna Maria Hofmann from Ullrichstein at Eberstadt, probably the
6302 Eberstadt-Lich. No proof firmly connects either Henrich Kölsch
to the 1709er (HJ).

Johann Henrich Kölsch made his first appearance on the Hunter
Lists 4 Oct 1710 with 1 pers. over 10 yrs. of age. On the cumulative entry for 24 Dec 1711 he was called Johannes Kelsch.

MARCUS KÖNIG (Hunter Lists #396)

J. Marcus Koning, printer of N.Y. of the principality of Halberstadt, md. 15 Sept 1713 Susanna, wid/o the late Herman Schoeck-
mann - potter at Kipsberry (N.Y. City Luth. Chbk.). This Palatine
printer was documented at 6348 Herborn (22 km. n.e. of Westerburg;
Chbks. begin 1638). Johann Marcus König, printer-fellow here and
s/o the late Johann Konigs - trabanten bey Churf. Durchl. zu Bran-
denburg, md. Anna Eliesabeth, wid/o the late Johannes Hugen (?)
... at home 4 April 1701. Joh. Markus König, Halberstadensis,
Buchdruckergeselle, was listed as #3371 of the Matrikel of the
Hoheschule in Herborn in 1691. Joh. Marcus Koenig, his wife, and
3 ch., from Halberstadt and now living at Herborn as a book printer,
petitioned to leave in 1709 (Nassau-Dillenburg Petitions). Johan
Markus Keüning, his wife, and 3 ch. were in the 6th party of Palatines in Holland in 1709 (Rotterdam Lists).

Marcus König made his initial appearance on the Hunter Lists
4 July 1710 with 4 pers. over 10 yrs. of age. Johann Marx Konig
was noted with 2 over 10 and 2 under 10 yrs. on 4 Aug 1710. He was
recorded with 4 pers. over 10 yrs. on 24 June 1711, and 3 over 10
and 1 under 10 on 29 Sept 1711. Johann Marcus King of N.Y., printer,
was nat. 8 Nov 1715 at N.Y. City (Denizations, Naturalizations,
and Oaths of Allegiance in Colonial N.Y., p. 39). Marcus Konig
Buchdrucker and his wife with 2 ch. were at Neu Yorck ca. 1716/17
(Simmendinger Register). Joh. Marc. Konig subscribed money to the
church in 1727 (N.Y. City Luth. Protocol). He was mentioned in a

letter from Rev. Johann A. Wolf at Rareton to the Rev. Michael C. Knoll 2 Nov 1736 (Luth. Church in N.Y. and N.J., p. 127). Markas King was noted in the Janeway Accounts May 1736 - March 1744/45. The ch. of Marcus[1] König and his wife Anna Elisabetha (who was a- live as late as 24 Feb 1712/13 when she joined the N.Y. City Ref. Church as w/o J[S] M[S] Koning of Herborn) were:

1) Johann David[2], bpt. 21 Jan 1702 - sp.: Johann David Andrae, printer-fellow here (Herborn Chbk.). David Konig subscribed £1 in 1727 (N.Y. City Luth. Protocol). He also was recorded in the Janeway Accounts, sometimes with his father. David, Marcus, Johann, and Luke King (Koenig) were all vestrymen at St. Paul's Church, Pluckemin in various yrs. during the 1767 - 1772 period (Letter From John P. Dern to HJ, 29 April 1977). David Coning, single man of Germany, md. 22 Nov 1724 Catharina Thiple, single woman of Germany (N.Y. City Ref. Chbk.). They had issue:

   i) Marcus[3], bpt. 27 Jan 1725 - sp.: Bartholomeüs Miller and Maria (N.Y. City Ref. Chbk.). He may have been the Markos Konig who signed the Articles of Faith of the New Germantown Church in 1767 (Chambers, p. 432).

   ii) Johannes[3], b. 2 April 1727 - sp.: Marcus Konig and the w/o Bartheld Miller (N.Y. City Luth. Chbk.).

   iii) Elisabetha[3], b. 25 Sept 1729 - sp.: Jacob Kuhn and Liesabeth Erb (N.Y. City Luth. Chbk.).

   iv) Lucas[3], bpt. 21 April 1733/34 aged ... old - sp.: Lucas Dippel and wife Maria (N.Y. City Luth. Chbk.).

2) Catharina Elisabetha[2], bpt. 12 Jan 1705 - sp.: Catharina Eliesabetha, d/o H. Nicolaus Andrä (Herborn Chbk.). Per- haps she is related to the Elisabeth Koning, wid/o George Perker, and Maria Koning, wife of Benjamin Sjervis, who both joined the N.Y. City Ref. Church 21 Aug 1739 (HJ).

3) Johann Philipp[2], b. 2 Sept 1708 - sp.: Johann Philipp Nies, citizen at Herborn (Herborn Chbk.).

JACOB KOPFF (Hunter Lists #397)

A Hans Jacob Kopf and wife Anna Barbara had a daughter Eva b. 1706 at 6901 Schönau; however, no firm connective has been est- ablished from this family to the 1709er (HJ). Jacob Kop, his wife, and 4 ch. were on Capt. William Koby's ship 6 July 1709 in the 5th party of Palatines in Holland (Rotterdam Lists).

Jacob Kopff made his initial appearance on the Hunter Lists 4 Oct 1710 with 1 pers. over 10 yrs.; the entry for Anna Sybilla Kabsin that date adds vid Kopff. Jacob Kopff had 4 pers. over 10

yrs. and 2 under 10 on 31 Dec 1710. His entry for 29 Sept 1711 read
5 over 10 and 1 under 10 yrs., for 24 Dec 1711 showed 4 over 10
yrs. and 1 under 10, and for 24 June 1712 recorded 6 pers. over 10
yrs. of age. Jacob Cup of Haysbury was a soldier in 1711 (Palatine
Volunteers To Canada). Jacob Kop was nat. 11 Oct 1715 (Albany
Nats.). He came to the Tulpehocken region after 13 May 1723, but
before 1725, because on 10 Jan of that yr. his name was on the 1st
tax list compilied for that section ("Early Tulpehocken Settlers",
by Charles Adam Fisher in 1723 - 1973 Anniversary Magazine of the
Tulpehocken). In this area he settled on a farm in the s.w. part
of Plumpton Manor. This farm contained 149 acres and 65 perches,
and was purchased from John Page on 5 Dec 1739 for the sum of £59,
15 sh. (From Edgar H. Berge's fine study of the original Tulpehocken
landowners, published in Die Shilgrut, Vol. VI, No. 1, Nov 1975).
The will of Jacob Kope of Tulpehocken in Lancester Co. was dated
3 Feb 1741/42 (Philadelphia Co. Will Bk. F, p. 279). In his will,
Jacob[1] specifically stated that Adam Lesh, Georg Lesh, and Elisabeth Madelina Braun were his step-children and mentioned his wife
Susanna; this shows that he md. Susanna Philippina, the wid/o the
emigrant 1709er Johann Balthasar Lesch (HJ). The known issue of
Jacob[1] Kopff were:

> 1) Anna Sophia[2], called my own child in his 1741 will. The
> Tulpehocken Chbk. noted that Anna Sophia, d/o John Jacob
> Kapp and w/o Johann Adam Lesch, was b. 13 Oct 1695 and was
> bur. as a wid. 10 March 1771, aged 76 yrs. and 4 months.
> Anna Sophia Kopp sp. Gerhardt Schaeffer in 1710 (West Camp
> Luth. Chbk.).

The Johann Adam Kopp, sp. in 1717 at West Camp, probably was
Johann Adam Lesch, step-son of Jacob[1] Kopf (HJ).

PETER JACOB KORNMANN (Hunter Lists #398)

John Dietrich Wannenmacher of Leheim in Darmstad md. 29 Nov
1710 Anna Kunigunda Kernmann, d/o Johann of the same place (West
Camp Luth. Chbk.). The German ancestral home of the family was 6086
Leeheim (6 km. e. of Oppenheim; Chbks. begin 1611, but gaps). The
grandfather of the N.Y. settler was Caspar Kornmann from Reinhard-
shain near Grünberg. His widow Barbara was bur. 24 July 1652. They
had issue:

> + Georg, conf. as s/o Caspar in 1648.
>
> Hans, conf. as s/o Caspar in 1650.

Peter Jacob, s/o Georg Kornmann and his wife Catharina, was bpt. 30
Nov 1659 - sp.: Peter Schüssler from Zwingenberg and Jacob Winter
here. Peter Jacob Kornmann, s/o Georg Kornmann, was conf. in 1674.
Peter Jacob, s/o Georg Kornmann - Gemeinsmann here, md. 8 Jan 1684

Anna Kunigunda, d/o Dönges Bonn - Gemeinsmann here. Peter Jacob
Kornmann aged 50, his wife, a son aged 20, a daughter aged 19,
Luth., wheelwright, were in the 2nd arrivals in England in 1709
(London Lists).

Peter Jacob Kornmann made his initial appearance on the Hunter Lists 4 Aug 1710 with 3 pers. over 10 yrs. of age; he was
called Johann Jacob Kornmann 4 Oct 1710 with 4 pers. over 10 yrs.
Peter Jacob Kornman aged 51 dead, Anna Conigunda Kornman aged 52
dead, Anna Conig Kornman aged 24, and John Christopher Kornman
aged 12A, were in N.Y. City in 1710/11 (Palatines In N.Y. City).
The ch. of Peter Jacob[1] and Anna Kunigunda Kornmann were:

> 1) Anna Kunigunda[2], b. 5 Oct 1684 - sp.: Anna Kun. Frick (?)
>   (Leeheim Chbk.). She md. 29 Nov 1710 Dieterich Wannenmacher.
> 2) Jost[2], b. 20 Jan 1688 - sp.: Jost Kornmann (Leeheim Chbk.).
> 3) Johann Christopher[2] (Palatines In N.Y. City).

JOHANN HENRICH KORN (Hunter Lists #399)

Johann Henrich Korn made his first appearance on the Hunter
Lists 4 Oct 1710 with 1 pers. over 10 yrs. of age. On 24 June 1711
he was registered with Cathar: Dreuth in his household with 2 pers.
over 10 yrs. and 1 pers. under 10 yrs. of age. The 25 March 1712
entry read 1 pers. over 10 and 1 pers. under 10 yrs. of age, and
the 24 June 1712 recording noted 2 over 10 and 1 under 10 yrs.
Hendrik Koorn sp. Dirk Hagedoorn in 1723 (Albany Ref. Chbk.).
Hendrik and Anna Koorn sp. Gysbert Van Zanten in 1742, and Henderick and Margarieta Carn sp. Albert Brat in 1757 (both Albany Ref.
Chbk.). The ch. of Johann Henrich[1] Korn were:

> 1) Elisabetha[2] (HJ), md. Geurt Brad 15 Sept 1737 (Albany Ref.
>   Chbk.).
> 2) Margaretha[2] (HJ), md. Gysbert Van Zanten 22 Feb 1739/40
>   (Albany Ref. Chbk.).
> 3) Anna[2] (HJ), md. Albert Brad 24 Nov 1743 (Albany Ref.
>   Chbk.).

There were several unplaced Carn-Kerns in colonial N.Y.: 1)
Maria Christ: Carn md. Christ Ernst Niemand 14 Feb 1760 (Stone
Arabia Ref. Chbk.); 2) Hans Georg Kirn and wife Anna Maria had
ch. bpt. at Stone Arabia Luth. beginning in 1753; 3) Hans Jacob
Kern and wife Eva had a son Jacob bpt. in 1759 at Loonenburg Luth.
Church; and 4) Johannes Kern and wife Eva Nagel had ch. bpt. at
Germantown Luth., Katsbaan Ref., Catskill Ref., and Loonenburg
Luth. Churches 1761 - 1773 (HJ).

NICLAUS KÖRNER (Hunter Lists #400)

John Nicol Körner aged 50, his wife, sons aged 6 and 3, daughters aged 9 and ¼, Ref., husbandman and vinedresser, were in the 3rd arrivals in England in 1709 (London Lists).

Niclaus Körner made his first appearance on the Hunter Lists 30 June 1710 with 2 pers. over 10 yrs. of age and 4 pers. under 10 yrs. The family size changed to 2 over 10 and 3 under 10 yrs. on the 4 Oct 1710 entry. The notation for 24 June 1711 read 4 over 10 and 1 under 10, for 29 Sept 1711 showed 3 over 10 and 2 under 10, for 24 Dec 1711 recorded 4 over 10 yrs. and 2 under 10, for 25 March 1712 registered 3 over 10 and 2 under 10, and for 24 June 1712 was 4 pers. over 10 yrs. and 1 pers. under 10 yrs. of age. Nicolaus Kerner: 1 man, 1 lad aged 9 - 15 yrs., 1 boy aged 8 yrs. and under, 1 woman, and 1 maid aged 9 - 15 yrs., were in Ulster Co. in 1710/11 (West Camp Census). Nicolas Kerner was nat. next to Andries and Andries Lodewyck Kerner on 8 and 9 Sept 1715 (Kingston Nats.). Nicolaus Körner and Magdalena with 4 ch. were at Beckmansland ca. 1716/17 (Simmendinger Register). Necolas Karner first appeared on the tax rolls of the North Ward in 1718/19 and then ceased being entered after 1720/21 (Dutchess Co. Tax Lists). Niclaus[1] Körner and wife Anna Magdalena had issue:

1) Anna Maria[2] (HJ), md. as a single woman b. Germany in 1719 Jan Van Gelder (Kingston Ref. Chbk.).

2) Andreas[2] (HJ), nat. with Nicolaus[1] in 1715 at Kingston. He md. as a single man b. Germany, living at Westenhoeck 8 Dec 1726 Elisabetha Stiever, b. Germany (Linlithgo Ref. Chbk.). They had issue:

   i) Nicolaus[3], bpt. 13 (?) Feb 1727 - sp.: Lodewyk Kerner and Sara Schott (Claverack Ref. Chbk.).

   ii) Jacob[3], bpt. 19 Oct 1729 - sp.: Margriet Whieler and Jacob Stuywer (Kinderhook Ref. Chbk.).

   iii) Magdalena[3], bpt. 2 Oct 1737 - sp.: Johannes Spoor and Mary Spoor (Kinderhook Ref. Chbk.).

   iv) Maria[3], bpt. 16 Aug 1741 - sp.: Jacob Spoor and Anna Maria Preis (Linlithgo Ref. Chbk.).

3) Ludwig[2] (HJ), nat. with Nicolaus[1] in 1715 at Kingston. He md. Catharina (--) and had ch.:

   i) Jacob[3], bpt. 30 June 1734 - sp.: Lauwrens Van Alen Jr. and Eytie Borghaart (Kinderhook Ref. Chbk.).

   ii) Jannet[3], bpt. 3½ months old 18 April 1738 at Goghkamke - sp.: Hannes Rauw and wife Catharina (Loonenburg Luth. Chbk.).

   iii) Nicolaus[3], bpt. 6 months old 15 May 1740 at Goghkem.

- sp.: Hannes Rausch and wife Catharina (Loonenburg
Luth. Chbk.).

iv) Magdalena[3], b. 5 Oct 1741 and bpt. Goghkameko, Ankrom
- sp.: Hendryk Brasy and wife Lisab. (Loonenburg Luth.
Chbk.).

v) Wynche[3], bpt. 29 Jan 1744 - sp.: J. Philipp and Catharina Philipp (Germantown Ref. Chbk.).

vi) Andreas[3], b. 15 Nov 1748 and bpt. Westehoek called
Sheffield - sp.: Andries Carner and wife Cathar.
(Loonenburg Luth. Chbk.).

4) Johann Adam[2], b. 21 July 1711 - sp.: Johann Francke and
Adam Hertel (West Camp Luth. Chbk.).

5) Catharina Elisabetha[2], b. 30 April 1714 - sp.: Catharina
Elisabetha Rau and Johann Mattheus Jung (West Camp Luth.
Chbk.).

ANNA URSULA KRAFFTIN (Hunter Lists #401)

Anna Ursula Krafftin made her only appearance on the Hunter
Lists 4 Oct 1710 with 1 pers. over 10 yrs. of age.

There was an unplaced Maria Catharina Krafft who md. Johann
Jost Schnell by 1734 (HJ).

JOHANNES KRÄMER (Hunter Lists #402)

Johan kramer, his wife, and 1 child were on Capt. Georg Brouwell's ship in Holland 5 June 1709 in the 3rd party of Palatines
(Rotterdam Lists). John Krämer aged 30, his wife, a daughter aged
2, Catholic, baker, were in the 3rd arrivals in England later
that yr. (London Lists).

Johannes Krämer made his first appearance on the Hunter Lists
4 July 1710 with 2 pers. over 10 yrs. and 1 pers. under 10; the
entry for 29 Sept 1711 read 2 over 10 and 2 under 10 yrs. On 25
March 1712, he was recorded with 1 pers. over 10, and then on 24
June 1712 Krämer was noted with 1 over 10 and 2 under 10 yrs.
Johannes Kramer and his wife Anna Margretha with 3 ch. were at
Neu-Heidelberg ca. 1716/17 (Simmendinger Register). A Johannes
Kremer (another man? - HJ) was a Palatine Debtor on the Manor of
Livingston in 1718 (Livingston Debt Lists); a letter from Phil:
Livingston dated 8 Feb 1717 mentioned that Johannis Kremmer who
put me of(f) the first now says he bought the goods on account
(Livingston Papers, Reel #3). A child of Johannes[1] Krämer was:

1) Elisabetha Barbara[2], bpt. 14 Aug 1714 - sp.: Pieter and
Elizabeth Knyskerk and Elizabeth Hoanghin (Albany Ref.
Chbk.).

A Peter, Joost, and John Cremer were enrolled in Lt. Goshin Van Alstein's Company in 1763 (Report of the State Historian, Vol. II, p. 797). Perhaps the latter man was the Johannes Kramer mentioned in Penrose's Mohawk Valley in the Revolution, pp. 128, 129, & 274 (HJ).

ANTHONI KRÄMER (Hunter Lists #403)

Antoni Kramer, widower of Altzheim on the lower Rhine, md. Gertrauda, wid/o Paul Elsaster of Fishborn in the earldom of Isenburg, 23 Jan 1711 (West Camp Luth. Chbk.). The registers at 6526 Alsheim, home of several other 1709ers, were examined, but the emigrant Kramer was not found there (HJ).

Anthoni Krämer made his first appearance on the Hunter Lists 1 July 1710 with 1 pers. over 10 yrs. and 1 pers. under 10 yrs. in the family. The entry for 25 March 1711 showed 2 over 10 and 1 under 10 yrs., and the notation for 24 June 1711 said 3 pers. over 10 and 1 under 10 yrs. Kramer's entry for 29 Sept 1711 was 3 pers. over 10 yrs. of age. Anthon Kraemer, Epis(copal), joined the church at N.Y. 19 July 1710 (West Camp Luth. Chbk.). Anthony Kremer: 1 man, 1 woman, were in Ulster Co. in 1710/11 (West Camp Census). Anthony Cramer was nat. 8 and 9 Sept 1715 (Kingston Nats.). Antonius Krämer and his wife Gertraud with 1 child were at Heessburg ca. 1716/17 (Simmendinger Register). Anthony Cremere made his initial appearance on tax rolls in the North Ward in 1717/18 and continued until 1722 (Dutchess Co. Tax Lists). His wife Gertraud md. for a 3rd time, as the St. Peter's Luth. Family Book at Rhinebeck records Ludwig Leysering, Gertraut his wife, Joh. Cramer his step-son, and Gertraut Cramerin ca. 1734 (HJ). The ch. of Anthoni[1] Krämer were:

1) Johanna Maria[2] (HJ), conf. at Reinbeeck 3 Sept 1719 (N.Y. City Luth. Chbk.).

2) Johann Henrich[2], bpt. 2 Nov 1712 - sp.: Johan Hendrik Scheerman (Kingston Ref. Chbk.). Henr. Kramer aged 17 yrs. was conf. in 1731 among the Germans at Beekman's Land (N.Y. City Luth. Chbk.).

3) Johannes[2], b. 15 April 1715 - sp.: Johann Henrich Scharmann (West Camp Luth. Chbk.). Johannes Cramer was taxed at Rhinebeck beginning in 1742/43 until 1755, when his farm was taxed (Dutchess Co. Tax Lists). He md. Catharina Flegeler (HJ) and had issue:

   i) Gertraud[3], bpt. 19 Jan 1746 - sp.: Jan Lodewyck Leystenreng and Geertruy Scherman (Rhinebeck Flats Ref. Chbk.).

   ii) Johannes[3], b. 19 Oct 1747 - sp.: Johannes Eckard and

Eva Top (Rhinebeck Luth. Chbk.). He md. Catharina Hamm (HJ). The will of John Cramer of Staatsburg in Rhinebeck Precinct was dated 1781 (Dutchess Co. Will Bk. A).

iii) Catharina[3], b. 12 Aug 1750 - sp.: Friedrich Ham and Catharina, and Peter Froelich (Rhinebeck Luth. Chbk.). She md. Bernhard Overhauser (HJ).

iv) Zacharias[3], b. 26 March 1753 - sp.: Zacharias Flegelaar and his wife (Rhinebeck Flats Ref. Chbk.).

v) Philip[3], b. 12 July 1758 - sp.: Philip S. Flegelar and Grietje Dop (Hopewell Ref. Chbk.).

vi) Magdalena[3], bpt. 17 Nov 1763 - sp.: Pieter Dop and Geertruy Krymer (New Hackensack Ref. Chbk.).

vii) Maria[3], b. 2 Dec 1769 - sp.: Joost Bosch and wife Maria Demoet (New Hackensack Ref. Chbk.).

4) Gertraud[2], bpt. 12 Jan 1718 - sp.: Niclaas Rouw and Geertruy Rouw (Kingston Ref. Chbk.). She md. Peter Dopp (HJ).

5) Nicolaus[2], b. latter Jan 1721 at Rheinbeeck - sp.: Niclaes Rau and wife Gertrud (N.Y. City Luth. Chbk.).

ANNA MARIA KRÄMERIN - MICHAEL KRÄMER (Hunter Lists #404)

Anna Maria Krämerin with 4 pers. over 10 and 3 under 10 yrs. made her initial appearance on the Hunter Lists 4 Aug 1710; the entry for 4 Oct 1710 read 3 over 10 and 3 under 10, for 24 June 1711 showed 4 over 10 and 3 under 10, for 24 Dec 1711 gave 3 over 10 and 3 under 10, and for 25 March 1712 noted 2 over 10 and 3 under 10. Michael Krämer was recorded 24 June 1712 as head of the family. Anna Maria Cramerin - wid. aged 38, (--) Cramerin her eldest sone x aged 18, Maria Eliz Cramerin aged 12, John Hendrich Cramerin aged 7, Anna Catharina Cramerin aged 5, and Juliana Maria Cramerin aged 1½, were in N.Y. City ca. 1710/11 (Palatines In N.Y. City). Anna Maria Krämerin, a wid. with 7 ch., was in Neu-Yorck ca. 1716/17 (Simmendinger Register). Anna Maria Nob, wid/o Wm Kramer, md. Samuel Rikbie, single man of Old Eng, 3 Jan 1719 (N.Y. City Ref. Chbk.). The ch. of Wilhelm and Anna Maria[1] Krämer were:

1) Michael[2] (HJ), noted in Hunter in 1712, probably the unnamed son listed in N.Y. City in 1710/11 (HJ). Michael Cramer of N.Y., boatman, was nat. at N.Y. City 22 Nov 1715 (Denizations, Naturalizations, and Oaths of Allegiance in Colonial N.Y., p. 21). There was a will for a Michael Kramer dated 1759 in Pa. (Lancaster Co. Will Bk. J).

2) Adam[2], called s/o Anna Maria Creiner 25 Sept 1710 when he was bound to Jos: Hunt, Jr. of Westchester at aged 13 (Apprenticeship Lists). A correspondent, Joseph Cramer, revealed that Adam[2] md. 28 Jan 1724/25 Miriam Cleaveland

at Norwich, Conn. (HJ).

3) <u>Maria Elisabetha</u>[2] (Palatines In N.Y. City).

4) <u>Johann Henrich</u>[2] (Palatines In N.Y. City). Perhaps he may
   have been the Johann Henrich Kramer who md. Anna Maria
   (--) and had issue Maria Christina bpt. 1754 (Catskill
   Ref. Chbk.) and Dorothea Margaretha bpt. 1756 (Loonenburg
   Luth. Chbk.) (HJ).

5) <u>Anna Catharina</u>[2] (Palatines In N.Y. City).

6) <u>Juliana Maria</u>[2] (Palatines In N.Y. City).

JOHANN HENRICH KRANTZ (Hunter Lists #405)

A Joh. Henr. Crantz and his wife left without release, returned, and were banished in 1709; they were from Seilhofen in Amt.
<u>Driedorf</u> (Nassau-Dillenburg Petitions). He probably was the Hen-
rich Krantz, s/o Johann Jost Krantz of Guntersdorf, who md. 10
June 1697 Anna Catharina, d/o Johann Jacob Immels at Rabenscheid
(Driedorf Chbk.). However, the emigrant 1709er was not this man
from Driedorf, but another individual (HJ). Johann Heinrich Krantz,
widower from the commune Isenburg, md. Anna Catharina Schaurmann,
d/o Heinrich in the commune of Isenburg, 25 July 1710 (West Camp
Luth. Chbk.). Johann Henrich[1] Krantz was found in Isenburg at 6484
<u>Fischborn</u> (14 km. n.w. of Schlüchtern), also home of his father-
in-law Henrich[1] Schaarmann. The records of this village are in
the registers of 6484 <u>Unterreichenbach</u> (1½ km. s. of Fischborn;
Chbks. begin 1599, but gaps). The father of the emigrant Johann
Henrich[1] Krantz was <u>Ernst Krantz</u>, mentioned as a court-servant at
Unterreichenbach in 1664. Joh. Henrich Krantz, a tailor, was sp.
to the child of his brother Tönges Cranz, cowherd at Oberreichen-
bach, 20 March 1708. Johann Henrich[1] disappeared from Fischborn
records after April 1709 (HJ).

Johann Henrich Krantz made his initial appearance on the Hunter Subsistence Lists 1 July 1710 with 1 pers. over 10 yrs. of age
and 2 pers. under 10 in the family. The family was recorded with
2 pers. over 10 yrs. and 2 under 10 on 4 Oct 1710, with 4 over 10
yrs. on 24 June 1711, with 3 over 10 and 1 under 10 yrs. on 29
Sept 1711, and with 4 pers. over 10 yrs. of age 24 Dec 1711. Jno.
Hen. Krantz: 1 man, 1 boy aged 8 and under, 1 woman, and 1 maid
aged 9 - 15 yrs., were in Ulster Co. in 1710/11 (West Camp Census).
Henrich Krantz was nat. next to Michel Krantz 8 and 9 Sept 1715
(Kingston Nats.). Heinrich Krantz and Anna Catharina with 4 ch.
were at Heessberg ca. 1716/17 (Simmendinger Register). He was taxed
£5 in 1718/19 and £7 in 1720/21 at Kingston (Ulster Co. Tax Lists).
The Kingston Trustees Records mention Hendrick Krans in Bk. 1, Part
C, pp. 2&3. The ch. of Johann Henrich[1] Krantz were:

1) <u>Elisabetha</u>² (HJ), probably the maid aged 9 - 15 yrs. at West Camp in 1710/11 (HJ). She sp. Johann Wilhelm Brandau in 1715, and Brandau's wife sp. Johann Henrich¹ Krantz in 1717 (both West Camp Luth. Chbk.). An Elisabetha Krantz md. Georg Adam Zufeldt by 1727 (HJ).

2) <u>Michael</u>² (HJ), nat. next to Henrich¹ Krantz 8 and 9 Sept 1715 (Kingston Nats.). He md. 12 Sept 1726 Charlotte Frolich, both b. in Germany (Kingston Ref. Chbk.). Issue:

    i) <u>Henrich</u>³ (HJ), md. Barbara Gernreich (HJ). The will of a Henry Cranss, farmer, of Montgomery, was dated 15 Feb 1787 and probated 28 Jan 1788 (Ulster Co. Will Bk. A).

    ii) <u>Johannes</u>³ (HJ), md. Catharina Alsdorf (HJ). They had a son Michael bpt. in 1756 (Montgomery Ref. Chbk.).

    iii) <u>Jacob</u>³, bpt. 11 Feb 1733 - sp.: Christoffel Muyl and Antjen Muyl (Kinston Ref. Chbk.). Perhaps he was the Jacob Krans who md. Catharina Theis, both found in the registers at Montgomery Ref. and Hebron Churches (HJ); a Mrs. Cath. Crance d. 18 July 1815, aged 79 yrs. in Montgomery (<u>Salem North Post</u> 17 Aug 1815).

    iv) <u>Michael</u>³, bpt. 16 April 1735 - sp.: Johannes Crist and Elisabeth Slemmer (Montgomery Ref. Chbk.). Michael Crans, aged 24, a weaver b. in Ulster Co., 5' 5½" with a dark complexion and brown eyes and hair, was in Capt. Clinton's Company in Ulster Co., April 1761 (<u>Report of the State Historian</u>, Vol. II, p. 651).

    v) <u>Nicolaus</u>³, bpt. 19 Oct 1736 - sp.: Nicholas Melsbach and Catharine Maul (Montgomery Ref. Chbk.).

    vi) <u>Valentin</u>³, b. 11 June 1738 and bpt. on the Walenkill at Hans Mullers - sp.: Hans Vrölich, and in his place Hans Muller, and Geertje Neukirch - w/o Johannis (N.Y. City Luth. Chbk.).

    vii) <u>Anna</u>³, bpt. 7 Oct 1740 - sp.: Christopher Maul and wife Anna Juliana Segins (Montgomery Ref. Chbk.).

    viii) <u>Gertraud</u>³, bpt. 7 May 1742 - sp.: Johannis Neukirk and Geertje Klaarwater (Montgomery Ref. Chbk.).

    ix) <u>Lydia</u>³, bpt. 22 May 1744 - sp.: Bernard Frolich and Lydia Delong (Montgomery Ref. Chbk.).

3) <u>Sebastian</u>², bpt. 8 Nov 1705 - sp.: Sebastian - s/o the late Clas Bechtols (Unterreichenbach Chbk.).

4) <u>Johannes</u>², bpt. 2 April 1709 - sp.: Johannes - s/o the late Johan Sommers (Unterreichenbach Chbk.).

5) <u>Johann Henrich</u>², b. 26 Jan 1712 - sp.: Johann Henrich Scharmann. The entry was then crossed out and a "+" entered

beneath the name of the child (West Camp Luth. Chbk.).

6) Johannes², b. 18 Feb 1713 - sp.: Johannes Straub (West Camp
Luth. Chbk.). Johannis Krans, single man of Elisabethtown,
md. 23 Oct 1734 Elisabeth Klaarwater, single woman b. New
Paltz (Montgomery Ref. Chbk.). He md. 2nd Anna Christina
Melsbach; one source says they were md. at Montgomery Ref.
March 1741/42, but this probably is an error (HJ). The
will of Johannis Krans of the Precinct of Hanover, naming
ch. from both marriages, was dated 17 April 1775 and probated 5 July 1777 (Ulster Co. Deed Bk. HH). Issue from
1st marriage:

   i) Henrich³, bpt. 7 Oct 1735 - sp.: Henricus Christ and
   Julia Edschel (Montgomery Ref. Chbk.).

   ii) Jacobus³, bpt. 30 Jan 1737 - sp.: Johannes Maul and
   Rachel Klaarwater (Kingston Ref. Chbk.).

   iii) Christopher³, bpt. 10 Oct 1738 - sp.: Christopher Mauk
   and Anna Julia Segius (Montgomery Ref. Chbk.).

   iv) Catharina³, bpt. 7 Oct 1740 - sp.: William Krans and
   Catharine Muller (Montgomery Ref. Chbk.).

   v) Elisabetha³, bpt. 7 Feb 1743 - sp.: Johannis Nieukirk
   and wife Geertje Klaarwater (Montgomery Ref. Chbk.).

By his 2nd marriage, the ch. of Johannes² were:

   vi) Matthias³, bpt. 22 May 1744 - sp.: Mathys Melsbach
   and wife Anna Eve Bush (Montgomery Ref. Chbk.).

   vii) Petrus³, bpt. 5 May 1747 - sp.: Petrus Melsbach and
   Lisabeth Griller (Montgomery Ref. Chbk.). (See Ulster
   Co. in the Revolution, p. 46, concerning him).

   viii) Henrich Christ.³, b. 18 Oct 1749 - sp.: Wilhelm Crantz
   and wife Elisab. Christina Anna (Rhinebeck Luth.
   Chbk.).

   ix) Wilhelm³, twin to the above, b. 18 Oct 1749 - sp.:
   Stephan Christ and Anna Sophronia (Rhinebeck Luth.
   Chbk.).

   x) Adam³, bpt. 9 Sept 1753 - sp.: Adam Nieukirk and Elsje
   Maria Schmidt (Montgomery Ref. Chbk.).

   xi) Susanna³, bpt. 23 Nov 1756 - sp.: Pieter Melsbach and
   Susanna Melsbach (Montgomery Ref. Chbk.).

   xii) Maria³, bpt. 7 June 1760 - sp.: Johannis Maul and wife
   Maria Catharine Menges (Montgomery Ref. Chbk.).

7) Maria Elisabetha², b. 1 July 1715 - sp.: Johann Straup and
his wife Maria Elisabetha (West Camp Luth. Chbk.).

8) Johann Wilhelm², b. 13 Dec 1717 - sp.: Jerg Wilhelm Kehl,
Peter Oberbach, and Elisabetha Catharina Brandau (West
Camp Luth. Chbk.). He md. 25 Oct 1740 Elisabetha (Christina

Anna) Müller (Montgomery Ref. Chbk.). They had ch.:

    i) <u>Catharina</u>[3], bpt. 11 Oct 1741 - sp.: Jacob Sensebach and Catharine Muller (Montgomery Ref. Chbk.).

    ii) <u>Anna</u>[3], bpt. 7 June 1748 - sp.: Johannis Krans and wife Christina Melsbach (Montgomery Ref. Chbk.).

    iii) <u>Philip</u>[3], bpt. 18 Aug 1752 - sp.: Barnard Muller and Elisabeth Jongbloet (Montgomery Ref. Chbk.).

8) <u>Johann Henrich</u>[2], b. 22 March 1720 and bpt. at Newtown in Albany Co. - sp.: Joh. Henrich Neukircken and wife Anna Cath., in place of Gertrude Kramer (N.Y. City Luth. Chbk.).

There were several unplaced Krantzes in colonial N.Y.: 1) a Petrus Krantz md. Elisabetha Kreller and had issue bpt. at Red Hook Luth. Church 1745 - 52; they were sp. there in 1745 by Georg Adam Zufeld; 2) a Henrich, s/o Johannes Krantz, md. 10 Nov 1765 Elisabetha, d/o Joh. Georg Müller (Red Hook Luth. Chbk.); and 3) a Stephanus Krantz sp. Joh: Mart: Krist in 1741 (Montgomery Ref. Chbk.).

<u>CONRAD KRANTZ</u> (Hunter Lists #406)

Elisabetha, wid/o Conrad Krantz of the commune Zigenheim in Hesten, md. 18 Dec 1711 Johann Michael Emmerich of Delckenheim in the commune Epstein in Darmstatt (West Camp Luth. Chbk.). A matching Conrad Krantz was found at 3579 <u>Wasenberg</u> in Amt Ziegenhain (16 km. n.w. of Alsfeld; Chbks. begin 1572). The father of this Conrad Krantz was one Bräunig Krantz who md. 5 Aug 1675 Catharina Moisch (?). They had ch.:

<u>Johannes</u>, bpt. 1676.

<u>Johann Jost</u>, bpt. 1682. He md. Anna Elisabetha Lünemann from Obergrenzebach 7 Feb 1704.

<u>Otto</u>, b. 5 Feb 1687 - sp.: Otto Krantz, brother of the father.

+ <u>Conrad</u>, bpt. as Curt Krantz 1 Nov 1687 - sp.: the s/o Johs. Stauffenberger.

Koenraat krants, his wife, and 1 child, were on Capt. Robbert Bülman's ship in the 4th party of Palatines in Holland in 1709 (Rotterdam Lists). Conrad Krantz aged 23, his wife, and a daughter aged 1, Ref., husbandman and vinedresser, were in the 4th arrivals in England later that yr. (London Lists).

Conrad Krantz made his first appearance on the Hunter Lists 1 July 1710 with 2 pers. over 10 yrs. and 1 pers. under 10. Conrad Krantz's wid[W] was noted with 1 pers. over 10 yrs. of age 25 March 1711 on the Subsistence Lists.

JOHANNES KREMBS (Hunter Lists #407)

Johannes Kremps, a shepherd auf dem Hainer Hof, was documented at 6086 Leeheim (6 km. e. of Oppenheim; Chbks. begin 1611, but gaps). Johannes Krems, his wife, with Anna Kristina and 1 child, were on Capt. Boüwel's ship in the 2nd party in Holland in 1709 (Rotterdam Lists). John Krems aged 29, his wife, and a son aged 4, Rom. Catholic, husbandman and vinedresser, were in the 2nd arrivals later that yr. in England (London Lists).

Johannes Krembs made his initial appearance on the Hunter Lists 4 Aug 1710 with 2 pers. over 10 yrs.; the entry for 24 Dec 1711 read 2 over 10 and 1 under 10, and for 25 March 1712 noted 2 pers. over 10 yrs. and 2 under 10. Johannis Krem was nat. 28 Feb 1715/16 (Albany Nats.). Johannes Krembs and his wife Apolonia were recorded at Neu-Quunsberg ca. 1716/17 with 1 child in the family (Simmendinger Register). Johannes Krems was a patentee in 1723 (Stone Arabia Patent). He was a director in the task of building a new Ref. church at Stone Arabia in 1733 (History of Montgomery & Fulton Counties, N.Y., p. 155). The Gramps Family Bible gives him dates of 1680 - 1770 (N.Y. State D.A.R. Bible Records, Vol 12, p. 101). The ch. of Johannes[1] Krembs were:

1) Johann Nicolaus[2], b. 27 Feb 1705 - sp.: Joh. Niclaus Schäfer on the Hainer Hof (Leeheim Chbk.).

2) Wilhelm[2], bpt. 1 June 1710 on the ship Midfort - sp.: Wm. Fowles, Capt. of the ship (West Camp Luth. Chbk.).

3) Peter[2] (HJ), md. Anna Elisabetha Emgen, who d. 8 Feb 1793, aged 76-4-8 (Stone Arabia Ref. Chbk.). Petter Kremps was in Soffrines Deychert's Company in 1757 and later was a Lieutenant in several Mohawk regiments in the 1760's (Report of the State Historian, Vol. II, pp. 783, 786, 882, & 891). Peter Craims was a freeholder at Stonrabie in 1763 (Albany Co. Freeholders). The will of Peter Kremps of Stone Arabia was dated 30 June 1801 and probated 24 July 1807 (Montgomery Co. Will Bk. I). He had ch.:

   i) Peter[3] (Will).

   ii) Anna Margaretha[3], bpt. 14 Oct 1739 - sp.: Hendrich Crems and Markreta Crems and Cristina Emge (Stone Arabia Ref. Chbk.). She md. Johannes Keyser 6 Nov 1759 (Schoharie Luth. Chbk.) (Will).

   iii) Dorothea[3], bpt. 1740 - sp.: Jacob Schuls and his wife (Stone Arabia Ref. Chbk.). She md. Philip Fuchs (Fox) 26 March 1761 (Stone Arabia Ref. Chbk.) (Will).

   iv) Anna Eva[3], bpt. 23 Oct 1743 - sp.: Stoffell Schuls and his wife Eva (Stone Arabia Ref. Chbk.).

v) <u>Catharina</u>³ (Will), md. Johannes Leymann (Will).

vi) <u>Elisabetha</u>³ (HJ), md. 8 Jan 1767 Johannes Eisenlord (Stone Arabia Ref. Chbk.). (Will).

vii) <u>Johannes</u>³, b. or bpt. 29 June 1756 - sp.: Hannes Emige and wife Elisabeth (Stone Arabia Luth. Chbk.). He may have been the John P. Crems who d. 8 Aug 1819, aged 61 ... (Stone Arabia Ref. Chbk.).

4) <u>Johann Henrich</u>² (HJ), dates in the Gramps Family Bible 1722 - Aug 1808. Hendrick Kremps was in Soffrines Deychert's Company in 1757 (<u>Report of the State Historian</u>, Vol II, p. 784). Hendrick Craims was a freeholder of Stonrabie in 1763 (Albany Co. Freeholders).He md. Christina Emgen, who d. 22 Aug 1796, aged 78 yrs. (Stone Arabia Ref. Chbk.). They had ch.:

i) <u>Maria Elisabetha</u>³, a sp. in 1760 (Stone Arabia Ref. Chbk.).

ii) <u>Elisabetha</u>³, a sp. in 1760 (Stone Arabia Ref. Chbk.).

iii) <u>Margaretha</u>³, bpt. 29 Dec 1751 - sp.: Willhelm Ömge and Margaretha Lauchs (Stone Arabia Ref. Chbk.).

iv) <u>Johann Henrich</u>³ (Gramps Family Bible). The Bible gives him dates 13 Feb 1755 - 19 March 1837.

v) <u>Anna Eva</u>³, bpt. 9 July 1756 - sp.: Christoph Schulz and wife Anna Eva (Stone Arabia Luth. Chbk.).

vi) <u>Anna</u>³, b. 19 March 1763 - sp.: Mar. - w/o Jacob Boss-her (Stone Arabia Ref. Chbk.).

vii) <u>Catharina</u>³, b. 15 Dec 1764 (Stone Arabia Ref. Chbk.).

5) <u>Maria Margaretha</u>² (HJ), md. Wilhelm Laux by 1751 (HJ).

6?) <u>Anna Dorothea</u>² (HJ), whom sp. strongly suggest may have md. Johann Jacob Schultz (HJ).

A Barbara Krems md. Johann Isaac Emgie 23 March 1762 (Stone Arabia Ref. Chbk.); she probably was a d/o either Peter² or Johann Henrich² Krembs (HJ).

JOHANNES KUGEL (Hunter Lists #408)

Anna Margaretha, wid/o Johann Kugel of Unter-Owisheim in the commune of Maulbronner in the duchy of Wuremberg, md. Adam Baumann 6 March 1711 (West Camp Luth. Chbk.). The town of origin actually was 7527 <u>Unteröwisheim</u> near Bruchsal (28 km. s. of Heidelberg; Chbks. begin 1577, but gaps). Johann Kugel, a cooper-fellow from Anspach, md. Margaretha, d/o Hans Georg Lapp - citizen and carpenter here, in 1707.

Johannes Kugel made his first appearance on the Hunter Lists 1 July 1710 with 2 pers. over 10 yrs.; on 4 Oct 1710 he was noted

next to Agnes Lapp. The ch. of Johannes[1] Kugel and his wife Anna
Margaretha Lapp were:

1) Anna Maria[2], bpt. 28 June 1707 - sp.: Jacob Banz - Innkeeper at the Crown, and Anna Maria Descher ... (Unteröwisheim Chbk.). The child d. 2 Nov 1707, aged 4 months and
4 days (Unteröwisheim Chbk.).

2) Hans Caspar[2], b. 23 May 1708 - sp.: Caspar Brenner - cooper
from Niederstätten in Frankenland, Catharina - w/o Michel
Boltz - cooper here, Michel Kümling - butcher here, and
Anna Maria - w/o Hs. Jacob Buntz - Innkeeper at the Crown
(Unteröwisheim Chbk.). He d. 18 Jan 1709, aged 8 months
and 2 weeks (Unteröwisheim Chbk.).

3) Maria Catharina[2], twin to the above, b. 23 May 1708 - same
sp. (Unteröwisheim Chbk.). She d. 29 May 1708, aged 6
days (Unteröwisheim Chbk.).

JOHANNES KUHLMER (Hunter Lists #409)

Johan Kühlman aged 50, his wife, daughters aged 20, 12, 9, 7,
and 2, Ref., husbandman and vinedresser, were the first family
listed in the 3rd arrivals in England in 1709 (London Lists).

Johannes Kuhlmann made his initial appearance on the Hunter
Lists 4 July 1710 with 3 pers. over 10 yrs. of age and 3 pers. under 10 yrs. The ages of the family increased to 4 over 10 yrs. and
2 under 10 yrs. of age on 4 Oct 1710. He sp. Martin Netzbacher in
1715 (West Camp Luth. Chbk.). Johannes Kolmann and Juliana with 3
ch. were at Quunsberg ca. 1716/17 (Simmendinger Register). A Catharina Kuhlmann sp. Johannes Straup in 1719 (West Camp Luth. Chbk.).
Johannes Coleman was a Palatine Debtor in 1721 (Livingston Debt
Lists). Johannes Kollman was a Palatine willing to remain on the
Manor 26 Aug 1724 and was one of the four patentees granted land
at Germantown (Doc. Hist. of N.Y., Vol. III, p. 724).

GEORG KUHLMANN (Hunter Lists #410)

The founder of the Hudson Valley Kilmer family was indeed
Georg[1] Kuhlmann/Kilmer. Some published genealogies relating to the
family mistakenly give one Philipp Kilmer as the first generation
in America; however, this non-existent Philipp came into being
through a misreading of the emigrant Philip[1] Helmer's name found on
the West Camp Census of 1710/11 (HJ). Georg Kuhlmann made his first
appearance on the Hunter Lists 4 July 1710 with 2 pers. over 10
yrs. of age and 3 pers. under 10. He was recorded with 4 pers. over
10 and 3 under 10 yrs. on 4 Aug 1710, with 6 pers. over 10 and 1
under 10 on 24 June 1712, and with 6 over 10 and 2 under 10 on 13

Sept 1712. Jurich Kelmer was nat. 17 Jan 1715/16 (Albany Nats.).
Hans Jury Kolemer was on the roll of the Independent Company of
the Manor of Livingston 30 Nov 1715 (Report of the State Historian, Vol. I, p. 523). Georg Colmer with wife and ch. was at Heessberg ca. 1716/17 (Simmendinger Register). The mark of Jury Coolmer was recorded on an old mss. dated 1718/19 (Livingston Papers,
Reel #4). Jury Coelmer/Coolmer was a Palatine Debtor in 1718, 1719,
1722, and 1726 (Livingston Debt Lists). His wife was called Anna
Margaretha in 1720 (N.Y. City Luth. Chbk.) and Eva Margaretha in
1725 and 1728 (West Camp Luth. Chbk. and N.Y. City Luth. Chbk.).
The ch. of Georg[1] Kuhlmann/Kilmer were:

1) Elisabetha[2] (HJ), md. Johann Wilhelm Kuhn (HJ).

2) Simon[2] (HJ), as Syms Coolmer a Palatine Debtor in 1726
   (Livingston Debt Lists). Simon Kilmer appeared on tax
   rolls in North East Precinct from Feb 1745 - 1779 (Dutchess Co. Tax Lists). The will of Simon Kilmer of the little Nine Partners was dated 5 June 1787 and probated 28
   March 1788 (Dutchess Co. Will Bk. A). Simon[2] md. Elisabetha Funck (HJ) and had issue:

   i) Christina[3], bpt. 6 Feb 1726 - sp.: Willem Koen and
      Elisabeth Kilmar (Kingston Ref. Chbk.).

   ii) Catharina[3], md. as d/o Simon 18 Aug 1747 Jacob Mil-
       lius (Germantown Ref. Chbk.).

   iii) Georg[3], md. as s/o Simon 8 Aug 1748 Eva Gertraud
        Dings (Germantown Ref. Chbk.). They had ch. bpt. at
        Gallatin Ref., Rhinebeck Luth., and Churchtown Luth.
        Churches (HJ).

   iv) Elisabetha[3], bpt. 1731 - sp.: Hendrick Kuhn and Eliz-
       abeth Kuhn (Red Hook Luth. Chbk.). She md. Georg
       Hoffmann (Will).

   v) Peter[3], md. as s/o Simon 22 Nov 1757 Maria Ellen
      (Red Hook Luth. Chbk.). He was on Rhinebeck tax rolls
      from 1758 - 1778 (Dutchess Co. Tax Lists). They had
      ch. bpt. at Red Hook Luth, Gallatin Ref., Rhinebeck
      Luth., and Rhinebeck Flats Ref. Churches (HJ).

   vi) Margaretha[3] (Will), md. 1st Nicolaus Stickel (HJ)
       and 2nd Henrich Weaver (Will).

   vii) Johann Wilhelm[3], bpt. 16 March 1735 - sp.: Johan Wil-
        helm Kuhn and Gertruit (Red Hook Luth. Chbk.). Will-
        iam and Peter Killmor were on a list of deserters
        from Capt. Arnout Viele's Company at Fort Edward in
        Aug 1757 (Report of the State Historian, Vol. II, p.
        785). Johann Wilhelm[3] md. Eva Kohler (HJ) and had
        ch. bpt. at Rhinebeck Luth., Manorton Luth., Red Hook

Luth., and Linlithgo Ref. Churches (HJ).

viii) Christina[3], bpt. 6 Feb 1737 - sp.: Nikkel Philip and
Christina Fonk (Katsbaan Ref. Chbk.). She md. Georg
Schäffer (Will).

ix) Johannes[3], b. 16 May 1739 and bpt. at Goghkameko (An-
cram) - sp.: Hannes Kilmer and wife Anna Veronica
(Loonenburg Luth. Chbk.). He md. 7 May 1764 Elisabetha
Ellen (Allen) (Red Hook Luth. Chbk.) and had ch. bpt.
at Pine Plains, Red Hook Luth., and Gallatin Ref.
Churches (HJ). He probably was the Johannes Kilmer
buried in 1820, aged 83 yrs. at Gallatin Ref. Cem.
(HJ).

x) Simon[3], bpt. 27 Jan 1741 - sp.: Simon Koen and Engel
Klom (Germantown Ref. Chbk.).

xi) Adam[3], bpt. 12 Dec 1742 - sp.: Adam Bitzer and Catharina Bitzer (Red Hook Luth. Chbk.). He md. 30 Sept
1766 Catharina Doll (Red Hook Luth. Chbk.). Adam[3] was
on North East tax rolls beginning in 1767 (Dutchess
Co. Tax Lists) and had ch. bpt. at Red Hook Luth. (HJ).

xii) Jacob[3] (HJ). Although not his Simon's will, sp. firmly cement him to Simon's family (HJ). Jacob[3] md. 1st
Anna Ellen (HJ) and md. 2nd Anna Maria Heiseroth 3
Dec 1770 (Germantown Ref. Chbk.). Jacob d. in 1831,
aged 88 yrs., and Anna Maria d. in 1830, aged 82 yrs.
(both Gallatin Ref. Cem.).

xiii) Nicolaus[3], bpt. 8 Jan 1749 - sp.: Nicolass Philipp and
Christin Philipp (Gallatin Ref. Chbk.). He was on
North East tax rolls in 1775 (Dutchess Co. Tax Lists).
Nicolaus[3] md. Catharina Hess (HJ) and had issue bpt.
at the Red Hook Luth. Church (HJ).

xiv?) Agnes[3] (HJ), who with husband John Williams sp. Peter[3]
Kilmer at Red Hook Luth. in 1776 (HJ).

3) Johannes[2] (HJ), md. Anna Veronica Becker (HJ) and had ch:
i) Maria[3] (HJ), md. Johannes Greber (Grever) (HJ).

ii) Elisabetha[3], bpt. 28 April 1734 - sp.: George Kelmer
and Elizabetha Becker (Germantown Ref. Chbk.). She
md. David Minckeler (HJ) and probably was the Elisabetha Minkler who d. 22 July 1827, aged 92 yrs. and
18 days (Germantown Ref. Cem.).

iii) Anna[3], bpt. 16 July 1736 - sp.: Georg Kilmer and Anna
Becker (Katsbaan Ref. Chbk.). She md. Joseph Rau (HJ).

iv) Johannes[3], bpt. 27 Aug 1739 - sp.: Johannes Jager and
Catharina Botzer (Germantown Ref. Chbk.). He md. 23
Oct 1764 Catharina Leick (Germantown Ref. Chbk.).

The will of a John Kilmer was dated 23 Sept 1795 and probated 30 Nov 1802 (Rensselaer Co. Will Bk. 2). Johannes[3] and Catharina had ch. bpt. at Germantown Ref. Church (HJ).

    v) <u>Margaretha[3]</u>, bpt. as Cretche 3 Sept 1742 - sp.: Pieter Bitzer and Cretche Kuhn (Red Hook Luth. Chbk.). She md. Henrich Kuhn (HJ).

   vi) <u>Wilhelm[3]</u>, bpt. 22 June 1746 - sp.: Wilm. Funck and Gritgen Kilmer (Red Hook Luth. Chbk.). He md. Catharina Linck (HJ) and had ch. bpt. at Germantown Ref. and Gilead Luth. at Centre Brunswick Churches (HJ). The will of a William Killmore was dated 17 Feb 1807 and probated 14 May 1808 (Rensselaer Co. Will Bk. 3).

  vii) <u>Catharina[3]</u>, bpt. 13 Aug 1749 - sp.: David Stiever and Catharina Stiver (Germantown Ref. Chbk.).

 viii) <u>Gertraud[3]</u>, bpt. 20 Oct 1751 - sp.: Simon Kuhn and Gertraut Kuhn (Germantown Ref. Chbk.). She md. Wilhelm Schneider (HJ).

4) <u>Philip[2]</u> (HJ), md. 1st Anna Margaretha Stiever (Stuber) (HJ) and probably 2nd Eva (--) (HJ). David Glenn Kilmer's book <u>The Family of John George Kilmer</u> mentions that many of this family's descendants migrated to Malahide Twp., Elgin Co., Ontario, Canada. The ch. of Philip[2] and Anna Margaretha were:

    i) <u>Catharina[3]</u>, b. 27 March 1738 and bpt. at Camp - sp.: Wilhelm Kuhn and Cathar. Kischer (Loonenburg Luth. Chbk.). She appears to have md. Friederich Fell at a very young age (HJ).

   ii) <u>Henrich[3]</u> (HJ), listed next to Philip Killmore on the List of Taxables at Claverack in 1779 (Lansing Collection, Manuscripts & History Section, N.Y. State Library, Albany). He md. Rosina Neher (HJ).

  iii) <u>Georg[3]</u>, bpt. 21 Oct 1744 - sp.: Friederick Ham and Jannetje Prussie (Linlithgo Ref. Chbk.). George and Hendrick Killmore were listed together in Capt. Johannis Hogeboom's Company in 1767 (<u>Report of the State Historian</u>, Vol. II, p. 871).

5) <u>Georg[2]</u> (HJ), md. 20 April 1738 Anna Margaretha Falckenberger (Loonenburg Luth. Chbk.). They had issue:

    i) <u>Johannes[3]</u>, b. 9 Feb 1739 and bpt. at Teerbosch - sp.: Hannes Kilmer and Gertrud Kuhn (Loonenburg Luth. Chbk.). He md. Elisabetha Michel (HJ) and had ch. bpt. at Germantown Ref. and Linlithgo Ref. Churches (HJ).

   ii) <u>Wilhelm[3]</u>, bpt. 19 May 1741 - sp.: Willem Coen and

Elizabeth Koen (Germantown Ref. Chbk.). He md. 27 Oct
1767 Gertraud Pulver (Germantown Ref. Chbk.) and had
ch. bpt. at Germantown Ref. Church (HJ).

  iii) Maria³, bpt. 12 May 1743 - sp.: Hieronimus Falckenburg
and wife Mareitje Meyer (Germantown Ref. Chbk.). She
md. 1st Caspar Minckeler and 2nd 10 Feb 1767 Wilhelm
Schneider (Germantown Ref. Chbk.).

  iv) Catharina³, bpt. 23 April 1749 - sp.: Peter Cilmer
and Catharina Fritz (Germantown Ref. Chbk.).

6) Abraham² (HJ), md. Anna Eva Laucks (HJ), who md. after Abraham's death to Johnn Michael Muchie. She joined the Red
Hook Luth. Church in 1742. The ch. of Abraham² Kilmer were:

  i) Nicolaus³, bpt. 8 Dec 1741 - sp.: Nicolaas Louck and
Lisabeth (Germantown Ref. Chbk.).

  ii) Emmerich³, bpt. 23 Jan 1743 - sp.: Emmerich Schauermann and Catterina Schertz (Red Hook Luth. Chbk.).

  iii) Elisabetha³, bpt. 5 Feb 1744 - sp.: Nicklas Laucks and
Elizabeth Laucks (Red Hook Luth. Chbk.). She md. Petrus Meyer 5 Nov 1764 (Linlithgo Ref. Chbk.).

  iv) Catharina³, bpt. 9 Feb 1746 - sp.: Abraham Devu and
Maria Catterina Reiffenberg (Red Hook Luth. Chbk.).

  v) Adam³, bpt. 6 March 1748 - sp.: Adam Reiffenberger
and Agnes John (Germantown Ref. Chbk.). He md. Catharina Kohl (HJ). They had ch. bpt. at Germantown Ref.
and a son Abraham bpt. at Manorton Luth. (HJ).

  vi) Nicolaus³, bpt. 13 April 1750 - sp.: Niclaes Tingebach
and Catharina Althuyser (Linlithgo Ref. Chbk.).

  vii) Wilhelm³, bpt. 17 June 1752 - sp.: Willem Jacobi and
wife Eva Schuk (Germantown Ref. Chbk.). He md. Jannet
Ellen (Allen) (HJ). They had a son bpt. at Manorton
Luth. Church (HJ).

7) Anna Barbara², b. 22 Dec 1720 at Camp - sp.: Parents and
Anna Barbara Loscher (N.Y. City Luth. Chbk.). She md.
Philip Speichermann (HJ).

8) Catharina² (HJ), md. David Stiever (Stuber) (HJ).

9) Johann Wilhelm², bpt. 7 weeks old 28 Nov 1725 - sp.: Johann Wilhelm Kunz (West Camp Luth. Chbk.).

10) Henrich², bpt. 3 months old at Kamp 5 May 1728 - sp.:
Henr. Winter and Liesabeth Kilmer (N.Y. City Luth. Chbk.).

Among the unplaced Kilmers along the Hudson were 1) Abraham
Gilmer, a sp. to Arndt Decker in 1769 at the Manorton Luth. Church;
2) Georg Kohlman who md. Maria Kohl and sp. at Germantown Ref. in
1774; 3) John Kilmer who md. Eleanor Dufly and had a ch. bpt. in
1773 at Gallatin Ref. Church; and 4) the Georg Kilmer who had an

illegitimate child with Catharina Milius named Georg, bpt. 2 April
1749 (Gallatin Ref. Chbk.); a comparison with the way this bpt.
was entered in the registers with other entries at the same time
and place confirms the illegitimacy (HJ).

JOHANN JACOB KUHN (Hunter Lists #411)

Hans Jacob Kun, his wife, and 5 ch., were in the 6th party of
Palatines in Holland in 1709 (Rotterdam Lists). There was a Johann Jacob Kuhn aus der Schweitz von Balcken Zürcher Gebieth who,
as he was called a cowherd, a swineherd, and a daylabourer, was
found in several Chbks. in the Pfalz. This Johann Jacob Kuhn and
wife Maria Elisabetha had ch. bpt. at several villages where other
1709ers were found: 1) Johann Wilhelm, bpt. 27 Nov 1695 at 6661
Rieschweiler; 2) Johann Jacob, bpt. 12 July 1697 at 6661 Rieschweiler; 3) Hanß Simon, bpt. 1 April 1703 at 6653 Webenheim; and
4) Anna Gertraud, bpt. Jan 1706 at Walsheim a/Blies. Another possible emigrant was the Johann Jacob Chun who md. 8 Dec 1676 to Anna
Elisabetha, d/o Wilhelm Mannschmied from Münster at 6251 Runkel,
another point of origin for many N.Y. settlers; this couple had a
son Johann Wilhelm b. 18 May 1686 at Runkel. However, no firm proof
has been found cementing either of these Johann Jacob Kuhns with
one of the American 1709ers of that name (HJ).

The Hunter secretary also noted #417 Jacob Kuntz 1st and
#418 Jacob Kuntz[d] on the subsistence rolls, making organization of
these emigrants extremely difficult. However, I believe that #418
Jacob Kuntz 2[d] and Johann Jacob Kuhn, #411 above, were entries for
the same emigrant: both were recorded near the Monin, Briegel, and
German families at various times on the lists, and the entries
never overlapped (HJ). #418 Jacob Kuntz 2[d] had but one entry on
the Hunter Lists on 4 July 1710 with 2 pers. over 10 yrs. of age
and 1 pers. under 10 yrs.; #411 Johann Jacob Kuhn had 3 over 10 yrs.
beginning 4 Aug 1710. Jacob Kuhn of Queensbury was noted as a Palatine soldier in 1711 (Palatine Volunteers To Canada). Jacob Koens
was on the roll of the Independent Company of the Manor of Livingston 30 Nov 1715 (Report of the State Historian, Vol. I, p. 522).
Jacob Kuhn with wife and ch. was at Heessberg ca. 1716/17 (Simmendinger Register); he was recorded directly next to Georg Colmer's
family (HJ). Jacob Koen was a Palatine Debtor in 1719 and 1721
(when he was recorded next to Wm. Koen) (Livingston Debt Lists);
there were other entries for a Jacob Koen on these lists, but I
believe they belong to Johann Jacob[2], s/o the emigrant 1709er
#420 Mathias[1] Kuntz (HJ). William S. Coons, in his classic Koon-
Coons Families of Eastern N.Y., appears not to have had access

to either the Hunter Lists or the Simmendinger Register until his manuscript was ready for publication, and thus has placed several ch. of Johann Jacob[1] Kuhn in the family of Samuel[1] Kuhn. After carefully weighing all the evidence, including German data on Samuel[1] Kuhn, the juxtaposition of Jacob and Wm. Koen's names on the Livingston Debt Lists, and especially the close association of Johann Jacob[1] Kuhn and Georg[1] Kilmer beginning in 1710 when they were near each other on the Hunter Lists and continuing to 1716/17 when they were next to each other on Simmendinger's roll, I am convinced that the ch. of Johann Jacob[1] Kuhn were:

1) Johann Wilhelm[2] (HJ), md. Elisabetha Kilmer (HJ), whose family had been noted near Johann Jacob[1] Kuhn on various Palatine mss. since their arrival in 1710. Willem Coen sp. Dirk Gelmer (Georg Kilmer - HJ) in 1723 with a Cath: Coen; perhaps she was his mother (HJ). Wm Koen was a Palatine Debtor in 1719, 1721 (next to Jacob Koen), 1722, and 1726 (Livingston Debt Lists). A William Coun was entered on tax rolls in the Middle Ward in 1728/29 (Dutchess Co. Tax Lists). The ch. of Johann Wilhelm[2] and Elisabetha were:

   i) Elisabetha[3], b. 1 April 1720 at Central Camp on the East Bank - sp.: Simon Calmer and Elisabeth Funck (N.Y. City Luth. Chbk.). Simon, Elisabeth, and Anna Margritha Kun joined the Germantown Ref. Church 7 June 1742. She md. 21 April 1747 Johannes Linck (Germantown Ref. Chbk.).

   ii) Simon[3], b. March 1721 at Camp - sp.: Simon Kelmer and Catharina Funck (N.Y. City Luth. Chbk.). He md. Catharina Linck (HJ) and had ch. bpt. at Germantown Ref., Rhinebeck Luth., and Red Hook Luth. Churches (HJ).

   iii) Maria Elisabetha[3] (HJ), md. Johannes Jager (HJ).

   iv) Anna Margaretha[3], bpt. 26 June 1726 - sp.: Tjerk Kermer and Elisabeth Kortenaar (Kingston Ref. Chbk.). She md. Johannes Michael 8 Nov 1743 (Loonenburg Luth. Chbk.).

   v) Johann Henrich[3], b. 30 March 1734 - sp.: Henrich Kun and wife Gertrut (Rhinebeck Luth. Chbk.). He md. Margaretha Kilmer (HJ) and had ch. bpt. at Rhinebeck Luth. and Germantown Ref. Churches (HJ).

   vi) Georg[3] (HJ), md. Anna Maria Plass (HJ) and had ch. bpt. at Churchtown Luth., Germantown Ref., and Manorton Luth. Churches (HJ).

2) Henrich[2] (HJ), who sp. Johann Wilhelm[2] in 1734 at Rhinebeck Luth. Church and was himself sp. many times by members of the Kilmer family. He md. Anna Gertraud Falckenberg (HJ)

494

and had ch.:

i) Anna³, bpt. 5 Oct 1735 - sp.: Jurrie Cilmer and Anna Volckenburgh (Germantown Ref. Chbk.).

ii) Simon³, md. as s/o Henrich of Camp 12 Dec 1758 Elisabetha Minckler (Germantown Ref. Chbk.). They had ch. bpt. at Germantown Ref. Church (HJ).

iii) Anna³, bpt. 12 Jan 1741 - sp.: Adam Reiffenberger and Angenietje Falkenburg (Red Hook Luth. Chbk.). She md. as d/o Henrich 20 March 1759 Henrich Gerretson (Germantown Ref. Chbk.).

iv) Catharina³, bpt. 23 June 1745 - sp.: Gorg Kilmer and Catterina Linck (Red Hook Luth. Chbk.). She md. as d/o Henrich 26 Nov 1765 Jacob Minckler (Germantown Ref. Chbk.).

v) Anna Margaretha³, bpt. 30 Aug 1747 - sp.: Jurg Kilmer and Anna Margaretha Kilmer (Germantown Ref. Chbk.). She md. 5 Dec 1770 Nicolaus Bauer (Germantown Ref. Chbk.).

vi) Wilhelm³ (HJ), md. 1st Elisabeth Elik or Ellen 21 April 1772 (Germantown Ref. Chbk.) and 2nd Elsjen Schneider (HJ).

vii) Maria Elisabetha³, bpt. 15 April 1750 - sp.: Johannes Jager and Mari Liess Jager (Germantown Ref. Chbk.).

viii) Susanna³, bpt. 12 Nov 1752 - sp.: Pieter Pulver and wife Susanna Trom (Germantown Ref. Chbk.).

ix) Henrich³, bpt. 9 Jan 1759 - sp.: Henricus Kuhn and Gertgen Petzer (Germantown Ref. Chbk.).

There was a Wilhelm Kuhn who md. Margaretha Bitzer by 1773 who seems to belong in this family, perhaps as a s/o Johann Wilhelm² (HJ). There also was an Elisabetha Kuhn who md. Hermann Bitzer by 1755 probably connected to this group (HJ).

SAMUEL KUHN (Hunter Lists #412)

The German origins of this family were with so many other N.Y. 1709ers at 6451 Hüttengesäß (13 km. n.e. of Hanau), entries for this village at 6456 Langenselbold (3 km. further s.; Chbks. begin 1563). The earliest known ancestor of the emigrant was his father Hans Kuhn, bur. 19 March 1693, aged 70 yrs; his wife Catharina d. at Hüttengesäß and was bur. 13 Nov 1679, aged 50 yrs. They had ch.:

Anna, md. 1st Georg Brüning and 2nd 25 Nov 1685 the N.Y. 1709er Nicolaus Bellinger.

Anna Margaretha, bpt. 11 Aug 1661 - the w/o (?) Henrich Kuhn von Lüden named Anna Margaret.

+ <u>Samuel</u>, b. in Hüttengesäß and bpt. 11 April 1664 - sp. Samuel
Reichert.

<u>Johannes</u>, b. in Hüttengesäß and bpt. 7 Nov 1666 - sp.: Johann
- s/o Caspar Reydel.

<u>Catharina</u>, b. in Hüttengesäß and bpt. Dna Oculi: 1668 - sp.:
Catharina - w/o Hans Kunesen (Kuhn?) of Marköbel.

<u>Johannes</u>, b. in Hüttengesäß and bpt. 21 Aug 1670 - sp.: Johan
Neidart ... Marköbel.

<u>Hermann</u>, b. in Hüttengesäß and bpt. 28 Jan 1672 - sp.: H.
Hermann Tollitzen.

<u>Johann Cyriax</u>, twin to the above, bpt. 28 Jan 1672 - sp.: H.
Cyriax Krähen.

In a list dated 30 Sept 1693 in the Birstein Archives, Nicklas
Böllinger and Samuel Kuhn each had 1 horse and ½ car at Hüttenge-
säß. Samuel, s/o Hans Kuhn at Hüttengesäß, md. Magdalena, d/o
Conrad Berthen, 1 Nov 1688.

Samuel Kuhn made his initial appearance on the Hunter Lists
4 Aug 1710 with 6 pers. over 10 yrs. and 1 pers. under 10; he was
enrolled directly next to Niclaus Bellinger, his brother-in-law,
on this entry (HJ). He was registered with 5 over 10 yrs. on 25
March 1711, with 4 over 10 and 1 under 10 yrs. on 24 June 1711,
with 3 over 10 and 1 under 10 on 24 Dec 1711, with 3 over 10 yrs.
and 2 under 10 on 25 March 1712, and finally with 4 over 10 and
2 under 10 yrs. on 24 June 1712. Samuel Kuhn and Rosenzweigin
were noted on 24 June 1711 on the Hunter Lists. Samuel Kuhn of
Annsberg was a soldier in 1711 (Palatine Volunteers To Canada).
Samuel Kun and Elisabetha with 5 ch. were at Wormsdorff ca. 1716/
17 (Simmendinger Register). Samuel Koen was a Palatine Debtor in
1718, 1721, and 1726 (Livingston Debt Lists). The ch. of Samuel[1]
Kuhn and his first wife Magdalena Berthen were:

1) <u>Johann Valentin[2]</u>, b. at Hüttengesäß and bpt. 4 June 1690
- sp.: Valentin - surviving son of Samuel Heidart (Langenselbold Chbk.). Valentin Kuhn was entered next to Samuel Kuhn and Rosenzweigen on 24 June 1711 on the Hunter
Lists. Valtin Kuhn of Annsberg was a soldier in 1711 (Palatine Volunteers To Canada). Valentin Kuhn and Anna Catharina with 3 ch. were living next to Marx and Heinrich
Bellinger at Neu-Ansberg in 1716/17 (Simmendinger Register). In the bpt. of his son Samuel in 1718 at Schenectady
Ref. Church, he was called from Scoharry. Velten Koon was
enrolled on tax lists in 1725/26 (Dutchess Co. Tax Lists).
He md. 1st Anna Catharina Wies (HJ) with whom he had his
ch. and probably md. 2nd Catharina Manck or Mauck (HJ).
The ch. of Johann Valentin[2] Kuhn were:

     i) <u>Johanna Elisabetha Margaretha</u>³, b. 1 Nov 1711 - sp.:
Hermann Segendorst, Anna Elisabetha Wis, and Anna Mar-
garetha Schaester (West Camp Luth. Chbk.). She md.
Jacob Drom (HJ).

    ii) <u>Anna Elisabetha</u>³ (HJ), md. John Bois (HJ).

  iii) <u>Anna Catharina</u>³, b. 21 Nov 1715 and bpt. at Schoharie
- sp.: the d/o Niclaus Feller (West Camp Luth. Chbk.).
She md. Ephraim Weller (HJ).

   iv) <u>Samuel</u>³, bpt. 2 June 1718, the parents being from Scoharry - sp.: not given (Schenectady Ref. Chbk.). He
md. Elisabetha Löscher (HJ) and had ch. bpt. at Loonenburg Luth., Linlithgo Ref., and Germantown Ref.
Churches (HJ).

    v) <u>Henrich</u>³ (HJ), md. Susanna Hoffmann (HJ) and had ch.
bpt. at Red Hook Luth., Kingston Ref., and Germantown
Ref. Churches (HJ).

   vi) <u>Catharina</u>³ (HJ), md. Anthony Poucher (HJ).

  vii) <u>Jacob</u>³ (HJ), joined the Germantown Ref. Church 7 June
1747 with Hermann Kuhn. Jacob³ md. Maria Kohl (HJ)
and had ch. bpt. at Germantown Ref., Linlithgo Ref.,
Rhinebeck Flats Ref., and Manorton Luth. Churches (HJ).

 viii) <u>Peter</u>³, bpt. 9 April 1727 - sp.: Pieter Polver and
Anna Maria Steel (Kingston Ref. Chbk.). He md. Lea,
d/o Jacob Kohl, 27 Oct 1747 (Germantown Ref. Chbk.).

   ix) <u>Johann Hermann</u>³, b. 21 Aug 1732 and bpt. at Camp -
sp.: Herman Kuhn and Anna Maria Mor (Loonenburg Luth.
Chbk.). He md. Catharina Kreissler (HJ) and had issue
bpt. at Red Hook Luth., Linlithgo Ref., Rhinebeck
Luth., Manorton Luth., and Rhinebeck Flats Ref.
Churches (HJ).

2) <u>Johann Conrad</u>², b. at Hüttengesäß and bpt. 9 July 1693 -
sp.: the s/o Conrad Berthen (Langenselbold Chbk.). Conrad
Kuhn of Annsberg was a soldier in 1711 (Palatine Volunteers
To Canada). Conrad Kuhn and Anna Margretha with 2 ch. were
listed next to Johannes Wiss at Neu-Ansberg ca. 1716/17
(Simmendinger Register). The ch. of Johann Conrad² and
his wife Anna Margaretha (Schoharie Ref. Chbk. calls her
Koning, but I believe she may have been d/o the 1709er
Ludolph Curring - HJ) were:

     i) <u>Georg</u>³ (HJ), md. Anna Rosina Ehrhardt (HJ). George
Coon, aged 46, b. Albany, labourer, 5' 5 3/4", dark
complexion, brown eyes, black hair, was in Capt. Christopher Yates Company in 1760 in Albany (<u>Report of the
State Historian</u>, Vol. II, p. 587). Jeurre, Conradt,

Simon and John Coon were under the command of Lt.
John M: Veeder and Ensign Gerret Banker in the Colony of Rencelarswick in 1767 (Report of the State Historian, Vol. II, p. 820).

   ii) Anna Margaretha[3] (HJ), md. Ludwig Wanner (HJ).

  iii) Johanna Elisabetha[3] (HJ), md. Johann Henrich Laux
23 Feb 1739 (Schoharie Ref. Chbk.).

   iv) Elisabetha Barbara[3] (HJ), md. Rudolph Foore (Forrer)
(HJ).

    v) Johannes[3] (HJ), md. 28 Sept 1751 Hillitje Zeger (Al-
bany Ref. Chbk.). They had a son Coenradt bpt. at
Albany in 1757 (HJ).

   vi) Adam[3], bpt. 6 Oct 1731 - sp.: Adam Zee and Margrieta
Pellinger (Schoharie Ref. Chbk.). He md. Maria Vander
Hoef 13 Jan 1757 (Albany Ref. Chbk.).

3) Anna Barbara[2], b. Hüttengesäß and bpt. 4 Dec 1696 - sp.:
the d/o Johannes Köhler (Langenselbold Chbk.).

4) Barbara Elisabetha[2], b. Hüttengesäß and bpt. 18 Sept 1700
- sp.: Elisab. - d/o H. Schultheiss Clos Ziegen (Langen-
selbold Chbk.). Note that her bpt. sp. was simply named
Elisabetha, which probably was the name the child used
(HJ). Sp. firmly show that this Elisabetha[2] md. Sebastian
Löscher (HJ).

5) Anna Catharina[2], bpt. 19 Aug 1703 - sp.: Anna Catharina -
d/o George Horre (Hüttengesäß Chbk. or Langenselbold
Chbk.).

With his 2nd wife Elisabetha (Rosenzweig? - HJ), the ch. of Samuel[1] Kuhn were:

6) Johann Hermann[2] (HJ), md. as single man b. in the Camp
2 Sept 1735 Anna Catharina Segendorff (Kingston Ref.
Chbk.). He md. 2nd Sarah Younglove, wid/o Thomas Loomis,
10 Dec 1765 (Germantown Ref. Chbk.). Issue from 1st wife:

    i) Elisabetha Gertraud[3], b. 1 Jan 1738 and bpt. at the
Camp - sp.: Jurge Segendorff and Gertraud Berhard
(Loonenburg Luth. Chbk.). She md. Johann Peter Roos
(HJ).

   ii) Anna Margaretha[3], b. 31 Oct 1739 and bpt. Goghkem.
(Ancram) - sp.: Marcus Kuhn and wife Anna Margreta
(Loonenburg Luth. Chbk.). She probably md. Jacob Hen-
derer (HJ).

  iii) Elisabetha[3], bpt. 27 Aug 1741 - sp.: Bastian Lesher
and Lisabeth Coen (Germantown Ref. Chbk.). She md.
27 May 1760 Johannes Hochdiel (Gallatin Ref. Chbk.).

   iv) Samuel[3], bpt. 16 April 1745 - sp.: Pieter Segendorf

and Catharina Lascher (Germantown Ref. Chbk.). He md.
Elsje Schut (HJ) and had ch. bpt. at Linlithgo Ref.,
Claverack Ref., and Gallatin Ref. Churches (HJ).

v) Hermann[3] (HJ), md. 30 Nov 1769 Jannet Schut (Linlithgo
Ref. Chbk.). They had ch. bpt. at Gallatin Ref.
Church (HJ).

vi) Johann Marcus[3], bpt. 8 Jan 1749 - sp.: Marcus Kuhn
and Mareitgen Kuhn (Gallatin Ref. Chbk.). He md. Abigail Loomis (HJ). Papers in the Estate of Marks Coon
of Ancram were issued to Abigail Coon 2 Sept 1815
(Columbia Co. Administrations Bk. C).

vii) Anna Maria[3], bpt. 16 Dec 1750 - sp.: Georg Michel
Duns and Anna Maria Duns (Gallatin Ref. Chbk.).

viii) Johann Adam[3], bpt. 7 July 1754 - sp.: Adam Segendorf
and Margritje Lesser (Germantown Ref. Chbk.). He d.
in 1825, aged 72 yrs. (Gallatin Ref. Cem.).

ix) Johann Peter[3], bpt. 28 Jan 1756 - sp.: Johannes Peter
Schneider and Anna Magdalena Herkersdorf (Gallatin
Ref. Chbk.).

7) Marcus[2], b. 30 July 1714 - sp.: Marcus Bellinger (West
Camp Luth. Chbk.). He md. Anna Maria Löscher (HJ); she
may have been the Marx Kuhn's wife who d. 8 Nov 1793 (Manorton Luth. Chbk.).

There were Kuhns in the area of Dover, N.Y. who belong in
this Samuel[1] family, such as Capt. Peter Coon of Dover who d. 6
Sept 1795 in his 73rd yr.; William S. Coons places him in the family of Johann Conrad[2], but I believe a bit more proof is needed
to cement this connective (HJ).

CONRAD KUHN now his son VALENTIN (Hunter Lists #413)

Koenraet Koen, his wife, (sons) Hans Veldekoen, Hans Deterkoen, Hans Jürgekoen, and one (other) child, were in Holland in
the 2nd party of 1709 (Rotterdam Lists). Conrad Kühn aged 40, his
wife, sons aged 14, 11, 8, and 2, Ref., husbandman and vinedresser,
were in the 2nd arrivals in England in 1709 (London Lists).

Conrad Kuhn made his first appearance on the Hunter Lists 4
Aug 1710 with 2 over 10 yrs. and 1 under 10. Although the heading
in the Ledger section notes his son Valentin, the Journal entries
mention only Conrad Kuhn: he had 2 over 10 on 25 March 1711, 1
over 10 yrs. on 25 March 1712, and 2 over 10 on 24 June 1712.
The ch. of Conrad[1] Kuhn were:

1) Johann Veltin[2] (Rotterdam Lists & Hunter Ledger), the Hans
Ffellacoons aged 15, orphan, apprenticed to one Caleb

Heathcote of Scarsdale on 22 Sept 1710 (Apprenticeship
Lists).

2) <u>Johann Peter²</u> (HJ), probably the Hans Deterkoen at Rotterdam in 1709 (HJ).

3) <u>Johann Georg²</u> (Rotterdam Lists). Hans Jerick Coons aged 6,
an orphan, was bound to Saml. Mulford at East Hampton also
on 22 Sept 1710 (Apprenticeship Lists).

An article "The Coon (Coan) Family of Guilford, Conn.", a letter from Virginia Coan Wiles, published in <u>Connecticut Ancestry</u>
(The Stamford Genealogical Society), Vol. 17, No. 4, May 1975,
mentions this family. An excellent volume chronicling this group
is Ruth Coan Fulton's <u>Coan Genealogy 1697 - 1982</u> which details the
descendants of Peter and Georg Coan of Guilford, Conn. (HJ).

VALENTIN KUHN (Hunter Lists #414)

It appears that the Hunter secretary may have mixed up two
Valentin Kuhns under #414 (HJ): Valentin Kuhn was listed next to
Anna Margaretha Kuhnin modo Phil: Laux's wife on 4 Oct 1710 with
1 pers. over 10 yrs. in his family. On 31 Dec 1710 he was listed
with 2 over 10 yrs. next to Georg Laux and one name from Marx Bellinger, whose mother was sister to the 1709er Samuel Kuhn (HJ).
From that point on, he appears to have been noted near members of
the Samuel Kuhn and Bellinger family; on 25 March 1712, Valentin
Kuhn was listed with 2 over 10 and 1 under 10 yrs. in the household. Thus there may have been two Valentin Kuhns under one heading: one who was brother of Anna Margaretha Kuhn, who md. the
step-son of Georg Laux named Philip (Laux) Launhardt, and the other
who was s/o the emigrant Samuel¹ Kuhn of Langenselbold (HJ). As if
to confuse the issue, on the Debit side of the Ledger section in
Hunter, the heading reads Valentin Kuhn - s/o Conrad Kuhn!

BENEDICT KUHNER (Hunter Lists #415)

The origins of this emigrant were at 6733 <u>Haßloch</u> (8 km. e.
of Neustadt a. d. Weinstraße; Chbks. begin 1700, Ref.). Benedict
Kuhner was a farmer in 1703. Bendik Kindr, his wife, and 3 ch.,
were on Capt. Jno. Blouwer's ship 3 July 1709 in the 5th party of
Palatines (Rotterdam Lists).

He made his first appearance on the Hunter Lists 30 June 1710
as #333 Benedict <u>H</u>uner with 2 pers. over 10 and 2 under 10 yrs.
Benedict <u>K</u>uner was recorded 4 Oct 1710 with 2 over 10 yrs. and 2
under 10 in the family. Benedictus Kuhner aged 36, Anna Felice Kuhner aged 40, Jacob A. Kuhner aged 4, and Eva Barbara Kuhner aged
9, were in N.Y. City in 1710/11 (Palatines In N.Y. City). Benedict

Kiner and his wife with 2 ch. were auf dem Rarendantz ca. 1716/17
(Simmendinger Register). The ch. of Benedict[1] Kuhner and wife
Felicitas (so-called at Haßloch) were:

1) <u>Eva Barbara</u>[2], bpt. 12 June 1701 - sp.: Eva Barbara - w/o
   Hanns Nebbers (?) (Haßloch Chbk.).
2) <u>Margaretha</u>[2], bpt. as Maria Cretha 23 Dec 1703 - sp.: Maria
   Cretha - w/o Georg Würth (Haßloch Chbk.).
3) <u>Anna Catharina</u>[2], bpt. 26 April 1705 - sp.: Anna Cath. -
   single d/o Georg Lochmann (Haßloch Chbk.).
4) <u>Johann Jacob</u>[2], b. at Böhl and bpt. 6 Nov 1707 - sp.: Joh.
   Jacob Wurth (Haßloch Chbk.).

My friend Annette Burgert of Worthington, Ohio was the first
to pinpoint the ancestral town of Benedict Kuhner.

MATHEUS KUNDY'S WIDDOW (Hunter Lists #416)

Matheus Gundy made his initial appearance on the Hunter Lists
30 June 1710 with 2 pers. over 10 yrs. of age. His entry for 4 Aug
1710 read 3 over 10 yrs. of age. Mathias Kundy's Wid[W] was noted
31 Dec 1710 with 2 over 10, and again on 25 March 1711 with 1 pers.
over 10 yrs. of age. On 24 June 1711 Jost Laux and Math: Kuhn's
wid[W] were noted on Hunter, but this probably refers to one of the
Matthias Kuhns and not Matheus Kundy (HJ).

A Martin Cundy was recorded in Franconia, Philadelphia Co.
in 1734 (<u>Genealogical Society of Pa. Publications</u>, Vol. I, 1895 -
1899, p. 170); as Martin and Mattheus sometimes interchanged as
Palatine Christian names in the 18th century, perhaps this Martin
Cundy was a descendant of the emigrant (HJ). A Christian Gondy
took the Oath of Allegiance to Pa. in 1739 (<u>Statutes At Large Of
Pa.</u>, Vol. IV, p. 327). A Joh[S] Freder[k] Kunter md. Cornel[ia] Coelie
24 Jan 1729 (N.Y. City Ref. Chbk.).

JACOB KUNTZ 1ST (Hunter Lists #417)

Jacob Kuntz made his initial appearance on the Hunter Lists
1 July 1710 with 2 over 10 yrs.; the entry for 4 Aug 1710 read 1
pers. over 10, for 4 Oct 1710 noted 2 over 10, and for 31 Dec 1710
recorded Jacob Kuntz's Wid[W] with 3 over 10 yrs. A study of the
juxtaposition of names near her on Hunter and at West Camp (i.e.
Hieronymus Schaib) suggests she was the Anna Maria Kuntz: 1 woman,
in Ulster Co. in 1710/11 (West Camp Census) (HJ).

JACOB KUNTZ 2ND (Hunter Lists #418)

See #411 Johann Jacob Kuhn (HJ).

JOHANNES KUNTZ (Hunter Lists #419)

A John Cunitz aged 33, his wife, sons aged 15 and 5, daughter
aged 1, Catholic, husbandman and vinedresser, were in the 2nd arrivals in England in 1709 (London Lists).

Johannes Kuntz made his first appearance on the Hunter Lists
4 Aug 1710 with 1 pers. over 10 and 1 pers. under 10. His entry
for 4 Oct 1710 read 1 pers. over 10 yrs. of age. The family was
recorded with 4 over 10 yrs. on 24 June 1711, with 4 over 10 and
1 under 10 on 24 Dec 1711, and with 6 pers. over 10 yrs. in the
cumulative entry 24 Dec 1711. He was the Johannes Kuatz noted next
to Maria Cath: Hebmannin (his future wife - HJ) in N.Y. City in
1710/11; his age was given as 40 yrs. in that mss. (Palatines In
N.Y. City). Johannis Coens was nat. 31 Jan 1715/16 (Albany Nats.).
Johannes Cuntz and Maria Catharina with 4 ch. were at Neu-Ansberg
ca. 1716/17 (Simmendinger Register). Maria Catherine Koens (a widow) was a patentee on the n. side of the Mohawk 30 April 1725,
and Lodwick Kones was a patentee on the s. side of the Mohawk on
that date (both Burnetsfield Patent). Pastor Sommer recorded one
Maria Catharina Contz at the Fall ca. 1744 (Schoharie Luth.
Chbk.). Joh[S] Coens, a widower of Cenr. Pals of Alssey, md. Maria
Catharina Vogelezang, wid/o Michiel Hüpman of the Graafschap Hardenberg, 23 Jan 1711 (N.Y. City Ref. Chbk.) and had issue:
1) Ludwig[2], b. 6 Dec 1711 - sp.: Ludwig Berscht (West Camp
Luth. Chbk.). He was a patentee in 1725 (Burnetsfield
Patent).

MATHIAS KUNTZ (Hunter Lists #420)

Philipp Henrich Cuntz, s/o Mattheus of Queensberg (and) of
Bischmusen near Saarbruecken, md. Maria Elisabetha Manngen, d/o
Ferdinand of Ansberg (and) of Wollbergshofen near Colln in the
commune of Neuburg, 25 June 1716 (West Camp Luth. Chbk.). The correct ancestral home of Mathias[1] Kuntz was 6601 Bischmisheim (3
km. e. of Saarbrücken; Registers are copies made by Pfr. Rug in
1930/31 from the original Chbks. which were lost during World War
II and copied again by Ludwig Luckenbill). It appears as if William S. Coons in his Koon-Coons Families of Eastern N.Y. had access
only to Vol. II of the Chbks. (HJ): Vol. I begins in 1672 and
from the copy made of this old register a more detailed history
of the American family emerges. The father of Mathias[1] Kuntz was
Johann Nickel Cuntz, bur. 23 Nov 1693, aged 68 yrs.; his wife was
Maria Clara, bur. 27 Feb 1694 aged 57 (67?) yrs. and md. 43 yrs.
according to her obituary. Johann Nickel Cuntz and his wife Maria
Clara had ch.:

+ <u>Matthias</u>, conf. 1681, aged 16 yrs.

<u>Hanß Jacob</u>, conf. as s/o Hans Nickel in 1682, aged nearly 14.
He md. Anna Eva Wolff 28 April 1697 and was bur. 14 Sept 1701.

<u>Anna Maria</u>, conf. as d/o Hans Nickel in 1685, aged nearly
13 yrs.

<u>Johann Georg</u>, conf. as s/o Johan Nickel in 1690, aged 14½ yrs.

<u>Johann Nikolaus</u> (?), conf. with no father named in 1696.

<u>Johann Bartholomäus</u> (?), conf. in 1696 with no father named.

<u>Johann Leonhardt</u>, called brother to Matthias in 1688.

Matthias Kuntz, s/o Joh. Nickel Kuntz, md. Anna Margaretha, d/o
Johann Lücken, 26 Jan 1687. Johannes Lück, Gerichtsmann and Bruder-
meister (?), was bur. 20 Dec 1693, aged 76 yrs.; Katharina Klein,
mother-in-law of Hanns Lücken, d. 24 April 1686. Anna Margaretha,
w/o Matthis Cuntz, was bur. 2 Feb 1704. Matthias Cuntz, widower,
md. Anna Margareth Spitz, single woman from Frankfurt, 1 Oct 1704.
Matteus Runtz, his wife, and 6 ch. were on Capt. Enrit's ship in
Holland in the 5th party of 1709 (Rotterdam Lists); he was but
one name away from Daniel Schumager, who also came from Bischmisheim (HJ).

Mathias Kuntz made his initial appearance on the Hunter Lists
4 July 1710 with 5 pers. over 10 yrs. of age and 1 pers. under 10
yrs. The family was recorded with 6 pers. over 10 on 4 Oct 1710,
4 over 10 yrs. and 2 under 10 on 24 June 1711, 2 over 10 and 2 under
10 on 25 March 1712, and 3 over 10 yrs. of age and 2 under 10 yrs.
on 24 June 1712. Mattheus Kuntz was a soldier from Queensbury in
1711 (Palatine Volunteers To Canada). Mathys Coens was nat. 17 Jan
1715/16 (Albany Nats.). Matthäus Cuntz and Anna Margretha with 5
ch. were at Quunsberg ca. 1716/17 (Simmendinger Register). Matys
Koens was a Palatine Debtor in 1718 and 1719 (at Kingsberry); Margriet Koons was a Palatine Debtor in 1721 (Livingston Debt Lists).
The ch. of Mathias[1] Kuntz and his first wife Anna Margaretha Lücken
were:

1) <u>Johann Leonhardt</u>[2], b. 4 Jan 1688 - sp.: Johann Leonhard
   Kuntz the brother, Hans Wendel Wund from Dutweiler, and
   Frau Eva Magdalena - w/o Master Hans Jacob Rotsch, the miller of the Brettbacher mill (Bischmisheim Chbk.). He was
   conf. as s/o Matthias in 1701 (Bischmisheim Chbk.).

2) <u>Anna Margaretha</u>[2], b. 31 March 1689 - sp.: Hans Michael -
   s/o Matthis Scherer, Anna Margaretha - single d/o the Pfr.
   G. Grath, and Anna Maria - d/o the late Barthel Kuntz
   (Bischmisheim Chbk.). She was conf. as a d/o Matth. Kuntz
   in 1704, aged 15 yrs. (Bischmisheim Chbk.). Anna Margaretha[2]
   md. the N.Y. 1709er Nicolaus Bohnenstiehl (HJ).

3) <u>Johann Jacob</u>[2], bpt. 16 April 1690 - sp.: Barthel Maurer,

Hanß Jacob Ludt - both Gemeinsmen here, and Anna Maria -
d/o Hannß Franz Ludt here (Bischmisheim Chbk.). He was conf.
in 1706 as a s/o Matth. Kuntz (Bischmisheim Chbk.). Johann
Jacob Cuntz, s/o Matheus of Bishmisten in the earldom of
Nastau-Sarbruck, md. Susanna Michel, d/o Henrich of the
commune of Maussenheim in Zweybruck, 2 Nov 1714 (West Camp
Luth. Chbk.). Jacob Coens was nat. next to Philip Coens
14 Feb 1715/16 (Albany Nats.). Jacob Cuntz and Susanna with
1 child were at Hunderston ca. 1716/17 (Simmendinger Register). Jacob Koens was a Palatine Debtor in 1718, 1719,
1721 and 1722 (Livingston Debt Lists); there was also one
of that name in 1726 on the Debt Lists, however, that man
probably was one of the several other Jacob Kuntz-Kuhns
in the Hudson Valley at that time (HJ). Susanna, wid/o Johann Jacob Koens, md. Christoffel Snyder in Feb 1724 (Linlithgo Ref. Chbk.). The child of Johann Jacob² and Susanna
was:

    i) Johann Henrich³, b. the beginning of Oct 1721 at Camp
       Queensberry - sp.: J. Henrich Michel, Joh: Henrich
       Haydoorn, and Anna Cath. Schneider (N.Y. City Luth.
       Chbk.).

4) Johann Georg², bpt. 4 Nov 1691 - sp.: Hannß Jakob - s/o
  Hanns Nickel Kuntz, Hans Georg - s/o Hanß Dietsch here,
  and Frau Anna Juliane - w/o Matthis Maurer the trouser-
  knitter here (Bischmisheim Chbk.). He was conf. as a s/o
  Matth. Kuntz in 1706 (Bischmisheim Chbk.). He probably was
  the Johann Georg Kuhns who md. as a single man 9 Oct 1739
  Anna Margaretha Buck in the Highland in the Kloof at Bach-
  wayk (N.Y. City Luth. Chbk.) and had issue:

    i) Anna Margaretha³, b. 9 Sept 1740 and bpt. at Niclaas
       Emig's - sp.: Jurgen Niclaas Kuhns and wife Agnese
       Catharina (N.Y. City Luth. Chbk.).

    ii) Martinus³, b. 18 Oct 1742 and bpt. in the Klove at
       Bachwaij - sp.: Martin Buck - in his place Nicolaus
       Kuhns, and Gertrude Buck (N.Y. City Luth. Chbk.).

    iii) Philip³, b. 20 Jan 1745 and bpt. in the Klove at Bach-
       way - sp.: Salomon Vliegler and wife Anna Margaretha
       (N.Y. City Luth. Chbk.).

    iv) Gertraud³ (per William S. Coons).

5) Philip Henrich², bpt. 31 May 1693 - sp.: Philips Bräuninger
  - Hirtheissicher Hoffmann at Fechingen, Henrich Pech - the
  innkeeper there, and Sybilla - w/o the honourable Peter
  Müller at Eschringen (Bischmisheim Chbk.). He md. 1st Maria
  Elisabetha, d/o Ferdinand Manngen, 26 June 1716 (West Camp

Luth. Chbk.) and 2nd Anna Barbara (--) (HJ). Philip Coens
was nat. next to Jacob Coens 14 Feb 1715/16 (Albany Nats.).
He was a Palatine Debtor in 1718, 1722, and 1726 (Livingston Debt Lists). His family appeared on the Family List
at St. Peter's Luth. Church at Rhinebeck ca. 1734. A letter from Philip Livingston to Robert Livingston dated 1
June 1745 mentioned Philip Coons and said that he was a
good man who deserved more than many other tenants in the
Manor (Livingston Papers, Reel #7). The will of Philipp
Koons of Livingston Manor was dated 16 Feb 1769 and probated 21 June 1769 (Fernow Wills #984). The ch. of Philip
Henrich[2] Kuntz and his 1st wife Maria Elisabetha were:

   i) Nicolaus[3] (HJ), md. 30 Oct 1745 Anna Margaretha Wied-
      erwachs (Loonenburg Luth. Chbk.). They had ch. bpt.
      at Germantown Ref., Gallatin Ref., Rhinebeck Luth.,
      and Churchtown Luth. Churches (HJ).

  ii) Catharina[3], b. 6 Feb 1721 at Tachkana and bpt. at
      Claverack - sp.: Jacob Stubber and wife Catharina
      (N.Y. City Luth. Chbk.). Catharina and Niclas Kuhn
      were conf. together at Goghkameka in 1738 (Loonenburg
      Luth. Chbk.). She md. Conrad Roschmann 21 Nov 1751
      (Rhinebeck Luth. Chbk.).

 iii) Ferdinand[3], md. as s/o Philip Henrich 29 May 1747
      Maria Silbernagel (Rhinebeck Luth. Chbk.). He was
      conf. 29 May 1739 at Goghkameka (Loonenburg Luth.
      Chbk.).

  iv) Margaretha[3], bpt. in 1725 - sp.: Christoffel Snyder
      and Marg. Bayer (Linlithgo Ref. Chbk.). She was conf.
      in Goghkam. 15 May 1740 (Loonenburg Luth. Chbk.).
      Margaretha md. 16 Sept 1746 Carl Treber (Rhinebeck
      Luth. Chbk.).

   v) Johann Georg[3], bpt. 21 May 1727 - sp.: Hans Kleyn and
      Nickel Coens (Linlithgo Ref. Chbk.). Joh. Jurge Kuhns
      was conf. at Ankrum 3 May 1744 (Loonenburg Luth.
      Chbk.). He md. Catharina (--) (HJ).

  vi) Clara[3], md. as d/o Philip Henrich 23 June 1748 Johan-
      nes Treber (Rhinebeck Luth. Chbk.). She was conf. 23
      May 1745 at Ankrum (Loonenburg Luth. Chbk.).

 vii) Matthias[3] (St. Peter's Luth. Family List).

viii) Philip[3] (St. Peter's Luth. Family List).

  ix) Adam[3], b. 30 March 1735 - sp.: Adam Dings and wife
      Eva (Rhinebeck Luth. Chbk.).

   x) Johannes[3], b. 19 Sept 1737 and bpt. Ancram - sp.:
      Bastian Loscher and wife Lisabeth (Loonenburg Luth.

Chbk.). He was conf. at Ancram 18 Aug 1750, aged 12
(Rhinebeck Luth. Chbk.). He md. Anna (--) (HJ).

6) Anna Maria², b. or bpt. auf dem Königstag: 1696 - sp.:
Conrad Ziegler, Anna Catharina - w/o Simon from Brechbach,
and Anna Maria Maul from Dutweiler (Bischmisheim Chbk.).

7) Johann Wilhelm², bpt. 23 Feb 1698 - sp.: Hans Wilhelm Ziegler, Hans Georg - s/o Adolff Diener, and Anna Margaretha
- wid/o Johann Leonhard Cuntz (Bischmisheim Chbk.).

8) Georg Nicolaus², bpt. as Georg Michel 21 March 1700 - sp.:
Hans Nickel Wölflinger and me, Georg Albrecht Beltzer -
the Pastor here, and Anna Elisab. Scherer - single woman
(Bischmisheim Chbk.). George Nicholas Koens was nat. 4
May 1731 (Ulster Co. Deed Bk. DD-130). Nicolas Kounse was
taxed in Rhinebeck in 1727 - 1731, and then taxed in Beekman from 1732 until his death; his wife was called a widow
on the rolls in 1774 (Dutchess Co. Tax Lists). He md. Agnes Catharina (Buck? - HJ), and William S. Coons suggests
that he may have md. someone else before her. Agnesa Catharina, w/o Jurge Nic. Kuhn, was conf. 20 June 1731 at Pieter Lassing's in the Highland (N.Y. Luth. Chbk.). The ch.
of Georg Nicolaus² and Agnes Catharina were:

   i) Matthias³, b. 29 Aug 1732 and bpt. at Pieter Lassings
     - sp.: Philip Emig and Anna Maria Emig (Loonenburg
     Luth. Chbk.).

  ii) Christina³, b. 13 Jan 1735 and bpt. in the Highland
     at P. Lassing's - sp.: Hans Jurgen Kuhns and Chris-
     tina Buck (N.Y. City Luth. Chbk.).

 iii) Martinus³, b. 1 April 1739 and bpt. in the father's
     house due to the illness of the child - sp.: Martin
     Buck and wife Mareitje (N.Y. City Luth. Chbk.).

  iv) Nicolaus³, b. 26 May 1742 and bpt. Pacquesien - sp.:
     Young Niclaas Bonenstiel and Liesabeth Bock (N.Y.
     City Luth. Chbk.).

   v) Gertraud³, b. 11 Sept 1745 and bpt. Bachgway - sp.:
     Barend Thalheimer and Christina (N.Y. City Luth.
     Chbk.).

William S. Coons adds several other ch. to the family of
Georg Nicolaus² including Christophel and possibly an Adam
and Wilhelm; he may be correct in his assumption, but I
believe further proof is needed on these added ch. to firmly cement them to this line (HJ).

9) Johann Peter², bpt. 16 July 1702 - sp.: Maria Margaretha -
w/o Hans Wendel Wunn at Duttweiler, Hans Peter Lorentz -
miller-servant from Hellenhausen, and Hans Jakob Ehrstein

from Sulz near Weißenburg - miller servant at Brebach. He
was bur. 23 July 1708, aged 6 yrs. (Bischmisheim Chbk.).
With his 2nd wife Anna Margaretha Spitz, the ch. of Matthias[1] were:

10) <u>Anna Barbara</u>[2], bpt. 29 Aug 1706 - sp.: Anna Cath. - single
d/o Adloff Diener here, Anna Barbara - surviving d/o Johann
Nickel Lücken, and Hans Peter - single surviving s/o the
late Johann Leonhard Kuntz (Bischmisheim Chbk.).

11) <u>Anna Catharina</u>[2], bpt. Dom. XVIII p. Trin.: 1708 - sp.:
Maria Catharina - d/o Hans Conrad Kläger from Bubingen,
Anna Catharina - d/o Jacob Klein here, and Hans Davidt -
single s/o Bernhard Jungk (Bischmisheim Chbk.).

12) <u>Johann David</u>[2], bpt. 24 June 1711 - sp.: Johann Bernhard,
J. David Ifland, and Anna Barbara Schumacher (West Camp
Luth. Chbk.). David Kuhns was conf. at Pieter Lassing's
DNIA II p. Trin.: 1737 (N.Y. City Luth. Chbk.). He md.
Catharina Hagedorn (HJ) and eventually settled in Rensselaer Co. (per William S. Coons). His ch. were:

   i) <u>Wilhelmus</u>[3], bpt. 6 March 1743 - sp.: Wilm. Hagedorn
and Anna Magreda Widerwax (Red Hook Luth. Chbk.).

  ii) <u>Johann Petrus</u>[3], b. 5 May 1745 - sp.: Petrus Hagedorn
and Anna Barbara (N.Y. City Luth. Chbk.).

 iii) <u>Philip Henrich</u>[3], b. 10 Oct 1750 and bpt. Ancram -
sp.: Philip Cuntz and wife Anna Barbara (Rhinebeck
Luth. Chbk.).

  iv) <u>Johann Jacob</u>[3], b. 13 May 1753 - sp.: Christian Lub
and Maria Lub (Schoharie Luth. Chbk.).

   v) <u>Abraham</u>[3], b. 17 Feb 1756 - sp.: Jan Ebbertse and Mareitje (Loonenburg Luth. Chbk.).

  vi) <u>David</u>[3] (per William S. Coons).

There were other Kuhns-Cuntz in the middle colonies in the
18th century: 1) Jacob Kuhn (Kien, King) md. 11 Jan 1730 Elisabetha Erving (Erbin? - HJ) (N.Y. City Ref. Chbk.) and had issue
bpt. in the period 1730 - 1744 at N.Y. City Luth. Church (HJ);
2) Johannes Cons of Lebanon, Hunterdon Co., N.J. had a will dated
10 April 1751 and probated 16 March 1769 (N.J. Wills: Lib. 14, p.
39); 3) Johannes Kuhns md. Anna Gertraut Kuhn and had issue bpt.
at Churchtown Luth., Gallatin Ref., Germantown Ref., and Linlithgo
Ref. Churches in the period 1763 - 1773 (HJ); 4) a Nicolaus Coons
had ch. Elisabetha, Adam, and Michael mentioned in the Janeway
Accts 1735 - 1744 in N.J.; and 5) a Thomas Coons had ch. bpt. at
New Brunswick, N.J. in the 1730's (HJ).

Even though he didn't have access to German records clarifying the earliest generations of the various families, William S.
Coons's <u>Koon-Coons Families of Eastern N.Y.</u> remains as a model of

its type and one of the finest Palatine genealogies ever written; his use of documented sources is especially noteworthy, and I recommend the book highly, particularly in regard to later generations of the family (HJ).

MATHEUS KUNTZ (Hunter Lists #421)

Mattheus Koen, his wife, and 1 child, were in the 2nd party of Palatines on Capt. Bouwel's ship in Holland (Rotterdam Lists). Matthew Kühn aged 34, his wife, and a son aged 2, Catholic, husbandman and vinedresser, were in the 2nd arrivals in England later in 1709 (London Lists). However, the above emigrant probably was not #421 on the Hunter Lists, as Mattheus Kun, his wife, and 1 child were returned to Holland in 1709 (P.R.O. T/1 119, 136 - 153).

Matheus Kuntz was entered once on the Hunter Lists on 4 Oct 1710 with 3 pers. over 10 yrs. of age in the family. On 24 June 1711, Jost Laux and Math: Kuhn's Wid^W were registered.

JOHANN CHRISTOPH KURTZ (Hunter Lists #422)

The German origins of this Hudson Valley family were at 7060 Schorndorf (16 km. n.e. of Esslingen; Chbks. begin 1569) and at 7062 Rudersberg (9 km. n. of Schorndorf; Chbks. begin 1633). The earliest known ancestor of Johann Christoph[1] was Johannes Kurtz, bur. 30 Dec 1677, aged 74 yrs., 9 months, less 7 days; his obituary stated that he was Burgomaster for 30 yrs. (Schorndorf Chbk.). Anna Maria, wid/o the Burgomaster Herr Johannes Kurtz, was bur. 25 Aug 1695, aged 78 yrs. less 3 months (Schorndorf Chbk.). A child of Johannes Kurtz Sr. and Anna Maria was Johannes Kurtz Jr. Johannes Kurtz, butcher and eldest s/o Herr Johann Kurtz the Burgomaster here, md. 23 April 1672 Anna Elisabetha, wid/o the late Augustin Walther - formerly citizen and merchant at Stuttgart (Schorndorf Chbk.). Anna Maria (sic), w/o the butcher Johannes Kurtz, was bur. 20 May 1688, aged 48 yrs. less 2 months (Schorndorf Chbk.). Johannes Kurtz, butcher and widower here, md. Anna Catharina, d/o Adam Soldner - daylabourer here, 13 Nov 1688 (Schorndorf Chbk.). Johannes Kurtz, formerly citizen, butcher and gate-keeper here, was bur. 17 May 1694, aged 56 yrs., 6 months, and 13 days (Schorndorf Chbk.); his widow Anna Catharina then md. Hannß David Mayer 26 Oct 1695 (Schorndorf Chbk.). The ch. of Johannes Kurtz Jr. and Anna Elisabetha Walther, his wife, were:

> Johannes, bpt. 3 July 1673 - d. 5 Aug 1674 (Schorndorf Chbk.).
>
> Johannes, bpt. 11 Sept 1674 - d. 13 Sept 1674 (Schorndorf Chbk.).
>
> + Johann Christoph, bpt. 2 Nov 1675 - sp.: Johannes Agricola,

Master Joh. Jacob Neuber - Weißgerber, and Margaretha - wid/o
the late Georg Kurz the Rittmeister, for her Maria Margaretha
- w/o Joh. Leonhardt Michel (Schorndorf Chbk.)
Maria Elisabetha, bpt. 4 March 1677 - d. 3 June 1677 (Schorndorf Chbk.).

Herr Johann Christoph Kurtz, surviving s/o the late Johannes Kurtz
- citizen and butcher at Schorndorf, md. Maria Margaretha, d/o the
late Conrad Kuhn, 22 June 1700 (Rudersberg Chbk.). Maria Margaretha, d/o Johann Conrad Kuhn and wife Anna Maria, was bpt. 28 April
1680 - sp.: H. Johann Jacob Lutz, Anna Margaretha Hartmann, and
Hans Beurlin here (Rudersberg Chbk.). Herr Johan Conrad Kuhn the
innkeeper here was bur. 28 Jan 1686 (Rudersberg Chbk.); his wid.
Anna Maria then md. Samuel Köllin 8 Feb 1687 (Rudersberg Chbk.).
Herr Johann Christoph Kurtz was called a Barbierer or Balbierer
at Großaspach in 1703 and 1706 (Großaspach Chbk.). Johan Kristoffel kurts was listed with his wife and 2 ch. in the 6th party of
Palatines in Holland in 1709 (Rotterdam Lists).

Johann Christoph Kurtz made his initial appearance on the
Hunter Lists 29 Sept 1711 with 2 over 10 yrs. and 2 under 10 yrs.
A mss. mentioning Drs. Kurtz and Ruger (now missing? - HJ) was
noted in N.Y. Col. Mss., Vol. LIV, p. 66, 16 Sept 1710. A letter
from Phil: Livingston told of money due him from John Christopher
Corts 13 June 1712 (Livingston Papers, Reel #3). Johan Christopher
Kurtz was nat. 8 and 9 Sept 1715 (Kingston Nats.). Under Palatine
Debtors were recorded Christ Curts' Wid in 1718, Wid^W Curts in
1719 (at Kingsberry), and Margreta Curtz in 1721 and 1726 (Livingston Debt Lists). Marg., former w/o Dr. Curtz, now intermarried
with Hanneman Sallbagh, was aged 41 in a deposition dated 1721/22
(Livingston Papers, Reel #4). The ch. of Johann Christoph[1] were:

1) Johann Christoph[2], b. 3 Oct 1701 - sp.: Mattes Kurz in
   Schorndorf, Johann Friedrich Pfeifer, Hans Rappen ...,
   Anna ..., and Hans Hartmann's ... (Rudersberg Chbk.). He
   was bur. 17 Feb 1704 a long-time ill (Großaspach Chbk.).

2) Christoph Friederich[2], bpt. 2 Dec 1703 - sp.: H. Johann
   Friedrich Pfeifern - balbierer at Rudersberg, Hans Michael
   Langbein - innkeeper at Backnang, Anna - w/o Hans Rappen
   the cooper at Rudersberg, and Veronica - single d/o H.
   Johann Daniel Hartmann, formerly Pfarrer at Rudersberg
   (Großaspach Chbk.).

3) Johannes[2], bpt. 14 Nov 1706 - sp.: H. Johann Friedrich
   Pfifferer (?) - barbierer, the others as above (Großaspach
   Chbk.). An old mss. mentions a trip by John Curtz and Cat-
   arina Ogilby on the Sloop Alida in 1726 (Livingston Papers,
   Reel #11). Johannes Kurtz, s/o Joh: Christoph Kurtz, md.

Elisabetha Bernhardt, d/o Hannes Bernhard, in 1727 - all
living in Heisberg (N.Y. City Luth. Chbk.). Johannes[2] was
prominent in Luth. affairs along the Hudson and was often
mentioned in the Albany Protocol (see pp. 41, 47 - 48, 74,
86, 101, 162, 182, 184, 206, 510, 524, and 534 - 36). He
was an overseer or executor of Pastor Berkenmeyer's will
(Fernow Wills #76). Johannes Curst was a freeholder at
East Camp in 1763 (Albany Co. Freeholders). The will of
John Kortz of German Camp was dated 20 June 1783 and probated 7 June 1785 (Fernow Wills #1004). The ch. of Johannes[2] Kurtz and Elisabetha were:

i) Johann Friederich[3], b. 20 March 1730 and bpt. at Haneman Saalbach's at Kamp (the child very sick) - sp.:
Johan Jost Bernhard and Anna Maria Löscher; in their
place was Jacob Scheffer and the grandmother (N.Y.
City Luth. Chbk.). Frederick Kortz, Capt., Christopher Kortz, Ensign, and John Kortz, Jr., were all
in Capt. Frederick Kortz's Company at East Camp in
1767 (Report of the State Historian, Vol. II, pp.
869 and 870).

ii) Christoph[3] (Will).

iii) Anna Margaretha[3], b. 22 Nov 1737 and bpt. at Camp -
sp.: Haneman Sallbach and Anna Margr. - the gr-parents (Loonenburg Luth. Chbk.).

iv) Elisabetha[3], b. 7 July 1740, one of twins - the other
still-born, and bpt. at the Camp - sp.: Hannes Saalbach Jr. and Lisabeth Silbernagel (Loonenburg Luth.
Chbk.).

v) Christina[3], b. Jan 1742 and bpt. at Teerbosch - sp.:
Jacob Pulver and wife Christina (Loonenburg Luth.
Chbk.).

vi) Johannes[3], bpt. 8 Dec 1747 - sp.: Johannes Lescher
and wife (Germantown Ref. Chbk.). He md. Maria Kerl
(HJ). Papers in the administration of the estate of
John Kortz, merchant, deceased, were granted to James
and John Kortz 24 Aug 1795 (Columbia Co. Administration Book B); papers in the estate of Mary Kertz,
deceased, were granted to John Kortz of Columbia Co.
and James Kertz of Ulster Co., merchants, her sons,
4 Feb 1799 (Columbia Co. Administration Book B).

A Maria Elisabetha Kurgtzin was at Hackensack ca. 1716/17
(Simmendinger Register). Anna Margaretha Coert was the w/o Johannes Reisdorf by 1716 (HJ). A Widow Barbara Kurtz md. Peter Blass
17 May 1758 (Germantown Ref. Chbk.).

JOHANNES LABACH (Hunter Lists #423)

An Adam Labag, his wife, and 5 ch., were on Capt. Leonard Allan's ship in the 5th party at Rotterdam in 1709, and a Reinhart Lÿbak, his wife, and 3 ch., were on Capt. Wilken's ship in the 3rd party in Holland that yr. (both Rotterdam Lists).

Johannes Labach made his only appearance on the Hunter Lists 1 July 1710 with 2 pers. over 10 yrs. of age. Johannes Labbach, single man, md. Rachel Meyer, single woman, 19 May 1727, and both lived Hackensack (Hackensack Ref. Chbk.). Hannes Labach sp. Martin Meyer in 1729 at Hakk. (N.Y. City Luth. Chbk.). The ch. of Johannes[1] Labach and Rachel were:

1) Catharina[2], bpt. 28 Jan 1728 - sp.: Hendrik Labbah and Elisabeth Lesse, md. people (Hackensack Ref. Chbk.).

2) Abraham[2], bpt. 30 June 1734 - sp.: Samuel Brevoort and wife (Hackensack Ref. Chbk.).

An elder brother of Johannes[1] Labach appears to have been Henrich Labach (HJ). Hendrik Labach, single man of Germany, md. Elisabetha Lesser (Löscher), single woman of Germany, 17 May 1724 (N.Y. City Ref. Chbk.). Joseph North was apprenticed to the cooper Mr. Henry Labagh 19 July 1725 (Indentures Of Apprentices 1718 - 1727, p. 177). The ch. of Henrich Labach and Elisabetha were:

1) Magdalena, bpt. 27 Jan 1725 - sp.: Gÿsbert Gerretse and Catharina Lesser (N.Y. City Ref. Chbk.).

2) Henrich, bpt. 11 May 1726 - sp.: Johannes Lesser and Eva Pendering (N.Y. City Ref. Chbk.).

3) Catharina, bpt. 15 Oct 1727 - sp.: Joris Walgraaf and wife Magdalena Lisart (Hackensack Ref. Chbk.).

4) Jacob, bpt. 25 Feb 1730 - sp.: Jacob Bos and wife Magdalena Bos (N.Y. City Ref. Chbk.).

5) Petrus, bpt. 10 Jan 1731 - sp.: Jacobus Bertholf and Elisabeth Van Emburgh (Hackensack Ref. Chbk.).

6) Johannes, bpt. 25 May 1732 - sp.: Dirk Pettit and wife Weintje Brouwer (Hackensack Ref. Chbk.).

7) Isaac, bpt. 30 June 1734 - sp.: Hendrik Van Giesen and wife (Hackensack Ref. Chbk.).

8) Catrientje, so bpt. 6 March 1737 - sp.: Perregrim Van Imburg and Catrientje Van Imburg (Hackensack Ref. Chbk.).

9) Abraham, bpt. 22 Feb 1739 - sp.: Abraham Varik and wife Annaetjen (Hackensack Ref. Chbk.).

JOHANN CASPAR LAIB (Hunter Lists #424)

Johan Leib, his wife, and 4 ch., were on Capt. John Sewell's ship in Holland with the 4th party of Palatines in 1709

Rotterdam Lists). John Leib aged 43, his wife, a son aged 10 yrs., daughters aged 14 and ½, Ref., husbandman and vinedresser, were in the 4th arrivals in England in 1709 (London Lists).

Johann Caspar Laib made his only appearance on the Hunter Lists 4 Oct 1710 with 1 pers. over 10 yrs. and 1 pers. under 10 yrs. of age; an added entry under that date noted extra subsistence for the previous days. After studying the Lipe family structure, noting how the family disappears after but one entry on Hunter, is missing from Simmendinger, and especially how Caspar has ch. into the mid-18th century, I believe that Johann Caspar mentioned on the Hunter Lists actually was Johann Caspar², the son aged 10 listed with John Leib in London in 1709 (HJ). If indeed this is the case, I strongly believe the ch. of Johannes¹ Leib were:

1) Anna² (HJ), probably the daughter aged 14 at London in 1709 (HJ). She md. 21 Oct 1721 Caspar Hamm (Albany Ref. Chbk.). They were sp. by Casper Leyb in 1724 (Albany Ref. Chbk.).

2) Johann Caspar² (HJ), probably the son aged 10 at London in 1709 (HJ). Hans Casper Liepe was nat. 31 Jan 1715/16 (Albany Nats.). Casper Lipe was a freeholder at Canajoharrie in 1763 (Albany Co. Freeholders). The will of Caspar Lipe of Conajohary in Tryon Co. was dated 4 Aug 1775 and probated 16 Nov 1782 (Fernow Wills #1057). The w/o Johann Caspar was called Catharina in 1733 (Schoharie Ref. or Luth. Chbk.). Issue:

   i) Jost³ (Will).

   ii) Catharina³, bpt. 20 March 1733 - sp.: Ludwig Rickert and Catharina (Schoharie Ref. or Luth. Chbk.).

   iii) Adam³ (Will), md. as s/o Casper Leib of Canajoharie 15 Dec 1761 Elisabetha, d/o Conrad Mathaeus (Stone Arabia Ref. Chbk.). The will of Adam Lipe of Minden was dated 27 Feb 1804 and probated 11 Nov 1805 (Montgomery Co. Will Bk. I). Maryly B. Penrose quotes dates for Adam³ based on the Fort Plain Chbk. as 3 Nov 1736 - 14 July 1805 (Mohawk Valley in the Revolution, p. 280).

   iv) Johannes³ (Will). The revolutionary war activities of Johannes Lipe of Minden are discussed in History of Montgomery & Fulton Counties, N.Y., pp. 129 - 131). The will of Johannes Lipe was probated 19 Dec 1814 (Mohawk Valley in the Revolution, p. 280).

   v) Anna Maria³ (Will), md. Jacob van der Werken (Will).

   vi) Maria Elisabetha³ (Will).

vii) <u>Anna</u>³ (Will), md. 6 Oct 1767 Jacob Mathees (Stone
Arabia Ref. Chbk.).

viii) <u>Margaretha</u>³ (Will), md. Adam Conderman (Countryman)
(Will).

JOHANNES LAHMEYER (Hunter Lists #425)

The European origins of this family were with the Bellingers,
Dygerts, Kuhns, and so many other N.Y. Palatines at 6451 <u>Hüttenge-</u>
<u>säß</u> (13 km. n.e. of Hanau), entries for this village at 6456
<u>Langenselbold</u> (3 km. further s.; Chbks. begin 1563). The earliest
known forefather of the N.Y. settler was his grandfather <u>Georg</u>
<u>Lahmeyer</u>, a teacher at Hüttengesäß, who md. after the death of
his 1st wife Barbara, who d. 1699, aged 64, to widow Gertraud Scha-
den, 12 Aug 1700. Marcus Lahmeyer, s/o the teacher Jörg Lahmeyer
at Hüttengesäß, md. 16 Nov 1681 Magdalena, d/o Clos Jacobs - also
inhabitant there. Magdalena, w/o Marcus Lohmeyer, was bur. 16 July
1687 at Hitzkirchen near Birstein, where she was on a journey for
medical treatment. Marcus Lohmeyer, widower and linenweaver, md.
19 Nov 1691 Engel, d/o Hans Deichert; she was sister of the N.Y.
1709er Werner Deichert (HJ). The ch. of <u>Marcus Lahmeyer</u> and his
1st wife Magdalena were:

+ <u>Anna Elisabetha</u>, bpt. 10 Sept 1682 - sp.: the d/o the late
Hanß Ebenauer, a this time maid at Hanaw.
+ <u>Johannes</u>, bpt. 6 Jan 1684 - sp.: Johannes Köhler.
<u>Anna Catharina</u>, bpt. 14 Oct 1686 - sp.: the d/o Clos Jacobs,
sister of the mother.

By his 2nd wife Engel Deichert, the ch. of Marcus Lahmeyer were:
<u>Anna Barbara</u>, bpt. 13 Oct 1692 - sp.: Anna Ursula, sister of
the child's father.
<u>Johann Gregorius</u>, bpt. 18 March 1694 - sp.: Jörg Lohmeyer,
the child's grandfather, a teacher from the Palatinate.
<u>Anna Magdalena</u>, bpt. 19 July 1696 - sp.: the d/o Jost Reidel.
<u>Johann Henrich</u>, bpt. 4 May 1697 - sp.: Joh. Henrich - s/o Hen-
rich Euler from Berckheim. He was bur. 16 April 1699.
<u>Johann Henrich</u>, bpt. 30 April 1699 - sp.: Joh. Henr. Reichart,
single man from Eckartshausen.

Johannes Lahmeyer made his initial appearance on the Hunter
Lists 4 July 1710 with 1 pers. over 10 yrs. On all his entries in
1710, he was noted next to Johannes (Jost) Schneider, suggesting
that Elisabetha Meyert, w/o Johannes Schneider, may have been the
Anna Elisabetha Lahmeyer bpt. in 1682 (HJ). On 4 Oct 1710, Johannes
Lahmeyer was but a few names from Werner Deuchert and others from
Hüttengesäß (HJ). Hance Lemire was recorded near Necoshehopin in

513

1734 ("Landholders of Philadelphia Co., 1734" in Genealogical Society of Pa. Publications, Vol. I, 1895 - 99).

ELIZABETH LAMBERTIN (Hunter Lists #426)

Johan[S] Bampert, his wife, and (ch.) Anna Krita, Gysbert,
Frans Adam, and 2 (other) ch., were in the 2nd party of Palatines
in Holland in 1709 (Rotterdam Lists). John Lambert aged 65, his
wife, sons aged 11 and 8, daughters aged 13 and 9, Roman Catholic,
husbandman and vinedresser, were in the 2nd arrivals in England
later that yr. (London Lists). There is no proof, but perhaps an
early marriage for the emigrant was 14 Nov 1665 when Johannes Lambert, citizen and joiner here from Amsterdam, md. Anna Maria Hanauer in the German Ref. Church at 6800 Mannheim; a Jois Lampert
and wife Anna Margaretha had a son Adrianus bpt. 1 Dec 1693 at
6508 Alzey also. However, it should be remembered that American
sources give the Darmstadt region as his ancestral home (HJ).

Elizabeth Lambertin made her first appearance on the Hunter
Lists 4 Aug 1710 with 3 pers. over 10 yrs. and 1 pers. under 10
yrs. The entry for 4 Oct 1710 read 4 pers. over 10 yrs. of age,
and the notation for 29 Sept 1711 recorded 2 over 10 yrs. Elisabeth Engler, wid/o Joh[S] Lambert of Darmstaderland, joined the N.Y.
City Ref. Church 29 May 1711; after this entry was written "dead."
Eliz. Lambertin, a wid. aged 47, Erhard A. Lampertin aged 13, and
Frantz Adam A. Lampertin aged 11, were listed as Palatines still
in N.Y. City in 1710/11 (Palatines In N.Y. City). Elisabetha Engeler, wid/o Johannes Lampert of Darmstaderland, md. Francois Lucas 9 Aug 1711 (N.Y. City Ref. Chbk.). The ch. of Johannes and
Elisabetha[1] Lambert were:

1) Anna Margaretha[2] (Rotterdam Lists). Anna Margt Lamberton
   aged 13, d/o Elizth Lamberton, was bound to Jno Deane of
   N.Y. 22 Sept 1710 (Apprenticeship Lists).
2) Gerhardt[2] (Apprenticeship Lists), probably the Gysbert
   Bampert in Holland in 1709 and also the Erhard A. Lampertin in N.Y. City in 1710/11 (HJ). Garrit Lamberton aged
   12, s/o Wid. Lamberton, was bound to Michl Hawdon of N.Y.
   23 Oct 1710 (Apprenticeship Lists). A Gerritt Lambartse
   was registered in Capt. Thomas Stillwell's Company in the
   King's Co. Militia in 1715 (Report of the State Historian,
   Vol. I, p. 485).
3) Frantz Adam[2] (Rotterdam Lists), the Frantz Adam A. Lampertin aged 11 in N.Y. City in 1710/11 (HJ). Ffrances Lamberton aged 10, s/o Wid. Lamberton, was bound to John Hicks
   of Flushing 1 Nov 1710 (Apprenticeship Lists).

JOHANNES LAMET (Hunter Lists #427)

Johannes Lamet made his first appearance on the Hunter Lists 1 July 1710 with 2 pers. over 10 yrs. of age in the household. He was recorded with 3 over 10 on 24 Dec 1711, and then with 2 over 10 yrs. again 24 June 1712. John Lamert was nat. 8 and 9 Sept 1715 (Kingston Nats.). Johannes Lamert with his wife and ch. was at Beckmansland ca. 1716/17 (Simmendinger Register). Hans Lambert was on tax rolls for the North Ward and then Rhinebeck from 1717/ 18 to 1778 (Dutchess Co. Tax Lists). He was an overseer of ye King's Highway in the North Ward in 1725, and in 1730 was a surveyor of ye fences in the North Ward (Dutchess Co. Supervisor's Records). Johannes Lambert had one slave in Rhinebeck in 1755 (History of Rhinebeck, by Edward M. Smith, p. 50). Johannes[1] md. Elisabetha (Vogel? - HJ, see Kingston Ref. bpt. #3956). His son was:

1) Johannes[2] (HJ), perhaps mixed up on some mss. with Johannes[1] (HJ). Hannes Lahmer was conf. at Rynbeck 12 Jan 1732, aged 20 (Loonenberg Luth. Chbk.), md. Anna Sybilla Zufelt (HJ) and had issue:

   i) Johannes[3], bpt. 14 April 1740 - sp.: Johannes Weller and Catharina Zufelt (Red Hook Luth. Chbk.).

   ii) Georg[3], bpt. 31 Oct 1742 - sp.: George Zufelt and Catharina Zufelt (Red Hook Luth. Chbk.). He was on Rhinebeck tax rolls 1771 - 1778 (Dutchess Co. Tax Lists). Georg[3] md. Elisabetha Zitzer (HJ).

   iii) Johann Adam[3], bpt. 9 Feb 1746 - sp.: Gorg Adam Zufelt and Anna Catterina Reisdorf (Red Hook Luth. Chbk.).

   iv) Anna Maria[3], b. 10 May 1748 - sp.: Laurentius Thiel and wife Anna Maria (Rhinebeck Luth. Chbk.). She md. Martin Zitzer (HJ).

JOHANNES LÄNCKER (Hunter Lists #428)

Johannes Lenker made his initial appearance on the Hunter Lists 30 June 1710 with 2 pers. over 10 yrs. of age in the family. His final appearance with the same numbers was 4 Aug 1710.

PETER LAMPMANN (Hunter Lists #429)

The German origins of the N.Y. Lampmann family were documented at several locales: 1) at 6473 Gedern (32 km. n.e. of Bad Nauheim; Chbks. begin 1674); 2) at 6470 Düdelsheim (18 km. n. of Hanau; Chbks. begin 1636); 3) at 6470 Rohrbach (3 km. n. of Düdelsheim; Chbks. begin 1699); and at 6475 Stockheim (2 km. further

n.). The father of the emigrant Peter[1] Lampmann was <u>Balthasar Lamp-</u>
<u>mann the elder</u>, bur. 14 Jan 1692 (Gedern Chbk.); Sabina Margaretha
Arnold, wid/o Balthes Lambman, was bur. 15 Dec 1709, aged 78 3/4
yrs. old (Gedern Chbk.). They had ch.:

> <u>Johannes</u>, b. April 1667, md. 12 Nov 1696 Margaretha Schupp,
> and d. 22 Nov 1737 (all Gedern Chbk. Family Book).
>
> <u>Philip</u>, b. Sept 1672, md. 8 April 1706 Anna Barbara Günter,
> and d. 8 June 1741 (all Gedern Chbk. Family Book).
>
> <u>Catharina</u>, b. Nov 1675.
>
> + <u>Peter</u>, a communicant at Gedern in 1692 (Gedern Chbk.).
>
> <u>Anna Maria</u>, b. March 1681, md. Lorenz Giermann von der Hütte,
> d. 11 Dec 1726, aged 45 yrs. (Gedern Chbk. Family Book).

A permit for Peter Lambmann of Gedern to go to Stockheim by paying
10 gulden was granted 7 July 1698 (Ortenberg Castle Archives, Bk.
Akte X G 436, p. 9, cited in Supplement #1 to the 3rd edition of
<u>Imprints on the Sands of Time</u>, by Henry R. Kelly, p. 6). Peter
Landtmann of Gedern, s/o the late Balthasar Landtmann of Gedern,
md. Catharina, wid/o Cunradt Frikk, at Stockheim 20 July 1698 (Düdelsheim Chbk.). Conradt Frikk md. 11 Nov 1685 Catharina, d/o Conrad Deckmann; Cunradt Frikk was bur. 24 Oct 1692, aged 37 yrs.
(both Düdelsheim Chbk.). Catharina, d/o Conrad Degmann, was bpt.
at Stockheim 6 Jan 1665 - sp.: his sister, the d/o Peter Degman
from Bleichenbach (Düdelsheim Chbk.). The 1st wife of Cunradt
Deckmann d. at Stockheim in 1674, aged 35 yrs. (Düdelsheim Chbk.);
her name was Juliana, for Conrad Deckmann, s/o Peter Deckmann, md.
Juliana, d/o Georg Stroh of Stockheim, 23 Oct 1662 (Bleichenbach
Chbk.). Anna, w/o Peter Deckmann, was bur. 15 March 1652 (Nidda
Chbk.). The Deckmanns were also related to the 1709er Conrads
and Windeckers, showing yet again how emigrant families often were
connected in Europe (HJ). Peter[1] Lampmanns petition to emigrate
in 1709 is fully transcribed in the section on #107 Anna Conrad
(HJ).

Peter Lampmann made his initial appearance on the Hunter Lists
30 June 1710 with 3 pers. over 10 yrs. and 2 under 10; the entry
read 3 over 10 and 1 under 10 on 24 June 1711, 2 over 10 yrs. and
1 under 10 on 25 March 1712, and finally 3 over 10 yrs. and 1 under 10 yrs. on 24 June 1712. Peter Lautman was nat. 17 Jan 1715/16
(Albany Nats.). Peter Lampmann and Catharina with 2 ch. were at
Wormsdorff ca. 1716/17 (Simmendinger Register). Peter Lantman was
a Palatine Debtor in 1718, 1719 (at Kingsberry), 1721, and 1726
(Livingston Debt Lists). Peter Lamp Man was a Palatine willing to
remain on the Manor 26 Aug 1724 (<u>Doc. Hist. of N.Y.</u>, Vol. III, p.
724). He and wife Catharina were in the St. Peter's Luth. Family
Book ca. 1734 (Rhinebeck Luth. Chbk.), and their ch. were:

1) <u>Johann Peter²</u>, b. 5 April 1700 at Stockheim - sp.: Michael
Dinges (Rohrbach Chbk.). Peter Landmann was conf. 23 March
1712 at Queensberg (West Camp Luth. Chbk.). Peter Landman,
s/o Peter of Stakheim in the commune of Litting-Isenburg,
md. Johanna Elisabetha Planck, d/o Johann of Dausenau in
the commune of Nastau, 24 Feb 1719 (West Camp Luth.
Chbk.). He (or his father) was a member of the Church
Council called by Berkenmeyer 27 Aug 1732 (<u>Albany Proto-
col</u>, p. 40). Johann Peter² and Johanna Elisabetha had ch.:

   i) <u>Peter³</u>, md. as s/o Peter Lampman of Hoseck 21 April
1745 at Kisk. Elisabetha Schmid (Loonenburg Luth.
Chbk.). N.Y.State D.A.R. Bible Records, Vol. 69, contains data on this family; it gives Peter³ a birthdate of July 1721 and his wife Elisabetha a birthdate of 26 March 1727. Peter, Stephanis, and Hendier-
ieck Lantman were in Capt. Jacob Halenbeck's Company
in 1767 (<u>Report of the State Historian</u>, Vol. II, p.
829). His ch. were bpt. at Loonenburg Luth. Church.

  ii) <u>Friederich³</u>, md. as s/o Peter Lampman 6 Nov 1748
Catharina Schram (Loonenburg Luth. Chbk.). Fredrieck
Lantman was a Sargent in Capt. Jacob Halenbeck's
Company in 1767 (<u>Report of the State Historian</u>, Vol.
II, p. 827). Friederich's ch. were bpt. at Loonen-
burg Luth. Church (HJ).

 iii) <u>Catharina³</u> (HJ), conf. together with Pieter and Friderich Lampmann at Albany 6 June 1742 (Loonenburg
Luth. Chbk.). She md. Henrich Jung (HJ).

  iv) <u>Henrich³</u>, b. 22 Aug 1727 - sp.: Henrich Ludwig and
Anna Maria Maul (Loonenburg Luth. Chbk.). He was
conf. 19 Feb 1748/49 (Loonenburg Luth. Chbk.). He
md. Maria Schmidt 25 Feb 1750 (Loonenburg Luth.
Chbk.) and had ch. bpt. at Loonenburg Luth. Church.

   v) <u>Johann Michael³</u>, b. 28 Nov 1729 and bpt. Kisket. -
sp.: Johan Michael Plank and Lisabeth Reutern (Loonenburg Luth. Chbk.). He md. 6 Oct 1751 Maria Brouwer,
both being of Hosack (Albany Ref. Chbk.). They had
issue bpt. at Albany Ref. Church (HJ).

  vi) <u>Johannes³</u>, b. 20 Jan 1732 and bpt. Kisket. - sp.:
Hannes Eberhard and wife Anna Sybilla (Loonenburg
Luth. Chbk.). John Lantman was noted as above Poesten
Kill in Capt. Van Aernam's Company in 1767 (<u>Report
of the State Historian</u>, Vol. II, p. 812). He md.
Susannah Letscher (HJ) and had ch. bpt. at Albany
Ref. and Trinity, N.Y. City Churches (HJ).

vii) <u>Maria³</u>, b. 21 April 1734 and bpt. at Kisket in Adam
Spoon's barn - sp.: Adam Spoon and wife Anna Maria
(Loonenburg Luth. Chbk.). She md. Peter Schram 24 Feb
1758 (Loonenburg Luth. Chbk.).

viii) <u>Stephanus³</u>, bpt. 28 Nov 1736 - sp.: Step. and Elyz
V: Rensselaar (Albany Ref. Chbk.). He md. Maria Brando (HJ) and ch. bpt. at Catskill Ref. Church (HJ).

ix) <u>Abraham³</u>, bpt. 10 Jan 1738/39 - sp.: Abraham and Alida Van Aarnem (Albany Ref. Chbk.).

x) <u>Elisabetha³</u>, bpt. 15 Feb 1741 - sp.: Stevanus and Elizabeth Van Renzelaar (Albany Ref. Chbk.). She md.
Nicolaus Schmidt 29 Dec 1761 (Loonenburg Luth. Chbk.).

2) <u>Anna Elisabetha²</u>, b. 5 Aug 1701 - sp.: Anna Elisabeth -
d/o Class Windecker (Rohrbach Chbk.). The child d. 29 May
1704 (Rohrbach Chbk.).

3) <u>Johann Caspar²</u>, b. 21 Oct 1705 at Stockheim - sp.: Johann
Casper Deckmann and wife Elisabeth (Rohrbach Chbk., little
record book of the Pastor). Casper Laupmann was conf. in
1722 (N.Y. City Luth. Chbk., transcribed from the late Mr.
Falckner's handboek). He and his family appeared on the
Family List of 1734 at St. Peter's Luth. (Rhinebeck Luth.
Chbk.). Johann Caspar² md. Elisabetha Rau or Rausch (HJ).
They had ch.:

i) <u>Catharina³</u> (St. Peter's Family List), md. Henrich Janssen Witbeek (HJ).

ii) <u>Anna³</u> (St. Peter's Family List).

iii) <u>Elisabetha³</u>, bpt. 25 Feb 1732 - sp.: Johan Schiffer
and Anna Elizabeth Schiffer (Germantown Ref. Chbk.).

iv) <u>Maria Barbara³</u>, b. 13 June 1734 - sp.: Joh: Georg Wid-
derwax and Maria Barbara Netzbach (Rhinebeck Luth.
Chbk.). Maria Barbel and Cath. Lampman were conf. 17
June 1750 at Theerbosch (Loonenburg Luth. Chbk.). A
Maria Lampmann md. Arent Wm. Junckmann 19 Oct 1755
(Germantown Ref. Chbk.).

v) <u>Anna Margaretha³</u>, b. 23 Feb 1736 - sp.: Mart: Widderwax and Anna Margret: Wand (Rhinebeck Luth. Chbk.).

vi) <u>Magdalena³</u>, b. Oct 1741 and bpt. Teerbosch - sp.:
Thomas Scheidewich and wife Lisabeth (Loonenburg Luth.
Chbk.). She md. David Williams 15 Dec 1759 (Rhinebeck
Flats Ref. Chbk.).

vii) <u>Johann Caspar³</u>, bpt. 13 weeks old 3 May 1744 at Ankrum
- sp.: Jo. Jurge Wiederwachs and Catharina Kuntz
(Loonenburg Luth. Chbk.).

viii) <u>Henrich³</u> (HJ), found at Churchtown Luth. Church (HJ).

ix) <u>Peter</u>[3], bpt. 5 Nov 1749 - sp.: Peter Stoppelbein and
wife (Germantown Ref. Chbk.).

x) <u>Anna</u>[3], bpt. 31 May 1753 - sp.: Jurg Scherts and wife
Catharina West (Germantown Ref. Chbk.).

<u>Imprints on the Sands of Time Left by Certain Kelly's, Lamp-
man's, Craig's, Ferguson's</u>, by Henry R. Kelly, with its various
editions and supplements, is a fine work that contains more detailed data on the family (HJ).

GEORG LANDGRAFF (Hunter Lists #430)

A Hans Georg Landgraf and wife Anna Margaretha had a son Michael b. 5 Aug 1689 - sp.: Michael Nungesser at Auerbach at 6140
<u>Schwanheim</u>; the father was called Schultheiss at Fehlen (Fehlheim?
- HJ) in the entry. More evidence is needed to prove the Schwanheim man was the 1709er (HJ).

Georg Landgraff made his initial appearance on the Hunter
Lists 1 July 1710 with 4 pers. over 10 yrs. of age. The family was
recorded with 6 over 10 on 4 Aug 1710, with 5 over 10 yrs. on 4
Oct 1710, with 3 pers. over 10 on 25 March 1711, with 4 over 10
yrs. on 24 June 1711, and with 3 over 10 yrs. 25 March 1712. The
entry for 24 June 1712 was back up to 4 over 10 yrs. of age. He
and his daughter Anna Elisabetha sp. Martin Seibert in 1716 at
Schoharie (West Camp Luth. Chbk.). Georg Landgraff and his wife
Elisabetha Catharina with 1 child were at Neu-Heidelberg ca. 1716/
17 (Simmendinger Register). Issue:

1) <u>Anna Elisabetha</u>[2] (West Camp Luth. Chbk.), a sp. in 1716.
2?) <u>Maria Elisabetha</u>[2], md. Henrich Schraemling, according to
an un-named source in <u>N.Y. State D.A.R. Bible Records</u>,
Vol. 7).

MAGDALENA LANGIN (Hunter Lists #431)

Magdalena Langin's only entry on the Hunter Lists was dated
4 Oct 1710, with 1 pers. over 10 yrs. of age and 2 pers. under 10
yrs.

There were many Langs in colonial N.Y., but no proof has been
found of their relationship to #431 Magdalena Langin: 1) a Jan
Lange and wife Magdalena had ch. bpt. in the N.Y. City Luth. Chbk.
in 1722 and 1730; 2) a Peter Lange and wife Eva Elisabetha had
a son bpt. in 1730 at N.Y. City Luth. Church (the aforementioned
two men appear to have been "<u>De</u> Langs" - HJ); and 3) Christ: Lange
and wife Baartje had ch. bpt. in 1734 and 1742 at Albany Ref.
Church, and he may have been the Christiaen Lang nat. 17 Jan 1715/
16 at Albany, if this nat. really wasn't for Christian[1] Bauch (HJ).

ABRAHAM LANGER ALIAS LE LONG (Hunter Lists #432)

A family that seems to match the 1709er was found at 6710
Frankenthal (7 km. n. of Ludwigshafen; Chbks. begin 1622, Wallonische Gemeinde) and at Oggersheim (4 km. s. of Frankenthal; Chbks.
begin 1698, Ref.). Abraham, s/o Charles le Long and wife Marie
des Marets, was bpt. 28 June 1668 - sp.: Jean de Marets - Gautier
à Manheim, Jean des Marets - le jeune demeurant dans cette ville,
Sara Bonnet - femme du dit Gautier demeurant à Manheim, and Georg-
ine le long, jeune fille (Frankenthal Wallonische Chbk.). Abraham
Le lon md. Anna Barbara Dorthel 2 Dec 1698 (Oggersheim Chbk.).
Ab^m Lang, his wife, and 3 ch., were on Capt. Jno. Untank's ship
in Holland (near a Johan Lang and wife) in the 5th party of Palatines (Rotterdam Lists).

Abraham Langer made his initial appearance on the Hunter
Lists 30 June 1710 with 2 over 10 yrs. and 1 under 10 in his family. The size increased to 5 pers. over 10 and 1 under 10 yrs.
on 4 Oct 1710. The entry for 24 June 1711 read 4 pers. over 10 and
2 under 10 yrs., and the notation for 25 March 1712 showed 3 pers.
over 10 and 2 under 10. The entry for 24 June 1712 recorded 5 pers.
over 10 yrs. of age. Abraham Langen was a soldier from Haysbury
in 1711 (Palatine Volunteers To Canada). Abraham Langer was nat.
17 Jan 1715/16 (Albany Nats.). Abraham Lang and Anna Maria with
4 ch. were at Hessberg ca. 1716/17 (Simmendinger Register); they
were recorded next to Michael (actually Nicolaus) Laux on the
register, and, as Maria Catharina - w/o Abraham Lang sp. Abraham
Lauck in 1711 at West Camp, I think there is a strong possibility
that Abraham Langer's 2nd wife might have been related to these
Laucks (HJ). Abraham Langh was a Palatine Debtor in 1718, 1719
(on our land), 1721 and 1722 (Livingston Debt Lists). The ch. of
the family of the Abraham found near Frankenthal were:

1) Peter², b. 2 Aug 1699 at Hemshof (Oggersheim Chbk.). The
   father was called le Long on the entry.
2) Peter², b. at Friesenheim and bpt. 25 April 1707 (Oggersheim Chbk.). The father was called Abraham le lonn, Gemeinsmann at Friesenheim, on this entry.

An Abraham Long had a daughter Elizabeth b. 14 Nov 1731 and
bpt. at Oley - sp.: Peter Long and wife Elizabeth (Stoever Chbks.).
Is this the family noted in #431 Magdalena Langin? (HJ).

ANNA CATHARINA LANTIN (Hunter Lists #433)

This family probably was noted in Holland as Felten Lant (or
Lantr), his wife, and 4 ch., on Capt. Jno. Untank's ship in the
5th party of Palatines (Rotterdam Lists).

Anna Catharina Lantin made her first appearance on the Hunter Lists 1 July 1710 with 3 pers. over 10 yrs. of age and 1 pers. under 10. The 4 Oct 1710 entry read 4 over 10 and 1 under 10 yrs., and the 31 Dec 1710 notation showed 5 over 10 and 1 under 10 yrs. The 24 June 1711 entry recorded 6 over 10 yrs., the 25 March 1712 entry showed 5 over 10 yrs., the 24 June 1712 recording mentioned 6 over 10, and the 13 Sept 1712 entry noted 5 over 10 yrs. of age. Anna Catharine Lant, wid., had land on the n. side of the Mohawk 30 April 1725 (Burnetsfield Patent); John Veldelent and Anna Veldelant also each had land on the n. side of the Mohawk on that date (Burnetsfield Patent). The ch. of Anna Catharina[1] Lant were:

1) <u>Christina</u>[2] (HJ), md. Georg Adam Schmidt (HJ). Their eldest son was named Johann Valentin, bpt. at N.Y. City Luth. in 1721 (HJ).

2) <u>Johann Valentin</u>[2]. He appears to have been known also as Johannes Lant (HJ). Johannes Lant was a freeholder at Claverack in 1763 (Albany Co. Freeholders). The will of Johannes Landt of Claverack, yeoman, was dated 7 Nov in the 13th yr. of the reign of Lord George III and probated 8 Aug 1791 (Columbia Co. Will Bk. A). Issue:

    i) <u>Johannes</u>[3] (Will), md. Sarah Winnen (HJ). Johannes[3] sometimes was called Jr. at bpts. of his ch. They had issue bpt. at Loonenburg Luth., Claverack Ref., and Albany Ref. Churches (HJ).

    ii) <u>Friederich</u>[3] (Will), md. as s/o Hans Velti Land 5 July 1747 Christina, d/o Georg Adam Schmidt (Germantown Ref. Chbk.). Frederick, Lowerence, and Felter Lant were in Capt. Johannis Van Hoesen's Company at Claverack 9 May 1767 (<u>Report of the State Historian</u>, Vol. II, p. 858). Friederich[3] had issue bpt. at Claverack Ref., Loonenburg Luth., and Schoharie Luth. Churches (HJ).

    iii) <u>Catharina</u>[3] (Will), md. 15 Sept 1758 Johannes Rohrbach (Claverack Ref. Chbk.).

    iv) <u>Lorentz</u>[3] (Will), md. 12 Sept 1761 Christina Schult (Germantown Ref. Chbk.). The will of Lawrence Landt of Claverack, yeoman, was dated 29 Aug 1797 and probated 29 May 1798 (Columbia Co. Will Bk. A). They had ch. bpt. at Kinderhook Ref. and Claverack Ref. Churches (HJ).

    v) <u>Jeremias</u>[3] (Will), md. as b. in the Jerseys in 1769 Catharina Maul, both live Claverack (Linlithgo Ref. Chbk.).

    vi) <u>Johann Valentin</u>[3] (Will, but abstract notes daughter

Falta - HJ). He md. Elisabetha Philip, although there
may be some confusion with the w/o Johann Valentin[2]
(HJ). They had ch. bpt. at Claverack Ref. and Kinderhook Ref. Churches (HJ).

   vii) Elisabetha[3] (Will).

   viii) Maria[3] (Will).

  3?) Anna Margaretha[2], a sp. to Henrich Spohn at Schoharie in
     1716 (West Camp Luth. Chbk.).

AGNES LAPPIN (Hunter Lists #434)

The origins of this Palatine family were at 7527 Unteröwi-
sheim (25 km. s. of Heidelberg; Chbks. begin 1577, but gaps). The
husband of Agnes[1] Lapp was Georg Lapp, citizen at carpenter at
Unteröwisheim. Görg Lab, his wife, and 2 ch. were on Capt Leonard
Allan's ship in the 5th party of Palatines in Holland in 1709
(Rotterdam Lists).

Agnes Lappin made her initial appearance on the Hunter Lists
1 July 1710 with 2 pers. over 10 yrs. of age in the family. The
31 Dec 1710 entry showed 3 over 10 yrs., and the 24 June 1711 not-
ation read 1 pers. over 10 yrs. of age. A notation mentioning
Lappin and an allowance for barrels of flour is in N.Y. Col. Mss.,
Vol. LIV, p. 174. and dated 1710. Agnus Lapin: 2 women, were in
Ulster Co. in 1710/11 (West Camp Census). The ch. of Georg and
Agnes[1] Lapp were:

  1) Anna[2], md. as d/o Hans Georg Lapp the carpenter 27 April
     1706 Hans Peter Schneider, s/o the late Johann Elias
     Schneider (Unteröwisheim Chbk.).

  2) Margaretha[2], md. as d/o Hans Georg Lapp the carpenter in
     1707 Johannes Kugel (Unteröwisheim Chbk.). Agnes Lappin was
     recorded next to Johannes Kugel on the Hunter Lists dated
     4 Oct 1710 (HJ).

  3) Catharina[2] (HJ), md. the 1709er Ludwig Bretsch or Bersch
     by 1711 (HJ). Agnes Lappin was one name from Ludwig Börsch
     on 4 Oct 1710 in the Hunter Lists (HJ).

An Anna Urzula Lapp md. Harmen Philipsen 18 April 1712 (Albany Ref. Chbk.). She may belong in this family, or perhaps in the
Laib group (HJ).

JOHANN JACOB LAUCK'S WID[W] ELIZAB: (Hunter Lists #435)

Elisabetha, wid/o Johann Jacob Lauck of Nurstatt in Darmstadt,
md. Thomas Ehmann, widower of Schornbach in Wurtemberg, 26 June
1711 (West Camp Luth. Chbk.). Perhaps he was the Jacob Laux found
by Frau Mittelstaedt-Kubaseck at 6840 Lampertheim, or the Johann

Jacob Lauck who md. Anna Elisabeth Stemler 29 Oct 1709 at 6238
Wallau, home of #436 Abraham Lauck. The town of origin for this
1709er as listed in the Kocherthal records at West Camp is difficult to decipher; the locale actually may be Berstadt or a vari-
ant spelling (HJ).

Johann Jacob Lauck made his first appearance on the Hunter
Lists 4 Oct 1710 with 2 over 10 yrs. in the household; he was 6
names from Johann Niclaus Laux and 23 names from Abraham Lauck
(HJ). Jacob Laux Wid^W Elizabeth was noted 24 June 1711 with 1 pers.
over 10 yrs. of age. On page 74 of the Journal, Wilhelm Laux's
Wid^W Elizab: vid. after Th: Eheman was noted 24 June 1711. Anna
Elizabeth Laukin aged 42 was in N.Y. City in 1710/11 (Palatines
In N.Y. City).

ABRAHAM LAUCK (Hunter Lists #436)

Abraham Lauck of the commune of Epstein in Darmstadt md. Anna
Catharina Becker, d/o Johann Henrich of Weerheim in the commune of
Dillenburg, 27 Sept 1710 (West Camp Luth. Chbk.). The origins of
this family were documented at 6238 Wallau (10 km. s.e. of Wiesbaden; Chbks. begin 1658, but poor and partially destroyed). The
grandfather of Abraham[1] Lauck was Hans Lauck, bur. 9 Nov 1666,
aged 55 yrs.; Catharina, wid/o Hans Lauck, d. 20 July 1683, aged
80 yrs. They had issue:

> Jacob, conf. as s/o the late Hans Lauck in 1667. He md. Elis-
> abetha Margretha Stiglitz 8 Jan 1678.

> + Johann Valentin, conf. as s/o the late Joh. Lauck in 1672,
> aged 13 yrs.

Velten Lauck, s/o the late Hans Lauck, md. Anna Catharina, d/o
Henrich Rühl, 8 Nov 1681. Anna Catharina, d/o Henrich Rühl, was
conf. in 1670. Henrich Rühl, s/o Best Rühl and an inhab. and widower at Wallau, md. Elisabeth, d/o Lorentz Schneider at Medenbach,
1 July 1656; Henrich Rühl was bur. 4 Jan 1689, aged 62 yrs., and
Elisabetha, w/o Henrich Rühl, was bur. 9 June 1686, aged 49 yrs.
and 11 months after she was ill 9 days. Catarina, w/o Best Rühl,
was bur. 18 Feb 1665, aged 79 yrs. and called the mother of Henrich Rühl in her obituary. A note in the Wallau Chbk. mentions
that Velten Lauck with wife and 4 ch. went to Ireland in 1708, because they couldn't go to the New Land. The issue of Johann Valentin Lauck and wife Anna Catharina Rühl were:

> Johann Jacob, bpt. as Johan Jacobum 5 April 1683 - sp.: Jo-
> hannes Rübsam, and Johann Jacob - s/o Henrich Rühl and the
> brother of the mother

> Maria Christina, bpt. 9 Dec 1684 - sp.: Anna Christina - w/o

Johannes Lang, and Maria - w/o Hans Häuser the carpenter.
She d. 19 Jan 1685.

Elisabetha Margaretha, bpt. 21 Dec 1686 - sp.: Ottilia Mar-
greth - w/o Johan Georg Stiglitz, and Anna Elisab. - w/o Joh.
Henrich Hess. She may have been the d/o Val. Lauck bur. 20
June 1690 at Wallau (HJ).

Johann Reinhardt, bpt. 12 Trin.: 1689 - sp.: Joh. Best Zig-
ler at Breckenheim, and Joh. Renis (?) Schumacher at Norden-
statt, both single.

+ Johann Abraham, bpt. Dom. Invocavit.: 1691 - sp.: Abraham
Nieß - Bleydenstättischer Hofmann, and Paul Wiekenhofer. He
was conf. at Wallau in 1702, aged 15 (sic) yrs.

Johann Michael, bpt. 5 June 1694 - d. 19 Nov 1695.

+ Elisabetha Catharina, bpt. 7 Oct 1696. She md. Johann Michael Schauer in 1717 (Tulpehocken Chbk. entry after the
event).

+ Elisabetha Christina (HJ), bpt. not found in the badly-dam-
aged Wallau Chbks. She md. Joh: Hannessen Van Husum 11 April
1720 at Claverack (N.Y. City Luth. Chbk.).

Abraham Lauck made his initial appearance on the Hunter Lists
4 Oct 1710 with 2 pers. over 10 yrs. of age and 1 pers. under 10
yrs. The family size increased to 2 over 10 and 2 under 10 on 31
Dec 1710. The entry read 4 pers. over 10 yrs. on 24 June 1711,
4 over 10 and 1 under 10 on 29 Sept 1711, 5 over 10 on 24 Dec
1711, 3 pers. over 10 yrs. and 1 under 10 on 25 March 1712, and
4 over 10 and 1 under 10 on 24 June 1712. Abraham Lauck was nat.
31 Jan 1715/16 (Albany Nats.). Abraham Lauck with wife and ch.
was at Heessberg ca. 1716/17 (Simmendinger Register). Abram Luyke
was a freeholder of the Northpart Livingston in 1720 (Albany Co.
Freeholders). Abrah: Luyk was a Palatine Debtor in 1718, 1719, and
1722 (Livingston Debt Lists). Abraham[1] first came to the Tulpehocken region after 13 May 1723, but prior to 10 Jan 1725, when
the first tax list for the section was compiled, and ca. 1732
owned a tract of land ca. 3 miles n. of the old Ried's Luth.
Church (1723 - 1973 Anniversary Magazine of the Tulpehocken, p.
52). Abraham Lauck deeded land to St. Daniel's (Eck) Luth. Church
congregation 31 May 1751; this was part of a tract of 94¼ acres
granted to Abraham Luke by deed dated 29 Oct 1746 by William Allen and his wife (Letter from Annette Burgert to the author).
Abraham Lauk, s/o Valentine Lauck, was b. in 1686 in the Electorate of Mayns and bur. 10 Aug 1771, aged 88 yrs (Tulpehocken
Chbk.). The will of Abraham Louck of Heidelberg Twp. was dated
28 Jan 1771 and files 15 Aug 1772 (Berks Co. Will Bk. 2, p. 115).
The ch. of Abraham[1] Lauck and Anna Catharina Becker were:

1) <u>Maria Catharina</u>[2], b. 7 Sept 1711 - sp.: J. Georg Stump,
Maria Catharina - w/o Niclaus Schaefer, and Maria Catharina - w/o Abraham Lang (?) (West Camp Luth. Chbk.). She
md. 1st Jacob Mountz, a tailor, and 2nd by 1761 John Tieter (Berks Co. Orphan's Court Records Bk. 1, pp. 21 - 25).

2) <u>Anna Christina</u>[2], b. 24 Oct 1715 - sp.: Philipp Wilhelm
Moor and his wife (West Camp Luth. Chbk.). She md. Georg
Peter Zerbe (HJ).

3) <u>Anna Catharina</u>[2], b. Oct 1721 at Taar boss - sp.: Johann
Friederick Propert and Anna Cath. Simons (N.Y. City Luth.
Chbk.). She md. Lazarus Wenger 10 Nov 1738 (Christ Little
Tulpehocken Chbk.).

4) <u>Johann Georg</u>[2] (Will), md. Susannah (--) (HJ). John Georg
and Abraham Lauk were on the list of members at Tulpehock-
en in 1743. The will of Georg Louck of Heidelberg was dated 22 March 1783 and probated 10 Feb 1784 (Berks Co. Will
Bk. B, p. 103). His ch. were:
   i) <u>Anna</u>[3], b. 24 March 1742 (St. Daniel's Chbk.). She md.
   Georg Jägly (Will).
   ii) <u>Johann Georg</u>[3], b. 24 May 1745 (St. Daniel's Chbk.).
   iii) <u>Anna Christina</u>[3], b. 6 Aug 1749 (St. Daniel's Chbk.).
   She md. Henry Walters (Will).
   iv) <u>Maria Catharina</u>[3], b. 8 Nov 1751 (St. Daniel's Chbk.).
   v) <u>Abraham</u>[3], b. 20 Nov ... (St. Daniel's Chbk.).
   vi) <u>Maria Catharina</u>[3], b. 1 Jan 1757 (St. Daniel's Chbk.).
   She md. Jacob Freitz (Will).
   vii) <u>Johannes</u>[3], b. 3 May 1761 (St. Daniel's Chbk.).

5) <u>Abraham</u>[2] (Will), md. 9 April 1754 Anna Margaretha Elber-
scheid (Host Church, Womelsdorf Chbk.).

6) <u>Elisabetha</u>[2] (Will), md. Peter Zerbe (Will).

There was a Peter Laucks who md. Anna Barbara Kuerschner 28
June 1743 at Tulpehocken (Stoever Chbks.); no connection has been
found as of this writing with Abraham[1] Lauck and this man (HJ).

JOHANN NICLAUS LAUCKS (Hunter Lists #437)

There may have been a relationship between Johann Niclaus[1]
Laucks and #436 Abraham Lauck (HJ): 1) both lived at Heessberg
according to Simmendinger, and 2) Abraham appears to have been the
name of Johann Niclaus's first-born son. The name of Nicolaus also
was prominent at 6238 <u>Wallau</u>, proven home of Abraham[1]: 1) Nicolaus
Lauck was bur. in Nov 1706, aged 76 yrs.; 2) This Nicolaus had a
son Philip Lauck, who then had a son Nicol bpt. Jubilate: 1689 at
Wallau; and 3) Nicolaus bur. 1706 also had a son named Johann

Michael who md. Anna Christina Hess 8 Jan 1684 at Wallau and had
a son Nicol bpt. 4 April 1690 there. More information is needed
before #437 Johann Niclaus[1] Lauck may be cemented firmly to the
Wallau group (HJ). Hans Nikel Locks, his wife, and 3 ch., were on
Capt. Jno. Blouwer's ship in the 5th party of Palatines in Holland
in 1709 (Rotterdam Lists).

Johann Niclaus Laucks made his first appearance on the Hunter
Lists 30 June 1710 with 2 pers. over 10 yrs. of age. The family
was recorded with 3 over 10 on 24 June 1711 (with a note saying
omitted), then with 2 pers. over 10 yrs. and 1 pers. under 10 on
29 Sept 1711. Niclaus Laux of Haysbury was a soldier in 1711 (Palatine Volunteers To Canada). Nicolas Loakes was nat. 8 and 9 Sept
1715 (Kingston Nats.). Michael Laux and Anna Elisabetha with 3 ch.
were at Heessberg ca. 1716/17 (Simmendinger Register). A deposition of Eliz., w/o Nic. Luyk, was found in Reel #4 of the Livingston Papers; on this old mss., she was aged 34 in the yr. 1721/22.
The signature of Nicol Luyk also survives on this same reel, dated
1727. Nicolas Luyk was a Palatine Debtor in 1718, 1719 (at Haysberry), 1721, and 1726 (Livingston Debt Lists). Necklas Laux was
a Palatine willing to continue 26 Aug 1724 (Doc. Hist. Of N.Y.,
Vol. III, p. 724). Nicholas Luycks appeared on tax rolls beginning
in 1730/31 and continued until 1758 (Dutchess Co. Tax Lists). The
ch. of Johann Niclaus[1] Laucks and Anna Elisabetha were:

1) Elisabetha[2] (HJ), md. Peter Althauser (HJ). They were sp.
   in 1742 by Christian[2] Laucks and in 1744 by Nicolaus[2]
   Laucks at Red Hook Luth. Church (HJ).

2) Abraham[2] (HJ), md. Anna Margaretha Reiffenberger 23 Dec
   1732 (Catskill Ref. Chbk.). He was on tax rolls for Rhinebeck 1733 - 1747/48 (Dutchess Co. Tax Lists). Issue:

   i?) Johannes[3], md. Anna (--). They had ch. bpt. at Pine
       Plains, Churchtown Luth., and Hillsdale Ref. Churches
       (HJ); one of their ch. was Abraham, bpt. 1 April 1771
       at Pine Plains.

   ii) Eva[3] (HJ), md. James Decker (HJ).

   iii) Maria Elisabetha[3] (HJ), a sp. to James and Eva Decker
        in 1758 at Linlithgo Ref. Church.

   iv) Jacob[3], bpt. 19 May 1741 - sp.: Jacob L(--)k and Anna
       Margretha Koen (Germantown Ref. Chbk.). He md. Cath-
       arina Fell (HJ), and they had a son Abraham bpt. at
       Churchtown Luth. 7 Dec 1760 (HJ).

   v) Abraham[3], bpt. 1 Jan 1745 - sp.: Abraham Kilmer and
      Mareitgen Haug (Red Hook Luth. Chbk.). A man of this
      name is mentioned in Reid's Loyalists In Ontario,
      p. 183.

vi) <u>Elisabetha</u>³, bpt. 23 Nov 1746 - sp.: Elisabeth Reiffenberger and Daniel (Reiffenberger) (Germantown Ref. Chbk.).

vii) <u>Christina</u>³, bpt. 1 March 1749 - sp.: Henrich Hocstetter and Christina Hockstetter (Germantown Ref. Chbk.).

viii) <u>Nicolaus</u>³, bpt. 15 July 1751 - sp.: Jurg Reiffenberger and Catharina Schurtz (Germantown Ref. Chbk.). Reid mentions a man of this name in <u>Loyalists In Ontario</u>, p. 184.

3) <u>Johann Wilhelm</u>², b. 30 Dec 1715 - sp.: Johann Wilhelm Hambuch, Sebastian Spickermann, and the w/o Ulrich Weniger (West Camp Luth. Chbk.).

4) <u>Anna Eva</u>² (HJ), md. 1st Abraham Kilmer (HJ), and 2nd Joh. Michael Mochie 29 Sept 1756 (Germantown Ref. Chbk.).

5) <u>Jacob</u>², b. latter part of Dec 1719 at East Camp - sp.: Jacob Dings and wife Gertrud (N.Y. City Luth. Chbk.).

6) <u>Johann Christian</u>² (HJ), taxed in Rhinebeck 1739/40 - 1743/44 (Dutchess Co. Tax Lists). He md. Christina Decker (HJ) and had issue:

i) <u>Margaretha</u>³, bpt. as Grit 16 Oct 1743 - sp.: Jacob Laucks and Grit Drom (Red Hook Luth. Chbk.).

ii) <u>Gertraud</u>³, bpt. 11 Jan 1746 - sp.: Henricus Janse Witbeck and Beliche Decker (Germantown Ref. Chbk.).

iii) <u>Gerhardt</u>³, bpt. 5 Feb 1747 - sp.: Herman Best and wife (Germantown Ref. Chbk.).

iv) <u>Nicolaus</u>³, b. 1 Jan 1752 - sp.: Gabriel Dekker and Catharina Dekker (Rhinebeck Flats Ref. Chbk.).

v) <u>Abraham</u>³, bpt. 14 March 1756 - sp.: Cornelius Feinhard and Cristina Prisei (Red Hook Luth. Chbk.).

vi) <u>Anna Maria</u>³, bpt. 11 Sept 1757 - sp.: Johan Joost Proper and wife Anna Maria Widerwachs (Linlithgo Ref. Chbk.).

vii) <u>Abraham</u>³, bpt. 25 May 1760 - sp.: Niclaes Shurz and wife Marytje Shoets (Linlithgo Ref. Chbk.).

7) <u>Jacob</u>², b. March 1722 at Camp Queensberry - sp.: Jacob Dings and Gertrude Dings (N.Y. City Luth. Chbk.). Jacob Laucks joined the Red Hook Luth. Church 2 Jan 1743. He was taxed at Rhinebeck from 1744/45 - 1769 (Dutchess Co. Tax Lists). He md. 1st Anna Jungbloet (HJ) and had ch.:

i) <u>Anna Maria</u>³, b. 25 Dec 1746 (?) - sp.: Joh: Thiel Jungblut and wife (Rhinebeck Luth. Chbk.). She md. as d/o Jacob 17 Sept 1765 Henrich Muller (Red Hook Luth. Chbk.).

ii) Jacob³, bpt. 18 May 1752 - sp.: Jurg Mauser and Mareitje Mauser (Red Hook Luth. Chbk.). He md. Catharina Patrick (HJ).

By his 2nd wife Catharina Waldorff, Jacob² Laucks had:

iii) Elisabetha³, bpt. 16 March 1755 - sp.: Christian
Fritz and Lisabeth Walthorff (Red Hook Luth. Chbk.).

iv) Catharina³, bpt. 6 June 1756 - sp.: Engelbertus Waldorff and Gerdraut Junkblut (Red Hook Luth. Chbk.).

Jacob² md. 3rd Anna Striebel 7 June 1757 (Red Hook Luth.
Chbk.) and had issue:

v) Margaretha³, bpt. 26 Feb 1758 - sp.: Nicolaus Laux
and Gretgen Reifenberger (Red Hook Luth. Chbk.).

vi) Elisabetha³, b. 8 May 1762 - sp.: Andreas Stickel
and wife Elisabeth Bitzer (Rhinebeck Luth. Chbk.).

vii) Petrus³, bpt. 17 Feb 1765 - sp.: Petrus Heermans and
wife Maria Van Wagenen (Red Hook Luth. Chbk.).

viii) Wilhelmus³, bpt. 15 May 1767 - sp.: Willh: Bitzer
and Eva Tonsbach (Red Hook Luth. Chbk.).

ix) Johannes³, bpt. 18 June 1769 - sp.: Johannes Striebel and wife Marytjen Dings (Red Hook Luth. Chbk.).

x) Adam³, b. 2 May 1775 - sp.: Adam Segendorf and wife
Catharina Stikkel (Red Hook Luth. Chbk.).

8) Nicolaus² (HJ), as Nicklas Laucks Jr. joined the Red Hook
Luth. Church 24 Dec 1743. Nicholas Luyk Junr., aged 33,
b. Albany County, farmer, 5' 6" tall, was in Capt. John
Van Ness's Company in May 1760 (Report of the State Historian, Vol. II, p. 559). He md. Anna Maria Waldorff (HJ)
and had issue:

i) Anna Barbara³, bpt. 2 Oct 1748 - sp.: Wilhelm Waldorff and Anna Barbara Gerenreuch (Germantown Ref.
Chbk.).

ii) Elisabetha³, bpt. 20 Jan 1751 - sp.: Philip Kester
and Lisabeth Waltorph (Germantown Ref. Chbk.).

iii) Catharina³, bpt. 28 Nov 1752 - sp.: Hermen Fritz and
Cattarina Waldorf (Red Hook Luth. Chbk.).

iv) Anna³, bpt. 15 Dec 1754 - sp.: Johannes Staats and
Catharina Priester (Rhinebeck Flats Ref. Chbk.).

v) Christina³, bpt. 29 Oct 1756 - sp.: Peter Kempel and
Cristina Lahm (Red Hook Luth. Chbk.).

vi) Henrich³, bpt. 28 Jan 1759 - sp.: Henricus Waldorff
and Catharina Fritz (Red Hook Luth. Chbk.).

vii) Johannes³, b. 3 Aug 1761 - sp.: Wilhelmus Heermansen
and wife (Rhinebeck Flats Ref. Chbk.).

viii) Michael³, bpt. 6 Oct 1763 - sp.: Johan Michel Mugge

and wife Eva Laubrie (Linlithgo Ref. Chbk.).

ix) Jacob[3], b. 11 Nov 1766 - sp.: Jacob Laucks and wife
Anna (Rhinebeck Luth. Chbk.).

x) Adam[3], bpt. 16 Oct 1768 - sp.: Adam Kilmer and Anna
Margriet Wagenaer (Gallatin Ref. Chbk.).

A Georg Lauck sp. Adam Reifenberger in 1755 at Germantown
Ref. Church. He md. 1 Sept 1757 as being b. in Dutchess Co. Cornelia Bresie (Linlithgo Ref. Chbk.) and had issue bpt. at Linlithgo Ref. and Churchtown Luth. Churches (HJ); due to the Reiffenberger connection, he may have been an elder s/o Abraham[2] Laucks
(HJ).

PHILIPP LAUX (Hunter Lists #438)
(KNOWN AS PHILIP LAUNHARDT - HJ)

Johann Georg Launert, s/o the late Philipp of the earldom of
Ustingen, md. Anna Catharina Schneider, d/o Joh Dietrich of the
earldom of Hachenburg, 7 June 1715 (West Camp Luth. Chbk.). The
family was documented at 6394 Grävenwiesbach (13 km. s.w. of Butzbach; Chbks. begin 1641). The grandfather of the emigrant was
Johannes Launert, who md. Elisabetha (--) 27 April 1651, and had
issue:

Anna Catharina, bpt. 25 March 1652 - sp.: Philipp Reinhard
from Menstet (?), Crain - w/o Johann Launert from Gemünden,
and Crain - d/o Adam Bauch.

Johann Christ, bpt. 26 June 1653 - sp.: Christ Lang from
Langenbach, and Elisab. - d/o Cunrad Ohle from Naunstat.

Margaretha, bpt. 24 Oct 1654 - sp.: Margreth - d/o Hans Enders Stein, and Hans Volpert.

Johann Nicolaus, bpt. 25 Dec 1656 - sp.: Johann Niclas Engel,
and Margreth Heupel.

+ Philip, bpt. 18 Oct 1659 - sp.: Philip Launert and Eilge -
w/o Johann Enders Ernst. He was conf. in 1673, aged 13 3/4.

Maria, twin to the above, bpt. 18 Oct 1659 - sp.: Cunrad Mehl
from Emrichshausen, and Maria - d/o Jonas Moses.

Johann Bernhard, bpt. 14 Dec 1662 - sp.: Johann Claß Launerts, and Anna - w/o Claß Velten from Naunstat.

Conrad, bpt. 19 March 1665 - sp.: Conrad Launert from Gemünd-
en, and Anna Catharina Jäger.

Anna, bpt. 20 March 1670 - sp.: Elisabetha - d/o Johan Lang
from Niederlauken, Anna - w/o Wilhelm Riel, and Hans Nickel
Moses.

Philipp Launhart at Haintzenberg md. Anna Eva (--) 25 June 1690;
Kingston Ref. Chbk. and Grävenwiesbach sp. show her name to be

Saltz or Sals (HJ). Anna Eva, wid/o the late Philip Launerts at
Haintzenberg, md. Dom. 19 Trin.: 1698 Johann Georg Laux; this explains why #438 Philipp[1] Laux became known as Philip Launhardt also, and why his brother Johann Georg mentioned "brother Peter Laux"
in his will (HJ). The ch. of Philipp Launhert and Anna Eva were:

+ Anna Christina, bpt. 12 July 1691 - sp.: Christina - w/o Hans
  Adam Sieber from Usingen, Anna - w/o Claß Velten from Naunstat, and Bernhard Launert. She md. Philip Wilhelm Mohr (HJ).

+ Johann Philip, bpt. 4 Oct 1693 - sp.: Johann Saltz from Wenden, and Margaretha - w/o Hans Adam Sieber, the Landbereuter
  from Usingen.

+ Johann Georg, bpt. 14 April 1697 - sp.: Hans Georg Sölmser
  the Gerichtsschöffe, and Anna Eulalia - wid/o Jacob Bothoff.
  Johann Georg Baunert was conf. at Queensberg in 1714 (West
  Camp Luth. Chbk.). Jurich Loundert was nat. 14 Feb 1715/16
  (Albany Nats.). Johann Georg Launert with wife and ch., and
  mother Eva Lauxin were at Heessberg ca. 1716/17 (Simmendinger
  Register). Jurrie Loonart made his initial appearance on tax
  rolls in the North Ward in 1717/18 and continued until June
  1768 (Dutchess Co. Tax Lists). The will of Johan George Launert of Witenkley's Kill was dated 14 May 1768 and probated
  15 Aug 1768 (Fernow Wills #1045). He and wife Anna Catharina
  Schneider had no surviving ch. (HJ).

Philipp Laux made his first appearance on the Hunter Lists 30
June 1710 with 1 pers. in the family. On page 39 of the Journal,
Anna Margretha Kuhnin moda Phil: Laux wife was noted 4 Oct 1710,
next to Valentin Kuhn and near Johann Hermann Klein; as Veltin
Kuhn, son of Samuel[1] Kuhn, was enrolled still next to Klein on the
Simmendinger Register in 1716/17, this may point to the possibilty
that Anna Margaretha Kuhn Launhardt was related to Samuel[1] Kuhn
(HJ). Phil. Lounhert was nat. 8 and 9 Sept 1715 (Kingston Nats.).
Phillip Loonart made his first appearance on tax rolls in the North
Ward in 1718/19 and continued until June 1767 at Rhinebeck (Dutchess Co. Tax Lists). Philip Laundert was a Palatine Debtor in 1718,
while his brother Johann Georg was one in 1718, 1719, 1721, and
1722 (Livingston Debt Lists). Georg Launhart and Phillip Launhart
with ch. Peter, Catharina, and Eva were on the St. Peter's Luth.
Family List ca. 1734 (Rhinebeck Luth. Chbk.). The will of Philipp
Lounhart of Rinebeck Precinct was dated 17 March 1768 and probated
16 May 1768 (Fernow Wills #1044). Philip[1] md. 2nd 7 Sept 1744 Catharina, wid/o Georg Schmidt of Kisk. (Loonenburg Luth. Chbk.). By
his 1st wife Anna Margaretha Kuhn, the ch. of Philip[1] (Laux) Launhardt were:

1) <u>Anna Catharina</u>², b. 24 Sept 1715 - sp.: Jerg Launert and
his wife Anna Catharina (West Camp Luth. Chbk.). She md.
Nicolaus Treber (Will).

2) <u>Philip</u>², b. 23 Jan 1719 - sp.: Philip Mohr and Anna Maria
- w/o Dietrich Schneider (West Camp Luth. Chbk.).

3) <u>Eva</u>², b. 7 Oct 1720 and bpt. at Camp - sp.: Christian Dietrich and Eva Druphagel (N.Y. City Luth. Chbk.). She md.
Johannes Best (Will).

4) <u>Peter</u>², banns to marry as s/o Philip of Rhynbek in 1744
Catharina, d/o Adam Spohn of Bakoven (Loonenburg Luth.
Chbk.). On a list of leases in the Livingston Papers Reel
#10 is one to Peter Londhart dated 1744. An Ancient Docu-
ment dated 1774 numbered 10763 mentions one Peter Lounhart. The will of Peter Loundhart of the Manor of Livingston was dated 25 Nov 1784 and probated 16 March 1793 (Columbia Co. Will Bk. A). No ch. were mentioned (HJ).

JOHANN PHILIPP LAUX (Hunter Lists #439)

It is difficult to sort out the different items on various mss.
for #438 Philipp Laux and #439 Johann Philipp Laux (HJ). #439 Johann Philipp¹ made his initial appearance 4 Oct 1710 with 3 pers.
over 10 yrs.; his entry read 3 over 10 and 1 under 10 31 Dec 1710
and 2 over 10 yrs. and 2 under 10 on 24 June 1711. Phillip Laux
of Haysbury was a soldier in 1711 (Palatine Volunteers To Canada).
Philip Loucks was nat. 17 Jan 1715/16 (Albany Nats.). Philipp Laux
with wife and ch. was at Beckmansland ca. 1716/17 (Simmendinger
Register). He md. Magdalena (--); due to sp. at Albany Ref. Church
in 1734 and 1742 between Laux and Christian Lang, this may point
to the possibility of his wife being #431 Magdalena Langin (HJ).
The ch. of (Johann) Philipp¹ Laux and wife Magdalena:

1) <u>Anna Maria</u>², bpt. 31 March 1717 - sp.: Andries Bratt and
Wyntie Roos (Albany Ref. Chbk.).

2) <u>Jacob</u>², bpt. 4 May 1718 - sp.: Andries Bratt and Wyntie
Roos (Albany Ref. Chbk.). He md. 1st Alida Goewey 2 Nov
1754 (Albany Ref. Chbk.). They had issue:
   i) <u>Philip</u>³, bpt. 23 Oct 1755 - sp.: Johannes and Jeesje
     Lock (Albany Ref. Chbk.).
   ii) <u>Salomon</u>³, bpt. 23 Oct 1755 - sp.: Salomon and Sara
     Holly (Albany Ref. Chbk.).
Jacob² md. Wid. Rachel Hogen 28 May 1757 (Albany Ref.
Chbk.) and had a child:
   iii) <u>Alida</u>³, bpt. 1 July 1759 - sp.: Pieter and Maria Goe-
     wey (Albany Ref. Chbk.).

3) <u>Anna Maria</u>², bpt. 2 Oct 1720 - sp.: Casper Ham and Anna

Leyb (Albany Ref. Chbk.). She md. Henrich Van Wie (HJ).

4) Johannes² (HJ), md. 27 April 1753 Geesje Legrange (Albany
Ref. Chbk.). They had issue:

   i) Philip³, bpt. 9 Dec 1753 - sp.: Jacob and Magdalena
Loeck (Albany Ref. Chbk.).

   ii) Maria³, bpt. 5 March 1758 - sp.: Henderick and Maria
Van Wie (Albany Ref. Chbk.).

5) Magdalena², bpt. 5 Dec 1726 - sp.: Corn. V. Dyk and Bar.
Spoor (Albany Ref. Chbk.). She md. 8 Aug 1759 Johannis
Van Wie (Albany Ref. Chbk.).

6) Conrad² (HJ), md. as a single man of Albany Co. 6 Oct 1751
Gertraud Van Deusen (Albany Ref. Chbk.). Conradt Loock
was in Leut. John M: Veeder's Company in the Colony of
Rencelarswick in 1767 (Report of the State Historian, Vol.
II, p. 820). The ch. of Conrad² Laux were:

   i) Philip³, bpt. 17 June 1753 - sp.: Henderick Van Wie
and Maria Loeck (Albany Ref. Chbk.).

   ii) Engel³, bpt. 30 May 1756 - sp.: Jan Van Deusen and
Maria Winne (Albany Ref. Chbk.).

JOHANN JOST LAUX (Hunter Lists #440)

Maria Elizabetha Laux, d/o Johann Just of Weiher in the earldom of Runckel, md. Johann Jacob Becker, s/o the late Johann of
Darmbach in the earldom of Runckel, 24 Jan 1716 (West Camp Luth.
Chbk.). As Johann Jost¹ Laux was a shepherd, the family was documented in several villages and towns as he wandered around the
Nassau - Runkel area tending his flock: 1) at 6257 Kirberg (11
km. s. of Runkel; Chbks. begin 1650); 2) at 5429 Kördorf/Lahn
(8 km. s.e. of Nassau; Chbks. begin 1655, partially destroyed by
water); and 3) at 5421 Dachsenhausen (7 km. s.w. of Nassau; Chbks.
begin 1639, in poor condition). He was called a shepherd at Ohren
in 1686 and 1688 (Kirberg Chbk.), at Kirberg in 1693 and 1696
(Kirberg Chbk.), at Attenhausen in 1699 and 1702 (Kördorf Chbk.
and Nassau Chbk., resp.), and at Scheuern in 1708 (Dachsenhausen
Chbk.). Sp. strongly suggest that Johann Jost¹ originally came
from 6394 Grävenwiesbach (HJ).

Johann Jost Laux made his initial appearance on the Hunter
Lists with Johannes Laux 1 July 1710; the entry recorded 2 pers.
over 10 yrs. of age. The entry for 4 Aug 1710 read 4 pers. over
10 yrs., for 4 Oct 1710 registered 3 over 10, for 31 Dec 1710
noted 3 over 10 and 1 under 10 yrs., and for 25 March 1711 was 2
over 10 yrs. of age. Jost Laux and Math: Kuhn's Wid^W were listed
24 June 1711, and Jost Laux and Elizab: Schwedin were recorded

29 Sept 1711 with 5 pers. over 10 yrs. of age. The ledger section
of Hunter mentioned that Anna Elizabeth Schwedin md. John Jost
Laux. 2 boards to make a coffin for the w/o Jost Laux were allo-
cated 7 May 1711 (N.Y. Colonial Mss., Vol. 55, p. 20 a-h). Johann
Just Laux and his wife Maria were recorded at Neu-Heessberg ca.
1716/17 (Simmendinger Register). The ch. of Johann Jost[1] Laux and
his 1st wife Maria Catharina, who sp. Johannes[1] Laux at Nassau
in 1702, were:

1) Maria Margaretha[2], bpt. 18 April 1686 - sp.: Anna Maria
   - w/o Peter Laux from Münster, Margaretha - w/o Hans Wilhelm Villing from Heringen, and Joh. Kuhn from Kalt. -
   Holzhausen (Kirberg Chbk.). Maria Margaretha Laux, the
   d/o the shepherd at Scheurn, md. the emigrant Philipp
   Peter Wagner 2 March 1708 (Dachsenhausen Chbk.).

2) Johannes[2], bpt. 12 Feb 1688 - sp.: Joh. Ernst of Heisten-
   berg near Usingen, Joh. Laux from Weier near Niedersel-
   ters, and Anna Catharina Kaltwasser (Kirberg Chbk.). There
   is a slight possibility that #441 Johannes Laux was this
   son to Johann Jost[1], but I believe a far more likely relationship between Johann Jost[1] and #441 Johannes Laux
   would be as brothers (HJ).

3) Johann Peter[2], bpt. 7 May 1693 - sp.: Joh. Peter Laux -
   his brother, Johann Dathumb, and Anna Maria - w/o Peter
   Peis the hofmann (Kirberg Chbk.).

4) Anna Dorothea[2], bpt. 30 Dec 1694 - sp.: Anna Dorothea -
   w/o Philipp the cowherd from Itstein (?), Anna Magdalena
   - d/o the late Conrad Trinckmann, and Huppert Frankenfeld
   (Kirberg Chbk.). She was bur. 15 Nov 1695, aged 11 months
   (Kirberg Chbk.).

5) Johann Jost[2], bpt. between 19 and 30 Aug 1696 - sp.: Joh.
   Jost Horn, Johann Henrich Ludwig from Gräbenwiesbach, and
   Maria Catharina Wagner (Kirberg Chbk.). He was bur. 22
   Aug 1704, aged 8 yrs. (Nassau Chbk.).

6) Maria Elisabetha[2], b. at Attenhausen and bpt. 26 May 1699
   - sp.: Joh. Nicolaus Schumacher, Johannes Laux at Weyer
   at the Long Hedge, Maria Elisab. Bingel, and Maria Catharina ... (Kördorf Chbk.). She md. Johann Jacob Becker
   24 Jan 1716 (West Camp Luth. Chbk.).

There was a Jost Laux, shepherd at Naunstatt, who had a son
Johann Tönies bpt. 21 Sept 1679 (no wife mentioned) - sp.: Johan
Tönies Laux - shepherd at Grevenwiesbach, and Anna Maria - w/o
Peter Saldenberger (Grävenwiesbach Chbk.). If this man was the
emigrant 1709er, it would make him a bit older than heretofore
thought (HJ).

JOHANNES LAUX (Hunter Lists #441)

This 1709er also had his roots at 6394 Grävenwiesbach, and
he was documented at 6252 Diez (18 km. s.w. of Weilburg; Chbks.
begin 1660, Ref.) and at 5408 Nassau (38 km. n.w. of Wiesbaden;
Chbks. begin 1673, Ref.). Johannes Laux, surviving s/o Thönges
Laux - formerly shepherd at Gräfen-Wiesbach near Usingen, md.
Elisabetha, d/o Wilhelm Holwein at Heistenbach, 5 Oct 1699 (Diez
Chbk.). He was called a shepherd at Scheuren in 1700 and at Ober-
wies in 1702, 1704, and 1705 (Nassau Chbk.). A Johan Louck came
alone on Capt. William Newton's ship in the 5th party of Palatines
in Holland in 1709 (Rotterdam Lists); however, he probably was
not #441 (HJ).

Johannes Laux made his initial appearance on the Hunter Lists
1 July 1710 with 2 pers. over 10 yrs. of age, recorded with Johann Jost Laux. The entry read 1 pers. over 10 yrs. of age 25
March 1711 and then returned to 2 over 10 yrs. 24 June 1711. Johannes Laux and Anna Elisabetha were auf dem Rarendantz ca. 1716/
17 (Simmendinger Register). He was a neighbor on the w. of Henry
Bost ca. 1720 in the Amwell region (A History of East Amwell 1700
- 1800, p. 16). Johannes Loux was nat. 8 July 1730 (N.J. Nats.).
Joannes Lokes was a freeholder of Amwell in 1741 (Hunterdon Co.
Freeholders). The will of Johan Laux of Amwell in Hunterdon Co.
was dated 19 May 1752 and probated 22 Sept 1752 (N.J. Wills: Lib.
7, p. 395). He left his personal estate to his wife Mary as sole
heiress and a legacy to his brother Derrick's oldest son (HJ).
The ch. of Johannes[1] Laux and wife Elisabetha Holwein were:

1) Johann Tönges[2], b. at Scheuern and bpt. 5 Sept 1700 - sp.:
   Tönges Laux - shepherd at Hübingen, Susanna - d/o Gröller
   from Heisterbach, and Peter Ackermann from Heistenbach
   (Nassau Chbk.).

2) Maria Catharina[2], bpt. 14 May 1702 - sp.: the w/o Jost
   Laux at Attenhausen, the son-in-law of Georg Lenhard from
   Eberwies, and Anna Maria - w/o Henrich Holtzhäuser from
   Heisterbach (Nassau Chbk.).

3) Johann Wilhelm[2], bpt. 1 Feb 1704 - sp.: Wilhelm Holwein
   - the grandfather of the child, Tönges Heymann, and the
   w/o Melchior Mey from ... (Nassau Chbk.).

4) Johann Christoph[2], bpt. 25 Dec 1705 - sp.: Johann Christ.
   Weiss, Johann Christoph Schmidt, and Anna Eva Maj (Nassau
   Chbk.).

Again, as I mentioned in section #440 on Johann Jost Laux,
I believe there is a slight possibility that #441 may have been
the s/o Johann Jost[1] named Johannes bpt. in 1688; however, as

the name of his wife was Elisabetha in Germany and on the Simmendinger Register and as no further record of the Johannes Laux who
md. in Diez in 1699 and had ch. bpt. at Nassau has been found after 1709, I believe it far more likely that the Diez - Nassau man
was indeed the emigrant Johannes[1] Laux (HJ).

GEORG LAUX (Hunter Lists #442)

The German roots of this family were at 6394 Grävenwiesbach
(13 km. s.w. of Butzbach; Chbks. begin 1641). Johann Georg Laux
md. Anna Eva, wid/o the late Philip Launert at Haintzenberg, Dom.
19 Trin.: 1698 (see section #438 on Philipp Laux for more on the
Launhardt family - HJ). Johann Georg[1] seems to have had ch. from
an earlier marriage, as Anna Christina Laucks, d/o Johan Georg
Laux from Heinzenberg, was conf. in 1704 at 6273 Steinfischbach
(HJ); indeed he may have been the Hans Georg Laux who md. Anna
Juliana (--) 19 Oct 1669 at Grävenwiesbach. His un-named wife was
bur. 6 June 1698 at 6292 Weilmünster.

Georg Laux made his initial appearance on the Hunter Lists
31 Dec 1710 with 6 pers. over 10 yrs. of age. The entry read 4
over 10 yrs. and 1 under 10 on 24 June 1711, 4 over 10 yrs. on
25 March 1712, and 5 over 10 yrs. of age on 24 June 1712. He often was enrolled not too many names away from Jost and Johannes
Laux on the Hunter Lists. Eva Zout, b. Germany and wid/o Hans Juriaan Louks, md. Johannes Traphagen 25 Jan 1718 (Kingston Ref.
Chbk.); sp. and later entries at Kingston show her name probably
was Saltz (HJ). The ch. of Georg[1] Laux and Anna Eva were:

1) "A Stillborn Son"[2], bpt. 22 Oct 1699 (Grävenwiesbach
   Chbk.).
2) Johann Peter[2], bpt. 5 June 1701 - sp.: Johannes Laux dwelling at Weyher near Runkel - Ref. religion, Peter Bley-
   bach - the bricklayer living at Langenbächer Mühl, and
   Anna - w/o Johann Henrich Schneider the Censor at Haintzenberg (Grävenwiesbach Chbk.). Johann Peter Laux was conf.
   with Joh: Georg Baunert Easter 1714 at Queensberg (West
   Camp Luth. Chbk.). Peter Loaks was nat. 8 and 9 Sept 1715
   (Kingston Nats.). Banns for the marriage of Pieter Luyks,
   single man b. Germany, and Neeltje Leg, single woman b.
   Kingston, were dated 19 May 1722 (Kingston Ref. Chbk.).
   Neeltje, w/o Peter Laux, joined the church Dom. Leetare
   1736/37 (Loonenburg Luth. Chbk.). Peter[2] was a member of
   Berkenmeyer's church council in 1735 (Albany Protocol, p.
   115). Cornelia Laux d. 13 June 1776, aged 76 yrs., and
   Peter[2] d. 12 Sept 1787, aged 89 yrs. (both Schoharie

Luth. Chbk.). The ch. of Johann Peter[2] and Neeltje were:

i) Johannes[3], bpt. 23 June 1723 - sp.: Johannes Traphag-
en and Eva Sals (Kingston Ref. Chbk.). He md. Elisa-
betha Straub 22 Sept 1743 (Loonenburg Luth. Chbk.).
They had issue bpt. at Katsbaan Ref. and Loonenburg
Luth. Churches (HJ). The will of Johannes Lauck of
Beaver Creek was dated 26 May 1788 and probated 10
Feb 1789 (Ulster Co. Wills).

ii) Anna[3], bpt. 28 March 1725 - sp.: Jan Leg and Annetjen
Fynhout (Kingston Ref. Chbk.). She md. 12 March 1744
Philip Spoon (Loonenburg Luth. Chbk.).

iii) Margaretha[3], bpt. 28 May 1727 - sp.: Philip Lonard
and Margriet Coensens (Kingston Ref. Chbk.). Margret-
je, Annatje, and Johannes Laux were conf. at Newton
31 Oct 1742 (Loonenburg Luth. Chbk.). She md. 17 Dec
1749 Wilhelmus Emmerich (Loonenburg Luth. Chbk.).

iv) Wilhelm[3], bpt. 8 June 1729 - sp.: Willem Leg Jr. and
Zusanna Leg (Kingston Ref. Chbk.). He was conf. 19
Feb 1748/49 (Loonenburg Luth. Chbk.). He md. at Kisk.
11 Sept 1751 Elisabetha Elig (Loonenburg Luth. Chbk.).
They had ch. bpt. at Loonenburg Luth. and Germantown
Ref. Churches (HJ).

v) Eva[3], bpt. 4 May 1731 - sp.: Philiph Moor and Christina Moor (Katsbaan Ref. Chbk.).

vi) Petrus[3], b. 29 Dec 1732 - sp.: Jan Legk and Sarah
Legk (Loonenburg Luth. Chbk.).

vii) Johann Georg[3], b. 3 Dec 1733 and bpt. Newton - sp.:
Hans Jurge Launert and wife Cath., but as the river
was impass., mother held child (Loonenburg Luth.
Chbk.).

viii) Neeltje[3], bpt. 4 April 1736 - sp.: John Leg and Sara
Leg (Katsbaan Ref. Chbk.).

ix) Petrus[3], b. 4 Aug 1738 and bpt. Kisket. - sp.: Peter
Maurer and wife Anna Catharina (Loonenburg Luth.
Chbk.).

x) Catharina[3], b. 13 March 1741 and bpt. Piet Laux' house
- sp.: Hans Jurge Launer and wife Anna Catharina
(Loonenburg Luth. Chbk.). She md. Andreas Elig 26 Jan
1762 (Loonenburg Luth. Chbk.).

xi) Andreas[3], b. 13 May 1743 and bpt. Newton - sp.: And-
reas Elid and wife Sophia (Loonenburg Luth. Chbk.).
He md. Catharina Hummeling 11 Nov 1763 (Loonenburg
Luth. Chbk.); she d. 11 Feb 1821, aged 79 (Schoharie
Luth. Chbk.). They had ch. bpt. at Germantown Luth.

and Schoharie Luth. Churches (HJ).

xii) Cornelius[3], b. 4 Feb 1746 and bpt. Kisket. - sp.: Jan
Laux and wife Lisabeth (Loonenburg Luth. Chbk.). He
md. Maria Merckle in 1768 (Schoharie Luth. Chbk.).
They had ch. bpt. at Schoharie Luth. Church (HJ).

DIETRICH LAUX (Hunter Lists #443)
JOHANN DIETRICH LAUX (Hunter Lists #444)

The will of Johan Laux of Amwell Twp. in Hunterdon Co., N.J.
dated 19 May 1752 and probated 22 Sept 1752 mentions a legacy to
his brother Derrick's oldest son, if he calls for it (N.J. Wills:
Lib. 7, p. 395). Evidence strongly points to #441 Johann Laux of
Hunterdon Co., N.J. being the Johannes Laux, s/o the late Thönges
Laux - formerly shepherd at Gräfen-Wiesbach (6394 Grävenwiesbach
- HJ), who md. Elisabetha Holwein 5 Oct 1699 at Nassau. As Derrick
was a common nickname for the more proper Dieterich in German settlements in colonial America, and as the will of Johannes[1] seemed
to imply that Derrick and his son lived some distance from N.J.
(but probably in America, by its tone), this seems to point to
the strong probability that Dieterich[1] Laux of the Mohawk Valley,
the only man so-named that I know of in the American colonies in
the 18th century, was then brother to Johannes[1] Laux of Amwell
and s/o Thönges Laux of Grävenwiesbach (HJ).

Dietrich Laux, #443 on the Hunter Lists, made only one appearance on these rolls: on 1 July 1710 he had 2 over 10 yrs. and 1
under 10 in his household. #444 Johann Dietrich Laux then was entered 4 Aug 1710 with the same number in the family; on 31 Dec
1710 he had 3 over 10 yrs. and 1 under 10, on 25 March 1711 the
family was recorded with 2 over 10 and 1 under 10 yrs., and on 24
June 1711 the Laux household showed 2 pers. over 10 yrs. of age.
Diedrich Loucks was nat. 31 Jan 1715/16 (Albany Nats.). Johann
Dieterich and his wife Maria Catharina with 2 ch. were at Neu-
Cassel ca. 1716/17 (Simmendinger Register); as the names match with
Johann Dieterich[1] Laux so well, and as the family was listed next
to Johann Jacob Becker and wife Maria Elisabetha, d/o Johann Jost[1]
Laux, on the Simmendinger publication, I am sure this Johann Diet-
erich entry refers to Johann Dieterich[1] Laux (HJ). Dietrich and
Henry Loucks signed a 1743 agreement on behalf of the Stone Arabia
Ref. Church, as Johann Dieterich was an elder there that yr. (His-
tory of Montgomery & Fulton Counties, N.Y., p. 155). Johann Dieterich[1] md. Maria Catharina (--) and had issue:

1) Jost[2], bpt. 29 Sept 1709 - sp.: Joost Luijckesz and Neeltie Engele (Rotterdam Ref. Chbk., Holland). The parents

on this fascinating entry were Dirck Luijckasz and wife
Maria Couweriagt, noted as outside the East Gate, coming
from the Paltz, going to England.

2) Johann Adam², b. 28 Dec 1715 and bpt. at Schoharie - sp.:
   Adam Starring and wife (West Camp Luth. Chbk.). He md.
   Catharina Elisabetha Schnell 16 Oct 1739 (Stone Arabia
   Ref. Chbk.). Their death record at Stone Arabia Ref. noted
   that Adam² was b. 15 Dec 1715 at Scohary and d. 14 Feb
   1790, aged 74 yrs. and 2 months, and that Catharina Elisabetha d. 14 Feb 1797, aged 76 yrs. and 2 months (or 13
   Feb 1797, aged 78 yrs., according to one transcript of the
   Stone Arabia Ref. Cem. - HJ). Penrose's Mohawk Valley in
   the Revolution has much on various descendants of this
   line. The ch. of Johann Adam² Laux and Catharina Elisabetha were:

     i) Dieterich³, bpt. 1740 - sp.: Hendrich Laux and Marÿa
        Lisabet Schnel (Stone Arabia Ref. Chbk.).
    ii) Johannes³, bpt. 1742 - sp.: Johannes Schnuell and his
        wife (Stone Arabia Ref. Chbk.).
   iii) Elisabetha³, b. 22 Dec 1744 - sp.: Görg Cobernoll and
        his wife Lisabet (Stone Arabia Ref. Chbk.).
    iv) Adam³, b. 27 May 1747 - sp.: Nicklas Felling and Lis-
        abet Schnell (Stone Arabia Ref. Chbk.).
     v) Catharina³, bpt. 26 Feb 1750 - sp.: Andereas Finck
        and Catterina (Stone Arabia Ref. Chbk.).
    vi) Anna Eva³, bpt. 29 Sept 1752 - sp.: Marcus Petri and
        wife Anna Eva (Stone Arabia Ref. Chbk.).
   vii) Peter³, bpt. 21 March 1755 - sp.: Petter Krembs and
        Elisabetta Empie (Stone Arabia Ref. Chbk.).
  viii) Jost³, b. 15 Sept 1756 - sp.: Willem Emgie and Mar-
        greth (Stone Arabia Ref. Chbk.).
    ix) Johann Georg³, b. 6 May 1759 - sp.: Goerg Snell and
        wife Maria (Stone Arabia Ref. Chbk.).
     x) Henrich³, b. 22 Nov 1761 - sp.: Henrich Frei and wife
        Margretha (Stone Arabia Ref. Chbk.).
    xi) Jacob³, b. 16 Sept 1764 - sp.: Jacob Ecker and Cath-
        arina Finck (Stone Arabia Ref. Chbk.).
   xii) Maria³, b. 8 March 1767 and d. 8 March 1767 (Stone
        Arabia Ref. Chbk.).

3) Anna Elisabetha² (HJ), md. Georg Coppernail 28 Jan 1740
   (Stone Arabia Ref. Chbk.).

4) Catharina² (HJ), md. Andreas Finck 14 Dec 1742 (Stone Arabia Ref. Chbk.). Her obituary at Stone Arabia gives dates
   11 March 1720 - 31 March 1790.

5) <u>Henrich²</u> (HJ), called Henrich D. Laux at his marriage 10
Oct 1749 to Maria Elisabetha Kräus (Stone Arabia Ref.
Chbk.). Hend'k D: Laux was in Soffrines Deychert's Company
in 1757, and Henry and Peter Laux were recorded in Lieut.
Goshin Van Alstein's Company in 1763 (<u>Report of the State
Historian</u>, Vol. II, pp. 783 & 797). Hendrick Lucks was a
freeholder at Stonrabie in 1763 (Albany Co. Freeholders).
He d. either 8 Feb 1795, aged 78-10-23, or 27 May 1812,
aged 87 and some months (both Stone Arabia Ref. Chbk.);
the correct Henrich D. Laux probably was the man who d.
in 1812, as the Stone Arabia Ref. Chbks. show a Henrich
conf. in 1740 there (HJ). The ch. of Henrich² and Maria
Elisabetha Laux were:

 i) <u>Catharina³</u>, bpt. 13 Sept 1751 - sp.: Adam Lauchs and
  Maria Catharina, his wife (Stone Arabia Ref. Chbk.).

 ii) <u>Elisabetha³</u>, bpt. 22 May 1753 - sp.: Gorg Cober Noll
  and Elisabetta Laucks (Stone Arabia Ref. Chbk.).

 iii) <u>Anna Eva³</u>, b. 13 Feb 1756 - sp.: Anna Eva - w/o Marcus Petri (Stone Arabia Ref. Chbk.).

 iv) <u>Anna³</u>, b. 15 Aug 1760 - sp.: Anna - single d/o Jacob
  Kraus, and Dieterich Laux - single (Stone Arabia Ref.
  Chbk.).

 v) <u>Jacob³</u>, b. 10 June 1762 - sp.: Jacob Kraus and wife
  Gertraud (Stone Arabia Ref. Chbk.).

 vi) <u>Dieterich³</u>, b. 23 July 1764 - sp.: Dieterich Lauchs
  and Dorothea Fox (Stone Arabia Ref. Chbk.).

 vii) <u>Maria³</u>, b. 14 Feb 1767 - sp.: Maria Margretha and
  Wilhelm Emgie (Stone Arabia Ref. Chbk.).

6?) <u>Peter²</u>, conf. in 1740 (Stone Arabia Ref. Chbk.).

7) <u>Dieterich²</u> (HJ), conf. in 1749 and a sp. in 1753 as Jr.
(both Stone Arabia Ref. Chbk.).

8?) <u>Margaretha²</u>, conf. in 1749 (Stone Arabia Ref. Chbk.).

  As the chbks. of Pastor Hager and others who serviced the
Schoharie - Mohawk region are missing, sorting out all the Lauxes
in the area is extremely difficult. <u>Johann Henrich Laux</u>, an early
settler in the Mohawk, obviously was a relative of some kind of
Johann Jost¹ and Johann Dieterich¹ Laux; however, sp. between Johann Henrich's family and the others are almost non-existent, il-
lustrating the somewhat separate identity of Johann Henrich's
group (HJ). Johan Hendrick Loucks was nat. 3 Jan 1715/16 (Albany
Nats.). Heinrich Laux and his wife Anna Margretha with 2 ch. were
at Neu-Heessberg ca. 1716/17 (Simmendinger Register). The name Henrich survives prominently in the offspring of the ch. of <u>Johann
Henrich Laux</u>:

1) <u>Johann Henrich</u>[2] (HJ), banns to marry as a single man 23
   Feb 1739 Johanna Elisabetha Kuhn (Schoharie Ref. Chbk.).
   They had ch.:

    i) <u>Elisabetha Barbara</u>[3], bpt. 7 Feb 1739/40 - sp.: Johan-
   nes Finck and Elisa Barbara Coen (Schoharie Ref.
   Chbk.).

    ii) <u>Maria Elisabetha</u>[3], md. as d/o Henrich[2] 28 Oct 1760
   Adam Huthmacher (Stone Arabia Ref. Chbk.).

    iii) <u>Margaretha</u>[3], bpt. 22 May 1743 - sp.: Coenraad Richt-
   meyer and Elizabeth Rigtmeyer (Albany Ref. Chbk.).
   She md. as d/o Henrich[2] 4 Dec 1759 Johannes Schäffer
   (Stone Arabia Ref. Chbk.).

    iv) <u>Johann Peter</u>[3], bpt. 25 Aug 1745 - sp.: Hannes and
   Anna Barb. Boom (Albany Ref. Chbk.). He sp. Adam Hut-
   macher at Stone Arabia Ref. Church in 1762 along with
   Catharina, single d/o Wilhelm[2] Laux (HJ).

    v) <u>Magdalena</u>[3] (HJ), a sp. at Stone Arabia Ref. in 1765
   with Peter[3] Laux.

    vi) <u>Catharina</u>[3], bpt. 23 Jan 1753 - sp.: Peter Schnell and
   Margaretha Deigert (Stone Arabia Ref. Chbk.).

    vii) <u>Anna</u>[3], bpt. 7 May 1755 - sp.: Werner Teigert and wife
   Magdalena (Stone Arabia Luth. Chbk.).

    viii) <u>Elisabetha</u>[3], b. 25 June 1762 - sp.: Elisabeth Ecker
   and Johannes Flack (Stone Arabia Ref. Chbk.).

2) <u>Maria Cunigunda</u>[2] (HJ), conf. in 1742 at Stone Arabia Ref.
   Church. She md. Theobald Deigert (HJ), and they had a son
   Henrich bpt. in 1746 at Schoharie Luth. Church.

3) <u>Wilhelm</u>[2] (HJ), conf. in 1742 at Stone Arabia Ref. Church.
   Willem Laux was in Soffrines Deychert's Company in 1757
   and 1763 (<u>Report of the State Historian</u>, Vol. II, pp. 783
   & 792). William Lucks was a freeholder at Stonrabie in
   1763 (Albany Co. Freeholders). Perhaps he was the Wilhelm
   Laux who d. 20 April 1787 (Stone Arabia Ref. Chbk.). Wilhelm[2] md. Maria Margaretha Krembs and had issue:

    i) <u>Catharina</u>[3], a sp. in 1762 at Stone Arabia Ref. Church.

    ii) <u>Christina</u>[3], bpt. 28 Dec 1751 - sp.: Jacob Schultes
   and wife (Stone Arabia Ref. Chbk.).

    iii) <u>Magdalena</u>[3], bpt. May 1755 - sp.: Johannes Wallrath
   and wife Malli (Stone Arabia Luth. Chbk.).

    iv) <u>Johann Henrich</u>[3], b. 23 June 1760 - sp.: Johannes
   Schumacher and wife Catharina (Stone Arabia Ref.
   Chbk.).

4) <u>Maria Barbara</u>[2] (HJ), md. Jacob Bratt (HJ). They sp. Maria
   Cunigunda Laux Deigert in 1754 at Stone Arabia Ref. (HJ).

5) Johann Georg² (HJ), conf. in 1745 at Stone Arabia Ref. Church. He md. Gertraud Deigert (HJ) and had ch.:

    i) Johann Peter³, bpt. 2 April 1752 - sp.: Johann Peter Deigert and wife Anna Elisabetha Fuchs (Stone Arabia Ref. Chbk.).

    ii) Johann Jost³, bpt. 1 March 1754 - sp.: Deobald Teuger and Maria Kinget Laux (Stone Arabia Ref. Chbk.). This child's bpt. name may provide a clue as to the ancestral line (HJ).

    iii) Wilhelm³, b. or bpt. 8 July 1756 - sp.: Wilm Laucks and wife Margaretha (Stone Arabia Luth. Chbk.).

    iv) Henrich³, b. 18 Oct 1761 - sp.: Peter Laux, and Pieter Laux (sic), and Elisabetha - single d/o Adam Laux (Stone Arabia Ref. Chbk.).

    v) Anna Elisabetha³, b. 24 Nov 1763 - sp.: Margretha and Henrich Wohleben (Stone Arabia Ref. Chbk.).

    vi) Georg³, b. 8 Feb 1766 - sp.: Georg Klock J. and Cath. Laux (Stone Arabia Ref. Chbk.).

    vii) Suphrenius³, b. 9 Oct 1770 - sp.: Severines Tyghart J. and Gertraud (Stone Arabia Ref. Chbk.).

6?) Margaretha², conf. in 1749 at Stone Arabia Ref. Church.

7?) Gertraud², conf. in 1752 at Stone Arabia Ref. Church.

8?) Peter², conf. in 1757 at Stone Arabia Ref. Church.

9?) Maria², conf. in 1757 at Stone Arabia Ref. Church.

PETER LAWER (Hunter Lists #445)

The German home of this family was at 5551 Veldenz (7 km s. of Traben-Trarbach; Chbks. begin 1646, but gaps). The grandfather of the emigrant was Jost Lauer. On 12 May 1657 Matthias Lauer, s/o Jost Lauer at Burgen, md. Barbara, d/o the late Matthias Reitz - formerly citizen at Burgen. They had issue:

    Johann Nicolaus, bpt. 28 Feb 1658 - sp.: Johann Marcus Weinet - single, Nicolaus Holl, and Catharina - w/o Peter Auler. He was bur. 22 Nov 1696, aged 38 yrs.

    Anna Catharina, bpt. 31 March 1661 - sp.: Catharina Peltz, Anna Magdalena Reitz, and Hans Adam Hag.

+ Johann Peter, bpt. 25 Sept 1664 - sp.: Hans Peltzer, Hans Peter Aulen, and Johannet - w/o Jost Lauer.

Anna Barbara, (1st) w/o Hans Peter Lauer, was bur. 25 Nov 1693, aged 23 yrs. Hans Peter Lauer, a widower, md. Anna Catharina Weimens, d/o Marx Weimens - citizen at Burgen, 2 July 1694. Johan Peter Laue, his wife, and 4 ch., were in the 6th party of Palatines in Holland in 1709 (Rotterdam Lists); he was noted on the same page as Mattys Bron and Johan Nikel Jung from Veldenz (HJ).

Peter Lawer made his initial appearance on the Hunter Lists
4 July 1710 with 3 pers. over 10 yrs. of age and 1 pers. under 10
yrs., and this entry remained the same until Sept 1712. Johan Peter Lawer of Dutchess Co., yeoman, was nat. at N.Y. City 1 Nov
1715 (Minutes of the Mayor's Court, N.Y. City). Peter Lauer and
Anna Catharina with 2 ch. were at Hunderston ca. 1716/17 (Simmendinger Register). Peter Lauer was a Palatine Debtor in 1718 and
1726 (Livingston Debt Lists). Johan Peter Lauer was a Palatine
willing to continue 26 Aug 1724 (<u>Doc. Hist. of N.Y.</u>, Vol. III, p.
724). His family was registered on the St. Peter's Luth. Family
List ca. 1734 (Rhinebeck Luth. Chbk.). A letter from Rev. Johannes
Weyerman, pastor in Veldenz, to Peter[1] Lauer survives dated 10
June 1733 in the Amsterdam Luth. Church Archives (Portfolio America):

My dear Father and our dear Godfather and much beloved
Friend:
We, all together, inform you, first, that we duly received your letter which you sent us several times, from
which we learned with joy that you are still hale and
well and that you live on such a good farm, with a fine
meadow at your door, and that you have such a goodly
number of sheep, cows and horses. Also, that you enjoy
such a good reputation among all the High Germans and
that our Luth. congregation has a faithful pastor and
a precentor. It is commendable in you that in your old
age you still cling to this so precious religion and
do not allow yourself to be led astray. As the temporary
pastor of the place where you used to live, I have learned this with great joy; only remain steadfast, which,
by virtue of my office I faithfullv admonish you to do.
I have inquired about your affairs and because of your
solicitude called your relatives to account and with
the entire consistory insisted on it that you receive
satisfaction, especially as your object is to get, not
money, but a good Luth. Bible. The matter then, has advanced so far that everything you wished will be sent
to you next year, together with the interest. With your
books, we shall send you some more Luth. books and give
you full power to hand them out to good Christian people,
but not to any Calvinists, we tell you. You will then
further hear what we are ordering. May our Lord give a
reasonable amount toward that. I shall take care of everything in the best manner and send things to Amsterdam
and the Luth. Consistory; then it will no doubt all get
into your hands. We shall address things to N.Y., to the
Luth. pastor, and now take the better care of you, because we hear that you are such a faithful member of our
church. There is (no) news. Commending you to divine protection, I remain,
Your most willing servant,
JOHANNES WEYERMAN
From Veldenz on the Moselle, 10 June 1733.

The ch. of Peter[1] Lawer and his 2nd wife Anna Catharina were:

1) <u>Johann Peter[2]</u>, bpt. 11 Sept 1695 and bur. 3 July 1707,
aged 12 yrs. (Veldenz Chbk.).

2) <u>Maria Margaretha[2]</u>, bpt. 23 Feb 1698 (Veldenz Chbk.). She

md. Matthias Auffensand (HJ).

3) <u>Johann Michael[2]</u>, bpt. 7 March 1700 and bur. 13 Aug 1702, aged 2 yrs. and 5 months (Veldenz Chbk.).

4) <u>Johann Mattheus[2]</u>, bpt. 15 April 1702 (Veldenz Chbk.). Johann Mattheus Lauer was conf. Easter 1715 at Queensberg (West Camp Luth. Chbk.). Johan Mathias Lawer (s/o Johan Peter Lawer) was nat. at N.Y. City 1 Nov 1715 (Minutes of the Mayor's Court, N.Y. City). He md. Anna Margaretha Rausch in 1728 (Kinderhook Ref. Chbk.). Anna Margareta Raus, w/o Joh. Matt: Laurer, was conf. 15 April 1729 at Newton (N.Y. City Luth. Chbk.). The ch. of Johann Mattheus[2] and Anna Margaretha Lauer were:

   i) <u>Christina[3]</u>, bpt. 14 Sept 1729 - sp.: Peter Lodewyk and Christyn (Kinderhook Ref. Chbk.). She was with her father on the St. Peter's Luth. Family List ca. 1734 (Rhinebeck Luth. Chbk.). Christina Laurer was conf. 3 May 1744 at Ankrum (Loonenburg Luth. Chbk.). She md. David Sorenberger (HJ).

   ii) <u>Maria[3]</u>, bpt. 27 May 1733 - sp.: Johan Caspar Rouws Jr. and Maria Margt. Louer (Kinderhook Ref. Chbk.). She also was on the St. Peter's List ca. 1734.

   iii) <u>Peter[3]</u>, b. 23 Jan 1736 - sp.: Peter Hagedorn and Cath: Link - d/o J. N. (Rhinebeck Luth. Chbk.). Peeter, Kasper, and Mikel Louwer were enrolled next to Phillip Ousensent on Capt. Joacham Staats' Company in 1767 (<u>Report of the State Historian</u>, Vol. II, p. 807). He md. Jannetje Springsteen (HJ) and had ch. bpt. at Kinderhook Ref. and Shodack Ref. Churches (HJ).

   iv) <u>Johann Caspar[3]</u>, b. 2 Jan 1738 - sp.: Hannes Kurtz and Lineri Catharina Kisler (Loonenburg Luth. Chbk.). He md. Catharina Schneider (HJ).

   v) <u>Johann Nicolaus[3]</u>, b. 13 Feb 1740 and bpt. at Ancram - sp.: Jo: Nic: Rausch and wife Anna Marg. (Loonenburg Luth. Chbk.).

   vi) <u>Johann Michael[3]</u>, b. 1 Oct 1743 and bpt. Rhinebeck - sp.: Michel Rauw and wife Anna Maria (Loonenburg Luth. Chbk.).

5) <u>Johann Michael[2]</u>, bpt. 25 Jan 1705 (Veldenz Chbk.).

A Maria Agnes Laur, d/o the late Arnold Laur of gebler near Creutzenech in the Pfaltz, md. 20 Nov 1710 Johann Crump, a gardiner of Bristol, England (West Camp Luth. Chbk.). No connective has been found between Maria Agnes Laur and Peter[1] Lawer in N.Y. records (HJ).

WILHELM LEHEMANN (Hunter Lists #446)

Clemens Lehman, step-son of Joh Henrich Schmid of Newtown,
md. Anna Gertraud Wolf, d/o the late Bertram of Gershofen in the
commune Dordorst in the earldom of Runckel, 3 Nov 1713 (West Camp
Luth. Chbk.). Henrich Schmidt aged 54, (wife) Anna Eliz aged 54,
Clements aged 24, Wilhelm aged 20, Hans George aged 13, John Niclaus aged 9, and Anna Maria aged 18, were in N.Y. City in 1710/
11 (Palatines In N.Y. City); the first two ch. on this roll were
Clement[1] and Wilhelm[1] Lehemann (HJ). Wilhelm Lehemann had but one
entry on the Hunter Lists: on 13 Sept 1712 with 2 pers. over 10
yrs. of age and 1 pers. under 10 yrs. Wilhelm Leman was nat. 8
and 9 Sept 1715 (Kingston Nats.). Clement Lehman (his mark) and
Willem Lehman were members of the church council at Kisketamenesy
in 1735 (Albany Protocol, p. 127). William Laymant was a freeholder at Caterskill and Cats Kill in 1763 (Albany Co. Freeholders).
He md. Maria Eva, wid/o Christian Eigeler (HJ), and they appear
to have had no ch. (HJ).

Cleman Leman was nat. 8 and 9 Sept 1715, next to Nicolas
Smith (Kingston Nats.). He was a member of the church council in
1732 (Albany Protocol, p. 40). The issue of Clement[1] and Anna Gertraud Lehemann were:

1) Johann Wilhelm[2], b. 13 Aug 1714 - sp.: Johann Wilhelm Lehman and Anna Maria Klein (West Camp Luth. Chbk.). A child
   of Clemens Lehmann d. 25 Aug 1714 (West Camp Luth. Chbk.).

2) Anna Margaretha[2], b. 21 Sept 1715 - sp.: Philipp Mueller
   and his wife Anna Margretha (West Camp Luth. Chbk.). Anna
   Margr., (d/o) Clement Lehman, was conf. 14 Jan 1730 at
   And. Elig's house at Newtown, aged 15 yrs. (N.Y. City
   Luth. Chbk.). She md. Johannes Frolich 1 April 1734 (Loon-
   enburg Luth. Chbk.).

3) Anna Elisabetha[2], b. 8 Dec 1717 - sp.: Niclaus Schmid and
   Anna Margretha Wolst (West Camp Luth. Chbk.). She was
   conf. 14 Jan 1730, aged 13 yrs. at Newtown with her sis-
   ter (N.Y. City Luth. Chbk.). She md. 1st Jacob Straub 18
   April 1737, and 2nd Georg Oberbach 15 Sept 1743 (both
   Loonenburg Luth. Chbk.).

4) Catharina[2], b. 12 Feb 1720 at Caterskill and bpt. Lonen-
   burg - sp.: Jurgen Schmidt and wife Catharina (N.Y. City
   Luth. Chbk.). She was conf. at Kisket in 1735 (Loonenburg
   Luth. Chbk.). Catharina[2] md. Johann Wilhelm Schramm 23
   Nov 1745 (Loonenburg Luth. Chbk.).

5) Georg[2], md. as s/o Clement[1] 23 April 1744 Agneta Williams
   (Loonenburg Luth. Chbk.). He was conf. at Kisket 23 Feb

1738/39 (Loonenburg Luth. Chbk.). His wife was conf. at
Newton 3 June 1744 (Loonenburg Luth. Chbk.). Jury Laman
was a 1st Lieutenant in the Albany Co. Militia in 1770
(Report of the State Historian, Vol. II, p. 763). The ch.
of Georg[2] and Agneta were:

  i) Wilhelm[3], b. 19 Jan 1745 and bpt. Kisket. - sp.: Jo:
Wilh. Lehman and Marytje Eiglern (Loonenburg Luth.
Chbk.).

  ii) Gertraud[3], b. 14 Jan 1747 and bpt. Kisket. - sp.: Clem
Lehman and Gertruyd, grandparents (Loonenburg Luth.
Chbk.).

  iii) Clement[3], b. 30 Oct 1748 and bpt. Kisket. - sp.: Andreas Eigler and Maria Schramm (Loonenburg Luth.
Chbk.).

  iv) Jacob[3], b. 10 Feb 1751 - sp.: Jacob Lehman and Lisabeth Spoon (Loonenburg Luth. Chbk.).

  v) Maria[3], b. 12 June 1754 - sp.: Velten Schram and Mareitje Eagler (Loonenburg Luth. Chbk.).

  vi) Anna[3], b. 7 April 1757 - sp.: Niclaas Smidt and Anna
Elisabeth, in their place, Wilhelmus Lehman and Jannetje (Loonenburg Luth. Chbk.).

  vii) Mattheus[3], b. 1 April 1759 - sp.: Wilhelmus Lehman
and Jannetje (Loonenburg Luth. Chbk.).

  viii) Andreas[3], b. 24 Oct 1761 - sp.: Andrees Euyler and
Liesabeth (Loonenburg Luth. Chbk.).

6) Wilhelm[2], md. as s/o Clement[1] 8 Feb 1746 Jannetje Schermerhoorn (Loonenburg Luth. Chbk.). He was conf. at Kisket 25
April 1742 (Loonenburg Luth. Chbk.). Issue:

  i) Clement[3], b. 29 Nov 1746 and bpt. Kisket. - sp.: Clem-
ent Lehman and Gertruyd, grandparents (Loonenburg
Luth. Chbk.). He md. Elisabetha Pulver 12 Jan 1767
(Germantown Ref. Chbk.).

  ii) Jacob[3], b. 13 April 1749 and bpt. Newton - sp.: Jacob
Lehman and Lisabeth Fuhrer (Loonenburg Luth. Chbk.).

  iii) Georg[3], b. 16 April 1752 - sp.: Jurgen Lehman and Ag-
neetje (Loonenburg Luth. Chbk.).

  iv) Cornelius[3], b. 29 Feb 1756 and bpt. as Cornelia -
sp.: Fried: Schram and Christina (Loonenburg Luth.
Chbk.).

  v) Johannes[3], b. 5 April 1758 - sp.: Velten Frolich and
Geertje Schermerhoorn (Loonenburg Luth. Chbk.).

7) Christina[2], md. as d/o Clement[1] 23 Dec 1746 Friederich
Schramm (Loonenburg Luth. Chbk.). She was conf. at Kisket
23 June 1745 (Loonenburg Luth. Chbk.).

8) <u>Anna Maria²</u>, b. 4 April 1728 - sp.: Andreas Eichler and
Anna Maria Schef (West Camp Luth. Chbk.).

9) <u>Jacob²</u>, b. 12 March 1733 at Newton - sp.: Jacob Maul and
wife Anna Dorothea (Loonenburg Luth. Chbk.). He was conf.
at Kisket 17 April 1748 (Loonenburg Luth. Chbk.). Jacob,
Jacob Jr., Wilhelmus, Jurye, Willem Jr., and Chlement Le-
ment were in Capt. Cornelus Dubois's Company at Caskill
9 April 1767 (<u>Report of the State Historian</u>, Vol. II, p.
877). Jacob² md. 26 ... 1751 Margaretha Schramm (Katsbaan
Ref. Chbk.). The ch. of Jacob² and Margaretha Schramm Lehmann were:

    i) <u>Anna Maria³</u>, b. 28 Dec 1752 - sp.: Velten Schram and
Annaatje Lehman (Loonenburg Luth. Chbk.).

   ii) <u>Clement³</u>, b. 7 Aug 1754 - sp.: Wilhelmus Lehman and
Gerdruyt Lehman (Loonenburg Luth. Chbk.).

  iii) <u>Friederich³</u>, b. 17 Aug 1756 - sp.: Joh: Wilhelm
Schram and Catharina (Loonenburg Luth. Chbk.).

   iv) <u>Gertraud³</u>, b. 10 Dec 1758 - sp.: Fried: Lampman and
Christina (Loonenburg Luth. Chbk.).

    v) <u>Anna³</u>, b. 16 Jan 1761 - sp.: Velten Schram and Ger-
truyd Lehman (Loonenburg Luth. Chbk.).

   vi) <u>Catharina³</u>, b. 11 Feb 1763 - sp.: Hinrich Schram
and Anna (Loonenburg Luth. Chbk.).

  vii) <u>Jeremias³</u>, bpt. 1765 - sp.: Jurri Leman and Angeniet
Leman (Catskill Ref. Chbk.).

 viii) <u>Wilhelmus³</u>, bpt. 21 Feb 1767 - sp.: Willem Leman and
Elizabeth Schram (Catskill Ref. Chbk.).

10) <u>Maria²</u>, b. 15 Nov 1735 and bpt. Kisket. - sp.: Friderich
Martin and Maria Eva Spoohns (Loonenburg Luth. Chbk.).

11) <u>Anna²</u>, b. 27 June 1739 and bpt. Kisket. - sp.: Philip
Spohn and Agnesa Borter (Loonenburg Luth. Chbk.). She
md. in 1754 Hieronymus Brando (Catskill Ref. Chbk.).

There was a Jeremiah Leaming who md. Elizabeth Peck by license dated 30 Oct 1755 (N.Y. Col. Marriage Licenses); perhaps he
was the Jeremiah Leaming mentioned as an executor with John Livingston in the 1768 estate of St. George Talbot (<u>Genealogical Data
From Colonial N.Y. Newspapers</u>, p. 129). This family and other
branches are discussed in Donna Valley Stuart's "The Lehmann/La-
man/Layman Family of Greene Co., N.Y." in the <u>N.Y. Genealogical
& Biographical Record</u>, Vol. 110, No. 2, April 1979.

<u>JOHANNES LEHR</u> (Hunter Lists #447)

A Johan Luur, his wife, (son) Kornelis, and 2 (other) ch.

were in the 2nd party of Palatines in Holland in 1709 (Rotterdam
Lists); however, he probably was the Johannes Lauer returned to
Holland in 1709 with 3 ch. (HJ). A Johannes Lehr was conf. in
1663, aged 13½ yrs. at 6394 Grävenwiesbach, home of several other
N.Y. 1709ers. A Johannes, s/o Hans Jacob Lehr of Wörsdorf, md. Anna Elisabetha, d/o Hans Jacob Beringer from Isenheim (?) in the
Pfalz, 24 Nov 1705 at 6200 Wiesbaden; this couple had a son Tobias
bpt. there in 1708. There also was a Master Johannes Löhr, shoemaker, who md. Maria Sybilla Veronica, d/o the late Herr Conrad
Gross at Kirchheim bey Bolanden, 23 Sept 1704 at Kleinbockenheim;
they had ch. Johann Peter b. 9 Dec 1706, and Gottfried b. 26 Feb
1708 there.

Johannes Lehr made his initial appearance on the Hunter Lists
30 June 1710 with 3 pers. over 10 yrs. and 2 under 10 yrs. The
family was recorded with 5 pers. over 10 yrs. 24 June 1711, 4 pers.
over 10 and 1 under 10 yrs. on 29 Sept 1711, 5 over 10 on 24 Dec
1711, 4 over 10 yrs. on 25 March 1712, 5 over 10 yrs. 24 June
1711, and 5 pers. over 10 yrs. of age and 1 pers. under 10 on 13
Sept 1712. Jno. Leher: 1 man, 1 lad aged 9 - 15 yrs., 1 woman, 1
maid aged 9 - 15, and 1 girl aged 8 yrs. and under were in Ulster
Co. in 1710/11 (West Camp Census). Johan Leyer of Queensbury was
a soldier in 1711 (Palatine Volunteers To Canada). Johann Lehr and
his wife Sibylla Catharina with 5 ch. were at Neu-Cassel ca. 1716/
17 (Simmendinger Register). Johanes Leer was a Palatine Debtor in
1718 (Livingston Debt Lists). The ch. of Johannes[1] Lehr and his
wife Sibylla Catharina were:

1) Friederich Wilhelm[2] (HJ), probably the lad aged 9 - 15
   yrs. mentioned in the West Camp Census of 1710/11 (HJ).
   Frederick Willem Leer was nat. 31 Jan 1715/16 (Albany
   Nats.). Frederick Leer was a freeholder at the Falls in
   1763 (Albany Co. Freeholders).
2) Anna Margaretha[2], b. 8 July 1712 - sp.: Johann Becker, Anna Margretha Gerlach, and Maria Margretha Wagner (West
   Camp Luth. Chbk.).
3) Ottilia Helena[2], b. 9 May 1717 and bpt. at Schoharie -
   sp.: Johann Adam Wallrath, Magdalena Eckhard, and Ottilia
   Curring (West Camp Luth. Chbk.). Perhaps she was the Helena Lehrin who sp. David Bottmann and wife Elisabetha Lehr
   in 1751 at Stone Arabia Ref. Church (HJ).

There were several unplaced Lehr - Leers in the Mohawk Valley: 1) Elisabetha, wid/o Georg Leer of the Falls, md. Joseph Her-
din of Canada 4 Dec 1761 (Stone Arabia Ref. Chbk.); 2) Elisabetha
Lehr md. David Bottmann (HJ); and 3) Eva Lehr md. Henrich Louis
(HJ).

HENRICH LEICHT (Hunter Lists #448)
LUDWIG LEICHT (Hunter Lists #449)

Georg Ludwig Leich, widower of Bernsfeld in Darmstatt, md.
Maria Martha, wid/o Johann Peter Emmerich of Neustad on the Hard,
26 June 1711 (West Camp Luth. Chbk.). The origins of this Palatine family were at 6315 Bernsfeld (14 km. n. of Laubach), entries
in registers at 6315 Nieder-Ohmen (4 km. s.e. of Bernsfeld; Chbks.
begin 1641). The grandfather of the emigrant Georg Ludwig[1] Leicht
was Johannes Leicht, called the old smith at Wettsassen at his
burial 13 June 1669, aged 76 yrs.; Maria, wid/o Johannes Leicht,
was bur. 14 Aug 1677, aged 81 yrs. Their son was Henrich Leicht
who md. Gela, d/o Hans Schlemmer 30 April 1649. Henrich Leicht
was bur. 15 April 1679, aged 57 yrs. and 7 weeks; Gela, wid/o Henrich Leicht, was bur. 9 March 1710. They had issue:

Susanna, bpt. 12 May 1650 - sp.: Susanna, d/o Johannes Mohr
at Niederohmen.
Eckhart, bpt. 7 p. Trin.: 1651 - sp.: Hans Schlemmer at N'
ohmen. He d. 1654, aged 3 yrs.
Georg Philip, bpt. 18 Dec 1653 - sp.: Jörg Philips at Elpen-
rod. He md. Barbara Opffermann 2 Nov 1680.
Catharina, bpt. Do. Judica: 1656 - sp.: Catharina - d/o Eck-
hart Fuchs at N.O. She md. Johan Jost Hornmann 24 Aug 1676.
Anna Maria, bpt. 6 p. Trin.: 1658 - sp.: the father's mother
Merga, w/o Johannes Leicht. She md. Johannes Köhler 24 Oct
1677.
Henrich, bur. 28 Jan 1670, aged 9 yrs. as s/o Henrich Leicht.
Johannes, md. 1684 as s/o Henrich Leicht to Eva Beer.
Peter, bpt. Lichtmess: 1665 - sp.: the s/o Henrich Peter. He
was bur. 3 June 1665.
+ Georg Ludwig, bpt. 13 May 1666 - sp.: Henrich, s/o the for-
ester at Elpenrod.
Anna Elisabetha, bpt. 13 June 1669 - sp.: the child's grand-
mother, the old smith's wife. She md. Claß Beer 7 June 1688.
Anna Gertraud, bpt. 6 March 1673 - sp.: Anna Gertr. - the d/o
the Pastor. She md. Henrich, s/o Hans Caspar Conrad, 23 Feb
1691 at Wettsasen.
Susanna, bpt. 8 Sept 1676 - sp.: Susanna, maiden-servant of
Johannes Mertz at Ilsdorf. She md. (this same) Johan Henrich
Conrad 26 April 1695.

Georg Ludwig Leicht md. Margaretha, wid/o Johann Henrich Wilhelm,
29 Oct 1685 at Bernfels; Johan Henrich Wilhelm had md. Margaretha,
d/o Henrich Köhler, 20 Jan 1670. A Lewis Leucht aged 54, his wife,
a son aged 22, Luth., smith, were in the 1st arrivals in England
in 1709 (London Lists).

548

Ludwig Leicht made his initial appearance on the Hunter Lists
next to Henrich Leicht 4 Aug 1710 with 2 pers. over 10 yrs. of age
in the household. The family showed 1 pers. over 10 on 24 June
1711, and 3 pers. over 10 on 29 Sept 1711. George Ludwig Leicht
aged 66, Anna Margatta Leicht aged 58, Johan Henrich Leicht aged
24, and Anna Eliz Leicht aged 20, were in N.Y. City in 1710/11
(Palatines In N.Y. City). Lodewÿk Layk, widower of the Pals, md.
Veronica Walen, wid/o Matthÿs Swiegen of the Pals, 7 Dec 1713 (N.Y.
City Ref. Chbk.). Ludwig[1] sp. Engel Hoef in the Highlands with his
step-daughter Mrs. Mann in 1716 (N.Y. City Luth. Chbk.). The child
of Georg Ludwig[1] Leicht and his wife Margaretha Köhler was:

1) **Johann Henrich[2]**, bpt. 20 Nov 1687 at Bernsfeld - sp.: Johannes Kappes, s/o the late Curt Kappes (Nieder-Ohmen
Chbk.). Johan Henrich Leich, s/o Jürgen Ludwig of Heppenheim auf der Wiesen im Amt Frensheim, md. Anna Elisabeth
Schmied, d/o Henrich Schmid of Armsheim in Oberamt Alzey,
17 July 1709 (London Churchbooks and the German Emigration
of 1709, by John P. Dern, p. 23). Henrich Leicht, #448 on
the Hunter Rolls, had 2 pers. over 10 yrs. of age 4 Aug
1710. The family was registered with 3 over 10 on 24 June
1711, and with 2 over 10 and 1 under 10 yrs. on 29 Sept
1711. Johann Henrich[2] md. 2nd Anna Eulalia, wid/o Johannes
Bernhardt, as Joh: Jurgen Bernhard, s/o the late Jan Bernhard and his mother Anna Elatia, now md. to Hinrich Leith-
en, residing at Bedfort, was conf. at P. Lassing's in 1739
(N.Y. City Luth. Chbk.). By his 1st wife, the ch. of Johann Henrich[2] Leicht were:

i) **Philip[3]**, b. 15 July 1711 - sp.: Philipp Peter Grauberger (West Camp Luth. Chbk.).
ii) **Ludwig[3]**, b. 13 Feb 1716 in Highlands and bpt. N.Y.
- sp.: Ludwig Leich, in his absence, Michael Pfeffer
and Margaret Mosemin (N.Y. City Luth. Chbk.).
iii) **Johannes[3]**, b. 31 Aug 1717 in Highland and bpt. at
Quaseck - sp.: Johannes Visscher and wife Mary (N.Y.
City Luth. Chbk.). A Johannes Leidt, single man b.
Dutchess Co., md. 5 Sept 1747 Treintje Slegt (Kingston Ref. Chbk.).
iv) **Quirinius[3]**, b. Sept 1719 at Badford and bpt. N.Y. -
sp.: Quirinus Neiddebber and wife Maria Elisabeth
(N.Y. City Luth. Chbk.). He was conf. as Quirinus
Light DNIA XVI, p.t.: 1740 (N.Y. City Luth. Chbk.).
v) **Elisabetha[3]**, bpt. 26 June 1722 - sp.: Willem Hemmen
and wife Esther (Tarrytown Ref. Chbk.). Elisabeth
Scherer, w/o Hans Scherer and d/o Hinr. Light, was

conf. 15 Sept 1741 at the home of And. Fr. Pick (N. Y. City Luth. Chbk.).

vi) Susanna³, bpt. 13 June 1724 - sp.: Marckus Moseman and Zusanna Storm (Tarrytown Ref. Chbk.). She was conf. 4 June 1740 at Pieter Lassing's (N.Y. City Luth. Chbk.). She md. Bernhardus Scherer 5 Oct 1742 (N.Y. City Luth. Chbk.).

vii) Johann Henrich³ (HJ), md. Catharina (--) (HJ).

By his 2nd wife Maria Martha, a child of Georg Ludwig¹ Leicht was:

2) Johann Eberhardt², b. 4 Sept 1712 - sp.: Johann Eberhard Jung (West Camp Luth. Chbk.).

JOHANNES LEICK (Hunter Lists #450)

There was a John Lichte aged 40, with his wife, daughters aged 5 and 2, Ref., shoemaker, in the 3rd arrivals in England in 1709 (London Lists); however, there is no proof he was the N.Y. settler (HJ).

Johannes Leick made his initial appearance on the Hunter Lists 1 July 1710 with 2 pers. over 10 yrs. of age. His entry for 4 Aug 1710 read 2 over 10 and 1 under 10 yrs., and for 4 Oct 1710 showed 2 over 10 yrs. of age. The household was registered with 3 pers. over 10 yrs. of age 31 Dec 1710, with 2 over 10 and 1 under 10 yrs. on 24 Dec 1711, and then back to 3 over 10 yrs. on 25 March 1712. Johannis Leek was nat. 17 Jan 1715/16 (Albany Nats.). Johannes Leyck and Anna Barbara with 3 ch. were at Wormsdorff ca. 1716/17 (Simmendinger Register). There was also a Hanss Leick with wife and ch. at Heessberg ca. 1716/17 according to Simmendinger; however, as this family was recorded next to Eberhard Jung (who md. a Schmidt) this Heessberg Leick probably was either #448 or #449 Georg Ludwig¹ or Henrich¹ Leicht (HJ). Hannes Luyk was a Palatine Debtor in 1718, 1719 (at Kingsberry), 1721 and 1726 (Livingston Debt Lists). Johanes Leuck was a Palatine willing to continue on the Manor 26 Aug 1724 (Doc. Hist. of N.Y., Vol III, p. 724). The family appeared on the St. Peter's Luth. Family List ca. 1734 as Joh. Linck, Anna Barbara - his wife, (ch.) Martinus, Johannes, Maria, and Catharina (Rhinebeck Luth. Chbk.). Johannes Like was a freeholder at East Camp in 1763 (Albany Co. Freeholders). The ch. of Johannes¹ Leick and his wife Maria Barbara were:

1) Anna Magdalena², bpt. 27 Sept 1709 - sp.: Leenhard Reichard, Anna Mag: Freet, and Marg: Mankenmüller (Rotterdam Luth. Chbk., Holland). The parents were named as Johannes Leuik and wife Anna Barb: Freet on this entry.

2) <u>Martin</u>² (St. Peter's Luth. Family List). He was on Rhine-
beck tax rolls 1743/44 - June 1748 (Dutchess Co. Tax Lists).
Martin and Baurent Lyck were in Capt. Frederick Kortz's
Company at East Camp in 1767 (<u>Report of the State Histor-
ian</u>, Vol. II, p. 869). The will of Martin Luyck of German
Camp was dated 13 June 1787 and probated 13 Aug 1789 (Col-
umbia Co. Will Bk. A). Martin² md. Anna Margaretha Finckel
(HJ), and they had issue:

  i) <u>Eva</u>³, md. as d/o Martin² 19 Nov 1765 Peter Blass (Germantown Ref. Chbk.).

  ii) <u>Johannes</u>³ (Will), md. Margaretha Schmidt (HJ) and had
  ch. bpt. at Manorton Luth. Church (HJ). He may have
  md. earlier to a Catharina (--) and had issue bpt. at
  Churchtown 1760 - 1767 (HJ).

  iii) <u>Catharina</u>³, bpt. 1 Sept 1745 - sp.: Zacharias Philipp
  and Catharina (Germantown Ref. Chbk.). She md. Isaac
  Wagener (HJ).

  iv) <u>Bernhardt</u>³ (Will), sometimes known as Barent, who md.
  Barbara (--) 9 June 1767 (Germantown Ref. Chbk.).
  They had ch. bpt. at Churchtown Luth. Church.

  v) <u>Anna Margaretha</u>³, bpt. 14 Aug 1748 - sp.: Henry Batz
  and Anna Margareth Batz (Germantown Ref. Chbk.). She
  md. Zacharias Holtzapfel 27 May 1766 (Germantown Ref.
  Chbk.).

  vi) <u>Joseph</u>³, b. 2 Jan 1751 - sp.: Joseph Neher and wife
  Eva (Rhinebeck Luth. Chbk.). He md. Polly (Bali) Hal-
  lenbeck 12 Feb 1771 (Germantown Ref. Chbk.). They had
  ch. bpt. at Manorton Luth. Church.

  vii) <u>Petrus</u>³, bpt. 23 Sept 1753 - sp.: Pieter Herder and
  Marytje Schever (Rhinebeck Flats Ref. Chbk.). He d.
  in 1832, aged 80 yrs. (Irish Farm Cem., Chatham).

  viii) <u>Henrich</u>³ (Will).

  ix) <u>Maria</u>³, bpt. 25 Dec 1756 - sp.: Henrich Bernhardt and
  wife Mareitgen Harter (Germantown Ref. Chbk.).

  x) <u>Martin</u>³ (Will).

  xi) <u>Anna</u>³, b. 4 March 1763 - sp.: Hen: Beckker and Anna
  Schneider (Germantown Luth. Chbk.).

3) <u>Johannes</u>² (St. Peter's Luth. Family List), conf. 2 Feb (?)
1738 at Camp (Loonenburg Luth. Chbk.). He md. Catharina
Laurie, who md. (2nd) Peter Hamm 27 March 1758 (Germantown
Ref. Chbk.). The ch. of Johannes² and Catharina were:

  i) <u>Catharina</u>³, bpt. 14 days old 15 July 1744 at Camp -
  sp.: Kilian Stoppelbain and Ursel Laurers (Loonenburg
  Luth. Chbk.). She md. Johannes Kilmer Jr. 23 Oct 1764

(Germantown Ref. Chbk.).

    ii) <u>Magdalena</u>[3], bpt. as Marlena 18 Aug 1745 - sp.: Frid.
Haber and wife Anna Cath. (Loonenburg Luth. Chbk.).

    iii) <u>Johannes</u>[3], bpt. 1 April 1750 - sp.: Hannes Leick and
Maria Barbel Leick (Germantown Ref. Chbk.).

    iv) <u>Eva</u>[3], bpt. 20 March 1753 - sp.: Johannes Pieter Lau-
rie and Eva Holtzappel (Germantown Ref. Chbk.).

  4) <u>Anna Maria</u>[2], b. 19 July 1714 - sp.: Anna Maria Winter
(West Camp Luth. Chbk.). She md. Georg Reiffenberger (HJ).

  5) <u>Anna Catharina</u>[2], b. 7 April 1717 - sp.: Johann Hoener and
wife Anna Catharina (West Camp Luth. Chbk.). She md.
Friederich Haber (HJ).

<u>CONRAD LEIN</u> (Hunter Lists #451)

The German roots of this N.J. family have yet to be proved
definitely. However, Conrad[1] Lein often was noted on the Hunter
Lists near Ludwig[1] Schmidt and Georg Ludwig[1] and Johann Henrich[2]
Leicht, who were documented at 6315 <u>Ober-Ohmen</u>. A Conrad, s/o
Henrich Lein, was b. in Ruppertenrod and bpt. 19 July 1656 - sp.:
Conrad Kirchhöfen Sr. here (Ober-Ohmen Chbk.). The name Conrad
Lein was an old one in the neighboring villages of Lardenbach and
Groß-Eichen, and an elder Chunrath Lein was bur. at Ober-Ohmen
9 p. Trin.: 1642, aged 72 yrs.

Conrad Lein first appeared on the Hunter Lists 1 July 1710
with 4 pers. over 10 yrs. of age and 3 pers. under 10. On 4 Oct
1710 the entry read 5 over 10 yrs. and 3 under 10 yrs., and on
24 June 1711 the family was recorded with 6 pers. over 10 yrs.
and 1 under 10. The household was registered with 4 over 10 and
1 under 10 on 25 March 1712, and with 5 pers. over 10 and 1 under
10 yrs. of age on 24 June 1712. Conrad Lein aged 56, Maria Marga.
Lein aged 46, Juliana Lein aged 18, Margareta Lein aged 14, Anna
Maria Lein aged 12, Abraham Lein aged 10, and Conrad Lein aged 7.
were in N.Y. City in 1710/11 (Palatines In N.Y. City). Conrad[1]
was mentioned in a vague reference in N.Y. Col. Mss. Vol. 57, p.
189b dated 1712. Conrad Lynus bought or leased 200 acres of land
in 1713/14 on the Ramapo Tract in Bergen Co., N.J., and he bought
several purchases of wheat, rye, peas, sugar, as well as a cow,
horse, and a wagon that yr. (Ramapo Account Book). Conrad Lein
and his wife Margretha with 6 ch. were at Hackensack ca. 1716/17
(Simmendinger Register). Papers in the estate of Conradt Lyne of
Bergen Co., N.J. were issued 1 May 1738 and an inventory made of
his personal property (N.J. Wills: Lib. C, p. 194). The ch. of
Conrad[1] Lein and his wife were:

1) Anna Juliana[2] (Palatines In N.Y. City), md. Joseph Bertram (HJ).

2) Margaretha[2] (Palatines In N.Y. City), conf. 12 June 1712 at Newtown (West Camp Luth. Chbk.). She md. Anthony Beem (Böhm) in Dec 1719 (Hackensack Ref. Chbk.).

3) Anna Maria[2] (Palatines In N.Y. City), conf. in 1717 (N.Y. City Luth. Chbk.). She md. Peter Sloats (Data from Valoe Brink).

4) Abraham[2] (Palatines In N.Y. City), conf. in 1717 (N.Y. City Luth. Chbk.). The will of Abraham Lynn of Saddle River in Bergen Co., N.J. was dated 30 Jan 1767 and probated 1 June 1771 (N.J. Wills). Abraham[2] md. Maria (--) and had issue:

    i) Johannes[3], bpt. 1740 - sp.: Joseph Bethren and Anna (Pompton Plains Ref. Chbk.).

    ii) Maria[3], bpt. 1743 - sp.: Coenraet Lyn and Tryntje (Pompton Plains Ref. Chbk.).

    iii) Catharina[3], bpt. 9 March 1746 - sp.: Coenraad Beem and Catharina (Pompton Plains Ref. Chbk.).

    iv) Margaretha[3] (Will).

    v) Anna[3] (Will).

    vi) Rachel[3] (Will).

    vii) Magdalena[3] (Will).

    viii) Elisabetha[3] (Will).

5) Conrad[2] (Palatines In N.Y. City). He md. Catharina Rutan, a wid. (HJ); in his will, Conrad[2] mentioned Coonrad Liens (alias Rutan), a son that my wife had before I md. her, as well as Alice Rutan. The will of Coonrad Liens of Saddle River Precinct, Bergen Co., yeoman, was dated 23 Sept 1755 and probated 12 Oct 1769 (N.J. Wills: Lib. K, p. 137). The ch. of Conrad[2] and Catharina were:

    i) Daniel[3] (Will).

    ii) Abraham[3], bpt. 26 Oct 1746 - sp.: Pieter Post and Anna (Pompton Plains Ref. Chbk.).

    iii) Henrich[3], bpt. 4 Dec 1748 - sp.: Joost Beem and Catharina (Pompton Plains Ref. Chbk.).

    iv) Peter[3] (Will).

    v) Johannes[3] (Will).

    vi) Rachel[3] (Will).

    vii) Margaretha[3] (Will).

    viii) Magdalena[3] (Will).

    ix) Catharina[3] (Will).

    x) Anthony[3] (Will).

6) Johann Peter[2], b. 1 Aug 1712 - sp.: Johann Peter Gerlach

and wife, and Anna Maria Lisemus (West Camp Luth. Chbk.).

Valoe Brink of La Verne, Calif. is planning a novel based on the German and American activities of Conrad[1] Lein and his descendants, and I eagerly look forward to its publication. She has been an ardent and enthusiastic supporter of this project (see her article "The Great American Novel!" in The Palatine Immigrant, Vol. VII, No. 3, Winter, 1982).

MARIA CATHARINA LENCKIN son (Hunter Lists #452)

Maria Catharina Lenkin was listed only once on 1 July 1710 with 1 pers. over 10 yrs. of age. Other entries on her page in the Ledger concern Johannes Lenker and a Johannes Lenck, and perhaps should have been filed by the Hunter secretaries under #428 (HJ).

PHILIPP HERMANN LEPPER'S WIDDOW (Hunter Lists #453)

This family was documented at 6340 Dillenburg (6 km. n. of Herborn; Chbks. begin 1646) and later at 5455 Rengsdorf (7 km. n. of Neuwied; Chbks. begin 1677). The father of the emigrant was Hans Lepper, citizen at Dillenburg. Philips Hermann Lepper, s/o Hans Lepper - citizen here, md. Maria Christina, d/o Herr Oberstruht (?) - late of Dillenburg, 12 Feb 1682 (Dillenburg Chbk.). Philipp Hermann[1] later moved to Rengsdorf where a relative, Andreas Ludwig Lepper, was Pastor there. The Fürstliches Archiv zu Wied has a mss. listing owners of goats at Rengsdorf 1699 - 1706, and among the names is Philipp Lepper. Philippüs Herman lepper, his wife, and 5 ch., were on Capt. Johan Enrit's ship in Holland in the 5th party of 1709 (Rotterdam Lists). Philippüs Hermann Lepper was a Listenmeister in London 5 Dec 1709, signing Pastor Hager's endorsement that date.

Anna Catharina Lepperin was recorded with 1 pers. over 10 yrs. of age 4 Oct 1710; an additional notation that date mentioned an entry for his daughters for 2 pers. over 10 yrs. of age. The ch. of Philipp Hermann[1] Lepper and Maria Christina were:
1) Johann Wilhelm[2], b. 13 Feb 1683 - sp.: Wilhelm Lepper - citizen, and Anna Julian - w/o Frank Karcher (Dillenburg Chbk.).
2) Anna Gertraud[2], b. 10 Aug 1685 - sp.: Anna Gertraudt - wid/o Hans Lepper and grandmother of the child (Dillenburg Chbk.).
3) Johannes[2], b. 7 Dec 1688 - sp.: H. Johs. Volsberg, and Maria - w/o Herr Andreas Ludwig Lepper, Pastor at Rengsdorf (Dillenburg Chbk.). There was a John Lebo nat. in 1718 in Lancaster Co., Pa. (Pa. Naturalizations).

4) <u>Anna Catharina</u>[2], b. 29 July 1690 - sp.: Catharina - w/o Johan Baldes the younger here (Dillenburg Chbk.). A Hanna Catrina Laparing aged 16, orphan, was bound to Andw Mead of N.Y. 27 Sept 1710 (Apprenticeship Lists).

5) <u>Johann Wilhelm</u>[2], b. 16 Nov 1693 - sp.: Jost Wilhelm Bennerm - citizen here, and Elisabetha - w/o Johannes Hazfeld - citizen here (Dillenburg Chbk.).

6) <u>Anna Christina</u>[2], b. 26 April 1695 - sp.: Anna Enn - w/o Jacob Butt (?), citizen here (Dillenburg Chbk.). Perhaps it was she who was apprenticed to Andw Mead in 1710 (HJ).

7) <u>Johann Philip</u>[2], b. 14 Aug 1696 - sp.: Johann Philipps Kring, citizen here (Dillenburg Chbk.). John Philip Lepper aged 12, an orphan, was bound to John Hallock of Brookhaven 31 Aug 1710 (Apprenticeship Lists).

8) <u>Christina</u>[2], b. 2 June 1699 - sp.: Andreas Ludwig Lepper - Pastor at Ringsdorf, and Christina - w/o Friedrich Hardt, citizen at Dillenburg (Dillenburg Chbk.). She d. 8 Sept 1699 (Dillenburg Chbk.).

9) <u>Anna Elisbetha</u>[2], b. 1 Oct 1700 - sp.: Anna Elisabetha Katz - d/o Johs. Katz, citizen at Dillenburg (Dillenburg Chbk.). She was bur. 24 Sept 1704, aged 4 yrs. (Rengsdorf Chbk.).

10) <u>Johann Wigand</u>[2], bpt. 6 May 1703 - sp.: Johann Wigand Lepper, pastoris loci filius (Rengsdorf Chbk.).

11) <u>Amelia</u>[2], bpt. 22 Sept 1706 - sp.: Amelia - w/o Joh. Henrich Lindner the teacher (Rengsdorf Chbk.).

There was a Johannes Lepper who, with wife Catharina, sp. a child of Joh: Haldron and Marytie Lepper in 1742 at the Tappan Ref. Church; there also was a Conrad Lepper who had a son Jacob Lepper, and both appeared in the Stone Arabia Ref. Chbk. in 1760.

<u>BALTHASAR LESCH HIS WIDDOW SUSANNA</u> (Hunter Lists #454)

The European roots of this N.Y. - Pa. family were in several towns along the Rhine: 1) at 6097 <u>Trebur</u> (17 km. s.e. of Wiesbaden; Chbks. begin 1592, but gaps); 2) at 6095 <u>Ginsheim-Gustavsburg</u> (10 km. s.e. of Wiesbaden; Chbks. begin 1664); and 3) at 6521 <u>Gimbsheim</u> (9 km s. of Oppenheim; Chbks. begin 1699). The grandfather of Balthasar[1] Lesch was <u>Jacob Lösch</u>. Hans Jacob Lösch, s/o Jacob Lösch, md. Anna Margaretha, d/o Wendel Latheimer (?) - Gerichtsmann at Wießheim an dem Heipt (?), 16 Nov 1658 (Trebur Chbk.). The ch. of <u>Hans Jacob Lösch</u> and Anna Margaretha were:

<u>Antonius</u>, b. 8 Sept 1659 (Trebur Chbk.).

<u>Catharina,</u> bpt. 29 Sept 1663 - sp.: Catharina - surviving d/o

Hans Lösch the Gerichtsmann (Trebur Chbk.).

Johannes, b. 30 July 1666 - sp.: Johannes, s/o Hans Luley the
elder (Trebur Chbk.).

Johann Adam, b. 10 Feb 1668 - sp.: Adam Ruby (Trebur Chbk.).
Johann Adam Lösch, single man from Trebur, md. Anna Barbara,
wid/o Johan Adam Traupel, 24 May 1692 (Ginsheim-Gustavsburg
Chbk.).

+ Johann Balthasar, b. 10 Aug 1671 - sp.: Hans Balthes, Friedr.
... auf dem Moltzhagen (?) (Trebur Chbk.).
Johan Balthasar Lösch, surviving s/o Hans Jacob Lösch - Gemeinsmann
at Trebur, md. Susanna, d/o the late Hans Georg Gering - shepherd
in Bischofsheim, 18 June 1694 (Ginsheim-Gustavsburg Chbk.). Balthasar Lesch was a Luth. inhabitant of Gimbsheim 27 Feb 1698 (Alzey
Census of 1698). Balter Zeÿps, his wife, and 4 ch. were on Capt.
Wilken's ship in the 3rd party in Holland in 1709 (Rotterdam
Lists); by a close study of the juxtaposition of names near this
emigrant (i.e. Johannes Joost Braun and hendrig Matheÿs) with those
surrounding Balzar Lesch at London, it is evident that Zeÿps was
actually Lösch (HJ). Balzar Lesch aged 38, his wife, sons aged 14,
8, and 2, a daughter aged 9, Luth., husbandman and vinedresser,
were in the 3rd arrivals at London in 1709 (London Lists).

Balthasar Lesch was first noted on the Hunter Lists 1 July
1710 with 2 pers. over 10 yrs. of age and 3 pers. under 10. The
entry read 3 over 10 and 2 under 10 on 4 Aug 1710, and 4 pers. o-
ver 10 yrs. and 2 under 10 on 4 Oct 1710. The cumulative entry for
24 Dec 1711 recorded Susanna Leschin with 3 pers. over 10 yrs. of
age and 1 pers. under 10. The will of Jacob Kopf of Tulpehocken
mentions his wife Susanna and his step-children Adam and Georg
Lesch, and Elisabetha Madelina Braun (Philadelphia Co. Will Bk. F,
p. 279, dated 1741); this shows that Susanna, wid/o Balthasar[1]
Lesch, md. 2nd Jacob Kopf (HJ). The ch. of Balthasar[1] Lesch and
wife Susanna were:

1) Johann Adam[2], the son b. 23 May 1695 - sp.: Johan Adam Neu,
single (Ginsheim-Gustavsburg Chbk.). He sp. Johannes Zech
in 1710 (West Camp Luth. Chbk.) and probably was the Joh.
Adam Kopp who sp. Theobald Jung at Schoharie in 1717, according to Kocherthal's register (HJ). Pastor Frederick S.
Weiser states the tombstone for Johann Adam Lesch shows
dates 1695 - 1768. Johann Adam[2] appeared on the first tax
list for Tulpehocken 10 Jan 1725 and was a landowner in the
valley ca. the yr. 1732, his tract being ca. a mile n. of
Rieds Luth. Church between the lands of Jacob Kopp and
Philip Brown (1723 - 1973 Anniversary Magazine of the Tulpehocken, p. 52). He was noted on the 1743 list of members

in the Tulpehocken Chbk. Johann Adam[2] md. Anna Sophia Kopf, b. 13 Oct 1695 - bur. 10 March 1771, aged 76 yrs. and 4 months (Tulpehocken Chbk.). The will of Adam Lesh was dated 26 Jan 1768 and probated 25 March 1768, and the will of Sophia Lesh was dated 29 Aug 1770 and probated 25 March 1771 (Lancaster Co. Wills: Bk. Y, Vol. 2, pp. 397 & 398). The ch. of Johann Adam[2] Lesch and Anna Sophia were:

  i) <u>Jacob[3]</u> (Wills). Papers in the estate of Jacob Lesh of Tulpehocken were granted to his widow Maria Catharine 17 May 1756 (Berks Co. Administrations: Bk. 1, p. 49); see also Berks Co. Orphan's Court Minutes pp. 9 - 12.

  ii) <u>Susanna[3]</u> (Wills). She md. Valentin Viehmann (HJ).

  iii) <u>Catharina Elisabetha[3]</u> (Adam's Will), md. Johann Michael Ehrhardt 27 May 1740 at Tulpehocken (Stoever Chbks.).

  iv) <u>Anna Christina[3]</u> (Wills, although the abstract of Adam's calls the child Christian). Anna Christina[3] md. Abraham Neff 8 June 1742 at Tulpehocken (Stoever Chbks.).

  v) <u>Margaretha[3]</u> (Adam's Will).

  vi) <u>Anna[3]</u> (Wills).

  vii) <u>Maria Elisabetha[3]</u>, conf. as d/o Adam[2] 9 Oct 1748, aged 15 yrs. (Tulpehocken Chbk.).

  viii) <u>Anna Sophia[3]</u>, conf. as d/o Adam[2] in 1753, aged 16 yrs. (Tulpehocken Chbk.).

  ix) <u>Anna Maria[3]</u> (Wills).

There is some minor disagreement as to the correct bpt. names of some of the female ch. of Johann Adam[2] Lesch (HJ).

2) <u>Johann Georg[2]</u> (Will of Jacob Kopf). Pastor Frederick Weiser gives his birthdate as 23 April 1699. Joh: Jurgen Lösch joined the church at Tschoghari in the so-called Weiserts-Dorp in 1720 and was listed again in 1721 (N.Y. City Luth. Chbk.). In 1745 George Loesch and his wife were admitted to fellowship in the Moravian Church and were instrumental in founding congregations at Heidelburg Twp., Quittopehille (now Lebanon), Nazareth and Bethlehem in Pa., and also at Bethania, N.C. The old Georg Lesches sold their home in Berks Co. and removed to Gnadenthal near Nazareth, Northampton Co., Pa. and celebrated their 50th wedding anniversary 15 Dec 1771. Johann Georg[2] Lesch d. 15 Aug 1790, aged 92 yrs., and his wife Christina Walborn d. 17 Dec 1782 (<u>Some Descendants of Balthaser & Susanna Phillipina Loesch</u>, by William W. Lesh, 1914, pp. 10 & 11). The registers at

Reed's Church contain much family material on Johann Georg[2] and his offspring, who were:

 i) Johann Jacob[3], b. 10 Nov 1722 - sp.: Johann Jacob Kop and wife (Reed's Chbk.).

 ii) Susanna Philipina[3], b. 12 June 1724 - sp.: Jacob Kop and wife (Reed's Chbk.).

 iii) Hermanus Walborn[3], b. 4 March 1726 - sp.: Hermanus Walborn (Reed's Chbk.).

 iv) Maria Elisabetha[3], b. 12 Feb 1728 - sp.: Martin Battorf and his wife (Reed's Chbk.).

 v) Maria Catharina[3], b. 24 Feb 1730 - sp.: Maria Catharina Schell (Reed's Chbk.).

 vi) Christina Elisabetha[3], b. 14 Jan 1732 - sp.: Philip Braun and wife (Reed's Chbk.).

 vii) Johann Balthasar[3], b. 19 March 1734 - sp.: Baltzar Anspach and wife (Reed's Chbk.).

 viii) Margaretha Elisabetha[3], b. 20 March 1736 - sp.: Margaretha Elisabetha Schell (Reed's Chbk.).

 ix) Johann Georg[3], b. 13 Feb 1738 - sp.: Christian Walborn and wife (Reed's Chbk.).

 x) Johann Adam[3], b. 6 June 1741 - sp.: Adam Walborn (Reed's Chbk.).

 xi) Maria Barbara[3], b. 25 Sept 1744 - sp.: Michael Rieth and his wife (Reed's Chbk.).

3) Elisabetha Magdalena[2], bpt. 18 Oct 1700 - sp.: Elisabeth - w/o Johannes Waicker (Gimbsheim Chbk.). Elisabetha Losch was conf. 23 March 1712 at Queensberg (West Camp Luth. Chbk.). She md. Philip Braun (Will of Jacob Kopf).

4) Susanna[2], bpt. 18 July 1706 - sp.: Susanna Grelt from Güntsheimb aus dem Darmstedter Landt (Gimbsheim Chbk.). Susanna, d/o Baltzer Lösch, was bur. 10 Feb 1707 (Gimbsheim Chbk.).

5) "A Son"[2], bpt. 27 Nov 1707 - sp.: Martinus Gabriel, inhabitant here at Gimbsheim (Gimbsheim Chbk.).

There was a Johan Adam Loss, s/o Hiob, who md. Cathrina Würtz, d/o Michel Würtz, 10 July 1709 (London Churchbooks and the German Emigration of 1709, by John P. Dern, p. 23); also a Maria Barbara Lasch, d/o Jacob of Kemmede in Ansbachschen, md. Johan Conradt Jordan, s/o Johannes of Mernhahn, 3 July 1709 (Ibid., p. 22). A John Losch (or Jan Lusk) md. Margaretha Heintgen (HJ) and had issue bpt. at Red Hook Luth. and Kingston Ref. Churches (HJ). However, none of these families appear to have any connection whatsoever with the family of Balthasar[1] Lesch (HJ).

MAGDALENA LESCHERIN (Hunter Lists #455)

A Magdalena lesorin was in the 3rd party of Palatines in Holland on Capt. Robb[t] Breene's ship in 1709 (Rotterdam Lists). Magdalen Lescherin aged 34, with a son aged 18, Ref., widow, was in the 3rd arrivals at London later that yr. (London Lists).

Magdalena Lescherin made her first appearance on the Hunter Lists 1 July 1710 with 3 pers. over 10 yrs. of age and 2 pers. under 10 yrs. The family was recorded with 1 over 10 and 2 under 10 on 4 Aug 1710, with 5 over 10 and 1 under 10 yrs. on 4 Oct 1710, and with 1 over 10 yrs. and 1 under 10 yrs. on 29 Sept 1711. Magdalena Santbergen, wid/o Jacob Leffjerin of Germany, md. Jacob Bosch 28 Feb 1714 (N.Y. City Ref. Chbk.). The ch. of Jacob and Magdalena[1] Lescher were:

1) __Anna Catharina__[2] (Apprenticeship Lists). Catrina Lizard, 15, d/o Widow Lizard, was bound to Isaac Stoutenburgh of N.Y. 24 Oct 1710 (Apprenticeship Lists). She md. 1st Tharmer Widder and 2nd James Makbrok (HJ).

2) __Magdalena__[2] (Apprenticeship Lists). Magdalena Lizard, 13, d/o Widow Lizard, was bound to Wellm Vandewater of N.Y. 24 Oct 1710 (Apprenticeship Lists). Magdalena Lesser md. Joris Walgraf 10 March 1724 (N.Y. City Ref. Chbk.). She joined the N.Y. City Ref. Church 26 Aug 1729.

3) __Elisabetha__[2] (Apprenticeship Lists). Elizabeth Lizard, 13, d/o Widow Lizard, was bound to James Leigh of N.Y. 24 Oct 1710 (Apprenticeship Lists). She md. Henrich Labach 17 May 1724 (N.Y. City Ref. Chbk.).

4) __Johann Gerhard__[2] (Apprenticeship Lists). Hans Gerrit Lizard, 10, s/o Widow Lizard, was bound to John Symons of N.Y. 24 Oct 1710 (Apprenticeship Lists).

5) __Johannes__[2] (HJ), md. 3 June 1722 as single man b. Germany Eva Binder (N.Y. City Ref. Chbk.). Johannes Lesser and his wife Eva Binder joined the N.Y. City Ref. Church 19 Nov 1723. They had issue:

   i) __Johannes__[3], bpt. 4 March 1724 - sp.: Matheus Binder and Magdalena Lesser (N.Y. City Ref. Chbk.).

   ii) __Maria__[3], bpt. 18 Dec 1726 - sp.: Jacob Bos, and Magdalena Shamberger - wid/o Jacob Lesser (N.Y. City Ref. Chbk.).

   iii) __Friederich__[3], bpt. 15 Dec 1728 - sp.: Johan Fredrik Jenter and Catharina Lesscher (N.Y. City Ref. Chbk.).

   iv) __Jacob__[3], bpt. 10 Jan 1731 - sp.: Joris Walgraaf, and Margareta Lesier - w/o Gysbert Gerritse (N.Y. City Ref. Chbk.).

v) <u>Magdalena³</u>, bpt. 25 March 1733 - sp.: Gÿsbert Gerrit-
sze and Hester Sibo (N.Y. City Ref. Chbk.).

6) <u>Margaretha²</u> (HJ). Margareta Lesser, w/o Gysbert Gerritse,
joined the N.Y. City Ref. Church 26 Aug 1729.

<u>JOHANNES LEYER</u> (Hunter Lists #456)

Johannes Leyer made his initial appearance on the Hunter
Lists 4 Oct 1710 with 4 pers. over 10 yrs. of age in the family.
The family then was registered with 3 over 10 yrs. 31 Dec 1710,
and with 2 over 10 and 1 under 10 yrs. 13 Sept 1712. Johannes Le-
yer and Elisabetha with 2 ch. were at Neu-Stuttgardt ca. 1716/17
(Simmendinger Register). <u>Simms' History of Schoharie Co. & Border
Wars of N.Y.</u>, p. 94, mentions a bond from John Andrews of Scorre
(Schoharie) to John Lawer for £26, 3 shillings, corrant money of
N.Y., and dated 3 May 1720 - the earliest date of any paper Simms
had seen dealing with the Schoharie Valley. John Lawyer was a
Justice of the Peace ca. 1725 (Albany Co. Deeds, Vol. 6, p. 140).
John Lawyer was a patentee in 1723 (Stone Arabia Patent). <u>Simms'
History of Schoharie</u> also calls him the first merchant among the
German settlers (p. 23). Simms adds on pp. 99 - 100:

> John Lawyer, named in the bond of 1720, and the father
> of one of the first white ch. b. in Schoharie, was one
> of the principal settlers at Bruna dorf: and was the
> first merchant among those Germans - trading near the
> present residence of Andrew Beller, ½ mile s. of the
> Court House. He is said to have been a flax-hatcheler
> in Germany: and we must suppose, from the state of his
> finances on his arrival in the Schoharie valley, that
> he commenced a very limited business. The natives were
> among his most profitable customers; as he bartered
> blankets, Indian trinkets, calicoes, ammunition, rum,
> etc., with them, for valuable furs, dressed deer-skins,
> and other commodities of the times. He was one of the
> best informed among the Germans who settled the county;
> and before his death became an extensive land-holder.
> He was quite a business man and a useful citizen, aiding
> many who purchased land in making their payments; and
> acquired the reputation of a fair and honorable dealer.
> He became a widower when ca. 80 yrs. old, and md. a wid.
> in N.Y. City. Arriving at Albany he sent word to have
> one of his sons come after him: but they were so offend-
> ed to think he should marry at that age, that neither
> of them would go. One Dominick took the happy couple to
> Schoharie; where, we take it for granted, they spent
> the honeymoon. It has been stated that Lawyer had sev-
> eral ch. by this late marriage. Judge Brown assured the
> author he had indeed, but that they were many yrs. old
> when he md. their mother. A well executed family por-
> trait of this father of the Lawyers, in the fashion of
> that day, is now to be seen at the dwelling of the late
> Wm. G. Michaels, near the Court House. It was painted
> in N.Y., and tells credibly for the state of the fine
> arts at that period.

This old picture, now in the Abby Aldrich Rockefeller Folk Art

Collection in Williamsburg, Va., has been reproduced on the cover
of the Schoharie Co. Historical Review, Vol. XXIX, No. 1, Spring-
Summer, 1965; this fine periodical also has an article on "The
Lawyer Family of Schoharie and Cobleskill", by George S. Van
Schaick, in the Oct 1952 issue. Berkenmeyer mentions a visit with
Johannes[1] Lawyer in Albany Protocol, pp. 98 - 100, dated 1734:

> We continued our trip. The people met at the home of
> Hannes Lawyer, where I got off my horse. Hannes Lawyer
> received us with coolness; his wife did not speak to us.
> On the way I had been told that two ch. were to be bpt,
> whose names I entered. Then I stated to H[annes] Lawyer
> and the deacons that I brought them two messages, one
> concerning the call [from the Luth. congregations in
> the Schoharie and Mohawk villages] and the other about
> the collection [for the church at Stone Arabia] from the
> brethren at Scoghary. The first I would present at the
> church service and the other in a home after the service.
> H[annes] Lawyer spoke first, saying that one pastor must
> first be dismissed before another could be called. I re-
> plied that this was the point about which I desired to
> speak with the people. Finally it was decided to have
> both the talk [about the call] and the [request for] the
> collection made from the pulpit.
> We then went to the church, and H[annes] L[awyer] in-
> vited me to have my meal with him. I accept this grate-
> fully and after having greeted H[annes] Scheffer at the
> door of the church I entered. The singing was as bad as
> beyond the Falls. After I preached the sermon, the peop-
> le were admonished [to give] to the collection. But the
> Ref. members left at once. Hannes Lawyer and H[annes]
> Scheffer said, "We are not accustomed to such long ser-
> mons, and since not all the people are present it would
> be better for the people to make the rounds themselves
> [for the collection]."
> "Well," I replied, "I did my part. Let me hear what the
> brethren intend to do about the call." They said that
> they were willing to have their own pastor but that they
> wanted to speak first with Mr. Van Dieren and then with
> the other brethren. I replied that this was also the op-
> inion of the other brethren who want to ask Mr. V. D[ie-
> ren] whether he will remain. H[annes] Lawyer interrupted,
> "That will serve no purpose, for he will not be willing
> to let his family down. But he is coming here once more
> this autumn." I replied, "I cannot do more. You saw my
> willingness to advise you. Let me know your decision so
> that I may serve you further." Then I left, and Schup-
> pius asked [for the collection] from some Luth. people
> who were still standing there. They promised two bush-
> els of corn each.
> On leaving, I got to thinking about the many tears I
> had shed in my prayers a week ago. My weeping must have
> occurred because I saw how far Scoghary still was from
> our Luth. Jerusalem, since they would neither acknow-
> ledge nor consider what could serve them for their
> peace.
> Coming home, H[annes] L[awyer] asked if I would like a
> dram. And when I replied Yes, if he had one, he laughed
> and ordered a cup...

The family of Johannes[1] Lawyer appears on a partially destroyed
section of Pastor Sommer's Family List (Schoharie Luth. Chbk.).
Johannes Lawyer's first wife, the old Mrs. Lawyer, d. 30 May

1760, aged 76 yrs. (Schoharie Luth. Chbk.). A license to marry was
issued to Johannes Lawyer and Anna Maria Michael 6 July 1761 (N.Y.
Marriage Licenses). The old Mr. Johannes Lawyer d. 29 Nov 1762
(Schoharie Luth. Chbk.). The will of Johannes Lawyer of Schoharry
in Albany Co. was dated 10 March 1760 and probated 29 Jan 1765
(Fernow Wills #1035). Mention of this disputed estate also is found
in Genealogical Data from Administration Papers, p. 187. Johannes
Lawyer's name was noted as one who was a freeholder at Schoharrie
in 1763 (Albany Co. Freeholders); this even after his death (HJ).
The ch. of Johannes[1] Lawyer and his 1st wife Elisabetha were:

1) Anna Sophia[2] (Will), md. 29 Oct 1733 Jost Bellinger (Schoharie Ref. Chbk.). She md. 2nd Christian Zeh (Will).

2) Elisabetha[2] (Will), called by Simms one of the first ch.
b. to the Palatines in the Schoharie Valley (Simms' History of Schoharie, p. 51). She md. 1st Marcus Rickert and
2nd Henrich Hayns (both Will).

3) Johannes[2] (Will). Johannes Lawyer Jr. was a freeholder in
Schoharrie in 1763 (Albany Co. Freeholders). Lt. Col. Johannis Lawyer was in Col. Jacob Starnberg's Regiment to
comprehend all Scohare Brekabeen and the settlements ad-
jacent (Report of the State Historian, Vol. II, p. 881).
The dates on his stone at the Schoharie Cem. read 1725 -
1795; his obituary in the Albany Register notes he d. 14
Aug 1794, aged 80 yrs. Johannes[2] md. 1st Catharina Vroman
1 Oct 1745 (Schoharie Luth. Chbk.). They had issue:

i) Elisabetha[3], b. 5 Nov 1746 - sp.: Mr. Lawyer and his
wife (Schoharie Luth. Chbk.). She md. Peter Zilly 8
Jan 1765 (Schoharie Luth. Chbk.).

ii) Catharina[3], b. 27 Aug 1748 - sp.: Peter Vroman and
his wife (Schoharie Luth. Chbk.).

Johannes[2] md. 2nd 27 Feb 1750 Christina Sternberg (Schoharie Luth. Chbk.), and they had issue:

iii) Johannes[3], b. 8 May 1751 - sp.: Johannes Rickert and
Elisabet Barbara Sternberg (Schoharie Luth. Chbk.).

iv) Rebecca[3], b. 26 Nov 1752 - sp.: Lambert Sternberg
and his wife (Schoharie Luth. Chbk.). She md. Dr.
Daniel Budd 10 March 1774 (Schoharie Luth. Chbk.).

v) Jacob[3], b. 1 Nov 1754 - sp.: Jacob Fr. Lawyer and
his wife (Schoharie Luth. Chbk.).

vi) David[3], b. 29 June 1757 - sp.: Adam Sternberg and his
wife (Schoharie Luth. Chbk.). He d. 10 July 1773,
aged 16 yrs. (Schoharie Luth. Chbk.).

vii) Abraham[3], b. 19 June 1759 - sp.: Abraham Sternberg
and Anna Rickert (Schoharie Luth. Chbk.). He d. 20

Jan 1825, aged 66 yrs. (Schoharie Cem., Schoharie).

viii) Lambert[3], b. 26 Dec 1761 - sp.: Lambert Sternberg
and wife (Schoharie Luth. Chbk.).

ix) Peter[3], b. 1 May 1764 - sp.: Peter Nicolas Sommer
and wife (Schoharie Luth. Chbk.).

x) Maria[3], b. 24 Oct 1766 - sp.: Jacob Heens and Maria
Catharina Sternberg (Schoharie Luth. Chbk.).

xi) Christian[3], b. 25 Dec 1768 - sp.: Johannes Lawyer Jr.
and wife (Schoharie Luth. Chbk.).

xii) Henrich[3], b. 23 Sept 1771 - sp.: Henrich Heens Jr.
and Maria Borst (Schoharie Luth. Chbk.).

4) Jacob Friederich[2] (Will), md 1 Oct 1745 Elisabeth Sternberg (Schoharie Luth. Chbk.). The w/o T. F. Lawyer d. 1796
(Schoharie Cem., Schoharie). Jacob F: Lawyer, Hannes Lawyer jun:, and Jacob Laweyer, were in Capt. Jacob Sternberger's Company at Schohare 2 May 1767 (Report of the
State Historian, Vol. II, p. 843). The will of Jacob Frederick Lawyer of Schoharie, farmer, was dated 27 May 1793
and probated 15 March 1804 (Schoharie Co. Will Bk. A); it
was also probated 26 Sept 1804 in Montgomery Co. (Montgomery Co. Will Bk. I). The ch. of Jacob Friederich[2] and Elisabetha were:

i) Johannes[3], b. 8 July 1746 - sp.: Mr. Johannes Lawyer
and wife (Schoharie Luth. Chbk.). He md. Anna Bauch
22 Sept 1767 (Schoharie Luth. Chbk.). He d. 28 June
1800, aged 54 yrs. and 21 days (Schoharie Cem., Schoharie).

ii) Jacob[3], b. 13 Aug 1748 - sp.: Jacob Sternberg and his
wife (Schoharie Luth. Chbk.). He d. 3 Feb 1827, aged
78 yrs. (Schoharie Luth. Chbk.).

iii) Lorentz[3], b. 10 Oct 1750 - sp.: Lorentz Lawyer and
his wife (Schoharie Luth. Chbk.). He md. Elisabetha
Lawyer 9 Nov 1773 (Schoharie Luth. Chbk.).

iv) Friederich[3], b. 26 Dec 1752 0 sp.: Lambert Sternberg
and his wife (Schoharie Luth. Chbk.). He d. 16 April
1757 of the small pox (Schoharie Luth. Chbk.).

v) Lambert[3], b. 26 May 1755 - sp.: Lambert Sternberg and
his wife (Schoharie Luth. Chbk.). He d. 20 April 1757
of the small pox (Schoharie Luth. Chbk.).

vi) Nicolaus[3], b. 3 Jan 1758 - sp.: Nicolas Sternberg and
Catharina Rickert (Schoharie Luth. Chbk.).

vii) David[3], b. 15 Jan 1760 - sp.: David Sternberg and
Catharina Sternberg (Schoharie Luth. Chbk.).

viii) Elisabetha[3], b. 24 June 1762 - sp.: Henrich Heens and wife Elisabeth (Schoharie Luth. Chbk.).

   ix) Adam[3], b. 21 Sept 1764 - sp.: Abraham Sternberg and
Sophia Sternberg (Schoharie Luth. Chbk.).

   x) Lambert[3], b. 17 Feb 1767 - sp.: Johannes Lawyer and
wife (Schoharie Luth. Chbk.).

   xi) Catharina[3], b. 19 March 1769 - sp.: Catharina - w/o
Johannes Rickert (Schoharie Luth. Chbk.).

5) Lorentz[2] (Will), md. 27 Oct 1747 Elisabetha Berg (Schoharie Luth. Chbk.). Lourance Lawyer was a freeholder at Schoharrie in 1763 (Albany Co. Freeholders). Lowrance Lawyer
was a soldier in Capt. Thomas Ackeson's Company in 1767
(Report of the State Historian, Vol. II, p. 846). Papers
in the estate of Lawrence Lawyer of Middleburg, deceased,
who d. ca. 10 yrs. ago, were filed 30 Nov 1811 and granted
to his son Abraham Lawyer (Schoharie Co. Will Bk. A). The
issue of Lorentz[2] and Elisabetha Lawyer were:

   i) Johannes[3], b. 4 Sept 1748 - sp.: Johannes Lawyer Jr.
and the old Mrs. Lawyer (Schoharie Luth. Chbk.). He
md. Eva Sternberg 25 May 1773 (Schoharie Luth. Chbk.).

   ii) Catharina[3], b. 24 Nov 1749 - sp.: Abraham Berg and
his wife (Schoharie Luth. Chbk.).

   iii) Elisabetha[3], b. 21 Dec 1752 - sp.: Henrich Häns and
his wife (Schoharie Luth. Chbk.). She md. Lorentz
Lawyer 9 Nov 1773 (Schoharie Luth. Chbk.).

   iv) Johann Philip[3], b. 2 Dec 1755 - sp.: Philip Berg and
his wife (Schoharie Luth. Chbk.). A little boy of Lorentz Lawyer d. 10 Sept 1757 (Schoharie Luth. Chbk.).

   v) Abraham[3], b. 3 Sept 1758 - sp.: Abraham Berg and his
wife (Schoharie Luth. Chbk.). He d. 10 Sept 1839,
aged 81 yrs. and 17 days (Middleburg Cem.).

   vi) Lorentz[3], b. 23 July 1763 - sp.: Wilhelm Bauch and
wife (Schoharie Luth. Chbk.).

   vii) Maria[3], b. 14 Sept 1765 - sp.: Lorentz - s/o Jacob
Fried. Lawyer, and Maria Kayser (Schoharie Luth.
Chbk.).

6) Catharina[2] (HJ), d. 26 Aug 1748, aged 21 yrs. (Schoharie
Luth. Chbk.).

BERNHARD LICKARD (Hunter Lists #457)

Bernhart Lingeret, his wife, and 1 child were on Capt Leonard Allan's ship in the 5th party of Palatines in Holland in 1709
(Rotterdam Lists).

Bernhard Lickard made his initial appearance on the Hunter

Lists 1 July 1710 with 2 pers. over 10 yrs. of age in the family.
The entry read 3 pers. over 10 yrs. 24 June 1711, and then re-
turned to 2 over 10 yrs. 29 Sept 1711. A special entry for Sibilla
Gieserin was included in the family 24 Dec 1711. Bernhard Lickhard
aged 25, and Justina Lickard aged 32 were in N.Y. City in 1710/11
(Palatines In N.Y. City). Johan Barent Lighthert was nat. 8 and 9
Sept 1715 (Kingston Nats.). Bernhard Lieckhart and Justina nebft
1 child were at Beckmansland ca. 1716/17 (Simmendinger Register).
Barent Lighthart was a Palatine Debtor in 1718 (Livingston Debt
Lists). B. Lighthart was mentioned often in the 1740's in the
collection of Dutchess Co. Ancient Documents (see #'s 425, 602,
1633, and 1848). Barent Legthart appeared on tax rolls at Beekman's Precinct beginning in 1738/39, as did his son (un-named) in
1739/40 (Dutchess Co. Tax Lists). The ch. of Bernhard[1] Lickhard
and Justina were:

1) <u>Johann Wilhelm[2]</u>, bpt. 3 June 1711 in the Upper German Colonies - sp.: Johann Wilhelm Stueckenrad (West Camp Luth.
   Chbk.).

2) <u>Johannes[2]</u>, b. 7 Nov 1712 - sp.: Johann Emmerich (West Camp
   Luth. Chbk.).

3) <u>Johann Daniel[2]</u>, b. 13 Feb 1715 - sp.: Johannes Fuehrer
   and Daniel Tastuh (West Camp Luth. Chbk.). There is an
   Ancient Document in Dutchess Co. (#3986) relating to him.
   Reid's <u>The Loyalists In Ontario</u>, p. 180, notes a Daniel
   Lightheart family of Adolphustown, Ernestown, and Darling-
   ton. Johann Daniel[2] md. Maria (--) (HJ) and had issue:

   i) <u>Anna Justina[3]</u>, b. 24 June 1739 and bpt. at Niclaas
      Emig's - sp.: Bernhard Lickhardt and wife Anna Jus-
      tina (N.Y. City Luth. Chbk.).

   ii) <u>Margaretha[3]</u>, b. 30 Nov 1741 and bpt. Pacquesien -
      sp.: Philip Salomon and Greetje (N.Y. City Luth.
      Chbk.).

   iii?) <u>Daniel[3]</u>, md. Maria Heens (HJ) and had issue bpt. at
      Schaghticoke Ref. Church (HJ).

   iv) <u>Anna[3]</u>, b. 15 April 1746 - sp.: Berend and Justina
      Lickhardt (N.Y. City Luth. Chbk.).

   v) <u>Elisabetha[3]</u>, b. 17 Oct 1752 - sp.: Andrees Berger
      and Liesabeth (Loonenburg Luth. Chbk.).

4) <u>Johann Peter[2]</u>, b. 10 Nov 1716 - sp.: Peter Burckhard and
   Amelia Klein (West Camp Luth. Chbk.). A child of Bernhard
   Luckhard d. 1 Sept 1717 (West Camp Luth. Chbk.).

5?) <u>Christina[2]</u>, a sp. with Johann Daniel[2] Likhard at Bachway
   in 1744 to Nette Dijmand, according to the registers of
   the N.Y. City Luth. Church.

JOHANN WILHELM LINCKEN (Hunter Lists #458)

This Hudson Valley family was documented at 5232 Flammersfeld (23 km. n. of Neuwied; Chbks. begin 1669, but gaps) and at 5231 Birnbach (7 km. further n.e.; Chbks. begin 1666, but gaps). The grandfather of the emigrant 1709er was Peter Linck. The emigrant's father was Jost Linck, whom we know to be a s/o Peter: a child of Gerhard, s/o Pitter Linck, was bpt. 16 Oct 1667 - sp.: Jost, s/o Pitter Linck (Birnbach Chbk.). Johann Wilhelm, eldest s/o Jost Linck at Hemmelzen, md. Anna Eva, d/o the late Johannes Firsbach from Berg, 2 June 1709 (Flammersfeld Chbk.). Johannes Firsbach from Berg d. 19 Feb 1706, aged 70 yrs., and Margaretha, wid/o Johannes Firsbach from Berg, d. 22 Feb 1707, aged 60 yrs. (both Flammersfeld Chbk.). Their daughter Anna Eva was bpt. 30 Sept 1685 - sp.: Hans Theiss Albach, Anna Maria - w/o Conradt Mehren, and Eva - w/o Michael Rocklius (?) of the parish Herschen (Sieg) (Flammersfeld Chbk.). Jan Willem lenken and his wife were passengers on Capt. Johan Facit's ship in Holland in the 5th party of 1709 (Rotterdam Lists).

Johann Wilhelm Lincken made his first appearance on the Hunter Lists 1 July 1710, but with no number, no monies mentioned, and no number of persons listed. On 4 Aug 1710 he had 2 pers. over 10 yrs. of age, and on 31 Dec 1710 was enrolled with 2 over 10 yrs. and 2 under 10 in the household. On 25 March 1711, he was recorded with 2 over 10 yrs. and 1 under 10, on 25 March 1712 with 1 over 10 and 1 under 10, and on 24 June 1712 with 2 pers. over 10 yrs. and 2 under 10 yrs. of age. Jno. Wm. Linck of Annsberg was a Palatine Volunteer in 1711 (Palatine Volunteers To Canada). Willem Linck was nat. 14 Feb 1715/16 (Albany Nats.). Johannes Linck and his wife with 3 ch. were noted at Wormsdorff ca. 1716/17 (Simmendinger Register). Willem Ling(h) was a Palatine Debtor in 1718, 1721, and 1726 (Livingston Debt Lists). William Linge registered his livestock mark in Dutchess Co. as WL ca. 1730 (Dutchess Co. Supervisor's Records). William Linke was a freeholder at East Camp in 1763 (Albany Co. Freeholders). The ch. of Johann Wilhelm[1] Linck and wife Anna Eva were:

1) Johann Nicolaus[2] (Loonenburg Luth. Chbk. in 1738 sp.), md. 13 May 1735 Anna Catharina Schmidt (Catskill Ref. Chbk.). The will of Nicholas Linck of the Manor of Livingston was dated 12 Feb 1772 and probated 29 Oct 1788 (Columbia Co. Will Bk. A). The ch. of Johann Nicolaus[2] and Anna Catharina were:

i) Anna Catharina[3], b. 2 Jan 1736 - sp.: Willhelm Link and Susanna Smid, d/o Bernhard (Rhinebeck Luth.

Chbk.). She md. Martin Holzapfel (Will).

ii) <u>Anna Eva³</u>, b. 5 March 1738 and bpt. at Camp - sp.: Jo: Wilh. Linck and Anna Eva, grandparents (Loonenburg Luth. Chbk.). She md. Andreas Pulver 20 Dec 1757 (Germantown Ref. Chbk.).

iii) <u>Maria Susanna³</u>, b. 27 Feb 1740 and bpt. at Teerbosch - sp.: Jo: Wilh Linck and Maria Susanna Schnid (Loonenburg Luth. Chbk.). She md. Gerrit Holzapfel (Will).

iv) <u>Anna³</u> (Will), md. Christophel Schneider (Will).

v) <u>Johann Wilhelm³</u>, bpt. 19 Feb 1749 - sp.: Wilhelm Linck and Anna Eva (Germantown Ref. Chbk.). He md. 11 May 1767 Zyllia Maria Blass (Germantown Ref. Chbk.). They had ch. bpt. at Germantown Ref. Church (HJ).

2) <u>Anna Gertraud²</u>, b. 1 June 1714 - sp.: Johann Grad, Gerdraut Schuch, and Anna Margretha Winter (West Camp Luth. Chbk.). She md. Philip Finckel (HJ).

3) <u>Zyllia Maria²</u> (HJ), md. Peter Plass (HJ).

4) <u>Johann Wilhelm²</u>, b. 7 Jan 1721 at Camp - sp.: Johan Willh. Schneider and Margareta Wiesborn (N.Y. City Luth. Chbk.). He md. Susanna Schmidt (HJ); he was dead by 1747 when his widow Susanna had md. Nicolaus Schäffer (HJ). A child of Johann Wilhelm² Linck and Susanna Schmidt was:

i) <u>Johann Wilhelm³</u>, bpt. 20 Oct 1742 - sp.: Willem Linck and Anna Eva (Germantown Ref. Chbk.). He md. 1st Elisabetha Schedewick (Chadwick) 11 July 1764 (Germantown Ref. Chbk.) and had issue bpt. there (HJ). He then md. Maria (--) (HJ) and had ch. bpt. at Manorton Luth., Churchtown Luth., and Gilead Luth. Churches.

5) <u>Catharina²</u> (HJ), md. Simon Kuhn (HJ).

6) <u>Maria Margaretha²</u>, md. as a d/o Johann Wilhelm¹ 21 April 1747 Johann Wilhelm Herter (Germantown Ref. Chbk.).

7) <u>Johannes²</u>, md. as a s/o Johann Wilhelm¹ 21 April 1747 Anna Elisabetha Kuhn (Germantown Ref. Chbk.). Johannes Link joined the Germantown Ref. Church 11 May 1743. He was on tax rolls at North East from Feb 1753 - 1779 (Dutchess Co. Tax Lists). John Link was on a list of deserters from Capt. Arnout Viele's Company 14 Aug 1757 (<u>Report of the State Historian</u>, Vol. II, p. 785). The ch. of Johannes² Linck and Anna Elisabetha Kuhn were:

i) <u>Anna³</u>, bpt. 10 April 1748 - sp.: Philip Linck and Lisabeth Kuhn (Germantown Ref. Chbk.). She md. Johannes Philip 27 Nov 1764 (Red Hook Luth. Chbk.).

ii) <u>Eva³</u>, bpt. 8 July 1750 - sp.: Wilhelm Linck and Eva

(Germantown Ref. Chbk.). She md. Johannes Reiffenberger (HJ).

  iii) Wilhelm³, bpt. 24 April 1753 - sp.: Willem Coen and
Elisabeth Coen (Red Hook Luth. Chbk.). He md. Maria
Kilmer (HJ).

  iv) Catharina³, bpt. 29 Feb 1756 - sp.: Simon Kuhn and
Catharina Linck (Red Hook Luth. Chbk.). She md. Conrad Milhem (HJ).

   v) Susanna³, bpt. 29 Oct 1758 - sp.: Herr Kuhn and Susanna Linck (Germantown Ref. Chbk.).

  vi) Henrich³ (from will of Johannes Linke of North East
dated 3 June 1801 and probated 28 July 1801 in Dutchess Co. Will Bk. B). He md. Catharina Linck (HJ).

 vii) Johannes³, b. 25 Dec 1762 - sp.: Hanes Kilmer and
Anna Kuhn (Rhinebeck Luth. Chbk.). He md. Anna Kupper (HJ).

viii) Zacharias³, bpt. 29 Dec 1765 - sp.: Zacharias Ditter
and Christina Kulmer (Red Hook Luth. Chbk.). He md.
Elisabetha Linck (HJ).

  ix) Maria³, bpt. 4 Dec 1768 - sp.: Georg Kuhn and wife
Maria Blass (Red Hook Luth. Chbk.).

   x) Susanna³, bpt. 15 March 1772 - sp.: Gerhard Holtzappel and wife Susanna Linck (Red Hook Luth. Chbk.).

  xi) Philip³, bpt. 23 June 1776 - sp.: Phillip Linck and
wife Catharina Pulver (Red Hook Luth. Chbk.).

8) Anna Elisabetha², bpt. 4 June 1727 or 1728 - sp.: Zachar-
ias Smith and Anna Elis. Schever (Linlithgo Ref. Chbk.).
She joined the Germantown Ref. Church 11 May 1743, and md.
Petrus Betzer 9 Dec 1746 (Germantown Ref. Chbk.).

9) Johann Philip², bpt. 17 weeks old 9 April 1730 at Saal-
bach's at Kamp - sp.: Philipp Scheffer and wife Anna Elis-
abeth (N.Y. City Luth. Chbk.). He joined the Germantown
Ref. Church 7 June 1747. Philip Linck md. Catharina, d/o
Peter Pulver, in 1751 (Germantown Ref. Chbk.). The will
of Philip Linck of Clermont in Columbia Co. was dated 22
Dec 1791 and probated 19 March 1792 (Columbia Co. Will Bk.
A). The ch. of Johann Philip² and Catharina were:

   i) Catharina³, bpt. 12 Nov 1752 - sp.: Conrad Pulver and
Catharina Link (Germantown Ref. Chbk.). She md. Wilhelm Kilmer (HJ).

  ii) Eva³, bpt. 4 June 1754 - sp.: William Link and wife
Eva (Germantown Ref. Chbk.). She md. Henrich Plass
(HJ).

 iii) Susanna³, bpt. 4 Feb 1756 - sp.: Peter Pulver and

wife Susanna Drum (Germantown Ref. Chbk.).

iv) Johann Wilhelm[3], bpt. 15 April 1758 - sp.: Joh: Wilh: Linck and wife Anna Eva Fursbach (Germantown Ref. Chbk.). He md. 1st Lena Rockefeller (HJ) and md. 2nd Anna Foland (HJ). Johann Wilhelm[3] d. 19 June 1846, aged 88-3-10 (Old Ghent Cem.).

v) Christina[3], b. 9 Sept 1760 - sp.: Jacob Pulver and Chr: (Germantown Luth. Chbk.). She md. Philip Klum (HJ).

vi) Petrus[3] (Will).

vii) Philip[3], bpt. 14 April 1765 - sp.: Phillip Harter and Elisabeth Pulver (Germantown Ref. Chbk.). He md. Christina Batz (HJ). Philip[3] d. 14 Feb 1827, aged 62 yrs. (Germantown Ref. Cem.).

viii) Susanna[3], bpt. 28 May 1767 - sp.: Peter Pulver and wife Susanna Trom (Germantown Ref. Chbk.).

ix) Johannes[3], bpt. 20 Jan 1771 - sp.: Johannes Linck and wife Anna Elisabeth Kuhn (Germantown Ref. Chbk.).

x) Gertraud[3] (Will).

10?) Anna Maria[2], a sp. to Peter Plass and Anna Elisabetha Linck in 1747 at Germantown Ref. Church.

Mr. Paul W. Prindle of Orleans, Mass. has been helpful in sorting out the complexities of the 2nd and 3rd generations of this family.

APPOLONIA LINSIN (Hunter Lists #459)

Appolonia Linsin made her initial appearance on the Hunter Lists 30 June 1710 with 3 pers. over 10 yrs. of age and 1 pers. under 10 yrs. The family was recorded with 4 over 10 yrs. and 1 under 10 on 4 Oct 1710, then with 3 over 10 yrs. on 29 Sept 1711, and 3 over 10 yrs. of age and 1 under 10 yrs. in N.Y. City on 25 March 1712. Apollonia Lintzin, wid., aged 40, Anna Catha Lintzin aged 16, Anna Margt. Lintzin aged 13, and Anna Eva Lintzin aged 6, were in N.Y. City in 1710/11 (Palatines In N.Y. City). Apolonia Linsin, a wid. with 3 ch., was in Neu-Yorck ca. 1716/17 (Simmendinger Register). Her maiden name was Houser, as Apolonia Houser, wid/o Marten Lins of Alsey, joined the N.Y. City Ref. Church 28 Aug 1711. Ch. of Martin and Appolonia[1] Lins were:

1) Anna Catharina[2] (Palatines In N.Y. City), md. Barthel Müller 25 June 1720 (N.Y. City Ref. Chbk.).

2) Anna Margaretha[2] (Palatines In N.Y. City), md. Hend: Harmanse 28 June 1724 (N.Y. City Ref. Chbk.).

3) Anna Eva[2] (Palatines In N.Y. City).

JOHANNES LORENTZ (Hunter Lists #460)

The ancestral origins of the N.J. Lorentz family were at
6729 **Bellheim** (6 km. s.w. of Germersheim; Chbks. begin 1684,
Cath., and 1706, Ref.). Joes Lorentz from Bellheim md. Anna Margaretha Heiliger, d/o Jois Heliger from Oberlustat, 13 Feb 1691
(Bellheim Cath. Chbk.). Johannes Loùrens and his wife, with (ch.)
Anna Lys, Anna Margriet, Magdelena, and 3 (additional) ch., were
passengers of Capt. Boùwel's ship in Holland in 1709 (Rotterdam
Lists). John Lorentz aged 39, with his wife, a son aged 2, and
daughters aged 14, 12, 10, 5 and 5, Ref., husbandman and vinedres-
ser, were in the Palatine group in England later that yr. (London
Lists).

Johannes Lorentz made his initial appearance on the Hunter
Lists 4 Aug 1710 with 5 pers. over 10 yrs. of age and 1 pers. under 10 yrs. Johannes Lohrentz aged 43, Anna Margaretta Lohrentz
aged 39, Anna Eliz Lohrentz aged 15, Magdalena Lohrentz aged 13,
Anna Barbara Lohrentz aged 11, and Alexander Lohrentz aged ½, were
in N.Y. City in 1710/11 (Palatines In N.Y. City). Joh[S] Laurens
and Anne Margrite his wife, with Anne Elisabeth their daughter,
from Germersheim, joined the N.Y. City Ref. Church 28 Aug 1711.
Johannes Lorentz and Anna Margretha with 6 ch. were auf dem Rarendantz ca. 1716/17 (Simmendinger Register). A lease from John Johnston and George Willocks of Perth Amboy, N.J. to Johanis Lowrance
of the Co. of Sumerset dated 1 March 1721 survives in the N.J.
Historical Society Mss., Folder 4 M 9 - 16. Johannes[1] sp. at the
Somerville Ref. and New Brunswick Ref. Churches in the 1720's.
The original family Bible of Johannes[1] survives, a copy of Sauer's
American Bible printed in 1743. The first entry in the family record reads I, Johannis Laurenz, bought this Bible for 27 shillings
in 1744; the family record there begins I was b. in 1661 md. Anna
Margaretta in 1691, and then lists the names of his ch. The will
of Johanous Lowrance of Pepack in the Co. of Sumersett, miller,
was dated 12 July 1745 and probated 3 Dec 1745 (Trenton Lib. 1,
fol. 16, also Somerset 84 R, or Will Bk. D, p. 345). It is fascinating to compare the names of the ch. and sp. at Bellheim with
those entered in the family Bible after the event (HJ). The ch.
of Johannes[1] Lorentz and his wife Anna Margaretha were:

1) Anna Apollonia[2], bpt. 12 Jan 1692 - sp.: Johannes Rohr-
   bacher and Anna Apollonia Rohrbach of Bellheim (Bellheim
   Cath. Chbk.). The Family Bible notes she was bpt. in Dec
   1692 and sp. by Felder Slenderwine in one translation and
   John Forbecker/Worbeck in another.
2) Anna Elisabetha[2], bpt. 1 March 1695 - sp.: Valentin

Schlindwein and Anna Elisabetha Schlindwein (Bellheim
Cath. Chbk.). The Family Bible notes she was b. 6 March
and bpt. 8 March 1695 - sp.: Felder Slenderwine. She md.
Bernhard Kötter (Getter, Kealer) (HJ & Will). Johannes[1]
sp. Bern: Kotter and Lisabeth in 1725 (Somerville Ref.
Chbk.).

3) Magdalena[2], bpt. 30 Jan 1698 - sp.: Magdalena - w/o Martin
Eswein of Belheim (Bellheim Cath. Chbk.). The Family Bible
gives Magalena or Matilda b. 1697 and bpt. 28 Jan 1698 -
sp.: Martin Ellerbin/Esterbein. She md. Johannes Mohr
(HJ & Will). Johannes[1] sp. Joh: Moor and Magdalena in 1721
(New Brunswick Ref. Chbk.).

4) Anna Barbara[2], bpt. 5 Sept 1700 - sp.: Hans Philipp Thyll
(Bellheim Cath. Chbk.). The Family Bible mentions she was
b. Sept 1699 and bpt. 3 Sept 1700 - sp.: Philip Steyel/
Dyel. She md. Jacob Bescherer (HJ & Will). Johannes[1] sp.
Jacob Pescheerer and Barbara in 1725 (Somerville Ref.
Chbk.).

5) Susanna[2], bpt. 22 April 1704 - sp.: Patrini Mayne and his
wife Susanna (Bellheim Cath. Chbk.).

6) Anna Margaretha[2], bpt. 22 April 1704 - sp.: Anna Margaretha Wölff (Bellheim Cath. Chbk.). These twins are not
found in the Family Bible entries (HJ).

7) Johann Jacob[2], b. 23 Aug 1707 - sp.: Hans Jacob - single
person from Zeißkam, and Anna Sybilla Klein - single person from Bellheim (Bellheim Ref. Chbk.). This child is
not found in the Family Bible.

8) Alexander[2], bpt. 11 July 1710 at N.Y. - sp.: Alex. Rosen-
quest and Elisabetha Esswein (West Camp Luth. Chbk.). The
Family Bible records his birth as 1708 & bpt. 6 or 16 Aug
1710 on the ship "Medford" - sp.: Alexander Rosinwater/
Austin, the ship's master. He was mentioned in the Janeway
Accts. 1735 - 40/41 as brother of Daniel Lorentz. Alexan-
der, John, and Daniel Lawrence are noted in the Journals
of Andrew Johnston 1743 - 1762, now in the N.J. Historical
Society. Richard and Margaret King sold land to Alexander
Lowrance of Rowan Co., N.C. 26 May 1756 (Rowan Co. Deeds:
Vol. 3, p. 315).

9) Daniel[2], b. 13 Dec 1713 - sp.: Daniel Shoemaker (Family
Bible). He md. Elisabeth Drake, d/o Abraham Drake and De-
liverance Wooden (Letter from John L. Ely).

10) Johannes[2], bpt. 15 Feb 1716 - sp.: Johannes Peter (Family
Bible). He md. Mary Perkins 1719 - 1760 and d. 23 April
1781 in Rowan Co., N.C. (Letter from John L. Ely). His will

dated 1781 is found in Rowan Co., N.C. Wills: B, 128).
Johannes was bur. in the Thyatira Presyterian Church Cem.
(John L. Fly).

The Janeway Accounts describe John Eveland, s/o the 1709er
Johann David[1] Ifflandt, as son-in-law to Hannis Lowrance and brother-in-law to John Lowrance and Jacob Wolf in an entry dated
March 1742/43; just how this entry ties into the family of Johannes[1] Lorentz is difficult to establish, as it would appear that
all of the daughters of Johannes[1] would have been listed in the
old Bible or his will (HJ).

Mr. John L. Ely of West Orange, N.J. has been of great help
in gathering data on this family, especially on those ch. of Johannes[1] Lorentz who moved away from N.J.

SEBASTIAN LÖSCHER (Hunter Lists #461)

The German origins of this prominent and prolific N.Y. family were at 6755 Hochspeyer (8 km. e. of Kaiserslautern), entries
for this town in the registers of 6719 Wattenheim (15 n.e. of
Hochspeyer; Chbks. begin 1688) and of 6753 Alsenborn (10 km. n.e.
of Kaiserslautern; Chbks. begin 1663). Bastiaen Leiser, his wife,
and (ch.) Johan Jacob, Anna Margreet, Anna Lys, Anna Bastiaens,
Hans Jury, and 5 (other) ch., were on Capt. Bouwel's ship in the
2nd party in Holland in 1709 (Rotterdam Lists). Sebastian Lescher
aged 40, his wife, sons aged 20, 14, 10, 8, and 6, daughters aged
15, 12, 6, 4, and 1, Luth., husbandman and vinedresser, were in
the 2nd arrivals in England later that yr. (London Lists).

Sebastian Löscher made his first appearance on the Hunter
Lists 4 Aug 1710 with 5 pers. over 10 yrs. of age and 4 pers. under 10 yrs. The entry read 6 over 10 and 4 under 10 yrs. on 4 Oct
1710, and 6 pers. over 10 yrs. and 3 under 10 on 31 Dec 1710. On
24 June 1711, the family was recorded with 9 pers. over 10 yrs.,
on 29 Sept 1711 with 8 pers. over 10, and on 24 Dec 1711 with 6
over 10 yrs. and 2 under 10. On 25 March 1712, Löscher was registered with 6 over 10 and 3 under 10, and on his last entry 13 Sept
1712 the emigrant was recorded with 5 pers. over 10 yrs. and 3 under 10 yrs. of age in the household. Sebastian Lescher and Elisabetha with 6 ch. were at Wormsdorff ca. 1716/17 (Simmendinger Register). Bastiaen Loeser/Losser was a Palatine Debtor in 1718, 1719
(at Kingsberry), 1721 and 1726 (Livingston Debt Lists). Bastian
Lesche was a Palatine willing to continue on the Manor 26 Aug 1724
(Doc. Hist. Of N.Y., Vol. III, p. 724). He was noted in the St.
Peter's Luth. Family List ca. 1734 (Rhinebeck Luth Chbk.). The ch.
of Sebastian[1] Löscher and (Maria) Elisabetha were:

1) <u>Johann Jacob²</u> (Rotterdam Lists).

2) <u>Anna Margaretha²</u> (Rotterdam Lists). Anna Margreth Lösch-
   erin of Hochspeyer was conf. Fest Pentecost: 1708 (Wattenheim Chbk.). She md. John (Jan) Wheeler (HJ).

3) <u>Anna Elisabetha²</u>, bpt. 3 Feb 1695 to Sebastian Lochner
   (poorly written) and Elisabeth from Hochspejer - sp.: Johannes Thebald from Hochspejer, and Anna Elisabeth - d/o
   Caspar Frantz from Alsenborn (Alsenborn Chbk.).

4) <u>Sebastian²</u> (Rotterdam Lists, as Anna Bastiaens). Sebastian
   Löscher from Germany was conf. at Albany in 1713 (N.Y.
   City Luth. Chbk.). Bast. Loser Jr. was a Palatine Debtor
   in 1718 and 1721 (Livingston Debt Lists). Sebastian² md.
   (Barbara) Elisabetha, d/o Samuel Kuhn (HJ). The will of
   Bastiaen Lesher of Livingston Manor was dated 11 June 1775
   and probated 1 Feb 1776 (<u>Fernow Wills</u> #1058). The ch. of
   Sebastian² Löscher and (Barbara) Elisabetha were:

   i) <u>Elisabetha³</u>, b. 29 Sept 1719 and bpt. at Lonenburg
   - sp.: Casper Rausch, and Pieter Ludwig and wife
   Christina (N.Y. City Luth. Chbk.). She md. Samuel
   Kuhn (HJ).

   ii) <u>Magdalena³</u> (Will), md. 4 Sept 1744 Georg Rossmann
   (Loonenburg Luth. Chbk.).

   iii) <u>Anna³</u> (Will), md. as d/o Sebastian² 23 June 1747 Peter Ben (Bain) (Germantown Ref. Chbk.).

   iv) <u>Catharina³</u>, bpt. 30 Oct 1725 - sp.: Dirck Gardenier
   and Cathrien Koens (Kinderhook Ref. Chbk.). She md.
   as d/o Sebastian² 18 Oct 1748 Johannes Rau (Germantown Ref. Chbk.).

   v) <u>Sebastian³</u>, bpt. 24 Sept 1727 - sp.: Hendrik Gardenier and Grietis (Kinderhook Ref. Chbk.). He md.
   Elisabeth Livingston (HJ).

   vi) <u>Maria³</u>, bpt. 17 Jan 1731 - sp.: Arje Gardenier and
   Engeltje V Slyck (Kinderhook Ref. Chbk.).

   vii) <u>Engel³</u>, bpt. 21 Jan 1733 - sp.: Cornelis Schermerhoorn and Lysbeth Gardenier (Kinderhook Ref. Chbk.).

   viii) <u>Samuel³</u>, b. 2 July 1735 - sp.: Markus Kuns and Anna
   Maria Loscher (Rhinebeck Luth. Chbk.). Samuel Lasher
   appeared on North East tax rolls June 1761 - June
   1765 (Dutchess Co. Tax Lists). He md. Elisabetha
   Gerritson, who d. 5 Sept 1807, aged 73-6-5 ("Pilt"
   Church Cem., Manorton). They had issue bpt. at Gallatin Ref., Linlithgo Ref., Germantown Ref., and Manorton Luth. Churches (HJ).

   ix) <u>Valentin³</u>, b. 7 May 1738 and bpt. in the father's

house at Rurian's Kill - sp.: Velten Kuhn and wife
Maria (Loonenburg Luth. Chbk.).

x) Friederich³, also b. 7 May 1738 and bpt. in father's
house at Rurian's Kill - sp.: Friderich Proper and
wife Susanna (Loonenburg Luth. Chbk.).

xi) Johann Marcus³, b. 14 March 1740 and bpt. at Teerbosch - sp.: Jo: Marcus Kuhn and wife Anna Margr.
(Loonenburg Luth. Chbk.). He md. Elisabetha Doll (HJ)
and had ch. bpt. at Manorton Luth., Gallatin Ref.,
and Linlithgo Ref. Churches (HJ).

xii) Johann Hermann³, b. 4 June 1742 and bpt. at Teerbosch
- sp.: Joh: Herman Kuhn and wife Catharina (Loonenburg Luth. Chbk.).

5) Johann Georg², md. as s/o Bastian¹ Loescher at the Camp
2 Feb 1726 Elisabetha Hemmer, an orphan (N.Y. City Luth.
Chbk.). Johann Georg Loscher was conf. at Queensberg 23
March 1712 (West Camp Luth. Chbk.). Hans Jury Losser was
a Palatine Debtor in 1726 (Livingston Debt Lists). The
ch. of Johann Georg² and Elisabetha Löscher were:

i) Elisabetha³, bpt. 19 March 1727 - sp.: Pieter Pouwer
and Elisabeth Lesser (Kingston Ref. Chbk.). She md.
12 Aug 1746 Philip Hanemann Salbach (Rhinebeck Luth.
Chbk.).

ii) Johann Sebastian³, bpt. 3 weeks old Nov 1728 at Kamp
- sp.: Johann Bastian Löscher and the w/o Conrad
Löscher (N.Y. City Luth. Chbk.). He md. Gertraud
Schultheiss (Schultes) (HJ), and they had issue bpt.
at Germantown Ref. and Germantown Luth. Churches
(HJ).

iii) Henrich³ (St. Peter's Luth. Family List), d. April
1818, aged 90 yrs. (Germantown Luth. Chbk.).

iv) Anna Maria³, bpt. 8 weeks old 11 Jan 1732 at Taar-
bosch - sp.: Johannes Bernhard Jr. and Maria Loscher (Loonenburg Luth. Chbk.). She md. Henrich Schultheiss (Schultes) (HJ).

v) Johann Georg³, b. 13 July 1735 - sp.: Georg Klum and
wife Anna Maria (Rhinebeck Luth. Chbk.). He d. 11
Sept 1831, aged 97 yrs. (Germantown Luth. Chbk.).

vi) Catharina³ (HJ), md. Peter Krein (HJ).

vii) Veronica³, bpt. 4 weeks old 2 Feb 1739 at Newton -
sp.: Philip Glum and wife Veronica (Loonenburg Luth.
Chbk.). She md. Bernhardt Schultheiss (Schultes)
(HJ).

viii) Engel³, bpt. 27 Aug 1741 - sp.: Conrad Löscher and

Engeltje Winneger (Germantown Ref. Chbk.). She md. Friederich Kramer (HJ).

ix) <u>Christina</u>[3] (HJ), md. 9 June 1767 Johannes Rau (Germantown Ref. Chbk.).

x) <u>Conrad</u>[3], b. 19 Feb 1746 - sp.: Cunrath Loescher and Elisabeth (Germantown Luth. Chbk.). He md. 24 Nov 1767 Lydia Fuhrer (Fiero) (Germantown Ref. Chbk.). They had ch. bpt. at Rhinebeck Luth. and Germantown Ref. Churches (HJ). Papers in the estate of Conuradt Lasher, late farmer of Rhinebeck, were issued to wid. Lydia and son George Lasher 16 Sept 1794 (Dutchess Co. Administrations Bk. A).

6) <u>Johann Conrad</u>[2], b. 14 Sept 1699 - sp.: Johan Conrad Becker and his wife, Hofleute auf dem Münchhof bey Hochspeyer (Wattenheim Chbk.). Conrad Loscher was conf. Easter 1714 at Queensberg (West Camp Luth. Chbk.). Coenradt Losser was a Palatine Debtor in 1726 (Livingston Debt Lists). Coenrat Lasser was a freeholder at East Camp in 1763 (Albany Co. Freeholders). He md. Anna Engel Wenniger (HJ) and had issue:

i) <u>Sebastian</u>[3], md. as s/o Conrad[2] 4 April 1749 Maria Schumacher (Germantown Ref. Chbk.). He was the eldest s/o Conrad[2] on the entries for the family on St. Peter's Luth. Family List ca. 1734 (Rhinebeck Luth. Chbk.). Sebastian[3] and (Anna) Maria had issue bpt. at Germantown Ref., Linlithgo Ref., Germantown Luth., and Loonenburg Luth. Churches (HJ).

ii) <u>Johannes</u>[3], bpt. 7 weeks old 11 Aug 1726 at Haneman Saalbachs at Kamp - sp.: Jos. Bast. Loscher - paternal grandfather, and Anna Winniger - maternal grandmother (N.Y. City Luth. Chbk.). He md. Anna Maria Dillenbach 27 Sept 1763 (Stone Arabia Ref. Chbk.), and they had among their ch. a son Conrad (HJ).

iii) <u>Johann Conrad</u>[3], bpt. 6 weeks old 18 Jan 1731 at Camp - sp.: Conrad Schneider - standing for him the father Henr. Schneider, and A. M. Loschers (Loonenburg Luth. Chbk.). He md. Christina Batz (Potts) (HJ). Papers in the estate of Conrad Lasher, deceased, farmer, were issued to Christina Lasher, wid., 14 April 1796 (Columbia Co. Administrations Bk. B).

iv) <u>Johann Gerhardt</u>[3], b. 29 Dec 1732 and bpt. Newton - sp.: Gerrit Weiniger and Margrete Sneider (Loonenburg Luth. Chbk.). Gerret Lesher was in Soverinus Deyger's Company at German Flatts 24 July 1763 (<u>Report of the</u>

State Historian, Vol. II, p. 793). He md. Catharina
Dillenbach (HJ).

v) Anna Maria³, b. 17 Feb 1735 - sp.: Christ. Diederich and wife Anna Maria (Rhinebeck Luth. Chbk.). She
d. single 15 March 1813, aged 77 yrs. (Germantown
Luth. Chbk.).

vi) Veronica³, md. as d/o Conrad² 31 Jan 1758 Georg Batz
(Potts) (Germantown Ref. Chbk.).

vii) Johann Georg³, b. 1 Jan 1739 and bpt. Newton - sp.:
Jurge Löscher and wife Lisabeth (Loonenburg Luth.
Chbk.). He md. Barbara Batz (Potts) (HJ). They had
issue bpt. at Germantown Ref. and Luth. Churches (HJ).

7) Anna Maria², b. 30 Jan 1702 and bpt. at Hochspeyer - sp.:
Johan Dietrich Billig the shepherd at Keysers Laudtern
and Anna Maria, his wife (Wattenheim Chbk.). She md. Marcus Kuhn (HJ); the w/o Marx Kuhn d. 8 Nov 1793 (Manorton
Chbk.).

8) Anna Barbara² (HJ), md. 9 Nov 1724 Andreas Wiederwachs
(Kingston Ref. Chbk.).

9) Johann Melchior², b. 8 April 1706 - sp.: Melchior Löscher
and Maria Elisabeth, a couple at Rothenbach bey Keysers
Lauthern (Wattenheim Chbk.).

10) Anna Catharina², b. 15 June 1708 - sp.: Wilhelm Wieser
the hunter, and Anna Catharina Wieser at Frankenstein
(Wattenheim Chbk.).

11) Maria Elisabetha², bpt. 1 June 1710 on the ship Midfort
- sp.: Johann Müller and wife Elisabeth (West Camp Luth.
Chbk.). A Maris Litser joined the Kinderhook Ref. Church
26 March 1723, and an Elyz: Lescher joined the same congregation 5 Sept 1724 (Kinderhook Ref. Chbk.). Eileen
Lasher Powers states she md. Cornelius Van Buren.

12) Johannes² (HJ), conf. as Hannes Löscher on Misericordia
Sunday 1726 at the Kamp (N.Y. City Luth. Chbk.). Johannes
may have been the Johann Melchior² bpt. in 1706, however,
his conf. date and advanced age when he sired his last
ch. make him fit better as the youngest ch. of Sebastian¹
(HJ). Johannes² was still listed in the family of Sebas-
tian¹ ca. 1734 in the St. Peter's Luth. Family List
(Rhinebeck Luth. Chbk.). Johannes Lesser was a freeholder
at East Camp in 1763 (Albany Co. Freeholders). Johannes,
Adam, and Philip Lescher were enrolled in Capt. Frederick
Kortz's Company at East Camp 12 May 1767 (Report of the
State Historian, Vol. II, p. 869). The will of Johannis
Lasher of Germantown was dated 3 Aug 1795 and probated

16 Nov 1796 (Columbia Co. Will Bk. A). Johannes[2] md. 1st
Anna Maria Klum (HJ) and had ch.:

   i) <u>Veronica[3]</u>, b. 5 April 1738 and bpt. at the Camp -
      sp.: Philip Glum and wife Veronica (Loonenburg Luth.
      Chbk.). She possibly md. Wilhelm Batz (Potts) (HJ).

  ii) <u>Elisabetha[3]</u>, b. 9 Nov 1739 and bpt. at Newton - sp.:
      Hans Jurge Loscher and Anna Maria (Loonenburg Luth.
      Chbk.). She md. Peter Zipperle (HJ).

 iii) <u>Philip[3]</u>, bpt. 7 Oct 1741 - sp.: Philippus Klom and
      wife Veronica Klom (Germantown Ref. Chbk.). A Philip
      Lescher md. Gertraud Blass, wid., 16 April 1770, and
      a Philip Lescher md. Elisabeth Schumacher 8 Oct 1771
      (both Germantown Ref. Chbk.).

  iv) <u>Anna Margaretha[3]</u>, b. 25 April 1743 and bpt. the Camp
      - sp.: Henr. Glum and Gritje Conradse (Loonenburg
      Luth. Chbk.). She md. Dieterich Schultheiss (Schul-
      tes) (HJ).

   v) <u>Anna Maria[3]</u>, bpt. 24 May 1746 - sp.: Marcus Kuhn and
      Anna Maria Kuhn (Germantown Ref. Chbk.).

  vi) <u>Adam[3]</u> (HJ), md. 1st Elisabetha (--) (HJ), and md.
      2nd Catharina Schumacher (HJ). This family appears
      in N.Y. State D.A.R. Bible Records Vol. 49 (HJ).

 vii) <u>Catharina[3]</u>, bpt. 23 July 1749 - sp.: Philip Klum and
      Catharina Klum (Germantown Ref. Chbk.). She probably
      md. Wilhelm Kramer (HJ).

viii) <u>Johann Sebastian[3]</u>, b. 3 Oct 1752 - sp.: John C. Hart-
      wick and Maria Loescher (Germantown Luth. Chbk.).

Johannes[2] Löscher md. 2nd as a widower Christina Holzapfel
6 April 1756 (Germantown Ref. Chbk.). This couple often
sp. children of Johannes[2] from his 1st marriage. The ch.
of Johannes[2] and his 2nd wife Christina were:

  ix) <u>Johannes[3]</u> (Will) (There is some question as to just
      which mother Johannes[3] had: Anna Maria or Christina?
      - HJ).

   x) <u>Wilhelm[3]</u>, b. 24 Jan 1762 - sp.: Wm: Holtzapfel and
      E. Blass (Germantown Luth. Chbk.).

  xi) <u>Marcus[3]</u>, b. 4 Jan 1764 - sp.: Marc: Kuhn and Ann
      (Germantown Luth. Chbk.).

 xii) <u>Petrus[3]</u>, b. 12 July 1765 - sp.: Johannes Blass and
      his wife Gertraut Holtzappel (Germantown Ref. Chbk.).

xiii) <u>Gertraud[3]</u>, bpt. 22 Jan 1769 - sp.: Wilhelmus Holtz-
      appel and Gerdraut Holtzappel (Germantown Ref. Chbk.).

 xiv) <u>Zacharias[3]</u>, bpt. 14 Dec 1771 - sp.: Zacharias Holtz-
      appel and wife Gritjen Leick (Germantown Ref. Chbk.).

xv) <u>Christina</u>³, bpt. 8 Jan 1774 - sp.: Wilh: Rakkefeller
and wife Margaretha Bahr (Germantown Ref. Chbk.).

xvi) <u>Conrad</u>³, bpt. 11 April 1775 - sp.: Conrad Lescher
and wife Engel Winniger (Germantown Ref. Chbk.).

Eileen Lasher Powers has published a detailed history of
this interesting family: <u>Lasher Lineage</u>. She and David Jay Webber are to be congratulated for their efforts in sorting out the
family lines of this group, probably the most complex and prolific of all the 847 families who arrived in colonial N.Y. in
1710 (HJ).

JACOB LÖSCHER (Hunter Lists #462)

The European roots of this family were at 6663 <u>Dellfeld</u> (8
km. e. of Zweibrücken), entries in the registers of 6661 <u>Riesch-
weiler</u> (2 km. n. of Dellfeld; Chbks. begin 1683). Johann Jacob
Löscher, s/o the late Samuel Löscher - weaver in Dellfeldt, md.
8 Nov 1698 Susanna, d/o the late Stephan Schläppy of St. Stephan
in Berner Gebiets in the Eydt-Genossenschaft. Hanß Jacob Loescher
from Dellfeld was on an emigrant list from the Duchy of Zweibrück-
en, 1709 (<u>Emigrants from the Palatinate to the American Colonies
in the 18th Century</u>, by Krebs and Rubincam, p. 31). The Rieschweiler Chbks. called Johann Jacob Löscher a linenweaver in 1703.

Johann Jacob Lescher made his initial appearance on the Hunter Lists 4 July 1710 with 2 pers. over 10 yrs. of age and 2 pers.
under 10 yrs. The entry for 24 June 1712 read 2 pers. over 10
and 3 pers. under 10 yrs. of age in the household. Jacob Löscher's
Wid. with 4 ch. was at Heessberg ca. 1716/17 (Simmendinger Register). The ch. of Jacob¹ Löscher and Susanna were:

1) <u>Johann Jacob</u>², b. Dellfeld and bpt. 13 Aug 1699 - sp.:
Joh. Thomas - s/o H. Thomas Senden the weaver in Dell-
feld, Jacob - s/o Stephan Schlappß from S. Stephan in
Berner Gebiet, and Apollonia - w/o Henrich Buchman the
Gemeinsmann in Delfeldt (Rieschweiler Chbk.).

2) <u>Anna Elisabetha</u>², bpt. 20 Dec 1701 - sp.: Joh. Adam -
s/o Joh. Jacob Rothhaar the Censor at Dellf., Joh. Daniel
- s/o Benedict Brüderlein from Kießbach, Anna Elisabeth
- d/o Adam Thaal from Contwig, and Anna Apollonia - w/o
Ulrich Schmidt from Dietrichingen (Rieschweiler Chbk.).

3) <u>Anna Maria</u>², bpt. 1 April 1703 - sp.: Anna Maria - w/o
Joh. Jacob Weydhess (?) the linenweaver at Rieschweiler,
Anna Maria, d/o the late Thomas Gelane (?) at Dellfeld,
Henrich Buchmann - Gemeinsmann there, and Martin Schärer
the Gemeinsmann at Mühlbach (Rieschweiler Chbk.). As I

noted in the section on #461 Sebastian[1] Löscher, a Maris
Litser was conf. 26 March 1723 at Kinderhook Ref. Church;
it is difficult to establish to which family she belongs
(HJ).

4) Susanna[2], bpt. 21 Sept 1704 - sp.: Görg Frantz - ...
bricklayer, Anna Ottilia - d/o Ulrich Schmidt from Dietrichingen, and Benedicta - d/o the late Stephan Schlappy
from St. Stephan in Berner Herrschaft (Rieschweiler
Chbk.).

5) Johann Adam[2], bpt. 11 Sept 1707 - sp.: M. Joh. Jacob Weyd-
tler - linenweaver and Gerichtsschöffe at Rieschweiler,
Adam Thegal (?) - Gemeinsmann in Contwig, Benedict Brüderlein at Kießbach (?), Anna Ottilia - w/o the linenweaver
M. Joh. Thomas Sindten at Nünschweiler, and Maria Margaretha - w/o Joh. Jacob Gelan at Dellfeldt (Rieschweiler
Chbk.).

6) Henrich[2] (HJ), a sp. with Susanna Litcher to Petrus Jeral-
man and Elisabeth Litscher in 1751/52 at Kinderhook Ref.
Church. He md. Anna Huyck (HJ) and had issue:
   i) Susanna[3], bpt. 28 May 1737 - sp.: J. Witbeek and M.
      Wyngaart (Albany Ref. Chbk.).
   ii) Gertraud[3], bpt. 18 Jan 1739 at Sch. - sp.: Willem
       Lievense and Magiel Quackenbos (Albany Ref. Chbk.).
   iii) Catharina[3], bpt. 7 June 1741 - sp.: Andries Huyk and
        Elizabeth Van Renzelaar (Albany Ref. Chbk.).
   iv) Maria[3], bpt. 11 Jan 1743/44 - sp.: Hendrik Bovie and
       Catharina Huyk (Albany Ref. Chbk.).
   v?) Jacob[3]. Jacob and Cornelis Letcher were listed above
       Poesten Kill in Capt. Abraham Van Aernam's Company
       in 1767 (Report of the State Historian, Vol. II, p.
       811).
   vi) Cornelius[3], bpt. 29 Feb 1749 - sp.: Pieter Van Buren
       Jr. and Margareeta Van Schaak (Kinderhook Ref.
       Chbk.).
   vii) Christina[3], bpt. 29 May 1752 - sp.: Gerrit Bovie
        and Christina Huyck (Albany Ref. Chbk.).
   viii) Johannes[3], bpt. 19 March 1758 - sp.: Johannis Hogen
         and Catharina Lansing (Albany Ref. Chbk.).
7) Anna Elisabetha[2], bpt. 1715 - 1718 - sp.: Robbert Wielaer
   and Maryia (Kinderhook Ref. Chbk.). She md. Peter Jeral-
   mann (HJ).

Later generations of this family are found in the chbks. of
Gilead Luth. at Centre Brunswick and Schaghticoke Ref. Churches
(HJ).

ANNA CATHARINA LOTTIN (Hunter Lists #463)

Anna Catharina, wid/o Johann Peter Lutt of Wald-Lebersheim
near Bingen in the earldom Schomburg, md. Johann Wilhelm Hanbuch,
widower of Nider Biber in the commune of Neuwid, 2 July 1717 (West
Camp Luth. Chbk.). The ancestral village was 6531 Waldlaubersheim
(5 km. s.w. of Bingen; Chbks. begin 1576, Luth.). The earliest
known ancestor of the American line was Johannes Lüth, Gerichtsmann at Schweppenhausen. Nicolaus Lüth, s/o Johannes Lüth - Gerichtsmann at Schweppenhausen, md. Anna Catharina, d/o Peter Wolt
- Gerichtsmann there, 2 Feb 1669 at Schweppenhausen. Hanß Peter
Lud from Schweppenhausen, s/o the Schultheiß Niclaß Lud, was conf.
in 1691. Hanß Peter Lud, s/o Niclaß Lud from Schweppenhausen, md.
Anna Catharina, d/o Johannes Coblentzer, 23 Sept 1704; this probably was a 2nd marriage for Hanß Peter[1] Lud (HJ). Anna Catharina,
d/o Joh. Coblentzer, was bpt. 24 June 1666 - sp.: Thielmann
Schultheiß, his wife Catharina, and Anna - w/o Joh. Urban. Anna
Catharina Coblentzer from Waldlaubersheim was conf. in 1685. Johannes, s/o Godhard Coblentzer, md. Elisabetha, d/o Niclas Schwei-
sen (?) at ..., 3 July 1662. Gotthard Coblentzer was bur. 10 Oct
1690, aged 91 yrs., and his wife Maria was bur. 10 Jan 1673. Other
Coblentzers came to America, as Elisabetha Margretha Coblentzer,
d/o the late Johann Peter by Bingen, md. Peter Schmidt 1 Aug 1710
(West Camp Luth. Chbk.); Peter Schmidt sp. Balthasar[2] Lott in 1729
at Kamp (N.Y. City Luth. Chbk.). The Waldlaubersheim registers
show that Hans Peter Coblentzer md. Margreth, d/o Peter Poß, 24
Jan 1671, and that Johan Peter Coblentzer was bur. 9 May 1691,
aged 44 yrs.; his daughter Elisabetha Margaretha Coblentzer was
conf. in 1698. Hans Peter Loet and his wife, with (ch.) Balthazer
Loet and 2 (additional) ch., were on Capt Bouwel's ship in Holland
in the 2nd party of 1709 (Rotterdam Lists). John Peter Lutt aged
29, with his wife, a son aged 11, daughters aged 3 and ½, Luth.,
husbandman and vinedresser, were in the 2nd arrivals in England
later that yr. (London Lists).

Anna Catharina Lothin made her initial appearance on the Hunter Lists 4 Aug 1710 with 2 pers. over 10 yrs. of age and 2 pers.
under 10 yrs. Anna Catharina Lutin, a wid. with 3 ch., was at
Heessberg ca. 1716/17 (Simmendinger Register). She and her 2nd
husband appeared on the St. Peter's Luth. Family List ca. 1734
(Rhinebeck Luth. Chbk.). A child of Hanß Peter[1] Lutt, probably by
a 1st wife, was:

1) Balthasar[2] (Rotterdam Lists), conf. as Barthas Lutt 30 A-
pril 1711 at the new German colony (West Camp Luth. Chbk.).
Baltus Lott was nat. 8 and 9 Sept 1715 (Kingston Nats.).

Baltus Lott was a Palatine Debtor in 1721 (Livingston Debt
Lists). Baltus Lott made his first appearance on tax rolls
in the Middle Ward in 1726/27; he was enrolled in 1745/46
at Crum Elbow, and from Feb 1753 to Feb 1756 at North
East, when his wid. took over the entry (all Dutchess Co.
Tax Lists). He and his family appeared on the St. Peter's
Luth. Family List ca. 1734, next to Michael Rau and family
(Rhinebeck Luth. Chbk.). Balthasar[2] md. Elisabetha (--);
she possibly was a Rau, judging from a sp. at Pine Plains
in 1774 (HJ). They had issue:

i) <u>Andreas[3]</u> (St. Peter's Family List), conf. as Andreas
Lot 15 May 1740 at Goghamek. (Loonenburg Luth Chbk.).
He was on Crum Elbow tax rolls in 1745/46, and on
rolls at North East from Feb 1753 until June 1760,
when his farm was listed (all Dutchess Co. Tax
Lists). He md. 1st Christina (--), and md. 2nd Anna
Maria Sarenberger 24 May 1752 (Rhinebeck Luth. Chbk.).
Andreas[3] had issue bpt. at Loonenburg Luth., Rhine-
beck Luth., Churchtown Luth., and Gallatin Ref.
Churches (HJ).

ii) <u>Sophia[3]</u> (St. Peter's Luth. Family List), conf. as
Sophia Lootin 12 May 1743 at Ankrum (Loonenburg Luth.
Chbk.). She md. Philip Rau 10 Jan 1748 (Germantown
Ref. Chbk.).

iii) <u>Maria[3]</u>, bpt 21 May 1727 - sp.: Joost Bernhardt and
Marytje Lott (Linlithgo Ref. Chbk.). She was conf. at
Ankrum 3 May 1744 (Loonenburg Luth. Chbk.). She md.
Friederich Sarenberger (HJ).

iv) <u>Peter[3]</u>, bpt. 5 weeks old 3 May 1729 at Kamp - sp.:
Peter Schmid and wife Liesabeth (N.Y. City Luth.
Chbk.).

v) <u>Elisabetha[3]</u>, md. as d/o Balthas[2] 10 Feb 1754 Johannes
Deder (Rhinebeck Luth. Chbk.). Lisabeth and Catharina
Lottin were conf. at Theerbosch 16 Sept 1750 (Loonen-
burg Luth. Chbk.).

vi) <u>Anna Catharina[3]</u>, b. Feb 1735 - sp.: Carl Tenerly and
wife Maria Utalia (Rhinebeck Luth. Chbk.). She md.
Georg Sarenberger (HJ).

vii) <u>Margaretha[3]</u>, bpt. 3 months old 30 Oct 1737 - sp.:
Catharina - d/o Andreas Bartels, and Jo. Philip
Spickerman (Loonenburg Luth. Chbk.). She md. Johannes
Bartel (HJ).

viii) <u>Philip[3]</u>, b. 24 March 1740 and bpt. Goghkem. - sp.:
Philip Neiss and Maria Catharina Schmid (Loonenburg

Luth. Chbk.). He was on tax rolls at North East 1774 - 1779 (Dutchess Co. Tax Lists). He md. Elisabetha Sarenberger (HJ), and they had ch. bpt. at Gallatin Ref. and Pine Plains Churches (HJ).

    ix) <u>Johannes[3]</u>, b. 10 April 1743 and bpt. Ankrum - sp.: Henr. Balth. Bartels and Lisabeth Bartels (Loonenburg Luth. Chbk.). John Loot was in Capt. Jeremiah Hogeboom's Company in 1767 (<u>Report of the State Historian</u>, Vol. II, p. 863). Reid's <u>Loyalists In Ontario</u>, pp. 182 - 183, notes a John Lott Sr. of Thurlow and Sidney. Johannes[3] md. Eva (--) (HJ).

    x) <u>Susanna[3]</u>, b. 8 Dec 1746 - sp.: Nicolas Raw and wife Susanna, and Henrich Wineger (Rhinebeck Luth. Chbk.).

Hanß Peter[1] Lutt and his wife Anna Catharina[1] had ch.:

    2) <u>Anna Maria[2]</u>, bpt. 9 Aug 1705 - sp.: Johann Niclas Lud - his brother from Schweppenhausen, Anna Maria Ebert (?), and Anna Lucia Heintz, all three single (Waldlaubersheim Chbk.). Anna Maria and Maria Otelia Looten were conf. together Misericordia Sunday: 1726 at the Kamp (N.Y. City Luth. Chbk.). She md. Michael Rau (HJ).

    3) <u>Maria Ottilia[2]</u>, bpt. 13 May 1708 - sp.: Hans Henrich Grätz and his wife Anna Ottilia, and the Widow Margaretha Indox (Waldlaubersheim Chbk.). She md. Charles Dannerly (Tenderly) 15 June 1728 (Kingston Ref. Chbk.). They were listed on the St. Peter's Luth. Family List ca. 1734 (Rhinebeck Luth. Chbk.).

GEORG LUCAS (Hunter Lists #464)

Hans Görg lukas, his wife, and 7 ch. were on Capt. Leonard Allan's ship in the 5th party of Palatines in Holland in 1709 (Rotterdam Lists).

Georg Lucas made his initial appearance on the Hunter Lists 1 July 1710 with 2 pers. over 10 yrs. and 1 pers. under 10 yrs. of age. The entry for 4 Aug 1710 showed 3 over 10 and 1 under 10 yrs., and the notation for 4 Oct 1710 read 6 pers. over 10 yrs. and 1 under 10 yrs.

There are several unplaced Lucases who may have descended from Georg[1]: 1) a Johann Dewald Lucas and wife Christyne had a son Johann Daniel b. 16 March 1733 and bpt. at Newton - sp.: Johann Daniel Lickhard and Gritge Maurer (Loonenburg Luth. Chbk.); they were mentioned in a dispute in <u>Albany Protocol</u>; 2) a Johannes Lucas md. as a widower of Heidelberg 12 Oct 1728 Elisabeth Pipes, wid/o Timoth[S] Paerker of Pa. (N.Y. City Ref. Chbk.); and

3) a Jan Stevense Luykas, who sp. Sam: Berrie in 1723 (N.Y. City
Ref. Chbk.). There were Lucasz family members who arrived pre-1709
also (HJ).

FRANCOIS LUCAS (Hunter Lists #465)

This Huguenot - Palatine family was documented at 6754 <u>Otter-</u>
<u>berg</u> (6 km. n. of Kaiserslautern; Chbks. begin 1657, French-Ref.)
and at 6800 <u>Seckenheim/Mannheim</u> (18 km. n. of Speyer; Chbks. begin 1641, Erlöser-Kirche Ref.). The father of the 1709er was <u>Jean</u>
<u>Lucas</u>, who md. Elizabeth Rollaire. They had ch.:

<u>Marie</u>, b. 21 July 1657 - sp.: Jean Profit et Thomas Samler,
Marie Colliner femme au dit Jean profit (Otterberg Chbk.).
She d. as veuve de defunt Danjel Bonquian 2 Dec 1720, aged
63 yrs. and 4 months (Otterberg Chbk.).

<u>Jean</u>, b. 24 May 1661 - sp.: Jean Dupont et ... la femme à
Thomas Hamlet (?), and Marguirite Collet - jeune fille (Otterberg Chbk.).

+ <u>Francois</u>, b. 8 Aug 1663 - sp.: Francois Maumont, Philippe
Rolar, and Marie Jeanne Rousin, femme de Jean Bodet (Otterberg Chbk.).

Francois Lucas, heune homme, md. Marie Baudouin, jeune fille, in
Nov 1688 (Otterberg Chbk.). Marie Baudouin, d/o Arnolt Baudouin
and Marie Menton, was b. 29 March 1668 - sp.: Johannes Leib, Jean
Hubert, Catharine lourbié - femme à Paul Baudouin, and Susanne -
femme à Michel Heitmiller (Otterberg Chbk.). Arnoult Baudouin d.
25 Jan 1681, aged 43 yrs. (Otterberg Chbk.). In the Seckenheim
Chbk. in 1696, Franz Lucas was called from Otterberg; in the Otterberg Chbk. in 1709, he was called of Frankenthal. Francis Lucas
aged 46, his wife, sons aged 17 and 11, daughters aged 19, 8, 6,
3, and 3 (twins), Ref., cloth and linnenweaver, were in the 1st
arrivals in England in 1709 (London Lists).

Francois Lucas made his first appearance on the Hunter Lists
with 3 pers. over 10 yrs. of age and 3 pers. under 10 on 4 Aug
1710. His entry in N.Y. City on 25 March 1712 read 5 over 10 yrs.
and 3 under 10, and on 24 June 1712 in N.Y. City was 4 over 10
and 3 under 10 yrs. He had a special subsistence 23 Sept 1713
for 77 ddies at 4 over 10 and 3 under 10 yrs. of age. Frantz Lucas
aged 38 was at New Rochelle with Mr. Chadden, with Maria Eliz.
Lucas, his daughter, aged 20, Frantz Lucas aged 13, Anna Maria Lucas aged 9, Anne Lucas aged 7, and Anna Catharina Lucas aged 4,
in 1710/11 (Palatines In N.Y. City). Francois Lucas, widower of
Pals, md. Elisabeth Engeler, wid/o J^S Lampert, 9 Aug 1711 (N.Y.
City Ref. Chbk.). Frantz Lucas, a widower with 5 ch., was auf dem

Rarendantz ca. 1716/17 (Simmendinger Register). The ch. of Francois[1] Lucas were:

1) <u>Maria Elisabetha</u>[2] (Palatines In N.Y. City). She sp. the bpt. of Maria Elizabeth, d/o Jeremias Schletzer and his wife Maria Bisscher, 7 April 1709 in Holland (Rotterdam Luth. Chbk.). Maria Elisabetha Lucas, single woman of Frankendaal, md. Herman Rickman 11 Dec 1712 (N.Y. City Ref. Chbk.).

2) <u>Isaac</u>[2], bpt. 12 Aug 1696 - sp.: Isaac Besancon - bachelor at Neu-Mannheim, and Maria - d/o Joseph Bleude the smith at Seckenheim (Seckenheim Chbk.). Franz and Maria Lucas were called from Otterberg in this bpt. entry (HJ).

3) <u>Frantz Jacob</u>[2], bpt. 8 Dec 1697 - sp.: Franz Jacob Erhart - s/o the late Erhard the gardener, and Anna Ursula Müller - d/o the late Müller, all at Seckenheim (Seckenheim Chbk.). Jacob Lucas, fils de Francois Lucas - demeurant à Frankenthal, sp. in the family Bonqueau in Feb 1709 at Otterberg. He was noted in the Janeway Accounts 1735 - 1746. Frantz (Jacob)[2] md. Jannetje Aten (HJ) and had ch.:

   i) <u>Aaron</u>[3], called s/o Francis in the Janeway Accounts.
   ii) <u>Maria</u>[3], bpt. 20 Feb 1723 (Somerville Ref. Chbk.).
   iii) <u>Elsche</u>[3], so bpt. 29 Aug 1725 (Somerville Ref. Chbk.).
   iv) <u>Frantz</u>[3], bpt. 17 Sept 1727 (Somerville Ref. Chbk.). Perhaps he was the Frans Lucas who md. Elizabeth (--) and had issue bpt. at Readington in 1748/49 (HJ).
   v) <u>Elisabetha</u>[3], bpt. 25 Aug 1733 (Somerville Ref. Chbk.).
   vi) <u>Abraham</u>[3], bpt. 16 Feb 1735/36 (Somerville Ref. Chbk.).
   vii) <u>Hilletje</u>[3], bpt. 2 Sept 1744 (Readington Ref. Chbk.).
   viii) <u>Hilletje</u>[3], bpt. 3 May 1747 (Readington Ref. Chbk.). Chambers adds a son <u>Thomas</u>[3], bpt. 6 Sept 1730, and a daughter <u>Elsye</u>[3], bpt. 4 Dec 1737, both at Somerville Ref. Church (HJ).

4) <u>Anna Maria</u>[2] (Palatines In N.Y. City).
5) <u>Anna</u>[2] (Palatines In N.Y. City).
6) <u>Anna Catharina</u>[2] (Palatines In N.Y. City).

There was a Jan Lafas and wife Francentje who had a son Isaac bpt. 12 June 1723 (Somerville Ref. Chbk.); no connective has been found between this couple and the emigrant Francois[1] Lucas (HJ).

JOHANN HENRICH LUDWIG (Hunter Lists #466)

Henrig lodewÿk, his wife, and 4 ch. were on Capt. Thomas
Keÿ's ship in Holland in the 5th party of Palatines in 1709 (Rotterdam Lists). However, the emigrant who arrived in colonial N.Y.
probably was the Johan Henrig Ludwig with wife and 2 ch. in the
4th party on the Rotterdam Lists (HJ). Henry Ludwig aged 40, his
wife, and sons aged 18 and 10, Luth., husbandman and vinedresser,
were in the 4th arrivals in England later that yr. (London Lists);
this Henry Ludwig was but a few names from Jacob Eschwein in the
4th arrivals at London, and the N.Y. Johann Henrich[1] Ludwig was
listed next to Jacob Eschwein's family on the Simmendinger Register ca. 1716/17. The juxtaposition of names near Johann Henrich[1]
on originals of the Hunter Lists (i.e. Niclaus Michael, Philipp
Laux, Balthasar Anspach) strongly suggest his German origins were
in the Taunus/Weilburg region of Germany (HJ). A man perfectly
matching the age of the Henry Ludwig at London was found in the
home village of so many other N.Y. emigrants at 6394 Grävenwiesbach, the home of Philipp (Launhardt) Laux in the heart of the
theorized area. The father of this Grävenwiesbach man was Nickel
Ludwig, conf. in 1665 at the age of 12½. Nickel Ludwig, a boy of
15 yrs., md. Elisabetha, a girl also of 15 yrs., 28 Jan 1668; they
had a son Johann Henrich b. at Mönstat and bpt. at Grävenwiesbach
20 Nov 1670. Johann Henrich Ludwig, a shepherd from Grävenwiesbach,
had daughters Maria Elisabeth, bpt. 8 March 1702, and Anna Elisabeth, bpt. 14 Dec 1704, at 6251 Oberneisen near Diez. I feel a bit
more proof still is needed to verify that the Grävenwiesbach Henry[1]
was indeed the N.Y. settler, but circumstantial evidence looks
good at this point that they were the same man (HJ).

Johann Henrich Ludwig made his first appearance on the Hunter
Lists 30 June 1710 with 2 pers. over 10 yrs. in the household. The
entry for 25 March 1711 read 4 pers. over 10 yrs, for 24 June 1711
showed 3 over 10 and 1 under 10, and for 25 March 1712 noted 2
pers. over 10 and 1 under 10 in the family. The 24 June 1712 entry
recorded 3 pers. over 10 yrs. and 1 under 10 yrs. of age. Hendrick
Lodwick was nat. 17 Jan 1715/16 (Albany Nats.). Heinrich Ludwig
with wife and ch. was at Hunderston ca. 1716/17 (Simmendinger Register). Hendrik Lodwik was a Palatine Debtor in 1718, 1721, and
1726 (Livingston Debt Lists). Hendrick Lodowick was a freeholder
of Albany Co. at Claverack in 1720 (Albany Co. Freeholders). Hen.
Lodwick was recorded on a list of cattle sold in 1722 on Reel #5
of the Livingston Papers. The ch. of the N.Y. Johann Henrich[1] Ludwig were:

1) Johann Peter[2], (HJ), nat. 28 Feb 1715/16 (Albany Nats.).

He md. Christina Rausch (HJ) and had issue:

    i) Caspar[3] (HJ), md. 18 July 1751 Maria Spoor (Albany Ref. Chbk.). Maria Spoor, w/o Casparus Lodewyk joined the Kinderhook Ref. Church 17 Feb 1753. They had ch. bpt. at Kinderhook Ref. and Shodack Ref. Churches (HJ).

Johann Peter[2] md. 2nd Maria Schantz (HJ) and had a child:

    ii) Andreas[3], bpt. 8 Nov 1744 - sp.: ... and Catharina Schans (Kinderhook Ref. Chbk.).

2?) Elisabetha[2], md. Joseph Steppins by 1725 (HJ).

MAGDALENA LUTZIN (Hunter Lists #467)

Anna Magdalena, wid/o Johann Christoph Lutz of Klingen-Munster in the Pfaltz, md. Johann Peter Glopp, tailor of Horn in the commune of Simmern in the Pfaltz, 12 Sept 1711 (West Camp Luth. Chbk.). Christoph Lutz (alone) aged 36, Ref., cooper and brewer, was in the 2nd arrivals in England with the Palatines of 1709 (London Lists).

Magdalena Lutzin made her initial appearance on the Hunter Lists 4 Oct 1710 with 2 pers. over 10 yrs. of age in the household.

ANNA BARBARA LUTZIN (Hunter Lists #468)

Anna Barbara Lutzin had but two entries in the Journal section of the Hunter Lists: on 31 Dec 1710 and 25 March 1711 with 2 pers. over 10 yrs. of age in the family.

A Mathys Luys (?) and wife Catharine Lasher had a daughter Catharina bpt. 7 Feb 1743 (?) at the Poughkeepsie Ref. Church, but no connective between him and any Lutz 1709er has been established (HJ).

ELEONORA MADEBACHIN (Hunter Lists #469)

Perhaps this N.Y. woman was a survivor of the family of Dirk Maybag, his wife, and 3 ch., in the 4th party in Holland in 1709 (HJ).

Eleonora Madebachin had but one listing on the Hunter Rolls: 4 Oct 1710 with 1 pers. over 10 yrs. of age.

CONRAD MAISINGER (Hunter Lists #470)

Koenraat Meinsinger, his wife, and 1 child, were recorded amidst other N.J. 1709ers (i.e. Johan Deis, Kristiaan Worms, Peter Wannemager, Bastiaan Minsinger, and Johan Philips Riger) on

Capt. Leonard Allan's ship in Holland in 1709 (Rotterdam Lists).

Conrad Maisinger made his initial appearance on the Hunter Lists 1 July 1710 with 2 pers. over 10 yrs. of age. His entry on 31 Dec 1710 read 2 over 10 and 1 under 10, and for 25 March 1711 was 2 over 10 yrs. On 24 June 1711 the family was recorded with 2 pers. over 10 yrs. and 2 pers. under 10, on 24 June 1712 with 2 over 10 and 3 under 10 yrs., and finally on 13 Sept 1712 with 3 over 10 and 3 under 10 yrs. Cond. Maisinger of Annsberg was a soldier in 1711 (Palatine Volunteers To Canada). The name of Conrard Meissinger appears often in the Ramapo Tract Account Book. Conrad Meusinger and Anna Margretha with 5 ch. were listed next to Nicolaus Meusinger ca. 1716/17 at Hackensack (Simmendinger Register). They sp. many ch. in N.J. over the yrs. One sp. in the Hackensack Chbk. in 1714 mentions Margrita, w/o Koenraet Miggiel, and the same bpt. as entered in the N.Y. City Luth. Chbk. notes Anna Margareta Meysingers; this strongly suggests that the father of Conrad[1] Maisinger was named Michael (HJ). Conrad[1] Maisinger md. Anna Margaretha, d/o Adam Wannemacher, (HJ) and had ch.:

1) <u>Peter[2]</u> (Janeway Account Book). He md. Charlotta (--) (HJ) and had a son:

    i) <u>Conrad[3]</u>, b. 12 Nov 1738 and bpt. at Raretons at Daniel Schomachers - sp.: Conrad Meisinger and Anna Margaretha (N.Y. City Luth. Chbk.).

2) <u>Johanna Margaretha[2]</u>, b. 20 May 1714 at Remoboech, N.J. - sp.: Johannes Miller, Janje - w/o Lucas Kiersteed, and Anna Marg. Gerlach (N.Y. City Luth. Chbk.).

3) <u>Anna Kunigunda[2]</u>, b. 5 April 1716 on island of Rembuch - sp.: Cunrad Friederick and Anna Kunigunda Wannemachers (N.Y. City Luth. Chbk.).

4) <u>Nicolaus[2]</u>, b. 22 July 1717 at Remobuch and bpt. Hackinsack - sp.: Niclaes Meyssinger and Anna Catharina Smiths (N.Y. City Luth. Chbk.). Nicolaes and Anneke, both children of Conraad Meisinger, were conf. together 21 April 1734 (N.Y. City Luth. Chbk.).

5) <u>Johann Conrad[2]</u>, b. 25 July 1720 and bpt. at Hackinsack - sp.: Cunrad Friedrich Jr. and Anna Maria Streyd (N.Y. City Luth. Chbk.).

6) <u>Johann Henrich[2]</u>, bpt. 18 Feb 1722 - sp.: Hendrik Smidt and wife Anna Catryn (Hackensack Ref. Chbk.).

7) <u>Sebastian[2]</u>, bpt. 22 Dec 1723 - sp.: Michiel Schort and wife Elisabeth (Hackensack Ref. Chbk.).

8) <u>Johann Dieterich[2]</u>, bpt. 17 Dec 1727 - sp.: Diderik Wannemaker and Anna Kinnie Wannemaker (Hackensack Ref. Chbk.).

SEBASTIAN MAISINGER'S SON NICHOLAS (Hunter Lists #471)

Bastiaan Minsinger, his wife, and 3 ch., were on Capt. Leonard Allan's ship in the 5th party of emigrants in 1709 (Rotterdam Lists).

Sebastian Maisinger made his initial appearance on the Hunter Lists 1 July 1710 with 1 pers. over 10 yrs. and 1 pers. under 10 yrs. of age; his entry for 4 Aug 1710 read 3 pers. over 10 yrs. Niclaus Maisinger then took over as head of the family 4 Oct 1710 when he was listed with 1 pers. over 10 yrs. of age. Niclaus Maisinger, s/o Sebastian, was noted 24 June 1711 with 2 pers. over 10 yrs. of age. Nicholas Meissinger was recorded in records of the Ramapo Tract. Nicolaus Meusinger and Anna Maria with 2 ch. were at Hackensack ca. 1716/17 (Simmendinger Register); they were enrolled next to Conrad Meusinger and his family on this census. This couple sp. Joh[S] Pielesvelt in 1743 and 1746 at Pompton Plains. The ch. of Nicholas[1] (technically, he was Nicholas[2] - HJ) and his wife Anna Maria (was she perhaps a Streit? - HJ) were:

1) Anna Margaretha[2], b. 2 Aug 1713 at Remaboeck in N.J. - sp.: Joh. Cunrad Meusinger and wife Anna Margareta (N.Y. City Luth. Chbk.).
2) Johann Michael[2], b. 30 April 1716 at Remobuch - sp.: Michel Stor and Magdalena Gerlachs (N.Y. City Luth. Chbk.).
3) Anna Maria[2], b. 5 Oct 1718 at Romerbuch - sp.: Christian Strydt and Anna Maria Fredericks (N.Y. City Luth. Chbk.).
4) Conrad[2], bpt. 18 June 1721 - sp.: Koenraet Muysiger and Margrit Sleygerr (Hackensack Ref. Chbk.).

JACOB MANCK (Hunter Lists #472)

Anna Veronica Manck, d/o Master Jacob of Urbach in the commune of Neuwied, md. Johann Mattheus Jung, s/o the late Jerg Hanss of Gernheim in the commune of Stromberg in the Pfaltz, 28 Sept 1714 (West Camp Luth. Chbk.). The origins of this family then were at 5419 Urbach (16 km. n. of Neuwied; Chbks. begin 1694, Ref.), and they were also documented at 5455 Rengsdorf (8 km. n. of Neuwied; Chbks. begin 1677). There were two early Jacob Mancks in the overall Neuwied region: 1) Jacob, the illegitimate s/o Herbert Manck of Harschbach (?) in the parish of Urbach, who md. 1st Anna Catharina Noll 2 April 1679 at 5450 Niederbieber and md. 2nd Barbara, wid/o Frantz Jost, 3 Jan 1716 there; this Jacob was bur. 16 May 1732, aged 87 yrs. at Niederbieber; and 2) the emigrant Jacob[1] Manck, called a tailor at Hartert in 1703, whose wife was called Anna Margaretha, agreeing with American data, in the Rengsdorf Chbk. Ancient mss. in the Fürstliches Archiv zu Wied note that

Jacob Manck was on a list of Dienstgeld im Amt Bonefeldt in 1708 and on a roll titled Römer-Monate of the parish Rengsdorf later that yr., when he was called Jacob Manck of Bonefeld. Jacob Manik, his wife, and 3 ch., were on Capt. Robbert Lourens's ship in the 3rd party of Palatines in Holland (Rotterdam Lists). Jacob Manck aged 39, his wife, and daughters aged 17, 9, and 3, Ref., husband-man and vinedresser, were in the 3rd arrivals in England later that yr. (London Lists).

Jacob Manck made his first appearance on the Hunter Lists 4 July 1710 with 3 pers. over 10 yrs. and 2 pers. under 10 in the household. The family was registered with 2 pers. over 10 and 3 under 10 yrs. on 4 Aug 1710, with 4 over 10 and 1 under 10 on 4 Oct 1710, and with 2 over 10 yrs. of age and 3 under 10 yrs. on 31 Dec 1710. On 24 June 1711, the family was recorded with 4 pers. over 10 yrs. and 1 under 10, on 29 Sept 1711 with 4 over 10 and 2 under 10, and on 24 Dec 1711 with 2 over 10 yrs. and 1 under 10. On 25 March 1712, the Jacob Manck family had 5 over 10 yrs. of age, and on 24 June 1712 the household was noted with 6 over 10. Jacob Mand: 1 man, 2 women, and 2 maids aged 9 - 15 yrs. were in Ulster Co. in 1710/11 (West Camp Census). Jacob Manck was nat. 8 and 9 Sept 1715 (Kingston Nats.). Jacob Manck and Anna Margretha were at Beckmansland ca. 1716/17 (Simmendinger Register). The ch. of Jacob[1] Manck and Anna Margaretha were:

1) Anna Veronica[2], md. as d/o Jacob[1] 28 Sept 1714 Johann Mattheus Jung (West Camp Luth. Chbk.).
2) "A Child[2]", d. 6 July 1703, aged 11 yrs. (Rengsdorf Chbk.).
3) "A Son[2]", d. 9 Sept 1704, aged 9 yrs. (Rengsdorf Chbk.).
4) Eva Catharina[2] (HJ). As Catharina Manck, she md. 1st Johannes Martin (HJ). She md. 2nd Johannes Kreisseler (HJ). Eva Catharina[2] md. 3rd Valentin Kuhn (HJ).
5) Anna Barbara[2], bpt. 3 Sept 1702 - sp.: Anna Barbara Fackert and Georg Runckel from Harttert (Rengsdorf Chbk.). A little girl of Jacob Manck at Harttert d. 10 Sept 1704 (Rengsdorf Chbk.).
6) Eva Maria[2], bpt. 28 Feb 1706 - sp.: Theiss Hofmann, Eva Anhauser, and Maria Gertrud Moll (Rengsdorf Chbk.).
7) "A Child[2]", d. 30 March 1715 (West Camp Luth. Chbk.). Perhaps this child was Eva Maria[2] (HJ).
8) Anna Elisabetha[2] (HJ), md. Henrich Meyer (HJ).

David Kendall Martin of Mouse Hill, West Chazy, N.Y. has written an interesting article "The Wife of Johannes Kreisler" dealing with the Mancks in the N.Y. Genealogical & Biographical

Record, Vol. 106, No. 4, Oct 1975.

HENRICH MANN (Hunter Lists #473)

Henrich Mann made his initial appearance on the Hunter Rolls 4 July 1710 with 2 pers. over 10 yrs. of age. The family was listed with 2 over 10 and 1 under 10 yrs. on 29 Sept 1711. Henrich Mann: 1 man and 1 woman were in Ulster Co. in 1710/11 (West Camp Census). Heinrich Mann and his wife Elisabetha Margretha with 2 ch. were at Neu-Cassel ca. 1716/17 (Simmendinger Register). Pastor Berkenmeyer mentioned a visit with the Manns in 1736 in his Albany Protocol, p. 188:

> On Monday evening, Henrich Kneskern and Peter Man arrived to take me to Scoghare. We left on the 15th and arrived there about seven o'clock. At the home of Henrich Man I found Messrs. Kneskern and Sternberger, so I rode with Mr. Jo[hann] Pe[ter] Kneskern to his home. Toward evening of the 16th we visited Mr. Henrich Stuberauch, who complained that he as well as Mr. Henrich Man had been misled with the letter, which was read to them without the corrections made in N.Y. and which made him very unhappy. According to Hannes La[w]yer's wishes, he had only signed that he would pay 3 shillings in order to settle the Van Di[eren] affair.

Henr[ich] Man and Peter Man, his son, communed at Fontyndorp in Schoharie later in Berkenmeyer's visit. By his wife who was named Maria Elisabetha, a child of Johann Henrich[1] Mann was:

1) Johann Peter[2], b. 23 July 1711 - sp.: Johann Peter Maurer, and the w/o Peter Wagner (West Camp Luth. Chbk.). His family appeared on Pastor Sommer's List of Schoharie families ca. 1744. Peter Man was a freeholder at Schoharrie in 1763 (Albany Co. Freeholders). Simms mentions the aged father of Capt. Mann being alive during the revolution (p. 249). A Peter Mann d. 29 May 1790 (Schoharie Luth. Chbk.); his will was proved 23 June 1790 (Albany Co. Wills Bk. I, p. 278). The ch. of Johann Peter[2] and Anna Margaretha were:

   i) Georg Henrich[3] (Sommer's Family List). He md. Christina Hauck 11 April 1760 (Schoharie Luth. Chbk.). Sgt. Georg H:, Corp. Pitter Jr., and Wilhelm Man were all in Capt. Jacob Sternberger's Company at Schohare in 1767 (Report of the State Historian, Vol. II, pp. 842 & 843). Georg Henrich[3] d. 6 Jan 1817, aged 82 yrs. (Zion Evangelical Luth. Chbk., Cobleskill).

   ii) Maria Elisabetha[3], b. 6 Oct 1737 and bpt. Schohari - sp.: Henrich Man and Maria Liese, the grandparents (Loonenburg Luth. Chbk.). She had banns to marry Jacob Ball 4 Nov 1753 (Schoharie Ref. Chbk.).

   iii) Johann Peter[3], bpt. (?) Feb 1739/40 - sp.: Pieter

Sneider, Elisachatarin Sneider, and Johannes Vinck
(Schoharie Ref. Chbk.). He md. Maria Kniskern 24 Sept
1765 (Schoharie Luth. Chbk.).

iv) Johannes[3], bpt. 19 March 1741/42 - sp.: Johannes Bat,
John Jacob Zimmer, and Margaretta Elisab: Schnyder
(Schoharie Ref. Chbk.). He probably d. 11 March 1758
(Schoharie Luth. Chbk.).

v) Elisabetha[3], b. 11 Aug 1744 - sp.: Jacob Schneider
and his wife (Schoharie Luth. Chbk.). She md. Jacob
Schyder 22 Oct 1769 (Schoharie Ref. Chbk.).

vi) Johann Wilhelm[3], b. 8 Nov 1746 - sp.: Johan Henrich
Mann, Wilhelm Schneider, and Eva Sternberg (Schoharie
Luth. Chbk.). He md. Catharina Borst 20 Nov 1774
(Schoharie Luth. Chbk.). Johann Wilhelm[3] d. 19 Oct
1816, aged 70 yrs. (Old Stone Fort Cem., Schoharie).

vii) Jacob[3], b. 25 July 1750 - sp.: Jacob Zimmer and Catharina Zimmer (Schoharie Luth. Chbk.). He md. Magdalena Werner 14 April 1771 (Schoharie Luth. Chbk.).
Jacob[3] d. 12 March 1829, aged 79 yrs. (Schoharie Cem.,
Schoharie). The Albany Argus of 31 March 1829 notes
that he d. by mistake, taking saltpetre for salt.

There was a Hendrick Man who joined the Schoharie Ref. Church
14 May 1740; he probably was the emigrant Henrich[1], unless there
was a Henrich[2] (the 2nd child listed in Simmendinger in 1716/17?
- HJ).

ALBRECHT DIETRICH MARTERSTOCK (Hunter Lists #474)

Albrecht Dietrich Marterstock, widower of Lamsheim in the
commune Neustatt in the Pfaltz, md. Elisabetha, wid/o Matthes Ru-
benich of Sittern near Birckenfeld in Westerich, 5 Sept 1710 (West
Camp Luth. Chbk.). The registers of 6715 Lambsheim were examined,
but he was not documented therein (HJ).

Albrecht Dietrich Marterstock made his initial appearance on
the Hunter Lists 30 June 1710 with 1 pers. over 10 yrs. of age.
On 4 Oct 1710 he was entered with 2 pers. over 10 yrs., and on 24
Dec 1711 the household showed 2 pers. over 10 yrs. and 1 pers. under 10 yrs. of age. Alb. Ffrid Marsterstork: 1 man and 1 woman
were in Ulster Co. in 1710/11 (West Camp Census). Dedrich Materstock was nat. 8 and 9 Sept 1715 (Kingston Nats.). Albrecht Marterstock and his wife Elisabetha were at Heessberg ca. 1716/17
(Simmendinger Register). Albany Co. Deeds Vol. 6, p. 255 mentions
land granted by Dederich Materstock of Albany Co. to Nicolaus Hoffman of Ulster Co. 14 Sept 1730. Dieterich Matestok (his mark) was

a leader of the Luth. congregation at Kisketamenesy 3 April 1735, according to a document he signed that date (Albany Protocol, p. 127). The ch. of Albrecht Dieterich[1] and Elisabetha were:

1) Johann Dieterich[2], b. 26 Nov 1711 - sp.: Dietrich Castelmann and Margretha Weidknecht (West Camp Luth. Chbk.). Diet. Matestok was conf. 1 April 1733, aged 21, at Newton (Loonenburg Luth. Chbk.). He md. Fva Maria Hertel 4 Jan 1736 at Newton (Loonenburg Luth. Chbk.). Dederick Materstock was a freeholder at Sagerties in 1763 (Albany Co. Freeholders). The issue of Johann Dieterich[2] was:

   i) Elisabetha[3], bpt. 16 Jan 1737 aged 11 weeks old at Newton - sp.: Hannes Hertel and Christina Matestock (Loonenburg Luth. Chbk.).

   ii) Johannes[3], b. 1 April 1739 and bpt. Newton - sp.: Jacob Eigener and wife Anna Margr. (Loonenburg Luth. Chbk.).

   iii) Adam[3], b. 18 Aug 1740 and bpt. Newton - sp.: Adam Hertel and Gertrud, grandparents (Loonenburg Luth. Chbk.). He md. Catharina Eigener 2nd Pasch: 1761 at Newtown (Loonenburg Luth. Chbk.). Adam, Dederick, Jacob, and Daniel Materstock were in Capt. Cornelus Dubois' Company at Caskill 9 April 1767 (Report of the State Historian, Vol. II, p. 877). He had issue bpt. at Loonenburg Luth. and Katsbaan Ref. Churches (HJ).

   iv) Jacob[3], b. 9 July 1743 and bpt. at Kisket. - sp.: Jo: Jacob Eigener and wife Anna Margr. (Loonenburg Luth. Chbk.).

   v) Elisabetha[3], bpt. 1 April 1746 - sp.: Diederich Marterstok and wife Lisabeth Marterstok (Katsbaan Ref. Chbk.). She md. Peter Eigener (HJ).

   vi) Maria[3], b. 31 Aug 1749 and bpt. Newton - sp.: John Laux and wife Lisab. (Loonenburg Luth. Chbk.).

   vii) Wilhelmus[3], b. 22 Nov 1753 - sp.: Wilhelm Behr and Neeltje Laux (Loonenburg Luth. Chbk.).

   viii) Johannes[3], b. 20 June 1756 - sp.: Johannes Maurer and Susanna (Loonenburg Luth. Chbk.).

2) Johanna Maria Sophia[2], b. 17 Dec 1714 - sp.: Gottfrid Wulsten Sr. and his wife, and Maria Barbara Testu (West Camp Luth. Chbk.).

3) Daniel[2], b. 23 Dec 1716 - sp.: Daniel Destuh and wife Barbara (West Camp Luth. Chbk.). Daniel Matestock aged 20, and Christina Matestock aged 17 were conf. at Newton in 1735/36 (Loonenburg Luth. Chbk.).

4) Maria Christina[2], b. 17 March 1719 - sp.: Wilhelm Brandau

and wife, and Christina Brunck (West Camp Luth. Chbk.).
She md. Francis Mac Durmond 1 Dec 1739 at Newton (Loonenburg Luth. Chbk.).

JOHANN CONRAD MARTIN (Hunter Lists #475)

The European roots of this family were at 6349 Eisemroth (8
km. e. of Dillenburg; Chbks. begin 1662). The grandfather of the
emigrant was Johann Henrich Merten. Johann Henrich, s/o the couple
Johan Henrich Mertens and Cathrin from Isenroth, md. Gilgen, d/o
Georg Pinstock and Cremien (Cathrin?) from Isemroth, 13 May 1666.
The ch. of Johann Henrich Merten the younger and his 1st wife were:
    Johann Georg, b. 30 May 1667 - sp.: Johann Jacob Mertens, Jo-
    han Görg - s/o Joh. Henrich Mertens, and Anna Juliana - w/o
    Joh. Gorg Diepels - all from Isemroth.
    Johann Philip, bpt. 28 Nov 1675 - sp.: Johan Jost Görg, Phil-
    ip Braun, and Susanna - d/o the late Joh. Henr. Mertens, all
    from Isenroth.
    Johannes, b. 9 Aug 1669 - sp.: Joh. Henrich Heylandt, Joh.
    Peter the teacher, Anna Elbeth - d/o Joh. Petzer, and Elbeth
    - d/o Johannes Peters, all from Isenrod.
Johann Henrich Mertens, widower, md. Catharina, d/o the late Andreas Rodenbach - formerly miller at Übernthal - and his wife Angels, 3 Oct 1676. The ch. of Johann Henrich Mertens the younger and
his 2nd wife Catharina were:
  + Johann Conrad, b. 23 July 1677 - sp.: Johann Jost - surviving
    s/o Andreas Rodenbach from Offenbach, Conrad Jacob from Off-
    enbach, and Maria - w/o Philip Braun from Osenrod.
    "Twins, a son & daughter", bpt. 18 April 1680 - sp.: Jacob
    Schröder, Anna Cathrin - d/o Adam Seiberts, Philipp Mertens,
    and Anna Cathrin - w/o Jost Thomas, all from Isemrod.
    Johann Enners, bpt. 28 Jan 1683 - sp.: Johannes Schneider,·
    Caspar Rodenbach from Offenbach, Anna Juliana - w/o Joh. Dan-
    iel Schmitt from Isenrod, and Catharina - w/o Dönges.
    Johannes, b. as a twin, the other d., bpt. 11 July 1684 -
    sp.: Johannes Sommer the younger, and Margaretha - w/o Phil-
    ipp Merten from Eyenr.
Johann Conrad Merten, s/o the couple Johann Henrich Merten and
Catharina from Eysemrot, md. Anna Catharina, d/o the late couple
Johann Sommers and Elsbeth also from Eysenrot, 25 Sept 1701. Johann, s/o the couple Johannes Sommers and Angels from Isemroth,
md. Elsbeth, d/o the couple Johann Peters and Cathrin from Isemroth, 12 Jan 1675. Joh. Conrad Merte, Joh^S Merten, and Hanß and
Hanß Georg Schäfer, each with wife and altogether 8 ch., petitioned to emigrate from Eisemroth in Amt Tringenstein in 1709 (Nassau-

Dillenburg Petitions).

Johann Conrad Martin first was noted on the Hunter Lists
with 1 pers. over 10 yrs. and 1 pers. under 10 on 30 June 1710.
The household showed 2 over 10 and 2 under 10 yrs. on 31 Dec 1710.
The family was recorded with 4 pers. over 10 yrs. of age 24 June
1711. Conrad Merdin: 2 men; 1 lad 9 - 15 yrs.; 1 woman were in
Ulster Co. in 1710/11 (West Camp Census). Conrad Merten and Anna
Maria with 3 ch. were at Beckmansland ca. 1716/17 (Simmendinger
Register). The ch. of Johann Conrad[1] Martin and Anna Catharina,
his 1st wife, were:

1) Johannes[2], bpt. 10 Sept 1702 - sp.: Johannes Merten and
   die Frau Kellerin Agnes Catharina Beckmänning from Dillenburg, and Anna Margr. - d/o Joh. Sommers from Eysen-
   roth (Eisemroth Chbk.). A Johanis Merte was nat. 8 and 9
   Sept 1715 (Kingston Nats.); possibly this was the emigrant, Johann Conrad[1] Martin, rather than his son (HJ).
   Johannes[2] md. Catharina Manck (HJ) and had a son:
   i) Jacob[3], bpt. 30 Aug 1724 - sp.: Jacob Mank and Maria
      Marthen (Kingston Ref. Chbk.). Johan Jacob Merten
      joined the Red Hook Luth. Church 14 April 1745. Ja-
      cob[3] md. Anna Barbara Stickel (HJ). They had ch. bpt.
      at Germantown Ref., Red Hook Luth., and Rhinebeck
      Luth. Churches, many of whom were sp. by members of
      the Kreisseler family, as (Eva) Catharina Manck,
      mother of Jacob[3] Martin, md. 2nd to Johannes Kreis-
      seler (HJ).

2) Anna Catharina[2], bpt. 14 Oct 1708 - sp.: Johann Philipp
   Mertens, Anna Catharina - single d/o Joh. Philipp Merten,
   and Anna Julian - w/o Johannes Sohn, all from Eys. (Eisemroth Chbk.).

3) Johann Friederich[2], b. 16 March 1713 - sp.: Johann Fridrich Haeger (West Camp Luth. Chbk.). He md. (Maria) Eva
   Maria Spohn 23 May 1737 (Loonenburg Luth. Chbk.). She md.
   2nd as wid/o Johann Friederich[2] 5 May 1747 Hermanus Behr
   (Loonenburg Luth. Chbk.). The ch. of Johann Friederich[2]
   Martin and his wife were:
   i) Christina[3], b. 30 Dec 1737 and bpt. Kisket. - sp.:
      Henrich Fees and wife Christina (Loonenburg Luth.
      Chbk.).
   ii) Wilhelmus[3], bpt. 5 days old 20 Aug 1739 at his fa-
       ther's house - sp.: Jo. Wilh. Elig and wife Margar-
       etha (Loonenburg Luth. Chbk.).
   iii) Johann Friederich[3], b. 15 Aug 1740 and bpt. Kisket.
        - sp.: Henr. Fees and wife Christina (Loonenburg

Luth. Chbk.). He md. 25 April 1769 Margaretha Dieterich (Germantown Ref. Chbk.). They had issue bpt. at
Germantown Ref. and Katsbaan Ref. Churches (HJ).

4) <u>Johann Henrich²</u>, b. 30 Jan 1715 - sp.: Hieronymus Weller,
Heinrich Schramm, and Catharina Schaib (West Camp Luth.
Chbk.). He md. Elisabetha Emmerich 6 April 1736, both b.
and residing in Nuton (Katsbaan Ref. Chbk.). Hendrick Mar-
tin was a taxpayer at Rhinebeck from June 1753 - Feb 1754
(Dutchess Co. Tax Lists). The ch. of Johann Henrich² and
Elisabetha Martin were:

   i) <u>Margaretha³</u>, bpt. as Grietje 6 Feb 1737 - sp.: Hen-
rich Brom ... (?) and Grietje ... (?) (Katsbaan Ref.
Chbk.). There was a Gritjen Martin who md. Petrus
Hommel 12 Jan 1771 (Red Hook Luth. Chbk.).

  ii) <u>Henrich³</u>, b. 21 Jan 1739 and bpt. Newton - sp.: Henr.
Fees and wife Christiana (Loonenburg Luth. Chbk.).

 iii) <u>Maria³</u>, bpt. 21 Sept 1740 at Newton - sp.: Hendryk
Brouwer and Margritje Emmerichs (Loonenburg Luth.
Chbk.). It is probable that she md. Peter Burckhardt
(HJ).

  iv) <u>Johannes³</u>, b. 1 Feb 1743 and bpt. at Kisket. - sp.:
Christian Fuhrer and wife Catharina Elisabetha (Loon-
enburg Luth. Chbk.). Johannes Merten joined the Red
Hook Luth. Church 15 May 1760. He md. 27 March 1764
Elisabetha Simon (Red Hook Luth. Chbk.). They had
ch. bpt. at Rhinebeck Luth. Church (HJ).

   v) <u>Gottlieb³</u> (HJ), md. Anna Schumacher (HJ). They had
ch. bpt. at Red Hook Luth. and Rhinebeck Luth.
Churches (HJ). He d. 2 Nov 1832, aged 86 yrs. and 10
months (St. Peter's Luth. Cem., Rhinebeck).

  vi) <u>David³</u> (HJ), md. Catharina Becker (HJ).

 vii) <u>Anna³</u>, b. 24 Sept 1753 - sp.: Philip Bohnenstiel and
wife Elisabetha (Rhinebeck Luth. Chbk.). She md.
Andreas Kohms (HJ).

5) <u>Catharina Elisabetha²</u> (HJ), md. 19 June 1739 1st Johannes
Emmerich Jr., and then 2nd 16 Feb 1740 Christian Fuhrer
(both Loonenburg Luth. Chbk.).

There were several unplaced Martins along the Hudson: 1) Anna
Vry, wid/o Joannis Martyn, md. Andries Plum 7 April 1723 (Tarrytown Ref. Chbk.); 2) Magdalena Martin md. Johannes Hauch in Sept
1771 (Red Hook Luth. Chbk.); 3) Dyrk Marten and wife Anna had ch.
bpt. at Loonenburg 1744 - 1749 and was mentioned in <u>Albany Proto-
col</u>; and 4) Joseph Martin md. Anna Dorothea Sax 8 April 1760 (Katsbaan Ref. Chbk.).

MARIA MAGDALENA MARXIN (Hunter Lists #476)

Maria Magdalena Marxin was listed once on the Hunter Lists, 4 July 1710 with 1 pers. over 10 yrs. of age. Perhaps she was related to Mathew Marx in the 2nd arrivals in London, or to Joseph Marks in the 3rd party at Rotterdam (HJ).

ANNA MATHESIN (Hunter Lists #477)

Maria Apolonia Matthes, d/o the late Peter of Eckersweil near Zweybrucken, md. Carl Nahr, widower and tanner of Bieckenfeld in Westerich, 29 Aug 1710 (West Camp Luth. Chbk.). The ancestral village of origin was 6589 Eckersweiler (8 km. n.w. of Kusel), entries in registers of 5180 Eschweiler (Chbks. begin 1616) and 6587 Baumholder (10 km. n. of Kusel; Chbks. begin 1679, Ref.). Pitter, s/o Jacob Matheis, was bpt. 6 May 1657 - sp.: Issak Nierstrass, Johann Steffens, and Catharina Frommery (Eschweiler Chbk.). A Peter Matthes sp. the 1709er Michael Hindescheit in 1706 at 6759 Reipoltskirchen Catholic Church. Peter Mattÿs Widow and her ch., a total of 4 in the family, were on Capt. Johan Ranneld's ship in the 3rd party of emigrants in Holland in 1709 (Rotterdam Lists). Anna Mathesin aged 53, with daughters aged 23, 20, and 18, Ref., Widow, was in the 3rd arrivals in England later that yr. (London Lists).

Anna Mathesin made her initial appearance on the Hunter Lists 1 July 1710 with 2 pers. over 10 yrs. of age in the family. The entry for 4 Aug 1710 read 4 pers. over 10 yrs., for 24 Dec 1711 showed 3 over 10 and 1 under 10, and for 24 June 1712 noted 3 pers. over 10 yrs. of age. An Anna Madesa was a Palatine Debtor in 1718 (Livingston Debt Lists). The ch. of Peter and Anna[1] Mathes were:

1) Hans Jacob[2], bpt. 3 Feb 1682 - sp.: Johannes Köhl - s/o Hans Michel Köhl from Mettweiler, Jacob Kunzel from Eckersweiler, and Anna Maria - d/o Clos Schäffer at Mettw. (Baumholder Chbk.). The parents were called from Eckersweiler on all the Baumholder bpts. (HJ).

2) Maria Barbara[2], bpt. 3 Feb 1686 - sp.: Maria Barbel ..., Johannes Albert - s/o Bäff (?) Albert at Mettw., Michel ..., Catharina - w/o Nickel Meyß, ..., and Dorothea - wid/o Hans Jacob Kohl (Baumholder Chbk.). Maria Barb: Mat(u)s was a Palatine Debtor in 1718 (Livingston Debt Lists).

3) Anna Maria[2], bpt. 19 Nov 1689 - sp.: Anna - ... Johannes Kirsch at Berschweiler, H. Nickel Albert - Schultheiß at Berschw., Laux Rothfuchs from Fohren, Anna Eva - w/o Laux Bihr from Fohren, and Maria - w/o Hanß Nickel Kohan at Mettw. (Baumholder Chbk.). She md. Georg Schäffer 28 Oct

1714 (West Camp Luth. Chbk.).

4) Maria Apollonia[2], md. as d/o Peter 29 Aug 1710 Carl Neher (West Camp Luth. Chbk.).

JOHANN MARTIN MATHEUS (Hunter Lists #478)

Martin Matheus, his wife, and 4 ch. were on Capt. Robbert Bulman's ship in the 4th party of 1709 (Rotterdam Lists). Marcus Matthes aged 88, and a daughter aged 24, Ref., stockingweaver, were in the 4th arrivals in England later that yr. (London Lists).

Johann Martin Matheus first made his appearance on the Hunter Lists 30 June 1710 with 1 pers. over 10 yrs. of age. He was enrolled 1 name from Georg Matheus 31 Dec 1710. Martin Mattheus Widow (should this be Widower? - HJ) "is 110 yrs. old" was noted at Neu-Quunsberg next to Georg Mattheus ca. 1716/17 (Simmendinger Register).

ANDREAS MATHEUS (Hunter Lists #479)

Andreas Matheus made his first appearance on the Hunter Rolls 4 July 1710 with 1 pers. over 10 yrs. of age in the family. Andreas Mathus was at Wormsdorff ca. 1716/17 (Simmendinger Register). Andr: Mattys was a Palatine Debtor in 1718/ 1719 (at Kingsberry), and 1721 (Livingston Debt Lists). The will of Andreas Mathys was dated 24 Oct 1726 and witnessed by Joh: Bernhard, John Kurtz, Geo. Adam Zufeld, W. C. Berckenmeyer, and Nic. Raw (Albany Co. Deeds: Vol. 6, p. 370). Andreas Mathes appeared on the St. Peter's Luth. Family List ca. 1734 (Rhinebeck Luth. Chbk.).

GEORG MATHEUS-MATTHIAS (Hunter Lists #480)

Georg Matthes aged 32, his wife, and a son aged 3, stockingweaver, Ref., were listed next to Marcus Matthes in the 4th arrivals in England in 1709 (London Lists). As he did not appear on the 4th Rotterdam party Lists, Georg was probably the s/o #478 Johann Martin Matheus (HJ).

Georg Matheus made his first appearance on the Hunter Lists 4 Aug 1710 with 2 pers. over 10 yrs.; he often was recorded near Johann Martin[1] Matheus (HJ). The family showed 1 pers. over 10 yrs. 25 March 1712, and then returned to 2 over 10 on the 24 June 1712 entry. Geo. Mathias of Queensbury was a soldier in 1711 (Palatine Volunteers To Canada). Jury Mathys was nat. 28 Feb 1715/16 (Albany Nats.). Georg Mattheus, his wife Catharina, and 1 child, were registered next to Martin Mattheus at Neu-Quunsberg ca. 1716/17 (Simmendinger Register). The ch. of Georg[1] Matheus and his wife Maria Catharina were:

1) Johann Jacob², b. 2 Dec 1715 and bpt. at Schoharie - sp.: Jacob Weber, Peter Bellinger, and Anna Maria Ifland (West Camp Luth. Chbk.).

2) Conrad², b. 10 May 1717 and bpt. at Schoharie - sp.: Conrad Weisser, Conrad Schuetz, and Anna Maria Bell (West Camp Luth. Chbk.).

HENRICH MATHIAS - MATHEUS (Hunter Lists #481)

Sabina Mattheus, d/o the late Henrich of Dinheim Bemeltem, md. Conrad Becker, s/o the late Sebastian of Altzheim on the lower Rhine in the commune Altzheim in the Pfaltz, 4 June 1717 at Schoharie (West Camp Luth. Chbk.). The town of origin for the Mattice family of Schoharie was 6501 Dienheim (2 km. s. of Oppenheim; Chbks. begin 1689, Ref.). As there was only one family named Matheus appearing in the old registers there, the father of the emigrant Henrich¹ most probably was Caspar Matheus (Matthäuß), Gemeinsmann at Rudelsheim. The w/o Caspar undoubtedly was the Widow Margaretha Matthais bur. 12 Feb 1701, aged ca. 65 yrs. of the Ref. religion. The ch. of Caspar Matthäuß were:

Adolph, bur. as surviving s/o the late Caspar Matheus 22 April 1698.

Stephan, md. as s/o the late Caspar Mattheiß - Gemeinsmann at Rudelsheim 12 Sept 1702 Anna Margaretha, d/o Marx Lauz (?) - inhabitant here at Dienheim. Stephan Mattheis was bur. 7 Feb 1709, aged 39 yrs.

+ Henrich (HJ).

Henrich¹ md. Catharina Melchior, as shown by the 1706 sp. of their son Johann Jost, who was sp. by Johann Jost Melchior of Leheim, mother's brother. The chbks. at 6086 Leeheim show that Catharina and Johann Jost Melchior were children of Peter Melchior, who d. 17 Aug 1679; Margretha, wid/o Peter Melchior, md. Christoffel Mohr at Leeheim 12 May 1680. Hendrig Matheys, his wife, and 6 ch. were on Capt. Wilkens's ship in the 3rd party in Holland in 1709 (Rotterdam Lists). Henry Mathes aged 42, his wife, sons aged 8, 6, and 1, daughters aged 13, 10, and 6, Ref., husbandman and vinedresser, were in the 3rd arrivals in England later that yr. (London Lists).

Henrich Mathias made his first appearance on the Hunter Rolls 1 July 1710 with 4 pers. over 10 yrs. of age and 3 pers. under 10. The lists showed 3 over 10 and 4 under 10 on 4 Oct 1710, and then 4 pers. over 10 yrs. and 3 under 10 31 Dec 1710. Henr. Mathous of Queensbury was a soldier in 1711 (Palatine Volunteers To Canada).

Heinrich Matthäus and Catharina with 4 ch. were at Neu-Stuttgardt
ca. 1716/17 (Simmendinger Register). The ch. of Henrich[1] Matheus
and Catharina were:

1) Maria Sybilla[2], conf. as d/o Henrich[1] 1708 (Dienheim
   Chbk.). She sp. Henrich Meyer in 1711 (West Camp Luth.
   Chbk.).

2) Sabina[2], bpt. 15 March 1699 - sp.: Sabina Bender - d/o the
   churchelder and Gerichtsverwandten Martin Bender and her
   bridegroom Stephan Trebur (Dienheim Chbk.). She md. Conrad
   Becker 4 June 1717 (West Camp Luth. Chbk.).

3) Nicolaus[2], bpt. 13 Feb 1701 - sp.: Nicolaus Vollert from
   Leheim - single, and Anna Margaretha - single servant at
   Nierstein (Dienheim Chbk.). He md. Elisabetha Kast, d/o
   Georg Kast (Fernow Wills #971). She probably was the Anna
   Elisabetha Matthes noted on Pastor Sommer's List of Scho-
   harie Families ca. 1744 (HJ). Nicholas Mathys was a free-
   holder at Schoharrie in 1763 (Albany Co. Freeholders).
   Nicclas Matice was a Sergeant in Capt. Thomas Ackeson's
   Company in 1767; others of that surname in that Company
   were Handryck, Hannicle, Fradryck, Joseph, Joseph Jr., Jo-
   hannis, Handrick, Adam, and Counrate Matice (Report of the
   State Historian, Vol. II, pp. 845 - 847. The ch. of Nicolaus[2] and Elisabetha Matheus were:

   i) Anna Dorothea[3], md. as d/o Nicolaus[2] 3 Dec 1745 Johann
      Georg Werner (Schoharie Luth. Chbk.).

   ii) Anna[3] (HJ), md. 14 July 1747 Johannes Freymäuer (Scho-
       harie Luth. Chbk.).

   iii) Henrich[3] (HJ), md. Maria Magdalena Ingold (HJ).

   iv) Johann Nicolaus[3], md. as s/o Nicolaus[2] 29 Sept 1753
       Sophia Ingold (Schoharie Ref. Chbk.). Catharina,
       Nicholas, and Sara Matheese were conf. 15 April 1750
       (Schoharie Ref. Chbk.).

   v) Catharina[3] (HJ), conf. with Nicholas and Sara in 1750.

   vi) Sarah[3] (HJ), conf. with Nicholas and Catharina in
       1750.

   vii) Friederich[3] (HJ), md. Gertraud Zimmer 2 June 1758
        (Schoharie Ref. Chbk.).

   viii) Elisabetha[3], bpt. 18 Nov 1737 - sp.: Markus Rickert
         and Elisabeth Layer (Schoharie Ref. Chbk.). She md.
         Wilhelm Bauch 2 April 1758 (Schoharie Ref. Chbk.).

   ix) Gertraud[3], bpt. 21 April 1739 - sp.: Hannes Enckhoold
       and wife Anna Margareeth Beckker (Schoharie Ref.
       Chbk.). She md. 7 Oct 1760 Jacob Schnell (Stone Ara-
       bia Ref. Chbk.).

x) Johannes³, bpt. 10 Jan 1741 - sp.: Markus Rickert and Elisabeth Layer (Schoharie Ref. Chbk.).

xi) Conrad³, bpt. 9 Sept 1744 - sp.: Niclaas Beckker and wife Elisabeth (Schoharie Ref. Chbk.). He md. 20 Nov 1766 Eva Hager (Schoharie Ref. Chbk.). See Penrose's Mohawk Valley in the Revolution, p. 283, for more on this man.

xii) Jost³ (HJ), md. Catharina Zimmer 22 March 1766 (Schoharie Luth. Chbk.).

xiii) Johannes³, bpt. 25 Dec 1750 - sp.: Georg Regtmayer and wife Anna Maria (Schoharie Ref. Chbk.). He md. Dorothea Hager 5 March 1775 (Schoharie Ref. Chbk.).

xiv) Adam³, md. as s/o Nicolaus² 28 March 1778 Anna Swart (Schoharie Ref. Chbk.). Reid's Loyalists In Ontario, p. 219, mentions an Adam, John, Nicholas, and William Mattice.

4) Elisabetha², b. 29 Oct 1703 - sp.: Elisabetha - the maid-servant in Oppenheim (Dienheim Chbk.).

5) Johann Jost², b. 27 March 1706 - sp.: Johann Jost Melchior - the mother's brother, inhabitant at Leheim (Dienheim Chbk.). He md. Margaretha Bauch (HJ); she probably was the Margaretha Matthes mentioned in Pastor Sommer's Family List ca. 1744 in the Schoharie Luth. Chbk. (HJ). A deed to Jost Matys from Hen. Matys survives dated 1742 for land at Schoharie (Manuscripts & History Section, N.Y. State Library at Albany, #13A9691). Joost Matys was a freeholder at Schoharrie in 1763 (Albany Co. Freeholders). His ch. were:

i) Catharina³, bpt. 5 March 1736 or 1738 - sp.: J. Marten Borst and Catharina Borst (Schoharie Luth. or Ref. Chbk.). She md. Arend Veeder 17 Aug 1762 (Schoharie Luth. Chbk.).

ii) Anna³ (HJ), md. Michael Braun 11 April 1758 (Schoharie Luth. Chbk.).

iii) Jost³ (HJ), md. Anna Rickert 5 March 1761 (Schoharie Ref. Chbk.).

iv) "A Child³", bpt. 30 Aug 1747 (Schoharie Ref. Chbk.).

v) Henrich³, md. as s/o Jost² 12 Nov 1775 Margarit Johnson (Schoharie Ref. Chbk.).

6) Johann Henrich², b. 14 Dec 1708 - sp.: Johann Henrich Hahn - Gemeinsmann here (Dienheim Chbk.).

7) Maria² (HJ), md. Dirk Hagedoorn (HJ).

8) Catharina² (HJ), whom Simms calls one of the 1st 4 ch. b. in the Schoharie settlements (p. 51). She md. 1st Johann

Martin Borst, and then md. 2nd 18 Aug 1747 Henrich Oyens (Schoharie Ref. Chbk.).

The Mattice Family History, by Rex G. Matice, should be consulted when studying this Schoharie Valley family, as it contains additional data on the group from private family sources.

JOHANN FRIDERICH MAUL (Hunter Lists #482)

The German home of the various N.Y. Maul families was 6349 Driedorf (9 km. s.w. of Herborn; Chbks. begin 1671). The grandfather of Johann Friederich[1] Maul was Paulus Maul, bur. 2 April 1686; Anna (Engen), wid/o Paulus Maul in Driedorf, was bur. 18 Sept 1689. They had issue:

Johannes (Emigrant #483 - see his section).

+ Johann Martin.

Johann Märten, s/o the citizen Paulus Maul in Driedorf, md. Anna Catharina, d/o the late Henrich Posthen at Heiligenborn, 31 Jan 1671. Johann Martin Maul at Heiligenborn was bur. 2 June 1697. The ch. of Johann Martin Maul and Anna Catharina were:

"A Child", bpt. 14 April 1672 - sp.: Jost Henrich Cuntz in Driedorf, Jost the herdsman from ..., and Cathar. Elisabeth - d/o Jost Henrich Cuntz in Driedorff. This child probably was the Jost Henrich Maul, s/o Johan Martin Maul at Heiligborn, who md. 19 Feb 1692 Anna Margr., d/o Johannes Henrich (HJ).

"A Child", bpt. 25 July 1675 - sp.: Johann Jost Maul, and Anna - w/o Henrich Posth at Hohroth.

"A Child", b. at Heiligenborn and bpt. 24 June 1677 - sp.: 'Johann Friedrich Posthen at Gusternhain, Johannes Henrich at Heiligborn, and Anursel - d/o Johan Frantz ... there.

"A Child", bpt. 6 April 1679 - sp.: Anna Margreth - d/o Paulus Maul in Driedorf, and Johann Friedrich - s/o Jost Held also here. (Sp. strongly suggest that either the child b. in 1677 or the one b. in 1679 was the emigrant Johann Friederich[1] (HJ).

"A Child", bpt. 24 Oct 1680 - sp.: Johannes Kuntz - single man in Driedorf, and Anna Dorth - d/o Johan Frantz Weiss at Heiligborn. It should be noted that the Driedorf registers remark that Johann Martin Maul at Heiligborn bur. a child 10 Feb 1681, and another child 21 March 1681 (HJ).

"A Child", bpt. 5 June 1682 - sp.: Görg Maul - single, and Anursel - d/o the late Johann Deubig, all in Driedorff.

"A Daughter", bpt. 1 May 1687 - sp.: Julian - w/o Johannes Maul at Hohroth, Anna Julian - d/o the late Paulus Maul in

Driedorff, and Johannes Schäffer from Manderbach - single
servant.

Johann Friedrich Maul, s/o the late Johan Martin Maul at Heiligborn, md. Anna Ursula, d/o Jacob Friess - Eltesten at Gusternhain,
7 Nov 1699. Joh. Friedr. Maul, his wife, and ch., petitioned to
emigrate from Heiligenborn in Amt. Driedorf in 1709 (Nassau -
Dillenburg Petitions). fredrig Maul, his wife, and 2 ch., were
in the 6th party of Palatines in 1709 in Holland (Rotterdam
Lists).

Johann Friderich Maul made his first appearance on the Hunter Rolls 4 Aug 1710 with 2 pers. over 10 yrs. of age and 2 pers.
under 10 yrs. The entry changed to 3 over 10 and 2 under 10 yrs.
4 Oct 1710, showed 4 over 10 and 1 under 10 24 Dec 1711, and then
4 pers. over 10 yrs. and 2 under 10 13 Sept 1712. A special notation was made 4 Aug 1710 for 1 pers. over 10 for the subsistence
of a young child. On many of his entries in Hunter, Johann Friederich[1] Maul was enrolled next to Johannes and Christoph Maul (HJ).
Frederick Maul aged 31, Anna Ursula Maul aged 31, John Jacob Maul
aged 4, Anna Catharina Maul aged 5, and John Paul Maul, orph.,
aged 12, were in N.Y. City in 1710/11 (Palatines In N.Y. City).
Due to the juxtaposition of names on certain old Palatine mss.,
and mutual sp. between the Maul and Schmidt families, I believe
there is a strong possibility that the John Paul Maul listed as
an orphan aged 12 in N.Y. City in 1710/11 may have become the
Johann Paul Schmidt who seems to have appeared out of nowhere in
the Katsbaan region and md. Christina Trombauer (HJ). Fred[k] Moule
was nat. 8 and 9 Sept 1715 (Kingston Nats.). Friederich Maul and
Anna Ursula with 4 ch. were at Beckmansland ca. 1716/17 (Simmendinger Register). Frederik Maul was a Palatine Debtor in 1718
(Livingston Debt Lists). Johann Friederich[1] and Anna Ursula Maul
were alive as late as 1742 when they sp. at Red Hook Luth. Church.
The ch. of Johann Friederich[1] and Anna Ursula Maul were:

1) "A Child"[2], bpt. 24 Sept 1701 - sp.: Anna Elisab. from
   Gusterhain - still single, and Jost Post, also single
   (Driedorf Chbk.).

2) "A Child"[2], bpt. 22 Dec 1702 - sp.: Anna Urs. - w/o Joh.
   Henrich ..., Anna Catharina - d/o Joh. Adam Han (?) from
   Waldaubach, and Johann Jost Schm... from Gusterhain (Drie-
   dorf Chbk.).

3) Anna Catharina[2] (Palatines In N.Y. City), md. 28 Feb 1721
   Friederich Streit (Kingston Ref. Chbk.).

4) Johann Jacob[2] (Palatines In N.Y. City). Jacob Moule was
   nat. 8 and 9 Sept 1715 (Kingston Nats.). He md. 16 April
   1730 at Newton Anna Dorothea, d/o Nicolaus Trombauer (N.Y.

City Luth. Chbk.). Dorothy Moul, w/o Jacob, d. 28 Oct 1760, aged 45 yrs. (German Church at Pink's Corners Cem.). Jacob Maul md. 2nd in 1761 the Widow Elisabetha Overbach (Catskill Ref. Chbk.). He appeared on Rhinebeck tax rolls 1736/37 - 1778 (Dutchess Co. Tax Lists). Jacob Maul d. 27 Nov 1783, aged 77 yrs. (German Church at Pink's Corners Cem.). The ch. of Johann Jacob[2] Maul and Anna Dorothea were:

   i) Friederich[3], b. 6 Jan 1733 and bpt. at Kisket. - sp.: Frid. Maul and Marlene Trombauer (Loonenburg Luth. Chbk.).

  ii) Margaretha[3], bpt. 16 Feb 1735 - sp.: Johannes Drumbauer and Margaretha Maul (Catskill Ref. Chbk.).

 iii) Johannes[3], bpt. 5 June 1737 - sp.: Johannes Muyl and Elisabeth Trombo (Kingston Ref. Chbk.).

  iv) Catharina[3], bpt. 27 Jan 1740 - sp.: Frederik Stryk and Catrina Mouwel (Kingston Ref. Chbk.).

   v) Elisabetha[3], bpt. 2 March 1742 - sp.: Jurge Streit and Elizabeth Trombauer (Red Hook Luth. Chbk.). She md. as d/o Johann Jacob[2] 28 Feb 1758 Jost Bauer (Red Hook Luth. Chbk.).

  vi) Johannes[3], bpt. 15 April 1744 - sp.: Johannes Maul and wife Elisabeth (Red Hook Luth. Chbk.).

 vii) Margaretha[3], b. 6 July 1746 - sp.: Zach Haber and wife Anna Fuhrer (Rhinebeck Luth. Chbk.). She md. as d/o Johann Jacob[2] (3)1 March 1765 Wilhelm Klum (Red Hook Luth. Chbk.).

viii) Jacob[3], b. 16 Dec 1748 - sp.: Johannes Maul and wife Elisabetha (Rhinebeck Luth. Chbk.). He d. 12 Nov 1805, aged 56-11-7 (German Church at Pink's Corners Cem.).

  ix) Friederich[3], b. 16 Sept 1751 - sp.: Johannes Benner and wife Magdalena (Rhinebeck Luth. Chbk.). He md. Maria Hamm (HJ). Frederick Moul d. 22 April 1824, aged 72-7-5, and Mary, his wife, d. 11 Aug 1846, aged 90-11-28 (German Church at Pink's Corners Cem.).

5) Anna Maria[2], b. 25 July 1712 - sp.: Christoph Maul, Anna Barbara Grauberger, and Anna Maria Neukirch (West Camp Luth. Chbk.). She md. Johann Peter Schneider 11 Feb 1735 (Kingston Ref. Chbk.).

6) Johannes[2], b. 3 Feb 1716 - sp.: Johannes Stahl, Johann Neukirch, and Juliana Reuter (West Camp Luth. Chbk.). Johannes[2] md. Elisabetha Trombauer (HJ). Johannis Moul was in Capt. Jeremiah Hogeboom's Company in 1767 (Report of the State Historian, Vol. II, p. 865). His ch. were:

i) Johannes³, bpt. 6 Nov 1738 - sp.: Johannes Trombauer and Lisabeth Maul (Red Hook Luth. Chbk.).

ii) Friederich³, bpt. 5 weeks old 20 July 1740 at Newton - sp.: Frid: Streit and wife Anna Cath., in their place Frid: Maul and Ursula, the gr-parents (Loonenburg Luth. Chbk.). Friederich³ md. 5 May 1763 Gertraud Scherp (Germantown Ref. Chbk.); the Claverack Ref. Chbk. calls the date 14 April 1763 (HJ). They had ch. bpt. at Claverack Ref. and Germantown Ref. Churches (HJ).

iii) Catharina³, bpt. 17 April 1743 - sp.: Jacob Maul and Anna Durt Trumbaur (Red Hook Luth. Chbk.). She md. Jeremias Landt in 1769 (Linlithgo Ref. Chbk.).

iv) Anna Maria³, bpt. 1 Sept 1745 - sp.: Andreas Drenbourgh and Anna Maria Strydt (Germantown Ref. Chbk.). She md. Tiel Rockefeller 16 June 1761 (Kingston Ref. Chbk.).

v) Jacob³, b. 15 March 1748 - sp.: Jacob Maul and Anna D: (Germantown Luth. Chbk.).

vi) Margaretha³, bpt. 3 Feb 1751 - sp.: Caspar Ham and Margriet Stoyt (Linlithgo Ref. Chbk.).

vii) Magdalena³, b. 4 Aug 1752 - sp.: Johannes Bender and Magdalena Streit (Rhinebeck Flats Ref. Chbk.). She md. Jan Herder 11 Sept 1768 (Linlithgo Ref. Chbk.).

viii) Johannes³, bpt. 19 May 1755 - sp.: Johannes Tromphouwer and Cristina Fiure (Germantown Ref. Chbk.).

ix) Elisabetha³, bpt. 16 Nov 1758 - sp.: Henr: Schuldt and Eliesabetha Schuldt (Germantown Ref. Chbk.).

x) Jacob³, b. 30 Aug 1760 - sp.: Jacob Maul and Anna D: (Germantown Luth. Chbk.).

7) Anna Margaretha², b. 20 Nov 1718 - sp.: Dietrich Sutz and Anna Margretha Emerich (West Camp Luth. Chbk.). She md. 8 June 1736 Martin Ham (Loonenburg Luth. Chbk., entry only mentions parents' name).

8) Elisabetha², bpt. 7 Jan 1722 - sp.: Christoffel Mouw and Antjen Mouw (Kingston Ref. Chbk.).

JOHANNES MAUL now his widdow (Hunter Lists #483)
CHRISTOPH MAUL (Hunter Lists #484)

As with #482 Johann Friderich¹ Maul, the point of origin for this Palatine family was 6349 Driedorf (9 km. s.w. of Herborn; Chbks. begin 1671). Paulus Maul, bur. 2 April 1686, and Anna (Engen), bur. 18 Sept 1689, were the parents of Johannes¹ Maul.

Johannes Maul, s/o the late Paulus Maul in Driedorf, md. Anna Juliana, d/o Niclas Theiss at Hohroth, 9 Feb 1687. Anna Julian, w/o Johannes Maul at Hochroth, d. at Hohenroth and was bur. 21 April 1693. Johannes Maul, widower at Hohenroth, md. Elsbeth, d/o Johann Georg Drisch there, 28 Nov 1693. Anursel, w/o Johann Görg Drisch at Hohenroth, was bur. 19 April 1677. Johannes Maul and family from Hohenroth in Amt. Driedorf petitioned to emigrate in 1709 (Nassau-Dillenburg Petitions). Johan Maul, his wife, and 7 ch., were listed next to Philip Sargusch and his family in the 6th party of Palatines in Holland in 1709 (Rotterdam Lists).

Johannes Maul made his initial appearance on the Hunter Lists 4 July 1710 with 2 pers. over 10 yrs. of age and 4 pers. under 10 yrs.; the same entry was recorded 4 Aug 1710, but this time he was listed next to Christoph Maul (HJ). The Johannes Maul family read 5 pers. over 10 and 1 under 10 yrs. 4 Oct 1710. On 24 June 1711, Johann Maul's Wid[W] Elizabeth was recorded next to Christoph and Friderich Maul; she was registered with 4 pers. over 10 yrs. of age and 1 under 10 yrs. Anna Eliz Maulin, wid., aged 42, Anna Catharina Maulin aged 13, Anna Ursula Maulin aged 16, Catharina Maulin aged 12, and Anna Maria Maulin aged 5, were all in N.Y. City in 1710/11 (Palatines In N.Y. City). Elisabetha Maunlin, a Wid. with 4 ch., was in Neu-Yorck ca. 1716/17 (Simmendinger Register). The ch. of Johannes[1] Maul and his 1st wife Anna Juliana were:

1) Christoph[2] (HJ), bpt. as "a child" 15 Jan 1688 - sp.: Christoffel Theiss - single man, and Anna Julian Maul - also single (Driedorf Chbk.). Christoph[2] md. Anna Juliana Sergius, d/o the Philip Sargusch listed next to Johannes[1] Maul in Holland in 1709 (HJ). Philip Sargusch, his wife, and 5 ch., were noted in the 6th party (Rotterdam Lists). Philip Sargus with 6 in his family were returned to Holland on board the John, John Chambers the Commander, in 1710 (PRO T1/125,203); the missing person in Sergius's family was his daughter Anna Juliana, who probably md. Christoph[2] Maul somewhere on the trip (HJ). Philippus Sergius md. Maria Elisabeth, d/o the Oberschultheiss Johann Wilhelm Andreas, 14 Nov 1682 at 5418 Nordhofen; their daughter Anna Juliana was bpt. 24 March 1689 - sp.: Anna Lovisa - w/o Hans Peter Hördts at Mogendorf, Maria Juliana - w/o Bertram Bergs, and Johann Thil Scheyer (?) from Selters (Nordhofen Chbk.). Sp. strongly suggest that Philip Sergius was s/o Pastor Wernerus Sergius, who md. Anna Catharina Vieger Whit Tuesday: 1656 at 6208 Langenschwalbach. The family Sergius was documented also at 6348 Herborn and

5419 Rückeroth (where Wernerus Sergius was Pastor), as
well as 6300 Wetzlar. Christoph[2] was #484 on the Hunter
Lists, making his first appearance 4 Aug 1710 with 2 pers.
over 10 yrs. of age; he was recorded next to Johannes[1]
Maul on this entry (HJ). Christoffel Moule was nat. 8 and
9 Sept 1715 (Kingston Nats.). Christoffill Moull was in
the company of Capt. Wittaker in the regiment of Jacob Rut-
sen in Ulster Co. in 1715 (Report of the State Historian,
Vol. I, p. 557). Christoph Maul with wife and ch. was at
Heessberg ca. 1716/17 (Simmendinger Register). Christoffel
Moul was taxed £3 in 1718/19 and £5 in 1720/21 in Kingston
(Ulster Co. Tax Lists). The Kingston Court Records show a
reference to him in Book I, Part C, pp. 29 & 30. Stuffel
Moll was in the Company of the Wall-a-kill in the Ulster
Co. Militia in 1738 (Report of the State Historian, Vol.
I, p. 608). He and Anna Juliana were alive as late as 1751
when they sp. at Montgomery Ref. Church (HJ). The ch. of
Christoph[2] and Anna Juliana Maul were:

    i) Dewertjen[3], bpt. 7 Sept 1712 - sp.: Gysbert Van Den
       Berg and Diewertjen Masten (Kingston Ref. Chbk.). She
       md. Andreas Decker 12 April 1730 (Kingston Ref. Chbk.)

    ii) Margaretha[3], bpt. 19 Sept 1714 - sp.: Frederik Mool
       and Margriet Snyder (Kingston Ref. Chbk.). She md. 26
       Aug 1739 Benjamin Constable (Kingston Ref. Chbk.).

    iii) Anna Catharina[3], bpt. 3 Nov 1717 - sp.: Henderik Fees,
       Anna Catryna Moul, and Anna Catryna Weeden (Kingston
       Ref. Chbk.). She md. Henrich Weller 26 Aug 1739
       (Kingston Ref. Chbk.).

    iv) Johannes[3], bpt. 31 July 1720 - sp.: Frederik Mool and
       Ossertjen (Kingston Ref. Chbk.). He md. Maria Catha-
       rina Menges 6 Sept 1743 (Montgomery Ref. Chbk.). He
       d. 15 March 1804, aged 83-7-15 (Montgomery Ref. Cem.).

    v) Elisabetha[3] (HJ), a sp. with Johannes[3] at Deerpark
       Ref. Church in 1745. She md. William Comfort (HJ).

    vi) Maria[3] (HJ), md. John Mac Lean (HJ).

    vii) Philip[3] (HJ), md. Susanna Hui (HJ).

    viii) Anna[3], bpt. 17 April 1734 - sp.: Henrick Christ and
       Maria Elisabeth Christ (Montgomery Ref. Chbk.). She
       md. John Comfort (HJ).

2) "A Child"[2], bpt. 29 May 1690 - sp.: Barb - w/o Johannes
   Göbels, Gorg Theiss - single, and Anna Kath. - w/o Johannes Stahl at Mademühlen (Driedorf Chbk.).

3) "A Child"[2], bpt. 10 April 1692 - sp.: Johann Christ. Theiss
   there, Johann Thonges - s/o Claus the Hainberger at

Rabenscheid, and Anna Margret - w/o Jost Henrich Maul at
Heiligenborn (Driedorf Chbk.).

By his 2nd wife Elisabetha, the ch. of Johannes[1] Maul were:

4) Anna Ursula[2] (Palatines In N.Y. City), probably the child
bpt. 2 Nov 1694 - sp.: Anna Kath. - w/o Henrich ... at
Rabenscheid, Johan Christ. Betz at Hohroth, Johann Henrich
Drisch - single, and Elsbeth - single d/o Johann Jost Betz
at Mademühlen (Driedorf Chbk.). She md. Nicolaus Sein 1
Oct 1724 (N.Y. City Ref. Chbk.).

5) "A Child"[2], bpt. 10 May 1696 - sp.: Engel - d/o Johann
Driesch, Anna Catharin - d/o the Posth. (?), and Johann
Jost Maul at Heiligborn (Driedorf Chbk.).

6) Anna Catharina[2] (Palatines In N.Y. City), probably the
child bpt. 24 Jan 1698 - sp.: Ursell - w/o Görg Maul in
Driedorf, Anna Kath. - w/o Johann Tönges Sahm at Hohroth,
and Peter Driesch - single (Driedorf Chbk.). Anna Catharina and Caatje Mouwlin were noted as joining the N.Y. City
Ref. Church 19 Feb 1718; their mother Elisabeth had joined
26 Feb 1712, and their sister Ursula had joined 31 May
1715 (HJ). Anna Catharina[2] md. Johann Peter Zenger 11 Sept
1722 (N.Y. City Ref. Chbk.).

7) Catharina[2] (Palatines In N.Y. City), probably the child
bpt. 12 March 1700 - sp.: Anna Julia Driesch - single,
Anna Catharin - w/o Johan Christ Betz, and Johan Henrich
Grün at ... (Driedorf Chbk.). She md. 1st Michael Mon-
cleur, and 2nd 8 June 1723 Jacob Vollenweyler (both N.Y.
City Ref. Chbk.).

8) "A Child"[2], bpt. 19 Jan 1703 - sp.: Anna Catharina - w/o
Georg Theiss, Anna Elis. - w/o ... Grün from ..., and Jo-
han Jacob Wulf from Hohroth (Driedorf Chbk.). A child of
Johannes Maul at Hochroth was bur. 12 May 1704 (Driedorf
Chbk.).

9) Anna Maria[2] (Palatines In N.Y. City), probably the child
bpt. 26 April 1704 - sp.: Johan Christ Göbeler - single,
Johann Görg Driesch - single, An Ursell - w/o Johann Christ
Driesch, and Anna Maria - d/o the Hainberger Conrad at
Donsbach (Driedorf Chbk.). Anna Maria Moulin was conf. 26
Aug 1729; she md. Jacobus Meet 23 June 1738 (both N.Y.
City Ref. Chbk.).

10) Johannes[2], b. in Hohenroth and bpt. 12 Jan 1709 - sp.:
Johannes Maul - s/o the late Johann Jost Maul in Dridorf,
Johan Christ Petz - s/o Johann Christ Betz from Hohnrod,
and Anna-Dorth - w/o Christianus Clas from Mademühlen
(Driedorf Chbk.).

GEORG MAUER (Hunter Lists #485)

The German origins of this family were at 6950 Mosbach/Baden
(18 km. s.e. of Eberbach; Chbks. begin 1626, Ref., and 1696,
Luth., but gaps). Georg Maurer, s/o Bartholomäus Maurer - citizen
and hunter at Adelsheim, md. Apollonia Dorothea, d/o Philip Buchi
- barber here, 29 Nov 1695 (Mosbach Ref. Chbk.).

Georg Mauer (Maurer) made his initial appearance on the Hunter Lists 1 July 1710 with 3 pers. over 10 yrs. of age. It is difficult to separate references for #485 Georg[1] Mauer and #486 Johann Georg[1] Maurer (HJ). Jurick Mower was nat. 17 Jan 1716/16 (Albany Nats.). Georg Maurer and Apolonia with 1 child were at Hunderston ca. 1716 (Simmendinger Register); on this roll they were
listed next to Conrad Hoffman and his family, who sp. Georg[1] Maurer and his (2nd) wife Maria Elisabetha in 1728 at Kamp (HJ). Hans
Jury Maurer was a Palatine Debtor in 1718, 1719 (at Hunterstown),
1721, and 1726 (Livingston Debt Lists). The ch. of Georg[1] Maurer
and his 1st wife Apolonia Dorothea were:

1) Lorentz[2], b. 27 June/7 July 1699 - sp.: Lorentz Reichard
   - s/o the late Danckers-miller here (Mosbach Luth. Chbk.).
   The father was called a gardener in this bpt. entry (HJ).

2) Anna Clara[2], b. 11 Feb 1702 - sp.: Georg Bernhard Bugy -
   s/o ... Philip Bugy, and Anna Clara - single d/o Bartholomäus Maurer - hunter at Bergfelder (?) (Mosbach Luth.
   Chbk.).

3) Georg Peter[2], b. 6 Jan 1704 - sp.: Peter Bender - citizen
   and cooper here (Mosbach Luth. Chbk.).

With his 2nd wife Maria Elisabetha, the ch. of Georg[1] Maurer were:

4) Johann Matthias[2], b. Aug 1720 at Hunterstown and bpt. Pre-
   vwenhoeck at Claverack - sp.: J. Matthias Lauer, J. Matthias Bender, and A. Cath. Hoffmann (N.Y. City Luth.
   Chbk.). A Matthy Moorer was on the Rhinebeck tax rolls Feb
   1756 - Feb 1758 (Dutchess Co. Tax Lists). This Dutchess
   Co. man md. Frena Basset (HJ) and had ch.:

   i) Maria[3], bpt. 5 May 1754 - sp.: Johannes Doom and his
      wife (Rhinebeck Flats Ref. Chbk.).

   ii) Friederich[3], b. 12 Nov 1755 - sp.: Frederic Hillegas
       and Grietje Heillgas (Rhinebeck Flats Ref. Chbk.).

5) Susanna[2], md. as surviving d/o Georg[1] 14 March 1749 Andreas Rees at Taghinak (Loonenburg Luth. Chbk.).

6) Conrad[2], bpt. 8 weeks (?) old 5 May 1728 at Kamp - sp.:
   Conrad Hofman and Liesabeth, Peter Henser's wife, and
   Anna Margreta Koch (N.Y. City Luth. Chbk.). He joined the
   Germantown Ref. Church in 1746. Conrat Mouer was in Capt.

Jeremiah Hogeboom's Company in 1767 (Report of the State Historian, Vol. II, p. 865). He md. Gertraud Schmidt (HJ) and had ch.:

   i?) Georg Adam[3], bpt. 16 April 1755 - sp.: Henderik Stobbelbeen and Elsje Smith (Claverack Ref. Chbk.). These parents & sp. may be reversed, according to Arthur C.M. Kelly.

   ii) Bernhardus[3], bpt. 24 July 1757 - sp.: Thys Emmerik and wife Marytje Smith (Claverack Ref. Chbk.).

   iii) Henrich[3], bpt. 26 July 1761 - sp.: Gerret Bouwman and Marytje Philip (Claverack Ref. Chbk.).

   iv) Petrus[3], bpt. 17 March 1765 - sp.: Andries Rees and Susanna Mauer (Claverack Ref. Chbk.).

   v) Johannes[3], bpt. 8 Nov 1767 - sp.: Johannes Holzappel and wife Marytje Schultis (Claverack Ref. Chbk.).

JOHANN GEORG MAURER (Hunter Lists #486)

A Georg Mauer aged 32, Luth., mason, was at London in the 4th arrivals in 1709 (London Lists).

Johann Georg Maurer made his first appearance on the Hunter Lists 30 June 1710 with 2 pers. over 10 yrs. of age in the family. The family showed 3 pers. over 10 yrs. 24 June 1711. Georg Maurer was auf dem Rarendantz ca. 1716/17 (Simmendinger Register).

PETER MAURER (Hunter Lists #487)

Peter Maurer made his first appearance on the Hunter Lists 4 July 1710 with 3 pers. over 10 yrs. of age. The entry for 13 Sept 1712 showed 3 pers. over 10 yrs. and 1 under 10 yrs. in the household. Peter Mauer: 1 man and 2 women were in Ulster Co. in 1710/11 (West Camp Census). Peter Mouwer was nat. 8 and 9 Sept 1715 (Kingston Nats.). Peter Maurer and Catharina with 2 ch. were at Beckmansland ca. 1716/17 (Simmendinger Register). Peter Mouerse was a freeholder at Kingston in 1728 (Ulster Co. Freeholders). The Kingston Trustees Records refer to Pieter Mowerse in Book I, Part C, pp. 135 - 137, and in Book II, pp. 130 & 131. He was a member of Berkenmeyer's Church Council in 1735 (Albany Protocol, p. 127). The ch. of Peter[1] Maurer and his wife Anna Catharina were:

   1) Anna Margaretha[2], b. 13 Aug 1712 - sp.: Henrich Mann and Anna Margretha Mueller (West Camp Luth. Chbk.). She was conf. 14 Jan 1730, aged 17 yrs. at And. Elig's house at Newtown (N.Y. City Luth. Chbk.). She md. Johann Jacob Eigener (HJ).

2) Johannes², b. 12 Jan 1716 - sp.: Reichart Backus and wife
   Elisabetha Catharina (West Camp Luth. Chbk.). Hannes Maurer was conf. 1 April 1733, aged 17 yrs. at Newton (Loonenburg Luth. Chbk.). He md. Susanna Eigener 19 Jan 1739
   (Loonenburg Luth. Chbk.). They had issue:
   i) Petrus³, b. 26 Dec 1738 and bpt. Newton at Peter Eig-
      ener's - sp.: Johan Jacob Eigener and Margreta (Loon-
      enburg Luth. Chbk.).
   ii) Catharina³, b. 24 March 1740 and bpt. Newton - sp.:
       Frid. Eigener and wife Christina (Loonenburg Luth.
       Chbk.). She md. Johann Georg Behr 19 June 1763
       (Loonenburg Luth. Chbk.).
   iii) Jacobus³, b. 20 Jan 1742 and bpt. Kisket. - sp.: Jo.
        Jacob Eigener and wife Anna Margreta (Loonenburg
        Luth. Chbk.). He md. Maria (--) (HJ); they had ch.
        bpt. at Catskill Ref. Church (HJ).
   iv) Margaretha³, b. 18 July 1744 and bpt. Newton - sp.:
       Peter Eigener and Margr., gr-parents (Loonenburg
       Luth. Chbk.).
   v) Johannes³, b. 6 Aug 1746 and bpt. at Newton - sp.:
      Peter Maurer and Cathar., gr-parents (Loonenburg
      Luth. Chbk.). A man of that name d. 6 May 1816, aged
      68 yrs. (Freese Farm Cem., Asbury, Saugerties).
   vi) Peter³, b. 19 Feb 1749 and bpt. in father's house -
       sp.: Pieter Laux and wife Neeltje (Loonenburg Luth.
       Chbk.). Petrus Maurer md. 23 May 1769 in Kaetsbaen
       Catharina Devenport (Germantown Ref. Chbk.).
   vii) Maria³, b. 6 March 1751 - sp.: Dieter Matestok and
        wife Eva Maria (Loonenburg Luth. Chbk.).
   viii) Leonhardt³, b. 11 Trin.: 1753 - sp.: Leenert Lucas
         and Julana Lucas (Loonenburg Luth. Chbk.).
   ix) Nicolaus³, b. 24 Jan 1756 - sp.: Petrus Eigener and
       Neeltje (Loonenburg Luth. Chbk.).
   x) Abraham³, b. 6 Aug 1761 - sp.: Adam Matestock and
      Catharina (Loonenburg Luth. Chbk.).
3) Christina², bpt. 7 Jan 1722 - sp.: Niclaas Brandauw and
   Christina Stryk (Kingston Ref. Chbk.). Christina Maurer
   de Bruyn was conf. Dom. 1 Adv.: 1739 at Newton (Loonenburg Luth. Chbk.). She md. Johann Friederich Eigener 2
   Dec 1739 (Loonenburg Luth. Chbk.).

JOHANN GEORG MAUSER (Hunter Lists #488)

A Hans Georg Mauser and wife Anna Barbara had a son Philipp
Jacob b. 20 Oct 1703 at 6361 Reichelsheim; however, no firm proof

exists that he was the emigrant 1709er (HJ).

Johann Georg Mauser (sometimes written Mayser) made his first appearance on the Hunter Rolls 30 June 1710 with 2 pers. over 10 yrs. of age and 2 pers. under 10. The entry for 4 Aug 1710 read 3 pers. over 10 yrs. and 1 under 10. Johannes Georg Mayser's Widd^W was enrolled in the cumulative entry on 24 Dec 1711 with 2 pers. over 10 yrs. of age and 1 under 10 yrs.

EVA MAUSIN (Hunter Lists #489)

The German origins of this woman were at 5431 Mogendorf (20 km. n.e. of Neuwied), entries in registers of 5418 Nordhofen (2 km. further n.; Chbks. begin 1659). Her father was Augustinus Maus from Mogendorf, who md. 11 Nov 1672 Anna Margaretha Schramme (?). The ch. of this couple were:

Hans Wilhelm, bpt. 5 March 1666.

Anna Gertraud, md. 11 Feb 1705 David Kröllens.

+ Anna Eva, called d/o Augustinus Maus at Nordhofen in 1707 when she sp. in the family Tröller.

Eva Maus made her initial appearance on the Hunter Lists 4 July 1710 with 1 pers. over 10 yrs. of age in the family. Anna Eva Meysen from Mogendorf joined the N.Y. City Ref. Church 28 Feb 1710/11. She md. Jacob Risch (HJ).

CHRISTOPH MAY'S WIDDOW (Hunter Lists #490)

A Christoph May, widower, md. Anna Catharina, d/o the late Georg Nöller, 14 Nov 1693 at 6102 Pfungstadt; however, no connective to the 1709er has been established with this man (HJ). Kristoffel Mig (?), his wife, and 2 ch., were on Capt. Frans Robbinson's ship in Holland in 1709 (Rotterdam Lists). Christoph Mey aged 35, his wife, and a daughter aged 3, Ref., husbandman and vinedresser, were in the 3rd arrivals in England later that yr. (London Lists).

Christoph May's Widdow had but one entry on the Hunter Lists, on 4 July 1710 with 1 pers. over 10 yrs.; a note in the Ledger section of these rolls notes she md. with Frederic Merckel. (Merckel's wife was named Anna Barbara Alman - HJ).

OTTILIA MAYIN (Hunter Lists #491)

Perhaps this emigrant was the Ottilia Traupel, d/o Class Traupel and wid/o Christoffel Haff, who md. Hans Mayss 29 Nov 1684 at 6095 Ginsheim-Gustavsburg; or perhaps she was the Anna Ottilia, wid/o Hans Jacquet - Gemeinsmann at Eussertahl, who md. 16 Feb

1706 at Queichhambach Johannes Mey, a Luth. from the Gerwilen (?) at 6747 <u>Annweiler</u> (HJ).

Ottilia Mayin had but one entry on the Hunter Lists: on the cumulative notation 24 Dec 1711 with 1 pers. over 10 yrs. of age.

<u>PETER MAY</u> (Hunter Lists #492)

The origins of this family were at 6551 <u>Niederhausen</u> (7 km. s.w. of Bad Kreuznach) and probably at 6521 <u>Dalsheim</u> (12 km. w. of Worms). Peter Mey, Catholic, was a resident of Niederhausen in 1698 (Alzey Census of 1698). As he often was surrounded by 1709ers from the Kreuznach - Worms area on extant Palatine mss., he probably moved ca. 1702 to Dalsheim, where he is found in the registers there (HJ). A Johann Peeter May, his wife, and 2 ch., were on Capt. Francois Warens's ship in the 5th party in Holland (Rotterdam Lists); however, this family was returned to Holland in the later part of that yr. (PRO T1/119, 136-153). The N.Y. emigrant family was the Peter May, his wife, and 4 ch., on Capt. Johan Rannelds's ship in the 3rd party in Holland in 1709 (Rotterdam Lists); on this ship's roll, he was registered next to Reysdorff and his family, and a Johannes Reisdorff was documented at 6551 <u>Waldböckelheim</u>, a town almost next to Niederhausen (HJ).

Johann Peter Mayy made his first appearance on the Hunter Lists 4 Aug 1710 with 2 pers. over 10 yrs. of age and 3 pers. under 10 yrs. The family showed 3 over 10 and 3 under 10 yrs. on 31 Dec 1710, 3 pers. over 10 and 2 under 10 on 25 March 1711, and 2 pers. over 10 and 2 under 10 yrs. 29 Sept 1711. The 25 March 1712 entry went down to 1 over 10 and 2 under 10 yrs., and then returned to 2 over 10 yrs. and 2 under 10 on 24 June 1712. Peter May was nat. 8 and 9 Sept 1715 (Kingston Nats.). Peter Mayen's Widow was noted with 3 ch. at Hunderston ca. 1716/17 (Simmendinger Register). Doritee Mayen was a Palatine Debtor in 1718 and 1721 (Livingston Debt Lists). The Dalsheim registers, which begin in 1692 for Ref. and 1706 for Luth., call the w/o Johann Peter May Magdalena. By his 1st marriage, the ch. of Peter[1] May were:

1) <u>Peter</u>[2] (HJ), md. as single man b. Germany 29 Sept 1723 (Jo)anna Catharina Susanna Kieffer (Kingston Ref. Chbk.). They had issue:
   i) <u>Balthasar</u>[3] (HJ), conf. with Christina and Johannes May 31 Oct 1742 at Newton (Loonenburg Luth. Chbk.).
   ii) <u>Christina</u>[3], md. as d/o Peter[2] 13 Aug 1745 Johann Henrich Schmidt (Loonenburg Luth. Chbk.).
   iii) <u>Johannes</u>[3] (HJ), conf. with Balthasar[3] and Christina[3] in 1742 at Loonenburg Luth. Church.

iv) <u>Catharina</u>³, md. as a d/o Peter² 13 Aug 1751 Johann
Friederich Kreisseler (Loonenburg Luth. Chbk.).

v) <u>Elisabetha</u>³, b. 3 March 1730 and bpt. at Kisket. -
sp.: Johan Jacob Maul and Lisabeth Emmerichs (Loonenburg Luth. Chbk.). Cathar. and Lisabeth May were
conf. at Newton 21 March 1747 (Loonenburg Luth.
Chbk.). She md. Johannes Werner 7 Jan 1754 or 1755
(Loonenburg Luth. Chbk.).

vi) <u>Anna</u>³, b. 15 April 1732 and bpt. at Newton - sp.:
Henrich Fees and Anna Christina (Loonenburg Luth.
Chbk.).

vii) <u>Maria</u>³, b. 29 Dec 1734 and bpt. at Kisket - sp.:
Friedrich Schram and wife Marytje (Loonenburg Luth.
Chbk.). She md. Nicolaus Kreisseler in 1757 (Loon-
enburg Luth. Chbk.).

viii) <u>Margaretha</u>³, b. 10 May 1736 and bpt. at Kisket. -
sp.: Hendryk Brouwer and wife Anna Margreta (Loonenburg Luth. Chbk.). She md. Johann Christian Pleto
(Bledau) 19 Oct 1762 (Loonenburg Luth. Chbk.).

ix) <u>Wilhelm</u>³, b. 25 Feb 1738 and bpt. at Kisket. - sp.:
Joh: Wilhelm Schram and Christina Fuhrer (Loonenburg
Luth. Chbk.).

x) <u>Wilhelm</u>³, b. 20 Nov 1743 and bpt. at Pieter May's
house - sp.: Wilhelm Kieffer and Maria Schramm, Jr.
(Loonenburg Luth. Chbk.). Wilhelm³ md. Magdalena
Janssen 5 April 1765 (Loonenburg Luth. Chbk.).
They had issue bpt. at Coxsackie Ref. and Loonenburg
Luth.Churches (HJ). Wilhelm³ was a Loyalist and
fought in Butler's Rangers; he and a J. May were at
Niagara 17 Sept 1787 (Information from Major Donald
C. Holmes of Kanata, Ontario).

2) <u>Johann Philip</u>², bpt. 24 Sept 1702 - sp.: Herr Johann Philipp Orb, the Schultheiss at Pfeddersheim (Dalsheim
Chbk.).

3) <u>Johann Jacob</u>², bpt. 22 March 1705 - sp.: Johann Jacob
Birb, single man (Dalsheim Chbk.).

4) <u>Christian Ludwig</u>², bpt. 23 Oct 1707 - sp.: H. Christian
Ludwig Freye, Ref. Pastor here (Dalsheim Chbk.).

Major Donald C. Holmes, an active member of many Canadian
genealogical and historical associations, has been a lively correspondent over the years on the Mays, Hainers, Schmidts, and
other Palatine families. His sharing of Loyalist materials especially has been appreciated in the course of this project (HJ).

ANNA MARIA MENGELIN (Hunter Lists #493)

Hans Wendel Megel, his wife, and 2 ch., were on Capt. John Howlentzen's ship in Holland in the 4th party of 1709 (Rotterdam Lists). Wendel Mengel aged 27, his wife, a son aged 3, daughters aged 5 and 2 days, Ref., husbandman and vinedresser, were in the 4th arrivals in England later that yr. (London Lists).

Anna Maria Menglin made her first appearance on the Hunter Lists 4 July 1710 with 1 pers. over 10 yrs. and 1 pers. under 10 yrs. of age. The family was recorded with 1 pers. over 10 and 3 under 10 yrs. on 4 Aug 1710, where the head of the household was called Wendel Mengel's Wid[W]. Anna Maria Mengelsin, a Wid. aged 27, John Carolus Mengelsin aged 3, Anna Maria Mengelsin aged 5, and Juliana Mengelsin aged 1½, were in N.Y. City in 1710/11 (Palatines In N.Y. City). Anna Maria Mengelsin joined the N.Y. City Ref. Church 26 Feb 1712, and then was noted as departed. Anna Maria Mengesin, a Widow with 3 ch., was at Neu-Yorck ca. 1716/17 (Simmendinger Register). Marytie Becker, wid/o Wendel Mengely, b. in Stadycken in the Paltz in Germany, had banns to marry John De Vries, single man b. at Tappan, 10 Jan 1719 (Tappan Ref. Chbk.). The ch. of Johann Wendel[1] Mengel and Anna Maria were:

1) Anna Maria[2] (Palatines In N.Y. City). Maria Mangley, d/o Anna Maria M., a child aged 8 was bound to Kathe Provost of N.Y. 2 May 1712 (Apprenticeship Lists).
2) Johann Carl[2] (Palatines In N.Y. City). Charles Mangley, s/o Anna Maria M., a child aged 6 was bound to Ffredk Seabringh of Kings 2 May 1712 (Apprenticeship Lists). Sp. at Tappan show that he was the Johannes Mangel who md. Maria Retan (HJ). They had issue:
   i) Elisabetha[3], b. 11 Jan 1738 - sp.: Abraham Retan and Elisabedt Retan (Tappan Ref. Chbk.).
   ii) Maria[3], b. 29 Feb 1740 - sp.: Johannes De Vries and wife Marytie (Tappan Ref. Chbk.).
3) Anna Juliana[2] (Palatines In N.Y. City).

There was a Catharina Mangel, w/o Matt[S] Forber, who joined the N.Y. City Ref. Church 20 Nov 1715; however, no firm connective between her and the family of Johann Wendel[1] Mengel has been established (HJ).

JOHANNES MENGES (Hunter Lists #494)

The foreign roots of this family were at 6930 Eberbach (18 km. n.w. of Mosbach; Chbks. begin 1615, Ref.). Through the kindness of James L. Powell of Seattle, Washington and his Mingus Family Association, a history of the family in Eberbach has been

given to me. The earliest known Menges in the town was <u>Hans Men-</u>
<u>ges</u>, b. ca. 1430, appearing on the Eberbach tax list of 1459. His
son was <u>Claus Menges</u>, ca. 1462 - 1516, appearing on Eberbach tax
lists 1487 - 1516. The s/o Claus Menges was <u>Jost Menges</u>, b. ca.
1510 and called the Mayor on various old mss. Jost's son was named
<u>Matthias Menges</u>, b. ca. 1542, and the s/o Matthias was called <u>Hans</u>
<u>Menges</u>, b. ca. 1566. The s/o Hans Menges was <u>Wilhelm Menges</u>, b.
ca. 1602 who md. Margaretha Kern 4 Sept 1627; their son was <u>Leon-</u>
<u>hardt Menges</u>, the father of the emigrant 1709er, b. 26 Jan 1634.
The 2nd w/o Leonhardt Menges was Elisabetha Schell, whom he md. 20
Sept 1659; she was the d/o Hans Schell and wife Bertha Koch, and
Elisabetha Schell Menges' dates were 7 Sept 1634 - 20 Nov 1679.
The emigrant Johannes[1] Menges was the s/o Leonhardt and Elisabetha
Menges and b. 24 June 1674. (Herein ends the material furnished
by the Mingus Family Association). Johannes[1] md. Susanna (--), who
d. 24 Aug 1702, aged 20 and 3/4 yrs. old, after suffering from con-
sumption for ½ a yr. The honourable Hanß Menges, citizen and carpenter here and widower, md. (2nd) 28 Nov 1702 Maria Eva, d/o the
also honourable Valentin Schölch - citizen and raftsman here.
Maria Eva, d/o H. Veltin Schelche and wife Anna Margrita, was b.
3 Feb 1678 - sp.: Eva - w/o Hans Phil. Bus, citizen and raftsman.
Hannß Valentin Schelche, s/o Georg Schelch - citizen and raftsman,
md. Anna Margaretha, single d/o the late Hans Stumpf - citizen
and raftsman here, 8 May 1677. John Menges aged 35, his wife, and
sons aged 9, 3, and ¼, Ref., carpenter, were in England in the
3rd arrivals of 1709 (London Lists).

Johannes Menges made his initial appearance on the Hunter
Lists 1 July 1710 with 3 pers. over 10 yrs. and 2 under 10. The
household showed 3 over 10 and 1 under 10 yrs. 31 Dec 1710, 3 over
10 on 25 March 1711, 2 pers. over 10 yrs. and 1 under 10 25 March
1712, and 3 over 10 yrs. of age on 24 June 1712. Johanis Menges
was nat. 8 and 9 Sept 1715 (Kingston Nats.). Johannis Mingas was
taxed £15 in Kingston in 1718/19 and 1720/21 (Ulster Co. Tax
Lists). The Kingston Trustees Records mention Johannis Minges in
Book I, Part B, pp. 99 - 101, and Book I, Part C, pp. 5 & 6. John
Mings was in the Company of the Wall-a-kill in the Ulster Co. Militia in 1738 (<u>Report of the State Historian</u>, Vol. I, p. 609). Johannes Mingus was said to have built a grist mill in the old village of Montgomery and later sold the 200 acres of land upon which
the village of Montgomery was built (<u>History of Orange Co.</u>, by
Russell Headley, p. 311, per James L. Powell). The 3rd w/o Johannes[1] Menges was Anna Eva Busch (HJ). She was bpt. Dominica, p.
Trin. 18: 1686 at 5455 <u>Rengsdorf</u>; her parents were the Herman

Busch, s/o Bartholomei Busch of Heinsen in the State of Hanover,
and Elisabetha, d/o the late Wilhelm Schlemer of Melsbach, who md.
at Rengsdorf Dom. V. p.t.: 1679/80. Herman Busch aged 54 with a
son aged 4 and a daughter aged 24, Luth., husbandman and vinedresser, was in the 3rd arrivals at London amongst all the other Neuwied area Palatines in 1709 (London Lists); his wife (Maria) Elisabetha had d. the 1st week of Nov 1698 at Rengsdorf. The child of
Johannes[1] Menges and his 1st wife Susanna was:

    1) <u>Hieronymus</u>[2], b. 7 Oct 1700 - sp.: Hieronymus - single s/o
       Hans Peter Neuen, citizen and merchant here (Eberbach
       Chbk.). Hieronymus Menges was nat. next to Johanis Menges
       8 and 9 Sept 1715 (Kingston Nats.). Jeronemus Mingers
       testified concerning a felony supposedly committed by John
       Nealy 11 Feb 1728/29 (Ulster Co. N.Y. Court Records in
       <u>National Genealogical Society Quarterly</u>, 1973). He md. as
       a single man b. Germany and resides at the Walkill 8 May
       1731 Maria Hoff (Kingston Ref. Chbk.).

By his 2nd wife Maria Eva, the ch. of Johannes[1] Menges were:

    2) <u>Maria Barbara</u>[2], b. 4 July 1703 - sp.: Hans Michel Stumpf
       (Eberbach Chbk.).
    3) <u>Susanna</u>[2], b. 23 July 1704 and bur. Aug 1704, aged 14 days
       - sp.: Anna Barbara - w/o Hans Michel Stumpf the tailor
       (Eberbach Chbk.).
    4) <u>Johann Leonhardt</u>[2], b. 13 Oct 1706 - sp.: Hans Michel Stumpf
       - citizen and tailor here (Eberbach Chbk.).
    5) <u>Johann Michael</u>[2], b. 23 April 1709 - sp.: same as before
       (Eberbach Chbk.).

By his 3rd wife Anna Eva Busch (who md. Matthias Melsbach after
the death of Johannes[1] Menges - HJ), Johannes[1] had issue:

    6) <u>Anna</u>[2] (HJ), sometimes called Anna Veronica, who md. Steph-
       anus Christ (HJ).
    7) <u>Anna Elisabetha</u>[2], b. 21 July 1715 - sp.: Mattheus Schle-
       mer, and Anna Elisabetha - w/o Peter Becker (West Camp
       Luth. Chbk.). She md. Lorentz Christ 7 Oct 1735 (Montgom-
       ery Ref. Chbk.).
    8) <u>Gertraud</u>[2], b. 6 Jan 1718 - sp.: Peter Gistler, Anna Ger-
       draut Meyer, and Gerdraut Kehl (West. Camp Luth. Chbk.).
    9) <u>Christian</u>[2], bpt. 8 Jan 1721 - sp.: Christiaan Meyer and
       Anna-Geertruy Meyer (Kingston Ref. Chbk.). He md. Maria
       Robertson (HJ) and had issue:
       i) <u>Elisabetha</u>[3], bpt. 12 Aug 1746 - sp.: Lawrence Krist
          and wife Elisabeth Menges (Montgomery Ref. Chbk.).
       ii) <u>Maria</u>[3], bpt. 20 Jan 1748 at Shawangunk - sp.: Fred-
          erich Gimberg and Maria Borde (Kingston Ref. Chbk.).

    iii) <u>Johannes</u>³, bpt. 15 Oct 1751 - sp.: John Roberson and
        wife Catharine Muller (Montgomery Ref. Chbk.).
    iv) <u>Hieronymus</u>³, bpt. 28 Oct 1753 - sp.: Hieronymus Men-
        ges and Maria Menges (Montgomery Ref. Chbk.).
    v) <u>Jacobus</u>³, bpt. 15 May 1756 - sp.: Johannis Maul and
        wife Maria Menges (Montgomery Ref. Chbk.).
    vi) <u>Moses</u>³, bpt. Nov 1759 (Montgomery Goodwill Church,
        per James L. Powell).
  10) <u>Maria Catharina</u>² (HJ), md. Johannes Maul 6 Sept 1743
      (Montgomery Ref. Chbk.).

<u>FERDINAND MENTGEN</u> (Hunter Lists #495)

    Maria Elisabetha Manngen, d/o Ferdinand of Ansberg (formerly)
of Wollbergshofen near Colln in the commune of Neuburg, md. Philipp Henrich Cuntz, s/o Mattheus of Queensberg (formerly) of Bischmusen near Saarbruecken, 25 June 1716 (West Camp Luth. Chbk.).
The village of origin actually was 5227 <u>Wilberhofen/Windeck</u> (5 km.
s.e. of Ruppichteroth). Entries on this nomadic family were found
at 5227 <u>Dattenfeld</u> (2 km. s. of Wilberhofen; Chbks. begin 1619,
Cath.), at 5202 <u>Geistingen/Hennef</u> (4 km. s.e. of St. Augustin;
Chbks. begin 1667, Cath.), at 5419 <u>Dierdorf</u> (19 km. n.e. of Neuwied; Chbks. begin 1676, Ref.) and at 5231 <u>Mehren</u> (10 km. w. of
Altenkirchen; Chbks. begin 1680). The father of Ferdinand¹ Mentgen is not known for certain, however, he may have been the Hermann Mentgen Sr., the Johann Mentgen, or the Henrich Mentgen mentioned early in the Dattenfeld Cath. registers (HJ). Ferdinant
Mentgen from Dattenfelt md. Clara from Stoßdorf 21 Jan 1693; the
sp. were Gerhard Heyen and Jacobo Heußer (Geistingen Cath. Chbk.).
In 1701 the Mehren Chbk. called Ferdinand Mängen a poor man from
the parish Geistingen who is staying on the Heuberg. In 1704 the
Dierdorf registers called Ferdinand and Clara a couple aus dem
Bergischen, and in 1707 they were called of Giershofen in this
same chbk. Ferdinand Mönd, his wife, and 4 ch. were on Capt Leonard Allan's ship in the 5th party of Palatines in Holland (Rotterdam Lists).

    Ferdinand Mentgen made his initial appearance on the Hunter
Lists 1 July 1710 with 4 pers. over 10 yrs. and 1 pers. under 10.
The family was recorded with 4 pers. over 10 yrs. of age 4 Oct
1710, 4 over 10 and 1 under 10 24 June 1712, and then 4 pers. over
10 yrs. 13 Sept 1712. Ferdo Mentegen was a soldier from Annsberg
in 1711 (Palatine Volunteers To Canada). Firdinard Menti was nat.
17 Jan 1715/16 (Albany Nats.). Ferdinand Mängen and Anna Clara
with 2 ch. were at Wormsdorff ca. 1716/17 (Simmendinger Register).

Ferdnand Menti was a Palatine Debtor in 1718, 1719 (at Kingsberry),
1721, and 1726 (Livingston Debt Lists). A receipt signed by Ferdinand Monti mentioning Harm[e] Pitzer dated 5 Feb 1722 is in the
Livingston Papers, Reel #11. A Faerneis Maemis subscribed 6 shillings in 1727 (N.Y. City Luth. Protocol). The ch. of Ferdinand[1]
Mentgen and Anna Clara were:

1) Anna Barbara[2], bpt. 31 Dec 1693 - sp.: Wilhelm Schomacher
   (?) at Stoßdorf, and Elisabetha - w/o Petrus Kremer at
   Geistingen (Geistingen Chbk.); the father is called Fer-
   dinandus ex Stoßdorffen on this bpt. (HJ). She md. Peter
   Hagedorn (HJ); for further evidence of this see bpt. #99
   in 1740 at Rhinebeck Flats Ref. Church, when Pieter Hagedoorn and Barber Man(_y) sp. Johannes Wever (HJ).

2) Maria Elisabetha[2], md. as d/o Ferdinand[1] 25 June 1716
   Philip Henrich Cuntz (West Camp Luth. Chbk.).

3) "A Daughter"[2], bpt. 29 May 1701 - sp.: Hermann auf dem
   Herberg, Thrin (?) - a wid. there, and Anna Immel - wid/o
   Ludwig Zimmerman there (Mehren Chbk.).

4) Johann Peter[2], b. 22 Feb 1704 at Giershofen - sp.: Peter
   - s/o the late Servatius Jungblut at Giershofen (Dierdorf
   Chbk.). He d. 14 Sept 1708 (Dierdorf Chbk.).

5) Johann Leonhardt[2], b. 1 April 1707 - sp.: Frantz Schäfer
   and Maria Gertraud - w/o Bertram Wolf (Dierdorf Chbk.).

6) Johann Georg[2], d. 18 Sept 1708 (Dierdorf Chbk.).

FRIDERICH MERCKEL (Hunter Lists #496)

The ancestral home of this family was at 6733 Haßloch (7 km.
e. of Neustadt a.d. Weinstraße; Chbks. begin 1700, Ref.). The name
of the 1st w/o Friederich[1] Merckel was Anna Barbara, according to
the Haßloch registers.

Friderich Merckel made his first entry on the Hunter Lists
4 July 1710 with 3 pers. over 10 yrs. and 2 under 10. The notation
for 4 Aug 1710 mentions the same number in the household, and then
records a special entry for his wife, the Wid. Mayin; the Ledger
section adds Christoph May's Widdow md. with Frederic Merckel. The
family showed 4 over 10 and 2 under 10 4 Oct 1710; they were entered next to Philipp Helmer on this date, and Helmer originated
near Haßloch at Neustadt a.d. Weinstraße (HJ). The household was
noted with 5 pers. over 10 and 2 under 10 on 31 Dec 1710, with 6
over 10 and 1 under 10 yrs. on 24 June 1711, with 7 over 10 yrs.
on 29 Sept 1711, with 7 over 10 and 1 under 10 on 24 Dec 1711,
and finally with 6 pers. over 10 yrs. and 1 pers. under 10 yrs.
13 Sept 1712. Fred Mirckle: 1 man, 2 lads aged 9 - 15 yrs., 1

woman, 3 maids aged 9 - 15 yrs., were in Ulster Co. in 1710/11
(West Camp Census). Fred[k] Markel was nat. 8 and 9 Sept 1715
(Kingston Nats.). Friederich ... (some translations give
"M..ue..") and Anna Barbara, with 6 ch. were at Beckmansland ca.
1716/17 (Simmendinger Register). Ffredrick Markel was taxed £10
in Kingston in 1718/19, and £12 there in 1720/21 (Ulster Co. Tax
Lists). Frederik Merkel was a freeholder of Kingston in 1728 (Ulster Co. Freeholders). The Kingston Trustees Records mention him
in Book I, Part B, pp. 96 & 97, and in Book II, pp. 13 & 14. With
his 1st wife Anna Barbara in Germany, the ch. of Friederich[1] Merckel were:

1) Anna[2] (HJ), md. 25 Nov 1720 Peter Winne (Kingston Ref.
   Chbk.).

2) Lorentz[2] (HJ), md. 6 April 1724 Sibylla Catharina Kehl
   (Kingston Ref. Chbk.). The Kingston Trustees Records mention Lowrens Merkel in Book I, Part C, pp. 118 & 119.
   Lowrens Merkell was a freeholder of Kingston in 1728 (Ulster Co. Freeholders). The ch. of Lorentz[2] were:

   i) Maria[3], bpt. 14 Feb 1725 - sp.: Manus Hommel and
      Marytjen Markel (Kingston Ref. Chbk.).

   ii) Gertraud[3], bpt. 26 June 1726 - sp.: Jury Keel and
       Geertruy Wenne (Kingston Ref. Chbk.).

   iii) Elisabetha[3], bpt. 21 April 1728 - sp.: Mathys Merkel
        and Elisabeth Keel (Kingston Ref. Chbk.).

3) Anna Maria[2], bpt. 21 Dec 1701 - sp.: Anna Maria - d/o
   Jacob Rümlin the carpenter here (Haßloch Chbk.). A Maria
   Merckel md. Johann Michael Planck 20 Nov 1738 (Katsbaan
   Ref. Chbk.).

4) Johann Matthias[2], bpt. 20 June 1703 - sp.: Joh. Mathes
   Löffler (?) - Gemeinsmann and butcher here (Haßloch
   Chbk.). Mattys Merkell was in the foot Company of the
   Kingston, Ulster Co. Militia in 1738 (Report of the State
   Historian, Vol. I, p. 604). Martininus Marckell was nat.
   Oct 1740, and called a farmer of Ulster Co. at his nat.
   (Denizations, Naturalizations, & Oaths of Allegiance in
   Colonial N.Y., by Kenneth Scott and Kenn Stryker-Rodda,
   p. 44). He md. Margaretha Kehl (HJ) and had issue:

   i) Friederich[3], bpt. 30 June 1734 - sp.: Coenraat Regt-
      meyer and Barbara Alman (Kingston Ref. Chbk.). A
      Friederich Merckel md. Lea Schmidt (HJ), and they
      had issue bpt. at Kingston Ref. and Marbletown Ref.
      Churches; perhaps this man was Friederich[3], s/o Jo-
      hann Matthias[2], or perhaps the man who md. Lea was
      a Friederich[2] Jr., s/o the emigrant Friederich[1] (HJ).

ii.) Wilhelm[3], bpt. 30 May 1737 - sp.: Barent Markel and
Saartje Nieukirk (Katsbaan Ref. Chbk.). He probably
md. Rachel Becker and had issue bpt. at Katsbaan Ref.
Church (HJ).

iii) Anna[3], bpt. 14 Oct 1739 - sp.: Pieter Wenne and Antje
Merkel (Kingston Ref. Chbk.). She md. Henrich Hend-
rixen 26 Nov 1756 (Kingston Ref. Chbk.).

iv) Gertraud[3], bpt. 20 June 1742 - sp.: Peter Wenne Jr.
and Geertje Langedyk (Kingston Ref. Chbk.). She md.
Valentin Schramm 28 Dec 1761 (Kingston Ref. Chbk.).

v) Johannes[3], bpt. 10 Sept 1744 - sp.: Jan Wulfin and
wife Grietje Miller (Katsbaan Ref. Chbk.). A Johannes
Merckel md. Jantje Wennie 29 Nov 1775 (Kingston Ref.
Chbk.).

vi) Mattheus[3], bpt. 22 Nov 1747 - sp.: Frederich Wenne
and Jannetje Kort (Kingston Ref. Chbk.).

vii) Margaretha[3], bpt. 25 June 1750 - sp.: Arend Winne and
Annaatje Winne (Katsbaan Ref. Chbk.).

viii) Maria[3], bpt. 14 Oct 1752 - sp.: Laurents Wenne and
Marretje Osterhout (Katsbaan Ref. Chbk.).

ix) Lorentz[3], bpt. 19 April 1756 - sp.: Willem Regtmeyer
and wife Antje Hommel (Katsbaan Ref. Chbk.).

5) Elisabetha[2], bpt. 24 Dec 1704 - sp.: Elisab. - w/o Ludwig
Würth (Haßloch Chbk.).

6) Johann Andreas[2], bpt. 5 Sept 1706 - sp.: Joh. Andr. Schab-
ebauer here (Haßloch Chbk.).

7) Margaretha Philippina[2], bpt. 23 Dec 1708 (Haßloch Chbk.).
By his 2nd wife Anna Barbara Alman, wid/o Christoph May, the ch.
of Friederich[1] Merckel were:

8) Johann Adam[2], b. 10 Dec 1711 - sp.: Johann Adam Friderich
and wife Regina (West Camp Luth. Chbk.).

9) Maria Elisabetha[2], b. 16 Feb 1713 - sp.: Maria Elisabetha
Straub (West Camp Luth. Chbk.). She md. Jacob Brink 22 Dec
1732 (Kingston Ref. Chbk.).

10) Bernhardt[2], bpt. as Barent 5 June 1715 - sp.: Barent Bor-
hans and Margriet Jansz (Kingston Ref. Chbk.). The case of
Barent Merkel vs. Jurjan Tappan was recorded in the Court
of Common Pleas at Kingston in 1741. Barnet, Wilhelmus,
Petrus, Benj'n, and William Mercle were all on the roll of
Capt. Stephen Nottingham in 1758 (Report of the State Historian, Vol. I, pp. 836 - 838). Barent[2] md. 1st Cornelia
Van Der Merken, and md. 2nd Barbara Van Der Merken 13 Sept
1747 (both Kingston Ref. Chbk.). By his 1st wife Cornelia
he had issue:

i) <u>Benjamin</u>[3], bpt. 14 Oct 1739 - sp.: Joh: Van Wagening and Rachel Van Der Merken (Kingston Ref. Chbk.). A Benjamin Merkel md. Margaretha Neukirch (HJ). Papers in the estate of Benjamin Merkle, late of Rochester, were issued 19 June 1789 (Ulster Co. Administrations Book A). He is mentioned in <u>Ulster Co. in the Revolution</u>, p. 155).

ii) <u>Elias</u>[3], bpt. 17 Oct 1742 - sp.: Wilhelmus Merkel and Barbara Van Der Merken (Kingston Ref. Chbk.).

iii) <u>Catharina</u>[3], bpt. 23 June 1745 - sp.: Hans Vandermerken and Susanna Bosch (Kingston Ref. Chbk.).

11) <u>Eva</u>[2], b. 21 Dec 1716 - sp.: Eva Mueller (West Camp Luth. Chbk.). She md. Jeremias Kittel 16 Sept 1739 (Kingston Ref. Chbk.).

12) <u>Elisabetha</u>[2], b. 16 Feb 1719 - sp.: Johann Klein and wife (West Camp Luth. Chbk.). She md. Thomas Bosch 9 March 1739 (Kingston Ref. Chbk.).

13) <u>Johannes</u>[2], bpt. 25 Sept 1720 - sp.: Christoffel Mouwel and Annetjen Mouwel (Kingston Ref. Chbk.). A Johannes Merckel, single man b. Kingston and lives at Smithsfield, md. Anna Elisabetha Schnaub, single woman b. Punstadt, Germany, 10 Sept 1746 (Walpeck Ref. Chbk.).

14) <u>Wilhelmus</u>[2], bpt. 22 July 1722 - sp.: Wilhelmus Brandouw and Elisabeth Brandouw (Kingston Ref. Chbk.). He md. Sarah Koch (Kok) 4 April 1752 (Kingston Ref. Chbk.). They had issue:

i) <u>James</u>[3], bpt. 21 Jan 1753 - sp.: James Scot and Susanna Bettis (Kingston Ref. Chbk.).

ii) <u>Wilhelmus</u>[3], bpt. 22 Jan 1754 - sp.: Barent Merkel and Grietje Hoffman (Marbletown Ref. Chbk.).

iii) <u>Johannes</u>[3], bpt. 17 Oct 1755 - sp.: Samuell Kock and Marritje Kock (Marbletown Ref. Chbk.).

iv) <u>Friederich</u>[3], bpt. 19 Dec 1756 - sp.: Jacob Nottingham and Magdalena Kok (Kingston Ref. Chbk.).

v) <u>Petrus</u>[3], bpt. 29 Oct 1758 - sp.: Petrus Merkel and his wife Sara West Broek (Kingston Ref. Chbk.).

vi) <u>Sarah</u>[3], bpt. 24 Nov 1761 - sp.: Cornelius Coole and wife Maria Schoonmaker (Marbletown Ref. Chbk.).

vii) <u>Alexander</u>[3], bpt. 17 July 1763 - sp.: Johannis Schomaker and Cathrina Schomaker (Marbletown Ref. Chbk.).

viii) <u>Benjamin</u>[3], bpt. 16 Dec 1764 - sp.: Benjamin Markel and Barbara Bosch (Kingston Ref. Chbk.).

ix) <u>Jacob</u>[3], bpt. 21 Sept 1766 - sp.: Frederick Busch and wife Jane (Marbletown Ref. Chbk.).

x) <u>Gerrebraggie</u>³, bpt. 30 Oct 1768 (Marbletown Ref. Chbk.).

xi) <u>Abraham</u>³, bpt. 26 Dec 1770 (Marbletown Ref. Chbk.).

15) <u>Petrus</u>², bpt. 14 Feb 1725 - sp.: Pieter Overbag and Maria Overbag (Kingston Ref. Chbk.).

16) <u>Petrus</u>², bpt. 25 Sept 1726 - sp.: Manus Hommel and Grietjen Snyder (Kingston Ref. Chbk.). He md. Sarah Westbrook (HJ), and they had ch.:

    i) <u>Johannes</u>³, bpt. 27 Jan 1760 - sp.: Thomas Bosch (Kingston Ref. Chbk.).

    ii) <u>Catharina</u>³, bpt. 11 April 1762 - sp.: Johannes Van Wagenen and wife Lena Kittel (Kingston Ref. Chbk.).

    iii) <u>Jacob</u>³, bpt. 1764 - sp.: Jacob Keator Jr. and Sara Ennist (Marbletown Ref. Chbk.).

    iv) <u>Elisabetha</u>³, bpt. 3 June 1766 -sp.: Jacobus Bos and Maria Bos (Kingston Ref. Chbk.).

    v) <u>Lea</u>³, bpt. 10 Oct 1770 (Kingston Ref. Chbk.).

    vi) <u>Friederich</u>³, bpt. 26 Dec 1772 (Marbletown Ref. Chbk.).

17) <u>Anna</u>², bpt. 18 May 1729 - sp.: Zacharias Bakker and Maria Merkel (Kingston Ref. Chbk.). She probably md. Jacobus Bosch Jr. 13 Oct 1745 (Kingston Ref. Chbk.).

<u>ANNA CATHARINA MERTZIN</u> (Hunter Lists #497)

Anna Catharina, wid/o Johann Mertz, md. Johann Hermann Speicherman, widower of (near) Otterberg, 27 July 1710 (West Camp Luth. Chbk.). There was a Johannes Mertz, teacher in Langenhayn, who had a daughter Maria Catharina bpt. 14 Nov 1705 at 6238 <u>Lorsbach</u>; however I have no proof he was the 1709er (HJ).

Anna Catharina Mertzin made her initial appearance on the Hunter Lists 30 June 1710 with 1 pers. over 10 yrs. and 3 pers. under 10. The entry for 4 Aug 1710 showed 2 pers. over 10 yrs. and 2 pers. under 10 in the household. The ch. of Johannes[1] Mertz were:

1) <u>Sophia Elisabetha Margaretha</u>² (HJ), conf. by Pastor Kocherthal 23 March 1712 at Queensberg (West Camp Luth. Chbk.). She md. Andreas Barthel (HJ).

2) <u>Elisabetha</u>² (HJ), conf. 14 April 1717 at Kingsberg (West Camp Luth. Chbk.).

3) <u>Maria Kunigunda</u>² (HJ), md. Philip Balthasar Barthel 6 May 1725 (Linlithgo Ref. Chbk.).

<u>HENRICH MESS</u> (Hunter Lists #498)

The German ancestral home of this Palatine family was at

5450 <u>Niederbieber</u> (2 km. n. of Neuwied; Chbks. begin 1655). The
parents of the emigrant were <u>Johannes Meess</u> and his wife Gertraut
of Segendorff; their ch. were:

<u>Catharina</u>, md. as d/o Johannes Meess at Segendorf 14 May 1691
Johannes, s/o the late Christ Ersfeldt; Johannes Ersfeld at
Segendorf was bur. 26 Dec 1698. Catharina md. 2nd 9 Nov 1699
Hans Wilhelm, s/o Thönges Kämmer (Johann Wilhelm[1] Kämmer was
an emigrant 1709er who settled in Schoharie - HJ).

+ <u>Johann Henrich</u>, bpt. 26 Feb 1671 - sp.: Johann Jacob Mees -
brother of the child's father, Henrich Bauer, and Margaretha
- w/o Theiss Zempers.

<u>Johann Jacob</u>, a sp. in 1671.

Henrig Meis, his wife, and 3 ch., were on Capt. Frans Robbenson's
ship in the 3rd party of Palatines in Holland (Rotterdam Lists).
Henry Meiss aged 38, his wife, sons 3 and $\frac{1}{4}$, Ref., smith, were in
the 3rd arrivals in England later that yr. (London Lists).

Henrich Mess made his initial appearance on the Hunter Lists
1 July 1710 with 2 pers. over 10 yrs. of age in the household. The
entry for 4 Oct 1710 showed 3 pers. over 10, and the notation for
24 June 1711 recorded 2 pers. over 10 yrs. of age. Henrick Mace
was in Col. Thomas Ffarmar's Regiment, 5th Company, in N.J. in
1715 (<u>Report of the State Historian</u>, Vol. I, p. 534). Heinrich
Ress and Magdalena with 2 ch. were auf dem Rarendantz ca. 1716/17
(Simmendinger Register); some translations give the surname as
Mesz (HJ). Francis Quick sold a 150 acre tract in what is now Raritan Twp. in 1724 to Hendrick Mees, a blacksmith (<u>A History of</u>
<u>East Amwell</u>, 1700 - 1800, p. 53). A child of Henrich[1] Mess was:

1) <u>Magdalena</u>[2] (HJ), who joined the N.Y. City Ref. Church 22
May 1739 as Magdalena Mees, w/o Dirk Ammerman of Amwel.

<u>ANNA MARGRETHA MESSERIN</u> (Hunter Lists #499)
(INCLUDING THE WIMMER FAMILY - HJ)

The European home of this family was 6927 <u>Bonfeld</u> (5 km w.
of Bad Wimpfen; Chbks. begin 1607). As U.S. descendants of this
family were known as Wimmer, I shall emphasize this branch in Germany (HJ). The earliest known Wimmer ancestor of the American line
was <u>Hans Winner</u> from Fürfeld. Sebastian Winner, s/o Hans Winner
from Fürfeld, md. Elisabetha, d/o Jeremias Eremer (Berner?) -
Gerichts from A... (?), 23 Feb 1661. Hanß Bastian Wemmer was noted
on a Schatzungseinnahmen for Bonfeld in 1687 (Generallandesarchiv
Karlsruhe 125/3094). The ch. of <u>Sebastian Wimmer</u> (sometimes written Winner) and his 1st wife Elisabetha were:

<u>Hans Jeremias</u>, bpt. 14 Dec 1661 - sp.: Jeremias Klempt and

Hans Landvatter.

Eva Margaretha, bpt. 22 Feb 1663 - sp.: Apollonia Klemp, and
Sophia - w/o Hans Landvetter the innkeeper here. Eva Margaretha - d/o Seb. Wimmer, was bur. 9 Feb 1665.

Adam, bpt. 28 April 1667 - sp.: Samuel Bürger - landlord and
innkeeper here. He was bur. 4 May 1667.

Eva Margaretha, bpt. 8 July 1668 - sp.: Eva Marg. - w/o Adolph
Dölling, and Eva Egler from Murrhardt - now cook in the castle. She d. 16 Sept 1668.

Adam, bpt. 22 July 1669 - sp.: Samuel Bürger the landlord
here, and Eva Marg. - w/o Adolf Dölling for her husband. He
md. 27 April 1697 at Gemmingen.

Maria Sophia, bpt. 5 March 1672 - sp.: Sophia - w/o Samuel
Bürger the inkeeper here, and Maria Cath. - surviving d/o
Michael Tholl.

Sophia Catharina, bpt. 19 July 1675 - sp.: Sophia - w/o Sam.
Bürger the innkeeper here, and Maria Cath. - w/o Wolf Kürr-
schelter the cartwright here. She was conf. with her sister
Maria Sophia in 1689. Sophia Catharina md. Joh. Michael Metz-
läcker 24 Nov 1705.

Elisabetha, w/o H. Seb. Winner, d. 21 Dec 1677, aged 40 yrs. Hans
Sebastian Winner md. Margaretha, d/o the late Lorentz Wollhauf 14
July 1678. Barbara, w/o Lorentz Walauf the shepherd here, was bur.
28 Oct 1674, aged 60 yrs. The ch. of Hans Sebastian Winner and his
2nd wife Margaretha were:

+ Catharina Christina, b. 6 Jan 1684. She md. (the 1709er - HJ)
  Johann Simon Vogt 17 Aug (?) 1707.

  Anna Margaretha, b. 10 Oct 1686 - sp.: Catharina - w/o Hans
  Stopp (?) at Fürfeld, and Anna Christina - w/o Hans Röther at
  Rappenau. She was bur. 25 March 1689, aged 3½ yrs.

  Johann Abraham, b. 28 April 1689 - sp.: Johann Roth - citizen
  and bricklayer at Rappenau, and Abrah. Klotz - single man.

  Bernhard Andreas, bpt. 26 Feb 1691 - sp.: Andreas Klotz -
  bricklayer and Gerichts here and Hans Bernhard Hess. He d.
  20 Dec 1691.

+ Johannes, b. 30 June 1696 - sp.: Johann Jacob Braun the sadler,
  Hans Bernhard Hess, and Joh. Georg Salomon the cooper.

Joh. Sebastian Winner d. 14 March 1699, aged 61 yrs. Maria Margaretha, wid/o Joh. Sebastian Wimmer, md. Martin Mesner of Alti
(Württ) - widower, 9 Nov 1700. Sebastian Wimmer's Widow with her
ch. were listed as leaving Bonfeld in the Chbk. there in a section
dated 1710 and called Emigrants From This Village. Margreeta Mees-
terin and 2 ch. were on Capt. William Newton's ship in the 5th party in Holland in 1709 (Rotterdam Lists).

Anna Margretha Messerin made her initial appearance on the Hunter Lists 30 June 1710 with 2 pers. over 10 yrs. and 1 under 10 yrs. of age. The family showed 3 over 10 yrs. on 24 June 1711, 2 over 10 and 1 under 10 yrs. on 29 Sept 1711, and then 3 over 10 yrs. 24 Dec 1711. Margaret Meserin, a Widow aged 50, Johannes Meserin aged 15, and Susan Cath Meserin aged 10, were in N.Y. City in 1710/11 (Palatines In N.Y. City). Hanss Metzger is Just Langmann's step-son, and Just Langinann and his wife were listed next to each other at Hackensack ca. 1716/17 (Simmendinger Register); this shows that Anna Margaretha Wohlauf Wimmer Messer md. for a 3rd time to Just Langmann (HJ). The ch. of Anna Margaretha[1] Messer (Metzger et var) who reached America were:

1) Johannes[2], b. 30 June 1696 (Bonfeld Chbk.). For the early part of his life in America he was called Johannes Messer or Metzger, as evidenced by the list of Palatines in N.Y. City in 1710/11 and the Simmendinger Register. However, even as early as 1714 when he sp. his sister Christina's child by Simeon Vogt, he was known also as Johannes Wimmer. Margareta Langmansen in the place of Johannes Wimmer sp. the Vogts in 1716 (N.Y. City Luth. Chbk.). Johannes Wimmer was a freeholder at Amwell in 1741 (Hunterdon Co. Freeholders). Johannes Wimmer of West Jersey purchased 425 acres of land in Frederick Co., Md. 5 Sept 1761. The will of Johannes Wimmer of Bedford Co., Va. was dated 20 June 1780 and proved 23 Oct 1780 (Bedford Co. Wills: Liber I, p. 378). Johannes[2] Wimmer md. Wyntje, d/o Barent and Apollonia Simons (HJ). Their ch. were:

    i) Maria[3], bpt. 6 March 1725/26 (Staten Island Ref. Chbk.).

    ii) Johannes[3], bpt. 19 March 1727 - sp.: Barent Simonsen and wife Appolonia (Readington Ref. Chbk.).

    iii) Maria[3], bpt. 1 Jan 1729 (Readington Ref. Chbk.).

    iv) Abraham[3] (Will).

    v) Isaac[3] (Will).

    vi) Jacob[3] (Will).

    vii) Christina[3] (Lyle G. Wimmer data).

    viii) Martha[3] (Lyle G. Wimmer data).

    ix) Catharina[3] (Lyle G. Wimmer data).

    x) Adam[3] (Will).

2) Susanna Catharina[2] (Palatines In N.Y. City); her bpt. was not found at Bonfeld (HJ). Catharina Messner sp. the Vogts twice at N.Y. City Luth. Church.

Mr. Lyle G. Wimmer of West Hartford, Conn. has been most generous in sharing his documented data on this family (HJ).

Receipt : Accompt of the Provision[s] To the Palatins : from

Date		Loaves of Bread	Bushels of Pease	Barrels of Porke	from whom Recew'd	Where laid up
Months	days					
July	10th	194	. . . . .	. . . . .	From Capt Walters	Distributed pres[ently]
		157	. . . . .	. . . .	Mr Thurman	Ditto
		145	. . . . .	. . .	Mr Hook	Do
		. . .	24	4	Mr Hoogland	Do
		496	24	4		
	11	181	. . . .	. . .	Mr Thurman	} Dist. presently
		315	. . . .	. . .	Capt Walters	
		496	. . . .	. . .		